darina allen's

ballymaloe cookery course

with photographs by ray main
and peter cassidy

kyle cathie limited

for Myrtle Allen

acknowledgements

Running the cookery school has been a wonderful voyage of discovery during which many, many people (including my students) have contributed to my culinary knowledge. The school was started with the inspiration of my parents-in-law, Ivan and Myrtle Allen, and the support of family and friends including my brother Rory O'Connell, Pauline and Neil O'Kennedy and of course my own dear mother Elizabeth O'Connell.

When students do a 12-week Certificate course here at the Cookery School they leave with seven or eight lever-arch files of recipes and notes on food-related subjects. This book is an attempt to condense all that information between the covers of one book – an impossible task, given that if it was the size it should be, you would need a wheelbarrow to get it into the kitchen.

Despite the fact that I have written fourteen cookbooks I still cannot type or use a word processor so I am deeply indebted to Adrienne Forbes who has laboured tirelessly to decipher my writing and corrected and recorrected each draft. A special thanks also to Anne Morrissey and Rosalie Dunne who have kept the show on the road while Adrienne and I struggled to finish. We are extremely grateful for the help of Margot Heskin, Truss Boelhouwer-Grifhorst and Marianne Jongma who supported us particularly in the final weeks when the pressure was really on. Patrick Treacy was enormously patient in waiting for me to write the recipes for the second edition. Thank you to my team of teachers and assistants who have tested the recipes and who suggested a tweak here or there as they observed their pitfalls in the kitchen due to insufficient explanation on my part. A heartfelt thank you to my garden angels and my farm manager who are responsible for the abundance of wonderful fresh produce throughout the seasons.

A very special thank you to the many guest chefs who have delighted us over the years. Each and every one has added to our repertoire and

foreword to second edition

shared their knowledge and passion with us. Some of their recipes have been reproduced in this book and I am deeply grateful for that generosity. Influences have come from many people over the years and we have tried to attribute wherever possible – please forgive us for those we have inadvertently overlooked.

My greatest debt of gratitude must surely go to my mother-in-law, Myrtle Allen, who pioneered the style of cooking for which Ballymaloe is now famous.

A special thank you to Mary Dowey, who contributed the excellent wine section, and gave stoic editorial help in the early days of this book. Huge thanks to my dear and special friend, Julia Wight, who conspired with my publisher, Kyle Cathie, to lock me into the drawing room of her London home so that this book would eventually be 'finished' – history repeated itself when Jenny and Laura Wheatley had to use the same tactics to get the second edition organised! And to my agent, Jacqueline Korn, who has encouraged me at every turn.

A big hug for Janie Suthering, who cooked every morsel of the food for Ray Main's delicious photographs, and special thanks to Peter Cassidy and Linda Tubby for the wonderful pictures in the new edition. Also to my editors Helen Woodhall, Sheila Davies, Stephanie Evans, Elaine Koster and James Bridgeman, along with Esme West and Sarah Epton, who have literally worked from dawn till dusk to lick this manuscript into shape. And the quite inspirational dedication and forbearance of my publisher Kyle Cathie who has had to use all her physical endurance and psychology to keep each and every one of us on track – most authors I know endlessly moan about their publishers – I am full of admiration for my publisher – she is truly heroic.

Last but not least my family and my long-suffering husband Tim, who not only runs the School with me but continues to support me every step of the way, for which I am truly grateful.

When I wrote this book back in 2000 my passion about the importance of eating organic and locally produced food may have seemed a little 'alternative'. Now, almost ten years later, these ideas have become a lot more mainstream. On a recent trip to the West Coast of America, I was thrilled to find that organic is now a given and, better still, that the word 'local' is even sexier than 'organic'. Everywhere I went people were talking about the provenance of their food and were very keen to eat food that was grown in their neighbourhood. Chefs were going out of their way to link up more with local farmers and producers and some were even growing their own vegetables.

The gathering momentum of this movement is very exciting, and I'm more convinced than ever before of the importance of using top-quality ingredients in cooking. There are a lot of talented chefs who can run rings around me when it comes to technique, but who just can't get food to sing as it should because their ingredients aren't up to scratch. Our big task nowadays as chefs and cooks is the sourcing of top-quality ingredients – finding fresh, local produce from organic sources.

I hope you enjoy this new edition of *Ballymaloe Cookery Course*. Since the book was first published many new recipes have entered into our repertoire from students and guest chefs and I am always picking up new ideas on my travels – somehow we have managed to squeeze all of these in! The new recipes reflect the latest food trends and use ingredients that are becoming easier to get hold of – offal, for example. Anyone can slap a steak on a pan but I think chefs and cooks are finding it's much more fun to take cheap cuts of meat and really make something delicious from them.

We've revamped the design of the book and have reorganised things a little to make it more user friendly. Plus we have some new fab photographs from Peter Cassidy. Enjoy!

contents

introduction

introduction

Myrtle Allen is my greatest inspiration and I feel deeply fortunate that our paths in life crossed. When I graduated from hotel school in Dublin in the late 1960s, you could count the number of good restaurants in Ireland on one hand (with a finger or two left over). Most of them wrote the menu when they opened and it was still the same 10 years later. And most didn't want a woman in the kitchen. Myrtle was different – a woman with no time for tins and packets, she wrote the menu for Ballymaloe House Hotel every day, seen as an amateurish thing to do back then, but something that seemed completely logical to her. She would use what was best and freshest in the garden, as well as the fresh fish that came in on the boats at Ballycotton. I was impressed by what I heard about this farmer's wife who cooked with the seasons in the wilds of East Cork. I sent off a letter and was offered a job in Myrtle's kitchens. The first person I met when I arrived was her son Timmy, to whom I am now married.

When I started out at Ballymaloe, every day was an adventure. I was like a sponge, soaking up as much exciting new information as I possibly could. With Myrtle, I came to realise the importance of good-quality produce, and I could see quite clearly that cooking good produce using simple techniques made great dishes. Myrtle continues to be an inspiration for me, and to this day I still go to Myrtle to get her advice or to ask her opinion. She is a pioneer, and I often think that I have got some of the credit for many of the things she has achieved. Many of the recipes in this book are recipes that Myrtle originally taught me in the Ballymaloe kitchen and we now pass them on to our students at the School.

Myrtle has always been delighted with the opportunities offered to me and her support and encouragement have meant that I have been able to go on and do other things. We now work together to champion the cause of the small artisanal producers, stimulating debate about food policies that we see as unsustainable or hygiene regulations that are out of proportion to the risks involved. In doing so we support our local food producers, whom we depend on absolutely for the quality produce that is essential to create the food for which Ballymaloe has become famous.

Many other people have influenced me and contributed to my culinary knowledge thus far. My own mother, Elizabeth O'Connell, taught me how to cook as I pulled at her apron strings; I feel very lucky to have been handed down the joy of cooking from her, and for the central part it has always played in my family life. My brother, Rory O'Connell, worked with me in the School in the early days and has always been tremendously supportive and generous with ideas and suggestions.

Then there are the books of Elizabeth David, Jane Grigson, Margaret Costa and particularly Alice Waters, whose whole philosophy I completely identify with; she's had the courage to motivate and inspire an entire generation of cooks, and has worked with farmers and food producers, helping them to connect with chefs. Over the years people have been so generous – cooking schools the world over have generously opened their doors to me enabling me to forge strong friendships with those who share my commitment to culinary education. I have been able to keep abreast of international food trends, thanks to my travels, and to meeting my colleagues at the conferences of the organisations of which I am a member – Slow Food, IACP and Euro Toque.

One of the great joys for me through the years has been to pick up the phone and invite some of the people I admire most to come and teach at the School as guest chefs: John Ash, Rick Bayless, Frances Bissell, John Desmond, Ursula Ferrigno, Rose Gray, Jane Grigson, Sophie Grigson, Marcella Hazan, Deh-ta Hsiung, Madhur Jaffrey, Alastair Little, Shermin Mustafa, Kevin Orbell McSean, Rory O'Connell, Sri Owen, Ada Parasiliti, Paul and Jeanne Rankin, Alicia Rios-Ivars, Claudia Roden, Ruth Rogers, Nina Simonds, Rick Stein, Anne Willan and Antony Worrall Thompson have all inspired us with their enormous dedication and enthusiasm and have contributed to our repertoire. TV chef Rachel Allen, originally a student at the cookery school, comes to us and teaches on a regular basis, and in recent years we have been lucky enough to have Peter Gordon, Skye Gyngell, Sam Clarke, Diane Kennedy and Eric Treuille visit.

Ballymaloe cookery school
Founded in 1983, the school's philosophy has always been to cook fresh, locally produced food with the seasons. We cook it simply to enhance the natural flavours, creating food that looks and tastes delicious. Having the School right in the middle of a farm and close to the sea is a huge bonus; the farm and gardens provide produce for the school, as well as for Ballymaloe House and the local farmers' market. Both the gardens and the farm are organic because I am passionately committed to healthy and wholesome food. What we don't produce ourselves we source locally. The farm across the road produces wonderful soft fruit and rhubarb when ours run out, and delicious potatoes too. We get wonderful fresh fish from the boats at Ballycotton, and local farmers' wives rear organic chickens, ducks, geese and turkeys for us. When Nora Ahearne delivers her free-range ducks we introduce her to the students saying, 'this is the person who reared those wonderful ducks for you'. When our local butchers, Frank Murphy and Kevin Day come, they share their knowledge and expertise as second-generation butchers. Local fish-smokers and farmhouse cheesemakers add to the bounty.

12-week course
We now run our 12-week courses three times a year – in January, April and September. Students come from the four corners of the earth and we take them on a journey from 'this is a wooden spoon' to being able to earn their living from cooking. We welcome students who have a passion for food, who really want to learn and who are prepared to work hard for three busy months.

The course not only provides a thorough grounding in cookery technique, it is also a total food experience for the student to become immersed in. On the first day we introduce the new students to our gardeners, Eileen, Haulie and Kay, who will produce much of what they will cook during their 12-week stay. I show them a barrow full of rich soil (some of them look askance at this eccentric grey-haired hippy woman on a mission) and I tell them about the millions of organisms and bacteria all working away underground to enrich it. I run my hands through it saying: 'Remember this is where it all starts, in the good earth, and if you don't have clean fertile soil you won't have good food or pure water.' Then they get their first recipe – how to make compost...

After we've had our composting lesson, we walk to the pastures where the Kerry cows, Herefords and Shorthorn cattle graze contentedly. We added two Jersey cows to our menagerie on the farm a few years ago, so that we can have wonderful unpasteurised Jersey milk for the family and grandchildren. The students have the opportunity to learn how to milk a cow which they queue up to do... not necessarily an essential life skill but 'can milk a cow' looks good on their CVs and certainly gets the conversation started!

We come round the corner to see the foraging Saddleback pigs, and from there to the greenhouses, where Rupert and Eileen show them how to sow seeds. For me this is a very important initiation to the course – I know of no better way to give people a respect for food than for them to plant a seed and watch it grow. Each and every student gets a broccoli or lettuce plant which they label and sow in the greenhouse and during the next 12 weeks they watch it grow. Farmers and people who grow their own food get disheartened when people don't respect their efforts; they understandably want people to appreciate the energy, passion and hard work that have gone into growing the food. And suddenly the students realise why...

I'm really keen for students to see the wider picture of food production. Trimmings and scraps from their cooking going either into the stock pot, to the hens or into the composting bin. The stock pot creates the basis for many wonderful soups, stews and

'Remember this is where it all starts, in the good earth, and if you don't have clean fertile soil you won't have good food or pure water.'

sauces; the scraps that go to the hens come back as eggs a few days later; and what goes into the compost bin is eventually returned to enrich the soil. We encourage our students to appreciate and value the work of the gardeners by learning how and when to harvest food. In doing so they get an insight into how long it takes to grow good food, and they won't dare to boil the hell out of a carrot when they realise it's taken three months to grow! They begin to see that everything is inter-connected and part of a holistic cycle, and learn about how things can be recycled beneficially.

Different cooking schools have different philosophies, and because ours is residential, it seems logical to teach in meals. Instead of doing a whole lesson on boiling techniques or making soufflés, each day we cook through a menu incorporating the relevant lessons, from basic principles to advanced professional techniques. People learn to cook almost without realising it. There is a demonstration every afternoon after which the students taste what's been cooked so that when they cook it themselves the following morning they know what they're aiming for. At lunchtime students and teachers all sit down together to enjoy the fruits of the morning's labour. It may come as a surprise that many students lose weight rather than gaining it (although those who visit the pub every night tend to put it on!).

On the 12-week course students can go into the kitchens at Ballymaloe House to watch the chefs. Often they are amazed to see them using exactly the same recipes as we use in the School – we pool knowledge and share ideas. Ballymaloe House is unique because their chefs always work to recipes (other chefs may think that's not macho). Years ago chefs did apprenticeships for five to six years and honed their palates; nowadays staff move about so quickly that it's essential to have a repertoire of tried-and-tested recipes that enable trainees to get consistent results. Trainee chefs and cooks start off by following the recipes faithfully, and when they become more skilled and confident they use their creativity to introduce their own twists.

Short courses

We also run a whole range of short courses on all types of topics, from one day to a week in duration. Our short courses are in keeping with the principles of the 12-week course and cover an extensive range of cooking techniques including bread-making, butchery, fish filleting, freezing, pickling and preserving, as well as courses linked to food trends of the moment: Tea – 'the new Black', Tapas, Offal Fest, Pickling and Preserving. I also love to introduce courses that are inspired by my travels – A Day in India, A Day in Mexico, A Day in Morocco. Other courses carry our underlying philosophies: Sustainable Seafood, Slow Food, Basic Home Butchery, Foraging...

We have recently introduced a series of Forgotten Skills courses for the growing number of people who are eager to learn how to produce their own food. These cover growing vegetables, keeping chickens in your garden, bee-keeping, making butter, yoghurt and cheese, and how to build a smokehouse and smoke your own food – we make pizzas, calzone, panzarotti and piadina in the wood burning oven and the stoves.

We also run lectures on menu-planning and entertaining, food costing, food hygiene and career options in the culinary world. And we really enjoy hosting wine tastings, where we teach people how to serve and appreciate wines, and how to choose wines to go with a meal.

shopping

It sounds extraordinary but in reality about 80 per cent of good food is about shopping, so the fundamental message we need to get across to our students is the importance of putting time and effort into sourcing good-quality ingredients. If one starts off with good, fresh, naturally produced food in season, one needs to do so little to make it taste good. If, on the other hand, the basis of the meal is mass-produced de-natured food which has travelled hundreds, even thousands of miles, one needs to be a magician to make it taste good. This is where chefs need to use all their culinary wizardry – to camouflage the original lack of flavour.

People who want their food wrapped in plastic or on polystyrene trays are very well catered for in this day and age; they can find everything they want in the shops or supermarkets. Alternatively, sourcing fresh local food that is in season can be far more of a challenge. In fact, the problem has been exacerbated in recent years as supermarkets have adopted a central distribution system for fresh produce as well as for dry goods.

At Ballymaloe we realise how extremely fortunate we are to be surrounded by such a wonderful pool of local produce, and that for many people sourcing such high-quality ingredients is far more difficult. Since I started the School 24 years ago, I've become increasingly concerned about how the majority of food is produced and where it comes from. Like it or not, we are going to be forced to think about the disastrous consequences of pushing animals and plants further and further beyond their natural limits. There is an indisputable link between disease and excessively intensive factory farming. BSE is the obvious example, as well as stronger and stronger strains of salmonella, e-coli, camphylobacter, and so on. I welcome the fact that these issues have stimulated many strong debates among our students about the way food is produced and increased in them the conviction that it is time for a new way forward.

The first thing I would advise anyone to do is grow your own food in a vegetable garden or an allotment – increasing numbers of people seem to be getting hooked on the magic of planting even a few tomato plants or herbs. The next best thing is to head for your local farmers' market. At these markets one can buy fresh local seasonal food directly from the producer. At last the market culture is taking off in the UK and Ireland – I started a farmers' market in our local town of Midleton in 1999 and it has continued to gather momentum ever since. Students at the School who are interested in the farmers' markets have the opportunity to come with us on Saturday morning to Midleton. There they learn how to set up and operate a stall and identify opportunities. They love the banter and the camaraderie among the stall-holders.

Remember that top-quality, health-giving food comes at a price. We somehow have an unreasonable assumption that cheap food is our right and so supermarkets in turn demand low-cost produce from their suppliers. This has resulted in food being unrealistically cheap. The repercussions of this have forced many farmers and food producers either to go out of business or to intensify their farming methods further. We are all losers in this situation. Research clearly shows that an ever-more intensive production system contributes to the spread of diseases and often results in poor-quality food.

Top tips for buying top-quality ingredients:
• Demand traceability – always find out the variety and source of food, particularly meat, poultry, vegetables and fruit.
• Buy fresh, organic and local produce with the seasons – research the farmers' markets and box schemes operating in your area.
• Taste whenever possible – be observant and uncompromising in your pursuit of quality.
• Look carefully for signs of deterioration (but remember that physical perfection does not necessarily mean best flavour).
• Demand that irradiated food is identified and labelled clearly.

local food

In the first edition of this book I predicted that 'local' would be the buzzword for the future. Ten years on, it is indeed a word on the lips of most conscientious shoppers – even big-chain supermarkets are promoting and labelling the local produce they stock. Supporting local producers is something I now feel more passionate about than ever. It simply makes no sense to buy expensive imported food that has travelled for thousands of miles. As far as I am concerned, local produce wins hands down every time, because it is so fresh and therefore tastes better and is much more nutritious. How wonderful to eat food plucked from a tree or pulled from the earth literally a matter of hours before it passes your lips! Local food is also a green choice – the transportation of food around the world (which is happening increasingly by air) has a significant impact on the diminishing fuel reserves and carbon emissions that are contributing to the current environmental crisis we face.

Italy is a shining example of a nation of people who have their priorities right. In their markets all local produce is marked 'nostrano' and Italians are prepared to pay more for local food because they know it will be fresher and of better quality.

Food for the future

Ballymaloe food is special because of the quality of the ingredients we have from the farmers and producers around us. If we were working with de-natured food there would be no point of difference. Occasionally people in the School say to me, 'Darina, get real, where are the students going to find food of this quality when they leave? Shouldn't you just be using normal food from the supermarket?' My response is that it's really important to cook using the best-quality produce so that the students can build up a taste memory against which to measure flavours when they leave the School – something to aim for when they're cooking in the future. The students appreciate this fundamental point –

after twelve weeks with us, they shop in a different way. They look for fresh and local produce, think in terms of the seasons, and always note varieties. They learn which varieties of apples, plums and cherries to buy again. They don't bother to buy tasteless, irradiated strawberries or French beans flown from the other side of the world in winter. When the students leave they not only make a determined effort to continue to source the same quality of produce, but many start to grow their own herbs and vegetables. Some even keep their own hens because they can't imagine life without them! Those going into the restaurant or catering business are encouraged to set up a network of small local producers just as we have done here so that they can get locally grown food with real traceability. This has a double benefit – not only do they know where the food comes from and how it is produced but they are also supporting their local community and thereby generating goodwill for their own business.

I believe that the future of Irish agriculture and tourism depends on us embracing this opportunity to produce top-quality, naturally produced food as a nation. We seem to be the obvious country to lead the way for Europe in organic production – the country with a clean green image that Bord Bia (the Irish Food Board) so proudly promotes as 'Ireland – Food Island'. What is needed is a visionary in government who can see sustainable agriculture as the way forward for Ireland. To support this movement we as consumers need to appreciate, support, protect and cherish the small artisan-producers who labour with passion and often little financial reward. We also need to encourage farmers who want to farm in a less intensive way. Perhaps most importantly we need to be willing to pay for the quality of food that we say we want.

why cook?

It's cool to cook

One of the exciting things for me at the moment is realising how many young people think it is cool to cook. Isaac, our son, says some of his friends who wouldn't have been 'caught dead' in a kitchen until recently are now desperate to learn how to cook. It's hip to entertain casually and whip up a little feast. No need for matching cutlery or fancy place settings – cooking is a social occasion. Get your friends involved in shelling the broad beans, cooking together and having fun. This trend owes a lot to young TV stars, such as Nigella Lawson and Jamie Oliver. Interestingly, the most hip thing of all nowadays is growing your own food, and then sharing and cooking it with your friends.

Why is it so important to be able to cook?

To many people cooking is an unimportant skill: why would you bother to take time out to learn to cook when you could be furthering your career or having fun in the pub? I would argue that it's hugely important to learn how to cook, for lots of different reasons, not least because so much depends on the food we eat – our health, our energy, our vitality, our ability to concentrate... We can't do much about our genes but we can take responsibility for our own health by controlling the food we eat. Health goes in through our mouths, and my father-in-law, Ivan, always used to say, our brains too.

If you can't cook, you're at the mercy of others for what you eat, and if you are fortunate enough to have delicious, healthy, wholesome food cooked for you, you're one in a million. Otherwise, the only alternative is to drop into the local deli, buy ready-prepared meals or make regular trips to restaurants which will prove to be an expensive business. If you can cook, it doesn't matter where you are in the world, you can gather a few ingredients together and conjure up a little meal for yourself and your friends. It's certainly the easiest way to win friends and influence people. I remember once when I was staying with friends in America, I made a loaf of soda bread, and while it was cooking, created a little raspberry jam from a punnet of raspberries in the fridge – they thought I was a complete magician. In the end, the way to everyone's heart is through their tummy – no matter how beautiful you are people soon get fed up with burnt sausages and leathery hamburgers. I always tell doctors, pilots, priests – anyone who'll listen – how important it is to take time out to learn how to cook, because no matter what else you do every day we all need to eat. Learn some cooking skills and take control of your life.

taste, taste, & taste again

I can't stress enough the importance of tasting continually as you cook. It doesn't matter if you've been cooking all your life, ingredients literally change every day. You need to taste at the beginning, in the middle and at the end. When cooking, think about flavour and, as you cook, imagine yourself eating it and that will help you get the proportions right. Always season with your fingers and never with a spoon, because then you are in touch and you are more likely to get the quantity right. Here I stress, taste, taste, taste. Carrots taste hugely different at different times of the year – in early spring they need more seasoning. In early summer when just pulled from the ground, they are meltingly delicious just boiled for a very few minutes and tossed in a little butter and freshly ground black pepper and salt. Here at the School one of the experiments we do to illustrate the importance of sourcing is to cook two pans of carrots side by side using exactly the same method. One pan contains freshly pulled carrots which arrived with the soil still on and the other contains pre-washed carrots that came in a plastic bag. Try this yourself – taste and learn from the flavour.

Tasting helps to develop your palate and build up your taste memory. Take every opportunity when you eat out or when you travel abroad to taste foods at source. Taste the ingredients as they are meant to be and then when you find them at home you will be able to judge whether they are of good quality. One of the most difficult things for a beginner in the kitchen is to judge whether more seasoning is needed or not. If in doubt, follow the advice that Myrtle gave me years ago when I was in doubt about a soup: take out a little bit in a cup, add some seasoning and if that improves the flavour, go ahead and season the whole pot.

herbs & spices

Fresh herbs add magic to your cooking. In fact, now that I think about it, they are absolutely essential to the flavour of Ballymaloe food. If you don't have access to fresh herbs in your garden or local shop, it's time to think about a little gardening. You don't need a garden – a window box on the windowsill or a wooden tub on a balcony is all you need. Get started with parsley, either flat-leaf or curly or both, add chives, then perennial mint. French tarragon, lemon balm, annual marjoram, dill, fennel, the list is endless... Herbs have been used both as food and medicine since man first walked on this earth. More recently the interest in herbs has gathered momentum not only among cooks and chefs but also among those who are interested in pursuing a healthier lifestyle and exploring herbal remedies and alternative medicines.

Spices too are essential. Having a few jars of fresh spices to hand is like having a Pandora's box to dip into when the fancy takes you. As a general rule, buy spices whole – with the possible exception of turmeric, and ginger when making gingerbread. Whole spices have infinitely more flavour than ground. As soon as spices are ground the flavour starts to tick away so use them as quickly as possible.

proportion

Buy in small quantities, use quickly and store away from direct light. Proportion is important yet it is one of the most difficult things to get right. There's a little trick that helps – imagine yourself eating it and you are more likely to get it right. Don't drown a dish with too much sauce or skimp with too little. It's strange how rare it is to get a sandwich with the right amount of filling.

There are several reasons to get the portion size right:

1. Many of us dislike having too much to eat on our plates. It causes the dilemma of being rude by leaving food behind and in my case I have real problems if I leave food, because my host immediately thinks that it wasn't good. Which leads me to the eternal problem of trying to slip it into my handbag or eating more than I want.

2. People leave it behind and it's wasted.

3. It makes no sense for restaurants to give over-large helpings because their guests will be too full to order a pudding. Serve reasonable size helpings; at Ballymaloe we serve slightly on the small side, with a table d'hôte menu of five courses plus cheese and coffee with petit fours. There's plenty to eat and every diner is offered seconds. In America helpings have become obscenely enormous; what used to be large a couple of years ago has been doubled into super-helpings. Obesity is growing – over 50 per cent of the American population is classified as obese and in Ireland it's 10 per cent and rising.

I've generally tried to give the amounts for average portions throughout this book. In general we multiply up quite accurately when taking a recipe for 6 and cooking it for a party of 24. For 48 people, multiply by 5 rather than 8 and reduce the butter and cream a bit.

family meals

Changes in lifestyle have led to an inevitable loss of family meals. As the 'grab, gobble and go' culture gathers momentum we have more dashboard dining, TV meals, and eating on the run. If we stop to think about it, many of our happiest childhood recollections are connected with sharing food around the kitchen table. This is what memories are made of. Nowadays, with everybody's busy lifestyle, it takes a real effort, but it is vital to understand how important it is to hang on to the tradition of eating together. It might not be possible every day but make a pledge to sit down together at least twice a week. Even if there are arguments, everyone is still communicating which has to be good! Cooking together is fun; get everyone involved in the chopping, peeling and grating. Many people find cooking relaxing after a busy day. Keep it simple. It doesn't have to be a feast, maybe just a boiled egg and fresh soda bread – and get the telly out of the kitchen!

at the table

Our students lay the table for lunch at the School each day. The place setting depends on the menu and the number of courses but the basic setting is a fork and two knives. Add a pudding spoon – and for dessert pastries you'll need a fork too. If the main course is meat or steak you may want to lay a serrated knife. For fish, the more traditional fish knives and forks have now been largely dropped from modern place settings. For pudding, the spoon and fork can go above the place setting with the fork underneath and its handle to the left and the spoon on top with its handle to the right. The soup spoon goes on the outside right-hand side. The butter knife should be laid either on the place setting or directly on the side plate. In more formal place settings, as our mums told us, 'always work from the outside in'. In that case, the bread knife will be on the outside. Don't get too fussed about all this, but at least try to have a fork and two knives.

Glasses

Normally the water glass is laid closest to the knife tip, then the white wine glass, then the red wine glass either in a triangle or a line. If there is a whole line of glasses, you know you're in for a good night!

Table manners – a few guidelines

Break bread rolls rather than cutting them. Tilt the bowl away from you when eating soup from an old-fashioned, shallow soup plate. Leaving your fork and knife crossed in the centre of your plate indicates that you haven't finished – when placed together in the centre of the plate this indicates you've finished. Don't pick up your potato on a fork and peel it obviously; do this discreetly. Once upon a time, instead of being allowed to ask for salt and pepper, one had to offer it to one's neighbour and hopefully the penny would drop that you actually needed it yourself. And then of course there's afternoon tea manners but that's more for history books. Always try to be considerate and anticipate your neighbours' needs.

Serve a finger bowl with foods that need to be eaten with the fingers, such as sweetcorn, quail, whole prawns or globe artichokes. Fill a small bowl with warm water and add a slice of lemon, and rose petals if you want. When you have finished nibbling the delicious morsels, dip your fingers into the bowl and dry discreetly on your napkin. And of course don't speak with your mouth full. Many a sophisticated elegantly dressed person lets themselves down with bad manners. And don't put your elbows on the table until you're an auntie! Be restrained and don't pile one food on top of another – it's an insult to the cook to be overly greedy and then leave food on the plate.

Clearing the table

Don't clear the table until everyone's finished eating. Clear discreetly and from the left (serve from the right). Hold the plate on your hand resting on the three middle fingers, secured by the thumb and little finger; place the fork upside down and slide the knife underneath. Place the next plate on your wrist where palm meets arm, and stack plates there. Clear debris discreetly to the lower plate. Stack up to three or four plates.

fashion in food

There's fashion in food just like everything else, and while it's important to keep in touch, don't fall into the trap of slavishly following trends for the sake of impressing people. It takes real courage to serve fresh, locally produced and seasonal food without any bobbles and bows and smarties on top. I truly believe that simply cooked food can be very sophisticated – Alice Waters of Chez Panisse in Berkeley, California has been known to serve a juicy, succulent heirloom peach as the pudding in a no-choice menu, which is as much a gastronomic treat as something which has taken hours to prepare with over-complex flavours.

Having said that, for the latest in culinary innovation, the place to be is the annual International Gastronomy Summit in Spain – 'Madrid Fusion'. The 'high priest' of the molecular gastronomy movement is the energetic alchemist Ferran Adrià, whose revolutionary cooking has made El Bulli the most famous restaurant in the world, and something of a pilgrimage for foodies. He creates startling combinations of taste, temperature and texture to provoke, surprise and delight the diner. Molecular gastronomy is rather a macho phenomenon – boys with their toys in laboratories beside their kitchens. I feel this kind of creation does not have immediate connection to the type of food we do at Ballymaloe, but I nonetheless find it intriguing and exciting.

Raw foodism is another growing movement, promoting the consumption of uncooked, unprocessed and organic foods. It is particularly popular in health- (and image-) conscious parts of the US. While I certainly support eating unprocessed and organic food, I feel this is a challenging regime to follow unless you have ingredients of superb quality at your fingertips.

The Slow Food Movement continues to go from strength to strength – founded in Italy 18 years ago by a group of leftist intellectuals as an antidote to the growing fast food trend, it has developed into a vibrant international movement with more than 100,000 members in 40 countries. The East Cork Slow Food Convivium is based at the Cookery School, and we are proud to host regular events in which the students participate.

The most exciting trend I'm seeing today is in artisan, hand-crafted food made in a time-honoured way – food with a story. Many chefs are growing their own produce in order to have the top-quality ingredients they desire, and the creation of home-cooked flavours such as pickles, jams and jellies (which chefs wouldn't be seen dead cooking some years ago) is really popular. Offal has even become tremendously fashionable as well as cuts of meat such as belly of pork… fat is good again! All sorts of people are curing their own bacon, chorizo and hams. I also think the home-cooked flavours of Poland and other Nordic countries are going to have their moment. And tea is very cool right now. All the trendy places offer an extensive tea menu and we recently had Sean Mahon at the School talking about tea as the 'new black'! I am also seeing a craze for cupcakes!

food & health

As each new food scandal breaks, people are beginning to take food issues more seriously, and question how their food is produced and where it comes from. When I first heard about food allergies in America about 25 years ago, in my ignorance I shrugged my shoulders, dismissing the Americans as neurotic. But now it's difficult to find anyone who doesn't know someone who has lumps or bumps or some sort of rash that can be linked to the food they're eating. Heart disease, cancers, asthma, diabetes and gluten intolerance are all on a rising curve. More and more research links these problems to the food we're eating and how it's produced. It's time to stop and think. We need to find a new way forward. In the words of Lady Eve Balfour: 'Agriculture should be looked on as the primary health service.' Our food should be our medicine.

kitchen safety

1. Keep knives sharp – sharp knives are safer than blunt knives.

2. Never, ever, leave a sharp knife in the sink.

3. Keep your knife by your side as you walk in a busy kitchen otherwise you may inadvertently stab someone if they suddenly reverse into your path.

4. Put a piece of wet kitchen paper underneath your chopping board to prevent it from slipping.

5. Turn handles of saucepans inwards on the cooker top (but not over a hot ring or flame).

6. Do not put wet food into a deep fryer; the water will boil and may cause the deep fryer to overflow and cause a fire.

As chefs, cooks and food handlers, we have a responsibility to operate in a way that does not endanger the health of others. Before you cook, understand the principles of food hygiene and operate to the highest standards at all times. Always wash your hands after a visit to the toilet. Wash your hands before you handle foods and regularly as you cook.

Try to source locally produced food in season, so that it is fresh. If possible, wash vegetables with soil on them in an outside sink. Use separate chopping boards for raw and cooked foods. If you are handling high-risk foods such as intensively produced chicken or pork, wash, scrub and dry the board and knives carefully before using them again. Cloths and tea towels can be a major source of cross contamination in a kitchen so be aware where they hang and how they are used, and change regularly – at least once a day and much more regularly in a busy restaurant kitchen. Ensure that the fridge and freezers are operating to the correct temperature: the fridge at no higher than 5°C, ideally 4°C, and the freezer no higher than –18°C.

Store cooked meat above raw meat in a fridge. It's best to keep food covered as far as possible. This also prevents transfers of flavours. In a restaurant business, you will be required to have separate fridges for different foods, particularly raw and cooked foods. Consult your Environmental Health Officer and local Health Authority for guidelines and regulations for your area.

Washing up

We have big signs all through the kitchens at the School: 'Use the absolute minimum of detergent'. When we use much more than is needed all we are doing is pouring more chemicals than necessary down the drain, bunging up our sewage systems and septic tanks. If possible, have two sinks: wash in one and rinse in the other. Rinsing is really important because the soap residue can be left on the plate and affect the food to be served on it. Use eco-friendly detergent, and only then if you have really greasy plates to wash. If you have a greasy old pan, wipe it out with kitchen paper and then you won't need so much detergent. For a burnt saucepan, put a fistful of salt into it, fill with cold water and gently bring to the boil to loosen the burnt layer. If you have top-quality stainless-steel saucepans, you can use a knife. For some people dishwashers may seem to be a luxury but they do sterilise the crockery and cutlery which in a catering situation is essential. Again, be prudent with detergent and rinse aid – it's rarely necessary to use as much as we think.

Anti-bacterial products

I am also concerned about the numerous products that we are continually encouraged to use by manufacturers who in many ways are capitalising on the public's paranoia about bacteria: 'magic' cleaners, air fresheners and bleaches of every sort are flooding the market. The fact that the use of these products is recommended as best practice by the health authorities is a worry because in my opinion the overuse of them can be counter-productive in several ways. They not only kill off bad bacteria but good ones too, and as a result there is evidence that stronger and stronger strains of bacteria are emerging. These chemicals also lull people into a false sense of security where they imagine that just a squirt will combat the dirt. In reality, the standards of hygiene these days are lower because people rarely roll up their sleeves and scrub into the corners as they used to.

store cupboard basics

Busy people who want to be able to whizz up meals in minutes will need to ensure that their store cupboard is always well stocked. The following are some suggestions for items that we find invaluable.

Store cupboard

onions

garlic

potatoes

carrots

flour: plain, self-raising, strong brown, strong white,
  wholemeal

pitta bread (in the freezer)

tortillas (in the freezer)

cream crackers

pasta: spaghetti, shells, penne, macaroni, noodles

rice: Basmati, Thai fragrant, brown, arborio

grains: oatmeal, couscous, bulgar, polenta,
  quinoa

tinned beans: chickpeas, flageolets, kidney beans,
  black-eyed beans, cannellini beans

tinned fish: sardines, tuna fish, anchovies

tinned sweetcorn

tinned tomatoes

sea salt (preferably Maldon)

black peppercorns

chicken/vegetable stock

extra-virgin olive oil

groundnut oil

sunflower oil

sesame oil

red and white wine vinegar

English mustard powder

French mustard

Ballymaloe Tomato Relish

Ballymaloe Jalapeño Relish

soy sauce (preferably Kikkoman)

harissa or chilli sauce

nam pla (fish sauce)

oyster sauce

plum sauce

olives

pesto

tapenade

salami

chorizo

butter

eggs

cheese: mature Cheddar, Parmesan

whole spices e.g. coriander, cardamom, nutmeg,
  cumin, cloves

nuts: hazelnuts, walnuts, almonds

dried fruit, especially apricots

homemade jam

local honey

marmalade

good-quality chocolate

A few treats

truffle oil

salted capers

Patum Peperium (Gentleman's Relish)

Panneforte di Siena

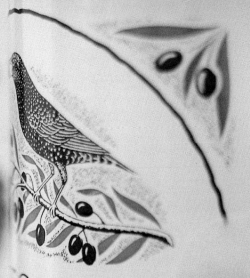

ORNEI

RGIN OLIVE
IC FARMING

_____ System

_ organically grown
_ na Olives

_ BY VEA S.A.
_ NIA, SPAIN

_ ML (25.3 FL.OZ.)

essential kitchen equipment

Knives

1 set of knives: buy the best you can afford

1 chopping knife (cook's or chef's knife)

1 filleting knife

1 vegetable or fruit paring knife

1 serrated vegetable or fruit knife

1 carving knife and 1 carving fork

1 large and 1 small palette knife

Tools

1 swivel-top peeler

1 sharpening steel

1 melon baller (not essential but handy)

1 zester (not essential but handy)

1 meat thermometer (not essential but handy)

1 skewer

1 stainless-steel grater

2 sieves (1 tin or stainless steel, 1 plastic)

1 bottle opener

1 corkscrew

1 perforated spoon

4 wooden spoons (2 large, 1 small, 1 straight ended to get into corners of pans)

2 plastic spatulas (1 large, 1 small)

2 whisks (1 coil, 1 balloon)

2 fish slices (1 plastic, 1 metal)

1 bendy metal spatula (not essential but brilliant)

2 flat pastry brushes

1 piping bag and set of nozzles (not essential but handy)

1 potato masher

1 ladle

1 rolling pin

1 pepper mill

1 salt crock (not essential but handy)

Measuring spoons

1 teaspoon

1 dessertspoon

1 tablespoon

We measure with ordinary spoons that most people have in their kitchen drawers. Unless otherwise stated we measure in rounded spoonfuls – a rounded spoonful has exactly the same amount on top as underneath. A heaped teaspoon has as much of the ingredient as the spoon will hold. A level teaspoon is just that and is the equivalent of a half rounded teaspoon. If you are using standard measuring spoons, always use level measurements. Our rounded measurements are the exact equivalent of a level measuring spoon. Also note that our tablespoon is the equivalent of four teaspoons whereas a standard measuring spoon holds just three teaspoons.

Boards

2 heavy wooden chopping boards

1 small garlic board (not essential but handy)

Mark the boards so that you know which surface to use. Of the first board, mark one side for raw meat and the other for onions. Of the second board, mark one side for cooked food and the other for fruit. If you have just one chopping board, mark one side 'R' for raw and 'O' for onion and garlic and the other side 'C' for cooked food and 'F' for fruit.

Saucepans

Buy the best heavy stainless steel saucepans you can afford. Some have a 50-year guarantee and you will be able to pass them onto your grandchildren. They don't burn or stick and do wonders for your cooking and your temper!

1 large saucepan and lid

1 medium saucepan and lid

1 small saucepan and lid

1 high-sided sauté pan

1 low-sided sauté pan

1 small saucepan (for boiling eggs, not essential but handy)

1 large casserole with lid

1 oval casserole with lid

1 small oval casserole with lid

1 non-stick frying pan

1 iron pan

1 grill-pan

Tins

1 quiche tin with removable base (size to fit requirements)

1 tart tin (size to fit requirements)

1 Swiss roll tin

Bowls

1 set of 5 stainless-steel mixing bowls, graded sizes

1 set of 3 Pyrex bowls, graded sizes

3–4 plastic bowls

1 Pyrex plate for tarts (not essential but handy)

1 pie dish

2 Pyrex measuring jugs

Machines

1 juicer (electric if possible for large quantities)

1 food processor

1 food mixer or hand-held mixer

1 liquidiser

1 coffee grinder

1 spice grinder

Indulgent but great!

dishwasher

pasta rolling machine

using the freezer

Freezing can be a very successful method of preserving food. It retains more of the quality, character and nutritive value of the food than methods such as bottling, canning and drying. Nonetheless as a guiding principle you should only freeze food when essential – it does not *improve* its quality.

Buy the smallest freezer possible. If you buy one larger than you need you will be tempted to fill it to capacity and unless you are supremely well-organised, much of the food you put in it will be forgotten about and eventually thrown away.

A full freezer costs less to run than a half empty one. The faster the food is frozen the smaller the ice crystals will be. Large ice crystals which result from slow freezing damage the cell walls of the food meaning that juice and soluble nutrients are lost when the food is thawed.

A home freezer is normally kept at –18°C. At this temperature both pathogenic and food spoilage micro-organisms are dormant. However, over time, an enzyme action takes place which results in the gradual deterioration of quality, flavour and colour. For that reason it is a good maxim to get food in and out of the freezer as fast as is practical.

Guidelines for freezing food

1. Food must be in perfect condition before it is frozen. Stale or contaminated food will not be improved by freezing.

2. Do not freeze more than one-tenth of the capacity of your freezer in 24 hours.

3. Use your freezer intelligently. Freeze pasta sauces, stews and soups in two-portion tubs that can be defrosted in a matter of 10 minutes. That way you'll never be stuck when impromptu guests show up. Food should be packed in small packets and should be separated while freezing in order to allow the cold air to circulate around them.

4. For best results the freezer should be set at the lowest temperature or 'super freeze' for 8–12 hours before freezing, particularly meat and vegetables. The packs should be put into the coldest compartment of the freezer. Once frozen, pack them tightly in an appropriate part of the freezer.

5. Do not put anything slightly warm into the freezer as it will bring up the temperature and may cause other foods to deteriorate slightly.

6. Vegetables freeze very well but should be cooked immediately after they are thawed. They may be frozen without blanching but their storage time will be much less, so for that reason it is worth blanching and refreshing green vegetables first to prevent enzyme activity.

7. If at all possible 'tray freeze' vegetables and fruit to keep them separate. This is done by spreading the fruit or blanched and refreshed vegetables in a single layer on a tray, they will then freeze individually and can be packed into bags or boxes. If food is 'tray frozen' first it will be less damaged and will thaw more quickly later.

Foods that benefit from being tray frozen include homemade sausages or sausage rolls, cheese croquettes, stuffed pancakes, filo pastry, hamburgers and bread rolls. Cakes should be frozen until the decoration is hard and then wrapped.

Foods that do not freeze well

Some foods cannot be successfully frozen because their texture can be spoiled by freezing, e.g. foods with a high water content. However, in some cases they may be used in soups, purées or jams.

1. Eggs cannot be frozen in the shell. Egg whites freeze very well; 25g (1oz) = 1 egg white when using them later. They will keep for up to 6 months in the freezer. Lightly whisked whole egg also freezes well. Egg yolks are not so successful. Hard-boiled eggs become tough and the white turns grey. Egg custard will separate in a freezer.

2. Cheese: Hard cheese or blue-veined cheese freeze well, either grated or in a piece. Cottage and cream cheese are not very satisfactory frozen. Camembert or Brie can be frozen but they should be ripened first.

3. Cream will separate if frozen unless it has been slightly whipped first.

4. Mayonnaise, Hollandaise, Béarnaise Sauce do not freeze well; like egg custard, they tend to separate when thawed.

5. Roux-based sauces freeze fairly well. Whisk slightly during reheating if possible. It's also a good idea to err on the side of having the sauce a little too thin rather than too thick, then a little extra roux can be whisked in during reheating.

6. Gelatine-based desserts e.g. mousses, soufflés and cheesecakes may be frozen but become slightly rubbery. They should be used within a month. Jellies, both sweet and savoury, lose their texture when frozen.

7. Melon has too high a water content for successful freezing.

8. Strawberries keep their colour and flavour well, but collapse when thawed. However, if you have a glut, the good varieties are still worth freezing to make jams, sorbets and fruit coulis.

9. Tomatoes may be frozen whole but, like strawberries, lose their structure when thawed. However, they are very useful for soups and stews and have the great advantage that they peel easily if dropped in cold or hot water for a few seconds. We freeze large quantities of tomato purée and find it invaluable.

10. Mashed potato may be piped around pre-prepared meat and fish dishes and frozen quite successfully. Potatoes cooked whole go leathery.

11. Foods with a very high fat content go rancid after several months in the freezer.

Wrapping

All food should be carefully wrapped before freezing. If food is not properly wrapped it will dry out and get 'freezer burn', this looks dry and unattractive although the food may still be safe to eat.

1. Good-quality plastic bags or plastic boxes should be used.

2. Recycled food containers e.g. ice-cream, yoghurt, milk or margarine cartons can be used but must be thoroughly cleaned first. Liquids, such as stock, can be poured into polythene bags and put into square plastic containers and frozen, remove later and easily stacked. We use 2 litre (3½ pint) plastic milk cartons for stock; they are 'free' and if you are in a hurry you can just cut the container without too many guilt pangs. Do not fill right to the top: allow a little space for expansion when freezing liquids.

Labelling

1. Label all packs going into the freezer with name, date and where appropriate, weight.

2. Keep a record of the content of the freezer in a book or on a chart. We use a large chart divided into sections roughly corresponding to where the food is kept in the freezer. Headings will vary according to your lifestyle. Ours are:

Soups

Meat – cooked

Vegetables – cooked

Fish – cooked

Stocks

Pastry

Cakes and biscuits

Ice-creams and sorbets

Miscellaneous – e.g. breadcrumbs, pine nuts, coffee beans

Food we find convenient to have in the freezer

Soups and stocks

Puff and filo pastry

Fresh nuts, coffee beans and breadcrumbs

Ice-creams and sorbets

Cooked dishes with piped potatoes e.g. Ham Morvandelle,
    Plaice with Mussels and Shrimps, Scallops Mornay,
    Spiced Lamb Pies, Stews, Vegetable Stews, Piperonata,
    Tomato Fondue etc...

Flan cases

A cake or two and maybe scones

A loaf or two of white yeast bread

Cheese biscuits

Thawing and re-freezing food

The safest way to thaw frozen food is in a fridge. Some foods may be cooked from frozen, but it is essential, particularly for meat, to ensure that it is fully cooked.

All poultry must be completely thawed before being cooked. A 1.3kg (3lb) chicken will take about 9 hours to thaw fully, whereas a 6kg (13.5lb) turkey will take 24 hours. It is now recommended to thaw poultry at room temperature. I still feel that a fridge is safer.

People worry about re-freezing food and indeed it is good to err on the side of being cautious. However, partially frozen food may be re-frozen provided it still has ice crystals in it. Thawed stocks should be reboiled for 5 minutes and allowed to get quite cold before re-freezing. Meat can be defrosted and then cooked, e.g. in a stew and then refrozen without any danger. Breadcrumbs may be re-frozen without ill effect.

Emergencies

1. Power cuts

In the event of a power cut, do nothing. Provided your freezer is fairly full, food should stay frozen for at least 12 hours. At all costs, resist the temptation to keep peeping in to check because you will allow warm air into the freezer and so speed up the defrosting.

It is well worth the effort to put a note on the freezer plug to make sure that no one turns it off by accident. Put masking tape over the plug.

2. Electrical faults

In the case of an electrical fault, telephone the service engineer, most companies have a 24-hour answering service for freezer owners.

3. Moving house

Ask the removers to transport the locked freezer fully loaded to your new house. Check there is an appropriate socket to plug it into when it arrives. The freezer should be last on and first off the removal van. Contents of the freezer should keep in perfectly good condition for 9–10 hours.

wine essentials by Mary Dowey

Now that wine is an everyday pleasure for so many people, anybody capable of rustling up the most casual supper needs to know the basics. It's important to understand how to buy wisely, how to store wine in the best conditions and how to serve it with confidence and style. More rewarding still is the process of learning about food-and-wine matching. And it may be useful to have some idea about the latest wine trends.

First, a few words about buying wine. Avoid the very cheapest. Think of the costs that find their way into every bottle: taxes, transportation, packaging, marketing, trade margins. In an extremely inexpensive bottle, the value of the wine itself will account for only a small fraction of the total. That is why so many so-called 'bargains' are bad buys. By paying just a little bit more, you may well end up with a bottle in which the wine itself is worth twice as much – simply because so many of those ancillary costs are fixed. At the other end of the spectrum, expensive wines aren't always as memorable as their hefty price tag might suggest. The law of supply and demand exerts a grim influence on the upper end of the market. For the best price:value ratio, the middle ground is often the most fruitful. When you do find a wine that you really like, consider buying it by the case as most wine merchants offer a case discount.

Although research indicates that over 90 per cent of wine is purchased to be consumed almost instantly, prudent cooks will probably plan a little further ahead. This being so, it is important to store wine carefully, including in the short term. It needs a cool, even temperature – ideally between 10–15°C (19–22°F), but a slightly higher temperature should do no harm, provided there are no major fluctuations. Light and vibrations also damage wine so put it somewhere not just cool but dark – well away from the hum of the heating system.

Glasses play a key role in the enjoyment of wine. Wine lovers like to see the colour of their drink clearly so that they can admire its depth or ponder the clues it gives to the wine's age. For this reason, plain, clear glass is preferable to cut crystal; coloured glass gets an emphatic thumbs-down. Glass shape is equally crucial. Since more of the sensory pleasure of wine comes from its smell than its taste (try drinking with a clothes peg on your nose if you doubt that), the drinker should be able to release the precious aromas by swirling the wine around. This is only possible with a glass that tapers in a little at the top, holding both the swirling liquid and its evanescent perfume in place. Pick tulips, in other words, rather than lilies! The glasses made by the specialist Austrian manufacturer Riedel are considered impeccable in terms of shape, weight and style.

Although many producers are now sealing their wines with screwcaps, synthetic closures or the elegant glass Vinolok stopper to avoid the risk of cork taint (more about this below), traditional corks are still widely used – so it's worth investing in a good corkscrew. Before you use it, remove the top of the foil from the metal capsule on the bottle with a foil cutter or pen-knife. When the cork has been drawn, pour a little wine into your own glass first and have a serious sniff before serving anybody else. If it is corked (as an estimated 5 per cent of wines currently are) it will smell slightly musty – like damp cardboard or a dank garden shed. Next have a good sip, because true cork taint will make a wine taste even mustier than it smells.

If the wine seems fine, start pouring – taking care not to fill glasses more than half full despite your generous impulses. The pleasurable sniffing and swirling ritual is simply impossible with a well-filled glass. Remember to hold the bottle with the label uppermost so that your guests can see what they are about to drink. Drips can be prevented by giving the bottle a quick turn to the right just as you stop pouring.

I have left decanting to the end of this brief gallop through the main points about serving wine because relatively few wines need to be decanted. Only the oldest and youngest call for this procedure – which isn't half as complicated as it sounds. Mature red wines and vintage ports are decanted in order to separate the wine from any sediment which has accumulated at the bottom of the bottle. As very old wines tend to be fragile, it is best not to decant them until just before they are to be drunk. Pour the wine slowly into the decanter, stopping the second you see that sediment is about to come out. (Purists hold a candle or light beneath the bottle as they pour, to see this more clearly.)

Young wines which still taste astringent also benefit from decanting. Exposing them to the air during pouring helps to soften them and open them up. All you have to do is empty the bottle into a jug, then pour the wine back into its bottle. This achieves far more than the standard practice of opening a wine a few hours before use and leaving the bottle 'to breathe'. Since the area of wine exposed to the air is no bigger than a coin, not much breathing is done!

Too much exposure to air does wine no favours. Leftovers deteriorate fairly quickly. White wines usually taste less appealing after a single day; red wines survive better, often keeping well for several days. For best results, decant leftovers into a clean half bottle or quarter bottle, filling it to the neck to reduce air contact. If this is not possible, using a wine vacuum pump and rubber bung to remove the air from a half-empty bottle is better than nothing. (Vacuvin is the leading brand.) Another useful tip is to freeze leftover wine in ice cube trays. Wine cubes, stored in plastic bags in the freezer, can be useful when you need to add a drop of wine to a sauce.

Now to the most fascinating aspect of wine – its potential to enhance the flavours of food. The principle sounds devastatingly simple. Pair the right bottle with the right dish and you have instant magic – a blissful fusion of complementary flavours. Choose the wrong wine – one which just doesn't go with the food – and both dish and drink taste lacklustre.

With so many wine grapes and wine styles, all with their distinctive flavours – not to mention the infinite variety of tastes coming our way from the global kitchen – picking successful partnerships can seem complicated. Books and articles have been written explaining at painful length all the factors which should be borne in mind when attempting this mating game – sweetness, acidity, tannin, and so on. My view is that, rather than get bogged down in theory, it's best to follow a few basic principles, along with the instincts which your tastebuds will soon help you to develop.

The first thing to think about is weight – light wines with light foods, heavier wines with heavier foods. Lobster, for instance, will suit a much richer white wine than would a delicate fish like plaice – choose something like a buttery, oaked new-world Chardonnay rather than a crisp and elegant Chablis. Depending on how they are cooked, meaty fish like salmon and tuna may taste better with a light red wine (a young Pinot Noir, perhaps) than with a white of any kind. (This is especially true if, for instance, the salmon is seared in pungent spices, or the tuna served with a robust Mediterranean sauce.) The more substantial a dish, the greater the need will be for a substantial wine. Take venison, for example. Those intense, gamey flavours which would overpower a light or medium-bodied red meet their match in the heavy hitters of the wine world – a strapping Australian Shiraz or a gloriously rich Amarone.

After you have thought about weight, consider the main flavours on the plate and try to choose a wine that will complement them. The herbaceous tang of Sauvignon Blanc brilliantly echoes the grassy character of young goat's cheese. The touch of sweetness in a generously fruity white wine like Viognier perfectly parallels the element of sweetness in crab. Peppery red Zinfandel picks up on the punchy flavours in spicy sausages, with all the roundness and lusciousness that spice needs to slip down comfortably with wine. Indian, Chinese and Thai dishes, often laden with chillies, ginger, spices and other pungent ingredients, go best with wines that are fruitier and a touch sweeter than you might normally choose.

On the whole, white wines work better than reds with hot and spicy dishes, particularly with Thai food. New World blends of Semillon and Sauvignon and the richer Australian Rieslings are worth trying, but so too is an Alsace Pinot Gris and ample southern French versions of Marsanne, Roussanne or Viognier. The hottest Indian dishes, especially those involving meat, taste best with round, fruity New World reds. Indeed, it's worth remembering that New World wines are generally more spice- and fusion-friendly than their European counterparts.

Eggs can be difficult with wine, particularly when still slightly runny, because the yolk coats the tongue. A good excuse to splash out on champagne or a good sparkling wine: both have marvellous palate-cleansing properties. Chinese food is often accused of a similar tongue-coating effect. The same painless remedy works!

At the sweet end of the menu, chocolate is sometimes viewed as problematic – but usually only by people who haven't yet sampled it with sweet red wines. Try a wickedly rich, dark chocolate pud with Banyuls or Maury, the Grenache-based sweet reds from Roussillon in the south of France, or with a glass of Late Bottled Vintage port, and see how much better it tastes than with a sweet white wine like Sauternes.

At least, that's what I think. The most important thing is for you to make up your own mind. Keep experimenting with new combinations – not difficult when wine producers the world over are experimenting themselves with different grapes and different styles. A fashion pendulum swings through the wine world with surprising force. When the first edition of this book was published the 'big four' grape varieties, Chardonnay, Sauvignon Blanc, Cabernet Sauvignon and Merlot, were almost inescapable. Although these are still popular, Rhône varieties, especially Syrah/Shiraz, are now moving centre stage, along with Pinot Noir, while the Spanish red grapes Tempranillo and Garnacha wave from the wings. Among the whites, Riesling and Pinot Gris are on the rise internationally while Austria makes a splash with Grüner Veltliner. Rosé of all

descriptions is back in fashion – thank goodness, as it is so food-friendly. And we're all drinking more sparkling wines, especially Italy's light, frothy prosecco.

Lightness – there's another new trend. After two decades during which the success of ripe, fruity New World wines encouraged producers everywhere to pick their grapes later – resulting in higher sugar levels, hence higher alcohol – a reaction has set in. Soon we will see more wines of 12–13 per cent alcohol by volume and fewer at the 13–14.5 per cent level which has become the norm. Most wine enthusiasts will be happy to see lighter, more elegant styles replacing head-splitting blockbusters.

This reversal has been prompted partly by mounting concern about alcohol consumption. Yes, wine can carry certain health benefits – but only when drunk in moderation and preferably with food. What does moderation mean? Most medical authorities suggest a maximum of 21 units of alcohol per week for men and 14 units per week for women. Since an average glass of an average wine today typically equates to at least 1.5 units of alcohol, it is remarkably easy to exceed the 'safe' guidelines without feeling remotely guilty of excess. Lower alcohol levels allow a little more leeway – but your liver still needs at least one alcohol-free day a week for its well-being.

On a more cheerful note, wine lovers stand to gain from the steady growth of organic and biodynamic wines. More and more producers are abandoning the use of chemical fertilisers and pesticides in the vineyard and a long list of permitted additives in the cellar. While the health benefits of this approach seem beyond doubt, the purity of flavour achieved by the most skilled is unquestionably life-enhancing.

So let's remember the deeply rooted belief of Anselme Brillat-Savarin, the famous French epicurean who paved the way for modern food writers over 200 years ago: 'A meal without wine is like a day without sunshine.' More than any other drink, this one is fascinating, reviving, civilising.

stocks & soups

Making stock is really just an attitude of mind. Instead of absent-mindedly flinging things into the bin, keep your carcasses, giblets and vegetable trimmings and use them for your stock pot. Nowadays some supermarkets and poulterers are happy to give you chicken carcasses and often giblets as well, just for the asking, because there is so little demand. I personally like to use the carcasses of free-range organic poultry which have not had hormones, antibiotics, bone strengtheners or antidepressants in their feed.

General Stock-making Tips

Stock will keep for several days in the refrigerator. If you need to keep it for longer, boil it up again for 5–6 minutes every couple of days; allow it to get cold and refrigerate again. Stock also freezes perfectly. Use large yoghurt cartons or plastic milk bottles – you can cut them off the frozen stock without a conscience if you need to defrost it in a hurry!

In restaurants, the stock is usually allowed to simmer uncovered so it will be as clear as possible but we advise people to cover the pot when making stock at home, otherwise the whole house is likely to smell of stock and that may put you off making it on a regular basis.

Chicken livers shouldn't go into the stock pot because they become bitter on prolonged cooking. Unsuitable vegetables include potatoes (they soak up flavour and make the stock cloudy); parsnips (too strong); beetroot (too strong also, and the dye would turn the stock red); cabbage or other brassicas (they give an off-taste when cooked for a long time). A little white turnip is sometimes an asset, but it is very easy to overdo. I also ban bay leaves from my chicken stocks because I find that the flavour can predominate and make different soups made from the stock all taste the same. Salt is another ingredient that you will not find in my stock recipes. Why? Because, if I want to reduce the stock later to make a sauce, it can become incredibly salty.

Vegetable Stock

Makes about 1.75 litres (3 pints)

This is just a rough guide – you can use whatever vegetables you have available except those listed to the left, but don't use too much of any one vegetable unless you want that flavour to predominate.

1 small white turnip
2 onions, roughly sliced
green parts of 2–3 leeks
3 sticks celery, washed and roughly chopped
3 large carrots, scrubbed and roughly chopped
½ fennel bulb, roughly chopped
110g (4oz) mushrooms or mushroom stalks
4–6 parsley stalks
bouquet garni
a few peppercorns
2.3 litres (4 pints) cold water

Put all the ingredients into a large saucepan, add the cold water, bring to the boil, then reduce the heat, cover and allow to simmer for 1–2 hours. Strain through a sieve.

Master Recipe
Chicken Stock

Makes about 3 litres (5 pints)

2–3 raw or cooked chicken carcasses (or both)
giblets from the chicken, i.e. neck, heart, gizzard (save the liver for another dish)
1 onion, sliced
1 leek, split in two
1 outside stick of celery or 1 lovage leaf
1 carrot, sliced
a few parsley stalks
sprig of thyme
6 peppercorns
3.6 litres (6 pints) cold water

Chop up the carcasses as much as possible. Put all the ingredients into a saucepan and cover with cold water. Bring to the boil and skim off any surface fat with a tablespoon. Simmer for 3–5 hours. Strain and remove any remaining fat. If you need a stronger flavour, boil down the liquid in an open pan to reduce by one-third to one-half the volume. Do not add salt.

> TIP: If you have just one carcass and do not want to make a small quantity of stock, freeze it and when you have saved up 6–7 carcasses plus giblets, you can make a really big pot of stock and get good value from your fuel.

Turkey Stock

Make in the same way as chicken stock, and use in turkey or chicken recipes.

Game Stock

Make in the same way as chicken stock; use appropriately.

Goose and Duck Stock

Make in the same way as chicken stock. Some chefs like to brown the carcasses first to produce darker stock with a richer flavour. Use in goose and duck recipes.

Master Recipe
Brown Beef Stock

Makes about 4 litres (7 pints)

2.3–2.75kg (5–6lb) beef bones, preferably with some scraps of meat on, cut into small pieces
3 large onions, quartered
3 large carrots, quartered
4 stalks celery, cut into 2.5cm (1in) pieces
large bouquet garni, including parsley stalks, sprigs of thyme, a bay leaf and sprig of tarragon
10 peppercorns
2 cloves
4 garlic cloves, unpeeled
1 teaspoon tomato purée
5 litres (8¾ pints) water

Preheat the oven to 230°C/450°F/gas 8. Put the bones into a roasting tin and roast for 30 minutes or until well browned. Add the onions, carrots and celery and return to the oven until the vegetables are also browned. Transfer the bones and vegetables to the stock pot with a metal spoon. Add the bouquet garni, peppercorns, cloves, garlic and tomato purée. De-grease the roasting pan and de-glaze with some water, bring to the boil and pour over the bones and vegetables. Add the rest of the water and bring slowly to the boil. Skim the fat off the stock and simmer gently for 5–6 hours. Strain, allow to cool, and skim any remaining fat off before use.

Veal Stock

Make the same way as Brown Beef Stock. Use for dishes such as Osso Buco.

Lamb Stock

Make in the same way as Brown Beef Stock. Use for lamb dishes such as Irish Stew.

Master Recipe
Basic Fish Stock

Makes about 1.75 litres (3 pints)

Takes only 20 minutes to make. If you can get lots of nice fresh fish bones from your fishmonger, it's well worth making two or three times this stock recipe, because it freezes perfectly. You will then have fish stock at the ready.

900g (2lb) fish bones, preferably sole, turbot or brill
7–15g (¼–½oz) butter
110g (4oz) onions, finely sliced
125–225ml (4–8fl oz) dry white wine
2.3 litres (4 pints) cold water
4 peppercorns
large bouquet garni containing sprig of thyme, 4–5 parsley stalks, small piece of celery and a tiny scrap of bay leaf

Wash the fish bones thoroughly under cold running water until no traces of blood remain, and chop into pieces. In a large stainless steel saucepan, melt the butter, add the onions, toss and sweat over a gentle heat until soft, but not coloured. Add the bones to the pan, stir and cook very briefly with the onions. Add the dry white wine and boil until nearly all the wine has evaporated. Cover with cold water, add the peppercorns and bouquet garni. Bring to the boil and simmer for 20 minutes, skimming often. Strain. Allow to cool, de-grease if necessary and refrigerate.

Household Fish Stock

Fish heads with the gills removed, fish skin and shellfish or mollusc shells, if available, may be added to the fish stock. It will be slightly darker in colour and less delicate in flavour. Cook for 30 minutes.

Shellfish Stock

A selection of crustacean and mollusc shells, e.g. prawns, shrimps, mussels, crab or lobster may be used. Cook for 30 minutes.

Demi-glaze

Reduce the strained fish stock by half to intensify the flavour, chill and refrigerate or freeze.

Glace de Poisson

Reduce the stock until it becomes thick and syrupy, then chill. It will set into a firm jelly which has a very concentrated fish flavour – excellent for adding to fish sauces or soups to enhance the flavour.

Master Recipe
Light Dashi

Dashi (bonito fish stock) is essential in many Japanese dishes. It provides a savoury flavour which cannot be attained by using seasoning only and it is much easier to make than meat or fish stock. The two main ingredients are the bonito flakes and konbu, a member of the kelp family that grows to amazing heights – some of 450m (1500ft) have been known. There is a really distinctive smell of the sea to this stock. Bonito flakes are sold dried. Konbu is also available in dried form.

425ml (¾ pint) water
10cm (4in) piece konbu (dried kelp)
5–7g (⅛–¼oz) dried bonito flakes

Wipe and clean the konbu with a dry cloth. Do not wipe off the white powder on the surface, as that is the one element that provides a unique savoury flavour.

Put the water in a saucepan and soak the konbu for 30 minutes before turning on the heat. Remove any scum that forms on the surface. When the water begins to bubble, just before boiling, take out the konbu. Do not overcook or it will become slimy and the flavour of the stock too strong. Add the bonito flakes, bring back to the boil, turn off the heat and set aside until the bonito flakes sink to the bottom. Strain through very fine muslin and discard the bonito flakes. Use fresh or freeze immediately.

Heavy Dashi

Follow the Master Recipe but increase the quantity of bonito flakes to 15–25g (½–1oz) and the water to 1.5 litres (2½ pints). Add two thirds of the bonito flakes and simmer the mixture uncovered for 20 minutes. Add the remaining bonito flakes and proceed as above. Keeps in the fridge for 3 days.

Instant Dashi

Instant dashi can be found in the form of a liquid extract as well as a powder. Just dissolve a liquid dashi or powdered dashi in boiling water. But the flavour is far from that of homemade dashi.

Bouquet Garni

A small bunch of fresh herbs used to flavour stews, casseroles, stocks or soups, usually consisting of parsley stalks, a sprig of thyme, perhaps a bay leaf and an outside stalk of celery, tied together with a little string. Sometimes chefs tie the bouquet garni to the handle of the saucepan for easy removal. Take out before serving.

Basic Chinese Stock

Makes about 2 litres (3½ pints)

This stock forms the essential basis of many delicious light fish or meat soups.

900g (2lb) chicken giblets, wings, necks, hearts, gizzards etc.
900g (2lb) pork spare ribs (or a total of 1.8kg (4lb) either chicken pieces or ribs)
4cm (1½in) fresh ginger root, unpeeled and thinly sliced
6 large spring onions
4.8–6 litres (8–10 pints) light Chicken Stock (see page 36)
4 tablespoons Shao Hsing rice wine

Put all the ingredients except the rice wine in a large saucepan and cover with cold water. Bring to the boil and skim off any scum. Reduce the heat, cover and simmer gently for about 4 hours, skimming regularly. Add the rice wine 5 minutes before the end of the cooking time. Strain the stock, cool, then refrigerate.

Remove the solidified fat from the top of the stock before use. The stock will keep in the refrigerator for several days; thereafter boil it every 2 or 3 days. It also freezes perfectly.

Ballymaloe Basic Vegetable Soup Technique

Well over half the soups we make at Ballymaloe are made to this simple ratio – 1:1:3:4.

1 part onion
1 part potato
3 parts any vegetable, or a mixture of vegetables
4 parts stock, a mixture of stock and milk, or water
seasoning

Chopping Fresh Herbs

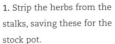

1. Strip the herbs from the stalks, saving these for the stock pot.

Use a very sharp chef's knife or chopping knife. The herbs should be dry, otherwise they will bruise as they are chopped.

2. Gather the herbs into a little ball on the chopping board with your fingers. Using your knuckles as a guide, keep the tip of the chef's knife on the board and slide the knife forward to chop the herbs roughly.

3. Then change the angle of the knife to a horizontal position. Hold the tip and continue to move the blade backwards and forwards until the herbs are chopped to the required texture. Use the blade of the knife to lift the chopped herbs off the board.

Note: A Chinese chopper or a mezzaluna is also excellent for chopping. This two-handled Italian blade is used in a rocking movement backwards and forwards across the board.

You can use chicken or vegetable stock, and season simply with salt and freshly ground pepper. Complementary fresh herbs or spices may also be added. Don't weigh the ingredients; it is their volume that is important rather than their weight – we use a 225ml (8fl oz) cup to measure out all the ingredients.

The great advantage is that you can make an enormous repertoire of different soups depending on what's fresh, in season and available. If potatoes and onions are the only option, it's still possible to make two delicious soups by increasing one or the other, and then adding one or several herbs. We have even used broad bean tops, radish leaves and nettles in season.

Example

Serves 6

50g (2oz) butter
1 cup potatoes, peeled and cut into 1cm (½in) cubes
1 cup onions, cut into 1cm (½in) cubes
salt and freshly ground pepper
3 cups vegetables of your choice, cut into 1cm (⅓in) cubes
4 cups homemade Chicken Stock (see page 36), or stock and creamy milk

Melt the butter in a heavy saucepan. When it foams, add the potatoes and onions, and turn them until well coated. Sprinkle with salt and pepper. Cover and sweat on a gentle heat for 10 minutes. Add the vegetables and stock. Boil until soft, liquidise, sieve or put through a mouli. Do not overcook or the vegetables will lose their flavour. Adjust the seasoning.

Master Recipe
Potato and Fresh Herb Soup

Serves 6

Most people have potatoes and onions in the house even when the cupboard is otherwise bare, so this delicious soup can be made at a moment's notice. While the vegetables are sweating, pop a few White Soda Scones or Cheddar Cheese Scones (page 476) into the oven and wow – won't everybody be impressed.

50g (2oz) butter
425g (15oz) potatoes, peeled and cut into 1cm (½in) cubes
110g (4oz) onions, cut into 1cm (½in) cubes
1 teaspoon salt
freshly ground pepper
1–2 tablespoons in total of the following: freshly chopped parsley, thyme, lemon balm, chives
850ml (1½ pints) homemade Chicken or Vegetable Stock (see page 36)
125ml (4fl oz) creamy milk

Garnish
herbs, freshly chopped, and some chive or thyme flowers in season

Melt the butter in a heavy saucepan. When it foams, add the potatoes and onions, and toss them in the butter until well coated. Sprinkle with salt and a few grinds of pepper. Cover with a butter wrapper or paper lid and the lid of the saucepan. Sweat over a gentle heat for about 10 minutes. Meanwhile, bring the stock to the boil. When the vegetables are soft but not coloured, add the freshly chopped herbs and stock, and continue to cook until the vegetables are soft. Purée the soup in a blender or food processor. Taste and adjust the seasoning. Thin with creamy milk to the required consistency. Garnish and serve.

Variations
Potato and Lovage Soup
Follow the Master Recipe, using just lovage, and garnish with freshly snipped lovage.

Potato and Parsley Soup
Follow the Master Recipe, omitting the herbs and adding 2–3 tablespoons of freshly chopped parsley just before blending.

Potato Soup with Parsley Pesto
My chef brother Rory O'Connell embellishes potato soup by drizzling a little Parsley Pesto (see page 589) over the top of each bowl just as it goes to the table.

Potato and Mint Soup
Follow the Master Recipe, omitting the herbs and adding 2–3 tablespoons chopped spearmint or Bowles' mint just before blending. Serve with a little Mint Cream (see page 386).

Potato and Tarragon Soup
Follow the Master Recipe, omitting the herbs and instead adding 1½ tablespoons of tarragon to the soup with the stock. Purée and finish as in the Master Recipe. Sprinkle a little fresh tarragon over the soup. A zig zag of soft cream is also delicious.

Potato, Chorizo and Parsley Soup
Follow the Master Recipe, omitting the herbs. Just before serving, cook about 18 slices of chorizo for a minute or two on each side on a non-stick pan. Serve 3 slices of chorizo on top of each bowl with a few sprigs of flat-leaf parsley and a few drops of chorizo oil. Serve immediately.

Potato and Melted Leek Soup
Follow the Master Recipe, but serve a teaspoonful of Melted Leeks (see page 173) on top of each helping. Scatter with snipped chives and chive flowers in season.

Potato and Smoky Bacon Soup
Follow the Master Recipe, omitting the herbs, and add 150g (5oz) smoky bacon cut into lardons and fried until crisp.

Potato and Roasted Red Pepper Soup
Potato and Fresh Herb Soup (see Master Recipe)
4 red peppers

Garnish
sprigs of flat-leaf parsley

Follow the Master Recipe, omitting the herbs.

Roast or chargrill the peppers, then peel and de-seed them, saving the sweet juices carefully. Purée the flesh with the juices. Taste and adjust the seasoning if necessary. Just before serving, swirl the red pepper purée through the soup or simply drizzle on top of each bowl. Top with some parsley. You might try adding one or two roast chillies to the pepper for a little extra buzz – Serrano or Jalapeño are good.

Winter Leek and Potato Soup

Serves 6–8

50g (2oz) butter
450g (1lb) potatoes, peeled and finely diced
110g (4oz) onions, finely diced
350g (12oz) white parts of the leeks, sliced (save the green tops for another soup or stock)
salt and freshly ground pepper
850ml (1½ pints) light homemade Chicken Stock (see page 36)
125ml (4fl oz) cream
125ml (4fl oz) milk

Garnish
chives, finely chopped
cream

Melt the butter in a heavy saucepan. When it foams, add the potatoes, onions and leeks, turning them in the butter until well coated. Sprinkle with salt and pepper. Cover with a paper lid (to keep in the steam) and the saucepan lid. Sweat on a gentle heat for 10 minutes or until the vegetables are soft but not coloured. Discard the paper lid. Add the stock, bring to the boil and simmer until the vegetables are just cooked. Do not overcook or the vegetables will lose their flavour. Liquidise until smooth and silky, then taste and adjust the seasoning. Add cream or creamy milk to taste. Garnish with swirls of cream and chives.

Chopping an Onion

1. Cut the onion in half from top to bottom.

2. Peel back the skin and trim the base but leave the root intact to hold the onion together as it is chopped.

3. Lay one half of the onion cut-side down on a chopping board.

4. With a sharp knife, make a series of horizontal cuts towards but not through the root. (The thickness of the slices will determine the size of the dice.)

5. Then, with the tip of the knife just in front of the root, cut the onion lengthways, almost to the root but not through it.

6. Finally, using your knuckles as a guide, cut the onion crossways into dice.

Note: If the chopped onion is not to be cooked immediately put the dice into a sieve and run under cold water to halt the enzyme action which gradually turns a cut onion sour. Otherwise the flavour of the dish you plan to cook may be spoilt.

Irish Colcannon Soup

Serves 6

Colcannon is one of Ireland's best loved traditional dishes – made from fluffy mashed potato flecked with cooked cabbage or kale. Here the same ingredients are used to make a delicious soup.

50g (2oz) butter
425g (15oz) potatoes, peeled and cut into 1cm (½in) cubes
110g (4oz) onions, diced
salt and freshly ground pepper
1.2 litres (2 pints) homemade Chicken or Vegetable Stock (see page 36)
450g (1lb) cabbage
25g (1oz) butter plus a knob
125ml (4fl oz) creamy milk

Melt the butter in a heavy saucepan. When it foams, add the potatoes and onions and toss them in the butter until well coated. Sprinkle with salt and pepper. Cover and sweat over a gentle heat for 10 minutes, add the stock, bring to the boil and simmer until the vegetables are soft.

Meanwhile make the buttered cabbage. Remove the tough outer leaves. Divide the cabbage into 4, cut out the stalks and finely shred across the grain. Put 2–3 tablespoons of water into a wide saucepan with the second quantity of butter and a pinch of salt. Bring to the boil, add the cabbage and toss constantly over a high heat, then cover for a few minutes. Toss again, add some more salt, freshly ground pepper and a knob of butter. Add the cabbage to the soup, then purée in a blender or food processor. Taste and adjust the seasoning.

Thin with creamy milk to the required consistency.

Potato and Sweetcorn Chowder

Serves 4–6

A satisfying and filling soup made in a short time. This could become a supper dish if eaten with a few scones and followed by a salad.

25g (1oz) butter
2–3 medium potatoes, parboiled for 10 minutes, drained, peeled and finely chopped
175g (6oz) onion, finely chopped
300ml (½ pint) homemade Chicken Stock (see page 36)
300ml (½ pint) milk
450g (1lb) sweetcorn kernels
salt and freshly ground pepper
225ml (8fl oz) light cream or creamy milk

Garnish
roasted red pepper dice or crispy bacon dice
sprigs of flat-leaf parsley

Melt the butter in a heavy-bottomed saucepan, add the onion and potato and sweat until soft but not coloured. Gradually add in the stock and milk, stirring all the time, and bring to the boil. Simmer for a few minutes, add the corn, season with salt and freshly ground pepper, cover and cook gently for 10–15 minutes or until the potatoes are cooked. Add the cream and heat through gently without boiling.

Serve in hot bowls with a little dice of roasted red pepper or crispy bacon and parsley on top.

Note: If the soup is too thick, thin it out with a little extra chicken or vegetable stock.

Master Recipe
Carrot Soup

Serves 6

This soup may be served either hot or cold. Don't hesitate to put in a good pinch of sugar – it brings out the flavour.

35g (1½oz) butter
600g (1¼lb) carrots, chopped
110g (4oz) onion, cut into 1cm (½in) cubes
150g (5oz) potatoes, peeled and cut into 1cm (½in) cubes
salt and freshly ground pepper
pinch of sugar
1.2 litres (2 pints) homemade light Chicken or Vegetable Stock (see page 36)
a little creamy milk (optional)

Garnish
a little lightly whipped cream or crème fraîche
sprigs of mint (optional)

Melt the butter. When it foams add the chopped vegetables, season with salt, pepper and sugar. Cover with a butter paper lid (to retain the steam) and a tight fitting lid. Leave to sweat gently on a low heat for about 10 minutes. Remove the lid, add the stock and boil until the vegetables are soft (5–8 minutes). Pour the soup into the liquidiser and purée until smooth. Add a little creamy milk if necessary. Taste and adjust the seasoning. Garnish with a swirl of cream or crème fraîche and sprigs of fresh mint if desired.

> TIP: Buy unwashed, local, organic carrots whenever possible. They have immeasurably better flavour than pre-washed ones and keep longer, too. Heirloom seeds are said to have more vitality and food value than F1 hybrids.

Variations
Carrot and Mint Soup
Add a sprig of spearmint to the Master Recipe when sweating the vegetables. Remove it and add 1 tablespoon of freshly chopped mint before puréeing the soup. A few crispy croûtons are good scattered over the soup. Serve with Mint Cream (see page 386).

Carrot and Cumin Soup
Make the soup as in the Master Recipe adding 2 teaspoons of freshly roasted and crushed cumin to the vegetables. Garnish each bowl of soup with a swirl of crème fraîche or yoghurt, a little freshly roasted and ground cumin and some coriander leaves. Breadsticks (see page 487) are delicious dunked in this soup.

Carrot and Coriander Soup
Substitute 2 teaspoons freshly roasted and crushed coriander seeds for cumin in the recipe above.

Carrot and Orange Soup
Add the freshly grated rind of 2 unwaxed oranges just before the soup is puréed. If unwaxed oranges aren't available, scrub the oranges well before grating to remove the wax from the skin.

Carrot, Parsnip and Lovage Soup
Follow the Master Recipe, replacing one third of the quantity of chopped carrots with chopped parsnips. Add 2 tablespoons freshly snipped lovage at the same time as the stock. Serve sprinkled with chopped lovage and, if you are feeling flamboyant, a tiny blob of softly whipped cream or crème fraîche.

How to Chop Root Vegetables (Carrots, Parsnips, Potatoes)

Wash and peel the vegetables, preferably using a swivel-top peeler. Cut a slice off one side or all four sides if a perfectly even dice is required. Cut the vegetable into slices. (The thickness of these will determine the size of the dice.) Flip over onto the flat side and then cut downwards into slices. Finally cut across to produce dice of the required size, 5mm (¼ in), 3mm (⅛ in), or 2mm (1/16 in) for Brunoise.

Curried Parsnip Soup

Serves 6–8

This delicious soup was adapted from Jane Grigson's recipe in her book *Good Things*. Flour may be omitted for coeliacs.

50g (2oz) butter
110g (4oz) onion, chopped
1 garlic clove, crushed
375g (13oz) parsnips, peeled and chopped
salt and freshly ground pepper
1 tablespoon flour
1 teaspoon curry powder
1.2 litres (2 pints) Chicken or Vegetable Stock
  (see page 36)
150ml (¼ pint) creamy milk

Garnish
Crispy Croûtons (see page 225)
chives or parsley, finely chopped

Melt the butter in a heavy saucepan, add the onion, garlic and parsnip, season with salt and pepper, and toss until well coated. Cover and cook over a gentle heat until soft and tender, about 10 minutes. Stir in the flour and curry powder and gradually incorporate the hot stock. Simmer until the parsnip is fully cooked, strain and liquidise. Correct the seasoning and add the creamy milk. Serve with crispy croûtons and sprinkle with chives or parsley.

Fennel and Parsnip Soup

Serves 8

This unexpectedly delicious combination of winter flavours is guaranteed to convert even the most ardent parsnip hater!

50g (2oz) butter
175g (6oz) onion, diced
450g (1lb) parsnips, washed, peeled and diced
450g (1lb) fennel bulb, finely diced
salt and freshly ground pepper
1.2 litres (2 pints) homemade Chicken or
  Vegetable Stock (see page 36)

125ml (4fl oz) milk
125ml (4fl oz) cream

Garnish
herb fennel or bulb fennel tops, finely chopped

Melt the butter and toss the onion, parsnips and fennel in it. Season with salt and pepper. Cover with a butter wrapper or paper lid and the lid of the saucepan. Cook on a gentle heat for 10–15 minutes or until soft but not coloured. Heat the stock and add, simmering for about 20 minutes or until the vegetables are completely tender. Add the milk and cream. Liquidise and taste for seasoning. Serve in bowls or a soup tureen sprinkled with the fennel.

Betty Hayes' Yellow Squash Soup

Serves 8

I look forward to Autumn to taste Betty's yellow squash soup – I couldn't believe my luck when she shared the recipe with me!

25g (1oz) butter
1 medium onion, chopped
¼ lemon, sliced and pips removed
40g (1½oz) white flour
1.2 litres (2 pints) chicken stock
700g (1½lb) butternut squash, peeled
  and diced
1 teaspoon salt and ¼ teaspoon white pepper
225ml (8fl oz) cream

Melt the butter in a saucepan, add the onion and lemon and sweat gently for 5–6 minutes. Sprinkle with flour, stir well and leave for 2–3 minutes until the flour is cooked.

Add the chicken stock gradually, then the squash. Stir and simmer gently until the squash is soft – about 25 minutes. Purée in a blender or food processor. Season with salt and pepper and then whisk in the cream with a wire whisk.

Taste and correct the seasoning if required.

Spiced Pumpkin Soup

Serves 6–8

900g (2lb) pumpkin or winter squash, peeled,
  de-seeded and cut into 1cm (½in) cubes
175g (6oz) onion, peeled and chopped
2 garlic cloves, crushed
25g (1oz) butter
1 sprig thyme
450g (1lb) very ripe tomatoes, skinned and
  chopped, or 1 x 400g (14oz) tin tomatoes
  de-seeded and roughly chopped
1 tablespoon tomato purée
1.2 litres (2 pints) homemade Chicken Stock
  (see page 36)
salt and freshly ground pepper
pinch of nutmeg
35g (1½oz) butter
½ teaspoon cumin seeds
½ teaspoon coriander seeds
½ teaspoon black peppercorns
1 teaspoon white mustard seeds
5cm (2in) piece of cinnamon stick

Put the pumpkin or squash into a pan with the onion, garlic, butter and thyme. Cover and sweat over a low heat for 10 minutes, stirring once or twice. Add the chopped tomatoes (plus ½–1 teaspoon sugar if using tinned tomatoes) and tomato purée, and cook until dissolved into a thick sauce. Stir in the stock, salt, pepper and a little nutmeg and simmer until the squash is very tender. Discard the thyme stalk, then liquidise the soup in several batches and return to the pan. You may need to add a little more stock or water if the soup is too thick. Taste and adjust the seasoning. Just before serving, gently reheat the soup and pour into a warm serving bowl. Heat the coriander, cumin and peppercorns, and crush coarsely. Melt the butter in a small saucepan and, when foaming, add the crushed spices, mustard seeds and cinnamon. Stir for a few seconds until the mustard seeds start to pop. Remove the cinnamon and quickly pour over the soup. Serve, mixing in the spiced butter as you ladle it out.

RIGHT: Spiced Pumpkin Soup

Butternut Squash Soup
Serves 8

Butternut squash is possibly the tastiest of all the squashes, but you could substitute several others such as Acorn squash.

50g (2oz) butter
600g (1¼lb) onions, chopped
125g (4½oz) celery, chopped
175g (6oz) carrots, chopped
35g (1½oz) fresh ginger root, peeled and chopped or grated
4 large garlic cloves, peeled and crushed
750g (1½lb) squash, peeled and cut into 1cm (½in) cubes (weighed after peeling)
salt and white pepper to taste
600ml (1 pint) homemade Chicken Stock (see page 36)
600ml (1 pint) water
125ml (4fl oz) milk
125ml (4fl oz) cream

Garnish
flat-leaf parsley, freshly chopped

Melt the butter in a heavy saucepan. When it foams, add the onions, celery, carrots, ginger, garlic and squash, and toss until well coated. Sprinkle with salt and pepper. Cover and sweat on a gentle heat for 10 minutes. Add the stock and water. Bring to the boil and cook until the vegetables are soft. Do not overcook or the vegetables will lose their flavour. Liquidise, adding the milk and cream as required. Taste and correct the seasoning. Sprinkle with the parsley.

White Turnip and Marjoram Soup
Serves 6

White turnip and marjoram is a wonderful flavour combination. Kohlrabi could also be used here.

50g (2oz) butter
150g (5oz) potatoes, peeled and chopped
110g (4oz) onions, finely diced
350g (12oz) white turnips, peeled and finely diced
salt and freshly ground pepper
1.2 litres (2 pints) homemade Chicken Stock (see page 36)
2 tablespoons chopped annual marjoram
150ml (¼ pint) creamy milk

Melt the butter in a heavy saucepan. When it foams, add the potatoes, onions and white turnips. Turn them until well coated. Sprinkle with salt and pepper. Cover and sweat on a gentle heat for 10 minutes. Add the stock and half of the marjoram. Bring to the boil and cook until soft. Add the remainder of the marjoram. Liquidise until smooth and silky, adding some creamy milk and perhaps a little more stock if necessary. Do not overcook or the soup will lose its fresh flavour. Taste and adjust the seasoning.

Master Recipe
Jerusalem Artichoke Soup
Serves 8–10

Jerusalem artichokes are a sadly neglected winter vegetable. They look like knobbly potatoes and are a nuisance to peel, but, if fresh, all they need is a good scrub. Delicious in soups and gratins, they are also a real gem from the gardener's point of view because their foliage grows into a hedge, providing shelter for compost heaps and pheasants!

50g (2oz) butter
600g (1¼lb) onions, chopped
600g (1¼lb) potatoes, peeled and chopped
1.1kg (2½lb) artichokes, peeled and chopped
salt and freshly ground pepper
1.2 litres (2 pints) light Chicken Stock (see page 36)
600ml (1 pint) creamy milk

Garnish
parsley, freshly chopped
crisp, golden croûtons

Melt the butter in a heavy saucepan, add the onions, potatoes and artichokes. Season with salt and pepper, cover and sweat gently for about 10 minutes. Add the stock and cook until the vegetables are soft. Liquidise and return to the heat. Thin to the required consistency with creamy milk, and adjust the seasoning. Garnish with parsley and crisp, golden croûtons.

Note: This soup may need more stock depending on how thick you like it.

Variations
Jerusalem Artichoke Soup with Crispy Bacon Croûtons
Cut 50g (2oz) streaky bacon into lardons and fry in a little oil until crisp and golden. Drain on kitchen paper. Mix with the croûtons and add to the Master Recipe just before serving.

Jerusalem Artichoke Soup with Mussels
Garnish the Master Recipe with 30 or so cooked mussels (see page 255) and some snipped fennel leaves. Mussels and artichokes have a wonderful affinity.

Celeriac and Hazelnut Soup
Serves 6

Celeriac, relatively new in our shops, is in fact a root celery which looks a bit like a muddy turnip. Peel it thickly and use for soups or in salads, or simply as a vegetable. This recipe is a deliciously light soup at Christmas time, great served in espresso cups at a drinks party.

50g (2oz) butter
140g (5oz) potatoes, cut into 5mm (¼in) dice
110g (4oz) onions, cut into 5mm (¼in) dice
salt and freshly ground pepper
425g (15oz) celeriac, cut into 5mm (¼in) dice

ABOVE: Beetroot Soup with Chive Cream

Serve the soup piping hot with a little blob of whipped cream on top. Sprinkle with the chopped hazelnuts and a sprig of chervil or flat-leaf parsley.

Master Recipe
Beetroot Soup with Chive Cream
Serves 8–10

900g (2lb) beetroot
25g (1oz) butter
225g (8oz) onions, chopped
salt and freshly ground pepper
1.2 litres (2 pints) homemade Chicken or
    Vegetable Stock (see page 36)
125ml (4fl oz) creamy milk

Chive Cream
125ml (4fl oz) sour cream or crème fraîche
chives, finely chopped

Wash the beetroot carefully under a cold tap. Do not scrub them – simply rub off the clay with your fingers. You do not want to damage the skin or cut off the tops or tails, otherwise the beetroot will 'bleed' while cooking. Put into cold water, bring to the boil and simmer, covered, for anything from 20 minutes to 2 hours depending on the size and age of your beetroots. They are cooked when their skins rub off easily. Remove these, and top and tail the beetroots.

Meanwhile, heat the butter in a pan and gently sweat the onions. Chop the cooked beetroot and add to the onions. Season with salt and pepper. In a separate pan, bring the stock to simmering point. Pour into a liquidiser with the vegetables, and blend until quite smooth. Reheat, add some creamy milk, taste and adjust the seasoning; it may be necessary to add a little more stock or creamy milk.

Serve garnished with swirls of sour cream and a sprinkling of chives.

1.2 litres (2 pints) homemade Chicken Stock,
    Vegetable Stock or water (see page 36)
100–225 ml (4–8floz) creamy milk (optional)

Garnish
2 tablespoons skinned, toasted and
    chopped hazelnuts
a few tablespoons whipped cream
sprigs of chervil or flat-leaf parsley

Melt the butter in a heavy saucepan. When it foams add the potatoes and onions and toss them in the butter until evenly coated. Season with salt and pepper. Cover with a paper lid (to keep in the steam) and the saucepan lid, and sweat over a gentle heat for about 10 minutes, until the vegetables are soft but not coloured. Discard the paper lid. Add the celeriac and chicken stock and cook until the celeriac is soft, about 8–10 minutes. Liquidise the soup and add a little more stock or creamy milk to create the required consistency. Taste and correct seasoning.

To prepare the hazelnuts: Put the hazelnuts into an oven (200°C/400°F/gas 6) on a baking sheet for about 10–15 minutes or until the skins loosen. Remove the skins by rubbing the nuts in the corner of a tea towel. If they are not sufficiently toasted, return them to the oven until golden brown. Chop and set aside to garnish.

Variations

Golden Beetroot Soup

Follow the Master Recipe using golden Chioggio beetroot.

Chilled Beetroot Soup

Follow the Master Recipe up to the point where you season it. Liquidise, with just enough stock to cover, until smooth and silky. Season with salt and pepper. Fold in some cream and yoghurt. Serve well chilled with little swirls of yoghurt and finely chopped chives.

Swede and Bacon Soup

Serves 6–8

1 tablespoon sunflower or groundnut oil
150g (5oz) rindless streaky bacon, cut into 1cm (½in) dice
350g (12oz) swedes, diced
110g (4oz) onions, chopped
150g (5oz) potatoes, diced
salt and freshly ground pepper
850ml (1½ pints) homemade Chicken Stock (see page 36)
cream or creamy milk to taste

Garnish
fried diced bacon
tiny croûtons
parsley, freshly chopped

Heat the oil in a saucepan, add the bacon and cook on a gentle heat until crisp and golden. Remove to a plate with a slotted spoon. Toss the swede, onion and potato in the bacon fat and season. Cover with a paper lid and sweat over a gentle heat until soft but not coloured, about 10 minutes. Add the stock, bring to the boil and simmer until the vegetables are fully cooked. Liquidise, taste, add a little cream or creamy milk and extra seasoning if necessary. Serve with a mixture of crispy bacon, tiny croûtons and chopped parsley sprinkled on top.

Green soups

There is an extra dimension to green soups. It's worth taking care to preserve the bright green colour as well as the lively, fresh taste.

First, remember not to overcook the green vegetables. Many greens – lettuce, kale, cabbage, spinach, watercress, for instance – cook very quickly, so they should not be added until the base vegetables are fully cooked in the stock. Then boil the soup rapidly without the lid on for only a few minutes until the greens are just cooked. Whizz in a blender and serve immediately or cool quickly and reheat just before serving. Green soups lose their fresh colour if they are kept hot indefinitely.

Beetroot and chard tops, turnip greens, pea and broad bean shoots and radish leaves all make delicious green soups.

Spiced Cabbage Soup

Serves 6

Another winter soup from Rory O'Connell.

50g (2oz) butter
150g (5oz) potatoes, chopped
110g (4oz) onions, chopped
salt and freshly ground pepper
850ml (1½ pints) homemade Chicken Stock (see page 36)
250g (9oz) spring cabbage leaves, chopped and stalks removed
50–125ml (2–4fl oz) cream or creamy milk

Spice Mixture
4 tablespoons vegetable oil
1 tablespoon whole black mustard seeds
4 garlic cloves, peeled and very finely chopped
½–1 hot, dried red chilli, coarsely crushed
½ teaspoon sugar
freshly ground pepper

Garnish
softly whipped cream
fresh coriander leaves

Melt the butter in a heavy pan. When it foams, add the potatoes and onions and turn them in the butter until well coated. Sprinkle with salt and pepper. Cover and sweat over a gentle heat for 10 minutes. Add the stock (pre-heat it if you want to speed things up) and boil until the potatoes are soft. Add the cabbage and cook, uncovered, for 4–5 minutes. (Keeping the lid off retains the green colour.) Purée immediately and add the creamy milk.

Now heat the oil in a large frying pan over a medium flame. When hot, put in the mustard seeds. As soon as they begin to pop, add the garlic. Stir the garlic pieces around until they turn light brown (be careful not to burn or it will spoil the flavour). Put in the crushed red chilli and stir for a few seconds. Add this spice mixture to the puréed soup with the seasoning. Taste and correct as necessary. Serve piping hot with a blob of whipped cream and a few coriander leaves.

Brussels Sprout Soup

Serves 6

500g (18oz) fresh Brussels sprouts, trimmed and quartered
30g (1oz) butter
110g (4oz) onions, finely chopped
2 large garlic cloves, chopped
1 tablespoon white flour
1.4 litres (2 pints) hot Chicken or Vegetable Stock (see page 36)
120ml (4fl oz) double cream or crème fraiche
salt and freshly ground pepper

Garnish
croûtons
almond flakes, toasted
110g (4oz) crispy lardons (optional)

Cook the sprouts in boiling water for 2–3 minutes in well salted water (use 3 teaspoons salt to 1.4 litres/2 pints of water). Drain.

Heat the butter in a saucepan and add the chopped onion and garlic. Cover, toss and sweat on a gentle heat for 4–5 minutes. Add the flour, stir and continue to cook for 1–2 minutes. Add the sprouts and the hot stock. Season with salt, pepper and nutmeg. Bring back to the boil and continue to cook for 5–6 minutes or until the sprouts are cooked. Add the cream and purée in a liquidiser. Taste and correct the seasoning.

Variation

Yummy as it is, one could embellish each bowl with a garnish of toasted almond flakes and some crispy bacon lardons or some shredded crispy duck confit.

How to String Spinach

Fold the leaf in half lengthways with the stalk pointing upwards and the ridge facing outwards.

Pull the stalk from top to bottom so that it tears off the leaf.

The stalks of spinach and similar vegetables may be cut into short lengths, cooked in boiling salted water and tossed with a little butter or olive oil – very nutritious and delicious! Kale stalks can be a little tough, however.

Spinach and Rosemary Soup

Serves 6–8

For a simple spinach soup, omit the rosemary and add a little freshly grated nutmeg with the seasoning. Instead of spinach, you can also use mustard greens or a combination of mustard greens and red Russian kale.

50g (2oz) butter
110g (4oz) onions, chopped
150g (5oz) potatoes, peeled and chopped
salt and freshly ground pepper
600ml (1 pint) homemade Chicken or Vegetable Stock (see page 36) or water

425–600ml (³/₄–1 pint) creamy milk
225–350g (8–12oz) spinach, de-stalked and chopped
1 tablespoon freshly chopped rosemary

Garnish
2 tablespoons whipped cream (optional)
sprig of rosemary or rosemary flowers

Accompaniments
Cheddar Cheese Scones (see page 476)

Melt the butter in a heavy saucepan. When it foams, add the onions and potatoes, and turn them until well coated. Sprinkle with salt and pepper. Cover and sweat over a gentle heat for 10 minutes. In separate pans, bring the stock and milk to the boil, and add to the vegetables. Bring back to the boil and simmer until the potatoes and onions are fully cooked. Add the spinach and boil with the lid off for 3–5 minutes, until the spinach is tender. Do not overcook. Add the chopped rosemary. Liquidise and taste. Serve garnished with a blob of cream and rosemary. If you have a pretty rosemary bush in bloom, sprinkle a few flowers over the top for extra pizzazz.

> TIP: The trick with green soups is not to add the greens until the last minute, otherwise they will overcook, and the soup will lose its fresh taste and bright green colour. Also, if you need to reheat, do so at the last minute. If the soup sits in a bain-marie or hostess trolley, its colour will go.

Green Pea Soup with Fresh Mint Cream

Serves 6–8

This soup tastes of summer. If you are using fresh peas, use the pods to make a vegetable stock as the basis for your soup. Having said that, best-quality frozen peas also make a delicious soup. Either way, be careful not to overcook them.

850ml (1½ pints) homemade Chicken Stock (see page 36) or water
25g (1oz) lean ham or bacon
10g (½oz) butter
2 medium spring onions, chopped
700g (1½lb) podded peas, fresh or frozen
outside leaves of a head of lettuce, shredded
sprig of mint
salt, freshly ground pepper and sugar
2 tablespoons thick cream

Garnish
cream, softly whipped
mint leaves, freshly chopped

Heat the stock.

Cut the bacon into very fine shreds. Melt the butter and sweat the bacon for about 5 minutes, add the spring onion and cook for a further 1–2 minutes. Then add the peas, lettuce, mint and the hot stock or water. Season with salt, pepper and sugar. Bring to the boil with the lid off and cook for about 5 minutes until the peas are just tender.

Liquidise and add a little cream to taste. Serve hot or chilled with a blob of whipped cream mixed with the mint.

If the soup is made ahead, reheat uncovered then serve immediately. It will lose its fresh taste and bright lively colour if it sits in a bain-marie or simmers at length in a pan.

Pea and Coriander Soup

Serves 6

This utterly delicious soup has a perky zing with the addition of fresh chilli. It can also be served cold.

850ml (1½ pints) homemade Chicken Stock (see page 36)
50g (2oz) butter
150g (5oz) onion, finely chopped
2 garlic cloves, peeled and chopped
1 green chilli, de-seeded and finely chopped

*450g (1lb) peas (good-quality frozen ones
   are fine)*
2 tablespoons freshly chopped coriander
salt, freshly ground pepper and sugar

Garnish
softly whipped cream
fresh coriander leaves

Heat the stock. Meanwhile, melt the butter
on a gentle heat and add the onion, garlic
and chilli. Season with salt and pepper and
sweat for 3–4 minutes. Add the peas and
cover with hot stock. Bring to the boil and
simmer for 5–8 minutes. Add the coriander
and liquidise. Check the seasoning and
add a pinch of sugar which enhances
the flavour.

Serve with a swirl of cream and a few fresh
coriander leaves on top.

Variation
Broad Bean and Savory Soup
Substitute peeled broad beans and savory
for the peas and coriander and proceed
as above.

Lettuce, Pea and Mint Soup
Serves 6–8

Mint is more fragrant at the height of
summer than towards autumn, so it may
be necessary to use more at the end of the
season. Use outside lettuce leaves for soup
and the tender inside for green salads.

50g (2oz) butter
175g (6oz) potatoes, peeled and diced
150g (5oz) onions, peeled
1 teaspoon salt
freshly ground pepper
*850ml–1.2 litres (1½–2 pints) homemade
   Chicken or Vegetable Stock (see page 36)*
225g (8oz) peas
*175g (6oz) lettuce leaves, chopped and stalks
   removed*
1 tablespoon cream (optional)
2 teaspoons mint, freshly chopped

Garnish
50g (2oz) cream, softly whipped
sprigs of mint

Melt the butter in a heavy saucepan. When
it foams add the potatoes and onions, and
turn them until well coated. Sprinkle with
the salt and pepper. Cover and sweat over
a gentle heat for 10 minutes. Add the
stock, bring to the boil and cook until the
potatoes and onions are softened. Add the
peas and cook for 4–5 minutes. Add the
lettuce, and boil with the lid off until the
lettuce is cooked (2–3 minutes). Do not
overcook or the soup will lose its fresh
green colour. Add the cream and mint, and
liquidise. Serve garnished with a blob of
whipped cream and a little mint.

> TIP: Freshly chopped dill is also great
> with lettuce soup.

Watercress Soup
Serves 6–8

There are references to watercress in
many early Irish manuscripts. It formed
part of the diet of hermits and holy men,
who valued its special properties. Legend
has it that it was watercress that enabled
St. Brendan to live to the ripe old age of
180! In Birr Castle in Co. Offaly, Lord and
Lady Rosse still serve soup made from
the watercress gathered from around St.
Brendan's well, just below the castle walls.

45g (1¾oz) butter
150g (5oz) potatoes, peeled and chopped
110g (4oz) onion, peeled and chopped
salt and freshly ground pepper
*600ml (1 pint) water or homemade Chicken or
   Vegetable Stock (see page 36)*
600ml (1 pint) creamy milk
*225g (8oz) chopped watercress (coarse stalks
   removed)*

Melt the butter in heavy saucepan and,
when it foams, add the potatoes and
onions and toss them until well coated.
Sprinkle with salt and pepper. Cover and
sweat over a gentle heat for 10 minutes.
Meanwhile prepare the watercress. When
the vegetables are almost soft but not
coloured, add the stock and milk, bring to
the boil and cook until the potatoes and
onions are tender. Add the watercress and
boil with the lid off for about 4–5 minutes
until the watercress is cooked. Do not
overcook or the soup will lose its fresh
green colour. Purée the soup in a liquidiser
or food processor. Taste and correct the
seasoning; serve immediately.

Variation
Coriander Soup
Substitute 225g (8oz) fresh coriander leaves
for watercress in the above recipe. This
Mexican recipe is a brilliant way to use up
lots of fresh coriander.

Irish Nettle Soup
Serves 6

Stinging nettles grow in great profusion
and are at their young and tender best in
spring. With their high iron content, they
were much used in folk medicine. Many
older people still like to eat nettles several
times during spring to purify the blood
and prevent arthritis over the coming
year. Don't forget to use gloves when
gathering them!

35g (1½oz) butter
*275g (10oz) potatoes, peeled and cut into 1cm
   (½in) cubes*
110g (4oz) onions, chopped
110g (4oz) leeks, chopped
salt and freshly ground pepper
*1 litre (1¾ pints) homemade Chicken Stock
   (see page 36)*
*150g (5oz) young nettle leaves, washed
   and chopped*
150ml (¼ pint) cream

ABOVE: French Onion Soup with Gruyère Toasts

Melt the butter in a heavy saucepan. When it foams, add the potatoes, onions and leeks, tossing them in the butter until well coated. Sprinkle with salt and pepper. Cover with a paper lid (to keep in the steam) and the saucepan lid, and sweat on a gentle heat for 10 minutes, or until the vegetables are soft but not coloured. Discard the paper lid, add the stock and boil until the vegetables are just cooked. Add the nettle leaves. Simmer uncovered for just 2–3 minutes. Do not overcook or the vegetables will lose their flavour. Add the cream or creamy milk and liquidise. Taste and correct seasoning if necessary. Serve hot.

Variation
Wild Garlic Soup

Substitute wild garlic leaves (*Allium ursinum*) for nettles in the recipe above. Garnish with wild garlic flowers.

French Onion Soup with Gruyère Toasts
Serves 6

French onion soup is probably the best known and loved of all French soups. It was a favourite for breakfast in the cafés beside the old markets at Les Halles in Paris and is still a favourite on bistro menus at Rungis market. In France, this soup is served in special white porcelain tureens. Enjoy it with a glass of gutsy French vin de table.

50g (2oz) butter
1.3kg (3lb) onions, thinly sliced
1.8 litres (3 pints) good homemade Beef,
  Chicken or Vegetable Stock (see page 36)
salt and freshly ground pepper

To Finish
6 slices French bread (baguette), 1cm (½in)
  thick, toasted
75g (3oz) Gruyère cheese, grated

Melt the butter in a saucepan. Add the onions and cook over a low heat for about 40–60 minutes with the lid off, stirring frequently – the onions should be dark and well caramelised but not burnt.

Add the stock, season with salt and freshly ground pepper, bring to the boil and cook for a further 10 minutes. Ladle into deep soup bowls, and put a piece of toasted baguette covered with grated cheese on top of each one. Pop under a medium grill until the cheese melts and turns golden. Serve immediately but beware – it will be very hot. Bon appetit!

TIP: Hold your nerve: the onions must be very well caramelised, otherwise the soup will be too weak and sweet.

Onion and Thyme Leaf Soup

Serves 6

45g (1³/₄oz) butter
450g (1lb) onions, cut into 1cm (¹/₂in) cubes
225g (8oz) potatoes, peeled and cut into
   1cm (¹/₂in) cubes
1–2 teaspoons fresh thyme leaves
salt and freshly ground pepper
850ml (1¹/₂ pints) homemade Chicken Stock or
   Vegetable Stock (see page 36)
150ml (¹/₄ pint) cream or cream and milk mixed

Garnish
a little whipped cream (optional)
fresh thyme leaves and thyme or chive flowers

Melt the butter in a heavy saucepan. As soon as it foams, add the onions and potatoes, and stir until they are well coated with butter. Add the thyme leaves, season with salt and freshly ground pepper. Place a paper lid directly on top of the vegetables to keep in the steam, cover the saucepan with a tight-fitting lid and sweat on a low heat for about 10 minutes. The potatoes and onions should be soft but not coloured. Add the stock, bring to the boil and simmer until the potatoes are cooked (5–8 minutes). Liquidise the soup and add a little cream or creamy milk. Taste and correct the seasoning if necessary. Serve garnished with a blob of whipped cream and sprinkled with thyme leaves and thyme or chive flowers.

Cauliflower and Cheddar Cheese Soup

Serves 6

Broccoli, Romanesco or calabrese can be used in place of cauliflower.

1 handsome head of cauliflower, about 900g
   (2lb) weighed with green outer leaves still on
600ml (1 pint) Cheddar Cheese Sauce
   (see page 580)
salt and freshly ground pepper

Garnish
50–75g (2–3oz) Irish cheddar cheese, grated
2 tablespoons freshly chopped parsley
Crispy Croûtons (see page 225)

Chop up all the outer green leaves of the cauliflower, put them in a saucepan and barely cover with cold water. Bring to the boil and simmer for about 45 minutes until you have a well-flavoured cauliflower stock. Chop up the cauliflower head, place in a saucepan and cover with the cauliflower stock, reserving any leftover liquid for later. Bring to the boil and cook, covered, until the cauliflower is tender (5–8 minutes). Liquidise the cauliflower to get a smooth purée. Mix the cauliflower purée and cheese sauce together, adding enough cauliflower or chicken stock to obtain a nice consistency. Taste and season. Serve with croûtons, cheese and parsley.

Mushroom Soup

Serves 8–9

Mushroom soup is the fastest of all soups to make and one of the all-time favourites. It is best made with flat mushrooms or button mushrooms which are a few days old and have developed a slightly stronger flavour. Wild mushrooms appear every few years after a good warm summer – it's either a feast or a famine! Surpluses can be used to make the base of the soup and the purée frozen (to take less room in the freezer). Add stock and milk to reconstitute just before serving.

25g (1oz) butter
110g (4oz) onions, rinsed under cold, running
   water and finely chopped
450g (1lb) mushrooms
600ml (1 pint) homemade Chicken or Vegetable
   Stock (see page 36)
600ml (1 pint) milk
25g (1oz) flour
salt and freshly ground pepper

Melt the butter in a saucepan over a gentle heat and toss the onions in it. Cover and sweat until soft and completely cooked.

Meanwhile, chop up the mushrooms very finely. Add to the saucepan and cook over a high heat for 4–5 minutes. In separate pans, bring the stock and milk to the boil (this is important: the milk may curdle if added to the soup cold). Stir the flour into the mushroom mixture, cook over a low heat for 2–3 minutes. Season with salt and freshly ground pepper, then add the hot stock and milk gradually, stirring all the time. Increase the heat and bring to the boil. Taste and add a dash of cream if necessary. Serve immediately or cool and reheat later.

> TIP: When chopping mushrooms put the chopping board on a tray and chop a few at a time until very fine. The tray catches all the pieces that scatter as you chop fast.

Vine-ripened Tomato Purée

900g (2lb) vine-ripened tomatoes
1 small onion, chopped
good pinch of salt
a few twists of freshly ground pepper
good pinch of sugar (optional)

Cut the very ripe tomatoes into quarters and put into a stainless steel saucepan with the onion, salt, pepper and sugar. Cook on a gentle heat until the tomatoes are soft (no water is needed). Put through the fine blade of the mouli-légume or a nylon sieve. Allow to cool and refrigerate or freeze.

> TIP: This is one of the very best ways of preserving the flavour of ripe summer tomatoes for the winter. Use for soups, stews, casseroles etc.

How to Peel Tomatoes

Choose tomatoes that are very ripe but still firm. Prick the base of each one. Put them into a deep bowl and completely cover with boiling water. Count to 10 slowly before pouring off the water. The skins will then peel off easily.

How to Seed Tomatoes

Halve the tomatoes crossways and, holding the halves over a bowl with the cut side down, squeeze them gently. Most of the seeds will fall out. If any remain, remove them with a teaspoon.

How to Make Tomato Concassé

Peel the tomatoes (see above), cut into quarters, then remove the seeds and divisions with a small knife or sharp spoon. Cut the flesh into small, even-sized dice. Don't forget to season with salt, pepper and perhaps a little sugar before using.

Master Recipe
Vine-ripened Tomato and Spearmint Soup
Serves 5

Tomato is to soup what apple is to puddings – top of the list of all-time favourites. And the marvellous thing about this recipe is that you can easily vary it in so many different ways, making it almost seem like a different soup each time. Of course, it's best to use a purée made from vine-ripened tomatoes in season. Good-quality tinned tomatoes (a must for your store cupboard) also produce a really good result but, because they are rather more acidic than fresh tomatoes, you need to add extra sugar.

10g (1/2oz) butter
1 small onion, finely chopped
700ml (1 1/4 pints) homemade Tomato Purée
  (see recipe next page) or 2 x 400g (14oz)
  tinned tomatoes, liquidised and sieved
225ml (8fl oz) Béchamel sauce (see page 580)
225ml (8fl oz) homemade Chicken Stock or
  Vegetable Stock (see page 36)
2 tablespoons freshly chopped spearmint
salt and freshly ground pepper
1–2 tablespoons sugar
125ml (4fl oz) cream (optional)

Garnish
whipped cream
spearmint, freshly chopped

Melt the butter over a gentle heat. Add the onion, cover and cook until soft but not coloured. Add the homemade tomato purée or the puréed and sieved tinned tomatoes, the Béchamel sauce and stock, the mint, salt and pepper, plus sugar if you are using tinned tomatoes – otherwise just a pinch. Bring to the boil and simmer for a few minutes. Liquidise and, if necessary, dilute with extra chicken stock. Bring back to the boil, correct the seasoning and serve with the addition of a little cream, if you choose. Garnish with spearmint and a blob of whipped cream.

TIPS: This soup needs to be tasted carefully. You may need to adjust the seasoning depending on the intensity of the tomato purée and the stock.

Like most soups, this one re-heats very well and can of course be frozen.

Variations
Tomato and Basil Soup
Add 2 tablespoons freshly torn basil leaves instead of mint.

Tomato and Coriander Soup
Add 2 tablespoons freshly chopped coriander instead of mint.

Tomato and Orange Soup
Add the finely grated rind of 1 unwaxed orange instead of mint.

Tomato and Rosemary Soup
Add 1 tablespoon freshly chopped rosemary instead of mint.

Tomato Soup with Pesto
Replace the garnish with a drizzle of lightly whipped cream and pesto. Serve with an accompaniment, either croûtons cut into square, star or tiny heart shapes and fried in olive oil, or Tapenade Toasts (see page 221).

Spiced Courgette and Green Pepper Soup with Roasted Red Pepper Cream
Serves 9

25g (1oz) butter
110g (4oz) onions, diced
150g (5oz) potatoes, peeled and diced
250g (9oz) courgettes, diced
200g (7oz) green pepper, diced
1/2 chilli, de-seeded and chopped
1.3 litres (2 1/4 pints) homemade Chicken Stock
  (see page 36)
1 level teaspoon each of cumin seed, cardamom
  seed and ground ginger
a little creamy milk

Heat the butter in a saucepan, and sweat the onions and potatoes over a low heat for 10 minutes, covered with buttered paper and a tight-fitting lid. Add the courgettes, green pepper and chilli. Cover with chicken stock and simmer until soft. Meanwhile, warm the spices in the oven to develop the flavour, then grind them. When the vegetables are soft, liquidise them, adding the spices and seasoning. Leave to infuse for a little while. Finish the soup by adding more chicken stock or creamy milk to achieve the required consistency. Serve hot with a garnish of Roasted Red Pepper Cream (see over page).

Roasted Red Pepper Cream

1 large red pepper
125ml (4fl oz) cream, softly whipped or
    crème fraîche
pinch of salt

Roast the red pepper in a moderate oven (180°C/350°F/gas 4) with a drizzle of olive oil until tender and collapsed, about 25 minutes. Remove and place in a sealed plastic bag. When cool, peel and de-seed the pepper. Chop the pepper flesh finely and mix into the softly whipped cream with the salt.

Red Pepper Soup with Avocado and Coriander Salsa

Serves 4–6

Rory O'Connell serves the salsa as an embellishment to this soup. A spoonful of Tomato and Chilli Sauce (see page 591) is also terrific with it.

25g (1oz) butter
2 tablespoons olive oil
2 medium onions, about 275g (10oz)
2 star anise
4 red or yellow peppers, de-seeded and chopped
salt, freshly ground pepper and sugar
600ml (1 pint) homemade Chicken Stock (see page 36), enough to cover

Melt the butter, add the oil and sweat the onions until they start to soften. Add the star anise together with the peppers. Season with salt, pepper and sugar, and sweat until the peppers become 'oily' and start to soften. Barely cover with chicken stock and simmer until the peppers are tender. Discard the star anise. Liquidise until smooth and allow to cool. Serve chilled in small bowls with a spoonful of Avocado and Coriander Salsa (see page 592) on top.

Spiced Aubergine Soup with Roast Pepper and Coriander Cream

Serves 8–10

We grow several different varieties of aubergine. The Slim Jim is our favourite for this recipe, but any type will do. Rory O'Connell taught this recipe to the students on his course here at Ballymaloe Cookery School.

2 tablespoons olive oil
175g (6oz) onion, chopped
8 garlic cloves, chopped
1 tablespoon cumin seeds, roasted and ground
1 tablespoon fennel seeds, roasted and ground
900g (2lb) aubergines, cut into 2cm (3/4in) cubes
salt and freshly ground pepper
1.5 litres (2½ pints) homemade Chicken Stock (see page 36)
freshly squeezed lemon or lime juice to taste
creamy milk, if necessary

Garnish
1–2 roasted red peppers, peeled, de-seeded and diced (see page 83)
2 tablespoons coarsely chopped coriander
150ml (¼ pint) whipped cream
coriander leaves

Gently sweat the onions with the garlic and spices in the olive oil until soft, about 10 minutes. Add aubergines, season with salt and freshly ground pepper and sweat until wilted, about 30 minutes. Pour in the chicken stock, bring to the boil and cook until tender, approximately 5 minutes. Liquidise, taste and correct the seasoning. You may need to add a little lemon or lime juice or a little creamy milk. Just before serving, fold the red peppers and coriander into the cream, reserving some to garnish each bowl with the coriander leaves.

Aztec Soup

Serves 6

In Mexico there are lots of variations on this theme.

2 chillies, roasted, peeled and torn into strips
1 tablespoon vegetable oil
1 onion, chopped
2 garlic cloves, finely chopped
1.2 litres (2 pints) homemade Chicken Stock (see page 36)
3–4 dashes Tabasco sauce
1 chicken breast
salt and freshly ground pepper
1 avocado
2 tomatoes, skinned, de-seeded and diced
¼ cup coriander leaves, chopped

Garnish
fresh coriander leaves
corn Tortilla Chips, torn into strips (see page 494)

First roast the chillies: put either over an open flame or under a grill until quite black and bubbly. Put in a bowl and cover with clingfilm for 5 minutes. Peel off the black skins with your fingers and pull into little strips for garnish.

Heat the oil in a stainless steel pan and sweat the onion until soft. Add the garlic and cook for another 1–2 minutes. Add the chicken stock and Tabasco and simmer for 5 minutes. Meanwhile, remove the skin from the chicken if necessary. Cut it into 1.25cm (½in) strips. Season well with salt and pepper. Add the chicken to the simmering broth and simmer for 3–4 minutes until white all the way through. Add the avocado and tomato, the coriander and the strips of roasted chillies. Do not overcook or the avocado will dissolve. Garnish with fresh coriander leaves and strips of corn Tortilla Chips (see page 494).

Asparagus Soup with Chervil

Serves 6

Asparagus is much more widely available now but is still the aristocrat of vegetables. If you grow your own you may have enough to allow yourself the luxury of making soup. A beautiful plant for the garden and if you can spare some of the feathery foliage, it is wonderful for flower arrangements.

560g (1⅓lb) asparagus, chopped
50g (2oz) butter
110g (4oz) onion, chopped
freshly ground pepper
850ml (1½ pints) homemade Chicken Stock
150–300ml (¼–½ pint) creamy milk

Garnish
1–2 teaspoons chervil
a few asparagus tips saved from the soup
Crispy Croûtons (see page 225), optional

Peel the root ends of the asparagus with a swivel top peeler, and chop the spears into 1cm (½ inch) pieces. Keep some of the tips for garnish.

Melt the butter in a heavy bottomed saucepan and, when it foams, add the onions and toss until well coated. Sprinkle with salt and pepper, cover with a butter wrapper and tight-fitting lid, and sweat over a gentle heat for 10 minutes.

Add the asparagus and stock and boil uncovered until soft (about 8–10 minutes). Liquidise, add creamy milk to taste and correct the seasoning. Stir in the chopped chervil just before serving. Boil the asparagus tips in salted water for 8–10 minutes and drain. Add to the soup as a garnish. Crispy Croûtons make a delicious accompaniment.

Spiced Chickpea Soup with Coriander Cream and Pitta Crisps

Serves 4–6

A speedier version of this delicious soup can be made with a tin of chickpeas.

225g (8oz) chickpeas, soaked overnight in plenty of cold water
1.5 litres (2½ pints) homemade Chicken or Vegetable Stock (see page 36)
2–3 teaspoons coriander seeds
2–3 teaspoons cumin seeds
50g (2oz) butter
175g (6oz) onions, finely chopped
5 large garlic cloves, peeled and finely chopped
1–2 small red chillies, halved, de-seeded and chopped
½ teaspoon ground turmeric
75ml (3fl oz) cream
salt and freshly ground pepper
freshly squeezed lemon juice

Garnish
crème fraîche
fresh coriander leaves
Pitta Crisps (see right)

Drain the chickpeas and put them in a saucepan, cover with the stock and bring to the boil. Cover and simmer gently for 45–60 minutes, or until soft and tender. Strain, reserving the liquid. Meanwhile, dry-roast the coriander and cumin seeds in a frying pan over medium heat for 2–3 minutes, then crush in a pestle and mortar or spice grinder. Melt the butter in a saucepan, add the onion, spices, garlic and chilli. Cook gently for 4–5 minutes, add the turmeric, stir and cook for another 1–2 minutes.

Remove from the heat, add the chickpeas and mix well. Season. Now liquidise the chickpeas with the cooking liquid and cream. Place in a saucepan and simmer for 10–20 minutes. If the soup is a little too thick, thin out with extra stock. Taste and, if necessary, sharpen with lemon juice. Serve with a blob of crème fraîche, coriander leaves and Pitta Crisps.

Pitta Crisps

3 mini pitta breads, about 8cm (3in) in diameter, halved crossways
4 teaspoons extra-virgin olive oil
1 teaspoon freshly ground cumin
½ teaspoon salt

Preheat the oven to 200°C/400°F/gas 6. Cut the pieces of pitta into triangles. Brush evenly with olive oil and sprinkle with cumin and salt. Spread pitta pieces in a single layer on a baking tray and bake in the middle of the oven for 3 minutes or until crisp and golden. Serve immediately.

Tojo's Lentil Soup

Serves 8–10

Tojo cooked in the Garden Café at the Ballymaloe Cookery School one summer, and he created some memorable dishes. He uses no stock for his soups since many of his guests are vegan or vegetarian. This soup is incredibly simple to make.

125ml (4fl oz) extra-virgin olive oil
6 large onions, chopped
125ml (4fl oz) soy sauce
4 garlic cloves
salt and pepper to taste
500g (18oz) Puy lentils
2.4 litres (4 pints) water

Garnish
flat-leaf parsley
extra-virgin olive oil

Heat the extra-virgin olive oil in a medium-sized pot, add the onions, soy sauce, garlic, salt and pepper. Place over a fairly high flame for about 10 minutes, then lower the heat and simmer until the onions have a slightly sweet taste. Add the water and lentils and simmer for about 45 minutes. When the lentils are cooked, taste and correct the seasoning. Be careful not to let the lentils get mushy – it's nice if there is a slight bite to them. Serve in wide soup bowls with parsley and drizzled with your best extra-virgin olive oil.

Fasolatha (Greek Bean Soup)
Serves 6

This staple rustic soup, which is wonderfully filling and easy to make, has nourished generations of Greeks. It also re-heats well and improves with keeping.

350g (12oz) haricot or cannelloni beans, soaked in plenty of cold water overnight, or 1 x 400g (14oz) tin cooked beans
1.2 litres (2 pints) water or homemade Chicken Stock (see page 36)
1 large onion, thinly sliced
1 leek, thinly sliced
2 carrots, finely diced
2 stalks of celery with leaves, finely chopped
1 x 400g (14oz) tin of tomatoes
1 tablespoon tomato purée
2 garlic cloves, chopped
150ml (1/4 pint) olive oil
salt, freshly ground pepper and sugar
1 tablespoon chopped marjoram
1 tablespoon chopped thyme leaves

Garnish
2 tablespoons freshly chopped flat-leaf parsley

Rinse the beans and drain them. Cover with fresh cold water, bring to the boil and simmer for 5 minutes. Drain, then add all other ingredients except the parsley. Cook for 40–50 minutes or until the beans are just soft and the vegetables cooked. Taste and correct the seasoning. Garnish with the parsley and serve drizzled with a little extra-virgin olive oil.

Avgolemono
Serves 4–6

Avgolemono may be served hot or cold.

1.2 litres (2 pints) homemade Chicken Stock (see page 36)
4 organic eggs
juice of 1–2 small lemons
1–2 tablespoons freshly chopped dill

Bring the chicken stock to the boil. Whisk the eggs in a bowl with the lemon juice. Gradually add the boiling stock, whisking all the time, return to the saucepan and put back on the heat, stir and cook until it thickens to a light coating consistency. It must not boil or it will curdle. Add the dill, taste and correct the seasoning.

You can simmer 25–50g (1–2oz) of rice in the stock, but you will need to allow extra stock because the rice soaks up quite a lot.

Stacciatella
Serves 4-6

This classic Italian soup is flavoured with saffron and is made in minutes.

2 organic eggs
50g (2oz) finely grated Parmesan cheese
2 tablespoons chopped flat-leaf parsley
1 litre chicken stock
1 teaspoon saffron threads soaked in 125ml (4fl oz) water

Parmesan Toasts
4 slices good ciabatta or country bread
2–3 tablespoons extra-virgin olive oil
freshly grated Parmesan cheese
sea salt and freshly ground pepper

Preheat the oven to 200°C/400°F/gas 6.

First make the Parmesan toasts: drizzle the bread with extra-virgin olive oil and top with grated Parmesan and freshly ground pepper. Cook on a baking tray for 5–6 minutes or until golden brown and set aside.

Whisk the eggs in a bowl with the cheese and the parsley. Bring the chicken stock to the boil, add the saffron and water. Pour in the egg mixture, whisking constantly. Reduce the heat and simmer for 1–2 minutes. Season with sea salt and pepper.

Put a Parmesan toast into each soup bowl, ladle over the soup and sprinkle the remaining cheese on top. Alternatively the Parmesan toasts may be served separately.

Aki Ishibashi's Miso Soup
Serves 4

Students now come from the four corners of the world to our little cooking school in Shanagarry. Aki, who came from Japan, was already a brilliant cook when she arrived.

600ml (1 pint) Dashi (see page 37)
3–4 generous tablespoons miso paste
175g (6oz) tofu, cut into 1cm (1/2in) cubes
1 dessertspoon wakame (dried seaweed)

Garnish
1 spring onion, thinly sliced

Heat the dashi, and dissolve the miso paste by stirring it into the dashi. When it has dissolved completely, add the tofu cubes and wakame. Bring it to the boil. As soon as it starts to boil, turn off the heat. Ladle miso soup into warmed individual soup bowls and garnish with spring onion.

Add any of the following to the basic soup:
Daikon (white radish) and radish leaves
Clams and spring onions
Potato and spring onions
Shiitake mushrooms and spring onions

Ballymaloe Mussel Soup
Serves 8

Because stale shellfish can cause illness, it is vital to sort the mussels carefully, discarding any that refuse to close tightly after they have been gently tapped. The maxim is, if in doubt, throw it out.

3.6–4.5kg (8–10lb) mussels, scrubbed under cold running water
425ml (3/4 pint) dry white wine
8 tablespoons chopped shallots
1 garlic clove, mashed
8 parsley sprigs, 1/2 bay leaf, 1/4 teaspoon fresh thyme leaves, a sprig of fresh fennel

lots of freshly ground pepper
1/4 teaspoon curry powder (optional)
Roux, made from 75g (3oz) butter and 75g
  (3oz) flour (see page 580)
600ml–1.2litres (1–2 pints) boiling milk
a little cream if necessary

Garnish
chopped parsley or chervil
croûtons

Clean the mussels (see page 255). Put the wine, shallots, garlic, fresh herbs and curry powder into a stainless steel saucepan, add the mussels, cover and simmer gently. Remove the mussels as they open. Shell the mussels, saving a few in the shell for a garnish. Remove the beards, open and place them in a bowl. Strain the mussel cooking liquid into a stainless steel saucepan and boil rapidly over a high heat to concentrate the flavour. Taste frequently as it boils; if it reduces too much, the salt content will be overpowering. Whisk the roux into the mussel liquid to thicken. Add the boiling milk to thin out the soup to a light consistency. Just before serving, add the mussels and a little cream. Decorate with chopped parsley or chervil and mussels in their shells. Serve croûtons separately.

> TIP: The milk must be boiling when added to the soup, otherwise it may curdle because of the acidity in the wine.

Variation
Cockle and Mussel Soup
Use half cockles and half mussels and proceed as above.

Seafood Chowder
See page 264

Mediterranean Fish Soup with Rouille
Serves 6–8

This gutsy fish soup is a labour of love and worth every minute. Fish soups can be made with all sorts and combinations of fish. Don't worry if you lack the exact ingredients I suggest – use a combination of whole fish and shellfish. The crab does add an almost essential richness in my opinion.

2.45kg (5½lb) mixed fish, e.g. 1 whole plaice,
  ½ cod, 2 small whiting, 3 swimming crab or
  1 common crab, 6–8 mussels, 8–10 shrimps
  or prawns, 2 fish heads
150ml (¼ pint) olive oil
1 large garlic clove, crushed
275g (10oz) onions, chopped
5 large, very ripe tomatoes or 1 x 400g (14oz)
  tin of chopped tomatoes
5 sprigs of fennel
2 sprigs of thyme
1 bay leaf
fish stock or water barely to cover
¼ teaspoon saffron
salt and freshly ground pepper
pinch of cayenne

Rouille
1 piece of French bread (baguette), 5cm (2in) long
6 tablespoons hot fish soup
4 garlic cloves
1 organic egg yolk
pinch of whole saffron stamens
salt and freshly ground pepper
6 tablespoons extra-virgin olive oil

Croûtons
8 slices French bread (baguette), 1cm (½in) thick
75–110g (3–4oz) Gruyère cheese, grated

Garnish
parsley, freshly chopped

Cut the fish into chunks, bones, head and all (remove gills first). Heat the olive oil until smoking, add the garlic and onions, toss for a minute or two, add the tomatoes, herbs and fish including shells. Cook for 10 minutes, then add enough fish stock or water to barely cover. Bring to a fast boil

and cook for a further 10 minutes. Add more liquid if it reduces too much. Soak the saffron strands in a little fish stock.

Pick out and discard the mussel shells. Taste, add salt, pepper, cayenne, saffron and the soaking liquid. Push the soup through a mouli (this may seem like an impossible task but you'll be surprised how effective it will be – there will be just a mass of dry bones left, which you discard).

Next make the rouille. Cut the bread into cubes and soak in some hot fish soup. Squeeze out the excess liquid and mix to a mush in a bowl. Crush the garlic to a fine paste in a pestle and mortar, add the egg yolk, the saffron and the soggy bread. Season with salt and pepper.

Mix well and add in the oil drip by drip as in making mayonnaise. If the mixture looks too thick or oily add 2 tablespoons of hot fish soup and continue to stir.

Toast slices of French bread slowly until they are dry and crisp. Bring the soup back to the boil. Spread the slices with rouille and sprinkle with Gruyère cheese, float a croûton in each plate of Mediterranean fish soup. Garnish with parsley and serve.

Mackerel and Dill Soup
Serves 10

This soup may sound unlikely but I was delighted to find this Scandinavian recipe. It is delicious and very cheap to make. Use very fresh whole mackerel — the bones are essential to the flavour of the soup.

2 large or 3 medium-sized very fresh mackerel
1.5 litres (2½ pints) water
a handful of dill stalks
1–2 teaspoons salt
10 whole white peppercorns
2–4 tablespoons finely chopped fresh dill
60ml (2½fl oz) cream
2 organic egg yolks
juice of 1 lemon

Gut the mackerel, wash well and remove the heads. Cut into 2.5cm (1 inch) pieces. Put the mackerel into a saucepan with the water, dill stalks, salt and peppercorns.

Bring to the boil, simmer for 5 minutes and strain. Discard the peppercorns and dill stalks, then carefully remove the mackerel flesh from the bones. Put the flesh back into the saucepan with the mackerel broth and add the dill, half the cream and half the lemon juice. Simmer for a few minutes.

Mix the remainder of the cream with the egg yolks. Whisk a little of the simmering liquid into the liaison of egg and cream and stir into the remainder of the mackerel soup. Taste and correct the seasoning and add more lemon juice if necessary. Serve hot with crusty white bread.

Chinese Fish Soup with Chilli and Coriander

Serves 6

We adore these light fish soups. Consider this recipe as a formula and vary the fish and shellfish depending on what you have available – mussels and white crabmeat are particularly delicious. Lemongrass and a dice of cucumber also work well.

225g (8oz) lemon sole or plaice fillets, skinned
iceberg lettuce heart, finely shredded
1.2 litres (2 pints) very well-flavoured Chinese Stock (see right)
salt and lots of freshly ground white pepper
1/2–1 red or green chilli, thinly sliced
18 prawns or 30 shrimps (we use Atlantic shrimps; if using the larger Pacific ones, use less), cooked and peeled

Garnish
6 teaspoons spring onion, finely sliced at an angle
coriander or flat-leaf parsley, freshly chopped
prawn or shrimp roe, if available

Cut the fish fillets into pieces at an angle, each about 4cm (1½in). Shred the lettuce heart very finely: you will need about 12 generous tablespoons.

When ready to eat, bring the stock to the boil, add the salt, sliced chilli and fish. Simmer for 1 minute. Add the prawns or shrimps and allow to heat through.

Put 2 tablespoons of the shredded lettuce into each soup bowl. Season generously with white pepper and immediately ladle the boiling soup over it. Garnish with spring onions, prawn or shrimp roe and lots of fresh coriander. Serve very hot.

Vietnamese Prawn Soup

Serves 4

The fresh clean taste of Asian soups like this one is soothing and addictive.

225g (8oz) shrimps or tiger prawns, unpeeled
1 stick lemongrass
2 x 2.5cm (1in) pieces fresh root ginger, peeled
850ml (1½ pints) light Chicken Stock (see page 36)
3 teaspoon lime juice, freshly squeezed
1/2 teaspoon crushed dried chilli or 1/4 teaspoon red chilli paste
3 teaspoons fish sauce (nam pla)
75–110g (3–4oz) Chinese leaves or butterhead lettuce, shredded

Garnish
coriander leaves

Peel the tiger prawns or shrimps, put the shells into the saucepan with the lemon grass, ginger and stock, bring to the boil and simmer for 10 minutes. Strain, return the liquid to the saucepan. Add the lime juice, dried chilli or chilli paste and nam pla and simmer for 2 minutes. Add the tiger prawns or shrimps and simmer for 4 or 5 minutes.

Divide the Chinese leaves between the bowls. Ladle in the boiling soup. Garnish and serve at once.

Thai Chicken, Galangal and Coriander Soup

Serves 8

This is a particularly delicious example of how fast and easy a Thai soup can be – and it looks great dished up in Chinese porcelain bowls. The kaffir lime leaves and galangal are served for dramatic effect but not eaten. The chilli may of course be nibbled!

850ml (1½ pints) homemade Chicken Stock (see page 36)
4 fresh kaffir lime leaves
5cm (2in) piece of galangal, peeled and sliced, or less of fresh ginger
4 tablespoons fish sauce (nam pla)
6 tablespoons lemon juice, freshly squeezed
225g (8oz) organic chicken breast, finely sliced
225ml (8fl oz) coconut milk
1–3 Thai red chillies
5 tablespoons fresh coriander leaves

Put the chicken stock, lime leaves, galangal, fish sauce and lemon juice into a saucepan. Bring to the boil, stirring all the time, then add the finely shredded chicken and coconut milk. Continue to cook over a high heat until the chicken is just cooked, about 1–2 minutes. Crush the chillies with a knife or Chinese chopper and add to the soup with the coriander leaves. Cook for just a few seconds and serve immediately.

Note: We usually use just one red Thai chilli. The quantity will depend on your taste and how hot the chillies are.

TIP: Blanched and refreshed rice noodles are also great added to this soup.

RIGHT: Thai Chicken, Galangal and Coriander Soup

Portuguese Chicken Soup with Mint and Lemon
Serves 6

A great little soup – food for the soul!

1.8 litres (3 pints) well-flavoured homemade
    Chicken Stock (see page 36)
2 chicken breasts
1 unwaxed lemon
1–2 tablespoons freshly chopped mint
175g (6oz) rice or orzo
salt and freshly ground pepper

Put the stock into a saucepan, add the chicken and finely pared strips of lemon peel (no pith). Bring slowly to the boil and simmer for 5 minutes. Remove the chicken, cool, and slice into thin shreds. Add the rice (or orzo), the juice from the lemon, and the mint. Season with salt and pepper.

Bring back to the boil and simmer until the rice or orzo is cooked. Add the shredded chicken again. Taste and correct the seasoning; add more lemon juice if necessary. Serve immediately.

French Peasant Soup
Serves 6

Here is another very substantial soup – it has 'eating and drinking' in it and would certainly be a meal in itself if you grate some Cheddar cheese over the top. Myrtle Allen called this soup Connemara Broth when she served it at La Ferme Irlandaise in Paris.

175g (6oz) unsmoked streaky bacon (in
    the piece)
olive or sunflower oil
150g (5oz) potatoes, peeled and cut into 5mm
    (¼in) dice
50g (2oz) onions, finely chopped
1 small garlic clove (optional)
450g (1lb) very ripe tomatoes, peeled and diced,
    or 1 x 400g (14oz) tin of tomatoes and juice

salt and freshly ground pepper
½–1 teaspoon sugar
850ml (1½ pints) homemade Chicken or
    Vegetable Stock (see page 36)
50g (2oz) cabbage (Savoy is best), finely chopped

Garnish
flat-leaf parsley, freshly chopped

Remove the rind from the bacon if necessary. Prepare the vegetables and cut the bacon into 5mm (¼in) cubes.

Blanch the cubes in cold water to remove some of the salt, drain and dry on kitchen paper, sauté in a little olive or sunflower oil until the fat runs and the bacon is crisp and golden. Add potatoes, onions and crushed garlic, sweat for 10 minutes and then add diced tomatoes and any juice.

Season with salt, pepper and sugar. Cover with stock and cook for 5 minutes. Add the finely chopped cabbage and continue to simmer just until the cabbage is cooked. Taste and adjust seasoning.

Sprinkle with lots of chopped parsley and serve.

Variation
Mediterranean Peasant Soup
Add half a thinly sliced Kabanos sausage to the soup with the potato. For a more robust soup, add 110g (4oz) cooked haricot beans with the cabbage.

Butterbean, Chorizo and Cabbage Soup
Serves 6

2 tablespoons extra-virgin olive oil
175g (6oz) onion, chopped
175g (6oz) chorizo or Kabanos sausage, sliced
400g (14oz) tin of Italian tomatoes
salt, freshly ground pepper and sugar
1.2 litres (2 pints) homemade Chicken Stock
    (see page 36)
1 x 400g (14oz) tin butter beans, haricot beans
    or black-eyed beans

½ Savoy cabbage
4 tablespoons freshly chopped flat-leaf parsley

Heat the oil in a sauté pan over a medium heat, add the onion, cover and sweat until soft but not coloured. Slice the chorizo or Kabanos and toss for 2–3 minutes or until it begins to crisp slightly – the fat should run. Chop the tomatoes fairly finely and add with all the juice to the pan, season with salt, freshly ground pepper and sugar.

Bring to the boil and cook on a high heat for 5–6 minutes, then add the boiling stock and butter beans. Bring back to the boil, thinly slice the cabbage and add. Cook for another 2–3 minutes, add the chopped parsley.

Taste and correct the seasoning and serve with lots of crusty bread.

Winter Vegetable and Bean Soup with Spicy Sausage
Serves 8–9

We make huge pots of this in the winter, and I usually keep some in the freezer. Kabanos is a thin sausage now widely available. It gives a gutsy slightly smoky flavour to the soup which, although satisfying, is by no means essential.

225g (8oz) rindless streaky bacon, cut into
    5mm (¼in) dice
2 tablespoons olive oil
225g (8oz) onions, chopped
275g (10oz) carrot, cut into 5mm (¼in) dice
200g (7oz) celery, chopped into 5mm (¼in) dice
125g (4½oz) parsnips, chopped into 5mm
    (¼in) dice
200g (7oz) white part of 1 leek, cut into 5mm
    (¼in) slices
1 Kabanos sausage (optional), cut into 5mm
    (¼in) slices
1 x 400g (14oz) tin of Italian tomatoes
225g (8oz) haricot beans, soaked and cooked
    (see below)

salt, freshly ground pepper and sugar
1.8 litres (3 pints) homemade Chicken Stock
* (see page 36)*

Garnish
2 tablespoons freshly chopped flat-leaf parsley

Blanch the bacon, refresh, and dry well.
Prepare the vegetables. Put the olive oil in
a saucepan, add the bacon and sauté over
a medium heat until it becomes crisp
and golden, then add the chopped onion,
carrots and celery. Cover and sweat for
5 minutes, then add the parsnip and finely
sliced leeks. Cover and sweat for a further
5 minutes.

Slice the Kabanos sausage thinly, if using,
and add. Chop the tomatoes and add to
the rest of the vegetables with the beans.
Season with salt, freshly ground pepper
and sugar, add the chicken stock. Allow to
cook until all the vegetables are tender,
which takes about 20 minutes. Taste and
correct the seasoning. Sprinkle with
chopped parsley and serve with lots of
crusty brown bread.

To prepare the haricot beans: soak
overnight in plenty of cold water. The next
day, strain the beans and cover with fresh
cold water, add a bouquet garni, carrot and
onion, cover and simmer until the beans
are soft but not mushy – this can take
30–60 minutes. Just before the end of
cooking, add salt. Remove the bouquet
garni and vegetables and discard.

Beef Consommé
Serves 4

A chef is always proud of a sparklingly
clear, well flavoured consommé. It needs
to be made with great care and attention.
In Ballymaloe, we buy a well hung shin of
beef from our butcher, Frank Murphy. We
use the bones to make a rich beef stock
and then use the meat to flavour the
consommé.

350g (3/4lb) boneless shin of beef (free of any
* fat), finely chopped*
1 small carrot, very finely chopped
green tops of 2 leeks, finely chopped
2 stalks of celery, very finely chopped
2 ripe tomatoes, quartered and de-seeded
3 organic egg whites
1.8 litres (3 pints) well-flavoured Beef Stock
* (see page 36)*
salt and freshly ground pepper
1–2 tablespoons medium or dry sherry
* (optional)*

Mix the chopped beef, carrots, leeks, celery,
tomatoes and egg whites in a bowl. Pour
on the cold stock, whisk well and season.
Pour into a stainless steel saucepan. Bring
slowly to the boil over a low heat, whisking
constantly (should take about 10 minutes).
As soon as the mixture looks cloudy and
slightly milky, stop whisking. Allow the
filter of egg whites to rise slowly to the top
of the saucepan. DO NOT STIR. Allow to
simmer gently for 45–60 minutes to extract
all the flavour from the beef and
vegetables. Add sherry if desired.

Put a filter or a jelly bag into a strainer,
then gently ladle the consommé into it,
being careful not to disturb the filter. Do
not press the sediment in the filter or the
consommé will not be sparkling clear.
Strain it through the cloth or filter a
second time if necessary. If serving the
consommé hot, bring it almost to a boil
and add any flavourings and garnish just
before serving. Do not cook the garnish in
the consommé as it will become cloudy. Do
not allow to boil.

Consommé en Gelée
This cool refreshing starter is perfect for a
summer meal. If consommé is allowed to
go cold it should become jellied. Chill and
just before serving spoon into chilled bowls.
Garnish with chives or wild garlic flowers
if available; sometimes we use marigold
petals and chervil – pretty and delicious.
Serve with freshly made Melba Toast (see
page 78).

1 small onion, diced
salt and freshly ground pepper
1 tablespoon freshly chopped mint

Put the tomatoes, vinegar, breadcrumbs, garlic, tomato juice, roasted red pepper, onion, cucumber, olive oil and mayonnaise into a food processor or blender. Season with salt and freshly ground pepper and sugar. Whizz until smooth. Dilute with water and chill, taste and correct the seasoning.

Mix all the ingredients for the garnish together in a separate bowl. Each guest helps themselves; the soup should be thick with garnish. Drizzle with extra-virgin olive oil; on a very hot day you can add an ice cube or two if you wish.

Cold soups

So refreshing are cold soups as an introduction to summer meals that the number of possibilities keeps increasing. Spanish gaspacho – perhaps the best known of them all – is especially cooling with the addition of ice or iced water before serving. Chilled, jellied consommé served with melba toast is also a classic. Lebanese cold cucumber soup is one of the yoghurt-based cold soups which has long been a favourite at Ballymaloe.

Some soups like Pea and Mint or Beetroot can taste equally delicious served hot or cold, but you may have to make some minor adjustments if you choose the latter option. Remember, cold dulls flavour, so taste and correct the seasoning just before serving. You may also want to add some fresh herbs. Many soups are served rather thicker when cold than when hot. (Most thicken naturally as they cool.) Fresh vegetable juices or tomato water are served thin and chilled.

Gaspacho
Serves 4–6

700g (1½lb) very ripe tomatoes, peeled and
  finely chopped
1 tablespoon red wine vinegar
3 thick slices good-quality stale bread made
  into breadcrumbs
2–3 garlic cloves, crushed
425ml (15fl oz) Fresh Tomato Juice (see page 571)
2 roast and peeled red peppers
110g (4oz) onion, peeled and chopped
1 medium cucumber, chopped
4 tablespoons extra-virgin olive oil
2 tablespoons homemade Mayonnaise
  (see page 584), optional
1 teaspoon salt
freshly ground pepper and sugar

Garnish
2 red peppers, finely diced
1 small cucumber, finely diced
4 very ripe tomatoes, finely diced
4 slices bread made into tiny croûtons and fried
  in olive oil
2 tablespoons diced black olives or small
  whole olives

Chilled Avocado Soup with Tomato and Pepper Salsa
Serves 4

This tasty soup is best made with fresh tomato juice. However, if you have any juices left from a tomato salad, tomato fondue, or a ratatouille, you could use those. Alternatively, simply purée a few tomatoes, seasoned nicely with salt, pepper and sugar.

1 very ripe avocado
½ small onion
½ teaspoon freshly squeezed lemon juice
150ml (¼ pint) homemade Chicken Stock
  (see page 36)
50ml (2fl oz) very good French Dressing
  (see page 226)
150ml (¼ pint) Fresh Tomato Juice
  (see page 571)

Garnish
Roasted Red Pepper, Tomato and Basil Salsa
  (see page 592)

Peel the avocado. Grate the onion on a very fine grater and scrape up enough pulp to measure ½ teaspoon. Put with the remaining ingredients in a liquidiser. Process to a purée, taste. Salt and pepper should not be needed. Fill 4 small serving bowls and chill. Put a spoonful of salsa into each small bowl and serve.

Pappa al Pomodoro
Serves 5–6

This Tuscan bread soup may not seem like a soup as we 'know' it. Made with really sweet ripe tomatoes, good bread and extra-virgin olive oil it is the most sublime comfort food. It can be eaten hot or cold.

extra-virgin olive oil
2 garlic cloves, peeled and chopped
2.2kg (5lb) very ripe sweet tomatoes, skinned, seeded and roughly chopped
2½ tins x 400g (14oz) organic chopped plum tomatoes
sea salt and freshly ground pepper and a pinch of sugar
2 loaves stale sourdough bread
lots of fresh basil
75ml (3fl oz) exra-virgin olive oil

Put the olive oil into a heavy saucepan over a medium heat. Add the garlic and cook gently for a few minutes. Just as the garlic begins to turn golden, add all the tomatoes. Simmer for about 30 minutes, stirring occasionally, until the tomatoes become rich and concentrated. Season with salt, pepper and sugar. Add 300ml (½ pint) water and bring to the boil.

Cut most of the crust off the loaves of bread. Break or cut into large chunks. Add the bread to the tomato mixture and stir until the bread absorbs the liquid – add more boiling water if it is too thick. Remove from the heat and let cool slightly.

Tear the basil leaves into pieces. Stir into the soup with 50–75ml (2–3fl oz) of the extra-virgin olive oil. Allow to sit for 5–10 minutes before serving to allow the bread to absorb the flavour of the basil and the delicious olive oil. Drizzle a little more olive oil over each bowl.

Vichyssoise
Serves 8–10

This cold soup was developed in 1917 by Louis Diat, chef of the Ritz Carlton in New York. It is based on the potage bonne femme recipe. You need a garden to get good leeks in late summer and perhaps it is worth using a few baby leeks for this tasty soup. This soup is very rich and needs to be served in small portions.

50g (2oz) butter
1 onion, finely chopped
whites of 4 leeks, cleaned and finely sliced
600g (1¼lb) potatoes, peeled and finely diced
salt and freshly ground pepper
1.2 litres (2 pints) homemade Chicken Stock (see page 36)
225ml (8fl oz) cream
1 tablespoon finely snipped chives

Melt the butter in a heavy saucepan, and as soon as it foams add the onion, leeks and potatoes. Season with salt and pepper. Cover with a butter wrapper and tightly fitting lid and sweat until soft but not coloured – about 5–8 minutes over a medium heat.

Meanwhile, heat the stock and add it to the pan. Bring back to the boil and simmer, covered, for 8–10 minutes, until the vegetables are cooked. Turn into a liquidiser and add a quarter of the cream. Whizz until very smooth and set aside to cool. This soup should be absolutely silky smooth; if it is not, put it through a sieve.

When cold, stir in the rest of the cream and refrigerate until well-chilled. Stir in the chives just before serving.

Note: Taste the soup and add the cream judiciously; it may not be necessary to add it all.

Lebanese Cold Cucumber Soup
Serves 8

This is a cooling summer soup which can be made in almost the time it takes to grate the cucumber. If you haven't got time to chill the soup, pop the bowls into the freezer while you make it. Serve small portions because this soup is rich.

1 large crisp cucumber
175ml (6fl oz) light cream
175ml (6fl oz) natural yoghurt (preferably organic)
scant 2 tablespoons tarragon or white wine vinegar
½–1 garlic clove, crushed
2 tablespoons finely chopped fresh mint
salt and freshly ground pepper
24–32 shrimps, peeled and freshly cooked (optional)

Garnish
sprigs of mint

Coarsely grate the cucumber. Stir in all other ingredients and season well. Serve chilled in small bowls garnished with mint. A few freshly cooked shrimps are a delicious addition, if available, but the soup is quite wonderful served without any embellishment. It can even be made a day ahead and kept covered in the fridge.

TIP: If this soup tastes a bit flat, a little pinch of salt works wonders.

starters

starters

The purpose of a starter is to whet the palate and set the mood for the rest of the meal. Above all, the starter should be light, and not so substantial as to blunt the appetite before the main course.

Menu Planning

In many ways menu planning is just common sense, but it is better to follow a few guiding principles in order to avoid potential pitfalls. In general, it is easiest to select a main course first, then choose a starter and dessert to complement.

The Occasion

The occasion is an important factor when choosing a menu and laying the table. For anniversaries or romantic evenings one might incorporate heart-shaped treats. For a welcome party for foreign guests it's a good idea to cook a traditional meal. Christmas, Hallowe'en and birthdays will also, of course, influence the choice. It can be fun to plan a meal on a particular colour scheme – green and red for Christmas or even the colours of your favourite sports team at a victory dinner.

Pleasing Your Guests

Do some research to avoid serving dishes that your guests are unable or unwilling to eat, whether for religious, moral or health reasons. Similarly, it is not usually wise to present anything too challenging or unusual. If you are unsure of your guests' tastes, it may be better to err on the side of caution. The golden rule is to be considerate. Many people find offal awful, and very hot curries and spicy food are not always appreciated. Corn on the cob might present problems for older people and squid, sea urchins, prawns in the shell and globe artichokes are sometimes an unwelcome challenge!

Season and Weather

People need and can digest much heartier meals in winter than in summer, so keep rich soups, stews and cassoulets for chilly days. Serve cold soups and sunny Mediterranean salads in summer.

Availability of Fresh Ingredients

It makes sense to use fresh food in season when it is at its cheapest and best – and very little sense to incorporate a dish that includes an expensive imported ingredient that may well be past its best by the time you get it. We are all becoming increasingly concerned about our carbon footprint, so let's make a resolution to reduce food miles and eliminate jet-lagged food from our menu as far as possible.

Don't forget about simple, everyday foods which are seldom found on restaurant menus, but which people often love to eat. My examples include cabbage, parsnips, swedes, whiting, rhubarb and carrigeen. At Ballymaloe we are passionate about cooking fresh and seasonal local food.

Budget

It is perfectly possible to prepare exciting meals on a small budget. Plan meals around beans and pulses, cheaper cuts of meat or less well-known fish. Egg-based dishes such as frittatas are economical too.

Food Value and Nutrition

More than ever, people are aware of the importance of eating fresh and nutritious food. Include a green salad in your meal and keep cream, butter and alcohol to the minimum. Use all fresh food if at all possible and eliminate processed foods entirely from your menu and your diet.

Number of Dishes

The number of dishes served will depend on various factors. The first is the skill of the cook: don't be over ambitious, and certainly don't cook anything new and complicated for guests. The second is the time available – make sure the menu is realistic, and write down a running order if necessary. Run through the menu to work out whether any special equipment is needed. If you are cooking in an unfamiliar kitchen, check that all the equipment you will need is available, before you start. Consider the help available: if entertaining single-handed or with little help, plan the menu so that as much as possible can be prepared ahead, particularly any complex dishes. The number of dishes will also depend on the type of service available – whether silver service, plate service, or a self-service buffet.

Balance

In the menu itself there should be contrasts in ingredients, colour, texture and flavour.

Ingredients: It's all too easy to repeat ingredients in your menu, particularly with an ingredient such as eggs:

> Cheese Soufflé
> French Onion Tart
> Tomato and Mint Salad, Green Salad
> Crème Caramel with Caramel Shards

On the face of it, the menu above looks balanced enough but your guests will actually be consuming about five eggs each!

Colour: Look for contrasting and attractive colour combinations. Try not to repeat colours unless you are working to a colour scheme. In particular, guard against an all-white plate: Cod with Cream and Bay Leaves, Buttered Cucumber and Scallion Potatoes sounds delicious but it would look completely unappetising. The addition of Tomato Fondue, for example, or at least a sprig of chervil, fennel or watercress would make all the difference.

Texture: Contrast crisp, soft, chewy and firm textures, e.g. buttered crumbs on fish pie, or creamy soup with croûtons. Also think about balancing light with heavy. A green salad with a meal has magical properties – it certainly makes me feel less full so I have room for dessert.

Flavour: Contrasts of flavour are important, e.g. mild with spicy (cucumber raita with curry), sharp with bland (blue cheese sauce on pasta or salad), sweet with sour (carrot and apple crudités with sweet and sour dressing).

Cooking methods: Vary the cooking methods you use the temperature of foods. Avoid lots of grills and sautés, for example:

> Grilled Mackerel with Maitre d'Hôtel Butter
> Steak with Béarnaise Sauce
> Apple Fritters

Sauces: Don't fall into the trap of serving similar sauces, by choosing mother and daughter sauces which seem to be different but have the same basis.

Garnishes: To a great extent we 'eat' with our eyes so garnishing is immensely important. Vary garnishes as far as possible. If you have a herb garden you will have access not only to herbs, but also to herb flowers which are edible and make pretty garnishes. Remember the golden rule – flavour is of paramount importance and garnishes should be relevant and edible.

Seasonings: Confine strong flavouring or spices to one dish in the menu unless you are cooking a specifically Indian or Chinese meal, in which case make sure not to repeat the same spices in each course.

Restaurant Menus

I feel passionately that a menu should reflect the food in the locality. Nowadays, menus are very often divided into many more categories than simply starter, main course and dessert. The main types of menu are as follows:

A la carte: each item priced separately.

Table d'hôte: a set menu with a fixed price with perhaps a choice of three or four items on each course.

Menu de gestation or tasting menu: a menu of seven or eight tiny courses so the diner has the opportunity to taste many of the chef's specialities.

No-choice menu: a menu chosen by the chef based on the freshest and best produce available on the day.

Master Recipe
Bruschetta with Chargrilled Peppers and Parma Ham

Serves 2

This toasted or chargrilled bread rubbed with garlic and drizzled with olive oil is found right across Italy from Tuscany to Apulia. Once the traditional lunch of shepherds and peasants, it has now become a fashionable appetiser – not surprising as, made with really good bread and extra-virgin olive oil, it becomes addictive. In Tuscany, it is called Fett'unta, meaning 'oiled slice', and in the south very ripe tomato is also rubbed into the chargrilled bread.

2 slices country bread or good-quality baguette,
  about 1cm (1/2in) thick
1 garlic clove, peeled and cut in half
extra-virgin olive oil
a little Tapenade (see page 590)
wild rocket leaves
a few strips roast red and yellow pepper,
  peeled, de-seeded and chargrilled
1–2 slices Parma ham

Garnish
basil leaves

Chargrill the slices of bread. Rub both sides of the bread with the cut sides of the garlic and drizzle with gorgeous extra-virgin olive oil.

Pop onto warm plates and spread with a little Tapenade.

Lay a few leaves of wild rocket and some red and yellow pepper on top. Drizzle with extra-virgin olive oil. Lay a ruffle of Parma ham and a leaf or two of basil on top. Serve immediately.

Variations
Garden Café Bruschetta with Mushrooms and Slivers of Parmesan

Serves 1

This was Katie's speciality at the Garden Café, which is beside the Ballymaloe Cookery School.

2 flat mushrooms
sea salt and freshly cracked pepper
a little extra-virgin olive oil
a little fresh marjoram
1 slice country bread
1 garlic clove, peeled and cut in two
Pesto (see page 589)
4–5 rocket leaves
shavings of Parmesan cheese (preferably
  Parmigiano Reggiano)

Garnish
5 olives, chopped finely
marigold petals (optional)

Season the mushrooms with salt, pepper, olive oil and a few leaves of marjoram and cook in a frying pan with a little olive oil over a medium heat. Cover with a lid and cook for 3–4 minutes, turning them half way through.

Meanwhile chargrill or toast the bread. Rub with the cut sides of the garlic. Spread a little pesto on the bread and cover with a few rocket leaves. Lay the sizzling mushrooms on top. Season with sea salt and pepper and some fresh marjoram. Put a few slivers of Parmesan on top.

Garnish the plate with a circle of chopped olives and marigold petals.

Serve immediately.

Goat's Cheese and Rocket Bruschetta with Tomato and Chilli Jam

Serves 1

1 slice Italian bread or 1 thick 2cm (3/4in) slice
  good-quality French baguette
1 garlic clove, peeled and cut in half
a little extra-virgin olive oil
a few rocket leaves
a few slices of fresh goat's cheese (e.g. St Tola,
  Ardsallagh, Min Gabhair)
Tomato and Chilli Jam (see page 513)

Garnish
a few olives
freshly cracked pepper

Chargrill or toast the bread. Rub the surface with the cut sides of the garlic, then drizzle with olive oil. Put a few rocket leaves on the bruschetta and top generously with the goat's cheese. Drizzle with Tomato and Chilli Jam.

Pop on to a large plate, add a few olives and some freshly cracked pepper. Serve immediately.

Some other good toppings
Tapenade (see page 590)

Spicy roast peppers

Olives, chillies and capers

Rosemary and Parsley Pesto (see page 589)

Spiced aubergines

White beans with rosemary

Courgettes with Tomato and Cumin
  (see page 71)

RIGHT: Crostini with Potatoes, Goat's Cheese and Rocket Leaves

Crostini with Potatoes, Goat's Cheese and Rocket Leaves

Serves 4

Crostini come from the same derivation as croûtons. We use Ardsallagh goat's cheese. Fresh kale pesto is also worth trying with this recipe.

4 potatoes (Golden Wonders or Kerr's Pinks)
extra-virgin olive oil for deep frying
4 slices homemade white country bread
salt and freshly ground pepper

Ballymaloe French Dressing (see page 226)
4 slices goat's cheese

Garnish
Tapenade (see page 590)
Parsley or Rocket Pesto (see page 589)
a few rocket leaves

Scrub the potatoes but do not peel. Cook in boiling salted water in their jackets until almost cooked. Pour off most of the water, cover the saucepan and steam over a low heat until fully cooked.

To make the crostini: heat 2.5–4cm (1–1½in) olive oil in a small sauté pan. When the oil is very hot but not smoking, add the bread and cook for just a few seconds until golden on one side. Quickly flip over with tongs and cook the other side. Drain and put on to kitchen paper. Keep warm.

Just before eating, peel the potatoes and slice thickly into scant 1cm (½in) slices. Season with salt and pepper, and gently toss in a little Ballymaloe French Dressing.

Pop a warm crostini on a plate, top with overlapping slices of warm potato and lay 1 or 2 slices of goat's cheese on top.

Put a few little dollops of Tapenade around the edge. Drizzle Parsley or Rocket Pesto here and there. Scatter 3 or 4 rocket leaves over the crostini and serve immediately.

A Plate of Mezzes

Mezze means appetiser in Arabic. These little starters are a traditional feature of Middle Eastern food and are often served with an anise-flavoured drink like arak or raki, or the Moroccan mahia made with dates or figs. You may want to prepare an assortment for a communal starter, or simply choose a selection to offer on individual plates. Choose from the following:

Claudia Roden's Hummus bi Tahina
Dukkah
Smoked Cod's Roe
Dolmades
Tzatziki
Taramasalata
Lamajun with Sesame and Thyme Leaves
Courgettes with Tomato and Cumin
Broad Bean and Mint Dip
Aubergine Purée
Roasted Red Pepper, Caper and Preserved
   Lemon Salad (see page 218)
Carrot and Mint Salad (see page 219)

Claudia Roden's Hummus bi Tahina

Serves 6–10 (depending on how it is served)

Hummus bi Tahina, with its rich earthy taste, has quite a cult following. Strange to the palate when first encountered, it soon becomes addictive. It makes an excellent starter served as a dip with pitta bread. It is also delicious with kebabs or as a salad with a main dish. Claudia showed us how to make this when she taught at the school in October 1985.

110–175g (4–6oz) chickpeas, cooked or tinned
juice of 2–3 lemons, or to taste, freshly
   squeezed
2–3 garlic cloves, crushed
150ml (¼ pint) tahini paste (available from
   health food shops and delicatessens)
2 tablespoons extra-virgin olive oil
salt

Garnish
1 tablespoon olive oil
1 teaspoon paprika
1 tablespoon finely chopped flat-leaf parsley
cumin (optional)
a few cooked chickpeas

Drain the chickpeas and keep a few whole ones aside to garnish the dish. Whizz up the remainder in an electric mixer or blender or food processor with a little of the cooking liquid to make a smooth paste. Add the lemon, garlic, tahini paste, olive oil and salt to taste. Blend to a soft creamy texture. Taste and continue to add lemon juice and salt until you are happy with the flavour. Pour into a serving dish, mix the paprika with a little olive oil and dribble over the surface in a cross. Do the same with the parsley. Cumin is also a delicious addition; use 1–1½ teaspoons. Sprinkle with a few cooked chickpeas and serve with pitta bread or any crusty white bread.

Hummus with Lamb and Pine Nuts

Serves 6–10

Hummus Bi Tahina (see left)
450g (1lb) lean leg or shoulder of lamb, cut into
   5mm (¼in) cubes
50g (2oz) pine nuts
1–2 tablespoons olive oil
salt and freshly ground pepper
½–1 teaspoon freshly roasted cumin seed
fresh coriander leaves

Preheat the oven to 180°C/350°F/gas 4.

Toast the pine nuts in the oven for about 5 minutes, turning regularly.

Heat the olive oil in a pan, toss in the meat, season well with salt, pepper and cumin. Cook for 3–4 minutes and add the pine nuts. Put the hummus into a bowl, pile the meat and pine nuts on top. Sprinkle with a few shredded fresh coriander leaves. Serve with pitta or other flat breads.

Dukkah

Serves 20 (depending on use)

Dukkah is an Egyptian spice mix that's much loved and even used for breakfast. The mixture of spices varies from family to family. Serve with crudités, warm pitta bread and a bowl of best olive oil. Just dip a piece of crisp vegetable or a strip of bread first into the olive oil and then into the Dukkah.

Store any leftover in a screw-top jar. Dukkah is delicious with all manner of things, even hard-boiled eggs, or sprinkle over grilled meats as seasoning.

50g (2oz) hazelnuts, toasted and finely chopped
4 tablespoons sesame seeds
2 tablespoons whole coriander seeds
1½ tablespoons whole cumin seeds
½ tablespoon black peppercorns
pinch of ground cinnamon
pinch of salt

Preheat the oven to 200°C/400°F/gas 6. Roast the hazelnuts for about 10 minutes, allow to cool, and rub off the loose skins.

Heat a small, heavy frying pan over a medium heat and toast the sesame seeds. Shake gently until they turn a shade darker and smell nutty, then tip them into a bowl. Repeat with the coriander and cumin seeds. Place the roast spices, sesame and peppercorns in a clean spice or coffee grinder and whizz quickly to give a coarse, dry powder. Add the pinches of cinnamon and salt.

Chop the hazelnuts finely or whizz them for just a few seconds in a spice grinder or food processor, taking care not to overprocess or the nuts will blend into a paste. Mix the chopped nuts with the rest of the ingredients and taste.

Smoked Cod's Roe

Serves 4

50–75g (2–3oz) smoked cod's roe
olive oil
segments of lemon

Slice the chilled cod's roe into 3mm (1/8in) slices. Arrange on a serving plate. Pop a few segments of lemon on the side. Serve soon with lots of flat bread or freshly made toast.

Botargo (the dried roe of the grey mullet) is also delicious served in this way.

Dolmades

Makes 30–36

No Greek mezze is complete without a dish of dolmades. The olive stall in Cork market sells stuffed vine leaves all year round. But if you grow a vine – easier than you think – everyone can have fun making stuffed vine leaves! They're in season in summer but vine leaves preserved in brine are always available.

36 fresh vine leaves or 225g (8oz) preserved vine leaves
225g (8oz) Basmati rice
175g (6oz) onion, finely chopped
2 tablespoons freshly chopped flat-leaf parsley
2 tablespoons freshly chopped mint
2 tablespoons freshly chopped dill
50g (2oz) raisins
50g (2oz) pine nuts, toasted
1/4 teaspoon cinnamon
pinch of allspice
salt and freshly ground pepper
150ml (1/4 pint) olive oil
150ml (1/4 pint) water
pinch saffron or turmeric (optional)
1 teaspoon sugar
juice of 1 freshly squeezed lemon

Plunge a few fresh vine leaves at a time into boiling water for about 30 seconds. They will become limp and pliable. Spread on a clean tea towel. If using preserved vine leaves, drain off the brine, put the leaves into a bowl, cover with boiling water and allow to soak for about 15 minutes. Drain, then cover with cold water. Repeat this procedure once or twice more depending on how salty they are.

Pour boiling water over the rice, stir, then drain; wash it in cold water and drain again. Mix the rice with the onion, parsley, mint, dill, raisins and pine nuts. Add the cinnamon and allspice. Season with salt and pepper.

To stuff the leaves: place a leaf on a clean work top or chopping board, vein side upwards and stem end towards you (trim off the stem if necessary). Put a heaped teaspoon of filling in the centre of the leaf at the base end. Fold the stem end over the filling, then fold in both sides neatly and roll up tightly like a cigar, tucking the seam underneath. Stuff the remaining leaves in the same way. Line a saucepan with vine leaves, arrange the dolmades tightly in a circle in the pot.

Mix the olive oil with the water, add the saffron or turmeric if using, then add the sugar and lemon juice and pour over the arranged vine leaves. Put a small inverted plate on top to keep them in place and to prevent them from unravelling. Cover the saucepan and simmer gently for 50–60 minutes or until the dolmades are thoroughly cooked. Add a little more water if necessary during cooking. Cool in the saucepan and serve cold.

Note: Dolmades may be refrigerated for several days. Vine leaves which are stuffed with minced lamb as well as rice are often served with Avgolemono Soup (page 54).

Tzatziki

Serves 8–10 (depending on use)

This Greek speciality is a delicious cucumber and yoghurt mixture which can be served as part of a mezze, as an accompanying salad or as a sauce to serve with grilled fish or meat. Greek yoghurt is usually made with sheep's milk and is wonderfully thick and creamy.

1 crisp cucumber, peeled and diced into 3–5mm (1/8–1/4in) dice
salt
1–2 garlic cloves, crushed
a dash of white wine vinegar or lemon juice
425ml (3/4 pint) Greek yoghurt or best-quality natural yoghurt
4 tablespoons cream (optional)
1 heaped tablespoon freshly chopped mint
sugar, salt and freshly ground pepper

Put the cucumber dice into a sieve, sprinkle with salt and allow to drain for about 30 minutes. Dry the cucumber on kitchen paper, put into a bowl and mix with the garlic, vinegar or lemon juice, yoghurt and cream. Stir in the mint and taste. It may need seasoning with salt, pepper and a little sugar.

Variation
Follow the Master Recipe but substitute dill for the mint.

LEFT: Lamajun with Sesame and Thyme Leaves

Lamajun with Sesame and Thyme Leaves
Serves 6–8

I first tasted this version of Lebanese flat bread Lamajun in the market on Rue Pierre de Serbie, close to the Musée d'Arte Moderne in Paris. They are cooked on a concave stove called a sag which looks like an upturned wok. The beaming cook, who turned these lamajun out like hot cakes, had a little roller that he dipped in the zahtar, sesame and thyme mixture and used to cover the base evenly at the speed of light.

Topping
150 ml (¼ pint) extra-virgin olive oil
2 tablespoons dried thyme
4 tablespoons sesame seeds, toasted
½–1 teaspoon sea salt

Dough
275g (10oz) plain flour
225ml (8fl oz) natural yoghurt

Mix all the ingredients for the topping in a bowl.

Preheat a heavy iron frying pan and the grill.

Mix the flour with the yoghurt to form a soft dough. Take about 50g (2oz) of the dough and roll until it's as thin as possible, using lots of flour. Spread the topping evenly over the dough, a brush works well. Put onto the hot pan (no oil needed) and cook for about 2 minutes or until golden on the bottom. Remove from the pan and slide on a hot baking sheet under the hot grill and cook for another 2–3 minutes.

Serve alone or with Hummus (see page 68) and Tabouleh (see page 136).

Taramasalata
Serves 4–8

Tarama is Greek and Turkish for fish roe. Traditionally, the Greek speciality taramasalata is made with the roe of grey mullet, but today smoked cod's roe is more commonly used. It is available in winter for a few months. Taramasalata is really easy to make and paler in colour than the disconcertingly bright pink ready-made equivalent.

3–4 slices good-quality white bread
250g (9oz) smoked cod roe
juice of 1–2 lemons, or to taste
50ml (2fl oz) sunflower oil
50ml (2fl oz) extra-virgin olive oil

Cut the crusts off the bread and soak the bread in water. Squeeze dry. Skin the cod's roe and put it into the food processor with the bread and the lemon juice. Flick on the motor. Trickle in the oil gradually as though you are making mayonnaise. Transfer to a bowl, cover and refrigerate. The mixture will firm up as it cools.

Courgettes with Tomato and Cumin
Serves 6–8

3 tablespoons extra-virgin olive oil
2 garlic cloves, crushed
2 large onions, finely chopped
1 teaspoon freshly chopped cumin
450g (1lb) courgettes, sliced 1cm (½in) thick
salt and freshly ground pepper
2 tablespoons white wine vinegar
chilli powder
450g (1lb) very ripe tomatoes, peeled and
   chopped
a little sugar

Heat the olive oil in a casserole, add the crushed garlic, onions and cumin. Sweat for 4–5 minutes, add the courgettes, salt, pepper, vinegar and chilli powder.

Toss gently in the oil, add the chopped tomatoes, season with a little sugar. Cover and cook for 8–10 minutes or until the courgettes and tomato are soft.

Taste, correct the seasoning and serve at room temperature as part of a selection of mezzes or with lamb.

Broad Bean and Mint Dip
Serves 4

A fresh-tasting dip best made with fresh young broad beans, but frozen ones will do at a push. Serve with crudités or bread.

450g (1lb) fresh broad beans, shelled
leaves from 6–8 mint sprigs
3–4 tablespoons extra-virgin olive oil
about 2 tablespoons lemon juice, freshly
   squeezed
salt and freshly ground pepper

Garnish
sprigs of mint

Cook the broad beans in boiling water until tender (just a few minutes). Drain, reserving the cooking liquid. Rinse to refresh under running cold water. Put the beans into a food processor or blender. Add the mint, olive oil and lemon juice and mix to a purée, adding enough of the reserved cooking liquid to give a soft consistency. Season to taste with salt and pepper. Taste and adjust the levels of lemon and oil if necessary.

Transfer the dip to a small serving dish. Serve at room temperature, garnished with sprigs of mint.

How to Chargrill Aubergines

There are several ways to do this. Each method produces a slightly different taste.

1. Prick the aubergines in a few places. Roast whole in a hot oven for about 30 minutes, turning over from time to time – they will collapse and soften.

2. Prick the aubergines as above. Put them on a wire rack under the grill and turn them regularly until the skin is black and charred.

3. Chargrill the aubergines over an open fire or barbecue – delicious.

4. For almost the most delicious flavour of all, chargrill the aubergines over an open gas flame, turning regularly until blistered, charred and soft and miserable looking. Allow to cool, peel and use as desired.

Master Recipe
Aubergine Purée with Olive Oil and Lemon
Serves 6

This is one of my absolute favourite ways to eat aubergine. It is served all through the southern Mediterranean, and there are many delicious variations.

4 large aubergines
4–5 tablespoons extra-virgin olive oil
juice of 1–2 lemons, or to taste
salt and freshly ground pepper

Roast or grill the aubergines depending on the flavour you like (see below). Allow to cool. Peel thinly, taking care to save every little morsel of flesh. Discard the skins and drain the flesh in a sieve or colander.

Transfer to a bowl, mash the purée with a fork or chop with a knife depending on the texture you like.

Add the olive oil and lemon juice, salt and pepper to taste.

Variations
Freshly crushed garlic may be added.

In Turkey some thick Greek yoghurt is often added. For this quantity of aubergine purée, allow 5–6 tablespoons yoghurt, and reduce the olive oil by half.

Mix with ricotta and freshly chopped herbs, e.g. marjoram. This makes a delicious 'sauce' for pasta.

A spicier version from Morocco. Add 1 teaspoon Harissa (see page 596), 1 teaspoon freshly ground cumin and 2 tablespoons coarsely chopped coriander leaves.

Add some pomegranate molasses, as they do in Syria. About 3–4 tablespoons could be substituted for the fresh lemon juice.

Julia Wight's Aubergine Purée
Follow the Master Recipe, adding:

2 small garlic cloves, finely chopped
½–1 teaspoon freshly ground and
   roasted cumin
1–2 tablespoons chiffonade of mint
juice of ½–1 lemon, freshly squeezed
freshly ground pepper or Chilli Pepper Oil
   (see page 227)

Mix well together and season to taste.

Pink Grapefruit and Pomegranate Sorbet
Serves 4–5

The jewel-like seeds of pomegranates look like glistening rubies, so appear festive. This sorbet is very versatile and may be served at the beginning, middle or end of a meal.

1 litre (1¾ pints) pink grapefruit juice (about 10 grapefruit)
about 225g (8oz) caster sugar
1 organic egg white (optional)
1–2 pomegranates

Garnish
2 pink grapefruit, cut into segments
pomegranate seeds
a little sugar
fresh mint leaves

8 chilled white side plates

Put the freshly squeezed grapefruit into a bowl, add the sugar and dissolve by stirring it into the juice. Taste. The juice should seem rather too sweet to drink: it will taste less sweet after the freezing. Cut the pomegranates in half around the 'equator'. Open out and carefully flick the seeds into a bowl, discard the skin and all the yellow membrane.

Make the sorbet in one of the following 3 ways:

Method 1
Pour into the drum of an ice-cream maker or sorbetière and freeze for 20–25 minutes. Fold in the pomegranate seeds. Scoop out and serve immediately or store in a covered bowl in the freezer until needed.

Method 2
Pour the juice into a stainless steel or plastic container and put into the freezer. After about 4–5 hours when the sorbet is semi frozen, remove and whisk until granular. Return to freezer. Repeat several times. When almost frozen fold in the pomegranate seeds. Keep covered in the freezer until needed.

Method 3
If you have a food processor, simply freeze the sorbet completely in a covered stainless steel or plastic bowl, then break into large pieces and whizz for a few seconds. Add one slightly beaten egg white, whizz again for another few seconds, then return to the bowl. Fold in the pomegranate seeds. Freeze again until needed.

Before serving, chill the plates in a fridge or freezer. Then, put 1–2 scoops of sorbet on chilled plate, garnish with a few segments of pink grapefruit. Sprinkle with pomegranate seeds, spoon a little grapefruit juice over the segments, decorate with fresh mint leaves and serve immediately.

Note: For straight Pink Grapefruit Sorbet, simply omit the pomegranate seeds.

Segmenting Citrus Fruit

1. With a sharp, preferably serrated knife, cut a slice off the top and bottom of the fruit in as far as the flesh.

2. Remove the skin and pith either in a spiral as though peeling an apple, or from the top to bottom in four or five pieces (easier, but more wasteful: holding the knife perpendicular, you need to follow the line of the pith).

When every scrap of pith is removed hold the citrus fruit crossways in the palm of your hand over a bowl.

3. Cut in front of the membrane to, but not through, the centre. Then push the knife forward to remove the segment cleanly from the membrane. Cut in front of the next membrane, hold back the membrane with your thumb to give more leverage, then push the knife forward toward the outer edge of the fruit to remove the segment; it will drop into the bowl.

4. When all the segments have been removed, squeeze the membrane tightly in your hand over the bowl to catch the final drops of juice. If the segments are not needed immediately, store in a bowl just large enough to hold them. Cover with plastic film and refrigerate, otherwise those exposed to the air will oxidise and become bitter.

LEFT: Pink Grapefruit and Pomegranate Sorbet

Grape and Grapefruit with Lovage or Mint

Serves 6

Fruit and fresh herb starters are popular at Ballymaloe. Pomelo, sweeties, ugli fruit or ordinary grapefruit can also be used.

3 pink grapefruit, peeled and segmented
30 grapes, peeled and de-seeded
3 teaspoons mint, finely chopped or 3 teaspoons
    lovage, finely chopped
about 3 teaspoons caster sugar

Combine the grapefruit and grapes in a bowl. Sprinkle with mint or lovage and sugar. Taste, and add more sugar if necessary. Chill before serving in a pretty white bowl with a sprig of mint on top.

Radishes with Butter, Crusty Bread and Sea Salt

When I was just 19, alone and frightened in Besançon in eastern France, a French girl took pity on me and invited me to have lunch with her in a café. We had a plate of charcuterie and radishes. I watched in fascination as she buttered her radishes, dipped them in sea salt and ate them greedily. I followed suit – I've never forgotten the flavour.

fresh radishes complete with leaves
butter pats
sea salt
crusty bread

Gently wash the radishes, trim the tail and the top of the leaves if they are large. Cut a chunk of butter into 1cm (¹/₂in) cubes. If you have butter pats, soak them in cold water and then roll each cube into a butter ball; drop them into a bowl of iced water.

To serve: put 7 or 8 chilled radishes on each plate, add 2 or 3 butter balls and a little mound of sea salt. Serve fresh crusty bread as an accompaniment.

Master Recipe
Asparagus on Toast with Hollandaise Sauce

Serves 4

This is a simple and gorgeous way to serve fresh asparagus during its short season in late spring. We feast on it in every possible way for those precious weeks – roast, chargrilled, in soups, frittatas, quiches… Don't forget to dip some freshly cooked spears in a soft boiled egg for a simple luxury! This was my father-in-law's favourite way to eat Irish asparagus.

One can buy a special, tall asparagus cooking pot – a real luxury but certainly worth the money if you cook asparagus regularly – however you can survive quite well with an oval casserole dish.

16–20 spears fresh green asparagus
4 slices homemade White Yeast Bread
  (see page 481)
butter
a little Hollandaise Sauce (see page 581)

Garnish
sprigs of chervil

Hold each spear of asparagus over your index finger down near the root end. It will snap at the point where it begins to get tough. Some people like to peel asparagus but we rarely do. Cook in about 2.5cm (1in) of boiling salted water in an oval cast iron casserole for 4–8 minutes or until a knife tip will pierce the root end easily.

Meanwhile toast the bread, spread with butter and remove the crusts. Place a piece of toast on a hot plate, put the asparagus on top and spoon a little Hollandaise sauce over. Garnish with a sprig of chervil and serve immediately.

Maltaise sauce (see page 582) is also a classic accompaniment to asparagus.

Seakale on Toast with Hollandaise Sauce

Serves 4–6

Seakale is an 'old-fashioned' perennial vegetable, often found in country house gardens. We look forward with great anticipation to its delicate flavour in spring. Quite apart from its gastronomic value, it is altogether a beautiful plant with its profusion of white flowers in Summer and bobbly seed heads in Autumn. Seek it out – it deserves to be better-known. Seakale tastes divine with wild salmon or Dublin bay prawns, and is delicious on toast with Hollandaise Sauce.

Follow the Master Recipe, but use:
450g (1lb) seakale
600ml (1 pint) water
1 teaspoon salt
50–75g (2–3oz) butter
toast
Hollandaise Sauce (see page 581) or melted
  butter

Wash the seakale gently and trim into manageable lengths – say 10cm (4in). Bring the water to a fast boil and add the salt. Add the seakale, cover and boil until tender – about 15 minutes.

Just as soon as a knife will pierce the seakale easily, drain and serve on hot plates with a little Hollandaise Sauce (see page 581) or melted butter and lots of toast.

Melon Sorbet with Lime Syrup
See page 403

Ballymaloe Chutney Eggs
See page 100

Oeufs Mimosa
See page 101

Almspurses with Tomato Sauce
See page 118

Rory's 'Blinis'
See page 118

Warm Salads (Salades Tièdes)

Salades tièdes, or warm salads, are a legacy of the Nouvelle Cuisine movement which began in the early 1970s in France led by Michel Guérard. Even though they are called warm salads, salades tièdes have a base of lettuces and salad leaves that are tossed in a chosen dressing and topped with a few morsels of something hot and delicious, e.g. a few fat prawns, some scallops, goat's cheese, roast vegetables, chicken or duck livers, bacon lardons, thinly sliced duck breast or duck confit, lamb's kidney...the variety is endless. Roast vegetables or crispy potatoes or vegetable crisps may be added for contrast of texture and flavour.

Choose a selection of lettuces and salad leaves as a base; these will vary from season to season and can include finely shredded red cabbage in the winter. Some fresh herbs and herb flowers will enliven the flavour. Wash and dry and keep fresh in the fridge. The dressing can be made with olive, hazelnut, walnut or sesame oil and the vinegars may vary too – red or white wine, sherry, balsamic, rice vinegar – depending on the flavours in the salad.

The salad and dressings may be prepared ahead, as of course may vegetable crisps or caramelised shallots. However, they need to be tossed and assembled just before serving and the hot toppings cooked and added at the last minute.

Some good combinations:

Spicy chicken, rustic roast potatoes and mango relish

Lamb's kidney tossed in marjoram, with oyster mushrooms and pink peppercorns

Chicken livers with julienne of apple and toasted hazelnuts

Salt and pepper squid with matchstick potatoes and sweet chilli sauce

Smoked Mackerel Salad with Beetroot and Horseradish Sauce on Baby Salad Leaves

Serve some 2.5cm (1in) pieces of smoked mackerel on a mixture of baby salad leaves, with 1cm (1/2in) dice of pickled beetroot (see page 514) and a few little blobs of horseradish sauce – a delicious combination dreamed up by Rory O'Connell at Ballymaloe.

Peppered Venison Salad with Horseradish Cream, Pommes Allumettes and Red Onions and Chives

Serves 4

A bit cheffy – one needs to do a bit of mise en place before putting this together but the combination of flavours is so worth the effort. A great starter but also a perfect light main course.

Dressing
2 tablespoons extra-virgin olive oil
1 tablespoon sunflower oil
1 tablespoon wine vinegar
pinch of sea salt and pepper
pinch of sugar
pinch of English mustard powder

Pommes Allumettes (see page 185)

450g (1lb) loin of venison, trimmed of all fat and gristle and cut into 5mm (1/4in) thick slices
4 tablespoons cracked pepper
extra-virgin olive oil for frying
salt to taste

4 handfuls of mixed salad leaves
1/2 red onion, thinly sliced and marinaded in 3 tablespoons sugar and 2 tablespoons vinegar and a pinch of salt for 10–15 minutes

Garnish
Horseradish Cream (see page 586)
2 tablespoons finely chopped chives

First make the dressing by whisking all the ingredients together. Store in a glass jar and shake to re-emulsify before use if necessary.

Cook the Pommes Allumettes and drain on kitchen paper and keep warm.

Brush one side of each slice of venison with olive oil and dip into the freshly cracked pepper. Season with salt. Heat a frying pan and when it is really hot sauté the venison in a little olive oil, cooking it for a few seconds on each side – until just medium.

Toss the salad leaves and divide between 4 large plates or 1 large serving dish. Place the cooked pommes allumettes on top of the leaves to form a 'nest'. When the venison is cooked place on top of the potatoes. Arrange a few slices of red onion around the salad. Drizzle with horseradish cream and sprinkle with chopped chives. Serve immediately.

Master Recipe
Warm Salad with Duck Livers and Marigold Petals

Serves 4

selection of lettuce and salad leaves e.g. butterhead, iceberg, oakleaf, lollo rosso, curly endive and mysticana
1 dessert apple, peeled, cored and diced
10g (1/2 oz) butter
4–6 fresh duck livers, organic if possible, or if unavailable, chicken livers
salt and freshly ground pepper
10g (1/2oz) butter

Dressing
3 tablespoons extra-virgin olive oil
1 tablespoon red wine vinegar
a little Dijon mustard
salt and freshly ground pepper

Garnish
1 tablespoon freshly chopped chives
chive flowers
marigold petals

Wash and dry the salad leaves and tear into bite-sized pieces. Whisk together the ingredients for the dressing. Fry the apple in a little butter until just soft and almost golden and taste – it may need a pinch of sugar. Keep warm. Wash and dry the livers and divide each into 2 pieces.

Just before serving, melt the second quantity of butter in a sauté pan, season the livers with salt and pepper and cook over a gentle heat, turning to cook on all sides – 5 minutes in all. While the livers are cooking, toss the salad leaves in just enough dressing to make them glisten.

Divide the salad between 4 large plates, sprinkle with the apple dice, divide the hot livers evenly between each salad. (They are very good slightly pink in the centre, but only if you like them that way!) Sprinkle with chives, chive flowers and marigold petals and serve immediately.

Variations

One can do lots of variations on this starter. One could also cook the fillet pieces from duck breasts quickly on a pan and slice them onto the salad.

Duck Confit Salad
Serves 4

Ingredients as Master Recipe but substitute 2 preserved duck legs (Confit de Canard, see page 291) for the livers.

Preheat the oven to 180°C/350°F/gas 4. Remove the duck legs from the fat (it may be necessary to melt some of it). Roast for 15–20 minutes and then cook for 4–5 minutes on a hot grill pan to crisp the skin.

Strip the crispy duck from the bones and divide between the 4 plates of salad. Sprinkle with chopped chives, chive flowers and marigold petals as described above. Serve immediately.

Warm Salad of Lamb Kidneys, Glazed Shallots and Straw Potatoes
Serves 4

Kidneys from spring lamb are best because they are mild and tender. They are also inexpensive and cook in a few minutes. They will keep better if you buy them in their jackets of white fat as this seals them against the air.

Caramelised Shallots
450g (1lb) shallots, peeled
50g (2oz) butter
125ml (4fl oz) water
1–2 tablespoons sugar
salt and pepper
sprig of thyme or rosemary

Hazelnut Oil Dressing
3 tablespoons hazelnut oil
3 tablespoons sunflower oil
2 tablespoons white wine vinegar
¼ teaspoon Dijon mustard
salt, freshly ground pepper and a pinch
  of sugar

Selection of lettuces (e.g. butterhead, lollo rosso,
  curly endive, rocket, winter purslane,
  watercress etc.) – allow a generous handful
  per person for a starter portion

oil, for deep frying
1 large potato, 110–175g (4–6oz)

2 tablespoons olive oil
4 lamb's kidneys trimmed of all fat and gristle
  and cut into 2cm (³⁄₄in) dice
salt and freshly ground pepper
1 tablespoon marjoram or thyme leaves

First prepare the shallots: put them with the butter, water, sugar, salt, pepper and herbs into a small saucepan. Bring to the boil and simmer, covered, until the shallots are nearly tender. Remove the lid and allow the juices to evaporate and caramelise, taking care they don't burn.

Whisk together the ingredients for the dressing and set aside. Wash and dry the lettuces and salad leaves if necessary, break into bite-sized pieces and place into a deep salad bowl.

Heat good-quality oil in a deep fryer to 200°C (400°F). Peel the potato and cut into fine julienne strips on a mandolin, in a food processor or by hand. Wash off the excess starch with cold water, drain and pat dry. Deep fry the potato strips until they are golden brown, then keep warm to serve with the salad.

Finally, heat the olive oil in a frying pan and when hot, add the kidneys.

Season with salt and pepper, add the marjoram or thyme and cook over a medium heat until just cooked (some people like them slightly pink). Don't over-cook the kidneys or they will become tough.

While the kidneys are cooking, toss the lettuces with the dressing and divide between 4 plates. Put the warm shallots around each pile of salad, arrange the fried potato carefully on top of each shallot in a little pile. Finally sprinkle on the cooked kidneys straight from the pan. Serve immediately.

Warm Salad of Chicken Livers
We sometimes toss chicken livers in a little foaming butter and grated ginger. Spoon over a mixture of salad leaves. Garnish with Game Chips (see page 185), wild garlic flowers and marigold petals.

Warm Salad of Goat's Cheese with Walnut Dressing
See page 212

Warm Salad of Bacon with Poached Egg and Cheese
See page 100

Seared Beef Salad with Horseradish Mayonnaise and French Fried Onions
See page 212

Smoked Mackerel Pâté with Fennel on Melba Toast

Serves 4

Cooked smoked salmon, fresh salmon, trout or herring may be substituted in this recipe.

110g (4oz) undyed smoked mackerel, free of
  skin and bone
50–75g (2–3oz) softened butter
1/4 teaspoon finely snipped fennel
1/2 teaspoon lemon juice
1/2–1 garlic clove, crushed to a paste
salt and freshly ground pepper
Melba toast (see below)

Garnish
sprigs of chervil and tomato concassé

Whizz all the ingredients in a food processor or by hand. Season with salt and pepper to taste. Add more lemon juice and garlic if necessary – it should be well seasoned. Serve in little individual pots or in slices if a larger quantity is made and set in a loaf tin.

This pâté can be piped in rosettes onto 5mm (1/4in) thick slices of cucumber, Melba toast, crisp croûtons or savoury biscuits. Garnish each with a sprig of fennel and fennel or chervil flowers, if available.

Crab Pâté with Cucumber and Dill Salad

Serves 8–10

This pâté, which is made in a flash once you have the crab meat to hand, can be served in lots of different ways (see Little Pots of Pâté, page 79). We make it into a cylinder and roll it in chopped parsley for extra posh! If it is set in a loaf tin it can be sliced and served with a salad.

150g (5oz) mixed brown and white cooked
  crab meat
110g (4oz) softened butter
1–2 teaspoons flat-leaf parsley, finely chopped
1 medium garlic clove, crushed
few grinds black pepper
fresh lemon juice to taste
Ballymaloe Tomato Relish (see page 271) or
  tomato chutney (optional)
3 tablespoons finely chopped flat-leaf parsley

Cucumber and Dill Salad (see right)

Garnish
flat-leaf parsley, fennel or chervil
fennel or chive flowers, if available

Mix all ingredients together in a bowl or, better still, whizz them in a food processor. Taste carefully and continue to season until you are happy with the flavour: it may need a little more lemon juice or garlic. Form the pâté into a cylinder, roll up in greaseproof paper, twist the ends like a Christmas cracker and chill until almost firm.

Spread one-quarter sheet of greaseproof paper out on the work top, sprinkle the chopped parsley over the paper, unwrap the pâté and roll it in the parsley so that the surface is evenly coated. Wrap it up again and refrigerate until needed.

Make the Cucumber and Dill Salad. Then arrange circles of cucumber slices on chilled plates and put 1 or more 5mm (1/4in) thick slices of pâté in the centre of each. Garnish with parsley, fennel or chervil and fennel or chive flowers if available. Serve with crusty white bread or hot toast.

Cucumber and Dill Salad

1 medium cucumber
2–4 teaspoons white wine vinegar
1/2 teaspoon dill or 1 teaspoon finely chopped
  fennel (herb)
salt, freshly ground pepper and lots of sugar

Finely slice the cucumber. Sprinkle with wine vinegar and season with salt, pepper and a good pinch of sugar. Stir in the snipped dill or fennel and taste.

Smoked Salmon Pâté

Allow 25g (1oz) per person

Don't waste your money on poor-quality smoked salmon. Do some homework before you shop (Bill Casey smokes wonderful Shanagarry salmon on our farm...), and build up a relationship with your fishmonger. This is a delicious way to use up smoked salmon trimmings.

smoked salmon trimmings
softened butter, unsalted
clarified butter (see page 105)
freshly ground pepper
lemon juice, to taste

Making Melba Toast

Preheat the grill to maximum. White bread, sliced about 5mm (1/4in) thick, is best for melba toast. Slide an oven rack under the grill as close to the element as possible.

Toast the bread on both sides. Lower the oven rack, it should be about 12.5cm (5in) from the element. Work quickly and while the toast is still hot, cut off the crusts and split the bread in half horizontally. Cut each slice into 2 or 4 triangles. Replace under the grill on the rack or oven tray. It will curl up within seconds, be careful not to let it burn.

The second stage may also be done in a low oven 150°C/300°F/gas 2. Melba toast will keep in an airtight tin for a day or two but it is much the best if served immediately.

Remove any skin or bones from the fish. Weigh the flesh. Add three-quarters the weight in butter, plus the pepper and lemon juice. Blend to a smooth purée. Fill into pots and run clarified butter over the top. (Alternatively, use a loaf tin.) Turn out and cut in slices when set. Serve with crusty white bread, a little green salad and perhaps some well seasoned tomato concasse, cucumber pickle or tomato salsa.

Pâté de Campagne with Celeriac Rémoulade and Redcurrant Sauce

Serves 10

Every charcuterie in France proudly sells its own version of Pâté de Campagne. They vary enormously in content and makeup – some are made with rabbit, game and even sweetbreads. A certain proportion of fat is essential, otherwise the terrine will be dry and dull. It is meant to be rough textured so the mixture should not be too finely minced. Resist cutting the terrine for a few days to allow the flavours to mature. Pâté de Campagne keeps very well, certainly for up to a week. Do try to find free-range organic pork.

225g (8oz) fresh chicken livers
2 tablespoons brandy
1/2 teaspoon ground white pepper (yes, all of it!)
225g (8oz) rindless, streaky rashers, very thinly sliced (you may need more if they are not very thinly sliced) or better still, barding fat*
1 medium onion, finely chopped
10g (1/2oz) butter
450g (1lb) rindless streaky pork, minced
225g (8oz) veal or chicken meat, minced
2 garlic cloves, finely chopped
1/4–1/2 teaspoon ground allspice (pimento)
good pinch of ground cloves
1–2 teaspoons freshly chopped annual marjoram (optional)
2 small organic eggs, beaten
salt, freshly ground pepper and nutmeg

50g (2oz) pistachios, shelled
175–225g (6–8oz) piece of cooked ham, cut in thick strips
a bay leaf
a couple of sprigs of thyme
Luting Paste (see right) or tin foil

1.8 litre (3 pint) terrine or casserole with a tight-fitting lid

Celeriac Rémoulade (see page 178)
Redcurrant Sauce (see page 598)

*A pork butcher will supply barding fat and caul fat to order. Both can be frozen. Barding fat is the name for the very thinly sliced pork or bacon used to line terrines and pâtés and to enclose food for cooking. The caul of pigs is used by butchers to encase minced offal, such as haggis and faggots.

Wash the chicken livers, separate the lobes and remove any trace of green. Marinade in the brandy and freshly ground white pepper for 2 hours.

Preheat the oven to 180°C/350°F/gas 4.

Line a terrine or casserole with very thinly sliced stretched bacon or barding fat, keeping a few slices for the top.

Sweat the onion gently in the butter until soft but not coloured. Mix the onion with the pork, veal, garlic, allspice, cloves, marjoram, eggs and the brandy from the chicken liver marinade. Season with salt, freshly ground pepper and lots of grated nutmeg and the marinade. Mix very thoroughly. Fry a little piece and taste for seasoning – it should taste quite spicy and highly seasoned. Add the pistachios and beat until the mixture holds together.

Spread a third of the pork mixture in the lined terrine, add a layer of ham strips (roughly half the quantity) interspersed with half the chicken livers, then cover with another third of the pork mixture. Add the remaining ham and livers and cover with the last third of pork. Lay the reserved barding fat or bacon slices on top, trimming the edges if necessary. Set the bay leaf and the sprigs of thyme on top and cover with the lid. Seal the lid and the

steam hole with luting paste or else place a sheet of tinfoil under the lid.

Cook in a bain-marie in the oven for 1 1/4–1 1/2 hours or until a skewer inserted for 1/2 minute into the mixture is hot to the touch when taken out. If you are still in doubt, remove the lid and check: the pâté should also have shrunk in from the sides of the terrine and the juices should be clear.

Cool until tepid, remove the luting paste or tinfoil and lid and press the terrine with a board and a 900g (2lb) weight until cold. This helps to compact the layers so that it will cut more easily. Keep for 2–3 days before serving to allow the terrine to mature. It may be frozen for up to 2 months.

To serve: unmould the terrine, cut into thick slices as needed and serve with Celeriac Rémoulade and Redcurrant Sauce and a good green salad. Gherkins and olives are often served as an accompaniment also, and don't forget some crusty white bread and a glass of red wine!

Luting Paste

225g (8oz) flour
150–175ml (5–6fl oz) water

Mix the flour and water into a dough firm enough to handle, roll into a rope and use to seal the lid onto the casserole to prevent the steam from escaping during cooking.

Little Pots of Pâté

A fun way to serve pâté is to offer 3 or even 5 tiny pots of different pâtés as a starter or summer lunch. We often include potted shrimps (see page 81) or a potted meat depending on what's available. Simply fill each little pot with a different pâté and decorate each with a different herb or herb flower – e.g. thyme leaves and flowers on the chicken liver pâté, a little fennel or dill plus the flowers if available on the fish pâtés. Flat-leaf parsley or chervil are decorative, while knotty marjoram would complement many potted meats. Serve with lots of crusty bread, hot thin toast or Melba toast.

Tiny Rosettes of Pâté

All the smooth pâtés, e.g. chicken liver, smoked salmon, mackerel, herring or potted crab, can be piped in rosettes on to 5mm (¼in) thick slices of cucumber, triangles of Melba toast, crisp croûtons, savoury biscuits or tiny tartlets. Garnish each with a little sprig of relevant fresh herb or flower e.g. chervil and perhaps tomato concassé.

Ballymaloe Chicken Liver Pâté with Melba Toast

Serves 10–12 (depending on how it is served)

This recipe has certainly stood the test of time. It has been our pâté maison at Ballymaloe since the opening of the restaurant in 1965. It is served in many different ways: its success depends upon being generous with good Irish butter.

225g (8oz) fresh organic chicken livers
butter for frying
2 tablespoons brandy
225–350g (8–12oz) butter (depending on how
    strong the chicken livers are)
1 teaspoon fresh thyme leaves
1 large garlic clove, crushed
salt and freshly ground pepper
clarified butter (see page 105) to seal the top

Wash the livers and remove any membrane or green-tinged bits. Melt a little butter in a frying pan. When it foams, add in the livers and cook over a gentle heat. Be careful not to overcook them or the outsides will get crusty – but all trace of pink should be gone. Put the livers through a sieve or into a food processor. De-glaze the pan with brandy, allow to flame, add the garlic and thyme leaves and then scrape off with a spatula and add to the livers. Purée for a few seconds. Allow to cool.

Add 225g (8oz) butter. Purée until smooth Season carefully, taste and add more butter, cut into cubes, if necessary. This pâté should taste fairly mild* and be quite smooth in texture. Put into pots or into one large terrine. Knock out any air bubbles. Run a little clarified butter over the top of the pâté to seal.

Serve with Melba toast (see page 78) or hot white bread. This pâté will keep for 4–5 days in a refrigerator.

* It should taste milder than you feel it should, just after it is made. The flavour will intensify on keeping.

Serving suggestions

1. In little ramekins accompanied by hot, crusty white bread.

2. As 'Little Pots of Pâté' (see page 79).

3. Fill the pâté into a loaf tin lined with clingfilm. When it is set, arrange slices on individual plates with a little dice of well-seasoned tomato concassé and then garnish with chervil or lemon balm.

4. For a buffet, the loaf-shaped pâté may be covered with a thin layer of soft butter, then decorated with tiny rosettes of butter and thyme leaves and flowers. The whole pâté is arranged on a bed of salad leaves and garnished with herbs in flower.

5. Rosettes of pâté may be piped onto tiny triangles of melba toast, Ballymaloe cheese biscuits, or slices of cucumber. These rosettes are very pretty but must be served within an hour of being prepared, otherwise they oxidise and become bitter (see tip). Garnish with a spot of tomato concassé and a little chervil.

6. Pâté may be formed into a roll, wrapped in clingfilm or greaseproof paper and refrigerated. Later the paper is removed and the roll of pâté decorated. It can be coated in finely chopped herbs and decorated with herb flowers.

TIP: It is essential to cover chicken liver pâté with a layer of clarified or even just-melted butter, otherwise it will oxidise and become bitter in taste and grey in colour.

Terrine of Chicken

Serves 10–20

A fiddle to make but so worthwhile. A recipe taught to my mother-in-law Myrtle Allen by Simone Beck. She passed it on to me.

225g (8oz) organic chicken livers
100ml (3½fl oz) brandy or madeira
salt to taste and 2 teaspoons ground white
    pepper (yes, use all of it)
1.1–1.3kg (2½–3lb) organic chicken
225g (8oz) streaky bacon, trimmed and
    de-rinded
225g (8oz) cooked ham, thickly sliced
marjoram, thyme, bay leaves
1 organic egg, beaten
a 'crepine' or sheet of bacon fat to cover the
    terrine or chicken skin all in one piece

a terrine dish or a small oval casserole dish
    roughly 18 x 12.5 x 8cm (7 x 5 x 3in)

Wash the livers, pat dry on kitchen paper, then put them in a flat dish with the brandy or madeira. Pepper generously with ground white pepper. Leave to marinate for 2 hours if possible.

Preheat the oven to 190°C/375°F/gas 5.

Clean the chicken in the normal way. Place the chicken, breast-side down on a board. Skin the chicken, beginning by making an incision down the back, lifting the skin with your fingers in order to separate it from the limbs. Detach limbs in order to debone them, keeping the breasts intact. Scrape all the meat from the bones and put through a mincer or food processor to produce a fine purée. Do the same thing with the bacon.

Cut the ham into long strips the length of the terrine. Use your hands to mix the meats well in a large bowl, add herbs, beaten egg and marinade from the livers. This mixture is called the farce in France. Line the terrine with chicken skin or a bard of bacon (see page 378).

Spread one-third of the farce on bottom of terrine, then arrange in the middle half the well-seasoned breasts, interspersed with strips of ham and chicken livers, on top. Repeat by covering with another layer of farce, chicken breasts, ham and livers. Cover with rest of farce and then with the ends of the chicken skin or bard of bacon.

Add a sprig of thyme and bay leaf. Cover the terrine and seal with flour and water-luting paste (see page 79).

Place the terrine in a bain-marie with hot water around it to come up to a third of the height of the terrine. Bring to the boil on the top of the oven, then transfer to the oven and cook for about 2 hours. Watch that it does not boil dry. Top up the water as necessary to prevent it from boiling dry.

Cooking time varies according to the constituents of the terrine. If you examine the fat coming to the surface during cooking it will show exactly what point the cooking has reached. If the fat appears cloudy, it is not yet cooked, if the fat is clear the terrine is fully cooked. Any juices should also be clear. Remove from the tin, allow to cool, then press with a board and leave for at least 3 days to mature.

Serve with green salad, lots of crusty bread and a glass of red wine.

Pork, Spinach and Herb Terrine

Serves about 20 – makes two loaves
  of terrine

This terrine tastes different every time we make it, depending on the variety of herbs used. It should be highly seasoned before it is cooked otherwise it may taste bland when cold. Use organically produced spinach, meat and herbs if possible.

700g (1½lb) spinach
900g (2lb) streaky pork
225g (8oz) pig's liver
175g (6oz) gammon or smoked lean bacon
175g (6oz) streaky bacon
2 medium onions, finely chopped
10g (½oz) butter
2 medium garlic cloves, peeled and chopped
2 organic beaten eggs
salt, freshly ground pepper and grated nutmeg, to taste
4 tablespoons freshly chopped mixed herbs – rosemary, thyme, basil, marjoram, parsley and chives

2 terrines or two 20 x 10cm (8 x 4in) loaf tins

Preheat the oven to 180°C/350°F/gas 4.

String and cook the spinach (see page 47) until soft, drain very well, then chop it up. Mince the meat and sweat the onions in the butter. Mix together all the remaining ingredients thoroughly, and add the beaten egg, seasoning and herbs. Fry a tiny piece of the mixture in a pan and taste. It should taste highly seasoned at this stage. Correct the seasoning if necessary.

Divide evenly between the terrines, cover with a lid or tin foil and bake for about 1 hour. The terrine is cooked when it shrinks in from the sides of the dish, and the juices are clear. Remove the cover 15 minutes before the end of cooking time to allow the top to brown slightly. Serve warm or cold.

Potted Prawns, Shrimps or Lobster

Serves 4

Here is a way to preserve some shrimps and use up some little morsels of prawns and lobster. We also use this recipe as one of the layers of the Ballymaloe Fish Terrine (see page 260).

When the shrimp boats arrived in the harbour, the fishermen's wives were ready to cook the shrimps in the boiling sea water. Then they were shelled and dropped into vats of boiling butter and flavoured sometimes with a little mace.

½ garlic clove
salt and freshly ground pepper
50–75g (2–3oz) clarified butter (see page 105)
1 teaspoon freshly chopped thyme leaves or annual marjoram
110g (4oz) shelled shrimps or diced lobster meat or shelled prawns
1–2 teaspoons lemon juice

Crush the garlic to a paste with a little salt. Bring the clarified butter to the boil with the thyme leaves and garlic. Add the shellfish and simmer together for 5 minutes, then leave to rest. Season carefully with the pepper and lemon juice. Pack into pots and run more clarified butter over the top, put into the fridge and allow to set. Serve at room temperature with Melba toast (see page 78) or crusty bread.

Note: Potted shrimps will keep in the fridge for 3–4 days. A little mace or Quatre Epices (see page 374) can be delicious instead of the herbs.

Potted Venison with Juniper Berries

Serves 6–8

'Potted' is a culinary term used in various types of preparation incorporating a pot, and may or may not be a preserve. Roast or spiced beef, lamb, leftover game or pheasant, pigeon, rabbit, hare or wild duck can be used in this recipe instead of venison. You won't need to use the juniper berries with spiced beef; if you like, add more butter and omit the cream. Potted meats keep better without cream.

225g (8oz) cooked venison
75g (3oz) butter
1 large shallot
1 small garlic clove
1 tablespoon brandy or gin
5 plump juniper berries
150ml (¼ pint) cream
salt and freshly ground pepper
clarified butter (see page 105)

Cut the meat into small pieces and whizz for a few seconds in a food processor; the texture should still be rough. Melt the butter in a saucepan, sweat the shallot and garlic until soft but not coloured.

Add the brandy or gin and allow to flame, cooking off the alcohol. Then add the juniper berries and squash with a wooden spoon in the hot pan. Allow to cool, then scrape the contents of the saucepan into the food processor with the venison. Season with salt and pepper. Whizz until smooth.

Whisk the cream until stiff, fold into the venison, taste and correct the seasoning. Fill a terrine, cover with a thin layer of clarified butter and leave for 24 hours.

Serve with hot thin toast or crusty white rolls.

Roasted Red Pepper Tart
Serves 4–6

A very delicious tart, perfect for a starter or a Summer lunch.

Shortcrust Pastry
Use half the amount in the recipe on page 112

3 red peppers (Spanish, if available)
1–2 tablespoons sunflower oil
salt and freshly ground pepper
1 organic egg and 2 egg yolks
225ml (8fl oz) double cream
fresh basil leaves (optional)

20 x 4cm (8 x 1½in) quiche tin with
*   removable base*

Preheat the oven to 250°C/475°F/gas 9.

Roast the oiled red peppers in the hot oven for 20–30 minutes. Put in a bowl, cover with clingfilm and leave until cool enough to handle. Peel and de-seed but do not wash. Cut the flesh into 1cm (½in) dice. Season with salt and freshly ground pepper. Allow to cool.

Reduce the oven temperature to 180°C/350°F/gas 4. Make the shortcrust pastry (see page 112). Chill for 15 minutes, then roll out to line the quiche tin. Line with greaseproof paper and fill to the top with dried beans. Rest for 15 minutes then bake for 20–25 minutes. Remove the beans and paper, brush a little of the egg over the base to seal it, and return to the oven for 1–2 minutes.

Whisk the egg and egg yolks with the cream, add the cooled peppers and a few leaves of torn basil if using. Pour into the pastry case and bake in a moderate oven for 30–35 minutes or until just set and slightly golden on top. Serve with a salad of rocket leaves or a good green salad.

Goat's Cheese, Roasted Red Pepper and Aubergine Tart
Serves 8–10

175g (6oz) plain white flour
75g (3oz) cold butter
pinch of salt
1 tablespoon poppy seeds (optional)
2 organic egg yolks
2 tablespoons extra-virgin olive oil
2 red peppers
1 large aubergine
olive oil, for frying
175–225g (6–8oz) goat's cheese (we use our
*   local cheese, Ardsallagh)*
salt and freshly ground pepper
½ quantity Tomato Fondue (see page 200)
Pesto (see page 589) or basil oil

25 x 4cm (10 x 1½in) flan ring or quiche tin

Preheat the oven to 250°C/475°F/gas 9.

Put the flour, butter and a pinch of salt into the food processor, whizz for a few seconds until the butter is roughly blended in. Add the poppy seeds, if using, and then the egg yolks and oil. Whizz for a few seconds again until the pastry comes together. Flatten into a round, wrap in clingfilm and chill.

Meanwhile roast the peppers in the hot oven for 20–30 minutes. Put in a bowl, cover with clingfilm and leave until cool enough to handle. Peel and de-seed but do not wash.

Slice the aubergines into 5mm (¼in) slices, sprinkle with salt and stack on a wire rack. Heat the olive oil in a frying pan, wash and dry the aubergine slices and fry until golden on both sides, drain.

Lower the oven temperature to 180°C/350F°/gas 4. Roll out the pastry and line the quiche, then bake blind. Line with greaseproof paper and fill with dried beans. Rest for 15 minutes, then bake for 20–25 minutes. Remove the beans and paper, brush a little egg over the base to seal it, and return to the oven for 1–2 minutes.

Cover the base of the pastry with slices of goat's cheese, arrange a layer of roasted red pepper on top. Season with salt and pepper. Spread a layer of aubergine slices on top then cover with Tomato Fondue.

Return to the oven for 10–15 minutes or until hot and bubbly. Drizzle generously with Pesto or basil oil and serve immediately with a good green salad.

Gruyère and Dill Tart
See page 113

French Onion Tart
See page 113

Mushroom and Thyme Leaf Tart
See page 114

Ballymaloe Quiche Lorraine
See page 114

Asparagus and Spring Onion Tart
See page 115

Crab, Tomato and Ginger Tart
See pages 115

Leek, Yellow Pepper and Marjoram Tart
See page 173

RIGHT: Buddy the Dog

Slicing Raw Peppers

Insert the knife under the stalk. Cut around the sides and the base of the pepper.

Open out from the bottom. The core may then be removed intact, so there is virtually no waste. Shake out any remaining seeds. Depending on the recipe you may want to remove the paler protruding flesh.

Cut the pepper into quarters and slice at an angle so that the slices are not too long.

How to Roast Peppers

There are three alternative methods:

1. Preheat the grill or better still use a charcoal grill or barbecue. Grill the peppers on all sides, turning them when necessary – they can be quite charred.

2. Preheat the oven to 250°C/475°F/gas 9. Put the peppers on a baking tray and bake for 20–30 minutes until the skin blisters and the flesh is soft.

3. Put a wire rack over a mild gas jet, roast the peppers on all sides. When they are charred, remove.

Whichever way you cook them, the next step is to put them into a bowl and cover tightly with clingfilm for a few minutes; this will make them much easier to peel. Pull the skin off the peppers, remove the stalks and seeds. Do not wash or you will lose the precious sweet juices. Divide each into 2 or 3 pieces along the natural division. Use as desired.

Aileen Murphy's Tomato and Spinach Tart with Goat's Cheese and Tapenade

Serves 4

225–275g (8–10oz) Puff Pastry (see page 456)
8 tablespoons Tomato Fondue (see page 200)
4 teaspoons Tapenade (see page 590)
225g (8oz) fresh spinach leaves, stringed, blanched and refreshed
4 tablespoons freshly grated Parmesan (Parmigiano Reggiano is best)
110g (4oz) mature goat's cheese
freshly ground pepper
olive oil
few black olives

Preheat the oven to 180°C/350°F/gas 4.

Roll out the pastry to the thickness of a coin. Cut out 4 rounds (18–20cm/7–8in) and perforate the surface all over with a fork. Spread each tart base with 2 tablespoons of Tomato Fondue and 1 teaspoon of tapenade. Divide the spinach between the tarts. Sprinkle Parmesan on top and place thin slices of goat's cheese, overlapping, on top of the tarts. Season each layer with pepper. Place on parchment paper discs. Cook for 10–15 minutes. Serve immediately with a drizzle of olive oil and some olives.

Alison Henderson's Cheddar Cheese, Onion and Potato Tart

Serves 6–8

Another permanent favourite at Ballymaloe Café.

Savoury Pastry (to line 2 tart tins)
275g (10oz) plain flour
175g (6oz) butter, chilled and diced
pinch of salt
2 teaspoons icing sugar
1 organic egg, beaten
butter and oil, for frying

1 onion, sliced thinly, lengthways
1 bunch spring onions, chopped
2 leeks, trimmed and sliced
10g (1/2oz) butter and olive oil, for sautéing
12 waxy, new potatoes, boiled and halved
150g (5oz) mature Cheddar cheese, grated (Alison uses local Imokilly Cheddar)
5 organic eggs, beaten
about 300ml (1/2 pint) cream
a little Parmesan cheese, grated
salt and freshly ground pepper

28cm (11in) tart tin

Pulse the flour, butter, salt and icing sugar in a food processor to give a coarse breadcrumb texture. Add the egg and pulse again, until it comes together. Then tip the dough onto a length of clingfilm, shape into a log, wrap and refrigerate overnight.

The next day preheat the oven to 200°C/400°F/gas 6. Line the tart tin with the dough and blind bake (without foil or beans) at for 5–6 minutes. Keep an eye on it and remove it from the oven before it dries out too much. Leave the oven on, turning it down to 180°C/350°F/gas 4.

Melt a little butter and oil in a pan and fry the onions with salt and pepper to take the rawness off. Don't allow to colour. Similarly, soften the leeks in a little butter and oil over a moderate heat. Add a splash of cream, stir and continue to cook until the leeks are melting. Remove and cool. Sauté the halved potatoes so the cut surfaces are gold. Drain.

Sprinkle a little cheese on the pastry base and top with onions. Mix the eggs with the cream, and fold in the leeks and most of the cheese. Season. Scatter the potatoes over the onions, so part of them protrudes out of the tart, and carefully pour over the custard. Sprinkle with any remaining cheese and bake in the oven for 25–30 minutes until set and golden round the edge. Allow to cool slightly. Sprinkle with Parmesan.

Shallot Tarte Tatin

Serves 2–4

110g (4oz) unsalted butter
600g (11/4lb) shallots, soaked in boiling water for 5 minutes, drained, peeled and trimmed
12 garlic cloves, peeled
300ml (1/2 pint) fresh Vegetable Stock (page 36)
225g (8oz) puff pastry
2 tablespoons caster sugar
1 tablespoon balsamic vinegar
salt and freshly ground pepper
fresh leaf salad, to serve

23cm (9in) ovenproof frying or sauté pan

Preheat the oven to 190°C/375°F/gas 5.

Melt 40g (2oz) of the butter in the frying pan. Add the shallots and cook until golden, for about 10 minutes, tossing occasionally so they colour evenly. After 5 minutes add the garlic cloves. Pour in the stock and simmer for 5–10 minutes, depending on the size of the shallots. When they are tender but still hold their shape, remove with a slotted spoon and drain well. Save the remaining stock for sauces or soup. Allow the shallots and garlic to cool completely.

Meanwhile, roll out the pastry and cut a 25cm (10in) circle. Transfer to a baking tray and refrigerate for at least 30 minutes to allow the pastry to rest.

Melt the rest of the butter in the ovenproof, non-stick frying pan. Sprinkle the sugar into the pan and cook for a few minutes until caramelised. Add the vinegar and then the shallots and garlic. Toss until well coated. Remove from the heat. Now arrange the garlic neatly in between the shallots. Season generously with salt and pepper. Place the cooled pastry on top, tucking the edges down the side of the pan. Prick with a fork and bake for about 30 minutes or until the pastry has risen and is golden brown. Allow to sit for a few minutes before loosening the sides with a knife and inverting onto a flat plate. Serve warm or cold, cut into slices and with a rocket or watercress salad.

Tomato Tarte Tatin
Serves 8

Mary-Jo Wendel served this recipe in her superb neighbourhood restaurant in Oxford, Ohio.

Paté Brisé
175g (6oz) plain white flour
pinch of salt
75–110g (3–4oz) butter
1 organic egg yolk
2–4 tablespoons water
50g (2oz) butter
350g (12oz) onion, chopped
½–1 red chilli
2 garlic cloves, crushed
900g (2lb) very ripe tomatoes peeled, seeded, and chopped
salt and freshly ground pepper
torn fresh basil, about 6 leaves

450–700g (1–1½lb) tomatoes, peeled, seeded, salted and drained, then sliced
salt
50g (2oz) goat's cheese or Parmesan

23cm (9in) diameter ceramic tart dish
melted butter for greasing

Preheat the oven to 190°C/375°F/gas 5.

Make the pastry. Sieve the flour with the salt and rub in the butter. Beat the egg yolk with 2 tablespoons of water and bind the mixture with just enough liquid to bring the pastry together. You may need a little more water, but do not make the pastry too wet – it should come away cleanly from the bowl. Flatten into a round, wrap in clingfilm and rest for 15 minutes.

Meanwhile melt the butter, add the onion, chilli and garlic. Cook until soft and slightly caramelised. Add the chopped tomatoes. Add salt and pepper to taste. Simmer until reduced almost to a paste. Stir in some torn fresh basil leaves.

Line the bottom of a ceramic tart or quiche dish with a circle of silicone paper. Brush generously with melted butter. Pack in a neat layer of tomato slices. Spread the cooked filling evenly over the tomato slices. Crumble the goat's cheese over the tart or sprinkle with grated Parmesan. Roll out the pastry to the size of the dish and cover the tomato and cheese.

Bake in a hot oven, until the crust is browned and cooked through. Cool a little before carefully turning out onto a warm plate and peel away the silicone paper. The tart may be cooked ahead and reheated before serving.

Smoked Mackerel Tart
Serves 4

Shortcrust Pastry (see page 112)

Filling
1 small onion, finely chopped
25g (1oz) butter
2–3 large smoked mackerel, filleted and skinned (smoked salmon can be substituted)
2 organic eggs
300ml (½ pint) double cream
1 organic egg yolk
3 ripe firm tomatoes made into concassé
1 tablespoon freshly chopped chives
½ tablespoon freshly chopped tarragon
salt and pepper

20cm (8in) x 4cm (1½in) quiche tin

Preheat the oven to 180°C/350°F/gas 4.

Make the shortcrust pastry. Chill for 15 minutes, then roll out to line the flan ring or quiche tin. Line with greaseproof paper and fill to the top with dried beans. Rest for 15 minutes then bake for 20–25 minutes. Remove the beans and paper, brush a little egg over the base to seal it, and return to the oven for 1–2 minutes.

Meanwhile make the filling. Sweat the onion in the butter, then allow to cool. Flake the mackerel, but don't break it up too much. Mix together all the tart ingredients and check the seasoning. Fill the tart shell and return to the oven for 20–25 minutes until just set.

Smoked Salmon Tart
Substitute smoked salmon for mackerel in the above recipe.

A Plate of Smoked Fish with Horseradish Sauce and Dill Mayonnaise
Serves 4

Occasionally we serve 3 different types of smoked fish – for example salmon, mussels and trout – on tiny rounds of Ballymaloe Brown Yeast Bread (see page 478) topped with a little frill of fresh lollo rosso. A little dollop of Sweet Cucumber Pickle goes with the smoked salmon, a dollop of homemade Mayonnaise is delicious with marinated smoked mussels and a blob of Horseradish Sauce and a sprig of watercress complements the pink smoked trout. These 3 delicious morsels make a perfect light starter. Most smoked fish is available all year round but sprats and herring are winter treats.

selection of smoked fish, e.g. smoked salmon, smoked mussels, smoked mackerel, smoked trout, smoked eel, smoked tuna, smoked hake, smoked sprats

Horseradish Sauce (see page 586)
Dill Mayonnaise (see page 585)
Sweet Cucumber Pickle (see page 514)

Garnish
segments of lemon
sprigs of watercress or rocket leaves

First make the Horseradish Sauce and Sweet Dill Mayonnaise and Sweet Cucumber Pickle.

Slice the salmon into thin slices down onto the skin, allowing 1 slice per person. Cut the mackerel into diamond-shaped pieces, divide the trout into large flakes. Skin and slice the eel. Thinly slice the tuna and hake.

To serve: choose 4 large white plates. Drizzle each with Sweet Dill Mayonnaise, then divide the smoked fish between the plates. Put a teaspoonful of Horseradish Sauce and Sweet Cucumber Pickle on each plate. Garnish with a lemon wedge and sprigs of watercress or rocket.

Gravlax with Mustard and Dill Mayonnaise

Serves 24–30

The Swedish way of pickling raw salmon, using salt, sugar and herbs, may also be used for trout or sea trout. The Finns make many exciting variations on the basic technique, and flavour their Gravlax with beetroot, black and even pink peppercorns. The Norwegians use beer. We've also used the basic mixture to pickle cod, hake and mackerel with tremendous success. Fillets of mackerel only take 2 or 3 hours to pickle and are absolutely delicious served with Mustard and Dill Mayonnaise. Pickled salmon keeps for up to a week. Fresh dill is essential in this recipe.

2 fillets fresh wild salmon
2 heaped tablespoons sea salt or dairy salt

2 heaped tablespoons sugar
2 teaspoons freshly ground pepper
4 tablespoons finely chopped dill

double quantity of Mustard and Dill
  Mayonnaise (see below)

If necessary, fillet the salmon and remove all the pin bones with tweezers. Do not skin.

Mix the salt, sugar, pepper and dill together in a bowl. Place 1 fillet of fish skin side down on a piece of clingfilm on a long dish. Scatter the mixture over the surface of the fish. Lay the second fillet on top skin side up. Wrap tightly with clingfilm and refrigerate for 24–36 hours. We usually turn it over every 12 hours.

To serve: wipe the dill mixture off the salmon and slice thinly down to the skin. Arrange on a plate, barely overlapping the slices. Zigzag with Mustard and Dill Mayonnaise. Alternatively arrange the salmon slices in a rosette shape. Fill the centre of the rosette with Mustard and Dill Mayonnaise. Garnish with fresh dill. Serve with brown bread and butter.

Mustard and Dill Mayonnaise

Serves 8–10

1 large organic egg yolk
2 tablespoons French mustard
1 tablespoon white sugar
150ml (¼ pint) ground nut or sunflower oil
1 tablespoon white wine vinegar
1 tablespoon finely chopped dill
salt and white pepper

Whisk the egg yolk with the mustard and sugar in a medium-sized glass bowl, drip in the oil drop by drop whisking all the time until the mixture has emulsifed, then add the vinegar and dill and season with salt and white pepper.

TIP: Gravlax is also great served with Sweet Cucumber Pickle (see page 514) and Egg Mayonnaise (see page 100).

Salting and Brining

Salt is one of the oldest preservatives. There are two basic methods of preserving with salt – dry-salting and brining. Both can be used for fish, meat and vegetables. Use sea salt, rock salt or dairy salt – do not use salt that has chemicals or anti-caking agent. Fresh food gives best results. Salting not only preserves but also enhances flavour. Food writers in the US are urging their readers to brine chicken and pork to improve the eating quality of what is invariably intensively reared meat. Dry-salting involves rubbing salt into the food. This draws out moisture which produces a brine. In the second method – brining – the food is immersed in a salt solution which must be strong enough to penetrate the food and extract the juices. A 20 per cent salt solution is recommended. This can be measured with a salometer but the traditional method was to add salt to the water until a fresh egg will float on the solution. Use pure fresh water, the chemicals in tap water may interfere with the curing. Use these proportions:

3.1kg (7lb) salt
2.4–4.2 litres (4–7 pints) water
900g (2lb) sugar

Traditional stoneware crocks are best for brining, but plastic is also fine. Metal or timber may affect the flavour of the food. Injecting the brine into meat speeds up the process. Particular care needs to be taken close to the bone where the meat starts to decay first.

Carpaccio of Smoked Salmon or Tuna with Avocado, Red Onion, Dill and Horseradish Cream

Serves 8

ABOVE: Carpaccio of Smoked Salmon or Tuna with Avocado, Red Onion, Dill and Horseradish Cream

Arrigo Cipriani of Harry's Bar in Venice created Filetto al Carpaccio in 1961, naming it after the painter, whose work was being exhibited at the time. It is cooked and sliced fillet. The name 'carpaccio' has been purloined to apply to sliced and raw meats, and fish as here.

175–225g (6–8oz) smoked salmon or very fresh blue or yellow fin tuna, very thinly sliced
1–2 avocados
1 small red onion, finely diced
1 tablespoon finely snipped chives
1 tablespoon finely chopped dill
1 tablespoon chopped chervil or flat-leaf parsley
freshly cracked pepper
Horseradish Sauce (see page 586)

First make the Horseradish Sauce but do not whip the cream in this instance.

To serve: arrange the smoked salmon or tuna in a single layer on 4 large chilled plates. Peel and cut the avocado into 5mm (¼in) dice. Drizzle some Horseradish Cream over the salmon or tuna, then sprinkle with avocado and red onion dice. Garnish with snipped chives, chopped dill and chervil or flat-leaf parsley sprigs.

Finally add a little freshly cracked pepper. Serve with crusty brown yeast bread.

Salt Cod Buñuelos
Serves 8 – makes about 40

Now that cod is becoming scarce we also use salt ling and hake in this recipe.

225g (8oz) skinned, boned and dried salt cod
450g (1lb) small potatoes, well scrubbed
2 garlic cloves, crushed
1 tablespoon freshly chopped flat-leaf parsley
a little freshly ground pepper
2 organic egg yolks
oil, for deep frying

Soak the cod in several changes of cold water for 24–36 hours depending on how salty it is. Drain. Put the potatoes and cod into a saucepan, cover with water, bring to the boil, cover and simmer for 30 minutes or until the potatoes are cooked. Drain, peel and push the potatoes through a ricer into a bowl. Remove the skin from the cod, flake the flesh and mix with the potatoes. Add garlic, parsley, pepper and egg yolks. Mix well. Taste and add salt if necessary.

To cook the buñuelos: drop teaspoons of the mixture into hot oil. They will puff up crisp on all sides. Drain on kitchen paper. Keep warm while you cook the remainder. Serve with hot Aïoli (see page 584) and Tomato Sauce (see page 591) or Tomato Fondue (see page 200).

Salmon with Tomato and Ginger in Filo
Serves 8

8 sheets filo pastry
75g (3oz) melted butter
8 x 50g (2oz) pieces wild Irish salmon
2 tablespoons peeled and grated fresh ginger
4 tablespoons Tomato Concassé (see page 51),
    seasoned with salt, freshly ground pepper
    and sugar
salt and freshly ground pepper

egg wash: 1 organic egg beaten with a pinch
    of salt
Hollandaise Sauce (see page 581)

Garnish
sprigs of flat-leaf parsley or fennel
well-seasoned Tomato Concassé

Preheat the oven to 230°C/450°F/gas 8.

Unfold the pastry and brush the a sheet with melted butter. Put a piece of salmon in the centre of the short end of the pastry and season with salt and pepper. Sprinkle with a little ginger and 2 teaspoons of tomato concassé.

Roll the pastry from the end once, then fold in the long sides and then roll over and over into a parcel. Brush with melted butter and put onto a baking tray. Repeat with the other 7 sheets.* Brush with egg wash just before baking. Cook in the oven for 10–12 minutes.

Meanwhile, make the Hollandaise sauce. Arrange the filo parcels on a hot plate with a little sauce, garnish with sprigs of flat-leaf parsley or fennel and a little Tomato Concassé.

*May be prepared ahead to this point.

Crab Filos with Thai Dipping Sauce
Serves 4

Another multi-purpose recipe! This makes a terrific starter and delicious canapes.

225g (8oz) cooked white crab meat
1 teaspoon fresh ginger, grated
1 garlic clove, crushed
1 tablespoon freshly chopped coriander
½ Thai chilli, finely chopped
1 teaspoon Thai fish sauce (nam pla)
salt and freshly ground pepper
3–4 sheets of filo pastry, depending on size
a little melted butter
egg wash: 1 organic egg beaten with a pinch
    of salt

Thai Dipping Sauce
3 tablespoons Thai fish sauce (nam pla)
3 tablespoons lime or lemon juice, freshly
    squeezed

2 tablespoons sugar, or more to taste
3 tablespoons warm water
1 garlic clove, crushed
3–4 fresh hot red or green chillies

Garnish
fresh coriander

Preheat the oven to 220°C/425°F/gas 7.

Put the crabmeat into a bowl, checking that there are no pieces of shell included. Add the ginger, garlic, coriander, chilli and nam pla. Mix well, taste and add seasoning, going easy with the salt – nam pla is very salty.

Unwrap the filo pastry. Lay 1 sheet down on the worktop, brush with melted butter. Lay a 2.5cm (1in) strip of the crabmeat mixture about 4cm (1½in) in from the edge of the longer side. Roll over and over to form a sausage. Brush with melted butter and chill. Repeat this exercise until all the filling has been used up.

Now make the Thai Dipping Sauce: combine the nam pla, lime or lemon juice, sugar and warm water in a jar, then add the crushed garlic. Mix well and pour into 4 little, individual bowls. Cut the chillies crossways into very thin rounds and divide them between the bowls.

Egg wash the rolls of filo and cut them with a sharp knife into pieces roughly 3cm (1¼in). Bake in the oven for about 10 minutes until crispy and golden. Garnish with fresh coriander and serve warm with Thai Dipping Sauce.

Vietnamese Spring Rolls with Peanut Dipping Sauce
Serves 4 – makes about 8

These are fun to make and yummy to eat! Nina Simonds, author of many wonderful books on Asian food, gave me this version when she came to teach at the school. *Banh trang* (rice papers) break easily so

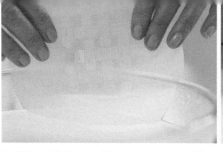

handle them carefully. You can buy circular or triangular ones; here I use the circular. They come in three sizes and this is the medium one.

Spring Rolls

50g (2oz) thin rice vermicelli noodles

1 large carrot or cucumber, peeled and cut into julienne strips or coarsely grated

salt

1 teaspoon sugar

8 lettuce leaves (preferably butterhead)

4 tablespoons fresh mint leaves

16 Chinese garlic chives (optional)

2 tablespoons fresh coriander leaves

8 large cooked pacific prawns or tiger prawns or 32 shrimps, cooked and shelled

8 rice paper wrappers (banh trang), 20cm (8in) in diameter

Peanut Dipping Sauce

1 teaspoon sugar

1 tablespoon rice wine vinegar

1 teaspoon carrot, finely grated

4 tablespoons hoisin sauce

2 tablespoons water

1 tablespoon peanut butter

1 red chilli, de-seeded and finely chopped

First make the Peanut Dipping Sauce: mix the sugar with the rice wine vinegar in a bowl, add the carrot and marinade for 15 minutes. Drain and squeeze the moisture from the carrot. Put the hoisin sauce into a small saucepan with the water and heat for a few minutes until thick and reduced. Add the peanut butter, stir, and simmer for a second or two. Cool. Stir in the chilli and carrot, then transfer to little serving bowls.

To prepare for making the spring rolls, soak the noodles in warm water for 15–20 minutes. Drain. Put the carrot into a bowl and sprinkle with salt and sugar. Put the lettuce, mint leaves, Chinese chives and coriander leaves on a plate. If the prawns are large, cut them in half.

Make spring rolls as shown right. Serve with the dipping sauce.

1. Fill a wide bowl with very hot water. Dip a banh trang (rice paper) into the hot water; it will soften in a second or two.

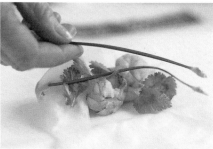

2. Remove, shake off excess moisture and put onto a clean tea towel. Lay a piece of lettuce over the bottom third of the rice paper, add a tablespoon of noodles, some shredded carrot and several mint leaves.

3. Roll the rice paper over half way into a cylinder, then fold in the sides.

4. Arrange 2 half prawns or 3 or 4 small shrimps along the top with a few coriander leaves, add a couple of garlic chives, allowing them to peep out from one end. Continue to roll up and press to seal.

Spring rolls may be made several hours ahead and kept covered. The general idea is that people dip their rolls in the sauce as they eat. Serve with lettuce leaves and sprig of fresh mint. Some people like to wrap the spring rolls in lettuce leaves before dipping.

Three-minute Fish

Serves 4

This is the fastest fish recipe I know and certainly one of the most delicious. It's fun to mix pink- and white-fleshed fish on the same plate (like salmon and sea bass).

450g (1lb) very fresh fish (wild Irish salmon, cod, turbot, large sole, sea bass or grey sea mullet)
olive oil or melted butter
flat-leaf parsley, thyme, chives, finely chopped
salt and freshly ground pepper

4 ovenproof main course plates

Season the fish about half an hour before cutting. Chill in the fridge to stiffen it.

Preheat the oven to 230°C/450°F/gas 8.

While the oven is heating, brush the plates with oil or melted butter. Put the fillet of fish on a chopping board skin-side down; cut the flesh into scant 5mm (¼in) thin slices down onto the skin. Arrange the slices on the plates but don't allow them to overlap or they will cook unevenly. Brush the fish with more oil or melted butter, season with salt and pepper and sprinkle each plate with a little freshly chopped herbs. Put the plates in the preheated oven and cook for 3 minutes; you might like to check after 2 minutes if the slices are very thin. The fish is cooked when it looks opaque.

Rush it to the table and serve with crusty white bread, a green salad and white wine.

Seared Fresh Salmon with Vine-ripened Tomato and Herbs

See page 241

Ballymaloe Fish Mousse with Shrimp Butter Sauce

See page 261

Smoked Eel with Brown Bread and Lemon

See page 249

ABOVE: Sweet Pea Guacamole on Warm Tortillas

Tortilla Chips with Guacamole and Salsa

Serves 4–6

For me, Mexican food is utterly irresistible – as indeed, are all things Mexican. Tortilla chips can now be found even in local shops and newsagents. However, most are rather too highly flavoured.

4–6 tortillas
salt
Guacamole (see page 594)
Tomatillo Salsa (see page 592) or Tomato and Coriander Salsa (see page 592)

Use the tortillas to make tortilla chips (see page 494). Sprinkle with a little salt. Serve with Guacamole and Salsa.

Sweet Pea Guacamole on Warm Tortillas

Makes about 16, depending on size

Guacamole (see page 594) is a Mexican dip made from very ripe avocados. I came across this fresh-tasting variation in California, served on tiny warm tortillas (see page 493). Little pancakes are also very good, however, and easier to make! Allow about 3 per person as a starter or simply serve as finger food.

16 warm tortillas, about 6cm (2½in)
450g (1lb) fresh or frozen peas, shelled
2 tablespoons extra-virgin olive oil
2 tablespoons lime juice, freshly squeezed
2 tablespoons finely chopped coriander
½–1 fresh chilli, de-seeded and finely chopped
¼–½ teaspoon freshly ground cumin
2 tablespoons freshly chopped flat-leaf parsley
½–1 teaspoon salt
½ teaspoon ground coriander

Garnish

crème fraîche or thick natural yoghurt
fresh coriander leaves

If you are using fresh peas, cook them in boiling, salted water for 3–4 minutes. Refresh under cold water and drain. Whizz the olive oil with the lime juice, coriander and chilli in a food processor for 1 minute. Add the peas, cumin, parsley, ground coriander and salt and blend until almost smooth. Taste, correct the seasoning, put into a bowl and cover until needed.

Serve on tiny hot tortillas or pancakes with a blob of crème fraîche or thick natural yoghurt if liked. Garnish with coriander.

Tostadas
Serves 8

Tostadas are a favourite snack in Mexico, the filling varies according to the area, it can be beef, chicken, pork, turkey, crab or just vegetables. They are quite a challenge to eat elegantly but, what the heck, they taste delicious!

8 tortillas, they ought to be corn but wheat
*   flour tortillas can be substituted*
225g (8oz) refried beans (see page 139),
*   (optional)*
⅓ iceberg lettuce, shredded
110–150g (4–6oz) cooked chicken breast,
*   shredded*
1 sliced chilli (optional)
4 very ripe tomatoes, sliced
1 avocado or Guacamole (see page 594)
4 tablespoons chopped spring onion
3 tablespoons sour cream
50–110g (2–4oz) Cheddar cheese, grated

Deep-fry the tortillas in hot oil until crisp and golden, drain on kitchen paper. Put each tortilla on a hot plate, spread with a little warm refried beans and then top with some crunchy lettuce, shredded chicken breast, guacamole and so on. Finish off with a blob of sour cream and a sprinkling of cheddar cheese and chives. Serve immediately. In Mexico, Tostados are considered to be finger food – you'll need both hands!

Master Recipe
Quesadillas
Serves 4

Quesadillas are massively popular in Mexico. On Sundays in Oaxaca there are little stalls on the streets and squares with women making and selling these delicious stuffed tortillas. They cooked them on a comal (a type of griddle pan) over a charcoal brazier. One of my favourites was flavoured with an aromatic leaf called *hoja santa*, then filled with shredded cornfed chicken and fiery tomato sauce. Choose either flour or corn tortillas, depending on your taste.

8 corn or wheat flour tortillas
110–225g (4–8oz) queso fresca or mild
*   Cheddar, grated or a mixture of Cheddar and*
*   mozzarella*
4 spring onions, sliced
2 green chillies, cut in strips or slices (optional)

Tomatillo Salsa (see page 592)

First make the Tomatillo Salsa.

Next heat a cast iron pan or griddle and proceed with the quesadillas. There are two ways of making them. One resembles a sandwich, the other a turnover. To make the sandwich type, lay a tortilla on the hot pan, spread about 25g (1oz) cheese over the top, keeping it a little from the edge. Sprinkle a few spring onions and some chilli strips on top. Cover with another tortilla. Cook for a minute or two, then carefully turn over. Serve, just as it is or cut into quarters, with the Tomatillo Salsa.

If you want to make the turnover-style quesadillas, lay a tortilla on the worktop, put a little filling onto 1 half, again keeping it in slightly from the edges, fold over and press gently to seal. Cook for 3–4 minutes on each side on a preheated pan or griddle. (It should be medium–hot, otherwise the outside will burn before the inside is cooked.) Then stand it upright so that the fold is also cooked. Serve as soon as possible with the Salsa.

Variations
Quesadillas with Tomato and Coriander Salsa and Guacamole
Follow the Master Recipe. Serve the quesadillas with Tomato and Coriander Salsa (see page 592) and Guacamole (see page 594) instead of Tomatilla Salsa.

Quesadillas with Cheese and Courgette Blossoms
A favourite filling for quesadillas in Oaxaca is simply grated Oaxacan string cheese (mozzarella is our nearest equivalent) and fresh squash or courgette blossoms. Thinly sliced green chilli is sometimes added for extra excitement! Accompany with Guacamole (see page 594) and Tomato and Coriander Salsa (see page 592).

Quesadillas with Spicy Chicken or Pork and Slices of Avocado
Add spicy chicken or pork and slices of avocado to the Master Recipe.

Quesadillas with Shredded or Smoked Chicken, Mango, Brie and Lime
Substitute brie slices for the cheddar cheese in the Master Recipe and add some shredded chicken and diced mango and lime.

Seafood Quesadillas
Shrimps, prawns or strips of smoked salmon can also be delicious.

Quesadillas with Chorizo and Spring Onion
Chop some chorizo, sprinkle over the cheese and scatter some chopped spring onion and perhaps a few slices of chilli.

Quesadillas with Mozzarella and Tapenade or Pesto
Spread quesadillas with Tapenade (see page 590), Pesto (see page 589) or Anchoiade (see page 593) and top with mozzarella.

Nachos with Melted Cheese

Serves 4 as a starter

Nachos are fried tortilla chips, in their native Mexico served with melted cheese, and for more substantial dishes with frijoles refritos (refried beans, see page 139) and other toppings.

8 tortillas (corn tortillas are more authentic but wheat flour ones are also delicious)
oil, for frying
salt
2–3 green chillies, finely sliced
110g (4oz) buffalo mozzarella cheese, grated, or half mozzarella, half Cheddar

Tomato and Coriander Salsa (see page 592)

Cut the tortillas into sixths or eighths depending on size. Heat some oil – a deep fat fryer is easiest but you can manage with a frying pan. The oil should be hot – 200°C/400°F. Fry the tortilla pieces until pale golden, remove with a slotted spoon, drain on kitchen paper and sprinkle with salt.

Just before serving, arrange on heatproof plates, allowing about eight nachos per person as a starter. Add some sliced chilli to each and top with a little grated cheese. Flash under a grill or pop into a hot oven (230°C/450°F/gas 8) until the cheese melts. Serve with Tomato and Coriander Salsa.

Pimentos de Padron

Serves 2

Pimentos de Padron are small green peppers named after a town in Galicia where they have been grown for over 400 years. In the summer, plates of these little green peppers are served in tapas bars all over Spain. They are fried in olive oil and sprinkled with coarse sea salt... delicious and addictive! Eating them is like playing Russian roulette – once in a while you get a fiery one that tastes volcanic!

250g (½lb) fresh pimentos de Padron
2 tablespoons Spanish extra-virgin olive oil
coarse sea salt, to taste

Heat the olive oil in a frying pan over a high heat. Add the whole pimentos. Toss continually with a wooden spoon until they puff up or until lightly browned in spots. Remove with a slotted spoon, drain well and transfer to a hot plate. Sprinkle with coarse sea salt and eat immediately.

Indian Spiced Vegetable Pakoras

Serves 4–6

These crispy vegetables in a spicy batter are also good served with Mango Relish (see page 92) and a Yoghurt Raita (see page 142).

1 thin aubergine, cut into 5mm (¼in) slices
salt
2 medium courgettes, cut into 2.5cm (1in) slices if they are very large, then cut the slices into quarters or batons
12 cauliflower florets
6 large or 12 small flat mushrooms, cut in half
spring onions, cut into 8–10cm (3–4in) lengths

Batter
175g (6oz) chickpea or plain flour
1 tablespoon freshly chopped coriander
1 scant teaspoon salt
2 teaspoons curry powder
1 tablespoon olive oil
1 tablespoon lemon juice, freshly squeezed
175–225ml (6–8fl oz) iced water
vegetable oil, for deep frying

Garnish
lemon wedges
coriander or flat-leaf parsley
Mango Relish (see right)

Put the aubergine slices into a colander, sprinkle with the salt and leave to drain while preparing the other vegetables. Blanch the courgettes and cauliflower separately in boiling, salted water for

2 minutes. Drain, refresh under cold water and dry well. Halve the mushrooms if necessary. Rinse the aubergine slices and pat dry.

Next make the batter: put the flour, coriander, salt and curry powder into a large bowl. Gradually whisk in the oil, lemon juice and water until the batter is the consistency of thick cream.

Heat good-quality oil to 180°C/350°F in a deep fryer. Lightly whisk the batter and dip the vegetables in batches of 5 or 6. Slip them carefully into the hot oil. Fry the pakoras for 2–3 minutes on each side, turning them with a slotted spoon. Drain on kitchen paper and keep warm in a moderate oven (uncovered) while you cook the remainder. Allow the oil to come back to 180°C/350°F between batches. When all the vegetable fritters are ready, garnish with lemon wedges and fresh or deep-fried coriander or parsley. Serve at once with Mango Relish.

Mango Relish

50ml (2fl oz) medium sherry
50ml (2fl oz) water
50ml (2fl oz) white wine vinegar
2 tablespoons sugar
½ cinnamon stick
2 star anise
½ teaspoon salt
pinch of ground mace
1 mango, peeled and diced
1 small red pepper, de-seeded and diced
1 tablespoon lemon juice

Put the sherry, water, vinegar, sugar, cinnamon, star anise, salt and mace into a small, heavy saucepan. Bring to the boil and simmer over medium heat for 5 minutes. Add the mango, pepper and lemon juice, lower the heat and simmer for 5 minutes more. Remove from the heat and leave to cool completely. Spoon into a screw-top jar and refrigerate until required (it will keep for up to 10 days).

Onion Chrysanthemums

Serves 6

6 medium onions
milk
flour, well seasoned with salt
cayenne pepper or smoked paprika

Orly Sauce (see page 585) or Tomato and Chilli
    Sauce (see page 591)

Place the onions upright on a chopping
board and peel. Cut in half, then quarters,
eighths, sixteenths, down to the root but
not through it. By now the onion will
vaguely resemble a chrysanthemum. Put
the onions into a large bowl of iced water
to open further. Drain well.

Heat the oil in a deep-fryer to 180°C/350°F.
Dip the onion in milk then in flour
seasoned with salt and cayenne or
smoked paprika. Sprinkle more flour over
the top and in between the 'petals'. Deep-
fry until crisp and golden. Serve with Orly
Sauce or Tomato and Chilli Sauce.

Yuk Sum

Serves 4

Don't let the name put you off! I came
across this extraordinary sounding dish
on a menu in a Chinese restaurant in
Birmingham and couldn't resist the
temptation. It turned out to be a delicious
pork dish served on lettuce leaves, and
this is my interpretation which, though
not authentic Cantonese, gets lots of
compliments.

2 tablespoons extra-virgin olive oil
1 teaspoon ginger, peeled and freshly grated
2 tablespoons chopped spring onion
225g (8oz) minced streaky pork
50g (2oz) mushrooms, chopped
25g (1oz) celery, finely chopped
1 tablespoon oyster sauce
salt and freshly ground black pepper

iceberg lettuce leaves

Garnish
1/3 cucumber approx. cut into a 5mm (1/4in)
    thick julienne
8 spring onion 'sweeping brushes'

Heat a wok until very hot, add the olive
oil, then add the grated ginger and spring
onion and toss for a second or two. Add
the pork, cook over a high heat until
almost cooked, then push the pork up to
the side of the wok. Add the chopped
mushrooms and toss until cooked. Add the
celery and mix with the mushrooms and
pork. Season with salt and freshly ground
pepper and add the oyster sauce. Toss for a
minute or two more. Taste and correct the
seasoning.

Arrange crisp iceberg lettuce on each of
the plates and spoon 1–2 tablespoons of
the pork mixture into the centre of each.
Garnish with the julienne of cucumber and
a couple of spring onion 'sweeping
brushes'.

Eat immediately by wrapping the pork,
cucumber and spring onion in the lettuce
to make a parcel.

eggs

eggs

I am passionate about hens. In fact, I can't imagine life without them. Ever since I was a child, we've always had our own – happy, lazy hens that range freely and enjoy dust baths in the sun. They are part of our way of life, part of our holistic system...

The scraps from the kitchen go to the hens and come back as eggs a few days later – a very satisfactory arrangement! There are few things better in life than getting up and going out to the hen house to collect lovely freshly laid eggs for breakfast.

Several times a year a hen will return from the woods with a little clutch of chicks. It doesn't matter whether you come from Tipperary or Tokyo, baby chicks – like puppies and kittens – delight everyone. And on Easter Sunday our hens even lay eggs with names on them(!) – thrilling our grandchildren Joshua, Luca, Willow and India and the guest children who stay in the cottages over Easter.

Egg Aesthetics

The breed of hen determines the colour of the egg shell. The Hepden Blacks and Speckledys we breed at Ballymaloe lay brown and speckledy eggs. From our collection of more rare breeds – Araucana, Bantam, Leghorn, Light Sussex, Maran, Minorca, Old English Game, Orpington, Polish, Silkie and Wyandotte, we get a variety of eggs; some white, some brown, some speckled. The Araucanas occasionally lay beautiful blue eggs when the fancy takes them and the Bantams lay the most wonderfully tasty and tiny eggs, which are perfect for children's breakfasts. All the birds are beautiful, and strut around the 'Palais des Poulets' looking haughty and decorative.

The colour of the yolk depends on diet and the time of year, becoming a richer yellow in the summer months when the hens have had access to lots of fresh green grass. Occasionally you come across a double-yolk egg. This happens when hens are coming to the end of their laying careers, but it is nothing to worry about – rather, something to celebrate.

Organic Free-range Eggs

Those of us who are fortunate enough to have some space to keep hens are blessed indeed. Our eggs have white curdy albumen and rich yellow yolks. Simply boiled, these eggs are a real treat.

If you do not have your own hens, wherever possible, buy organic free-range eggs – these are produced by birds raised under strict regulations, including the following:

1. Continual access to the great outdoors
2. Flocks of no more than 500
3. Feed that is antibiotic free and 100 per cent organic
4. No de-beaking

Note that organic eggs are always free-range, but free-range eggs are not necessarily organic. Do read the labels. Unfortunately, roughly 80 per cent of commercially produced eggs are from **battery chickens**. Avoid them at all costs! I cannot emphasise enough the virtues of organic eggs.

As true organic eggs are produced in smaller quantities than battery eggs you should be prepared to pay more for them. (They will still be better value for money than the equivalent amount of meat.)

Other Types of Eggs

Tiny **quail** eggs can be fried, poached, soft or hard-boiled in the same way as hen eggs. They have beautiful speckled shells and are delicious for canapés, starters or for children's breakfasts. **Duck** eggs (wash them well first) work very well in sponge cakes. **Turkey** eggs are very similar in flavour to hen eggs. **Pheasant** and other wild bird eggs can also be eaten, but people are reluctant to do so nowadays (and in some cases it is illegal), as many wild bird populations are threatened and in decline.

Relative Weights

Quail	20g (3/4oz)
Guinea fowl	25g (1oz)
Duck	50g (2oz)
Hen (large)	50g (2oz)
Turkey	75g (3oz)
Goose	200g (7oz)
Ostrich	500–550g (18–20oz)

Buying and Storage

The official advice is that eggs should be consumed within 21 days of being laid, but I suggest within seven days – the quality deteriorates rapidly. If you're buying them from a shop, look for ones that have been date-stamped and never buy cracked eggs.

For boiling eggs do not use eggs more than a day or two old; for baking 4–5 day-old eggs are fine, and for whipping week-old egg whites are better as fresh ones don't whip up so well.

It's probably best to store your eggs in the fridge because chilling slows deterioration, but do allow them to return to room temperature before use. If you are unsure about the freshness of your eggs, put them in a bowl of water. If they sink to the bottom, they are fresh; if not, the gas in them will cause them to rise to the surface. When you crack really fresh eggs onto a plate, you should be able to see three distinct layers – as they deteriorate, the albumen becomes more watery, and you will only see two.

Buttered Eggs

If you have your own hens, you can extend the shelf life of your eggs by rubbing the newly laid, still warm shells with a tiny scrap of butter to seal the pores. This old-fashioned way of preserving eggs is traditional in my part of the country and buttered eggs can still be bought in the Cork market. Stored in a cool place, the eggs will keep for several weeks and have a wonderful curdy texture, reminiscent of a newly laid egg.

Nutrition and Health

With all the media attention on cholesterol, it's easy to lose sight of the fact that eggs are a nutrient-rich, affordable contribution to a healthy diet. They are an excellent source of protein, containing all the essential amino acids needed by the human body, and they contain most of the recognised vitamins (with the exception of vitamin C). They are also rich in minerals, particularly iodine, phosphorus and zinc are are relatively low in calories.

Salmonella

Salmonella continues to make headlines despite the fact that, since 1998, cases of salmonella poisoning in Britain have dropped by half. This drop is due in part to recommendations made by the Government's Advisory Committee on the Microbiological Safety of Food, that eggs should be maintained at a temperature below 20°C (68°F) and consumed within 21 days.

Many countries have also devised symbols of quality – a shamrock in Ireland and a red lion in the UK – which are stamped on eggs, along with a 'best before' date, to indicate that they are fresh and from vaccinated hens. As a precaution, do not eat raw eggs, and do not give lightly cooked eggs to infants, the elderly or to pregnant women. Unfortunately buying organic does not necessarily guarantee disease-free eggs, although studies suggest that salmonella is less common in organic chickens than conventional birds.

We have our own hens at Ballymaloe, living in luxury in the Palais des Poulets. They roam outside, scratching in the vegetable patch and in the fields around the school – genuine free-rangers.

The hens provide yet another way for the students to learn about how food is produced. Each term we hatch a batch of chicks in our incubator for the students on the 12-week course (most of whom have never seen the magic of a chick emerging from an egg).

Many become so attached to the hens and are so impressed by the quality of their eggs that they decide to keep a few hens when they leave.

To encourage the growing number of people who want to know how to produce organic free-range eggs for themselves we've been offering a course on keeping chickens in your garden at the Cookery School.

The recipes here all call for medium eggs, unless otherwise stated.

How to Boil an Egg

Far be it for me to sound too dramatic but there's absolutely no point in serving either a boiled or poached egg unless you can get really fresh organic eggs. Allow the eggs to reach room temperature if they have been in the fridge. Bring a small saucepan of water to the boil, add a little salt, then lower the eggs gently into the water on a spoon. The eggs must be covered with water. Bring the water back to the boil and simmer gently for up to 6 minutes, according to your taste. A 4-minute egg will be still quite soft. Five minutes will almost set the white while the yolk will still be runny. Six minutes will produce a boiled egg with a soft yolk and a solid white.

Freshly Boiled Eggs and Soldiers
Serves 2

Mothers all over the country cut up fingers of toast for children to dip into soft-boiled eggs. In our family we call them 'dippies'.

4 organic eggs
2 slices of fresh quality white bread
a few pats of butter
salt and freshly ground pepper

Boil the eggs as above.

Meanwhile toast the bread, cut off the crusts and spread the slices with butter. Cut into fingers. Immediately the eggs are cooked, pop them into egg cups and put the dippies on the side. Serve with sea salt, a pepper mill and a few pats of butter.

Variations
Spread the hot buttered toast with Marmite or Vegemite and cut, dip and enjoy.

When asparagus is in season in May we dip freshly cooked spears into the egg yolk – delicious!

Molly Eggs
Serves 3–6

Oeufs Mollet – peeled soft-boiled eggs – are affectionately known as Molly Eggs in the Ballymaloe kitchen. They can be served with a variety of different sauces. A favourite is Alsacienne.

Alsacienne Sauce
1 soft-boiled organic egg
¼ teaspoon French mustard
¼ teaspoon salt
2 teaspoons freshly squeezed lemon juice
125ml (4fl oz) light olive oil
60–125ml (2–4fl oz) chicken stock
2 teaspoons finely chopped shallots or spring onion
2 teaspoons chopped herbs (mixture of parsley, thyme and chives)

6 fresh organic eggs
6 freshly cooked crostini (see page 67)

To make the sauce, carefully peel the soft-boiled egg and drop the yolk into a medium-sized Pyrex bowl. Save the egg white. Add the mustard, salt and lemon juice. Gradually whisk in the oil to create an emulsion as one would for mayonnaise. Add the chicken stock, chopped egg white, shallots and fresh herbs. Place the bowl over boiling water and stir until the sauce thickens slightly and the sauce is warm to the touch.

Soft-boil the eggs for 4–5 minutes, remove from the water and peel carefully.

To serve: put the freshly cooked crostini onto a warm plate and place a warm egg on top of each crostini. Spoon the sauce over the top and serve immediately.

Oeufs Florentine
See page 171

How to Poach Eggs

No fancy egg poachers or moulds are required to produce a perfect result. All you need is a really fresh egg from a happy, lazy hen. Bring a small saucepan of water to the boil, add a little salt, reduce the heat, swirl the water, crack the egg and slip gently into the whirlpool in the centre. For perfection the water should not boil again but bubble very gently just below boiling point. Continue to cook for 3–4 minutes until the white is set and the yolk still soft and runny. Lift out gently on a slotted spoon, and drain thoroughly. Serve on hot toast.

Alternatively, slip the poached egg into a bowl of cold water. Unlikely as it may sound, poached eggs reheat very well when popped back into barely simmering water (to compensate, slightly undercook them in the initial stage).

Eggs Benedict
Serves 4

Rich and gorgeous, this is often eaten for breakfast or brunch. The quality of the components can lift it from the mundane to the extraordinary. You can use smoked salmon, Serrano or Pata negra ham.

½ quantity Hollandaise sauce (see page 581)
sunflower oil
4–8 slices crispy bacon or 4 slices cooked ham, slightly smoked, is good too
4 organic eggs
2 English muffins, toasted, or 4 rounds toast made from good-quality bread
butter

First make the Hollandaise sauce. If using bacon, heat a spot of sunflower oil in a hot frying pan. Cook the bacon until crisp. Drain on kitchen paper. Meanwhile poach the eggs as above, and toast and butter the muffins or bread. Put 2 slices of bacon or 1 slice of ham on each piece. Top with the poached egg and coat with the sauce. Serve extra hot toast and sauce separately.

Warm Salad of Bacon with Poached Egg and Cheese

Serves 4

This gorgeous little salad depends totally on good ingredients. Make it with battery-produced eggs and indifferent bacon and you'll wonder why you bothered. We use Gubbeen bacon, which is cured and smoked by a brilliant young Irish artisan producer called Fingal Ferguson – the son of Tom and Giana Ferguson, from West Cork, who make the famous Gubbeen farmhouse cheese. If you can't lay your hands on this, look out for the best-quality smoked bacon you can find. We also use Gabriel cheese, a hard cheese made by the Fergusons' neighbour, Bill Hogan. A good nutty Parmesan may be used instead.

Caesar Salad dressing (see page 208)
olive or sunflower oil
175g (6oz) smoked bacon lardons
4 organic eggs, poached
a mixture of salad leaves
25g (1oz) hard cheese (such as Gabriel or a
    good Parmesan, e.g. Parmigiano Reggiano),
    freshly grated
parsley, freshly chopped

First make the dressing – you will have more than you need for this recipe but it keeps for several weeks so save it in the fridge for another time.

Meanwhile heat a frying pan, add a little olive or sunflower oil and cook the bacon until crispy. Poach the eggs (see page 99).

To assemble: put a little dressing on the plates. Arrange a selection of lettuce and salad leaves on top (we also add freshly cooked asparagus or chicory in season, or some chard or beet greens). Sprinkle the sizzling bacon over the salad and top with a poached egg. Drizzle more dressing over the eggs and salad leaves. Sprinkle with the cheese and parsley and serve immediately.

How to Hard-boil Eggs

Eggs that were laid a few days ago are ideal for hard-boiling. Very fresh eggs tend to be more difficult to peel. Eggs sold in the average shop or supermarket tend to be about a week old so there will be no need to worry about them being too fresh! Lower the eggs gently into boiling salted water, bring the water back to the boil and cook the eggs for 10 minutes (or 7–8 for a slightly soft centre). Drain and put immediately into a bowl of cold water. (Eggs with a black ring around the yolk have been overcooked.)

Ballymaloe Chutney Eggs

Serves 6

6 hard-boiled organic eggs
50g (2oz) soft butter
1 tablespoon Apple and Tomato Chutney (see
    page 512) or Ballymaloe Country Relish
salt and freshly ground pepper

Garnish
tiny sprigs of watercress or chervil

When the eggs are cold, shell them and slice in half lengthways. Sieve the yolks into a bowl, add the soft butter and chutney and mix well. Taste the mixture – it may need a little seasoning. Fill into a piping bag with a 2.5cm (1in) star nozzle. Pipe a rosette of the mixture into each egg white. Garnish with the watercress or chervil. Serve as a starter on a little bed of salad leaves. Alternatively, serve one as part of a selection of stuffed eggs.

Master Recipe
Egg Mayonnaise

Makes 8

Egg mayonnaise has a ring of the 1950s and 1960s about it, since it used to be such a staple on country hotel menus. The usual offering was an overcooked, hard-boiled egg, cut in half lengthways, smothered in commercial mayonnaise and sprinkled with a little parsley and paprika. This lighter, more labour-intensive version is one of the favourites on the buffet at Ballymaloe House. We also serve it in combination with smoked salmon and cucumber pickle as a starter.

4 hard-boiled organic eggs
3–4 tablespoons Mayonnaise (see page 584)
1/2 teaspoon finely chopped chives
salt and freshly ground pepper
salad leaves

Garnish
parsley or chervil

When the eggs are cold, shell them and cut in half lengthways. Sieve the yolks into a bowl, mix with mayonnaise, add the chives and salt and pepper to taste. Fill into a piping bag with a large star nozzle and pipe into the whites. Garnish with a sprig of parsley or chervil and serve on a bed of lettuce.

Variations
Egg Mayonnaise with Black Olives

Follow the Master Recipe. Chop 4–6 stoned Kalamata olives into fine dice, add to the sieved egg yolk and mayonnaise. Omit the chives if you wish. Garnish each with a sprig of chervil.

Anchovy Egg Mayonnaise

Follow the Master Recipe. Mash 4–6 salted anchovies in a bowl, add to the sieved egg yolk and mayonnaise. Omit the chives.

Oeufs Mimosa

Serves 4

In this very superior version of stuffed eggs, each one has a fat prawn or a few shrimps hiding inside. Be sure to tell people that there is shellfish involved, in case anyone has a seafood allergy. Oeufs Mimosa is great as a starter, or as part of a plate of stuffed eggs, or on a cold buffet. The sprinkled sieved egg yolk on top resembles the mimosa flower, hence the name.

4 hard-boiled organic eggs
8 cooked prawns or 16 shrimps
150ml (¼ pint) Mayonnaise (see page 584)
a few lettuce leaves
salt and freshly ground pepper

Garnish
sprigs of watercress
a few whole shrimps or prawns

When the eggs are cold, shell them and cut in half lengthways. Sieve the yolks into a bowl, reserve a little for the mimosa garnish, and mix the remainder with 3–4 tablespoons of the mayonnaise.

Add salt and pepper and taste to check the seasoning. Put a fat prawn or 1 or 2 cooked shrimps into each egg white and spoon some egg mayonnaise mixture into each one. Round off the top, so that the shape resembles a whole egg. Thin the remaining mayonnaise with cold water to coating consistency and coat the eggs carefully.

Sprinkle with the reserved egg yolk. Serve on a bed of lettuce and garnish with sprigs of watercress and a few shrimps or prawns.

Khai Loog Kheoy (Son-in-Law's Eggs)

Serves 6

This delicious version of Son-in-Law's Eggs was given to us by Wasinee Beech who was born in Thailand but now lives in Clonakilty in Co. Cork. Her food is absolutely delicious.

6 organic eggs, cooked and shelled
2 dried red chillies
5 tablespoons vegetable oil
8 shallots, sliced thinly
5 fresh or dried Chinese or shiitake mushrooms
3 garlic cloves, crushed and chopped finely
110g (4oz) free-range pork, minced
2½ tablespoons palm sugar
2 tablespoons fish sauce (nam pla)
2 tablespoons tamarind water (see right)
1 tablespoon lemon juice, freshly squeezed
3 spring onions, sliced in 1cm (½in) slices

Garnish
fresh coriander leaves

Boil the eggs gently for 7 minutes in salted water. Cool and remove the shells. Roast the chillies until fragrant but not burnt. Heat the oil in a pan, fry the shallots until crispy, drain on kitchen paper and reserve the oil.

If you are using dried Chinese mushrooms, soak them for 20 minutes, slice them and reserve the soaking water for use later.

Heat 3 tablespoons of the reserved oil in a wok, add the eggs and fry until all sides are golden brown and slightly crispy. Cut each egg in half and arrange on a serving dish. Clean the wok and add the rest of the oil. Stir-fry the garlic until golden. Add the pork and mushrooms and stir until the pork is cooked (about 5 minutes). Add the palm sugar, nam pla, tamarind water and lemon juice. If more liquid is required, add a little bit of water from the soaked mushrooms.

Taste and correct the seasoning, add the spring onions, give a quick stir and spoon the sauce over the eggs with the crispy shallots and chillies. Garnish with fresh coriander and serve with plain boiled rice (see page 124).

How to Make Tamarind Water

Tamarind is a souring agent used extensively in Indian and Asian cooking. It is very easy to use and gives dishes a special bitter-sweet flavour. The most common form of tamarind found in the West comes in a block of dark, sticky pulp which can be kept without refrigeration. Tamarind water keeps in a jar in the fridge for up to a week.

a piece of tamarind pulp the size of a table tennis ball
150ml (¼ pint) hot water

Put the pulp and hot water together into a small bowl. Leave to soak for 30 minutes. Squeeze the softened pulp between your fingers and when you feel the pips, remove and discard them. Pour the tamarind pulp and the liquid into a sieve, press to extract as much flavour as possible, then discard the fibrous remains. Use the tamarind water as required.

How to Fry an Egg

Choose very fresh organic eggs. Never buy cracked eggs. Put a frying pan on a low heat, melt a little butter and break the egg into the pan, then cover with a Pyrex plate. After a few minutes the egg yolk will film over. Serve immediately.

Sunny Side Up

Fry the egg in a little melted butter for 4–5 minutes on a low heat without flipping over. Serve immediately.

Basted Fried Eggs

Melt quite a large knob of butter or a few tablespoons of bacon fat in a pan, turn the heat to medium, allow the egg to cook for about a minute, then baste with the hot fat or butter. Serve as soon as the yolk has filmed over.

Easy Over

Fry the egg for 1–2 minutes and as soon as it is firm enough, slide an egg slice underneath and gently flip it over. Cook for a minute or two more. Serve immediately.

Deep-fried Eggs

Heat 2.5cm (1in) oil (sunflower or pure olive) in a frying pan, or use a deep fryer. The oil should be hot enough to brown a cube of bread in 30 seconds. Crack the egg and drop gently into the oil. Alternatively crack the egg into a cup first and then slide gently into the oil.

Immediately, using 2 wooden spatulas or perforated spoons, fold the egg white over the yolk to cover it. When the egg yolk is completely covered, allow the egg to cook for a minute or so until the white is firm and crisp and the yolk is still soft. Lift out with a perforated spoon. Drain on kitchen paper and serve immediately.

Deep-fried eggs are delicious with a spicy tomato sauce, or on top of a mixture of salad leaves as in Warm Salad of Bacon (see page 100).

Master Recipe
Scrambled Eggs

Serves 2

Perfectly scrambled eggs are rare indeed. I've had positively horrendous concoctions served up for breakfast in some posh hotels. On one particularly memorable occasion they arrived in a solid mound garnished with a sprig of redcurrants. For a perfect result, really fresh organic eggs are essential. Perfectly scrambled, these need no further embellishment, except perhaps a couple of slices of hot thin toast or fresh bread – but it's fun to experiment with variations all the same.

4 organic eggs
4 tablespoons creamy milk
salt and freshly ground pepper
a knob of butter

Break the eggs into a bowl, add the milk and season with salt and pepper. Whisk until the whites and yolks are well mixed. Put a knob of butter into a cold saucepan, pour in the egg mixture and stir continuously, preferably with a flat-bottomed wooden spatula over a low heat, until the butter melts and eggs have scrambled into soft creamy curds. Serve immediately on warm plates with lots of hot buttered toast or fresh soda bread.

> TIP: Don't heat the plates too much or the scrambled eggs will actually overcook between the stove and the table.

Variations
Scrambled Eggs with Tomato

Follow the Master Recipe. A few seconds before the eggs are fully scrambled, add 1 very ripe, peeled tomato which has been finely chopped and seasoned with salt, pepper and a pinch of sugar. Stir once or twice and serve immediately.

Scrambled Eggs with Tarragon and Basil

Follow the Master Recipe. Add 1 teaspoon freshly chopped tarragon and basil a few seconds before the eggs are fully scrambled. Serve immediately.

Scrambled Eggs with Chives

Follow the Master Recipe. Add 1–2 teaspoons freshly chopped chives a few seconds before the eggs are fully scrambled. Cold scrambled egg with chives makes the best egg sandwiches.

Scrambled Eggs with Asparagus

Follow the Master Recipe. Add 2–4 stalks freshly cooked, diced asparagus a few seconds before the eggs are fully scrambled.

Scrambled Eggs with Smoked Salmon

Some hotels serve this for breakfast but I rather prefer it for supper on a tray beside the fire. Follow the Master Recipe. A few seconds before the eggs are fully scrambled, add 2–3 tablespoons diced smoked salmon trimmings, stir once or twice, sprinkle with a little chopped parsley and serve immediately.

Scrambled Eggs with Smoked Bacon

Follow the Master Recipe. Cook 2–3 tablespoons of bacon dice in 1 tablespoon olive oil until crisp and golden. Add to the scrambled eggs with 2 teaspoons chopped parsley a few seconds before the eggs are fully scrambled, and serve immediately.

Spanish Scrambled Eggs with Chorizo

Follow the Master Recipe but use extra-virgin olive oil instead of butter. Cook 110g (4oz) diced chorizo in 1 tablespoon of olive oil until it begins to crisp and the fat runs. Add to the scrambled egg with 2 teaspoons of chopped parsley a few seconds before the eggs are fully scrambled, and serve immediately. Smoked bacon or prosciutto crisped in olive oil is a yummy alternative.

Matzo Scrambled Eggs

Serves 3–4

Zayne Stewart made this Jewish speciality for me in her apartment in Marbella. It sounded distinctly unpromising but tasted delicious.

4 fresh matzos
4 large organic eggs
¾–1 teaspoon salt
75g (3oz) unsalted butter

Crumble the matzos in smallish pieces and place in a large sieve. Hold under cold running water until the matzos are soft but not completely disintegrated (about 10–15 seconds). Whisk the eggs, add salt and stir in the matzos and any loose crumbs.

Heat the butter in a pan over a moderate heat. When foaming, add the matzo and egg mixture and cook, stirring constantly, until the eggs are scrambled and the matzo has begun to crisp.

Serve immediately on warm plates.

Cholita's Mexican Scrambled Eggs

Serves 4

Cholita Diaz, a wonderful Oaxacan cook, showed me how to make this favourite Mexican breakfast dish. One mouthful transports me back to Oaxaca, one of the most magical places in the entire world.

35g (1½oz) butter (in Mexico they use lard)
1 small onion, finely chopped
1–2 chillies (serrano or jalapeño), de-seeded and finely chopped (the amount depends on how much excitement you would like in your life!)
1–2 very ripe tomatoes, finely chopped
8 organic eggs
1 teaspoon salt

Melt the butter in a heavy saucepan over a medium heat, and cook the onion and chillies until the onion is soft but not coloured. Add the tomato and cook gently for a few more minutes. Meanwhile whisk the eggs and salt together well, add them to the saucepan and scramble, stirring all the time until cooked to your taste. Serve immediately on warm plates, preferably with tortillas.

Master Recipe
Baked Eggs

Serves 4

Oeufs en cocotte sounds so much more exotic than baked eggs – or shirred eggs, as they are known in the United States. Whatever the name, they make a tasty starter or snack and there are countless variations. Timing is critical, and once again the quality and freshness of the eggs really matter.

6–8 tablespoons cream
4 organic eggs
salt and freshly ground pepper

4 small ramekins
10g (½oz) butter, for greasing

Lightly butter the 4 ramekins. Heat the cream, then spoon about 1 tablespoon into each ramekin and break an egg into each, too. Season with salt and freshly ground pepper. Spoon the remainder of the cream over the top of the eggs.

Place the ramekins in a bain-marie (see glossary) of hot water, cover with tin foil or a lid and bring to simmering point on top of the stove. Continue to cook either gently on top of the stove, or in a moderate oven, 180°C/350°F/gas 4, for about 12 minutes for a soft egg, 15 minutes for a medium egg and 18–20 minutes for a hard egg. Serve immediately.

Variations
Baked Eggs with Cheese

Follow the Master Recipe, sprinkling ½–1 tablespoon finely grated cheese – Parmesan, Gruyère or Cheddar – on top of each egg. Bake uncovered in a bain-marie in the oven if preferred.

Baked Eggs with Tomato and Chilli Fondue

Follow the Master Recipe. Put 1 tablespoon Tomato and Chilli Fondue (see page 200) underneath each egg in the ramekins. Proceed with or without adding cheese. Omit the chilli from the tomato fondue if you prefer your baked eggs less perky.

Baked Eggs with Piperonata

Follow the Master Recipe. Put 1 tablespoon of Piperonata (see page 199) underneath each egg in the ramekins. Spoon 1 tablespoon cream over each egg. Sprinkle ½–1 tablespoon finely grated cheese on top of each egg; a little cooked bacon may also be added. Bake uncovered in a bain-marie in the oven if preferred.

Baked Eggs with Fresh Herbs and Dijon Mustard

Follow the Master Recipe. Use a total of 3 tablespoons freshly chopped parsley, tarragon, chives and chervil. Mix the herbs and 2 teaspoons mustard into the cream and proceed as in the basic recipe.

Baked Eggs with Smoked Salmon, Smoked Mackerel or Smoked Haddock

Follow the Master Recipe. Put 1 tablespoon chopped smoked salmon, flaked smoked mackerel or smoked haddock in the base of each ramekin. (If you are using smoked haddock, it should be gently cooked in milk first because the haddock is cold-smoked and as a result, still semi-raw.) Add 1–2 tablespoons chopped parsley to the cream and proceed as in the basic recipe.

Baked Egg with Chorizo

Follow the Master Recipe. Add some diced chorizo to the ramekin with or without Tomato and Chilli Fondue (see page 200).

Omelettes

Omelettes appear in different guises all around the world. There are three main types – folded French omelettes, flat omelettes and soufflé omelettes, both sweet and savoury. The folded omelette may be made simply with a seasoning of salt and freshly ground pepper or a sprinkling of fresh herbs or freshly grated cheese. Alternatively a filling such as hot Mushroom à la Crème, Piperonata, Tomato Fondue or seafood may be added just before the omelette is folded.

Flat omelettes are quite different, however. The eggs help to bind other ingredients, such as potatoes, leeks or peppers. Cheese is often added as are freshly chopped herbs. Flat omelettes are found all over the world, from Provence in France to the tortillas of Spain, the kuku of the Middle East and the frittatas of Italy. The fluffy Danish omelette is a variation on this theme. It is usually cooked in a deep frying pan over a very low heat without stirring until just set and slightly puffed.

Some people favour starting a frittata on top of the stove and then transferring it to a preheated oven at 150°C/300°F/gas 2, until just set. Asian omelettes are usually cooked in a wok and include shrimps and fresh herbs. They are often folded in half and may be served with a volcanic chilli sauce. In Japan, cooks use special rectangular pans to make omelettes that are shaped into neat rolls to slice for sushi or into thin shreds for garnishing soups. In China thin omelettes are used as wrappers for other ingredients but are also occasionally filled with vegetables.

Soufflé omelettes may be sweet or savoury. The eggs are separated and the fluffy, beaten egg whites are folded into the beaten egg yolks and sugar (in the case of a sweet omelette). Don't cook on too high a heat, otherwise the outside will be burnt before the inside is set.

French Omelette

Serves 1

An omelette is the quintessential fast food but many a travesty is served in its name. The whole secret is to have the pan hot enough and to use clarified butter if at all possible. Ordinary butter will burn if your pan is as hot as it ought to be. The omelette should be made in half the time it takes to read this recipe! Your first omelette may not be a joy to behold, but persevere. Practice makes perfect. The best tender golden omelette takes no more than 30 seconds to cook – or 45 seconds if you are adding a filling. If it is cooked too slowly, it will be tough and leathery and may be pale in colour rather than lightly browned. Time yourself. You'll be amazed! Note that the size of pan suggested below is just right for a two-egg omelette. If you use more eggs, the proportions of the omelette and the timing will be altered.

2 organic eggs
2 teaspoons water or milk
2 teaspoons clarified butter (see page 105) or
*   olive oil*
filling of your choice
salt and freshly ground pepper

23cm (9in) omelette pan, preferably non-stick

Warm a plate in the oven. Whisk the eggs with the water or milk in a bowl until thoroughly mixed but not too fluffy. (You can use either a fork or a hand whisk.) Season with salt and pepper. Put the warm plate beside the cooker. Have the filling also to hand, hot if necessary, with a spoon at the ready.

Heat the omelette pan over a high heat. When it is very hot, add the clarified butter; it should sizzle immediately. Pour in the egg mixture. It will start to cook instantly, so quickly pull the edges of the omelette towards the centre using a plastic or metal spatula, tilting the pan so that the uncooked egg runs to the sides 4 or 5 times. Continue until most of the egg is set and will not run easily any more. The centre will still be soft and uncooked at this point but will continue to cook on the plate. If you are using a filling, spoon the hot mixture in a line across the centre at this point.

To fold the omelette: flip the edge that is just below the handle of the pan into the centre, then hold the pan almost perpendicular over the plate so that the omelette flips over again. Half roll, half slide the omelette onto the plate so that it lands folded in three. Serve immediately.

Variations
Fines Herbes
Add 1 teaspoon each of freshly chopped parsley, chives, chervil and tarragon to the eggs just before cooking or scatter over the omelette just before folding.

Suggested Fillings
Smoked Salmon or Smoked Mackerel
Use diced or flaked fish and perhaps a little finely chopped parsley or dill.

Kidneys
Use one cleaned and diced lamb's kidney, cooked gently in a little butter, and add 1 teaspoon freshly chopped parsley.

Crispy bacon, diced cooked ham or chorizo sausage

Mushroom à la Crème (see page 201) **with crispy bacon**

Goat's cheese, grated Cheddar, Gruyère, Parmesan or a mixture of cheeses

Tomato Fondue, with or without pesto (see page 200)

Piperonata (see page 199)

Clarified Butter and Ghee

Clarified butter is butter with the salt and milk particles removed. It is excellent for cooking because it can withstand higher temperatures than normal butter. It will also keep for several weeks in a fridge. **To make clarified butter** melt 225g (8oz) butter gently in a saucepan or in the oven. Allow to stand for a few minutes. Spoon the crusty white layer of salt particles off the top; underneath is the clear liquid butter known as clarified butter. The milky liquid at the bottom can be discarded.

Ghee is a clarified butter widely used in India and some Arab countries (where it is called *samna*). The butter is first melted then simmered until the moisture evaporates and the butter caramelises producing a sweet nutty flavour.

Omelette Sambo

Serves 1

Needless to say, this technique can be applied to a whole host of different fillings, so you can let your imagination run riot – but don't use it as a dustbin for leftovers.

½ baguette
French omelette, Fines Herbes variation
* (see left)*
2 tablespoons Tomato Fondue (see page 200) or
* Mushroom à la Crème (see page 201)*
pesto, herb-flavoured oil or chilli oil

To Serve
flat-leaf parsley, rocket leaves, tiny spinach or
* ruby chard leaves*
red and yellow cherry tomatoes

Crisp the baguette by putting it briefly in a hot oven if necessary. Meanwhile, make a well-seasoned herb omelette (see page 104). Fill with Tomato Fondue or Mushroom à la Crème (see page 201) and roll it up. Split open the baguette and smear with pesto, herb-flavoured oil or chilli oil. Pop the rolled omelette inside and close up again. Leave it whole, or cut it in half or into slices. Serve immediately with a nice mixture of salad leaves, a few cherry tomatoes and a drizzle of herb-flavoured oil.

Cheese Soufflé Omelette

Serves 1–2

A perfect soufflé omelette is a special treat. It takes a little longer to make than a French one but it is well worth the effort. Irish farmhouse cheeses such as Coolea, Desmond or Gabriel from West Cork are utterly delicious in this recipe. If you can't get these, use Gruyère or Parmesan.

3 organic eggs, separated
2–4 tablespoons finely grated Irish farmhouse
* cheese, or use Gruyère, Parmesan or a mixture*
1 teaspoon finely chopped chives or spring
* onion tops (optional)*
25g (1oz) butter
a little extra grated cheese (optional)
salt and freshly ground pepper

23cm (9in) omelette pan, preferably non-stick

Whisk the egg yolks until light, season well, and add the cheese and chives. Whisk the egg whites until they hold a stiff peak, stir a little of the whites into the yolks, then very lightly and carefully fold in the rest with a metal spoon. Melt the butter in the frying pan, shaking it gently so that the sides are covered with butter too. As it foams, turn in the egg mixture and level it off with a palette knife. Cook very gently for 3–4 minutes. When you lift the omelette with the palette knife, the bottom should be golden, and it should have started to rise.

Put the pan under the grill, about 10cm (4in) from the element, and cook very gently for a further 3–4 minutes until the omelette is well risen and just set. Remove at once, loosen the edges with the palette knife and, if you wish, fold it over, score lightly across the centre. Transfer to a hot plate and sprinkle with extra cheese. Serve immediately with a good green salad.

Fluffy Danish Omelette

Serves 1–2

This delicious omelette is also very good with smoked salmon or smoked mackerel. A vegetarian version can be made with red or green peppers, tomatoes and aubergine.

8 organic eggs
60ml (2½fl oz) water
salt and freshly ground pepper
10g (½oz) butter
4–6 slices of streaky bacon (smoked or
* unsmoked)*
a little oil
6 very ripe tomatoes or 12 cherry tomatoes
2 tablespoons chives or tarragon, freshly
* chopped*
2 tablespoons parsley, freshly chopped

23cm (9in) omelette pan, preferably non-stick

Put the eggs, water and seasoning into a bowl. Whisk until really fluffy and light – they should froth up to 3 or 4 times their original volume. Meanwhile put the pan on to heat and melt the butter. As soon as it foams, add the egg mixture and turn down the heat to the minimum. You may want to use a heat-diffusing mat.

Meanwhile, fry the bacon until crisp and golden in a little oil. Drain on kitchen paper, cut into 2cm (¾in) pieces and keep warm.

Cut the tomatoes into quarters, and then quarters again (or halve, if using cherry tomatoes). Season with salt and pepper.

When the bottom of the omelette is set, scatter the tomatoes and hot crispy bacon on top. They will lightly sink into the fluffy top. Sprinkle with fresh herbs and serve immediately, cut into segments or with a good green salad.

Provençal Terrine with Tomato Sauce

Serves 10–12

One of my favourite vegetarian terrines is really a multi-layered omelette. It makes a sensational starter or main course for a summer lunch party, and you can vary the flavouring if you want to. The secret to success is to prepare all the ingredients first, then cook one layer after the other very quickly.

Courgette Layer
2 tablespoons extra-virgin olive oil
350g (12oz) courgettes, grated on the coarsest part of a grater and lightly sprinkled with sea salt
3 organic eggs
1 tablespoon cream or milk
salt and freshly ground pepper
2 teaspoons freshly chopped annual marjoram

Tomato Layer
2 tablespoons extra-virgin olive oil
400g (14oz) very ripe tomatoes, peeled, de-seeded and chopped
salt, freshly ground pepper and a pinch of sugar
pinch of fresh thyme leaves

3 organic eggs
1 tablespoon cream or milk

Olive Layer
3 organic eggs
1 tablespoon cream or milk
2 tablespoons black olives, stoned and chopped
2 teaspoons finely chopped parsley
salt and freshly ground pepper

Spinach Layer
1 tablespoon melted butter
110g (4oz) cooked spinach, or 200g (7oz) fresh spinach
salt, freshly ground pepper and freshly grated nutmeg
3 organic eggs
1 tablespoon cream or milk
25g (1oz) grated Gruyère

extra-virgin olive oil

Accompaniments
fresh Tomato Sauce (see page 590) or Tomato Fondue (see page 200)

23 x 12.5 x 5cm (9 x 5 x 2in) loaf tin, lined with silicone paper

First prepare all the ingredients, and preheat the oven to 180°C/350°F/gas 4.

To make the courgette layer: heat 2 tablespoons of oil in a frying pan and cook the courgettes until soft but still bright green, then drain. Whisk the eggs, add the cream or milk, salt, pepper, marjoram and courgettes. Set aside.

To make the tomato layer: heat the oil in a pan, add the tomatoes, season with salt, pepper, sugar and thyme. Cook until you have a soft, very thick and concentrated paste. Whisk the eggs with the cream or milk, add the tomato paste, taste and correct seasoning. Set aside.

Make the olive layer: whisk the eggs, add the cream or milk, olives and parsley, season with pepper and a very little salt. Set aside.

LEFT: Provençal Terrine with Tomato Sauce

To make the spinach layer: cook the spinach if raw in the melted butter in a frying pan until soft and wilted. Season with salt, pepper and a generous grating of nutmeg. Drain, press out every single drop of liquid and chop finely. Whisk the eggs, add the cream or milk, stir in the spinach, taste and add more salt and pepper if necessary.

To assemble: when all the preparation is done, cook the layers one after the other. Heat 1 tablespoon of olive oil in a 20.5cm (8in) non-stick pan. Pour in the courgette mixture, stir around for about 30–60 seconds until the texture is just like a softly scrambled egg, pour immediately into the lined loaf tin. Continue with the other layers, cooking each in 1 tablespoon of olive oil. Sprinkle the spinach layer with Gruyère cheese and cover the top with a piece of silicone paper. Cook in a bain-marie in the oven for 10–15 minutes or until set – it should feel firm in the centre and a skewer should come out clean. Allow to cool.

Serve lukewarm or cold with hot or cold Tomato Sauce, lots of crusty bread and a good green salad (see page 223).

Note: Sweet little individual 'terrines' can be made in small ramekins – they take about 10 minutes to cook.

How to Whisk Egg Whites

Choose a large bowl, preferably with a round bottom. Unlined copper is best, but stainless steel, glass or delph porcelain are also fine (although the whites tend to detach from the sides of glass or delph bowls). Plastic is least successful because it is difficult to remove all traces of grease and detergent residue, both of which prevent the whites from fluffing up. Make sure that the bowl is spotlessly clean and dry. Similarly, the egg whites must be free of any egg yolk, oil, grease or water.

A pinch of salt or cream of tartar (Bextartar) added to the egg whites at the beginning will help to increase the volume. Caster sugar added at the end of whisking will help to stabilise the foam. This is called 'meringuing' the egg whites.

To whisk: put the egg whites into the bowl. Using a light balloon whisk or a coil whisk, turn the bowl onto its side and start to whisk, slowly at first and then faster until the egg whites are stiffly beaten. They will form a stiff peak on the end of the whisk when lifted out of the bowl. At this point change the angle of the whisk and stir in a full circular movement to tighten the egg white and make it more stable. If using caster sugar in a sweet soufflé, add a little just before this stage and then 'tighten' the egg whites. It should be possible to turn the bowl upside down at this stage without the egg whites falling out. Over-whisked egg white will become granular. If egg whites separate and become grainy, add 1 unbeaten egg white for every 4 whites in the bowl and continue to whisk for 30 seconds. This should re-emulsify the problem egg whites.

Egg whites may of course be whisked in an electric food mixer but this method does not result in as great a volume as those hand-whisked in a copper bowl. These can achieve up to eight times their own volume. Stiffly beaten egg whites should be used immediately as they deflate very quickly.

Note: slightly stale egg whites whip up better than very fresh ones. Egg whites that have been frozen whisk well. (1 egg white = 30ml/1fl oz.)

To prepare a copper bowl: before whisking egg whites the bowl needs to be carefully cleaned to remove any toxic copper carbonate. Put about 2 tablespoons of salt into the bowl, then add a few tablespoons of plain white vinegar. Alternatively use a cut lemon. Clean the entire inside of the bowl very well; it will turn a bright pinkish copper colour. Rinse and dry well. Clean again in two hours if necessary.

Folding Egg Whites

The technique of folding egg whites into a base mixture is a crucially important one for many dishes. Whisked egg whites are the lightest of all ingredients. When sugar is added, as in meringue, they tend to be firmer. The lighter the base mixture, the easier it is to fold in the egg whites. Stir about a quarter of the whites into a firmer mixture to lighten it before folding in the remainder of the egg whites. Then gently pour this mixture onto the top of the stiffly beaten egg whites in the bowl. Using a long-handled spatula or a metal spoon, cut down into the centre of the bowl and lift the mixture up and over, turning the bowl anti-clockwise at the same time as you repeat the motion. Stop as soon as all the egg whites are incorporated.

TIP: If there is a spot of yolk in the white the easiest way to remove it is with the edge of the egg shell (it has an affinity to the shell) before whisking.

Master Recipe
Basic Frittata
Serves 2–4

Frittata, kuku and tortilla all sound much more exciting than a flat omelette although that's basically what they are. Unlike its soft and creamy French cousin, this type of omelette is cooked slowly over a very low heat during which time you can be whipping up a delicious salad to accompany it! A frittata is cooked gently on both sides and cut into wedges like a piece of cake. The basic recipe, flavoured with grated cheese and a generous sprinkling of herbs, is delicious, but you may add anything that takes your fancy.

All the frittate here can be cooked in a non-stick frying pan with an 18cm (7in) base, sloping sides and a 23cm (9in) rim.

8 large organic eggs
2 teaspoons chopped parsley
2 teaspoons torn basil or chopped marjoram
1 teaspoon thyme leaves
75g (3oz) Gruyère, grated
25g (1oz) Parmesan, grated
25g (1oz) butter
1 teaspoon salt
lots of freshly ground pepper

Whisk the eggs in a bowl, add the fresh herbs, salt, pepper and grated cheese into the eggs. Melt the butter in the frying pan. As soon as it starts to foam, tip in the eggs. Turn down the heat, as low as it will go. Leave the eggs to cook gently for 12 minutes on a heat diffuser mat, or until the underneath is set. The top should still be slightly runny.

Meanwhile, preheat the grill. Pop the pan under the grill for a minute to set but don't brown the top.

Slide a palette knife under the frittata to free it from the pan. Slide onto a warm plate. Serve cut in wedges with a good green salad (see page 223) and perhaps a Tomato Salad (see page 220).

Variations
Mushroom Frittata
Clean, slice and quickly fry 450g (1lb) flat mushrooms in a little olive oil, cooking until they are slightly golden. Season with salt and pepper. Add to the basic frittata mixture and proceed as in the Master Recipe. A mixture of wild mushrooms is divine.

> TIP: Slice the mushroom stalks into thin rounds up to the cap, then lay the mushroom, gills down, on the chopping board and slice. Use both stalk and caps for extra flavour and less waste. Alternatively put the stalks into a vegetable stock.

Smoked Salmon and Goat's Cheese Frittata
Follow the Master Recipe, adding to the egg mixture just before cooking: 3 slices smoked salmon, diced, and substituting a mild goat's cheese for half the Gruyère, crumbling it into the mixture.

Courgette and Herb Frittata
Follow the Master Recipe, adding to the egg mixture just before cooking: 4 green or golden courgettes (or a mixture), 1 crushed garlic clove and 2–3 tablespoons of freshly chopped herbs (mint, marjoram or torn basil leaves), fried in a little olive oil for 3–4 minutes.

Tomato, Goat's Cheese and Chorizo Frittata
Follow the Master Recipe, adding to the egg mixture just before cooking: 450g (1lb) ripe cherry tomatoes roasted for 10–15 minutes and cooled before adding), 110–175g (4–6oz) chorizo, thickly sliced then quartered. Instead of grated Gruyère, use 110g (4oz) soft goat's cheese: divide it into walnut-sized pieces and, as the egg cooks, drop them in at regular intervals.

Asparagus, Rocket and Wild Garlic Frittata
Serves 6

This is an example of how we incorporate seasonal ingredients into a frittata.

225g (8oz) thin asparagus, tough ends trimmed
8 organic eggs
50g (2oz) Parmesan (Parmigano Reggiano if possible), freshly grated
2–3 tablespoons wild garlic and rocket leaves, roughly chopped
2 tablespoons olive oil
1 teaspoon salt
lots of freshly ground pepper
wild garlic and rocket leaves and flowers, to garnish

Bring 2.5cm (1in) salted water to the boil in an oval casserole. Blanch the asparagus for 3–4 minutes until just tender. Drain. Slice the end of the spears evenly at an angle, keeping 4cm (1½in) of the tips intact. Reserve. Whisk the eggs in a bowl, add the asparagus, most of the Parmesan and wild garlic leaves. Season with salt and pepper.

Preheat the grill. Heat the oil in the pan, add the egg mixture and reduce the heat to the bare minimum, using a heat diffuser mat if necessary. Continue to cook over a gentle heat until just set, about 15 minutes.

Arrange the asparagus on the top. Sprinkle with the remaining Parmesan. Pop under the grill for a few minutes, making sure the pan is at least 10cm (4in) from the element. The frittata should be set and lightly golden. Turn out onto a warm plate, cut into wedges and garnish with the wild garlic and rocket. Serve immediately with a good green salad.

Thai Omelette with Chilli Sauce
Serves 4–6

In Thailand, this omelette is made in a wok, often over a charcoal brazier. It is served with a volcanic chilli garlic sauce called Sri Racha, available in Asian shops.

4 organic eggs
1 tablespoon fish sauce (nam pla)
1 teaspoon water
50ml (2fl oz) vegetable oil (sunflower or peanut)
Sri Racha sauce or Hot Chilli Sauce (see
page 592)

Whisk the eggs, fish sauce and water in a bowl until well blended. Heat the oil in a non-stick pan. When very hot, pour in the eggs and tilt the pan to spread them evenly. The eggs will begin to sizzle and puff up. Pull the edges in towards the centre with a plastic or metal slice and keep tilting the pan until no runny egg remains. When the edges are golden and the top is almost set, gently flip the omelette over and brown the other side.

Turn the omelette out onto a plate and serve with small saucers of Sri Racha.

Variation

Thai Omelette with Pork, Spring Onions and Coriander

Add 110g (4oz) minced pork, 1 tablespoon sliced spring onions and 1 tablespoon freshly chopped coriander to the beaten eggs. Cook the omelette in the same way but a little longer.

Spicy Indian Omelette

Serves 1

Every culture has its own version of an omelette – I came across this one in Delhi.

2 organic eggs
1 heaped tablespoon finely chopped onion
1 heaped tablespoon chopped coriander
1 large tomato, finely chopped
½ teaspoon freshly roasted cumin
salt and lots of freshly ground pepper

sunflower oil or clarified butter (see page 105)

Heat a frying pan on a high heat. Whisk the eggs in a bowl. Add the remainder of the ingredients, season well with salt and freshly ground pepper. Put a little oil into

the pan – it should be very hot. Pour in the egg mixture. It will start to cook immediately so quickly pull the edges of the omelette towards the centre with a plastic or metal slice, tilting the pan so that the uncooked eggs runs to the sides. Continue to tilt the pan until most of the egg is set and will not run any more. The omelette may need to cook for a further 5 seconds to brown the bottom. The centre should still be soft and moist.

To fold the omelette: flip the edge below the handle of the pan into the centre, then hold the pan almost perpendicular over the plate so that the omelette will flip over again, then half roll, half slide the omelette onto the plate so that it lands folded into three. It should take no more than 30 seconds in all to make the omelette.

Serve immediately or use in sandwiches.

Tortilla de Patatas (Spanish Potato Omelette)

Serves 6

In Spain, you must understand, tortilla is not just a dish: it is a way of life. Tortillas – not to be confused with Mexican tortilla which is a flat bread – or flat omelettes are beloved by Spaniards and tourists alike. You'll be offered them in every Spanish home, in the most elegant of restaurants and the most run-down establishments. No Spanish picnic would be complete without a tortilla and every tapas bar will have them on display. People even eat them at the cinema! *Tortilla de Patatas* may sound deceptively simple but it's not as easy to make to perfection as you might think. The secret of success is to use enough oil.

Spanish olive oil, such as Lerida
225g (8oz) potatoes, peeled and thinly sliced or cut into uneven dice
150g (5oz) onions, thinly sliced

8 organic eggs
1 teaspoon sea salt
freshly ground pepper

18–20cm (7–8in) frying pan, non-stick
if possible

Put a generous 2.5cm (1in) of olive oil into the frying pan, then cook the onions and potatoes over a medium heat until crisp and golden. This can take up to 20 minutes. Drain off the oil and reserve.

Whisk the eggs in a bowl, season with salt and pepper, add the potato and onion. Put 2 tablespoons oil back into the pan. Once it begins to sizzle, pour in the egg mixture, then lower the heat. When the egg begins to cook, loosen the edges and continue to cook, shaking the pan occasionally, and tidying the edges to keep them rounded.

When the tortilla is well set and golden underneath, cover the pan with an oiled plate and turn the tortilla upside down on to it, taking care not to burn your hand. Add a little more oil to the frying pan if needed. Slide the tortilla back in. Cook until the lower side is golden and the whole is firm but still slightly moist in the centre. Serve hot or at room temperature cut into wedges or squares.

> TIP: The quality of the eggs really matters here. Keep the heat low or the tortilla will be tough.

Variations

Add spinach, chorizo and courgettes to the base mixture.

Present as finger food by using a cocktail stick to anchor a rocket leaf and cherry tomato on top of each slice.

Omelette Arnold Bennett

Serves 1–2 as a main course

Theatre critic, playwright and author, Arnold Bennett, was staying at the Savoy Hotel to write his novel, *The Imperial Palace*, when he asked the chefs to make this dish for him. It is another flat omelette, but this time the egg white is folded in to give a light, fluffy texture. This delicious omelette is also very good made with smoked salmon, smoked mackerel or chorizo sausage. Roast red and yellow pepper, blanched and refreshed broccoli florets or asparagus are lovely, too.

50–75g (2–3oz) smoked haddock
a little milk
25g (1oz) butter
150ml (¼ pint) cream
3 organic eggs, separated
2–3 tablespoons Parmesan (preferably
    Parmigiano Reggiano), grated
salt and freshly ground pepper

Garnish
parsley, freshly chopped

non-stick omelette pan with a 20cm (8in) base,
    sloping sides and a 25cm (10in) rim

Put the smoked haddock into a small saucepan. Cover with milk and simmer gently until it is cooked enough to separate into flakes (about 10 minutes). Drain. Toss the flaked haddock over a moderate heat with half the butter and 2 tablespoons of the cream and set aside. Separate the eggs, beat the yolks with a tablespoon of the cream and season with salt and freshly ground pepper. Whip the egg whites stiffly. Fold the yolks into the haddock mixture and add half the grated Parmesan. Fold in the egg whites, the haddock and egg yolk mixture.

Preheat the grill. Melt the remaining butter in the omelette pan. Pour the mixture in gently and cook over a medium heat until the base of the omelette is golden. Spoon the remaining cream over the top and sprinkle with the rest of the finely grated Parmesan. Pop under a hot grill for a minute or so until golden and bubbly. Slide on to a hot dish, sprinkle with parsley and serve immediately with a good green salad (see page 223).

> TIP: Avoid smoked haddock which is bright orange. The colour has much more to do with dye than smoke.

How to Make a Hot Soufflé

Even for a seasoned chef, a perfect, well-risen soufflé, puffed and golden, is a source of considerable pride and satisfaction – the ultimate triumph of the chef's art. But don't be intimidated. Essentially, it is simply a well-seasoned sauce or purée, enriched with egg yolks and lightened with stiffly beaten egg whites. When cooked, the mixture expands in the hot oven, hence the impressive height.

11 key points about soufflés:

1. The egg whites should be stiffly whisked just before using (see page 107) in a bowl which is dry, spotlessly clean and free from all grease. A copper bowl is best; glass, stainless-steel and porcelain are satisfactory; plastic is less successful.

2. Use a thin, flat-bladed spoon or long-handled spatula to fold the egg whites carefully into the base mixture. A thick wooden spoon may knock out some of the precious air that you have so carefully incorporated as you whisked the egg whites.

3. The base for savoury soufflés is usually Béchamel or Velouté sauce (see pages 580 and 581), flavoured with vegetable or fish purée. The base mixture must be highly flavoured or seasoned because egg white tends to dull flavour. The soufflé base must be the correct consistency – soft enough to fold in the egg whites easily. If it is too firm, stir a little stiffly beaten egg white in to lighten it, then fold in the remainder gently but firmly.

4. To increase the volume, 1 or 2 extra egg whites are added to many soufflés. The final volume should be at least double the base mixture.

5. The volume will decrease in varying degrees when the egg whites are folded in, depending on the content of the base mixture. The oil in chocolate tends to deflate egg whites dramatically, so it is essential to work fast and get the soufflé into the oven without delay. The cooked soufflé will increase by at least 50 per cent in volume and may even increase by 100 per cent.

6. A classic soufflé is best baked in a straight-sided soufflé dish or dishes. For a professional result, fill the dish to within 1cm (½in) of the top. Individual soufflés are best filled right to the top and smoothed with a palette knife. Chefs often run a clean thumb around the inner edge of the filled soufflé mould to make a groove. This creates a 'top hat' effect in the oven. Most soufflés, except chocolate, may be refrigerated at this stage for an hour or two, but must be served as soon as they are baked.

7. When baking a large soufflé, place the mould low in the oven to allow space for expansion. Some chefs like to bake savoury soufflés, particularly cheese ones, in a bain-marie.

8. Try to avoid opening the oven door while the soufflé is cooking. Whereas a soufflé will probably not sink if you do this half way through the cooking time (to turn it so that it cooks evenly), it is best to avoid draughts.

9. The soufflé is ready when the top is brown and puffed and the centre is slightly soft and creamy when shaken gently. Serve on a hot plate, immediately. The cool air will cause the soufflé to shrink within 3–5 minutes.

10. Soufflés that are cooked at a higher temperature rise faster and fall faster.

11. A soufflé mixture may also be cooked on a Swiss roll tin and rolled up like a roulade.

Note: A cold soufflé is not a real soufflé at all, but a mousse-like mixture lightened with egg whites and set in a soufflé dish with a high collar to give the impression of a risen soufflé.

Parmesan and Gruyère Cheese Soufflé

Serves 8–10

Well-risen soufflés always produce a gasp of admiration when brought to the table. Don't imagine for one moment that you can't master the technique – soufflés are much more good-humoured than you may think and can even be frozen when they are ready for the oven. The French create infinite variations on the theme, both sweet and savoury.

35g (1½oz) butter
25g (1oz) flour
300ml (½ pint) milk
4 organic eggs, separated
50g (2oz) Gruyère, finely grated
50g (2oz) Parmesan, freshly grated
pinch of cayenne pepper
freshly grated nutmeg
salt and freshly ground pepper

8–10 individual soufflé dishes, 7.5cm (3in)
  diameter x 4cm (1½in) deep, or one large dish
  15cm (6in) diameter x 6cm (2½in) high

For the dishes
knob of butter, melted
10g (½oz) Parmesan (optional)

Prepare the soufflé dish or dishes: brush evenly with melted butter and dust with a little Parmesan if liked. Preheat the oven to 200°C/400°F/gas 6 and heat a baking sheet.

Melt the butter in a heavy saucepan, stir in the flour and cook over a gentle heat for 1–2 minutes. Draw off the heat and whisk in the milk. Return to the heat, whisk as it comes to the boil, cover and simmer gently for 4–5 minutes. Remove from the heat. Separate the eggs and put the whites into a large copper, glass or stainless steel bowl, making sure it is spotlessly clean and dry. Whisk the yolks one by one into the white sauce and add the cheese. Season with salt, pepper, cayenne and freshly grated nutmeg and stir over a gentle heat for a few seconds until the cheese melts. Remove from the heat. *

Whisk the egg whites with a little pinch of salt, slowly at first and then faster until they are light and hold a stiff peak when you lift up the whisk. Stir a few tablespoons into the cheese mixture to lighten it and then carefully fold in the rest with a spatula or tablespoon. Fill the mixture into the soufflé dishes (if you fill them three-quarters full you will get about 10 but if you smooth the tops you will have about 8). Bake in the oven for 8–9 minutes for the individual soufflés or 20–25 minutes for the large one. For the latter you will need to reduce the temperature to 180°C/350°F/gas 4, after 15 minutes. Serve immediately.

* Can be made ahead up to this point. Individual frozen soufflés may be baked from frozen but will take a few minutes longer to cook.

Goat's Cheese and Thyme Leaf Soufflé

Serves 6

We bake this soufflé golden and puffy in a shallow, oval dish instead of the traditional soufflé bowl.

300ml (½ pint) cream
300ml (½ pint) milk
a few slices of carrot
1 small onion, quartered
sprig of thyme, a few parsley stalks and a little
  piece of bay leaf
4–5 black peppercorns
75g (3oz) butter
35g (1½oz) flour
5 organic eggs, separated
110g (4oz) goat's cheese, crumbled (we use St.
  Tola or Ardsallagh)
75g (3oz) Gruyère, grated
50g (2oz) mature Cheddar (Coolea, Desmond),
  Parmesan or Regato may also be used, grated
a good pinch of salt, freshly ground pepper,
  cayenne and nutmeg
2 teaspoons fresh thyme leaves

Garnish
thyme flowers, if available

30cm (12in) shallow oval dish (not a soufflé
  dish) or 6 individual wide soup bowls with
  a rim
melted butter, for greasing

Preheat the oven to 230°C/450°F/gas 8.

Brush the bottom and sides of the dish with melted butter. Put the cream and milk into a saucepan, add the carrot, onion, herbs and peppercorns. Bring slowly to the boil and allow to infuse for 10 minutes. Strain and discard the flavourings.

Melt the butter, add the flour and cook for 1–2 minutes. Whisk in the strained cream and milk, bring to the boil and continue whisking until it thickens. Cool slightly. Add the egg yolks, goat's cheese, Gruyère and most of the Cheddar (or Parmesan if using). Season with salt, pepper, cayenne and nutmeg. Taste and correct the seasoning. Whisk the egg whites stiffly and fold them gently into the mixture with a flat spatula to make a loose consistency. Put the mixture into the prepared dish, scatter the thyme leaves on top and sprinkle with the remaining cheese.

Cook for 12–15 minutes, or until the sides and top are nicely puffed up and golden. The centre should still be creamy. Garnish with thyme flowers. Serve immediately on warm plates with a good green salad (see page 223).

TIP: Don't open the oven during cooking as the soufflé may collapse. If this *does* happen, the best course of action is to turn it out into a dish, pour some cream over it, sprinkle with grated Parmesan and pop it back into the oven for 5–10 minutes, depending on whether it's hot or cold. It will puff up amazingly. Call it a twice-baked soufflé, and serve!

Shortcrust Pastry for Savoury Flans and Quiches

Water gives a perfectly good texture but egg makes the pastry a little richer.

225g (8oz) plain white flour, spelt or sifted wholemeal flour
110g (4oz) butter*
water or beaten organic egg mixed with a little water

Keep everything as cool as possible; if the fat is allowed to melt, the finished pastry may be tough. Sift the flour into a large bowl. Cut the butter into cubes and rub into the flour with your fingertips. When the mixture looks like coarse breadcrumbs, stop. Take a fork or a knife – whichever you feel most comfortable with – and add just enough water or egg with a little water to bring the pastry together, then discard the fork and collect the pastry into a ball with your hands. This way you can judge more accurately whether you need a few more drops of liquid. Although rather damp pastry is easier to handle and roll out, the resulting crust can be tough and may well shrink out of shape as the water evaporates in the oven. Drier and slightly more difficult-to-handle pastry will give a crisper, 'shorter' crust.

Cover the pastry with clingfilm and leave to rest in the fridge for a minimum of 15 minutes. This will make the pastry much less elastic and easier to roll.

* 150–175g (5–6oz) butter will produce a richer pastry, but beginners would be wise to use half butter to flour for ease of handling.

How to Line a Flan Ring

Use either a flan ring or a tin with a removable base. It should be at least 5cm (2in) deep.

Pastry made with:
110g (4oz) flour will line a 15–18cm (6–7in) flan ring
175g (6oz) flour will line a 23cm (9in) flan ring
225g (8oz) flour will line a 25–30cm (10–12in) flan ring

Lightly sprinkle the worktop and rolling pin with flour and roll out the pastry quite thinly, making sure to keep it in a circular shape. The pastry should be 4–5cm (1½–2in) wider than the flan ring itself.

Sprinkle the pastry with flour, fold in half and then into quarters and then lift on to the ring. Alternatively, roll the pastry over the pin and unroll into the ring. Gently press the pastry on to the base of the tin and right into the edges or, if you are using a flan ring, onto the baking sheet. Next press some of the overhanging pastry forward and cut off the rim by pressing it down on to the edge of the tin with your thumb. Tuck the cut edge in against the sides of the tin or flan ring and decorate the resulting rounded edge with a knife or pastry crimpers. Make sure that no pastry sticks to the outer edge or it will be difficult to remove the tin later. Prick the base of the pastry lightly with a fork.

How to Bake Blind

Line the empty pastry case with greaseproof paper and fill it to the top with dried beans (keep them in a screw top jar for the purpose) to hold the pastry in place while the tart shell is being baked. Bake for 15–20 minutes at 180°C/350°F/gas 4.

Gruyère and Dill Tart
Serves 8

Mervyn Mark from Just Desserts in San Francisco gave me this recipe after I waxed lyrical about its flavour and texture.

Shortcrust pastry
175g (6oz) plain white flour
75g (3oz) butter (if using unsalted butter, add a pinch of salt)
50ml (2fl oz) water (approx.)

Filling
4 organic eggs
350ml (12fl oz) cream
75g (3oz) Gruyère or Emmenthal, freshly grated
25g (1oz) Parmesan (Parmigiano Reggiano if possible), freshly grated
1–2 generous tablespoons fresh dill, chopped
1 teaspoon salt
lots of freshly ground pepper
freshly grated nutmeg

23cm (9in) tart tin

Preheat the oven to 180°C/350°F/gas 4.

First make the pastry in the usual way (see left). Flatten into a small round, cover with greaseproof paper and leave to rest in the fridge for a minimum of 15 minutes. Roll it out on a lightly floured board until 2mm (¹/₁₆in) thick, then fit into the tin, bringing the pastry just a little above the rim. Rest in the fridge for a further 15 minutes. Bake the tart shell blind (see left) for 20 minutes. Take out of the oven, then remove the beans and paper. Brush the tart shell with a little beaten egg and return to the oven for 1–2 minutes to seal the base. Set aside to cool.

Now make the filling: whisk the eggs and the cream together in a bowl, add the Gruyère and Parmesan and the dill. Season with salt, pepper and nutmeg. Pour the filling into the tart shell and bake for 30 minutes, or until the filling is slightly puffy and golden brown. Serve with Tomato Salad (see page 220) and a good green salad (see page 223).

> TIP: Buy a chunk of cheese, wrap it well, store in the fridge and grate when needed it. Ready-grated cheese does not taste nearly as good.

French Onion Tart
Serves 6

Here the pastry is richer than in the previous recipe. Organic onions are not sprayed with an anti-sprouting mixture. Seek them out if you can.

Shortcrust Pastry
110g (4oz) flour
pinch of salt
75g (3oz) cold butter
1 organic egg yolk
2 teaspoons cold water

Filling
20g (³/₄oz) butter
2 teaspoons olive oil
400g (14oz) onions, finely chopped
2 whole organic eggs and 1 egg yolk
225ml (8fl oz) cream
salt and freshly ground pepper
freshly grated nutmeg

18cm (7in) tart tin, or individual tart tins

Preheat the oven to 180°C/350°F/gas 4.

First make the pastry: sift the flour with the salt into a large bowl. Cut the butter into cubes, toss into the flour, then rub in with your fingertips until the mixture resembles coarse breadcrumbs. Whisk the egg yolk with the cold water and bind the mixture with this. You may need a little more water, but do not make the pastry too wet – it should come away cleanly from the bowl. Flatten into a round, wrap in clingfilm and leave to rest in the fridge for 15 minutes.

Roll it out thinly on a lightly floured board and line the tart tin. Line the empty pastry case with greaseproof paper and fill to the top with dried beans. Rest for 15 minutes in the fridge. Bake the tart shell blind (see

left) for about 15 minutes or until pale and golden. Remove the beans and paper. Brush the tart shell with a little beaten egg and return to the oven for 1–2 minutes to seal the base. Set aside to cool.

Now make the filling: melt the butter with the oil in a heavy saucepan. Add the onions, cover and cook over a low heat until they are quite soft, transparent and pale golden colour, about 10 minutes. Cool.

Whisk the eggs and egg yolk with the cream and mix thoroughly into the onions. Season with salt, pepper and a little nutmeg. Taste. Pour the filling into the tart shell, bake in the preheated oven for about 20 minutes. Serve with tomato and basil salad and a good green salad (see page 223).

Variation
Add 1–2 tablespoons of chopped marjoram or thyme leaves to the onions with the eggs and cream.

> TIP: If you want a wonderfully rich flavour, cook the onions until they are a rich golden colour, almost caramelised.

How to Line Tartlets

Roll the pastry thinly: the smaller the pastry tin, the thinner the pastry needs to be. If the tartlets are 10cm (4in) in diameter, it's worth lining each individually with pastry, then greaseproof paper, filling with baking beans and baking blind if necessary (see page 112). However, smaller tins can be lined by laying a single sheet of pastry over them.

Press the pastry gently into each tin and then run a rolling pin over the lot to cut off the unwanted pastry.

Instead of filling each one with paper and a few beans, you can stack the tins up in piles of two or three, placing an empty tin on top. This helps the tartlets to keep their shape while cooking. Remember to chill for at least 10 minutes before cooking to avoid shrinkage. Tarts or tartlets may be frozen either cooked or uncooked and kept for up to 4 weeks.

Mushroom and Thyme Leaf Tart
Serves 6

This really flavoursome tart is one of the few that tastes superb warm or cold. Buy your Parmesan (preferably Parmigiano Reggiano) in a piece if at all possible, because ready-grated cheese is frequently rancid and may spoil the recipe. May I also respectfully suggest that you use cream. Both the flavour and texture are quite different if milk is substituted.

Rich Shortcrust Pastry
110g (4oz) plain white flour
50–75g (2–3oz) butter
a little water or beaten organic egg mixed with
*　a little water*

Filling
10g (½oz) butter
225g (8oz) mushrooms, flat if possible, finely
*　chopped*
1 teaspoon fresh thyme leaves
sea salt
freshly ground black pepper
225ml (8fl oz) cream
2 organic eggs and 1 egg yolk
50g (2oz) Parmesan (preferably Parmigiano
*　Reggiano), freshly grated*
a good pinch of cayenne

18cm (7in) flan ring or tin with removable base

Preheat the oven to 180°C/350°F/gas 4.

Make the shortcrust pastry in the usual way (see page 112), allow to rest, line the flan ring and bake blind (see page 112). Meanwhile, melt the butter in a pan and fry the mushrooms over a very high heat. Add thyme leaves and season with salt and pepper. Cook until all the juice has been absorbed. Cool.

Whisk the cream in a bowl with the eggs and egg yolk, stir in the mushrooms and most of the Parmesan. Taste, and add the pinch of cayenne and more seasoning as necessary. Pour into the tart shell. Sprinkle with the remainder of the cheese. Bake in

the oven for about 30–40 minutes or until the filling is set and the top delicately brown. Serve with a good green salad (see page 223).

Note: Tiny mushroom quiches may be served straight from the oven as appetisers before dinner or for a drinks party.

Master Recipe
Ballymaloe Quiche Lorraine
Serves 6

This may also be made with rich shortcrust pastry.

½ quantity Shortcrust Pastry (see page 112)

Filling
110–175g (4–6oz) rindless streaky bacon
*　rashers (green or slightly smoked)*
1 tablespoon olive or sunflower oil
110g (4oz) chopped onion
2 large organic eggs and 1 egg yolk
300ml (½ pint) double cream or half milk,
*　half cream*
1 teaspoon freshly chopped parsley
½ teaspoon freshly chopped chives
75g (3oz) freshly grated Cheddar or 50g (2oz)
*　freshly grated mature Gruyère*
salt and freshly ground pepper

18 x 3cm (7 x 1¼in) quiche tin or flan ring

Preheat the oven to 180°C/350°F/gas 4.

First make the pastry in the usual way (see page 112). Chill for 15 minutes, then roll out to line the flan ring or quiche tin.

Line the empty pastry case with greaseproof paper and fill it to the top with dried beans. Rest for 15 minutes then bake blind for 20–25 minutes. Remove the beans and paper, brush a little egg over the base to seal it, and return to the oven for 1–2 minutes.

Cut the bacon into 1cm (½in) lardons, blanch and refresh if necessary. Dry on kitchen paper. Heat the oil and crisp off the bacon, remove and set aside. Sweat the onions gently in the oil and bacon fat for about 10 minutes. Cool.

Meanwhile, whisk the eggs and egg yolk, add the cream (or cream and milk), herbs, cheese, and cooled bacon and onions. Season and taste.

Pour the filling into the tart shell and return to the oven for 30–40 minutes, or until the centre is just set and the top golden (don't overcook or the filling will be slightly scrambled).

Serve warm with a good green salad (see page 223).

Variations
Smoky Bacon, Flat Mushroom and Chive Quiche
Follow the Master Recipe adding 110g (4oz) sliced and sautéed flat mushrooms to the egg mix with the smoky bacon (be sure to cool before adding). Increase the amount of chives to 1 tablespoon.

Tomato Quiche
Follow the Master Recipe, but reduce the quantity of cream to 225ml (8fl oz) and make up with 275g (10oz) Tomato Fondue (see page 200). Strain the Tomato Fondue first so it is not too runny. Use 2 teaspoons chopped marjoram or 1 tablespoon chopped basil instead of the parsley and chives. Bacon and onions may still be added if liked.

Piperonata Quiche
Follow the Master Recipe, but reduce the quantity of cream to 225ml (8fl oz) and make up with 275g (10oz) concentrated Piperonata (see page 199). Drain the Piperonta well before using so it is not too runny. The bacon, onions and herbs in the Master Recipe are optional.

Asparagus and Spring Onion Tart
Serves 6

My children and their friends reckon that Tim makes the best quiches in the whole world. They're not biased – he does. Try this one in early summer when asparagus is in season.

½ quantity Shortcrust Pastry (see page 112)

Filling
25g (1oz) butter
1 tablespoon olive oil
250g (9oz) onion, finely chopped (we use about half spring onion, complete with green tops, and half ordinary onion)
150g (5oz) fresh asparagus, trimmed, and with ends peeled
3 organic eggs
125ml (4fl oz) double cream
110g (4oz) Cheddar, grated
salt and freshly ground pepper

18cm (7in) quiche tin or flan ring

Preheat the oven to 180°C/350°F/gas 4.

First make the pastry in the usual way (see page 112). Chill for 15 minutes, then roll out to line the quiche tin or flan ring to a thickness of about 3mm (⅛in). Line the empty pastry case with greaseproof paper and fill to the top with dried beans. Rest for 15 minutes and bake blind for 20 minutes. Remove the beans and paper, wash a little of the egg over the base then return the tart shell to the oven for 1–2 minutes. This seals the pastry and helps to avoid a 'soggy bottom'.

Melt the butter in a pan, add the olive oil and onions; sweat the onions with a good pinch of salt until soft but not coloured.

Cook the asparagus in boiling salted water until 'al dente' (4–5 minutes, depending on the thickness of the asparagus), then drain. When it is cool enough to handle cut into 1cm (½in) pieces.

Whisk the eggs in a bowl, add the cream, most of the cheese, the onion and cooked asparagus. Season. Pour the filling into the tart shell, top with the remaining cheese and return to the oven for 40–45 minutes. Serve warm.

Crab, Tomato and Ginger Tart
Serves 6

This recipe comes from my brother, Rory O'Connell, who used to be the chef at Ballymaloe House.

½ quantity Shortcrust Pastry (see page 112)

225g (8oz) fresh cooked crab meat, brown and white
5 ripe tomatoes, peeled, quartered and made into concassé (see page 51)
2 organic eggs and 1 egg yolk, beaten
225ml (8fl oz) cream
2 tablespoons finely chopped chives
1 teaspoon freshly grated green ginger
salt and freshly ground pepper

18cm (7in) quiche tin or flan ring

Preheat the oven to 180°C/350°F/gas 4.

First make the pastry in the usual way (see page 112). Chill for 15 minutes, then roll out to line the quiche tin or flan ring to a thickness of about 3mm (⅛in). Line with greaseproof paper and fill to the top with dried beans. Rest for 15 minutes then bake blind for 20 minutes. Remove the beans and paper, and brush a little of the egg over the base and return to the oven for 1–2 minutes. This seals the pastry and helps to avoid a 'soggy bottom'.

Gently combine all the ingredients for the filling in a bowl, and season to taste. Pour the filling into the tart shell and return it to the oven. Cook until the top is golden coloured and the filling is just set – about 30–40 minutes. It is delicious served warm with a tossed good green salad (see page 223) and perhaps a little Hollandaise Sauce (see page 581).

How to Cook Crêpes

Choose an iron or non-stick crêpe pan. Heat on a brisk flame. Batter made from half milk and half water produces a lighter, lacier crêpe. Be sure to whisk melted butter into the batter. This will help to prevent the crêpes from sticking to the pan and will save you the trouble of greasing the pan between each one. Choose a small ladle that holds just enough batter to cover the base of the pan with a thin film. Alternatively put the batter into a measuring jug with a good pouring lip. When the pan is really hot, pour just enough batter in to cover the base when the pan is tilted from side to side. If the pan is as hot as it ought to be, the crêpe should be ready to turn almost immediately. Loosen the pancake around the edge. (A flexible plastic spatula is best for this.) Turn over quickly – a few seconds will be enough to cook the other side. (The crêpe should be just flecked with brown spots.) Slide on to a plate and continue to cook the remainder of the batter. The crêpes may be stacked on top of each other and peeled apart later. Crêpes stored in this way may be kept in the fridge and used hours or even days later. They will peel off each other easily.

Ballymaloe Crêpes Suzette

Serves about 4 (makes 8 pancakes)

Crêpes Suzette are the aristocrats of the pancake family, served in smart restaurants by the head waiter from a trolley. We serve them in Ballymaloe House on Shrove Tuesday. Myrtle Allen flambés them at the table. She once caused considerable consternation by setting her hair ablaze as she did this a little too enthusiastically! This recipe comes from *The Ballymaloe Cookbook* with her permisson.

Batter
50g (2oz) plain flour
1 tablespoon oil
1 organic egg and 1 egg yolk
2 teaspoons orange Curaçao liqueur
150ml (¼ pint) milk

Sauce
225g (8oz) large ripe oranges
75g (3oz) softened butter
50g (2oz) caster sugar
generous tablespoon each of brandy and orange Curaçao

First make the batter: put the flour in a bowl and make a well in the centre. Into this pour the oil, egg, egg yolk and orange curaçao. Stir, gradually drawing in the flour from the sides. Add the milk slowly until it is the consistency of thin cream. Set aside in the refrigerator for 30 minutes. Then make the crêpes by putting a small ladleful of batter at a time into a hot non-stick frying pan; as soon as bubbles rise to the surface, flip over and cook the other side. Keep the crêpes ready for use later.

For the sauce: grate the rind of the oranges very carefully so as not to penetrate the pith. Add to the butter and sugar, and cream vigorously until smooth.

To finish: put the frying pan over a high heat. Melt about 10g (½oz) of the orange butter in it. When bubbling, put a cooked crêpe in and heat through, turning so that both sides get warm. Fold it into a fan shape and rest it against the side of the pan. Continue in the same way with the remaining pancakes. Sprinkle them with caster sugar. Pour over the brandy and curaçao. Set alight, to burn off the alcohol, keeping your face away from the flames. Tilt the pan and spoon the juices over the pancakes until the flames subside. Serve immediately on hot plates.

Crawford Café Spinach and Mushroom Crêpes

Serves 6–7

The Crawford Café in Cork, run by my son, Isaac Allen, cannot take these crêpes off the lunch menu or there would be a riot! There are lots of variations, but this is a particularly delicious version.

450g (1lb) spinach (weighed after stalks have been removed)

Mushroom à la Crème (see page 201)

Soda Water Crêpe Batter (see page 118)

Hollandaise Sauce (see page 581)

25cm (10in) non-stick pan

To make the filling: remove the stalks from the spinach and cook as for Buttered Spinach (see page 171). Mix the Mushroom à la Crème with the spinach. Taste and correct the seasoning.

Make the crêpes (see left).

Lay a pancake on a clean worktop. Put 2 generous tablespoons of filling in the middle, fold in the sides and fold over the ends to make a parcel. Repeat with the others.

Serve with a little light Hollandaise Sauce and a good green salad (see page 223).

Some Other Good Fillings
Mushroom and Ginger à la Crème (see page 201)

Cooked chicken or ham

Mussels, prawns or shrimps

Chunks of cooked salmon or scallops

LEFT: Ballymaloe Crêpes Suzette

Soda Water Crêpe Batter
Makes 12–14 crêpes

325g (11oz) flour
pinch of salt
6 organic eggs
650ml (22fl oz) milk
1 small bottle (113ml) soda water
1 tablespoon oil

20cm (10in) non-stick pan

To make the batter: sift the flour and salt into a bowl, make a well in the centre and drop in the lightly beaten eggs. With a whisk or wooden spoon, starting in the centre, mix the egg and gradually bring in the flour. Add the milk and soda water and beat until the batter is covered with bubbles, then add the oil. Let the batter stand in a cold place for an hour or so – longer will do no harm. Alternatively put all the ingredients into a liquidiser or food processor and whizz for a minute or so. Cook small ladlefuls of the batter on a hot, non-stick pan. Stack the crêpes one on top of another, ready for use.

Almspurses with Tomato Sauce
Makes 12 pancakes

This is a fun way to serve savoury pancakes. Serve 1 as a starter or 3, each with a different filling, for a substantial main course. The filling can include meat, fish or just a juicy vegetable mixture.

1 x Savoury or Herb Pancake Batter (see right)

Suggested Fillings
Piperonata (see page 199)
Mushroom à la Crème (see page 201)
Tomato Fondue (see page 200)
Creamed Spinach (see page 171)
seafood
chicken and ham

long chives for tying
Tomato Sauce (see page 591)

Lay a pancake on the worktop. Put two heaped teaspoons of your hot chosen filling into the centre. Gather the edges together and then tie into a purse with a blanched and refreshed chive. Serve on a hot plate surrounded by homemade Tomato Sauce.

Savoury or Herb Pancake Batter
Makes 12 pancakes

175g (6oz) white flour, preferably unbleached
a good pinch of salt
2 large organic eggs and 1–2 egg yolks
425ml (3/4 pint) milk or, for very light and crisp pancakes, milk and water mixed
2 tablespoons freshly chopped herbs (e.g. parsley, thyme, chives), optional
6–8 teaspoons melted butter

30cm (12in) non-stick pan

Sift the flour and salt into a bowl, make a well in the centre and drop in the lightly beaten eggs. With a whisk or wooden spoon, starting in the centre, mix the egg and gradually bring in the flour. Add the liquid slowly and beat until the batter is covered with bubbles. Stir in the herbs, if using. Let the batter stand in a cold place for an hour or so – longer will do no harm.

Just before you cook the pancakes, stir in the melted butter into the batter. This will make all the difference to the flavour and texture of the pancakes and will make it possible to cook them without greasing the pan each time.

Heat a heavy cast-iron crêpe pan or non-stick pan to very hot. Pour in just enough batter to cover the base of the pan thinly. Loosen the pancake around the edge, flip over with a spatula or thin egg slice, cook for a second or two on the other side and slide off the pan on to a plate. The pancakes may be stacked on top of each other and peeled apart later. They will keep in the fridge for several days and also freeze perfectly. For freezing, place a sheeet of silicone paper between each pancake.

Rory's 'Blinis'
Makes about 30

These are really cheat blinis (sometimes called crumpets or pikelets), but they are really quick to make and you can choose from a whole array of yummy toppings. Serve an assortment as a starter or just nibble them with drinks.

225g (8oz) white flour
1/4 teaspoon salt
1/2 teaspoon bicarbonate of soda
1 teaspoon cream of tartar (bextartar)
25g (1oz) butter
2 organic eggs
175–225ml (6–8fl oz) milk
1 tablespoon chopped parsley

30cm (12in) non-stick pan

Sift the dry ingredients into a bowl and rub in the butter. Drop the eggs into the centre, add a little of the milk and stir rapidly with a whisk allowing the flour to drop gradually in from the sides. When half the milk is added, beat until bubbles rise. Add the remainder of the milk and allow to stand for an hour if possible. Then add the parsley.

Drop a good teaspoonful of the batter into a hottish pan and cook until bubbles appear and start to burst on the top. (It usually takes a bit of trial and error to get the temperature right.) Flip over and cook until golden on the other side. Cool on a wire rack and serve as soon as possible with a mixture of toppings.

Suggested Toppings
Smoked salmon, crème fraîche and dill or chives

Smoked mussels, crème fraîche and cucumber pickle

Roast red and yellow pepper and pesto or basil leaves

Chopped hard-boiled egg, mayonnaise and chives

Cream cheese with Chilli and Red Pepper Relish (see page 514)

Salami and Guacamole (see page 593)

Spiced beef, avocado and rocket leaves

Bread Pudding with Asparagus and Fontina

Serves 8

Mary Risley from Tante Marie's Cooking School in San Francisco shared this delicious recipe with us. The technique can be used with many ingredients if it's not asparagus season – mushrooms, tomatoes, roast peppers, and so on.

12–16 thick slices of best-quality white bread
butter

4 organic eggs
600ml (1 pint) milk OR 425ml (15fl oz) milk
*   plus 150ml (5fl oz) buttermilk*
450g (1lb) asparagus, trimmed
1 teaspoon salt
1 teaspoon pepper, freshly ground
20g (³/₄oz) Parmesan (Parmigiano Reggiano if
*   possible), freshly grated*
225g (8oz) Fontina, Swiss cheese or other white
*   cheese, roughly grated*
10g (¹/₂oz) butter

25 x 20cm (10 x 8in) lasagne dish,
*   buttered*

Preheat the oven to 180°C/350°F/gas 4.

Butter the bread. Whisk the eggs with the milk. Bring a little water to the boil in a heavy oval casserole and add salt. Add the asparagus and cook for 3–4 minutes or until al dente. Drain and refresh under cold water. Cut in thin diagonal slivers.

Pour a little of the egg and milk mixture into the base of the lasagne dish. Arrange a layer of bread on top. Sprinkle half the asparagus over the bread. Season well with salt and pepper. Strew one third of each of the cheeses on top. Pour some of the egg mixture on this layer then repeat the layers and seasoning and finish with a layer of bread. Pour the remainder of the liquid evenly over the top. Sprinkle with the remaining cheese. Bake in a bain-marie in the oven for about 45 minutes or until crisp and golden on top. Serve with a good green salad (see page 223).

Variation

Try courgettes, lots of basil and a well-seasoned cheese sauce with lots of Parmesan. Or Tomato Sauce (see page 591) with lots of Parmesan.

rice, other grains & pulses

rice, other grains & pulses

Grains and pulses have been an important staple food for thousands of years. When fully ripe, harvested and dried, they can be stored for several months, providing reliable winter food. Grains and pulses, as well as dried peas and beans, provide an alternative and relatively inexpensive source of protein.

Rice

Rice has to be one of the world's greatest staples, and one of the most versatile cooking ingredients. With around 2,500 different varieties, there's plenty of scope for choice. All varieties of rice have their own unique characteristics. The trick is to use the right type of rice for the dish you are making, and I advise buying organic or biodynamically grown rice wherever possible.

White or Brown?

White and brown rice are both delicious but differ in terms of flavour and texture. Nutritionally speaking, brown rice is superior – lots of good B vitamins come with its rich, earthy flavour. It is unrefined, so it's got a shelf life of around 6 months only. White rice, on the other hand, is refined – meaning that the outer bran layers and the germ have been removed – and as a result it has a longer shelf life of between 2 and 3 years (although best eaten when fresh). It has a more delicate and aromatic flavour than brown rice.

Short Grain Rice

Use for risotto, sushi, paella and rice pudding. The grains are almost round and the amylopectin within them causes them to stick together when cooked. They absorb much more liquid than long grain rice.

Risotto rice is plump, white rice that can absorb lots of water without getting mushy. The best comes from Italy, Aborio being the most well-regarded.

Sushi rice is sticky, white short grain rice, similar in appearance to Italian risotto rice but not as starchy.

Glutinous rice, sometimes called sweet, sticky or Japanese-style rice, is used in Southeast Asia for sweet and savoury dishes. Ironically, it doesn't contain gluten. The grains are flat and rounded and should be soaked before steaming. When cooked, the little round grains stay separate but they can be pressed together into little balls or rolls. Ideal for sushi and with Thai or Chinese food.

Black glutinous rice is unrefined and the grains are long and wide. It cooks like glutinous rice and can be used for both sweet and savoury dishes.

Calasparra is my absolute favourite for paella. A short grain rice grown in Spain with plump grains that can absorb extra water and take on more flavour while remaining firm.

Long Grain Rice

Long grain rice is used for savoury dishes, pilafs, pullaos, salads and stuffings. Properly cooked, the grains will stay separate and fluffy (if overcooked they will stick together and become mush).

Basmati, the aristocrat of long grain rice, is available in white and brown (brown basmati takes less time to cook than other brown rice). Tilda is one of the finest basmati – delicious in Indian pullaos, pilvâs and biryanis and definitely worth the extra price you pay for its fine flavour.

Thai fragrant/jasmine rice is deliciously aromatic and slightly sticky when cooked. Wonderful hot or cold.

Red rice is unrefined and grown in small quantities in France. It is very popular and tastes similar to brown rice.

Wild Rice

This is not actually a rice but a long grain marsh grass. The full flavour emerges when the grains burst after 50–60 minutes of nice slow cooking by the absorption method (boiled rather than steamed).

Storage and Cooking of Rice

Buy rice little and often from a shop with a quick turnover. Store it in glass jars in a cool, dry place. Eat it within a year. And no, it doesn't improve with age!

50g (2oz) of rice (dry weight) per person is usually about right, but if your guests are hungry they will easily polish off 75–110g (3–4oz) each. Of course you can boil rice in a pot of water or cook it in a steamer but many respected chefs, including Sri Owen, Madhur Jaffrey and Deh-Ta Hsiung, swear by electric rice cookers and say they're foolproof.

Re-using Cooked Rice

Cooked rice is excellent for fried rice, salads and stuffings. Of course it is best to use freshly cooked rice but if you have leftover rice, pop it in the fridge as soon as it's cooled down. Eat within 2–3 days because cooked rice is susceptible to *Bascillus cereus*, which causes severe stomach cramps and diarrhoea. If you need it hot, reheat cooked rice very thoroughly: *Bascillus cereus* cannot survive temperatures lower than 4°C/39°F or higher than 60°C/140°F. Some use a microwave, but I prefer to throw the rice in some boiling water for 1 minute only, or to steam it over boiling water. Serve it in a nice hot dish and no one will be any the wiser!

Other Grains

Botanically, grains are the fruit of cereal plants in the grass family. There are about 8,000 species of grain, but only a few are commonly used in the kitchen. Harvested grains are significantly dehydrated and are only palatable after they have absorbed water and been cooked. Water is usually used for cooking, but stock or milk is also used in some cases. Many of the grains are cooked in the form of pilafs, and some need soaking.

Wheat is perhaps the most important and widely used grain. It is most commonly processed into flour. **Wheat berries or kernels** are grains which have had the husks removed. These are cooked as pilaf and are excellent in salads with other grains. **Cracked wheat** (including bulgar which is the basis of tabouleh) comes in fine, medium and coarse grain. The finer grains can be used for bread and batter, the coarser for pilaf. Semolina is made from a hard durum wheat and its flour is used in pasta, gnocchi and milk puddings. **Couscous** is not actually a grain, but a pasta made from durum wheat. It appears in this chapter because it is always cooked like a grain.

Corn is divided into two main types – field corn and sweet corn. Field corn is harder and has more starch. It is used for animal feed and is also processed into cornflour and cornmeal for breads, pancakes and polenta. **Polenta** can be made from yellow or white cornmeal. Rich meat stews are often served with yellow polenta, and white polenta is best with fish. **Sweetcorn** is used for popcorn and specific types, such as blue corn and white corn, are ground and used in bread or corn chips.

Barley is used for brewing beer and the hulled, polished grain of pearl barley is a great thickener in stews and soups (add it towards the end as it needs no pre-cooking). It is also used in salads.

Oats are sold in various forms (pinhead, rolled or flaked) and are used for porridge, breakfast cereals, biscuits and oatcakes.

Rye is mostly grown for flour and is used in dark breads. The whole grains may be cooked as a pilaf and are sometimes used in soups and casseroles.

Quinoa, amaranth and **buckwheat** are called pseudograins because of their similarities to grain in flavour and preparation techniques. They are dicot plant seeds, and contain protein that is unusually complete for plant sources. They are also a good source of dietary fibre, phosphorus, magnesium and iron, and are gluten-free.

Pulses

Pulses, the dried seeds of different varieties of peas and beans, have been a staple for thousands of years – they were even found beside the graves in the pyramids, meant as food for the pharaohs in the afterlife. It's easy to see why they are still so popular: they're cheap, earthy and versatile. They're great for salads, but also good for absorbing gutsy flavours like tangy sausage, fresh herbs and spices, and also go well with a piece of salt pork or lamb. They are an important source of protein and roughage, and are a vital part of a vegetarian or vegan diet.

Chickpeas are the main ingredient in hummus and are also used in stews and casseroles. **Lentils,** or dahl, come in a range of colours and are used in numerous Indian dishes. **Mung beans** and **alfalfa** are most familiar in the form of bean sprouts.

Split peas are usually puréed (as in pease pudding) and can also be used in soups. Dried **marrowfat peas,** with their slightly minty taste, were the bane of my life when I was a child, but now that they're harder to come by, I love them! They're used in soups and stocks and are served with fish and chips in the form of mushy peas.

Red kidney beans are one of the most popular beans, valued for their flavour and colour. They are an essential ingredient in chilli con carne. Other dried beans, such as **borlotti, flageolets, haricots, lima, pinto** and **dried broad beans,** are used in stews and salads.

Storage and Preparation of Pulses

Though very long-lasting, pulses will not last forever and the older they are, the longer they will take to cook. So, as with rice, buy dried pulses little and often and make sure they are stored in a cool, dry place.

Pulses should be rinsed and soaked before cooking. Place them in a large bowl of fresh water and allow them to soak for about 6–8 hours, or overnight. Soaking more or less doubles their size. Allow 1.2 litres (2 pints) of water per 450g (1lb). If any pulses float to the surface during soaking, they should be thrown away as they are not good. Once they have been soaked, they are ready to be simmered slowly until cooked. It is imperative that red kidney beans, in addition to soaking, are boiled vigorously for 10 minutes at the start of their cooking time, in order to destroy toxins.

Emergency Measures

If you get really stuck and haven't had time to soak them, pop the pulses in cold water and bring to the boil as slowly as you can, as they will need to cook for longer. Do not add salt until the end of the cooking time.

Plan Ahead

When you're cooking peas and beans, soak twice the amount you need and, once cooked, pop half of them in a plastic box in the freezer for when you next need them. They will last for months. Keep the water or liquid you cooked them in as well – it's ideal for stocks and stews.

Master Recipe
Plain Boiled Rice

Serves 8

I find this way of cooking rice in what we call 'unlimited water' to be very satisfactory for plain boiled rice – even, dare I say, foolproof. The grains stay separate and it will keep happily covered in the oven for up to half an hour.

4.8 litres (8 pints) cold water
2 teaspoons salt
450g (1lb) best-quality long grain rice, preferably Basmati rice, or Thai fragrant rice
a few little knobs of butter (optional)

Bring the water to a fast boil in a large saucepan. Add the salt. Sprinkle in the rice and stir at once to ensure that the grains don't stick. Boil rapidly, uncovered.

After 4–5 minutes, depending on the rice, test by biting a few grains between your teeth – they should still have a slightly resistant core. If the rice overcooks at this stage, the grains will stick together later. Strain well through a sieve or fine strainer.

Put into a warm serving dish, dot with butter if using, cover with tin foil or a lid and put in a very low oven, 140°C/275°F/gas 1, for at least 15 minutes. Remove the lid, fluff up with a fork and serve.

Variation
Basmati Rice with Parsley
Follow the Master Recipe, tossing in 2–4 tablespoons freshly chopped parsley when the rice is cooked.

Jewelled Christmas Rice with Pomegranate Seeds and Sultanas
Soak 50g (2oz) sultanas in boiling water for at least 30 minutes. Remove the seeds from 1 small or 1/2 a large pomegranate. Add the sultanas, pomegranate seeds and 2 tablespoons of freshly snipped flat-leaf parsley or coriander leaves to the cooked rice just before serving.

Fried Rice

Serves 6

Fried rice is a terrific and very nutritious way of using up leftovers. It can be ready to eat in just a few minutes. There are dozens of variations of fried rice in China. Some cooks like to add the eggs to the wok first, followed by the rice. My family favour adding the egg at the later stage for a moister result. Other tasty bits, such as bamboo shoots, bean sprouts and Chinese mushrooms may be added.

2 organic eggs, lightly beaten
2 tablespoons chopped spring onion, green and white parts
1 teaspoon salt
3 tablespoons sunflower or olive oil
110g (4oz) mushrooms, chopped
110g (4oz) cooked meat; chicken, pork, ham or spicy sausage, cut into small dice or 110g (4oz) peeled prawns or shrimps
110g (4oz) cooked green peas or green pepper
450g (1lb) Plain Cooked Rice (see left)
1–2 tablespoons light soy sauce

Whisk the eggs with the spring onion and lots of salt. Heat the oil in a very hot wok, add the mushrooms and stir-fry for 1–2 minutes, then add the meat or shrimps and peas. Continue to stir-fry for another minute or so. Add the rice and soy sauce, continue to stir-fry, add the eggs and stir-fry for about 2 minutes until the eggs are set. Stir to make sure that each grain of rice is separate. Taste, correct the seasoning and serve immediately.

Variation
Bacon, Egg and Sausage Fried Rice
Proceed as above, replacing the mushrooms, shrimps and peas with 4 rashers of bacon (cooked and sliced) and 4 juicy sausages (cooked and sliced) or 110g (4oz) chorizo. Finish by adding a small fistful of coarsely chopped flat-leaf parsley. I also love to add 6–9 cherry tomatoes cut in half.

Thai Jasmine Rice

Serves 4–6

Thai fragrant rice, a plain long grain variety, has a slight jasmine scent and is perfect for South-east Asian meals. When cooked, it is shiny with just a slight hint of stickiness.

350ml (12fl oz) Thai fragrant rice
350ml (12fl oz) water

Put the rice and water into a heavy saucepan, bring to the boil, stir once, cover with a tight-fitting lid and lower the heat to the absolute minimum – use a heat diffuser mat if possible. Continue to cook on the lowest heat for 15 minutes. Do not uncover during cooking. Remove from the heat, keep covered and allow to sit for 5 minutes before serving. The rice will stay warm for several hours, if necessary.

Note: Cover with tin foil if the saucepan lid is really not tight-fitting.

Coconut Rice

Serves 4–6

This is a delicious way to cook rice that we enjoyed in Asia.

450g (1lb) Thai fragrant or Basmati rice
2 tablespoons butter
850ml (1 1/2 pints) coconut milk (Chaokoh)
1 teaspoon salt
1 pandanus leaf or, if unavailable, 1 bay leaf

Soak the rice for 1 hour, drain well. Melt the butter in a casserole over a medium heat, add the rice, toss and cook for 2–3 minutes. Add the coconut milk, salt and the pandanus leaf or bay leaf. Bring to the boil and cook until all the coconut milk has been absorbed. Cover, reduce the heat to absolute minimum and cook for a further 10 minutes. Serve hot.

Persian Rice

Serves 8

Serve with pan-grilled chicken (see page 271) and Harissa (see page 596).

¹/₂ teaspoon saffron

1 tablespoon boiling water

2 tablespoons salt

275g (10oz) Basmati rice

3 tablespoons olive oil

175g (6oz) onion, peeled and chopped

¹/₄ teaspoon freshly ground cardamom

¹/₂ teaspoon freshly ground coriander seeds

50g (2oz) dried cranberries

25g (1oz) dried cherries

110g (4oz) raisins

50g (2oz) pistachio nuts, roughly chopped

2 tablespoons freshly chopped coriander leaves

salt and freshly ground pepper

Put the saffron in a little bowl and cover with the boiling water. Bring 4.8 litres (8 pints) cold water to the boil, add the 2 tablespoons of salt. Sprinkle in the Basmati rice, stirring all the time. Bring back to the boil and cook for 6–7 minutes, by which time the grain should have doubled in size and be slightly 'al dente'. Drain, put into a bowl, add the saffron and the soaking liquid. Mix well and allow to cool.

Meanwhile, heat the oil in a sauté pan, add the onions and cook until crisp and golden, then add the freshly ground spices. Cook for 3–4 minutes, add the dried cranberries, dried cherries and raisins. Cook for a further 1–2 minutes. Then add the rice. Season, add the pistachio nuts and toss well. Taste and correct the seasoning. Sprinkle with the freshly chopped coriander.

Pilaf Rice
Serves 8

Pilaf (also known as *pilâv* or *pilau*) is the national dish of Turkey and many versions are found in the Middle East. A pilaf looks after itself once the initial cooking is underway, and is very is versatile – serve it on its own or with meat, fish and herbs. Beware, however, of using pilaf as a dustbin – all additions should be carefully seasoned and balanced.

25g (1oz) butter or ghee (see page 105)

2 tablespoons finely chopped onion or shallot

400g (14oz) long grain rice, preferably Basmati

scant 1 litre (1³/₄ pints) homemade Chicken Stock (see page 36)

2 tablespoons finely chopped herbs (e.g. parsley, thyme, chives), optional

salt and freshly ground pepper

Melt the butter or ghee in a casserole, add the onion and sweat for 2–3 minutes. Add the rice and toss for 1–2 minutes, just long enough for the grains to change colour.

Season with salt and pepper, add the stock, cover and bring to the boil. Reduce the heat to a minimum and then simmer on top of the stove or in the oven (170°C/325°F/gas 3) for about 10 minutes. By then the rice should be just cooked and all the liquid absorbed. Just before serving, stir in the fresh herbs if using.

Note: Basmati rice cooks quite quickly; other types of rice may take up to 15 minutes.

Mary Jo's Pilaf Rice
Serves 6–8

In this version of pilaf, the rice is cooked separately from the other ingredients.

300g (11oz) Basmati rice

10g (¹/₂ oz) ghee (see page 105) or 1 tablespoon extra-virgin olive oil

¹/₂ small onion, finely chopped

1 teaspoon coriander seeds

1cm (¹/₂ in) cinnamon stick

small pinch of turmeric or powdered saffron

¹/₂ teaspoon salt

450ml (16fl oz) soaking water

Wash the rice in cold water, changing the water twice. Drain, cover with fresh water and soak for 20–30 minutes. Meanwhile, melt the ghee in a heavy saucepan (with a tight-fitting lid) and sauté the onion gently along with the coriander seeds, cinnamon, and turmeric.

Drain the rice, retaining 450ml (16fl oz) of the soaking water. Stir the rice and salt

into the onion mixture, pour in the retained water and stir again to dissolve the salt. Cover, bring to a simmer and cook over a low heat for 10 minutes, or until the water is absorbed.

Fluff with a fork, place a clean tea towel between the rice and the lid to absorb moisture and allow to rest covered for at least 10 minutes before serving.

Sticky Rice
Serves 4–6

Sticky or glutinous rice, sometimes called sweet rice, is the daily staple of Laos and the millions of Thais of Laotian heritage who live in northern and north-eastern Thailand. This chewy, satisfying rice is soaked for several hours or overnight and then steamed until it is sticky and soft. It is eaten with the fingers, starting with a fist-sized portion and pinching off a walnut-size lump, which is rolled into a small ball with one hand. It is paired with meat or vegetables, dipped into a pungent sauce, or eaten as it is.

Sticky rice is presented in beautiful hand woven baskets for special occasions; family meals are served on a large plate along with accompanying dishes. Since sticky rice can be served hot, warm or at room temperature; it's particularly great for picnics and outdoor meals. This recipe comes from Nancie McDermott's *Real Thai*.

400g (14oz) sticky rice

Put the rice into a bowl. Cover with cold water by 5cm (2in) and soak for at least 3 hours, or overnight. Fill the bottom of a steamer pan, wok or saucepan with water. Place a steamer rack or tray about 2.5cm (1in) or more above the water, cover the steamer and bring the water to a rolling boil over high heat.

Drain the rice and transfer to a traditional bamboo, sticky rice-steaming basket, or any steamer such as a colander or even a strainer suspended above boiling water.

Uncover the pan and place the rice-filled steaming basket on the rack over the steam, taking care not to burn your hands. Reduce the heat to maintain a steady flow of steam through the rice and cook for about 30–45 minutes until the grains swell and glisten and are sticky enough to be squeezed into small lumps. Add boiling water to the steamer pan as required to maintain the original level.

As soon as the rice is cooked, turn it out onto a baking sheet and gently spread it into a shallow layer with a wet wooden spoon. This will release some of the steam and moisture. As soon as it cools enough to touch, gather the rice gently into a large lump and transfer to a basket or a plate. Serve hot, warm or at room temperature.

Note: The cooking time for sticky rice depends on how long the rice soaks. The longer you soak it, the faster it will cook.

Isaac's Sushi Rice

450g (1lb) sushi rice
600ml (1 pint) water

Sweet Vinegar Water
50ml (2fl oz) rice wine vinegar
1½ tablespoons sugar
2½ teaspoons salt

Rinse the rice for 10 minutes in a colander or sieve under cold running water, or until the water becomes clear.

'Wake up' the rice by placing it in a pan with 600ml (1 pint) cold water for 30–45 minutes. Then bring to the boil (in the same water) and cook for 10 minutes until all the water has been absorbed. Do not stir; do not even take off the lid. Turn up the heat for 10 seconds before turning the heat off. Remove the lid, place a tea towel over the rice, replace the lid and leave it for 20 minutes.

Mix the vinegar, sugar and salt together in a bowl until dissolved. Turn the rice out onto a big, flat plate (preferably wooden).

While the rice is still hot, pour the vinegar solution over the rice and mix the rice and vinegar together in a slicing action with the aid of a wooden spoon. Don't stir. You must do it quickly, ideally fanning the rice with a fan (this is much easier if you have a helper!). Allow to cool on the plate and cover with kitchen paper or a tea towel. (It will soak up the liquid as it cools.)

Shermin's California Rolls (Inside-Out Sushi)
Makes 7–8 rolls (6–8 pieces in each roll)

bamboo rolling mat
7–8 sheets nori seaweed
vinegar water (see Gunkan Maki, right)
450g (1lb) freshly cooked sushi rice (see Isaac's Sushi Rice, left)
110g (4oz) wild smoked salmon, cut into oblong pieces 1cm (½ in) wide
1 large, ripe avocado, cut into long pieces, similar in size to the salmon
50g (2oz) sesame seeds (lightly toasted)

To Serve
pickled ginger
wasabi paste
soy sauce

Place the bamboo mat on the worktop with the bamboo lines running horizontally. Wave a sheet of nori seaweed over a gas flame until soft and pliable (8–10 seconds). Lay the seaweed on the bamboo mat, shiny side down and grain running horizontally. Dip your hands in the vinegar water to prevent the rice from sticking to them.

Using your finger tips, press enough rice onto the seaweed to cover it evenly and thinly. Lift the seaweed with the rice attached and turn the whole thing upside down and place back on the bamboo mat (the rice will be on the outside of the finished sushi roll). Lay a strip of salmon and a line of avocado pieces horizontally across the seaweed. Roll the rice over the

filling, tucking the end in. Continue rolling up, pressing firmly on the bamboo mat.

Sprinkle an even layer of sesame seeds on the worktop. Roll the sushi in the seeds until evenly covered. Make all the rolls in the same way.

To serve, wet a sharp knife and cut into 6–8 even-sized pieces using a sawing motion. Serve with pickled ginger, wasabi paste and a little bowl of soy sauce.

Gunkan Maki (Battleship Sushi)
Makes 18 pieces

Vinegar Water
2 tablespoons rice vinegar
225ml (8fl oz) water

Sushi
3 sheets nori seaweed, each cut into 6 x 2.5cm (1in) strips
½ x quantity freshly cooked sushi rice (see Isaac's Sushi Rice, left)
wasabi paste
110g (4oz) of flying fish roe (dyed green, red or natural colour) or salmon roe

Mix the vinegar and water in a small bowl. Dip your hands in it to prevent the rice from sticking to them. Shape about a tablespoon of sushi rice into an oval ball. Dry your hands and pick up a strip of nori. Wrap it around the rice ball with the smooth side of the nori facing outwards.

Crush a grain of cooked rice at the end of the strip of nori so that it seals the nori where it overlaps to form a ring around the rice. The nori should come up about 4mm (⅙ in) higher than the rice so that it creates a little container for the topping.

Dab a little wasabi paste onto the rice and flatten slightly. Spoon the topping onto the rice, keeping it inside the crown of nori.

Serve as soon as possible as part of a sushi plate.

RIGHT: Shermin's California Rolls

Risotto Rice

Italians love their rice, and grow it in the north, in the Po valley. The rice used must be medium grain white, with the ability to absorb the liquid in which it cooks. Of the 4 types of rice – superfino, fino, semifino and ordinario – only use the first 2 for risotto. Arborio is a superfino type, as are Roma Carnaroli and Maratelli. Vialone, with grains a little shorter than Arborio, is a fino type. These rice varieties are rich in starch, which dissolves in cooking.

Risotto is often considered to be a sort of dustbin to use up leftovers. Nothing, in fact, could be further from the truth. A perfectly cooked risotto made with the right rice is a feast. The technique is altogether different to the Indian pilafs and for perfection it should be served the moment it is cooked.

Master Recipe
Risotto alla Parmigiana (Risotto with Parmesan)
Serves 6

The rice dishes of Italy's Veneto, the region around Venice, are famous. Rice was introduced there by the Arabs and many varieties of short grain rice still grow in the marsh lands around the river Po.

In Venice, risotto is made almost liquid, its great quality being its immense versatility. The Veneto is richer in vegetables than any other area so all sorts of vegetables and combinations of vegetables are included in the dish as well as herbs, poultry, game, chicken livers or shellfish. There is a famous black risotto, made with squid ink, and another with pine kernels and raisins – a legacy of the Arabs.

1–1.3 litres (1/3/4–2 1/4 pints) homemade
   Chicken Stock (see page 36)
50g (2oz) butter
2 tablespoons olive oil
1 onion, finely chopped
400g (14oz) risotto rice
50g (2oz) Parmigiano Reggiano, freshly grated
sea salt

First bring the stock to the boil, turn down the heat and keep it simmering. Melt half the butter in a heavy saucepan with the oil, add the onion and sweat over a gentle heat for 4–5 minutes until soft but not coloured.

Add the rice and stir until well-coated (so far the technique is the same as for a pilaf and this is where people become confused). Cook for 1 minute or so and then add 150ml (1/4 pint) of the simmering stock, stir continuously and, as soon as the liquid is absorbed, add another 150ml (1/4 pint) stock.

Continue to cook, stirring continuously. The heat should be brisk, but if it's too hot the rice will be soft outside but still chewy inside. If it's too slow, the rice will be gluey. It's difficult to know which is worse so the trick is to regulate the heat so that the rice bubbles continuously. The risotto should take about 25–30 minutes to cook.

After about 20 minutes, reduce the additions of stock to about 4 tablespoons at a time, using a small ladle. Watch it very carefully from here on. The risotto is done when the rice is cooked but is still ever so slightly 'al dente'. It should be soft and creamy and quite loose, rather than thick and dry. The moment you are happy with the texture, stir in the remaining butter and Parmesan, taste and add more salt if necessary. Serve immediately.

TIP: Risotto does not benefit from hanging around.

Variations
Risotto con Ragu
Follow the Master Recipe, but add 300ml (1/2 pint) Ragu (see page 150) to the rice just before you add the stock (taste carefully – you may not need all the cheese). Continue as in the basic recipe.

Risotto with Chicken Liver Sauce
Follow the Master Recipe. Pour into a hot serving dish and fill the centre with Chicken Liver Sauce (see page 153). Serve immediately.

Risotto with Dried Mushrooms
This is one of the very best ways to get maximum value from some precious, expensive dried mushrooms such as porcini, boletus or cêpes. You will need 7g (1/4oz) of mushrooms and only 25g (1oz) of freshly grated Parmesan. Soak the dried mushrooms in 425ml (3/4 pint) of lukewarm water for 30 minutes, strain and filter off the dark liquid and save. Wash the mushrooms well to make sure there is no grit left.

Follow the Master Recipe. When the rice has cooked for about 12 minutes, add the mushrooms and 150ml (1/4 pint) of the strained liquid. Continue to add the mushroom liquid until it is all used up and then revert to the simmering stock until the rice is cooked. Serve with extra Parmesan.

Risotto with Fresh Mushrooms
Melt 25g (1oz) butter in a saucepan and, just as it foams, add in 225g (8oz) sliced mushrooms and season with salt and pepper. Reduce the heat and cook long and slow until the mushrooms are dark and concentrated in flavour. This method of cooking mushrooms makes them taste like wild mushrooms.

Follow the Master Recipe. When it has been cooking for about 20 minutes, add in the cooked mushrooms and continue.

Risotto with Pumpkin and Rosemary Butter

Serves 4

300g (10oz) pumpkin (we like Cherokee and
   Sweet Mama)
1 onion, finely chopped
1 tablespoon extra-virgin olive oil
salt and freshly ground pepper
350g (12oz) risotto rice
50g (2oz) butter
1–2 tablespoons freshly chopped rosemary
Parmigiano Reggiano, freshly grated

Peel the pumpkin, remove the seeds and
fibres and cut into small cubes. Fry the
onion in the oil until soft, but not coloured.
Add the pumpkin dice, season with salt
and freshly ground pepper and cover.
Simmer gently until the pumpkin is tender
but not breaking up (this takes 5–15
minutes depending on the variety).

Meanwhile, cook the risotto, following the
Master Recipe on page 128). When almost
cooked, add the pumpkin. Finally, mix the
butter with the rosemary and stir into the
risotto. Taste, correct the seasoning and
serve immediately on hot plates.

Risotto with Courgettes and their Blossoms

Serves 4–6

110g (4oz) small courgettes
150g (5oz) butter
1 medium onion, about 110g (4oz)
1.5–1.8 litres (2½–3 pints) homemade Chicken
   Stock (see page 36)
400g (14oz) risotto rice
150ml (5fl oz) dry white wine
6–8 courgette blossoms
2 tablespoons chopped annual marjoram
50g (2oz) Parmigiano Reggiano, freshly grated
   plus extra for sprinkling
salt and freshly ground pepper

Cut the courgettes in half lengthwise and
then into 5mm (¼in) thick slices at an
angle. Alternatively, simply cut them into
dice. Melt about 50g (2oz) of melted butter
in a frying pan and cook the courgette
until 'al dente'. Set aside.

Melt another 50g (2oz) butter in a heavy
saucepan, add the onion and sweat over a
gentle heat for a few minutes.

In another saucepan, bring the stock to
the boil, turn down the heat and keep it
simmering. Add the rice to the onions, stir
for 1–2 minutes until well-coated, then add
the wine and continue to cook until the
wine is almost fully absorbed. Season well
with salt and freshly ground pepper.

Then begin to add small ladlefuls of
simmering stock, stirring all the time, and
ensuring that the last addition has been
almost absorbed before adding the next
ladleful.

After about 12 minutes, when the rice is
beginning to soften, add the courgettes and
cook for a few more minutes. When you are
happy that it is just right, stir in the
courgette blossoms and marjoram and
finally the remaining butter and Parmesan.
Taste – it should be exquisite. Correct the
seasoning if necessary. Serve immediately
in warm bowls with an extra sprinkling of
Parmesan.

Risotto with Broad Beans, Peas, Asparagus and Sugar Snaps

Serves 8

600ml water
225g (½lb) broad beans
110g (4oz) sugar snaps
6 stalks green asparagus
225g (½lb) peas
1.8–2 litres (3–3½ pints) homemade Chicken
   Stock (see page 36)

35g (1½oz) butter
110g (4oz) onions, chopped
400g (14oz) risotto rice
5–6 tablespoons dry white wine
25g (1oz) freshly grated Parmigiano Reggiano
salt and freshly ground pepper

Bring the water to the boil in a large
saucepan, add salt, and the broad beans
and cook for 2–3 minutes until almost
tender. Drain and refresh in cold water.

Slip the beans out of their shells and set
aside. Meanwhile cook the sugar snaps,
again in boiling salted water until 'al
dente', drain and refresh, then cook the
asparagus for just 4–5 minutes and finally
the peas for 3–4 minutes, drain and
refresh. Do this while cooking the risotto
if you can keep your eye on several pots
at the same time!

To start the risotto, first bring the stock to
the boil, turn down the heat and keep it
simmering. Melt 25g (1oz) of the butter in a
heavy saucepan, add the finely chopped
onion and cook over a medium heat until
soft but not coloured. Add the rice and a
generous pinch of salt. Stir the rice over
the heat for 2–3 minutes or until it turns
translucent, then increase the heat and add
the dry white wine. When the wine has
evaporated, add a couple of ladlefuls of
stock, stir and reduce the heat to medium,
keep stirring and as soon as the liquid has
been almost absorbed, add another ladleful
and so on, stirring all the time.

After about 10 minutes, add the beans,
peas, sugar snaps and continue to ladle in
more stock as it is absorbed. After about 5
minutes, taste the rice, it should be just
cooked, stir in the remainder of the butter,
freshly grated Parmesan and the asparagus
sliced into 5cm (2in) pieces at an angle.
Add a little more stock if necessary; the
risotto should be soft and loose.

Taste and correct the seasoning. Serve
immediately in hot bowls with extra
Parmesan to sprinkle over the top.

Supplì
Serves 6, makes about 24

These delicious Roman specialities are little crispy balls of rice with a centre of molten mozzarella (the full name is from *supplì al telefono*, because the hot cheese is stringy, like telephone wires). When you make risotto, it's worth making twice the basic amount, just to be sure you have enough left over to make Supplì.

1 x quantity Risotto alla Parmigiana
  (see page 128)
1 organic egg, beaten
salt and freshly ground pepper

Filling
175g (6oz) mozzarella cheese, diced
50g (2oz) Parmigiano Reggiano, freshly grated

egg wash (2 organic eggs beaten with a pinch
  of salt)
Crisp Breadcrumbs (see page 318)
olive or sunflower oil for deep-frying
rocket leaves, to serve

Mix the cold risotto with the egg, taste and correct the seasoning if necessary. Mix the mozzarella with the Parmesan. Take about 1 tablespoon of rice and flatten it on the palm of your hand, put a generous teaspoon of cheese into the centre and gather the rice around the filling to shape into a ball or an oval about 5cm (2in) long. The rice should be a thin shell not more than 1cm (½in) thick. Put onto a baking tray lined with silicone paper.

When all the supplì have been shaped, dip in eggwash and then in Crisp Breadcrumbs. Just before serving, heat the oil to 190°C/375°F in a deep fryer. Cook the supplì a few at a time until crisp and golden. Drain on kitchen paper. Serve immediately on a bed of rocket leaves.

Alternative Filling
Follow the recipe above, making the filling by mixing 110g (4oz) diced mozzarella, 110g (4oz) Parma ham or crumbled crispy rashers, 2 tablespoons chopped flat-leaf parsley (or half parsley/half chives) and ½–1 finely chopped chilli.

Mexican-style Rice
Serves 8

350g (12oz) long grain white rice
1 onion, chopped
2 garlic cloves, chopped
450g (1lb) ripe tomatoes, peeled, deseeded and
  coarsely chopped
4 tablespoons sunflower oil
850ml (1½ pints) homemade Chicken Stock
  (see page 36), left to cool
150g (5oz) cooked green peas
salt and freshly ground pepper

Garnish
4–6 small red chillies
fresh coriander sprigs

Soak the rice in a bowl of hot water for 15 minutes. Drain, rinse well under cold running water, drain again and set aside.

Combine the onion, garlic and tomatoes in a food processor to make a purée. Heat the oil in a large frying pan. Add the drained rice and sauté until it is golden brown. Using a slotted spoon, transfer the rice to a saucepan. Reheat the oil remaining in the pan and cook the tomato purée for 2–3 minutes. Tip it into the saucepan with the rice and pour in the cold stock. Season to taste. Bring to the boil, reduce the heat to the lowest possible setting, cover the pan and cook for 15–20 minutes until almost all the liquid has been absorbed.

Meanwhile, slice the red chillies from tip to stem end into four or five sections. Place in a bowl of iced water until they curl back to form flowers, then drain.

Stir the peas into the rice mixture and cook, without a lid, until all the liquid has been absorbed and the rice is tender. Stir the mixture from time to time.

Transfer the rice to a serving dish and garnish with the chilli flowers and coriander. Warn diners that the 'flowers' are hot and should be approached with caution!

Rice and Lentils with Crispy Onions
Serves 6

The Lebanese restaurant Le Mignon in London's Camden Town makes what they call *moujadara* – delicious comfort food. There are versions of this from Syria to Egypt. Serve it alone or as part of a mezze.

I'm very happy to say that since the first edition of this book was published, Hussien Dekmak of Le Mignon has written his *Lebanese Cookbook*, so at last I have his recipe for *moujadara*, which is printed here with his kind permission. He says that brown or green lentils can be used, but brown lentils give a much better result.

225g (8oz) brown or green dried lentils, rinsed
4 tablespoons olive oil
½ small onion, finely chopped
110g (4oz) Basmati rice
1 teaspoon cumin
salt and freshly ground pepper

Crispy Onions
vegetable oil
4 tablespoons sliced onion

Place the lentils in a deep pan, cover with water and bring to the boil. Boil for 20 minutes, then drain and set aside.

Heat the olive oil in a pan, add the onion and fry until browned. Add the rice, cooked lentils, salt, pepper and cumin and just enough water to cover. Cover and bring to the boil, then reduce the heat and stir occasionally for 15 minutes or until the rice is cooked. Place in a serving dish.

To make the crispy onions: pour vegetable oil into a deep frying pan to the depth of about 5cm (2in). Heat well and deep-fry the sliced onion until brown and crispy. Remove from the pan and arrange on top of the lentil and rice mixture. Serve hot.

RIGHT: Rice and Lentils with Crispy Onions

How to Cook Couscous

The commercial varieties of couscous we get here are pre-cooked and instant. You do not need to steam it in the traditional way, in fact it's no advantage to do so. Once the grain has absorbed an equal volume of water, all you need to do is heat it through. Claudia Roden's advice is:

For 6 people, put 500g (1lb 2oz) of medium-ground couscous in a Pyrex or pottery bowl. Gradually add 600ml (1 pint) of warm salted water (1/2–1 teaspoon salt), stirring so that it gets absorbed evenly. After about 10 minutes, when the grain has become a little plump and tender, add 3 tablespoons of sunflower oil and rub the grain between your hands to air it and break up any lumps. Heat it through in the oven, covered with tin foil. A small quantity for 2 or 3 can be heated in a saucepan, stirring so as not to burn the bottom, or in the microwave. Before serving, break up any lumps very thoroughly and work in 2 tablespoons of butter or sunflower oil.

Moroccan Couscous
Serves 4–6

This is the basic Moroccan Couscous recipe that Claudia Roden made for us at the school, and around which you can improvise. Claudia explained: 'This dish can be varied indefinitely. Fry the meat and chopped onions in oil on top of the stove before adding the other ingredients if you like. Add baby onions, sliced green peppers and a slice of pumpkin, small shredded white cabbage, a few pitted dates, or, as Algerians sometimes do, runner beans and peas. Colour the stew with tomato concentrate and paprika and make it fiery with cayenne or harissa. Or add a little cinnamon and rose water to the butter when you melt it into the couscous.'

In Morocco the untreated couscous would be steamed over the stew. I've always had a huge complex about my couscous – I simply can't get it anything like as light and fluffy gorgeous as the couscous I've had in Morocco. Claudia cheered me up by explaining that it is virtually impossible to get untreated couscous over here and that even in Morocco many people settle for the pre-cooked couscous. I have to tell you, though, it's not a patch on the real thing… I suppose I will just have to go to Morocco to taste at the source.

900g (2lb) lean stewing lamb or 450g (1lb) lamb, 225g (8oz) beef and 225g (8oz) chicken
2 onions, chopped
50g (2oz) chickpeas, soaked overnight
2 turnips, quartered
2 large carrots, sliced
2 tablespoons olive oil
1/4 teaspoon ground ginger (optional)
1/4 teaspoon saffron (optional)
50–110g (2–4oz) raisins
3 courgettes, sliced, or 1/2 marrow, cut in pieces
110g (4oz) fresh shelled or frozen broad beans
2 tomatoes
a bunch of parsley, finely chopped
a bunch of coriander, finely chopped
cayenne or chilli pepper
1 teaspoon paprika
salt and freshly ground pepper

450g (1lb) prepared couscous (see left)

Put the meat, chicken if using, onions, chickpeas, turnips and carrots – all the ingredients which require longer cooking – in the bottom part of the pan. Cover with water, add the oil, pepper, ginger and saffron if you like, bring to the boil and simmer for about 1 hour. Add salt only when the chickpeas have softened. Add raisins, courgettes or marrow, broad beans, tomatoes, parsley and coriander to the simmering stew. Cook for a further 1/2 hour.

Take a good cupful of sauce from the stew and stir in cayenne or chilli pepper, and a little paprika – enough to make it very fiery.

Pile the couscous onto a large dish, preferably wooden or earthenware. Arrange the meat and vegetables over the couscous and pour the broth over it. Pass the hot, peppery sauce round separately in a little bowl.

Alternatively, serve the couscous, the meat and vegetables, the broth and the peppery sauce in separate bowls.

Israeli Couscous with Shiitake Mushrooms and Coolea Cheese
Serves 6

Israeli couscous is made from the same toasted semolina as regular couscous but comes in little round balls about the size of whole peppercorns. Coolea is one of the best-loved Irish farmhouse cheeses. Aged Gouda or Parmesan can be substituted.

2 tablespoons olive oil
1 medium onion, chopped
2 shallots, chopped
1 garlic clove, crushed
110g (4oz) shiitake mushrooms or button mushrooms, sliced
450g (1lb) Israeli couscous
125ml (4fl oz) dry white wine
1 litre (1 3/4 pints) homemade Chicken or Vegetable stock (see page 36)
finely grated zest of 1 unwaxed lemon
3–4 firm ripe tomatoes, de-seeded and diced or 2 roasted red peppers, peeled, de-seeded and cut into strips
2 tablespoons chopped chives
1 tablespoon parsley
50g (2oz) Coolea farmhouse cheese (or Gouda or Parmesan), freshly grated

Topping
sautéed fresh shiitake or ordinary mushrooms
Roast Spring Onions (see page 187)
a few drops of truffle oil (optional)

Garnish
sprigs of flat-leaf parsley

Heat the oil in a medium saucepan, add the onion, shallots, garlic and mushrooms and sauté until lightly coloured. Add the couscous and cook for 1 minute. Add the wine and 225ml (8fl oz) stock, and cook, stirring occasionally until the liquid is absorbed. Add the remaining stock by the ladle and continue to cook and stir occasionally until the stock is almost absorbed (about 10 minutes). Stir in the lemon zest, tomatoes or roasted peppers, herbs and cheese and serve immediately in warm bowls, topped with sautéed mushrooms and grilled spring onions. If you have a bottle of truffle oil, drizzle some over the top for extra zizz. Garnish with some sprigs of flat-leaf parsley.

Couscous with Vegetables and Coriander
Serves 8

225–350g (8–12oz) couscous
6–10 tablespoons olive oil
350g (12oz) onions, chopped
350g (12oz) carrots, diced into 5mm (1/4in) dice
2 garlic cloves, mashed
1/2 –1 tablespoon coriander seeds, freshly ground
450g (1lb) very ripe tomatoes, peeled and chopped or 1 x 400g (14oz) tin tomatoes and their juice
1–2 fresh chillies, cut into thin slices
350g (12oz) courgettes, sliced into 5mm (1/4in) rounds
4 tablespoons melted butter (optional)
110–175g (4–6oz) peas
150ml (1/4 pint) homemade Vegetable Stock (see page 36) or water
2 tablespoons freshly chopped parsley
3–4 tablespoons fresh coriander leaves
50g (2oz) black olives (optional)
salt and freshly ground pepper

Preheat the oven to 180°C/350°F/gas 4.

Measure the volume of couscous and soak in an equal volume of warm water for about 15 minutes or until all the water has been absorbed.

Heat 4 tablespoons of olive oil in a saucepan, add the onions, carrots, garlic and coriander, cover and sweat over a gentle heat until soft but not coloured. Add the tomatoes and the chillies, season with salt and pepper and cook, uncovered, for a further 10–15 minutes. Meanwhile toss the courgettes in 2 tablespoons of olive oil, add to the vegetable mixture and take off the heat.

Season the couscous with salt and pepper and stir in about 4 tablespoons of olive oil or 4 tablespoons of melted butter. Put into an ovenproof dish and cover with foil and a tight-fitting lid. Place in the oven for about 20 minutes or until heated through. Cook the peas in the boiling stock or salted water and add both peas and liquid to the vegetables, with a tablespoon of parsley. Taste and correct the seasoning. Taste the vegetables and add a tablespoon of fresh coriander.

Spread the couscous on a hot serving dish and make a well in the centre. Add 2 tablespoons of fresh coriander to the hot vegetables and fill into the centre. Sprinkle with the remainder of the coriander, parsley and the olives, if using. Serve immediately.

Couscous Salad with Capers, Olives, Pine Nuts and Currants
Serves 6–8

450ml (16fl oz) water
75g (3oz) currants or raisins
3/4 teaspoon salt
4 tablespoons extra-virgin olive oil
250g (9oz) couscous
110g (4oz) onion, finely chopped
2 large garlic cloves, minced
2 tablespoons red wine vinegar
75g (3oz) green olives, drained and sliced thinly
2 tablespoons capers, drained
75g (3oz) pine nuts, toasted lightly
2 tablespoons finely chopped flat-leaf parsley
2 tablespoons finely chopped mint
salt and freshly ground pepper

Put the water with the currants or raisins, salt and 1 tablespoon of oil into a saucepan and bring to the boil. Stir in the couscous, cover and allow to stand, off the heat, for 5 minutes. Fluff up the couscous with a fork and transfer to a bowl.

Sweat the onion and garlic in 2 tablespoons of olive oil until soft and golden. Stir the onion mixture into the couscous with the vinegar, olives, capers, toasted pine nuts, parsley, mint and the remaining oil. Season with salt and pepper to taste.

This salad may be made a day ahead. Cover and refrigerate but allow it to come back to room temperature before serving.

Quinoa with Herbs
Serves 6

Quinoa (pronounced keen-wah) is an ancient Incan staple and one of the oldest grains on earth. Most quinoa comes from South America and is readily available in health food shops. Quinoa is one of the best grain-based sources of protein, calcium and iron. This nutritional wonder grain cooks quickly and gives texture and crunch to salads, soups and baked dishes.

250g (9oz) quinoa
450g (1lb) homemade Vegetable or Chicken Stock (see page 36)
2 tablespoons extra-virgin olive oil
sea salt and freshly ground pepper
2 tablespoons freshly chopped herbs

Put the quinoa in a sieve and wash with cold water for 2 minutes to remove the natural bitter coating. Bring the stock to the boil in a saucepan, stir in the quinoa and simmer uncovered for approximately 20 minutes or until translucent and all the liquid is absorbed. Add the olive oil and fresh herbs and season with salt and pepper. Serve warm or cold.

Master Recipe
Creamy Polenta
Serves 6–8

1.8 litres (3 pints) water
2 teaspoons salt
225g (8oz) coarse polenta flour (e.g. Bramata)
110g (4oz) butter
75–110g (3–4oz) Parmigiano Reggiano,
   freshly grated
sea salt and freshly ground pepper

Put the water into a deep, heavy saucepan and bring to the boil, add salt, then sprinkle in the polenta flour very slowly, letting it slip gradually through your fingers, whisking all the time (this should take 3–4 minutes). Bring to the boil and when it starts to 'erupt like a volcano' turn the heat down to the absolute minimum – use a heat diffuser mat if you have one.

Cook for about 40 minutes stirring regularly* (I use a whisk at the beginning but as soon as the polenta comes to the boil I change to a flat-bottomed wooden spoon.) The polenta is cooked when it is very thick but not solid and comes away from the sides of the pot as you stir.

As soon as the polenta is cooked, stir in the butter, Parmesan and lots of pepper. Taste and add a little more sea salt if necessary. It should be soft and flowing; if it is too stiff, add a little boiling water.

*If you stir constantly on a slightly higher heat, the cooking time can be reduced to about 20 minutes but it is more digestible if cooked more slowly over a longer period.

Variations
Polenta with Fresh Herbs
Follow the Master Recipe, and add 2–4 tablespoons of freshly chopped herbs e.g. parsley, chives, thyme leaves, sage or rosemary, into the cooked polenta.

LEFT: Chargrilled Polenta with Rocket and Roasted Red and Yellow Peppers

White Polenta
Use white polenta flour instead of regular and proceed as above.

Chargrilled Polenta
Polenta can be served the moment it's ready or it can be turned into a wet dish and allowed to get cold. It can then be sliced and chargrilled, pan-grilled, toasted or fried and served with all sorts of toppings. It can even be cut into thin slices and layered with a sauce, just like lasagne.

Follow the Master Recipe but omit the butter and Parmesan. Pour the cooked polenta into a wet dish – I use a 23 x 18 x 5cm (9 x 7 x 2in) lasagne dish, which is just perfect for this quantity, but you could use a Swiss roll tin and cut it into squares or diamonds when it is cold). Allow to get completely cold. Polenta can be stored like this, covered in the fridge, for several days. It makes the most delicious snack or you can make a sophisticated starter for a dinner party in just a few minutes.

To serve: cut into slices 1–2cm (1/2–3/4in) thick and chargrill, pan-grill or fry. Put it directly onto the bars of the grill on the highest heat without oil and cook until it is hot through and grill-marked on each side. (If the polenta is to be sautéed, use a little olive oil or butter.) Serve the slices of grilled polenta as an accompaniment to meat or fish dishes. There are countless other possibilities. Use your imagination!

Chargrilled Polenta with Caramelised Onions and Pesto
Follow the Chargrilled Polenta recipe, then spread a slice of grilled polenta with Warm Caramelised Onions (see page 188) and top with a teaspoonful of Pesto (see page 589).

Chargrilled Polenta with Rocket and Tapenade or Roasted Red and Yellow Peppers
Follow the Chargrilled Polenta recipe, arranging some fresh rocket leaves on the grilled polenta, and topping with Tapenade (see page 590) and/or roasted red and yellow peppers (see page 191). A slice or two of prosciutto is also delicious.

Chargrilled Polenta with Tomato Fondue and Pesto
Follow the Chargrilled Polenta recipe, spreading 1 tablespoon of hot Tomato Fondue (see page 200) on the grilled polenta and topping with a teaspoonful of pesto.

Chargrilled Polenta with Gorgonzola, Cashel Blue or Goat's Cheese
Follow the Chargrilled Polenta recipe, spreading the hot grilled polenta with Gorgonzola, Cashel Blue or goat's cheese and serve immediately.

Tabouleh

Serves 6–12, as a starter or main course

This refreshing and highly nutritious Middle Eastern salad can be served on its own but we love it with chargrilled lamb or lamb kebabs.

110g (4oz) bulgar (cracked wheat)
75ml (3fl oz) extra-virgin olive oil
juice of 2 freshly squeezed organic lemons or more if you need it
salt and freshly ground pepper
25–50g (1–2oz) freshly chopped parsley
25–50g (1–2oz) freshly chopped mint
50–110g (2–4oz) spring onion, green and white parts, chopped

Garnish
6 very ripe firm tomatoes (a combination of red and yellow looks great), de-seeded, diced and sprinkled with a little salt, pepper and sugar
1 firm crisp cucumber, cut into 5mm (1/4in) dice
rocket leaves or flat-leaf parsley
black olives (optional)

Soak the bulgar in cold water for about 30 minutes, drain and squeeze well to remove any excess water. Stir in the olive oil and some of the lemon juice. Season with salt and pepper and leave aside to absorb the dressing while you chop the parsley, mint and spring onions. Just before serving, mix the herbs with the bulgar, taste and add more lemon juice if necessary. It should taste fresh and lively.

Arrange on a serving plate with little dishes of well-seasoned tomato and cucumber dice. Garnish with rocket or flat-leaf parsley. A few black olives wouldn't go amiss either, and warm pitta or Middle Eastern flatbread is the perfect accompaniment.

Bulgar Wheat and Pecan Nut Salad

See page 214

LEFT: Tabouleh

Master Recipe
Haricot or Flageolet Beans with Tomato and Rosemary

Serves 4–6

Serve as an accompaniment to roast lamb.

225g (1/2lb) dried haricot beans or flageolet
  beans
bouquet garni (see page 37)
1 carrot, chopped
1 onion, chopped
3 tablespoons olive oil
175g (6oz) onions, chopped
4 large garlic cloves, crushed
1 x 400g (14oz) tin tomatoes
large sprig of rosemary, chopped
salt, freshly ground pepper and sugar

Soak the beans overnight in plenty of cold water. Next day, drain the beans, put them in a large saucepan and cover with fresh cold water. Add the bouquet garni, carrot and onion, bring to the boil over high heat, cover and simmer until the beans are soft but not mushy – anything from 30–60 minutes. Just before the end of cooking, add 1 teaspoon of salt. Remove the bouquet garni and vegetables and discard.

Meanwhile, heat the oil in a wide saucepan and sweat the onions gently until soft but not coloured; add the garlic and cook for 1–2 minutes. Add the tomatoes and their juice, the beans, and rosemary. Simmer for 10–15 minutes, using some of the bean liquid if necessary, and season well.

Note: The mixture should be juicy but not swimming in liquid.

Variations
Gratin of Haricot Beans with Tomato and Rosemary
Follow the Master Recipe, and put the mixture into a shallow ovenproof dish. Scatter a mixture of Buttered Crumbs (see page 248) and grated cheese over the top

and put into a hot oven (230°C/450°F/gas 8) or flash under a grill until crisp and golden on top.

Bean Stew with Spicy Sausage
Follow the Master Recipe, but add 2 sliced chorizo or Kabanos sausages to the stew with the beans. Then proceed as before.

Mary Jo's Greek-style Butterbeans

Serves 6

225g (8oz) butterbeans, soaked overnight,
  rinsed
225g (8oz) loin bacon
2 tablespoons extra-virgin olive oil
225g (8oz) onions, peeled and chopped
110g (4oz) carrots, peeled and diced
1–2 tablespoons chopped fresh chilli, seeds
  included
2–3 garlic cloves, finely chopped
1 teaspoon dried oregano
1 teaspoon freshly chopped rosemary
1 x 400g (14oz) tin tomatoes, chopped
salt

Soak the butter beans overnight in a large bowl covered with lots of cold water.

The next day, drain and rinse the beans and transfer to a saucepan. Cover with fresh water, bring to the boil and cook for 45 minutes to 1 hour until very tender. Reserve the cooking liquid.

Trim the rind from the bacon, cut into small dice and brown in 1 tablespoon of olive oil. Remove the bacon, add a second spoonful of oil if needed and gently sauté the chopped onions and carrots until tender. Add the chilli and garlic and cook until fragrant. Stir in the chopped herbs, tomatoes, and reserved bacon. Add the drained beans and enough bean liquid to allow the mixture to simmer gently without sticking. Season with salt, cover and simmer for 30 minutes, stirring occasionally. Serve warm or at room temperature.

Soaking and Cooking Pulses

Soak pulses overnight in plenty of cold water. Next day, drain the pulses and cover with fresh water. Add a carrot, an onion and a bouquet garni (see page 37). Cover and cook for 1/2–3/4 hour or until the pulses are soft but not mushy. Add salt. Drain and discard the vegetables and bouquet garni. Save the cooking water for vegetable stock.

Windowsill Cooking: Sprouting Seeds for Bean Sprouts

Use approximately 2 tablespoons of seeds or 4 tablespoons of legumes (such as alfalfa, mung beans or soya beans). Put the seeds in a large jar, cover with warm water and soak for 8 hours. Drain off the liquid, rinse the seeds and drain again. Now lay the jar on its side. Rinse the sprouts 2–3 times a day and replace the jar on its side. Do not let the sprouts sit too long in water or dry out as this will spoil the crop.

Keep the sprout jar in a dark place for the first 2–3 days and bring it out in the light on the last day when the chlorophyll develops. This process generally produces nice green sprouts. Within 3–4 days the sprouts will have developed completely and will be ready to eat and/or refrigerate.

Buy legumes and seeds for sprouting from natural food stores and health food shops. We particularly recommend using alfalfa seeds because of their delicate taste. But you can also use mung or soya beans.

Cassoulet (French Bean Stew)

Serves 8

I am one of Elizabeth David's greatest fans, but it took me years to gather up the courage to try cassoulet after I had read and reread the descriptions of different types in *French Provincial Cooking*. My mouth watered – I longed to try this most comforting of winter stews – but I felt I would never manage to get all those ingredients together at one time. Eventually, I realised that it's really just a bean stew. At its most basic it can consist simply of sausage and beans and everything else is a bonus. It also reheats very well and, unless it's my imagination, it gets better and better. Use Polish sausage, Italian Zampone or Cotechino, or Saucisson de Toulouse.

700g (1¹/₂lb) haricot beans
1 carrot
1 onion studded with 2 cloves
2 Bouquet Garni (see page 37)
225g (¹/₂lb) streaky bacon or pickled pork
3 tablespoons olive oil
3 onions, sliced

5 garlic cloves, crushed
6–8 very ripe tomatoes, peeled and sliced
salt and freshly ground pepper
1.2 litres (2 pints) homemade Chicken Stock (see page 36), left to cool
4 legs of confit de canard (duck) or 2 pieces of confit d'oie (goose) or 4 fresh duck legs
450g (1lb) shoulder of lamb, cut into 4 thick chops
350–450g (³/₄–1lb) coarse pork sausages
50g (2oz) breadcrumbs

Garnish
chopped parsley

Soak the beans overnight in plenty of cold water. The next day, cover with fresh water, add the carrot, the clove-studded onion and one of the bouquet garni. Cover and cook for ¹/₂–³/₄ hour or until the beans are three-quarters cooked. Drain and discard the vegetables and bouquet garni.

Meanwhile, preheat the oven to 150°C/300°F/gas 2. Cut the bacon into 2.5cm (1in) squares. Heat the olive oil in a casserole or pot, add the bacon and fry until beginning to turn golden, add the onions, garlic, tomatoes, salt, pepper and a new bouquet garni. Cook for 1–2 minutes, add the cold stock and allow to simmer for 15 minutes.

Discard the bouquet garni, then add the duck or goose, the lamb, sausage and finally put the beans on top. Bring the cassoulet to the boil, then spread a layer of breadcrumbs over the top. Put the casserole into the oven, and continue to cook for 1–1¹/₂ hours or until the beans and meat are cooked. By this time, a crust will have formed and the beans will have absorbed most of the stock; if they haven't, remove the lid from the saucepan and cook uncovered for a further 15 minutes or so.

Sprinkle with chopped parsley and serve from the casserole (if you have cooked it in an earthenware pot all the better). Serve with a good green salad (see page 223).

LEFT: Cassoulet

Mediterranean Bean Stew

Serves 6–8

This is a delicious rustic bean stew, cheap to make yet wonderfully filling and nutritious, and a particularly good dish for vegetarians. Do not add the salt to the beans until near the end of the cooking time, otherwise they seem to harden.

350g (12oz) haricot, kidney or black-eyed beans, or a mixture – but cook separately as they all cook at different rates
1–3 carrots
1–3 onions
1–3 bouquet garni (see page 37)

2 tablespoons extra-virgin olive oil
225g (8oz) onions, sliced
1 chilli, de-seeded and diced (optional)
1 large red pepper, cored, de-seeded and sliced
1 large green pepper, cored, de-seeded and sliced
2 garlic cloves, crushed
1 x 400g (14oz) tin of tomatoes, or 450g (1lb) peeled, very ripe tomatoes, chopped
2 tablespoons concentrated tomato pureé
1 tablespoon chopped marjoram, thyme or basil
1 Bouquet Garni (see page 37)
salt, freshly ground pepper and sugar
50g (2oz) black olives
2 tablespoons freshly chopped parsley

Prepare and cook the dried beans separately (see page 137). When tender but not mushy, strain and reserve 300ml (¹/₂ pint) of the liquid and discard the vegetables and bouquet garni.

Heat the oil in a casserole and sweat the onions and chilli on a low heat for about 5 minutes. Add the peppers and garlic, cover and continue to sweat gently for 10 minutes. Stir in the tomatoes with their juice, tomato pureé, herbs, beans, bouquet garni, reserved cooking liquid, salt, pepper and a pinch of sugar. Cover and simmer for about 20 minutes, or until the beans and peppers are cooked.

Five minutes before the end of cooking time, add the olives and freshly chopped parsley. Remove the bouquet garni, taste and correct the seasoning. Serve with rice.

Variation
Mediterranean Bean Stew with Chorizo or Bacon

Follow the Master Recipe, but add 110g (4oz) sliced chorizo or streaky bacon (blanched, de-rinded, and cut into cubes) with the beans and proceed as in the Master Recipe.

Black Bean, Avocado, Tomato and Corn Salad with Chilli and Coriander

Serves 4

Serve either as a course on its own or as an accompaniment to a piece of pan-grilled steak, chicken breast or fish.

175g (6oz) black beans
1 teaspoon salt

Dressing
175ml (6fl oz) extra-virgin olive oil
4–5 tablespoons lime or lemon juice
2 tablespoons chopped parsley

4 vine-ripened tomatoes
2 avocados, peeled and diced
1 red onion, sliced into rings
2 chillies (Jalapeño or Serrano), sliced
110g (4oz) cooked, fresh or frozen sweetcorn or corn niblets
4 tablespoons freshly chopped coriander
salt, freshly ground pepper and sugar

Prepare and cook the beans (see page 137) Add the salt only at the end of the cooking. To make the dressing: mix the olive oil with the lime or lemon juice and parsley and season well with salt and pepper. When the beans are fully cooked, drain and toss immediately in half of the dressing.

Cut the tomatoes into quarters and then each quarter in half crossways. Sprinkle with salt, freshly ground pepper and sugar. Combine the tomatoes, avocados, red onion and chillies in a bowl, season gently, toss with the corn and the remainder of the dressing in a bowl, add the beans and coriander. Taste, correct the seasoning and serve immediately.

Frijoles de Olla

Serves 6–8

Beans cooked simply like this and the Frijoles Refritos that are made from them are virtually a staple in Mexico, served at almost every meal including breakfast. In Mexico, the markets are often divided into two sections: on one side the regular stalls serving all manner of things, and the eating side where people eat simply and cheaply at large tables covered in colourful oil cloth. Hundreds of people eat these beans every day with some coarse salt, hot green chillies and a stack of tortillas, and maybe a few small pieces of creamy cheese melting over them. They keep well and taste even better the next day or two days after.

450g (1lb) dried black beans or red kidney or pinto beans
1–2 tablespoons good-quality pork lard or butter
1 small onion, chopped
1 teaspoon salt, approx.
1–2 sprigs of epazote or Mexican tea – a green herb used in Mexican cooking (optional)

Cover the beans generously with cold water and soak overnight. Alternatively, if you are in a hurry, bring the beans to the boil, cook for 3–4 minutes, then take off the heat and leave aside for an hour or so.

Either way, drain the beans, cover with fresh water (about 1.5 litres/ 2½ pints), add the lard or butter and onion, but not the salt. Bring to the boil and simmer gently for 1–2 hours, depending on the

beans. About ½ hour before the end of the cooking, add the salt and the sprig of epazote, if you have it.

Ensure that the beans are always covered while they cook; top up with boiling water to cover them by about 1cm (½in). When cooked, the beans should be completely soft and the liquid slightly thickish and soupy.

Frijoles Refritos (Refried Beans)

50–75g (2–3oz) best-quality pork lard or butter
1 medium onion, finely chopped
225g (8oz) Frijoles de Olla (see left)

Heat the lard or butter in a heavy frying pan and cook the onion until soft and brown. Increase the heat and add about a third of the beans and their broth to the pan and cook over a high heat, mashing them as you stir. Gradually add in the rest of the beans until you have a thick, coarse purée. Taste and season if necessary. This process takes less than 10 minutes. The beans are ready when the purée begins to dry out and sizzle at the edges.

Frijoles Refritos keep well and may be reheated many times in a saucepan over a medium heat. They accompany many snacks, including Mexican scrambled eggs.

Molettas

If you've got some leftover refried beans this is a yummy way to use them up, as served for breakfast in a hotel in Mexico City. Split squishy white rolls and spread each one with warm refried beans. Top with grated cheese and pop under the grill or into a hot oven until the cheese melts. Serve with tomato salsa and guacamole.

Borlotti or Cannellini Beans

Serves 8

Serve with slow-roasted or grilled meals.

450g (1lb) borlotti or cannellini beans
4 tablespoons extra-virgin olive oil plus extra
    for drizzling
6 garlic cloves, cut in half
1 red chilli (optional)
2 very ripe tomatoes
10 sage leaves or 4–6 sprigs of thyme
salt and freshly ground pepper

Cover the beans generously with cold water and allow to soak overnight. The next day, discard the water. Put the beans into a saucepan. Cover with fresh water and add 4 tablespoons of olive oil, the garlic, chilli, tomatoes and sage or thyme. Bring to the boil and skim and then simmer for 1–1½ hours or until the beans are tender.

Remove the chilli, tomatoes, herbs and garlic. Drain the beans and save the water for soups or stews. Season with salt and freshly ground pepper. Drizzle with best-quality extra-virgin olive oil. Taste and correct the seasoning, and serve.

Note: If not using the beans immediately it's best to leave them sitting in the water until ready to use. Season with salt and pepper.

Variation

Tuscan Bean Purée

We sometimes purée the beans coarsely and then drizzle with extra-virgin olive oil or alternatively purée a ladleful with the cooking liquid and mix that with the remainder of the beans to give a creamy soupy texture. Drizzle with extra-virgin olive oil or chilli oil and decorate with freshly snipped flat-leaf parsley.

Black Bean, Corn and Roasted Red Pepper Salad

See page 207

Salad of Fresh and Dried Beans

Serves 8

110g (4oz) haricot beans
110g (4oz) red kidney beans
110g (4oz) flageolet beans
110g (4oz) black-eyed beans
450g (1lb) fresh French beans
4 tablespoons well-seasoned French dressing
    (see page 226)
2 tablespoons chopped parsley
2 tablespoons freshly chopped coriander
75–110g (3–4oz) toasted hazelnuts, roughly
    chopped

Garnish
coarsely chopped fresh coriander

Prepare and cook the beans (see page 137), remembering to soak the different varieties separately. Drain and save the cooking water for soup. Cook the French beans in lightly salted boiling water for 3–4 minutes, then drain and refresh.

Toss the beans in well-flavoured dressing while still warm. Add the parsley and coriander and season well. Scatter with hazelnuts and garnish with coriander.

Falafel with Hummus and Tzatziki

Serves 8

Even if it's well seasoned, falafel can be a little hard going, but it is transformed with lashings of good hummus and tzatziki.

450g (1lb) chickpeas
175g (6oz) onion, finely chopped
2 garlic cloves, crushed
1–2 tablespoons freshly ground cumin
1 tablespoon freshly ground coriander
4 tablespoons chopped parsley
2 tablespoons freshly chopped coriander leaves
salt and freshly ground pepper
¼–½ tablespoon chilli powder
vegetable oil for deep-frying

Salad
110g (4oz) French beans
6 tomatoes, peeled, quartered and de-seeded
½ cucumber, diced
1 tablespoon freshly chopped mint
1 red onion, finely sliced
a mixture of salad leaves

Dressing
6 tablespoons extra-virgin olive oil
2 tablespoons white wine vinegar or
    2 tablespoons lemon juice
salt, freshly ground pepper and sugar

Accompaniments
Tzatziki (see page 69)
Hummus bi Tahina (see page 68)

Soak the chickpeas in plenty of cold water overnight. The next day, drain and discard the water. Whizz the chickpeas in a food processor, add the onion, garlic, spices, herbs, salt, pepper and chilli powder. Continue to whizz until the mixture is puréed but still slightly grainy.

Heat the oil in a deep fryer to 180°C/350°F. Shape about 1 tablespoon of the mixture into a flat pattie – this amount should make about 24 falafel. Cook until crisp and a rich golden brown. Taste, correct the seasoning and continue to shape the remainder. Fry a few falafel at a time.

Cook the French beans into lightly salted boiling water for 3–4 minutes, then drain and refresh. Toss the tomatoes, cucumber and beans in a little dressing. Season with salt, pepper and sugar. Sprinkle over the mint and red onion.

To serve: Put 3 little blobs of hummus on each plate, put a hot, crispy falafel on top of each one, toss the salad leaves in dressing and place on top. Serve immediately with bowls of Tzatziki and the salad.

RIGHT: My lovely daughter Lydia

Chickpeas with Fresh Spices

Serves 8–10

A few little jars of fresh spices are a must for your store cupboard, they add zest and lots of exotic flavour to your food.

450g (1lb) chickpeas
2 fresh green chillies
5cm (2in) piece fresh ginger, peeled and roughly chopped
4 garlic cloves
4 tablespoons olive oil
225g (8oz) onion, finely chopped
1 teaspoon whole cumin seeds, crushed
2 teaspoons whole coriander seeds, crushed
1–2 teaspoons chilli powder
8 very ripe tomatoes, peeled and chopped
salt and freshly ground pepper

Garnish
2 tablespoons freshly chopped coriander leaves
1 tablespoon fresh mint leaves

Soak the chickpeas in plenty of cold water overnight. The next day, drain and discard the water. Cover the chickpeas with fresh water and cook until tender – anything from 30–60 minutes, depending on the quality. Drain and reserve the cooking liquid. Meanwhile, discard the seeds from the chillies and grind to a paste in a pestle and mortar or food processor with the ginger and garlic.

Heat the oil in a heavy sauté pan, sweat the onions until soft but not coloured, add the chilli paste together with the cumin, coriander seeds and the chilli powder. Cook for 1–2 minutes, then add the tomatoes, chickpeas and a little of the liquid (save the rest for soup), and simmer gently for about 10 minutes until the flavours have mingled.

Taste, season with salt and pepper. Sprinkle with the coriander and mint and serve immediately. This is quite delicious served either hot or cold.

Master Recipe
Puy Lentils

Serves 4–6

Green speckled lentilles du Puy are the aristocrats of the lentil family: in France they are recognised by their own *appellation d'origine*, as are French wines. They cook in minutes and can star or play a supporting role in many dishes. Try them just as a vegetable with a crispy duck breast or toss in some pieces of cooked ham or bacon and a few cubes of dessert apple cooked in butter for a complete meal.

225g (8oz) Puy lentils
1 carrot
1 onion, stuck with 2 cloves
1 bouquet garni (see page 37)
butter or extra-virgin olive oil
a large handful of freshly chopped herbs (e.g. fresh oregano, annual marjoram or parsley)
juice of 1/2–1 freshly squeezed lemon, to taste
sea salt and freshly ground pepper

Wash the lentils and put them into a large saucepan. Fill with cold water, add the carrot, onion and bouquet garni, bring slowly to the boil, reduce the heat and simmer very gently for 10–15 minutes, testing regularly. The lentils should be 'al dente' but not hard. Drain, remove and discard the carrot, onion and bouquet garni.

Season the lentils while warm with a good knob of butter or some extra-virgin olive oil, then add lots of freshly squeezed lemon juice and some finely chopped herbs. Season with sea salt and freshly ground pepper. Serve immediately.

Variation
Spiced Puy Lentils

Substitute 2 tablespoons of fresh coriander for the herbs in the above recipe, add to the lentils with 1 large or 2 small chillies and proceed as above.

Spicy Lentil Burgers with Cucumber and Coriander Raita

Serves 5–10, makes 10 burgers

2 tablespoons olive oil
1 garlic clove, crushed
1 large onion, finely chopped
2 carrots, finely chopped
1 celery stick, finely chopped
225g (8oz) green lentils, boiled for 25–30 minutes and drained
1 1/2 teaspoons ground cumin
2 teaspoons ground coriander
6 tablespoons freshly chopped parsley
1 tablespoon lemon juice
1 organic egg, beaten
50g (2oz) white breadcrumbs
seasoned white flour
salt and freshly ground pepper
vegetable oil for shallow-frying

Cucumber and Coriander Raita (see page 594)
Tomato and Chilli Jam (see page 513)

Heat the oil in a frying pan, sauté the garlic, onion, carrots and celery for 10–12 minutes over a medium heat until softened and lightly browned. Add the lentils, spices, parsley, lemon juice and seasoning. Cook for 5 minutes. Put the lentil mixture into a food processor, add the egg and breadcrumbs and pureé until it holds together, but still has a coarse texture.

Transfer the mixture to a large bowl. Cover a baking tray with silicone paper. With wet hands, shape the mixture into 10 burgers and dip in the seasoned flour. Place them on the baking sheet, cover and chill for 30 minutes.

Heat the oil in a frying pan. Cook the burgers in batches for 5–7 minutes on each side. Drain on kitchen paper. Serve with Raita (see page 595) or Tomato and Chilli Jam (see page 513) with a little roasted and ground coriander, chunky homemade chips, a tomato salad and a good green salad (see page 225).

Dal Makhani (Spiced Lentils and Kidney Beans)

Serves 4–6

A gem of a recipe from Alison Henderson.

6 green cardamom pods
3 bay leaves
2 garlic cloves, peeled
2.5cm (1in) piece fresh ginger, peeled
1 cinnamon stick
2 teaspoons coriander seeds
175g (6oz) Puy lentils, rinsed
75g (3oz) kidney beans (dried or tinned)
1 onion, finely sliced
2 tablespoons cream
25g (1oz) butter
salt and freshly ground pepper

Dressing
25g (1oz) butter
1 teaspoon cumin seeds
2 garlic cloves, sliced
1 small onion, finely chopped
2 tomatoes, peeled, de-seeded and chopped
1 green chilli, finely chopped

Tie the cardamoms, bay leaves, garlic, ginger, cinnamon and coriander in a piece of muslin (as you would for a bouquet garni). Put the lentils and the kidney beans into a deep saucepan with double their volume of water, add the onion and the spice bag and bring to the boil. (If you are using tinned kidney beans, do not add them at this stage.) Lower the heat and simmer the pulses for about 1 hour until soft but not mushy – you may have to add more water. When the lentils are soft, stir in the butter and half the cream. The tinned kidney beans can now be stirred in.

To make the dressing: melt the butter in a small frying pan and add the cumin seeds and the garlic. When the spices start to colour, add the onion and fry for a few more minutes, then add the tomatoes and green chilli. Simmer for 1–2 minutes, then pour into the pulses with the remaining cream. Add salt and seasoning to taste.

Rosemary Kearney's Gluten-Free Spicy Lentil Lasagne

Serves 8–10

Spicy Lentil Mixture
350g (12oz) cooked Puy lentils (see page 142)
1 carrot
1 onion
bouquet garni (see page 37)
4 tablespoons extra-virgin olive oil
2 teaspoons freshly ground cumin
2 teaspoons freshly ground coriander
1 teaspoon paprika
1 teaspoon freshly ground cinnamon
salt and freshly ground pepper

1 x gluten-free Béchamel Sauce (see page 581)
Buttered Spinach (see page 171)
3 red peppers
1 x Tomato Fondue (see page 200)
10–12 sheets gluten-free lasagne
2 x 150g (5oz) balls buffalo mozzarella
freshly grated Parmigiano Reggiano
a little butter

28 x 20cm (11 x 8in) lasagne dish

Preheat the oven to 250°C/475°F/gas 9.

First make the gluten-free Béchamel sauce and set aside.

Cook the spinach according to the buttered spinach recipe and allow to cool.

Rub the whole peppers with a little olive oil. Place on a baking tray and roast them in the oven for 20–30 minutes until they are soft and the skin blisters. Put them into a bowl, cover with clingfilm and allow to cool before peeling and de-seeding.

Reduce the temperature of the oven to 180°C/350°F/gas 4.

Make the Tomato Fondue.

Cook the Puy lentils as in the Master recipe (page 142). Drain, remove and discard the carrot, onion and bouquet garni. Mix the extra-virgin olive oil with the spices and pour over the lentils which should be still warm. Season with salt and pepper.

To assemble: spread half of the tomato fondue over the base of the lasagne dish. Pour all the spicy lentils over the first layer of fondue, then top with the remaining fondue.

Blanch the gluten-free lasagne sheets in a large saucepan of boiling salted water for 2 minutes. Drain on kitchen paper.

Place a layer of the blanched lasagne sheets on top of the tomato fondue.

Next put on a layer of the buttered spinach and then the peppers. (Don't be tempted to wash the roasted peppers or you will lose all the lovely flavours.)

Cut the mozzarella balls into 6 slices and arrange over the roasted pepper layer. Repeat with another layer of lasagne, then cover with a layer of Béchamel sauce. Sprinkle generously with grated Parmesan. Dot with a few knobs of butter and wipe the edges of the dish clean. Bake for 40 minutes or until the lasagne is golden and bubbly on top.

pasta & noodles

pasta & noodles

My first tentative effort at making my own pasta was in 1970 – I had just come across a recipe in *Gourmet,* the American food and travel magazine, and was so excited I couldn't wait to try it. Soon the kitchen was festooned with sheets of pasta drying on the front of the Aga and it was so delicious that we were all immediately hooked.

Homemade Pasta

Making homemade pasta is surprisingly easy, but the rolling is unquestionably laborious. You might want to consider investing in a pasta machine – even the most basic ones will simplify the process. Pasta machines with a zillion attachments that promise to make lots of different shapes are rarely worth the money – the results from these machines often disappoint. Once you've rolled out some sheets of pasta there are a myriad of possibilities crafting shapes yourself. All you have to do is decide what you fancy – from simple noodles to lasagne or pappardelle, plump ravioli, cappelletti or tortellini...

Dried Pasta

Tender, homemade pasta is one of life's little luxuries, but it's certainly not the only option. If you haven't the time or the inclination to make your own, don't be disheartened. Lots of delis and speciality food stores produce a variety of pasta that is almost as good as homemade, so you can cheat a little. There's also an ever-increasing range of quality dried pasta. The Italians have never been sniffy about dried pasta. Their view is that while homemade pasta is best for some dishes, dried is better for others. Good dried pasta (try to buy brands made to Italian specifications) is also a better option than poor-quality fresh pasta.

In the early 1980s, I longed to learn more about Italian food, so I went to Marcella Hazan's classes in Bologna. I've always believed that if you want to learn the cuisine of a particular country, you need to go there and immerse yourself in the culture, visit the markets and taste the ingredients. You can't begin to reproduce the flavours, or even think of teaching it to others, before you know what the food is meant to taste like.

Pasta is an Italian word which means 'paste'. Wheat grows in northern Italy, so in Tuscany pasta is made with wheat flour, eggs and no salt. Further south it is made with durum semolina.

Serving Pasta

Pasta is the ultimate fast food. Low in fat and high in carbohydrates, it's certainly much better for you than running down to the local burger bar, and it can be prepared in less time than it would take for the speediest of takeaways to arrive. Everyone needs to have a few packets of pasta stashed in their store cupboard. Combined with even the simplest of tomato sauces you can whip up a delicious little supper in a few minutes. Pasta's brilliant for casual and spontaneous entertaining – there's nothing quite like it for feeding a crowd of friends in the minimum of time with little fuss and virtually no washing up. Most of the dishes in this chapter are quick and easy to make. Of course, some pasta recipes will take a little more time to prepare (ragu sauce can take several hours to cook down to a luscious, juicy taste sensation), but they're worth it for a special treat.

Remember that with dishes like lasagne, although it's great to stick to the traditional recipe, it should be viewed as a formula. Experiment with different combinations of flavours – fish or vegetable lasagnes are equally delicious, made all the nicer by the fact that they're a little unusual.

The same applies equally to the stuffed pastas, like ravioli, cappelletti and tortellini. Once you've made the classic version a couple of times, you can move on to experiment and have fun with all sorts of fillings.

Which Sauce?

There are hundreds of different pasta shapes available, so be sure to choose a shape and sauce that complement each other. As a general rule, serve light, thin sauces with delicate pastas (like capellini or spaghetti), and heavier sauces with thicker shapes (like penne). Pasta shapes with holes or ridges, like rigatoni, are perfect for chunky sauces.

Cooking Pasta

Pasta, whether fresh or dried, needs to be cooked in a large saucepan of salted boiling water. Take it off the heat while it still has a slight bite ('al dente'). Drain, but not too meticulously. Toss immediately with extra-virgin olive oil. This, combined with the few remaining tablespoons of cooking water, will prevent the pasta from sticking together. Serve immediately, or reheat the pasta in the sauce later and then serve.

Freshly grated Parmesan is wonderful with pasta, but not compulsory. Experiment with different cheeses. (In Italy, cheese is never served with shellfish pasta.)

For the best flavour in pasta salads, it's crucial to toss the freshly cooked pasta in a well-flavoured dressing while still warm.

Leftover pasta can be reheated. The Italians would be appalled, but one can fry off cooked pasta and add it to an omelette.

Storage and Freezing

Dried, uncooked pasta can be stored for a year or two if kept in a cool, dry place in a sealed packet or covered container. Fresh pasta will keep for 3–4 days if refrigerated, and can be frozen for up to a month.

Cooked pasta can be kept refrigerated in an airtight container for 2–3 days. Add a little olive oil to prevent the pasta from sticking.

Pasta dishes like lasagne, canelloni and ravioli freeze well. For the best results, prepare the recipe, cover, and freeze it before baking. Defrost and bake when needed.

Nutrition

Pasta is high in fibre, low in fat and is sodium- and cholesterol-free. It is full of complex carbohydrates which give a slow and steady release of energy. Most bought pasta is now enriched with folic acid (which helps to prevent some birth defects and may protect against heart disease and some types of cancer), iron, thiamin, riboflavin and niacin.

Wholewheat pasta is unrefined and provides the same quantity of energy as processed white pasta but contains more fibre and much more magnesium.

Coeliacs, who have a gluten intolerance (the protein found in wheat, rye and barley) and therefore have to follow a gluten-free diet, need not avoid pasta. Although the majority of pasta is made from durum wheat flour or semolina, gluten-free options do exist. Alternatives include rice, corn, soya and buckwheat pasta and noodles made from peas, lentils and mung beans. Rice and soya pasta is wheat- and gluten-free, and is one of the most complete protein foods.

Noodles

Asian noodles are a brilliant discovery. They are usually dried and made from four different types of flour: **wheat flour** (Japanese somen, udon and Chinese wheat flour noodles – incuding flavoured noodles and egg noodles), **rice flour** (vermicelli), **mung-bean flour** (cellophane noodles) and **buckwheat flour** (Japanese soba).

Cellophane noodles have little or no taste and absorb the flavours of the ingredients that are cooked with. They are prized for their texture. **Chinese wheat flour noodles** are the oldest form of noodles. They vary in thickness and may be round or flat. The thinnest are used in light soups, whereas the thicker varieties stand up to heartier soups and casseroles. **Vermicelli** are thin and delicate noodles used in soups, salads and stir-fries. The dried noodles are also deep-fried and used as 'nests' for stir-fried foods. **Soba noodles** have a nutty flavour and are rich in both protein and fibre. They are most commonly served cold with a dipping sauce or hot in soups. Soba may also be flavoured with green tea, lemon zest or black sesame seeds. **Somen** are the most delicate Japanese noodles. Like soba, they are served cold with a dipping sauce, but they also make a light and delicate garnish for hot soups. **Udon** are fat, white, slippery noodles, used for hearty soups and casseroles.

Leftover noodles are yummy fried like a cake in a frying pan until they are crispy on the bottom.

Master Recipe
Homemade Pasta
Makes 600g (1lb 5oz)

In Tuscany, fresh pasta is made just with flour and eggs – no water and usually no salt.

400g (14oz) plain white flour
1 teaspoon salt (optional)
3–4 organic eggs

Sift the flour into a bowl and add the salt if using. Whisk the eggs together, make a well in the centre of the flour and add in most of the egg. Mix into a dough with your hand, adding the remainder of the egg only if you need it. If it is much too wet it is very difficult to get it right; the pasta should just come together but shouldn't stick to your hand – if it does, add a little more flour.

Knead for a few minutes until smooth and then put on a plate covered with an upturned bowl for 1 hour to relax. Divide the dough in half and roll out one piece at a time as thinly as possible, keeping the other piece covered. You ought to be able to read the print on a matchbox through the pasta.

A long, thin rolling pin is a great advantage but you can manage perfectly well with an ordinary domestic rolling pin.

Pasta can be flavoured and coloured in all sorts of ways. Add anything from tomato purée for orange pasta to squid ink for designer black pasta (the latter is not worth the trouble, I assure you!).

Variations
Pasta with Fresh Herbs
Mix 3 tablespoons finely chopped fresh herbs (e.g. parsley, chives, thyme, marjoram or a mixture) with the flour and continue as in the Master Recipe.

Tomato Pasta
Add 2 tablespoons tomato paste with most of the beaten eggs and continue as in the Master Recipe.

Black Pepper Pasta
Add 2 tablespoons freshly ground pepper to the flour and proceed as above.

Pasta Verde

150g (5oz) cooked spinach (about 225g (8oz)
*   raw spinach, stalks removed, should yield*
*   the cooked amount)*
225g (8oz) plain white flour
2 organic eggs

Use a potato masher to squeeze every single drop of water out of the spinach, chop well or purée, add the spinach to the flour with the eggs and continue as for basic pasta dough (you may not need all the egg). Rest for just 10 minutes and then roll out and proceed as in the Master Recipe.

How to Make Long Strands of Pasta

Allow the rolled-out pasta to dry for about 30 minutes, or until just dry to the touch. Roll up from one end like a Swiss roll and slice with a chopping knife into whatever thickness you need (see below). You can use the rolling pin as a guide for your knife. Open out and let it run through your fingers to separate the strands. Use immediately or allow to dry on a lightly floured tray.

Tagliatelle or noodles: 5mm (1/4in) wide

Fettuccini: 3mm (1/8in) wide

Pappardelle: 1.5cm (2/3in) wide – cut
                     with a pasta wheel

How to Cook Pasta

Fresh pasta cooks very quickly indeed. It should take only 1–2 minutes to be perfectly cooked but still have bite – al dente, as the Italians say.

For dried pasta, be guided by the instructions on the packet but start to test about 2–3 minutes before the suggested time.

Choose a large, deep saucepan; two handles are an advantage for ease of lifting. To cook 500g (1lb 2oz) pasta, use 2 tablespoons of dairy salt or sea salt to 4.8 litres (8 pints) of water. Bring the water to the boil before adding the salt. Tip the pasta in all at once and stir well to ensure the strands are separate, then cover the pan just long enough to bring the water back to the boil. Cook, uncovered, until al dente.

Drain the pasta immediately it is cooked. Don't overdrain. Fresh pasta, and all long pasta, should still be still wet and slippery: toss the sauce in immediately. Pasta shapes need to be thoroughly drained, otherwise the water they contain may dilute the sauce too much. It is a good idea to keep aside a few tablespoons of the pasta water to adjust the consistency of the sauce.

Fresh or Dried?

A recent myth that needs to be de-bunked once and for all is that fresh pasta is better or preferable to dried pasta. Neither is superior, they are quite simply different. There are two types of dried pasta: plain pasta made from egg, durum semolina flour and water, and egg pasta made from durum wheat and eggs.

Oil-based sauces are usually served with plain pasta, while butter or cream-based sauces are usually served with egg pasta.

Which Pasta?

Bucatini – thick hollow strands
Conchiglie – little shells
Cannelloni – thick tubes
Farfalle – bow ties or butterflies
Fettuccini – 'small ribbons' – medium egg noodles
Fusilli – twisted spaghetti
Gnocchetti – ridged shell-shaped pasta
Macaroni – thicker hollow strands
Orecchiette – 'little ears', medium saucer-shaped shells
Orzo – rice-shaped pasta
Pappardelle – broad egg noodles
Penne – pasta cut diagonally into quills, smooth or ridged
Rigatoni – large ridged tubes
Rotini – spirals or twists
Spaghetti – 'length of cord' – thin strands
Spaghettini – thinner strands
Tagliatelle – medium egg noodles
Taglierini – thinner noodles
Vermicelli – 'little worms'

Which Sauce?

Spaghettini and spaghetti are best served with olive oil sauces, but the flatter ribbon noodles of varying widths may also be served with butter, cream, egg and cheese, and meat-based sauces.

When serving pasta shapes and tubes, the chunkier the sauce the larger the pasta shapes need to be.

Pasta Portion Size

Depends on appetite! As a rough guideline we use:

Dried pasta
60g (2½oz) for a starter
110g (4oz) for a main course

Fresh pasta
110g (4oz) for a starter
150g (5oz) for a main course

Sauces

Roasted Red Pepper Sauce
Makes sufficient for 450g (1lb) of pasta

4 red peppers
vegetable oil
50g (2oz) freshly grated Parmesan (preferably Parmigiano Reggiano)
1 teaspoon balsamic vinegar
25g (1oz) ground almonds
½ garlic clove, crushed
¼–½ teaspoon lemon zest
salt and freshly ground pepper

Preheat the oven to 200°C/400°F/gas 6.

Rub a little oil onto the skins of the peppers, and roast for about 18 minutes or until the skin is wrinkly and the peppers are slightly soft. Put into a bowl, cover with clingfilm or a tea towel for about 5 minutes. Then peel and de-seed but do not wash.

Whizz the peppers, Parmesan, salt, pepper, almonds, garlic, lemon zest and balsamic vinegar in a food processor. Taste and correct the seasoning. The sauce can be stored in the fridge under a film of oil. Toss freshly cooked pasta in the sauce, serve with plenty of basil and shavings of Parmesan.

Tomato, Mint and Caper Sauce

Serves 4: sufficient for 450g (1lb) fettucini, spaghetti or penne

600ml (1 pint) Tomato Fondue (see page 200)
2 garlic cloves, crushed
2 tablespoons capers, roughly chopped
1–2 tablespoons freshly chopped mint
25–50g (1–2oz) freshly grated Parmesan
   (preferably Parmigiano Reggiano)

While the pasta is cooking, heat the Tomato Fondue, add the garlic, capers and mint and simmer for 4–5 minutes. Drain the pasta, toss with the sauce, add a little Parmesan and serve immediately with the rest of the pasta.

Variation

25g (1oz) diced Chorizo or Kabanos sausage can be substituted for capers.

Gorgonzola Sauce

Serves 4: Sufficient for 450g (1lb) fettucini, spaghetti or penne

Florets of cooked broccoli (about 225g/8oz) are delicious added to this dish.

10g (½oz) butter
200g (7oz) Gorgonzola or Cashel Blue
200ml (7fl oz) cream or 125ml (4fl oz) cream
   and 75ml (3fl oz) milk
freshly ground pepper
freshly grated nutmeg

While the pasta is cooking, melt the butter in a little saucepan, add the crumbled cheese and cream or the cream and milk. Stir over a low heat until smooth and creamy, season with freshly ground pepper and a little nutmeg. Toss with the cooked pasta and serve immediately.

Tapenade Cream Sauce

Mix Tapenade (see page 590) with thick, rich cream – about equal quantities. Toss with freshly cooked pasta and chopped parsley.

Master Recipe
Alfredo Sauce

Serves 4 as a main course: sufficient for 225g (8oz) tagliatelle

We use this recipe as the basis for dozens of delicious creamy sauces – add whatever takes your fancy, depending on the season.

25g (1oz) butter
175g (6oz) best-quality cream
50g (2oz) freshly grated Parmesan (preferably
   Parmigiano Reggiano)
freshly ground pepper, sea salt and nutmeg

Melt the butter in a wide saucepan, add half the cream, simmer for a couple of minutes until the cream thickens slightly, then add the hot, drained tagliatelle, the rest of the cream and the cheese. Season with pepper, nutmeg and sea salt. Toss briefly to coat the pasta, taste and add a little more seasoning if necessary. Serve immediately on hot plates.

Variations
Alfredo with Smoked Salmon and Parsley

Omit the Parmesan from the Master Recipe. Add 50–110g (2–4oz) smoked salmon, cut into cubes, and 2 tablespoons of freshly chopped flat-leaf parsley.

Alfredo with Roasted Pumpkin

Follow the Master Recipe, adding 225g (8oz) of roasted pumpkin and a few toasted pine nuts with the hot, drained tagliatelle.

Alfredo with Red Pepper and Rocket

Follow the Master Recipe, adding strips of roasted red pepper and a few rocket leaves to the hot, drained tagliatelle.

Alfredo with Broad Beans or Peas

Follow the Master Recipe, adding shelled and cooked broad beans or peas to the hot, drained tagliatelle. Rocket is also good.

Master Recipe
Ragu Sauce (Bolognese Sauce)

Serves 6

I've been told that if you want to make your way to an Italian man's heart, it is essential to be able to make a good ragu. This is a wonderfully versatile sauce – the classic Bolognese sauce for Tagliatelle alla Bolognese, indispensable for lasagne and also delicious with polenta and gnocchi. I have been making Marcella Hazan's version for many years from her *Classic Italian Cookbook*. Marcella says it should be cooked for at least 3½ hours at the merest simmer and that 5 hours would be better, but I find you get a very good result with even 1½ hours' cooking on a heat diffuser mat. Ragu can be made ahead and freezes very well.

35g (1½oz) butter
3 tablespoons extra-virgin olive oil
2 tablespoons finely chopped onion
2 tablespoons finely chopped celery
2 tablespoons finely chopped carrot
350g (12oz) minced lean beef, preferably chuck
   or neck meat
salt
300ml (½ pint) dry white wine
125ml (4fl oz) milk
⅛ teaspoon freshly grated nutmeg
1 x 400g (14oz) tin Italian tomatoes, roughly
   chopped with their own juice

In Italy, they sometimes use an earthenware pot for making ragu, but I find that a heavy, enamelled cast-iron casserole with high sides works very well. Heat the butter with the oil and sauté the onion briefly over medium heat until just translucent. Add the celery and carrot and cook gently for 2 minutes. Next add the minced beef, crumbling it in the pot with a fork. Add salt to taste, stir and cook only until the meat has lost its raw red colour (Marcella says that if it browns it will lose its delicacy).

Add the wine, turn the heat up to medium-high and cook, stirring occasionally, until all the wine has evaporated, stirring every now and then. Lower the heat to medium, add in the milk and the nutmeg and cook until the milk has evaporated, stirring every now and then. Next add the chopped tomatoes and stir well. When the tomatoes have started to bubble, turn the heat down to the very lowest so that the sauce cooks at the gentlest simmer – just an occasional bubble. I use a heat diffuser mat for this.

Cook uncovered for a minimum of 1½ hours (better still 2 or even 3 depending on how concentrated you like it), stirring occasionally. If it reduces too much add a little water and continue to cook. When it is finally cooked, taste and correct the seasoning. Because of the length of time involved in cooking this, I feel it would be worthwhile to make at least twice the recipe.

Pasta with Chanterelles, Tapenade and Flat-leaf Parsley
Serves 4–6

225g (8oz) penne, conchiglie or farfalle
225–450g (8oz–1lb) chanterelles
25g (1oz) butter
125ml (4fl oz) cream
2–3 tablespoons Tapenade (see page 590)
2 tablespoons freshly chopped flat-leaf parsley
salt and freshly ground pepper

Cook the pasta until al dente. Meanwhile, quickly but gently wash the chanterelles under cold running water. Trim the base of the stalks and discard. Slice thickly.

Melt the butter in a sauté pan on a high heat. When it foams, add the chanterelles. Season with salt and pepper. Cook on a hight heat, letting the juices exude at first and then cook until the chanterelles re-absorb them. Add the cream and bubble for a minute or two. Stir in the Tapenade. Strain the pasta and drain well, put back into the saucepan and add the sauce. Sprinkle with parsley, toss gently, then put into a hot bowl and serve immediately.

Taglierini al Profumo di Limone (Fresh Noodles with Lemon)
Serves 6

This recipe was given to me by Mimmo Baldi, the chef-owner of Il Vescovino in Panzano. His restaurant, overlooking many of the best vineyards in Chianti, serves some of the most inspired food I have tasted in Italy – certainly worth a detour.

200g (7oz) fresh or dried taglierini
2 lemons, preferably unwaxed
150ml (5fl oz) very fresh cream
knob of butter
salt and freshly ground pepper

If the lemons are not unwaxed, scrub gently to remove any wax, then grate the lemon zest on the finest part of a stainless-steel grater, add it to the cream, cover the bowl and leave to infuse in the fridge for 5–6 hours.

Cook the pasta in plenty of boiling, salted water until al dente, drain well and put into a hot pasta dish, adding the cream and lemon mixture. Season with salt and freshly ground pepper, add a knob of butter and toss well. Serve instantly. This sauce should not be thick.

Master Recipe
Spaghetti with Mussels
Serves 6

450g (1lb) spaghetti
4 tablespoons olive oil
2.6kg (6lb) cleaned mussels (weight in shells)
3 large garlic cloves, finely chopped
1 red chilli, chopped, or 1 teaspoon chilli flakes
125ml (4fl oz) dry white wine
900g (2lb) very ripe tomatoes, peeled, seeded and chopped
2 tablespoons freshly chopped marjoram, oregano or basil leaves
salt, freshly ground pepper, sugar
2 tablespoons freshly chopped flat-leaf parsley
extra-virgin olive oil, for drizzling

Heat 2 tablespoons of the olive oil in a wide sauté pan, add the washed mussels. Cover and cook for a few minutes or until just opened. Scoop out the mussels onto a tray to cool. Strain the liquid and return to the pan to reduce by half. When the mussels are cool, remove from the shells (discard the beard and shells) and add the mussels to the concentrated liquid.

Heat the remaining 2 tablespoons of olive oil in another pan, add the garlic and chilli and cook for a couple of minutes. Add the wine and cook to reduce by half. Then add the tomatoes, season with salt, freshly ground pepper and a pinch of sugar. Add the marjoram and cook for 10–15 minutes or until the sauce is reduced. Add the mussels and the cooking liquid.

Cook the pasta until almost al dente. Drain. Add the pasta to the bubbling sauce, continue to cook for a couple of minutes. Serve on hot plates, sprinkled with chopped parsley and drizzled with oil.

Variations
Spaghetti with Mussels and Courgettes
Add 450g (1lb) sliced courgettes, softened in olive oil, to the Master Recipe.

Spaghetti with Squid
Substitute 4 medium squid (about 600–700g /1¼–1½lb, after cleaning) for the mussels. Slice the body and wings into 1cm (½in) strips, separate the tentacles. Be careful not to overcook the squid. Add to the tomato sauce just before serving. Serve as soon as the squid turns opaque.

TIP: Although freshly grated Parmesan is wonderful with every type of pasta, in Italy cheese is never served with shellfish pasta.

Spaghetti with Chilli, Shrimps and Parsley

Serves 4

225–450g (8oz–1lb) spaghetti
3 tablespoons extra-virgin olive oil
1 garlic clove
2 fleshy red peppers, diced
225g (8oz) cooked, peeled shrimps
red pepper flakes (optional)
175ml (6fl oz) cream
2–4 tablespoons freshly chopped
  flat-leaf parsley
salt and freshly ground pepper

Heat the olive oil in a sauté pan, add the garlic and peppers, season with salt and pepper and cover and sweat on a gentle heat until tender but not coloured.

Cook the pasta in plenty of boiling salted water. When it is almost al dente, add the shrimps to the pepper, toss for a minute or two to heat through and add the cream and pepper flakes, if using. Bubble up and taste for seasoning. As soon as the pasta is al dente, drain well, add to the pan and toss in the sauce over the heat until well coated.

Turn into a hot pasta dish, sprinkle with chopped parsley and serve immediately .

Variation

Chunks of tuna or salmon may be substituted for shrimps in this recipe, as can crispy bacon, Kabanos or Chorizo sausage.

Pasta with Sardines, Pine Nuts and Raisins

Serves 6

Purists would be very sniffy about my use of tinned rather than fresh sardines in this classic Sicilian dish. However, I make no apologies: it tastes delicious – and anyway, fresh sardines are thin on the ground in Ballycotton, not to speak of Cullohill! Dried, toasted breadcrumbs, incidentally, were once the poor man's Parmesan in Sicily.

350g (12oz) spaghetti or tagliatelle
2 tablespoons olive oil
110g (4oz) onion, chopped
50g (2oz) pine nuts, lightly toasted
50g (2oz) raisins, plumped up in hot water
2–4 tablespoons chopped fennel leaves
2 tins best-quality sardines in olive oil
6 tablespoons fine, dried breadcrumbs or
  3 tablespoons freshly grated Parmesan
  (preferably Parmigiano Reggiano)

Cook the pasta in plenty of boiling, salted water.

Heat the olive oil in a sauté pan, add the onion and cook on a gentle heat until soft and golden, add the toasted pine kernels, raisins and fennel and toss well. When the pasta is almost cooked, add the sardines to the sauce. Drain the pasta, drizzle with a little extra-virgin olive oil, add the sardine mixture and toss gently. Taste and correct the seasoning.

Turn into a hot serving dish and serve immediately sprinkled with fine, dried breadcrumbs or grated Parmesan.

Variation
Pasta with Mackerel
Substitute pan-grilled mackerel for the sardines in the recipe above.

Penne with Tomatoes, Spicy Sausage and Cream

Serves 6

This makes a tasty autumn or winter supper or lunch dish.

450g (1lb) penne
25g (1oz) butter
1 teaspoon finely chopped rosemary
700g (1½lb) fresh ripe tomatoes, peeled,
  de-seeded and cut into 1cm (½in) dice or
  1½ x 400g (14oz) tins tomatoes, chopped
175–225g (6–8oz) Chorizo or Kabanos sausage
pinch of crushed chillies
125–175ml (4–6fl oz) cream
2 tablespoons finely chopped flat-leaf parsley
4 tablespoons freshly grated Parmesan
  (preferably Parmigiano Reggiano)
extra flat-leaf parsley, snipped
salt, freshly ground pepper and sugar

Melt the butter in a large sauté pan, add the chopped rosemary and diced tomatoes.

LEFT: Spaghetti with Chilli, Shrimps and Parsley

Season with salt, freshly ground pepper and sugar. Cook until the tomatoes have just begun to soften into a sauce, which takes about 5 minutes.

Slice the sausage into 5mm (1/4in) rounds, add to the pan with the crushed chillies and season with salt (not too much as the sausage may be salty). Add the cream and chopped parsley, allow to bubble for 3–4 minutes, stirring frequently until the cream has reduced by about half. Remove the pan from the heat and set aside.

Cook the pasta until it is al dente, drain and toss with the sauce, add the grated Parmesan. Toss again, check the seasoning. and serve sprinkled with the parsley.

Cheat's Method of Cooking Dried Pasta

We developed this method of cooking pasta when we taught a survival course for students in bedsits or small apartments with limited cooking facilities. Italians are usually shocked but it works perfectly.

Bring a large saucepan of salted water to the boil, add the pasta, stir, put the lid on the saucepan and bring back to the boil. Cook for 2 minutes for spaghetti and tagliatelle, or 4 minutes for penne, small shells, etc. Keep the pan covered. Then turn off the heat and allow the pasta to continue to cook for the time indicated on the packet. Test, drain and proceed as usual.

Note: Pasta made by this method is good, and does not overcook as easily as pasta made by the conventional method.

Orzo Salad

Pasta, Bocconcini and Tomato Salad

Tuna, Bean and Pasta Salad

Tuscan Pepper and Pasta Salad
See page 206

Tagliatelle alla Bolognese
Serves 6

Italians wince when we talk about Spaghetti Bolognese. They say there's no such thing – that Bolognese sauce should not be served with spaghetti but with tagliatelle instead!

450g (1lb) Homemade Pasta (see page 148),
    cut into tagliatelle or noodles
Ragu recipe (see page 150)
25g (1oz) butter
35–50g (1½–2oz) freshly grated Parmesan
    (preferably Parmigiano Reggiano)

Heat the ragu, adding a little water if it is too thick. Cook the pasta until it is al dente and strain immediately. Put a little sauce in a warm serving dish, top with the hot tagliatelle or noodles and pour over the remainder of the sauce. Dot with butter, sprinkle with Parmesan, toss well, and serve immediately with extra Parmesan.

Spaghetti Carbonara
Serves 4

4.8 litres (8 pints) water
1–2 tablespoons salt
450g (1lb) spaghetti
4 tablespoons extra-virgin olive oil
200g (7oz) thick sliced smoked streaky bacon or
    pancetta, cut into strips 1cm (1/2in) wide
1/2 teaspoon freshly ground pepper
3–4 organic eggs, lightly beaten
2 tablespoons crème fraîche
2 tablespoons finely chopped parsley
90g (3½oz) freshly grated Parmesan
    (preferably Parmigiano Reggiano)
flat-leaf parsley, freshly chopped

Cook the pasta in plenty of boiling, salted water. Drain well.

Heat the olive oil in a large sauté pan over a medium heat. Add the smoky bacon or pancetta and cook, stirring frequently for 5–6 minutes, until coloured and slightly crispy. Add the black pepper and cook for

another minute. Add the spaghetti and toss with the smoky bacon or pancetta and oil until warmed through.

Combine the eggs, crème fraîche and parsley and add to the pan. Remove from the heat and stir constantly for 1 minute to allow the heat from the oil and spaghetti to cook the eggs. Stir in three-quarters of the freshly grated Parmesan.

Transfer the hot pasta to a large shallow bowl and sprinkle with the remaining Parmesan and freshly chopped parsley.

Marcella Hazan's Pappardelle with Chicken Liver Sauce
Serves 4

It was Marcella Hazan who first introduced me to classic Italian cooking and she has become a legend in her lifetime. This recipe is one of my favourites from her *Classic Italian Cookbook*.

275g (10oz) pappardelle or noodles
225g (8oz) fresh chicken livers
3 tablespoons extra-virgin olive oil
25g (1oz) butter
35g (1½oz) diced pancetta or prosciutto (I use
    unsmoked streaky bacon)
2 tablespoons chopped shallot or onion
1/4 garlic clove, peeled and finely chopped
1½ teaspoons fresh sage leaves
110g (4oz) minced lean beef
salt and 6–8 grinds of freshly ground pepper
1 teaspoon concentrated tomato purée dissolved
    in 4 tablespoons dry white vermouth

freshly grated Parmesan (preferably Parmigiano
    Reggiano)

Wash the chicken livers, trim off any fat or traces of green and cut them into 3 or 4 pieces. Dry thoroughly on kitchen paper.

Heat the oil and half the butter in a small saucepan, add the diced streaky bacon and fry gently until it begins to crisp, then remove to a plate. Add the rest of the butter and sauté the onions over a medium heat until translucent, add the garlic, stir 2 or 3 times, add back in the bacon and the sage leaves, then add the minced meat, crumbling it with a fork, and cook until it has lost its raw red colour.

Season with salt and freshly ground pepper, turn the heat up to medium high and add the chicken livers. Stir and cook until they have lost their raw colour, add the tomato purée and vermouth and cook for 9–10 minutes. Taste.

Meanwhile, cook the pasta or noodles in plenty of boiling salted water. The moment the pasta is drained, transfer to a warm dish, add the sauce, toss thoroughly and serve immediately with grated Parmesan, if desired. This sauce is also delicious served with Risotto (see page 128).

Aileen's Pappardelle with Roast Pumpkin, Pine Nuts and Rocket
Serves 4 as main course

A gorgeous Autumn pasta dish conjured up by Aileen Murphy, one of the bright young chefs in the Ballymaloe kitchen.

450g (1lb) fresh pappardelle
225g (8oz) pumpkin
3 tablespoons butter, plus a little melted butter
2 tablespoons pine nuts, lightly toasted
250ml (8fl oz) cream
75g (3oz) freshly grated Parmesan (preferably Parmigiano Reggiano)
grating of nutmeg
16–24 rocket leaves, depending on size
salt and freshly ground pepper

Preheat the oven to 180°C/350°F/gas 4. Season the wedge of pumpkin with salt and freshly ground pepper. Drizzle with melted butter, cover loosely with tin foil and roast for about 20–25 minutes or until the pumpkin is tender. Cut into 2.5cm (1in) cubes, and keep warm. Toast the pine kernels until golden either in the oven or under a grill.

Put the cream and 3 tablespoons of butter in a saucepan and simmer over a medium heat for less than 1 minute, by which time the butter and cream will have slightly thickened. Add most of the Parmesan, salt and freshly ground pepper and a grating of nutmeg. Remove from the heat and set aside until required.

Cook the pasta in plenty of boiling salted water. While the pasta is cooking, reheat the sauce gently and add the cubed pumpkin and toasted pine nuts.

Drain the pasta and toss it carefully in the sauce. Taste and correct the seasoning. Finally, add the rocket leaves and allow them to wilt slightly. Serve immediately, sprinkled with the remaining Parmesan and some fresh rocket leaves.

Pappardelle with Broad Beans and Rocket Leaves
Serves 4

450g (1lb) pappardelle
8 tablespoons Broad Bean Purée (see page 193)
225g (8oz) broad beans, shelled
4 tablespoons extra-virgin olive oil, approx.
fistful of rocket leaves
sea salt and lots of freshly ground pepper

First make the Broad Bean Purée and cook and keep warm the shelled broad beans.

Cook the pappardelle until al dente. Drain quickly. Add a little extra-virgin olive oil to the pan, add the broad beans, pasta and rocket leaves and toss well. Season with lots of pepper and some sea salt. Put 2 tablespoons of Broad Bean Purée onto each plate. Put a portion of pasta on top and serve immediately.

Ballycotton Seafood Lasagne
See page 263

Master Recipe
Lasagne Verde (Green Lasagne)
Serves 12

As a recipe, lasagne has all the virtues – it is mildly exotic, suitable for large numbers, not too expensive and it can be made ahead and reheated very successfully. It's best made with homemade Pasta Verde (see page 148) but can also be made with good-quality dried pasta. You can use the lasagne technique with all sorts of fillings (see variations).

In my experience, the 'no-cook' lasagne benefits from being blanched and refreshed first, but whichever type you use, be particularly careful not to overcook it. Mushy lasagne is all too common.

450g (1lb) Spinach Pasta or Egg Pasta
600ml (1 pint) Ragu (see page 150) or chosen filling
1.2 litres (2 pints) well-flavoured Béchamel Sauce (see page 580)
75–110g (3–4oz) freshly grated Parmesan (preferably Parmigiano Reggiano)
a few knobs of butter

2 medium 20 x 25cm (8 x 10in) lasagne dishes, or 1 large one, 25 x 30cm (10 x 12in)

First prepare the Ragu and Béchamel sauces and set aside.

If using homemade pasta, make it and allow to rest. Roll it out and cut into rectangular strips about 10 x 23cm (4 x 9in).

Preheat the oven to 230°C/450°F/gas 8.

Cook 3 or 4 strips of pasta at a time, stir and cook for just 30 seconds after the water comes back to the boil. Remove and put into a bowl of cold water, then drain on a tea towel.

Taste each sauce; they should be well seasoned. Grease the lasagne dishes, spread a little béchamel on the base, cover with a layer of barely overlapping sheets of pasta. Spread a little of the chosen filling

on the pasta, just enough to dot it with meat (ragu is a very rich and concentrated sauce). Spread a layer of béchamel over the ragu, sprinkle lightly with freshly grated Parmesan, then continue with another layer of pasta and so on up to within 2.5cm (1in) of the top of the dish (don't make more than 6 layers). Finish with a layer of pasta coated with béchamel, sprinkle with the remainder of the cheese and dot with a few little knobs of butter.*

Wipe the edges clean. Bake for 10–15 minutes or for 30 minutes if using dried, bought pasta – don't overcook. Allow to rest for about 10 minutes so that the layers compact slightly. Serve from the dish – it should be bubbly and golden on top.

*It may be prepared ahead to this point and kept in the fridge for several days or frozen for up to 3 months.

Variations

Lasagne with Ragu and Piperonata
We make a variation on the above by substituting Piperonata (see page 199) for Ragu in one or two of the layers.

Chicken Pilaf and Spinach Lasagne
Alternate Chicken Pilaf (see page 275) and cooked spinach in the layers.

Seafood Lasagne
Monkfish or Scallops Mornay (see page 252) make a delicious seafood lasagne.

Lasagne with Courgettes
Serves 6

If yellow courgettes are available, this looks pretty made with half green and half yellow.

Homemade pasta dough made with 2 organic eggs (see page 148) or bought lasagne, blanched
1.3kg (3lb) courgettes

2 tablespoons extra-virgin olive oil
25g (1oz) butter
1 teaspoon finely chopped garlic
1 tablespoon finely chopped flat-leaf parsley
2–3 tablespoons freshly chopped marjoram
1½ x Béchamel Sauce (see page 580)
⅛ teaspoon freshly grated nutmeg
75g (3oz) freshly grated Parmesan (preferably Parmigiano Reggiano)
salt and freshly ground pepper

Trim the courgettes and cut them in half lengthways. Lay the halves cut-side down, and slice crossways into 5mm (¼in) semi-circles. Put the olive oil, butter and garlic in a large sauté pan over a medium heat. When the garlic begins to change colour, add the parsley and marjoram and stir well.

Mix in the courgettes, season with salt and black pepper and continue cooking, stirring from time to time until tender. Remove the courgette and herb mixture using a slotted spoon and set it aside.

Make the Béchamel Sauce. Pour about four-fifths of it into a bowl, add the courgette mixture, freshly grated nutmeg and 50g (2oz) of the Parmesan and stir.

Preheat the oven to 200°C/400°F/gas 6.

Smear the bottom of the baking dish with half of the remaining Béchamel sauce and cover with a layer of pasta. Cover the pasta with a thin layer of the Béchamel and courgette sauce. Continue layering the

ABOVE: Lasagne with Courgettes

pasta and the sauce until there are at least 5 layers. Spread the remaining Béchamel and the courgette mixture over the final layer of pasta so that it is dotted with courgettes. Sprinkle the remaining Parmesan on top.

Place on the upper shelf of the oven. Bake for 15–20 minutes or until a light golden crust forms on top. Remove from the oven and allow to rest for 10 minutes before serving.

Vegetarian Lasagne
Serves 12

450g (1lb) fresh Homemade Lasagne Verde (see page 148) or 375g (13oz) dried plain or spinach lasagne
1.8 litres (3 pints) milk made into well-seasoned Béchamel Sauce (see page 580)
Piperonata (see page 199)
225g (8oz) freshly grated Parmesan (preferably Parmigiano Reggiano) or mature Cheddar, or a mixture
2 x Mushroom à la Crème (see page 201)
salt and freshly ground pepper

2 dishes, 20 x 25cm (8 x 10in), or 1 large rectangular one, 25 x 30cm (10 x 12in)

First taste each component, to ensure it is delicious and well-seasoned. Ensure the Béchamel is not too thick for good coverage.

Blanch the lasagne pasta. Spread a little Béchamel sauce on the base of each dish, cover with strips of pasta and a layer of Piperonata. Add another layer of pasta. Spread with Béchamel sauce and sprinkle with grated cheese. Add the Mushroom à la crème next, then more pasta, Béchamel sauce, cheese and so on, ending with a layer of sauce and a good sprinkling of Parmesan. (Ensure all the pasta is under the sauce.) Cook as above. Serve with a good green salad (see page 223).

Variations

You can make vegetarian lasagne with many different layers, including:

Tomato Fondue (see page 200)
Creamed or Buttered Spinach (see page 171)
Fried Slices of Aubergine, Roasted Red Pepper Strips and Pesto
Mushroom à la Crème (see page 201)

Ravioli

Makes about 36, serves 6 as a starter, 4 as a main course

Ravioli, those tiny stuffed pockets of pasta, may be made ahead and kept covered for up to 3 days in the fridge, depending on the filling, or may be frozen. Ensure you defrost thoroughly before cooking.

225g (8oz) fresh, Homemade Pasta dough
  (see page 148)
chosen filling
110g (4oz) freshly grated Parmesan (preferably Parmigiano Reggiano)

fluted pastry wheel or ravioli cutter

Make the pasta dough as for the Master Recipe. Cover with an inverted bowl and leave to relax for ½–1 hour, so that the dough loses its elasticity. Roll out until paper thin and divide in half. Brush one

piece of dough lightly with water and put teaspoons of filling at 4cm (1½in) intervals. Cover with the remaining sheet of dough, press the top piece down gently to seal each mound of filling, ensuring that all the air is released. Cut into squares with a fluted pastry wheel or stamp out squares with a ravioli cutter. If they are not being cooked the same day, transfer to floured, greaseproof paper and leave for 5–6 hours to dry, depending on the filling.

Poach the ravioli for 8–10 minutes, or until al dente and drain. Serve the grated Parmesan separately.

Fillings
Chicken and Fresh Herb
Mix 225g (8oz) cooked chicken or a mixture of chicken and cooked ham with 4 tablespoons thick Béchamel Sauce (see page 580), Tomato Sauce (see page 590) or cream and 2 tablespoons freshly chopped flat-leaf parsley or other herbs, e.g. tarragon or marjoram. Bind with a lightly beaten egg and season to taste. Basil would be good with Tomato Sauce.

Spinach and Ricotta Ravioli
Wash 225g (8oz) fresh spinach without stems and cook in a covered saucepan on a low heat until the leaves wilt. Drain the spinach thoroughly and squeeze it dry. Allow it to cool, then chop it and mix with 110g (4oz) fresh ricotta cheese, ½ teaspoon freshly grated nutmeg and salt and pepper.

Cheese Ravioli
Mix together 50g (2oz) freshly grated Parmesan, 110g (4oz) fresh ricotta, 1 lightly beaten egg or 2 egg yolks, 1 tablespoon chopped fresh basil or parsley and salt and freshly ground black pepper to taste.

Variations
Ravioli in Sage Butter
Serve with Sage Butter (see page 588).

LEFT: Spinach and Ricotta Ravioli

Baked Ravioli in Cream Sauce
Make a Béchamel Sauce (see page 580) with 700ml (1¼ pints) milk. Add 150ml (¼ pint) double cream, taste for seasoning and keep warm.

Cook the ravioli in plenty of boiling, salted water, drain well and arrange in layers in a shallow, buttered baking dish with the sauce and ending with a layer of sauce. Sprinkle with 50g (2oz) freshly grated Parmesan. Bake at 180°C/350°F/gas 4 for 20–25 minutes until bubbling and golden brown on top. Ensure it is thoroughly heated, especially if the ravioli has been frozen.

Ravioli in Tomato Sauce
Make a Tomato Sauce (see page 590). Cook the ravioli in plenty of boiling, salted water until al dente, drain and layer with the Tomato Sauce in a shallow, buttered baking dish, ending with a layer of sauce. Sprinkle with 50g (2oz) freshly grated Parmesan and cook as above.

Cappelletti and Tortellini
Serves 15–20 people: makes 200–300

Cappelletti and tortellini are little stuffed pasta, very much a labour of love to make but quite delicious. I was interested to discover that it is a tradition to serve cappelletti in broth on Christmas and New Year's Day in parts of Emilia Romagna. On Christmas Eve, the entire family, from children to grannies, become involved – everyone sits around the kitchen table and shapes the little dumplings. In fact, children are often best at this because their fingers are so small and nimble. By the time several hundred have been made everyone has had lots of fun and the skill has unwittingly been passed from one generation to the next. This recipe, one of my great favourites, is adapted from *The Classic Italian Cookbook* by Marcella Hazan.

Homemade Pasta dough (see page 148)

Filling
25g (1oz) butter
110g (4oz) pork fillet, cut into 1cm (½in) dice
175g (6oz) chicken breast, cut into 1cm (½in) dice
35g (1½oz) garlic salami
250g (9oz) ricotta or sieved cottage cheese
1 organic egg yolk
100g (3½oz) freshly grated Parmesan (preferably Parmigiano Reggiano)
½ teaspoon freshly grated nutmeg
salt and freshly ground pepper

First make the pasta dough, cover and allow to rest while you make the filling.

Melt the butter in a heavy saucepan, add the diced pork, season with salt and pepper and cook gently until nicely browned and cooked through. Remove to a plate, then add the diced chicken breasts to the saucepan, season again and cool – they won't take so long: about 2–3 minutes. Add to the pork. Allow to cook while you prepare the other ingredients.

Chop the garlic salami very finely and mix with the cottage cheese, Parmesan and egg yolk. Chop the cooked pork and chicken very finely (you can do this in a food processor if you are very careful, using the pulse button, but don't let it reach a purée).

Add to the other ingredients, grate in the nutmeg, season with salt and pepper, mix well, taste and add more seasoning if necessary. Cover and keep in the fridge until you are ready to make the cappelletti.

Divide the dough in half, cover one piece and roll the other piece into a very thin sheet. Repeat with the other half. Then cut the pasta into 4.5cm (1¾in) squares for cappelletti or 5cm (2in) rounds for tortellini. (You will probably have to trim the edges quite a bit to get even strips and squares, but keep the trimmings. Cut them into noodles and you can cook them another time.)

The dough for stuffed pasta should not be dried, so gather your helpers around you and set to work right away. Put the equivalent of ¼ teaspoon of filling in the centre of each square (do this with your fingers – it's so much faster). Then fold the square in half diagonally to make a triangle, press down firmly to seal the sides, pick up the triangle by one end of its long base, hold it between your thumb and index fingers with tip of the triangle pointing towards your knuckle, catch the other end of the base with your other hand and wrap it around your index finger, press the two ends firmly together to seal, then slide the cappelletti off your finger and push the little peak ends upwards so they resemble those wondrous bonnets worn by nuns years ago.

Tortellini are made in a similar way, starting with a circle of pasta rather than a square. Fill as for the capelletti, fold up the edges so the little parcel looks like a plump tummy button. Both cappelletti and tortellini can of course be made slightly larger, depending on how you plan to serve them.

At this point, I reckon it's worth the effort to pause and cook two or three in a little boiling salted water to check the flavour. Although it's great fun, this is not exactly fast food and nothing could be more disappointing than to discover that they could have done with a little more seasoning when it's too late.

As you make the cappelletti or tortellini, put them out on clean, dry tea towels. You can cook them right away, but otherwise turn them every couple of hours until they are uniformly dry (in the Restaurant Diana in Bologna, they have a wooden frame with a perforated zinc base especially for drying the cappelletti). When they are dry they will keep for up to a week.

Cappelletti or Tortellini with Butter and Cream
Serves 8

150 cappelletti or tortellini (see page 157)
35g (1¹/₂oz) butter
150ml (5fl oz) cream
45g (1³/₄oz) freshly grated Parmesan
  (preferably Parmigiano Reggiano)
extra Parmesan, for sprinkling

First cook the pasta in boiling salted water: drop in the cappelletti, stir gently and, as soon as the water comes back to the boil, time them: fresh cappelletti will take 4–5 minutes but dry cappelletti may take up to 20 minutes. Have a colander ready.

Meanwhile, melt the butter and cream in a wide sauté pan. As soon as the cappelletti are cooked, scoop up and drain, add to the butter and cream, put on a low heat and toss gently in the sauce. Add the grated Parmesan and continue to toss until they are evenly coated. Turn into a hot serving dish and serve immediately on warmed plates with extra Parmesan.

Cannelloni
Makes 8
Serves 4 as a starter, 2 as a main course

Cannelloni are rolls of pasta with a delectable filling – the same filling may be used for lasagne or indeed cappelletti or tortellini. Like ravioli, cannelloni may be prepared ahead and reheated, provided each component is cold when it is put together so keep them in the fridge. They can also be frozen and will keep for 2 months. You can also adapt the components of the recipe to make Lasagne. This is a recipe I enjoy very much, based on one from the *French Cookery School Book* by Anne Willan and Jane Grigson.

110g (4oz) Homemade Pasta dough (see page 148)

Sauce
35g (1¹/₂oz) butter
35g (1¹/₂oz) flour
425ml (³/₄ pint) milk
salt, freshly ground pepper and nutmeg
300ml (¹/₂ pint) cream
10g (¹/₂oz) Parmigiano Reggiano

Filling
175g (6oz) stewing veal or chicken, minced
175g (6oz) lean pork, minced
2 small organic egg yolks
good pinch ground mace or freshly grated
  nutmeg
salt and freshly ground pepper

Topping
25g (1oz) freshly grated Parmesan (preferably
  Parmigiano Reggiano)
10g (¹/₂oz) butter

25 x 20cm (10 x 8in) lasagne dish

To make the pasta dough, follow the Master Recipe and rest for 30 minutes. Roll it out as thinly as possible with a rolling pin. Cut it into 10cm (4in) squares, spread it on kitchen paper and leave to dry while you prepare the other ingredients. If making ahead, pack the squares between sheets of greaseproof paper or silicone paper and store in a plastic bag in the fridge for up to 4 days.

Next make the sauce: melt the butter in a heavy-bottomed saucepan, stir in the flour and cook for 2 minutes, pour in the milk, bring to the boil, whisking all the time, season with salt, pepper and grated nutmeg and cook for 2 minutes. Add enough cream to make a fairly thick sauce and remove from the heat.

For the filling: mix the minced veal or chicken and pork together, add the egg yolks and 300ml (¹/₂ pint) of the sauce, season well with salt, freshly ground pepper and ground mace or nutmeg.

Put 4 litres (7 pints) of water in a large saucepan and bring to the boil. Add 2 tablespoons of salt. Cook the cannelloni squares for 1–2 minutes if very fresh or for longer if dried, until al dente. Drain and refresh in a bowl of cold water.

Preheat the oven to 180°C/350F°/gas 4.

To assemble: butter the lasagne dish lightly, drain the squares on kitchen paper and fill each one with 1–2 tablespoons of the filling, roll them up and place side by side in the dish. Reheat the sauce, stir in the remaining cream, stir in the freshly grated Parmesan and taste for seasoning. Spoon the sauce over the cannelloni – it should cover them completely. Top with Parmesan, dot with butter and bake for 40–45 minutes. Ten minutes before the end of cooking, remove the lid so that the cheese browns.

Master Recipe
Macaroni Cheese
Serves 6

Macaroni cheese is one of my children's favourite supper dishes. We use our local cheddar, which is made at Mitchelstown and matured, at Imokilly Creamery. We also often add cubes of cooked bacon or ham to the sauce.

3.6 litres (6 pints) water
2 teaspoons salt
225g (8oz) macaroni
50g (2oz) butter
50g (2oz) white flour, preferably unbleached
1 litre (1³/4 pints) boiling milk
3 teaspoons Dijon mustard
150g (5oz) mature Cheddar, grated
1 tablespoon freshly chopped parsley (optional)
salt and freshly ground pepper

1.2 litre (2 pint) capacity pie dish

Bring a large pot of water to the boil, add the salt. Sprinkle in the macaroni and stir to ensure it doesn't stick together. Cook for 10–15 minutes, until just soft, and drain well.

Meanwhile melt the butter, add in the flour and cook on a medium heat, stirring occasionally for 1–2 minutes. Remove from the heat and gradually whisk in the milk. Bring back to the boil, stirring all the time. Add the mustard, cheese and parsley if using, and season with salt and freshly ground pepper to taste. Add the cooked macaroni, bring back to the boil, taste, correct the seasoning and serve immediately.

Macaroni cheese reheats very successfully provided the pasta is not overcooked in the first place. It is very good served with cold meat, particularly ham.

> TIP: Macaroni soaks up an enormous amount of sauce. Add more sauce if making ahead to reheat later.

Variations
Macaroni Cheese with Smoked Salmon
Add 110g (4oz) smoked salmon pieces to the macaroni cheese.

Macaroni Cheese with Mushrooms and Courgettes
Add 225g (8oz) sliced sautéed mushrooms, and 225g (8oz) sliced courgettes cooked in olive oil with a little garlic, and marjoram or basil to the macaroni cheese. Toss gently, turn into a hot serving dish and scatter with grated cheese – delish.

Spicy Korean Beef and Tofu with Crispy Noodles
Serves 6

When Nina Simonds came to teach at the school in the summer of 1998, she charmed us all with her delicious recipes. This was one of our favourites, which I have adapted slightly for our ingredients.

450g (1lb) firm tofu
450g (1lb) freshly minced beef
3 tablespoons finely chopped spring onions, white parts only
1 tablespoon freshly grated ginger
2–3 garlic cloves, crushed
1¹/2 teaspoons toasted sesame oil
50g (2oz) thin rice noodles
2 tablespoons sunflower oil

vegetable oil for deep-frying

Sauce
scant 4 tablespoons Chinese ground bean sauce or sweet bean paste
3 tablespoons sugar
scant 2 tablespoons toasted sesame oil
1¹/2 teaspoon hot chilli paste

leaves of 1 Butterhead lettuce, washed, gently dried and arranged in a bowl on the table
fresh coriander leaves

Put the tofu into a dish, cover with a plate and weight it gently for about 30 minutes. Put the minced beef in a bowl, add the spring onions, ginger, garlic and sesame oil.

Heat the oil in a deep-fryer or wok. Put in a few rice noodles at a time – they puff up instantly. Remove immediately and drain on kitchen paper. Arrange on 6 serving plates.

Cut the pressed tofu into 5mm (¼in) cubes.

Mix all the ingredients for the sauce together. Heat the sunflower oil in a wok or pan until very hot, add the beef and stir-fry until it changes colour, tip into a sieve over a bowl to drain.

Wipe out the wok or pan. Heat the wok again, add the sauce mixture. Stir until it thickens, add the beef and tofu cubes and toss gently to coat with the sauce. Spoon over the noodles.

Garnish with some fresh coriander leaves. Each diner puts some of the noodles and sauce into a lettuce leaf, rolls it up and enjoys.

Indian Spicy Noodles with Tomato

Serves 4–6

A filling, vegetarian noodle dish where you wouldn't miss the meat! Whip up this addictive dish from a packet of those crispy noodles in your store cupboard.

110g (4oz) egg noodles, cooked
3 tablespoons sunflower oil
½ teaspoon cumin seeds
5 garlic cloves, finely chopped
1 green chilli, finely chopped
1 teaspoon freshly grated ginger
good pinch of ground asafoetida (optional)
¼ teaspoon ground turmeric
¼–½ teaspoon cayenne pepper
110g (4oz) onion, finely chopped
6 ripe tomatoes, peeled and coarsely chopped
salt, freshly ground pepper and sugar
3 tablespoons finely choppped coriander leaves

Cook the noodles according to the instructions on the packet. Drain and reserve.

Heat the oil in a wok or large, preferably non-stick, frying pan over a medium-high heat.

When hot, add the cumin seeds, stir for a few seconds. Add the garlic, chilli and ginger. Stir and fry for 2–3 minutes until the garlic begins to colour. Add the asafoetida, if using, turmeric and cayenne pepper. Stir very quickly and then add the onion and cook for 3–4 minutes on a medium heat. Then toss in the chopped tomatoes, season with salt, pepper and sugar and cook for 5–6 minutes, stirring frequently. Add the coriander, taste and correct the seasoning.

Simmer for 2–3 minutes or until the tomatoes are tender. Stir the noodles into the tomato mixture. Bubble for a minute or two to heat the noodles through. Serve immediately with lots of fresh coriander.

Below: Indian Spicy Noodles with Tomato

Rosemary Kearney's Chicken, Noodle and Coconut Laksa

Serves 6–8

Rosemary taught us this on her one-day course for coeliacs – it's now one of our favourite soups.

175g (6oz) fine rice noodles
2 chicken breasts
2 red chillies, chopped, with seeds
4 garlic cloves, finely chopped
2.5cm (1in) piece of ginger, peeled and finely chopped
175g (6oz) fresh coriander, leaves and stalks, coarsely chopped
juice of 1–2 limes
50ml (2fl oz) toasted sesame oil
2 x 400ml (14fl oz) tins coconut milk
generous 700ml (1¼ pints) homemade Chicken Stock (see page 36)
1 tablespoon fish sauce (nam pla)
salt and freshly ground pepper

Garnish
8 spring onions, peeled, trimmed and finely sliced at an angle
coriander leaves

Pour boiling water over the bowl of rice noodles and allow to soak until soft. Drain and cut into 5cm (2in) lengths. Thinly slice the chicken breasts at an angle and set aside. Put the chilli, garlic, ginger, coriander and the juice of 1 lime into a food processor and pulse to a coarse paste. Heat the sesame oil in a large saucepan and fry the chilli paste for 3 minutes. Add the coconut milk and chicken stock.

Bring to the boil, reduce the heat and simmer for 5 minutes. Add the thinly sliced chicken and simmer for a further 5 minutes or until the chicken is cooked through. Add the fish sauce, taste, and add more lime juice, salt and pepper if necessary.

Divide the noodles into serving bowls, ladle in the hot soup and garnish with spring onion and coriander leaves.

Asian Chicken and Noodle Salad

Serves 6–8

Dressing
1 tablespoon peanut butter
1 garlic clove, crushed
¼ teaspoon Chinese or English mustard
50ml (2fl oz) soy sauce
½ teaspoon sugar
50ml (2fl oz) rice wine vinegar
2 tablespoons Chilli Pepper Oil (see page 227)
50ml (2fl oz) sesame oil

700ml (¼ pint) homemade Chicken Stock
    (see page 36)
1 teaspoon salt
900g (2lb) chicken breasts
225g (8oz) Chinese noodles or fettuccini, cooked
1 tablespoon toasted sesame seeds
1 cucumber
2–3 celery stalks
2 spring onions
2 tablespoons freshly chopped coriander leaves

Mix all the dressing ingredients except the sesame oil in a bowl, then gradually whisk in the oil. Bring the chicken stock to the boil, add the salt and chicken breasts, cover and simmer gently for 10–12 minutes. Alternatively, simmer for 4 minutes, turn off the heat, cover and allow to finish cooking in the hot stock for 10–12 minutes.

Drain, allow to cool for a few minutes. Shred into long strips along the grain of the chicken breast, put into a large bowl. Add the cooked noodles.

Toast the sesame seeds in a dry pan over a medium heat for 2–3 minutes, stirring regularly, then allow to cool on a plate.

Halve the cucumber, remove the seeds and cut into 4cm (1½in) julienne or 5mm (¼in) slices cut at an angle, then add to the bowl. Cut the celery into 5mm (¼in) dice. Slice the spring onions at an angle and add these to the bowl.

Toss in the dressing. Taste and correct the seasoning. Serve sprinkled with toasted sesame seeds and fresh coriander leaves.

Phad Thai Mae Sawad (Fried Noodles Thai-style)

Serves 4–6

Wasinee Beech was born and brought up in Thailand. She and her family moved to Clonakilty in West Cork seven years ago. She teaches our students many wonderful Thai recipes. This is one of them.

2 tablespoons vegetable oil
200g (7oz) raw prawns, shelled and de-veined
10 shallots, thinly sliced
½–1 teaspoon freshly roasted ground chilli
25g (1oz) dried shrimps
1 tablespoon chopped dry radish (optional)
4 tablespoons palm sugar
2 tablespoons lemon juice
2 tablespoons tamarind juice
2–3 tablespoons fish sauce (nam pla),
    depending on how salty the dry shrimps are
250g (9oz) Thai rice noodles, soaked until soft
    (approx. 20 minutes) then drained
1–2 organic eggs (optional)
225g (8oz) beansprouts
4 spring onions or 5 Chinese chives, cut into
    2.5cm (1in) lengths
3–4 tablespoons freshly crushed roasted
    peanuts

Heat the oil in a wok. Drop in the prawns and quickly stir-fry. Remove with a slotted spoon and set aside. Add the shallots and stir-fry until they are golden brown. Add the chilli and stir quickly. Stirring all the time, add the dry prawns, radish, palm sugar, lemon juice, tamarind juice and fish sauce. Add the noodles and stir in well. Add the prawns and mix really well but being careful not to break up the noodles. Add the eggs, if using, and toss around gently. Finally add the beansprouts and spring onions. Sprinkle with peanuts and serve immediately.

Cellophane Noodle Salad with Chicken and Shrimps

See page 210

Crispy Noodle Pancake

Serves 4

225g (8oz) Chinese noodles or fettuccini
3 tablespoons extra-virgin olive oil, or 1½
    tablespoons chilli oil plus 1½ tablespoons
    olive oil, or 2 tablespoons soy sauce and
    1 tablespoon sesame oil or sunflower oil
2 tablespoons sunflower oil, for frying

Drop the noodles into a large pan of boiling, salted water and stir. Cook for 3–4 minutes or until al dente, then drain. Transfer to a bowl. Sprinkle with olive oil or chilli oil or a mixture of soy sauce and sesame oil.

Heat the 2 tablespoons of sunflower oil in a frying pan, add the noodles, flatten into a 'cake' 1cm (½in) thick. Cook for 4–5 minutes on one side or until crisp and golden. Flip over onto a plate and slide back into the pan to cook the other side. Drain on kitchen paper, and serve with a spicy sauce such as Tomato Fondue with Chilli (see page 200).

Note: The crispy noodle pancake can be reheated in a moderate oven.

vegetables

vegetables

The Ballymaloe Cookery School is in the midst of a 100-acre farm in East Cork, Ireland. Both the farm and gardens have organic certification with the Irish Organic Trust. We still have an acre of greenhouses – a legacy of days when we were horticulturalists, with 5 acres of tomatoes and cucumbers and 65 acres of apples. Originally the greenhouses were heated with oil but the oil crisis in the early 1970s, which resulted in 25 per cent inflation, finished all that.

Now, even though the greenhouses are no longer heated, we grow a wide range of crops year round. The extra protection of the glass makes it possible to grow early potatoes and carrots, a wonderful variety of kales, early beetroot, Swiss chard and leeks. Later in the year, we have 20 or 30 different types of tomatoes (including many heirloom varieties), cucumber, sweetcorn, beans, calabrese, spinach, tomatillas, aubergine, peppers, chillies, a variety of lettuces and salad leaves, coriander, rocket and a selection of tender herbs.

The potager in the old haggard, close to the school, is designed to be decorative as well as functional. The vegetables are planted in patterns to provide a contrast of texture, colour and flavour and are carefully rotated each year. The old herringbone brick paths bisect the garden and the vegetables are interplanted with edible flowers, which encourage beneficial insects into the garden to help with pollination.

The edible flowers – nasturtiums, marigolds, violas and even batchelor's buttons, are used in salads with chive flowers, pea shoots, purslane, mustard greens and oriental greens like mizuna and mibuna. We allow the seed heads of poppies and nigella to dry so we can collect the seeds to scatter over breads and biscuits.

When the broad beans reach the height of a couple of feet we pinch out the tops (this discourages black fly) and we have the extra bonus of being able to use the tender shoots in salads and for making a delicious soup.

Even though the vegetable garden is very small, probably less than half an acre, we grow a wide range of vegetables with many old and unusual varieties. We've got a particularly good strain of globe artichokes which came from Myrtle Allen's family garden in Rushbrooke, cut-and-come kale (*Brassica oleracea*) from the gardens at Glin Castle, Jerusalem artichokes from the walled garden at Ballymaloe and Chinese artichokes, a present from a professor at University College Cork.

Students on our 12-week course meet the gardeners at 8am on a rota basis. They go out with them to bring in the vegetables and herbs for the morning cooking. On short courses, it's a matter of choice. Some students understandably choose to roll over and sleep for another hour, while others find that the experience enhances their overall enjoyment of the course.

The gardeners, Eileen, Haulie and Kay, are deeply knowledgeable and enormously generous with their information so students who are interested in growing their own produce can get valuable tips and practical advice. This experience is an intrinsic part of the 12-week course at the Ballymaloe Cookery School. It gives the student a unique understanding of how food is produced and a respect for food and those who produce it, which in my opinion is vital for all good cooks and chefs. It also establishes a dialogue and understanding between the farmer and the chef, which is so often lacking. Considering that we are all interdependent it is extraordinary how rare this logical situation is.

What we don't produce ourselves we buy from a network of local farmers, particularly our neighbouring farm owned by the Walsh family, who grow a wide range of vegetables and fruit. Hopefully when the students leave, their experience at the school will encourage them to establish a network of small food producers to provide them with fresh, naturally produced, seasonal ingredients for their own businesses.

Buying Vegetables – Buy Local

Not surprisingly, my advice is to **buy fresh, local food, in season whenever possible**. For me they must be organic as there is just no point in ingesting heaps of residues from chemical sprays. However, faced with a decision of whether to buy organic carrots from abroad or local food in season grown with the minimum of sprays, I would always opt for the latter. Jet-lagged vegetables (even if they are organic) that may be several weeks old and have travelled several thousand miles before getting to us have practically no nutritional value and even less taste.

Always choose the freshest and liveliest-looking vegetables, and enquire about the source of the produce and the name of the producer. The demand is growing for information to be made available to the consumer about the level of pesticides and herbicides in fresh produce, and your shop or supermarket may well highlight local produce. With all this information you can then make an informed choice as to what to buy.

One sure-fire way of knowing exactly where your vegetables have come from, and how they were grown, is by shopping at your local **farmers' market**. There the producers will be able to answer all of your questions and will also be glad to have your feedback on their produce.

There are also many **box schemes** running nowadays – companies who deliver fresh, local and seasonal fruit and vegetables to your door. This is a great way to support ethical farming and is also very convenient if you have a busy lifestyle.

Vegetables – an Alternative to Meat

Vegetables add flavour, interest and colour to all meat and fish dishes, but whereas once they were viewed as purely optional side dishes, they are now celebrated in their own right as an inexpensive alternative to meat.

The variety of vegetables continues to grow as more and more people adopt a vegetarian or semi-vegetarian diet. Don't just stick to what you know – experiment with less-known varieties and the many 'exotic' vegetables, such as okra, bok choi, white cucumbers and sweet chillies, that are now available over here. Note the varieties you buy and compare flavours when you cook. Best of all, start to grow your own!

Health Benefits

Vegetables are high in vitamins, minerals, and fibre, and have a low fat and sodium content. There are strong links between increased consumption of fruit and vegetables and the decreased risk of chronic diseases such as heart disease, some types of cancer (such as cancer of the stomach, oesophagus and lung) and strokes – all of which are diet-related due to diets high in fat and too low in fruit and vegetables.

Numerous studies have shown how 'lesser' illnesses (like obesity) also benefit from a vegetable-enriched diet. As a result of these studies, there have been campaigns to raise awareness of the benefits of eating fruit and vegetables, and to encourage people to eat at least five servings a day. (The National Cancer Institute in America claim that people who eat five portions of fruit and vegetables a day have half the risk of developing cancer as those who eat only one or two servings.)

Many vegetables are delicious raw and also retain more of their nutritional value uncooked. Also, as a rule of thumb, the darker the colour of the vegetable the more nutritious it is (particularly in terms of beta-carotene which boosts immunity and is said to lower the risk of cancer and heart disease). Seek out veggies like beetroot, kale and spinach, carrots, sweet potatoes and sweet red pepper .

How to Cook Vegetables

There are six basic ways to cook vegetables:

1. In a saucepan full of salted water and no lid (e.g. french beans, broccoli and sugar peas). Use 3 teaspoons of salt for every 1.2 litres (2 pints) of water.

2. In a little water in a covered saucepan (e.g. cauliflower, carrots, Swiss chard and celery).

3. In a heavy casserole using no water except the drops that adhere after the vegetables have been washed (e.g. cucumber, Jerusalem artichokes, white turnips and leeks).

4. Steamed over well-salted water in a bamboo, metal or pottery steamer.

5. Roasted (e.g. carrots, parsnips, onions, potatoes, celeriac...)

6. Stir-fried quickly over a high heat.

Master Recipe
Green Broccoli, Calabrese or Romanesco

Serves 4

The secret of real flavour in broccoli, as in many other green vegetables, is not just freshness; it needs to be cooked in well-salted water. If you grow your own broccoli, cut out the central head but leave the plant intact and very soon you'll have lots of smaller florets. Romanesco is a variety of calabrese and is in season from summer to autumn.

450g (1lb) calabrese or romanesco
600ml (1 pint) water
1½ teaspoons salt
25–35g (1–1½oz) butter
lots of freshly ground pepper

Peel the stems of calabrese or romanesco with a knife or potato peeler to remove the tough outer skin. Cut the stalk close to the head and then cut into ½–1cm (¼–½in) pieces. If the heads are large divide the florets into small clusters.

Add the salt to the water and bring it to a fast rolling boil. First add the stalks and then the florets, and cook, uncovered, at a rolling boil for 5–6 minutes. Drain off the water while the broccoli still has a bite. * Melt 25g (1oz) butter in a saucepan until it foams and toss the broccoli in it gently. Taste, season with lots of freshly ground black pepper and serve immediately.

* Broccoli can be blanched and refreshed earlier in the day and reheated in a pan of boiling salted water just before serving.

Variations
Broccoli or Calabrese with Sugar Snaps and French Beans
Follow the Master Recipe. Cook the vegetables in separate pans. Sugar snaps and French beans are cooked in exactly the same way. They are delicious mixed together – toss them all in a little melted butter, taste and correct seasoning before serving.

Broccoli or Calabrese with Oyster Sauce
Follow the Master Recipe omitting the butter, cooking the calabrese until al dente. Douse with oyster sauce to taste and serve immediately.

Broccoli or Calabrese with Chilli and Garlic
Follow the Master Recipe, cooking the broccoli until al dente. Heat 3 tablespoons olive oil in a saucepan, add 1 or 2 chopped garlic cloves and 1 chopped and de-seeded chilli. Allow to sizzle for 1–2 minutes, pour over the hot broccoli and toss gently. Serve immediately.

Broccoli or Calabrese with Butter and Lemon
Follow the Master Recipe, cooking the broccoli until al dente. If you like lemon, add the juice of ½ a lemon to the foaming butter.

Sprouting Broccoli (green, purple or white)
A superb late winter vegetable. Follow the Master Recipe. No need to peel the stalks.

Master Recipe
Buttered Cabbage

Serves 4

Irish people usually boil cabbage for ages, so when I cooked it this way on my TV programme some years ago it caused a sensation. This method takes only a few minutes to cook but first the cabbage must be carefully sliced into fine shreds. It should be served the moment it is cooked.

450g (1lb) fresh Savoy cabbage
25–50g (1–2oz) butter
salt and freshly ground pepper
a knob of butter

Remove the tough outer leaves from the cabbage. Cut into quarters, remove the core, then slice into fine shreds across the grain. Put 2–3 tablespoons of water into a wide saucepan with the butter and a pinch of salt. Bring to the boil, add the cabbage and toss constantly over a high heat, then cover for a few minutes. Take care it doesn't boil dry. Toss again and add some more salt, freshly ground pepper and a knob of butter. Serve immediately.

Variation
Emily's Cabbage with Thyme Leaves
Add 3–4 teaspoons thyme leaves to the above just before serving.

Buttered Cabbage with Caraway Seeds
Add ½–1 tablespoon lightly crushed caraway seeds and 1–2 tablespoons freshly chopped parsley to the cabbage, toss constantly as above.

Creamed Savoy Cabbage

Serves 4

1 head Savoy cabbage
225ml (8fl oz) water or bacon water
50g (2oz) butter
350ml (12fl oz) cream
salt and freshly ground pepper

Remove the tough outer leaves from the cabbage. Cut into quarters, remove the core, then slice into fine shreds across the grain.

Bring the water to the boil in a wide saucepan, add the cabbage and season it well. Cover with a greaseproof paper lid and the saucepan lid and cook briskly until the cabbage is just tender. Drain off any excess water.

Add the cream to the cabbage and bring back to the boil to allow the cream to thicken slightly.

Now remove from the pot and purée to a coarse consistency. Check the seasoning and add the butter if you think it needs it. Reheat in a non-stick pan.

Chinese Seaweed (Deep-fried Cabbage)

Surprisingly, the 'crispy dried seaweed' served in many Chinese restaurants is no such thing – merely deep-fried cabbage shreds. This original way of cooking cabbage tastes absolutely delicious and once you start to eat it, just like peanuts or popcorn, it is quite addictive.

Savoy cabbage or spring green cabbage
salt
sugar

Remove the stalks from the outer leaves. Roll the dry leaves into a cigar shape and slice with a very sharp knife into the finest possible shreds.

Heat the oil in a deep-fryer to 180°C/350°F. Toss in some of the cabbage and cook for a few seconds. As soon as it starts to crisp, remove and drain on kitchen paper.

Sprinkle with salt and sugar, toss and serve cold.

Darina's Favourite Red Cabbage with Apples

Serves 6–8

This recipe, the simplest and best I've tasted, was given to us by a German neighbour, Elsa Schiller. She explained how she would first buy a red cabbage at a stall in their local farmers' market and then move onto another stall to buy the weight of the cabbage in cooking apples. Red cabbage is particularly good with duck, goose, venison or pork. Add a few plump sultanas occasionally to ring the changes.

450g (1lb) red cabbage
about 1 tablespoon wine vinegar
125ml (4fl oz) water
1 level teaspoon salt
about 2 heaped tablespoons sugar
450g (1lb) Bramley Seedling cooking apples

Remove any damaged outer leaves from the cabbage. Cut into quarters, remove the core and slice the cabbage finely across the grain. Put the wine vinegar, water, salt and sugar into a cast-iron casserole or stainless-steel saucepan. Add the cabbage and bring it to the boil.

Meanwhile, peel and core the apples and cut into quarters (no smaller). Lay them on top of the cabbage, cover and continue to cook gently until the cabbage is tender, 30–50 minutes. Do not overcook or the colour and flavour will be ruined. Taste for seasoning and add more sugar if necessary. Serve in a warm serving dish.

Note: Some varieties of red cabbage are quite tough and don't seem to soften much, even with prolonged cooking. Our favourite variety, Red Drummond, gives best results.

Master Recipe
Cauliflower Cheese

Serves 6–8

1 medium cauliflower with green leaves
salt

Mornay Sauce
600ml (1 pint) milk with a dash of cream
1 onion, sliced
3–4 slices of carrot
6 peppercorns
sprigs of thyme or parsley
Roux (see page 580)
150g (5oz) Cheddar or a mixture of Gruyère,
*   Parmesan and Cheddar, grated*
½ teaspoon English powder mustard
salt and freshly ground pepper

Garnish
parsley, chopped

Preheat the oven to 230°C/450°F/gas 8.

Prepare and cook the cauliflower (see page 169). Meanwhile make the Mornay Sauce. Put the cold milk into a saucepan with the onion, carrot, peppercorns and herb. Bring to the boil, simmer for 3–4 minutes, remove from the heat and leave to infuse for 10 minutes.

Strain out the vegetables, bring the milk back to the boil and thicken with roux to a light coating consistency. Add most of the cheese, reserving enough to sprinkle over the dish, and a little mustard. Season, taste and correct the seasoning if necessary. Spoon the sauce over the cauliflower and sprinkle with the remaining cheese. The dish may be prepared ahead to this point.

Put into the oven or under the grill to brown. If allowed to get completely cold, it will take 20–25 minutes in the oven. Serve sprinkled with chopped parsley.

Variation
Cauliflower Cheese Soup
Follow the Master Recipe but, instead of browning it, liquidise the lot with any leftover cauliflower cooking water and about 850ml (1½ pints) light chicken stock to make a nice consistency. Taste and correct the seasoning. Serve with croûtons, diced Cheddar and parsley.

Leeks au Gratin
Leeks are also delicious served in this way. For a more substantial meal wrap each cooked leek in a slice of cooked ham before coating them with the sauce.

Chicory au Gratin
Substitute cooked chicory (see page 173) for leeks in the above recipe.

TIP: Seek out organic vegetables in your local area. Why not buy a few packets of seeds and grow your own?

To Cook Cauliflower

Remove the outer leaves and wash both the cauliflower and the leaves well. Put no more than 2.5cm (1in) of water in a saucepan just large enough to take the cauliflower; add a little salt. Chop the leaves into small pieces and cut the cauliflower into quarters. Place the cauliflower on top of the green leaves in the saucepan, cover and simmer until the cauliflower is cooked, about 15 minutes. Test by piercing the stalk with a knife; there should be just a little resistance. Remove the cauliflower and the leaves to an ovenproof serving dish, depending on how it is being served.

Crunchy Cauliflower with Garlic Butter

Serves 4–6

1 medium cauliflower
50g (2oz) Garlic Butter (see page 588)
45g (1³/₄oz) butter
2 tablespoons olive oil
75g (3oz) white breadcrumbs

Prepare and cook the cauliflower as above. Melt the garlic butter in a frying pan and toss the cauliflower florets and chopped stalks in it. Put in a hot serving dish. Melt the butter and oil in the frying pan, toss in the crumbs and cook, tossing all the time, until golden. Sprinkle over the cauliflower and serve immediately.

Cauliflower Purée

Cook the cauliflower florets in the basic way. They should be quite soft. Drain and purée in a food processor with a good lump of butter and a generous dash of cream. Season well with salt, freshly ground pepper and a little mace or freshly ground nutmeg. Delicious as a sauce with steak or venison.

Cauliflower with Anchovy and Chilli

Serves 4–6

1 medium cauliflower
110g (4oz) onion, finely chopped
3 tablespoons olive oil
¹/₂–1 red chilli, de-seeded and finely chopped
4 anchovy fillets, chopped
2 tablespoons freshly chopped parsley
3 teaspoons red wine vinegar

Cook the cauliflower. Meanwhile, sweat the onion in the olive oil over a gentle heat for a few minutes. Add the chilli and continue to cook until the onion is soft but not coloured. Add the anchovies, parsley and vinegar, stir to heat through, pour over the hot cauliflower and serve immediately.

Roast Cauliflower

Serves 6–8

Seems rather peculiar at first but when cauliflower florets are blasted in a very hot oven it concentrates their natural sweetness and the flavour is addictive!

1 fresh cauliflower cut or divided into 4cm (1¹/₂ in) florets
4 tablespoons extra-virgin olive oil
sea salt

Preheat the oven to 230°C/450°F/gas 8. Put the florets into a deep bowl and sprinkle with olive oil and sea salt. Spread in a single layer on a baking sheet to roast. Cook for 15–20 minutes, tossing occasionally, until golden and tender.

Italian Cauliflower Fritters

Serves 6–8

An easy way to perk up cauliflower which, let's face it, can be a pretty tasteless vegetable without some help from a perky cheese sauce or some spices.

1 medium cauliflower (in florets, steamed)
well-seasoned flour
2 eggs, beaten
50g (2oz) Parmesan (preferably Parmigano Reggiano), freshly grated
olive oil, for deep-frying

Dip the steamed cauliflower florets into the seasoned flour one by one. Next dip in beaten egg and then in Parmesan. Fry the cauliflower florets in hot oil in a deep-fryer at 200°C/400°F until golden and crisp. Serve immediately.

Sicilian Green Cauliflower with Black Olives

Serves 8

Anna Tasca from Regaleali in Sicily gave me this recipe. We used Romanesco but in Sicily they use the wonderful green cauliflowers in season in the autumn.

2 heads green cauliflower or calabrese, about 900g (2lb)
110g (4oz) onion, finely chopped
125ml (4fl oz) extra-virgin olive oil
50g (2oz) black olives, pitted and sliced
salt and freshly ground pepper
25g (1oz) Parmesan (preferably Parmigano Reggiano)or pecorino, freshly grated
225g (8oz) mozzarella, grated (optional)

Preheat the oven to 200°C/400°F/gas 6. Cut the cauliflower or calabrese into 5cm (2in) florets and boil in well-salted water until al dente, about 5 minutes. Drain. Meanwhile, sauté the onion in half the olive oil until tender and slightly golden, about 3–4 minutes. Remove from the heat and add the olives. Set aside.

Spread out the cauliflower or calabrese in a large, flat dish and mix in the onion-olive mixture. Add the remaining olive oil, salt and pepper to taste, (remembering that the Parmesan may be salty). Toss the cauliflower or calabrese with about half of the Parmesan and top with the mozzarella if desired. Sprinkle the top with the remaining Parmesan and bake for 20–30 minutes or until the top is nice and golden. Serve warm or at room temperature.

Mary Jo's Indian-style Cauliflower and Cabbage with Tomato

This basic stir-fry and steaming method for vegetables may also be used with green beans, zucchini, Swiss chard...

2 tablespoons vegetable oil or 1 tablespoon
  ghee (see page 105) + l tablespoon oil
1/2 teaspoon black mustard seeds
1/2 cumin seeds
1 small onion, thinly sliced
1/2 red or green chilli, thinly sliced
1 tablespoon finely chopped fresh ginger
1/2 teaspoon tumeric
2 medium tomatoes, diced
l medium potato, peeled and diced
1/2 small cabbage, sliced
1/4 to 1/2 cauliflower, broken into florets
salt
dry mango powder (amchur) or lemon juice to
  taste
coriander leaves

In a large frying pan with a lid, heat the oil and ghee until it begins to shimmer. Add the mustard and cumin seeds, cover the pan, allow to pop and lower the heat.

Remove the lid, add the sliced onion and sauté until limp and golden. Add the sliced chilli, ginger and turmeric and stir while cooking briefly. Add the tomatoes and when they start to soften add the diced potato and sliced cabbage. Season with salt, cover, and half-cook. Mix in the cauliflower, adding a little water if necessary and continue to simmer until all the vegetables are tender. Season to taste with salt, dry mango powder or lemon juice. Garnish with coriander leaves.

Master Recipe
Brussels Sprouts
Serves 4–6

Not surprisingly many people hate Brussels sprouts because they are all too often overcooked.

The traditional way to cook sprouts was to cut a cross in the stalk so that they would, hopefully, cook more evenly. Fortunately I discovered quite by accident when I was in a mad rush one day, that if you cut the sprouts in half lengthways they cook much faster and taste infinitely more delicious so with this recipe I've managed to convert many ardent Brussels sprout haters! If they are enormous cut into quarters instead.

450g (1lb) Brussels sprouts, cut lengthways
600ml (1 pint) water
1 1/2 teaspoons salt
25–50g (1–2oz) butter
salt and freshly ground pepper

Choose even, medium-sized sprouts. Trim the outer leaves if necessary and cut them in half lengthways. Salt the water and bring to a fast rolling boil. Toss in the sprouts, cover the saucepan just for 1 minute until the water returns to the boil, then uncover and cook for 5–6 minutes or until the sprouts are tender but still have a slight bite. Pour off the water.*

Melt the butter in a saucepan, roll the sprouts gently in the butter, season with lots of pepper and salt. Taste and serve immediately in a hot serving dish.

Note: * If the sprouts are not to be served immediately, refresh them under cold water as soon as they are cooked. Just before serving, drop them into boiling salted water for a few seconds to heat through. Drain and toss in the butter, season and serve. This way they will taste almost as good as if they were freshly cooked: certainly much more delicious than sprouts kept warm for half an hour in an oven or a hostess trolley.

Variation
Brussels Sprouts with Buttered Almonds and Bacon
Follow the Master Recipe. Meanwhile melt 10g (1/2oz) butter in a frying pan, toss in about 25g (1oz) nibbed or flaked almonds and 50–110g (2–4oz) bacon lardons and cook for a few minutes or until golden. As soon as the sprouts are cooked, drain and toss with the buttered almonds and bacon. Serve immediately in a hot dish.

Brussels Sprouts with Thai Flavours
Serves 4–6

400ml (14fl oz) coconut milk
1 tablespoon green curry paste
1 green chilli, pounded
175ml (6fl oz) chicken stock
450g (1lb) Brussels sprouts, cut in half,
  blanched and refreshed in boiling salted water
2 kaffir lime leaves
1/2 tablespoon palm sugar or a little less of soft
  brown sugar
2 tablespoons fish sauce (nam pla)
20 basil leaves
1 large red chilli, pounded
1 tablespoon soy sauce

Heat a wok on a low heat. Pour 110ml (4fl oz) coconut milk into the wok. Add the green curry paste and the pounded green chilli, and mix well. Then add the stock, the remainder of the coconut milk, Brussels sprouts, kaffir lime leaves, palm sugar and fish sauce, half the basil leaves and pounded red chilli.

Stir constantly on a medium heat until the sauce boils and foams up. Reduce the heat and simmer, stirring constantly until cooked (about 12 minutes). Add the remainder of the basil leaves and soy sauce, and season to taste. Serve immediately.

Master Recipe
Bok Choi

Serves 4–6

450g (1lb) bok choi (pak choi)
1.2 litres (2 pints) water
2 teaspoons salt
freshly ground pepper
25g (1oz) butter

Cut the bok choi into about 2cm (³/₄in) squares. Steam or cook in boiling, salted water until tender – 3–5 minutes. Drain well. Melt the butter in the pan and toss the bok choi in it. Season with freshly ground pepper and serve immediately.

Variations
Bok Choi with Oyster Sauce

Follow the Master Recipe, omitting the butter. Douse in 2–3 tablespoons oyster sauce and serve immediately.

Bok Choi with Ginger, Garlic and Chilli

Follow the Master Recipe, omitting the butter. Heat 2–3 tablespoons sunflower oil in a hot wok, add 1 teaspoon grated ginger, 1 teaspoon chopped garlic and ¹/₂–1 sliced green chilli. Cook for 1–2 minutes in the hot oil, add the bok choi, toss gently to coat, taste and correct the seasoning – a few tablespoons sliced spring onion greens is a good addition.

Bok Choi with Tomato and Ginger

Follow the Master Recipe, omitting the butter. Just before serving, toss in a hot wok with ¹/₄–¹/₂ of the recipe for Tomato Fondue (see page 200) and 1 teaspoon freshly grated ginger. Finish with a few drops of toasted sesame oil.

Master Recipe
Buttered Spinach

Serves 4–6

Here are 3 different basic methods of cooking – all of them a huge improvement on the watery mush that, unfortunately, frozen spinach often ends up as.

900g (2lb) fresh spinach, weight without stalks
salt, freshly ground pepper and grated nutmeg
50–110g (2–4oz) butter

Method 1

Melt a scrap of butter in a wide frying pan, toss in as much spinach as will fit easily, season with salt and freshly ground pepper. As soon as the spinach wilts and becomes tender, strain off all the liquid, increase the heat and add some butter and freshly grated nutmeg. Serve immediately.

Method 2

Wash the prepared spinach and drain. Put into a heavy saucepan on a very low heat, season and cover tightly. After a few minutes, stir and replace the lid. As soon as the spinach is cooked, about 5–8 minutes, strain off the copious amount of liquid that spinach releases and press between two plates until almost dry. Chop, or purée in a food processor if you like a smooth texture, and return to the pan. Increase the heat, add butter, correct the seasoning and add a little freshly grated nutmeg to taste.

Method 3

Cook the spinach uncovered in a large saucepan of boiling salted water until soft, about 4–5 minutes. Drain and press out all the water. Continue as in method 2. Method 3 produces a brighter coloured spinach.

Variations
Caribbean Spinach with Dill

The little island of St Barths is a French-owned colony in the Caribbean. Just opposite the tiny airport building, Gucci, Versace, Cartier, Hermès all have shops to tempt the well-heeled tourists who frequent the island.

Virtually no food is produced there; it's all imported from France or neighbouring islands and even the milk and yoghurt is French. In general the food was expensive and bad. The last straw was when I asked for local fish in one of the restaurants and the waiter told me excitedly that there was no local fish but they had Dover sole which had just arrived from France. This spinach was almost the best thing we ate. Add half the recipe of Tomato Fondue (see page 200) to Buttered Spinach cooked by Method 1 in the Master Recipe. Just before serving, add 2–4 tablespoons freshly chopped dill. Taste and correct the seasoning. Serve with lamb or pan-grilled local fish.

Spinach with Raisins and Pine Nuts

Cook the spinach as in the Master Recipe. Soak 25–35g (1–1¹/₂oz) seedless raisins in boiling water for 10 minutes until they are plump and juicy. Toast 25–35g (1–1¹/₂oz) pine nuts until they are golden brown. Add the raisins and pine nuts to the spinach. Season well and allow to bubble for 4–5 minutes. Add a splash of balsamic vinegar and serve.

Creamed Spinach

Follow the Master Recipe, cooking the spinach by method 2 or 3; drain very well. Add 225–350ml (8–12fl oz) of cream to the spinach and bring to the boil, stir well and thicken with a little roux (see page 580) if desired, otherwise stir over the heat until the spinach has absorbed most of the cream. Season with salt, pepper and freshly grated nutmeg to taste. Creamed spinach may be cooked ahead of time and reheated.

Oeufs Florentine

A classic dish and one of the most delicious combinations, this is one of our favourite lunch or supper dishes. Serve freshly poached organic eggs on top of creamed spinach.

Saag
Serves 4–6

110g (4oz) onion, sliced
3 cloves garlic, crushed (optional)
1–2 chopped fresh Jalapeño chillies (or less of
    Thai)
2 tablespoons olive oil
450g (1lb) very ripe tomatoes
1.3kg (3lb) spinach, destalked and sliced
1 teaspoon garam masala
salt, freshly ground pepper and sugar

Sweat the sliced onions and garlic (if used)
and chilli in oil on a gentle heat. It is vital
for the success of this dish that the onions
are completely soft before the tomatoes
are added.

Remove the hard core from the tomatoes.
Put them into a deep bowl and cover them
with boiling water. After 10 seconds, pour
off the water immediately; peel off the
skins, chop and add to the onions. Season
with salt, freshly ground pepper and sugar.
Add the spinach, toss on a high heat, cover
for a few minutes. Add the garam masala
and continue to cook for 20–25 minutes
or until virtually no liquid remains. Cook
for just 10 minutes, or until the tomato
softens. Taste and correct the seasoning.
This may be served immediately or
reheated later.

Wilted Greens
Serves 4

2 tablespoons olive oil
1 garlic clove, chopped
¼–½ red chilli, de-seeded and chopped
about 1 fistful of leaves per person: a mixture
    of young vegetable leaves (young beetroot
    leaves, Swiss chard, spinach, sorrel, rocket)
salt and freshly ground pepper

Heat the olive oil in a pan, add in the garlic
and chilli, then the leaves, and toss well,
season with salt and freshly ground
pepper. Taste and serve immediately they
have just wilted.

Master Recipe
Ruby Chard or Swiss Chard with Butter
Serves 4

There are several ways of using the stalks
of chard including tossing them in
vinaigrette or olive oil and lemon juice.
Cook the green leaves as you would
spinach (see page 171). I often add in
the green leaf for a minute or two before
the end of cooking, then you have the best
of both worlds.

450g (1lb) Swiss chard stalks (weight after
    leaves are removed)
butter or olive oil
salt and freshly ground pepper

Pull the green leaves off the chard stalks
and wash and drain. Cut the chard stalks
into pieces about 5cm (2in) long. Cook in
boiling, salted water until they feel tender
when pierced with the tip of a knife. Drain
very well. Toss in a little melted butter or
olive oil, season and serve immediately.

Variation
Ruby Chard or Swiss Chard with Parmesan

Follow the Master Recipe, until the
draining stage. Grease a 25 x 20cm (10 x
8in) earthenware dish with a little butter,
arrange some of the chard stalks in a
single layer and season with salt and
pepper. Sprinkle with about 75g (3oz)
freshly grated Parmesan and dot with a
little butter. Repeat until the dish is full,
finally sprinkle the top layer generously
with the freshly grated Parmesan. Dot
with a little butter. Bake in a preheated
oven at 200°C/400°F/gas 6 for 15–20
minutes or until crisp and golden. This
also works well with fennel.

Master Recipe
Grilled Chicory or Radicchio
Serves 6

Marcella and Victor Hazan told me about
this delicious way to cook chicory while
we ate huge pizzas in a trattoria in Venice.
Serve hot or lukewarm, as an
accompanying vegetable or as part of a
starter. A plate of Italian antipasto might
include some char-grilled peppers with
basil, a slice or two of bresaola or Parma
ham, sun-dried tomatoes sprinkled with
parsley and garlic and drizzled with olive
oil, a few black olives and a slice of
bruschetta.

6 perfect plump heads of chicory or radicchio
    trevisano
extra-virgin olive oil
sea salt and freshly ground pepper

Preheat the grill.

Discard any discoloured or wilted leaves from the chicory or radicchio, trim the base and wash if needed. Cut them in half lengthways and make little cuts in the root part so that the heat and oil can penetrate. Arrange the halves cut-side up in the grill pan and paint with olive oil. Sprinkle with salt and pepper and put under the hot grill about 10cm (4in) from the heat.

After 7–8 minutes turn the chicory over and paint again with olive oil. Cook for a further 7–8 minutes and then turn again, basting with the oil in the grill pan and adding more if necessary. Cook for another 5–8 minutes, depending on size. The chicory or radicchio is cooked when the root end can be pierced easily with the tip of a knife. At this stage it will look slightly sad and blackened but will taste quite delicious.

Variation
Mimmo's Grilled Chicory with Gorgonzola and Walnuts
Follow the Master Recipe and just before serving put some gorgonzola and a very little finely chopped walnut on top of each piece. Exquisite hot or lukewarm!

Master Recipe
Braised Chicory
Serves 6

6 heads of chicory (tightly closed with no
    trace of green)
1.2 litres (2 pints) water
2 teaspoons salt
1 teaspoon sugar
good squeeze of lemon juice
10–25g (1/2–1oz) butter
freshly chopped flat-leaf parsley

Remove a thin slice from the root end of each chicory. Remove the centre root with the tip of a sharp knife if you find it too bitter. Bring the water to the boil, add the salt, sugar, a good squeeze of lemon juice and the chicory. Cook for about 45 minutes to 1 hour or until almost or completely tender, depending on how you intend to finish the cooking (when it is completely tender a knife tip will pierce the root end without resistance). Remove the chicory, drain well, then squeeze out all excess water (I do this in a clean tea towel).

Melt the butter in a wide sauté pan, put in the chicory in a single layer and cook over a very low heat turning occasionally until golden on all sides. This takes about 30–40 minutes. Serve in a hot serving dish sprinkled with a little parsley.

Variation
Chicory à la Crème
Follow the Master Recipe but add 6 tablespoons of cream to the chicory when it is golden, increase the heat and let it bubble for a few minutes.

Master Recipe
Melted Leeks
Serves 6–8

8 medium leeks
50g (2oz) butter
2 tablespoons water, if necessary
salt and freshly ground pepper
parsley or chervil, chopped

Cut off the dark green leaves from the top of the leeks. Slit the leeks about half way down the centre and wash well under cold running water. Slice into 5mm (1/4in) rounds.

Melt the butter in a heavy saucepan (we use an oval Le Creuset casserole). When it foams, add the sliced leeks and toss gently to coat with butter. Season with salt and pepper. Cover with a paper lid and a tight-fitting saucepan lid. Reduce the heat and cook very gently for about 10–20 minutes, or until soft and moist.*

Check and stir every now and then. Serve on a warm dish either plain or sprinkled with parsley or chervil.

* Frequently, we turn off the heat after 5–8 minutes and allow the leeks to finish cooking in the saucepan.

Note: The leeks may be cooked in the oven at 170°C/325°F/gas 3 if that is more convenient.

Leeks with Yellow Peppers and Marjoram
Serves 6

This mixture is also irresistible served in crispy shortcrust tartlets or filo triangles.

Melted Leeks (see left)
3 yellow peppers, sliced
1 tablespoon water
1–2 tablespoons freshly chopped annual
    marjoram or a mixture of parsley, basil and
    marjoram

Follow the Master Recipe and add the peppers to the melted leeks in the pan, toss and add a drop more water if necessary. Stir in half the herbs, cover and continue to cook until the peppers are soft. Taste, add the remainder of the herbs, correct the seasoning and serve.

Variation
Leeks with Yellow Peppers and Marjoram Tart
Fill a fully-baked savoury tart shell with the cooked vegetable mixture and serve immediately.

Master Recipe
Leek Vinaigrette

Serves 8

The secret of this recipe is to toss the leeks in vinaigrette while they are still warm. They are particularly good with chopped hard-boiled eggs, black olives and flat-leaf parsley.

8 medium leeks
3–4 tablespoons Ballymaloe French Dressing
  (see page 226)

Trim the leeks down to the pale end (save the trimmings for the stock pot). Clean them thoroughly under running water, and poach them gently in a little boiling salted water until just tender.

Alternatively cut the leeks into 1cm (1/2in) rounds at an angle. Poach in a covered saucepan in just a very little boiling salted water.

Remove the leeks from the water with a perforated spoon and allow to cool for a few minutes. Coat with French dressing while still warm and leave to marinate. The leeks may be served as a first course or an accompanying salad.

Variation
Leek Vinaigrette Terrine with Beetroot Sauce

Follow the Master Recipe. When the warm leeks have been tossed in vinaigrette arrange in layers in a lined terrine, cover and gently press with a board and light weight. Next day, turn out and cut into thick slices with the utmost care. Serve with lots of crusty white bread, and a beetroot sauce made from puréed Pickled Beetroot (see page 514), from which the onion has been omitted.

Coolea Cheese and Leek Fritters

Makes about 25, depending on size

Helene Willems cooked these little fritters over a camp stove in the open air at the Slow Food Convivium at Bill Hogan's in Schull, Co. Cork. They smelled tantalising and tasted delicious. Gouda can be used if you can't find Coolea, a West Cork farmhouse cheese.

25g (1oz) butter
400g (14oz) leeks, trimmed and thinly sliced
200g (7oz) flour
2 organic eggs
225ml (8fl oz) milk
200g (7oz) mature Coolea farmhouse cheese
  or Gouda, freshly grated
salt and freshly ground pepper
chilli pepper
freshly grated nutmeg

Melt the butter in a large pan, add the sliced leeks, cover and sweat on a gentle heat until soft but not coloured. This will take about 5 minutes. Cool.

Sift the flour into a bowl, make a well in the centre, add the eggs and break up with a whisk. Add the milk gradually, whisking all the time in a circular movement from the centre to the outside of the bowl. Add the cooled leeks and the grated cheese. Season with the salt, pepper, chilli pepper and nutmeg to taste.

Heat a frying pan, preferably non-stick, on a medium heat. Drop a small spoonful of the batter onto the pan, allow to cook until golden, flip over onto the other and cook for 1–2 minutes. Taste and correct the seasoning if necessary.

Cook the remainder in the same way. Serve hot on their own or with a little Tomato and Chilli Sauce (see page 591) or Tomato Fondue (see page 200).

Mashed Parsnips

Serves 4

In their valiant efforts to help the poor during the potato famines of 1845 and 1846, The Society of Friends encouraged the cultivation of parsnips, which had been grown in Ireland since early Christian times. In early writings there are many references to *meacan*, which scholars believe to be parsnips. Originally they would have been boiled and mashed with country butter. They are also delicious mixed with carrots, or cut into chunks and roasted, alone or around a joint of beef. Crispy parsnip cakes also make an irresistible and inexpensive treat.

700g (1 1/2lb) parsnips
50–75g (2–3oz) butter
salt and freshly ground pepper
chopped parsley

Peel the parsnips thinly. Cut off the tops and tails and cut them into wedges. Remove the inner core if it seems to be at all woody, cut the wedges into 2cm (3/4in) cubes. Cook them in boiling salted water for 15–20 minutes. They should be quite soft. Drain. Mash with a potato masher, add a nice bit of butter and season well with salt and freshly ground pepper. The texture should not be too smooth. Serve sprinkled with parsley.

Variation
Parsnip Cakes with Crispy Bacon

Follow the Master Recipe, allow to cool, then wet your hands and shape the mixture into 6 cakes. Dip each in flour, beaten egg and breadcrumbs. Heat a little olive oil with some butter in a wide frying pan, fry the cakes on a gentle heat until golden on both sides. Serve hot with lardons of crispy bacon or as an accompaniment to a main course.

Pan-roasted Parsnips

Serves 6–8

I have a real passion for pan-roasted parsnips – we eat them 3 or 4 times a week during the parsnip season.

4 parsnips
olive oil
salt and freshly ground pepper

Preheat the oven to 230°C/450°F/gas 8.

Peel the parsnips and cut them into quarters – the chunks should be quite large. Roast in olive oil in the hot oven for 30 minutes, turning them frequently so that they do not become too crusty. We often roast them in the same pan as Rustic Roast Potatoes (see page 181). Cooked this way they will be crisp outside and soft in the centre.

Saratoga Chips

Parsnips also make very good chips. Cook them in a deep-fryer using good-quality oil at 180°C/350°F.

Parsnip Crisps

See page 287 – brilliant for nibbles or to pile high on a salad or soup.

Soy-Glazed Parsnips with Sesame Seeds

Serves 4–6

Naranjan McCormack, from Malaysia but now living in Fermoy, Co. Cork, teaches this recipe to our students at an Asian class. Palm sugar, also known as 'Gula Melaka', is a hard brown sugar made from the sap of the Aaren palm. If not available, substitute with light muscovado sugar with a touch of maple syrup. The natural sweetness of parsnips, the intense savouriness of soy sauce and the crisp nuttiness of sesame seeds make an excellent combination in this inexpensive vegetable recipe.

450g (1lb) smallish parsnips, peeled and sliced
into strips
1 tablespoon groundnut oil
50g (2oz) palm sugar
3–4 tablespoons light soy sauce
2 tablespoons toasted sesame seeds

Put the parsnips in a heavy saucepan with the groundnut oil and cook them until halfway tender. Add the palm sugar and cook over a medium heat until the sugar has dissolved. Stir in the soy sauce and continue cooking until the parsnips are tender. Transfer to a hot serving dish and sprinkle with the toasted sesame seeds.

Note: Carrots, turnips, yams, mooli, sweet potato and other root vegetables can be cooked this way. A splash of rice vinegar or coconut vinegar adds a sweet and sour tang.

Kitty's Curried Oven Parsnips

This was the brainchild of Kitty Ahearne, who makes several large trays of this delicious recipe for Sunday lunch at Ballymaloe House.

Kitty's Curry Oil
300ml (½ pint) sunflower oil
1½ tablespoons curry powder
a squeeze of lemon juice

parsnips (number depends on size, one is
usually enough for 2 portions)

Preheat the oven to 180°C/350°F/gas 4. Prepare the curry oil by mixing all the ingredients in a bowl or jar. Scrub and peel the parsnips. Cut off the taper in one piece, then cut the remainder of the parsnips into quarters. Blanch in boiling salted water for 4–5 minutes. Drain, dry and allow to cool.

Toss the parsnips in a little of the curry oil, season with salt and freshly ground pepper, and toss again. Roast for 30–40 minutes, tossing occasionally until golden on all sides.

Kitty also roasts a mixture of winter root vegetables (carrots, parsnips and celeriac) in her curry oil, adding some quartered onions towards the end of cooking – delicious!

Roast Sweet Potatoes with Chipotle Butter

Serves 6

Chipotle in Adobo is a must-have chilli sauce that will liven up your store cupboard!

6 sweet potatoes

Chipotle Butter
75g (3oz) unsalted butter
3 tablespoons Chipotle in Adobo sauce

Preheat the oven to 230°C/450°F/gas 8.

Scrub and dry the sweet potatoes. Put into a roasting tin and cook for 45–60 minutes or until completely soft. Meanwhile whizz the soft butter and chipotle in adobo with a food processor (or mash it by hand). Serve with the sweet potatoes.

Chipotle butter is also delicious with pan-grilled fish and meat.

Master Recipe
Glazed Carrots

Serves 4–6

Unwashed carrots keep better and have infinitely more flavour than ready-washed ones. If you don't believe me experiment. Early Nantes and Autumn King have particularly good flavour. Cook some of each in exactly the same way in different saucepans and the difference in flavour is a revelation.

This method of cooking carrots takes a little vigilance but the resulting flavour is delicious.

450g (1lb) carrots, topped, tailed and cleaned
10g (1/2oz) butter
125ml (4fl oz) cold water
pinch of salt
good pinch of sugar

Garnish
parsley or mint, freshly chopped

Cut the carrots into slices 5mm (1/4in) thick, either straight across or at an angle. Leave very young carrots whole.

Put them in a saucepan with the butter, water, salt and sugar. Bring to the boil, cover and cook over a gentle heat until tender, by which time the liquid should have all been absorbed into the carrots. If not, remove the lid and increase the heat until all the water has evaporated. Taste and correct the seasoning.

Shake the saucepan so the carrots become coated with the buttery glaze. Serve sprinkled with parsley or mint.

Variation
Glazed Carrots with Cumin Seeds
Follow the Master Recipe, adding 1/2–1 teaspoon cumin just before all the water has evaporated. Garnish with freshly chopped parsley. Freshly roasted coriander is equally delicious.

Carrot and Potato with Cream and Fresh Spices
Serves 6

Fresh spices can add magic to your cooking – here they give an altogether new dimension to carrots and potatoes. Cardamom is a member of the ginger family and is also known as 'grains of paradise'. Often used in Indian curries, in Scandinavia it is used to flavour cakes and breads. Sophie Grigson introduced us to this dish when she was guest chef at the school.

900g (2lb) medium potatoes
450g (1lb) carrots
2 1/2 teaspoons cumin seed
3 teaspoons coriander seed
2.5cm (1in) cinnamon stick
1 teaspoon cardamom seed
8 cloves
1/4 teaspoon black peppercorns
10g (1/2oz) butter
1 large red onion, roughly diced
1 garlic clove, finely chopped
25g (1oz) fresh ginger, peeled and grated
1/4 teaspoon freshly grated nutmeg
1/2 teaspoon turmeric
1 teaspoon sugar
1/2 teaspoon salt
700g (1 1/2lb) very ripe tomatoes, peeled and chopped
175ml (6fl oz) yoghurt
125–225ml (4–8fl oz) creamy milk
1–2 tablespoons fresh coriander, chopped

Garnish
sprigs of fresh coriander
Ballymaloe Tomato Relish

Cook the potatoes, unpeeled, in boiling, salted water until just cooked. Scrape or thinly peel the carrots and cut into 1cm (1/2in) thick slices; cook in a little boiling, salted water until just tender.

Put the whole spices into a spice grinder or pestle and mortar and grind finely. Melt the butter in a saucepan and cook the onion until golden. Add the garlic, ginger, ground spices, nutmeg, turmeric, sugar and salt. Cook for 1–2 minutes, then add the tomato and finally the yoghurt, little by little, stirring well.

Peel the cooked potatoes and cut into 1cm (1/2in) slices. Add with the carrots to the sauce, stir in the milk, simmer until they have warmed through. Stir in the coriander, taste and correct the seasoning and serve immediately with a good green salad (see page 223).

Carrot, Parsnip and Cabbage with Mustard Seeds
Serves 6

3 tablespoons sunflower oil
1 tablespoon black mustard seeds
1 chilli, seeded and chopped
225g (8oz) carrots, coarsely grated
225g (8oz) parsnips, coarsely grated
225g (8oz) cabbage, finely shredded against the grain
2 tablespoons freshly chopped parsley
2 tablespoons freshly chopped mint
salt, freshly ground pepper and sugar
freshly squeezed lemon juice, to taste

Heat the oil in a sauté pan and add the mustard seeds. They will start to pop almost instantly. Add the chopped chilli and stir and cook for a minute or so. Add the carrots, parsnips and cabbage. Toss over a medium heat for 2 or 3 minutes, then add the parsley and mint and toss again. Season with salt, freshly ground pepper and a little sugar. Add the lemon juice, taste and correct seasoning. Serve immediately.

Celeriac and Apple Purée
Serves 4

Particularly delicious with game, celeriac is a knobbly root vegetable that can be dug from the ground all through the winter months when needed.

450g (1lb) celeriac (weight after peeling)
350g (12oz) dessert apples (Cox's Orange Pippin)
2 tablespoons chopped lovage (optional)
4 tablespoons cream
salt and freshly ground pepper

RIGHT: Carrot, Parsnip and Cabbage with Mustard Seeds

Peel the celeriac and cut it into large chunks. Drop into lightly salted boiling water and simmer until soft and tender, about 15 minutes.

Meanwhile, peel and core the apples, cut them into quarters and cook with a teaspoon of sugar and a very little water (about 1 dessertspoon) in a covered saucepan until soft. When the celeriac is cooked, drain and add it to the apple. Purée them in a food processor with the lovage, if using, until smooth and add the cream. Taste and season with salt and pepper.

This purée can be prepared ahead and reheated in the oven at 180°C/350°C/gas 4.

Celeriac Rémoulade
Serves 12–15

A favourite winter salad when I was an au pair in France. Use it in combination with other winter salads as a starter or as an accompaniment to Paté de Campagne (see page 79) or a game terrine.

700g (1½lb) celeriac
1 tablespoon Dijon mustard
350ml (12fl oz) homemade Mayonnaise
  (see page 100)
freshly ground pepper
lemon juice, freshly squeezed

Trim with a knife and peel the celeriac thickly. Grate it coarsely. Stir the Dijon mustard into the mayonnaise and add some to the celeriac (keep back a little in case not all is needed). It should be saucy but not too sloppy. Add lemon juice to taste and a little more seasoning if necessary.

Celeriac Crisps
Serve with game, sprinkle over *salades tièdes* (warm salads) or nibble with drinks.

1 celeriac root
acidulated water (see glossary)
oil for deep-frying
salt

Peel the celeriac. Leave whole or cut into quarters and drop into acidulated water until ready to cook.

Heat the oil in a deep-fryer to 150°C/330°F. Dry the celeriac and slice into paper thin slices on a mandolin. Fry a few at a time until pale golden. Drain on kitchen paper and sprinkle with a little salt.

Beetroot Crisps
Fry slices of beetroot as above. Carrots and parsnips also work well.

How to Cook Beetroot

Leave 5cm (2in) of leaf stalks on top and the whole root on the beet. Hold it under a running tap and wash off the mud with the palms of your hands, so that you don't damage the skin; otherwise the beetroot will bleed during cooking. Cover with cold water and add a little salt and sugar. Cover the pot, bring to the boil and simmer on top, or in an oven, for 1–2 hours depending on size. Beetroot are ready if they dent when pressed with a finger. If in doubt, test with a skewer or the tip of a knife.

Hot Beetroot
Serves 6

We all adore beetroot. In summer we eat them from the time they are walnut sized, when they cook in just 10 or 15 minutes and are sweet and tender. Serve with duck, beef or lamb. Hot beetroot is also divine with fish, particularly cod.

700g (1½lb) beetroot, cooked (see above)
10g (½oz) butter
125–175ml (4–6fl oz) cream
salt and freshly ground pepper
a sprinkling of sugar (may not be necessary)
1–2 teaspoons chives, finely chopped

Peel the cooked beetroot, using rubber gloves for this operation if you are vain. Chop the beetroot flesh into cubes. Melt the butter in a sauté pan, add the beetroot, toss, add the cream and allow to bubble for a few minutes. Season with salt, pepper and sugar if necessary. Sprinkle over the chives and serve immediately.

Roast Beetroot with Goat's Cheese and Balsamic Vinegar
Serves 4

6–12 baby beetroot, a mixture of red, golden and Chioggia would be wonderful
extra-virgin olive oil
balsamic vinegar
175g (6oz) goat's cheese
rocket and beetroot leaves
wild garlic leaves (if available)
sea salt and freshly cracked pepper

Preheat the oven to 230°C/450°F/gas 8.

Wrap the beetroot in tin foil and roast in the oven until soft and cooked through – between ½ and 1 hour, depending on size.

To serve: rub the skins off the beetroot and keep whole or cut into quarters. Toss in the extra-virgin olive oil. Scatter a few rocket and tiny beetroot leaves on each serving plate. Arrange a selection of warm beetroot on top. Drizzle with more olive oil and balsamic vinegar. Put 1 dessertspoonful of goat's cheese beside the beetroot. Sprinkle with sea salt and pepper and garnish with tiny beet greens or wild garlic flowers and serve.

Beetroot Tops

Beetroot tops are full of vitamins and minerals. They are often unnecessarily discarded – if you grow your own remember to cook them as well as the beetroot. When the leaves are tiny they make a really worthwhile addition to the salad bowl both in terms of nutrition and flavour.

RIGHT: Roast Beetroot with Goat's Cheese and Balsamic Vinegar

450g (1lb) fresh beetroot tops
butter or olive oil
salt and freshly ground pepper

Cut the stalks and leaves into 5cm (2in) pieces. Cook in boiling salted water (1.8 litres/3 pints water to 1½ teaspoons salt) for 6–8 minutes or until tender. Drain, season and toss in a little butter or olive oil. Serve immediately.

Swedes with Caramelised Onions
Serves 6

The humble swede is wonderfully perked up by being served with soft sweet onions.

900g (2lb) swedes
50–110g (2–4oz) butter
salt and freshly ground pepper

Garnish
parsley, finely chopped
Caramelised Onions (page 188)

Peel the swede thickly in order to remove the thick outer skin. Cut into 2cm (3/4in) cubes. Cover with water. Add a good pinch of salt, bring to the boil and cook until soft. Strain off the excess water, mash the swedes well and beat in the butter. Taste and season with plenty of freshly ground pepper and extra salt if necessary. Garnish with the parsley and serve piping hot with the Caramelised Onions.

Braised White Turnips with Marjoram
Serves 4–6

This recipe is sensational on its own but particularly delicious with duck.

450g (1lb) small white turnips
25g (1oz) butter
1–2 tablespoons freshly chopped oregano or annual marjoram
salt and freshly ground pepper

Wash and peel the white turnips and cut into 1cm (½in) slices. Melt the butter in a heavy-bottomed casserole. Add the sliced turnips and season with salt and freshly ground pepper. Add 1 tablespoon water and half the chopped marjoram. Cover and cook on a gentle heat until tender for 8–10 minutes, until the turnip is just tender.

Taste and correct seasoning and add a little more freshly chopped marjoram and serve immediately.

Variation
Kohl Rabi with Marjoram
Substitute Kohl Rabi for white turnips in the recipe above, using less marjoram so as not to overpower the delectable but delicate flavour.

Spiced White Turnips
Serves 4

White turnips deserve to be more popular. This Indian recipe has lots of zesty flavour.

2 tablespoons sunflower oil
1 large onion, chopped
1 garlic clove, crushed
½ teaspoon freshly grated ginger
2 fresh green chillies, chopped
2 ripe tomatoes, chopped
1 teaspoon cumin, freshly ground
1 teaspoon coriander, freshly ground
½ teaspoon turmeric
salt
350g (12oz) white turnips, peeled and diced
1 teaspoon cane or brown sugar
coriander leaves, roughly chopped

Heat the oil in a wok or heavy-bottomed sauté pan, add the onion and fry until it softens. Add the garlic, ginger, chillies, tomatoes, spices and salt, and stir well. Add the turnips and about 150ml (5fl oz) hot water. Stir well. Cover and bring to the boil, then reduce the heat and cook for about 20 minutes until the turnips are cooked.

Add the sugar, stir, taste and correct the seasoning if necessary. Sprinkle with the coriander leaves and serve immediately.

Roasted Jerusalem Artichokes
Serves 4–6

Just delectable, roast artichokes are high on my list of favourite winter vegetables – if you have any space at all pop a few into the ground; they grow and multiply really easily. The foliage grows to a height of 2.1–2.5m (7–8ft) in the summer; ideal to provide privacy from prying neighbours or to make a maze for children to play in. There are 'dwarf' varieties too.

450g (1lb) Jerusalem artichokes, well scrubbed and sliced into 1cm (½in) rounds
2 tablespoons sunflower or olive oil
salt and freshly ground pepper
sprigs of rosemary or thyme (optional)

Preheat the oven to 200°C/400°F/gas 6.

Toss the Jerusalem artichokes with the oil in a roasting tin. Season well with salt. Bake for 15–30 minutes depending on size. Test with a knife tip – they should be mostly tender but offer some resistance. Sprinkle with sprigs of thyme or rosemary. Season with pepper and serve.

Braised Jerusalem Artichokes
Serves 4

The flavour of Jerusalem artichokes is particularly good with game, beef or shellfish.

700g (1½lb) Jerusalem artichokes
25g (1oz) butter
1 dessertspoon water
salt and freshly ground pepper
parsley, chopped

Peel the artichokes thinly and slice them into 5mm (¼in) rounds. Melt the butter in a cast-iron casserole, toss the artichokes and season with salt and pepper. Add the water and cover with a paper lid to keep in the steam and the saucepan lid.

Put in a moderate oven (180°C/350°F/gas 4) until the artichokes are soft but still keep their shape; about 15–20 minutes. Toss every now and then during cooking. Serve sprinkled with parsley.

Master Recipe
Roast Potatoes

Everybody loves roast potatoes, yet people ask over and over again for the secret of golden crispy roast potatoes. Duck or goose fat gives a delicious flavour to roast potatoes. Good-quality pork fat or lard from free-range pigs is also worth saving carefully for roast or sauté potatoes. All three fats will keep for months in a cold larder or fridge. Good chicken fat and olive oil are also tasty for browning roast potatoes.

Buy good-quality 'old' potatoes. New potatoes are not brilliant for roasting. Cut the potatoes into similar sizes. For perfection peel them just before roasting. Do not leave them soaking in water or they will be soggy inside because of the water they absorb. This always applies, no matter how you cook potatoes. Unfortunately, many people have got into the habit of peeling and soaking potatoes even if they are just going to boil and mash them.

Dry the potatoes carefully, otherwise they will stick to the roasting tin, and when you turn them over you will lose the crispy bit underneath. If you have a fan oven it is best to blanch and refresh the potatoes first, then proceed as follows: heat the olive oil or fat in a roasting pan and toss the potatoes to make sure they are well coated. Roast in a hot oven (200°C/400°F/gas 6), basting occasionally, for 30–60 minutes depending on size.

Rustic Roast Potatoes
Serves 4–6

These are my children's favourite kind of roast spuds. They all love the crusty skin.

6 large 'old' potatoes
olive oil, duck or goose fat or beef dripping (unless for vegetarians)
sea salt

Preheat the oven to 230°C/450°F/gas 8.

Scrub the potatoes well, cut them into quarters lengthways or cut into thick rounds of about 2cm (¾in). Put into a roasting tin, drizzle with olive oil and toss so they are barely coated. Roast in the oven for 30–40 minutes depending on size. Sprinkle with sea salt and serve.

Variations
Rustic Roast Potatoes with Rosemary
Follow the Master Recipe, adding a few sprigs of rosemary or some coarsely chopped rosemary with the olive oil and proceed as above. Serve garnished with a fresh sprig of rosemary.

Rustic Roast Potatoes with Thyme
Follow the Master Recipe, substituting thyme for rosemary; marjoram is also gorgeous.

Rustic Roast Potatoes with Garlic Cloves
Follow the Master Recipe, adding 18 or more unpeeled garlic cloves after the potatoes have been cooking for 10–15 minutes. Toss in the oil. Keep an eye on the garlic cloves; they will probably be cooked before the potatoes, and, if so, remove and keep them warm in a serving dish. Press the soft sweet garlic out of the skins and eat it with the crispy potatoes.

BELOW: Rustic Roast Potatoes with Garlic Cloves

Master Recipe
Fluffy Mashed Potato
Serves 4

Duchesse is the rather posh French name for mashed potato enriched with boiling milk and egg.

900g (2lb) unpeeled potatoes (preferably Golden Wonder or Kerr's Pink)
300ml (½ pint) creamy milk
1–2 organic egg yolks or 1 whole egg and 1 egg yolk
25–50g (1–2 oz) butter
salt and freshly ground pepper

Scrub the potatoes well. Put them into a saucepan of cold water, add a good pinch of salt and bring to the boil. When the potatoes are about half cooked, say 15 minutes for 'old' potatoes, strain off two-thirds of the water, replace the lid on the saucepan, put on to a gentle heat and allow the potatoes to steam until they are cooked. Peel immediately by just pulling off the skins, so you have as little waste as possible, mash while hot. (If you have a large quantity, put the potatoes into the bowl of a food mixer (not a food processor) and beat with the spade).

While the potatoes are being peeled, bring the milk to the boil, add enough boiling creamy milk into the hot mashed potatoes, mix to get a soft light consistency suitable for piping, add the eggs, then beat in the butter, the amount depending on how rich you like your potatoes. Season with salt and freshly ground pepper. Taste and add more butter and seasoning if necessary.

Note: If the potatoes are not peeled and mashed while hot and if the boiling milk is not added immediately, the Duchesse potato will be lumpy and gluey. If you only have egg whites they will be fine and will make a deliciously light mashed potato also. Do not use a food processor or you will have gluey mashed potatoes.

Note: Mashed potatoes may be put aside and reheated later in a moderate oven, 180°C/350°F/gas 4. Cover with tin foil while it reheats so that it doesn't get a skin.

Variation
Rustic Mash
Just barely mash the potatoes, season, toss and serve.

Master Recipe
Scallion Champ or Mash
Serves 4

1.3kg (3lb) large 'old' potatoes
300–350ml (10–12fl oz) milk
110g (4oz) scallions (spring onions), chopped
50–110g (2–4oz) butter
salt and freshly ground white pepper

Scrub the potatoes but do not peel them. Cook in boiling salted water until cooked through. Drain off the water and return the potatoes to the pan. Cover with cold milk and bring slowly to the boil. Simmer for 3–4 minutes, turn off the heat and leave to infuse. Drain the potatoes, reserving the milk. Peel and mash the potatoes and, while hot, mix with the spring onions and the boiling milk, and beat in the butter. Season with salt and pepper.

Variations
Buttermilk Mash
Substitute buttermilk for ordinary milk in the Master Recipe, only barely heat it or it will curdle.

Scallion and Horseradish Mash
Follow the Master Recipe, adding 4 tablespoons grated horseradish with the spring onions.

Scallion and Potato Cakes
Shape leftover Scallion Mash into potato cakes and fry until golden on both sides in clarified butter or a mixture of butter and oil. Serve piping hot.

Wild Garlic Mash
Follow the Master Recipe, and add 50–75g (2–3oz) roughly chopped wild garlic leaves to the milk just as it comes to the boil.

Master Recipe
Parmesan and Olive Oil Mash
Serves 4

Fresh chicken livers cooked in a little butter with some fresh sage leaves are delicious served on top of olive oil mash.

900g (2lb) 'old' potatoes
225ml (8fl oz) boiling milk
75g (3oz) extra-virgin olive oil
50g (2oz) Parmesan (preferably Parmigiano Reggiano), freshly grated
salt and freshly ground pepper

Scrub the potatoes but do not peel them. Cook in boiling salted water until they are about three-quarters cooked. Pour off most of the water, cover and steam for the rest of the cooking.

Meanwhile bring the milk to the boil. Peel the potatoes as soon as they are cooked and mash while still hot using a hand masher or purée through a 'potato ricer'. Beat in half the hot milk, most of the olive oil and the Parmesan.

Finally add the remainder of the milk if necessary. The amount will depend on the variety of potato – some absorb more than others. It should be light and fluffy. Season with salt and freshly ground pepper and drizzle with a little extra-virgin olive oil. Taste and serve immediately.

Variations
Olive Oil Mash
Utterly delicious and frightfully fashionable. Follow the Master Recipe, but omit the Parmesan cheese. Garnish with a few chopped olives for extra pzazz.

Flavoured Oil Mash
Flavoured oils, e.g. chilli. porcini or roast garlic oil, are delicious drizzled onto mashed potato.

Master Recipe
Mustard Mash

Serves 4–6

1.3kg (3lb) 'old' potatoes
150ml (1/4 pint) milk
150ml (1/4 pint) cream
75g (3oz) unsalted butter
10g (1/2oz) dry English mustard powder or
    2 tablespoons Dijon mustard
salt and freshly cracked black pepper

Scrub the potatoes but do not peel them. Cook in boiling, salted water until cooked through. Drain, peel and mash immediately. Put the milk and cream into a saucepan and bring to boiling point, then add to the hot mashed potatoes, together with the butter and mustard. Season with salt and pepper. Taste and correct seasoning.

Variation
Mustard and Parsley Mash
Follow the Master Recipe, and add 1–2 tablespoons chopped parsley to the mash.

Master Recipe
Ulster Champ

Serves 8

Traditionally in this northern Irish dish, homemade country butter would have been used. Young nettle tops or leeks were also used instead of peas. This recipe was given to me by Deborah Shorley from Claragh.

1.8kg (4lb) 'old' potatoes
50–110g (2–4oz) butter
600ml (1 pint) milk
450g (1lb) young peas, weight after shelling
8 tablespoons chopped parsley
salt and freshly ground pepper

Cook the potatoes in boiling salted water until tender and drain well. Dry over the heat in the pan for a few minutes, then peel and mash with most of the butter while hot. Meanwhile bring the milk to the boil and simmer the peas in it until just cooked, about 8–10 minutes. Add the parsley for the final 2 minutes of cooking. Add the hot milk mixture to the potatoes. Season well, beat until creamy and smooth and serve piping hot with the remaining knob of butter melting in the centre.

West Cork Mash

Serves 6

West Cork Farmhouse cheesemaker, Giana Ferguson makes this delicious rustic mash. It's been a family favourite for generations and she calls it broken potatoes. Giana replaces the butter with lashings of Spanish extra-virgin olive oil in summer.

1.3kg (3lb) potatoes
milk
salt and freshly ground pepper
butter

Scrub the potatoes well, so that no trace of soil remains. Put into a saucepan, cover with salted water, bring to the boil, cover. When the potatoes are almost cooked, strain off two-thirds of the water, replace the lid and continue to cook over a gentle heat so that the potatoes steam until they are tender.

Bring the milk to the boil. Mash the potatoes while still hot using a hand masher. Add enough milk to soften. Season with salt and freshly ground pepper and heat a nice big knob of butter. Taste – this rustic mash will be flecked with the potato skins and taste quite delicious.

Colcannon

Serves about 8

Songs have been sung and poems have been written about Colcannon, a traditional Irish dish associated particularly with Halloween. Kale was used at first but now cabbage is more common. This comfort food at its very best has now been 'discovered' and is often on smart restaurant menus in London and New York.

'Did you ever eat colcannon
When 'twas made with yellow cream
And the kale and praties blended
Like a picture in a dream?
Did you ever scoop a hole on top
To hold the melting lake
Of the clover-flavoured butter
Which your mother used to make?'

900g–1.3kg (2–3lb) 'old' potatoes
450g (1lb) Savoy or spring cabbage
50g (2oz) butter
250ml (9fl oz) milk
25g (1oz) spring onion (optional)
salt and freshly ground pepper

Scrub the potatoes and put them in a saucepan of cold water. Add a good pinch of salt and bring them to the boil. When the potatoes are half cooked, about 15 minutes, strain off two-thirds of the water, replace the lid back, and cook over a gentle heat so that the potatoes steam until they are tender.

Remove the dark outer leaves from the cabbage. Wash the rest and cut into quarters, removing the core. Cut the cabbage finely across the grain. Boil in a little boiling water or bacon cooking water until soft. Drain and season with salt, pepper and a little butter.

When the potatoes are just cooked, put the milk and spring onion into a saucepan and bring to the boil. Peel the potatoes and mash them quickly while still warm, beating in enough boiling milk to make a fluffy purée. (If you have a large quantity, put the potatoes in the bowl of a food mixer and beat with the spade.) Then stir in the cooked cabbage and taste for seasoning. For perfection, serve immediately in a hot dish with a lump of butter melting in the centre. Colcannon may be prepared ahead and reheated in a moderate oven (180ºC/350ºF/ gas 4), for about 20–25 minutes. Cover while reheating so it doesn't get too crusty on top.

1   2   3   4   5   6

The Perfect Chip

1. Straw potatoes (pommes allumettes): finest possible strips about 6cm (2½in) long.

2. Matchstick: similar length but slightly thicker.

3. Mignonette: 5mm (¼in) thick x 6cm (2½in) long.

4. Pont Neuf: about 1cm (½in) thick and 6cm (2½in) long.

5. Jumbo: about 2.5cm (1in) thick and 6cm (2½in) long.

6. Buffalo: similar size to Jumbo but unpeeled.

How to Cook Chips

Sales of frozen and pre-prepared chips have rocketed in a relatively short time – so much so that I feel many people have forgotten how easy it is to make chips at home. Here are the simple secrets of really sensational chips:

1. Use good quality 'old' potatoes e.g. Golden Wonder or Kerr's Pink

2. Use best-quality oil, lard or beef fat for frying. We frequently use olive oil because its flavour is so good and because when properly looked after it can be used over and over again. Avoid poor-quality oils which have an unpleasant taste and a pervasive smell.

3. Scrub the potatoes well and peel or leave unpeeled according to taste. Cut into similar size chips so they will cook evenly.

4. Rinse quickly in cold water but do not soak. Dry meticiously with a damp tea towel or kitchen towel before cooking – otherwise the water will boil on contact with the oil in the deep frier, possibly making it overflow. Do not overload the basket, otherwise the temperature of the oil will be lowered, making for greasy rather than crisp chips. Shake the pan once or twice to separate the chips while cooking.

To cook the first three sizes: Fry quickly in oil at 195°C/385°C until crisp.

To cook the last three sizes: Fry first at 160°C/310°F until they are soft and just beginning to brown (the time will vary from 4–10 minutes depending on size). Drain, increase the heat to 190°C/375°F and cook for a further 1–2 minutes or until crisp and golden.

To serve: Shake the basket, drain well, toss onto kitchen paper, sprinkle with a little salt, turn onto a hot serving dish and serve immediately.

Master Recipe
Potato Crisps or Game Chips

A mandolin slicer is useful though not essential for slicing. Potato crisps are sliced on a plain cutter and game chips on a crinkled cutter.

Game chips are paper-thin rounds of potato which are deep-fried in extra-virgin olive oil at 180°C/350°F until absolutely crisp, drained on kitchen paper and sprinkled with salt. Serve hot or cold. Provided they are properly cooked they will keep perfectly in a tin box for several days. These crisps or game chips are the traditional accompaniment to roast pheasant or guinea fowl.

Variations
Garlic Crisps

Follow the Master Recipe, putting the crisps into a warmed serving dish. Melt some Garlic Butter (see page 588) and drizzle it over the crisps. Serve immediately as a snack or as an accompaniment to hamburgers or steaks or on a *salade tiède* (warm salad).

Volcanic Crisps

Follow the recipe above, adding 1–2 tablespoons of chilli flakes to the butter with the garlic and parsley.

Pommes Gaufrette

Follow the Master Recipe. A mandolin is essential for slicing these potatoes. Rotate the potatoes 90° between each cut so the slices are latticed. Deep-fry for 2–3 minutes at 190°C/375°F or until crisp and golden.

Soufflé Potatoes

Slice potatoes very thinly (2mm/1/16in) on a mandolin. Deep-fry at 180°C/350°F for 4–5 minutes or until just beginning to brown. Drain and cool. Just before serving re-fry at 195°C/385°F: they will puff up immediately. Cook for 1–2 minutes until crisp and golden.

Sauté Potatoes
Serves 4–6

900g (2lb) potatoes
25–50g (1–2oz) clarified butter (see page 105)
2 tablespoons olive oil
parsley, chopped
salt and freshly ground pepper

Scrub the potatoes and boil or steam them until just cooked. Drain and when they are cool, peel and cut into 1cm (1/2in) slices. Heat the butter and oil in a frying pan until foaming, put the potatoes in a single layer, and season with salt and freshly ground pepper. Fry on a medium heat until golden on one side and then turn over to brown on the other side. They are good served sprinkled with chopped parsley.

Variation
Peppered Pops

Add 1–2 tablespoons of freshly cracked pepper to the foaming butter and proceed as above.

Potatoes with Cumin and Ginger
Serves 6

900g (2lb) potatoes, cooked in their jackets
5 tablespoons extra-virgin olive oil
2 teaspoons ground cumin, freshly roasted
3 teaspoons ginger, freshly grated
1/2 teaspoon salt
1 teaspoon freshly ground pepper
1/2 teaspoon cayenne
3 tablespoons freshly chopped coriander

Peel the potatoes and cut into 2cm (3/4in) cubes. Heat a wide frying pan. Pour in the oil, and add the ground cumin, ginger, salt, pepper and cayenne. Stir and add the potatoes, toss gently and cook until the potatoes are hot and crusted with the spices. Sprinkle with chopped coriander. Taste. Correct seasoning.

Pommes Julienne
Serves 4–6

900g (2lb) potatoes, peeled
25–50g (1–2oz) butter
salt and freshly ground pepper

25.5cm (10in) shallow baking tin

Cut the peeled potatoes into julienne strips and dry well. Rub a thick even coating of butter over the base and sides of the tin. Press in a thick layer of potatoes to cover the base of the pan. Season. Cover with a butter wrapper and a tight-fitting lid. Cook on a gentle heat for about 20–30 minutes. Loosen the sides with a palette knife. Turn out onto a plate when the bottom is golden brown and crisp.

Variation
Julienne Tart with Smoked Salmon, Crème Fraîche and Crispy Capers

Follow the recipe above. When the potatoes are cooked invert the cake onto a hot serving plate and top with crème fraîche and chives. Place slices of smoked salmon on top, sprinkle with Deep-fried Capers (see page 225) and serve immediately.

Baked Potatoes
Serves 8

Best not to wrap baked potatoes in tin foil, it softens the skins and spoils the flavour; it can even make them wet and soapy.

8 x 225g (8oz) 'old' potatoes
sea salt and butter

Preheat the oven to 200°C/400°F/gas 6.

Scrub the potatoes well and prick them 3 or 4 times so the skins don't burst in the oven. Bake for about 1 hour depending on size.

When cooked, serve immediately while skins are still crisp and make sure to eat the skins with lots of butter and sea salt.

There are so many good things to eat with baked potatoes; here are just a few suggestions:

Garlic mayonnaise with tuna fish
Garlic butter with crispy rashers of bacon
Crème fraîche with chopped smoked salmon and chives
Crème fraîche with roasted peppers and a drizzle of pesto

Master Recipe
Gratin Dauphinois
Serves 4–6

There are many wonderful French potato gratins that I love, but if I were forced to choose one I think it would have to be this sinfully rich Gratin Dauphinois. This is a particularly good version of the classic recipe because it can be made ahead and reheated with great success.

900g (2lb) even-sized potatoes
salt and freshly ground pepper
250ml (9fl oz) milk
250ml (9fl oz) double cream
1 small garlic clove, crushed
freshly grated nutmeg

Preheat the oven to 200ºC/400ºF/gas 6.

Peel the potatoes and slice them into very thin rounds 3mm (1/8in) thick. Do not wash them but dab them dry with a cloth. Spread them out on the worktop and season with salt and freshly ground pepper, mixing it in with your hands.

Pour the milk into a saucepan, add the potatoes and bring to the boil. Cover, reduce the heat and simmer gently for 10 minutes.

Add the cream, garlic and a generous grating of nutmeg and continue to simmer for 20 minutes, stirring occasionally so that the potatoes do not stick to the saucepan. Just as soon as the potatoes are cooked take them out with a slotted spoon and put them into 1 large or 6 small ovenproof dishes. Pour the creamy liquid over them.*

Cook in a bain-marie in the oven, for 10–20 minutes or until they are bubbly and golden on top.

*Can be prepared ahead to this point.

Variations
Smoked Mackerel and Potato Gratin
Follow the Master Recipe. Remove the skin and bones from 225g (8oz) smoked mackerel and divide into chunky bits. Put a layer of smoked mackerel and a sprinkling of chopped parsley in the centre as you layer the gratin into the dishes.

Smoked Salmon and Dill Gratin
Follow the Master Recipe. Add 175g (6oz) smoked salmon, cut in small cubes, and 1 tablespoon of dill in between the layers of potato.

Potato and Chorizo Gratin
Follow the Master Recipe. Add 175–225g (6–8oz) of chorizo or Kabanos sausage in between the layers of potato. Crispy bacon, mussels, shrimps etc., may also be used.

Gratin of Potato and Mushroom
Serves 6

If you have a few wild mushrooms, chanterelles or field mushrooms, mix them with cultivated mushrooms for this gratin. If you can only find flat mushrooms no matter, one way or the other the gratin will be delectable. It is terrific with a pan-grilled lamb chop or a piece of steak.

700g (11/2lb) 'old' potatoes, peeled and thinly sliced
butter
1 garlic clove, finely chopped
225g (1/2lb) wild or cultivated mushrooms, or a mixture of cultivated, brown, oyster and shiitake, sliced
300ml (1/2 pint) single cream
3 tablespoons Parmesan (preferably Pamigiano Reggiano), grated
salt and freshly ground pepper

25 x 20cm (10 x 8in) ovenproof gratin dish

Preheat the oven to 180°C/350°F/gas 4.

Blanch and refresh the potato slices. Grease a shallow gratin dish generously with butter and sprinkle the garlic over it. Arrange half the potatoes in the bottom of the dish, season with salt and pepper and put in the mushrooms. Season again and finish off with a final layer of overlapping potatoes. Bring the cream almost to boiling point and pour over the potatoes. Sprinkle the cheese on top and bake for about an hour, until the gratin becomes crisp and golden brown with the cream bubbling up around the edges.

Gratin of Potato and Celeriac

Serves 4–6

1 large celeriac, peeled, quartered and thinly sliced
acidulated water (see glossary)
900g (2lb) waxy potatoes, thinly sliced
1 teaspoon chopped tarragon or marjoram
300ml (10fl oz) cream
salt and freshly ground pepper

Preheat the oven to 190°C/375°F/gas 5.

Put the celeriac slices into acidulated water to prevent it discolouring. Blanch and refresh both the potatoes and celeriac. Drain the slices and dry them thoroughly on kitchen paper. In a gratin dish, arrange alternate layers of potatoes and celeriac, ending with a layer of potato. Season each layer with salt and freshly ground pepper. Add the chopped tarragon and pour over the cream. Bake the gratin for about an hour until bubbly and golden.

Variation

Gratin of Potato and Vegetables

Experiment with parsnips, white turnips, Jerusalem artichokes...

Oven-roasted Winter Root Vegetables

about equal volumes of:
parsnips
swede turnips
celeriac
carrot

whole garlic cloves
olive oil
winter herbs (thyme, rosemary, chives and parsley), freshly chopped
salt and freshly ground pepper

Preheat the oven to 200°C/400°F/gas 6.

Cut all the vegetables into similar-sized pieces – 2cm (3/4in) cubes are a good size. Put all the vegetables into a large bowl with the garlic. Drizzle generously with olive oil and season with salt and pepper.

Spread them in a single layer on 1 or several roasting tins. Roast, uncovered, stirring occasionally until they are fully cooked and just beginning to caramelise. Be careful, a little colour makes them sweeter, but there is a narrow line between caramelising and burning. If they become too dark they will be bitter.

Serve sprinkled with the herbs.

Note: some freshly roasted and ground cumin or coriander is also a delicious addition just before the end of cooking.

Caramelised Onions

450g (1lb) onions, sliced
2–3 tablespoons olive oil

Caramelised onions take a long time to cook: allow about 30–45 minutes. Heat the olive oil in a heavy saucepan, toss in the onions and cook over a low heat for as long as it takes for the onions to soften and caramelise to a golden brown. Stir and scrape the base of the saucepan regularly as they cook.

Onion Bhajis with Tomato and Chilli Sauce

Serves 4 as a starter

Cheap, cheerful and delicious – ideal pub grub!

110g (4oz) plain flour
2 teaspoons baking powder
1 teaspoon chilli powder
2 eggs, beaten
150ml (1/4 pint) water
4 onions, thinly sliced
2 tablespoons snipped fresh chives
vegetable oil for deep-frying

Tomato and Chilli Sauce (see page 591)

First make the Tomato and Chilli Sauce.

Sift the flour, baking powder and chilli powder into a bowl. Make a well in the centre, add the eggs, gradually add in the water and mix to make a smooth batter. Stir in the onions and chives. Season well with salt and pepper.

Just before serving, heat the oil to about 170°C/325°F. Fry dessertspoons of the batter for 5 minutes on each side until crisp and golden, and drain on kitchen paper. Serve hot or cold with the Tomato and Chilli Sauce.

French Fried Onions

Serves 6

1 large onion
milk
seasoned flour
good quality oil or beef dripping for deep-frying

Slice the onion into 5mm (1/4in) rings around the equator. Separate the rings and cover with milk until needed. Just before serving heat the oil in a deep-fryer to 180°C/ 350°F. Toss the rings a few at a time in seasoned flour. Deep-fry until golden in the hot oil. Drain on kitchen paper and serve hot with steaks, hamburgers, etc.

LEFT: Onion Bhajis with Tomato and Chilli Sauce

Spicy French Fried Onions

Add some cayenne pepper to the seasoned flour in the above recipe.

Roast Onions

I'm always surprised that so few people cook onions in this ultra simple way. We call them roast onions but I suppose, strictly speaking, they are baked. Choose small or medium onions.

Preheat the oven to 200°C/400°F/gas 6.

Roast Whole Onions

Bake the unpeeled onions until soft; this can take anything from 10–30 minutes, depending on size. Serve in their jackets. The diner can pull off the root end, squeeze out the onion and eat it with butter and sea salt.

Roast Onion Halves

Split the unpeeled onions in half lengthwise. Put a little olive oil on the base of a roasting tin, sprinkle with sea salt, put the onions cut-side down into the tin and roast until golden on the cut side. Turn off the oven and continue to cook until soft.

Roast Onion Slices

Choose large onions, cut into thick slices around the equator, spear each side with a soaked kebab stick or a skewer. Roast in a little olive oil and sea salt as above. Turn half way through cooking.

Roast Spring Onions

Peel the outer layer from the spring onions. Toss in extra-virgin olive oil, then roast until tender, 8–20 minutes depending on size. Turn them regularly.

Oignons à la Monégasque

Serves 6–8

This gutsy French salad keeps for not just days but weeks and is delicious with cold meat or game or as part of a salad.

450g (1lb) button onions, spring onions, young summer onions or leeks, whole
350ml (12fl oz) water
125ml (4fl oz) white vinegar
1 tablespoon olive oil
2 tablespoons sugar
250ml (9fl oz) homemade Tomato Purée (see page 50) or 2 tablespoons tomato paste mixed with 250ml (9fl oz) water
1/2 bay leaf
1/2 teaspoon thyme
sprig of parsley
75g (3oz) seedless raisins
salt and freshly ground pepper

This can also be made with larger onions if they are cut lengthways so that each segment has a piece of root left on, which will hold the onion together. Simply put all the ingredients into a saucepan cover and stew gently until the onions are soft, anything from 20 minutes to 2 hours. Button onions take about 2 hours. Remove the lid after the first hour.

Note: We also use young Japanese onions in the spring for this recipe, and cook them whole with 7.5–10cm (3–4in) of the green shoot left on.

Aigre-doux Onions with Thyme Leaves

Serves 4–6

A basket of baby onions is a real treasure to have in the pantry. We save the small onions of the crop carefully; gorgeous for roasting, sweet and melting cooked whole in stews, or in an onion 'Tarte Tatin' and irresistible with a shiny sweet-sour glaze. *Aigre-doux* means sweet and sour, as does *agrodolce* in Italian.

450g (1lb) button onions
25g (1oz) butter
2 teaspoons thyme leaves
25g (1oz) sugar
50ml (2fl oz) white wine vinegar
salt and freshly ground pepper

Peel and trim the onions leaving root base intact. Melt the butter in a heavy saucepan and toss the onions in it. Add the thyme. Cover with a butter wrapper and a tight-fitting lid. Cook over a low heat until almost soft. Add the sugar and vinegar, increase the heat and cook until the salt, vinegar and onion juices make a syrupy glaze. Spoon into a hot serving dish and serve immediately.

'Sun-dried' Tomatoes

Sun-dried tomatoes can be bought at enormous expense preserved in olive oil but you can make your own quite easily. I find this method of drying them in the coolest oven of my 4-door Aga quite successful. A fan oven works well also.

very ripe tomatoes
sea salt
sugar
olive oil

Cut the tomatoes in half crossways, put on to a wire rack, season with sea salt and sugar and drizzle with olive oil. Leave in the coolest part of a 4-door Aga, or in a fan oven at the minimum temperature, until they are totally dried out and wizened. I leave them in for 24 hours depending on size (after about 1 hour turn upside down). Store in sterilised jars covered with olive oil. A few basil leaves or a couple of sprigs of rosemary, thyme or annual marjoram added to the oil make them especially delicious. Cover and keep in a cool, dry, preferably dark place. Use on salads, with pasta etc.

Oven-roasted Tomatoes

Proceed as above but remove and use tomatoes while they are still plump but have reduced in size by half.

RIGHT: 'Sun-dried' Tomatoes

Buttered Cucumber with Fennel

Serves 4–6

Many people love cucumber raw, but few think of cooking it as a vegetable. It is quite delicious prepared in this way, and particularly good with fish.

25g (1oz) butter
1 cucumber, peeled and cut into 1cm (1/2in) dice
1/2 teaspoon snipped fresh fennel fronds
salt and freshly ground pepper

Melt the butter in a heavy saucepan or casserole, toss in the cucumber and season with salt and freshly ground pepper. Cover and sweat over a low heat until just soft, which takes about 20 minutes.

Stir occasionally. Add some snipped fresh fennel. Taste, and correct the seasoning if necessary.

Cucumber Neapolitana

Serves 6

Cucumber Neapolitana is a terrifically versatile vegetable dish – it keeps for several days so can be made ahead and it reheats well. It is delicious served with rice or pasta. It makes a great stuffing for tomatoes and is particularly good with roast lamb.

10g (1/2oz) butter
1 medium onion, 110g (4oz), sliced
1 cucumber, peeled and cut into 1cm (1/2in) dice
4 very ripe tomatoes
60ml (21/2fl oz) cream
1 dessertspoon freshly chopped mint
Roux (see page 580), optional
salt, freshly ground pepper and sugar

Melt the butter in a heavy saucepan and when it foams add the onion. Cover and sweat for about 5 minutes until soft but not coloured. Add the cucumber to the onions, toss well and continue to cook. Meanwhile drop the tomatoes into boiling water for 10 seconds, peel them and slice into the casserole, season with salt, pepper and a pinch of sugar. Cover and cook for a few minutes until the cucumbers are tender and the tomatoes have softened. Stir in the cream and bring back to the boil. Add the mint. If the liquid is very thin, thicken it by carefully whisking in a little Roux.

Okra in Batter

Serves 4

Look for unblemished and deep green okra or Lady's fingers. Only add salt to okra dishes after cooking, as it causes the vegetable to sweat. Don't cook okra with water either, as it makes it slimy. There are 2 types of pod – the oblong gomba, essential to New Orleans gumbo, to which it has given its name, and the round bamya.

225g (8oz) fresh okra or lady's fingers
110g (4oz) flour
11/2 tablespoons ground rice or rice flour
1 tablespoon cayenne pepper
1/2 teaspoon ground cumin
1/2 teaspoon turmeric
1 teaspoon salt
1 teaspoon thyme leaves
olive oil for frying

Slice the caps off the okra and discard the rest. Cut into 1cm (1/2in) thick rounds. Sift the flour, rice flour, cayenne, cumin, turmeric and salt into a bowl. Add the thyme leaves, mix thoroughly and make a well in the centre. Add about 100ml (31/2 fl oz) water and whisk in a little at a time to make a light batter about the consistency of thick cream.

Heat the oil in a deep-fryer over a medium-low heat. Fold the slices of okra gently into the batter. Drop tablespoons of the okra gently into the oil. Fry, turning now and then, until the fritters are crisp and golden. This will take about 6–7 minutes. Serve immediately.

Master Recipe
Buttered Celery

Serves 4–6

When you arrive at the delicious tender leaves at the centre, do not cut off the base, simply break off, nibble or save for crudités. A little block of root remains. Trim this and taste; it resembles celeriac and is delicious, eaten raw or diced and cooked with the celery.

1 head of celery
150ml (1/4 pint) water
25g (1oz) butter
salt and freshly ground pepper

parsley, chopped

Pull the stalks off the head of celery. If the outer stalks seems a bit tough, peel the strings off with a swivel top peeler or simply save these tougher stalks for the stock pot. Cut the celery into 1cm (1/2in) chunks, preferably at an angle.

Bring the water to the boil in a saucepan. Add a little salt and the chopped celery. Cover and cook for 15–20 minutes or until a knife will go through the celery with ease. Drain, add the butter and season with salt and pepper. Serve garnished with parsley. A little snipped lovage is also a delicious addition.

Variation
Celery with Cream and Parsley or Lovage

Follow the Master Recipe until the celery is cooked then remove it, pour off most of the water and add 125–175ml (4–6fl oz) cream. Thicken with a little Roux (see page 580), add the celery back in and allow to bubble for a few minutes. Put into a hot serving dish, sprinkle with freshly chopped parsley or lovage and serve.

Chargrilled Red and Yellow Peppers

Serves 8

The sweet, slightly smoky flavour of roasted or char-grilled peppers makes this summery starter one of my absolute favourites. In fact every now and then I roast lots of peppers and store them peeled and de-seeded in a glass Kilner jar with a few fresh basil leaves and lots of extra-virgin olive oil. Then I can dip in whenever I fancy and eat them as they are, or use them in a salad or as an accompaniment to pan-grilled fish or meat, or with lentils and goat's cheese. They are also very good on tapenade toasts – toast some bruschetta and slather with tapenade (see page 590).

8 red and 8 yellow peppers (preferably Italian or Spanish)
2 garlic cloves, cut in very fine slivers (optional)
8 fresh basil leaves
extra-virgin olive oil
10–12 black Kalamata olives (optional)
sea salt and freshly cracked pepper

Preheat the grill or – better still – use a charcoal grill. Grill the peppers on all sides, turning them when necessary, until they are quite charred.

Alternatively preheat the oven to 250°C/475°F/gas 9; put the peppers on a baking tray and bake for 20–30 minutes until they are soft and the skin blistered.

Put them into a plastic bag to cool and seal the end – this will make them much easier to peel.

Peel the peppers then halve and remove stalks and seeds but don't wash. Choose a wide, shallow serving dish. Arrange the peeled peppers and what juices you can, add the garlic, basil and a good drizzle of olive oil. Scatter a few black olives over the top if liked.

How to Cook Sweetcorn

Bring a large saucepan of water to the boil, add salt.

Peel the ears of corn, trim both ends, drop into the water. Cover the saucepan and bring back to the boil, cook for just 3 minutes.

Drain, allow to cool and serve imediately with butter and salt.

Fresh Sweetcorn with Marjoram

Serves 6

6 ears of corn, freshly picked if possible
25–50g (1–2oz) butter
salt and freshly ground pepper
1–2 tablespoons freshly chopped annual marjoram

Prepare the sweetcorn as above, then slice the kernels vertically off the cob. Melt the butter in a saucepan and add the corn. Season, add the marjoram, stir briefly. Taste, correct the seasoning. Serve immediately.

Chargrilled Fennel

Fennel is very good baked, grilled or roasted. Grilling is a very quick way of preparing it.

1–2 fennel bulbs, trimmed (reserve the fronds) and cut into diagonal slices
extra-virgin olive oil
salt and freshly ground pepper

Drizzle the fennel with oil and turn gently to coat. Season with salt and pepper. Cook for 1–2 minutes on both sides on a chargrill or grill. Garnish with the trimmed feathery leaves and serve immediately.

Master Recipe
Globe Artichokes with Melted Butter

Serves 6 as a starter

Whole globe artichokes are quite fiddly to eat. First you pull off each leaf separately and dip in the sauce. Have plenty of bowls for the discarded part of the leaves. Eventually you are rewarded for your patience when you come to the heart. Don't forget to scrape off the tickly 'choke'; then cut the heart into manageable pieces, sprinkle it with a little sea salt before you dip it into the remainder of your sauce. Simply delicious!

6 globe artichokes
1.2 litres (2 pints) water
2 teaspoons salt
about 2 teaspoons white wine vinegar

175g (6oz) butter
juice of 1/4 lemon, freshly squeezed

Trim the base of the artichoke just before cooking so it will sit steadily on the plate and rub the cut end with lemon juice or vinegar to prevent it from discolouring. Prepare a large saucepan of boiling water and add 2 teaspoons salt and 2 teaspoons vinegar to every 1.2 litres (2 pints) water. Pop in the artichokes and bring back to the boil. Simmer steadily for about 25 minutes. Test after about 20 minutes to see if they are done by raising the artichoke out of the water and tugging off one of the larger leaves at the base; if cooked, it should come away easily; if not continue to cook for another 5–10 minutes. Remove and drain upside down on a plate.

While they are cooking, melt the butter and add lemon juice to taste.

To serve: put each warm artichoke onto a hot serving plate and serve the sauce or melted butter in a little bowl beside it. Artichokes are eaten with your fingers, so you might like to provide finger bowls of warm water with a slice of lemon.

Variations

Globe Artichokes with Vinaigrette Dressing

Follow the Master Recipe to cook the artichokes. Serve them with Vinaigrette (see page 226).

Globe Artichokes with Hollandaise Sauce

Follow the Master Recipe to cook the artichokes. Serve them with Hollandaise Sauce (see page 581).

Globe Artichoke Hearts Braised in Olive Oil

Serves 4

850ml (1½ pints) water
1 lemon
6 globe artichokes
6 tablespoons extra-virgin olive oil
1 onion, coarsely diced
2 garlic cloves, chopped
4 tablespoons coarsely chopped parsley
60ml (2½fl oz) water
salt and freshly ground black pepper

Preparing the artichokes is quite fiddly. Acidulate the water with the juice of the lemon and drop in the squeezed lemon halves. Cut a ring around the stalk where it meets the base of the artichoke. Break off the stalk and the toughest fibres will come with it. Then, with a sharp knife, starting from the base, ruthlessly cut off all the leaves and trim the top down as far as the heart. Scrape out the hairy choke, using the tip of a knife or a sharp-edged spoon. Work quickly and drop the trimmed hearts into the acidulated water, or they will discolour.

Heat the oil in a wide sauté pan, add the onion and garlic and sweat for a few minutes. Cut the artichoke hearts into quarters or eighths, add to the pan with the parsley. Season and toss well. Add the water, cover and cook for 10–15 minutes, until the artichokes are tender. Serve hot or at room temperature.

Cardoons with Cream and Parmesan

Serves 6

Cardoon plants look very like their cousins the globe artichokes but unlike the latter the cardoon is cultivated for its stalks, not its thistle-like flowers. We've been growing them for about a decade now, but only have about 8 or 10 plants so we tend to eat them in the same way every year – raw, cut into strips and dipped in a Bagna Cauda Sauce (see page 593) or cooked and then stewed in butter with some cream and lots of Parmesan.

1.8kg (4lb) cardoon ribs, trimmed
acidulated water (see recipe, left)
butter
Parmesan cheese (preferably Parmigiano
    Reggiano), freshly grated
cream
salt and freshly ground pepper

Preheat the oven to 200°C/400°F/gas 6.

Separate the stalks and heart. Use the tender heart for eating raw with Bagna Cauda if you like. Cut the stalks into manageable lengths, 8–10cm (3–4in), cook in acidulated water for 30–35 minutes. Drain and refresh in cold water and remove the strings from the outer stalks.

Smear a large, shallow dish with butter, arrange a layer of cardoons in the base, dot with butter, season with salt and pepper. Sprinkle with Parmesan, another layer of cardoons, butter, seasoning, Parmesan and continue until the dish is full, finishing with a layer of cardoons. Pour on a little cream and sprinkle the top with Parmesan cheese.

Bake in the oven for 15–20 minutes or until the cardoons are tender and the top is bubbling and golden.

Asparagus with Sauce Maltaise

Serves 4–6 as a starter

16–20 spears of very fresh green asparagus
Sauce Maltaise (see page 582)
chervil

Trim the root end of the asparagus, and peel if you wish (save the trimmings for soup). Cut into uniform lengths. Just before serving, cook the asparagus in boiling salted water. Depending on the thickness of the spears it may take from 4–8 minutes to cook. Test by putting the tip of a sharp knife through the thicker end. The knife should go through easily. Remove from the water and drain.

Put a spoonful of Sauce Maltaise on each warmed serving plate and place a few spears of asparagus beside it and garnish with a little chervil.

Master Recipe
French Beans

Serves 8

I find that French beans need a lot of salt in the cooking water to bring up the flavour. They don't benefit from being kept warm, so if you need to cook them ahead try the method I suggest below. I think it works very well.

900g (2lb) French beans
1.2 litres (2 pints) water
3 teaspoons sea salt
25–50g (1–2oz) butter
sea salt and freshly ground pepper

Top and tail the beans. If they are small and thin leave them whole, if they are larger cut them into 2.5–4cm (1–1½in) pieces at an angle. Bring the water to a fast rolling boil, add 2 teaspoons of salt then toss in the beans. Continue to boil very fast for 5–6 minutes or until just cooked (they should still retain a little bite). Drain immediately.*

Melt the butter in the saucepan, toss the beans in it, taste, season with pepper and a little sea salt if necessary.

* The beans may be refreshed under cold water at this point and kept aside for several hours.

Variations

French Beans with Fresh Chilli

Follow the Master Recipe until the beans are well drained. Heat 2 tablespoons olive oil in a wide sauté pan, and add 1 chopped garlic clove, 1 tablespoon coarsely chopped parsley and 1–2 chopped chillies. Toss over a medium heat for a few seconds, season well with salt and pepper, add the beans, taste and serve.

French Beans with Fresh Chilli and Anchovy

Add 6–8 chopped anchovies to the olive oil and proceed as above.

French Beans with Tomato Fondue

Follow the Master Recipe until the beans are well drained. Mix with 1 quantity of the recipe for Tomato Fondue (see page 200). Heat through and serve.

How to Cook Runner Beans

Runner beans need topping and tailing; they also need the strings removed. Cook as for French beans; though the flavour is different, some people just love runner beans with their colourful flowers. You will need to use 2 rather than 3 teaspoons salt to every 2 pints water when boiling them.

Slice at an angle or put through a traditional bean slicer.

Maharashtra Runner Beans with Mustard Seeds

Serves 4

This stir-fry is from Maharashtra in India, delicious on its own or with a pan-grilled lamb chop or steak. Top and tail the beans, remove the strings and chop finely to get the best flavour (you can also use French beans). Do not cover while cooking or you will lose the fresh green colour.

2 tablespoons sunflower oil
1 teaspoon black mustard seeds
150g (5oz) onion, finely chopped
1 teaspoon cumin seeds
350g (12oz) runner beans, sliced into 1cm
  (1/2in) pieces
salt and freshly ground pepper
pinch of sugar
2–3 tablespoons water
1 tablespoon freshly squeezed lemon juice
1–2 tablespoons desiccated coconut

Heat the oil in a wok or sauté pan and add the mustard seeds. As soon as they begin to pop, add the onion and cumin seeds. Stir and fry until the onion is soft.

Add the runner beans, salt, pepper, a pinch of sugar and a few tablespoons of water. Cook uncovered for 4 or 5 minutes until the beans are tender. Add the freshly squeezed lemon juice. Serve hot, sprinkled with fresh desiccated coconut.

Broad Beans with Olive Oil and Thyme Leaves

Serves 6

600ml (1 pint) water
1 teaspoon salt
700g (11/2lb) shelled broad beans
6 tablespoons olive oil
1 teaspoon thyme leaves

Bring the water to the boil, add the salt and beans, and cook for 6–8 minutes or until the beans are tender. Refresh in cold water. Drain the beans and peel off the outer skin. Pour the oil into a saucepan, toss in the beans and thyme leaves.

Cook for 2–3 minutes on a gentle heat – just long enough for the beans to heat through. Taste, add more salt if necessary and serve immediately.

Broad Beans with Summer Savory

Serves 8

Summer savory is a herb which has an extraordinary affinity with beans, seeming to make them taste more 'beany'. If you don't have any, simply leave it out.

150ml (1/4 pint) water
1 teaspoon sea salt
450g (1lb) shelled broad beans
sprig of summer savory
about 25g (1oz) butter
1–2 teaspoons freshly chopped summer savory
sea salt and freshly ground pepper

Bring the water to a rolling boil, add the sea salt, broad beans and a sprig of savory. Boil very fast for 3–4 minutes or until just cooked. Drain immediately.

Melt a little butter in a saucepan, toss in the broad beans and season with freshly ground pepper. Taste, add some more savory and a little sea salt if necessary.

Broad Bean Purée

Follow the recipe above, then slip the beans out of their skins. Add 2–3 tablespoons cream, then purée, check the seasoning and serve.

TIP: To reheat precooked beans: just before serving, plunge into boiling salted water for 1/2–1 minute, drain and toss in butter. Season and serve immediately.

Garden Peas with Fresh Mint

Serves 8

Really fresh peas from the garden are exquisite; it is difficult to resist eating them all raw as you pod them!

150ml (1/4 pint) water
1 teaspoon salt
1 teaspoon sugar
1 sprig mint
450g (1lb) garden peas or petit pois, freshly shelled
25g (1oz) butter
1–2 teaspoons freshly chopped mint

Bring the fresh cold water to the boil, add the salt, sugar, mint and the peas. Bring back to the boil over a high heat and simmer until the peas are cooked, 4–5 minutes at most. Strain, reserving the water for soup or gravy. Add some butter and the mint and a little extra seasoning if necessary. Eat immediately.

TIP: Frozen peas can be extraordinarily good. The cheaper brands tend to lack flavour so buy the best you can afford.

Sugar Peas or Snow Peas or Sugar Snaps

Serves 6

Beware – these can go on cooking after they've been drained so err on the side of undercooking.

450g (1lb) sugar peas, sugar snaps or snow peas
1.2 litres (2 pints) water
1 1/2 teaspoons salt
25–50g (1–2oz) butter
freshly ground pepper

String the sugar peas. Bring the water to a good rolling boil, add the salt and the peas and continue to boil furiously with the lid off until just cooked: this will take about 4–6 minutes. They should still have a slight crunch. Drain immediately.*

Toss in a little melted butter, taste and correct seasoning. Serve immediately in a hot serving dish.

* As with many green vegetables sugar peas, snow peas or sugar snaps can be refreshed with cold water at this point and reheated just before serving in boiling salted water.

Courgettes with Marjoram

Serves 4

I'm completely hooked on annual marjoram. The seed is sometimes difficult to track down because it can be called sweet marjoram or knotty marjoram, but if you have any little patch at all it's worth growing because it transforms so many dishes into a feast.

*1lb (450g) green or golden courgettes or a
  mixture, no more than 15cm (6in) in length
1–2 tablespoons extra–virgin olive oil
1–2 teaspoons annual marjoram or basil,
  chopped
salt and freshly ground pepper*

Top and tail the courgettes and cut them into scant 5mm (1/4in) slices. Heat the oil and toss in the courgettes so that they become coated. Cook on a medium heat until just tender (about 4–5 minutes). Add the marjoram or basil. Season with salt and freshly ground pepper. Turn into a hot dish and serve immediately.

Note: Courgettes are one of the trickier vegetables to cook. Like mangetout peas they seem to continue cooking at an alarming rate after you've taken them out of the pot, so whip them out while they are slightly al dente.

Mushroom Crostini with Rocket and Parmesan

Serves 2

This is a poshed-up version of mushrooms on toast. Virtually all fungi are delicious on toast so this can be very humble or exotic, depending on the variety chosen.

*extra-virgin olive oil
2 slices from a large good-quality baguette
butter (optional)
4–6 flat mushrooms or large oyster mushrooms
marjoram, thyme or rosemary
1 or 2 garlic cloves (optional)
rocket leaves
Parmesan (preferably Parmigiano Reggiano),
  freshly grated*

Heat 2.5cm (1in) olive oil in a frying pan until just below smoking point. Fry the pieces of bread one at a time, whip them out just as soon as they become golden, drain on kitchen paper and keep warm. (The oil may be strained and used again for another purpose.)

Heat a little olive oil or half olive oil and half butter in a frying pan. Remove the stalks from the mushrooms and place them skin side down in the pan in a single layer. Put a little dot of butter into each or better still use garlic or marjoram butter, made simply by mixing some chopped garlic and parsley or annual marjoram into a little butter. Alternatively, sprinkle with marjoram and some crushed garlic if you like. Season with salt and pepper.

Cook on 1 side for 3–6 minutes (depending on the size of the mushroom: it could be anything from 3–6 minutes), then turn over as soon as you notice that the gills are covered with droplets of juice. Cook on the other side until tender. Meanwhile, rub the surface of the warm crostini with a cut clove of garlic, put on 2 hot plates.

Arrange a few fresh rocket leaves on each one, top with overlapping mushrooms.

Sprinkle with Parmesan and serve immediately. If there are any buttery juices in the pan, spoon every drop over the mushrooms for extra deliciousness.

Portobella Mushrooms with Parsley Pesto and Balsamic Vinegar

Serves 6

*6 Portobella mushrooms or large meaty flats
2 large garlic cloves, crushed
olive oil
110g (4oz) cooked beetroot
60ml (2 1/2fl oz) homemade Chicken or
  Vegetable Stock (see page 36)
2 tablespoons cream
60ml (2 1/2fl oz) balsamic vinegar
salt and freshly ground pepper*

Parsley or Basil Pesto (see page 589)

*fresh thyme leaves and flowers or wild garlic
  flowers to garnish*

Preheat the oven to 250°C/475°F/gas 9.

If you are using Portobella mushrooms split them in half widthways and arrange on a baking tray in a single layer. Flats should be kept whole. Sprinkle with salt, a few grinds of pepper and the garlic. Drizzle with olive oil and roast in a fully preheated hot oven for 10–15 minutes or until cooked through.

Purée the beetroot with a little chicken or vegetable stock and the cream. Taste and correct seasoning.

When the mushrooms are almost cooked, put the balsamic vinegar in a small saucepan and boil to reduce until slightly syrupy. Sandwich the 2 pieces of each mushroom or 2 flats together with a dollop of Parsley or Basil Pesto. Arrange each in the centre of a hot plate. Drizzle balsamic vinegar and beetroot purée around the edge. Garnish with thyme leaves and flowers or wild garlic flowers.

Portobella Mushrooms with Goat's Cheese and Walnuts

Serves 8

275g (10oz) soft goat's cheese (Ardsallagh is good)
2 garlic cloves, roughly chopped
2 teaspoons freshly chopped thyme
2 tablespoons flat-leaf parsley plus extra sprigs
4 tablespoons extra-virgin olive oil
8 large Portobella or field mushrooms
16 walnut halves
salt and freshly ground black pepper

Preheat the oven to 220°C/420°F/gas 7.

Place the goat's cheese, garlic, thyme, parsley and 2 tablespoons of the olive oil in a blender and whizz to a smooth paste.

Season the mushrooms with salt and freshly ground black pepper, then drizzle over the remaining oil. Divide the goat's cheese mixture evenly between them. Cook for 15–20 minutes or until they are golden and the mushrooms are soft to the point of a knife. Meanwhile toast the walnuts, and sprinkle with extra sprigs of flat-leaf parsley over the mushrooms just before serving.

Portobella Mushroom Burger

Serves 2

Cook 2 large flat mushrooms on a pan-grill or in the oven drizzled with olive oil. Season with salt, freshly ground pepper, a little crushed garlic and some thyme leaves. Toast 2 hamburger buns, spread with goat's cheese and pesto or garlic butter. Top with the juicy portobella and the other half of the bun. Serve immediately.

Roast Pumpkin

a slice of pumpkin, seeds and fibres removed
olive oil or beef dripping
salt and freshly ground pepper
chopped parsley or grated Gruyère cheese

Preheat the oven to 180°C/350°F/gas 4.

Cut the pumpkin into chunks with a bit of skin on each piece. Season with salt and pepper. Toss in olive oil or melted dripping and roast in the oven for 3/4–1 hour depending on size, turn occasionally.

Serve either sprinkled with parsley or arrange in a dish, scatter with grated Gruyère cheese and flash under a grill until the cheese becomes bubbly and brown. If you then scatter it with crispy bacon and lots of chopped parsley you have a supper dish rather than just an accompanying vegetable.

Mary Jo's Roast Pumpkin

Serves 20

Great for a party. This makes a nice vegetarian/vegan dish served with a simple Pilaf Rice (see page 125).

2.2kg (5lb) peeled pumpkin cut in large chunks (thick fleshed white pumpkins are best)
2 medium onions, halved and thinly sliced

2 cloves garlic, peeled and finely chopped
l green or red chilli, chopped, seeds left in
1 teaspoon ground ginger
1 teaspoon cinnamon
1 teaspoon allspice
1/2 teaspoon turmeric
60ml (2¹/₂fl oz) extra-virgin olive oil
juice of 1 small lime
salt
coriander leaves

Preheat the oven to 220°C/425°F/gas 7.

Mix the pumpkin with the onions, garlic, chilli, dry spices and salt. Pour over the olive oil and combine. Scrape the entire mixture onto a baking tray and spread out evenly. Roast in the oven until tender and tinged with brown.

Carefully lift the pumpkin onto a warm serving platter and drizzle the caramelised liquid from the baking tray over the top. (If juices are too watery, pour into saucepan and reduce until syrupy.) Squeeze over the lime juice and sprinkle with coriander leaves.

Patty Pan Squash with Basil or Marjoram
Serves 6

12–18 patty pan squash or a mixture of patty pan squash and small green courgettes
olive oil
2 tablespoons freshly chopped marjoram or torn basil leaves
lemon juice (optional)
salt and freshly ground pepper

Trim the squash and cut each one into 6 or 8 pie-shaped pieces depending on size. Slice the courgettes on the diagonal into 7mm (1/3in) slices. Heat a few tablespoons of olive oil in a cast-iron pan or wok, add the patty pan squash and courgettes, if using. Season with salt and freshly ground pepper, toss rapidly over the heat, add the chopped or torn herbs. Toss for another minute or so.

Taste and correct seasoning. A few drops of lemon juice might be good. Serve immediately.

Stir-fried Vegetables
Serves 2–4

You can stir-fry a number of different vegetables but think about texture, colour and flavour before you make your choice. A wok is by far the most useful bit of kitchen equipment but useless unless you have a powerful gas cooker. Having said that, a good heavy frying pan will suffice for this recipe.

2 tablespoons spring onion, cut into thin slices at an angle
1 tablespoon grated or finely chopped fresh ginger
2–3 garlic cloves, chopped
50g (2oz) mushrooms, cut into quarters and sliced thinly
70g (2¹/₂oz) French beans, cut into 3cm (1¹/₄in) slices at an angle
75g (3oz) yellow or green courgettes, cut in half lengthways and sliced thinly
75g (3oz) mangetout peas, cut into small pieces approx. 1cm (¹/₂in) approx. at an angle
50g (2oz) broccoli, cut into tiny florets
25g (1oz) peanuts or cashew nuts (optional)
salt and freshly ground pepper
a pinch of sugar
1 tablespoon freshly chopped parsley
1 tablespoon freshly chopped mixed herbs (e.g. mint, chives, thyme or basil)

First prepare the vegetables.

Heat the wok until it smokes, add the oil and heat again. Add the spring onions, ginger and garlic, toss around, then add the vegetables one after the other in the order they are listed above, tossing between each addition. Season with salt, freshly ground pepper and sugar. Sprinkle with freshly chopped herbs, taste, correct the seasoning. Serve immediately in a hot serving dish.

Giant Courgette or Marrow in Cheddar Cheese Sauce
Serves 4–6

Most people who grow courgettes find it hard to eat them fast enough; when they turn into marrows try this – it is unexpectedly good.

1.3kg (3lb) large courgette or small marrows (should yield about 900g (2lb) prepared)
45g (1³/₄oz) butter
about 225ml (8fl oz) creamy milk
Roux (see page 580)
50g (2oz) mature Cheddar, grated
1 tablespoon freshly chopped parsley
salt and freshly ground pepper

Peel and de-seed the courgette or marrow and cut into 2.5cm (1in) chunks. Melt the butter in a heavy casserole, toss in the courgette or marrow and season. Cover with a butter wrapper and the lid of the saucepan. Cook over a low heat until soft and juicy, about 20 minutes.

Remove the marrow or courgette with a slotted spoon to a warm serving dish. Add the creamy milk to the juices in the casserole and bring to the boil. Whisk in enough roux to thicken the sauce. Add the cheese, taste and correct the seasoning. Pour the sauce over the courgettes and serve sprinkled with a little parsley.

Variations

1. Sprinkle a little extra grated cheese or a mixture of grated cheese and Buttered Crumbs (see page 244) on top and flash under the grill until crispy and golden.

2. Put a layer of shepherd's pie mixture in a deep ovenproof dish, top with marrow and cheese sauce and bake in a preheated oven (190°C/375°F/gas 5) for 30 minutes.

3. A layer of Tomato Fondue (see page 200) under the courgettes is also delicious.

Gratin of Aubergines and Tomato with Parmesan

Serves 4–6

You can find many recipes for this famous Italian dish – this one is from Ursula Ferrigno. Delicious as a vegetable course or as an accompaniment to a main course. You can use tinned tomatoes.

3 medium fresh aubergines
125ml (4fl oz) olive oil
1 medium onion, chopped
450g (1lb) very ripe tomatoes, peeled and
    chopped
3 sprigs rosemary
zest of 1 lemon, preferably unwaxed
lots of fresh basil leaves
50–110 g (2–4oz) Parmesan (preferably
    Parmigiano Reggiano), shaved or coarsely
    grated
sea salt, coarsely ground black pepper and a
    pinch of sugar

30 x 25cm (12 x 10in) earthenware dish

Preheat the oven to 200°C/400°F/gas 6.

Slice the aubergines into 5mm (¼in) thick rounds. Put into a colander. Sprinkle with salt and leave for 15 minutes to de-gorge. Meanwhile, make the tomato sauce: heat the olive oil in a saucepan and sweat the onion until soft but not coloured. Add the tomatoes. Season with salt, pepper and sugar. Bring to the boil and simmer gently with the lid on at first until rich tasting.

When the aubergines have de-gorged for 15 minutes, rinse in cold water and pat dry.

Brush a baking tray generously with olive oil and place the aubergines in a single layer on the tray. Sprinkle with rosemary, drizzle with oil and bake for about 10 minutes in the oven or until golden.

Add the lemon zest to the tomato sauce and mix well. Taste the sauce and adjust the seasonings as desired.

Arrange a layer of aubergines in an earthenware or gratin dish, sprinkle with torn basil leaves and slivers of Parmesan. Cover with a layer of tomato sauce followed by more aubergines, basil and Parmesan.

Continue layering in this way and finish with a sprinkle of Parmesan on top. Bake for 10 minutes or until bubbling and golden.

Tian of Mediterranean Vegetables Baked with Olive Oil and Herbs

Serves 8–10

A tian is a large, heavy earthenware pot made in Provence. You need one that measures 35 x 30cm (14 x 12in) or a large shallow ovenproof dish. Strictly speaking, Provençal tian is made of green vegetables – marrow, spinach, chard and perhaps peas. This is a more colourful version.

3 small aubergines, about 700g (1½lb)
900g (2lb) very ripe tomatoes, peeled
600g (1¼lb) courgettes
125–175ml (4–6fl oz) extra-virgin olive oil
4 spring onions, thinly sliced, or 1 onion, very
    thinly sliced
2–4 teaspoons freshly chopped herbs (e.g.
    rosemary, thyme or annual marjoram)
salt and freshly ground pepper

1–2 tablespoons freshly chopped parsley
    to garnish

Preheat the oven to 200°C/400°F/gas 6.

Prepare the vegetables: cut the aubergines into 1cm (½in) slices, sprinkle them with salt and leave to de-gorge for 15–20 minutes. Rinse and pat dry with kitchen paper. Drop the tomatoes in a bowl of boiling water for ten seconds then peel and cut in thick slices. Slice the courgettes at an angle in 1cm (½in) slices.

Drizzle a tian or shallow baking dish with half the olive oil, sprinkle in the spring

onions and some chopped herbs, arrange the aubergine slices alternately with tomatoes and courgettes. Season with salt and pepper, drizzle with the remaining oil and sprinkle over a little more marjoram. Bake for 25–30 minutes or until vegetables are cooked through. (Keep an eye on them: you may need to cover with tin foil if they are getting too charred.) Sprinkle with parsley and serve.

Variation
Gratin of Vegetables
Sprinkle Buttered Crumbs (see page 244) mixed with grated Parmesan, Cheddar or Gruyère on top and brown under the grill before serving.

Vegetarian Moussaka

Serves 8

This is a vegetarian version of a Greek peasant recipe served in almost every taverna in Greece. There are many variations on the theme, some of which include cooked potato and raisins.

350g (12oz) aubergines
350g (12oz) courgettes
400g (14 oz) tinned tomatoes or very ripe
    tomatoes in summer
1 onion, finely chopped (include some green
    part of spring onion if you have it)
4 garlic cloves, crushed
olive oil for frying
450g (1lb) mushrooms sliced and sautéed
2 teaspoons freshly chopped marjoram or fresh
    thyme
2 teaspoons freshly chopped parsley
pinch of grated nutmeg
2 teaspoons flour
2 boiled potatoes, sliced
salt and freshly ground pepper

Topping
35g (1½oz) butter
35g (1½oz) flour
600ml (1 pint) milk
1 bay leaf
2 organic egg yolks

2 tablespoons cream
110g (4oz) grated Gruyère or mature Cheddar
salt and freshly ground pepper

25 x 20cm (10 x 8in) earthenware dish

Preheat the oven to 180°C/350°F/gas 4.

Slice the aubergines and courgettes into
1cm (½in) slices, score the flesh with a
sharp knife and sprinkle with salt. Leave
for at least 15 minutes to de-gorge.
Roughly chop or cut up the tinned
tomatoes, peel and chop the fresh
tomatoes if using. Keep the juices.

Meanwhile in a heavy saucepan over a
gentle heat, soften the onions and garlic in
one tablespoon of olive oil. Add the
sautéed mushrooms, freshly chopped
herbs, and nutmeg to the onions. Stir in
the flour and cook for a minute or two
then pour in the tomatoes and their juice.
Bring to the boil, stirring, and simmer for
2–3 minutes. Season well.

Rinse and wipe the aubergines dry. Heat
1cm (½in) of olive oil in a frying pan. Fry
first the aubergines on both sides, then the
courgettes until light golden colour,
heating up more oil if necessary. As the
courgettes are done, put them into the
bottom of a shallow casserole. Add a layer
of sliced potato. Season with salt and
freshly ground pepper. Tip the mushroom
mixture onto the courgettes and potato,
then lay the fried aubergine on top of that.
Keep the top as flat as possible.

Melt the butter in a saucepan. Stir in the
flour. Cook, stirring, for 1 minute, then
draw off the heat. Add the milk slowly,
whisking out the lumps as you go. Add the
bay leaf. Return the pan to the heat and
stir until boiling. Season with salt and
pepper and simmer for 2 minutes. Mix the
egg yolk with the cream in a large bowl.
Pour the sauce on to this mixture, stirring
all the time. Add half the cheese and pour
over the casserole. Sprinkle the rest of the
cheese on top and bake for 30–35 minutes
until reheated and well browned.

Note: Moussaka can be made up in large
quantities ahead of time, cooled quickly
and frozen after it has been closely
covered with clingfilm.

Spiced Vegetable Pie
Serves 6

250g (9oz) onions, chopped
225g (8oz) potatoes, peeled and chopped
250g (9oz) carrots, chopped
225g (8oz) celeriac, peeled and chopped
110g (4oz) parsnip, peeled and chopped or/and
    110g (4oz) mushrooms, sliced and sautéd
2 tablespoons olive oil
2 teaspoons cumin seeds
3 teaspoons coriander seeds
½ teaspoon cardamom seeds
2 tablespoons flour
1 teaspoon turmeric
salt, freshly ground pepper and sugar
300ml (10fl oz) Vegetable Stock (see page 36)

Pastry
450g (1lb) flour
salt
250g (9oz) butter
175g (6fl oz) water

egg wash made with 1 organic egg, a little
    water and a pinch of salt

tart tin 20cm (8in) in diameter and 4cm (1½in)
    deep or individual tins

Preheat the oven to 230°C/450°F/gas 8.

Cut the vegetables into uniform-sized
cubes of about 2.5cm (1in). Heat the olive
oil in a wide sauté pan, add the onions,
potatoes, carrots, celeriac, parsnips and
mushrooms, if using. Season with salt and
freshly ground pepper, toss in the oil, cover
the pot and sweat on a gentle heat for 4–5
minutes. Meanwhile heat the cumin,
coriander and cardamom seeds on a pan
until they start to smell aromatic – it takes
just a few seconds. Crush lightly, add to
the vegetables. Cook for 1–2 minutes. Take
off the heat – sprinkle over the flour,
turmeric and a pinch of sugar, stir well.

Put back on the heat and add the vegetable
stock gradually, stirring all the time. Cover
the pot and simmer for 20–30 minutes or
until the vegetables are almost tender but
not mushy.

Meanwhile make the pastry. Sift the flour
and salt into a mixing bowl and make a
well in the centre. Dice the butter, put it
into a saucepan with the water and bring
to the boil. Pour the liquid all at once into
the flour and mix together quickly; beat
until smooth. At first the pastry will be
too soft to handle but as it cools it may
be rolled out 3–5mm/⅛–¼in thick, to fit
the tin. The pastry may be made into one
large pie or individual pies. Keep back one-
third of the pastry for lids.

Fill the pastry-lined tins with the vegetable
mixture which should be almost, but not
quite cooked, and cooled a little. Brush the
edges of the pastry with the egg wash and
put on the pastry lids, pinching them
tightly together. Roll out the trimmings to
make pastry leaves or twirls to decorate
the tops of the pies; make a hole in the
centre, egg-wash the lid and then egg-
wash the decoration also. Bake the pies
for 20–35 minutes, depending on size.

Ratatouille Niçoise (Mediterranean Vegetable Stew)
Serves 8–10

Ratatouille, perhaps the most famous
Mediterranean vegetable stew of all, can
be horrendously unappetising. In fact,
it's quite difficult to get a really good
result with the classic method unless
you stand over the pot. For some time
now I have been following Roger Vergé's
example, by cooking the aubergines and
courgettes separately and adding them
in at the end. You get far better results.
Ratatouille can be served hot or cold.

450g (1lb) medium aubergines, unpeeled

450g (1lb) courgettes, not more than 15cm (6in) long

extra-virgin olive oil

2 red peppers

1 green pepper

350g (12oz) large onions, sliced

2 large garlic cloves, crushed

450g (1lb) very ripe tomatoes or 1 x 400g (14 oz) tin Italian tomatoes

1/2 teaspoon coriander seeds, crushed

1 tablespoon freshly chopped basil or annual marjoram

salt, freshly ground pepper and sugar

Slice the aubergines and courgettes into 1cm (1/2in) rounds, sprinkle with a little salt and put into a colander. Leave for an hour to de-gorge, then rinse and pat dry with kitchen paper. Heat about 2cm (3/4in) olive oil in a frying pan, cook the aubergines and courgettes in a single layer until golden brown on each side and drain on a wire rack over an oven tray.

Cut the peppers in quarters, remove the stems and seeds and slice into 5mm (1/4in) strips at an angle.

Heat 2 tablespoons olive oil in a wide casserole, add the sliced onions and crushed garlic, cover and sweat on a gentle heat for about 5 minutes. As they begin to soften add the sliced peppers, cover and simmer for 10–12 minutes.

Meanwhile, peel and slice the tomatoes, add to the peppers and season with salt, pepper and sugar. Simmer without covering the pan until the vegetables are just cooked – about 6–8 minutes. Then add the aubergines and courgettes with the crushed coriander. Stir gently, add the basil or marjoram. Taste and correct the seasoning.

Caponata

Serves 4–6

1 large aubergine, unpeeled, cut into 1–2cm (1/2–3/4in) dice but not peeled

salt

5–6 tablespoons extra-virgin olive oil

5–6 celery stalks, chopped

1 large onion, chopped

1 x 400g (14oz) tin chopped tomatoes

1–11/2 tablespoons caster sugar

4 tablespoons red wine vinegar

1/2–1 teaspoon freshly ground coriander

1 teaspoon capers

12 black olives, pitted and roughly chopped

2 tablespoons coarsely chopped flat-leaf parsley

salt and freshly ground pepper

Sprinkle the aubergine dice with salt and leave to de-gorge for about 30 minutes. Rinse and gently dry with a clean tea towel or kitchen paper.

Heat 4 tablespoons of the oil in a wide sauté pan. Add the celery and cook slightly until browned. Transfer to a plate. Add the aubergine to the pan, with more oil if necessary, and sauté until golden and tender. Leave to cool.

Add another tablespoon of oil to the pan and sauté the onion until golden. Chop the tomatoes and add with their juice. Simmer for 15 minutes or so until thick. Add the sugar, wine vinegar and coriander. Cook for a further 10 minutes. Stir in the capers, olives, parsley, aubergine and celery. Season with salt and plenty of pepper. Taste and adjust seasoning, pour into a serving dish.

Serve warm or cool.

Master Recipe
Piperonata

Serves 6–8

This is one of the indispensable trio of vegetable stews that we always reckon to have to hand. We use it not only as a vegetable but also as a topping for pizzas, as a sauce for pasta, grilled fish or meat and as a filling for omelettes and pancakes. Try to find those knobbly misshapen Spanish peppers – they have far more flavour than most of the perfectly shaped peppers from Holland.

2 tablespoons extra-virgin olive oil

1 onion, sliced

1 garlic clove, crushed

2 red peppers

2 green peppers

6 large, very ripe tomatoes or 1 x 400g (14oz) tin Italian tomatoes

1/2–1 fresh green chilli

salt, freshly ground pepper and sugar

a few fresh basil leaves

Heat the olive oil in a casserole, add the onion, stir and cook for a few seconds, then add the garlic, toss and allow to soften over a gentle heat in the casserole, covered with the lid, while you prepare the peppers.

Halve the peppers, remove the seeds, cut into quarters and then into strips across rather than lengthways. The onion should be soft and tender by now so add the peppers, toss them in the oil then replace the lid and continue to cook.

Meanwhile, if using fresh tomatoes, drop them into boiling water for 10 seconds then remove and immediately peel. Slice the tomatoes and the chilli and add to the casserole, season with the salt, pepper and sugar and a few fresh basil leaves. Stir well. Cook until the vegetables are just soft – about 30 minutes. Piperonata keeps in the fridge for several days and freezes perfectly.

Master Recipe
Tomato Fondue

Serves 6

Tomato fondue is one of our great convertibles, it has a number of uses, we serve it as a vegetable, sauce, filling for omelettes, topping for pizza, stuffing, etc... Make this in the summer, when tomatoes are at their juicy best, or use tinned ones the rest of the year.

1 tablespoon extra-virgin olive oil
110g (4oz) onions, sliced
1 garlic clove, crushed
900g (2lb) very ripe tomatoes, peeled, or
   2¹/₂ x 400g (14oz) tins tomatoes
1 tablespoon, freshly chopped herbs (of any of
   the following, or a mixture: thyme, parsley,
   mint, basil, lemon balm, marjoram)
salt, freshly ground pepper and sugar

Heat the oil in a stainless-steel saucepan. Add the sliced onion and crushed garlic, toss until coated, cover and sweat on a gentle heat until soft but not coloured. It is vital for the success of this dish that the onions are completely soft before the tomatoes are added.

Slice the fresh peeled or tinned tomatoes and add with all the juice to the onions. Season with salt, freshly ground pepper and sugar (tinned tomatoes need lots of sugar because of their high acidity). Add a generous sprinkling of chopped mint or torn basil.

Cook uncovered for 10–30 minutes, or until the tomato softens. Cook fresh tomatoes for a shorter time to preserve the lively fresh flavour. Tinned tomatoes need to be cooked for longer depending on whether one wants to use the fondue as a vegetable, sauce or filling.

Variations
Tomato Fondue with Chilli
Add 1–2 chopped fresh chilli with the onions and garlic in the Master Recipe.

Tomato Fondue with Chilli and Basil
In addition to the chilli, use torn basil instead of mixed herbs in the Master Recipe.

Tomato Fondue with Chilli and Coriander
In addition to the chillies (we use Hungarian wax chillies), use lots of coarsely chopped coriander instead of mixed herbs in the Master Recipe.

Tomato Fondue with Cannellini Beans and Chorizo
Add 1 x 400g (14oz) tin of cooked cannellini to the Tomato Fondue with 110g (4oz) cooked chorizo, and continue to cook for a further 10 minutes.

Spicy Tomato Fondue with Brussels Sprouts
Add about 450g (1lb) blanched and refreshed brussels sprouts to the Tomato Fondue with Chilli above and garnish with lots of fresh chopped coriander.

Heirloom Tomato Fondue
Use a mixture of heirloom tomatoes and add the juice of ¹/₂ lemon and 2 teaspoons rice or balsamic vinegar.

Master Recipe
Mushroom à la Crème
Serves 4

Mushroom à la crème may be served as a vegetable, or as a filling for vol au vents, bouchées or pancakes. It may be used as an enrichment for casseroles and stews or, by adding a little more cream or stock, may be served as a sauce with beef, lamb, chicken or veal. A crushed clove of garlic may be added while the onions are sweating. Flat mushrooms are even better than buttons for this recipe.

10–25g (¹/₂–1oz) butter
75g (3oz) onion, finely chopped
225g (8oz) mushrooms, sliced
a little olive oil, for frying
salt and freshly ground pepper
squeeze of lemon juice
125ml (4fl oz) cream
freshly chopped parsley
¹/₂ tablespoon freshly chopped chives (optional)

Melt the butter in a heavy saucepan until it foams.

Add the chopped onions, cover and sweat on a gentle heat for 5–10 minutes or until quite soft but not coloured; remove the onions to a bowl. Meanwhile cook the sliced mushrooms in a little olive oil in a hot frying pan (in batches if necessary). Season each batch with salt, pepper and a tiny squeeze of lemon juice. Add the mushrooms to the onions in the saucepan, then add the cream and allow to bubble for a few minutes.

Taste and correct the seasoning, and add parsley and chives if used.

Mushroom à la Crème keeps well in the fridge for 4–5 days and freezes perfectly.

Variations
Mushroom and Ginger à la Crème
Add 2 teaspoons of peeled and grated ginger to the basic recipe.

Wild Mushroom à la Crème
Substitute wild field mushrooms or a mixture of mushrooms, e.g. oyster, enoki, shiitake, nameko, girolles or chanterelles for the mushrooms in the Master Recipe.

salads

salads

Salad is healthy, colourful and delicious, and there are so many possibilities! It is essential that the ingredients, where possible, are locally and organically grown (rather than hydroponically) in rich, fertile soil full of complex nutrients for optimum nutrition content and flavour. Try to avoid packaging (ideally go for loose produce) and watch out for bagged salad – the leaves are usually washed in chlorine before being sealed into the complex artificial atmospheres the bags provide to keep them 'fresh'.

Grow Your Own

It is such fun to grow your own salads – buy a couple of seeds and get started. Get the kids involved too, they'll love it. You'll be surprised at how productive even a few containers on a small balcony or window sill can be. Some lettuces, salad leaves and fresh herbs need very little space and one really gets a huge buzz from eating homegrown produce. The freshness and flavour will also be far superior to anything you can buy from a supermarket. Rather than harvesting the whole lettuce, just pick off the outside leaves as you need them and the plant will continue to flourish.

In the greenhouses here at the Ballymaloe Cookery School we grow many different salads leaves, including claytonia, lambs lettuce, mibuna, mizuna, mysticana, garland chrysanthemum, red orach, chickweed, purslane, bok choy, pak choi, texel greens and mustard greens – a big thank you to Joy Larkcom for introducing us to many of these. Quite a few weeds are edible too – chickweed, the bane of many gardeners lives, is one such plant. I even saw it for sale in New York City's Union Square farmers' market for several dollars a bunch! Ground elder (another garden pest) has quite a pungent taste, made all the sweeter for knowing it is a weed.

Treat Your Salad Gently

At Ballymaloe, one of the first things the students are taught is how to wash lettuce: fill a sink to the top with cold water, take the lettuce in your hands and break off the leaves one by one until you reach the tender heart. Gently wash the leaves in the water. If you are concerned about the possibility of slugs or green fly when washing organic salad leaves add a little salt to the washing water. Use a salad spinner to dry the leaves a few at a time (this step is important as water dilutes the dressing). When drying lettuce and salad leaves, be aware that you need to handle the leaves carefully. Don't give in to the temptation to put the washed lettuce in a tea towel and swing it around your head, like I used to do when I was a child! You will only bruise the leaves.

Salads All Year Round

At Ballymaloe, we serve a green salad with every lunch and dinner throughout the year. At the school we fill our huge Irish beech salad bowl (made by Keith Mosse from Bennetsbridge) with leaves and edible flowers that vary through the seasons. In summer there are marigolds, nasturtiums, daisies, bachelor's buttons, wild garlic flowers, courgette and chive flowers. In winter the more robust lettuces, a little chard, beetroot leaves, shredded white and red cabbage, wild and garden sorrel, purslane and lambs lettuce (which survives even in snow). In winter, dressings are often more robust than in summer, using red wine vinegar, honey and wholegrain mustard.

Warm Salad

Warm salads or salades tièdes, the legacy of nouvelle cuisine (the 1980s French food trend), have stood the test of time. They are an interesting combination of lettuce, salad and herb leaves topped with a few delicious hot morsels.

The Basic Ingredients
Making a good salad is, as ever, totally dependent on using good ingredients. Always use local, seasonal produce – avoid out of season, lacklustre fruit and vegetables that have been transported halfway across the world.

Salads aren't just about iceberg lettuce and slices of cucumber. Use your imagination. Be creative and spontaneous, using everything from fruit and seeds, to vegetables and pasta. Think carefully about how the flavours and textures will combine together, and choose a complementary dressing.

Green Salads
A green salad should be a mixture of lettuces and salad leaves with a contrast of colour, texture and flavour. For colour, add radicchio, copper oak leaf lettuces and orach leaves. A burst of flavour can be introduced with peppery hot rocket leaves, mustard greens and pungent golden marjoram. Including cos or a good iceberg will add a welcome crunch to your salad. Foraging for wild foods adds lots of extra excitement to a salad. Watercress, wild sorrell, salad burnet, fat hen and wild garlic are all delicious in season.

Salad Dressings
Many people seem to imagine that there is a mystery to making salad dressing. Well, let me demystify it for you. All you need is the finest quality oil, some good vinegar, a little freshly ground pepper and sea salt. Whisk three parts extra-virgin olive oil with one part wine vinegar, add a little freshly ground pepper and some sea salt. One could also add a little crushed garlic and a spot of Dijon or grainy mustard, a few chopped herbs, maybe even a little honey to ring the changes. But provided that the oil and vinegar are top quality, even a basic dressing will be delicious.

The best oils are cold-pressed (a natural, chemical-free process which produces a low acidity level). Extra-virgin olive oil is the result of the first pressing of olives and has the lowest acidity. A good cold-pressed extra-virgin olive oil is better for you than most other oils, and has even been shown to reduce harmful cholesterol.

Other types of oils, such as nut and seed oils, are also suitable for dressings. Try hazelnut, walnut, pistachio, sunflower, groundnut, rapeseed, grapeseed, sesame, pumpkin seed and even macadamia nut oil. Some of these are rich and aromatic and their distinctive flavours tend to dominate. They are best used in moderation and with a specific purpose in mind. Olive oils infused with herbs, chillies or truffles are also fun to experiment with.

I first tasted authentic balsamic vinegar in Italy in 1981. The making of traditional balsamic vinegar is a lengthy process which stretches over many generations. This precious vinegar made from the concentrated juice of the trebbiano grape is used sparingly and respectfully. Originally it was given as part of a bride's dowry. Nowadays, however, because it has become so fashionable, it is largely produced through the solera system of tiered barrels in a process similar to the making of sherry. The best wine vinegars are wood-aged, for example Spanish Forum Vinegar. Also look out for Chinese red vinegar which is delicious. Verjuice (an acidic juice made by pressing unripe grapes) is another super product to experiment with.

Dressing a Salad
Be careful not to use too much dressing – use just enough to make the leaves glisten. Dress at the last moment in a deep bowl and toss the salad gently.

The opposite is true for tomato salad; dress as soon as the tomatoes are cut to seal in the flavour. Whether for eight or eighty, the sliced tomatoes are best spread in a single layer. They can then be seasoned evenly. If they are in a deep bowl they are difficult to season properly and even gentle tossing can cause the seeds to fall out. Once the tomatoes have been seasoned with salt, freshly ground pepper and a little sugar and then dressed with extra-virgin olive oil and freshly squeezed lemon juice (or a few drops of vinegar), they can be transferred to a serving bowl, if you wish.

Ballymaloe Buffet
Every Sunday night at Ballymaloe House we have a special buffet dinner. The joints of meat are cooked and the fish is poached in the afternoon. Salads are freshly made and kept cool, but not refrigerated. (If you *have* to put a salad in the fridge always allow it to return to room temperature before serving.) When making salads for a buffet, think carefully about combinations, and try not to use a mumbo jumbo of ingredients. Make single ingredient salads, such as aubergine, cucumber, potato or mushroom and caramelised onion. Most people will mix the salads on their plates, so their flavours should complement each other.

A Little Secret
Serve a salad of lettuces and salad leaves with, or just after, the main course as it has a miraculous effect – you will suddenly feel less full and have room for pudding after all!

Tuscan Pepper and Pasta Salad

Serves 12–14

175ml (6fl oz) Ballymaloe French Dressing (see page 226)
2 tablespoons Pesto (see page 589)
225–450g (½–1lb) penne or pasta shells
1 yellow pepper, preferably Italian or Spanish
2 red peppers, preferably Italian or Spanish
1 large cucumber
8–10 very ripe tomatoes
1 red onion, sliced very thinly
1 tablespoon chopped parsley
2–4 tablespoons annual marjoram, chopped or basil, torn
sugar
50–110g (2–4oz) black olives
salt and freshly ground pepper

First make the dressing and whisk the Pesto into it. Cook the pasta until al dente in boiling, salted water. Cut the peppers in quarters, remove the seeds and cut into 4cm (1½in) strips on the bias. Halve the cucumber, remove the seeds and cut into 5cm (2in) batons. Cut the tomatoes into quarters or sixths, depending on the size.

Drain the pasta as soon as it is cooked. While it is still warm, toss it in a little of the dressing. Mix all the prepared ingredients in a bowl, along with the onion and the herbs. Season with salt, pepper and sugar to taste. (In winter this salad needs lots of sugar.) Pour over the rest of the dressing. Serve in a wide bowl, sprinkled with black olives and parsley.

Summer Pasta with Courgette, Sugar Snaps and Peas

Serves about 10

450g (1lb) green and golden courgettes, 10–15cm (4–6in) long
450g (1lb) sugar snaps
450g (1lb) penne
110g (4oz) peas
50g (2oz) butter
4 tablespoons extra-virgin olive oil
1 teaspoon chilli flakes (optional)
salt and freshly ground pepper
2 tablespoons freshly chopped parsley
50g (2oz) fresh basil leaves, torn, or marjoram, chopped
a few courgette blossoms, if available

Top and tail the courgettes and cut into 5mm (¼ in) thick slices at an angle. String the sugar snaps if necessary. Bring 12 pints of water to the boil in a large deep saucepan, add 2 tablespoons salt, and cook the pasta until al dente. Meanwhile shoot the sugar snaps into 1.2 litres (2 pints) of boiling water with 1½ teaspoons of salt and cook uncovered until crisp and al dente (about 3–4 minutes). Drain and refresh under cold water. Save the water and bring to the boil again. Add the peas and cook for a few minutes.

If you're adept at juggling and have enough stove space you can cook the courgettes while the pasta and sugar snaps are cooking. Heat the butter and olive oil in a sauté pan, add the chilli flakes if using, toss in the courgettes, increase the heat and continue to toss for 3–4 minutes. Season with salt and pepper, cover and reduce heat to medium for another few minutes by which time the courgettes should be tender but still al dente. Draw off the heat and allow to cool. By now if you're timing is good the pasta should be al dente so drain it quickly.

To assemble
Add the sugar snaps, peas, courgettes, chopped parsley and the torn basil or chopped marjoram to the pasta. Toss well with a little extra-virgin olive oil. Taste and correct seasoning if necessary. Turn into a pasta bowl and sprinkle a few courgette blossoms and basil leaves over the top

Variation

225g (8oz) diced smoked salmon is also delicious added to this salad.

Tuna Fish, Bean and Pasta Salad

Serves 8

The cooked pasta is soaked in French dressing while it is still warm so that it absorbs extra flavour.

75g (3oz) pasta shells (conchglie, orecchiette or fusilli)
oil and lemon for cooking
150ml (¼ pint) Ballymaloe French Dressing (see page 226)
1 x 200g (7oz) tin each of flageolet beans, borlotti beans and red kidney beans, rinsed and drained*
1 bunch spring onions, chopped diagonally
1 box mustard and cress*
1 tablespoon chives, freshly chopped
1 tablespoon parsley, finely chopped
lemon juice, freshly squeezed
1 x 200g (7oz) tin tuna fish, drained
15 small black Niçoise olives
salt and freshly ground black pepper

Cook the pasta in plenty of boiling, salted water with 1 tablespoon of oil and a slice of lemon until tender. This will take about 10 minutes. Drain thoroughly and rinse the pasta well under cold running water. Soak the pasta in the French dressing for about 30 minutes, seasoning well.

Mix the pasta with the cooked beans, spring onions, half the mustard and cress, half the chives, the parsley and some lemon juice. Add the tuna and mix gently so as not to break up the flesh too much. Pile into a serving dish and scatter over the black olives and the remaining herbs, and mustard and cress.

* We also use 75g (3oz) dried black-eyed beans, 75g (3oz) dried haricot beans and 75g (3oz) red kidney beans - soak them separately overnight in cold water. Next day cook each type in fresh water for about 30 minutes with a few slices of onion and carrot and a bouquet garni.

* If you don't have mustard and cress to hand omit it – the salad is still delicious, although it is more nutritious if included.

Black Bean, Corn and Roasted Red Pepper Salad

Serves 6–8

Substitute 110–225g (4–8oz) penne or orzo for rice if you prefer a pasta salad.

275g (10oz) dried black beans
1 garlic clove
dried chillies (chipotle)
1 large onion, halved
175g (6oz) long grain rice
1 tablespoon extra-virgin olive oil
225g (8oz) cooked corn (about 4 ears)
2 sweet red peppers, roasted, peeled, de-seeded
    and diced (see page 83)
2 tablespoons fresh coriander or mint
2 tablespoons fresh parsley
6 spring onions, chopped

Dressing
50ml (2fl oz) red wine vinegar
2 tablespoons lemon juice, freshly squeezed
1 clove garlic, crushed
1½ teaspoons toasted and ground cumin seed
½ teaspoon toasted and ground coriander
175ml (6fl oz) extra-virgin olive oil

Cover the beans with plenty of cold water and soak for at least 3 hours or overnight. Next day drain them. Place the beans in a large pot with the garlic, chillies and onion. Cover with plenty of fresh water and bring to the boil. Continue to simmer for 1–1½ hours or until the beans are tender.

While the beans are cooking, cook the rice: bring a large pot of salted water to the boil, add the rice and bring back to the boil for 5–10 minutes or until the rice is tender. Drain and toss in the olive oil. Make the dressing by whisking all the ingredients together in a jar. When the beans are tender but still intact, remove the onion, garlic and chillies. Drain and toss in the dressing while still warm.

In a large bowl, mix the beans with the rice, corn, red peppers, coriander or mint, parsley and spring onions, and more dressing. Taste and correct seasoning if necessary.

ABOVE: Black Bean, Corn and Roasted Red Pepper Salad

Arizona Rice and Black Bean Salad

Serves 4–6

450g (1lb) black beans
450g (1lb) Basmati rice
1.3kg (3lb) medium salsa
2 bunches of spring onions
450g (1lb) vine-ripened tomatoes, diced
10g (½oz) salt
¼ teaspoon cayenne pepper
25g (1oz) cumin, roasted and freshly cracked
50g (2oz) coriander, chopped
50g (2oz) lime juice, freshly squeezed

Wash the beans thoroughly. Cook the beans in boiling, salted water for 2–3 hours or until tender. Top up with boiling water if necessary. Drain and rinse with cold water.

Cook the rice in boiling, salted water until tender. Drain well.

Combine all ingredients in a large bowl and toss together gently. Mix well and check seasonings.

Orzo Salad with Pesto, Cherry Tomatoes and Knockalara Cheese

Serves 4–6

Orzo is one of my best discoveries in recent years. Essentially, it is pasta grain, which may be used in a whole variety of dishes, hot and cold. For this salad we use Knockalara cheese, made from ewe's milk in Cappoquin, Co. Waterford – but you could use Feta cheese instead.

225g (8oz) orzo
2 tablespoons Pesto (see page 589)
12 cherry tomatoes, red and yellow mixed, if possible
balsamic vinegar or red wine vinegar
pinch of sugar
salt and freshly ground pepper
25g (1oz) toasted pine kernels
75g (3oz) Knockalara or Feta cheese, cut into 2cm (³⁄₄in) cubes

Garnish
rocket leaves, if available
sprigs of basil

Cook the orzo for 10–12 minutes or until 'al dente'. Drain, rinse quickly under the tap and allow to cool. Put into a large bowl and toss with the pesto. Quarter the tomatoes, season with salt and freshly ground pepper, sprinkle with balsamic or red wine vinegar and sugar and toss well. Toast the pine kernels until golden.

Add the tomatoes and pine nuts to the orzo which should by now be cool. Toss gently. Add the cubes of cheese and toss one more time. Turn onto a serving dish, and garnish with rocket leaves and a sprig or two of basil. Eat immediately.

TIP: When making pasta salads, pasta should be tossed in a well-flavoured dressing while still warm.

Caesar Salad

Serves 4

This legendary salad, first made in Mexico by Caesar Cardini in the 1920s, has become all the rage. It takes only a few minutes to make at home. Serve it in deep bowls as they do in Australia or on chilled white plates.

1 large cos (Romaine) lettuce
2 tablespoons extra-virgin olive oil
10g (¹⁄₂oz) butter
2 slices white bread, cut into 2.5cm (1in) cubes
50g (2oz) Parmesan cheese (preferably Parmigiano Reggiano), freshly and coarsely grated

Dressing
50g (2oz) tin anchovies
2 organic egg yolks
1 garlic clove, crushed
2 tablespoons lemon juice, freshly squeezed
a generous pinch of English mustard powder
¹⁄₂ teaspoon salt
¹⁄₂–1 tablespoon Worcestershire sauce
¹⁄₂–1 tablespoon Tabasco sauce
175ml (6fl oz) sunflower oil
50ml (2fl oz) extra-virgin olive oil
50ml (2fl oz) cold water

Wash the lettuce leaves, dry really thoroughly, lightly wrap in a tea towel and chill in a bowl in the fridge while you make the dressing.

The dressing can be made in a food processor but is also quick to make by hand. Drain the anchovies and crush lightly with a fork. Put into a bowl with the egg yolks, garlic, lemon juice, mustard powder, salt, Worcestershire and Tabasco sauces. Whisk together and as you whisk, add the oils slowly at first, then a little faster as the emulsion forms. Finally whisk in the water to make a pouring consistency. Taste and season: this dressing should be highly flavoured.

To make croûtons heat the olive oil and butter in a frying pan over a medium heat. When the butter is melted, toss in the cubes of bread and cook for a few seconds on all sides until golden. Drain through a metal sieve and spread out on kitchen paper.

To serve, put 1 tablespoon of dressing per person in a big bowl, add in the chilled whole lettuce leaves, about half the croûtons and half the Parmesan. Toss the leaves gently but thoroughly in the dressing. (This is done most effectively using your hands, or use salad servers.) Add more dressing if necessary to coat the leaves. Arrange the dressed leaves on individual chilled plates. Add a few croûtons and sprinkle the remaining Parmesan on top. Serve immediately.

Note: The remaining dressing will keep covered in a fridge for several days.

Master Recipe
Salade Niçoise with Seared Tuna

Serves 6

In Provence there are many versions of this colourful salad, which makes a wonderful summer lunch. Some include crisp red and green peppers and some omit the potato. Now that we can get fresh tuna occasionally we sear it quickly and serve warm on the salad. Alternatively, use good-quality tinned tuna. Pan-grilled mackerel is also a delicious alternative.

8 medium new potatoes, cooked but still warm (I use Pink Fir Apple variety)
salt, freshly ground pepper and sugar
3–4 ripe tomatoes, peeled and quartered
110g (4oz) cooked French beans, topped and tailed and cut into 5cm (2in) lengths, blanched and refreshed
2 teaspoons chives
2 teaspoons parsley, chopped
2 teaspoons annual marjoram or thyme
350g (12oz) fresh tuna or 400g (14oz) tin tuna
1 crisp lettuce
3 hard-boiled organic eggs, shelled and quartered

12 black olives

1 teaspoon capers (optional)

1 tin anchovies

8 tiny spring onions

salt and freshly ground pepper

French dressing

50ml (2fl oz) white wine vinegar

175ml (6fl oz) extra-virgin olive oil

2 large garlic cloves, mashed

2 teaspoons Dijon mustard

good pinch of salt and freshly ground pepper

1 tablespoon parsley, chopped

1 tablespoon basil or annual marjoram

Mix all the ingredients for the dressing together in a screw-top jar – it must be very well-seasoned otherwise the salad will be bland.

Slice the new potatoes into 5mm (1/4in) slices and toss in some dressing while still warm. Season with salt and pepper. Toss the tomatoes and beans in some more dressing, season with salt, pepper and sugar and sprinkle with some chopped herbs.

Heat a grill-pan or frying pan. Cut the tuna into 2cm (3/4in) thick steaks. Season with salt and freshly ground pepper, and cook quickly on both sides; it should still be rare in the centre. Beware: tuna overcooks very easily and becomes dry and boring.

Line a shallow bowl with lettuce leaves. Arrange the potatoes on top, followed by the rest of the ingredients, finishing off with the olives, capers and chunks of tuna and/or the anchovies. Drizzle some more dressing over the top. Sprinkle over the remainder of the herbs and the spring onions and serve.

Variation
Vegetarian Salade Niçoise
Follow the Master Recipe but omit the tuna and anchovies. Add strips of roasted red and yellow peppers and chargrilled onions.

Soused Mackerel with Chickpea and Avocado Salad
Serves 8–10

Also delicious with fresh pan-grilled mackerel or sardines.

Soused Mackerel

8 fresh whole mackerel

1 onion, thinly sliced

1 teaspoon whole black peppercorns

6 whole cloves

1 teaspoon salt

1 teaspoon sugar

300ml (10fl oz) white wine vinegar

1 bay leaf

Chickpea and Avocado Salad

yolk of 1 hard-boiled organic egg, sieved

8 tablespoons extra-virgin olive oil

4 tablespoons red wine vinegar

1 red onion, finely chopped

2 garlic cloves, crushed

4 tablespoons flat leaf parsley, chopped

2 tablespoons small capers, drained and rinsed

2 x 400g (14oz) tins chickpeas, drained and rinsed

2 ripe avocados, peeled and chopped into chunky dice

salt and ground black pepper

flat-leaf parsley and lemon to garnish

Preheat the oven to 140°C/275°F/gas 1.

First make the soused mackerel. Gut, fillet and wash the mackerel, making sure there are no bones. Roll up the fillets skin-side out and pack tightly into a cast iron casserole. Sprinkle over thinly sliced onion, peppercorns, cloves, salt, sugar, vinegar and the bay leaf. Bring to the boil on top of the cooker and then pop into the oven for 30–40 minutes.

To make the salad, put the sieved egg yolk in a bowl and whisk in the olive oil and vinegar. Add the onion, garlic, parsley, capers, chickpeas and diced avocado. Season to taste with sea salt and pepper.

To serve, spoon some of the avocado salad onto each serving plate and place two soused mackerels on top. Garnish with flat-leaf parsley and a wedge of lemon.

Italian Seafood Salad
Serves 8

Seafood salad is possibly the most popular cold seafood dish around the coast of Italy. Every port has its own version and even though the content varies they are all tossed simply in a mixture of olive oil and fresh lemon juice. Tiny squid or calamare are also a favourite addition. In this recipe I've included some grilled red pepper, a dice of cucumber and a few black olives which are delicious if not very traditional.

450g (1lb) cooked salmon or monkfish (or a mixture of both), cut into 1cm (1/3in) flakes or chunks

450g (1lb) cooked prawns or shrimps, or a mixture of prawns and scallops

1.8kg (4lb) mussels, steamed, opened, and removed from the shells or 900g (2lb) mussels and 900g (2lb) cockles or clams

1 roasted red pepper, peeled and diced, optional

2 cucumbers, seeded and cut into 5mm (1/4in) dice, optional

8 black olives, pitted (optional)

1 tablespoon freshly chopped parsley

salt and freshly ground pepper

Dressing

75ml (3fl oz) extra-virgin olive oil

40ml (1 1/2fl oz) freshly squeezed lemon juice

1/2 garlic clove

1 tablespoon freshly chopped mixed herbs e.g. parsley, chives and annual marjoram

salt and freshly ground black pepper

Garnish

sprigs of flat-leaf parsley

lemon segments

a few whole prawns or shrimps

In a screw-top jar mix together all the ingredients for the dressing, adding salt and pepper to taste. Shake well to emulsify.

Put the fish and shellfish into a wide serving bowl and add the cucumber dice, roasted red pepper and pitted olives (if using). Season with salt and pepper.

Very gently toss the seafood salad in a few tablespoons of dressing – just enough to coat lightly, and sprinkle with chopped parsley. Marinate for 1 hour.

Just before serving, garnish with large sprigs of parsley, lemon wedges and a few whole cooked prawns or shrimps.

Thai Squid Seafood Salad

See page 248

Lobster and Mango Salad

See page 259

Cellophane Noodle Salad with Chicken and Shrimps

Serves 8 as a starter or 4 as a main course

Mooli is the South-east Asian white radish, also known as daikon. It is a root vegetable served raw in salads and has a cool sharp tang (which is lost when cooked).

7g (¼oz) Chinese mushrooms (wood ears)
600ml (1 pint) homemade Chicken Stock
  (see page 36)
2 skinless chicken breasts
200g (7oz) cellophane noodles
75g (3oz) mooli or French radishes
3 tablespoons fish sauce (nam pla)
3 tablespoons lime juice, freshly squeezed
1 scant tablespoon caster sugar
2–4 Thai red chillies, de-seeded and finely
  chopped
1 red onion, thinly sliced
2 spring onions, thinly sliced at an angle
a few tender celery leaves if available
32 cooked Pacific or Dublin Bay prawns or
  48 smaller shrimps
110g (4oz) coriander leaves
salt and freshly ground pepper

Garnish
sprigs of coriander and a couple of red and
  green chillies

Put the mushrooms into a bowl, cover with warm water and allow to reconstitute for about 15 minutes. Drain, rinse and trim off any hard bits. Slice into thin strips. Bring the chicken stock to the boil, add salt and slip in the chicken breasts; bring back to the boil and simmer gently for 8 minutes. Remove from the heat, cover and allow to cool. Then shred the chicken.

Put the noodles into another bowl, cover with boiling water and allow to stand for 5 minutes. Drain and cut into 8–10cm (3–4in) lengths with a knife or clean scissors. Peel the mooli and slice very thinly. Put in a bowl of iced water to crisp up.

Mix the fish sauce, lime juice, sugar and chillies in a large bowl. Add the onions, spring onions, celery leaves and mushrooms and mix well. Drain the mooli well and add with the noodles, shrimps, chicken and coriander to the other ingredients. Toss gently. Taste and correct seasoning. Serve garnished with coriander and a few slices of red and green chillies.

Smoked Turkey or Chicken Salad with Apple, Walnuts and Cranberries

Serves 6

225g (8oz) boneless smoked turkey or chicken,
  cut in julienne
1 large apple (Golden Delicious or Granny
  Smith), peeled, cut into wide matchsticks and
  tossed with 1 dessertspoon lemon juice
3 tablespoons dried cranberries, softened
  (or pomegranate seeds)
1 small red onion, peeled, thinly sliced into
  rings and macerated in 1 dessertspoon lemon
  or lime juice
75g (3oz) shelled walnuts, lightly toasted
250g (9oz) baby salad leaves

Lemon Honey Vinaigrette (see page 226)
sprigs of flat-leaf parsley or chervil, to decorate

Prepare each item as above (to soften dry cranberries, place in a bowl with 2 teaspoons water, cover and set in a low oven for 10 minutes, or microwave on low power for 1 minute). Just before serving toss the salad leaves in a little vinaigrette – just enough to make the leaves glisten. Divide between six deep plates, and sprinkle some smoked turkey or chicken, apple, onion rings, dried cranberries and toasted walnuts on top. Garnish with flat-leaf parsley or chervil if available.

Chicken Tonnata Salad

See page 278

Curried Chicken Salad with Mango and Roasted Cashew Nuts

See page 278

Thai Chicken and Coconut Salad

See page 278

Quail and Grape Salad

Serves 4

4 quails
4 generous teaspoons honey
sea salt and freshly ground pepper
20 grapes, black or green
4 tablespoons lardons of streaky bacon
1 tablespoon extra-virgin olive oil
selection of lettuces and salad leaves,
  about 200g (7oz)

Hazelnut Oil Dressing
3 tablespoons hazelnut oil
1 tablespoon sunflower oil
1 tablespoon vinegar
¼ teaspoon mustard
salt, freshly ground black pepper and sugar

RIGHT: Cellophane Noodle Salad with Chicken and Shrimps

Preheat the oven to 180°C/350°F/gas 4.

Brush each quail with 1 teaspoon of honey and season with sea salt and pepper. Place in a roasting tin in the oven and cook for 10–20 minutes, depending on the size of the quail. Baste while cooking. The birds are done when the juices run clear if you pierce the meat on the leg.

Meanwhile, halve the black grapes or peel and pip green ones. Make up the dressing and toss the grapes in 1 tablespoon of it. Blanch the lardons of bacon, pat dry and reserve. When the quail are cooked, joint them into 4 by removing the drumsticks and thighs together and the breasts in one portion each. Keep the quail warm. Sauté the blanched lardons in olive oil and keep warm.

Arrange the grapes around each plate. Toss the lettuces carefully in the hazelnut oil dressing and place in the centre of the plates. Sprinkle on the warm lardons of bacon and finally put the warm quail on top of the lettuces. Serve immediately.

Spicy Beef Salad with Thai Chilli Dressing

Serves 8 for light lunch or 16 as a starter

This is a great recipe from a recent trip to Australia.

1 red pepper
1 small red onion
2 spring onions
24 red cherry tomatoes or a mixture of red and yellow
2 handfuls each mint and coriander leaves
100g (3½oz) peanuts, roasted
700–900g (1½–2lb) beef fillet or sirloin
1 tablespoon extra-virgin olive oil
salt and freshly ground pepper

Chilli Dressing
2 garlic cloves, peeled and crushed
1–2 fresh red Thai chillies, de-seeded and roughly chopped
2 tablespoons light soy sauce
2 tablespoons lime juice, freshly squeezed
1 tablespoon fish sauce (nam pla)
25g (1oz) palm sugar or light soft brown sugar

First make the dressing: pound the garlic and chillies together in a pestle and mortar if available. Put into a bowl and add the soy sauce, lime juice, fish sauce and palm sugar, and mix well until dissolved. Taste and correct the balance if necessary.

Cut the pepper into quarters, de-seed, and cut into thin slices at an angle. Slice the red onion thinly, slice the green and white parts of the spring onions at an angle, and halve or quarter the cherry tomatoes. Mix it all in a bowl with the mint, coriander and peanuts. Toss gently and cover.

Preheat a grill-pan. Cut the beef into thick slices and season. Sprinkle with a little olive oil and cook until medium rare or medium. Allow to rest on an upturned plate for 5–10 minutes. Slice the beef thinly and add to the other ingredients. Spoon the dressing over the salad and toss gently. Serve immediately.

Thai Beef Salad

See page 348

Seared Beef Salad with Horseradish Mayonnaise and French Fried Onions

Serves 6 as a starter or light lunch

The crispy onions are best cooked at the last minute, but they may be cooked ahead and reheated just before serving. Strips of roast red pepper and crumbled blue cheese are also great on this salad.

6–18 slices of beef fillet, 5mm (¼in) thick (use 1 slice per person from the mid-fillet or 3 slices from the tapered end)
salt and freshly ground pepper

extra-virgin olive oil
selection of lettuce and salad leaves
Horseradish Mayonnaise (see page 586)
French Fried Onions (see page 187)
a few fresh rocket leaves
freshly cracked pepper

Dressing
4 tablespoons extra-virgin olive oil
1 tablespoon white wine vinegar
¼ teaspoon whole-grain mustard (we use Lakeshore)
1 teaspoon freshly chopped herbs; thyme, parsley, tarragon would be good
salt and freshly cracked pepper

First make the dressing by whisking all the ingredients together in a bowl. Season well. Wash and dry the salad leaves. Prepare and cook the French Fried Onions. Heat a grill-pan on a high heat and season the beef on both sides with salt and freshly ground pepper and a drizzle of olive oil. Sear the beef on the hot grill-pan, first in one direction and then the other to give a criss-cross effect.

Toss the salad leaves in just enough dressing to make the leaves glisten. Divide between six warm plates, piling them up in the centre. Arrange the seared beef around the salad. Dribble a little Horseradish Mayonnaise over each slice of beef. Put a clump of hot crispy onions on top of the salad. Serve immediately with a rocket leaf or two on each plate and a little sprinkling of freshly cracked pepper.

Warm Salad of Goat's Cheese with Walnut Oil Dressing

Serves 4

This is a perfect supper dish but you can equally serve it as a starter, main or cheese course. Include a few cherry tomatoes or a few strips of roast red pepper if you want to make it more substantial.

selection of lettuces, herb and salad leaves
  e.g. butterhead, frisée, oakleaf, radicchio
  treviano, rocket, salad burnet, golden
  marjoram
12 slices French bread, toasted
175–225g (6–8oz) fresh soft goat's cheese (our
  favourites are Ardsallagh, Croghan, St Tola,
  Lough Caum, or St Macha)
16–20 fresh walnut halves

Dressing
4 tablespoons walnut oil plus 2 tablespoons
  sunflower or groundnut oil, or 6 tablespoons
  extra-virgin olive oil
2 tablespoons white wine vinegar
dash of Dijon mustard

Garnish
chive or wild garlic flowers or marigold petals
  (Calendula officinalis) in season

Wash and dry the salad leaves, tear the larger ones into bite-sized pieces. Make the dressing by whisking all the ingredients together. Cover each piece of toasted French bread with a 2cm (3/4in) slice of goat's cheese. Just before serving, preheat the grill. Place the slices of bread and cheese under the grill and toast for 5–6 minutes or until the cheese is soft and slightly golden.

Meanwhile, toss the salad greens lightly in just enough dressing to make the leaves glisten, then put a small handful onto each plate. Place 1–3 hot goat's cheese croûtons onto each portion. Scatter with a few walnut pieces and decorative with chive or wild garlic flowers. Serve immediately.

For more warm salads, see Starters, pages 75–76:

Smoked Mackerel Salad with Beetroot and Horseradish Sauce on Baby Salad Leaves

Peppered Venison Salad with Horseradish Cream, Pommes Allumettes and Red Onions and Chives

Warm Salad with Duck Livers and Marigold Petals

Warm Salad of Lamb Kidneys, Glazed Shallots and Straw Potatoes

Warm Salad of Bacon with Poached Egg and Cheese
See page 100

Traditional Greek Salad with Marinated Feta
Serves 6

This salad is served in virtually every taverna in Greece. Buying good-quality feta can be difficult; try sourcing it in Cypriot delicatessens. Don't bother to make this salad unless the tomatoes are sweet and ripe, and the cucumbers are crisp and juicy. We use Mani, organic Greek extra-virgin olive oil.

75g (3oz) fresh feta, cubed (we sometimes use
  local Knockalara ewe's milk cheese)
1–2 tablespoons extra-virgin olive oil
1 tablespoon marjoram
1/2–1 crisp cucumber
1–2 red onions or 6 spring onions
6 very ripe tomatoes
12–18 Kalamata olives
2 tablespoons fresh annual marjoram, chopped
3 tablespoon extra-virgin olive oil
1 tablespoon lemon juice, freshly squeezed
salt, freshly cracked pepper and sugar

Garnish
sprigs of flat-leaf parsley

Cut the cheese into 2.5cm (1in) cubes. Drizzle with extra-virgin olive oil and some marjoram.

Just before serving, halve the cucumber lengthways and cut it into chunks. Slice the red onions or chop coarsely the green and white parts of the spring onions. Core the tomatoes and cut into wedges. Mix the cucumber, spring onions, tomatoes, olives and marjoram in a bowl. Sprinkle with olive oil and lemon juice. Season with salt, pepper and sugar and toss well. Sprinkle with cubes of cheese and parsley. Serve at once.

Variation
Greek Salad in Pitta Bread
Split a pitta bread in half across or lengthways. Fill with Greek salad drained of dressing, and shredded lettuce. Serve immediately. The filling should be spooned into the pitta bread just before it is to be eaten, otherwise the bread will go soggy.

Broccoli, Feta and Cherry Tomato Salad
Serves 4–6

450g (1lb) broccoli florets
150g (5oz) feta cut into 1cm (1/2in) cubes
275g (10oz) cherry tomatoes, halved
Ballymaloe French Dressing (see page 226)
1 tablespoon freshly chopped mint
sugar and freshly ground black pepper

Blanch the broccoli for 2–3 minutes, drain, refresh and put in a bowl with the feta and tomatoes. Sprinkle with dressing. Season, add the mint, and toss gently. It is unlikely the salad will need salt because of the feta.

Moroccan Chickpea Salad
Serves 4

Chickpeas have been grown since Roman times all over the Middle East and southern Europe. The white species (*garbanzos*), said to be the finest, is grown in Spain. It's always a good idea to keep a few tins of chickpeas in your larder.

5 tablespoons extra-virgin olive oil
110g (4oz) onion, finely chopped
2 garlic cloves, finely crushed
4cm (1½in) piece fresh ginger, peeled
   and grated
2 x 400g (14oz) tins chickpeas, drained
pinch of dried chilli flakes
juice and finely grated rind of 1½ lemons
leaves from a bunch of coriander, chopped
salt and freshly ground pepper

mixed ground cumin and paprika, to serve

Heat 1 tablespoon of the oil in a frying pan, add the onion, garlic and ginger and cook gently for 5–7 minutes, until soft and transparent. Add the chickpeas, chilli flakes and lemon rind and stir for about 30 seconds, then add the lemon juice and let the mixture bubble until it is almost dry. Add the coriander and season to taste with salt and pepper.

Turn the chickpea mixture into a warm serving bowl and pour over the remaining oil. Sprinkle a little ground cumin and paprika over the top.

Note: For dried chickpeas, use 225g (8oz) of chickpeas. Cover with cold water overnight. Next day discard the water. Cover with fresh water, bring to the boil and cook until tender – about 45 minutes.

Fattoush
Serves 6

There are many delicious ways of using up bread, particularly in the Mediterranean countries. Fattoush is a good example, as is Panzanella, or Tuscan bread salad, which you may see on menus in Italy. Marjoram or basil may be included or substituted for coriander. Sumac flakes give this salad a characteristic, slightly sour taste. If you can't get it, the salad will still taste delicious but not so authentic.

2 stale pitta breads or 2–3 thick slices of stale
   sourdough or good country bread
a little bunch of rocket or purslane

1 mild sweet red pepper (optional)
2–3 teaspoons sumac, if available
4 vine-ripened tomatoes, cut into quarters and
   then into halves crosswise
½ cucumber, coarsely chopped
3 spring onions, sliced at an angle
2–3 tablespoons freshly chopped parsley
2 tablespoons fresh coriander leaves
2–3 tablespoons fresh mint
salt and freshly ground pepper

Dressing
3 tablespoons freshly squeezed lemon juice
6 tablespoons extra-virgin olive oil
2 garlic cloves, crushed
salt and freshly ground pepper, maybe even a
   pinch of sugar or a dash of balsamic vinegar

If the bread isn't stale toast it until crisp. Cut into uneven-sized pieces. Chop the rocket or purslane coarsely. Cut the sweet red pepper into rounds or dice. Mix it all in a salad bowl with the tomato, cucumber, spring onions and herbs along with the sumac flakes (if using). Season.

Whisk the dressing ingredients together. Spoon over the salad, toss gently and taste. Allow the salad to sit for at least 30 minutes, or better still 1 hour before serving, so that the bread soaks up lots of yummy dressing and juice.

Bulgar Wheat and Pecan Nut Salad
Serves 8

1 litre (1¾ pints) homemade Chicken or
   Vegetable Stock (see page 36)
350g (12oz) bulgar wheat
110g (4oz) pecans, coarsely chopped
150g (5oz) currants
3 tablespoons freshly chopped flat-leaf parsley
1 tablespoon extra-virgin olive oil
grated zest of 1 orange
salt and freshly ground pepper

Bring the stock to the boil. Put the bulgar into a bowl and pour over the boiling stock. Allow to sit until the stock is absorbed and the bulgar is cool.

Add the pecans, currants, parsley, olive oil and orange zest. Season with salt and freshly ground pepper. Toss well and serve at room temperature.

Potato and Spring Onion Salad
Serves 4–6 as a side dish

The secret of delectable potato salad is simple – use good-quality potatoes, and peel and toss in them in French dressing whilst still warm. Use Golden Wonder or Kerr's Pinks (although many people prefer to use a waxy potato like Pink Fir Apple or Sharp's Express). Mayonnaise may be omitted if a less rich potato salad is your choice.

1kg (2¼lb) potatoes
2 tablespoons chives or spring onions, chopped
   or 2 teaspoons onion, chopped
2 tablespoons chopped parsley
salt and freshly ground pepper, to taste
125ml (4fl oz) Ballymaloe French Dressing
   (see page 226)
125ml (4fl oz) homemade Mayonnaise
   (see page 584)

Boil the potatoes in their jackets until tender; drain, cool and peel. Dice them while still hot. Mix immediately with onion, parsley, salt and pepper. Stir in the French dressing, and allow to cool. Finally add the mayonnaise. Keeps well for about 2 days.

Note: Potato salad may be used as a base for other salads; for example, add cubes of garlic salami, cooked Kabanos sausages or cooked mussels.

Variation
Potato and Thyme Leaf Salad
Cook the potatoes as above. Then coat in good olive oil. Season to taste and sprinkle liberally with fresh thyme leaves and flowers.

Soft Piped Potato Salad with Fresh Herbs

Serves 4–6

The first time we made this salad, it was out of necessity because we overcooked the potatoes. It was a great success and now we make it regularly by choice!

1 generous litre (1³/₄ pints) freshly mashed potato (see page 182)

Add Ballymaloe French Dressing (see page 226), finely chopped parsley, chives, mayonnaise and seasoning to the potato to taste. Pipe onto individual leaves of lettuce or use to garnish a starter salad or hors d'oeuvres.

Blood Orange, Beetroot and Rocket Salad

Serves 6

Pickled Beetroot (see page 514), preferably still warm
3–4 blood oranges
4 small fistfuls of rocket leaves
24 fresh walnut halves, slightly toasted

Dressing
zest of 1 orange, finely grated
1 small shallot, very finely diced
juice of ¹/₂ orange
3 tablespoons extra-virgin olive oil
1 teaspoon balsamic vinegar
sea salt and freshly ground pepper

To make the dressing, put the finely grated orange zest in a bowl with the shallot and orange juice. Whisk in the oil and vinegar. Season with salt and pepper. It should taste nice and perky.

Peel all the oranges and cut into thin slices. Divide the rocket between the plates. Top with sliced beetroot and blood orange slices and scatter with walnut halves. Drizzle a little dressing over and serve at once.

White Turnip and Oregano Salad

Serves 4 as a side dish

Use very small turnips; they taste sweeter and fresher than those left to grow to fairy-tale size. Delicious with most meats.

450g (1lb) white turnips
French dressing (see page 226)
2–3 tablespoons oregano or annual marjoram, chopped
salt and freshly ground pepper

Wash and peel the turnips (if necessary) and top and tail them. Cut into 5mm (¹/₄in) slices and cook in a very little boiling salted water until tender - this will take just a few minutes. Drain. Toss in dressing while still hot and sprinkle with oregano or marjoram. Correct the seasoning and eat warm.

Dunsandel Spiced Pumpkin Salad

Serves 6–8

Dunsandel store and Café is a few miles south of Christchurch on New Zealand's South Island. We dropped in for lunch and to our amazement found one of our students – Sinead Doran! She says this is the most popular salad at the store – she can't keep up with demand when the pumpkins are in season.

1 large pumpkin, peeled and cubed
extra-virgin olive oil
300g (10oz) red pepper, finely sliced
3 spring onions, chopped
150g (5oz) sweetcorn
lots of chopped parsley
salt and pepper
1 red chilli, chopped

Roast pumpkin in lots of olive oil, don't let it get mushy. While it is still warm add rest of the ingredients. Taste and correct seasoning.

Ballymaloe Cauliflower, Broccoli or Romanesco Salad

Serves 6 as a side dish

Cauliflower or broccoli salad is not an obvious choice but it is surprisingly delicious. The secret is to dip the florets in a good dressing while still warm so they really absorb the flavours.

1 head cauliflower
125ml (4fl oz) Ballymaloe French Dressing (see page 226)

Ideally this should be made with a slightly shot head (one that is starting to go to seed) at the end of season. Take a head with the leaves on and trim off the damaged ones. Wash and shred the remaining leaves and stalk. Split the cauliflower into about 8 pieces so it will cook evenly.

Take a saucepan that fits the cauliflower exactly and boil 2.5cm (1in) of water in it. Add a little salt, put in the shredded leaves and sit the cauliflower on top, stems down, and cover closely. Control the heat so that the pan does not boil dry. Remove from the pan when the stalks are barely tender.

Divide into florets and dip each into dressing while still warm. Arrange like a wheel on a round plate. Build up layer upon layer to reform the cauliflower head. This looks and tastes delicious on a cold buffet.

Note: Purple, white sprouting and green broccoli (calabrese) can also be cooked this way. A mixture of all three looks and tastes delicious.

Leek Vinaigrette
See page 174

Oignons a la Monégasque
See page 188

Aubergine Salad with Olives, Sun-dried Tomatoes and Rocket Leaves

Serves 8

We now grow several varieties of aubergine. Choose firm medium-sized aubergines and seek out the slim Indian varieties for extra flavour. If the aubergines are cooked in extra-virgin olive oil, they are also divine served as a simple salad with no embellishment.

4–8 aubergines, depending on size
extra-virgin olive oil for frying

Sun-dried Tomato Dressing
50g (2oz) 'Sun-dried' Tomatoes (see page 188)
50ml (2fl oz) extra-virgin olive oil
2 tablespoons parsley, chopped
1 tablespoon annual marjoram, chopped
salt and freshly ground pepper

Garnish
handful of rocket leaves
50–75g (2–3oz) tiny Tunisian black or picholine olives, stoned and chopped

Slice the aubergines into 1cm (½in) thick rounds. Sprinkle with salt and de-gorge for 15–20 minutes on a rack over a baking tray. Heat 2–2.5cm (¾–1in) of olive oil in a frying pan until very hot. Fry the aubergine slices in batches until golden brown on both sides. Drain on a wire rack.

While the aubergines are cooling make the dressing - chop the sun-dried tomatoes and add the olive oil, parsley and marjoram. Season to taste. Arrange the aubergine slices on a large serving dish and decorate with the rocket leaves. At the last minute drizzle the sun-dried tomato dressing over and around the salad and finally sprinkle with olives.

Avocado, Pomegranate and Wild Rocket Salad

Serves 4

The deep red pomegranate seeds give this salad a bright note on a wintry day and its sweet juiciness contrasts well with the peppery rocket, the smoothness of the avocado and the crunchy cucumber.

1 pomegranate
1 large avocado
squeeze of lemon juice
2–3 large handfuls wild rocket

Dressing
3 tablespoons extra-virgin olive oil or avocado oil
2 tablespoons sherry vinegar
salt and freshly ground black pepper
1 shallot, finely chopped
½ cucumber

Make the dressing by mixing the oil, vinegar, salt and pepper. Add the shallot when you are ready to prepare the salad.

Cut the cucumber in 4 lengthways, remove the seeds and cut each quarter into 2 strips. Cut the strips into dice, put them in a colander and sprinkle with salt. Cut the top from the pomegranate and pull it apart gently. Pick out the seeds and discard all the pith. Put the seeds and any juice into a bowl. Dice the avocado and sprinkle with lemon juice to prevent the flesh discolouring. Rinse the cucumber and dry on a clean tea towel.

To assemble, put the rocket into a salad bowl and scatter the cucumber, avocado and finally the pomegranate seeds over it. Add pomegranate juice to the dressing if you wish. Whisk the dressing and pour it over the salad.

Variation

Omit the shallot from the dressing and replace the cucumber with 50g (2oz) of toasted and skinned hazelnuts or toasted pine nuts.

Salad with Pomegranates, Persimmons and Pecans

Serves 8 as a starter

A delicious salad that I came across in California with Mary Risley.

3 ripe Fuyu persimmons (Diospyros kaki – little firm persimmons)
3 ripe pears (d'Anjou pears if you can find them)
1 lime, freshly squeezed
seeds from ½ pomegranate
a selection of frisée lettuce, watercress and rocket leaves
75–110g (3–4oz) pecans, freshly toasted

Vinaigrette
2 tablespoons balsamic or sherry vinegar
2 teaspoons Dijon mustard
2 shallots, finely chopped
salt and freshly ground pepper
5 tablespoons extra-virgin olive oil

Preheat the oven to 180°C/350°F/gas 4.

First make the vinaigrette: mix the vinegar, mustard, shallots, salt and pepper in a screw-top jar with the oil until emulsified.

Slice the persimmons and pears into slices about 1cm (½in) thick. Put into a bowl and sprinkle with the lime juice. Add the pomegranate seeds and toss gently.

Wash and dry the lettuces and store in a clean towel in the fridge until ready to use. Put the pecans onto a baking sheet in the oven for 5–6 minutes, tossing gently from time to time. Alternatively toast under a grill.

When ready to serve, toss the lettuce in some of the vinaigrette and arrange on eight plates. Toss the fruit mixture lightly in the remaining vinaigrette. Arrange on top of the greens and sprinkle with the toasted pecans. Serve immediately.

RIGHT: Salad with Pomegranates, Persimmons and Pecans

Mushroom and Caramelised Onion Salad

Serves 6–8 as an accompaniment

Great with cold meats or poached salmon. Best eaten on the day it is made, but also keeps for a day or two.

2 tablespoons extra-virgin olive oil
2 large onions, sliced
25–50g (1–2oz) butter
350g (12oz) mushrooms, thinly sliced
salt and freshly ground pepper
1 large garlic clove, crushed
lemon juice, freshly squeezed

Heat a little olive oil in a heavy saucepan and cook the onions gently over a low heat. Stir every few minutes so that they brown evenly. This operation may take 20–30 minutes until the onions are slightly caramelised to a rich gold.

Meanwhile, melt the butter in a wide pan, add the mushrooms and sauté for 4–5 minutes. Season with salt and pepper, a very little crushed garlic and a squeeze of lemon juice. Add the onions to the mushrooms as soon as they are cooked and taste. Correct seasoning, if necessary.

Like most salads, this is best served at room temperature.

Roasted Red Pepper, Caper and Preserved Lemon Salad

Serves 6

This is a delicious way to use Preserved Lemons (see page 515).

6 red peppers, ripe and fleshy
sea salt and freshly ground pepper
peel of ½–1 preserved lemon, very finely diced
1–2 tablespoons tiny capers
sprigs of flat-leaf parsley
4 tablespoons extra-virgin olive oil

Roast and peel the peppers (see page 83). Cut into strips about 2.5cm (1in) wide. Season with salt and pepper. Sprinkle on the preserved lemon peel, a few little capers and some sprigs of flat-leaf parsley. Drizzle with extra-virgin olive oil.

Lime and Pepper Salad

Serves 4 as a starter

Tim and I adore being invited to dinner by our students. Kelley Ryan-Bourgoise and her husband Don cooked a wonderful meal for us at their house overlooking the sea. This fresh tasting salad was our first course. It would also be delicious served as an accompaniment to a pan-grilled chicken breast or a piece of salmon.

1 red pepper
1 yellow pepper
1 orange pepper
3 ripe tomatoes, sliced
1 green jalapeño chilli pepper, finely chopped
2–3 tablespoons coarsely chopped coriander
2 avocados, peeled and sliced

Vinaigrette
3 tablespoons freshly squeezed lime juice
2 teaspoons grated lime zest
1 tablespoon honey
4 tablespoons extra-virgin olive oil
a few drops of Tabasco sauce (or any hot pepper sauce you like)
2 small garlic cloves, crushed
salt and freshly ground pepper

First make the vinaigrette. Put the freshly squeezed lime juice and half the zest in a bowl. Whisk in the honey, oil and Tabasco sauce, add the crushed garlic and season with salt and freshly ground pepper.

Slice the peppers into thin julienne strips and add the sliced tomatoes. Toss together with the chopped jalapeño chilli, coarsely chopped coriander and the rest of the lime zest. Add the vinaigrette and gently fold in the avocado. Taste and correct the seasoning. Serve on individual plates with crusty bread.

Courgette Salad with Olive Oil and Sea Salt

Serves 4 as a starter

This simple salad is perfection served warm with nothing more than a sprinkling of extra-virgin olive oil and a little sea salt.

8 small courgettes with flowers, if available (choose shiny, firm courgettes)
extra-virgin olive oil (the very best Italian oil)
sea salt and freshly ground pepper

Separate the flowers from the courgettes. Remove the stamens and little thorns from the base of the flowers. Plunge the courgettes into boiling, salted water and poach until barely tender. Remove from the pan and allow to cool slightly. While still warm slice them at an angle – 6 slices per courgette.

Season with sea salt and pepper and sprinkle with olive oil. Toss gently and serve immediately surrounded by courgette blossoms. Hot crusty bread is the only accompaniment needed.

Variation
Courgette and Prawn Salad
A few fat Dublin Bay prawns and some homemade mayonnaise turn this into a divine summer lunch or supper dish.

Bright's Celery and Cashew Nut Salad

Serves 6

This very simple salad is completely delicious, with a fresh and crunchy taste. It was given to me by Yu Long Bao ('Bright'), one of our Chinese students. Eat it on its own or as an accompaniment to cold meat or warm chicken.

1 head of fresh celery
600ml (1 pint) water
3 teaspoons salt
1 tablespoon extra-virgin olive oil
200g (7oz) cashew nuts
pinch of sugar

Slice the celery diagonally into pieces the size of a cashew nut. Bring the water to the boil in a saucepan and add 2 teaspoons of salt (salted water preserves the colour of the celery). Add the celery to the boiling water and immediately turn off the heat. Leave the celery in the hot water for 3 minutes.

Drain off the water. The celery should still be crisp. Heat the oil in a frying pan and swirl to coat the base of the pan. Add the cashew nuts and stir constantly for 1 minute taking care not to burn the nuts. When the nuts are golden and smell toasted add the celery to the pan. Toss well and season with 1 teaspoon salt and a pinch of sugar to taste. Serve hot or cold.

Korean Carrot Salad

Serves 6

One of my students, Aliona McKinnon, was taught how to make this delicious salad by her Aunt Svetlana.

5 medium carrots
1 large onion, sliced
6 cloves of garlic, chopped finely
2 teaspoons ground coriander, chopped finely
4 tablespoons extra-virgin olive oil
3 tablespoons vinegar
1 tablespoon sugar
salt and freshly ground pepper
3 teaspoons chopped coriander

Wash the carrots and grate on the coarse part of the grater. Fry the onion in olive oil in a large frying pan until golden. Add the carrot and stir. Put this mixture in a bowl with the remaining ingredients, mix together and add salt and pepper if required. Serve as a starter or as an accompaniment to Aliona's Plov (see page 306).

Carrot and Mint Salad

Serves 4

Serve as part of a plate of salads or mezze.

450g (1lb) carrots, peeled and coarsely grated
3 tablespoons olive oil
1 tablespoon lemon juice or white wine vinegar
salt, freshly ground pepper and sugar
1–2 tablespoons mint, freshly chopped
8 black olives (optional)

Put the coarsely grated carrot into a bowl. Whisk the oil and lemon juice or vinegar together, pour over the grated carrot, and season with salt, pepper and sugar. Sprinkle on 1 tablespoon of chopped mint. Mix well. Turn into a serving dish and garnish with the remainder of the mint and some black olives if desired.

Variations
Carrot, Cumin and Currant Salad
Follow the Master Recipe, omitting the mint and olives, and instead add 1/4–1/2 tablespoon ground freshly roasted cumin and 2 tablespoons currants. Taste and correct seasoning.

Moroccan Carrot Salad
Sprinkle the grated carrot with some lemon juice and a few drops of orange flower water. Season with salt and sugar and marinate for 1 hour. For a more robust salad, peel 4 oranges, cut them into chunks and mix with the carrots.

Coleslaw

Serves 16–24

Coleslaw is an American salad, the 'cole' being a general word for all true cabbages (*Brassica oleracea*).

450g (1lb) white cabbage (we use Drumhead), thinly sliced
1 large carrot, cleaned and roughly grated
1 onion, thinly sliced into rings
salt and freshly ground pepper
150–300ml (1/4–1/2 pint) homemade Mayonnaise (see page 584) or mayonnaise and yoghurt mixed
1 tablespoon chopped parsley

Mix the cabbage, carrot and onion together and season. Fold in the mayonnaise or mayonnaise and yoghurt mix. Taste and correct the seasoning. Sprinkle with parsley and serve immediately or keep refrigerated.

Variations

Add some diced or finely sliced celery stalks **or** 1 crisp eating apple tossed in 2 tablespoons lemon juice **or** 50g (2oz) sultanas and 1 tablespoon chopped mint.

Broadway Coleslaw

Serves 10

350g (12oz) red cabbage, cut into 5mm (1/4in) dice
350g (12oz) green cabbage, cut into 5mm (1/4in) dice
75g (3oz) red onion, cut into 5mm (1/4in) dice, rinsed under cold water
1/4–1/2 cucumber, cut into 5mm (1/4in) dice
1–2 apples, finely diced
1 tablespoon freshly chopped parsley
1 tablespoon freshly chopped mint
125ml (4fl oz) Ballymaloe French Dressing (see page 226)
salt, freshly ground pepper and sugar

Mix all the ingredients in a large bowl and toss in the dressing. Taste and correct seasoning (this salad often needs a good pinch of sugar).

Cucumber and Fennel Salad

Serves 4–6 as a side dish

This is gorgeous with Ballymaloe Crab Salad (see page 259).

1 medium cucumber
salt
2 teaspoons wine vinegar
1–2 tablespoons sugar
1 teaspoon fennel, finely chopped

Finely slice the cucumber (leave the peel on if you like it), sprinkle with salt, vinegar and lots of sugar, and stir in the snipped fennel.

Barossa Valley Cucumber Salad

Serves 6–8 as a side dish

2 cucumbers
salt
1 small onion, finely chopped
1 tablespoon white wine vinegar
freshly ground pepper and sugar
1–2 tablespoons double cream or crème fraîche

Peel and slice the cucumber into paper-thin slices. Spread on a large plate and sprinkle with salt. Allow to de-gorge for 30 minutes. Drain and put into a bowl. Add the finely chopped onion and sprinkle with the white wine vinegar. Season with freshly ground pepper and sugar. Cover and refrigerate. Just before serving stir in the cream. Taste for seasoning, and serve.

Shanagarry Summer Tomato Salad

Tomatoes have been grown in the greenhouses here in Shanagarry since my father-in-law, Ivan Allen, built his first timber house in the winter of 1934. For years the crops were grown commercially but for the past 8–10 years we have concentrated on growing as many varieties as we have space for, with the emphasis totally on flavour – yield is not a high priority and every tomato is vine-ripened on the plant. We even grow the tiny Tumbler variety in hanging baskets interspersed with herbs outside the cottages and around the school. Freshly picked, sweet-tasting tomatoes, piled high in baskets, are part of every day, and tomato salads made from a mixture of colours, shapes and varieties are part of almost every menu in late summer and early autumn.

Heirloom Tomato Salad

Use a mixture of vine-ripened heirloom tomatoes in the recipe above, and a combination of freshly squeezed lemon juice and extra-virgin olive oil enhances the flavour in a delicious way. Don't forget the seasoning. We grow a lot of heirloom varieties every year, all shapes, sizes and colours (red, green, black, orange and several streaky varieties). They make a divine salad in later summer and early autumn. This year we plan to grow 35 different tomatoes and will carefully taste, compare and eliminate the ones we feel are not justified on grounds of flavour.

TIP: Tomatoes must be dressed as soon as they are cut to seal in their flavour.

Tomato Salad

In the late summer when we have intensively sweet, vine-ripened tomatoes, we often serve a tomato salad as a first course. The flavour is so wonderful; it is a revelation to many people who have forgotten what a tomato should taste like.

8–12 tomatoes: use one variety, or a mixture, of very ripe red or yellow vine-ripened tomatoes (we enjoy Sweet 100's, Green Zebra, Ox Heart, Valencia, Golden Jubilee etc. Try to include some cherry tomatoes, pear-shaped, and if you can get them – the pretty striped Green Zebra, they look and taste particularly stunning)
salt, freshly ground pepper and sugar

Ballymaloe French dressing (see page 226) or balsamic vinegar/white wine vinegar and extra-virgin olive oil
2–4 teaspoons basil leaves or mint leaves

Cut the tomatoes in half or lengthwise or into wedges, or simply into 1cm (½in) thick slices depending on shape and size. Spread out in a single layer on a large flat plate, season with salt, pepper and a sprinkling of sugar. Sprinkle with dressing (sparingly with balsamic vinegar if using). Scatter with torn basil or mint leaves. Toss gently, just to coat the tomatoes. Serve either as a first course or as an accompanying salad.

TIP: Never store tomatoes in the fridge as this will have a detrimental effect on both the flavour and texture.

RIGHT: Tomato Salad

Tomato Salad with Mozzarella and Tapenade Toasts
Serves 4

Only make in summer when the tomatoes are superb.

4 small hand-rolled Mozzarella cheeses
Tomato Salad for 4 (see opposite)
Tapenade (see page 590)
4 crostini, freshly cooked in extra-virgin olive
* oil (see page 67)*
extra-virgin olive oil
freshly cracked pepper
basil leaves

Put a fresh, milky hand-rolled Mozzarella on each of 4 white plates, and arrange a helping of tomato salad beside it. Spoon tapenade onto a freshly cooked crostini and pop it decoratively on the side. Drizzle with your best extra-virgin olive oil and a sprinkling of pepper. Put a fresh basil leaf on top and serve immediately.

Rocket and Cherry or Sun-dried Tomato Salad
Serves 6

Serve with pan-grilled chicken breasts.

110g (4oz) fresh rocket leaves or a mixture of
* mysticana and rocket leaves*
'Sun-dried' Tomatoes (see page 188) or red and
* yellow cherry tomatoes*

Dressing
2 tablespoons white wine vinegar or white
* wine vinegar and balsamic vinegar mixed or*
* freshly squeezed lemon juice*
6 tablespoons extra-virgin olive oil
1 garlic clove, crushed
½ teaspoon Moutarde de Meaux or Lakeshore
* wholegrain and honey mustard*
salt and freshly ground pepper

Whisk all the ingredients together for the dressing. Wash and dry the salad leaves and tear into small pieces.

Just before serving, toss the salad leaves in just enough dressing to make the leaves glisten. Arrange in a wide serving dish. Cut the sun-dried tomatoes into quarters and scatter over the salad.

Isaac's Mimosa Salad

Serves 6 as a starter

This light and lovely salad has egg yolk on top and gives the effect of a Mimosa flower. We vary the lettuces in this recipe acording to the season and availability.

use one or a mixture of chicory, watercress, rocket or wild garlic leaves (we also use young pea shoots when available)
4 organic eggs
24 large black olives, preferably Kalamata
50–75g (2–3oz) Parmesan (Parmigiano Reggiano)

Dressing
50ml (2fl oz) extra-virgin olive oil
125ml (4fl oz) balsamic vinegar
1 garlic clove, crushed
pinch of sea salt, freshly cracked pepper and a large pinch of sugar

Hard-boil the eggs for 10 minutes in boiling salted water. Chill under a cold running tap. Peel the eggs and separate. Sieve the yolks and finely chop the whites. Stone the olives and chop finely.

Make the dressing by mixing the olive oil, balsamic vinegar and crushed garlic together. Season with salt, pepper and sugar.

Mix the greens in a large bowl and coat with enough dressing to make the leaves glisten. Place a bunch of the dressed leaves on each plate. Sprinkle the chopped egg whites and olives on top and finish with the sieved egg yolk and parmesan. Serve immediately.

Old-fashioned Salad with Shanagarry Cream Dressing

Serves 2–4

This simple old-fashioned salad, which is the sort of thing you might have had for tea on a visit to your Gran on a Sunday evening – perhaps with a slice of meat from the Sunday roast – is one of my absolute favourites. It can be quite delicious when it is made with crisp lettuce, good home-grown tomatoes and cucumbers, free-range eggs and home-preserved beetroot.

If, on the other hand, you make it with pale battery eggs, watery tomatoes, tired lettuce and cucumbers, and worst of all, vinegary beetroot from a jar, you'll wonder why you bothered.

We serve this traditional salad at Ballymaloe as a starter, with an old-fashioned dressing which would have been popular before the days of mass-produced mayonnaise.

Our recipe came from Lydia Strangman, a Quaker lady who was the previous occupant of our house.

lettuce leaves
2–4 tomatoes, quartered
2 hard boiled eggs, quartered
16 slices of cucumber
2–4 sliced radishes
4 slices of Pickled Beetroot (see page 514)
Shanagarry Cream Dressing (see page 220)

Garnish
4 tiny spring onions
sprigs of watercress
chopped parsley

Arrange a few lettuce leaves on each plate. Then scatter a few tomatoes, egg quarters, slices of cucumber, 1 radish and 2 slices of beetroot on top.

Garnish with spring onion, sprigs of watercress and the remaining egg white from the dressing and sprinkle some chopped parsley over the top.

Serve with a tiny bowl of dressing in the centre of each plate (and immediately while the salad is crisp and before the beetroot starts to run).

A Plate of Ballymaloe Garden Salads

We frequently serve a selection of vegetable salads on a plate as a starter or main course.

A summer selection might include:
Red and Yellow Tomato Salad with Mint or Basil
Cucumber Salad
Courgette Salad with Olive Oil and Sea Salt
A few radishes
Mushroom and Caramelised Onion Salad
Green Salad
Egg Mayonnaise
Potato and Spring Onion Salad

A winter selection might include:
Potato and Spring Onion Salad
Pickled Beetroot and Onion Salad
Cucumber Salad
Winter Green Salad
Carrot and Apple Salad
Onions or Leeks Monégasque
Egg Mayonnaise
Green Salad

Crudités with Aïoli

Crudités, meaning raw vegetables, is one of my favourite French starters: small helpings of very crisp vegetables with a homemade tapenade. It fulfils all my criteria for a first course: the plates look tempting, taste delicious and, provided you keep the helpings small, are not too filling. Better still it's actually good for you – so you can feel very virtuous at the same time!

Children also love crudités – they may not fancy tapenade but you can use other dips such as Garlic Mayonnaise (see page 584) or Guacamole (see page 593). Cut the vegetables into bite-sized pieces so they can be picked up easily. Use as many of the following vegetables as are in season:

tomatoes quartered, or left whole with the calyx on if they are freshly picked
purple sprouting broccoli, broken (not cut) into florets
calabrese, broken into florets
cauliflower, broken into florets
French beans or mangetout peas
baby carrots, or larger carrots cut into sticks about 5cm (2in) long
cucumber, cut into sticks about 5cm (2in) long
tiny spring onions, trimmed
celery, cut into sticks 5cm (2in) long approx.
chicory, in leaves
red, green or yellow peppers, cut into strips about 5cm (2in) long, and de-seeded
fresh fennel
very fresh Brussels sprouts, cut into halves or quarters
whole radishes, with green tops left on
parsley, finely chopped
thyme, finely chopped
chives, finely chopped
sprigs of watercress

Aïoli (see page 584)

A typical plate of crudités might include the following: 4 sticks of carrot, 2 or 3 sticks of red and green pepper, 2 or 3 sticks of celery, 2 or 3 sticks of cucumber, 1 mushroom cut in quarters, 1 whole radish with a little green leaf left on, 1 tiny tomato or 2 quarters, 1 Brussels sprout cut in quarters, and a little pile of chopped fresh herbs. Wash and prepare the vegetables. Arrange on individual plates in contrasting colours, with a little bowl of Aïoli or chosen sauce in the centre.

Alternatively, do a large dish or basket for the centre of the table. Pretty and edible sauce containers can be made from courgette flowers, hollowed-out tomatoes or cucumber.

La Grande Anchoïade

Anchoïade (see page 594) is a Provençal and Corsican dish of anchovies, tomatoes, almonds, herbs and olive oil pounded to a paste and seasoned with lemon juice. The Corsicans add figs and red peppers.

La Grande Anchoïade can be a meal in itself – anchoïade served with a basket of crudités and lots of crusty bread.

The crudités might include:
tomatoes
celery
radishes
carrots
cucumbers
peppers
tiny artichoke hearts
spring onions
fresh broad beans
young carrots
hard-boiled eggs
black olives

Pinzimonio

A Tuscan appetiser made up of fresh, crunchy vegetables (fresh fennel, asparagus, baby carrots, celery sticks…), dipped into a bowl of the finest Tuscan extra-virgin olive oil. Simple, but delicious!

Greek Green Salad
Serves 4

Cos or similar crisp lettuce, washed
sprigs of fresh dill, about 2–3 tablespoons
3–4 spring onions, sliced
1–2 tablespoons freshly squeezed lemon juice
4 tablespoons extra-virgin olive oil
salt and freshly ground pepper

Slice the lettuce across the grain, about 5mm (¼in) thick. Put into a bowl, sprinkle with spring onion and sprigs of dill. Just before serving mix the oil and lemon juice. Toss the salad, season and serve.

Italian Green Salad
Serves 4

selection of lettuces and salad leaves: romaine, radicchio, lollo rosso, rocket leaves, Buckler leaf sorrel, golden marjoram, courgette blossoms and dark opal basil

Italian Salad Dressing (see page 226)

First make the dressing. Then wash and dry the salad leaves. Just before serving, toss the salad with the dressing in a deep bowl and serve immediately.

Kinoith Summer Garden Salad with Ballymaloe French Dressing

selection of lettuces and salad leaves
e.g. butterhead, oakleaf, iceberg, lollo rosso, frisée, mizuna, mibuna, mesclun, saladisi, red orach, rocket (arugula), edible chrysanthemum leaves, wild sorrel leaves, buckler leaf sorrel, salad burnet, young nasturtium leaves, tiny chard and beetroot leaves

selection of herbs
e.g. golden marjoram, annual marjoram, tiny sprigs of dill, tarragon, mint, lemon balm, green pea shoots, broad bean tips, flat-leaf parsley

selection of flowers
e.g. chive flowers, wild garlic flowers, borage flowers, young nasturtium flowers marigold petals, courgette blossom

Ballymaloe French Dressing (see page 226)

First make the dressing. Then wash and dry the salad leaves and tear into bite-sized bits. Sprinkle with edible flowers and petals. Just before serving toss in a little dressing; just enough to coat the leaves lightly. Serve immediately.

Winter Green Salad with Honey and Wholegrain Mustard Dressing

For this salad, use a selection of winter lettuces and salad leaves (butterhead, iceberg, radicchio, endive, chicory, watercress, Buckler leaf sorrel, rocket leaves and winter purslane and mysticana). Tips of purple sprouting broccoli are also delicious and, if you feel like something more robust, use some finely shredded Savoy cabbage and maybe a few shreds of red cabbage too. Honey and Wholegrain Mustard Dressing (see page 226) goes beautifully.

Wash and dry the lettuces and other leaves very carefully in a large sink of cold water. If large tear into bite-sized pieces and put into a deep salad bowl. Cover with cling film and refrigerate if not to be served immediately. Just before serving, toss in the dressing – just enough to make the leaves glisten. Serve immediately.

Note: green salads must not be dressed until just before serving, otherwise they will be tired and unappetising.

Insalata di Campo

A delightful salad of wild leaves and flowers from the woods and hedgerows. It might include:

Wild Leaves
watercress
dandelion leaves
wood and field sorrel
salad burnet
red and green orach
chickweed
wild garlic leaves

LEFT: Insalata di Campo

Flowers
primroses
violets
wild garlic flowers
borage, blue and white

Wash and carefully dry the leaves. Choose a dressing – I like to use the Italian Salad Dressing (see page 226) with this salad. Toss the leaves in just enough dressing to make the leaves glisten. Scatter the flowers over the top and enjoy!

Bits and pieces to add to a basic green salad to make a meal

1. Roughly diced avocado, tomato, cucumber, lots of parsley and mint leaves.

2. Broccoli or sprouting broccoli florets.

3. Black olives.

4. Slivered Parmesan and rocket leaves. (Anchovy vinaigrette is particularly good with this salad.)

5. Orange segments, chicory leaves and black olives and perhaps some walnuts.

6. Blue cheese: crumble a piece of Blue Cheese (Cashel Blue, Stilton or Roquefort) over the salad and use Honey and Mustard Vinaigrette (see page 226).

7. Toasted pine nuts, pistachios, hazelnuts or slivered almonds sprinkled with a little sea salt.

8. Crispy Croûtons (see right).

9. Lardons of crispy bacon or chorizo. We use Gubbeen bacon and chorizo.

10. Shredded red cabbage and green Savoy cabbage, raisins and freshly chopped mint.

11. Cubes of Cheddar cheese tossed in Ballymaloe Relish or Apple and Tomato Chutney (see page 512).

12. Smoked trout with a dill horseradish dressing.

13. Slivers of smoked salmon and avocado.

14. Thinly shaved fennel and pomegranate seeds.

15. Herb Bundles (see below)

16. Deep-fried Capers (see below)

Herb Bundles
We love to serve little bunches of herb sprigs tossed in an appropriate dressing as a garnish or an accompaniment.

Crispy Croûtons
Makes enough for a salad for 4 people.

10g (1/2oz) butter
1 tablespoons extra-virgin olive oil
1 slice of slightly stale loaf bread, crusts removed and cut into a 5mm (1/4in) dice

Melt the butter in a clean frying pan with the olive oil. Turn up the heat, and add the diced bread. The pan should be quite hot at first, then reduce the heat to medium and keep tossing all the time until the croûtons are golden brown all over. Drain on kitchen paper towel.

Alternatively, cook a few croûtons at a time for a few seconds in hot olive oil in a clean frying pan. When the croûtons are pale golden, drain through a metal sieve, catching the oil in a Pyrex bowl. Turn the croûtons out onto kitchen paper to drain, and return the oil to the pan, reheat and fry the remaining batches. The oil may be filtered and used again.

Deep-fried Capers
If the capers have been packed in salt, wash in cold water, and if in brine, drain. Either way dry well. Delicious sprinkled over salads, smoked salmon or sea trout.

50g (2oz) capers
extra-virgin olive oil, for frying

Heat the oil in a deep fryer to 180°C/350°F. Fry the capers for 1–2 minutes until they puff up. Drain and serve immediately.

Salad Dressings

The flavour of your dressing will depend on the quality of your oils and vinegars. A basic French dressing is usually 3 or 4 parts oil to 1 part vinegar. There are many variations on the theme.

Master Recipe
Basic Vinaigrette or French Dressing

Makes enough to dress a salad for 4 people

6 tablespoons extra-virgin olive oil
2 tablespoons white wine vinegar
sea salt and freshly ground pepper

Whisk all the ingredients together just before the salad is to be eaten.

Variations
Mustard Vinaigrette

Follow the Master Recipe, and add ½–1 teaspoon Dijon or whole grain mustard and 1 teaspoon of finely chopped parsley.

Garlic Vinaigrette

Follow the Master Recipe, and add 1 small peeled and crushed garlic clove and ½–1 teaspoon of Dijon or whole grain mustard and 1 teaspoon of finely chopped parsley.

Honey and Mustard Vinaigrette

Follow the Master Recipe, and add 2 teaspoons of runny honey, 1 small peeled and crushed garlic clove and ½–1 teaspoon of Dijon mustard.

Herb Vinaigrette

Follow the Master Recipe, and add 1 tablespoon of freshly chopped herbs to the basic dressing; choose from parsley, chives, thyme and mint.

Herb and Garlic Vinaigrette

Follow the Master Recipe, and add 1 small peeled and crushed garlic clove and a spot of honey to the herb vinaigrette.

Anchovy Vinaigrette

Follow the Master Recipe, and add 2 mashed anchovy fillets, 1 teaspoon of chopped parsley and 1 peeled and crushed garlic clove.

Coriander and Ginger Vinaigrette

Follow the Master Recipe, and add 1 tablespoon of freshly chopped coriander leaves and 1 teaspoon of peeled and finely chopped ginger and 1 finely chopped spring onion.

Lemon Honey Vinagrette

Use lemon juice instead of white wine vinegar, and add 1 teaspoon runny honey and ½ teaspoon Irish grainy mustard.

Ballymaloe French Dressing

Makes 300ml (10fl oz) jar

Affectionately known as Billy's French dressing after a chef who has starred in Ballymaloe kitchens for almost 30 years.

175ml (6fl oz) extra-virgin olive oil or a mixture of olive and other oils e.g. sunflower and groundnut
50ml (2fl oz) white wine vinegar
1 level teaspoon mustard (Dijon or English)
1 level teaspoon salt
few grinds of black pepper
1 large garlic clove, peeled (and mashed if not using a blender)
sprig of parsley
1 small spring onion
sprig of watercress

Put all the ingredients into a blender and run at medium speed for about 1 minute. Alternatively mix the oil and vinegar in a bowl, and add the mustard, salt, pepper and garlic. Chop the parsley, spring onion and watercress finely and add in. Whisk before serving.

Honey and Wholegrain Mustard Dressing

Makes 300ml (10fl oz) jar

A delicious dressing – everyone's favourite at the Cookery School.

175ml (6fl oz) olive oil or a mixture of olive and other oils, e.g. sunflower and groundnut
50ml (2fl oz) white wine or cider vinegar
2 teaspoons runny honey
2 heaped teaspoons wholegrain honey mustard
2 garlic cloves, peeled and crushed
salt and freshly ground pepper

Mix all the ingredients together in a screw-top jar; shake thoroughly before use.

Italian Salad Dressing

Serves 4

If you choose to use lemon juice, remember that Italian lemons are much sweeter and juicier than the imported fruit we have access to, so it may be necessary to add sugar to the dressing.

1 tablespoon freshly squeezed lemon juice or balsamic vinegar
3 tablespoons Italian extra-virgin olive oil
sea salt and freshly cracked pepper

Combine the ingredients together in a screw-top jar.

Basil Dressing

Makes 300ml (10fl oz) jar

175ml (6fl oz) extra-virgin olive oil
50ml (2fl oz) white wine or rice wine vinegar
salt, freshly ground pepper and sugar
1 garlic clove
10–15 basil leaves
1 finely shopped shallot (optional)

Liquidise all the ingredients and store in a screw-top jar in a cool, dark place. It will keep for 3–4 days. Shake well before use.

Shanagarry Cream Dressing
Serves 4

2 hard-boiled eggs
1 tablespoon dark, soft brown sugar
pinch of salt
1 level teaspoon dry mustard
1 tablespoon brown malt vinegar
50–125ml (2–4fl oz) cream

Cut the eggs in half, sieve the yolks into a bowl, and add the sugar, salt and mustard. Blend in the vinegar and cream. Chop the egg whites and add some to the sauce. Keep the rest to scatter over the salad.

ABOVE: Basic Vinaigrette, Herb Vinaigrette, Coriander and Ginger Vinaigrette, Anchovy Vinaigrette, Mustard Vinaigrette

Blue Cheese Dressing
Serves 4

125ml (4fl oz) extra-virgin olive oil
4 teaspoons lemon juice
1/2 teaspoon runny honey
2 tablespoons Roquefort or Cashel Blue cheese, crumbled
freshly ground black pepper

Mix the oil, lemon juice and honey together, add the crumbled cheese, season with black pepper, taste and adjust if necessary.

Tapenade Oil

Add enough extra-virgin olive oil to the Tapenade recipe (see page 590) to make a pouring consistency. Use to drizzle on plates.

Chilli Pepper Oil
Makes about 450ml (16fl oz)

A condiment to add zizz to every dish! Try a few tablespoons in your bread dough or use it as a dip to dunk your bread in.

25g (1oz) chilli pepper flakes
450ml (16fl oz) sunflower or olive oil

Put the chilli pepper into a saucepan, cover with cold oil and gradually heat through – don't overheat or it will taste bitter. Turn off the heat and allow to cool. Strain into a sterilised bottle. Store in the fridge – it lasts almost indefinitely.

Porcini Oil

Put 25g (1oz) dried porcini into the oil and proceed as above. Don't strain.

fish & shellfish

fish & shellfish

The Ballymaloe Cookery School is within sight and smell of the sea – just two miles from the little fishing village of Ballycotton, where we get our fish. Every time I take a bite of deliciously fresh fish or a succulent Dublin Bay prawn, I bless the fishermen who labour in all kinds of weather to catch the fish for our delight. During the 12-week course I encourage the students to go over to Ballycotton to see the boats arriving with their catch of gleaming fish, so they too will be able to recognise really fresh fish and appreciate the labours of the fishermen who risk their lives to catch it.

The wonderful fresh fish we get from the boats in Ballycotton Harbour is a far cry from the fish I ate as a child. I lived in a country village called Cullohill, in Co. Laois. On Thursday, 'fresh fish' was dropped off in the village by a bus on a long journey from Dublin to Cork. People would flock to the village shop to buy whiting, smoked haddock or, occasionally, plaice as a special treat. I loved plaice, fried simply in butter – but that was until I tasted plaice at Ballymaloe.

On the evening I arrived, a local fisherman came to the kitchen door with a bucket full of shiny, stiff fresh plaice as a present. Myrtle and Tim showed me how to fillet the sparkling fish and then we cooked it 'à la meunière' under Myrtle's direction. The first bite was a complete revelation, meltingly tender, sweet and delicate. I simply couldn't believe it was the same fish that I had previously eaten and even enjoyed.

I now know that the fish of my youth was possibly a week old when I ate it. I also realised why so few people enjoy fish – the reality is that many people, particularly those who live inland, never taste really fresh fish and, as a result, can't quite understand why people wax lyrical about it.

The availability of fresh fish depends on the weather. The type of fish that we have access to from the boats varies through the seasons. In the winter, we have herrings, sprats, Dover sole, plaice, turbot, brill, John Dory, monkfish, squid, ling, hake, haddock, pollock and whitebait and, when the weather improves, the fishermen put out their pots to catch shrimps, prawns, crabs and lobsters.

As a result of overfishing and ill-conceived fishing policies in the EU in recent years, fish has got gradually scarcer and boats have had to go out further to find fish. Cod in particular has suffered, with populations currently in serious decline. We have therefore subsitiued cod in many of the recipes in this chapter in an effort to allow depleted stocks to recover. At Ballymaloe, we always use local and seaonal fish, and feel deeply fortunate to still be able to get a certain proportion of day-boat fish at a time when many boats have to stay out for anything from three days to a week to get to the fishing grounds and catch enough fish to make the trip worthwhile.

Not only do we have Ballycotton Harbour down the road, we also have a delivery every Friday from a treasured food supplier in Kilmackalogue Harbour on the Beara Peninsula. They bring an array of precious 'fruits de mer' including mussels, clams, palourdes, roghans, cockles, scallops and sea urchins.

Our other source of fish is the famous market in Cork city. Several fish stalls vie with each other to provide an extraordinary selection of fresh fish. The fish from the waters around our coast – mackerel, salt cod and sprats – jostle for space on the marble slabs with fish from around the world – mahi mahi, doctor fish, kelapia, ruby snapper, yellow fin tuna, snapper, orange roughy and red emperor.

Fast Food

Fish and shellfish are the quintessential fast food. So many delicious recipes can be cooked in minutes – pan-grilled, baked, roasted, boiled, steamed or cooked in a little butter in the pan. Keep it simple; there's no need to smother a piece of really fresh fish in a complicated sauce. Just enjoy its natural flavour.

Buying Fresh Fish and Shellfish

It is absolutely vital to be able to judge accurately whether fish is fresh or not, and for many people this is very difficult. For me, the most important thing to remember is that fresh fish doesn't smell fishy, it just has the merest scent of the sea, reminiscent of fresh seaweed. Really fresh fish looks bright, slippery and lively and not at all dull, whereas stale fish looks distinctly miserable. The eyes will be sunken and the skin can be gritty and dry, with a strong fishy smell.

That's all straightforward enough, but between the time fish is fresh and the time it is really stale there are several days during which it will be gradually deteriorating. It is during this period that it is most difficult to tell just what condition the fish is in, particularly if it has been cut into small pieces. You have to judge by the colour and smell. Check that the flesh of white fish is white and not at all discoloured. The underskin of flat fish should also be quite white and not yellowing.

It is worthwhile building up a good relationship with your local fishmonger, just as you do with your local butcher. Ask for help and take the opportunity to learn every time you go shopping. When you get some delicious fresh fish, remember to say how much you enjoyed it, but on the other hand if you get stale fish, hand it back gently but firmly. Most fishmongers are very conscientious and do all they can to get the fish to you in perfect condition – and this is easier said than done, because they are dealing with a very perishable product.

Remember also that fish have their seasons just as other fresh foods. For example, many of the flat fish such as plaice, sole and lemon sole are not worth eating in January and February because they are full of roe and the flesh tends to be soft and watery – look out for some delicious herring instead.

For those of you who live far from the sea, frozen fillets can be excellent. Good firms freeze their fish in prime condition within hours of being caught, so it is far preferable to fresh fish several days old.

Shellfish should, ideally, be purchased alive (prawns and scallops are the exception to the rule; they can be dead when you buy them, but should still smell fresh). Shells of live mussels may open naturally but will close tightly when tapped, indicating that they are alive. Throw away any dead ones.

Crabs and lobsters can be very lively, so be wary. Many will already have their pincers tied with rubber bands. Pick up lobsters from behind their heads with a good firm grip, and lift crabs by their small back legs, keeping your fingers well out of the way of their powerful pincers.

Freshly shucked oysters and scallops have a fresh sea-breeze smell and a clear, milky or light-grey liquid should surround them. All oysters are best when there is an 'r' in the month, although gigas oysters native to the Pacific can be eaten all year round (they don't normally spawn in the colder water around our coast). However, when the water is very warm in August and September the texture is unpleasantly soft and creamy.

Farmed Salmon versus Wild Salmon

There is indeed much debate surrounding salmon. At Ballymaloe, we only serve wild salmon in season which, in our area, lasts a short six weeks.

Ninety per cent of salmon sold is farmed, which means the fish are bred in small pens and most have antibiotics and anti-parasitic medicine added to their feed. They are also fed pigment-fortified pellets, to improve the colour of the flesh. There are environmental concerns too – intensive farming off the West coast of Ireland is blamed for the virtual extinction of the sea trout.

All of this is worrying, but the issue is not so cut-and-dry. It is made more confusing by the fact that wild salmon populations are in decline and some species are endangered. While most foodies would prefer wild salmon for taste and texture, if eating it contributes to their extinction, then questions need to be raised. A balance needs to be struck, and there needs to be a concerted push to clean up salmon aquaculture. When buying farmed salmon, look out for organic fish, raised to the Soil Association Standards and fed on organic feed.

Nutrition

Fish and shellfish sales have rocketed in recent years as concerns about cholesterol and food additives rise. Fish is a healthy option, being an excellent source of protein and low in saturated fat. Shellfish, fish and particularly fish oil, are also high in omega-3 (unsaturated fatty acids), which help to lower blood pressure, fend off heart disease and improve psoriasis, rheumatoid arthritis and kidney disease. The oilier, darker-fleshed fish like anchovies, salmon, mackerel and herring generally have more omega-3s than leaner types. Many dietitians recommend eating fish twice a week.

How to Cook a Whole Salmon or Sea Trout

A whole poached wild salmon, served hot or cold, is always a dish for a very special occasion. Long gone are the days when the servants in great houses complained bitterly if they had to eat salmon more than twice a week. To poach a salmon or sea trout whole, with the head and tail on, you really need a fish kettle. This is a long narrow saucepan which will hold a fish of 3.6kg (8lb) in weight. Most people do not have a fish kettle, so if you want to keep the fish whole, then the best solution is to bake it in the oven wrapped in tin-foil. Alternatively, you can cut the salmon into 3 pieces, and cook them separately in the way I describe for cooking a piece of salmon. Later, you can arrange the salmon on a board or serving dish, skin it and do a cosmetic job with rosettes of mayonnaise and lots of fresh herbs. A 3.6kg (8lb) salmon will feed 16 people very generously and it could quite easily be enough for 20. As salmon is very rich, 110–150g (4–5oz) cooked salmon is generally plenty to allow per person. Use any leftover bits for Salmon Pâté or Salmon Rillettes (see pages 78 and 554).

Poaching Fish

Most cookbooks will tell you to poach salmon in a 'court-bouillon' – a mixture of wine and water with some sliced carrots, onion, peppercorns and a bouquet garni including a bay leaf, but I feel very strongly that a beautiful salmon is at its best poached gently in just boiling, salted water. The proportion of salt to water is very important. *We use 1 rounded tablespoon salt to every 1.2 litres (2 pints) water.* The aim is to use the minimum amount of water to preserve the maximum flavour. The fish should be just covered so use a saucepan that will fit the fish exactly.

Other fish, such as cod, grey mullet, hake or sea bass may be poached in the same way, but you will need to adjust the time depending on size.

To Poach a Piece of Fish

Choose a saucepan that will just fit the piece of fish: an oval cast-iron saucepan is usually perfect. Half-fill with measured salted water (see above), bring to the boil and put in the piece of fish. Cover the saucepan, bring back to the boil and simmer gently for 20 minutes. Turn off the heat, allow to sit in the water for 4–5 minutes and serve within 15–20 minutes. *Never poach fish cutlets* because the maximum surface is exposed to the water giving maximum loss of flavour.

Wild salmon has a short season, which varies slightly from area to area. The tails and fins of farmed salmon are often damaged or deformed slightly, depending on the numbers in the cages. Depending on the production method, they tend to be fatter and flabbier than wild salmon. Look out for Organic Farmed Salmon which is reared to Soil Association standards and fed on organic feed. The colour of the salmon flesh is determined mostly by what the fish feeds on. The colour of farmed salmon can literally be chosen from a colour card, the feed is then made up and coloured to order.

Poached Whole Salmon or Sea Trout to be served cold

1 whole salmon or sea trout
water
salt

Garnish
crisp lettuce leaves
sprigs of watercress, lemon balm, fennel and
*   fennel flowers (if available)*
a segment of lemon for each person
Homemade Mayonnaise (see page 584)

fish kettle

Clean and gut the salmon carefully; do not remove the head, tail or scales. Carefully measure the water and half fill the fish kettle, adding 1 rounded tablespoon of salt to every 1.2 litres (2 pints). Cover the fish kettle and bring the water to the boil. Add the fish and allow the water to come back to the boil. Simmer for just 2 minutes and then turn off the heat. Keep the lid on and allow the fish to cool completely in the water (the fish should be just barely covered by the water).

To serve: when the fish is just cold, remove from the fish kettle and drain for a few minutes. Line a large serving dish with fresh, crisp lettuce leaves, top with sprigs of watercress, lemon balm and fennel and fennel flowers, if available. Carefully slide the salmon onto the dish. Just before serving, peel off the top skin, leaving the tail and head intact. (We don't scrape off the brown flesh in the centre because it tastes good.) Pipe a line of mayonnaise along the centre of the salmon lengthways and garnish with tiny sprigs of fennel and fennel flowers or very thin twists of cucumber. Put some segments of lemon around the dish between the lettuce and herbs. Resist the temptation to use any tomato or, horror of horrors, to put a slice of olive over the eye. The pale pink of the salmon flesh with the crisp lettuce and fresh herbs seems just perfect. Serve with a bowl of good homemade mayonnaise.

Poached Whole Salmon or Sea Trout to be served hot, warm or barely cold

1 whole salmon or sea trout
water
salt

Garnish
sprigs of fresh parsley, lemon balm and fennel
Hollandaise Sauce (see page 581)
a segment of lemon for each person

fish kettle

Clean and gut the salmon carefully; do not remove the head, tail or scales. Carefully measure the water and half-fill the fish kettle; add 1 rounded tablespoon of salt to every 1.2 litres (2 pints). Cover the fish kettle and bring the water to the boil. Add the salmon or sea trout and allow the water to come back to the boil. Cover and simmer gently for 20 minutes. Then turn off the heat and leave the salmon in the water for 4–5 minutes to settle. Remove from the water. It will keep hot for 20–30 minutes.

To serve: carefully lift the whole fish out of the fish kettle and leave to drain on the rack for a few minutes. Then slide onto a large, hot serving dish. Garnish with lots of parsley, lemon balm and fennel and 10–12 segments of lemon. I don't remove the skin until I am serving it at the table, then peel it back gradually as I serve; however, if you prefer, remove the skin at the last second before bringing it to the table. When you have served all the fish from the top, remove the bone as delicately as possible, put it aside and continue as before. Serve with Hollandaise sauce – a marriage made in heaven.

Whole Salmon or Sea Trout cooked in foil

3.6–4.2kg (8–9lb) salmon or sea trout, cleaned
110g (4oz) butter
sea salt and freshly ground pepper
sprig of fennel

Garnish
segments of lemon
sprigs of parsley or fennel

a large sheet of good-quality tin foil

Preheat the oven to 180°C/350°F/gas 4.

Put the tin foil on a large baking sheet, preferably with edges. Place the salmon in the centre. Smear butter on both sides of the fish and put a few lumps in the cavity. Season with salt and pepper and put a sprig of fennel in the centre if you have it. Be generous with the butter; it will mix with the juices to make a delicious sauce to spoon over the fish. Bring the tin foil together loosely and seal the edges well.

Bake for about 90 minutes (allow 10 minutes per 450g/1lb). Open the package, being careful of the steam. Test by lifting the flesh off the backbone at the thickest point where the flesh meets the head. The fish should lift off the bone easily and there should be no trace of blood; if there is, seal again and pop back in the oven for another 5–10 minutes (but be careful not to overcook it).

Serve hot or cold. If you are serving it hot, spoon the juices over each helping, or use the butter and juice to make a Hollandaise-type sauce by whisking the hot, melted butter and salmon juice gradually into 2 egg yolks, adding a little lemon juice to taste. Garnish with parsley and fennel. If the fish is to be eaten cold, serve with some freshly made salads and a bowl of Homemade Mayonnaise (see page 584).

Serve warm with asparagus or sea kale, or fresh green peas and new potatoes.

Baked Trout with Spinach Butter Sauce

Serves 4–6

We can sometimes get lovely fat, pink trout about 2 years old, which have wonderful taste – much better than the smaller ones. This is a horrendously rich-sounding sauce but it tastes delicious and the flavour is sublime.

2 x 900g (2lb) whole rainbow trout
25–50g (1–2oz) butter
salt and freshly ground pepper
sprig of fennel

Spinach Butter Sauce (see page 587)

tin foil

Preheat the oven to 190°C/ 375°F/gas 5.

Gut the trout and wash well, making sure to remove the line of blood from the inside near the back bone. Dry with kitchen paper, season inside and out with salt and freshly ground pepper. Put a blob of butter and a sprig of fennel into the centre of each trout. Take a large sheet of tin foil, smear a little butter on the centre, put the trout onto the buttered bit and fold over the edges into a papiotte shape. Seal well to ensure that none of the juices can escape. Repeat with the other trout.

Put the two tin foil parcels on a baking tray (make sure they are not touching), and bake for about 30 minutes. Meanwhile, make the Spinach Butter Sauce.

When the fish is cooked, open the parcels. There will be lots of delicious juices; use some of these to thin out the sauce. Put the two parcels onto a hot serving dish and bring to the table. Skin the fish and lift the juicy pink flesh onto hot plates.

Spoon the Spinach Butter Sauce over the fish and serve immediately.

Variation
Baked Turbot or Brill with Spinach Butter Sauce

Cook whole turbot or brill as for Baked Plaice (see page 236). Skin and carefully lift the fillets off the bone. Serve on hot plates with Spinach Butter Sauce. Rich but exquisite!

Poached Monkfish with Red Pepper Sauce

Serves 6 as a main course

A whole monkfish is quite a sight to behold – years ago fishermen were concerned that no one would want to eat this exceptionally good fish because of its ugly appearance, so they took the precaution of cutting off the head before they sent the tails to the fishmongers.

Monkfish has a similar texture to Dublin Bay prawns so it was regularly substituted for the latter before it became almost as expensive. In recent years, it has become one of the most highly regarded fish and they are now becoming scarce.

Monkfish are brilliantly designed – they have a huge mouth with a double row of teeth, and come equipped with what looks like a radar and a little fishing rod. The latter has what looks like a tiny fish on the end which attracts shoals of smaller fish to swim right into the monkfish's open mouth and chomp!

700g (1½lb) monkfish tails, carefully trimmed
  of skin and membrane, filleted
1.2 litres (2 pints) water
1 teaspoon salt

Note: measure the ingredients above carefully; it really matters.

Roasted Red Pepper Sauce (see page 149)

Garnish
sprigs of flat-leaf parsley or chervil

Cut the monkfish into 1cm (½in) slices and refrigerate until needed. Meanwhile, make the Red Pepper Sauce.

Bring the water to the boil and add the salt. Add the monkfish and simmer for 4–5 minutes or until completely white and no longer opaque.

Drain well. Arrange in a warm serving dish or on individual plates, coat with the Red Pepper Sauce, garnish with sprigs of flat-leaf parsley or chervil and serve immediately.

Master Recipe
Roast Salmon with Teriyaki Sauce

Serves about 20

Roasting salmon is so blissfully easy. In fact, it is one of the simplest dinner party dishes I know. It is also good at room temperature or even cold. Teriyaki is a Japanese sauce.

1 whole fresh salmon (about 4kg/9lb)
salt and freshly ground pepper
50g (2oz) butter, melted
4 tablespoons extra-virgin olive oil

Odette Rocha's Teriyaki Sauce
225ml (8fl oz) Kikkoman soy sauce
225ml (8fl oz) dry white wine
2 large garlic cloves, peeled and thinly sliced
4cm (1½in) piece root ginger, peeled and
  thinly sliced
2 tablespoons wholegrain mustard with honey
2 tablespoons soft brown sugar

Preheat the oven to 250°C/475°F/gas 9.

Put all the ingredients for the Teriyaki Sauce into a stainless steel saucepan. Bring to the boil and simmer for 4–5 minutes. Keep aside.

Descale the salmon, fillet and remove the pin bones. Line a baking tray with tin foil. Put the fillets of fish on top and season with salt and pepper. Brush with melted butter and oil. Roast the salmon in the oven for 20–25 minutes or until cooked and tender. Transfer to a hot serving dish. Spoon some Teriyaki Sauce over the hot salmon and serve immediately, with the remainder of the sauce served separately.

New potatoes and bok choy are good accompaniments.

Smaller quantity
Halve or quarter the amount of Teriyaki Sauce. Cut the salmon into 75g (3oz) portions and cook in a smaller ovenproof dish. Serve in the same way.

Variations

Roast Salmon with Dill Butter
Melt 225g (8oz) butter, add 4 tablespoons freshly chopped dill and spoon over the salmon as soon as it comes out of the oven. Serve with Tomato Fondue (see page 200) and new potatoes; divine!

Trout with Cream and Dill
Serves 4

Little rainbow trout are available in virtually every fish shop. This combination is surprisingly delicious and very fast to cook. If dill is difficult to find, use a mixture of fresh herbs. Mackerel can be used instead of the trout.

4 fresh trout
salt and freshly ground pepper
75g (3oz) butter
175ml (6fl oz) cream
1–2 tablespoons finely chopped fresh dill

Gut the trout, fillet carefully, wash and dry well. Season with salt and pepper. Melt the butter in a frying pan, and fry the fillets flesh-side down until golden brown. Turn over onto the skin side and add the cream and chopped dill. Simmer gently for 3–4 minutes or until the trout is cooked. Taste the sauce to check the seasoning and serve immediately.

Tronçon of Turbot with an Olive Oil Sauce Vièrge
Serves 4

Rick Stein charmed us all with his scrummy fish dishes when he came to the school in the summer of 2001. He describes his food as 'a bit simple' but it's just what we love – I can't wait to make another trip to his restaurant in Padstow in Cornwall.

4 x 175–225g (6–8oz) tronçons (fillets) of
* turbot*
75ml (3fl oz) extra-virgin olive oil, plus extra
* for brushing*
1 teaspoon chopped rosemary
1 teaspoon chopped thyme
1 bay leaf, very finely chopped
½ teaspoon crushed fennel seeds
1 teaspoon coarsely crushed black peppercorns
1 teaspoon sea salt flakes

Olive Oil Sauce Vièrge
83ml (3fl oz) extra-virgin olive oil
2 tablespooons lemon juice
1 plum tomato, de-seeded and diced
8 black olives, pitted and cut into fine strips
2 anchovy fillets in oil, drained and diced
1 garlic clove, finely chopped
1 heaped teaspoon coarsely chopped parsley
salt and freshly ground pepper

Preheat the grill to high.

Mix together the olive oil, chopped herbs, fennel seeds, crushed peppercorns and sea salt in a shallow dish. Add the pieces of turbot and turn them over in the mixture so that they are well coated. Place on an oiled baking tray, skin-side up, and grill for 7–8 minutes.

Meanwhile, make the sauce. Put everything except the chopped parsley and seasoning into a small pan. Just as the fish is ready, place over a very low heat just to warm through.

To serve, lift the pieces of fish into the centre of 4 warmed plates. Stir the parsley and seasoning into the sauce and spoon it around the fish. Brush the top of each piece of fish with a little more oil and sprinkle with a few flakes of sea salt.

> TIP: Turbot and brill are both flat fish and look very similar. Turbot is superior and more expensive, but brill can be really delicous when absolutely fresh. They are interchangeable in recipes. Turbot can be distinguished from brill by its slightly thorny or knobbly skin.

Baked Plaice or Sole with Herb Butter
Serves 4

This is a superb recipe devised by Myrtle Allen which can be used not only for plaice and sole but for all very fresh flat fish such as brill, turbot, dabs, flounder and lemon sole. Depending on the size of the fish, it may be served as a starter or a main course. A brilliant way to cook for those on a low-fat diet but for those who are not, accompany it with Herb Butter or another complementary sauce: Hollandaise, Mousseline, Beurre Blanc, Lobster or Champagne.

4 very fresh plaice or sole on the bone
salt and freshly ground pepper

Herb Butter
50–110g (2–4oz) butter
4 teaspoons finely chopped mixed herbs – fresh
parsley, chives, fennel and thyme leaves

Preheat the oven to 190°C/375°F/gas 5.

Turn the fish on its side and remove the head. Wash the fish and thoroughly clean the slit. With a sharp knife, cut through the skin right round the fish, just to where the fringe meets the flesh. Be careful to cut neatly and cross the side cuts at the tail or it will be difficult to remove the skin later.

Sprinkle the fish with salt and pepper and lay them in 5mm (¼in) of water in a shallow baking tin. Bake in the oven for 20–30 minutes according to the size of the fish. The water should have just evaporated as the fish is cooked. Check to see whether the fish is cooked by lifting the flesh from the bone; it should lift off the thickest part easily and be quite white with no trace of pink. Meanwhile, melt the butter and stir in the chopped herbs. Just before serving, catch the skin down near the tail and pull it off gently (the skin will tear badly if not properly cut). Lift the fish onto hot plates and spoon the Herb Butter over them. Serve immediately.

Roast Seabass with Olive Oil and Lemon
Serves 6

6 x 175g (6oz) fillets of seabass, cod or hake
extra-virgin olive oil
salt and freshly ground white pepper

Garnish
lemon-flavoured olive oil (we use Colonna
Granverde)
1–2 lemons
bunch of watercress

Preheat the oven to 230°C/450°F/gas 8.

Score the fish quite deeply on the skin side to prevent curling. Heat a thin film of olive oil in a non-stick pan to just before smoking point. Season the fillets and place skin-side down in the pan until a nice crust forms. Turn on the other side and complete the cooking in the oven. Arrange skin-side up on a serving dish, drizzle a little olive oil over the fish, and garnish with lemon wedges and watercress.

How to Fillet a Flat Fish (Plaice, Sole, Flounder, Turbot, Brill, Halibut etc.)

Use a sharp filleting knife with a flexible blade

1. Lay the fish on a chopping board, dark skin upwards with the head towards you. With the point of the knife cut down the centre of the fish, onto the bone, from tail to head just left of the spine. Keeping the knife almost flat, slide the knife between the flesh and the bone.

2. Using long sweeping strokes from tail to head, gradually detach the fillet.

3. Turn the fish around and slip the knife over the spine, cut from head to tail this time and remove the fillet in the same way.

4. Turn the fish over and repeat the process on the other side. Use the bones for a fish stock.

Master Recipe
Warm Skate Wing with Coriander Dressing

Serves 4 as a starter, 2 as a main course

The French are very fond of serving warm fish with a cold dressing.

1 medium skate wing
1 onion
2–3 sprigs of parsley
2 tablespoons white wine vinegar
pinch of salt

Coriander Dressing
4 tablespoons extra-virgin olive oil
2 tablespoons sunflower or groundnut oil
2 tablespoons sherry or balsamic vinegar
salt and freshly ground pepper
½ teaspoon Dijon mustard
1 teaspoon coriander seeds
1 tablespoon green spring onion, cut at an
   angle, or very thinly sliced red onion rings

Poach the skate wing (see page 232). Lift the flesh off the bone and divide it into 2 or 4 portions.

Meanwhile, make the dressing by combining the oils, vinegar, salt, freshly ground pepper and mustard. Warm the coriander seeds for a few minutes, crush in a pestle and mortar and add to the dressing. Just before serving, add the spring onion tops and spoon over the warm skate wing.

Serve immediately on warm plates. This dish is best eaten lukewarm.

Variation
Warm Skate Wing with Ballymaloe Herb Dressing
Follow the Master Recipe, replacing the Coriander Dressing with Ballymaloe French Dressing (see page 226). We serve this as part of a selection of fish and shellfish in a buffet, or as part of a seafood plate, but it is quite delicious served on its own with salads.

Warm Skate Wing with Dill Mayonnaise and Sweet Cucumber Pickle
Follow the Master Recipe to poach the skate wing. Spread a little Dill Mayonnaise (see page 585) onto a plate and place a portion of skate on top. Serve with Sweet Cucumber Pickle (see page 514).

Skate with Black Butter and Deep-fried Capers

Serves 2 as a main course

This classic recipe is one of the most delicious ways of serving a piece of really fresh skate wing.

1 medium skate (ray) wing weighing 600–700g
   (1¼–1½lb)
1 onion, sliced
a few sprigs of parsley
a little salt
2 tablespoons white wine vinegar

Black Butter
50g (2oz) butter
2 tablespoons white wine vinegar

Garnish
parsley, freshly chopped
Deep-fried Capers (see page 225)

Choose a pan wide enough for the skate to lie flat while cooking. Put the skate in, cover completely with cold water, and add the onion, parsley, salt and wine vinegar. Bring to the boil gently, cover, and barely simmer for 15–20 minutes. If the flesh lifts easily from the cartilage, the skate is cooked. Turn off the heat and transfer the fish onto a large serving plate. Skin and lift the flesh onto hot plates, first from one side of the cartilage, then the other, scraping off the white skin. Divide into 2 portions. Cover and keep hot.

Next make the Black Butter. Melt the butter in a hot pan, allow it to foam and just as it turns brown, add the wine vinegar; allow to bubble up again and then pour sizzling over the fish. Sprinkle with chopped parsley and serve immediately, garnished with crispy Deep-fried Capers.

Variation
Poached Skate Wing with Hollandaise Sauce and Buttered Cucumber
Follow the recipe as above to poach the skate wing. Serve on hot plates with Hollandaise Sauce (see page 581) and Buttered Cucumber (see page 190).

How to Skin Fish Fillets

Put the fillet of fish skin-side down onto the board.

Cut through the flesh down onto the skin at the tail end, with the knife at a 45° angle. Hold onto the skin and half push, half saw the flesh off the skin.

If the knife is at the right angle, there should be no waste. Use the skins for a fish stock.

Note: Do not remove the skin if you plan to pan-grill the fish.

How to Skin Dover Sole or Black Sole

1. Lay the fish on a chopping board, dark skin uppermost. With a sharp knife, cut across the skin where the tail joins the body. Lift the edge of the skin and run your index finger between the skin and the flesh to loosen it.

2. Grip the skin with a cloth in one hand, and use your other hand to hold down the tail end. Pull the skin towards the head. Turn the fish over, and repeat on the other side.

3. Alternatively, holding the fish by the head, continue to pull the skin down towards the tail.

Grilled Dover Sole on the Bone

Serves 1

Sole on the bone, the mainstay of many fish restaurants, is still my absolute favourite way to eat this fish. Surprisingly, sole is one of the fish that can be tough if it is too fresh; a day old is perfect. Dover sole is called 'black sole' in Ireland.

1 Dover sole, skinned
25–50g (1–2oz) butter, melted
salt and freshly ground pepper

Garnish
segment of lemon

About 30 minutes before cooking, sprinkle the fish on both sides with salt and brush liberally with butter.

Grill on both sides until cooked through; the length of time will depend on the size and thickness of the fish. Test by lifting a little of the flesh close to the head where it is thickest; it should lift easily from the bone and there should be no trace of blood. Transfer to a hot plate and serve immediately with the lemon and freshly ground pepper.

Grilled John Dory on the Bone

Serves 4

Johnny Dory (as the fisherman in our nearby port of Ballycotton call this ugly-looking flat fish) is one of the most exquisite fish in the sea. It is one of the two fish said to have the thumbprint of St. Peter clearly on the side. The other is the round fish haddock. St. Peter is supposed to have leant over the edge of his boat in the Sea of Galilee and picked them out of the water, hence they are blessed. John Dory is also very good pan-grilled or baked.

4 very fresh whole John Dory
salt and freshly ground pepper
butter
Herb Butter (see page 588)

Remove the head from the fish. Score the skin crossways on both sides, sprinkle with a little salt and pepper and spread butter on both sides of the fish. Grill for 10–12 minutes at a medium heat; you will need to turn the fish once during the cooking time. Serve immediately with a little Herb Butter.

Grilled Salmon Tortilla with Rocket, Tapenade and Aïoli

Serves 4 as a snack

A great recipe from Mary Risley who owns an inspirational cooking school called Tante Marie's in San Francisco.

450g (1lb) fresh wild salmon
extra-virgin olive oil
sea salt and freshly ground pepper
Tapenade (see page 590), made with 110g (4oz)
   Niçoise or Kalamata olives, stoned
4 flour tortillas
Aïoli (see page 584)
1 bunch rocket leaves
4 very ripe tomatoes, sliced and seasoned with
   salt, pepper, sugar and freshly chopped mint

To prepare the salmon, remove the pin bones if necessary, and divide into 4 portions. Sprinkle with salt and pepper and brush with extra-virgin olive oil.

Next make the Tapenade, keeping it as a chunky paste. Pan-grill the salmon over a moderately high heat until it is just cooked through. Remove from the heat. Quickly warm the tortillas on each side under the grill or on a pan. Put a piece of salmon, some rocket, a spoonful of Tapenade, and some Aïoli in the bottom half of each tortilla. Top with a few sliced tomatoes. Fold over the top and serve immediately.

RIGHT: Grilled John Dory on the Bone

How to Pan-grill Fish

A pan-grill is a cast iron frying pan with ridges. I pride myself on not being a gadget person but I find this piece of kitchen equipment indispensable not only for fish but also for meat, vegetables and even polenta. Here are two methods:

Method 1

Season the unskinned fish on both sides with salt and freshly ground pepper and brush the flesh side with extra-virgin olive oil.

Heat a cast-iron griddle pan. Place the fish fillet flesh-side down on the hot pan, cook for a minute or so and then revolve the fillet so there are criss-cross grill markings on the fish. Reduce the heat. Cook for a further 3–4 minutes, depending on the thickness of the fish. Turn over and continue to cook on the skin side until crisp and golden.

Method 2

Dip the fish fillets in flour seasoned with salt and freshly ground pepper. Shake off the excess and spread a little soft butter with a knife on the flesh side of the fish as though you were buttering a slice of bread rather meanly. When the grill is quite hot but not smoking, place the fish fillets, butter side down, on the grill; the fish should sizzle as soon as it touches the pan. Turn down the heat slightly and let the fish cook for 4–5 minutes. Turn and continue to cook on the other side until crisp and golden.

Note: You can pan-grill fish whole under 900g (2lb) such as mackerel, herring and brown trout. Fish over 900g (2lb) should be filleted and then cut across into portions. Large fish from 1.8–2.6kg (4–6lb) can be grilled whole. Cook for 10–15 minutes approx. on each side and then put in a hot oven (220°C/425°F/gas 7) for another 15 minutes or so to finish cooking.

Pan-grilled Mackerel with Maitre d'Hôtel Butter

See page 524

Pan-grilled Fish with Lemon and Parsley Butter

Serves 4 as a main course

A piece of perfectly cooked pan-grilled fish is hard to beat but it takes more care and skill than you might think to get it just right. Other flavoured butters may be used, depending on the fish.

8 fillets of very fresh fish e.g. mackerel, grey mullet, sea bass, cod, haddock or wild salmon (allow 175g/6oz fish for main course, 75g/3oz for a starter)
seasoned flour
small knob of butter
Parsley and Lemon Butter (see page 588)

Garnish
segments of lemon
parsley

Pan-grill the fish (see left, Method 2). When crisp and golden on both sides transfer to a hot plate, put a blob of butter on each and serve immediately.

The Parsley Butter may be served directly on the fish or, if you have a pretty shell e.g. a gigas oyster shell, place it at the side of the plate as a container for the butter. Garnish with parsley and a segment of lemon.

Try serving it with Scallion Mash (see page 182).

Pan-grilled Tuna with Tomato and Basil Salsa and a Herb Salad

Serves 6

Swordfish is also delicious in this recipe.

6 x 175g (6oz) tuna fillets (skin removed)
salt and freshly ground pepper
2 tablespoons extra-virgin olive oil, plus extra for herb salad

Tomato and Basil Salsa

6–8 very ripe tomatoes peeled and seeded and cut into 5mm (1/4in) dice
salt, freshly ground pepper and sugar
4 tablespoons extra-virgin olive oil
freshly squeezed lime juice
6–8 leaves of fresh basil

a mixture of fresh herbs such as flat-leaf parsley, chervil, mint, lemon balm, tarragon, golden marjoram

Preheat the grill. Make the Tomato and Basil Salsa – season the tomato dice with salt, pepper and sugar and add the olive oil, a squeeze of lime and torn basil leaves. Taste and correct the seasoning if necessary.

Season the tuna well with salt and freshly ground pepper, brush with oil and cook on both sides for 3–6 minutes. The centre should still be pink.

Meanwhile, warm the salsa slightly; it will probably be enough to put the bowl into the oven while you heat the plates.

Toss the herbs in a little extra olive oil and lemon juice. Season with a few flakes of sea salt.

Serve the tuna immediately onto hot plates with a little of the tomato salsa on top.

Pan-grilled Cod with Ulster Champ and Oven-roasted Tomatoes

Serves 8

8 fillets of cod (skin attached), or use haddock, grey sea mullet or sea bass
salt and freshly ground pepper
extra-virgin olive oil
24 or more sweet cherry tomatoes, or tomatoes on the vine (optional)
Ulster Champ (see page 183)
Parsley Pesto (see page 589)
Sun-dried Tomato Oil (see right)
sprigs of fresh chervil

First make the Ulster Champ. When it is ready, preheat the oven to 230°C/450°F/gas 8.

Pan-grill the cod, following Method 1 (see left).

Meanwhile, spread the tomatoes in a single layer in a roasting pan. Toss them in a little olive oil and season with salt and pepper. Roast in the hot oven for 4–5 minutes or until they begin to burst. It is also fun to roast them on the branch.

To serve: put a generous spoonful of soft Ulster Champ on 8 warmed serving plates. Arrange a piece of cod, skin-side up onto the potato. Drizzle a little parsley pesto around the edge and dot around a little sun-dried tomato oil. Add 3 roasted tomatoes, sprinkle with some sprigs of chervil and serve immediately.

Sun-dried Tomato Oil
Whizz a few really good-quality sun-dried tomatoes with extra-virgin olive oil or chilli oil in a blender or food processor; taste and season if necessary. Use to drizzle around fish or chicken or vegetable dishes.

Seared Fresh Salmon with Vine-ripened Tomatoes and Herbs
Serves 6

I love this simple, fresh-tasting dish which can be enjoyed as a starter or a main course.

350g–700g (³/₄–1¹/₂lb) fillet of wild fresh
  salmon, scales removed but skin on
salt and freshly ground pepper
a little extra-virgin olive oil or Clarified Butter
  (see page 105)

2–4 tablespoons freshly chopped basil,
  marjoram, mint and flat-leaf parsley,
3–6 very ripe tomatoes, peeled and coarsely
  chopped
pinch of sugar
60–150ml (2¹/₂–5fl oz) extra-virgin olive oil

Cut the salmon into strips 6–10cm (2¹/₂–4in) wide approximately. Season well with salt and pepper. Fry or pan-grill carefully in a little olive oil or clarified butter. Transfer to a serving dish, flesh-side up. Mix the herbs with the tomato dice, season with salt, pepper and sugar and add the olive oil. Spoon over the fish. Serve warm or cold.

Seared Tuna or Swordfish with Piperonata and Tapenade
Serves 6

The secret of cooking tuna is to undercook it like a rare steak, otherwise it becomes dry and dull. The sweetness of Piperonata and the gutsy taste of Tapenade are great with it.

6 x 175g (6oz) pieces of tuna or swordfish
  (remove the skin if necessary)
2 tablespoons extra-virgin olive oil
salt and freshly ground pepper
Piperonata (see page 199)
Tapenade (see page 590)

Garnish
6–8 leaves of flat-leaf parsley or basil

First make the Piperonata and Tapenade.

Preheat the pan-grill. Brush the fish with oil and season well with salt and freshly ground pepper. Sear the fish on the hot grill pan, first in one direction and then the other. Cook on both sides for 2–3 minutes. The centre should still be pink.

Meanwhile, reheat the Piperonata if necessary. Put a few tablespoons onto each plate, and place a piece of sizzling fish on top. Put a little Tapenade on top or dot irregularly around the edge of the Piperonata. Add a few sprigs of flat-leaf parsley or basil and serve immediately.

How to Fillet a Round Fish (Salmon, Cod, Haddock, Grey Mullet)

Use a sharp filleting knife with a flexible blade.

Put the gutted fish onto a chopping board.

First cut around the base of the head down to the bone with the point of the knife.

Slit the skin from the head to the tail just above the backbone, using the back fin as a guide.

Slide the knife across the bone in long, sweeping movements, keeping the blade as flat as possible.

Cut through the centre bones and detach the fillet.

Turn the fish over and detach the fillets from the other side.

Remove the pin bones with tweezers.

Cumin-crusted Fish with Olive and Chilli Salsa

Serves 6

2 tablespoons cumin seeds
6 fillets very fresh fish (haddock, hake, grey
  mullet, turbot, cod or salmon, approximately
  75g/3oz each)
sea salt and freshly ground pepper

Olive and Chilli Salsa

110g (4oz) Kalamata olives, stoned and
 roughly chopped
2 tablespoons freshly chopped flat-leaf parsley
2 chillies, de-seeded and finely chopped
1 garlic clove, crushed
125ml (4fl oz) olive oil
sea salt and freshly ground pepper
lemon juice (optional)

Garnish
rocket leaves

First make the Olive and Chilli Salsa: mix all the ingredients together. Taste; it may need a squeeze of lemon juice.

Dry-roast the cumin seeds in a pan over a medium heat and then grind in a pestle and mortar. Season both sides of the fish with salt and pepper. Dip the flesh side in cumin seeds. Just before serving, heat a pan-grill over a moderate to high heat. Cook the fish in a very little oil until crisp and golden on both sides. Serve on hot plates with a little of the Olive and Chilli Salsa sprinkled around the edge. Garnish with rocket leaves and serve immediately.

Mackerel with Tomatoes and Tapenade

Serves 4

4 large ripe tomatoes, thinly sliced
salt and freshly ground pepper
pinch of sugar

1 tablespoon thyme leaves
8 fresh mackerel fillets
Black and Green Tapenade (see page 590)

Garnish
flat-leaf parsley sprigs

Preheat the grill to the highest heat.

Arrange the tomato slices in a single layer on a lightly oiled baking tray. Season lightly with salt, pepper and a pinch of sugar, and sprinkle with the thyme leaves. Slash the skin of each mackerel fillet two or three times and place, skin-side up, on top of the tomatoes.

Grill the mackerel until the skin is crisp and the fish is cooked through and the tomatoes are warm (about 3–4 minutes).

Transfer the mackerel and tomato to warm plates. Drizzle a little tapenade over the top. Serve immediately with little sprigs of flat-leaf parsley.

Deh-Ta Hsiung's Steamed Grey Sea Mullet

Serves 4 as a main course

Deh-Ta Hsiung, a Chinese chef who came to the school to give us a 'Taste of China', was so excited by the flavour of grey sea mullet that he almost emigrated to Ireland. Here is his delicious recipe for steamed fish.

1 grey sea mullet 700–900g (1½–2lb), scaled
  and gutted (perch, sea bass or salmon trout
  can be used instead)
1 teaspoon salt
1 teaspoon sesame seed oil
4 spring onions
2–3 dried shiitake mushrooms, soaked and
  thinly shredded
50g (2oz) uncooked pork fillet or cooked ham,
  thinly shredded
2 tablespoons light soy sauce
1 tablespoon rice wine or sherry
4cm (1½in) piece ginger root, thinly shredded
2 tablespoons vegetable oil

Wash the fish under the cold tap and dry well, both inside and out, with kitchen paper. Trim the fins and tail with strong scissors and watch out for the very sharp spines.

Slash both sides of the fish diagonally as far as the bone at intervals of about 1cm (½in) with a sharp knife. Rub about half the salt and all the sesame oil inside the fish, and place it on top of 2 or 3 of the spring onions in an oval heatproof dish.

Mix the mushrooms and pork or ham with the remaining salt, a little of the soy sauce and wine.

Stuff about half of this mixture inside the fish and put the rest on top with the shredded ginger. Place in a hot Chinese steamer over a wok with sufficient water to come above the bottom of the steamer. Steam vigorously for 15 minutes.

Meanwhile, thinly shred the remaining spring onions and heat the vegetable oil in a little saucepan until bubbling. Remove the fish dish from the steamer, arrange the spring onion shreds on top, pour the remaining soy sauce over it and then the hot oil from head to tail. Serve hot.

If you don't possess a steamer big enough to hold a whole fish, wrap it in silver foil and bake in a preheated oven at 230°C/450°F/gas 8 for 20–25 minutes.

TIP: There are several good reasons for slashing both sides of the fish before cooking: first, if you are cooking the fish whole, the skin will burst unless it is scored; second, slashing allows the heat to penetrate more quickly and at the same time helps to diffuse the flavours of the seasoning and sauce. Also, because the Chinese never use a knife at the table, it is much easier to pick up pieces of flesh with just a pair of chopsticks.

Monkfish Spiedino with Salmoriglio Sauce

Serves 4

There are lots of variations you can do on the kebab theme. This Italian spiedino is quick, easy and irresistible. Use unsmoked bacon and leave out the peppercorns or vary the herbs if you like.

450g (1lb) monkfish, cut into 2.5cm (1in) cubes
4–6 smoked streaky bacon rashers, cut into 2.5cm (1in) squares
1 small red pepper, cut into 2.5cm (1in) squares
bulbs of tiny spring onions (optional)
1 level teaspoon whole black peppercorns
1 level teaspoon sea salt
2 tablespoons freshly chopped herb fennel
extra-virgin olive oil

Salmoriglio Sauce

2 heaped tablespoons annual marjoram leaves (with stalks removed)
1 scant level teaspoon sea salt
1 teaspoon sugar
1 tablespoon lemon juice
4–6 tablespoons extra-virgin olive oil
segments of lemon

First make the Salmoriglio Sauce: pound the marjoram with the sea salt and sugar in a pestle and mortar until completely crushed. Slowly add the lemon juice and olive oil as for mayonnaise. Set aside.

Thread the monkfish, bacon, pepper and spring onion alternately on 4 skewers. Crack the black peppercorns in a pestle and mortar, and add the sea salt and fennel. Spread this mixture out onto a work surface or plate and roll the filled skewers in it, then cover with clingfilm and refrigerate until the barbecue or chargrill is hot enough for cooking.

Brush the spiedini with a little olive oil – they usually take about 4–5 minutes on each side. Serve drizzled with Salmoriglio Sauce and garnished with lemon segments.

Note: The spiedino can be cooked under a radiant grill also. Serve with Beurre Blanc (see page 583) for a change.

Cod or Haddock Niçoise

Serves 6 as main course

This is an extremely simple fish dish with a rich, robust flavour. Virtually any round fish may be used, and it is just as suitable for a starter as for a main course, but remember to halve the quantities!

700g (1½lb) cod or haddock fillet, cut into 6 portions
salt and freshly ground pepper
450g (1lb) very ripe tomatoes, skinned, de-seeded, chopped and sprinkled with a little sugar
1–2 garlic cloves, crushed
1 tablespoon capers, rinsed
12 black olives, stoned and sliced
2 tablespoons freshly chopped parsley
1 teaspoon fresh thyme leaves
3 tablespoons extra-virgin olive oil

Preheat the oven to 200°C/400°F/gas 6.

Season the fish with salt and pepper. Prepare and mix all the remaining ingredients. Place the fish in a single layer in an oiled, ovenproof dish, spoon over the tomato mixture and bake until just cooked through – about 15 minutes. Serve with a good green salad and tiny new potatoes.

Master Recipe
Fish Cakes with Olive and Anchovy Butter

Makes 8

Originally an economical way of using up leftover scraps of boiled fish, fish cakes of all kinds are now a 'must have' on trendy menus. They are absolutely scrummy served hot with a small dollop of flavoured butter melting on top.

25g (1oz) butter
110g (4oz) onion, finely chopped
110g (4oz) mashed potato
225g (8oz) cold leftover fish e.g. salmon, cod, haddock, hake (a proportion of smoked fish such as haddock or mackerel is good), flaked
2 tablespoons fish sauce (nam pla), optional
1 organic egg yolk
1 tablespoon parsley, chopped
salt and freshly ground pepper
seasoned flour
1 organic egg, beaten
fresh white breadcrumbs
Clarified Butter (see page 105) or a mixture of butter and oil for frying

Olive and Anchovy Butter (see page 588)

First make the Olive and Anchovy Butter and refrigerate.

Next make the fish cakes: melt the butter in a saucepan, toss in the onion, cover and sweat over a gentle heat for 4–5 minutes, until soft but not coloured. Scrape the contents of the pan into a bowl, add the mashed potato and the flaked, cooked fish, fish sauce (if using), egg yolk and parsley. Season well with salt and pepper and taste.

Form the mixture into fish cakes about 50g (2oz) each. Coat them first in flour, then in beaten egg and finally in crumbs. Chill until needed, then cook on a medium heat in clarified butter until golden on both sides. Serve piping hot with Olive and Anchovy Butter. Accompany with Tomato Fondue (see page 200) and a good green salad.

Variations
Spicy Fish Cakes

Follow the Master Recipe adding 1–2 de-seeded and chopped chillies to the onion, and substituting freshly chopped coriander for parsley. Serve with Tomato and Chilli Sauce (see page 591) and garnish with sprigs of fresh coriander.

Tiny Fish Cakes

Follow the Master Recipe and form into tiny fish cakes. Serve as canapés.

Master Recipe
Haddock with Buttered Crumbs

Serves 6–8

Hake, pollock, ling, grey sea mullet or, in fact, any of the round fish may be used for this delicious recipe; it's a simple formula but so good, with lots of variations. Cod is also delicious, but we use less these days to allow the depleted stocks to recover. This dish can be served in individual dishes; scallop shells are a great idea – attractive, completely ovenproof and can be used over and over again.

900g (2lb) fillets of haddock, hake, ling,
*   haddock, grey sea mullet or pollock*
salt and freshly ground pepper

Mornay Sauce (see page 580)
110g (4oz) grated cheese

Buttered Crumbs
25g (1oz) butter
50g (2oz) soft, white breadcrumbs

900g (2lb) Fluffy Mashed Potato (see page 182)

Preheat the oven to 180°C/350°F/gas 4.

Make the Mornay Sauce, and mix in two-thirds of the grated cheese. Next make the Buttered Crumbs: melt the butter in a pan and stir in the breadcrumbs. Remove from the heat immediately and allow to cool.

Skin the fish and cut into portions: 175g (6oz) for a main course, 75g (3oz) for a starter. Season with salt and pepper. Coat the base of an ovenproof dish or individual dishes with the Mornay Sauce. Lay the pieces of fish on top. Top with another layer of sauce. Mix the remaining grated cheese with the buttered crumbs and sprinkle over the top. Pipe a ruff of fluffy Mashed Potato around the edge if you want to have a whole meal in one dish.

The dish can be prepared ahead to this point and cooked later, but because the fish is raw, it should be cooked on the same day.

Cook for 25–30 minutes or until the fish is cooked through and the top is golden brown and crispy. If necessary, flash under the grill for a minute or two before you serve to brown the edges of the potato.

Note: Buttered Crumbs are worth knowing about: keep a batch of them in your fridge (they keep for a week or more in a covered box). The crumbs crisp up in the oven and make a yummy crust. Use to scatter over gratins or creamy dishes or mix with grated cheese or fresh herbs as a coating for fish or meat.

> TIP: When assembling this dish, particularly in individual portions, be generous with the sauce and more sparing with the fish, the result will be juicy and delicious. If the cheese is sprinkled on top of the buttered crumbs it makes a tough crust, so mix together before sprinkling on top.

Variations

For pubs, cafés, restaurants, delicatessens or anyone who would like to prepare this fish dish and refrigerate or freeze it, follow this alternative method, using milk and roux instead of Mornay Sauce.

Skin the fish and cut into portions: 175g (6oz) for a main course, 75g (3oz) for a starter. Season with salt and pepper. Lay the pieces of fish in a lightly buttered sauté pan, and cover with 600ml (1 pint) cold milk. Bring to the boil and simmer for 4–5 minutes, or until the fish has changed colour. Remove the fish to a serving dish or dishes with a perforated spoon.

Bring the milk back to the boil and thicken with roux (see page 580) to a light coating consistency. Add 3 teaspoons of mustard (preferably Dijon) and two-thirds of the grated cheese; keep the remainder of the cheese for sprinkling over the top. Season with salt and pepper and taste. Add 1 tablespoon parsley (optional).

Next make the Buttered Crumbs. Coat the fish with the sauce. Mix the remaining grated cheese with the buttered crumbs and sprinkle over the top. Pipe a ruff of Fluffy Mashed Potato or Champ around the edge for a more substantial dish.

Cool and freeze or refrigerate and reheat later in a moderate oven for 15–20 minutes as above.

Haddock with Buttered Leeks
Sweat 450g (1lb) finely sliced leeks in 25g (1oz) butter in a covered casserole over a gentle heat until tender, and add in layers to the fish dish following the Master Recipe.

Haddock with Cucumber and Dill or Fennel
Peel 1 small cucumber and cut into 1cm (½in) dice. Sweat in a little butter. Add 1–2 teaspoons of dill or fennel. Layer with the fish in the Master Recipe.

Haddock with Tomato Fondue
Put a layer of Tomato Fondue (see page 200) under or over the fish and proceed as in the Master Recipe.

Haddock with Piperonata
Put a layer of Piperonata (see page 191) under or over the fish and proceed as in the Master Recipe.

Haddock with Mussels or Shrimps and Buttered Crumbs
Add 16–24 cooked mussels or shrimps to the dish before saucing and proceed as in the Master Recipe.

Haddock with Mushrooms
225g (8oz) mushrooms, sliced
10g (½oz) butter
salt and freshly ground pepper
1 tablespoon freshly chopped parsley (optional)

Sauté the mushrooms in foaming butter, season with salt and pepper, and add the parsley. Put a layer under the fish and proceed as in the Master Recipe.

Master Recipe
Fish and Chips

Serves 8

Fish and chips became famous because it can be utterly delicious. The fish needs to be spanking fresh, the batter crisp, the potatoes a good variety and most importantly the oil needs to be good quality. In Spain and Greece olive oil is frequently used, but sunflower or groundnut are excellent also.

8 very fresh fillets of cod, haddock, hake, plaice, lemon sole or monkfish

Beer Batter
250g (9oz) self-raising flour
good pinch salt
225ml (8fl oz) beer
225ml (8fl oz) cold water

Chips
8–16 potatoes, well scrubbed and unpeeled
oil for deep-frying

Garnish
1 lemon
vinegar

First make the batter: sieve the flour and salt into a bowl, make a well in the centre and gradually whisk in the beer and water. Allow to stand while you make the chips.

Cut the potatoes into chips, buffaloes if you like but basically any size you fancy (see page 184). Remember that the bigger they are, the longer they take to cook.

Heat the oil in a deep fryer with a basket to 180°C/350°F. Add the chips, making sure they are absolutely dry and don't cook too many together. Cook for a few minutes until they are just soft and drain.

Just before serving, dip the fish fillets in batter, allow excess to drip off and lower gently into the oil – 1 piece at a time. Cook until crisp and golden, drain on kitchen paper and keep warm. Increase the heat to 190°C/375°F. Put the chips back in and cook for a minute or two until really crisp. Drain on kitchen paper and sprinkle with salt. Serve the fish and chips immediately, either on a plate or in a cornet of newspaper. Serve vinegar as an accompaniment if you want to have really traditional fish and chips, or offer segments of lemon.

> TIP: Dip a tiny morsel of fish in batter, deep-fry and taste to check the seasoning; if necessary, add more salt to the batter. Shake the basket as the fish is lowered into the oil to prevent it sticking to the base of the pan.

Cheat's Beer Batter
I sometimes make an even faster batter by just whisking beer into flour to achieve a coating consistency. Add a pinch of salt to taste – works brilliantly.

Variations
Teeny Weeny Fish and Chips
It's fun to serve scaled-down fish and chips as canapés with drinks. Put freshly cooked goujons of plaice, sole or monkfish and freshly cooked fine chips in tiny cornets of plain paper and serve hot. Allow 175g (6oz) fish per person.

Monkfish with Tartare or Orly Sauce
Cut the monkfish tail into roughly 4cm (1½in) strips. Dip in batter or in flour, egg and breadcrumbs and deep-fry until crisp and golden. Serve with Tartare Sauce (see page 585) or Orly Sauce (see page 585). Allow 175g (6oz) fish per person. Exquisite!

Fish and Chips with Tartare Sauce and Ulster Champ
Serve freshly fried fish and chips with a bowl of Tartare Sauce (see page 585) and some Ulster Champ (see page 183).

How to Deep-fry

As ever, the quality of the oil is crucially important to the flavour of the food. At Ballymaloe House, we use beef fat and occasionally pure olive, groundnut or sunflower oil, depending on the food. Beef fat is high in vitamin D and gives a particularly delicious flavour to fish and chips. Lard from organically reared pigs also produces delicious results. It is important to realise that different oils and animal fats have a different 'smoking point'.
Animal fats: around 190°C/375°F.
Vegetable fats: 200°C/400°F, or even higher.

The 'smoking point' of 'all-purpose' oils will differ according to the blend and method of processing. Many have a low smoking point because they contain preservatives or emulsifiers. In general these oils are poor quality and in some cases the quality is downright disgraceful.

If possible, use a thermostatically controlled deep fryer. The temperature should not drop below 170°C/325°F or the food will be soggy and greasy. Raw fish, poultry, meat, croquettes, fritters and beignets are best fried at 180–190°C/350–375°F, while vegetables are best at the higher temperature. At smoking point, the structure of the fat changes, giving it an unpleasant taste and smell. It should not be used again, even at a lower temperature.

To deep-fry fish, heat the oil or fat to the correct temperature, dip the fish in the coating and drop individually into the hot oil, shaking the basket slightly so it doesn't stick to the bottom; this is particularly important with batter. Continue to cook until crisp on the outside and cooked through to the centre. For this reason, smaller pieces of fish are more suitable than large.

Deep-fried Whitebait with Chilli Mayonnaise

whitebait (defrosted)
seasoned flour
Red Chilli Mayonnaise (see page 585)

Toss the whitebait in seasoned flour and deep-fry for a few minutes until crisp. Serve with Red Chilli Mayonnaise.

Fritto Misto di Mare

Fritto Misto literally means 'mixed fry' and certainly sounds much better in Italian than in English. Fritto Misto di Mare is a mixture of fish which is either pan-fried or deep-fried and served with an appropriate sauce or sauces.

It is delicious only if you use a variety of very fresh fish and good olive oil to fry in. Don't use the atrociously poor-quality oil on general sale for deep-frying. It will ruin the flavour of even superb fish and the smell will permeate your hair and clothes and, if you don't shut the doors, your whole house as well! Invite your friends to eat in the kitchen for a fritto misto party. Serve straight from the fryer – it will be memorable.

A typical Fritto Misto might include the following deep-fried fish:
prawns, dipped in batter
mussels, dipped in batter or flour, egg and crumbs
monkfish strips dipped in batter or flour, egg and crumbs
fillets of plaice or sole dipped in batter or flour, egg and crumbs
squid rings dipped in batter, egg and crumbs, or in seasoned flour
panfried crab cakes
a slice of salmon pan-fried and served with Maître d'Hôtel Butter (see page 588)

Sauces
Tartare Sauce (see page 585)
Orly Sauce (see page 585)
Garlic Mayonnaise (see page 584)

Garnish
sprigs of parsley or watercress
segments of lemon

Put a selection of freshly fried fish on hot plates, garnish with parsley and lemon and serve with the selection of sauces. Some deep-fried vegetables, such as slices of courgette or courgette blossoms, are also delicious with the fritto and help to spin out the fish.

Spicy Goujons of Plaice or Lemon Sole with Coriander and Red Pepper Mayonnaise
Serves 4–6

Goujon is a French term to describe small fried strips of sole or plaice, possibly derived from gudgeon, a small tasty freshwater fish.

4–6 fillets plaice or lemon sole about 700g (1½lb), skinned

Spicy Seasoned Flour
175g (6oz) flour
1 teaspoon salt
3 tablespoons sesame seeds
2 teaspoons chilli powder
1 teaspoon freshly ground pepper
2 teaspoons curry powder

Roasted Red Pepper Mayonnaise (see page 585)
Tomato and Coriander Salsa (see page 592)

oil for frying
a little milk
sprigs of coriander

Skin the fillets of fish if the fishmonger won't do it for you. Cut them into 5mm (¼in) thick strips lengthwise or on the diagonal if the fillet is very long. They look great if they are 10–12.5cm (4–5in) long.

Mix together the ingredients for the seasoned flour in a wide pie dish. Make the Aïoli and the Salsa. Just before serving, heat the oil to 200°C (400°F), toss a few pieces of fish in milk, and then in the spicy flour. Deep-fry a few pieces at a time and serve immediately.

Pile up on warm plates with the Coriander and Roasted Red Pepper Mayonnaise (see page 585), and Tomato and Chilli Salsa (see page 592). Garnish with sprigs of fresh coriander.

Spicy Haddock and Squid Cakes with Thai Dipping Sauce
Makes 14–16 (serves 4 as a starter)

2cm (¾in) cube fresh ginger, peeled and grated
2 garlic cloves, roughly crushed
1 large bunch of fresh coriander, roots attached, roughly chopped
1½ tablespoons Thai green curry paste
250g (9oz) fresh haddock fillet, skin- and bone-free, cut into cubes
250g (9oz) squid, cleaned and roughly chopped
freshly squeezed juice of a lime
2 tablespoons fish sauce
sunflower oil, for frying
sea salt and freshly ground black pepper

Thai Dipping Sauce (see page 88)
lime wedges, to serve

Put the ginger, garlic, coriander and curry paste into a food-processor. Whizz until the mixture is very well processed. Stir and blend more if necessary. Next add the fresh haddock, squid, lime and fish sauce. Pulse in the processor – the mixture should not be completely smooth. Season with salt and pepper.

Heat the oil in a deep fryer or about 5cm (2in) in a deep frying pan. Cook a little piece of the mixture to check the seasoning. Divide the mixture into patties roughly 4cm (1½in) in diameter. Fry the fish cakes in batches of about six for 3–4 minutes until golden. Drain well on kitchen paper and keep warm while you cook the rest.

Serve with Thai dipping sauce, a wedge of lime and maybe a few fresh coriander leaves.

How to Prepare Squid

1. Cut off the tentacles just in front of the eyes.

2. Pull the entrails out of the sac and discard.

3. Remove the beak.

4. Catch the tip of the quill and pull it out of the sac.

5. Pull off the wings and scrape the purplish membrane off them and the sac. Wash the sac, wings and tentacles well.

6. Cut into 2cm (³/₄in) rounds or slices.

Thai Squid Salad

Serves 4–6 as a starter

Young squid are best for this salad. One must be careful not to cook for more than a few minutes or they become rubbery (unless you continue to cook for about 40 minutes).

700g (1¹/₂lb) small squid, cleaned
850 ml (1¹/₂ pints) water
¹/₂ teaspoon salt

Dressing
juice of 1 lime
1 tablespoon fish sauce (nam pla)
1 tablespoon light soy sauce
2 teaspoons rice vinegar
1–2 small red bird chillies, finely chopped
2 shallots, very finely sliced
2 teaspoons caster sugar
4 tablespoons warm water

1 cucumber
1 tablespoon freshly chopped coriander leaves
1 tablespoon chopped basil leaves

Slice the body of the squid into 5mm (¹/₄in) circles, divide the tentacles and slice the wings into thin strips at an angle. Bring the water to the boil and add the salt. Put the squid pieces into the boiling water and cook, with the water just bubbling a little, for 3–4 minutes. Drain immediately.

Mix all the ingredients for the dressing in a glass or pottery bowl. While the squid pieces are still warm, put them into the bowl with the dressing and mix well.

Cut the cucumber in half lengthwise, scoop out the seeds using a melon baller or teaspoon, then cut the flesh into thin half moon shapes. When the squid is cool, mix the coriander, basil leaves and cucumber slices into the salad. Taste and add more salt if necessary. Serve at room temperature.

Master Recipe
Salt and Pepper Squid with Sweet Chilli Sauce

Serves 6

Squid is immensely nibbleable – pile a plate high for a main course.

600g (1¹/₄lb) whole squid
110g (4oz) plain white flour
1 tablespoon salt, preferably sea salt
1 tablespoon freshly ground pepper
1–2 tablespoons chilli powder (depending on whether it is mild or hot)
peanut or sunflower oil, for deep-frying
8 sprigs of coriander

Garnish
lemon segments
sweet chilli sauce

Prepare the squid in the usual way (see left). Mix the flour, salt, pepper and chilli powder in a bowl. Heat the oil to 180°C/350°F in a deep-fryer. Toss the squid in the seasoned flour. Shake off any excess and drop one at a time into the hot oil (don't overcrowd the basket). Fry for 2 minutes then remove and drain on kitchen paper.

Put the coriander into the oil and cook for 1 minute. This has a tendency to spit so be careful. Drain on kitchen paper. Divide the squid between 4 plates. Top with the fried coriander. Garnish with a lemon wedge and serve with sweet chilli sauce.

Variations
Spicy Squid

Follow the Master Recipe but substitute freshly roasted cumin seed or five-spice powder for chilli powder. Panko crumbs, the crispy Japanese bread crumbs, make a delicious coating for squid. Serve with Tartare Sauce (see page 585) and Hot Chilli Sauce (see page 592).

Squid with Tomato and Herbs

Serves 6

A Julia Wight recipe.

4 medium-sized squid
5 tablespoons extra-virgin olive oil
2 large onions, sliced
2 garlic cloves, sliced
glass red, white or rosé wine
salt and freshly ground pepper
bouquet of herbs, including some fresh
  fennel
5 tomatoes, peeled, seeded and diced
a little paprika
Tomato Purée (see page 50)
2 teaspoons sugar
parsley, chopped

First prepare the squid (see left) and cut into 5mm (¼in) rounds.

Heat 4 tablespoons olive oil in a stew-pan, and in this melt the onion and garlic. Add in the squid, stir well and then pour in the wine. Let it bubble a minute, then season, turn down the heat and add the bouquet of herbs. Leave to simmer, covered, for 1–1½ hours until tender. This can be done on the hob or in the oven, very slowly.

Lift out the squid and keep warm. Reduce the sauce until fairly thick.

Meanwhile melt the tomatoes in 1 tablespoon of olive oil, uncovered. Season well and add about 2 teaspoons Tomato Purée, the same of sugar, and some paprika. Add the tomatoes to the wine sauce, pour over the squid, sprinkle with parsley, and serve very hot with plain, boiled rice.

Spaghetti with Squid
See page 151

Squid with Garlic Butter

Serves 4 as a starter, 2 as a main course

2 medium-sized squid
2 tablespoons Garlic Butter (see page 588)

Garnish
segments of lemon

First prepare the squid (see left). Just before serving, heat 4 plates. Melt the garlic butter in a frying pan, allow to foam, and toss in the squid (do it in two batches if necessary). Toss around for 30–60 seconds or until the pieces turn from opaque to white. Serve instantly on hot plates with a segment of lemon on each.

Octopus a la Galicia

Serves 8 people

Ismael Mesa, a student on our 12-week certificate course from Gran Canaria, made friends with the local fishermen in Ballycotton and managed to persuade them to land us some octopus. We then all had a wonderful lesson on how to cook 'pulpo', for which I am deeply grateful.

You can use frozen or fresh octopus (frozen is best). If you are using fresh, make sure you wash it very well. You will also need to use a mallet or rolling pin to tenderise the flesh.

1.3kg (3lb) octopus (don't use the head)
1 bay leaf
1 onion, peeled and whole
2 tablespoons paprika (sweet or spicy)
4 tablespoons good extra-virgin olive oil
coarse sea salt
crusty white bread

Fill a large saucepan with water and add the onion and bay leaf. As soon as the water has come to the boil, use tongs to dip the octopus in and out of the water rapidly 3 or 4 times so that the tentacles curl up. Then leave the octopus in the saucepan and continue to cook for about 40 minutes on a medium heat until it is tender (you can stick a fork into the flesh to check). Turn off the heat and allow the octopus to sit in the water for 5 minutes.

Remove the octopus from the water and shake off the excess water. Cut into 2.5cm (1in) pieces and place on a big serving dish. Drizzle with olive oil, and sprinkle with paprika and coarse sea salt and mix well. Serve warm with crusty white bread.

Octopus Salad in Vinaigrette (Pulpo en Vinagreta)
Serves 4 as a starter, 10 as tapas

450g (1lb) octopus

Dressing
½ green pepper, finely diced
½ red pepper, finely diced
1 spring onion, finely chopped
4–5 cherry tomatoes, quartered
2 tablespoons white wine vinegar
6 tablespoons extra-virgin olive oil

Cook the octopus as above and allow to cool completely. Cut into 2.5cm (1in) pieces. Meanwhile mix all the ingredients for the dressing in a jam jar. Serve on small plates and drizzle the dressing on top. Serve with crusty white bread.

Smoked Eel with Brown Bread and Lemon

Good smoked eel needs no embellishment.

freshly smoked eel
segments of lemon
green salad
brown bread

Skin the eel and cut into paper-thin 8–10cm (3–4in) lengths. Serve 2 or 3 pieces per person either on or off the bone. Garnish with a lemon wedge and a little green salad. Serve with fresh brown bread.

Ceviche

In Latin America, raw fish is marinated in lime or lemon juice, often with some sliced vegetables, peppers, chilli or sliced onion. The fish may be sliced in thin strips or cut into dice and then left in the marinade for anything from 4 to 24 hours. The acid in the lime or lemon juice 'cooks' the fish by acting on the albumen so the flesh turns whiter and firmer in texture – it has a clean fresh taste. The fish should always be very fresh and from unpolluted water. Extra freshly sliced vegetables are often added before serving for their texture and colour. Keep refrigerated until served.

Susie Noriega's Peruvian Ceviche

Serves 10–12 as a starter

900g (2lb) fillets of monkfish, cod, plaice, lemon
 sole or scallops
4 limes
2 lemons
2 garlic cloves, finely chopped
salt and freshly ground pepper
fresh coriander, chopped
1–2 fresh chillies
75g (3oz) onions, finely sliced
1 green pepper, finely diced
1 red pepper, finely diced

Garnish
crisp lettuce leaves
5–6 spring onions
sweetcorn (optional)
2 avocados
diced peppers

Skin the fish, slice or cube it into 1cm (½in) pieces, and put it into a deep, stainless steel or china bowl. Squeeze the juice from the limes and lemons and pour over the fish. Sprinkle with salt, pepper and garlic. Cover and leave to marinate for 2–3 hours in a fridge.

LEFT: Susie Noriega's Peruvian Ceviche

Next add the fresh coriander, onions, chillies and the red and green peppers. Cover and leave for 2½ hours in the fridge. Serve or keep covered until later.

To serve: arrange a few crisp lettuce leaves on a plate and place a tablespoon of ceviche in the centre. Decorate with slices of avocado, diced peppers, sweetcorn and spring onions. Serve it with crusty white bread or tortillas.

Finnish Beetroot-marinated Salmon

Serves 15–20

In Scandinavian countries, they do many variations on the basic Gravlax. I came across this version in Finland.

2 sides of salmon
3 tablespoons sea salt
3 tablespoons sugar
freshly ground pepper
400g (14oz) raw beetroot, grated
2 tablespoons grated horseradish (optional)
125ml (4fl oz) sunflower oil
50ml (2fl oz) vodka

Beetroot Sauce
400g (14oz) cooked beetroot, chopped
2 teaspoons Dijon mustard
2 tablespoons sugar
8 tablespoons red wine vinegar
225ml (8fl oz) vegetable oil
pinch of salt
freshly ground pepper

Garnish
sprigs of dill

Place one fillet of fish skin-side down in a dish, and sprinkle with salt, sugar and freshly ground pepper. Place the other fillet on top. Wrap tightly in clingfilm and marinate the salmon for 24 hours.

Mix the grated beetroot and horseradish together and add the oil and vodka. Spread the mixture evenly over the fish, sandwich together again and marinate in the fridge for one more day.

Next make the Beetroot Sauce: whizz the chopped beetroot, mustard and sugar in a blender. Add the vinegar and oil gradually and alternately. Season with salt and pepper. Wipe the vegetable mixture off the salmon and slice thinly. Arrange on a plate and drizzle sauce around them. Garnish with sprigs of dill.

Gravlax with Mustard and Dill Mayonnaise

See page 86

Soused Mackerel with Mustard and Dill Mayonaise

Serves 8 as a main course, 16 as a starter

Sousing is a form of pickling – steeping or cooking in vinegar or white wine. It is particularly suited to oily fish. Treat herrings this way too.

8 mackerel, about 175g (6oz) each, cleaned
1 onion, thinly sliced
1 teaspoon whole black peppercorns
6 whole cloves
1 teaspoon salt
1 teaspoon sugar
300ml (½ pint) white wine vinegar
1 bay leaf
Mustard and Dill Mayonnaise (see page 585)

Preheat the oven to 130°C/250°F/gas ½.

Fillet the mackerel, ensuring there are no bones (a tall order but do your best). Roll up the fillets skin-side out and pack tightly into a cast-iron casserole. Sprinkle with onion, peppercorns, cloves, salt, sugar, vinegar and the bay leaf. Bring to the boil on top of the stove and then put into the oven for 30–45 minutes. Leave the mackerel to get quite cold. It keeps for 7–10 days in the fridge.

To serve: put 1–2 fillets of soused mackerel on a plate and zig-zag Sweet Mustard and Dill Mayonnaise over the fish. Serve with fresh crusty bread.

Scallops in Mornay Sauce

Serves 12–14 as starter, 6–7 as main course

12 scallops
dry white wine and water to cover
75g (3oz) chopped shallots or onion
25g (1oz) butter
150–175g (5–6oz) chopped mushrooms
2 heaped tablespoons flour
creamy milk
salt and freshly ground pepper
50–75g (2–3oz) Cheddar, grated
1 heaped tablespoon chopped parsley
Fluffy Mashed Potato (see page 182) for piping
   around the shells (optional)

Put the scallops in a medium-sized stainless steel pan and cover in half white wine and half water. Poach for 3–5 minutes (be careful to simmer and not overcook). Remove the scallops and reduce the cooking liquid to about 300–350ml (10–12fl oz).

Sweat the shallots gently in butter until soft (about 5–6 minutes). Add the mushrooms and cook for a further 3–4 minutes. Stir in the flour and cook for a minute more. Add creamy milk to the scallop cooking liquid to make up to 600ml (1 pint) and add to the pan. Taste the sauce, reduce until the flavour is really good and season.

Cut the scallops into four and add to the sauce along with some of the cheese and parsley. Decorate individual scallop shells or a serving dish with Fluffy Mashed Potato, fill the centre with the scallop mixture and sprinkle the top with the remaining cheese.

Just before serving, reheat in a medium-hot oven (350°F/180°C) until just bubbling (about 20 minutes).

Variation
Monkfish Mornay
Substitute collops of monkfish for scallops in the above recipe.

Scallops with Jerusalem Artichokes and Beurre Blanc Sauce

Serves 2 as a main course

Jerusalem artichokes have a wonderful affinity with shellfish, particularly scallops and mussels. This is an exquisite dish and worth the little extra effort.

8 scallops
Beurre Blanc Sauce (see page 583)
2–4 Jerusalem artichokes, depending on size
25g (1oz) butter
lemon juice
salt and freshly ground pepper

Garnish
chervil or fennel sprigs

First prepare the scallops: wash and slice the nuggets in half horizontally, and keep the corals whole. Keep chilled.

Next make the Beurre Blanc Sauce and keep warm.

Wash and peel the artichokes and cut into 1cm (½in) rounds. Put them into a casserole with the butter and a squeeze of lemon juice (to prevent discolouration). Season with salt and freshly ground pepper, cover and cook gently until almost tender. Turn off the heat and allow to continue cooking in the casserole.

To assemble: season the scallops and cook in a non-stick pan until golden on each side. Put 2–3 tablespoons of Beurre Blanc Sauce onto each plate. Put 4 artichoke rounds on top of the sauce on each plate. Divide the cooked scallops between the 2 plates, placing them on top of the artichoke rounds. Put the coral in the centre and garnish with chervil or fennel and serve immediately.

Chargrilled Scallops with Aubergine and Pesto

Serves 4 or more as a starter

12 scallops
1–2 aubergines
Classic Pesto (see page 589) or a jar of
   good-quality bought pesto
salt and freshly ground pepper
extra-virgin olive oil

Garnish
sprigs of basil

Slice the aubergine lengthways into thin slices, sprinkle with salt and leave to degorge for 15–20 minutes. Meanwhile, make the pesto.

Wash the aubergine slices and pat dry with kitchen paper. Brush with a little olive oil and chargrill quickly on both sides either on a chargrill or on a very hot pan-grill.

Just before serving, season the scallops with salt and freshly ground pepper. Cook on the chargrill or pan-grill. Allow them to brown well on one side before turning over onto the other.

To serve, cover the base of the plate with aubergine slices, arrange 3 or 4 scallops and their coral on top, and put a blob of soft pesto between the scallops. Garnish with a sprig of fresh basil and serve.

Pan-grilled Scallops with Sweet Chilli Sauce and Crème Fraîche

Serves 4 as a starter

20 fresh scallops, dried on kitchen paper.
sea salt and freshly ground pepper
sweet chilli sauce
crème fraîche

Garnish
coriander leaves

Preheat a heavy (preferably cast iron) frying pan. Sear the scallops well on both sides. Season with sea salt and freshly cracked pepper. Toss quickly in sweet chilli sauce.

Arrange 5 scallops on each plate, and top each scallop with a little blob of crème fraiche and a sprig of fresh coriander. Serve as soon as possible. A little herb salad would be delish in the centre of each plate – perhaps chervil, flat-leaf parsley, tarragon and coriander.

Crispy Deep-fried Oysters with Wasabi Mayonnaise
Serves 4

12 Pacific oysters
Beer Batter (see page 246)
Wasabi Mayonnaise (see page 585)
oil for deep-frying

Garnish
4 segments of lime or lemon

First make the Wasabi Mayonnaise. Next make the Beer Batter.

Heat good-quality oil in a deep fryer.

Dip the oysters individually in batter and deep-fry until crisp and golden. Drain on absorbent paper. Serve immediately – 3 per person with a blob of Wasabi Mayonnaise and a segment of lime or lemon.

Hot Buttered Oysters

These wonderfully curvaceous oyster shells tend to topple over maddeningly on the plate so that the delicious juices escape. In the restaurant, we solve this problem by piping a little blob of Fluffy Mashed Potato (see page 182) on the plate to anchor each shell.

12 Pacific (gigas) oysters
25g (1oz) butter
1/2 teaspoon finely chopped parsley

To Serve
4 segments of lemon
4 ovals of hot buttered toast (optional)

Open the oysters and detach completely from their shells. Discard the top shell but keep the deep shell and reserve the liquid. Put the deep shells into a low oven to heat through.

Melt half the butter in a pan until it foams. Toss the oysters in the butter until hot through (about 1 minute). Put a hot oyster into each of the warm shells. Pour the reserved oyster liquid into the pan and boil up, whisking in the remaining butter and the parsley. Spoon the hot juices over the oysters and serve immediately on hot plates with a wedge of lemon.

Alternatively, discard the shells and just serve the oysters on the hot buttered toast. The toast will soak up the juice – simply delicious!

LEFT: Crispy Deep-fried Oysters with Wasabi Mayonnaise

Prawns Bretonne

Serves 8–10

Divine!

Bretonne Sauce (see page 582)
450g (1lb) fresh Dublin Bay prawns, shelled
110g (4oz) butter

First make the Bretonne Sauce.

Cook and shell the prawns (see right).

Heat the butter in a pan and, when it is sizzling, add the prawns. Toss them in the butter until heated through. Serve with Bretonne Sauce.

How to Cook Prawns

The secret of ensuring flavour in prawns and shrimps is to cook them in well-salted water so carefully calculate the salt to water ratio: use 1 tablespoon salt to every 1.2 litres (2 pints) of water. Bring a large pot of water to the boil and add the correct amount of salt. Put the prawns into the fast-boiling, salted water. As soon as the water returns to the boil, test a prawn to see if it is cooked. A cooked prawn should be firm and white, not opaque or mushy. Cooked prawns should rise to the top. When cooked, remove prawns immediately. Very large ones may take a little longer.

Do not cook too many prawns together, otherwise they may overcook before the water even comes back to the boil – better to cook them in batches.

Allow to cool on a tray in a single layer and then remove the shells. (Prawns yield about one-sixth of their original volume.)

> TIP: For sushi, thread the cooked prawns onto satay sticks lengthways to keep them straight.

How to Cook Shrimps

We get delicious briny shrimps from the fishermen in Ballycotton. Follow the method above and add the live shrimps. Cook until they have changed colour from grey to orangey pink and have no trace of black on the top of the head – this takes 2–4 minutes, depending on size.

How to Remove the Intestine from Dublin Bay Prawns

Remove the head of the raw prawns and discard or use for making fish stock. With the underside of the prawns uppermost, tug the little fan-shaped tail at either side and carefully draw out the trail (the trail is the intestine, so it is very important to remove it before cooking, regardless of whether the prawns are to be shelled or not).

Ballycotton Prawns or Shrimps with Homemade Mayonnaise

Serves 4

We eat Dublin Bay prawns in several ways but they are almost best just freshly cooked and served with Homemade Mayonnaise.

32 large very fresh prawns or 64 shrimps
4–8 tablespoons homemade Mayonnaise
  (see page 584)

Garnish
fresh watercress sprigs
4 segments of lemon

First cook the prawns or shrimps (see left). Put 8 cooked whole prawns on each plate. Spoon a tablespoon or two of homemade Mayonnaise into a little bowl or oyster shell on the side of the plate. Pop a segment of lemon on the plate. Garnish with some fresh watercress. Serve with crusty brown soda bread.

Variation
Prawns or Shrimps with Brown Bread and Homemade Mayonnaise

Stamp out a large round of thinly sliced Ballymaloe Brown Yeast Bread (see page 478) per person, spread with a little butter and add a frill of lollo rosso lettuce.

Peel the prawns or shrimps and arrange 6–8 in a circle on each piece of bread. Pipe a rosette of Homemade Mayonnaise in the centre, garnish with sprigs of chervil and fennel and perhaps a few fennel flowers.

They are also delicious with a little Sweet Cucumber Pickle or Dill Mayonnaise. Do individual ones for finger food.

Deh-ta Hsiung's Prawn Satay

Serves 4–6

Shrimps, prawns, or cubes of monkfish can be marinated in spices, then threaded onto bamboo satay sticks and cooked on the barbecue or under the grill. Satays are terrifically versatile. They may be served as a starter with drinks, or as a light meal when served with rice and salad. The marinade is also good for pork or chicken.

450g (1lb) raw shrimps or prawns
1 garlic clove, finely chopped
2 shallots, or 1 small onion, finely chopped
2 tablespoons light soy sauce
1 tablespoon sugar
1 tablespoon freshly ground coriander
1 tablespoon lemon juice or red wine vinegar

1–2 tablespoons vegetable oil, for brushing
225g (8oz) Pixie's Peanut Sauce (see page 591)

24–26 bamboo satay sticks (soak satay sticks in cold water for at least 30 minutes)

Peel and drain the shrimps or prawns, and marinate in the remaining ingredients for at least 1 hour. Thread the prawns onto bamboo satay sticks. Be careful to keep the prawns down to one end. Brush each satay with a little oil and chargrill until just cooked, turning frequently. Serve hot with Peanut Sauce.

Scampi with Tartare Sauce

Serves 8–10

Scampi (*Nephrops norvegicus*) is the Venetian name for what we commonly call Dublin Bay Prawns, although those fished from the Adriatic are twice the size. Scampi was the 'must have' starter of the 60s and 70s. It is utterly delicious when made with fresh prawns; sadly nowadays it is more often a travesty made with inferior, soggy, frozen ones. Pieces of fresh monkfish are also delectable.

450g (1lb) very fresh Dublin Bay prawns, peeled
Tartare Sauce (see page 585)

Batter
275g (10oz) plain white flour
3¼ tablespoons extra-virgin olive oil
2–3 organic egg whites
sea salt

Garnish
segments of lemon

Preheat oil to 180°C/350°F in a deep fryer. Then make the batter: sieve flour into a bowl, make a well in the centre, pour in the olive oil, stir, and add enough water to make a batter about the consistency of double cream. Allow to stand for at least 1 hour.

Just before serving, whisk the egg whites to a stiff peak and fold into the batter, adding a good pinch of salt.

Just before serving, dip the prawns individually in the batter and deep-fry until crisp and golden. Drain on kitchen paper. Serve immediately with a little bowl of Tartare Sauce and a segment of lemon.

How to Cook Mussels

Check that all the mussels are tightly shut. If open, tap the mussel on the work top; if it does not close within a few seconds, discard it. (The rule with shellfish is always, 'If in doubt, throw it out') Wild mussels occasionally have barnacles attached to the shells. Scrape them off the shells with the back of a knife. Wash the mussels well in several changes of cold water. Spread them in a single layer in a pan, covered with a folded tea towel or a lid and cook over a gentle heat. This usually takes 2–3 minutes, and the mussels are cooked just as soon as the shells open. Remove them from the pan immediately or they will shrink in size and become tough. Remove the beard (the little tuft of tough 'hair' which attached the mussel to the rock or rope it grew on). Discard one shell. Loosen the mussel from the other shell but leave it in the shell. Eat warm or cold.

Moules Provençales

Serves 6–8

Don't skimp on the garlic in the butter for this recipe or they will taste dull and 'bready'.

48 mussels, approx. 1.5–1.8kg (3¼–4lb)
Provençale Butter (see page 588)
50–75g (2–3oz) fresh, white breadcrumbs

Cook and cool the mussels (see left).

Meanwhile, make the Provençale Butter. If you have it made in advance, you will need it to be soft enough to spread evenly over the mussels in their shells. Dip each one into the breadcrumbs. They may be prepared ahead to this point and frozen in a covered box lined with clingfilm or tin foil.

Arrange in individual serving dishes. Brown under the grill and serve with crusty white bread to mop up the delicious juices.

Mussels with Thai Flavours

Serves 4

2kg (4½lb) mussels
2 tablespoons groundnut or sunflower oil
6 garlic cloves, crushed
1–2 red chillies, finely chopped
1 stalk lemongrass, finely chopped
1 tablespoons fish sauce (nam pla)
3–4 tablespoons chopped mint or coriander
3 kaffir lime leaves

Check the mussels carefully, discarding any broken or open shells. Wash well and drain. Heat the oil on a medium heat, add the garlic and chilli and fry for a minute or two. Add the lemongrass, fish sauce, kaffir lime leaves and then the mussels. Cover with a folded tea towel or saucepan lid . The mussels will open in a few minutes.

Discard one shell from each mussel, and remove the beards. Add the chopped mint or coriander to the mussel juices. Divide the mussels between four deep, wide bowls, pour the hot juices over and serve.

Cockles or Mussels in the Goan Style

Serves 6

36–48 mussels or cockles
4 tablespoons extra-virgin olive oil
225g (8oz) onion, finely chopped
2 teaspoons freshly grated ginger
6 garlic cloves, crushed or grated
1–2 fresh green chillies, thinly sliced
2 teaspoons freshly ground cumin
1/2 teaspoon ground turmeric
1/2 teaspoon salt
400ml (14fl oz) coconut milk
lots of fresh coriander

Check the mussels, discarding any open mussels that refuse to close when tapped on the worktop. Wash well.

Put the oil in a sauté pan and add the onion, garlic and ginger, and stir. Cover and cook on a gentle heat until soft but not coloured. Add the chilli, cumin, turmeric and salt and cook for 1–2 minutes. Add the coconut milk, stir and bring to the boil. Add the mussels and stir. Cover the sauté pan and increase the heat and cook for 4–5 minutes or until the shells have opened.

Serve in deep bowls with rice or crusty bread to soak up the delicious juices. Sprinkle lots of fresh coriander on top.

LEFT: Cockles or Mussels in the Goan Style

Lobster or Crayfish

Serves 2–4

The method described here is considered by the RSPCA to be the most humane way to cook lobster and certainly results in deliciously tender and juicy flesh. When we are cooking lobster, we judge by colour, or allow 15 minutes for the first 450g (1lb) and 10 minutes per 450g (1lb) after that.

2 x 900g (2lb) live lobsters

Court Bouillon
1 carrot
1 onion
600ml (1 pint) water
600ml (1 pint) dry white wine
bouquet garni: parsley stalks, sprig of thyme, celery stalks and a small bay leaf
6 peppercorns

Cover the lobsters with lukewarm salted water (4 tablespoons of salt to every 2.3 litres/4 pints of water). Put the saucepan over a low heat and bring slowly to simmering point: lobster and crab die at about 44°C (112°F) and by this stage the lobsters will be changing colour so remove them and discard all the cooking water.

Slice the carrot and onion and put with the water, wine, bouquet garni and peppercorns into a stainless steel saucepan and bring to the boil. Put in the lobsters and cover with a tight-fitting lid. Steam them until they change colour to bright red, or follow the time given for weight, and remove them from the pot. Strain the cooking liquid and reserve for a sauce.

Lobster:
A 1.1kg (2½lb) lobster will yield about 350g (12oz) meat, depending on the time of year.

Crayfish (Spiny Lobster):
A 2.2kg (5lb) crayfish will yield about 1.1kg (2½lb) meat. Crayfish is therefore less expensive in the long run.

Ballymaloe Hot Buttered Lobster

Serves 4 as a main course

Ballymaloe is famous for this dish. It is one of the most exquisite ways to eat fresh lobster but, for perfection, the lobster must come straight from the sea, not from a holding tank. Sadly, lobsters are becoming more scarce so enjoy them while you can. When buying lobster, do not buy undersized or female ones. Bord Iascaigh Mhara introduced a system whereby the fishermen cut a V-shaped notch in the tail of female lobster so they can be identified easily even when they do not have eggs. Do not accept female lobster in a restaurant; we all have a responsibility to conserve the stocks.

1.8 kg (4lb) live lobster
Court Bouillon (see recipe left)
110g (4oz) butter
lemon juice, freshly squeezed

Garnish
sprigs of watercress, flat-leaf parsley or fennel segments of lemon

Cook the lobsters in Court Bouillon (see recipe left).

As soon as they are cool enough to handle, split them in half and extract all the meat from the body, tail and large and small claws. Scrape out all the soft, greenish tomalley (liver) from the part of the shell nearest the head and put it with the rest of the meat into a warm bowl wrapped in a tea towel. Cut the meat into chunks.

Heat the lobster shells. Melt half the butter and, when it is foaming, toss the meat in it until it is cooked through and the juices turn pink. Spoon the meat into the hot shells. Put the remaining butter into the pan, heat and scrape up any bits. Add a squeeze of lemon juice. Pour the buttery juices into small, heated ramekins and serve beside the lobster on hot plates. Garnish with sprigs of watercress, flat-leaf parsley or fennel, and lemon segments. Eat immediately.

Ballymaloe Lobster with Cream and Fresh Herbs

Serves 4 as a main course, 8 as a starter

The filling may also be served in the lobster shells, or in a vol au vent case, or as a chunky lobster sauce for baked plaice, sole or turbot. Crawfish may be used in this recipe also.

50g (2oz) butter
225g (8oz) sliced button mushrooms
salt and freshly ground pepper
a little lemon juice
350g (12oz) cooked lobster meat
4 teaspoons shallot, finely chopped
50ml (2fl oz) dry white wine
225ml (8fl oz) Court Bouillon (see page 257)
225–350ml (8–12fl oz) cream
Roux (see page 580)
1 teaspoon thyme leaves
2 teaspoons freshly chopped parsley
1–2 tablespoons Hollandaise Sauce
  (see page 582)

Garnish
sprigs of watercress and fennel

Melt the butter in a wide sauté pan and toss the mushrooms on a high heat for a minute or two. Season and add a little lemon juice. Set aside.

Add a little more butter to the pan and toss the lobster meat and green juices in the foaming butter until the meat is cooked through and the juices turn pink. Remove the lobster meat and add to the mushrooms. Then cook the shallots gently in the sauté pan. After approx. 2 minutes, add the white wine and reduce by half. Now add the court bouillon and reduce again. Add the cream, whisk in some roux and add the mushrooms and lobster meat. Boil up the sauce for the last time and stir in the herbs and Hollandaise. Taste and correct the seasoning.

Reheat the lobster shells and fill with the lobster mixture. Garnish with the sprigs of watercress and fennel. Serve immediately.

Variation
Lobster Vol au Vents

Pile the creamy lobster mixture into buttery vol au vents – this is often served on the Sunday night buffet in Ballymaloe. Individual vol au vents made with puff pastry make a sensational starter.

Master Recipe
Lobster and Mango Salad

Serves 6

Choose a ripe, juicy perfumed mango to partner an exquisite lobster.

ABOVE: Lobster and Mango Salad

a selection of salad leaves e.g. lollo rosso,
  butterhead, iceberg, oakleaf, rocket,
  watercress
1 ripe mango
350g (12oz) lobster tail and claw meat –
  a 900g–1.1kg (2–2½lb) lobster should yield
  this quantity

Dressing
6 tablespoons extra-virgin olive oil
2 tablespoons lemon juice
salt and freshly ground pepper
pinch of sugar
2 teaspoons freshly chopped parsley

Garnish
sprigs of fennel, chervil and borage flowers

Wash and dry the salad leaves. Combine all the ingredients for the dressing. Peel the mango and cut into slices or dice depending on the desired presentation. Sprinkle with lemon juice.

To assemble: toss the salad leaves in just enough dressing to make the leaves glisten. Arrange a little mound on each plate, intersperse with slices or the dice of mango. Garnish with a few slices of lobster tail and perhaps a lobster claw. Brush a very little dressing over the lobster and garnish with sprigs of fennel, chervil and a few borage flowers, if available.

Variation

Lobster and Avocado Salad

Follow the Master Recipe and substitute avocado for the mango. Add some diced, unpeeled cucumber to the salad. Serve with homemade Mayonnaise (see page 584). The soft meat is delicious with homemade Mayonnaise served underneath the salad leaves.

Ballymaloe Crab Salad

Serves 4–6

We serve this as a starter or a main course.

white and brown meat of 2–3 medium crabs,
   freshly cooked
homemade Mayonnaise (see page 584)
Ballymaloe French Dressing (see page 226)
Soft Piped Potato Salad (see page 215)
Tomato Salad (see page 220)
Cucumber and Fennel Salad (see page 220) or
   Sweet Cucumber Pickle (see page 514)

First make all the accompaniments.

Mix the white meat with mayonnaise and the brown meat with French Dressing to taste. Serve with homemade Mayonnaise alongside the salads.

How to Cook Crab

Buying Crab

At Ballymaloe, we buy whole crabs rather than just claws, for fear of encouraging fishermen to pull off the claws and discard the bodies. If a crab loses 1 claw, it can feed itself and gradually grow another, but if both claws are removed, it will die slowly from hunger. The other consideration is that the crab meat in the body is really delicious!

Choose heavy, lively ones. Female crabs tend to yield more meat – they are easy to recognise because they have a broader flap of shell than the male. Meat yield varies, depending on the type and size of the crab and the time of year. Crabs should either be live or ready-cooked from your fishmonger. If a fresh crab shows no sign of life, do not risk using it.

Note: 450g (1lb) cooked crab in the shell yields about 175–225g (6–8oz) crab meat, depending on the time of the year.

Cooking Crab

Put the crab into a saucepan and cover with cold or barely lukewarm salted water: use 175g/6oz salt to every 2.4 litres (4 pints) water. This sounds like an incredible amount of salt but try it; the crab will taste deliciously sweet.

Cover, bring to the boil and then simmer, allowing 15 minutes for the first 450g (1lb) and 10 minutes for the second and third (I've never come across a crab bigger than that!). Pour off two-thirds of the water half-way through cooking, cover and steam the crab for the remainder of the time. As soon as it is cooked, remove it from the saucepan and allow to get cold.

To Extract the Crab Meat

First remove the large claws. Hold the crab with the underside upper-most and lever out the centre portion – I do this by catching the little lip of the projecting centre shell against the edge of the table and pressing down firmly. The Dead Man's Fingers (gills) usually stay attached and come out with this central piece, but check occasionally; if 1 or 2 remain in the body shell, remove and discard them.

Press your thumb down over the light shell just behind the eyes so that the shell cracks slightly, and then the sac which is underneath can be removed easily and discarded. Everything else inside the body of the crab is edible. The soft meat varies in colour from cream to coffee to dark tan, and towards the end of the season it can contain quite a bit of bright orange coral which is stronger in flavour than the rest. Scoop it all out and put it into a bowl. There will also be 1 or 2 teaspoonsful of soft meat in the centre portion attached to the small claws – add that to the bowl also.

Scrub the shell and keep it aside if you need it for dressed crab. Crack the large claws with a hammer and extract every bit of white meat from them. Poke out the meat from the small claws, using a lobster pick, skewer, or even the handle of a teaspoon. Mix the brown and white meat together or use separately, depending on the recipe.

Ivan Allen's Hot Dressed Crab

Serves 5–6 as a main course

When I first came to Shanagarry, crabs were considered a nuisance by most fishermen because they found their way into the lobster pots and were much less lucrative to sell. The legendary Tommy Sliney, who sold his fish from a donkey and cart on Ballycotton pier, occasionally brought us a few, and it was always a cause for celebration. We would prepare all the other ingredients and then my father-in-law, Ivan Allen, would mix and taste the Dressed Crab.

425g (15oz) crab meat, brown and white mixed
(2 or 3 crabs should yield this)
75–100g (3–3½oz) soft white breadcrumbs
2 teaspoons white wine vinegar
2 tablespoons tomato chutney or relish
25g (1oz) butter
generous pinch of dry mustard or 1 level
teaspoon French mustard
salt and freshly ground pepper
175ml (6fl oz) White Sauce (see page 580)

Topping
110g (4oz) Buttered Crumbs (see page 244)

Preheat the oven to 180°C/350°F/gas 4.

Thoroughly scrub the crab shells. Mix together all the ingredients except the buttered crumbs, taste carefully and correct the seasoning. Fill the shells and sprinkle the tops with the buttered crumbs.

Bake for about 15–20 minutes, or until heated through and brown on top. Flash under the grill if necessary to crisp the crumbs.

Crab Cakes

Crab cakes can be made with the same mixture. We add finely chopped chilli and lots of fresh coriander, then flour, egg, crumb and deep-fry. Serve with Tartare Sauce (see page 585) and Tomato and Coriander Salsa (see page 592).

Master Recipe
Tomatoes Stuffed with Crab Mayonnaise

Serves 6 as a starter

Crab Mayonnaise is versatile. It is delicious used as a filling for a cucumber or tomato ring as well as a stuffing for tomatoes. It also marries very well with a simple tomato salad or as a first course for a dinner party.

6 very ripe but firm tomatoes
150g (5oz) mixed white and brown freshly
cooked crab meat (1 medium-sized cooked
crab should yield enough)
salt and freshly ground pepper
175–225ml (6–8fl oz) homemade Mayonnaise
(see page 584) or a couple of tablespoons
French Dressing instead of some of the
mayonnaise
2 teaspoons finely grated onion

Garnish
small lettuce leaves
garden cress or watercress
edible flowers, such as chives

Cut the tops off the tomatoes, remove the seeds with a melon baller or a teaspoon, season inside with salt and turn upside down to drain while you prepare the filling.

Mix the crab meat with the homemade Mayonnaise, and add ½ teaspoon of the onion juice. Taste and season if necessary.

Fill the tomatoes with the crab mixture and replace the lids. Arrange a bed of lettuce and salad leaves on a white plate.

Serve 1 large or 2 small tomatoes per person, garnished with sprigs of fresh herbs and edible flowers.

Crab Pâté with Cucumber and Dill Salad

See page 78

Variation
Cherry Tomatoes Stuffed with Crab Mayonnaise

Follow the Master Recipe but use cherry tomatoes. Garnish with a sprig of fennel or chervil – a fiddle to do but delicious served as a canapé.

Ballymaloe Fish Terrine with Cherry Tomato Sauce

Serves 10–12 as a starter

A perfect starter for a summer lunch or wedding, it can be made several days ahead and freezes well. Most fish terrines are based on sole and, though they are delicious when served hot, they can be very dull and bland when cold. This layered fish pâté is a great favourite at Ballymaloe. Its content varies depending on the fish available to us.

Potted Shrimps or Prawns (see page 81)
Smoked Mackerel Pâté (see page 78)
Smoked Salmon Pâté (see page 78)
chopped parsley and chives

12.5 x 20cm (5 x 8in) bread tin or, better still, a
longer, thinner mould if available

Line the tin neatly with a double thickness of clingfilm.

Make the potted shrimps or prawns. Allow to cool, pour into the tin in an even layer, sprinkle with a little chopped parsley and chill while you prepare the next layer.

Make the smoked mackerel pâté. When the shrimps have set hard, spread an even layer of the mackerel on top. Sprinkle with a little more parsley or chopped chives and refrigerate.

Lastly, make the salmon pâté and spread this final layer onto the fish terrine. Cover with clingfilm to compact the layers and chill until needed.

Cherry Tomato Sauce

450g (1lb) very ripe cherry tomatoes
10g (½oz) onion, chopped
2 teaspoons balsamic vinegar
2 tablespoons extra-virgin olive oil
1 teaspoon salt
1 teaspoon sugar
freshly ground pepper
2 basil leaves or 4 fresh mint leaves

Chop the tomatoes and whizz briefly in a blender with the other ingredients. Sieve, taste and correct the seasoning.

To serve the terrine, turn out onto a chilled dish and remove the clingfilm. For a buffet, decorate with salad leaves and with any fresh herbs and herb flowers you can find. Serve in slices and offer a little Cherry Tomato Sauce with each helping. Alternatively, pour off the sauce onto individual white plates, place a slice of the fish terrine on top, and garnish with tiny sprigs of fennel or cress and fennel flowers if available. Serve with Melba Toast (see page 78).

Ballymaloe Fish Mousse with Shrimp Butter Sauce

Serves 16–20

This recipe makes a large number of light fish mousses. It is a favourite on the menu at Ballymaloe and can be served with many sauces. Although the mousse is light, it is also very rich so serve it in small ramekins. They can be done in several batches as the raw mixture keeps perfectly overnight, covered, in the fridge.

The fish must be absolutely spanking fresh for this recipe, otherwise it will taste stale as there is nothing to hide a taint. A teaspoon of salt may sound excessive but it is vital to season the raw mixture well, or the mousse will be bland.

350g (12oz) very fresh fillets of whiting
　or pollock, skinned and totally free of bone
　or membrane
1 teaspoon salt
pinch of freshly ground white pepper
1 organic egg and 1 egg white
700ml (generous 1¼ pints) double cream,
　chilled
Beurre Blanc recipe x 2 (see page 583)
225g (8oz) shrimps, cooked and peeled
7g (¼oz) butter

Garnish
sprigs of chervil
whole cooked shrimps (1–3 per person),
　optional

individual ramekins 60ml (2½fl oz) capacity,
　5cm (2in) diameter x 2.5cm (1in) deep

Chill the bowl of the food processor while you trim the fish.

Cut the fillets into small dice. Purée in the chilled bowl of the food processor. Add the salt and freshly ground pepper and then add the egg and egg white and continue to purée until it is well incorporated. Rest and chill in the fridge for 30 minutes.

Meanwhile heat the oven to 200°C/400°F/gas 6. Line the ramekins with clingfilm or brush with melted butter. When the fish has rested, pour in the cream, put the bowl back onto the food processor and whizz again until it is just incorporated. Taste and correct the seasoning. (If tasting raw fish doesn't appeal, poach a little blob in a pan of simmering water.)

Fill the ramekins with mousse and put them in a bain marie. Cover with a pricked sheet of tin foil or greaseproof paper. Pour boiling water into the bain marie. Put it in the oven and bake for 20–30 minutes. The mousses should feel just firm in the centre and will keep perfectly for 20–30 minutes in a plate-warming oven.

Meanwhile, make the Beurre Blanc Sauce and keep warm. When the mousses are cooked, remove them to a warm place. Toss the shrimps in a sauté pan in a very

little foaming butter until hot through, then add them to the sauce, taste and correct the seasoning: the sauce should be very thin and light.

To serve: unmould each mousse onto a warm plate. Spoon a little hot sauce on top and garnish with shrimps and sprigs of fresh chervil.

Seafood Okra Gumbo

Serves 6 as a main course

Say Gumbo and you immediately think of New Orleans. Summer is the time when all the main ingredients are at their best, though you can enjoy it all year round. As with most stews, gumbo is best prepared in advance (to the point before the shrimps are added) to allow the flavours to marry. When reheating, stir frequently and take care not to overcook the shrimps.

900g (2lb) fresh or frozen shrimps, heads on
2 small fresh crabs
3.6 litres (6 pints) water
2 tablespoons vegetable oil, for frying
500g (18oz) fresh okra, sliced into 2.5cm
　(1in) rounds
175ml (6fl oz) vegetable oil
110g (4oz) flour
225g (8oz) onion, chopped
150g (5oz) green pepper, chopped
75g (3oz) celery, chopped
1 garlic clove, peeled and finely chopped
1 x 400g (14oz) tin Italian tomatoes, chopped
2 bay leaves
2 teaspoons salt (to taste)
½ teaspoon black pepper
½ teaspoon white pepper
¼ teaspoon cayenne pepper

Peel and de-vein the shrimps (see page 254) and set aside, covered, in the fridge. Rinse the shells and heads and place in a large stainless-steel pan with 2.4 litres (4 pints) of cold water. Bring to boil, reduce the heat and simmer for 30–45 minutes. Strain, discard the shells and heads, and set the stock aside.

Meanwhile, wash the crabs under running water, drop into a pan of 1.2 litres (2 pints) of boiling water and simmer for 20–30 minutes. Strain, reserving the stock, and allow the crabs to cool. When you can handle the shells, snap off both claws, then break open the shell and extract all the meat. Set aside.

In a heavy-bottomed skillet or large frying pan, heat the oil and add the sliced okra. Sauté over a medium heat for 10–15 minutes or until soft but not soggy. Heat the remaining vegetable oil in a deep-sided, heavy-bottomed metal casserole and add the flour to make a roux (see page 580). Add the onions, pepper, celery and garlic and sauté, stirring occasionally, until tender. Don't be concerned if some of the vegetables stick to the bottom; their caramelised juices add flavour to the dish.

Add the tomatoes, bay leaves and the seasonings and cook for about 10 minutes before adding the okra slices. Cook gently for a further 10 minutes.

Add the reserved crab stock and half the shrimp stock. Bring to the boil, stirring constantly, then lower the heat, partially cover, and simmer for 30 minutes. If the gumbo becomes too thick, adjust with more shrimp stock. Check the seasoning. Add the crab meat and simmer for 10 minutes, then add the peeled shrimps, return to the boil, and simmer for a further 5 minutes, until the shrimps are firm and pink. Serve in large bowls with plain boiled rice.

Ballycotton Fish Pie

Serves 6–8

Many different types of really fresh fish may be used for a fish pie, so feel free to adapt this recipe a little to suit your needs. Periwinkles are a good and cheap addition and a little smoked haddock is tasty also, but use sparingly unless you want the smoky flavour to predominate. A little left-over Hollandaise Sauce will enrich the pie.

1.1kg (2½lb) fillets of cod, haddock, ling, hake, salmon, pollock or monkfish or a mixture (use up to 225g/½lb smoked haddock)
18 mussels (optional)
salt and freshly ground pepper
1 small onion, finely chopped
25g (1oz) butter
225g (8oz) mushrooms, preferably flat, sliced
600ml (1 pint) milk
Roux made with 25g (1oz) butter and 25g (1oz) flour (see page 580)
1–2 tablespoons double cream (optional)
2 tablespoons freshly chopped parsley
1 tablespoon freshly chopped dill
4 hard-boiled organic eggs, shelled and chopped (optional)
900g (2 lb) Fluffy Mashed Potato or Scallion Champ (see page 182)

Preheat the oven to 180°C/350°F/gas 4.

Cut the fish into 150g (5oz) chunks. Season with salt and freshly ground pepper.

Check that all the mussels are tightly shut. Wash them, put into a shallow pan in a single layer, cover, and cook over a medium heat just until the shells open – 3 or 4 minutes will do. Cool.

Meanwhile, sweat the onion in a little melted butter over a gentle heat until soft but not coloured, and remove to a plate. Increase the heat, sauté the sliced mushrooms in the hot pan, season with salt and freshly ground pepper and add to the onions. Put the fish into a wide sauté or frying pan in a single layer, cover with the milk, and season with salt and pepper. Cover and simmer gently until the fish is just cooked – no more than 3–4 minutes.

Remove the fish with a slotted spoon, carefully removing any bones or skin. Bring the liquid to the boil and thicken with roux, add a little cream and the parsley, dill, eggs, mushrooms, fish and mussels. Stir gently, taste and correct the seasoning.

Spoon into 1 large or 6–8 small dishes and pipe potato or Scallion Champ on top. The pie may be prepared ahead to this point.

Cook for 10–15 minutes if the filling and potato are warm, or 30 minutes if reheating the dish from cold. Flash under the grill if necessary to brown the top. Serve with Garlic Butter or Parsley Butter (see page 588).

Haddock, Sweet Potato and Coconut Stew

Serves 4–6

This one-pot stew, adapted from a recipe sourced by Philippa Davenport, comes from the Solomon Islands. Omit the brazil nuts if you wish, but they add a delicious crunch. You can use white- or orange-fleshed potatoes. It is very quick to prepare; ideal for a mid-week supper dish.

450g (1lb) haddock or monkfish (steaks or fillets)
450g (1lb) sweet potatoes, peeled and cut into 2.5cm (1in) chunks
2 tablespoons extra-virgin olive oil
1 medium onion, peeled and chopped
3 garlic cloves, peeled and finely chopped
2.5cm (1in) cube fresh ginger, peeled and finely chopped
600ml (1 pint) Fish Stock (see page 37)
150g (5oz) creamed coconut
1 x 400g (14oz) tin Italian tomatoes, chopped
35g (1½oz) shelled brazil nuts
10g (½oz) coriander, freshly chopped
salt and freshly ground pepper

Cut the fish into large chunks, removing any bones, and set aside on a plate at room temperature. Put the peeled chunks of sweet potato into cold water to prevent discolouration. Heat the oil in a deep-sided, heavy-bottomed cast-iron casserole and sweat the onion for 3 minutes until it is soft but not brown. Add the garlic and ginger and cook gently for a further 4–5 minutes.

Drain the sweet potato, add to the casserole and stir well to coat. Cook for about 3 minutes, then add the hot fish stock and creamed coconut. Cook over a low heat, covered, until the coconut has melted, stirring from time to time. Then add the tomatoes and simmer, uncovered, for 7–10 minutes, or until the sweet potato is just cooked.

Add the fish pieces and cook gently, covered, for a further 5 minutes, or until the fish is done. Taste and season. Meanwhile, roughly chop the brazil nuts (you may also toast them under a preheated grill for 3–5 minutes for extra flavour).

To serve: sprinkle the chopped brazil nuts and coriander over the stew. This makes a meal in itself, but you can serve with fresh, warm hunks of bread.

Ballycotton Seafood Lasagne

Serves 8

10–12 sheets of homemade lasagne (see page 148) or very thin commercial lasagne
1 teaspoon salt
2 tablespoons extra-virgin olive oil
110g (4oz) onion, finely chopped
1 large garlic clove, finely chopped
175g (6oz) mushrooms, sliced
2 tablespoons chopped parsley
1 glass white wine
175g (6oz) scallops (out of shells)
110–175g (4–6oz) cooked prawns or shrimps, shelled
12 mussels
225–275g (8–10oz) monkfish, cut into collops
salt and freshly ground pepper
creamy milk
Roux (see page 580)
Parmigiano Reggiano

Preheat the oven to 180°C/350°F/gas 4.

Bring a large pan of water to a fast rolling boil and add salt. Cook the sheets of pasta a few at a time until al dente,

about 1 minute for homemade pasta, about 5–8 minutes for shop-bought pasta. Drop immediately into a bowl of cold water, drain and lay out on tea towels in a single layer. Heat the olive oil in a sauté pan, add the onions and sweat until soft and just beginning to colour. Add the garlic and stir. Increase the heat, add the sliced mushrooms and toss for a minute or two. Remove from the pan and set aside.

Put the scallops into a small saucepan, cover with water and wine and poach gently for 4–5 minutes until just cooked. Remove with a slotted spoon and drain. Bring the liquid back to the boil, add the monkfish pieces and poach for 3–5 minutes until they change colour to white. Add to the scallops. Next, put the scrubbed mussels into the liquid and remove as soon as the shells open. Remove the beards and discard the shells. Add to the seafood mix.

If the prawns are raw, cook in a little butter until they turn pink, cut in half and add to the rest of the fish. If using cooked peeled prawns, just add to the fish.

Mix the fish with the mushroom mixture and add 2 tablespoons of parsley. Season with salt and pepper.

Make a sauce by measuring the cooking liquid and making it up to 1.2 litres (2 pints) with full cream milk. Bring to the boil, thicken with roux and allow to simmer gently for 5–6 minutes until the flavour is mellow and delicious.

To assemble: spread a little of the sauce on the base of an ovenproof dish and, keeping back a little for the top of the lasagne, mix the rest with the fish and mushrooms. Lay lasagne over the sauce in the bottom of the dish, spread some of the seafood sauce over the pasta and sprinkle with Parmesan. Continue until there are least 4 layers, finishing with a layer of pasta. Spread the reserved sauce over the top layer. Sprinkle with grated cheese and bake for 15–20 minutes until bubbly and golden on top. Allow to rest for 10 minutes before serving.

Isaac's Shellfish Paella

Serves 8–10

110g (4oz) butter
4 tablespoons extra-virgin olive oil
8 tablespoons sliced shallot
8 garlic cloves, mashed
24 each of large prawns, mussels, and clams
450g (1lb) squid, cleaned and cut into rings
    plus whole tentacles
400g (14oz) Paella rice
4 tablespoons dry white wine
600ml (1 pint) light Fish Stock (see page 37)
20 asparagus tips
450g (1lb) fresh peas or mange tout
450g (1lb) baby courgettes, sliced
a good few strands of saffron
juice of 1 lime
600ml (1 pint) vegetable cooking water
4 large tomatoes
4 tablespoons chopped parsley and chives
salt, freshly ground pepper, sugar

46cm (18in) paella pan

Melt the butter and olive oil in a paella pan, and sweat the shallot and garlic slowly until they are soft. Add the shelled prawns and raw squid and cook until they stiffen. Remove and set to one side.

Then add the rice and wine. Stir until the rice is completely coated with the wine and butter. Continue to cook until nearly all the liquid has been absorbed, then add half the fish stock. Stir gently and occasionally (you can over-stir this).

The temperature is critical; the mixture should be just barely bubbling and should continue this way until the dish is fully cooked. If it cooks too quickly or too slowly the rice will become stodgy and heavy. Allow the liquid to be absorbed before adding more stock and repeat until all the stock has been used.

Meanwhile, cook the asparagus and peas in a little boiling salted water. Use the same pan for both but cook separately. When cooked, rinse under cold water and set to one side. Keep the cooking water.

Cook the courgettes in a frying pan over a high flame with some olive oil, salt and pepper; again keep to one side.

Steam the mussels and clams in a covered pot until they open. Put aside and keep the juices. Sieve the mussel and clam juice, add the saffron, the lime juice and the vegetable cooking water. When all the fish stock has been used up, continue to add the vegetable water and shellfish and saffron liquid. The rice may not take all the liquid. You will know by the texture of the rice when it is cooked – there shouldn't be any bite. When the paella is fully cooked, gently fold the vegetables and shellfish in.

Sprinkle with chopped tomato, parsley and chives and serve from the paella dish.

Seafood Chowder

Serves 6

A chowder is a wonderfully substantial fish soup; in fact it could almost be classified as a stew. It is certainly a meal in itself and there are plenty of variations on the theme. Firm-fleshed fish works best. The base of the chowder can be prepared in advance.

1 tablespoon extra-virgin olive or sunflower oil
110g (4oz) streaky bacon, rind removed, cut
    into 5mm (¼in) dice
175–225g (6–8oz) onions, chopped
25g (1oz) flour
850ml (1½ pints) homemade Fish Stock (see
    page 37) or, as a last resort, water
425ml (¾ pint) milk
bouquet garni made up of 6 parsley stalks,
    2 sprigs of thyme and 1 bay leaf
6 medium-sized potatoes, e.g. Golden Wonder,
    cut into 5mm (¼in) dice
salt and freshly ground pepper
pinch of mace
pinch of cayenne pepper
700g (1½lb) haddock, monkfish, cod or other
    firm white fish (or a mixture), free of bones
    and skin
150ml (¼ pint) single cream

450g (1lb) mixed, cooked shellfish – mussels,
    clams, scallops, shrimps or prawns and the
    cooking liquor

Garnish
parsley and chives, freshly chopped

Heat the oil in a stainless-steel saucepan and brown the bacon well until it is crisp and golden. Add the onion, cover and sweat for a few minutes over a low heat. Stir in the flour and cook for 1–2 minutes. Add the fish stock or water gradually, then the milk, bouquet garni and potatoes. Season well with salt, pepper, mace and cayenne. Cover and simmer until the potatoes are almost cooked – this takes 5–6 minutes. The chowder may be prepared ahead up to this point.

Cut the fish into 2.5cm (1in) cubes. Add to the pot as soon as the tip of a knife will go through the potato. Simmer gently for 3–4 minutes, stir in the cream and add the shellfish and any liquor obtained from opening the mussels or clams. When the soup returns to the boil, remove from the heat.

Remember that the fish will continue to cook in the heat of the chowder, so make sure it is not overcooked. Taste, correct the seasoning and sprinkle with freshly chopped parsley and chives.

Crusty hot white bread or hot crackers are usually served with a chowder.

Variation

Try using 110g (4oz) smoked haddock in this recipe. Poach it gently in some of the milk first, and flake it. Add to the chowder with the shellfish.

TIP: Stir the chowder as little as possible once the fish has been added to avoid it breaking up. Be careful not to overcook the fish, particularly if using softer varieties like cod.

poultry

poultry

We have several flocks of free-range hens in the fields around the cookery school, some of which we rear for the table. Locally produced organic chicken is also now available at Midleton Farmers' Market. This market, which I started with a group of producers in June 2000, has been warmly welcomed by producers and consumers alike – local food for local people. The quality and taste are for many people a forgotten flavour, and for those brought up on mass-produced supermarket chickens, it is a revelation.

Nora Ahearne sells us wonderful free-range ducks, geese and turkeys. When she delivers them to the school I introduce her to the students so they can meet the person who rears this delicious poultry. Another local farmer rears us plump guinea fowl. The flavour of these birds is deliciously gamey. They are much sought after by local restauranteurs and are a favourite on our menu at Ballymaloe House.

Free-range versus Battery Chickens

Consumers are growing increasingly concerned as they become aware of the intensive rearing which produces the poultry on the supermarket shelves. Battery birds are kept in hideously crowded pens, which are stacked on top of each other with no natural light. They are fed a cocktail of meal, which can include antibiotics, hormones, anti-depressants, muscle strengtheners and growth promoters.

Free-range and organic chickens are becoming more widely available but beware of misleading labels. The term 'free-range' does not always guarantee that the chicken has led a contented life pecking around a farmyard. There are varying degrees of free-range, so ask lots of questions and keep looking until you find a good source. The description 'maize fed' can also be misleading. Unless specifically stated, they are simply intensively reared birds that have been partly fed on corn meal, and are not necessarily superior to other chickens.

To add to the confusion, a large percentage of the chicken sold at present in the European Union is imported from Thailand and Brazil. Once it arrives in the EU at a registered abattoir, it can then be re-labelled and miraculously turned into an 'Irish' or 'English' chicken. This causes deep resentment among producers and consumers who wish to be able to source and buy poultry that is reared in their own country.

A true free-range chicken must have access to grass and be able to range freely. Organic birds are always free-range and will, in addition, be fed on specially compounded meal made from organically grown grain. No poultry or fish protein supplements or growth stimulants are added to their diet and they are allowed to grow to full size naturally.

Poussins are intensively reared baby chickens – about 4 weeks old. Although they are tender, they often have little flavour, and even less meat. Having said that, I have tasted excellent French poussins.

Buying Organic

Seek out free-range, certified organic poultry where you can be sure that the birds were fed an additive-free diet, had access to open air and were free to range. It takes 37–41 days to produce a conventional chicken in an intensive system. It takes more than twice that long to rear an organic chicken. Consequently the feed and production cost is much higher. So, if you want this kind of bird, find a good local supplier and pay them what they need to produce the quality you seek. This might be double the price (or more) of a conventional supermarket chicken. The choice is yours. You get what you pay for.

Duck, guinea fowl, quail and turkey can also be intensively reared. Geese, on the other hand, are difficult to breed in this way and tend to be reared more extensively. You may want to ask questions about the content of their feed. When choosing poultry, look for meaty birds with skin that's creamy-white to yellow and that are free of bruises, feathers and torn or dry skin.

Giblets

Quite often nowadays poultry is sold without giblets – mostly because people don't know how to cope with them. This is a shame, as they're invaluable for making a flavoursome stock. The hearts and gizzards are also excellent added to a salade tiède.

Hanging

Free-range poultry needs to hang for slightly longer than intensively reared birds – because of their outdoor life they've had more exercise and can, therefore, be a little tougher.

Salmonella and Campylobacter

Besides being a relatively affordable and high-quality source of protein, poultry has been blamed for almost 25 per cent of food poisoning outbreaks in recent years – more than any other type of food. Although salmonella gets more press coverage, three times as many cases of campylobacter infection have been reported.

Neither campylobacter nor salmonella is usually fatal, but they can have serious implications for the very young, aged and pregnant – whose immune systems are less able to fight off infection.

Unfortunately buying organic does not necessarily mean that your meat will be disease-free. In a recent study, while salmonella was found to be less common in organic chickens than intensively reared birds, there was little difference in the occurrence of campylobacter.

Infection is usually contracted by eating food which has been contaminated by the bacterium and has not been properly stored or cooked. The best way to kill the bacteria is to ensure that poultry is cooked through thoroughly, and to wash your hands after touching uncooked meat. Further preventative precautions are outlined in the sections below.

Storing

Poultry, particulary chicken, should be used while it's fresh, within a day or two of purchase, or frozen straight away (organic birds keep considerably longer). If you've bought your poultry from a supermarket, take it out of the plastic wrapping as soon as you get home, put it on a plate, cover with clingfilm and store in the fridge. Try not to let it sit at room temperature for more than 15 minutes. Always store raw meat at the bottom of the fridge, to ensure that it can not drip down and cross-contaminate cooked meat and other foods.

Defrosting

Make sure that frozen poultry is fully defrosted before cooking it. Never leave it to thaw on a counter – ideally it should be allowed to defrost in the fridge. A quicker method is to submerge it inside a water-proof freezer bag in cold running water. If you use a microwave for defrosting, the bird should be cooked immediately after thawing as microwaving might well have already started the cooking process.

Food Hygiene

Scrub, wash and dry the chopping board and any utensils that you've used to prepare raw chicken before using them again. Try to keep one side of your chopping board for raw poultry only, and stick to the other side for any other food. In catering, separate boards are obligatory.

Cooking

It is essential that chicken is cooked through properly, in order to safe-guard against salmonella or campylobacter poisoning. To ensure that a roast is thoroughly cooked, roast it at 180°C (350°F/gas 4), to an internal temperature of 85°C (185°F). Allow it to cook without interruption. Many chefs now use a meat thermometer to check for readiness, but home cooks can judge by the colour of the juices, which should run clear when a skewer is inserted into the thickest part of the thigh. If you stuff your chicken, pack it loosely and ensure that the centre of the stuffing reaches 75°C (165°F). Never cook stuffed poultry in a microwave and ensure that leftover poultry and stuffing are refrigerated separately.

Poultry is remarkably versatile, and every part of it can be used. Be sure to keep the giblets, wing tips and carcasses to make stock for soups, stews, casseroles and sauces. On the continent, chickens come with their head and feet still on. When added to soups and stews, these bits give extra flavour and depth.

Many of the recipes for chicken, turkey and guinea fowl and pheasant are interchangeable – although you'll need to adjust the cooking time and quantities.

Ducks and geese are brown meat throughout. They're naturally fatty and some chefs suggest pricking the bird with a skewer before cooking to allow some of the fat to run out. We don't do that. I would simply recommend that you find a good-quality bird to begin with, then all you will need to do is rub a little salt over the breast before roasting it. Save the fat for roast or sauté potatoes and confit (it'll keep for months in your fridge). Many cooks value duck and goose fat so highly that they buy it in tins. We sell our surplus duck and goose fat at the Midleton Farmers' Market.

Master Recipe
Pan-grilled Chicken with Rosemary
Serves 8

A spice crust improves the flavour of chicken breasts immeasurably – a single spice or a combination of spices may be used as a marinade as in this recipe, or simply applied as a crust.

8 organic chicken breasts
1–2 tablespoons freshly chopped rosemary
4 tablespoons extra-virgin olive oil

Lemon Butter (see page 588)

Flatten the chicken breasts slightly and drizzle over the rosemary and olive oil. Cover and leave to marinate for 10–20 minutes.

Pan-grill the chicken breasts (see right) or barbecue them on an oiled rack about 12.5cm (5in) from the coals. Cook for several minutes each side, brushing with extra marinade while cooking. Serve with Lemon Butter, a good green salad and a Red Chilli Mayonnaise (see page 585).

Variations
Pan-grilled Chicken Breasts with Cardamom
Follow the Master Recipe and substitute the rosemary for 1 teaspoon each of cardamon seeds and black peppercorns, together with a pinch of cayenne pepper for. Pound the spices in a mortar and if time permits marinate for about 2 hours.

Note: Thyme and marjoram also greatly enhance the flavour of chicken breasts.

Serve with any of the following: Tomato and Chilli Jam (see page 513), Sweet Chilli Sauce (available in Asian groceries and many supermarkets), Chilli and Coriander Butter (see page 588) or chargrilled Mediterranean vegetables.

Cajun Chicken with Spicy Mayonnaise
Use six chicken breasts and substitute the following Cajun Spice mix for the rosemary in the Master Recipe.

1 teaspoon each salt, dried oregano and dried thyme leaves
1/2 teaspoon each freshly ground pepper, white pepper, onion powder, garlic powder, paprika and cayenne

Mix the spices. Brush the chicken breasts with oil and dip into the spices. Cook on a hot grill-pan. Serve with Red Chilli Mayonnaise (see page 585) or Tomato and Chilli Jam (see page 513).

Pan-grilled Chicken Breasts with Persian Rice
Follow the Master Recipe and serve it with Persian Rice (see page 124).

Pan-grilled Chicken Breasts with Tomato and Basil Sauce
Follow the Master Recipe and serve with Tomato and Basil Sauce (see page 587).

Cumin and Coriander-crusted Chicken with Cucumber and Mint Raita and Ballymaloe Tomato Relish
Follow the Master Recipe and substitute 3 tablespoons freshly roasted and ground cumin seeds and 3 tablespoons freshly roasted and ground coriander seeds for the rosemary. Serve with Cucumber and Mint Raita and Ballymaloe Tomato Relish.

Pan-grilled Chicken Breasts with Fire and Brimstone Sauce and Rustic Roast Potatoes
Follow the Master Recipe, and substitute Fire and Brimstone Sauce (see page 596) for the rosemary.

Fill a little bowl of sauce and put it on each plate for dipping. Serve with Rustic Roast Potatoes (see page 181) and garnish with a few sprigs of fresh coriander or flat-leaf parsley.

Note: Chicken fingers (the little inside fillet of the chicken breast), may be used as a substitute in any of the above recipes.

How to Pan-grill Chicken Breasts

Use skinless chicken breasts. (Remove the fillet, refrigerate, and save for another dish.)

Heat a cast-iron grill-pan until quite hot. Brush each chicken breast with olive oil, season with salt and freshly ground pepper. Place the chicken breasts on the hot grill-pan for about 1 minute, change to the opposite direction to get criss-cross markings on the chicken breast. Repeat on the other side. If the chicken breasts are very large, the grill-pan may now be transferred to a preheated moderate oven 180°C/350°F/gas 4. They can take from 8–15 minutes to cook depending on size.

LEFT: Pan-grilled Chicken Breasts with Parsley Salad and Sun-dried Tomatoes (page 272)

How to Prepare a Chicken Paillarde (Butterflied Chicken Breast)

An excellent way to prepare chicken breasts, particularly for the barbecue – they cook faster and more evenly.

Remove the fillet from each chicken breast and save for another dish. Slice each chicken breast from top to bottom, so that you can open it out like a book.

Flatten with the palm of your hand to ensure a good, flat shape.

Pan-grilled Chicken Breasts with Couscous, Raisins and Pistachio Nuts
Serves 8

Hot peppery Harissa (see page 596), a North African spice mixture, can be smeared over the pan-grilled chicken breasts to adds even more excitement to this dish.

350g (12oz) couscous
1–2 tablespoons extra-virgin olive oil
600ml (1 pint) well-flavoured homemade
*   Chicken Stock (see page 36)*
110g (4oz) raisins
45g (1³/₄ oz) peeled pistachio nuts, or toasted
*   pine nuts*
110g (4oz) split peeled almonds, toasted
salt and freshly ground pepper
8 organic chicken breasts
4 tablespoons extra-virgin olive oil
a little butter or extra-virgin olive oil (optional)
harissa (optional)

Garnish
sprigs of fresh coriander

Preheat the oven to 180°C/350°F/gas 4.

Put the couscous into a bowl. Sprinkle with a few drops of olive oil, and rub with fingers to coat the grains. Cover the couscous in its own volume of chicken stock or water (450ml/16fl oz) and allow to soak for 15 minutes, stirring every now and then. When the liquid has been absorbed, add the raisins and pistachio or pine nuts and almonds, and season with salt and pepper. Put into a heavy covered dish and heat through in the oven for about 20 minutes.

Brush the chicken breasts with olive oil and cook on a preheated grill-pan until just cooked through and golden on both sides and criss-crossed with markings from the grill-pan (see page 271 for technique). Season with salt and pepper.

Add butter or olive oil to the couscous to taste. Season with salt and freshly ground pepper. Spread a little harissa (if using) on the pan-grilled chicken breasts.

To serve, divide the couscous into hot deep plates. Put a chicken breast on top, de-grease the grill-pan and de-glaze with a little well-flavoured chicken stock. Garnish with sprigs of coriander and serve immediately.

Pan-grilled Chicken Breasts with Parsley Salad and Sun-dried Tomatoes
Serves 8

8 organic chicken breasts
olive oil
salt and freshly ground pepper

Basil Dressing (see page 226)

Parsley Salad
4 handfuls Italian and curly parsley, de-stalked
Worcestershire sauce
8 chopped Sun-Dried Tomatoes, (bought or
*   make your own, see page 188)*
slivers of Parmesan (preferably Parmigiano
*   Reggiano)*

First make the basil dressing.

Just before serving, brush the chicken breasts with olive oil. Cook on a preheated grill-pan until just cooked through and golden on both sides and criss-crossed with markings from the grill-pan. Season with salt and pepper.

To serve: put a pan-grilled chicken breast on each plate. Toss the parsley in a little of the basil dressing, and sprinkle with a little Worcestershire sauce. Put a portion of parsley salad on each plate, sprinkle with a few pieces of sun-dried tomato and slivers of parmesan cheese. Serve immediately with Rustic Roast Potatoes (see page 181) or Buffalo Chips (see page 184).

Chargrilled Chicken Paillarde with a Smoked Chilli Butter
Serves 8

A favourite recipe inspired by Belfast's super-chefs, Paul and Jeanne Rankin.

8 organic chicken breasts
4 tablespoons extra-virgin olive oil
2 tablespoons freshly chopped herbs (parsley, marjoram, rosemary, thyme)
salt and freshly cracked pepper

Smoked Chilli Butter
110g (4oz) soft butter at room temperature
2 teaspoons lemon juice, freshly squeezed
1 tablespoon freshly chopped coriander
2 anchovies, chopped
2 teaspoons chopped shallots
2 tablespoons smoked barbecue sauce (or smoked ketchup)
2 smoked jalepeño (chipotle) chillies or fresh chillies, sliced
salt and freshly ground pepper

To Serve
chargrilled vegetables

Garnish
fresh coriander leaves

Prepare the chicken paillarde (see left).

Mix the olive oil and herbs together in a shallow dish. Season each chicken paillarde with salt and pepper and coat both sides in the herbed oil.

Then make the Chilli Butter: put all the ingredients into a food processor and whizz for a few seconds until almost smooth.

Next chargrill the vegetables and keep warm. Cook the chicken on the chargrill or grill pan for approx. 4 minutes on each side, turning each after a few minutes to give a nice criss-cross effect.

Place a mixture of chargrilled vegetables in the middle of a warm plate, put a chicken paillarde on top and a blob of Smoked Chilli Butter. Garnish with fresh coriander leaves.

Master Recipe
Chicken Breasts with Mushrooms and Marjoram
Serves 4

Soaking the chicken breasts in milk gives them a tender and moist texture but it is not essential for this dish. We often serve this recipe with orzo, a pasta which looks like grains of rice and is all the rage in our house nowadays.

4 organic chicken breasts
milk (optional)
salt and freshly ground pepper
25g (1oz) butter
2 tablespoons chopped shallot or spring onion
110g (4oz) mushrooms, sliced
150ml (¼ pint) homemade Chicken Stock (see page 36)
150ml (¼ pint) cream
1 tablespoon freshly chopped parsley or marjoram

Garnish
sprigs of flat-leaf parsley

Soak the chicken breasts in milk, just enough to cover them, for about 1 hour. Discard the milk and dry with kitchen paper. Season with salt and pepper (this step is not essential).

Choose a sauté pan just large enough to take the chicken breasts in a single layer. Heat half the butter in the sauté pan until foaming, put in the chicken breasts and turn them in the butter; do not brown. Cover with a round of greaseproof paper and the lid. Cook on a gentle heat for 5–7 minutes or until just barely cooked.

Meanwhile, sweat the shallots gently in a pan in the remaining butter. Increase the heat, add the mushrooms, season with salt and pepper and cook for 3–4 minutes. They should be slightly golden. Set aside. When the chicken breasts are cooked remove to a warmed serving plate and keep hot. Add the chicken stock and cream to the saucepan.

Reduce the liquid by one-third over a medium heat; this will thicken the sauce slightly and intensify the flavour. When you are happy with the flavour and texture of the sauce, add the chicken breasts and mushroom mixture, together with the parsley or marjoram. Simmer for 1–2 minutes, taste and correct the seasoning. The dish may be prepared ahead to this point - cool quickly, cover, refrigerate and reheat later.

Serve with freshly cooked orzo and scatter some sprigs of parsley over the top.

Variations
Chicken with Mushrooms and Ginger
Follow the Master Recipe and add 1–2 teaspoons of freshly grated ginger to the mushrooms in the pan.

Chicken with Mushrooms and Rosemary
Follow the Master Recipe but tuck a sprig of rosemary in between the chicken breasts as they cook; discard later. Add 1 teaspoon of chopped rosemary to the mushrooms in the pan. Garnish with sprigs of rosemary. Serve with penne or orzo.

Bang Bang Chicken

Serves 6

This explosive-sounding chicken dish was made popular in restaurants like The Ivy and Le Caprice in London. There are lots of versions.

5 organic chicken breasts
110g (4oz) cellophane noodles
2 cucumbers, cut into thin strips

Poaching Stock
1.2 litres (2 pints) Chicken Stock (see page 36)
2 spring onions
1 chilli
4 garlic cloves
3 slices fresh ginger

Sauce
4 large garlic cloves, crushed
4 tablespoons freshly chopped coriander
175g (6oz) smooth peanut butter
4 tablespoons light soy sauce
2 tablespoons honey
1 teaspoon chilli oil
1 tablespoon Japanese rice vinegar
1 teaspoon dry sherry

Garnish
fresh coriander leaves
6 red chillies (optional)

Put all the ingredients for the poaching stock in a saucepan and add the chicken breasts. Bring slowly to the boil, simmer for 5 minutes and turn off the heat. Cover and allow to sit in the poaching liquid until fully cooked. Put the noodles in a bowl and cover with hot water. Leave for about 5 minutes and drain (they are served lukewarm).

Whizz all the ingredients for the sauce in a food processor or mix well in a bowl. If it appears very thick, thin to a coating consistency with water.

Peel the cucumbers and remove seeds and cut into 5cm (2in) julienne strips. Wash your hands, shred the chicken with your fingers or with two forks.

To serve: divide the noodles between the plates, top each one with cucumber julienne, then shredded chicken, and drizzle the sauce over the chicken and garnish with coriander and a whole chilli pepper.

Crispy Chicken Sandwich

Serves 4

4 organic chicken breasts
salt and freshly ground pepper
French mustard
4 slices Gruyère cheese or mature Cheddar
2–3 teaspoons freshly chopped parsley
4 slices cooked ham or 4 cooked streaky rashers
seasoned white flour, preferably unbleached
beaten egg
fine dry breadcrumbs
clarified butter, for frying (see page 105)

Detach the fillet from the chicken breasts and keep aside for another recipe. Carefully slit the chicken breast down the side and open out. Season with salt and pepper. Smear with a little French mustard, put a thin slice of Gruyère cheese or mature cheddar cheese lengthways on one side of the chicken breast, sprinkle with a little parsley and top with a slice of cooked ham or bacon rasher. Fold over the other side of each chicken breast, and press well to seal. Dip each one first in seasoned flour, then into beaten egg and then breadcrumbs. Press them in well again.

Fry until golden and cooked all the way through in some clarified butter in a shallow pan, or deep-fry in good quality oil at 170°C/325°F/gas 3 for 10–15 minutes depending on the size of the chicken breasts.

Serve whole or cut lengthways at an angle so the melted cheese begins to ooze out irresistibly. Serve immediately with a Rocket and Cherry Tomato Salad (see page 221) or Parsley Salad (see page 272).

Alternative Fillings

Salami, mozzarella and thyme leaves
Mozzarella, pesto and sun-dried tomato
Crushed garlic and chopped parsley
Prosciutto and Taleggio

Mexican Chilaquiles

Serves 4

We grow tomatillas and epazote in the greenhouse but if you can't find the pretty green tomatillas with their papery husk, use Tomato and Chilli sauce.

6–8 corn tortillas (stale is fine)
1 large chicken breast, cooked and shredded
salt and freshly ground pepper
350ml (12fl oz) Tomato and Chilli Sauce (see page 591) or Tomatillo Salsa (see page 592)
225ml (8fl oz) chicken broth
1 large sprig of epazote (optional)
4–8 tablespoons crumbled queso fresco or mozzarella and Cheddar, mixed

To Serve
2–4 tablespoons sour cream
1 onion, thinly sliced (optional)
fresh coriander leaves

20.5 x 12.5cm (8 x 5in) ovenproof dish

Preheat the oven to 230°C/450°F/gas 8.

Cut the tortillas into eighths. Dry them out in a moderate oven if they are moist; they are best stale and leathery for this dish. Heat oil in a deep-fryer and cook the tortilla pieces in batches until crisp and light golden. Drain on paper. Just before serving spread half the tortillas over the base of a deep-sided serving dish. Cover with the chicken and season. Put another layer of tortillas on top.

Thin out the sauce with a little chicken broth if too thick. Cover the tortillas with the hot sauce and a sprinkling of cheese.

Heat through in the oven for 5–10 minutes or until hot and bubbly. Serve with sour cream, more grated cheese for sprinkling, a little onion if liked and coriander.

Master Recipe
Chicken Pilaf
Serves 8

This recipe may sound dull but in fact it is a delicious and economical way to serve large numbers for a party. Serve with a Pilaf Rice and Tomato Fondue and garnish with sprigs of parsley or watercress. It may be prepared ahead of time and reheats well. Add the liaison just before serving, otherwise the sauce will curdle.

1 x 1.8–2kg (4–4½lb) boiling fowl or good
  free-range and organic chicken
1 large carrot, sliced
1 large onion, sliced
5 peppercorns
a bouquet garni made up of a sprig of thyme,
  parsley stalks, a tiny bay leaf, a stick of celery
425–600ml (¾–1 pint) water and white wine
  mixed or light Chicken Stock (see page 36)
25g (1oz) Roux (see page 580)
225–300ml (8–10fl oz) cream or creamy milk
salt and freshly ground pepper

Liaison
1 egg yolk
50ml (2fl oz) cream

Pilaf Rice (see page 125), full quantity

Season the chicken with salt and freshly ground pepper; put into a heavy casserole with the carrot, onion, bouquet garni and peppercorns. Pour in stock or water and wine mixture. Cover and bring to the boil and simmer either on top of the stove or in the oven for 1½–3 hours, depending on the age of the bird. When the bird is cooked, remove from the casserole.

Strain and de-grease the cooking liquid and return to the casserole. Discard the vegetables and the bouquet garni: they have already given their flavour to the cooking liquid. Reduce the liquid in an uncovered casserole for a few minutes. (If it tastes a little weak, add cream and reduce again.) Thicken to a light coating consistency with Roux. Taste and correct

ABOVE: Chicken Pilaf with Tomato Fondue

the seasoning. Skin the chicken and carve the flesh into 5cm (2in) pieces; add the meat to the sauce and allow it to heat through and bubble (the dish may be prepared ahead to this point).

Finally, just before serving mix the egg yolk and cream to make a liaison. Add some of the hot sauce to the liaison then carefully stir into the chicken mixture. Taste, correct the seasoning and stir well but do not allow to boil further or the sauce will curdle. Serve with Pilaf Rice.

Variations
Chicken and Mushroom Pilaf
Follow the Master Recipe, but add 450g (1lb) sautéed sliced mushroom to the Chicken Pilaf just before serving.

Chicken and Bacon Pilaf
Follow the Master Recipe and add cubes of cooked streaky bacon to either the original Chicken Pilaf, or the Chicken and Mushroom Pilaf, just before serving.

Note: Any of the above may be served as a pie, covered with pastry, mashed potato or champ. They can also be used as a filling for filo pies or parcels.

Tojo's Chicken Khorma with Basmati Rice and Poppadoms

Serves 8–12

1kg (2¼lb) organic chicken fillets
300ml (½ pint) natural yoghurt
25g (1oz) garlic cloves, crushed
25g (1oz) fresh ginger, peeled and grated
25g (1oz) fresh chilli, finely chopped

2 teaspoons freshly ground pepper
2 teaspoons whole cumin seeds
2 teaspoons whole coriander seeds
1 teaspoon cloves
1 teaspoon ground cinnamon
1 teaspoon turmeric
60g (2½oz) butter
450g (1lb) onions, sliced
300ml (10fl oz) coconut milk
450g (1lb) very ripe tomatoes, half the amount peeled and liquidised, the other half peeled and diced
1 tablespoon freshly chopped coriander
1 teaspoon salt

lime juice (optional)
cream

Cut the chicken fillets into 2.5cm (1in) cubes. Mix the yoghurt, garlic, ginger and chilli in a bowl, then add the chicken. Season, mix well, cover and allow to marinate in the fridge for at least 6 hours or overnight.

Later or the following day, preheat the oven to 250°C/475°F/gas 9. Warm all the spices except the cinnamon in a pan for 1–2 minutes and grind to a fine powder. Soften the onions in butter, add the freshly ground spices and cook for 5 minutes. Add the coconut milk little by little and continue to cook until the onions are completely softened. Then add the liquidised tomatoes.

Spread the chicken cubes on an oiled oven tray and cook for 10–15 minutes in the hot oven. Keep warm. Liquidise the onion and coconut milk mixture and return to the pot. Add the cooked chicken, diced tomatoes and coriander. Reheat.

Taste, correct the seasoning, adding a little lime juice if necessary. The curry should be mild and have a creamy consistency; add a little cream if needed.

Serve with Basmati Rice (see page 124) and Poppadoms.

Thai Green Chicken Curry with Thai Fragrant Rice

Serves 4

4 organic chicken breasts or thighs (450g/1lb after bones are removed)
225ml (8fl oz) coconut milk (we use Chaokoh)
3 tablespoons sunflower or peanut oil
2 garlic cloves, finely chopped
1–2 tablespoons Green Curry Paste (see right) – or use the ready-made Amoy brand
3 tablespoons fish sauce (nam pla)
1 teaspoon sugar
225ml (8fl oz) homemade Chicken Stock (see page 36)
4 fresh kaffir lime leaves (use more if they are frozen)
20 pea aubergines (if available) or ⅓ of 1 aubergine, cut into 20 pea-sized pieces
15 Thai basil leaves

First make the Green Curry Paste (see right).

Slice the chicken finely and keep aside.

Heat the coconut milk gently in a small saucepan but don't let it boil. Heat the oil in a wok or frying pan until almost smoking. Add the garlic and toss over once or twice for a few seconds until golden (watch out – the garlic can burn very easily). Add the curry paste and stir-fry for a few seconds, then add the warm coconut milk and stir until it curdles and thickens in the oil. Add the fish sauce and sugar.

Next mix in the chicken, stir well and cook until it changes colour (thighs will take longer to cook).

Add the stock, bring to the boil and cook for 2–3 minutes. Add the kaffir lime leaves, aubergines and basil. Cook for 1 minute, turn into a hot dish and serve immediately with Thai Jasmine Rice (see page 124).

Green Curry Paste

This is my favourite recipe for Green Curry Paste. It comes from *The Taste of Thailand* by Vatcharin Bhumichitr.

2 long green chillies, chopped
10 small green chillies, chopped
1 tablespoon chopped lemongrass
3 shallots, chopped
2 tablespoons chopped garlic (about 4 cloves)
2.5cm (1in) piece galangal, chopped
3 coriander roots, chopped
1 tablespoon coriander seeds, ground
½ teaspoon cumin, ground
½ teaspoon white pepper, ground
1 teaspoon kaffir lime juice or finely chopped lime leaves
2 teaspoons shrimp paste
1 teaspoon salt

Using a pestle and mortar, grind all the ingredients to a thick paste.

How to Poach Chicken or Turkey Breasts

Bring a saucepan of chicken stock to the boil, add the chicken breasts, and simmer gently for 5–7 minutes, depending on size. Turn off the heat, cover, and allow the chicken breasts to cool in the liquid. Remove with a slotted spoon. Use for chicken salads. Turkey breasts will take longer, depending on size.

Chicken Satay
Deh-Ta Hsiung
Serves 6–8, depending on the course

Cubes of tender meat, pork, beef, lamb or prawns may also be marinated in spices, threaded onto bamboo satay sticks and cooked on the barbecue or under the grill. Satays are terrifically versatile – they can be served as a starter, with drinks or as a light meal when served with rice and salad.

Marinade
1 garlic clove, crushed
2 shallots or 1 small onion, finely chopped
2 tablespoons light soy sauce
1 tablespoon sugar
1 tablespoon coriander seeds, freshly ground
1 tablespoon lemon juice or red wine vinegar

450g (1lb) organic chicken breast or thigh meat,
    boned and skinned
crispy lettuce leaves
coriander leaves
1–2 tablespoons vegetable oil
225g (8oz) Pixie's Peanut Sauce (see page 591)
24–36 bamboo skewers (soaked in cold water
    for a few hours or overnight to prevent them
    burning on the barbecue)

Mix all the ingredients for the marinade in a bowl. Cut the chicken into 2.5cm (1in) cubes and toss into the marinade. Leave for at least 1 hour.

Thread the meat cubes onto 1 end of the bamboo satay sticks. Brush each satay with a little oil and chargrill on a barbecue until just cooked, turning frequently.

Arrange some crispy lettuce and coriander leaves on plates, add the skewers and serve with a small bowl of peanut sauce.

Note: Chicken breasts may be cut into strips instead of cubes.

Jeanette Orrey's Real
Chicken Nuggets
Serves 6

This is a simple recipe made from local, free-range or organic chicken and a world away from the shop-bought chicken nuggets that have such a bad name. One adult portion will be roughly ten nuggets.

225g (8oz) fresh white breadcrumbs (or less
    if dried)
1 teaspoon garlic powder
1½ teaspoons paprika
1 organic egg
125ml (4fl oz) milk
900g (2lb) organic chicken breast, diced
Tomato Sauce (see page 591)

Preheat the oven to 200°C/400°F/gas 6.

Put the breadcrumbs into a bowl. Add the garlic powder and paprika and toss. Spread out onto a large tray. Whisk the egg with the milk in a large bowl. Coat the chicken pieces in batches. Transfer the chicken pieces to the tray of breadcrumbs. Toss to coat each piece evenly.

Arrange the crumbed chicken on a lightly oiled baking sheet. Bake in the oven for 10 minutes or until browned and crisp and cooked through. Serve with homemade Tomato Sauce.

Chicken Goujons with
Garlic Mayonnaise
Serves 4

2–3 organic chicken breasts, skinned
good-quality oil, for deep-frying
salt and freshly ground pepper

Olive Oil Batter
150g (5oz) plain white flour
2 tablespoons extra-virgin olive oil
1–1½ egg whites
sea salt

Garlic Mayonnaise (see page 584)

First make the batter. Sieve the flour into a bowl, make a well in the centre, pour in the olive oil, stir and add enough water to make a batter about the consistency of double cream. Allow to stand.

Just before cooking, whisk the egg whites until stiff and fold into the batter with sea salt to taste.

Heat the oil in a deep-frier. Cut the chicken breasts into 1cm (½in) strips on the bias and season. Drop individually into the batter and fry for 2–3 minutes or until crisp.

Drain on kitchen paper and serve immediately on a hot plate with a blob or bowl of well-seasoned garlic mayonnaise.

Preparing Buffalo Wings,
Mini-drumsticks, or
'Chicken Lollipops'

With a small knife cut through the skin just above the bone at the less fleshy end. Push the flesh upwards and turn inside out, pulling it up over the end of the bone so that it resembles a drumstick. Marinate the chicken wings, Chinese drumsticks or buffalo wings in a chosen marinade.

Chicken Tonnata Salad

Serves 8 as a main, 16 as a starter

Baby beetroot can be used instead of beans.

8 organic chicken breasts, skinned
salt and freshly ground pepper
225g (8oz) French beans
a little extra-virgin olive oil, for brushing

Tonnata Sauce
1 rounded tablespoon salted capers
2 salted anchovies
4 rounded tablespoons homemade Mayonnaise
   (see page 584)
75g (3oz) canned tuna in oil, plus 2 tablespoons
   of the oil
1 tablespoon lemon juice

Garnish
16–24 black olives
16 salted anchovies
16 salted capers
sprigs of flat-leaf parsley

First make the Tonnata Sauce: wash the capers and anchovies and pat dry. Put all the ingredients for the sauce in a food processor with a little pepper and whizz until smooth and then put into a bowl. Cover and set aside.

Season the chicken breasts with salt and pepper, then brush with oil. Heat a pan-grill and cook the chicken for 8–10 minutes on each side. Set aside to cool.

Top and tail the beans and halve at an angle if large. Bring a saucepan of water to the boil, add salt and cook the beans for 3–4 minutes or until tender but al dente. Drain, refresh under cold water and spread on a plate to dry. Put a little green salad on each plate and scatter some beans on top. Slice each chicken breast into 5 or 6 pieces, place on top of the leaves, and drizzle with the sauce. Garnish with capers, anchovies, a few olives and sprigs of parsley.

Variation

Turkey Tonnata Salad

Follow the Master Recipe, but substitute poached turkey breast for chicken.

Curried Chicken Salad with Mango and Roasted Cashew Nuts

Serves 8–10

If you are fortunate enough to find really ripe, perfumed mango, this is an excellent salad – typical of a New York deli.

1.3kg (3lb) organic chicken breasts
salt and freshly ground pepper
1.2 litres (2 pints) homemade Chicken Stock
   (see page 36)
1½ tablespoons lemon juice, freshly squeezed
2 ripe mangoes, peeled, stoned and cut into
   1cm (½in) pieces
175–225g (6–8oz) celery, chopped
4 spring onions, chopped, including green part
125ml (4fl oz) natural yoghurt
125ml (4fl oz) homemade Mayonnaise
   (see page 584)
1½ teaspoons curry powder
½ teaspoon freshly ground cumin seeds
150g (5oz) roasted cashew nuts

Garnish
2 tablespoons freshly chopped coriander

Season the chicken with salt and pepper and poach it in the stock for 5–7 minutes, until cooked (see page 276). Drain on a slotted spoon and cut into medium dice.

Mix the chicken with the lemon juice in a large bowl, and season well with salt and pepper. Add the mango, celery and spring onions.

Whisk the yoghurt into the mayonnaise. Toast the cumin seeds in a hot frying pan for a few seconds, add the curry powder and cook for a futher 1–2 seconds. Grind, cool and add to the yoghurt and mayonnaise. Mix and pour over the other ingredients. Toss gently. Taste and correct the seasoning.

Just before serving, add the roasted cashew nuts, scatter with coriander and serve.

Thai Chicken and Coconut Salad

Serves 4–6

1 x 400g (14oz) tin coconut milk (we use the
   Chaokoh brand)
50ml (2fl oz) fish sauce (nam pla)
45g (1³⁄₄oz) palm sugar or pale brown sugar
800g (1³⁄₄lb) organic chicken thighs, boned
4 kaffir lime leaves
2 red shallots or 1 small red onion, very
   finely sliced
1 red pepper, de-seeded and very finely sliced
2 medium Thai chillies, de-seeded and very
   thinly sliced
½–1 cucumber, de-seeded and cut in fine
   julienne strips
25g (1oz) fresh coriander leaves
1 tablespoon peanuts, unsalted and freshly
   roasted (see right)

1 banana leaf or some vine or lettuce leaves
   (optional)
a little sunflower oil

Garnish
fresh mint
coriander leaves
a few whole chillies

Put the coconut milk, fish sauce and palm sugar into a saucepan over a medium heat. Stir until the sugar dissolves. Add the chicken and bring slowly to the boil. Simmer, covered, for 4–5 minutes, then remove from the heat and allow to cool in the covered saucepan. The chicken will continue to cook but will be moist and tender.

Remove the centre rib from the kaffir lime leaves. Roll the leaves into a cigarette shape and slice as finely as humanly possible. Mix the sliced vegetables, shredded lime leaves, fresh coriander and peanuts in a bowl.

Drain the chicken and pour a generous amount of the coconut milk poaching liquid over the vegetables and toss gently. Cut the chicken into 1cm (½in) thick strips and toss gently again. Taste for seasoning.

If you happen to have a banana leaf, cut it into 4–6 large squares and polish with a little sunflower oil. Put on a plate and pile high with chicken salad, alternatively use vine leaves or a bed of lettuce. Drizzle with extra poaching liquid. Garnish with little sprigs of mint and coriander and perhaps a few whole chillies. Serve.

How to Roast Peanuts

Crushed, roasted peanuts are a common seasoning throughout most of south-east Asia. They add a nutty taste, a crunchy texture and protein to a dish. Raw peanuts are sold in every market in this region, usually still covered with their red inner skins.

To roast them at home, put them into an ungreased, well-heated, cast-iron wok or frying-pan over a medium heat. Stir the peanuts around until they are roasted, reducing the heat if necessary. The red skins will turn crisp and papery. When the peanuts have cooled, rub them with both hands and blow the skins away.

To crush them, lightly or finely as required, either whizz them for a few seconds in a clean coffee grinder or, if only a few tablespoons are needed, chop them up with a large knife.

Crispy Chicken Skin with Sweet Chilli Sauce

Don't attempt this unless you have a free-range, organic chicken.

Cut chicken skin into manageable sized pieces and lay it out on a wire rack. Sprinkle with a little sea salt. Cook for 3–4 hours in a fan oven at 50°C/100°F/gas ⅛. The fat will render out and the skin will crisp. Delicious served with a bowl of sweet chilli sauce for dipping.

How to Joint a Chicken (8 Pieces)

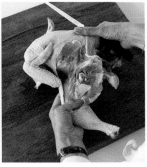

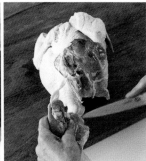

1. Place the chicken on the chopping board with the legs and cavity away from you. Remove the wish bone from the neck end (keep for the stock pot).

2. Turn the chicken around with the legs and cavity towards you. Cut through the loose skin between the left leg and the breast. Push the left leg down with your thumb and upwards with your four fingers to break the ball and socket joint.

3. Turn the bird onto its side and using your thumb as a guide, carefully cut around the oyster piece so that it remains attached to the leg. Ideally remove the drumstick, thigh and oyster in one piece, leaving as little meat as possible on the carcass.

4. Put the leg skin side down on the chopping board. Divide the leg into 2 portions by cutting through the line of fat at the knuckle between the thigh and drumstick. Repeat Steps 2–4 with the right leg.

5. Cut along the edge of the left side of the breastbone to loosen the white meat. Use long sweeping movements to remove the breast in one piece with the wing attached. (Alternatively, use poultry shears to cut through the breastbone and ribs – this adds extra flavour particularly for a casserole).

6. Cut the wing from the breast. If desired, detach the skin from the breast by pulling gently from the flesh. Chop off the pointed wing tips (discard if the chicken has been intensively reared, otherwise use in the stock pot or use for chicken wing recipe). Divide the breast pieces in two. Repeat Steps 5–6 with the right breast.

The chicken is now divided into four pieces of brown meat, four pieces of white meat and two wings. To joint a chicken into just 4 pieces don't separate the drumsticks from the thighs and do not cut the wings from the breasts. The remaining carcass can be used to make stock.

Master Recipe
Shanagarry Chicken Casserole
Serves 4–6

A good chicken casserole, even though it may sound 'old hat', always gets a hearty welcome from my family and friends. Sometimes I make an entire meal in a pot by covering the top with whole peeled potatoes just before it goes into the oven. Pheasant or rabbit may also be used.

1 organic chicken, about 1.8kg (4lb)
a little butter or oil, for sautéeing
350g (12oz) green streaky bacon (blanch it if salty)
450g (1lb) onions (baby onions are nicest)
350g (12oz) carrot, peeled and thickly sliced (if the carrots are small, leave whole, if large, cut in chunks)
sprig of thyme
700ml (1¼ pint) homemade Chicken Stock (see page 36)
Roux (see page 580), optional
Mushroom à la Crème (see page 201), optional

Garnish
1 tablespoon freshly chopped parsley

Preheat the oven to 180C°/350°F/gas 4.

Joint the chicken into 8 pieces (see page 279), season well with salt and pepper. Cut the rind off the bacon (use for stock) and cut the bacon into roughly 1cm (½in) cubes. Heat a little butter or oil in a frying pan and cook the bacon until crisp, remove and transfer to the casserole.

Add the chicken pieces to the pan 2 or 3 at a time and sauté until golden, and then remove to the casserole. Then toss the onion and carrot in the pan to coat them well, adding a little butter if necessary. Remove to the casserole.

De-grease the frying pan and de-glaze with stock, bring to the boil and pour into the casserole. Season well and add thyme. Put

the casserole over a medium heat and bring to a simmering point on top of the stove, then put into the oven for 30–45 minutes. When the chicken is just cooked, pour the whole casserole contents into a clean pan, straining off the cooking liquid. De-grease, and return the de-greased liquid to the casserole and bring to the boil over a high heat. Thicken with a little roux if necessary. Add the meat, carrots and onions back into the casserole and bring to the boil. Taste and correct the seasoning. The casserole is very good served at this point, but it's even more delicious if some Mushroom à la Crème is stirred in as an enrichment. Serve sprinkled with parsley and bubbling hot.

> TIP: Heat control is crucial here, the pan mustn't burn yet it must be hot enough to sauté the chicken. If it is too cool, the chicken pieces will stew rather than sauté and, as a result, the meat may be tough.

Variations
Shanagarry Chicken Casserole with Herb Crust

Follow the Master Recipe. Make half the quantity of the dough for Soda Bread (see page 474). Roll out the dough into 2cm (¾in) thick round and stamp into rounds with a 5cm (2in) cutter. When the casserole is almost cooked remove the lid and cover the top of the stew with slightly overlapping herb scones, brushed with egg wash and sprinkled with a little cheese if you wish. Increase the heat to 230°C/450°F/gas 8 for 10 minutes, then reduce the heat to 200°C/400°F/gas 6 for a further 20 minutes or until the crust is baked.

How to Stuff a Bird

A complementary stuffing not only adds flavour and interest to a roast bird but also helps to make it go a little further and keeps the breast meat moist.

Stuffing is usually based on breadcrumbs, potato or rice, flavoured with herbs and perhaps dried fruit such as apricots or prunes. A little chopped onion is often added but it needs to be sweated first in butter otherwise it may still be slightly raw when the bird is cooked. Chestnut stuffings are much loved, particularly in the UK and in the US. Oysters are added to the Thanksgiving stuffing for the turkey. Turkeys may be stuffed both in the cavity and at the neck (crop) end. Tuck the wing tips underneath the bird to keep the flap of skin in place to enclose the stuffing.

Potato-based stuffing is traditional with goose or duck in Ireland. Apple is sometimes added to cut the richness.

Watchpoint
Many cookery writers caution against putting the stuffing into a bird and suggest that it is safer to cook the stuffing separately in a tin foil parcel or in an ovenproof dish. There is in fact no problem about stuffing a bird provided you follow a few basic food safety rules:

1. Do not over-fill the cavity with stuffing; leave a space between the top of the stuffing and the breast bone to allow the heat to penetrate so that the bird can cook fully.

2. If a frozen bird is being used it should be fully defrosted before being stuffed.

3. Do not put warm stuffing into poultry or a joint of meat unless you plan to cook it immediately. If it is left uncooked, particularly at room temperature, even for a short time, you can provide perfect incubating conditions for bacteria to grow. The Food Safety Authority tell us to assume that poultry (particularly intensively reared birds) will be infected with salmonella so ensure that the birds and the stuffing are fully cooked and there will be no problem.

How to Carve a Chicken or Turkey

Allow the chicken to rest for 10 minutes in a warm place before carving. Put the chicken on a small chopping board, sitting on a tray in order to catch any juices; these may be added to the sauce or gravy later. Each portion of chicken should have some white and dark meat.

1.6kg (3¹/₂lb) chicken will yield 4 portions

 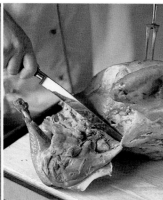  

1. Cut through the skin between the leg and the breast.

2. Turn the bird onto its side, break the ball and socket joint and carefully cut around the oyster piece so that it remains attached to the leg. Ideally remove the drumstick and thigh and oyster in 1 piece.

3. Halve the leg by cutting through the line of fat at the knuckle between the thigh and drumstick. Keep on a warm serving dish or on individual hot plates.

Carve off a generous piece of white meat with the wing still attached and serve with the thigh.

4. Carve the remainder of the white meat into slices and put with the drumstick.

Repeat on the other side.

2–2.2kg (4¹/₂–5lb) chicken will yield 6 portions

Cut off the leg as above. Put the legs skin-side down on the board. Separate the drumstick and thigh by cutting through the line of fat at the knuckle.

Put the thighs skin-side down and further divide the thigh into two pieces by cutting in half along the side of the thigh bone.

Put these three pieces of brown meat on a warm serving dish or separate plates. Carve a generous piece of white meat with the wing attached and combine with the piece of dark meat that has no bone.

Carve the remainder of the white meat into slices and divide between the drumstick and the thigh piece with the bone.

Now each portion has both dark and white meat plus some bone.

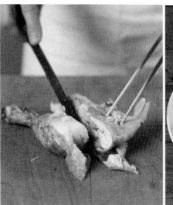 

Casserole Roasting

An excellent cooking method for turkey, chickens, pheasant or even a leg of pork. The joint of meat is cooked whole in the covered casserole with no added liquid. During the cooking process some of the juices escape into the casserole and are flavoured with the herbs or spices. This liquid forms the basis of the sauce.

Master Recipe
Casserole – Roast Chicken with Tarragon
Serves 4–6

There are two kinds of tarragon, French and Russian; we use French because it has the better flavour. Unfortunately, this is more difficult to grow because it is propagated by root cuttings – you can't grow it from seed as you can the Russian tarragon. French tarragon grows to a height of about 23cm (9in) whereas the Russian will grow to about 1.25m (4ft) in summer.

1 organic chicken, about 1.6kg (3½lb)
1 tablespoon freshly chopped French tarragon
  and 1 sprig of tarragon
25g (1oz) butter
150ml (¼ pint) cream
salt and freshly ground pepper
½–1 tablespoon freshly chopped French
  tarragon (for sauce)
150ml (¼ pint) homemade Chicken Stock
  (see page 36), optional
Roux (see page 580), optional

Garnish
sprigs of fresh tarragon

Preheat the oven to 180°C/350°F/gas 4.

Remove the wishbone and keep for the stock. Season the cavity of the chicken with salt and pepper and stuff a sprig of tarragon inside. Mix the chopped tarragon with two-thirds of the butter. Smear the remaining butter over the breast of the chicken, place breast side down in a casserole and allow it to brown slowly over a gentle heat. Turn the chicken breast-side up and smear the tarragon butter over the breast and legs. Season with salt and pepper. Cover the casserole and cook in the oven for 1¼–1½ hours. Remove to a carving dish in a warm oven and allow to rest for 10–15 minutes before carving.

Meanwhile spoon the surplus fat from the juices, add a little freshly chopped tarragon and cream (or just stock, if you prefer*) and boil up the sauce until it thickens slightly. Alternatively bring the liquid to the boil, whisk in just enough roux to thicken the sauce to a light coating consistency. Taste and correct the seasoning.

Carve the chicken, arrange on a serving dish, nap with the sauce and serve.

Note: Some chickens yield less juice than others. If you need more sauce, add a little more homemade Chicken Stock with the cream. If the sauce is thickened with roux this dish can be reheated.

* This dish is also delicious without cream, just using chicken juices, stock and fresh herbs.

TIP: To test if whole birds are cooked, pierce the flesh between the breast and the base of the thigh. This is the last place to cook, so if there is no trace of pink here and if the juices are clear, the chicken is certainly cooked.

Variations
Casserole – Roast Chicken with Marjoram
Substitute annual marjoram for tarragon in the recipe above.

Casserole – Roast Chicken with Rosemary
Substitute 1–2 tablespoons rosemary for tarragon in the Master Recipe.

Casserole – Roast Chicken with Summer Garden Herbs
Substitute 4–6 teaspoons of freshly chopped summer herbs e.g. parsely, thyme, tarragon, chervil, chives etc, for the tarragon in the recipe above.

Casserole – Roast Turkey with Marjoram and Piperonata
Serves 10–12

Provided you have a large enough pot, this is a fantastic way to cook turkey – vary the herbs or mixture of herbs to the season. Ideal for entertaining. There are several varieties of marjoram, the one we use for this recipe is the annual sweet marjoram (Origanum marjorana).

1 organic turkey, 4.4–5.3kg (10–12lb)
110g (4oz) butter
2–3 sprigs of marjoram
4 tablespoons finely chopped marjoram
850ml (1½ pints) light cream
salt and freshly ground pepper
Roux (see page 580), optional

Piperonata (see page 199)

Garnish
sprigs of marjoram

Follow the Master Recipe method, smearing the breast of the turkey with half the butter. Cook in the oven for about 2–2½ hours. Meanwhile, make the Piperonata.

Serve with Piperonata and garnish with sprigs of fresh marjoram.

Note: Use the turkey carcass to make stock, exactly as you would with a chicken.

LEFT: Roast Turkey with Marjoram and Piperonata

Master Recipe
Old-fashioned Roast Turkey with Fresh Herb Stuffing

Serves 10–12

This is my favourite roast stuffed turkey recipe. You may think the stuffing seems dull because it doesn't include exotic-sounding ingredients like chestnuts and spiced sausage meat, but in fact it is moist and full of the flavour of fresh herbs and the turkey juices. Cook a chicken in exactly the same way but use one-quarter of the stuffing quantity given.

1 organic turkey, with neck and giblets
  4.4–5.3kg (10–12lb)
225g (8oz) butter
large square of muslin (optional)

Garnish
large sprigs of fresh parsley or watercress

Fresh Herb Stuffing
350g (12oz) onions, chopped
175g (6oz) butter
400–450g (14–16oz) soft breadcrumbs
50g (2oz) freshly chopped herbs such as
  parsley, thyme, chives, marjoram, savory,
  lemon balm
salt and freshly ground pepper

Preheat the oven to 180°C/350°F/gas 4.

Remove the wishbone from the neck end of the turkey, for ease of carving later. Make a Turkey Stock (see page 36).

Next make the stuffing: sweat the onions gently in the butter until soft, remove from the heat, then stir in the crumbs, herbs and a little salt and pepper to taste. Allow it to get quite cold. If necessary wash and dry the cavity of the bird, then season and half-fill with cold stuffing. Put the remainder of the stuffing into the crop at the neck end.

Weigh the turkey and calculate the cooking time (15 minutes per 450g/1lb and 15 minutes over).

Melt 4 teaspoons of butter and soak a large piece of good quality muslin in the melted butter; cover the turkey completely with the muslin and roast in the oven for 3–3½ hours. There is no need to baste it because of the butter-soaked muslin. The turkey browns beautifully, but if you like it even browner, remove the muslin 10 minutes before the end of the cooking time.

The turkey is cooked when the juices run clear (see tip on page 283). Remove the turkey to a carving dish, keep warm and allow to rest.

Note: Alternatively, smear the breast, legs and crop well with soft butter, and season with salt and freshly ground pepper. If the turkey is not covered with butter-soaked muslin then it is a good idea to cover the whole dish with tin foil. However your turkey will then be semi-steamed, not roasted in the traditional sense of the word.

Present the turkey on your largest serving dish, surrounded by crispy roast potatoes, and garnished with large sprigs of parsley or watercress and maybe a sprig of holly (make sure no one eats the berries!). Serve with Cranberry Sauce (see page 597) and Bread Sauce (see page 594).

How to Prepare a Chicken, Pheasant, Turkey or Guinea Fowl for Roasting

First remove the wishbone from the neck end of the chicken; this isn't at all essential but it does make carving much easier later on. Tuck the wing tips underneath the chicken to make a neat shape. If necessary wash and dry the cavity of the bird, then season and half fill with cold stuffing. Tie a knot around the 'pope's nose' or 'parson's nose' and secure the legs with a bow. Season the breast and legs and smear with a little soft butter or olive oil.

Traditional Roast Chicken with Herb Stuffing and Gravy

Serves 4–6

1 organic chicken, 1.6–2.2kg (3½–5lb)

Stock
giblets, wing tips and wishbone (keep the liver
  for a pâté)
1 sliced carrot
1 sliced onion
1 stick celery
a few parsley stalks and a sprig of thyme

Stuffing
75g (3oz) onion, chopped
45g (1¾oz) butter
75–100g (3–3½oz) soft white breadcrumbs
2 tablespoons finely chopped fresh herbs e.g.
  parsley, lemon thyme, chives and annual
  marjoram
salt and freshly ground pepper

Garnish
large sprigs of fresh parsley or watercress

Follow the Master Recipe.

For the gravy, spoon off the surplus fat from the roasting pan. De-glaze the pan juices with the stock from the giblets and bones. Using a whisk, stir and scrape well to dissolve the caramelised meat juices from the roasting pan. Boil it up well, season and thicken with a little roux if you like. Taste and correct seasoning.

Boning Birds

All birds have a similar anatomy so they are boned in the same way. Sometimes they are partially boned, leaving the leg and wing bones intact to add shape when stuffing is added (this is more usual for small birds). For galantines or ballotines, the bird is boned completely. Choose a bird with the skin intact, so it can be kept whole to use for wrapping.

How to Bone a Chicken or Turkey

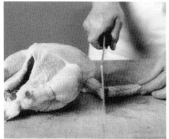
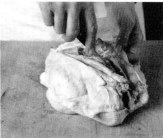

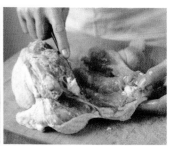

1. Using poultry shears or a Chinese chopper, cut off the wing tip and middle section leaving the largest wing bone. Alternatively, remove the wings altogether, or leave them intact and tuck them underneath the body of the bird later.

2. Put the bird breast side down, on the cutting board. Using a small knife with a pointed blade, slit the skin in a line down the backbone from neck to tail, exposing the backbone.

3. Using your thumb as a guide, cut the flesh and skin away from the carcass, working evenly with short sharp strokes of the knife. After each stroke, carefully ease the flesh and skin away from the carcass, using the fingers of your left hand.

4. Cut the flesh from the saber-shaped bone near the wing. As you reach the ball and socket joints connecting the wing and thigh bones to carcass, sever them. The wing and thigh are thus separated from the carcass but still attached to the skin.

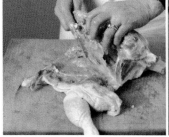

5. Using longer strokes of the knife, continue cutting the breast meat away from the bone until you reach the ridge of the breastbone where skin and bones meet. Take great care not to sever the skin here as it is very thin and close to the tip of the bone. Turn the bird around and repeat on the other side.

6. When the skin and meat have been freed from the carcass on both sides of the bird, they will remain attached to the carcass only along the breastbone. Lift up the carcass of the bird in one hand so that the skin and meat hang loosely from the breastbone.

7. Cut against the ridge of the breastbone to free the skin and flesh from the carcass. Be careful – the skin here is easily pierced or torn. Spread the chicken skin-side down on the cutting board. The bird is partially boned at this point, the wing and leg bones are still in place.

8. For the leg bone: holding the inside end of the thigh bone firmly in the left hand, cut through the tendons attaching the flesh to the bone. Use the knife to scrape the meat from the thigh bone, pushing the meat away from the end of the bone. When you reach the joint between the thigh and drumstick, stop, and start from the other end.

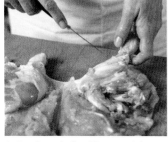

9. Cut through the skin around the claw end of the drumstick, then push the meat up towards the knuckle, loosening inside with your thumb. Be careful of the splinter bone, which runs downwards close to the bone.

10. Then, with the tip of a small sharp knife, cut the meat from around the knuckle joint; using your fingers as a guide, feel whether it is free.

11. Tug the thigh bone and drumstick and they should come out in 1 piece, drawing the skin inside out. Repeat on the other side. Push the skin from the legs and wings right side out. The completely boned bird will now be flat.

12. Season the inside well, and stuff the bird with your chosen stuffing. Re-form the bird into shape, sew up with cotton string, leaving a long piece to make removal easier later, and turn over. If you've kept the wings on, tuck them underneath at the neck end. Roast or casserole-roast as you prefer.

Arlene Hogan's Boned Chicken

Serves 8–10

1 chicken, 1.6–1.8kg (3½–4lb), boned
  (see page 285)

Stuffing
1 onion, chopped
1 garlic clove, crushed
25g (1oz) butter
1 chicken liver, chopped
175g (6oz) sausage meat
finely grated rind of 2 unwaxed lemons
2 tablespoons chopped herbs (parsley,
  tarragon, thyme, chives, marjoram, lemon
  balm)
50g (2oz) breadcrumbs
2 beaten organic eggs
1 dessertspoon brandy (optional)
freshly ground pepper and salt to taste

Gravy
850ml (1½ pints) homemade Chicken Stock
  (see page 36)

Preheat the oven to 200°C/400°F/gas 6.

Make the stuffing: sauté the onion and garlic in the butter, add the chicken liver and toss for 2–3 minutes. Cool. Mix with the other ingredients and bind with half a beaten egg. Fry a little knob of stuffing to test for seasoning.

Stuff the chicken, reshape and roast in the oven for 1¼–1½ hours. Reduce the temperature to 180°C/350°F/gas 4 if it is getting too brown. Allow to rest in a warm place for 10 minutes before carving.

Meanwhile make some Gravy (see page 594). Carefully slice the chicken into 5mm (¼in) thick slices. Serve immediately with chargrilled Mediterranean vegetables.

Variation

Use half the recipe of Duxelle Stuffing (see page 304) instead of the sausage meat stuffing. Add 50g (2oz) breadcrumbs and a beaten egg to the Duxelle.

Crunchy Chicken and Mushroom Filo Pies

Serves 6 as a main course

These pastries can be made in varying sizes as canapés or starters.

Mushroom à la Crème (see page 201)
225g (8oz) ham or bacon, cooked and diced
1 packet filo pastry – use what you need and
  carefully freeze the remainder
350g (12oz) organic chicken, poached and diced
Clarified Butter (see page 105)
organic egg wash

Preheat the oven 200°C/400°F/gas 6.

First make the Mushroom à la Crème. We use half milk and half cream to make a lighter sauce. Add the coarsely chopped cooked ham or bacon and cooked chicken to it. Taste and correct the seasoning of the filling.

Defrost the filo pastry (if necessary) and unfold. Use one sheet to make each pie and serve one pie per person.

To make the parcels: brush the top sheet of filo with melted butter. Put 1–2 tablespoons of the filling in the centre of the sheet, about 6cm (2½in) from the narrow end. Fold the pastry over the filling twice and then fold in one of the edges, roll over and then fold in the other side so there is even thickness of pastry at both sides. Continue to roll over to enclose the filling. Brush with egg wash and melted butter.

To make triangles: cut each sheet in 4 lengthwise, brush each strip with melted butter, put a heaped teaspoon of filling near the end of the strip. Fold over and over from side to side to form a triangle. Brush with melted butter and egg wash.

Bake in the oven for 15–20 minutes depending on size.

Serve with a good green salad and some spicy greens.

Roast Guinea Fowl with Parsnip Crisps and Redcurrant Sauce

Serves 4

The tart bittersweet flavour of the redcurrants is great with guinea fowl. I also love bread sauce with guinea fowl.

1 guinea fowl, 1.5–1.8kg (3½–4lb)
300ml (½ pint) homemade Game or Chicken
  Stock (see page 36)

Stuffing
45g (1½oz) butter
75g (3oz) onions, chopped
65g (scant 2½oz) white breadcrumbs
1 tablespoon freshly chopped herbs (parsley,
  thyme, chives, marjoram)
salt and freshly ground pepper

Parsnip Crisps (see below)
Redcurrant Sauce (see page 598)

4 large sprigs of watercress

Preheat the oven to 190°C/375°F/gas 5.

Eviscerate the guinea fowl if necessary and remove the 'crop' which is at the neck end; wash and dry well.

To make the stuffing: melt the butter and sweat the onions until soft but not coloured, then remove from the heat. Stir in the breadcrumbs and herbs, season with salt and pepper, and taste. Unless you are cooking the bird right away, allow the stuffing to get quite cold before putting it into the bird. Season the cavity with salt and freshly ground pepper and stuff the guinea fowl loosely. Smear the breast and legs with soft or melted butter. Roast in the oven, for about 1¼ hours. Test by pricking the leg at the thickest point: the juices should just run clear (see tip on page 283).

Meanwhile make the Sauce and the Crisps. Put the guinea fowl on a warmed serving dish and keep hot. Spoon off any surplus fat from the pan (keep it for roasting or sautéeing potatoes). De-glaze the pan with stock. Bring it to the boil and use a whisk to dislodge the caramelised juices so they can dissolve into the gravy. Season, taste and boil until you are happy with the flavour.

Carve the guinea fowl into four portions giving each person some brown and white meat. Spoon gravy over the meat. Pile some Parsnip Crisps over the top and garnish with watercress. Serve with Redcurrant Sauce.

Parsnip Crisps
Serves 6–8

We serve these delicious crisps as a garnish for roast pheasant or guinea fowl, on warm salads, and as a topping for parsnip or root vegetable pie.

1 large parsnip
sunflower or groundnut oil, for deep-frying
salt

Heat the oil in a deep fryer to 150°C/300°F. Scrub and peel the parsnips. Either slice into wafer-thin rounds or peel off long slivers lengthways with a swivel top peeler. Allow to dry off on kitchen paper.

Drop a few at a time into the hot oil. They colour and crisp up very quickly. Drain on kitchen paper and sprinkle with salt.

ABOVE: Roast Guinea Fowl with Parsnip Crisps and Redcurrant Sauce

Roast Goose with Potato Stuffing and Bramley Apple Sauce

Serves 8–10

This is one of my favourite winter meals. However, a word of warning! A goose looks enormous because it has a large carcass. Many people have been caught out by imagining that it will serve more people than it does. Allow 450g (1lb) cooked weight per person. This stuffing is also delicious with duck but use one quarter of the quantity given below.

1 organic goose, about 4.5kg (10lb)

Stock
neck, giblets and wishbone of goose
1 onion, sliced
1 carrot, sliced
Bouquet Garni (see page 37)

Potato Stuffing
25g (1oz) butter
450g (1lb) onions, chopped
450g (1lb) cooking apples, e.g. Bramley
  Seedling, peeled and chopped
1 teaspoon each thyme and lemon balm
2–3 tablespoons fresh orange juice
900g (2lb) potatoes
1/4 teaspoon finely grated orange rind
salt and freshly ground pepper

Bramley Apple Sauce (see page 597)

Preheat oven to 180°C/350°F/gas 4.

Combine the stock ingredients in a saucepan, cover with cold water and simmer for 1¹⁄₂–2 hours.

For the stuffing, melt the butter in a heavy saucepan. Add the onions, cover and sweat over a gentle heat for about 5 minutes; add the apples, herbs and orange juice. Cook, covered, until the apples are soft and fluffy.

Meanwhile, boil the potatoes in their skins until cooked, peel, mash and add to the fruit and onion mixture. Add the orange rind and seasoning. Allow it to get quite cold before stuffing the goose.

Season the cavity of the goose with salt and freshly ground pepper and rub a little salt into the skin also. Stuff the goose loosely and roast for about 2 hours in the moderate oven. Prick the thigh at the thickest part; the juices which run out should be clear. If they are still pink, the goose needs a little longer. When cooked, remove the goose to a serving dish and put it in a very low oven while you make the gravy.

To make the gravy, spoon off the surplus fat from the roasting tin (save for sautéeing or roasting potatoes – it keeps for months in a fridge). Add about 600ml (1 pint) of the strained giblet stock to the roasting tin and bring to the boil. Using a small whisk, scrape the tin well to dissolve the meaty deposits which are full of flavour. Taste for seasoning and thicken with a little Roux, if you like. If the gravy is weak, boil it for a few minutes to concentrate the flavour; if it's too strong, add a little water or stock. Strain and serve in a hot gravy boat.

Carve the goose and serve the Bramley Apple Sauce and gravy separately.

Roast Duck with Sage and Onion Stuffing and Red Cabbage

Serves 4

1 organic duck, 1.8kg (4lb)

Sage and Onion Stuffing
35g (1¹⁄₂oz) butter
75g (3oz) onion, finely chopped
1 scant tablespoon finely chopped sage
100g (3¹⁄₂oz) soft white breadcrumbs
salt and freshly ground pepper

Duck Stock
neck and giblets from duck
1 carrot, sliced
1 onion, quartered
bouquet garni (see page 37)

2–3 peppercorns
Red Cabbage (see page 167)
Bramley Apple Sauce (see page 597)

Preheat the oven to 180°C/350°F/gas 4.

To make the stock, put the neck, gizzard, heart and any other trimmings into a saucepan with the carrot and onion cut in quarters. Add the bouquet garni, cover with cold water and add the peppercorns but no salt. Bring slowly to the boil and simmer for 2–3 hours. This will make a delicious stock, which will be the basis of the gravy.

Meanwhile, make the stuffing: heat the butter in a heavy pan, sweat the onion over a gentle heat for 5–10 minutes until soft but not coloured, and add the breadcrumbs and sage. Season with salt and pepper to taste. Unless you plan to cook the duck immediately allow the stuffing to get cold.

When the stuffing is quite cold, season the cavity of the duck and spoon in the stuffing. Truss the duck loosely and roast in a moderate oven for about 1¹⁄₂ hours.

Then cook the Red Cabbage and Bramley Apple Sauce.

When the duck is cooked remove to a serving dish and allow to rest while you make the gravy. De-grease the cooking juices in the pan (keep the duck fat for roast or sauté potatoes). Add stock to the juices, bring to the boil, taste and season if necessary. Strain gravy into a sauceboat. Serve the duck accompanied by the Red Cabbage, gravy, and Bramley Apple Sauce.

Duck Roast with Honey and Rosemary and Salade Composée
Serves 4

We are very fortunate to have Nora Ahearne in the area. She rears the most wonderful free-range duck, geese and turkeys with the most incredible flavour.

1 organic duck, about 1.3–1.8kg (3–4lb)
2 tablespoons honey
2 teaspoons thyme leaves
2 teaspoons rosemary
2 tablespoons shallot or onion, chopped
2 garlic cloves, finely chopped
175ml (6fl oz) homemade Chicken Stock
  (see page 36)
25g (1oz) butter
sea salt and coarsely ground pepper

Salade Composée (see right)
Hazelnut or Walnut Vinaigrette (see right)

Garnish
2 oranges, segmented
sprigs of flat-leaf parsley

Preheat the oven to 180°C/350°F/gas 4.

Brush the duck with the honey. Season generously with sea salt and pepper. Sprinkle on the herbs, shallot and garlic. Roast in the oven for about 1 hour. Baste the duck regularly during cooking; it should develop a rich glaze. Remove the duck to another roasting tin for the remainder of the cooking time (about 30 minutes), reducing the heat to 170°C/325°F/gas 3 if it's browning a little too much.

Meanwhile make the gravy in the original roasting tin: de-grease the roasting pan and de-glaze the caramelised juices with chicken stock. Allow the stock to boil and simmer gently to dissolve the caramelised juices and to reduce slightly. When the duck is fully cooked allow to rest in a warm oven for 10–15 minutes.

Carve into 4 portions and arrange on a hot serving dish. Add the de-greased juices from the carving dish to the gravy. Return to the boil, whisk in the butter and spoon over the duck. Garnish with orange segments and sprigs of flat-leaf parsley or watercress and serve with a Salade Composée.

Salade Composée

8 croûtons of bread (small french stick if possible)
4 tablespoons lardons of bacon
a selection of salad leaves: butterhead, raddichio, cos or Chinese leaves, lambs lettuce, curly endives, watercress, rocket leaves, beet or Swiss chard leaves.
50g (2oz) fine French beans, blanched and refreshed
1–2 oranges, carefully segmented
a little duck fat

Preheat the oven to 180°C/350°F/gas 4.

Brush the croûtons with duck fat and place on a baking tray and cook until golden brown. Blanch the lardons of bacon for 15–20 minutes to remove the excess salt. Dry them and fry in a little sunflower oil until golden and crispy. Remove from pan and keep warm.

Carefully tear the lettuces into bite-sized pieces and toss with the beans in the dressing, until the leaves just glisten. Carve the duck and arrange on individual plates. Arrange some salad next to the duck, and the croûtons and orange segments around the salad. Sprinkle the warm lardons of bacon over the salad and serve immediately.

Hazelnut or Walnut Vinaigrette

2 tablespoons white wine vinegar
2 tablespoons sunflower or peanut oil
4 tablespoons hazelnut or walnut oil
pinch of mustard, salt, pepper and sugar

Combine all the ingredients to make the dressing in a screwtop jar and shake well.

Duck Legs with Onions and Thyme Leaves
Serves 2

This delicious recipe was described to me by John Desmond late one night after a delicious meal in his restaurant on Hare Island, just off Baltimore on the south coast of Ireland.

2 organic duck legs
very little vegetable oil
600g (1¼lb) medium-sized onions, peeled and cut into quarters
¼ teaspoon fresh thyme leaves
sea salt and freshly ground pepper

Garnish
sprigs of fresh thyme

Preheat the oven to 250°C/475°F/gas 9.

Season the duck legs all over with crushed sea salt. Heat a tiny drop of oil in a heavy casserole and cook the duck legs, skin-side down, over a medium heat until well-browned. Then turn and brown on the other side.

Remove the duck legs to a plate, increase the heat, and toss the quartered onions in the duck fat until slightly golden, pouring off some of the fat if there is an excessive amount. Sprinkle with a few thyme leaves and season with salt and freshly ground pepper. Put the duck legs back in on top of the onions, cover, and cook in the oven for 1 hour or until the duck is cooked through and the onions are soft and juicy. Check every now and then.

Serve the duck legs on the bed of onions. Garnish with sprigs of fresh thyme.

Variation
Duck Legs with Turnips
Substitute 900g (2lb) white turnips, peeled and cut into chunks, for the onions in the above recipe. The white turnips will soften and absorb the duck juices. Delicious.

How to Joint a Duck
(and make the most of every little morsel)

1. First remove the wishbone from the neck end.

2. Remove the wings – use these for the stockpot.

3. Remove the legs – roast or use for duck confit.

4. Remove the duck breasts. Tear off the inside fillet and use on a salade tiède.

How to render duck or goose fat
Trim excess fat off the duck breasts and save to render down for duck fat. Remove all the rest of the duck fat from the carcass – particularly the pieces near the tail end inside the carcass. Cut into small pieces and put onto a roasting tin in a low oven 100°C/200°F/gas ¼. The liquid fat will render out slowly, the skin will gradually become crisp and golden. Pour the fat into a stainless steel saucepan or Pyrex bowl.

Note: Save the crispy 'grillons' – in France these delicious morsels are sprinkled over a salad.

Making stock
Finally there is the duck carcass; if you have a cleaver, chop into smaller pieces and use for duck stock. Add the duck wings and giblets (except the liver) and lots of aromatic vegetables and seasoning. Save the duck liver for pâté or for a salade tiède.

Duck Rillettes
In France, I once ate delicious duck rillettes in a restaurant called La Treille in the Dordogne. The chef explained that he used the little pieces of meat from the duck and carcass, which had cooked in the stock. The shredded meat was seasoned with salt, pepper and quatre èpices, and mixed with duck fat and served with hot thin toast. It was absolutely delicious.

How to Pan-grill Duck Breasts – Magret de Canard

Score the fat of the duck breast. Put the duck breast-side down on a cold grill pan. Cook over a low heat for 15–20 minutes on the fat side, and when the fat is thin and crisp, turn over onto the flesh side. The duck breast should be about half cooked by then. Sprinkle with a little salt and continue to cook until it reaches the required degree of doneness – medium to well done is many people's preference. I personally find that rare duck, which was very fashionable when nouvelle cuisine was all the rage, can be unpleasant and tough.

How to Prepare a Duck or Goose for Roasting

First gut the bird if necessary and clean well.

Singe carefully over a gas jet.

Remove the wishbone from the neck end.

Duck: Use a sharp chopper to trim the wings just above the first joint, nearest the body. Chop off the knuckle just above the knee.

Goose: Tuck the wings in close to the body. Legs leave intact.

Season the cavity. Stuff with cold stuffing just before the bird goes into the oven. Truss loosely with cotton string.

Note: It is not absolutely essential to chop off the wings and legs of a duck unless you want a more formal restaurant presentation.

Confit de Canard (Preserved Duck Legs)
Makes 4

Confit is an almost exclusively French way of preserving. First the meat is salted and then it is cooked for a long time, and slowly, in fat. Originally, confit was made to preserve meat, particularly goose and duck, for the winter but nowadays this essentially peasant dish has become very fashionable.

4 duck legs (or 2 legs and 2 breasts, or the
   equivalent amount of goose)
1 garlic clove
1 tablespoon sea salt
1 teaspoon freshly cracked black peppercorns
a few gratings fresh nutmeg
1 teaspoon thyme leaves
1 crumbled bay leaf

900g (2lb) duck or goose fat
1 bay leaf
2 sprigs of thyme
sprigs of parsley
6 garlic cloves, unpeeled

Rub the duck legs all over with a cut clove of garlic. Mix the salt, pepper, nutmeg, thyme and bay leaf together and rub the duck legs with the mixture. Put into an earthenware dish, cover and leave overnight in a cold larder or fridge.

Cut every scrap of fat off the duck carcasses – you will need about 900g (2lb). Render the fat in a low oven, 100°C/200°F/gas ¼, strain and keep aside.

Next day, melt the fat over a low heat in a wide saucepan. Clean the salt cure off the duck legs and put them into the fat – there should be enough to cover the duck pieces. Bring to the boil, add the herbs and garlic and simmer over a low heat until the duck is very tender (about 1–1½ hours – a bamboo skewer should go through the thickest part of the leg with no resistance). Remove the duck legs from the fat. Strain it, leave it to rest for a few minutes and then pour the fat off the meat juices.

When the duck is cold pack it into a sterilised earthenware crock or jar, pour the cool fat over so that the pieces are completely submerged and store in the fridge until needed. (Leave for at least a week to mature. When needed melt the fat to remove the confit.)

Serve hot and crisp on a salad or add to cassoulet (see page 138) or serve simply with thickly sliced potatoes sautéed in duck fat and some Puy Lentils (see below).

Confit of Duck Legs with Puy Lentils
Serves 6 as a main course

6 large duck legs made into confit (see left)

450g (1lb) Puy lentils
1 carrot
1 onion, stuck with 2 cloves
bouquet garni
butter or extra-virgin olive oil
lots of lemon juice, freshly squeezed
2–3 tablespoons freshly chopped herbs (annual
   marjoram or parsley)
sea salt and freshly ground pepper

Garnish
whole garlic cloves and a sprig of rosemary

Preheat the oven to 230°C/450°F/gas 8.

Cook the lentils: put them into a saucepan and cover with cold water. Add the carrot, onion and bouquet garni, bring slowly to the boil, reduce the heat and simmer very gently for 10 minutes, testing regularly. The lentils should be al dente but not hard. Drain. Remove and discard the carrot, onion and bouquet garni. Season the lentils while warm with a good knob of butter or some olive oil, then add lots of lemon juice and the herbs. Season with sea salt and pepper.

Meanwhile, as the lentils are cooking, melt the duck fat and remove the confit. Roast the duck confit in the oven until hot and crisp (15 minutes approximately).

Put a portion of lentils on individual, warmed plates, top with a piece of duck confit. Serve with crispy Pan-roasted Parsnips (see page 175) and coarsely diced Rustic Roast Potatoes (see page 181). Garnish with whole garlic cloves and a sprig of rosemary.

Pan-grilled Duck Breast with Kumquat Compote
Serves 6

4 duck breasts
salt and freshly ground pepper
Kumquat Compote (see page 391)

Garnish
sprigs of fresh rosemary or flat-leaf parsley

First make the compôte.

Score the fat of the duck breasts. Pan-grill over a low heat (see opposite). When cooked season with salt and pepper and transfer to an upturned plate resting on a larger plate. This will catch any juices which may escape and will ensure that the meat is not sitting in a pool of liquid.

Reheat enough kumquat compôte to accompany the duck. Add the duck juices to the Kumquat Compote.

Cut the duck breasts into slices crosswise, and arrange on individual plates with 1–2 tablespoons of kumquat compote. Garnish each with a sprig of rosemary or flat-leaf parsley.

Duck Breast with Spiced Lentils and Caramelised Apples

Serves 4

4 duck breasts
salt and freshly ground pepper
225g (8oz) Puy lentils
1 large or 2 small chillies, finely chopped
2 tablespoons fresh coriander
lemon juice, freshly squeezed
extra-virgin olive oil

Caramelised Apples
2 eating apples (Cox's Orange Pippin or Golden
  Delicious)
25g (1oz) butter
1 tablespoon sugar
juice of 1/2 lemon
1 tablespoon Calvados (optional)

Garnish
sprigs of coriander or flat-leaf parsley

Season the duck breasts and score the fat with a sharp knife. Heat a pan-grill over a high heat; cook the duck fat-side down for 15–20 minutes, depending on thickness. Turn over and continue until fully cooked but still tender and juicy. Reduce the heat and cook on a low heat for 10–15 minutes until the fat is crisp and fully cooked. A lot of fat will run out and you may need to pour some off.

Cook the lentils (see page 142), and prepare the apples. Peel, core and cut into 5mm (1/4in) slices. Melt the butter in a non-stick frying pan, toss in the apple and cook gently for 5 minutes. Add the sugar and allow to caramelise slightly. Add the lemon juice and Calvados. Allow it to become syrupy, then remove from the pan and keep warm.

Heat the lentils and stir in the chilli, coriander, and a squeeze of lemon juice. Season with salt and pepper and some olive oil to taste. Divide the lentils between hot plates, arrange a crispy duck breast on top and garnish with apple, sprigs of coriander or flat-leaf parsley.

LEFT: Duck Breast with Spiced Lentils and
Caramelised Apples

Duck with Orange

Serves 4

1 duck 1.8kg (4lb) in weight
3 brightly coloured oranges
3 tablespoons granulated sugar
60ml (2 1/2fl oz) red wine vinegar
300ml (1/2 pint) Duck or Chicken Stock
  (see page 36)
60ml (2 1/2fl oz) red wine
125ml (4fl oz) Port
1/2–1 tablespoon Grand Marnier
salt, pepper and a few drops of lemon juice

Garnish
sprigs of parsley or watercress

Preheat the oven to 220°C/425°F/gas 7.

Scrub the oranges. Peel the zest from two and cut two thirds into fine julienne strips, blanch and refresh. Season the duck cavity and skin with salt and pepper. Put the remaining one third of the orange peel into the cavity and transfer the duck to the hot oven. After 30 minutes, reduce the temperature to 180°C/350°F/gas 4. Continue to roast for a further 30–45 minutes.

Meanwhile, make a sweet and sour caramel. Boil the sugar and vinegar over a moderately high heat for several minutes until the mixture has turned into a chestnut-brown coloured syrup. Remove from the heat immediately and pour in 150ml (1/4 pint) of the stock. Simmer for a minute, stirring to dissolve the caramel. Then add the rest of the stock, port, wine and juice of one orange. Simmer until the sauce is clear and lightly thickened; add the liqueur little by little. Add the remainder of the orange julienne. Taste, correct the seasoning and sharpen with lemon juice if necessary. Leave aside. Cut the remaining 2 oranges into neat segments and reserve for garnishing.

When the duck is cooked, let it rest in a warm oven for at least 10 minutes before carving. Spoon sauce over the top and garnish with orange segments and herbs.

Duck Tacos

Serves 6

A popular starter in several of my favourite restaurants in Mexico City.

2 organic duck legs, roasted or confit
sea salt and freshly ground pepper
12 small tortillas (see page 493)
Guacamole (see page 593)
1 onion, finely chopped
fresh coriander, chopped

Preheat the oven to 180°C/350°F/gas 4.

Wrap the tortillas in silver foil and warm in the oven for about 10 minutes. Remove the hot meat and crispy skin from the bone and chop into small pieces. Season with sea salt and freshly ground pepper. Place in a communal bowl in the centre of the table with tortillas (wrapped in a cotton napkin to keep them warm), and bowls of guacamole, onion and coriander as accompaniments. Each diner can roll their own tacos to their liking.

lamb

lamb

Easter Sunday at Ballymaloe would never be complete without a succulent roast leg of spring lamb, served with a mint sauce made from the very first tender leaves of the new season's mint.

Our local butcher provides us with the most delicious lamb. He buys his animals on the hoof from local farmers and keeps them on his own pasture until he deems them ready for slaughter. He hangs his lamb for a week or more and then brings it out to Ballymaloe. We usually buy the whole carcass and use every scrap in a variety of dishes.

Lamb, Hogget and Mutton
Spring lamb is approximately five months old and is in season for just a few weeks over Easter. From then on up until Chrismas, it is referred to as lamb. After Christmas, until the following Easter, it's called hogget. Mutton is two years old and has a distinctive flavour.

Ballymaloe is one of the few places where one finds hogget identified on a menu. It has a more pronounced flavour than lamb and, although you can roast it in the normal way, we find it responds particularly well to slow roasting or braising with the first of the wild garlic or winter vegetables. Mutton is stronger in flavour than hogget or lamb. It can be marginally tougher than lamb, if not cooked with care, but it has a wonderful if slightly more mature flavour. It is becoming increasingly rare in Ireland to find mutton, as most farmers can not afford to keep their lambs out at pasture for so long.

Breeds to Look For
Most sheep are grass fed; and the fine quality of Ireland's sweet, green grass is reflected in the excellent flavour of our lamb.

Mountain lamb is at long last getting the recognition that it deserves. It tends to be leaner than some of the other lowland breeds, and living on hilly pastures, they have access to a variety of grasses, heather, wild herbs and flowers on the hills, which give the meat a unique and delicious flavour. Lamb from the hills of Connemara, Wicklow, West Cork, Kerry and Donegal is now particularly sought after in Ireland.

Nowadays there is also a growing interest in rare breeds of lamb among chefs and other discerning consumers. In the UK, in the upland areas and the fells, there are superb Swaledale and Herdwick sheep. Many rare breed farmers have realised that there is a growing market for this type of lamb and now target the public directly and sell their meat through farmers' markets. They also understand the value of highlighting the name of the breeds, so look out for them – and if you've never tasted a rare breed, you really should. The meat might not be as lean as other breeds, but the flavour is distinctive and full of character.

Traceability
Supermarkets and independent butchers have responded to recent health scares and customer concerns by putting traceability schemes into operation and by identifying the source of their meat.

When I buy a joint of meat, I like to know where it's come from and how the animal has been reared. Fortunately for us, we have a very good and trustworthy local butcher, who has all the answers to my questions. Butchers who build up a bond of trust with their consumers by knowing the provenance of their meat, and by guaranteeing that it is both hormone- and antibiotic-free, are at a distinct advantage – they soon build up a loyal customer base.

Uses and Cooking

Unlike beef, every part of the lamb carcass can be roasted – from the shoulder down to the leg. The **neck** has lots of bone and is normally added to a stew together with, what we call here in Ireland, **rack chops**. These are chops from the shoulder and are known in the UK as **gigot chops**. Ask your butcher to cut them at least 2.5cm (1in) thick because if they are too thin there's a tendency for the meat to toughen a little bit during cooking.

The **shoulder** is less expensive than the leg or loin. It is most often used for stews or curries, but is absolutely delicious slow roasted. It's a bit more difficult to carve but the bone in the shoulder gives it extra sweetness and flavour. It has a little more fat but this merely enhances the flavour and adds succulence. Scrape up all the little gungy bits of caramelised sediment in the roasting pan to make delicious gravy. Slow-roasted shoulder of lamb with rosemary or coriander with a sprinkling of sea salt is, without a doubt, one of my favourite meals. One can also bone the shoulder and roll it up with your favourite stuffing or some gutsy tapenade. Or simply tie it up, pop a spot of rosemary and garlic on top and then roast it.

All of the loin – both the **centre loin** (where the chops have a T-bone) and the **side loin** (the cutlets) – can be roasted, pan-grilled, fried or sautéed. The end part, or '**breast of lamb**', can be cut into pieces, dipped in flour, egg and crumbs and made into little **epigrams** which are then roasted until beautifully plump and crispy. Alternatively, make lamb **riblets** by cutting the breast into thin slices with the bone still in. These can be marinated using one of the marinades in the barbecue chapter, or bought ready-marinated from many butchers, and simply roasted at home with no further fuss.

To prepare a **rack of lamb**, you'll need to buy the side loin – the part of the loin with the cutlet bones in it (ribs). Two prepared racks can be interlinked to create a '**guard of honour**' (see page 299) which is guaranteed to impress your guests. Even though it looks quite elaborate, it's easy to carve. Don't get too carried away when trimming the end of the cutlets. Nowadays posh restaurants seem to leave just the bare eye of the cutlet, and cut off the lovely streaky bit along the bone. Ironically, the more they trim off, the more they charge for it. It's a pity to lose all of that because it is sweet, juicy and good.

For a simple dinner, you can cut between the bones for lamb cutlets, but for an extra special dinner party, it's worth making a **crown roast of lamb**. When you're preparing the rack of lamb, follow the images on page 298 carefully. Saw along the top of the ribs where they meet the chine bone, then run your knife underneath the bone and lift it off. When it is cooked, you'll be able to carve through between the cutlets unimpeded.

The **leg** can, of course, be roasted whole, or cut into two joints. One can also barbecue or chargrill big thick, juicy steaks from the leg or use chunks of it in stews and curries – we like to use it in our Mild Madras Curry. **Lamb shanks**, cut from the front leg, are very fashionable today as people have discovered how succulent they are. Shanks are less expensive than many other cuts and are great for gutsy stews. They become meltingly tender with long, slow cooking. The meat should almost fall off the bone.

Saddle of Lamb and How to Prepare It

A saddle of lamb consists of both loins of the lamb, attached at the backbone, in the same way as a baron of beef.

First remove the papery outer skin with a small sharp knife. If the meat is well-chilled it should be possible to lift a corner of the skin and tug sharply to peel off. Trim off any excess fat from the edges of the saddle, but leave the back fat. Tuck the flaps underneath the saddle. Cut off the kidneys but keep them (they can be attached to the end of the saddle with wooden skewers 30 minutes before the end of the roasting time and roasted). With a sharp knife score the back fat all over in a fine criss-cross pattern.

To Prepare a Rack of Lamb or Lamb Cutlets

Chill the meat well first. Skin the best end: side loin or rack, lift a corner of the skin from the neck end with a small knife, hold it firmly and peel it off (use a cloth to get a good grip). Chine if the butcher has not already done so; this means to saw carefully through the chine bone (or spine) just where it meets the rib bones. Take care not to saw right through into the eye of the meat. Now remove the chine bone completely. Chop off the cutlet bones so that the length of the remaining bones is not more than twice the length of the eye of the meat. Remove the half-moon shaped piece of flexible cartilage found between the layers of fat and meat at the thicker end of the best end. This is the tip of the shoulder blade. It is simple to work out with a knife and your fingers.

If thin small cutlets are required cut between each bone as evenly as possible, splitting the rack into six or seven small cutlets. If thicker cutlets are required carefully ease out every other rib bone, then cut between the remaining bones into thick cutlets. Now trim the fat from the thick end of each cutlet, and scrape the rib bones free of any flesh or skin.

Epigrams

Cut off half the streaky meat at the end of the bones in one piece. Clean all the fat and scraps of meat off the bones, score the back fat. Use for epigrams.

Noisettes of Lamb

These are boneless cutlets, tied into a neat round shape with a string. They are made from the loin of best end. To prepare, first skin the meat: lift a corner of the skin with a small knife, holding it firmly (using a cloth to get a good grip), and pull it off or else trim off neatly with the knife. Now remove first the chine bone and then all the rib bones, easing them out with a short sharp knife.

Trim off most of the fat from the meat. Roll it up tightly, starting at the meaty thick side and working towards the thin flap. Tie the roll neatly with separate pieces of cotton string tied at 4cm (1½in) intervals. Trim the ragged ends of the roll to neaten them. Chill well, then cut the roll into slices, cutting accurately between each string. The average best end will give 4 good noisettes. The string from each noisette is removed after cooking. Noisettes are often served on a croûton of fried bread or a potato galette.

Crown Roast

Two racks (side loin) are needed. For a more impressive roast use three. Each side loin is prepared in the same way as for roast rack of lamb but the bones are left slightly longer. It is skinned, chined and the shoulder cartilage is removed. All fat is removed and the top 2.5–5cm (1–2in) of the bones are scraped in the same way.

Bend each best end into a semi-circle, with the fatty side of the ribs inside. To facilitate this it may be necessary to cut through the membrane about 2.5cm (1in), between each cutlet, from the thick end. Be careful not to cut into the fleshy part of the meat.

With fine cotton string sew the end of the racks together to make a circle with the meaty part forming the base of the crown. Tie a piece of string round the waist of the crown. Traditionally crown roast is stuffed, but this can result in undercooked inside fat unless it is completely trimmed before cooking.

Guard of Honour

Prepare 2 best end racks or side loins exactly as for the crown roast. Score the fat in a criss-cross pattern.

Hold the 2 best ends 1 in each hand facing each other with the meaty part of the racks on the board, and the fatty sides on the outside. Adjust them so the rib bones interlock and cross at the top.

Tie with cotton string in several places. Stuff the arch if required. Serve with cutlet frills on top of each bone for extra posh or retro look.

Lamb Roast with Rosemary and Garlic
Serves 8–10

Rosemary survives year round even in colder gardens. Spike your leg of lamb with this pungent herb and garlic – delicious hot, warm or at room temperature on a buffet. Loin of lamb, shoulder or rump may be cooked in the same way.

1 leg of lamb, 2.6–3.1kg (6–7lb)
4–5 garlic cloves
2 sprigs of rosemary
salt and freshly ground pepper
Gravy (see overleaf)
600ml (1 pint) stock, preferably homemade
   Lamb Stock (see page 36)
Roux (see page 580), optional

Preheat the oven to 180°C/350°F/gas 4.

Choose a good leg of lamb with a thin layer of fat. Ask the butcher to trim the knuckle and remove the aitch bone for ease of carving later, otherwise prepare it as on page 300. With the point of a sharp knife or skewer, make deep holes all over the lamb, about 2.5cm (1in) apart. It is a good idea not to do this on the underside of the joint, in case somebody insists on eating their lamb unflavoured.

Divide the rosemary sprigs into tufts of 3 or 4 leaves together. Peel the garlic cloves and cut them into little spikes about the same size as a matchstick broken into 3.

Stick a spike of garlic with a tuft of rosemary into each hole in the lamb. Cover and refrigerate for 1–2 hours if you have time. Alternatively, cook immediately.

Sprinkle the joint with salt and pepper and put it into a roasting tin in the oven.

Cook for a good 1 hour more for rare lamb, 1½ hours for medium and 1¾ hours for well done. Remove the joint to a serving dish and allow it to rest while you make the gravy.

Gravy

Spoon the fat off the roasting tin. Pour the stock into the cooking juices remaining in the tin. Boil for a few minutes, stirring and scraping the pan well, to dissolve the caramelised meat juices (I find a small whisk ideal for this). Thicken with a very little Roux if you like (see page 580).

Taste and add salt and pepper if necessary. Strain and serve the gravy separately in a gravy boat. Serve with Roast Potatoes (see page 181).

Variations

Roast Leg of Lamb with Marjoram and Garlic
Follow the Master Recipe but substitute little tufts of marjoram for rosemary.

Lamb Roast with Thyme and Garlic
Follow the Master Recipe but substitute little sprigs of thyme for rosemary.

Lamb Roast with Coriander Seeds
Follow the Master Recipe but omit the rosemary and substitute 2 tablespoons of coriander seeds. Insert garlic with a few seeds warmed in a pan and then crushed in a pestle and mortar. Drizzle the lamb with extra-virgin olive oil before roasting. Add 1 tablespoon freshly ground coriander to the gravy.

Lamb Roast with Cumin
Follow as for Lamb Roast with Coriander seeds but substitute freshly ground cumin for coriander. Alternatively mix cumin and coriander.

How to Prepare a Leg of Lamb for Roasting

Trimming the shank end of the leg is merely for appearance but the removal of the pelvic bone is essential because it makes carving so much easier. Your butcher may well do it for you but, armed with a sharp knife, it only takes a few minutes to do at home.

The pelvic bone is made up of the aitch bone and the hip bone. Because it is an irregular shaped bone at an angle to the leg bone, it makes carving difficult. It is attached by a ball and socket joint.

Place the leg of lamb on a chopping board, skin side down. Trace the outline of the bone with a sharp knife; cut deeper around the pelvic bone keeping the knife as close to the bone as possible. Free all the bones and then loosen and separate the ball and socket joint. Use this bone and the shank end to make a little stock for gravy.

To Trim the Shank End

Saw through the bone just above the knuckle. Trim the meat off the end of the bone. Add to the stockpot and cook for about 1½ minutes. In cooking, the meat will shrink a little further and leave the end of the bone exposed. A paper frill may be slipped over the end of the bone when serving.

Lamb Shanks

Lamb shanks come from the shoulder but one can also use the end of the leg joint. The latter take a shorter time to cook because they are less muscular.

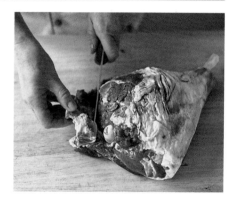

Removing the aitch bone for ease of carving.

Trimming the shank end of the leg with a saw.

Lamb shanks come from the foreleg or shoulder.

Lamb Roast with Garden Herbs

Serves: an average-weight leg of lamb 3.1–3.6 kg (7–8lb) will serve 8–10 people. Allow about 175g (6oz) per person.

I like to tie a little bunch of herbs onto the end of the bone just before I bring the roast to the table for carving.

1 leg of lamb, 2.6–3.1kg (6–7lb)

Herb Marinade
3 large garlic cloves
35g (1½oz) herbs (parsley, thyme, lemon balm, mint, tarragon, chives, rosemary and marjoram*), chopped
125–225ml (4–8fl oz) extra-virgin olive oil
salt and freshly ground pepper

Gravy
600ml (1 pint) homemade Lamb or Chicken Stock (see page 36)
2 teaspoons freshly chopped herbs, as above
Roux (see page 580)
25g (1oz) butter (optional)
salt and freshly ground pepper

*If you don't have access to such variety, use whatever fresh herbs you have e.g. parsley, chives, thyme and mint.

Preheat the oven to 180°C/350°F/gas 4.

First make the herb relish: peel and crush the garlic cloves and put them with the olive oil, salt and pepper and fresh herbs into a food processor and whizz for about 1 minute or until it becomes a soft green paste. Alternatively mix in a little bowl.

If possible remove the aitch bone from the top of the leg of lamb so that it will be easier to carve later, then trim the end of the leg. Score the fat lightly, rub in the herb mixture and leave to marinate for several hours if possible.

Roast for a good 1 hour for rare, 1½ hours for medium and 1¾ hours for well done meat. When the lamb is cooked, remove the joint to a carving dish. Rest the lamb for 10 minutes before carving.

To make the gravy: de-grease the juices in the roasting tin, add the stock, bring to the boil and thicken with a little Roux if desired. Just before serving, whisk in some knobs of butter to enrich the gravy. Taste for seasoning and add salt and pepper if necessary.

Serve with Ulster Champ (see page 183) and Oven-roasted Tomatoes (see page 188) **or** Chargrilled Peppers (see page 191) and Gratin Dauphinois (see page 186).

Roast Shoulder of Lamb with Tapenade

Serves 16–20

Monique Avril (wife of the vigneron Paul Avril) showed me how to make this delicious Provençal recipe on a sunny afternoon in Châteauneuf du Pape. You will need cotton string.

1 shoulder of lamb, 3.6kg (8lb) with bones and 3.1kg (7lb) without bones. Two small shoulders are even better.

Tapenade
175g (6oz) black olives, stoned
2 large garlic cloves, peeled and chopped
2 anchovies
2 tablespoons extra-virgin olive oil

Gravy
850ml (1½ pints) homemade Lamb or Chicken Stock (see page 36)

Preheat the oven to 180°C/350°F/gas 4.

Ask your butcher to bone the shoulder of lamb for you or do it yourself. Use the bones to make stock for the gravy.

To make the tapenade: put the olives, garlic, anchovies and olive oil into a food processor and whizz for a few seconds – just long enough to chop the olives fairly coarsely – it shouldn't be a purée.

Score the skin of the lamb lightly then put the meat skin side down on your worktop. Remove surplus fat from the inside, spread the olive mixture over the lamb and roll lengthways, tying at regular intervals with string. Sprinkle lightly with salt and roast in the oven, for about 1¼ hours. This will produce lamb with a faint pink tinge.

Remove to a carving dish and allow to rest while you make the gravy in the usual way (see page 594). Carve at the table and serve with a little gravy, some chargrilled vegetables and Rustic Roast Potatoes (see page 181).

Butterflied Leg of Lamb with Spices

Serves 8–10

1 leg of lamb, 2.2–2.6kg (5–6lb)

Marinade
2 teaspoons cumin seeds
1 teaspoon black peppercorns
1 teaspoon cardamom seeds
½ teaspoon chilli powder (optional)
1 teaspoon salt
5 tablespoons extra-virgin olive oil
1 tablespoon balsamic or wine vinegar or sherry
3 garlic cloves, peeled and crushed

Follow the instructions to butterfly the lamb (see right).

Thick pieces of meat may be slightly opened out by slitting part of the way with a sharp knife. It is not necessary to get the meat all the same thickness – one of the attractions of this dish is that it provides a mixture of well done and underdone pieces of meat. Remove any excess fat.

Roast the cumin seeds in a pan over a medium heat for 1–2 minutes and add the peppercorns and cardamom seeds. Remove from the heat and crush coarsely in a pestle and mortar. Mix the other marinade ingredients together in a bowl and add the ground spices. Put the lamb inside a large plastic bag and pour over the marinade; knot the end tightly. Leave in the fridge for 24 hours, turning from time to time.

Preheat the oven to 200°C/400°F/gas 6 and cook the lamb for 1–1½ hours, basting with marinade every 10 minutes. Rest the meat for 15–20 minutes before carving.

If you prefer to barbecue the lamb, light the barbecue and allow it to reach full heat. It's difficult to give a time for this – barbecues vary so much. Drain the lamb and arrange the rack at least 25.5cm (10in) from the coals, otherwise the inside will be raw while the outside is charred. It will take about 45 minutes to cook. Baste the lamb with marinade regularly during cooking.

Rest the meat for 15–20 minutes before carving.

Serve with crusty potatoes, a good green salad and maybe Apple and Mint Jelly (see page 507), Ballymaloe Country Relish or Apple and Tomato Chutney (see page 512).

How to Butterfly a Leg of Lamb

If the leg has already been boned, simply cut open from top to bottom and lay flat – it will roughly resemble the shape of a butterfly hence the name. Alternatively cut down along the leg and shank bone on the underside and carefully remove.

Open out the lamb as below. You will need to make a few further cuts to allow the lamb to lie flat on the board.

Boiled Mutton or Hogget with Caper Sauce

Serves 6–8

The correct terms for lamb go like this: spring lamb from Easter, then from Easter until Christmas it is lamb, and from Christmas until the following Easter it should be known as hogget. Mutton is from an older animal, and difficult to find these days.

This is a wonderful dish for a cold winter's evening. Ballymaloe House is one of the few places where hogget is on the menu – often braised with winter vegetables or wild garlic.

1 x 3kg (6½lb) leg of mutton or hogget
3 onions, peeled and halved
4–5 carrots, halved if large
2 sticks of celery, halved
6 peppercorns
sprig of thyme
1 bay leaf
salt and freshly ground pepper

Caper Sauce
25g (1oz) butter
1 tablespoon plain white flour
600ml (1 pint) milk
2 tablespoons capers, chopped
1 tablespoon chopped parsley (optional)

Ask your butcher to cut the leg at the shank end. Put the meat into a saucepan just large enough to fit it nicely. Cover with water, add a good sprinkle of salt and bring to the boil. Remove any scum that rises to the surface.

Add the vegetables and bay leaves. Cover the pan and simmer very gently. Allow 30 minutes for every 450g (1lb) plus 25 minutes.

Meanwhile make the Caper Sauce. Melt the butter in a saucepan, stir in the flour and cook for a minute or two.

Gradually mix in the milk, bring to the boil and simmer for 4–5 minutes. Season with salt and pepper and put aside.

Just before serving add 150ml (¼ pint) of de-greased broth from the saucepan to the sauce. Bring back to the boil, and add the roughly chopped capers and parsley. Taste and correct the seasoning.

Carve the meat into slices at the table and serve with Caper Sauce.

Lamb Cutlets with Tarragon Vinegar
Serves 4

A delicious simple dish. Sherry vinegar may be substituted for tarragon vinegar here.

8 lamb cutlets
salt and freshly ground pepper
25g (1oz) butter
50g (2oz) shallots, finely chopped
2 tablespoons tarragon vinegar
150ml (5fl oz) cream
sprigs of fresh tarragon

Ask your butcher to prepare the cutlets for you, leaving only the eye of the meat on the bone or just a little of the streaky part. Season them with salt and pepper.

Heat a cast-iron pan over a high heat. Add the butter and when foaming add the cutlets and cook until brown on both sides but still pink in the centre – you may need to cook them in 2 batches depending on the size of the frying pan. Put the lamb to rest on a plate and keep warm.

Add the shallots to the pan and toss for 1–2 minutes. Add the vinegar carefully; it will probably flame. Allow the fumes to burn off and then pour in the cream, allowing it to bubble for 1–2 minutes; taste and correct the seasoning. Spoon the sauce over the cutlets and serve immediately with sprigs of fresh tarragon. French beans or young broad beans go well.

Saddle of Lamb Chops with Three Sauces
Pan-grill the saddle lamb chops and serve with three sauces. Choose from Ballymaloe Mint Sauce (see page 594), Onion Sauce (see page 581) and Redcurrant Jelly or Sauce (see page 508 or 598 respectively).

Epigrams
Cheap and absolutely delicious. Remove the streaky part of the loin of lamb in one piece. Score the fat side and cut into strips about 8cm (3in) wide. Dip into flour, then beaten egg and then breadcrumbs. Roast in a hot oven, 200°C/400°F/gas 6, for 40–45 minutes.

BELOW: Butterflied Leg of Lamb with Spices

Master Recipe
Roast Loin of Lamb with Duxelle Stuffing and Mint Sauce
Serves 10–12

Irish lamb is still remarkably sweet and for the most part naturally reared. No lamb I've tasted on any of the starred restaurant menus on the continent could equal the flavour of the lamb I buy from my local butcher who rears his animals on rich old pastures full of wild flowers and herbs. There are still many conscientious butchers around the country so search them out and support them.

1 whole loin of lamb, about 2.8kg (6½lb).
    Allow 175–225g (6–8oz) boned loin per
    person
salt and freshly ground pepper

Duxelle Stuffing
110g (4oz) butter
225g (8oz) onion, chopped
450g (1lb) mushrooms, chopped
450g (1lb) cooked ham or bacon, chopped
2 tablespoons freshly chopped parsley, chives
    and fresh thyme leaves, mixed
salt and freshly ground pepper

Gravy
600ml (1 pint) homemade Lamb or Chicken
    Stock (see page 36)
Roux (see page 580)
1 tablespoon freshly chopped herbs (chives,
    thyme and parsley)

Preheat the oven to 180°C/350°F/gas 4.

First make the stuffing: melt the butter in a heavy saucepan on a low heat and add the onions. Sweat on a gentle heat until soft, about 6–8 minutes. Increase the heat, add the mushrooms, season with salt and pepper, and cook for 2–3 minutes until just tender. Add the ham and herbs. Taste and check seasoning. Allow the mixture to cool before stuffing the loin of lamb.

Bone the loin of lamb and put the bones into a saucepan with a few aromatic vegetables and a bouquet garni. Bring to the boil and simmer for a few hours to make a little stock for the gravy. Lightly score the fat side of the meat, turn over and trim off the excess flap (keep to make Epigrams, see page 303). Sprinkle the joint with salt and pepper. Spread the stuffing on the boned side and roll up like a Swiss roll. Tie with cotton string.

Roast for about 1½ hours. When the loin is cooked, remove from the roasting pan, place on a serving dish and keep warm.

To make the gravy: de-grease the roasting tin and de-glaze with the stock. Allow the stock to boil for a few minutes. Whisk in a little roux if a slightly thicker gravy is preferred. Season with salt and pepper and, if you have them, add a sprinkling of freshly chopped herbs.

Serve with Ballymaloe Mint Sauce (see page 594) or Apple and Mint Jelly (see page 507).

Lamb Chops Duxelle
Even a few simple lamb chops can be made into a feast with the Duxelle Stuffing from the Master Recipe. Preheat the oven to 200°C/400°F/gas 6. Cut a pocket in the eye of the chops, fill with a generous teaspoonful of Duxelle Stuffing. Dip the chops first in seasoned flour then in beaten egg and then in breadcrumbs. Bake on an oiled baking sheet in the oven for 25–30 minutes.

Braised Lamb Shanks with Garlic, Rosemary and Flageolet Beans
Serves 4

Antony Worrall Thompson cooked me lamb shanks when he came to teach at the school – a really gutsy, comforting dish.

4 lamb shanks, about 1.1kg (2½lb)
8 small sprigs of rosemary
8 slivers garlic
4 anchovy fillets, halved
salt and freshly ground pepper

Braising Ingredients
25g (1oz) goose or duck fat or olive oil
2 carrots, roughly chopped
2 celery stalks, roughly chopped
1 leek, roughly chopped
1 onion, roughly chopped
1 head garlic, halved horizontally
½ bottle good red wine
150ml (¼ pint) homemade Chicken or Lamb
    Stock (see page 36)
sprig of thyme
2 sprigs of rosemary
2 bay leaves
2 strips of dried orange peel

Sauce
2 tablespoons extra-virgin olive oil
110g (4oz) streaky bacon, cut into lardons and
    blanched
110g (4oz) carrot, finely diced
110g (4oz) celery stalk, finely diced
110g (4oz) onion, finely diced
6 garlic cloves
4 very ripe tomatoes, peeled and diced or
    200g (7oz) tinned tomatoes plus juice
2 sprigs of thyme
leaves from 2 sprigs of rosemary, chopped
1 x 400g (14oz) tin flageolet beans, drained or
    110–200g (4–7oz) dried flageolet beans,
    soaked overnight and then boiled rapidly for
    20 minutes
150ml (¼ pint) homemade Chicken or Lamb
    Stock (see page 36)

Garnish
sprigs of rosemary and thyme

Preheat the oven to 150°C/300°F/gas 2.

Remove most of the fat from each shank, then scrape the meat away from the bone to loosen it. Make 2 deep incisions in each joint and insert a sprig of rosemary and a sliver of garlic wrapped in half an anchovy fillet into each incision. Season the meat with salt and pepper. Heat the goose fat or olive oil in a heavy sauté pan or casserole and sauté the meat in it until well-browned on all sides. Remove the meat from the pan.

ABOVE: Braised Lamb Shanks with Garlic,
Rosemary and Flageolet Beans

Master Recipe
Roast Rack of Spring Lamb with Three Sauces

Serves 4–6

We use grass-fed lamb from our butcher, who buys his animals on the hoof from local farmers. He is our vital link with safe food because he knows on what the animals are fed and how they are reared.

2 racks of spring lamb (6 cutlets each, most
  butchers will prepare it for you)
salt and freshly ground pepper

Accompaniment
Fresh Mint Chutney (see page 594)
Onion Sauce (see page 581)
Redcurrant Sauce (see page 598)

Garnish
little sprigs of fresh mint

Preheat the oven to 220°C/425°F/gas 7.

Prepare the racks of lamb (see page 298). Remove the skin and score the fat. Refrigerate until needed.

Sprinkle the racks of lamb with salt and freshly ground pepper. Roast fat side upwards for 25–30 minutes depending on the age of the lamb and how well done you want it to be. When cooked, remove to a warm serving dish. Turn off the oven and allow the lamb to rest for 5–10 minutes before carving so that the juices re-distribute evenly through the meat.

Carve the lamb into cutlets, allowing 2–3 per person depending on size. Serve with fresh Mint Chutney, Onion Sauce and Redcurrant Sauce and lots of Rustic Roast Potatoes (see page 181).

Add the carrots, celery, leek, onion and garlic and cook over a high heat until well-browned. Add the red wine and bring to the boil and stir for 1–2 minutes. Add the stock, herbs and orange peel, then place the lamb shanks on top. Cover and cook in the oven for 2¼ hours.

Meanwhile, make the sauce: heat the olive oil in a saucepan and brown the bacon in it. Then reduce the heat and add the carrot, celery, onion and garlic and cook for about 8 minutes or until the vegetables have softened. Add the tomatoes, herbs, flageolets and enough stock to half-cover the beans. Cover and simmer for ½–1 hour.

When the lamb has finished cooking, remove the thyme, bay leaves and orange peel. Taste and correct seasoning. Serve in a hot, deep dish with the beans and vegetables poured over and around. Garnish with sprigs of fresh rosemary and thyme. Serve with Fluffy Mashed Potato (see page 182).

Stewing

Stewing involves long, slow, gentle cooking in a covered, heavy saucepan or casserole. It's worth remembering the old saying 'a stew boiled is a stew spoiled'. If a stew is allowed to boil fast for even a short time the protein and gelatine in the meat harden and the meat becomes tough and chewy rather than meltingly tender.

Less prime cuts are best for stewing. Meat should be well-trimmed of all fat and gristle. Cut into cubes up to 5cm (2in) in size, but certainly not smaller than 2.5cm (1in). Beef should be cut into larger cubes because it needs a particularly long, slow cooking. The meat is often tossed in well-seasoned flour and then quickly sealed in a hot pan; this adds another layer of flavour and helps to thicken and enhance the colour of the gravy.

Vegetables (such as onions and carrots) are cooked with the stew. Celery and cubes of root vegetables help to flavour and bulk up the stew. Fresh herbs, chilli and spices add excitement to the flavour.

The liquid can be water or stock, and occasionally tinned tomatoes and their juices are added. A proportion of red or white wine may also be added. White stews or blanquettes may be made from veal or pork – onions, leeks or mushrooms are added but no carrots. A blanquette of veal would be enriched with a liaison of egg yolk and cream at the end of cooking.

Every country has its stews – France has its ragoûts, navarins and daubes, Hungary has its famous goulash, Morocco its tagines, and Greece the estoufado. Some cooks add freshly cooked vegetables at the end of cooking, such as French beans or broccoli. In our experience it is best not to add mushrooms to the stew at the beginning – they can become bitter and dark with long, slow cooking. Add them to the stew close to the end of cooking in the form of sautéed, sliced mushrooms or Mushroom à la Crème (see page 201).

Stews may be cooked on a very gentle heat on top of the stove. Use a heat diffuser mat or cook in a low oven. Bring to boiling point on top of the stove before transferring to the oven. Stews usually improve in flavour if kept for a day or two.

Ballymaloe Irish Stew
Serves 4–6

Best in early summer, made with young lamb and new season's carrots and onions.

1.3kg (3lb) lamb chops not less than 2.5cm (1in) thick
6 medium or 12 baby onions
6 medium or 12 baby carrots
8–12 potatoes or more if you like (Golden Wonder or Kerr's Pink are excellent)
850ml (1½ pints) Stock (Lamb Stock if possible, see page 37) or water
sprig of thyme
about 1 tablespoon Roux (see page 580), optional

Garnish
1 tablespoon freshly chopped parsley
1 tablespoon freshly chopped chives

Preheat the oven to 180°C/350°F/gas 4.

Cut the chops in half and trim off some of the excess fat. Set aside. Render down the fat on a gentle heat in a heavy pan (discard the rendered down pieces).

Peel the onions and scrape or thinly peel the carrots (if they are young you could leave some of the green stalks on the onions and carrots). Cut the carrots into large chunks, or if young leave them whole. If the onions are large roughly chop them; if they are small they are best left whole.

Toss the meat in the hot fat until it is slightly brown. Set aside. Quickly toss the onions and carrots in the fat. Build the meat, carrots and onions up in layers in the casserole, carefully season each layer with salt and pepper.

De-glaze the pan with lamb stock and pour into the casserole. Peel the potatoes and lay them whole on top of the casserole, so they will steam while the stew cooks. Season the potatoes. Add a sprig of thyme, bring to the boil on top of the stove, cover and transfer to the oven or allow to simmer on top of the stove until the stew is cooked, about 1–2 hours, depending on meat.

When the stew is cooked, pour off the cooking liquid. Transfer the meat and vegetables to a clean pan. De-grease the juices and pour over the meat. Reheat and slightly thicken with a little Roux if you like. Check the seasoning. Bring back up to the boil, sprinkle with parsley and chives and serve from the pan. Alternatively transfer to a large pottery dish and then garnish.

Aliona's Plov
Serves 8–10

In Uzbekistan everyone has their own recipe for Plov. This is Aliona's version – delicious comforting food.

4–6 tablespoons extra-virgin olive oil
1kg (2¼lb) shoulder of lamb, cut into 2cm (¾in) cubes
2 large onions, chopped
3 large carrots, cut into 3cm (1¼in) sticks
1 teaspoon cumin seeds
1 teaspoon coriander seeds
1 teaspoon paprika
½ teaspoon chilli powder
5 garlic cloves, peeled and chopped
salt and freshly ground pepper
water
225g (8oz) basmati rice, washed
1 level teaspoon turmeric
1 whole garlic bulb

Heat the oil in a large casserole dish and brown the cubed meat over a medium heat. Add the onion, carrot, spices, garlic and seasoning. Add enough water to cover, bring to the boil, cover and cook until the meat is tender (about 15–20 minutes).

Add the washed rice and 200ml (7fl oz) more water and boil rapidly until the water evaporates. Sprinkle turmeric over the top and place the garlic bulb in the centre of the rice mixture. Cover with a lid and turn the heat right down. Using a heat-diffuser mat, cook for 30–40 minutes, by which time the rice should have absorbed all the liquid.

Serve with the Korean Carrot Salad (see page 219) and thinly sliced onion rings.

Asian Lamb Stew

Serves 8

1.3kg (3lb) lean leg or shoulder meat (trimmed of all fat)
4 fat leeks
475ml (¾ pint) homemade Lamb or Chicken Stock (see page 37) or water
2 tablespoons sunflower oil
50ml (2fl oz) soy sauce
50ml (2fl oz) dry sherry
3 teaspoons red wine vinegar
1½ tablespoons soft brown sugar
4 garlic cloves, crushed
5 star anise
½–1 teaspoon crushed red pepper flakes
3 strips of dried orange zest (from unwaxed oranges)
Roux (see page 580) or cornflour

Cut the meat into 5cm (2in) cubes. Trim and wash the leeks and cut into 5cm (2in) lengths at an angle. Heat a little sunflower oil in a sauté pan over a high heat. Brown the meat on all sides and transfer to a casserole. Add a little more oil if necessary, and toss in the leeks. Cook for 5 minutes and add to the meat in the casserole.

De-glaze the pan with the stock or water, bring to the boil and add to the meat and leeks. Add the soy sauce, sherry, vinegar, brown sugar and garlic. Tie the star anise, pepper flakes and orange zest in a piece of muslin or cheesecloth and add to the casserole. Bring to the boil, cover and simmer for 1 hour, or until the lamb is melting and tender. When cooked, discard the muslin bag and thicken the juices with a little Roux or cornflour mixed with 2 tablespoons of water.

Serve with a bowl of Plain Boiled Rice (see page 124).

Tagine of Lamb with Preserved Lemon

Serves 6

The word tagine refers both to the distinctive earthenware cooking pot with a shallow base and conical top and to a multitude of stew-like dishes cooked in it. These can be based on meat, fish, poultry or vegetables. I lugged my precious tagine all the way from Morocco. Without question it is the most expensive tagine in the whole of Ireland... even though it was a bargain in Medina I had to pay excess baggage at the airport and the Moroccans would not settle for my leftover dirhams – they wanted sterling or dollars and would let me have the tagine until they got them!

1 shoulder of lamb, 1.3kg (3lb)
½ tablespoon ground cinnamon
1 teaspoon ground ginger
1 teaspoon black peppercorns, freshly ground
generous pinch of saffron
50g (2oz) unsalted butter
2 onions, chopped
2 garlic cloves, finely chopped
salt
175g (6oz) raisins, soaked in water and drained
2 tablespoons honey
3 tablespoons freshly chopped coriander
1 tablespoon sunflower oil
50g (2oz) flaked almonds
1 Preserved Lemon (see page 515), half if large

couscous (see page 132)

Trim the lamb, discarding excess fat. Cut it into 4cm (1½in) cubes. Mix the cinnamon, ginger, pepper and saffron with 4 tablespoons of water. Toss the lamb in this mixture. If you have time, leave to marinate for up to 24 hours in the fridge.

Melt the butter in a tagine or wide pan. Add the lamb, onions, garlic, salt and enough water to come halfway up the meat. Bring to the boil, cover and reduce heat to a gentle simmer. Cook for about 1 hour, turning the lamb occasionally until the meat is meltingly tender. Add the

drained raisins, honey and half the coriander. Continue simmering for a further 30 minutes or so, uncovered until the sauce is thick and unctuous. Taste and adjust seasoning.

While the tagine is cooking, scoop the soft flesh out of the preserved lemon and chop up the peel. Fry the almonds gently in the oil until almost golden brown, then add the diced lemon and toss 2 or 3 times. Drain on kitchen paper. Sprinkle preserved lemon, almonds and the remaining coriander leaves over the lamb just before serving. Serve with couscous.

Preserved Lemons

Preserved lemons are one of the indispensable flavours in Moroccan cooking. Buy them loose in the souks or make them easily at home. You probably won't be able to source the Doqq or Boussers lemons used in Morocco but do try to use unwaxed lemons. Several presentation methods are used. The Moroccan Jews use olive oil and in the Safi area some spices and herbs are added. Use plain dairy salt with no chemicals. It is important to ensure that the salted lemons are completely covered with lemon juice otherwise they won't keep. The pickling liquid may be reused several times. See page 515 for recipe.

Babotie

Serves 8–10

This South African recipe was given to us by Alicia Wilkinson from Silwood Kitchens in Cape Town.

1¹/₂ teaspoons butter
generous 30ml (1fl oz) oil
2 onions, chopped
2 garlic cloves, crushed
450g (1lb) lamb, freshly minced
110g (4oz) carrot, grated
2 teaspoons curry powder
1 teaspoon ground coriander
2¹/₂ teaspoons ground ginger
3 teaspoons finely chopped mixed herbs
1 teaspoon turmeric
¹/₂ teaspoon cinnamon
sugar to taste – about 1 teaspoon
a piece of red chilli
1 teaspoon salt
1 teaspoon pepper
10g (¹/₂oz) almonds, chopped
some lemon leaves or ¹/₂ teaspoon lemon rind, finely grated
2 slices white bread, 2.5cm (1in) thick soaked in water, drained and squeezed dry
generous 15ml (¹/₂fl oz) wine vinegar

Topping
250ml (9fl oz) buttermilk
2 large organic eggs
salt and freshly ground pepper
2¹/₂ teaspoons turmeric

Preheat the oven to 180°C/350°F/gas 4.

Heat the butter and oil in a heavy pan over a medium heat, add the onions and garlic, and cook until soft. Add the mince and stir well, then the carrot, spices, herbs, sugar, chilli, seasoning, almonds and lemon rind. Stir well and continue to cook until the flavours mingle. Stir in the bread and wine vinegar. Mix well, taste and correct seasoning.

Put the meat into a shallow, rectangular baking dish and smooth over.

Make the topping by whisking all the ingredients together. Check the seasoning and strain over the meat through a coarse sieve. Bake at once in the oven until the topping is set and golden.

Mild Madras Curry with Fresh Spices

Serves 8

This is a korma curry made with nut milk and no chilli: it is deliciously spiced but not hot. Measure the spices meticulously because these proportions really work.

900g (2lb) boneless lamb or mutton (leg or shoulder is perfect)
1 tablespoon pounded fresh green ginger
salt

50g (2oz) ghee or clarified butter (see page 105)
4 onions, sliced in rings
4 garlic cloves
2 teaspoons coriander seed
¹/₂ teaspoon black peppercorns
1 teaspoon cardamom seeds (from whole green cardamom pods if possible)
8 cloves

Nut Milk
110g (4oz) almonds
450ml (16fl oz) single cream

1 tablespoon turmeric powder
¹/₂ teaspoon sugar
lime juice, freshly squeezed

First make the nut milk. Blanch, peel and chop up the almonds until they have the texture of nibbed almonds. Put them into a small saucepan with the cream and simmer for 4–5 minutes. Turn off the heat and leave to infuse for 15 minutes.

Meanwhile peel the ginger thinly with a vegetable peeler. Pound into a paste in a

pestle and mortar, or chop or grate finely. Cut the meat into 4cm (1¹/₂in) cubes and mix it with the ginger and a sprinkling of salt.

Melt the butter in a large saucepan and cook the onion rings and crushed garlic over a gentle heat for 5 minutes.

Remove the seeds from the cardamom pods and measure 1 teaspoon. Discard the pods. Grind the coriander, pepper, cardamom and cloves in a clean spice or coffee grinder. Add the spices to the onions and cook over a medium heat for 2–3 minutes.

Remove the onion mixture and add the meat to the saucepan. Stir over a high heat until the meat browns. Return the onion mixture to the pot. Add in the nut milk, turmeric and sugar. Stir well. Cover and simmer gently on top of the stove or better still in a low oven 170°C/325°F/gas 3, until the meat is cooked (about 1 hour).

Add lime juice to taste. Serve with plain boiled rice and segments of lime.

Notes: You can substitute 450ml (16fl oz) coconut milk for nut milk in this recipe.

For a hotter curry, add 1–2 chopped chillies with the onions and garlic.

Other suggested accompaniments:

Apple and Tomato Chutney (see page 512)

Hot Chilli Sauce (see page 592)

Banana and Cardamom Raita or Cucumber and Coriander Raita (see page 595)

Sliced bananas and chopped apples

Indian breads – Naan, Paratha or Poppadoms (see page 492)

Master Recipe
Shepherd's Pie with Garlic or Parsley Butter
Serves 6

I adore Shepherd's Pie. It is best made with leftover cooked roast lamb. Nowadays, however, people rarely cook large enough joints of meat to have much leftover so raw lamb mince is used instead – nothing like as delicious.

25g (1oz) butter
110g (4oz) onion, chopped
25g (1oz) flour
450ml (16fl oz) stock and leftover gravy
1 teaspoon tomato purée
2 teaspoons mushroom ketchup (optional)
2 teaspoons freshly chopped flat-leaf parsley
1 teaspoon thyme leaves
salt and freshly ground pepper
450g (1lb) cooked lamb, minced
900g (2lb) Fluffy Mashed Potatoes (see page 182) or Mashed Parsnips (see page 174)
Garlic or Parsley Butter (see page 588)

Preheat the oven to 180°C/350°F/gas 4.

Melt the butter in a small saucepan, add the onion, cover with a round of greased paper and cook over a slow heat for 5 minutes. Add the flour and cook until brown but take care not to burn it. Pour in the stock and gravy, bring to the boil and skim if necessary. Add the tomato purée, mushroom ketchup, parsley, thyme, salt and pepper and simmer for 5 minutes. Stir the minced meat into the sauce and bring to the boil. Taste and correct the seasoning.

Put in a pie dish. Cover with the mashed potatoes and score with a fork. Reheat in the oven for about 30 minutes until the potato is nicely browned. Serve with Garlic and Parsley Butter, melting in the centre.

Cottage Pie
Follow the Master Recipe but substitute beef for the lamb.

Arabian Shepherd's Pie
Serves 4

pinch of saffron stamens
3 tablespoons sultanas
2 tablespoons extra-virgin olive oil
110g (4oz) onion, chopped
2 carrots, grated
2 garlic cloves, crushed
2 teaspoons freshly ground coriander
2 teaspoons freshly ground cumin
450g (1lb) lamb, cooked and minced
450ml (1 pint) homemade Beef Stock (see page 36) or leftover gravy
1 x 400g (14oz) tin chickpeas
salt and freshly ground pepper
2 tablespoons freshly chopped coriander
1 lemon, freshly squeezed (optional)
900g (2lb) cooked mashed potato

Preheat the oven to 200°C/400°F/gas 6.

Put the saffron in a small bowl, add the sultanas and cover with a little boiling water, waiting for the sultanas to 'plump up'. Meanwhile prepare the remainder of the ingredients.

Heat the olive oil in a large saucepan and sweat the onion, carrot and garlic over a gentle heat for about 5 minutes. Add the spices, stir, and cook for a minute or two. Add the minced lamb, stock or leftover gravy and chickpeas, and season with salt and freshly ground pepper. Mix gently, and then add the sultanas in saffron water and fresh coriander. Taste and sharpen with lemon juice if necessary. Pile the mixture into an ovenproof dish. Add a little cumin to the mashed potato and spread roughly over the top. Bake for 15–20 minutes or until bubbly and golden on top.

Greek Moussaka
Serves 8

This is a Greek peasant recipe served in almost every taverna in Greece. There are many variations on the theme, some of which include a layer of cooked potato slices and raisins. I'm not sure if it is my imagination but I sometimes feel that moussaka is even better on the second day.

350g (12oz) aubergines
350g (12oz) courgettes
1 x 400g (14oz) tin tomatoes, or very ripe fresh tomatoes in summer
extra-virgin olive oil, for frying
1 onion, finely chopped (include some green part of spring onion if you have it)
1 garlic clove, crushed
450g (1lb) minced lamb, cooked
1 tablespoon freshly chopped marjoram or thyme
2 teaspoons freshly chopped parsley
1 bay leaf
pinch of grated nutmeg
2 teaspoons flour
salt and freshly ground pepper

For the topping
35g (1½oz) butter
35g (1½oz) flour
600ml (1 pint) milk
1 bay leaf
2 organic egg yolks
2 tablespoons cream
110g (4oz) grated Gruyère or mature Cheddar
salt and freshly ground pepper

25.5 x 20.5cm (10 x 8in) earthenware dish

Preheat the oven to 180°C/350°F/gas 4.

Slice the aubergines and courgettes into 1cm (½in) slices, score the flesh with a sharp knife and sprinkle with salt. Leave for half an hour. Roughly chop or cut up the tinned tomatoes, or peel and chop the fresh tomatoes finely if using. Keep the juices.

Heat 1 tablespoon of olive oil in a heavy saucepan over a gentle heat, add the onion and garlic, cover, and sweat for 4 minutes. Add the meat, herbs and nutmeg to the onions. Stir in the flour and cook for 2 minutes. Pour in the tomatoes and their juice. Bring to the boil, stirring, and simmer for 2–3 minutes. Season well.

Rinse and wipe the aubergines dry. Heat a generous amount of olive oil in a pan-grill until hot. Cook the aubergines on both sides until golden. Brush the courgettes with olive oil, pan-grill until light golden on each side. As the courgettes are done, put them into the bottom of a shallow casserole. Tip the meat mixture on top of the courgettes and add a layer of the aubergines. See that the top is as flat as possible and set aside.

Make the topping: melt the butter in a saucepan. Stir in the flour. Cook, stirring, for 1 minute, then draw off the heat and add the milk slowly, whisking out the lumps as you go. Add the bay leaf. Return the pan to the heat and stir until boiling. Season with salt and pepper and simmer for 2 minutes. Mix the egg yolks with the cream in a large bowl. Pour the sauce onto this mixture, stirring all the time. Add half the cheese and pour over the casserole. Sprinkle the rest of the cheese on top and bake for 30–35 minutes in the oven until completely reheated and well-browned on top.

Moussaka can be made up in large quantities ahead of time, cooled quickly and frozen after it has been closely covered with clingfilm.

Lamb Kebabs with Tzatziki
Serves 8

Choose kebab skewers carefully. They need to be flat and at least 3mm (¹⁄₈in) wide, better still 5mm (¹⁄₄in). If they are round, the meat will swivel as you try to turn it. Kebabs are best barbecued but may also be pan-grilled or cooked under a salamander.

900g (2lb) lean shoulder or leg of lamb

Marinade 1
300ml (¹⁄₂ pint) natural yoghurt
1 teaspoon ground coriander
1 teaspoon ground cumin
¹⁄₄ teaspoon freshly ground pepper
juice of ¹⁄₂ lemon

Marinade 2
6 tablespoons extra-virgin olive oil
juice of 1 lemon
1 tablespoon annual marjoram, rosemary or thyme leaves
2 large garlic cloves, crushed
salt and freshly ground pepper

Accompaniment
Tzatziki (see page 69)

metal skewers or kebab sticks

Mix either or both marinades. Cut the meat into 2.5cm (1in) cubes, season with salt and pepper and put into the marinades for 1 hour at least. Drain the meat and thread onto metal skewers or kebab sticks. Grill for 7–10 minutes over a barbecue, turning and basting with the marinade 2 or 3 times. Serve with a green salad and Tzatziki.

RIGHT: Lamb Kebabs with Tzatziki

Lamb Choila

Serves 4 as a starter

This delicious choila is served at Monty's of Kathmandu in Dublin.

2 whole lamb fillets
a little extra-virgin olive oil
1 red onion, thinly sliced
2 fresh chillies, coarsely chopped
2 tablespoons finely chopped spring onion
2 tablespoons coriander
1 tablespoon thinly sliced ginger
1 tablespoon garlic, chopped
juice of 1 lemon, freshly squeezed
salt and freshly ground pepper
1/4 tablespoon garam masala
3 tablespoons mustard oil
1/4 teaspoon fenugreek seed
dash of red wine

Garnish
fresh ginger, thinly sliced
3 tablespoons freshly snipped coriander

Dry the lamb fillets with kitchen paper. Heat a little olive oil in a non-stick frying pan over a medium heat and cook the lamb until it is browned all over (about 5–10 minutes) – the meat should still be slightly pink in the middle. Cut the fillets into cubes and set aside.

In a large bowl, thoroughly mix the onions, chillies, spring onions, coriander, ginger, garlic, lemon juice, salt and pepper, garam masala and diced up meat lamb.

Heat the mustard oil in a large frying pan. When hot, add the fenugreek seeds and fry for a minute or two until the seeds turn black. Pour the mustard oil with fenugreek seeds and the red wine over the spiced meat and and again mix thoroughly. Taste and correct the seasoning.

Serve on bed of crisp lettuce and garnish with fresh ginger and coriander.

Kerry Pies

Serves 6

Mutton pies, made in Kerry, were served at the famous Puck Fair in Killorglin in August and taken up the hills when men were herding all day. The original hot-water crust pastry was made with mutton fat but we have substituted butter for a really delicious crust.

450g (1lb) boneless lamb or mutton, shoulder
  or leg (keep bones for stock)
275g (91/2oz) onions, chopped
275g (91/2oz) carrots, chopped
2 tablespoons flour
300ml (8fl oz) mutton or lamb stock
1 teaspoon chopped parsley
1 teaspoon thyme leaves
salt and freshly ground pepper

Hot Water Crust Pastry
350g (12oz) white flour
pinch of salt
175g (6oz) butter, diced
125ml (4fl oz) water
1 organic egg, beaten with a pinch of salt
  to glaze

2 x 15cm (6in) diameter tins, 4cm (11/2in) high
  or 1 x 23cm (9in) tin

Trim all surplus fat from the meat and then neatly chop it into small pieces, about the size of a sugar lump. Render down the scraps of fat in a large, heavy saucepan until the fat runs and then discard the pieces. Toss the vegetables in the fat, leaving them to cook for 3–4 minutes.

Remove the vegetables and brown the meat in the remaining fat over a high heat. Stir in the flour and cook gently for 2 minutes, blending in the stock gradually. Bring to the boil, stirring occasionally. Return the vegetables to the pan with the parsley and thyme leaves, season and leave to simmer, covered. If using young lamb, 30 minutes will be sufficient; but mutton may take up to an hour.

Preheat the oven to 200°C/400°F/gas 6 and while the lamb is cooking and the oven is heating, make the pastry. Sieve the flour and salt into a mixing bowl and make a well in the centre. Dice the butter, put it into a saucepan with the water and bring to the boil. Pour the liquid into the flour and mix together quickly, beating until smooth. At first the pastry will be too soft to handle but as it cools it will become more workable. Roll out to 2.5–5mm (1/8–1/4inch) thick, to fit the large pie tin or small individual tins.

Fill the pastry-lined tins with the slightly cooled meat mixture. Make lids from the remaining pastry, brushing the outside edge with water and egg wash so that the pastry case is sealed tight when you pinch the lid and the base tightly together. Roll out the trimmings to make pastry leaves or twirls to decorate the tops of the pies and stick on with the remaining egg wash. Bake for about 40 minutes, or until the pastry is golden brown. Serve hot or cold.

Sam's Merguez Sausages

Makes about 20 thin sausages, each 20cm (8in) long

Sam Clark of Moro in London has been another of our guest chefs. This recipe comes from Samantha and Samuel Clark's book *Casa Moro*.

900g (2lb) lamb, shank or shoulder meat,
  boned and trimmed of skin and sinew
200g (7oz) lamb kidney fat (beef suet is an
  acceptable substitute)
2 rounded tablespoons sweet paprika
1/2 teaspoon black peppercorns, freshly ground
2 teaspoons rosewater
3/4 teaspoon ground cinnamon
2 tablespoons Harissa (see page 596) or
  11/2 tablespoons dried crushed chilli
1 teaspoon roughly ground fennel seeds
1 tablespoon cumin seeds, crushed
35g (11/2oz) fresh coriander, washed and stalks
  retained

5 whole garlic cloves, peeled

2–2¹/₂ teaspoons fine sea salt

8 metres lamb sausage casings (narrow
   sausage skins)

Soak the casings in cold water and run water through once or twice by putting the end of the casings over the cold tap. Combine all the other ingredients in a bowl and then put everything through a fine die on a mincer. Load the casing on to the nozzle of a sausage stuffer and form into 8in-long links the same thickness of your little finger. Grill the sausages over a high heat until just cooked through but blistered on the outside.

Lamb, Pork, or Chicken Satay

Serves 6–8

Satays are most versatile – they can be served as a starter, with drinks, or as a light meal alongside rice and salad.

450g (1lb) lean lamb leg or chicken breast or
   thigh meat (boned and skinned), chopped into
   2.5cm (1in) cubes

1 garlic clove, finely chopped

2 shallots or 1 small onion, finely chopped

2 tablespoons light soy sauce

1 tablespoon sugar

1 tablespoon ground coriander

1 tablespoon lemon juice or red wine vinegar

24–26 bamboo satay sticks (soak them
   in water for 30 minutes, otherwise they
   will burn)

1–2 tablespoons vegetable oil

225g (8oz) Pixie's Peanut Sauce (see page 591)

Chop the meat into 2.5cm (1in) cubes and then mix all the remaining ingredients in a large bowl. Coat the meat with the mixture and leave to marinate for at least 1 hour. Light the barbecue. Thread the meat onto the satay sticks and brush with a little oil. Place on the barbecue and chargrill for a few minutes, turning frequently. Serve hot with satay sauce.

Spicy Indian Meatballs with Banana and Cardamom Raita

Serves 6

These spicy meatballs have a secret centre.

450g (1lb) shoulder of lamb, minced

4 cardamom pods

1 teaspoon coriander seeds

1 clove

¹/₂–³/₄ teaspoon chilli powder

2 garlic cloves, crushed

salt and freshly ground pepper

1 organic egg

about 2 tablespoons curd cheese mixed with
   1 teaspoon chopped parsley

pork caul fat (if the meatballs are to be
   cooked on a barbecue)

Banana and Cardamom Raita (see page 595)

Remove the seeds from the cardamom and discard the pods. Grind the seeds with the coriander and clove.

In a large bowl, mix the lamb with the spices, chilli powder and garlic and add the beaten egg. Season with salt and pepper. Fry off a tiny bit to check the seasoning.

Divide the mixture into 6, shape each portion into a round, about 10cm (4in) in diameter. Put a full teaspoon of curd cheese and parsley into the centre of each round, and gather up the edges so that the filling is completely enclosed. Wrap loosely in caul fat if you are using a barbecue.

Cover and chill until required or barbecue or fry immediately on a medium heat in a barely oiled frying pan. They will take about 5 minutes on each side. Serve immediately with a green salad and Banana and Cardamom Raita.

pork & bacon

pork & bacon

At last chefs are discovering the different and exciting flavours and textures of traditional breeds of pork - on a recent trip to the New York, Black Berkshire Pork was on the menu at all three restaurants we ate in. Here on the farm at Ballymaloe, we rear a mixture of free-range and organic Saddleback, Red Duroc, Gloucestershire Old Spot, Tamworth and Black Berkshire pigs. They live outdoors and feed on organic meal with the bonus of scraps from the greenhouses and gardens when the end of a crop (e.g. lettuces or cabbages) is pulled out. The pork is absolutely delicious; sweet and juicy. It's relished by the family, students and guests at Ballymaloe House. We sell what surplus we have at the farmers' market in Midleton where the demand far outstrips our supply.

Male pigs, or boars, are usually kept for breeding. The females are divided into gilts (those yet to farrow their first litter) and sows (fully-grown). Pigs are usually slaughtered between the ages of four and seven months, although suckling pigs can be as young as 7 weeks – which accounts for their succulence and size.

Breeds
Old-fashioned or traditional rare breeds are worth searching for, and your local farmers' market is a good place to start. Both Saddleback and Duroc have great flavour, as do Tamworth and Berkshire. Tamworth is a reddish-gold coloured pig and one of the oldest British breeds. Its meat is lean and it produces lovely pork and very good bacon – in fact, it came top in a taste test carried out by Bristol University in the mid 1990s, using both commercial and rare breed pigs.

Berkshire pigs were originally bred for pork but are now also used for bacon and produce excellent joints, chops and crackling. The first 'Berkshire' pig ever recorded was bred by Queen Victoria. Other rare breeds include Middle White, Gloucestershire Old Spots (probably one of the best known of all the British rare breeds) and British Lop which is the most endangered of the native breeds – only 200 breeding females remain in the country.

The few small farmers around the country who are rearing these pigs have a growing number of very loyal private customers who appreciate the sweet and succulent pork that they are producing.

Pork
Pork is fresh pig meat and it comes in a variety of joints and cuts. It should be cooked and used up quickly while it's still fresh, because it's uncured. In our experience organic meat keeps for considerably longer than intensively cooked meat.

Bacon
Bacon can be any part of the pig, which is then brined or traditionally dry-cured. Ireland has always been famous for its ham and bacon. Increasingly, however, pigs are being reared indoors in very intensive units and fed on just a basic stock meal, which often has growth promoters, hormones and antibiotics in it. Many people feel that both the texture and flavour of the bacon has suffered as a result and complain that bacon rashers release a white gooey fluid (a combination of salt and nitrates) when you cook it. For the best quality, buy dry-cured bacon which is low in nitrates or, better still, has no nitrates at all. Bacon, like ham and gammon, can either be bought smoked or green (unsmoked).

Thankfully, some farmers and producers with a real passion for their product have started to respond to the demand for quality bacon. Fingal Ferguson, son of Tom and Giana Ferguson who produce the much loved Gubbeen cheese in West Cork, is producing really good bacon now. He buys his pigs from a local farmer who feeds them on a good, natural diet with no questionable additives. Fingal cures the bacon himself and smokes it in the smokery on the farm. In a relatively short time, his bacon has acquired what is akin to a cult following. The Rudd family in County Offaly also have a range of very good bacon products and Anthony Cresswell, famous for Ummera smoked salmon, has recently branched out into smoked bacon.

Ham and Gammon
Ham and gammon are both from the hind leg of a pig, and will have been cured either in brine (a wet cure), or by rubbing salt into the meat (a dry cure). Sometimes the hams are cured still attached to the leg, otherwise they are cut off first and then cured separately. The latter usually results in a stronger, saltier cure. Gammons are always cured separately.

Buying
Seek out good quality, free-range pork in your area. You will need to pay more for pork from pigs that have had plenty of space to roam and forage, and been fed a completely natural and organic diet, but it's well worth it. When buying pork or bacon, with the exception of fillet, we like to buy it with a little covering of fat on it (about 5–10mm). This is particularly important if you want to glaze a ham or loin of bacon. Of course, you don't have to eat the fat, but you should make sure that it is there to begin with, otherwise the meat will have very little flavour and won't be nice and juicy. Traditional breeds have more fat.

Cooking
When cooking **ham**, you will know it is not fully cooked if you can lift it up on a skewer. It is cooked if the skewer comes out very easily and the skin should also peel off without a problem. You can then glaze it with a little brown sugar, cloves and pineapple juice, mustard or even marmalade. On a recent trip to the US Momofuku Restaurant in Greenwich Village NY offered three different home-cured hams on their menu.

For a mouth-wateringly delicious **roast**, slow roast the shoulder or leg, which have the best flavour. Loin is also tender and succulent and makes wonderful crackling. The shoulder is the most economical joint.

Loin of bacon is a really good cut for a party because it carves very easily and you don't need any particular carving skills. A ham tends to take a bit more skill in the carving. Also delicious is the cut that we call the oyster cut, which is the piece between the loin and the leg. It's a really lean piece, almost like ham, and it's very good. The oyster cut is equivalent to the chump chop piece in lamb, and it can also be known as chump chops of pork.

Other Pork Products
Pork **sausages** are usually made from the shoulder or belly meat and come with different percentages of meat content. Speciality sausages, with ingredients such as leek, stilton, apple, or fresh herbs added, are increasingly popular.

Frank Krawczyk and Fingal Ferguson make us the most fantastic **salami** and **chorizo**, and we have recently had our own success making dry cured hams and a variety of salami and chorizo.

Parma ham (made in Italy) and **Serrano ham** (from Spain) are both cured and air-dried. Parma ham is served in paper-thin slices. **Pata Negra**, made from the dry cured hams of the Iberian pig, wildly fed on acorns in oak forests, is a truly sensational food.

One of the Forgotten Skills courses we now run at the school is How to cure a Pig in a Day. It's great fun – we take one of our own Gloucester Old Spot Pigs and work from the nose to the tail, producing everything from dry and wet-cured bacon and hams to tripe, pâtés, salami, chorizo, chistora and prosciutto.

Ballymaloe Bacon Chop with Irish Whiskey Sauce

Serves 6

In the restaurant at Ballymaloe, we serve Bacon Chop with Irish Whiskey Sauce; other good things to serve with it are fried banana or plantain, spiced peaches or Mango Relish (see page 92). Choose a piece of bacon with the rind still on and with a little covering of fat. Use freshly cured green bacon.

900g (2lb) loin of bacon (boneless and without the streaky end)

Coating
110g (4oz) seasoned flour
1 organic egg beaten with a little milk
50g (2oz) fresh, white breadcrumbs

For Frying
25g (1oz) Clarified Butter (see page 105) or 10g (½oz) butter and 1–2 tablespoons olive oil
Irish Whiskey Sauce (see recipe below right)

Put the piece of bacon into a deep pot and cover with cold water. Bring to the boil. If the bacon is salty, a layer of white froth will develop on the surface; discard the water and start again. You may need to do this twice or in extreme cases 3 times. After the blanching process, bring the water to the boil, cover the saucepan and continue to boil for 45–60 minutes or until fully cooked. Remove the rind and trim away excess fat – 1cm (½in) of fat is quite acceptable. Slice into chops 1–2cm (½–¾in) thick. Dip in seasoned flour, then in well beaten egg and finally coat with white breadcrumbs (see above right). Heat the clarified butter or oil in a heavy frying pan and fry the chops gently until they are cooked through and golden on both sides.

Serve with Irish Whiskey Sauce and Scallion Champ (see page 182).

> TIP: For a cheaper version, streaky bacon may be used instead of loin.

How to Make Breadcrumbs

Stale white bread makes better breadcrumbs. Cut the crusts off the bread. (If you don't object to brown specks in the breadcrumbs you can leave the crusts on.) Break into biggish chunks, and put a few chunks at a time into a food processor or liquidiser. Whizz for a few seconds or until the bread has been transformed into breadcrumbs.

Dry breadcrumbs
Bake bread crusts slowly in a cool oven (maximum 110°C/225°F/gas ¼) for several hours until dry and crisp. Whizz the crusts in a liquidiser and put through a sieve. Store in a covered jar – provided the crusts were well-toasted the crumbs seem to keep for months.

> TIP: Soft white breadcrumbs freeze brilliantly and can be used directly from the freezer. Breadcrumbs are invaluable to have in a freezer for stuffings, bread sauce, croquettes, etc.

Irish Whiskey Sauce

Serve with ham, bacon or ice cream. Keeps indefinitely in a covered jar.

225g (8oz) caster sugar
5 tablespoons cold water
4 tablespoons hot water
3 tablespoons Irish whiskey

Put the sugar and cold water into a small saucepan and stir over a gentle heat until the sugar dissolves and the syrup comes to the boil. Remove the spoon and do not stir. Continue to boil until it turns a nice chestnut-brown colour. Remove from the heat and immediately add the hot water. Allow to dissolve again and then add the Irish whiskey. Serve hot or cold.

Irish Whiskey and Banana Sauce
Sounds very 50s, but tastes great! Slice 2 bananas into the sauce above, and serve with bacon chop or glazed loin of bacon.

Breading: Coating with Seasoned Flour, Egg and Breadcrumbs

Delicate foods need to have a protective coating before they are pan-fried, deep-fried and sometimes before they are pan-grilled. The coating may be seasoned flour, cornmeal, a batter or a mixture of seasoned flour, beaten egg and breadcrumbs. Use 3 flat plates for a large quantity:

Plate 1 (seasoned flour)
Use 1 teaspoon of salt and 1 teaspoon of pepper to 110g (4oz) white flour.

Plate 2 (egg wash)
Whisk 2 eggs with 2 tablespoons of milk or water.

Plate 3 (breadcrumbs)
White breadcrumbs.

Dip the food in seasoned flour until evenly coated. Shake off any excess flour, then dip in beaten egg and drain off any excess. Finally toss in the breadcrumbs.

Deep-fry immediately or dry on a wire rack or on non-stick paper.

Do not pile several pieces on top of each other or they will stick together and the coating will come off when you attempt to separate the pieces.

Panko crumbs
Japanese breadcrumbs may also be used and give an even crisper coating.

Variations
Chilli powder or freshly ground spices, such as cumin or coriander, may be added to the seasoned flour. Chopped herbs may also be added to the breadcrumbs.

Bacon and Cabbage with Parsley Sauce

Serves 12–15

Without question Ireland's national dish – less known abroad but much more widely eaten, particularly in rural Ireland, than the legendary Irish Stew. Choose a piece of bacon with a nice covering of fat. Be careful with salt, the bacon water may be salty enough.

1.8–2.2kg (4–5lb) loin or shoulder of bacon, with a nice covering of fat
1 head cabbage, savoy, greyhound or spring cabbage, depending on the time of year
salt and freshly ground pepper
50–75g (2–3oz) butter

Parsley Sauce (see page 580)

Cover the bacon in cold water and bring slowly to the boil. If the bacon is very salty there will be white froth on top of the water, so discard this water and start again; it may be necessary to change the water several times depending on how salty the bacon is. Finally cover with hot water, bring to the boil, cover and continue to simmer, allowing 45 minutes to the kg (20 minutes to the lb).

Meanwhile, remove the outside leaves from the cabbage, cut into quarters and remove the centre core. Cut into thin strips across the grain. About 30 minutes before the bacon is cooked, add the cabbage and continue to cook until it is soft and tender and the bacon fully cooked through.

Meanwhile make the Parsley Sauce.

Remove the bacon to a hot plate, strain the water off the cabbage. Return the well-drained cabbage to the saucepan, add a good lump of butter and season well with pepper. Taste. Remove the rind from the bacon and serve with the cabbage and the Parsley Sauce. The traditional accompaniment would be lots of boiled floury potatoes.

TIP: An alternative way of cooking the cabbage is Buttered Cabbages (see page 166).

Loin of Pork Cooked in Milk

Serves 6–8

At the Cookery School we rear free-range, organic saddleback pigs – happy and lazy, they play in the field and eat windfall apples in the orchard in autumn. When Rose Grey and Ruth Rogers came to the School as guest chefs they cooked many of their trademark dishes, including this one. The meat we have now is even better than what we had access to then: succulent juicy pork – quite divine.

1.8–2.2kg (4–5lb) pork, rindless
sea salt and freshly ground pepper
dash of extra-virgin olive oil
1.5 litres (2½ pints) full cream milk
50g (2oz) butter
6 garlic cloves, peeled and split in half
2 unwaxed lemons

Season the pork on all sides with salt and pepper. Heat the oil in a large round casserole over medium heat. Slowly brown the meat all over then remove to a plate. Pour out any excess fat – save for roast or sauté potatoes. Do not wash the pan.

In a separate pan, bring the milk almost to boiling point. Melt the butter in the casserole then add the garlic and toss. Replace the meat and add enough hot milk to come half way up the pork. Bring to the boil. Use a swivel-top peeler to take off the peel from the lemon without removing any pith, and add to the milk.

Lower the heat to reduce the casserole to the merest simmer. Leave the pot partly uncovered and barely simmering for 1½–2 hours, by which time the milk will have curdled into a golden curd.

Carve the meat carefully and spoon some of the delicious curd over each slice.

Master Recipe
Glazed Ham with Pickled Kumquats

Serves 20–25

A perfectly glazed ham always looks stunning. Buy ham made from pigs that have ranged freely and have been fed organic feed so that the ham has a nice covering of fat (you will need to order well ahead). This is crucially important to the success of the following recipe. Ultra-lean hams are much less flavourful and juicy. A layer of fat is essential for glazing the ham. You don't have to eat it although it will be difficult to resist the sweet caramelised bits. A really sweet ham is irresistible hot or cold and works well with many accompaniments. Loin of bacon may be glazed in the same way and is easier to carve – both are perfect for effortless entertaining.

4.4–5.2kg (10–12lb) fresh or lightly smoked ham
4–6 tablespoons pineapple juice (from 1 small tin)
450g (1lb) brown demerara sugar
60–80 whole cloves, depending on the size of the diamonds

Pickled Kumquats (see page 513)

If the ham is salty, soak it in cold water overnight; next day discard the water. Cover the ham with fresh cold water and bring it slowly to the boil. If the meat is still salty there will be a white froth on top of the water. Discard the water, cover the ham with fresh cold water again and repeat the process. Finally, cover the ham with hot water and simmer until it is almost cooked. Allow 45 minutes to the kg (20 minutes to 1lb).

Meanwhile, make the Pickled Kumquats.

When the ham is fully cooked a skewer will come out effortlessly and the skin will peel off easily. Glaze the ham (see right) and serve hot or cold with Pickled Kumquats.

Variation
Glazed Loin of Bacon
Follow the Master Recipe, but use 1.8–2.2kg (4–5lb) loin of bacon, either smoked or green (unsmoked). Cook for 40 minutes to the kg (15 minutes to the lb).

Suggested Accompaniments to Hot Glazed Ham or Loin of Bacon

Tomato Fondue (see page 200)
Piperonata (see page 199)
Mushroom à la Crème (see page 201)
Ulster Champ (see page 183)
Colcannon (see page 183)
Fluffy Mashed Potato (see page 182)
Pickled Kumquats (see page 513)
Cumberland Sauce (see page 594)
Tomato and Chilli Sauce (see page 591)
Mango Relish (see page 92)

How to Glaze Ham or Bacon

Peel off the rind, cut the fat into a diamond pattern and stud each diamond with a whole clove. Blend some brown sugar to a thick paste with a little pineapple juice (be careful not to make it too liquid). Spread over the ham and bake in a hot oven, 250°C/475°F/gas 9, for 20 minutes or until the top has caramelised. While it is glazing, baste regularly with the syrup and juices.

LEFT: Glazed Ham with Pickled Kumquats

Ham Morvandelle

Serves about 20

This is a terrific recipe for a party. It freezes well and reheats perfectly. The recipe comes from the Burgundy area of France and takes its name from the Morvan forests. Loin or oyster cut of bacon may be used for this recipe.

3.6–4.4kg (8–10lb) whole ham
25g (1oz) butter
1 tablespoon vegetable oil
225g (8oz) carrots, sliced
225g (8oz) onions, sliced
12 sprigs of parsley
1 bay leaf
12 peppercorns
sprig of thyme
4 cloves
½ bottle of white Burgundy, Chablis (we use a
  Petit Chablis) or Pouilly Fuissé
850ml (1½ pints) homemade Chicken Stock
  (see page 36)

Sauce
4 tablespoons chopped onion or shallot
900g (2lb) mushrooms, sliced
salt and freshly ground pepper
500ml (18fl oz) cream
Roux (see page 580)

Liaison
3 organic egg yolks
60ml (2½fl oz) cream

Soak the ham in cold water overnight and discard the water the next day. Place the ham in a large saucepan and cover with fresh cold water. Bring it slowly to the boil and discard the water. Repeat the process once or twice more, depending on how salty the ham is. (This is particularly important if the dish is to be frozen because freezing seems to intensify the salty taste.)

Preheat the oven to 180°C/350°F/gas 4 if you are going to cook the ham in the oven.

Meanwhile, melt the butter and oil in a casserole large enough to take the ham.

Toss the sliced carrots and onions in the fat and sweat for about 10 minutes. Place the ham on top of the vegetables and add the parsley, bay leaf, peppercorns, thyme and cloves. Pour over the wine and stock; cover with the lid, bring to the boil and simmer on top of the stove or in the moderate oven, until the ham is cooked. Allow about 2½–3 hours for this weight, or 15 minutes per 450g (1lb) plus 15 minutes. You can test when the ham is cooked by lifting the skin: if it peels off easily, the ham is cooked. Check very carefully to make sure the ham is fully cooked before proceeding with the sauce.

To make the sauce cook the onion or shallot in a little butter on a low heat until soft. Remove from the pan. Sauté the mushrooms over a high heat and add to the onion. When the ham is cooked, remove it from the casserole and strain and de-grease the cooking liquid. Return the liquid to the casserole with the cream and bring to the boil. Thicken with prepared roux to a light coating consistency and simmer for 5 minutes. Add the mushrooms and onions and taste for seasoning. Skin the ham and slice carefully. Arrange in one or more serving dishes.

To make the liaison, mix the egg yolks with the cream and add a ladleful of the simmering sauce. Mix well and add back into the remaining sauce. Do not allow to boil again or it may curdle.

Spoon the sauce over the slices of ham in the serving dish. (The recipe may be prepared ahead to this point.) Cook in the oven for 20–30 minutes. It should be bubbling and slightly golden on top.

For a dinner party, you may want to pipe a border of Fluffy Mashed Potatoes (see page 182) around the outside of theserving dish. Tomato Fondue (see page 200), Piperonata (see page 199) and a good green salad make excellent accompaniments.

Master Recipe
Roast Pork with Crackling and Green Gooseberry Sauce

Serves 10–12

Pork has suffered more than almost any other meat from modern, intensive rearing methods. For years I longed and searched in vain for the sweet, juicy pork we ate as children. In despair, much to the great consternation of my husband and family I bought two saddleback pigs from West Cork and a black Berkshire boar from the Comeragh mountains. They live happily and completely naturally in our orchard and are fed on organic feed. They have produced several large litters of Bonhams, which delight us all. The boar would appear to be a descendant of the early Irish pig as he too can clear a fence with the greatest of ease – I've spent many hours chasing him around the immediate countryside. The pork is sweet and delicious! The acidity in green gooseberries cuts the richness of the pork deliciously.

1 loin of pork with the rind still on, 2.2kg (5lb)
salt and freshly ground pepper
sprigs of rosemary (optional)

Gravy
600ml (1 pint) homemade Chicken Stock
  (see page 36)
Roux (see page 580), optional
Green Gooseberry Sauce (see page 597)

Preheat the oven to 190°C/375°F/gas 5.

Place the pork skin side up on the work top and rub salt over the rind and into the fat. Turn the pork over (skin-side down) on the work top, season well with salt and pepper and perhaps a little chopped rosemary. Roll up tightly and tie with cotton string. Cook in a roasting tin on a trivet, allowing 25–28 minutes to 450g (1lb). Baste every now and then.

Just before the end of cooking time remove the pork to another roasting tin, replace in the oven and turn up the temperature to 230°C/450°F/gas 8, to get crisp crackling. When the joint is cooked the juices should run clear. One shouldn't eat pork pink. Put the pork onto a hot carving dish and allow to rest in a very cool oven while you make the gravy in the original roasting tin.

To make the gravy, de-grease the roasting pan (keep the delicious pork fat for sautéeing potatoes), put on a medium heat, add the chicken stock and whisk to dissolve the caramelised pork juices. Bring to the boil. Season and thicken with a little roux, if desired. Freshly chopped herbs may be added to the gravy. Serve with crispy roast potatoes and Green Gooseberry Sauce.

Variation
Roast Stuffed Pork with Sage and Onion Stuffing and Bramley Apple Sauce

Follow the Master Recipe. Make the Sage and Onion Stuffing (see page 288) and spread it over the flesh side. Roll up tightly and tie with cotton string. Serve with Bramley Apple Sauce (see page 597).

TIP: For really good crackling score the skin at 5mm (¼in) intervals running with the grain – you may want to ask your butcher do this because the skin can be quite tough. (This will also make it easier to carve later). Use a Stanley knife to score the rind at home.

Roast Suckling Pig with Apple and Jalapeno Jelly
Serves 10–12

1 suckling pig
salt and freshly ground pepper
3–4 tablespoons freshly chopped rosemary
   (optional)
a little extra-virgin olive oil

Sage and Onion Stuffing (see page 288 and
   use double the recipe)
sprigs of rosemary and watercress

Apple and Jalapeño Jelly (see page 507) or
Bramley Apple Sauce (see page 597)

Rub salt, pepper and rosemary over the skin and into the cavity of the pig. Allow to marinate overnight.

The next day preheat the oven to 180°C/350°F/gas 4.

Make the stuffing and fill the cavity loosely with it. Truss with skewers and lace over the skewers with cotton string to close the cavity. Truss the front and back legs loosely to keep a neat shape.

Use a sharp knife to make an incision along the backbone, then score the back diagonally at 2.5cm (1in) intervals from head to tail.

Roast the suckling pig on its belly in a large roasting tin, sprinkle a little more salt over the meat and drizzle with olive oil. Wrap the ears with tin foil to protect them from the direct heat – they burn easily.

Roast in the oven, basting every 30 minutes. It will take 2½ –3½ hours, depending on size. A 4.4kg (10lb) pig will be cooked in about 2½ hours. Allow 3 hours for 5.8kg (13lb) and 3½ hours for an 8kg (18lb) pig. The pig is ready to eat when the skin has turned to crisp golden crackling.

To serve: make gravy from the juices in the pan. Remove the skewers and trussing strings. Arrange on a large serving platter surrounded by crispy Roast Potatoes (see page 181) and sprigs of rosemary and watercress. Please, don't put an apple in its mouth! Serve with gravy, Apple and Jalapeño Jelly or Bramley Apple Sauce.

Roast Kassler

Serves 10–12

This delicious German speciality is fresh loin of pork marinated with pepper, cloves and juniper berries for 12–24 hours and then oak-smoked for a further 12 hours. It used to be quite difficult to find but is now becoming more widely available as many pork butchers produce their own. It is best roasted rather than boiled. It may be served hot, warm or cold.

2.2kg (5lb) Kassler

Preheat the oven to 180°C/350°F/gas 4.

Put the piece of Kassler onto a roasting tin and cook for about 1¾ hours or for 20 minutes per 450g (1lb). During cooking, baste once or twice with the fat which will render out. Test the meat: the juices should run clear when cooked. Turn off the oven or set to a very low heat; leave the meat to relax for about 20 minutes before carving. De-grease the pan and serve the sweet juices with the Kassler. Keep the pork fat to roast or sauté potatoes.

Belly of Pork with Star Anise and Savoy Cabbage

Serves 8

1.5kg (3.4lb) pork belly, rind on
2 large onions, sliced into rings
4 garlic cloves, chopped
3–4 sprigs of thyme
450ml (1 pint) Homemade Chicken Stock, cold
  (see page 36)
salt and freshly ground pepper
1–2 teaspoons five-spice powder
Savoy cabbage

Preheat the oven to 160°C/325°F/gas 3.

Score the rind of the pork belly at 2cm (¾in) intervals with a Stanley knife. Scatter the onion over the base of a roasting tin in a single layer and sprinkle with garlic and

thyme leaves. Pour in the cold stock and sit the pork belly on top. Sprinkle with salt, pepper and five-spice powder, rubbing the flavouring into the cuts in the pork. Cover with foil and cook in the oven for about 3 hours, basting occasionally, until the pork is very soft and juicy.

Pork en Croûte with Duxelle Stuffing and Bramley Apple Sauce

Serves 6

2 fresh pork steaks

Marinade
3 tablespoons extra-virgin olive oil
3 tablespoons lemon juice
3 sprigs of parsley
sprig of thyme or fennel
1 bay leaf
1 garlic clove, crushed
pinch of salt and freshly ground pepper

Duxelle Stuffing (see page 304); use a quarter
  of the recipe
225–275g (8–10oz) homemade Flaky Pastry
  (see page 413) or Puff Pastry (see page 456)
egg wash made with 1 organic egg and
  a pinch of salt

Bramley Apple Sauce (see page 597)

Preheat the oven to 220°C/425°F/gas 7.

Trim the pork steaks of all fat and trim the chain (the long thin strip of meat on the edge of the pork fillet). Mix all the ingredients for the marinade in a bowl and marinate the pork steaks for 3–4 hours. Meanwhile make the Duxelle Stuffing.

To assemble: split the pork steaks down one side and open out flat. Season with salt and pepper, divide the stuffing between both steaks, and fold the meat over.

Divide pastry in two, roll out each piece and cover the pork as though it was a parcel, decorate with pastry leaves. Egg wash and bake in the oven for 10 minutes,

then turn down heat to 180°C/350°F/gas 4 and cook for another 20 minutes. Serve with Bramley Apple Sauce.

Note: If the 'chain' has not already been removed by the butcher you can chop it up, cook it in a little butter and add it to the stuffing.

Casserole-Roast Pork with Normandy Mustard Sauce

Serves 12–15

Leg of pork can often be very dry, particularly if it is too lean, but casserole-roasting gives a much juicier result. This recipe is perfect for a dinner party because it can be made ahead and reheats perfectly. It is even better made with shoulder meat, which is less expensive.

2.6kg (6lb) boneless joint of pork, rindless but
  with the fat intact (leg, shoulder or loin)
2 tablespoons extra-virgin olive or sunflower oil
mirepoix of vegetables:
  2 onions, sliced
  2 carrots, sliced
  1 outside stalk of celery, sliced
  2 garlic cloves
  1 Bouquet Garni (see page 37)
300ml (½ pint) dry white wine or light Chicken
  Stock (see page 36) or a mixture of both
salt and freshly ground pepper

Sauce
150ml (¼ pint) cider vinegar
12 crushed peppercorns
600ml (1 pint) cream or creamy milk
salt and freshly ground pepper
4 teaspoon English mustard powder, mixed
  with 1 tablespoon water
salt
Roux (see page 580), optional

Garnish
freshly chopped flat-leaf parsley

Preheat the oven to 170°C/325°F/gas 3.

Remove the rind from the pork if necessary and discard. Tie the joint into a neat shape using cotton string. Select a casserole large enough to take the piece of meat without too much waste of space. Heat the oil in the casserole and brown the joint on all sides over medium heat. Remove the pork to a plate and pour off all but a couple of tablespoons of fat from the casserole.

Toss the vegetables and unpeeled garlic in the remaining fat, season, add the bouquet garni and place the joint of pork on top. Add the stock and/or dry white wine, cover and bring to the boil on top of the stove. Transfer to the oven for about 2–2½ hours, basting a couple of times during cooking.

To make the sauce, remove the meat to a warm serving dish, strain the cooking juices and vegetables through a sieve and de-grease.

Add the cider vinegar and peppercorns to the casserole and reduce to about 2–3 tablespoons. Add the de-greased juices and a few tablespoons of the sieved mirepoix. Add the cream and simmer for 5 minutes. Taste and add salt if necessary. Whisk in the mustard and simmer for a few more minutes. The sauce should be a light coating consistency – if it is too thin, thicken slightly by whisking in a little roux.

Taste again and correct seasoning. Strain into a sauce boat and serve with the pork. Alternatively, the pork may be carved onto a serving dish, coated with the sauce and reheated later. In this case pipe a border of Fluffy Mashed Potato (see page 182) around the dish. Serve sprinkled with the chopped parsley.

Sweet and Sour Pork with Prunes, Raisins and Pine Nuts
Serves 6

Jo Bettoja, whose food I adore, served us this rich, sweet and sour stew in her home in Rome. It's an old family recipe for wild boar that has been passed down through the generations. Tim and I loved the rich, gutsy flavour so she kindly shared her recipe.

1.8kg (4lb) boneless shoulder or leg of pork, cubed

Marinade
6 juniper berries
10 black peppercorns
2 bay leaves
½ teaspoon thyme leaves
1 carrot, chopped
1 onion, chopped
1 stick celery, chopped
750ml (24fl oz) or more dry red wine
50ml (2fl oz) red wine vinegar

5 tablespoons extra-virgin olive oil
sea salt
175ml (6fl oz) red wine vinegar
freshly ground pepper
36 prunes, soaked in water
50g (2oz) raisins, plumped in hot water
35g (1½oz) pine nuts, toasted
2 tablespoons sugar
45g (1¾oz) dark chocolate, grated

Accompaniment
Creamy Polenta (see page 135)

Mix all the ingredients for the marinade together in a bowl. Add the cubes of pork and stir well. Cover and marinade for 48 hours in the fridge. Stir every now and then during this period.

Drain the meat, reserving both the marinade and vegetables. Dry the meat on kitchen paper.

Preheat the oven to 170°C/325°F/gas 3.

Heat 4 tablespoons of olive oil in a frying pan on a high heat. Brown the meat on all sides, transfer to a casserole and season with salt. Add a little more oil to the pan and cook the marinated vegetables for 5–8 minutes or until the onion is soft; add a few tablespoons of the marinade to prevent the vegetables from burning if necessary. Add to the meat in the casserole. De-glaze the pan with the rest of the marinade plus 50ml (2fl oz) of red wine vinegar. Bring to the boil and scrape into the casserole.

Add ½ teaspoon pepper, bring back to the boil, cover, and cook in the oven for about 1½ hours until the meat is tender.

Remove the meat to a bowl and strain the sauce into a saucepan (one large enough to fit the meat). Press the vegetables through the sieve to get the last of the juices, and discard the vegetables. Add the prunes, raisins and pine nuts to the sauce.

In another small saucepan simmer 125ml (4fl oz) of red wine vinegar with 2 tablespoons sugar for 4 minutes, then add to the sauce with the chocolate and the meat. Bring slowly to the boil and simmer for 15 minutes. Taste and adjust the seasoning if necessary.

Serve with Creamy Polenta and follow with a good green salad.

How to Make Lard

Lard is made from pig fat that is rendered slowly in the oven at 110°C/225°F/gas ¼. Don't bother unless the pig is at least free-range, and better still, organic. It can be stored in the fridge for 2–3 months.

Portuguese Pork, Bean and Chorizo Stew

Serves about 10

600g (1¼lb) cannellini beans, haricot beans,
   butter beans or black beans
4 tablespoons extra-virgin olive oil
1.1kg (2½lb) streaky pork (belly pork)
700g (1½lb) streaky bacon or pancetta
450g (1lb) ham hocks
4 garlic cloves, sliced
450g (1lb) onions, roughly chopped
450g (1lb) carrots, cut into 7mm (⅓in) slices
2 green peppers, seeded and chopped
sprig of thyme
bay leaf
450g (1lb) very ripe tomatoes, peeled and
   chopped or 1 x 400g (14oz) tin Italian
   tomatoes
450g (1lb) chorizo, cut into 5mm (¼in) slices
freshly ground pepper
1 teaspoon hot or smoked paprika
bunch of parsley stalks as bouquet garni
fistful of fresh coriander or parsley leaves

Soak the beans overnight in plenty of
cold water.

Remove the pork and bacon rind and cut
the meat into 4–5cm (1½–2in) chunks.
Likewise cut the ham hock into chunks.

Heat a little oil in a frying pan, and brown
the pork, bacon and ham hocks on all sides
(a few at a time). Transfer to a large
casserole. Pour off the excess fat but leave
enough to fry off the garlic, onions, carrots
and pepper with the thyme and bay leaf -
cook on a gentle heat, stirring occasionally.

Transfer to the casserole, add the chopped
tomatoes, chorizo, pepper and paprika. De-
grease and de-glaze the pan with a little
water. When all the caramelised meat and
vegetable juices have dissolved, pour them
into the casserole, then add just enough
water to almost cover the meat. Bring to
the boil, add the parsley stalks if using,
and cover. Simmer gently on a low heat
for 2–2½ hours, or transfer to a moderate
oven, 170°C/325°F/gas 3.

Meanwhile, drain the soaked beans, cover
with fresh cold water, bring to the boil and
simmer until cooked. This takes about 40
minutes to 1½ hours, depending on the
type of bean. Add to the stew 15–20
minutes before the end of cooking. Check
the seasoning; it is unlikely to need salt.

Serve in deep wide soup bowls sprinkled
with lots of coarsely chopped coriander or
parsley. Mop up the juices with crusty
bread.

Pork Fillet with Gentle Spices

Serves 4–6

**An excellent dish for entertaining; serve
with a green vegetable and a bowl of orzo
or Pilaf Rice (see page 125). You can also
use chicken breasts.**

1–2 teaspoons whole cardamom pods
1 teaspoon whole coriander seeds
1 teaspoon whole cumin seeds
25g (1oz) butter
110g (4oz) onions, chopped
2 pork fillets or 700g (1½lb) pork leg or
   shoulder
salt and freshly ground pepper
150ml (¼ pint) homemade Chicken Stock
   (see page 36)
150ml (¼ pint) cream

Garnish
flat-leaf parsley or coriander

If using leg or shoulder preheat the oven to
150°C/300°F/gas 2.

Press the cardamom pods and extract
the seeds; grind to a fine powder with the
coriander and cumin seeds in a pestle and
mortar or in a spice grinder.

Melt the butter in a sauté pan, add the
onions and sweat over a gentle heat until
soft. Remove from the heat. Slice the pork
fillets into 2cm (¾in) slices. If using pork
leg or shoulder, cut into 2cm (¾in) cubes

and trim off the fat. Season with salt and
pepper, toss the meat in the ground spices,
add to the onion and sauté gently for a
few minutes. For pork fillet cover the pan
tightly and cook for 10–15 minutes. If leg or
shoulder is being used, transfer the sauté
pan to the oven for 20–40 minutes, or until
the pork pieces are cooked but still nice
and juicy. Remove the pork to a serving
dish and keep warm. (The dish may be
prepared ahead to this point – reheat in
a saucepan over a gentle heat until
piping hot.)

Put the casserole back onto the heat, add
the stock and cream and allow to bubble
for 3 or 4 minutes. Taste and adjust the
seasoning, add the pork pieces back into
the sauce, allow to reheat for 2 or more
minutes. Serve on a hot dish, garnished
with flat leaf parsley or coriander.

Spare Ribs with Ginger

Serves 4–6

900g (2lb) nice, meaty spare ribs
5cm (2in) piece fresh ginger, peeled and crushed
5 tablespoons dark soy sauce
5 tablespoons sugar
4 spring onions or scallions
3 tablespoons Chinese rice wine or dry sherry

Unless you are adept with a chopper, give
your butcher a big smile and ask him to
separate the spare ribs and chop each
into 8cm (3in) lengths.

Choose a wide sauté pan or frying pan, and
add the ginger, soy sauce, sugar, spring
onions, rice wine and water. Stir and add
the spare ribs. Bring to the boil, cover and
simmer over a medium heat. Stir every
now and then. After about 35 minutes
increase the heat. Remove and discard
the spring onions and ginger.

Cook for another 20–25 minutes until the
liquid is thick and syrupy. Turn the spare
ribs in the glaze until they are evenly
coated. Serve hot.

RIGHT: Pork Fillet with Gentle Spices

Carbonnade of Pork with Mushrooms

Serves 6–8

A quick and delicious recipe. If you haven't got any wine to hand, just add a little more stock. The same formula can be used for fillet steak or chicken breast but be careful not to overcook the meat.

900g (2lb) pork fillet
1–2 tablespoons extra-virgin olive or sunflower
* oil or a little butter*
110g (4oz) onion, finely chopped
60ml (2½fl oz) dry white wine
150ml (¼ pint) homemade Chicken Stock
* (see page 36)*
225g (8oz) mushrooms, sliced
300ml (½ pint) sour cream or light cream
Roux (see page 580)
juice of 1 lemon
salt and freshly ground pepper
2 tablespoons freshly chopped flat-leaf parsley

Garnish
6–8 heart-shaped croûtons made with white
* bread fried in clarified butter or olive oil*

Cut the pork into slices about 7mm (⅓in) thick. Pour a little oil into a very hot frying pan, sauté the pork pieces a few at a time until brown on both sides. Remove to a plate and keep warm.

Add a little more oil or butter and cook onions gently until soft and golden. De-glaze the pan with wine and bring to the boil, add the stock and boil again to reduce by a quarter.

Meanwhile sauté the sliced mushrooms in batches in a little butter and oil in a very hot pan and add to the pork.

Add the cream to the sauce, bring back to the boil and thicken with a little roux. Add the cooked pork and mushrooms. Taste, add a little lemon juice, and simmer gently for a couple of minutes.

Dip the tip of the croûtons in the sauce and then into the chopped parsley.

Add the remainder of the parsley to the sauce, taste again and correct seasoning if necessary. Pour into a hot serving dish and garnish with the crisp croûtons.

Filipino Pork with Peppers and Fresh Ginger

Serves 6

Oriental meat recipes make the most of a little meat. This delicious pork dish was cooked for me by Susie Noriega. Serve with Plain Boiled Rice (see page 124).

450g (1lb) pork fillet
2 tablespoons light soy sauce
freshly ground pepper
35g (1½oz) unsalted peanuts, shelled
1 fresh red or green chilli
35g (1½oz) bamboo shoots
2 small green peppers
2.5cm (1in) fresh ginger root
large garlic clove
4 large spring onions
2 tablespoons groundnut oil
1 teaspoon tapioca
60ml (2½fl oz) water, approx.
1 tablespoon Tabasco or oyster sauce
pinch of sugar

Cut the pork into 5mm (¼in) strips, marinate in light soy sauce, season with freshly ground pepper and leave aside. Put the peanuts on a baking sheet and roast for about 20 minutes in a moderate oven, 180°C/350°F/gas 4, until golden. Rub off the loose skins.

Halve the chilli and remove the seeds. Cut into small dice. Cut the bamboo shoots in pieces the same size as the pork. Halve and quarter the green pepper, remove the seeds and cut into similar-sized pieces.

Peel the ginger root and garlic and chop finely. Also chop the spring onions finely, at an angle.

Heat a wok, add half the oil and fry the garlic, ginger and spring onions for a few

seconds. Remove to a plate. Heat the wok to very hot, add the other tablespoon of oil, and toss the pork for 2 minutes maximum and then add in the rest of the vegetables. Season with salt and freshly ground pepper, add a drop of water, cover and cook for 3–4 minutes until the vegetables are cooked but still crunchy. Then add the chilli and roasted peanuts.

Dissolve the tapioca in about 60ml (2½fl oz) of water, add a dash of Tabasco or oyster sauce and a pinch of sugar. Add to the wok, bubble up again and serve immediately in a hot serving dish.

Joanna's Ginger Pork (or Beef)

Serves 3–4

300–450g (11–14oz) pork loin or beef steak,
* thinly sliced*

Marinade
1 tablespoon sake
2 tablespoons soy sauce
1 teaspoon ginger juice

Sauce
3 tablespoons mirin
2 tablespoons caster sugar
3 tablespoons soy sauce
1 tablespoon ginger juice (or more to taste)

Mix all the ingredients for the marinade in a bowl and add the meat, marinating for 5–7 minutes. Grate the ginger on a microplane and then squeeze a tablespoon's worth of juice out of the pulp (or use a garlic press).

Heat a large frying pan (not too hot) and add the mirin and sugar. When the sugar has dissolved and it starts to bubble, add the meat and soy sauce. If the pan is not big enough to comfortably hold everything, do it in two batches.

When the meat is cooked, the pan will be quite juicy. At this stage add the ginger juice, stir and turn off the heat. It can be served hot or at room temperature.

Pork Chop with Pineapple, Chilli and Coriander Salsa

Serves 8

8 pork chops, free-range if possible

Chilli and Rosemary Marinade
4 tablespoons finely chopped rosemary
4 cloves garlic, crushed
1 tablespoon freshly cracked peppercorns
1 teaspoon fennel seeds, crushed
1/4–1/2 chilli flakes
6 tablespoons extra-virgin olive oil

Pineapple, Chilli and Coriander Salsa
1/2–1 fresh pineapple, diced
1–2 red chillis, seeded and diced
1 medium red onion, finely diced
2 tablespoons finely chopped coriander or mint
grated zest of 1 lime
3–4 tablespoons lime juice, freshly squeezed
salt
pinch of sugar (optional)

Mix all the ingredients for the marinade together. Snip the fat off the chops. Dip both sides in the marinade, cover and leave to absorb the flavours for an hour or more.

Meanwhile make the salsa. Mix all the ingredients in a pottery or stainless steel bowl. Taste and correct seasoning. Allow the flavours to mingle for 15–30 minutes if possible.

Just before serving, season the pork chops with salt. Grill over a barbecue or on a pan-grill until cooked through. Serve with the salsa.

Thai Stir-fried Pork with Ginger and Coriander

Serves 4–6

The quantity of fresh ginger may seem extraordinary here but it tastes great so don't be tempted to reduce it.

450g (1lb) pork fillet
2 teaspoons cornflour
good pinch of salt
2 tablespoons sesame oil
3 tablespoons sunflower or ground nut oil
4 tablespoons fresh ginger, peeled and finely chopped
2 tablespoons fish sauce (nam pla)
2 tablespoons soy sauce
1 teaspoon sugar
freshly ground pepper

Garnish
fresh coriander leaves

Trim the pork fillet and cut into 5mm (1/4in) thick slices. Cut each slice into 4 chips. Put them into a bowl and toss well with the cornflour, salt and sesame oil. Leave to marinate for 20–30 minutes.

Just before eating, heat the sunflower oil in a wok, add the ginger, and stir-fry in the hot oil until just beginning to crisp (this may take 2–3 minutes but it's worth persevering). Add the pork and toss until it changes colour. Then add the fish sauce, soy sauce, sugar and lots of freshly ground pepper. Taste and correct the seasoning if necessary.

Turn into a hot serving dish, garnish with fresh coriander leaves and serve with rice and perhaps some mange tout peas.

Master Recipe
Homemade Sausages with Scallion Mash

Serves 6–8 (makes about 12–16)

Homemade sausages are just as easy to make as hamburgers and make a cheap and comforting meal. Use organic, free-range pork, and at least 1/4 fat to lean, better still 1/3, otherwise the sausages will be dry rather than juicy.

450g (1lb) good, fat, streaky pork
2–4 teaspoons mixed fresh herbs – parsley, thyme, chives, marjoram and rosemary or sage
1 large garlic clove, crushed
1 organic egg
60g (2 1/2oz) soft white breadcrumbs
salt and freshly ground pepper
a little vegetable oil

Mince the pork – once for coarse sausages, twice for a finer texture. Chop the herbs finely. Crush the garlic to a paste with a little salt. Whisk the egg, then mix all the ingredients together thoroughly in a bowl and season well.

Heat a frying pan, fry off a little knob of the mixture to check the seasoning, and correct it if necessary. Divide into 16 pieces and roll into sausages. Fry gently on a barely oiled pan until golden on all sides. These sausages are particularly delicious served with Bramley Apple Sauce (see page 597) and a big bowl of buttery Scallion Mash (see page 182).

TIP: Resist the temptation to make them too large, otherwise they are difficult to cook properly into the centre without burning the outside.

Variations

Homemade Sausages with Coriander and Thai Dipping Sauce

I recently substituted 2 tablespoons of fresh coriander for the mixed herbs in the sausage mixture and found it completely delicious. I also added a good pinch of sugar to enhance the sweetness in the oriental way. If you want to continue in that vein serve the sausages with Thai Dipping Sauce (see page 88), instead of the more traditional mash and apple sauce.

Chilli Bangers

Add 1–2 chopped chillies to the pork for extra excitement. Chilli flakes can be used if you have no chillies.

Vietnamese Pork and Lemongrass Patties

Serves 4–6 (makes 16 approx.)

450g (1lb) lean, minced pork
25g (1oz) shallots, chopped
2 stalks lemongrass, trimmed and very finely chopped
½ teaspoon salt
lots of freshly ground pepper

Put everything into a food processor, season well with salt and pepper, and whizz for just a few seconds. Heat a frying pan and cook a tiny piece to check the seasoning, adjusting if necessary.

Make the meat mixture into patties up to 8cm (3in) in diameter and pan-grill for 5 minutes on each side. Alternatively you can make the meat into small balls about 5cm (2in) in diameter and thread them onto well-soaked bamboo skewers and barbecue them for 10–15 minutes, turning on all sides. Serve with a Thai Dipping Sauce (see page 88).

RIGHT: Vietnamese Pork and Lemongrass Patties

beef

beef

Butchers

The art of a butcher does not merely involve killing and cutting up meat. The skill starts when he sees an animal in a field and judges whether it will kill out into good meat or not. Then there is the ability to keep the animals relaxed, to slaughter humanely, and the judgement involved in knowing how long to hang the meat (this is, of course, vitally important, but is only one of many factors). Finally there is the practical skill involved in cutting up the meat. Many craft butchers have learned the trade from their fathers and grandfathers, or they have been apprenticed to a good butcher. They understand and know every part of the process.

In an abattoir, on the other hand, there may be hundreds of people each having knowledge of only one or two parts of the production line. It seems completely incredible to me that we do not appreciate and value the small, conscientious local butchers more – they have such a wealth of knowledge and experience. It is these butchers who are virtually being hassled out of existence by EU and government regulations that would prefer to have only eight or ten abattoirs across the country, to make regulation easier. However, we are hopeful that with the reallocation of funds under CAP reforms towards rural development, the mindset at official level is becoming more supportive.

Breeds

Apart from the pasture the animals graze on, the flavour of the meat is determined by the breed. The breeds that I prefer for flavour are what I call the traditional breeds: Aberdeen Angus, or Aberdeen Angus crossed with Shorthorn, Hereford and Pole Angus. There are also a lot of delicious UK rare breeds, such as Devons, Longhorn and Ayrshires.

Here on the farm I have some Aberdeen Angus, Herefords and some crosses. I also have a small herd of beautiful, black Kerry cattle. Kerry is not really a beef breed (they are very good for dairy), but I've been rearing them because they were an endangered species and I wanted to help preserve the breed. They are the oldest Irish breed – possibly even the oldest in Europe. Timmy gave me my first Kerry cow about ten years ago as a birthday present. She came from an organic farmer called Ivan Ward from County Wexford.

In recent years, the principal emphasis in agriculture has been on producing food as cheaply as possible through maximum yields, and farmers have been encouraged and pressurised in this direction. The unfortunate consequence of this policy is that animals and plants are consistently pushed beyond their natural limit. In an effort to satisfy the unrealistic demands of supermarkets and consumers, farmers have sourced cheaper and cheaper protein for animal feeds, resulting in meal that contained not only meat and bone meal, but also wood pulp and even on occasion, faeces. The end result has been BSE in animals and CJD in humans. At present it is still very difficult to source animal feed that can be guaranteed GM free – a considerable concern for a growing number of farmers and consumers.

In Ireland, grass grows abundantly and many of our best foods, meat and dairy, are grass-based. Although most cattle are fed a little grain, I prefer the flavour of grass-fed to exclusively grain-fed beef (it has a rich golden fat and a really delicious beefy flavour).There is also a growing body of research highlighting the nutritional advantages of grass-fed beef.

Buying

Seek out local butchers who know exactly where their meat comes from and how the animals were reared – such butchers are a vital link with safe and quality meat. At Ballymaloe we buy from several local butchers including Frank Murphy and Michael McGrath who also have their own abattoirs. Engage with your local butcher – ask about breeds and feed every time you buy meat. Watch as he butchers so you can become familiar with the various cuts of meat. Ask for advise and don't forget to give feedback when you get something particularly delicious.

When buying your meat, choose meat with a little layer of fat – fat gives flavour and while a joint of meat is roasting, it renders out and bastes the meat, giving it an extra sweetness and succulence. Both the colour of the fat and the amount of marbling in the flesh is determined by the breed, age and diet of the animal. One doesn't have to eat the fat, but it does need to be on the meat originally for flavour. Dieticians are correct to caution us against eating too much fat, but don't get caught up in the low-fat mania. It is not only how much fat you eat, but the kind of fat that is important – a little quality fat is good for us. The main reason to be careful is that toxins from an animal's feed collect in its fat. If we eat too much of it, it can in turn be absorbed into our own fat tissue.

Cuts of Beef and How to Cook Them

The majority of the prime cuts are from the hind quarter, with most of the stewing and braising meat in the fore-quarter. Remember that the parts of the animal that are exercised the most tend to be the toughest, but they are also the cuts that have the best flavour. As with any meat much of the flavour comes from the bones. It is therefore very important, particularly for stews, casseroles and roasting, to include the bones when cooking.

A **T-bone steak**, found along the loin, should consist of the T-bone, sirloin, fillet and sometimes a little streaky piece on the end. **Sirloin** and **fillet** steaks are suitable for roasting, pan-grilling or sautéing. Fillet steaks are always tender but not necessarily full of beefy flavour. If you are not sure how many steaks you will need, buy the whole piece of sirloin or fillet and cut the steaks as you need them. Steak should be cut at least 2.5cm (1/2in) thick – unless they are medallions of fillet or minute steaks. Steaks are best eaten on the day they are cut (they pick up a 'fridge taste' if they are not consumed rapidly).

The shoulder and neck meat is lean and good for mincing and casseroles. **Mince** should always be eaten on the day it is minced, or alternativley freeze it in a flat block. **Prime rib** is excellent for roasting while the round, topside, silverside and brisket are best in **pot roasts**. Parts that are a little tougher, such as round steak, flank and shins have excellent flavour and benefit from being stewed or braised.

Cheaper cuts of meat e.g. short ribs, shin of beef, flank, flap and skirt are suitable for braising and slowly cooking and make truly delicious meals. Many creative chefs and home cooks derive much more satisfaction from making a dish from cheaper cuts – anyone can slap a fillet steak onto a pan but it takes much more skill to produce succulent short ribs or oxtail stew.

At Ballymaloe we occasionally serve **baby beef**, but we do not serve intensively reared veal. **Veal** is the meat from calves slaughtered at four or five months. In some systems, the calves are kept indoors all their lives and light is excluded, so the flesh is pale. They are milk-fed and their feed includes antibiotics. Baby beef are also milk-fed, but the flesh is not so pale and the flavour not so delicate. We find it sweet and delicious and our guests enjoy it very much.

Roasting time (see page 336) can only ever be a guideline, since it depends not only on the weight, but also on the thickness of the cut. When you calculate cooking time, be sure to incorporate some resting time as the internal temperature of the meat will continue to rise by a degree or two as it rests in a warm oven.

Corned and Spiced Beef

Corned beef has always been associated with Ireland – many people think that we live almost exclusively on corned beef and cabbage! This is not the case, though it can be truly delicious. Meat was originally corned (brined) or spiced to preserve it in the days before refrigeration. Many spices have preservative and antiseptic properties, so spiced beef lasts as long, if not longer, than corned beef. Enormous quantities of corned and spiced beef were exported from Cork and one can still buy both in the Cork market, all year round.

Hanging

Hanging meat is important because it both tenderises the flesh and develops flavour. The hanging time depends on several factors, including breed and age. Our local butcher hangs our beef for ten days before he delivers it to Ballymaloe, where we hang it in a cold room for a further week or so. It sounds quite short, but these are mostly maiden heifers (18 month-old females that have never calved), so they do not need to be hung as long as older carcasses.

You may want to order a large joint of prime beef well ahead and ask your butcher to hang it for you. A butcher's cold room is invariably a better environment for hanging meat than a domestic fridge. Well hung meat loses some weight and is darker on the outside where it is exposed to the air. This is desirable so don't be fooled into thinking that all meat should be bright red or pink in colour.

Traditional Roast Rib of Beef with Horseradish Sauce, Gravy and Yorkshire Pudding

Serves 8–10

Few people can resist a roast rib of beef with horseradish sauce, Yorkshire pudding, lots of gravy and crusty roast potatoes. Choose the meat carefully. Always buy beef on the bone for roasting; it will have much more flavour and it isn't difficult to carve. Ask your butcher for a traditional breed as these have the best flavour.

2.6–3.6kg (6–8lb) prime rib of beef on the bone
salt and freshly cracked pepper
Yorkshire Pudding (see page 338)
Horseradish Sauce (see page 586)

Gravy
600ml (1 pint) homemade Beef or Chicken Stock
   (see page 36)
Roux (see page 580), optional

Ask your butcher to saw through the upper chine bone so the 'feather bones' will be easy to remove before carving. Weigh the joint and calculate cooking time (see right).

Preheat the oven to 250°C/475°F/gas 9.

Score the fat and season with salt and pepper. Place the meat in a roasting tin with the fat side uppermost. As the fat renders in the heat of the oven, it will baste the meat. The bones provide a natural rack to hold the meat clear of the fat in the roasting pan.

Put the meat into a fully preheated oven; after 15 minutes turn down the heat to moderate (180°C/350°F/gas 4) until the meat is cooked to your taste.

Meanwhile, make the batter for the Yorkshire pudding and allow to rest. Make the Horseradish Sauce, cover and refrigerate.

When the meat is cooked, it should be allowed to rest on a plate in a cool oven for 15–30 minutes before carving, depending on the size of the roast. A plate-warming oven would be perfect. The internal temperature of the meat will continue to rise by as much as 2–3°C/5°F, so remove the roast from the oven while it is still slightly underdone.

Put the Yorkshire pudding into a hot oven to cook; it will take about 20 minutes.

Meanwhile make the gravy: tilt the roasting tin to the side and spoon off as much of the fat as possible. Pour the cold stock into the cooking juices remaining in the tin. The last globules of fat will solidify. Quickly remove them with a spoon, bring to the boil, stirring and scraping the pan well to dissolve the caramelised meat juices (I find a small whisk ideal for this). Thicken very slightly with a little Roux, if you like. Taste and add salt and pepper if necessary. Strain and serve in a warm gravy boat.

Carve the beef at the table and serve with Horseradish Sauce, Yorkshire pudding, gravy and lots of crusty Roast Potatoes (see page 181).

Roast Rib of Beef with Three Sauces

At Ballymaloe House we serve prime Rib of Beef with **Horseradish Sauce** (see page 586), **Béarnaise Sauce** (see page 586) and **Garlic Mayonnaise** (see page 584) and lots of crusty Roast Potatoes (see page 181) – a delicious combination.

Roasting Times

Since ovens vary enormously in efficiency, thermostats are not always accurate and some joints of meat are much thicker than others, these figures must be treated as guidelines rather than rules. The times below include the 15-minute searing time at a high heat.

Beef on the bone
Rare 10–12 minutes per 450g (1lb)
Medium 12–15 minutes per 450g (1lb)
Well-done 18–20 minutes per 450g (1lb)

Beef off the bone
Rare 8–10 minutes per 450g (1lb)
Medium 10–12 minutes per 450g (1lb)
Well-done 15–18 minutes per 450g (1lb)

How do I know when the meat is cooked?
There are various ways of checking. I usually put a skewer into the thickest part of the joint, leave it there for about 30–45 seconds and then put it against the back of my hand, if it still feels cool, the meat is rare, if it is warm it is medium rare, if it's hotter it's medium and if you can't keep the skewer against your hand for more than a second then you can bet it is well done. Also, if you check the colour of the juices you will find they are clear as opposed to red or pink for rare or medium.

If you own a meat thermometer, that will eliminate guesswork altogether but make sure the thermometer is not touching a bone when you are testing.

Beef is rare at an internal temperature of 60°C/140°F, medium at 70°C/145°F and well-done at 75°C/165°F.

Boning and Carving a Rib of Beef

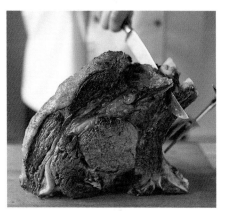  

For maximum flavour, cook the rib of beef with the chine bone still attached, and remove it before carving. You can also remove the meat from the ribs to faciliate carving. We prefer however to carve the meat while it is still on the bone. Be sure to have a really sharp carving knife.

Master Recipe
Yorkshire Pudding

Serves 8–10

Simply irresistible with lots of gravy! I cook individual ones which I'm sure would be very much frowned on in Yorkshire but, if you want to be more traditional, cook one large pudding in a roasting tin and cut it into squares.

110g (4oz) white flour, preferably unbleached
pinch of salt
2 organic eggs
300ml (1/2 pint) milk
10g (1/2oz) butter, melted
olive oil or pure beef dripping (unless for
    vegetarians) for greasing tins
deep bun tray

Sieve the flour and salt into a bowl, make a well in the centre and drop in the eggs.

Using a small whisk or wooden spoon, stir continuously, gradually drawing in flour from the sides, adding half the milk in a steady stream at the same time. When all the flour has been mixed in, whisk in the remainder of the milk and the cool melted butter. Allow to stand for 1 hour.

Grease a hot, deep bun tin with beef dripping or olive oil and fill half to two-thirds full with the batter. Bake in a hot oven for about 20 minutes. Remove from the tins and serve warm.

Variations
Olive Yorkshire Puddings
Follow the Master Recipe and grease the tins with olive oil. Drop 2 or 3 stoned olives into each pudding.

Mustard and Thyme Leaf Yorkshire Pudding
Follow the Master Recipe and add some thyme leaves to the mixture and English or French mustard to each pudding.

Toad in a Hole
Pop a freshly cooked chipolata into each bun tin before cooking.

Sirloin of Beef Roast with Cracked Peppercorns served with Olive Yorkshire Puddings

Serves 1

1.8kg (4lb) sirloin of beef, well hung
extra-virgin olive oil
25–50g (1–2oz) black peppercorns, cracked
sea salt

Olive Yorkshire Puddings (see above)
Gravy (see page 594)

Garnish
sprigs of rosemary, watercress or flat-leaf
    parsley

Preheat the oven to 250°C/475°F/gas 9.

An hour or so before you plan to cook the meat, score the fat lightly, brush the surface of the meat with olive oil and coat with freshly cracked black pepper.

Place the meat in a roasting tin, fat side up. Sprinkle with sea salt and put into the fully preheated oven. After 15 minutes, reduce the heat to moderate (180°C/350°F/gas 4). As the fat renders down, it will baste the meat. Roast until the beef is cooked to your taste. Transfer to a carving dish. Keep warm while you make the gravy. Taste the gravy and strain into a sauce boat.

Serve with a little Gravy and an Olive Yorkshire Pudding.

Serve Horseradish Sauce (see page 586) and Béarnaise Sauce (see page 586) separately. Salsa Verde (see page 593) makes a good accompaniment in summer; in winter Pan-roasted Parsnips (see page 175) go well.

How to Cook Steak

The approximate cooking times for each side of the steaks are:

	sirloin	fillet
rare	2 minutes	5 minutes
medium rare	3 minutes	6 minutes
medium	4 minutes	7 minutes
well done	5 minutes	8–9 minutes

Steak with Irish Whiskey Sauce

Serves 4

4 well-hung sirloin or fillet steaks
1 garlic clove
lots of freshly ground pepper
olive oil
salt
110–225g (4–8oz) mushrooms
2–4 tablespoons Irish whiskey
125ml (4fl oz) homemade Beef Stock
    (see page 36)
25ml (4fl oz) cream
1 tablespoon freshly chopped flat-leaf parsley

Cut the clove of garlic in half and rub the cut side over the steaks. Then crush the garlic and reserve for the sauce. Season the steaks with freshly ground pepper and drizzle over a litle olive oil.

Just before serving, sauté the mushrooms in a hot pan, season with salt and pepper and keep warm. Wash the pan out. Season the steaks with salt and cook to your taste. Remove to a plate. De-glaze the pan with whiskey and allow to flame; as the flames die away, add the garlic, stock, cream and parsley. Bring to the boil and simmer for a few minutes, add the mushrooms and continue to cook until the sauce tastes really good and lightly coats the back of a spoon. Put the steaks onto 4 warm plates. Pour any escaped juices into the sauce, taste and correct the seasoning. Spoon over the steaks and serve immediately.

From left to right: T-bone steak, sirloin steak, minute steak, fillet steak and medallions

Pan-grilled Steak with Béarnaise Sauce, French Fried Onions and Chips
Serves 6

Of all the sauces to serve with steak, Béarnaise is my absolute favourite. We find a heavy-ridged, cast-iron grill pan best for cooking steaks when you don't need to make a sauce in the pan.

6 x 175g (6oz) sirloin or fillet steaks
1 garlic clove, halved
a little olive oil
salt and freshly ground pepper

Béarnaise Sauce (see page 586)
French Fried Onions (see page 187)
Chips (see page 184)

Garnish
fresh watercress (optional)

Prepare the steaks about 1 hour before cooking. Rub both sides of each steak with the cut face of the garlic. Grind some black pepper over the steaks and sprinkle on a few drops of olive oil. Turn the steaks in the oil and set aside. If using sirloin steaks, score the fat at 2.5cm (1in) intervals.

Prepare the French Fried Onions and make the Béarnaise Sauce and keep warm. Just before serving, heat the pan-grill, season the steaks with a little salt and put them down onto the hot pan. Turn a sirloin steak over onto the fat and cook for 1–2 minutes or until the fat becomes crisp.

Put the steaks onto a plate and leave to rest for a few minutes in a warm place while you cook the Chips. Garnish with watercress and serve.

Sirloin Steak Sandwich with Bonnie Stern's Barbecued Onion Sauce
Serves 8

An extraordinary-sounding sauce, it really takes an act of faith to make it but it tastes delicious. Bonnie Stern is a fellow cook from Toronto whose *Heart Smart* books are full of little gems.

700g (1¹⁄₂lb) sirloin, cut into generous 2.5cm (1in) thick steaks
2 tablespoons balsamic vinegar
1 tablespoon Dijon mustard
¹⁄₂ teaspoon freshly ground pepper
2 garlic cloves, crushed
2 thin French sticks
handful of freshly chopped flat-leaf parsley

Bonnie Stern's Barbecued Onion Sauce
2 tablespoons olive oil
3 large onions, sliced
3 garlic cloves, chopped
110g (4oz) tinned tomatoes
100g (3¹⁄₂oz) brown sugar
125ml (4fl oz) rice vinegar or cider vinegar
125ml (4fl oz) strong coffee
1 tablespoon Worcestershire sauce

Pat the steak dry. Mix the balsamic vinegar, mustard, pepper and garlic in a small bowl. Rub all over the meat. Cover and refrigerate.

Make the onion sauce: heat the olive oil in a saucepan. Add the onions and garlic and cook until soft but not coloured. Add the tomatoes, sugar, rice vinegar, coffee and Worcestershire sauce. Bring to the boil and simmer gently for 15 minutes.

Just before serving, barbecue or pan-grill the steak, 4–6 minutes on each side for sirloin steak, depending on the thickness. Allow to rest for 5 minutes. Slice thinly. Cut the crusty French sticks into 8 equal lengths, slit each in half and make hot, juicy sandwiches with the steak and barbecued onion sauce. Sprinkle with lots of parsley and eat immediately.

Other Good Things to Serve with Steaks
Salsa Verde (see page 593)
Mushroom à la Crème (see page 201)
Sauce Beurre Rouge (see page 583)
Tapenade (see page 590)
Anchoïade (see page 594)
Olive and Anchovy Butter (see page 588)
Provençale Butter (see page 588)
Barbecue Sauce (see page 538)
Dijon and Grainy Mustard Cream (see page 586)
Chipotle Butter (see page 175)
Garlic Butter (see page 588)
Roasted Red Pepper Pesto (see page 590)

Seared Beef with Gorgonzola Polenta and Red Onion Marmalade

Serves 6

6 x 175g (6oz) fillet steaks

Red Onion Marmalade (see page 512)

Gorgonzola Polenta
1.5 litres (2½ pints) homemade Chicken Stock
  (see page 36)
175g (6oz) cornmeal
salt and freshly ground pepper
175g (6oz) Gorgonzola or Dolcelatte

Garnish
rocket leaves

First make the Red Onion Marmalade.

Next make the polenta: bring the chicken stock to the boil and whisk in the cornmeal. Turn the heat down to a minimum and cook for 30–35 minutes, stirring regularly. Remove from heat and stir in the cheese. Season to taste.

To serve, barbecue or pan-grill the steaks to your taste. Spoon a little soft polenta onto the centre of each plate.

Arrange a steak on top with a small spoonful of Red Onion Marmalade. Garnish with some rocket leaves.

Sirloin Steak with Chimichurri Sauce

Serves 6–8 and makes 225–250ml (8–9fl oz) sauce

Chimichurri is a hot and perky sauce from Argentina.

6 x 175g (6oz) sirloin steaks

Chimichurri Sauce
1 cup flat-leaf parsley
4 large garlic cloves, peeled and crushed
125ml (4fl oz) extra-virgin olive oil

50ml (2fl oz) red wine vinegar
2 tablespoons water
salt
1 red onion, finely chopped
½ chilli, de-seeded and chopped, or ¼ teaspoon chilli flakes

Chop the parsley finely with the garlic. (Alternatively, pulse in a food processor, scraping down the sides of the bowl, until well mixed.) Transfer to a bowl. Whisk in the oil, vinegar and water gradually. Add the red onion, chilli and salt. Taste and add more seasoning if necessary.

Pan-grill the steak, transfer to hot plates, spoon some chimichurri over the top and serve immediately with crusty fried potatoes or Rustic Roasts (see page 181).

Rib Eye Steak with Roquefort Cheese, Glazed Onions, Roasted Red Peppers and Rosemary on Soft Polenta

Serves 6

1 garlic clove
6 rib eye steaks
lots of freshly ground pepper
salt
4 roasted red peppers, skinned and peeled
4–6 onions
75g (3oz) Roquefort or Gorgonzola or Cashel Blue Cheese

Garnish
sprigs of flat-leaf parsley
sprigs of rosemary
sprigs of tarragon

Creamy Polenta (see page 135)

Cut the garlic clove in half and rub the cut side over the steaks. Season with salt and lots of freshly ground pepper.

Next make the Creamy Polenta.

Peel and slice the onion. Melt some butter and oil in a sauté pan and cook over a medium heat, stirring occasionally until soft and slightly caramelised. Keep both the onions and the thick strips of roasted red pepper warm.

Preheat a heavy grill pan. Season the steaks with salt and cook to perfection on the hot pan. Meanwhile, reheat the polenta if necessary. Taste and correct the seasoning.

Spoon some onto each hot plate and place a steak on top. Divide the hot caramelised onions and the pepper strips between each steak. Crumble some chunks of Roquefort, Gorgonzola or Cashel Blue cheese on top. Garnish with rosemary sprigs, tarragon and flat-leaf parsley.

Peppered Steak with Cauliflower Purée

Serves 6

Cauliflower Purée (see page 169)

6 x 175g–200g (6–7oz) well hung sirloin steaks
1 garlic clove, peeled and halved
2 tablespoons white peppercorns
2 tablespoons black peppercorns
olive oil
sea salt

First make the Cauliflower Purée.

Rub the steaks on both sides with the cut side of the garlic. Crush the peppercorns coarsely in a pestle and mortar or in a coffee grinder. Brush each steak lightly with olive oil and then dip into the peppercorns, coating both sides evenly.

Heat a frying pan until very hot and add a few tablespoons of oil. Season the steaks with sea salt, transfer to the pan, reduce the heat to medium and cook until a good thick crust has formed. Turn the steaks over and finish cooking to suit your taste.

Remove the steaks to hot plates and allow to rest. Serve the steaks on a bed of rocket with Sauté Potatoes (see page 185) and Cauliflower Purée.

Peppered Beef with Scallion and Horseradish Mash

Serves 4

4 x 175g (6oz) fillet steaks
freshly cracked black peppercorns
salt
1–2 tablespoons olive oil
50ml (2fl oz) brandy
125ml (4fl oz) homemade Beef Stock
  (see page 36)
175ml (6fl oz) cream
1½ tablespoons green peppercorns
rocket leaves
Scallion and Horseradish Mash (see page 182)

First cook the Scallion and Horseradish Mash.

Roll the fillet steaks in the cracked peppercorns and season with salt. Heat a heavy pan, add a little oil and seal the steaks on all sides. Reduce the heat and cook to the desired stage. Remove from the pan and rest in a warm place while you make the sauce: pour off any excess fat, de-glaze the pan with brandy, add the beef stock, cream and whole peppercorns. Reduce to a light pouring consistency.

Put a large spoonful of Scallion and Horseradish Mash on the plate, arrange the rocket leaves beside it and lay the steak on top. Spoon over some sauce.

Variation
Pan-grilled Steak with Grainy Mustard Butter, Scallion and Horseradish Mash
Pan-grill the steak, serve with Scallion and Horseradish Mash (see page 182) and a slice of Grainy Mustard Butter (see page 588) melting on top.

Stewing

The tougher cuts of meat are perfect for long, slow stewing which tenderises the meat. Cuts of meat suitable for stewing:

Lamb: neck, shoulder, breast
Beef: neck, shin, brisket, chuck chump, blade, flank, skirt
Veal: shank, flank, neck
Pork: neck, leg, shoulder

Daube de Boeuf Provençale (Beef Provençale)

Serves 8

This gutsy winter stew has a rich, robust flavour. It reheats perfectly and can also be made ahead and frozen.

1.3kg (3lb) lean stewing beef – use topside
  or chuck

Marinade
2 tablespoons olive oil
300ml (½ pint) dry white or red wine
1 teaspoon salt
½ teaspoon pepper
½ teaspoon thyme, sage or annual marjoram
1 bay leaf
2 garlic cloves, peeled and crushed
110g (4oz) carrots, thinly sliced
110g (4oz) onions, thinly sliced

450g (1lb) streaky bacon cut into 1cm (½in)
  lardons
1 x 400g (14oz) tin Italian tomatoes, chopped
150ml (¼ pint) Beef Stock (see page 36)
175g (6oz) sliced mushrooms
10 anchovy fillets
2 tablespoons capers
3 tablespoons white or red wine vinegar
2 tablespoons freshly chopped flat-leaf parsley
2 garlic cloves, mashed
Roux (see page 580), optional

Garnish
flat-leaf parsley, freshly chopped

Cut the beef into large chunks, about 8cm (3in). Mix the marinade ingredients in a bowl or large casserole. Add the meat, cover and marinate overnight in a fridge or cool larder. Transfer the meat to a plate. Strain the marinade, reserve the vegetables and the marinade.

Preheat the oven to 170°C/325°F/gas 3.

Heat the oil in a frying pan, cook the lardons until crisp, add to the casserole. Dry the meat with kitchen paper. Seal the meat on the hot pan, and add to the bacon with the marinated vegetables and tinned tomatoes.

De-grease the frying pan and de-glaze with the marinade and 150ml (¼ pint) good Beef Stock, then add to the casserole. Bring to the boil and either simmer very gently on top of the stove or transfer to the oven for about 1½–2 hours.

Meanwhile, sauté the sliced mushroom on a hot pan and set aside.

When the meat is soft and tender, liquidise the anchovies with the capers, parsley, wine vinegar and garlic. Add to the casserole with the mushrooms. Simmer gently for 8–10 minutes. Taste and correct the seasoning. De-grease and, if necessary, thicken the boiling liquid by whisking in a little roux.

Sprinkle with chopped parsley and serve with Fluffy Mashed Potatoes or Ulster Champ (see page 183).

Master Recipe
A Classic Boeuf Bourguignon
Serves 6

In Ireland, stew is generally regarded as something you feed the family, not your guests. Not so in France, where this most famous of all beef stews might be served for a special Sunday lunch or dinner with friends. After all, it is not cheap to make: you need top-quality, well-hung beef and the best part of a good bottle of red wine. As the name suggests, it used to be made with Burgundy, but with current Burgundy prices I might settle for a good Beaujolais or a full-bodied Côtes du Rhône.

1.3kg (3lb) best stewing beef, cut into 5cm (2in) cubes
175g (6oz) salt pork or streaky bacon
1–2 tablespoons extra-virgin olive oil
1 medium carrot, sliced
1 medium onion, sliced
2 tablespoons brandy (optional)
425–600ml (3/4–1 pint) full-bodied red wine
300–425ml (1/2–3/4 pint) homemade Brown Beef Stock (see page 36)
1 tablespoon tomato paste
5cm (2in) piece of dried orange peel (see below)
sprig of thyme
1 bay leaf
2–3 garlic cloves, peeled but left whole
salt and freshly ground pepper
Roux (see page 580), optional
18–24 small onions, depending on size
450g (1lb) fresh button or field mushrooms, cleaned and quartered
2 tablespoons freshly chopped parsley

Trim off the rind and cut the bacon into 1cm (1/2in) cubes. Blanch and refresh if salty, then dry well on kitchen paper. Heat the olive oil in a frying pan, sauté the bacon until crisp and golden and transfer it to a casserole. Turn up the heat so that the oil and fat from the bacon are almost smoking. Dry off the cubes of meat. Sauté a few pieces at a time until nicely browned on all sides, then add to the casserole with the bacon. Toss the sliced carrot and onion in the remaining fat and add these too.

If there is any fat left in the pan at this stage, pour it off. Add the brandy, if using, and flame it to burn off the alcohol. Then de-glaze the pan with the wine, scraping the little bits of sediment from the base of the pan until they dissolve. Bring to the boil and pour over the beef.

The casserole may be prepared ahead to this point. Allow it to get cold, cover and refrigerate overnight, or at least for a few hours. The wine will have a tenderising effect on the meat, and the other ingredients will add extra flavour as the meat marinates.

After marinating, bring the casserole to the boil, add enough stock to cover the meat, together with the tomato paste, orange peel, thyme, bayleaf and the cloves of garlic. Season with salt and freshly ground pepper. Bring to the boil, cover and simmer very gently either on top of the stove or in a low oven (170°C/325°F/gas 3) for 1 1/2–2 1/2 hours, depending on the cut of meat used. The meat should not fall apart but it should be tender enough to eat without too much chewing.

Meanwhile, cook the onions and mushrooms. Peel the onions (see tip right). Simmer gently in a covered casserole with about 1cm (1/2in) of water or beef stock – they will take about 30–35 minutes, depending on size. When cooked, a knife should pierce them easily. Toss the quartered mushrooms a few at a time in a little olive oil in a hot pan, and season with salt and freshly ground pepper.

When the meat is tender, pour everything into a strainer placed over a saucepan. Discard the herbs, carrot, onion and orange peel and return the meat to the casserole with the onions and mushrooms. Remove the fat from the liquid. There should be about 600ml (1 pint) sauce. Taste, bring back to the boil and simmer. If the sauce is too thin or too weak, reduce for a few minutes, otherwise thicken slightly by whisking in a little roux. Pour over the meat, mushrooms and onions, bring back to the boil, simmer for a few minutes until heated through, and correct the seasoning if necessary. Sprinkle with parsley and serve.

Note: A strip of dried orange peel is often added to stews in France and can really enhance the flavour. Use an unwaxed organic orange if possible. Otherwise scrub the skin well and remove thin strips of peel with a swivel-top peeler without the pith. Allow to dry overnight close to a radiator or an Aga. Dried orange peel may be stored in a screw-top jar and keeps for weeks.

Variation
Ostrich Stew
Follow the Master Recipe, substituting stewing ostrich meat for beef in the above recipe – it takes approx. 1 1/2 hours to cook.

TIP: Peeling small onions is made easier if you drop the onions into boiling water for 1 minute, run them under the cold tap, 'top and tail' them and then slip off the skins.

Master Recipe
Winter Beef Stew
Serves 6–8

A stew like this is great for family meals or perfect for a shooting lunch; robust and filling, it will even stand up to being reheated several times.

900g (2lb) good stewing beef (rump, shin or flank), well hung
25g (1oz) butter
3–4 tablespoons olive oil
225g (8oz) onion, sliced
225g (8oz) celery, chopped into 1cm (1/2in) dice
1 large carrot, sliced into 1cm (1/2in) pieces

110g (4oz) parsnip or swede turnip
175g (6oz) streaky bacon, rind removed, cut
  into 1cm (1/2in) dice
2 tablespoons seasoned flour
425–600ml (3/4–1 pint) homemade Beef Stock
  (see page 36)
bouquet garni
225g (8oz) mushrooms, sliced
salt and freshly ground pepper
Roux (see page 580), optional

Garnish
3–4 tablespoons freshly chopped flat-leaf parsley

Preheat the oven to 150ºC/300ºF/gas 2.

Trim the beef and cut into 2.5cm (1in)
cubes. Melt half the butter and olive oil in
a pan and lightly brown the onion. Then
add in all the other vegetables except the
mushrooms, toss in the oil and transfer
to a casserole.

Turn up the heat and add a little more
olive oil. Fry the bacon until crisp and add
to the casserole. Toss the meat lightly in
seasoned flour and cook in the pan in
batches until lightly brown on all sides.
Transfer to the casserole.

Pour the stock into the pan, bring to the
boil and scrape the pan to dissolve the bits
of sediment and caramelised juices. Pour
this over the meat, and add the bouquet
garni and season the casserole with salt
and pepper. Cover with the lid and simmer
in the oven for about 1½–2½ hours,
depending on the cut of meat.

Sauté the mushrooms in the remainder of
the butter, and add them to the casserole
about 20 minutes before the end of
cooking. When the meat is cooked, taste
the juice; if it is a little weak, strain it off
into another saucepan and reduce to
concentrate the flavour or, if it is too
liquid, whisk in a little roux. Remove the
bouquet garni. Correct the seasoning and
sprinkle with parsley.

Serve with potatoes and a winter green
salad.

Variations

Winter Beef Stew with Olives

Follow the Master Recipe. Add 50–75g (2–3oz) of stoned black or green olives to the stew, about 10 minutes from the end of cooking.

Winter Beef Stew with Herb Crust

Follow the Master Recipe. Roll out ½ quantity of White Soda Bread with Herbs dough (see page 474) into a 2cm (¾in) thick shape. Stamp into rounds with a 5cm (2in) cutter.

When the stew is almost cooked, remove the lid from the casserole and cover the top of the stew with slightly overlapping herb scones. Brush with egg wash and sprinkle with a little grated Cheddar cheese.

Cook in the oven, increasing the heat to 230°C/450°F/gas 8 for 10 minutes, then reducing the heat to 200°C/400°F/gas 6 for a further 20 minutes or until the crust is baked.

Chilli con Carne with Sour Cream, Cheddar Cheese and Tortillas

Serves 4–6

In the US every year there are huge chilli 'cook-offs' with passionate rivalry between the contestants, all of whom are determined that they make the best chilli. Even though it is usually associated with beef, chilli can also be made from lamb, pork or veal. Use stewing cuts; leftover cooked meat may be used but it's best to avoid mince. Cubed meat produces a far more appealing texture.

450–700g (1–1½lb) meat
2–3 tablespoons olive oil
1 large onion, chopped
2–3 garlic cloves, peeled and crushed
1 small green pepper, de-seeded and sliced

Hot Chilli Sauce (see page 592)
1 tablespoon tomato purée
1 teaspoon ground cumin
225g (8oz) red kidney beans, soaked and cooked
salt and brown sugar

Garnish
sour cream
sprigs of coriander
Cheddar, freshly grated

Trim the meat where necessary and cut into 1–2cm (½–¾in) cubes.

Heat a little oil in a frying pan and brown the meat. Transfer to a casserole. Brown the onion and garlic lightly in the same oil, and scrape out onto the meat. Add the peppers, Chilli Sauce and enough water to almost cover the ingredients. Cover tightly, bring to the boil and simmer gently until cooked. Check the liquid occasionally. By the end of the cooking time it should have reduced to a thick sauce. If it reduces too soon, add a little water.

Finally add the tomato purée, cumin, kidney beans, salt and brown sugar to taste. Simmer for a further 15 minutes. Serve in deep, wide soup bowls with a blob of sour cream in each.

Garnish with coriander and cheese, and serve with tacos, Guacamole (see page 593) and Tomato and Coriander Salsa (page 592).

Julia's Lithuanian Beef Goulash

Serves 8

1.1kg (2½lb) stewing beef, cut into 2.5cm (1in) cubes
3 garlic cloves, crushed
1 tablespoon paprika
½ teaspoon cayenne pepper
salt and freshly ground pepper
3 tablespoons sunflower oil
1 large or 2 medium onions, sliced
1 large carrot, cut into 1cm (½in) cubes
50g (2oz) plain flour
850ml (1½ pints) beef stock

Preheat the oven to 160°C/325°F/gas 3.

Put the beef in a bowl and add the garlic, paprika, cayenne, salt and pepper. Mix well and leave to rest while you prepare the other ingredients.

Heat a tablespoon of the sunflower oil in a frying pan, add the sliced onion and chopped carrot and fry for a few minutes until slightly soft. Remove from the pan and transfer to a casserole. Brown the meat in batches in a frying pan with a little oil and transfer to the casserole.

Put the casserole on a medium heat, add the flour, stir and cook for 1 minute. Gradually add the stock and bring to a simmer. Transfer to the oven and cook for 1½–2 hours (depending on the cut of meat) until meltingly tender. Serve with boiled potatoes or plain boiled rice.

Osso Bucco

Serves 4

In this classic Italian recipe, each piece of veal should include a piece of bone, with the delicious marrow intact. Traditionally the dish would be served with a Risotto Milanese.

2.2kg (5lb) shin of veal (baby beef), cut into 5cm (2in) thick pieces.
50g (2oz) butter
150ml (5fl oz) dry white wine
150ml (5fl oz) homemade Veal Stock (see page 37)
350g (12oz) ripe tomatoes
pinch of sugar (optional)
salt and freshly ground pepper

Gremolata
2 tablespoons freshly chopped flat-leaf parsley
1 unwaxed lemon
1 garlic clove, peeled

Melt the butter in a heavy-bottomed casserole, brown the veal on both sides a few at a time. Remove to a plate and continue until all the pieces have been browned, adding a little extra butter if necessary. Return all the meat to the casserole, arranging the pieces side by side so that they stay upright. This way, the precious marrow doesn't fall out during cooking.

Add the white wine and cook for 10 minutes. Meanwhile, skin, chop and deseed the tomatoes and add to the casserole with a pinch of sugar, depending on their sweetness. Add the stock, season, and cook for 1½–2 hours.

Shortly before serving, prepare the gremolata. Chop a handful of parsley with the garlic and the grated rind of half the lemon. Sprinkle the gremolata over the osso bucco just before serving.

Rose Veal Chop with Frizzled Sage Leaves
Serves 6

Humanely reared veal is often referred to as rose veal to distinguish it from its intensively reared counterpart. The Soil Association is spearheading a movement to rear organic veal calves, an initiative which is welcomed and supported by top chefs and cooks.

6 rose veal chops, 2.5cm (1in) thick
salt and freshly ground black pepper
extra-virgin olive oil
50g (2oz) butter
24–30 fresh sage leaves
6 segments of lemon

Heat a grill pan. Drizzle the chops with olive oil and season with sea salt and freshly ground pepper.Cook for 5–8 minutes on the hot grill pan.

Meanwhile, heat the butter in a frying pan. Dry the sage leaves if necessary, and add to the pan. Cook for 30 seconds to 1 minute until they frizzle up. Put the chops on to a hot serving plate and spoon the frizzled sage leaves over each chop.

Serve with a segment of lemon, Rustic Roast Potatoes (see page 181) and rocket leaves.

Mary Jo's Braised Short Ribs
Serves 10–12

Mary Jo has come to the School as a guest teacher on many occasions and contributed many gems to our repertoire.

6 cross-cut short ribs, trimmed – if possible, trim and salt the beef the night before cooking
225g (8oz) streaky bacon or duck fat
7–8 small onions
225g (8oz) carrot, diced
6–8 garlic cloves
1 chilli
175g (6oz) celery, diced
1–2 red or yellow peppers (optional)
2 level tablespoons tomato purée
a few sprigs of thyme
20–25ml (3/4–1fl oz) red wine

Optional Additions
homemade Beef or Chicken Stock for gravy (see page 36)
cinnamon stick
2–3 cloves
1 spiral of orange zest
1–2 bay leaves
10–12 black olives
10–12 prunes

Garnish
flat-leaf parsley, freshly chopped

Preheat the oven to 150°C/300°F/gas 2.

Trim and dice the bacon, saving the rind to cook with the beef as it adds gelatin to the sauce. In a wide sauté pan, render the fat from the bacon using a little olive oil or duck fat. Alternatively use all duck fat and omit the bacon. Remove the bacon and set aside.

Brown the beef in batches in the same pan and then set aside. Leave 2 tablespoons of fat in the sauté pan and sweat the onion, carrot and celery gently, stirring to dissolve all the browned bits that will add to the flavour. Add the garlic, optional pepper and sweat for 5–6 minutes before transferring to a casserole or heavy braising pot, preferably enamelled cast iron, together with the beef. Reserve the pan.

Add the tomato paste to the hot sauté pan and cook briefly. Add the wine and bring to boil, then pouring over the beef and add the thyme and as many of the optional ingredients as desired. Cover with a butter paper and tight fitting lid and braise in the oven for 2–4 hours until tender.

Remove the herbs and degrease if necessary. Add stock if needed and thicken with a little roux if desired. Scatter with flat-leaf parsley and serve with mashed potato.

Beef Stroganoff
Serves 6–8

Margot Heskin's delicious version of this much-loved recipe.

775g (1lb 11oz) fillet of beef, cut into very thin strips
50g (2oz) butter
2 tablespoons olive oil
1 large onion, finely chopped
225g (8oz) mushrooms, sliced
nutmeg, freshly grated
1 teaspoon Dijon mustard
200ml (7fl oz) sour cream
1 teaspoon paprika (optional)
salt and freshly ground pepper

Melt half the butter in a sauté pan with 1 tablespoon of the oil and add the onions. Season well with salt and pepper. Cook on a medium heat for about 10 minutes, until the onions are soft but not coloured.

While the onions are cooking, sauté the mushrooms in the remaining oil in another pan over a high heat. Add the mushrooms, season with salt, pepper and grated nutmeg.

When the onions and mushrooms are cooked, remove from the pan. Melt the remaining butter in the pan and, when it starts to foam, add the beef and stir-fry over a high heat until just cooked. Return the onions and mushrooms to the pan. Check the seasoning. Stir in the mustard, paprika and, finally, the sour cream. Continue to cook until the stroganoff is just bubbling.

Serve with Plain Boiled Rice (see page 124).

Fondue Bourguignonne

Serves 4

This meat fondue is fun for a small dinner party. Only cut up the beef just before you are about to cook, otherwise it will dry out. This is one of the national dishes of Switzerland and it is eaten communally, often on long, spiky, double-pronged forks. The cooking is done on a spirit stove, and the main cooking vessel is known as a caquelon, which is filled with oil in which to cook the meat. Fondue sets are available at a reasonable price and usually cook for up to 6 people. Many are the stories of fines raised on those who lose their meat in the fondue pot!

900g (2lb) fillet or sirloin of beef, trimmed and cut into 2.5cm (1in) cubes

extra-virgin olive oil

Sauces
Garlic Mayonnaise (see page 584)
Horseradish Sauce (see page 586)
Béarnaise Sauce (see page 586)

Half-fill the fondue pot with olive oil. Divide the cubes of meat between 4 bowls. Place the fondue lamp on the table, light it and put the saucepan of hot olive oil on top.

Provide each guest with a bowl of meat cubes and a plate and 1 or preferably 2 fondue forks in addition to their other cutlery. Pass around the 3 sauces separately. Each guest spears 1 cube of meat at a time on their fondue fork and cooks it to their taste – rare, medium, or well-done.

Accompany with a good green salad and plenty of crusty, home-baked bread or Chips (see page 184).

Stir-fried Beef with Oyster Sauce

Serves 6–8

Deh-Ta Hsiung has come to teach a Chinese cooking course at the Ballymaloe Cookery School several times. This is one of his favourite beef recipes, which we have been making ever since. A stir-fry is a terrific way to make a little beef go a long way.

350–400g (12–14oz) beef steak (rump for preference)
110g (4oz) bamboo shoots
110g (4oz) carrots
110g (4oz) broccoli, mange tout peas or courgettes (or a mixture)
110g (4oz) baby corn cobs (optional)
4–5 tablespoons sunflower or peanut oil
1–2 spring onions, cut into short lengths
1 teaspoon peeled and freshly grated ginger
1 scant teaspoon salt
1 teaspoon sugar
stock or water
2–3 tablespoons oyster sauce

Marinade
1 teaspoon sugar
1 tablespoon light soy sauce
2 tablespoons rice wine or dry sherry
2 teaspoons cornflour, mixed with 1 tablespoon water

Garnish
1 tablespoon freshly chopped flat-leaf parsley or coriander leaves

Cut the beef into thin slices across the grain, about the size of a large postage stamp. Mix the marinade ingredients in a bowl; add the beef slices, toss and allow to marinate for 25–30 minutes.

Meanwhile, prepare the vegetables: cut the bamboo shoots and carrots into roughly the same size as the beef; slice the broccoli or courgettes and corn cobs if using. Top and tail the mange tout peas (cut lengthwise at an angle if large).

Heat the oil in a preheated wok. Stir-fry the beef for about 30–40 seconds or until the colour changes and then quickly remove with a slotted spoon. In the same oil, add the spring onions, ginger and the vegetables; stir-fry for about 2–3 minutes, then add the salt, sugar and a little stock or water if necessary. Add the beef and oyster sauce and blend well. Stir for 1 more minute. Turn into a hot serving dish and sprinkle with parsley or coriander.

Using Mince

Minced meat is inexpensive and incredibly versatile – used in a wide variety of dishes from all over the world, from meat balls to hamburgers to Bolognaise sauce, to Middle Eastern kibbeh.

Pork, lamb, veal and chicken can be minced as well as the most familiar beef. Because mincing bruises the meat, it is crucially important that it is used when very fresh – I personally will only use meat that has been minced on the day, as I find that it sours quickly even when refrigerated.

The cuts of meat affect the quality of the mince, for beef mince it's useful to know that very lean cuts from the leg, such as round, can dry out in cooking. Flank, chuck and other cuts from the shoulder are fatter and have a sweeter flavour and juicier texture. Flank is also excellent but ensure that the connective tissue is removed otherwise the end result will be tough. The difference is not so noticeable in other meats.

If possible, buy a whole piece of meat and ask your butcher to mince it or, if you own a mincer, do it at home. Keep mince refrigerated; it keeps up to 2 days but the flavour deteriorates. Fresh mince may be frozen for 1–2 months. Freeze in shallow blocks so it defrosts quickly and use immediately.

Basic Hamburgers

Serves 4–6

The hamburger is the universal fast food, immortalised by the Americans and enjoyed by the rich and famous, the down and outs and all the rest of the world as well. It can be a feast or a travesty, simply a burger in a bun or an elaborate creation with lots of sauces and pickles. So, love them or hate them, hamburgers are here to stay and with a bit of effort they can be simply delicious. The secret of really good hamburgers is the quality of the meat. It doesn't need to be an expensive cut but it is essential to use the beef on the day it is minced. A very small percentage of fat in the mince will make the hamburgers sweet and juicy. The egg is not essential, although it helps to bind the burgers and increases the food value.

10g (¹/₂oz) butter
50g (2oz) onion, very finely chopped
450g (1lb) beef (flank, chump or shin would be
    perfect), freshly minced
¹/₂ teaspoon fresh thyme leaves
¹/₂ teaspoon finely chopped parsley
1 small organic egg, beaten
salt and freshly ground pepper
pork caul fat (optional)
oil or dripping

Melt the butter in a saucepan and toss in the onion, sweating until soft but not coloured. Leave to get cold. Meanwhile mix the mince with the herbs and beaten egg, season with salt and pepper, add the onions and mix well. Fry off a tiny bit in the pan to check the seasoning and correct if necessary. Then shape into hamburgers – 4–6, depending on the size you require. Wrap each in caul fat if using. Cook to your taste in a medium-hot pan or grill pan in a little oil, turning once.

Variations

There are endless ways to serve homemade hamburgers – with cheese, bacon, chilli, blue cheese, mushrooms...

The following are a few of our favourites, always served with lots of crispy Chips (see page 184).

Hamburgers with Caramelised Onions (see page 188) **and Pesto** (see page 589)

Hamburgers with Guacamole (see page 593) **and French Fried Onions** (see page 187)

Hamburgers with Mushroom à la Crème (see page 201)

Hamburgers with Bonnie Stern's Barbecued Onion Sauce (see page 339)

The Great American Hamburger, served in a bun with lettuce, sliced onions and tomato, gherkins, a dill pickle, mayonnaise and tomato sauce and, of course, lots of crispy chips.

> TIP: If the hamburgers are to be wrapped in caul fat, wrap loosely to allow for contraction during cooking.
>
> If cooking in batches, be sure to wash and dry the pan between batches.

Mexican Mince with Tacos and Tomato Salsa

Serves 6

Mince cooked in this Mexican way is absolutely addictive – I adore all the accompaniments. Serve with freshly cooked tortilla chips – *totopos.*

450g (1lb) beef, freshly minced
2 tablespoons sunflower oil
175g (6oz) onions, chopped
2 garlic cloves, crushed
1 teaspoon freshly ground cumin
2 teaspoons freshly ground annual marjoram
    or oregano
1 fresh chilli, de-seeded and chopped or a pinch
    of chilli powder or 1 teaspoon chilli sauce
good dash of soy sauce

salt, freshly ground pepper and a pinch
    of sugar

Heat the oil in a frying pan, add the chopped onion and garlic and cook over a medium heat until soft and slightly golden. Increase the heat, add the minced beef and stir until brown. Add the cumin, marjoram or oregano and chilli. Then shake in the soy sauce and season well with salt, freshly ground pepper and sugar. Be sure to taste as this mixture needs a surprising amount of salt.

Serve with Tomato and Coriander Salsa (see page 592), Guacamole (see page 593), shredded, crispy lettuce, sour cream, grated Cheddar cheese and tortillas (see page 493). Put them together in whatever combination you fancy and enjoy!

Spicy Koftas

Serves 4–6

This is a great way to use up leftovers.

900g (2lb) beef or lamb, finely minced
175g (6oz) onions, finely chopped
¹/₂ teaspoon ginger, freshly grated
2 teaspoons cumin seeds, freshly roasted and
    ground
1 teaspoon coriander seeds, freshly roasted
a good pinch cayenne
1 teaspoon paprika
1 organic egg
3 tablespoons freshly chopped parsley
3 tablespoons freshly chopped coriander
    or marjoram
salt and freshly ground pepper

Mix the mince with the spices, season well, cook a morsel on a frying pan and taste for seasoning, correcting if necessary. Allow to sit for an hour or so if possible. Shape the mince into sausage shapes around a flat skewer, not too large or they will break.

Brush with a little oil, then cook on a barbecue or a pan-grill turning on all sides until crisp and golden. Serve with a green salad and tzatziki.

Ballymaloe Spiced Beef

Serves 12–16

Although spiced beef is traditionally associated with Christmas, in Cork we eat it all year round! It may be served hot or cold and is a marvellous stand-by. This delicious recipe for spiced beef has been handed down through Myrtle Allen's family and, though I have tried several others, it is still my favourite. It includes saltpetre, nowadays regarded as a health hazard, so perhaps you should not live exclusively on it! Certainly people have lived on occasional meals of meats preserved in this way for generations.

The recipe below makes enough spice to cure 5 flanks of beef, each about 1.8kg (4lb) in size. Leftover spice mixture will keep for weeks or even months in a screwtop jar. If it is properly spiced and cooked, spiced beef will keep for 3–4 weeks in the fridge.

1.3–1.8kg (3–4lb) lean flank of beef or silverside

Ballymaloe Spice for Beef

225g (8oz) demerara sugar
350g (12oz) salt
10g (1/2oz) saltpetre (available from chemists)
75g (3oz) whole black peppercorns
75g (3oz) whole allspice (pimento or Jamaican pepper)
75g (3oz) whole juniper berries

Make the Ballymaloe Beef Spice by grinding all the ingredients (preferably in a food processor) until fairly fine.

To prepare the beef: if you are using flank of beef, remove the bones and trim away any unnecessary fat. Rub some of the spice well into every crevice of the beef. Put it into an earthenware dish and leave in a fridge or cold larder for 3–7 days, depending on the thickness of the meat. Turn it occasionally. (This is a dry spice, but after 1–2 days some liquid will come out of the meat.) The longer the meat is left in the spice, the longer it will last and the greater will be the spicy flavour.

Just before cooking the meat, roll and tie the joint neatly with cotton string into a compact shape, cover with cold water and simmer for 2–3 hours or until soft and cooked. Or, if the beef is to be eaten cold, remove it from the liquid, press by putting it on a flat tin or into an appropriate sized bread tin; cover it with a board and weight and leave for 12 hours.

Serving suggestions

Serve cut into thin slices with some freshly made salads and homemade chutneys, or use in sandwiches.

Spiced beef is delicious cold in paper-thin slices with a Potato and Spring Onion Salad (see page 214) and avocado and salad leaves, including rocket.

Spiced beef with Sweet Cucumber Pickle (see page 514) and Ballymaloe Country Relish or Apple and Tomato Chutney (see page 512).

Baby Beef Scallopini with Spinach, Raisins and Pine Nuts

Serves 6

We do not serve intensively reared veal either at Ballymaloe House or at the Cookery School but once or twice a year we have a naturally reared milk-fed calf from Sibylle Knoble or one of my own Kerry bull calves. The meat is not so pale as conventional veal but it is wonderfully sweet and delicious. This is one of Tim's favourite meals, reminding him of the Jersey baby beef of his childhood when his father was a Jersey breeder.

700g (1½lb) lean baby beef from the top round
salt and freshly ground pepper
seasoned flour
beaten organic egg
fresh white breadcrumbs
Clarified Butter (see page 105)

To Serve
lemon segments
Spinach with Raisins and Pine Nuts
  (see page 171)

With a very sharp knife, cut the top round into 5mm (1/4in) thick slices across the grain. Trim off any fat or sinews. Put between 2 sheets of clingfilm and flatten a little more with a meat pounder or rolling pin.

Dip each piece in well seasoned flour, beaten egg and soft white breadcrumbs. Pat off the excess. Melt 3 or 4 tablespoons of clarified butter in a wide frying pan. Fry the scallopini a few at a time until crisp and golden on one side, then flip over onto the other. Drain briefly on kitchen paper. Serve hot with segments of lemon and Spinach with Raisins and Pine Nuts (see page 171).

Seared Beef Salad

See page 212

Thai Beef Salad

Serves 4

Addictive!

400g (14oz) sirloin steak, cut into 2 steaks
  if more convenient
3 tablespoons soy sauce
2 garlic cloves, crushed
2 tablespoons lime juice, freshly squeezed
assorted lettuce leaves and salad leaves
1/2 cup fresh mint leaves
1/2 cup fresh basil leaves
1/2 cup fresh coriander leaves
1/2–1 cucumber, peeled, de-seeded and sliced

Dressing
2 red chillies, chopped
3 tablespoons soy sauce
2 tablespoons lime juice
2 teaspoons palm or brown sugar
2 kaffir lime leaves, finely shredded

Preheat a chargrill. Cook the steak (or steaks) for 2–3 minutes on each side or until cooked to your liking. They shouldn't be cooked more than medium rare. Cover the steak and leave to rest on a plate.

Mix the soy sauce, garlic and lime juice in a bowl and add the steak; leave to marinate for 10 minutes. Toss the lettuce, mint, basil, coriander and cucumber in a bowl. Arrange on serving plates.

To make the dressing: combine the chillies, soy sauce, lime juice, palm sugar and lime leaves. Taste and balance if necessary.

Just before serving, sprinkle some dressing over the salad leaves and toss. Slice the beef thinly and place on top of the salad. Serve at once.

Yakiniku

Serves 4

350g (12oz) beef fillet

Marinade
1 tablespoon apple, peeled and grated
2 tablespoons soy sauce
1 tablespoon garlic, crushed
1 tablespoon sesame oil
1 tablespoon sesame seeds

Slice the beef thinly into bite-size pieces. Mix the other ingredients in a bowl and marinate the beef in this mixture for 30 minutes. Heat a frying pan over a high heat and stir-fry the beef quickly. Serve with steamed rice and miso soup.

Carpaccio with Slivers of Desmond, Rocket and Chopped Olive

Serves 12

We use the wonderful Desmond cheese made by Bill Hogan in West Cork, but a nutty Parmesan or Grana Padana would also be superb.

ABOVE: Carpaccio with Slivers of Desmond, Rocket and Chopped Olive

450g (1lb) fillet of beef, preferably Aberdeen Angus (fresh not frozen)
rocket leaves, about 5 per person
4–5 very thin slivers Desmond or Parmesan cheese
sea salt and freshly cracked pepper
24–36 olives (we use Kalamata)
extra-virgin olive oil or truffle oil

Chill the meat, and stone and chop the olives. Just before serving, slice the beef as thinly as possible with a very sharp knife. Spread the slices of beef out on a piece of oiled clingfilm. Cover with another piece of oiled clingfilm. Roll gently with a rolling pin until the beef is almost transparent and has doubled in size. Peel the clingfilm off the top, invert the meat onto a chilled plate, and gently peel away the other piece of clingfilm. Put the rocket leaves of top of the beef and scatter the slivers of cheese over the top of the rocket. Put a little chopped olive around the edge and sprinkle with flakes of sea salt and freshly cracked pepper. Drizzle with your best extra-virgin olive oil or truffle oil and serve immediately with crusty bread.

offal

offal

Cork city has been a trading port since the time of the Phoenecians. The market in the centre of Cork is unique in Ireland. You can buy everything from sun-dried tomatoes, native and exotic fish and artisanal breads to offal (or variety meats, as the Americans call it). Side by side with nam pla, bok choi and mooli radishes are pigs' heads, tails, skirts, salted pigs' trotters (crubeens), offal bones and bodice (the ribs) which can be either salted or fresh.

It is fascinating to wander through the labyrinth of market stalls and see third and fourth-generation stall holders trading alongside new-age arrivals, each passionate about the food they are selling. Historically, Cork was the last port of call for ships and liners before they crossed the Atlantic. Thousands of Cork people were employed in the provisioning trade and part of their weekly wage was paid in offal, so to this day, Cork people eat more offal than in any other part of the country.

Offal is defined as every part of a dead animal – excluding the skin, hide and meat. Cuts such as liver, kidney, tongue, heart and sweetbreads (the pancreatic and thymus glands) are most regularly eaten, although brain, trotters, tripe, cheeks, ears and pig's head are also consumed.

Ironically, despite the fact that offal is now harder to come by (butchers are often forbidden to sell the innards because of concerns over BSE and foot and mouth), it has suddenly become enormously popular in posh restaurants. On a recent trip to the US, virtually every restaurant I visited had several offal dishes on the menu. In Casa Mono in Greenwich Village, smart New Yorkers were queuing up for duck hearts with favala beans, cocks combs with girolles and pigs' trotters with salsa verde. Momofuku was offering spicy honeycomb tripe, pigs' ears, beef cheek and warm veal head terrine or grilled veal sweetheart with pickled roasted chillis and lime. Marrow bones also featured on several menus.

Nutrition

Offal, and most particularly liver, is extremely nutritious and is rich in vitamins B12, A, C and D, folic acid, riboflavin and iron (which is needed to make red blood cells and helps to prevent fatigue and anaemia).

Buying and Cooking

Many people are squeamish about eating offal, or any part of an animal that is too recognisable. Others have been turned off offal remembering, with a shudder, the overcooked slabs of shoe-leather liver served in their schooldays. But really, the rules about buying and cooking offal are the same for any other cut of meat: seek out top-quality fresh meat and treat it with respect. You can make a feast out of the most unlikely ingredients. Beef or pigs' cheek and oxtail make some of the most satisfyingly rich stews. Of course, an added advantage of most offal is that, because demand for it tends to be lower, it's usually quite cheap. So you can rustle up a sustaining and inexpensive family meal with very little effort.

Haggis is the most traditional of all Scottish dishes, eaten on Burns Night (25th January) and at Hogmanay (New Year's Eve). It consists of a sheep or lambs' stomach, stuffed with oatmeal and liver. The finest haggis is made with deer's liver, but most are made with lamb's liver.

Pigs' intestines are used for homemade sausages, salamis and chorizo. Pigs' blood is a key ingredient in **black puddings**, for which Ireland is famous. **White puddings** contain no animal blood, hence the colour, and are a blend of pork, pigs' liver, bacon, grains, eggs, cornflour and spices. The old Irish blood pudding, **drisheen**, is still sold in the Cork market.

Tripe is made from the muscular lining of a cow's stomach. There are four types of tripe. Three come from different parts of the honeycomb (or second stomach) and one from the first stomach. Honeycomb tripe is the finest, but still very tough and needs to be cooked for at least 12 hours. It is glutinous but delectable. So is **spleen**. I remember, much to Timmy's disgust, eating yummy spleen sandwiches in soft baps with grated Parmegiano Reggiano in Palermo in Sicily some years ago.

Giblets, from chicken, turkey, duck and geese, are often used to flavour stocks and gravies. Chicken livers are used whole or in paté. One of my favourite salades tièdes includes hearts and gizzards – not for the faint-hearted! **Foie gras** and pâté de canard is made from the livers of geese and ducks that have been force-fed on a special diet – the subject of much controversy.

Storage

Fresh offal can be stored in the fridge for 1–2 days. It should be covered and kept in the coldest part of the fridge (usually near the bottom). Make sure that it cannot drip onto, and cross-contaminate, raw products such as vegetables. Offal can also be stored for up to a month in the freezer.

Oxtail Stew

Serves 4

Oxtail makes an extraordinarily rich and flavoursome winter stew. This is a humble dish which has recently been resurrected by trendy chefs who are capitalising on their customers' nostalgic craving for their gran's cooking. All the flavour comes if the meat melts off the bone so allow plenty of cooking time for a hearty stew.

110g (4oz) streaky bacon
2 oxtails
25g (1oz) beef dripping or 2 tablespoons
    olive oil
225g (8oz) onion, finely chopped
225g (8oz) carrots, cut into 2cm (³/₄in) cubes
50g (2oz) celery, chopped
1 bay leaf, sprig of thyme and parsley stalks
salt and freshly ground pepper
150ml (¹/₄ pint) red wine and 425ml (³/₄ pint)
    homemade Beef Stock (see page 36) OR
    600ml (1 pint) Beef Stock
1 tablespoon homemade Tomato Pureé
    (see page 49)
175g (6oz) mushrooms, sliced
5g (¹/₄oz) Roux (see page 580)
2 tablespoons freshly chopped parsley

Preheat the oven to 160°C/ 325°F/gas 3. Cut the bacon into cubes and cut the oxtail into joints. Heat the dripping or oil, add the bacon and sauté for 1–2 minutes. Then add the vegetables and cook for 2–3 minutes, stirring occasionally. Remove and reserve. Add the oxtail pieces and brown lightly all over.

Return the bacon and vegetables to the pan. Add the herbs, salt and pepper, wine, stock and tomato purée. Cover and cook very gently either on top of the stove or in the oven for 2–3 hours, or until the oxtail and vegetables are very tender.

Cook the mushrooms in a hot pan in the butter for 2–3 minutes. Stir into the oxtail stew and cook for about 5 minutes. Transfer the oxtail joints to a hot serving dish and keep warm. Remove the bay leaves, thyme and parsley stalks. Bring the liquid back to the boil, whisk in a little Roux and cook until slightly thickened. Add the oxtail back in with the parsley and bring to the boil. Taste and correct the seasoning and serve in the hot serving dish with lots of Champ (see page 182) or Colcannon (see page 183).

Scalloped Potato with Steak and Kidney

Serves 4–6

450g (1lb) well-hung stewing beef, cut into 1cm
    (¹/₂in) cubes
1 beef kidney
salt and freshly ground pepper
1.1–1.35kg (2¹/₂–3lb) 'old' potatoes, cut into
    5mm (¹/₄in) thick slices
350g (12oz) onion, chopped
50–60g (2–2¹/₂oz) butter
375ml (13fl oz) water or homemade stock
    (see page 36)

Garnish
parsley, freshly chopped

2.4 litre (4 pint) capacity gratin dish or
    casserole

Preheat the oven to 150°C/300°F/gas 2. Remove the skin and white core from the kidney and discard; cut the flesh into 1cm (¹/₂in) cubes, put them into the bowl, cover with cold water and sprinkle with a good pinch of salt.

Layer the base of the casserole with potato slices. Drain the kidney and mix with the beef, then scatter some of the meat and chopped onion over the layer of potato. Season well with salt and freshly ground pepper, dot with butter, add another layer of potato, more meat, onions and seasoning and continue right up to the top of the casserole. Finish with an overlapping layer of potato.

Pour in the stock, bring to the boil, and cover and cook in a preheated oven for 2–2¹/₂ hours or until the meat and potatoes are cooked. Sprinkle with parsley and serve from the casserole.

Pickled Ox Tongue with Oignons à la Monégasque

Serves 8–10

There's a great saying around the Cork area when someone is about to venture home after a night of liquid socialising: 'Ah, there'll be nothin' for you for dinner but hot tongue and cold shoulder'. Order a pickled ox tongue a week or so ahead from your butcher, unless you live near Cork Market where pickled ox and lamb's tongues are available all year round.

1 pickled ox tongue
cold water
Oignons à la Monégasque (see page 188)

In a narrow saucepan with high sides, cover the tongue with cold water, bring to the boil, cover the saucepan and simmer for 4–4¹/₂ hours until the tongue is tender and the skin will easily peel off the tip. Do not use salt; the tongue will be salty enough.

Remove from the pot and reserve the liquid. As soon as the tongue is cool enough to handle, peel off the skin and remove all the little bones at the neck end. Sometimes I use a skewer to prod the meat to make sure no bones are left behind. Curl the tongue and press into a small plastic bowl. Pour over a little of the cooking liquid.

Nowadays the butcher often removes all the little bones. If this is the case, the liquid may not set into a jelly without the help of gelatine – use 2 teaspoons or 2 leaves to 600ml (1 pint) of liquid. Put a side plate or saucer on top and weigh down. Cool and refrigerate. Serve thinly sliced with Oignons à la Monégasque and a green salad.

> TIP: pickled ox tongue, cooked and pressed, will keep for 5–6 days in the fridge.

Other Accompaniments

Sweet Cucumber Pickle (see page 514)
Redcurrant Jelly (see page 508)
Horseradish Sauce (see page 586)
Pickled Beetroot (see page 514)
Salsa Verde (see page 592)

Variation
Spiced Ox Tongue

'Spiced Tongue' was a common nineteenth century dish on the tables of the middle classes. It was spiced with cloves and flavoured with onion, thyme, parsley, salt and pepper. In Cork, spiced ox tongue is also seasonally available just before Christmas, when a few tongues are thrown into the spice barrel. Mr. Breslin in Cork Market spices tongues for me occasionally and they have been much enjoyed, not just at Christmas but for summer picnics also. Cook as for Pickled Ox Tongue (see page 353).

Sweetbreads

Sweetbreads are the thymus or pancreatic glands of young milk-fed animals, that is to say those of calves or lambs. Calves' sweetbreads are best. The sweetbreads tend to shrink and toughen when the animals' diet changes to grass and meal.

Sweetbreads come in pairs. The compact heart sweetbread is more highly prized because it slices more evenly than the looser, more elongated throat sweetbread. Choose sweetbreads that are white or pale pink in colour, not bruised and compact in texture. They are extremely perishable when raw, so should be prepared and pre-cooked immediately.

Put the sweetbreads into a bowl and cover with cold water. Soak for 2 hours and discard the water. Cut away any discoloured parts. Cover in fresh, cold water or chicken stock, bring to the boil and simmer for 3 minutes (lamb) and

LEFT: Warm Salad of Sweetbreads with Walnuts

5 minutes (calf) and then drain. Cool. Gently pull away any gristly bits, being careful that the sweetbreads don't come apart as some of the connective tissue will have dissolved during cooking. The sweetbreads need to be pressed between 2 plates with a weight not more than 900g (2lb) for 3–4 hours in the fridge before being sliced for further cooking.

Warm Salad of Sweetbreads with Walnuts

Serves 4

4 lamb sweetbreads
25g (1oz) butter
1 small carrot, diced
1 onion, diced
2 sticks celery, diced
bouquet garni
600ml (1 pint) Chicken Stock (see page 36)

French beans, cut in julienne, blanched and
   refreshed (optional)
8 walnuts, freshly shelled
salad leaves (iceberg, oakleaf, butterhead,
   radicchio, sorrel, endive, rocket, watercress)

seasoned flour
beaten organic egg
butter and oil, for sautéeing

Walnut Dressing
1 tablespoon white wine vinegar
1 tablespoon groundnut or sunflower oil
2 tablespoons walnut oil
1/4 teaspoon Dijon mustard
salt and freshly ground pepper

Garnish
chive flowers

Soak the sweetbreads in a bowl of cold water for 2 hours. Discard the water. Poach the sweetbreads in fresh water gently for about 5 minutes, depending on size. Cool, and carefully remove the gelatinous membranes and any fatty bits.

Melt the butter in a pan, add the vegetables and sweat to soften. Add the bouquet garni. Bring the chicken stock to the boil and add the vegetables.

Prepare the salad: wash and dry the lettuce leaves; prepare the French beans, if using.

Slice the sweetbreads into escalopes and dip in seasoned flour and then in beaten egg. Heat a little butter and oil in a heavy pan so it foams and sauté the sweetbreads until golden on both sides.

Shake together the ingredients for the dressing in a screw-top jar. Toss the salad leaves and walnuts in the walnut dressing, divide between 4 plates and lay the hot sweetbreads on top of the salad. Sprinkle with chive flowers and serve immediately.

Pig Tails with Swede Turnips

Serves 6

Paddy McDonnell's stall in the Cork market is just one of several that sell pig tails, skirts and kidneys and bodices. He tells me that he still sells about 200 a week, but he is concerned because they are becoming more scarce nowadays and most pigs reared in an intensive way have their tails docked. Pig tails are rather irreverently known in Cork as 'slash farts' or 'pigs' mud-guards'! Only last year I inquired of a customer at one of the stalls what she was going to do with her purchase and she replied without any hesitation, 'I've got ten in the family, I'll split them in half and boil them up with turnips and then they'll go further – the group of Americans I was showing around the market couldn't believe their ears!

6 pig tails
1 swede turnip, peeled and cut into 2.5cm
   (1in) cubes
butter
salt and freshly ground pepper

Cover the pig tails with cold water, bring to the boil and then drain, discarding the water. Cover with fresh water and bring to the boil again. Add the turnip to the pot, cover and continue to cook until the pig tails are soft and tender and the turnip is fully cooked (about 1 hour).

Remove the tails and keep warm. Mash the turnip with a generous lump of butter and season to taste. Put in a hot bowl and serve the pig tails on top.

Stuffed Ox Heart

Serves 6

This could be good for a Valentine's Day treat! Guaranteed to bring on a proposal!

1 ox heart

Stuffing
75g (3oz) butter
175g (6oz) onions, finely chopped
1 tablespoon chopped chives
1 tablespoon thyme leaves
1 tablespoon annual marjoram
1 tablespoon freshly chopped parsley
175g (6oz) white breadcrumbs
salt and freshly ground pepper

Gravy
600ml (1 pint) homemade Beef Stock
2–3 tablespoons mushroom ketchup (optional)
Roux (see page 582)

Preheat the oven to 180°C/350°F/gas 4.

Trim the heart and cut away any sinews to make a nice pocket. Wash thoroughly in cold, salted water and then dry well.

To make the stuffing, follow the master recipe from page 284. Allow to cool.

Season the inside of the heart and fill with the stuffing, piling the extra on the top. Cover with a butter wrapper and tie with cotton string if necessary. Put into a deep roasting tin or casserole and add the beef stock. Season again, cover and bake in the oven for 3–3½ hours or until tender.

When the beef heart is fully cooked, remove carefully to a serving dish. Bring the cooking liquid to the boil, thicken with a very little roux and correct the seasoning. Strain and serve with the sliced, stuffed heart.

How to Prepare Beef, Veal or Lamb Kidneys

Choose fresh kidneys that have no strong smell of ammonia. Richer tasting beef kidney is wonderful in stews and soup, whereas the more delicate veal kidneys are best sautéed or grilled. If you want to keep kidneys for a few days, buy them in their suet.

Beef suet, when trimmed of all traces of blood or meat, may be used in mince pies, plum puddings, suet pastries or suet puddings. Suet keeps for months in the fridge.

Beef Kidneys

1. Remove the kidneys from the suet.

2. Remove the ducting from the kidneys with scissors.

Lamb Kidneys

1. Remove suet and peel off the outer membrane.

2. Cut in half lengthways and remove the membrane.

3. Snip out the inner plumbing and cut into cubes or slices, depending on the dish.

Lamb Kidneys in their Jackets
Serves 2

Lamb kidneys cooked in their suet are one of our favourite naughty treats. Lamb kidneys are also delicious wrapped in caul fat and roasted.

2 kidneys
sea salt

Preheat the oven to 230°C/450°F/gas 8.

If there is an excessive amount of suet on the kidneys, trim them a little. Sprinkle with sea salt and cook in a roasting tin for 10–12 minutes, depending on size. The fat should be crispy on the outside and soft within and, when the kidneys are almost cooked, allow them to rest for a few minutes.

Serve with boiled potatoes and a green salad.

TIP: Overcooking toughens kidneys so don't cook for more than a few minutes.

Butterflied Lamb Kidneys with Rosemary
Serves 4 as a starter, 2–3 as a main course

Lamb kidneys are most delicate and delicious around Easter when they are still very young.

8 lamb kidneys
8–16 tough sprigs of rosemary, stripped of
*   most of the leaves but leave the tip intact*
salt and freshly ground pepper
8 flat mushrooms
1–2 tablespoons olive oil
1 tablespoon freshly chopped rosemary
4 slices country bread

Remove the skin from the kidneys just before cooking and season them.

Cut the kidneys from the base, open them out, but keep them attached at the top so they are butterflied. Remove all the core. Skewer each kidney with 1 or, if necessary, 2 rosemary sprigs. Season both kidneys and mushrooms with salt and pepper. Brush with olive oil and sprinkle with chopped rosemary. Grill or pan-grill the kidneys and mushrooms on both sides until cooked through, 3–5 minutes. Serve on toasted country bread.

Lamb or Veal Kidneys in Grainy Mustard Sauce

Serves 4 as a starter, 2–3 as a main course

Lamb kidneys are under-appreciated – we absolutely love them, so tender and so fast to cook. Veal kidneys are mild and delicate in flavour but less easy to come by.

8 lamb or 2 veal kidneys (buy fresh lamb
  kidneys still in the suet)
a little butter
4 dessertspoons wholegrain mustard
225ml (8fl oz) cream
salt and freshly ground pepper

Garnish
flat-leaf parsley, freshly snipped

Remove the skin, membrane and core from the kidneys and cut into bite-sized pieces. Sauté in a little butter in a pan, turn occasionally until nicely cooked, about 5 minutes over a medium heat. Season with salt and pepper. Add the cream and mustard, bring to the boil and simmer for 3–4 minutes, until the sauce thickens slightly. Taste and correct the seasoning.

Serve immediately on hot plates, scattered with parsley. Homemade noodles, rice or orzo are delicious with this dish for a main course. Serve with a good green salad.

How to Prepare Liver

Unless you plan to cook it immediately, buy the liver in a larger piece and slice just before cooking. Peel off the outer membrane. Cut the liver diagonally into slices and cook very quickly and eat immediately. Overcooking toughens the liver.

Lamb's Liver with Freshly Cracked Pepper

Serves 4 as a starter, 2 as a main course

450g (1lb) lamb's liver
flour seasoned with salt
freshly cracked pepper
25–50g (1–2oz) butter, clarified
rocket leaf salad

Slice the lamb's liver into 1cm (1/2in) thick slices. Dip the slices of liver in well-seasoned flour and lots of freshly cracked pepper, and shake off the excess.

Melt the butter in a frying pan. Cook gently in the foaming butter for 1–2 minutes on each side. It should still be slightly pink in the centre.

Serve immediately with a rocket leaf salad, and perhaps some toasted or chargrilled country bread.

Salad of Duck or Chicken Livers with Apples, Hazelnuts and Wild Garlic Flowers

Serves 4

1 dessert apple
4 duck or chicken livers
2 tablespoons hazelnuts, crushed
5g (1/4oz) butter
1 tablespoon olive oil

selection of lettuce leaves (butterhead, frisée,
  oakleaf, radicchio, rocket, salad burnet)
wild garlic flowers

Hazelnut Oil Dressing
4 tablespoons hazelnut oil
2 tablespoons sunflower oil
2 tablespoons white wine vinegar
2 teaspoons mustard
salt, pepper and sugar

First make the Hazelnut Oil Dressing by shaking all the ingredients together in a screw-top jar. Season with salt and freshly ground pepper.

Cut the apple into thin julienne strips, and mix with the hazelnuts and 1 tablespoon hazelnut oil dressing.

Melt the butter and oil in a frying pan and cook the livers gently until just tender. While the livers are cooking, toss the lettuces in enough dressing to make them just glisten and divide between 4 serving plates. Place a quarter of the apple julienne on top of each salad and finally the warm duck or chicken livers on top. Sprinkle with wild garlic flowers and serve immediately.

BELOW: Lamb or Veal Kidneys in Grainy Mustard Sauce

Crostini di Fegatini

Serves 10–20

Crostini comes from the same root as croûtons; in Italy they are served with various toppings. Chicken liver crostini are the best loved in Tuscany. Recipes vary but I particularly love this version which was given to me by Mimmo Baldi and is served at his restaurant 'Il Vescovino' in Panzano in Chianti. He likes to add a small tablespoon of chicken stock to each crostino just as soon as it is fried in olive oil. Mimmo then sprinkles them with a little freshly grated Parmesan, a generous amount of fegatini and serves them immediately – you always know when they have been served to a table because conversation stops and all one can hear is mmm, mmm!

225g (8oz) fresh chicken livers
salt and freshly ground pepper
3 tablespoons extra-virgin olive oil
1 carrot, finely chopped
1 onion, finely chopped
1 stick celery, finely chopped
3 anchovy fillets
20g (³/₄oz) capers
20g (³/₄oz) gherkins
1 stalk flat-leaf parsley
125ml (4fl oz) port, marsala or Vin Santo
125ml (4fl oz) good homemade Chicken Stock
  (see page 36)
25–50g (1–2oz) Parmigiano Reggiano, freshly
  grated
15–20 slices French bread, about 7cm (2³/₄in),
  chargrilled, toasted or fried in olive oil until
  golden brown on each side

Season the chicken livers with salt and pepper. Sauté the chicken livers in 1 tablespoon of the olive oil in a small sauté pan over a medium heat until they are just firm. Remove from the pan and drain in a sieve or colander for 10 minutes.

Meanwhile, prepare the vegetables. Heat the rest of the olive oil in the same saucepan, and add the carrot, onion and celery. Cover and cook until soft – about 5–6 minutes. Add the chicken livers and cook for about 10 minutes more, then let this mixture cool for 30 minutes.

Add the anchovies, capers, gherkins and parsley to the livers and either mash with a fork or roughly blend in a food processor. Reheat this mixture, add the alcohol and reduce until all the liquid has been absorbed, then add the chicken stock. The mixture should have a moist, creamy consistency. Taste and correct the seasoning.

Use the French bread to make the crostini, and just as soon as they are fried or toasted, sprinkle with Parmesan, spread with a generous amount of the fegatini mixture and serve immediately.

Serving suggestion: To make a more substantial plate, add a few ruffles of freshly sliced Parma ham and some rocket leaves – one of my favourite starters.

Pork Cheeks with Savoy Cabbage

Serves 4

125ml (4fl oz) extra-virgin olive oil
450g (1lb) pork cheeks
salt and freshly ground pepper
110g (4oz) streaky bacon
1 large onion, chopped
1 carrot, peeled and chopped
5 garlic cloves, peeled
225ml (8fl oz) cider
450ml (16fl oz) chicken stock
1 x 400g (14oz) tin tomatoes, roughly chopped
1 Savoy cabbage, cored and thinly sliced
110g (4oz) streaky bacon, cut in 5mm
  (¹/₄ in) dice
1 onion, finely chopped
salt and freshly ground pepper
1–2 tablespoons sugar
60ml (2¹/₂fl oz) red wine vinegar
2 tablespoons fresh thyme leaves
2 tablespoons coarsely chopped fresh parsley

Preheat the oven to 180°C/350°F/gas 4.

Heat the olive oil in a pan over a high heat. Add a couple of pork cheeks and sear on all sides - they need to be a rich golden brown. Repeat with the others but don't overcrowd the pan or they will stew rather than sear. Season well with salt and freshly ground pepper. Add the streaky bacon and cook for 3–4 minutes until the fat begins to run and the edges are crisp. Add the onion, carrot and whole garlic cloves and continue to cook for 3–4 minutes. Transfer to a casserole. Deglaze the pan with the cider and some stock and bring to the boil, stirring to dissolve any caramelised meat juices. Add to the pork cheeks in the casserole with the tomatoes and the remainder of the stock. Bring to the boil and transfer to the preheated oven for about an hour or until the meat is meltingly tender.

Heat 2 tablespoons extra-virgin olive oil in a wide sauté pan over a medium heat. Add the finely diced bacon, stir and cook until the fat runs and the bacon is crisp. Add the finely chopped onion, stir and cook for a minute or two more, then add the cabbage. Season with salt and freshly ground pepper and cook, tossing occasionally, for 4–5 minutes or until the cabbage is almost cooked. Add a sprinkle of sugar, a dash of red wine vinegar and the thyme. Toss, taste and continue to cook for 3–4 minutes.

When the pork cheeks are cooked, remove them to a serving dish or divide them between 4 deep plates. Add some cabbage and keep warm. Push the cooking liquid through a sieve, pressing well to extract as much flavour as possible. Reheat and add some fresh parsley. Correct the seasoning and pour some of the liquid over the pork cheeks. Serve immediately.

Brawn

Serves 16–20

My eldest son reckons to be very cool; like many of his generation nothing seems to faze him. However, one day when he lifted the lid off a pot on the Aga, he shrieked and uttered some quite unprintable expletives when he caught sight of the pig's head bubbling in the pot. My daughters continually count my happy bonhams in the orchard to make sure that none of them end up in brawn.

half a salted pig's head
1 boiling fowl or free-range chicken
2 carrots, sliced
2 onions, sliced
1 stick celery (optional)
sprig of thyme and a few parsley stalks
4 or 5 peppercorns
1 tablespoon freshly chopped parsley and
  thyme

2 x 1.2 litre (2 pint) pudding bowls

Wash the pig's head, remove the brain and discard. Put the head into a saucepan and cover with cold water. Bring to the boil then discard the water. Bring to the boil in fresh water and cook for 3–4 hours or until the meat is soft and tender and parting from the bones. Meanwhile, put the fowl or chicken into another saucepan. Add the carrots and onions, celery if you have it to spare, parsley stalks and a sprig of thyme. Add about 6cm (2½in) of cold water and a few peppercorns. Cover, bring to the boil and cook until the bird is tender.

When both meats are cooked, remove them from the cooking liquid and take the meat from the bones. Skin the chicken and chop it and the pig's head into pieces. Mix the meats together and add the chopped parsley and thyme leaves. Taste and correct the seasoning. Pack the meat into one large or two small pudding bowls and add a little of the cooking liquid from each pot. Press with a weight. When cold, turn out and serve in slices with a salad. Brawn will keep for several weeks in the fridge.

Tripe and Trotters with Chorizo

Serves 6–8

2 fresh pig's trotters
1kg (2¼lb) honeycomb tripe, cut into
  thin strips
salt
2 tablespoons extra-virgin olive oil
1 large onion, chopped
1 garlic clove, crushed
1 large red pepper, sliced
2 tomatoes, peeled, deseeded and chopped
½ teaspoon chilli powder
250g (9oz) cooked ham, chopped
250g (9oz) chorizo, cut into 5mm (¼in) slices

Garnish
4 tablespoons coarsely chopped parsley

Put the pig's trotters into a deep saucepan. Cover with cold water and bring to the boil, then cover and simmer for 2½ hours.

Drain and transfer the trotters into a saucepan with the tripe, barely cover with fresh water, add some salt and cook for 1½–2 hours or until tender and the meat is almost falling from the bones on the trotters. Remove the trotters and, when cool enough to handle, remove the bones and discard. Chop the meat coarsely and return to the pan with the tripe.

Heat the olive oil in a saucepan. Add the onions, then cover and sweat for 4–5 minutes. Add the garlic and pepper and season with salt. Add the tomato, and cook for 5–6 minutes or until soft. Add the chilli powder, ham and chorizo, stir well and cook for 5–6 minutes. Stir in the tripe and the trotters. Taste, correct the seasoning, then garnish with parsley and serve.

Black Pudding with Grainy Mustard and Apple Sauce

Serves 12 for canapés, 4–6 as a starter

The French serve their black pudding for lunch or dinner accompanied by mounds of fluffy, Golden Delicious apples and potato purée. It is also very good served on buttery croutons as a canapé or starter.

12 slices best-quality black pudding, about 1cm
  (⅓in) thick

Golden Delicious Apple Sauce (see page 597)

Croûtons
12 slices French bread
butter or extra-virgin olive oil
1 wholegrain mustard
1 teaspoon honey

Garnish
flat-leaf parsley or watercress

Preheat the oven to 180ºC/350ºF/gas 4.

While the oven is heating, make the apple sauce: peel, quarter and core the apples; cut the quarters into 2 and put them in a stainless steel or cast-iron saucepan with the sugar and water. Cover and cook on a very low heat until the apples break down into a fluff. Stir and taste for sweetness.

Brush both sides of the bread with butter or olive oil and then cook on a baking sheet until golden on both sides – about 20 minutes. Drain on kitchen paper and keep warm. Melt a very little butter in a frying pan and sauté the black pudding on both sides on a medium heat. Remove the skin from the black pudding.

Mix the mustard with the honey and spread on each warm croûton. Lay a piece of hot pudding on top and finish with a blob of apple sauce. Garnish with flat-leaf parsley or watercress.

game

game

My father-in-law, Ivan Allen, was a great ornothologist and a lover of birds in general. Consequently, we don't tend to serve a great deal of game at Ballymaloe. This year, for the first time, we had several clutches of pheasant chicks living on our farm – thanks to Tim who wouldn't allow the grass to be mown in the orchard until the end of July, by which time the pheasant chicks were independent, strong and hardy. However, our lands are preserved and we only shoot pigeons if they become a nuisance.

Many local estates rear pheasants for shooting and sometimes in winter we are given a brace of wild pheasant as a present. The flavour is rich and gamey and we savour every mouthful. Our venison also comes from a local estate, and game dealer Paul Fletcher sells a variety of game.

All game, whether feathered or furred, is wild and has usually been shot or stalked. Having said that, there is an increase in game farming. Chances are that if it does not look like it has been shot, then it probably hasn't – and it is also unlikely that it is truly wild. All game is shot during the winter months, never during the breeding season. Game seasons and guidelines are different in many parts of the world, so check in your area for local rules.

Venison
Because it is wild, venison is antibiotic and hormone free. Even if it is deer from a deer park it will have been reared in an extensive free-range way. Make sure that you buy venison from a reputable dealer, and not from the back of someone's car. In order to be sold, venison needs the game warden's seal. This guarantees a level of quality, and should indicate that the deer was inspected by a local vet for TB after it was killed. If it's just been shot somewhere up in the hills,

it's unlikely that this procedure has taken place. Ask how many times and where the deer was shot. Inspect the carcass thoroughly – it might be badly damaged from careless or bad shooting, and much of the meat rendered unusable. If the dealer is unable or unwilling to answer your questions, don't buy from them.

Venison is always very lean, so it will need to be wrapped in caul fat, or larded. The haunch and the saddle (the main loin part) are best for roasting. The shoulder is good braised or used for stewing, and should be marinated in olive oil to moisten it. You can mince the neck or use it for stock. The flank can be braised or used for the stockpot. The most important thing to know about venison is that it *must* be rare: do not over-cook it or it will be dry, tough and dull. The classic accompaniments for venison are gravy and redcurrant jelly.

Rabbit
Wild rabbit is not sold so much nowadays due to fears about myxomatosis. Fortunately we have a regular supply of wild rabbit from a local man who likes to shoot. Many (though it has to be said not all) of our students are delighted to have the opportunity to learn how to skin and prepare a wild rabbit. Farmed rabbit is usually more tender than wild rabbit. A tip for judging the age of rabbit: the ears of a young rabbit will tear easily, older rabbits are understandably tougher.

Duck
There are several different types of wild duck: mallard (quite often found in parks); widgeon, pochard and tufted duck, teal, pintail and shoveller – all of which taste a bit fishy. Widgeon is two-thirds the size of mallard, and teal is half the size of widgeon. You need to remove the oil glands from many wild duck, otherwise there'll be a musky flavour to the meat.

Wild Goose

Like duck, goose can taste a little fishy. To solve this problem, some people boil the goose before roasting it.

Snipe and Woodcock

Snipe makes a delectable starter or savoury course whilst woodcock, which are two or three times larger, can be used for a main course. Leave the head on – the traditional way to serve it is with the bill used as a skewer through the legs. Woodcock are generally cooked with a rasher wrapped around them and are served on a croûton of toast. They can be roasted quite rare, and you can use the pan juices to make gravy. Both snipe and woodcock are cooked undrawn (with the innards still inside), but do remove the gizzard before you cook them. Don't worry about the innards – they will disintegrate during the cooking, and become like a sauce around the bird, which will make your gravy delicious.

Pheasant

When buying pheasant, bear in mind that the hen has more breast meat than the cock. It is also useful to know that the spur at the back of a pheasant's leg indicates its age, growing longer as the bird ages.

Pigeons

Pigeons can be quite tough if not handled carefully in the cooking. If you are using the whole bird, use it in a game or pigeon pie; roasting wild pigeons really doesn't work as they're usually as tough as old boots. It's best to use just the breast meat and to pan or stir-fry it very quickly, or to poach it gently in stock (roasting the breasts, unless you baste every couple of minutes, usually ends in the meat becoming very dry and tough). We usually don't bother to pluck pigeons, preferring simply to remove the feathers with the skin from the breast, which we then discard with the legs and wings that have very little meat.

Hanging Game

If game is cooked soon after it has been killed (within 12 hours), it will be tender but have an undistinguished flavour. If it is allowed to hang for a few days, enzyme action in the flesh will tenderise the meat and give it a fuller 'gamey' flavour. The longer the meat is hung, the stronger the flavour will be.

Feathered game is hung by the head and furred game by the legs. Game should hang in a cool, dry, well-ventilated larder or refrigerated cold room (especially in the hotter months). In warmer weather, the meat will deteriorate more quickly; the cooler it is, the longer it can hang. Hanging times also depend on individual taste. I prefer my game to taste reasonably gamey, otherwise one may as well eat a chicken, but if you prefer a more natural flavour hang for minimum rather than maximum times. The following hanging times are guidelines:

Venison (gutted and bled)	2–3 weeks
Rabbit	2–3 days
Hare	7–14 days
Mallard and Teal	2–3 days
Wild Goose	2–3 weeks
Snipe	4–5 days
Woodcock	5–7 days
Grouse	5–7 days
Pheasant	3–5 days
Partridge	3–4 days

Game birds are hung in the feather (unplucked) and never in pairs. If they touch each other, they will start to deteriorate. Badly shot birds deteriorate faster, so examine them on a daily basis. You'll know when a bird is ready for plucking when it begins to smell a little 'high' or sweet.

Buying Game

Game birds are traditionally sold in the feather for various good reasons. They are more easily identifiable and the feathers keep the bird moist during hanging. However, feathers often hide where the bird has been shot, which can be in the poulterer's interest. Always ask how long the bird has been hanging. Ask to examine the bird yourself to see where it has been shot; if it has been shot through the breast or the leg, there will be a lot of waste, so it is best to buy birds that have been shot through the head, neck or wing. Badly shot or older birds are best used for pâtés or casseroles. If you don't wish to pluck and draw the game yourself, ask the poulterer to do it for you and to save the gizzard (which you can use for stock) and the liver (to use for pâté or terrines). There will be a charge for this service. Supermarkets are offering a wider selection of oven-ready game so be adventurous.

Freezing

If you are in the happy position of having an over-abundance of game, it is quite safe to freeze it, although it does have a slightly adverse effect on the taste and texture of the meat. Game should be hung for the minimum rather than the maximum time before freezing. It is not necessary to gut and pluck the birds before freezing, although you can if you prefer. Pack the game into thick polythene bags and expel the air before closing. Label clearly with contents and date of freezing: six months is the maximum time game should be frozen if you wish to preserve its flavour.

Game Broth with a Julienne of Vegetables

Serves 6

This delicious soup is based on stock made from a game carcass. If the stock tastes weak, put it into a wide saucepan and reduce it without a lid until the flavour has concentrated sufficiently.

300ml (½ pint) homemade Game Stock
  (see page 36)
50g (2oz) carrots, cut in fine julienne strips
50g (2oz) leeks, cut in fine julienne strips
1.2 litres (2 pints) well-flavoured homemade
  Game Stock (see page 36)
small sprigs of tarragon
50g (2oz) small button mushrooms,
  thinly sliced
2 tablespoons chopped spring onion (cut
  diagonally)
flat-leaf parsley, chopped
salt and freshly ground pepper

Bring the stock to the boil, add the julienne of carrot and simmer for 5 minutes. Then add the leeks. Season, and simmer for a further 3–4 minutes, or until the vegetables are tender (the carrots should still have a slight bite). Drain the vegetables, adding this stock to the well-flavoured stock. Keep the vegetables aside until needed.

Just before serving, bring the well-flavoured broth to the boil. Check the seasoning, add a couple of sprigs of tarragon with the julienne of vegetables and finely sliced mushrooms. Boil for 1 minute. Serve immediately, scattered with the spring onions and flat-leaf parsley.

George Gossip's Game Pie

Serves 6

This is an ideal way to use up old or damaged pheasants and the odd pigeon or the like for which you cannot think up a good use. It is really delicious and none the worse for being made from leftovers. Do try to use different types of game for this, as it dramatically improves the flavour. Hare is especially good, but do not use duck – its flavour doesn't marry well with pheasant.

225g (8oz) pickling onions (or sliced
  large onions)
10–25g (½–1oz) butter
2 garlic cloves, chopped
700g (1½lb) game meat, off the bone and
  sliced or diced: pheasant, pigeon, hare,
  venison or the like
225g (8oz) piece streaky bacon, cut into 5mm
  (¼in) dice
50g (2oz) flour
salt and freshly ground pepper
1–2 tablespoons vegetable oil
bay leaf
150ml (¼ pint) homemade Game Stock
  (see page 36), made from the bones of a hare
  for preference
150ml (¼ pint) red wine
225g (8oz) button mushrooms
350g (12oz) homemade Puff Pastry (see page
  456), rolled out thinly
1 organic egg, beaten with a little milk

Fry the onions lightly in butter until golden. Add the garlic and fry for a further minute. Sprinkle the meats and bacon with seasoned flour and brown them gently in a little oil in a heavy-bottomed saucepan. Add the onions, garlic, bay leaf, stock and wine and stew slowly, covered.

Making Julienne Strips or Matchsticks

Julienne strips are vegetables or citrus fruits cut into very fine, thin matchsticks. Generally a julienne of vegetables or citrus fruits is used as a garnish, but sometimes a much larger julienne may be used as a vegetable or part of a salad.

1. Wash and thinly peel the vegetables, preferably using a swivel-top peeler.

2. Square off the sides. (Use trimmings for the stock pot or for soup.)

3. Cut the vegetables crossways into 5cm (2in) lengths, or as required.

4. Cut lengthways into thin sticks.

5. Stack the slices and cut lengthways into thin strips.

Just before the meat is done, add the mushrooms and continue cooking until everything is tender. If there is too much sauce, strain and return the sauce to the heat and boil down rapidly until sufficiently reduced. Allow to cool.

This stage is best completed a day or so in advance for the flavours to intensify. It may also be made up in larger amounts and then frozen in the required portions.

Preheat the oven to 220°C/425°F/gas 7. Line a small pie dish with ¾ of the puff pastry. Fill with the mixture (having first checked the seasoning), cover with a lid made from the remaining pastry, decorate and glaze with an egg wash.

Bake in the hot oven until golden brown. Serve with baked or mashed potatoes, red cabbage, celery and redcurrant jelly.

George Gossip writes: 'Shooting trips are often an all-male affair, with a distinct lowering of standards. Personal memories involve enormous fried breakfasts, making full use of any leftover potatoes from the previous night; vast numbers of under-done kidneys, fried eggs either runny, or very over-cooked and leathery, a dozen eggs poaching all together in a saucepan, lots of fried bread, wonderful black puddings, made by the local butcher, in a roasting tin and cut in thick slices, like cake, and far, far too many rashers of bacon and sausages. Thick slices of bread, thickly buttered. Comparisons between each others' wives' marmalade. To drink, strong tea or even stronger coffee, made in a jug and filtered through a sieve with too wide a mesh. Beware the question 'Would you like a starter?' It probably means a glass of Paddy! Usually the dogs are allowed to lick the frying pans, before they are washed.'

Petits Pots de Gibier (Little Game Custards)

The recipe comes from Jane Grigson's *Food with the Famous*, the famous in this case being Lord and Lady Shaftesbury. Lady S. was given it by Emily Eden, a remarkable spinster lady who had accompanied her brother, Lord Auckland, when he went to India as Governor-General from 1835 to 1842, and wrote several books about her experiences there.

'For each person,' says George Gossip 'allow one (egg) yolk and 100ml (3½fl oz) skimmed, strained stock. Beat together, add seasoning and pour into buttered custard cups. Put on the lids, stand in a pan of simmering water on top of the stove, and leave it for half an hour. Serve with toast or with the sandwiches of the following recipe.'

Jane Grigson says the stock should be from pheasants or pigeons (and I have found it ideal from grouse, partridge or from a game stock including all of these – plus a very little hare). Jane says pigeons make a particularly good stock since most recipes only use the breasts, leaving a great deal of unused meat on the carcasses (but that assumes you can be bothered to pluck them).

She also says simmer with aromatics, a glass or two of wine, and beef stock to cover – while I use only game (but a good rich mixture). I also use sherry rather than wine. I put it in ramekins in a bain-marie, covered with tin foil, and cook in the oven for about 20 minutes. You have to watch it carefully as you don't want it too solid.

Jane Grigson suggests serving it with Ham Toast with Cheese: 'Sandwich slices of good ham between thin slices of bread – do not butter it – and cut away the crusts. Dip in clarified butter. Cut diagonally across into triangles and arrange closely together on a baking sheet. Sprinkle over with a layer of grated cheese – use well dried-out Cheddar or Lancashire – and bake in a hot oven until browned. Drain for a few minutes on kitchen paper, to get rid of any greasiness, and serve on a very hot dish.'

We find it best as a starter for a rather smart dinner party, usually accompanied by Melba Toast (see page 78).

How to Cut Up a Rabbit or Hare

For 6 or 7 pieces:

Detach the hind legs from the carcass, cut through the cartilage on the front of the leg.

Cut around the forelegs and remove also.

Chop the saddle into 2 or 3 pieces, so that you now have 6 or 7 pieces.

Discard the back passage.

For 8 or 9 pieces:

Follow the steps above, then divide the hind legs into 2 pieces.

West Cork Rabbit Casserole

Serves about 6

Rabbits and hare run wild all over Ireland. They are extremely prolific and though sweet and cuddly are considered to be a pest by the farmers, so don't feel guilty – tuck in!

350g (12oz) unsmoked streaky bacon
1.6–1.8kg (3½–4lb) rabbit, wild if possible
a little butter and oil
450g (1lb) onions (baby ones are nicest)
350g (12oz) carrot, peeled and thickly sliced
sprig of thyme
700ml (1¼ pints) homemade Chicken Stock
   (see page 36)
a little Roux (see page 580), optional

Mushroom à la Crème (see page 201), optional

Garnish
2 teaspoons freshly chopped parsley

De-rind the bacon and cut into cubes roughly 2.5cm (1in) square (blanch if salty) and dry on kitchen paper. Joint the rabbit into 8 pieces.

Preheat the oven to 80°C/350°F/gas 4. Heat a little oil in a sauté pan and sauté the bacon until crisp, remove and put in a casserole. Add the rabbit pieces to the pan and sauté until golden, then add to the bacon in the casserole. Heat control is crucial here: the pan mustn't burn, yet it must be hot enough to sauté the rabbit. If it is too cool, the rabbit pieces will stew rather than brown and, as a result, the meat may be tough.

Then sauté the onion and carrot, adding a little butter if necessary. Add to the casserole, de-grease the pan and de-glaze with stock, bring to the boil and pour over the rabbit mixture.

Season well, add a sprig of thyme and bring to simmering point on top of the stove, then put into the oven for 30–45 minutes. The cooking time depends on how long the rabbit pieces were sautéed. When the casserole is just cooked, strain off the cooking liquid, de-grease and return the de-greased liquid to the casserole and bring to the boil.

Thicken with a little Roux if necessary. Add back the meat, carrots and onions and bring to the boil. The casserole is very good served at this point, but even more delicious if some Mushroom à la crème is stirred in as an enrichment. Serve bubbling hot, sprinkled with chopped parsley.

Rabbit with Mustard and Sage Leaves

Serves 6

Many French peasants rear their own rabbits in hutches either beside or in their farmhouses. This recipe brings back memories of delicious rabbit stews I ate with Mamie and Papie Viénot in Lille-sur-le-Doube. I have a feeling that many of you may be a bit squeamish about eating rabbit, but this recipe is also very good made with chicken.

1 rabbit about 1–1.3kg (2½–3lb) or 1 chicken,
   the same weight
6 fresh sage leaves
2 teaspoons English mustard powder
2 teaspoons grainy mustard, e.g. Moutarde
   de Meaux
125ml (4fl oz) dry white wine
10g (½oz) butter
2 teaspoons olive oil
1 tablespoon wine vinegar
18 baby onions, peeled
225ml (8fl oz) crème fraîche or fresh cream and
   lemon juice
a little Roux (see page 580), optional
salt and freshly ground pepper

Garnish
fresh sage leaves

Joint the rabbit into 6 portions. Put it into a terrine with the chopped sage leaves. Mix half the mustard powder and half the grainy mustard with 50ml (2fl oz) water. Pour this and the wine over the rabbit and leave to marinate for about 1 hour. Drain the rabbit pieces and dry them on kitchen paper. Season well.

Put the butter and oil into a wide sauté pan over a medium heat and lightly brown the rabbit on all sides, then transfer to a casserole. De-grease the pan, de-glaze with the vinegar and pour this and the marinade onto the rabbit. Add the onions and the rest of the mustard. Add another 50ml (2fl oz) water, season and stir well. Cover and leave to cook gently for about 1 hour.

When the rabbit is tender, take out the pieces and arrange them on a hot plate with the onions (making sure the onions are fully cooked). De-grease the juices, add the cream to the pot and reduce over a high heat until it thickens, whisking in a little roux if necessary. Taste and sharpen with lemon juice if necessary. Pour the sauce over the rabbit pieces – through a sieve if you prefer a smoother sauce. Decorate with some sage leaves and serve immediately.

Jugged Hare

Serves 6

Jugged hare is the English equivalent of the famous French civet de lièvre. This is one of Jane Grigson's recipes from her splendid book *English Food*. The method was the obvious way of cooking game slowly in the days when most cooking was done over the hearth fire. Today, the dish is more usually cooked in a casserole. The blood of the hare is added, so this robust and comforting dish is not for the faint-hearted! Rabbit can be substituted for the hare.

1 hare, prepared and jointed
strips of pork or bacon fat for larding (optional)
salt, freshly ground pepper and ground mace
bouquet garni
1 onion, stuck with 3 cloves
110g (4oz) butter
150ml (¼ pint) white wine
1 anchovy, chopped
pinch of cayenne pepper
1 tablespoon butter
1 tablespoon flour
blood of the hare or rabbit (optional)
lemon juice (optional)

Garnish
triangles of fried bread

Unless your hare or rabbit is young and tender, you will be wise to lard it. Put the pieces into a large jug (the unlipped stoneware jugs still made in France, and widely sold in England are ideal) after rubbing them with salt, pepper and mace. Add the bouquet garni, onion and butter.

Cover the jug tightly and securely with kitchen foil tied with string to make sure it keeps in place. Stand the jug in a pan of boiling water and keep it simmering until the hare is cooked – about 3 hours, but the time depends on the age and toughness of the creature. This can either be done on top of the stove (a solution to the problems of slow cooking without an oven) or in the oven if this is more convenient.

Transfer the cooked pieces to a serving dish. Strain the juices into a pan. Add the wine, anchovy and pepper to taste. Thicken either with the flour and butter mashed together, and added in little knobs, or with the blood of the hare – in the latter case, mix a little of the sauce with the blood, then return it to the pan and stir over a low heat until thick. The sauce must not boil again once the blood has been added or it will curdle.

Sharpen with a little lemon juice if you like, and serve with the fried bread.

Stewed Hare, Rabbit, Woodpigeons or Venison with Forcemeat Balls
Serves 6

Another delicious recipe from George Gossip.

1 hare or rabbit, jointed, or six whole pigeons, or 1.5kg (3lb) stewing venison, cut in pieces
a little flour, seasoned
75g (3oz) lard
225g (8oz) streaky bacon, cut in strips
225g (8oz) onion, chopped
1 heaped teaspoon fresh thyme
1 heaped tablespoon freshly chopped parsley
½ bay leaf
homemade Game or Beef Stock (see page 36)
75ml (3fl oz) port
Redcurrant Jelly (see page 508)
salt and freshly ground pepper

Forcemeat Balls
110g (4oz) fresh white breadcrumbs
50g (2oz) chopped suet
1 tablespoon freshly chopped parsley
1 teaspoon fresh thyme
grated rind of ½ lemon
50g (2oz) bacon, finely chopped
salt and freshly ground pepper
1 large organic egg

Turn the joints, pigeons, or pieces of venison in seasoned flour (in the case of hare or rabbit, keep the brains, liver and blood for the final thickening) then brown them in the lard with the bacon and onion. Transfer to a casserole.

Put in the herbs and just enough stock to cover them. Simmer gently until the meat is tender and falls easily off the bone. Add the port, jelly and seasoning to taste.

To thicken the sauce, either mix some of the liquid with a little of the remaining seasoned flour (about a tablespoon) and return it to the pot, or mash the brains, liver and blood together. Pour on a little hot liquid and then return this mixture to the pot and cook without boiling for a few minutes until the sauce is thickened.

The second method produces the better flavour – a good game butcher will give you the blood of a hare or wild rabbit.

Meanwhile, mix the ingredients for the forcemeat balls, and shape them into balls about 2.5cm (1in) diameter. Fry them in lard until brown and add to the stew. They are also good in game soups, but in this case make them smaller. If you do not want to make forcemeat balls, serve the stew with triangles of fried bread.

Casserole-roast Pheasant with Apple and Calvados
Serves 2–3

This recipe comes from the Vallé d'Auge in Normandy in France, where they have wonderfully rich cream and delicious apples. Chicken or guinea fowl may also be used in this recipe.

1 plump young pheasant, about 725g–900g (1lb 10oz–2lb)
10g (½oz) butter
4–5 tablespoons Calvados
225ml (8fl oz) cream or 125ml (4fl oz) cream and 125ml (4fl oz) homemade Chicken Stock (see page 36)
Roux (see page 580), optional
salt and freshly ground pepper
25g (1oz) butter
2 dessert apples, e.g. Cox's Orange Pippin

Garnish
sprigs of watercress or chervil

Preheat the oven to 180°C/350°F/gas 4.

Heat a casserole, preferably oval, just large enough to fit the bird. Season the cavity, spread the butter over the breast and legs of the pheasant and place breast-side down into the casserole. Allow it to brown over a gentle heat, turn over and sprinkle with salt and pepper. Cover with a tight-fitting lid and cook in the oven for 40–45 minutes. Check to see that the pheasant is cooked (there should be no trace of pink juices coming out from a fork poked between the leg and the breast). Transfer the pheasant to a serving dish and keep warm.

Carefully strain and de-grease the juices in the casserole. Bring to the boil, add the Calvados and ignite it with a match. Shake the pan, and when the flames have gone out, add the cream (or stock and cream). Reduce by boiling until the sauce thickens, stirring occasionally; taste for seasoning.

Fry the peeled, cored and diced apple in butter until golden. Carve the pheasant and arrange on a hot serving dish or individual plates. Cover with the sauce. Put a little of the apple in the centre and garnish with watercress or chervil.

Note: Although many game recipes are very traditional, feel free to be creative with accompaniments. Roast pheasant or quail are wonderful with Chickpeas with Fresh Spices (see page 142), Caribbean Spinach (see page 171), spiced aubergines or roasted vegetables.

Roast Pheasant with Game Chips, Cranberry Sauce and Bread Sauce

Serves 2–3

A roast pheasant makes the perfect Christmas dinner for two and you'll probably have a little left over for a cold supper or lunch. This slightly unorthodox way of cooking the pheasant produces a moist, juicy bird. Guineafowl is also wonderful cooked and served in this way. You will need a piece of muslin or a new J-cloth.

1 plump young pheasant

Stuffing
35g (1¹/₂oz) butter
75g (3oz) onions, chopped
60g (2¹/₂oz) soft white breadcrumbs
1 tablespoon freshly chopped herbs (parsley, thyme, chives, marjoram)
50g (2oz) butter
salt and freshly ground pepper

Gravy
300ml (¹/₂ pint) Game or Chicken Stock (see page 36)
50g (2oz) butter

Game Chips (see page 185)
Cranberry Sauce (see page 597)
Bread Sauce (see page 594)

Preheat the oven to 190°C/375°F/gas 5.

Gut the pheasant, if necessary, and remove the crop, which is at the neck end; wash all over and dry well.

To make the stuffing: melt the butter and sweat the onions until soft but not coloured, then remove from the heat. Stir in the breadcrumbs and herbs, season with salt and pepper and taste.

Unless you are about to cook the bird right away, allow the stuffing to get quite cold before you use it.

Season the cavity of the pheasant with salt and pepper and fill it loosely with the stuffing. Sprinkle the breast with salt and pepper. Melt the butter and soak a piece of muslin or J-cloth in it. Wrap the pheasant completely in the muslin or J-cloth (fear not, the J-cloth will not melt: you can even wash it out and use it later!).

Roast in the preheated oven, for about 1¼ hours. Test by pricking the leg at the highest point: the juices should just run clear. Remove the muslin or J-cloth and keep the pheasant warm on a serving dish while you make the gravy.

Spoon off any surplus fat from the roasting pan (keep it for roasting or sautéing potatoes). De-glaze the pan with the Game or Chicken Stock. Bring it to the boil, and use a whisk to dislodge the crusty caramelised juices so they can dissolve into the gravy. Season with salt and pepper, taste and boil until you are happy with the flavour. Pour into a hot gravy boat.

Carve the pheasant and serve with stuffing, gravy, Game Chips, Cranberry Sauce and Bread Sauce.

Pheasant with Wild Mushrooms and Colcannon

Serves 6–8

2 plump pheasants, about 800g (1³/₄lb) each
1 tablespoon olive oil
110g (4oz) streaky bacon, diced
50–125ml (2–4fl oz) brandy
4 juniper berries, crushed
300ml (¹/₂ pint) dry white wine

900g (2lb) Wild Mushroom à la Crème (see page 201)
Colcannon (see page 183)

Garnish
flat-leaf parsley

Preheat the oven to 180°C/350°F/gas 4.

Season the pheasants inside and out with salt and pepper.

Heat the oil in an oval casserole just large enough to take the birds. Toss in the bacon and cook for a few minutes until it begins to crisp, remove the bacon and allow the pheasants to brown on the breast side. Turn them the other way up, add the bacon back in, pour in the brandy, flambé by lighting the brandy juices with a taper or match and boil for a few minutes to cook off the alcohol. Add the juniper berries. Cover the casserole, put in the oven, cook for about 40–45 minutes.

Meanwhile, make the Colcannon and Wild Mushroom à la Crème.

Remove the pheasants to a serving dish and keep warm. De-grease the cooking juices and add the white wine. Bring to the boil and reduce until slightly thickened.

Meanwhile, joint the pheasant and arrange it on a warmed serving plate, spoon the sauce over and garnish with flat-leaf parsley.

Serve with Colcannon and Wild Mushroom à la Crème.

Pheasant and Potato Pie

Serves 6–8

This was another of my favourite winter dishes at the Arbutus Lodge restaurant in Cork when the Ryan family were there.

350g (12oz) raw meat, using a combination of pheasant and chicken or pheasant, chicken and veal – for example, 175g (6oz) pheasant, 75g (3oz) chicken, 75g (3oz) veal
50g (2oz) shallots, finely chopped and sweated in 25g (1oz) of butter
1 tablespoon freshly chopped parsley
1 teaspoon thyme leaves
salt and freshly ground pepper
4 tablespoons white wine

225g (8oz) potatoes, peeled, very thinly sliced and left under a cold running tap to wash off all their starch

450g (1lb) Puff or Flaky Pastry (see pages 456 and 413)

organic egg wash

10 tablespoons cream, reduced to thicken slightly

Preheat the oven to 180°C/350°F/gas 4.

Chop up the meat into small pieces. Season the meat with the shallot, herbs, salt, pepper and white wine – it should be highly seasoned. Dry the washed, sliced potatoes and add to the meat.

Roll out 2 rounds of pastry – one 25.5cm (10in) and one 32cm (12in). Place the larger one on a baking sheet and put the filling on it. Egg-wash the edge of the pastry and then place the smaller piece of pastry on top to cover the filling. Fold the bottom piece of pastry up to enclose the pie and seal well. Scallop the edges of the pastry and egg-wash the whole pie. Make a small hole in the centre to allow the steam to escape.

Place in the oven and cook for approximately 45 minutes. Five minutes from the end of the cooking time, cut a 10cm (4in) lid in the top of the pie and pour in the reduced cream. Replace the lid and finish cooking. Serve the pie as soon as possible after it is cooked.

We serve a little Beurre Blanc sauce (see page 583) with it – decadent but delicious!

Faisinjan
Serves 4

The Grigsons have delicious ways of serving game. This recipe is from Sophie Grigson's *Ingredients Book*.

1 plump pheasant, cut into 8 portions

2 tablespoons vegetable oil

1 onion, chopped

225g (8oz) shelled walnuts, coarsely ground or very finely chopped

1 cinnamon stick

3 tablespoons pomegranate syrup

425ml (3/4 pint) water

salt and pepper

sugar

1 tablespoon freshly chopped parsley

fresh pomegranate seeds (optional)

Brown the pheasant pieces in the oil. Set aside, and fry the onion in the same oil until browned, stirring to prevent burning. Turn down the heat, add the walnuts and cinnamon and cook gently for a few minutes, stirring.

Mix in the pomegranate syrup, water and a little salt and pepper. Bring up to the boil, stirring occasionally, then add the pheasant pieces. Cover and simmer gently for 30 minutes.

Uncover and continue simmering for another 15–30 minutes until the meat is very tender and the sauce is thick. Taste and add more salt or pepper, or a little sugar to give a sweet and sour sauce. Sprinkle with the parsley and pomegranate seeds, if using, before serving.

BELOW: Faisinjan

Pheasant with Chorizo, Bacon and Tomatoes
Serves 6

George Gossip, who cooked this recipe on our Game Course, says it is an amalgamation of Elizabeth David's Pheasant with Spiced Rice, a chicken dish of Penelope Casas' and his own ideas.

175–225g (6–8oz) good-quality streaky bacon, diced into 1cm (½in) cubes
2 tablespoons extra-virgin olive oil
1 plump pheasant, cut into 4 portions
1 large onions, sliced
1 garlic clove, chopped
450g (1lb) ripe tomatoes, peeled and chopped, or 1 x 400g (14oz) tin chopped tomatoes
225g (8oz) chorizo sausage, sliced
sprig of thyme
2 tablespoons freshly chopped flat-leaf parsley
2 teaspoons good-quality paprika, preferably sweet Hungarian
salt and freshly ground pepper
300g (11oz) Pilaf rice (see page 125)

Fry the bacon in the olive oil in a heavy frying pan, add the pheasant and cook lightly. Remove and keep warm.

Add the sliced onions and the garlic to the pan, cover and sweat gently. When these are cooked, remove the lid, add the chopped tomatoes and increase the heat. Add the chorizo slices, the herbs and spice and cook rapidly to form a thick sauce. Season with salt and pepper.

Add the pheasant pieces to the tomato sauce and cook through. Add the wings and thigh pieces first, then the breast sections, which will require less cooking. Check the seasoning and, if the sauce has become too thick, dilute with a little water.

Serve on a bed of Pilaf Rice, accompanied by a green salad.

Pheasant with Jerusalem Artichokes
Serves 4

Pheasants adore Jerusalem artichokes, and many of the large estates specially plant a patch as a treat for them. It seemed logical therefore to cook them together and indeed it turns out to be a very good marriage of flavours. Casserole-roasting, the cooking method used here, is a particularly good way to cook pheasant, especially if it is not in the first flush of youth. Chicken or guinea fowl may also be cooked in this way.

1 plump pheasant
25g (1oz) butter
salt and freshly ground pepper
900g (2lb) Jerusalem artichokes

Garnish
parsley, freshly chopped or flat-leaf parsley sprigs

Preheat the oven to 180°C/350°F/gas 4.

Smear a little butter on the breast of the pheasant and brown it in the casserole over a gentle heat. Meanwhile, peel and slice the artichokes into 1cm (½in) pieces. Remove the pheasant, add a little butter to the casserole and toss the Jerusalem artichoke slices in the butter. Season, and sprinkle 1 tablespoon of water over the top. Return the pheasant, tucking it right down into the sliced artichokes so that they come up around the sides of the bird. Cover with a butter wrapper and the lid of the casserole. Cook for a further 1–1¼ hours.

Remove the pheasant as soon as it is cooked, strain and de-grease the cooking liquid if there is need but usually there is virtually no fat on it. The juices of the pheasant will have flavoured the artichokes deliciously. Arrange the artichokes on a hot serving dish, carve the pheasant into 4 portions and arrange on top.

The artichokes always break up a little – that is their nature. Spoon some juices over the pheasant and artichokes and serve scattered with parsley.

Pigeon or Squab Stew and Pie
Serves 10–12

This was a favourite recipe for winter house parties at Ballymaloe – brilliant for a shooting lunch. Tim and his brother Rory would bag a few dozen pigeons, doubly welcome because pigeons tend to breed at an incredible rate and damage crops on the farm.

4–6 pigeon or squab breasts
their weight in lean beef
half their weight in streaky bacon
bacon fat or olive oil, for frying
8 baby carrots or sticks of carrot
10–12 button onions
1 garlic clove
1–2 teaspoons flour
225ml (8fl oz) red wine
225ml (8fl oz) good stock
150ml (¼ pint) homemade Tomato Purée (see page 50) or smaller quantity of tinned purée or tomato paste: use according to concentration and make up with extra stock
Roux (see page 580), optional
2 teaspoons chopped thyme and parsley
salt and freshly ground pepper

225g (8oz) Mushroom à la Crème (see page 201)

For the Pie Topping
225g (8oz) Puff or Flaky Pastry (pages 456 and 413)

Preheat the oven to 150°C/300°F/gas 2.

Remove the rind from the bacon, cut into 'lardons' about 2.5cm (1in) wide, cut the beef and pigeon into similar size pieces. Heat some bacon fat or olive oil in a pan and fry until crisp and golden. Remove to a 2.4 litre (4 pint) casserole, add beef and pigeon a little at a time to the pan and toss until it changes colour.

Put into the casserole. Turn the carrots, onions and crushed garlic in the fat and add them to the meat in the casserole. Stir the flour into the fat in the pan, cook for a minute or so and then stir or whisk in the wine, stock and tomato purée.

Bring to the boil and thicken with roux if necessary. Pour over the meat and vegetables in the casserole. Season, add the thyme and parsley, return to the boil, then cover and cook for 1–2 hours, depending on the age of the pigeons, in the oven. When it is cooked, add the Mushroom à la Crème. Check the seasoning.* Allow to get quite cold as the flavour will improve overnight.

* The pigeon stew can be eaten at this point, served with fluffy mashed potatoes and a green vegetable, such as Buttered Cabbage (see page 166).

To assemble and bake the Pigeon Pie: as soon as the pigeon stew is cold, or the next day, fill into a pie dish, cover with Puff or Flaky Pastry lid and bake for 10 minutes at 230°C/450°F/gas 8, then for about 20 minutes at 190°C/375°F/gas 5.

Serve with a good green salad.

Pigeon Breasts with Juniper Berries

George Gossip is unquestionably the best game cook I know – and this is another of his recipes.

Pluck the breasts of the pigeon, then cut the breast, still attached to the breast bone, off the carcass. Discard the remainder of the carcass. Pack the breasts into a plastic box, cover with red wine, add a sliced onion, some thyme and a bay leaf. Cover and leave in the fridge for a couple of days (they will keep several weeks if necessary).

When you want to cook the pigeon breasts, take out the number required and slice the meat thinly.

Sauté a few lardons of fat, unsmoked bacon in a hot pan (blanch and refresh the bacon if very salty and sauté in a little oil). Remove when crisp, add a little butter if necessary, add and quickly toss the pigeon breast slices. They should still be pink. Add a good few crushed juniper berries and flambé in gin. Add back in the bacon and pour in some Game, Beef or Chicken Stock and allow to simmer for a couple of minutes. Taste and correct the seasoning. Enrich the pan juices with some knobs of butter.

Serve on very hot plates. Sprinkle with chervil or parsley. Serve as a first course with heart-shaped croûtons, or as a main course with a baked potato and a good green salad.

Warm Salad of Pigeon Breast with Spiced Pears and Mushrooms
Serves 12

6 small ripe pears, Conference or Doyenne de Comice
2½ cm (1in) piece of cinnamon stick
½ teaspoon allspice berries
1 teaspoon coriander seeds
1 star anise
¼ teaspoon black peppercorns
1 tablespoon sugar
grated rind of 1 orange
225g (8oz) flat mushrooms, sliced
25g (1oz) butter
2 tablespoons extra-virgin olive oil
12 pigeon breasts, skinned
enough salad leaves for 12 helpings
flat-parsley leaves

Dressing
1 tablespoon verjuice
1 tablespoon lemon juice
6 tablespoons extra-virgin olive oil
½ teaspoon Dijon mustard
1 teaspoon honey
salt and freshly ground pepper

Peel and quarter the pears. Put the cinnamon stick, allspice berries, coriander seeds, star anise, black peppercorns and sugar in a spice grinder, whizz to a powder and add the grated orange rind. Toss the pears in the spice mixture.

Make the dressing by whisking all the ingredients together in a bowl.

Heat the butter in a wide sauté pan, add the pears, toss and cook on a gentle heat until the pears are tender. Keep warm.

Heat a little olive oil in a frying pan, sauté the mushrooms over a high heat, season with a little salt and freshly ground pepper and keep warm. Clean the frying pan and heat a little olive oil on a very high heat. Season the pigeon breasts and fry very quickly – they should be sealed on the outside but still pink, otherwise they will be tough. Remove to a plate to rest while you dress the salad leaves. Toss the leaves in the dressing and divide between 12 plates. Divide the warm pears and mushrooms between the plates. Quickly slice the pigeon breasts and allow 1 per person. Scatter with flat-leaf parsley and serve immediately.

Quail Véronique
Serves 2 as a main course, 4 as a starter

4 quail
a little butter and oil
20 green grapes (peeled and seeded, being careful to reserve any juices)
4 tablespoons double cream
salt and freshly ground pepper

Preheat the oven to 180°C/350°F/gas 4.

Split the quail in half by cutting lengthways through the breastbone with a strong sharp knife. Season each bird. Heat butter and oil in a heavy-bottomed, ovenproof pan just big enough to fit the quail. Sauté until golden brown on the breast side; quail needs to be well-browned and almost crispy to enhance the flavour.

Cover the pan tightly with a lid and tin foil. It is important that the steam does not escape, otherwise the juices from the cooking birds will evaporate. Put the quail into the oven for about 10 minutes.

Remove the quail from the oven as soon as they are cooked, and keep them in a warm place. Remove any excess fat from the juices and put the pan on a low heat. Add the cream, peeled grapes and any grape juice. Simmer the sauce for 2–3 minutes. Finally check for seasoning.

To serve: spoon a little sauce and some grapes over and around the spatchcock quail on 2 or 4 plates.

Terrine of Wild Duck with Sultanas
Serves 8–10

A smooth and very rich game pâté as made by the inspirational chef, Michel Guérard. It should be made at least a day in advance. Chicken livers can successfully be substituted for duck livers in this terrine. We cooked individual ones in the smallest ramekins and they took 10 minutes. Individual soufflé dishes take 15–20 minutes. If you make it in a terrine, use a very sharp knife for slicing it to keep its shape. Alternatively, serve direct from the terrine with a spoon.

2 young mallards, about 1 kg (2¼lb) each
50g (2oz) best-quality sultanas
2½ tablespoons of Armagnac or best-quality brandy
salt and freshly ground pepper
1 tablespoon sunflower or groundnut oil

For the Forcemeat
190g (6½oz) very fat streaky bacon, rindless, and with no lean meat if possible
325g (11oz) wild duck or chicken livers (threads and any traces of green removed)
2 heaped teaspoons salt
¾ teaspoon pepper

pinch of Quatre Epices (see right)
225ml (8fl oz) double cream
4 organic egg yolks

You only need the breasts or 'supremes' of the ducks in this recipe, so remove the legs before cooking the ducks but leave the breasts on the carcass. The legs can be used for other recipes.

Wash the sultanas, pat dry and soak in the armagnac for about 1 hour. Set aside to add later.

Preheat the oven to 250°C/475°F/gas 9. Put the ducks, legs removed, into a small roasting pan, season with salt and pepper, sprinkle with oil and roast for 15–20 minutes. The flesh should still be pink.

Meanwhile, prepare the forcemeat. Cut the bacon into small chunks, put with the duck livers, salt, pepper and quatre épices in a liquidiser or food processor and blend to a smooth creamy consistency. Add the cream, egg yolks and strained armagnac and continue to blend until the mixture becomes liquid, perhaps 30 seconds. Push the mixture through a sieve into a bowl with the help of a spoon. Any small fibres from the bacon or livers will be caught in the mesh.

Remove the four breasts from the cooked ducks by sliding a flexible knife along the breast bone on either side and lifting the flesh away. Skin the fillets and cut them into dice, 5mm (¼in) across. Add the diced duck fillet and the sultanas to the liver mixture and mix thoroughly.

To cook the terrine, lower the oven heat to 200°C/400°F/gas 6. Pour the forcemeat mixture into an earthenware terrine. The pâté should be about 5cm (2in) thick. Cover with a sterilised board and weigh down to compact the layers, and cook in a bain-marie for 45–60 minutes. Leave in a cool place overnight.

The following day, serve the pâté with crusty white bread or thick slices of toast and a glass of red wine!

Quatre Epices

Quatre épices is a French spice blend used mainly in pork products. It can occasionally be found in shops outside France, but can easily be made up at home with:

125g (4½oz) pepper, freshly ground
4 teaspoons cloves, freshly ground
25g (1oz) ginger, freshly ground
35g (1½oz) nutmeg, freshly ground

Roast Wild Mallard
Serves 2

1 mallard
3–4 juniper berries
sprig of thyme
sprig of marjoram
4–5 slices rindless streaky bacon or butter
salt and freshly ground pepper
150ml (¼ pint) homemade Game or Chicken Stock (see page 36)
splash of red or white wine, or juice of 1 orange

Preheat the oven to 230°C/450°F/gas 8.

Trim the end off the wing tips at the first joint. Chop the ends off the legs just above the 'knee'. Remove the wish bone (make sure the crop has been removed). Season the cavity and add a few crushed juniper berries along with the herbs.

Smear the breast with butter or bard with bacon, then truss with string. Roast for about 20 minutes if you like it fairly rare or 30 minutes if you prefer it better done – be careful not to overcook or it will be dry. Note that duck which has been barded with bacon will take longer to cook – up to 10 minutes.

As soon as the duck is cooked, remove to a warm serving dish. De-grease the roasting pan and add some stock and a splash of

RIGHT: Terrine of Wild Duck with Sultanas

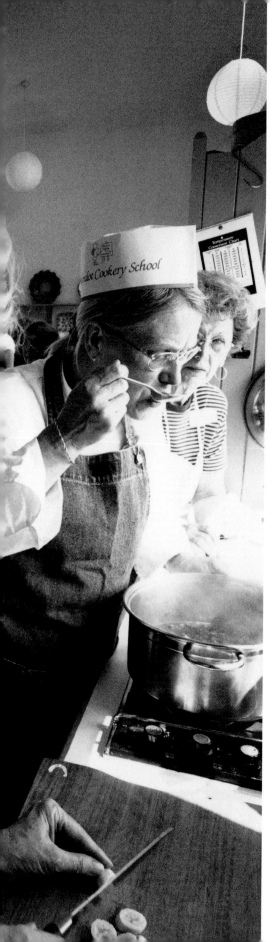

wine or the juice of an orange. Boil well, taste, correct the seasoning and strain. Carve the duck and serve the hot gravy with it.

Widgeon, Pintail or Shoveller can also be roasted in this way, cooking temperatures as above, for 13–20 minutes. Teal takes about 12–15 minutes.

Roast Woodcock or Snipe
Serves 4

Woodcock and snipe are highly regarded not only for their delicious flesh but also for their innards, with the exception of the gizzard, which is removed before the livers are roasted.

2 woodcock, or 4 snipe, gizzards removed
streaky bacon (optional)
25–50g (1–2oz) melted butter
4 croûtons, large enough for the birds to sit on
salt and freshly ground pepper

Garnish
sprigs of watercress or fresh herbs

Preheat the oven to 230°C/450°F/gas 8.

Remove the gizzard from the birds by making a small insertion in the thin abdominal skin, slightly to the right of the centre. Locate the hard lump of the gizzard with a skewer or trussing needle, remove and detach from the innards which should remain in the bird. Brush the birds with melted butter, season, and truss with their beaks. Alternatively, wrap in streaky bacon and truss with string.

Toast and butter 1 side of the bread, put the toast buttered side down on a baking tray, with the snipe or woodcock on top. Roast in the oven for 18–22 minutes for woodcock, depending on size, and half that time for snipe. The birds are usually cooked when the bacon is crispy! Remove the trussing string, if using, and serve the woodcock or snipe on the croûtons. Garnish with sprigs of watercress or herbs.

Note: If you want to make a sauce to serve with the birds, add a tablespoon of brandy to the juices in the roasting tin with the cooked mashed innards and season. Warm through but don't boil. Arrange the croûtons on a hot serving dish, spoon the sauce over and sit the birds on top, garnish and serve immediately. Medlar Jelly (see page 508) is very good with this dish.

Medallions of Ostrich with Celeriac and Redcurrant Sauce
Serves 6

This dish can also be made with loin of venison.

700g–900g (1½–2lb) loin of ostrich
salt and freshly ground pepper
extra-virgin olive oil

Celeriac and Purée (see page right) or Gratin of Potato and Celeriac (see page 187)
Redcurrant Sauce (see page 598)
watercress salad

First make the Celeriac Purée or Gratin and the Redcurrant Sauce. Trim any gristle or membrane from the eye of the loin. Just before serving slice the meat into 1cm (½in) thick medallions, season with salt and freshly ground pepper.

Heat a grill-pan or cast-iron frying pan. Drizzle the meat with a little olive oil. Sauté over a high heat for 1–2 minutes on each side. The centre of the medallions should still be rare.

Serve with the creamy gratin and a little Redcurrant Sauce. A peppery watercress salad is a perfect accompaniment.

Potted Venison with Juniper Berries
See page 81

Medallions of Venison with Blackberry Sauce
Serves 4

4 medallions of venison
butter, to fry
225g (8oz) blackberries, fresh or frozen
425ml (¾ pint) homemade Chicken Stock
  (see page 36)
75ml (3fl oz) port
4 tablespoons sloe gin or brandy
lemon juice, to taste
salt and freshly ground pepper

Garnish
fresh blackberries and sprigs of fresh herbs

Purée or liquidise and sieve the blackberries. If you are using frozen ones, they may need a little sugar. Put the stock and port into a stainless-steel saucepan and boil and reduce for a few minutes. Add the gin (or brandy) and fruit and boil until the sauce coats the back of a spoon.

Meanwhile, season the medallions of venison, fry in a very little butter on a hot pan for 2 minutes on each side.

Sharpen the sauce with a little lemon juice, taste and correct the seasoning. Put the medallions onto a hot plate, spoon over a little sauce and garnish with a few blackberries and a few sprigs of herbs.

Serve immediately with Gratin Dauphinois (see page 186) and a good green salad.

Venison with Celeriac Purée
Serves 4

This recipe was a favourite of Canice Sharkey's when he was chef at the much-loved Arbutus Lodge restaurant in Cork. As ever, it is important not to marinate the venison for too long, nor to overcook it, or it will be dry and dull. A little Redcurrant Jelly (see page 508) may be added to the sauce at the end, or served separately.

450g (1lb) loin of venison (makes 12 noisettes)
butter and oil, to pan-fry

Marinade
125ml (4fl oz) olive oil
125ml (4fl oz) white wine
dash of sherry vinegar
1 garlic clove
4 juniper berries
1 small onion, sliced
1 small carrot, sliced
bay leaf and thyme
a few knobs of butter

Sauce
1 tablespoon chopped shallot
dash of white wine
425ml (15fl oz) homemade Beef Stock
  (see page 36)

Celeriac Purée
1 head celeriac, peeled and chopped
milk
cream and a knob of butter
salt and freshly ground pepper
mashed potato

Garnish
sprigs of rosemary

Preheat the oven to 180°C/350°F/gas 4.

Make the celeriac purée: cook the celeriac in milk and, when cooked, drain and purée. Season with salt and pepper, and add a little cream or butter. Cut the purée with about ⅓ of the quantity of mashed potato and keep warm in the oven.

Meanwhile, place the whole loin of venison in the marinade for about 10–15 minutes. Take out and cut into noisettes about 2cm (¾in) thick. Pan-fry in butter and oil, until well-sealed. Place on a tray and put into a moderate oven to keep warm while you make the sauce.

Meanwhile, de-glaze the pan with a little white wine and add the shallots. Add the stock and reduce by half. Add a tablespoon of the marinade and whisk in a little butter.

Place 3 noisettes on each plate with 3 quenelles of celeriac purée. Pour some sauce over and garnish with rosemary.

Venison Chilli
Serves 6

A great way to use strong venison. I love Mexican flavours but if you can't get anchos or guajillo chillies use 2–3 chillies, seeded and chopped instead.

4 ancho or 2–3 chillies, seeded and chopped
3 tablespoons extra-virgin olive oil
2 onions, chopped
4 garlic cloves, chopped
900g (2lb) venison, diced (use shoulder
  or breast)
1½ teaspoons ground cumin
salt and freshly ground pepper
400g (14oz) tin chopped tomatoes
1 tablespoon tomato purée
500ml (18oz) beef stock
2 tablespoons red wine vinegar
800g (1lb12oz) tinned red kidney beans
2 tablespoons chopped marjoram

Heat a heavy iron frying pan or pan-grill. Toast the chillies over a moderate heat, turning them regularly with tongs, until they soften. It will take 5–10 minutes. Transfer them to a bowl and cover with boiling water, weighing them down with a saucer to keep the chillies submerged. Soak for 30 minutes. Remove them from the water and purée in a liquidizer with 225ml (8fl oz) of the soaking liquid.

Heat the olive oil in a casserole, add the onions and garlic, and cook over a medium heat until they start to brown. Add the venison, toss, and brown well. Add the cumin, salt, pepper, tomatoes, tomato purée and chilli purée. Stir and add the stock. Cover the pan tightly and simmer gently over a low heat for 1½–2 hours.

When the venison is cooked, stir in the vinegar, beans and chopped marjoram. Simmer uncovered for 10 minutes. Serve with fluffy rice.

Larding and Barding

Very lean meat is larded or barded to introduce fat to baste the meat during cooking.

Larding: You will need 225g (8oz) back fat or very fat streaky pork or pork caul fat, cut into 5mm (¼in) wide strips (or lardons).

Insert a larding needle into a strip, draw a lardon through the meat to make a stitch; trim the end.

Repeat the stitches at 2.5cm (1in) intervals to make horizontal rows, positioning each row about 1cm (½in) away from the previous row, repeat with the remainder of the fat.

Barding: Wrap the entire joint in organic caul fat (order from a pork butcher) or in a very thin sheet, or sheets, of pork back fat. Thin streaky rashers may also be used. Caul fat may be frozen – it is wonderful stuff!

Master Recipe
Roast Haunch of Venison with Potato and Mushroom Gratin

Serves about 16–20 people

A haunch of venison makes a splendid party dish. Calculate the cooking time carefully, as it is easy to overcook venison We like our venison slightly pink and still very juicy, so I usually turn off the oven at the end of the cooking time and leave the meat to relax for 20–30 minutes.

1 haunch venison, about 2.6–3.1kg (6–7lb)

To Lard or Bard the Venison
225g (8oz) back fat or very streaky pork or
*   pork caul fat, cut into 5mm (¼in) wide strips*

Marinade
1 dessertspoon mixed fresh herbs (thyme,
*   savory, marjoram, sage)*
4 tablespoons olive oil
125ml (4fl oz) dry white wine

Gravy
1.2 litres (2 pint) homemade Beef or Venison
*   Stock (see page 36)*
dry white wine, to taste (optional)
Roux (see page 580), optional

Gratin of Potato and Mushroom (see page 186)

Preheat the oven to 180°C/350°F/gas 4.

First lard the venison (see left). Put the haunch into a shallow stainless-steel or cast-iron dish (not tin or aluminium). Sprinkle it with the herbs. Pour the olive oil and wine over the meat.

Cover the dish and marinate the meat for about 4 hours at room temperature or in a refrigerator overnight, turning the meat occasionally. The marinade liquid will be used to baste the meat during cooking.

To cook: Weigh the venison and calculate 10 minutes for every 450g (1lb). During the cooking time, baste every 10 minutes with the oil and wine marinade and turn the joint over half way through. When the venison is cooked, remove it to a warmed serving dish while you make the gravy.

De-grease the roasting pan, add the stock and perhaps a dash of wine. Bring to the boil, scraping and dissolving the sediment and crusty bits from the pan. Thicken slightly with a little Roux, taste and correct the seasoning, and pour into a warm gravy boat. Serve with Gratin of Potato and Mushroom.

Note: It is very easy to overcook venison, mainly because it goes on cooking after the oven has been turned off.

Other Accompaniments

Gratin Dauphinois (see page 186)
Roast Potatoes (see page 181)
Darina's Favourite Red Cabbage with Apples (see page 167)
Celeriac Purée (see page 377)
Brussels Sprouts (see page 170)

Variation
Roast Haunch of Venison with Plum or Francatelli Sauce

Follow the Master Recipe.

Serve the haunch of venison on a large serving dish surrounded by roast potatoes, red cabbage, celeriac purée or brussels sprouts.

Carve onto very hot plates. Serve with Plum or Damson Sauce, or Francatelli sauce (see below).

Francatelli Sauce

This delicious sauce was invented by Queen Victoria's chef, Francatelli. It is very easy to make. You may need to double the quantity for 20 hungry people.

2 tablespoons port
225g (8oz) Redcurrant Jelly (see page 508)
small stick of cinnamon, bruised
thinly pared rind of 17 lemon

Simmer together for 5 minutes, stirring. Strain into a hot sauceboat.

Plum or Damson Sauce
Serves 10–15

Also delicious with duck.

450g (1lb) blood plums or damsons
225g (½lb) sugar
2 cloves
2.5cm (1in) piece cinnamon stick
25g (1oz) butter
2 tablespoons Redcurrant Jelly (see page 508)
125ml (4fl oz) port

Put the plums into a stainless steel saucepan with the sugar, cloves, cinnamon, one tablespoon of water and the butter. Cook slowly until reduced to a pulp. Push the fruit through a fine sieve and return the purée to a clean saucepan.

Add the Redcurrant Jelly and port, bring to the boil and simmer for a few minutes. The sauce may be served either hot or cold.

> TIP: Venison medallions cook in minutes and marry well with any of the sauces used for Haunch of Venison.

Venison Stew with Melted Leeks
Serves 8

When you buy venison, allow time for marinading, and remember that an ingredient like fat salt pork or fat unsmoked bacon is essential either for cooking with the meat (stew) or for larding (roasting or braising), unless the meat has been well hung.

1.3kg (3lb) shoulder of venison, trimmed and diced into 4cm (1½in) cubes
seasoned flour

Marinade
300–350ml (10–12fl oz) red wine
1 medium onion, sliced
3 tablespoons brandy
3 tablespoons olive oil
salt, lightly cracked pepper
bouquet garni

Sauce
225g (8oz) fat salt pork or unsmoked streaky bacon, diced
2 tablespoons olive oil
2 large onions, chopped
1 large carrot, diced
1 large garlic clove, crushed
425ml (¾ pint) homemade Beef or Game Stock (see page 36)
bouquet garni (see page 37)
24 small mushrooms, preferably wild ones
10g (½oz) lemon juice or Redcurrant Jelly (see page 508)
salt, freshly ground pepper, sugar
Melted Leeks (see page 173)

Season the venison and soak in the marinade ingredients for 24–48 hours. Drain the meat well (reserving the marinade), pat it dry on kitchen paper and turn in a little seasoned flour.

Preheat the oven to 150°C/300°F/gas 2. Brown the pork or bacon in olive oil in a frying pan, cooking it slowly at first to make the fat run, then raising the heat. Transfer to a casserole.

Brown the venison in the fat, then the onion, carrot and garlic. Do all this in batches, transferring each one to the casserole. Do not overheat or the fat will burn. Pour off any surplus fat, de-glaze the pan with the strained marinade and pour over the venison. Heat up enough stock to cover the ingredients in the casserole and pour it over. Add the bouquet garni, bring to a gentle simmer, then transfer to the preheated oven. Cover closely and leave until the venison is tender.

Test after 1½ hours, but allow 2½ hours cooking time. For best results, it is wise to cook this kind of dish one day in advance and then reheat it. This improves the flavour and gives you a chance to make sure that the venison is tender.

Sauté the sliced mushrooms in butter. Season with salt and pepper and add to the stew.

Finally taste the venison sauce. It will need seasoning and perhaps a little lemon juice. It also sometimes benefits from a pinch of sugar or just a little Redcurrant Jelly.

Serve with Melted Leeks, baked potatoes and perhaps a green vegetable: brussels sprouts, calabrese or cabbage.

Variation
Venison Pie
Serves 8

Venison Stew (see recipe left)

Pastry
350g (12oz) Puff or Flaky Pastry (see pages 456 and 413), rolled out thinly
organic egg wash

Preheat the oven to 250°C/475°F/gas 9.

Fill one large or several small, greased pie dishes with the stew and cover with pastry. Flute the edges, egg-wash and decorate with pastry leaves. Bake in the oven for 10 minutes and then reduce the heat to 180°C/350°F/gas 4 for 25–30 minutes or until pastry is crisp and golden and the pie is bubbling.

puddings

puddings

The sweet trolley at Ballymaloe House is legendary. It has been a highlight of dinner ever since the restaurant opened in 1963. There's always a homemade ice-cream served in an ice bowl, and a meringue gâteau filled with a complementary filling. The yolks of freshly laid eggs from our free-range hens are used to make the ice-cream, and the whites are used for the meringues. There will also be a compote of fruit in season: perhaps a mousse, a soufflé of Carrigeen moss or a fruit tart made with buttery homemade flaky or puff pastry. The choice changes with the seasons. Coming up to Christmas there are mince pies and Myrtle Allen's Plum Pudding with brandy butter, and if you are there in winter you may catch a steamed pudding or a blood orange tart. On Shrove Tuesday, Myrtle or Hazel make crêpes Suzettes at your table, and in autumn there will be crushed blueberries, wild berries and maybe some hazelnuts from the wood…

The art of the pastry chef is becoming ever more exciting. Using specialist pastry chocolate and sugar techniques, skilled chefs can create amazing confections, some so elaborate that one almost feels reluctant to eat them. Most of the desserts in this book are simple to master and won't make you feel guilty for tucking in.

Choosing Your Pudding
Of course pudding isn't obligatory, but many people have a sweet tooth so this could be the part of the meal that they most look forward to. Dessert is a special treat for most people (either because they're too busy, health- or weight-conscious), so it's worth putting some extra throught into creating something special.

The choice of pudding depends on the meal. Follow a rich main course with a compote of fruit or perfectly ripe fresh fruit salad of local summer berries or citrus fruits in season. A tart, luscious meringue or ice-cream will be enjoyable after a piece of simple pan-grilled fish or meat. Try to provide a contrast in terms of texture. Chocolate always seems to be a hit – regardless of what came before or how full one is!

Presentation
Many desserts need very little embellishment to look mouth-wateringly delicious – maybe just a sprig of mint or a light dusting of icing sugar. Others benefit from elaborate decorations and presentation. Dramatic results can be achieved relatively easily with simple techniques using chocolate leaves and curls, caramel shards, crystallised flowers, candied orange or julienne zest, brandy snap baskets, chocolate coffee beans and lashings of cream.

Cream
In Ireland we have wonderful rich cream but remember cream tastes different depending on how you serve it. Choose runny cream to serve with silky chocolate mousse and the like, and softly whipped cream (which barely holds the print of the whisk) to serve with most other puddings. Stiffly whipped cream has the least flavour of all, and don't even think about cream that comes squishing out of a can! At the Cookery School we have our own Jersey cream which we separate from the milk in an old Alfa-Laval separater – it's rich and delicious, such a luxury. The Kingstons from Glenilon in West Cork have also built up a tremendous following for their artisan cream.

The Ballymaloe Ice Bowl

The ice bowl was Myrtle Allen's brilliant solution to keeping the ice-cream cold during the evening on the sweet trolley in the restaurant. I quote from *The Ballymaloe Cookbook*, published by Gill and Macmillan:

'It took me twelve years to find the solution to keeping ice-cream cold on the sweet trolley in my restaurant. At first we used to unmould and decorate our ices on to a plate. This was alright on a busy night when they got eaten before melting. On quieter occasions the waitresses performed relay races from the dining-room to the deep freeze. I dreamed about nineteenth-century ice boxes filled from ice houses, to my husband's increasing scorn, and then I thought I had a solution. A young Irish glass blower produced beautiful hand-blown glass cylinders which I filled with ice-cream and fitted into beautiful tulip shaped glass bowls. These I filled with ice cubes. Six months later, however, due to either the stress of the ice or the stress of the waitresses, my bowls were gone and so was my money. In desperation I produced an ice bowl. It turned out to be a stunning and practical presentation for a restaurant trolley or a party buffet.'

To make a Ballymaloe Ice Bowl

Take two bowls, one about double the capacity of the other. Half fill the big bowl with cold water. Float the second bowl inside the first. Weigh it down with water or ice cubes until the rims are level. Place a square of fabric on top and secure it with a strong rubber band or string under the rim of the lower bowl, as one would tie on a jam pot cover. Adjust the small bowl to a central position. The cloth will hold it in place. Put the bowls on a Swiss roll tin and place in a deep freeze, re-adjusting the position of the small bowl if necessary as you put it in. After 24 hours or more take it out of the deep freeze.

Remove the cloth and leave for 15–20 minutes, by which time the small bowl should lift out easily. Then try to lift out the ice-bowl. It should be starting to melt slightly from the outside bowl, in which case it will slip out easily. If it isn't, then just leave for 5–10 minutes more. Don't attempt to run it under the hot or even cold tap, it may crack. If you are in a great rush, the best solution is to wring out a tea-towel in hot water and wrap that around the large bowl for a few minutes. The best course of action is to perform this operation early in the day, fill the ice bowl with scoops of ice-cream, and then store it in the freezer ready for serving. Put a folded serviette under the ice bowl on the serving dish to catch any drips. In the restaurant we make a new ice-bowl every night, but at home when the dessert would be on the table for barely half an hour, it should be possible to use the ice bowl several times. As soon as you have finished serving, give the bowl a quick wash under the cold tap and get it back into the freezer – this way you can use it two or three times. One more point: don't leave a serving spoon resting against the side of the bowl or it will melt a notch in the rim.

At Ballymaloe, Myrtle Allen surrounds the ice bowl with vine leaves in summer, scarlet Virginia creeper in autumn and red-berried holly at Christmas. I'm a bit less restrained – I can't resist surrounding it with flowers. However you present it, ice-cream served in a bowl of ice like this usually draws gasps of admiration when you bring it to the table.

Fresh Figs with Raspberry Sauce

Serves 8

8 fresh figs
Raspberry Sauce (see page 599)
whipped cream

Decoration
mint or lemon balm sprigs
fig leaves (optional)

Trim the stalk and cut a cross in each fig, cutting down almost to the base. Gently open out the fruit to resemble a flower unfurling. Make a nick just under the stalk, and peel off the skin in strips. If you can find any, put a fig leaf on each plate, a fig on top, then a dollop of cream in the centre. Spoon a little Raspberry Sauce over the top and serve the remainder in a bowl. Decorate with a sprig of mint or lemon balm. Eat immediately.

Agen Stuffed Prunes with Rosewater Cream

Serves 6

This ancient recipe from the Middle East will change your opinion of prunes. Claudia Roden introduced us to this pretty and delicious dish when she was guest chef at the school. Agen prunes are a variety from the southwest of France.

450g (1lb) Agen prunes, pitted
same number of fresh walnut halves
150ml (¼ pint) each water and red wine or
    more or 300ml (½ pint) water
300ml (½ pint) cream
2 tablespoons caster sugar
1 tablespoon rose blossom water

Decoration
a few chopped walnuts
rose petals (optional)

We've experimented with removing the stones from both soaked and dry prunes – dry work best. Use a small knife to cut out the stones and then stuff each prune with half a walnut. Arrange in a single layer in a sauté pan. Cover with a mixture of water and wine, if using. Put the lid on the pan and simmer for about 30 minutes. Add more liquid if they become a little dry. The prunes should be plump and soft.

Lift them gently onto a serving plate in a single layer and let them cool. Whip the cream to soft peaks, add the sugar and rose blossom water. Spoon dollops over the prunes and chill well.

Just before serving, scatter a few chopped walnuts over each dollop of cream, sprinkle with rose petals and serve well chilled. This dessert tastes even better the next day.

Mangoes in Lime Syrup

Serves 2

This simple recipe must be made with a perfectly ripe mango; if the fruit you buy is under-ripe, wrap it in newspaper and keep it in your kitchen for a few days. Papayas are also delicious served in exactly the same way.

1 ripe mango
110g (4oz) sugar
125ml (4fl oz) water
1 lime

Put the sugar and water into a saucepan, stir over a gentle heat until the sugar dissolves, bring to the boil and simmer for 2 minutes. Allow to cool.

Peel the mango and slice quite thinly down to the stone. Put the slices into a bowl and cover with the cold syrup.

Remove the zest from the lime either with a zester or a fine stainless-steel grater and add to the syrup with the juice of the lime. Leave to macerate for at least an hour. Serve chilled.

Variation
Bananas in Lime Syrup
Substitute 4 bananas for the mango in the above recipe – a brilliant little gem, made in minutes. Peaches, nectarines and papayas respond well to this recipe too.

Spiced Fruit with Star Anise

Serves 8

The syrup can be made well in advance and kept in the fridge until needed.

Syrup
400g (14oz) white granulated sugar
25g (1oz) star anise
1 small cinnamon stick
1 vanilla pod
750ml (26fl oz) water

1.6kg (3½lb) mixed fruit (such as strawberries,
    papaya and pineapple, blueberries, cherries)
lightly whipped cream, to serve

To make the syrup, put the sugar, spices and water into a saucepan. Boil until syrupy (about 7–10 minutes). Leave to cool.

Cut the larger fruits into equal-sized pieces and mix with the berries and cherries. Strain the syrup to remove the spices and then pour it over the fruits and allow to macerate for at least 30 minutes.

Serve with softly whipped cream.

A Simple Fresh Fruit Salad

Serves 6–8

Don't fall into the trap of using too much apple. Also it is surprisingly important to cut the fruit into nicely shaped pieces, otherwise it can look a mess. The sugar and lemon juice draw out the juice from the fruit and give a very fresh-tasting fruit salad.

1 ripe pear
1 ripe apple
2 ripe oranges
25g (1oz) caster sugar
freshly squeezed juice of 1 lemon
1 ripe banana

Optional extras
1 kiwi fruit
110g (4oz) peeled and pipped grapes
110g (4oz) fresh strawberries
1 peach or nectarine

Garnish
mint leaves
chopped chilli

Peel the pear and apple, cut into quarters, core and cut across the grain into slices less than 5mm (¼in) thick. Peel the oranges with a stainless-steel serrated knife as though you were peeling an apple, making sure to remove all the pith, then cut each segment individually and add to the apple and pear. Sprinkle with caster sugar and lemon juice. About 15 minutes before serving, add the sliced bananas, taste and add more juice or sugar if necessary. If using kiwi fruit, grapes or strawberries add them with the orange. Serve garnished with mint leaves and a little chopped chilli and pass around a bowl of lightly whipped cream.

Citrus Fruit Salad

Serves 6

In the winter when many fruits have abysmal flavour the citrus fruits are at their best. This delicious fresh-tasting salad uses a wide variety of the ever-expanding citrus family. It's particularly good when a few blood oranges are included. Ugli fruit, pomelos, tangelos and sweeties all add excitement and zing. A great palate-cleanser after a heavy winter meal.

225g (8oz) kumquats
350ml (12fl oz) water
200g (7oz) sugar
1 lime
225g (8oz) clementines
110–225g (4–8oz) tangerines or mandarins
1 pink grapefruit
2 blood oranges
lemon juice, if necessary

Slice the kumquats into 5mm (¼in) rounds and remove pips. Dissolve the sugar in the water over a low heat, and add the sliced kumquats. Cover and simmer for about 30 minutes or until tender. Remove from the heat. Allow to cool.

Remove the zest from the lime with a zester and add with the juice to the kumquats. Meanwhile peel the clementines and tangerines (or mandarins) and remove as much of the white pith and strings as possible. Slice into rounds 5mm (¼in) thick, and add to the syrup. Segment the grapefruit and blood oranges and add to the syrup also. Leave to macerate for at least 1 hour. Taste and add a squeeze of lemon juice if necessary. Serve chilled.

Fruit Chat (North Indian-style Fruit Salad)

Serves 8

Use a combination of fresh fruit such as mango, papaya, bananas, peaches, melon, kiwi, guava, strawberries, raspberries, blackberries and blueberries for this recipe. Jaggery is a raw cane sugar with a very special taste. If you can't find it, substitute soft brown or golden caster sugar instead.

450–700g (1–1½lb) prepared fruit
juice of 1–2 lemons
salt to taste
2 teaspoons chat masala (black salt)
2 teaspoons roasted cumin seeds, ground
½ teaspoon freshly ground black pepper
25g (1oz) freshly chopped mint leaves
1½ tablespoons fresh ginger, peeled and finely grated
8–12 hot green chilli, sliced (if that terrifies you, use much less)

Decoration
fresh mint and coriander
whole chillies
crushed jaggery

Prepare the fruit in generous-sized pieces and mix in a large platter. Add lemon juice, salt and chat masala, toss gently to mix, sprinkle over the other ingredients and toss again.

Serve the fruit salad over lettuce leaves, decorate with mint and chillies. Sprinkle cumin and jaggery over as needed.

Moroccan Orange Salad

Serves 4

6 juicy oranges, Navel or Valencia, organic or
  unwaxed
1–2 tablespoons orangeflower water
a little sugar

Scrub the oranges. Grate the zest carefully
from 1 of the oranges using the finest side
of the grater. Peel and remove all pith,
leaving 6 clean oranges. Slice them thinly
into a large bowl containing the zest.
Sprinkle the orangeflower water onto the
orange slices. Sprinkle with sugar, arrange
in overlapping slices on a wide platter.
Chill for as long as possible.

Summer Fruit Salad with Sweet Geranium Leaves

Serves 8–10

Sweet geranium (Pelargonium graveolens)
and many other varieties of scented
geraniums are ever present on our
window sills at Ballymaloe. We use the
delicious lemon-scented leaves in all sorts
of ways, and occasionally we use the
pretty purple flowers to enliven and add
magic to otherwise simple dishes. The
crystallised leaves, all frosty and crinkly,
are wonderful with fresh cream cheese
and fat juicy blackberries. I discovered this
recipe, which has now become a perennial
favourite, quite by accident a few
summers ago as I raced to make a
pudding in a hurry with the ingredients I
had at that moment.

110g (4oz) raspberries
110g (4oz) loganberries
110g (4oz) redcurrants
110g (4oz) blackcurrants
110g (4oz) small strawberries
110g (4oz) blueberries
110g (4oz) fraises des bois or tiny strawberries

Syrup
400g (14oz) sugar
450ml (16fl oz) water
6–8 large sweet geranium leaves

Put all the freshly picked berries into a
white china or glass bowl. Put the sugar,
water and sweet geranium leaves into a
stainless-steel saucepan and bring slowly to
the boil, stirring until the sugar dissolves.
Boil for just 2 minutes. Cool for 4–5 minutes
then pour the hot syrup over the fruit and
allow to macerate for several hours.

Remove the geranium leaves. Serve chilled,
with softly whipped cream or Vanilla
Ice-cream (see page 399), or just as it is,
decorated with a few fresh sweet geranium
leaves.

For a winter version, follow the Summer
Fruit Salad recipe but substitute best-
quality frozen berries and currants – pour
the boiling syrup over the frozen berries in
the bowl.

> TIP: The geranium syrup can be stored
> in the fridge or even frozen.

A Jelly of Fresh Raspberries with Fresh Mint Cream

Makes 10 ramekins

450g (1lb) fresh raspberries

Syrup
225g (8oz) sugar
225ml (8fl oz) water
4 sprigs fresh mint
1 dessertspoon framboise liqueur
1 tablespoon freshly squeezed lemon juice
3 rounded teaspoons gelatine
3 tablespoons water

Fresh Mint Cream
15 mint leaves
1 tablespoon freshly squeezed lemon juice
175ml (6fl oz) cream

10 ramekins or individual moulds, lined with
  clingfilm

Make a syrup by bringing sugar, water and
mint sprigs slowly to the boil. Simmer for
a few minutes, allow to cool, and add the
framboise and lemon juice.

Sponge the gelatine in the water in a small
bowl or pint measure, then place the bowl
in a pan of simmering water until the
gelatine completely dissolves. Remove the
mint leaves from the syrup, then pour the
syrup onto the gelatine and add to the
raspberries. Fill the lined moulds. Put into
the fridge and leave to set for 3–4 hours.

Meanwhile make the Fresh Mint Cream:
crush the mint leaves in a pestle and
mortar with the lemon juice, add the
cream and stir (the lemon juice will
thicken the cream, if the cream becomes
too thick add a little water).

To assemble: spread a little Fresh Mint
Cream on a white plate, turn out a raspberry
jelly and place in the centre. Place five mint
leaves on the cream around the jelly.
Decorate with a few perfect raspberries.
Repeat with the other jellies. Serve chilled.

Variation
Blueberry Jelly with a Fresh Mint Cream

Follow the recipe above, substituting 450g
(1lb) blueberries for the raspberries, and
add a dessertspoon of myrtle liqueur to
the syrup instead of the framboise.

RIGHT: A Jelly of Fresh Raspberries and
Blueberries with Fresh Mint Cream

Agar Agar

Agar Agar is a vegetarian product that works exactly like gelatine. It is derived from seaweed. It needs to be boiled with some or all of the liquid ingredients in the recipe before it will set. Use 2 teaspoons for 600ml (1 pint) of liquid.

Agar agar is available at health food shops.

Summer Fruit Jelly with Sweet Geranium Cream

Serves 10

450g (1lb) summer fruit, perhaps:
  225g (8oz) fresh raspberries
  110g (4oz) tiny strawberries
  110g (4oz) blueberries or blackcurrants

Syrup
225g (8oz) sugar
225ml (8fl oz) water
4 sweet geranium leaves
1 tablespoon freshly squeezed lemon juice

3 rounded teaspoons gelatine
3 tablespoons water

Sweet Geranium Cream
4–5 sweet geranium leaves
1 tablespoon lemon juice
175ml (6fl oz) cream
sugar to taste, optional

10 individual ramekin dishes or moulds, lined with clingfilm or brushed lightly with non-scented vegetable oil

Make a syrup by bringing sugar, water and sweet geranium leaves slowly to the boil. Simmer for a few minutes, allow to cool, then add lemon juice.

Sponge the gelatine in 3 tablespoons of water, then place the bowl over a pan of simmering water until the gelatine is completely dissolved.

Remove the sweet geranium leaves from the syrup, then pour the syrup onto the gelatine and then add to the fruit. Stir gently. Fill the lined moulds. Put into the fridge and leave to set for 3–4 hours.

Meanwhile make the Sweet Geranium Cream: crush the leaves in a pestle and mortar with the lemon juice, add the cream and stir. (The lemon juice will thicken the cream, so if it becomes too thick add a little water.) Taste, and add a little sugar if it is too bitter, but remember the sauce should be tart.

To serve: spread a little Sweet Geranium Cream onto a white plate, turn out a jelly and place in the centre. Place 3–5 tiny sweet geranium leaves on the cream. Decorate with a few perfect raspberries, serve chilled.

> TIP: You will need to use 4 teaspoons of gelatine to each 600ml (1 pint) of fruit and liquid.

Fresh Orange Jelly with Mint

Serves 6–8

This is best during the winter when citrus fruits are at their best.

6 oranges, organic or unwaxed
juice of 1 freshly squeezed lemon
225ml (8fl oz) syrup, made with 175ml (6fl oz) water and 175g (6oz) sugar
1 teaspoon Grand Marnier
2 rounded teaspoons gelatine
2 tablespoons water

Sauce
225ml (8fl oz) fresh orange juice, sweetened to taste with caster sugar
2 tablespoons freshly chopped mint

Decoration
sprigs of mint or lemon balm

1 terrine 850ml (1½ pint) capacity or 6–8 oval or round moulds 100ml (3½fl oz) capacity, lined with clingfilm or brushed with non-scented vegetable oil

Grate the rind from 2 of the oranges very carefully on a stainless-steel grater. Segment all six oranges and add the syrup, orange zest, lemon juice and Grand Marnier. Mix well. Then strain the liquid off the oranges again and measure 300ml (½ pint). Keep the remainder aside for the sauce.

Sponge the gelatine in 2 tablespoons of cold water in a small bowl for a few minutes. Put the bowl into a saucepan of simmering water until all the gelatine crystals are dissolved. Mix with the orange liquid, stirring carefully. Add the orange segments and fill into the individual moulds or terrine. Put in the fridge and allow 3–4 hours to set.

To make the sauce, measure the remaining orange liquid and make up to 225ml (8fl oz) with more freshly squeezed orange juice. Taste and sweeten if necessary, then add the freshly chopped mint.

To serve: turn out the jellies onto individual plates. Pour a little sauce around each jelly and decorate with mint leaves or lemon balm.

Variations

Blood Orange Jelly

Substitute 6–8 blood oranges and follow the above recipe.

Citrus Fruit Jelly with Mint

2 pink grapefruit
2 blood oranges or mandarins
2 oranges, organic or unwaxed
juice of ½ lemon
225ml (8fl oz) syrup, made with 175ml (6fl oz) water and 175g (6oz) sugar
2 rounded teaspoons gelatine
2 tablespoons water

Sauce
125ml (4fl oz) pink grapefruit juice
125ml (4fl oz) fresh orange juice, sweetened to taste with caster sugar

Decoration
sprigs of fresh mint

Follow the recipe for Fresh Orange Jelly, omitting the Grand Marnier. Make the sauce in the same way, but using freshly squeezed orange and grapefruit juice to make 225ml (8fl oz).

Summer Pudding
Serves 12–16

Everyone seems to become wistful when you mention Summer Pudding. Bursting with soft fruit and served with lots of softly whipped cream, it's one of the very best desserts of summer. We make our Summer Pudding with cake, although many people use slices of white bread to line the bowl. Summer Fruit Salad with Sweet Geranium Leaves (see page 386) also makes a successful filling, but you need to cook the blackcurrants and redcurrants until they burst before adding the soft fruit. Make sure the fruit and syrup is boiling when you pour it into the sponge-lined bowl, otherwise the syrup won't soak through the sponge properly.

2 x 18cm (7in) Great Grandmother's Cake
 (see page 452)
225g (8oz) blackcurrants
225g (8oz) redcurrants
450g (1lb) raspberries or 225g (8oz)
 raspberries and 225g (8 oz) strawberries
550g (1lb 4oz) granulated sugar
725ml (1½ pints) water
6–8 sweet geranium leaves, optional

1.8 litre (3 pint) pudding bowl

First make the sponge. Cut each round of sponge in half, horizontally. Line the bowl with the cake, crusty side inwards. It doesn't matter if it looks quite patched, as it will blend later.

Dissolve the sugar in the water, add the sweet geranium leaves (if using) and boil for 2 minutes. Add the blackcurrants and redcurrants and cook until the fruit bursts (about 3–4 minutes). Then add the raspberries (and strawberries if using).

Taste, and remove the sweet geranium leaves and discard. Immediately, ladle some of the hot liquid and fruit into the sponge-lined bowl. When about half full, if you have remaining scraps of cake, put them in the centre. Then fill to the top with fruit. Cover with a layer of sponge. Put a plate on top and press down with a heavy weight. Allow to get cold. Store in the refrigerator for a minimum of 24 hours before serving, but it will keep for 4–5 days.

To serve: unmould onto a deep serving dish and pour any leftover fruit and syrup over the top and around the side. Serve with lots of softly whipped cream.

Variation
Blackcurrant Summer Pudding
In winter, follow the recipe above, but use 900g (2lb) frozen blackcurrants, 600g (1lb 5oz) granulated sugar and 700ml (1¼ pints).

Poached Quince with Cloves
Serves 6

The Greeks adore quince and make all kinds of compote, jams and pastes with them (they also cook quince with meat). I adore this compote as it was cooked for me by Maria Katsiou-Maroulaki in Thessaloniki.

6 ripe quince
600ml (1 pint) water
225–350g (8–12oz) sugar
6–8 cloves
freshly squeezed lemon juice

To make the syrup, dissolve the sugar in the water and boil together for 2 minutes. Peel the quinces and cut into quarters or eighths depending on size. Put immediately into the hot syrup (otherwise they will go brown) with the cloves.

Cover and simmer for about 1 hour or until the fruit is tender, tasting about halfway through and adding more sugar or lemon juice as necessary. They will become a glorious deep red colour. Allow to get cold and serve chilled with some pouring cream.

Note: A vanilla pod could be substituted for cloves in this recipe.

Variations
Poached Quince with Vanilla
Substitute a vanilla pod for the cloves in the above recipe.

Poached Guava with Cinnamon
Poach 8 guava with a small cinnamon stick and follow the recipe above but simmer for only 20 minutes approximately.

Poached Plums
See page 522 – delicious with mascarpone.

Poached Blackcurrants with Icy Cold Cream

Serves 4

Divine!

350g (12oz) blackcurrants
Stock Syrup (see recipe page 568)
icy cold cream

warm Shortbread (see page 466)

Cover the blackcurrants with Stock Syrup. Bring to the boil and cook until the fruit bursts – this takes about 4–5 minutes. Serve with warm shortbread biscuits and icy cold cream.

Pears Poached in Saffron Syrup

Serves 4

Most exotic of the fruit compotes, pears cooked in this way turn a wonderful deep golden colour and are delicately infused with the flavours of saffron and cardamom, two of the world's most precious spices. We use Conference and Doyenne de Comice pears. This compote is rich, intensely sweet, and best served well-chilled.

200g (7oz) sugar
425ml (15fl oz) water
6 whole cardamom pods, lightly crushed
¼ teaspoon good quality saffron threads
3 tablespoons freshly squeezed lemon juice
4 firm pears

Put the sugar, water, cardamom pods, saffron and lemon juice into a shallow wide pan: we use a stainless-steel sauté pan. Stir to dissolve the sugar and bring to a simmer. Meanwhile, peel the pears, half and core them and immediately put them into the simmering syrup, cut side uppermost.

LEFT: Green Gooseberry and Elderflower Compote (slightly underdone!) with Elderflower Fritters

Cover with a paper lid and the lid of the pan and cook gently for 20–30 minutes, spooning the syrup over them every now and then. Carefully remove the pears and arrange in a single layer in a serving dish, cut side down. Pour the syrup over and allow to cool. This compôte keeps for several weeks, covered, in the fridge.

Green Gooseberry and Elderflower Compote with Elderflower Fritters

Serves 6–8

Elderflowers have an extraordinary affinity with green gooseberries and by a happy arrangement of nature they are both in season at the same time.

Compote
3–4 elderflower heads
450g (1lb) sugar
600ml (1 pint) cold water
900g (2lb) green gooseberries, topped and tailed

Elderflower Fritters
110g (4oz) white flour
pinch of salt
1 organic egg,
150ml (¼ pint) lukewarm water
caster sugar

First make the compote: tie the elderflower heads in a little square of muslin. Put into a stainless-steel saucepan, add the sugar and cover with cold water. Bring slowly to the boil and continue to boil for 2 minutes. Add the gooseberries and simmer just until the fruit bursts. It is essential to cook the fruit until it actually bursts, otherwise the compote will be too bitter. Allow to get cold.

To make the fritters: sift the flour and salt into a bowl. Make a well in the centre and drop in the egg. Using a whisk bring in the flour gradually from the edges slowly adding in the water at the same time. Heat the oil in a deep fry to 180°C/350°F.

Hold the flowers by the stalks and dip into the batter. Fry until golden brown in the hot oil. Drain on kitchen paper, toss in caster sugar and serve immediately with Gooseberry and Elderflower Compote.

Apricot and Cardamom Compote

Serves 4

450g (1lb) fresh apricots or 225g (8oz) best-quality dried apricots
12 cardamom pods
1.2 litres (2 pints) water
200–400g (7–14oz) sugar
2 tablespoons freshly squeezed lemon juice

If you are using dried apricots, soak them overnight in plenty of cold water. Crush the cardamom pods slightly. Put them with the water, sugar and lemon juice into a pan, bring to the boil, add the apricots and simmer until tender. The time varies depending on whether they are fresh or dried – between 15 and 30 minutes. Pour into a bowl, chill and serve. Alternatively remove the apricots and continue to simmer until the syrup is more reduced.

Serve chilled with Pannacotta (see page 406) or crème fraîche.

Kumquat Compote

Serves 6–8

Kumquats are the baby of the citrus family. This compote keeps for weeks in the fridge. You can serve it with Pannacotta (see page 406), but it is equally delicious with a duck breast, roast pork or gammon steak. Serve warm or cold.

1.5kg (3lb 5oz) kumquats
1 litre (1¾ pints) water
500g (1lb 2oz) sugar

Cut the kumquats into four lengthways and discard the pips. Put in a pan with the water and sugar and cook very gently, uncovered, for 30 minutes until tender.

Fruit Fools

Fools are old-fashioned and gorgeous and so quick to make. We serve fruit fools right through the seasons at Ballymaloe. They are essentially purées of sweetened fruit into which softly whipped cream is swirled. Soft fruits, such as raspberries, loganberries and strawberries, are usually left raw, whereas blackcurrants, gooseberries and apples are usually cooked in a stock syrup; rhubarb may need a little gelatine or it may otherwise be too runny. The amount of cream used depends on your own taste. A little stiffly beaten egg white may also be added to lighten the fool. It should be the texture of softly whipped cream. If it is too stiff, stir in a little milk rather than more cream.

Fools may be served immediately or chilled for several hours. Serve with Shortbread (see page 466) or Jane's Biscuits (see page 461). Leftover fool may be frozen into a simple parfait; some will be more crystalline than others, depending on the water content of the fruit. Serve in slices with a complementary sauce or compote.

Master Recipe
Green Gooseberry Fool

Serves 6

Tart green gooseberries picked in May make the best gooseberry fool. It will keep for several days covered in a fridge.

450g (1lb) hard green gooseberries
Stock Syrup (see page 568), made with 300ml
  (½ pint) cold water and 225g (8oz) sugar
softly whipped cream

Barely cover the green gooseberries with Stock Syrup. Bring to the boil and cook until the fruit bursts – about 5–6 minutes. Liquidise or purée the fruit and syrup and measure. When the purée has cooled completely, add half its volume of softly whipped cream or according to taste.

Variation
Green Gooseberry and Elderflower Fool

Add 3–4 elderflower heads tied in muslin with the gooseberries and proceed as above.

Blackberry and Apple Fool

Serves 4–5

275–500g (10–18oz) blackberries
cooking apples to make 250g (9oz) apple purée
  (see Bramley Apple Sauce, page 597)
110g (4oz) sugar
225ml (8fl oz) softly whipped cream

Pick over the blackberries and wash if necessary. Make a dry purée by cooking the apples in 1–2 tablespoons of water on a low heat. Liquidise or sieve and sweeten to taste while still hot. Allow to cool. Purée the raw blackberries and add them with the softly whipped cream to the apple purée.

Strawberry, Raspberry, Loganberry, Tayberry or Boysenberry Fool

450g (1lb) fruit
sugar to taste
425–600ml (15–20fl oz) soflty whipped cream

Simply crush the fruit, and add sugar to taste. Swirl in softly whipped cream. Taste and add more cream as necessary. Serve immediately.

Apricot and Cardamom Fool

Apricot and Cardamom Compote (page 391)
softly whipped cream

Purée the apricots with a little of the syrup. Fold in softly whipped cream into the thick purée to taste. Serve with scones and biscuits.

Master Recipe
Rhubarb Fool

Serves 6

450g (1lb) red rhubarb, cut into chunks
175–225g (6–8oz) sugar
2 tablespoons water
300ml (10fl oz) softly whipped cream

Put the rhubarb into a stainless-steel saucepan with the sugar and water, stir, cover, bring to the boil and simmer until soft, which takes about 20 minutes. Stir with a wooden spoon until the rhubarb dissolves into a mush. Allow to get quite cold. Fold in the softly whipped cream to taste.

Variation
Rhubarb and Strawberry Fool

Serves 6–8

A divine combination.

450g (1lb) red rhubarb, cut into chunks
225g (8oz) sugar
2 tablespoons water
225g (8oz) strawberries
300ml (½ pint) cream, whipped

Follow the recipe above for cooking the rhubarb, and allow it to get quite cold. Mash the strawberries and add to the rhubarb. Fold in the softly whipped cream to taste.

Blackcurrant Fool

Serves 6

My favourite fool.

350g (12oz) blackcurrants, fresh or frozen
Stock Syrup (see page 568)
softly whipped cream

Cover the blackcurrants with Stock Syrup. Bring to the boil and cook until the fruit bursts – about 4–5 minutes. Liquidise or purée the fruit and syrup, strain through a nylon sieve, and measure. When the purée has cooled, add up to equal quantity of softly whipped cream, according to taste.

An alternative presentation is to layer blackcurrant purée and softly whipped cream in tall sundae glasses. Finish your layers with one of cream, drizzle a little thinned purée on top, and serve chilled with Shortbread (see page 466).

Variation
Blackcurrant Ice-cream

Leftover blackcurrant fool makes a delicious ice-cream. Make a blackcurrant coulis by thinning the blackcurrant purée with a little more water or syrup. Set in loaf tins lined with clingfilm – a great recipe for a party and amazingly good for so little effort.

Meringues

There are few desserts that are as easy and impressive as meringues. The meringue bases will keep for several weeks in a tin, so you can assemble an impromptu filling with whatever you have to hand. There is no magic to making meringue, provided your mixing bowl is dry, free of grease and spotlessly clean, and that when you separate the eggs not a drop of yolk gets into the whites. If it does, no amount of whisking will get you fluffy white clouds of egg white – you'll have to start again. A copper bowl is best, stainless-steel and glass are also fine, but a plastic one should only be used as a last resort because it tends to hold grease and detergent residue unless meticulously washed and rinsed.

Master Recipe
Ballymaloe Break all the Rules Meringue
Serves 6–8

Unlike other meringue recipes, we just put everything into the same bowl rather than folding it in carefully. We think it's foolproof – as long as the bowl is spotlessly clean. Make double this amount if using a food processor, otherwise the whisk won't reach the egg white in the bottom of the bowl.

2 organic egg whites
110g (4oz) caster sugar
  or 125g (4½oz) icing sugar

2 baking sheets
silicone paper

Preheat the oven to 150°C/300°F/gas 2, or according to the individual recipe. Line 2 baking sheets with silicone paper. Draw 2 x 20cm (8in) circles or heart shapes on the silicone paper and set aside.

Check that your bowl is dry, free of grease and spotlessly clean. Break up the egg whites with the whisk and then add all the sugar in one go. Whisk at full speed until the mixture forms stiff dry peaks.

Divide the mixture between the circles or heart shapes and spread evenly with a palette knife. Bake immediately for 45–60 minutes or until crisp. The meringues should peel off the paper easily. Turn off the oven and allow to cool.

> TIP: The proportion of filling to meringue really matters. Too much and it will be too luscious; too little and it will appear dry. As a rough guide, the filling should be about the thickness of one disc of meringue.

Variations
Meringue Gâteau with Fruit
Follow the Master Recipe. Sandwich the meringues together with 300ml (½ pint) or whipped cream and 225g (8oz) fruit such as strawberries, kiwi fruit, peaches or nectarines. Chill for several hours before serving. Decorate with rosettes of whipped cream stuck with little pieces of fruit.

> TIP: Do not put hot meringues straight from the oven on to a cold surface as they will crack, or at least craze, if you do.

Strawberry Meringue Blobs
Serves 8

4 organic egg whites
225g (8oz) caster sugar
5–10g (¼–½oz) flaked almonds
300ml (½ pint) whipped cream
450g (1lb) strawberries

Decoration
sprigs of mint, lemon balm or sweet cicely

Follow the Master Recipe until the meringue mixture forms stiff dry peaks. Put 8 blobs of meringue on a prepared baking sheet, and scatter a few flaked almonds over each one. Bake in the preheated oven for 10–15 minutes. Allow the meringue to cool on the trays.

To assemble: pipe or spoon some whipped cream into each meringue. Top with sliced strawberries, and decorate with a mint, lemon balm or sweet cicely leaf if you have one to hand. Eat immediately!

Lemon Curd Meringue Blobs
Follow the recipe above and serve with whipped cream and homemade Lemon Curd (see page 511) and Crystallised Lemon Peel (see page 515).

Heart-shaped Lemon and Elderflower Curd Meringue
Follow the recipe above and divide the mixture between two heart shapes drawn on silicone paper. Bake immediately for about 45 minutes or until crisp. Allow to cool, in the oven if possible. When completely cold, sandwich the meringue discs together with Lemon and Elderflower Curd (see page 511) and whipped cream. Decorate with rosettes of cream and lemon balm or sweet geranium leaves.

Meringue Nests with Kiwi and Lime
Serves 6

Meringue
2 organic egg whites
125g (4½oz) icing sugar

Filling
225g (8oz) kiwi fruit
225g (8oz) whipped cream
juice of 1 lime

Decoration
whipped cream
fresh mint or lemon balm leaves

piping bag

Preheat the oven 150°C/300°F/gas 2. Draw out four 9cm (3½in) circles on silicone paper on a baking sheet. Follow the Master Recipe until the mixture forms stiff peaks. Put the meringue mixture into a piping bag with a number 5 rosette nozzle. Pipe a few blobs onto each circle and spread thinly with a palette knife. The meringue should not be more than 5mm (¼in) thick. Then carefully pipe a wall of meringue rosettes around the edge of each circle.Bake for 45 minutes or until the meringue nests lift easily off the paper. Turn off the oven and allow them to cool in the oven.

To assemble: peel the kiwi and cut them into wedges lengthways. Toss in freshly squeezed lime juice. Pipe some whipped cream into each nest and arrange the slices of kiwi on top. Top with tiny rosettes of cream and decorate with fresh mint or lemon balm leaves.

Almond Meringue with Chocolate and Rum Cream
Serves 6

We use this all-in-one meringue recipe for birthdays, anniversaries, Valentine's Day, or simply for a special dessert. If you chill the assembled dessert for an hour before serving it will be easier to cut. Almond meringue is particularly delicious with soft berry fruits, but peaches, nectarines, or kiwi fruit are also very good. Mango and passion fruit is irresistible.

Meringue
as for Master Recipe
35g (1½oz) whole unskinned almonds

Filling
25g (1oz) good quality dark chocolate
10g (½oz) unsweetened chocolate
1 tablespoon rum
1 tablespoon single cream
300ml (½ pint) whipped cream

Decoration
5 toasted almonds

Blanch and skin the almonds. Grind or chop them, not to a fine powder but until slightly coarse and gritty. Follow the Master Recipe until your mixture forms stiff dry peaks. Fold in the almonds. Divide the mixture between the circles or heart shapes and spread evenly with a palette knife. Bake immediately for 45 minutes or until crisp. The meringues should peel off the paper easily. Turn off the oven and allow to cool in the oven.

To make the filling, melt the chocolate with the rum and single cream very gently, either in a very cool oven, or over hot water. Cool and then fold the mixture into the whipped cream.

To assemble, sandwich the meringues together with the filling. Decorate with rosettes of chocolate and rum cream stuck with halved toasted almonds.

Almond Meringue with Strawberries and Cream
Follow the recipe above, then sandwich together the two meringues with 300ml (½ pint) whipped cream and 225g (8oz) sliced strawberries. Decorate with rosettes of whipped cream and strawberries, or with little sprigs of mint or lemon balm.

Almond Meringue with Loganberries or Raspberries
Follow the recipe above, using 225g (8oz) loganberries or raspberries.

Hazelnut Meringue with Raspberries and Cream
Follow the recipe above substitute 35g (1½oz) hazelnuts for the almonds.

Walnut or Brazil Nut Meringue with Pears
Serves 6

Meringue
as for Master Recipe
12 walnut or brazil nut kernels, chopped

Filling
1–2 ripe dessert pears
225ml (8fl oz) unsweetened whipped cream

Decoration
5 walnut halves

Follow the Master Recipe until your mixture forms stiff dry peaks. Gently fold in the chopped nuts. Bake in a very low oven 100°C/200°F/gas ½ for 3–4 hours. Turn off the oven and allow to get quite cold.

To assemble: put one of the meringue discs on a serving plate. Peel the pears, core and slice. Spread most of the cream over the meringue, arrange the pears on top of the cream and put the second disc of meringue on top of this. Decorate with rosettes of cream and walnut halves.

Ballymaloe Irish Coffee Meringue with Chocolate Coffee Beans
Serves 8

Meringue
2 organic egg whites
125g (4½oz) icing sugar
2 teaspoons instant coffee powder (not granules)

Filling
300ml (½ pint) whipped cream
1 tablespoon Irish whiskey

piping bag

Line 2 baking trays with silicone paper. Follow the Master Recipe, but keep back 2 tablespoons of icing sugar. Whisk until mixture stands in firm dry peaks – this may take 10–15 minutes. Sieve the coffee and the remaining icing sugar together and fold in carefully.

Use about half the meringue mixture to pipe 8 small rosettes onto the silicone paper. Spread the remainder of the mixture carefully with a tablespoon or a palette knife into 8 circles on the paper.

Bake in a low oven 150°C/300°F/gas 2 for approximately 1 hour or until crisp. The meringue discs should peel easily from the paper. Allow to get quite cold.

To serve: add the whiskey to the whipped cream. Put a meringue disc onto a serving plate, pipe or spoon a blob of whiskey-flavoured cream on top. Decorate with a meringue rosette and chocolate coffee beans if available. Dust with a little sieved coffee or cocoa.

Toffee Meringue with Caramel Shards

Serves 6

Meringue
2 organic egg whites
110g (4oz) soft brown sugar

Toffee Filling
10g (1/2oz) butter
20g (3/4oz) soft brown sugar
10g (1/2oz) caster sugar
30g (11/4oz) golden syrup
30ml (1fl oz) cream
a drop of pure vanilla extract

Decoration
150ml (1/4 pint) softly whipped cream
Caramel Shards (see below)

Preheat the oven to 150°C/300°F/gas 2.

Follow the Master Recipe until the mixture makes stiff peaks. Divide the meringue between the 2 circles and spread evenly with a palette knife. Bake for 45–60 minutes, or until crisp and firm. Peel off the paper. Cool on a wire rack.

To make the filling, melt the butter with the sugars and golden syrup, simmer for about 2 minutes. Stir in the cream and a drop of vanilla extract. Continue to stir on a low heat until smooth. Allow to get cold.

To assemble, spread a generous layer of whipped cream over the base of the meringue. Spoon an even layer of toffee filling on top. Cover with the second meringue disc. Decorate with a few rosettes of whipped cream and some shards of caramel.

Caramel Shards

Put a layer of silicone paper onto a baking sheet. Put 110g (4oz) sugar into a saucepan, stir over a medium heat until melted. Allow to caramelise to a pale chestnut colour. Take the pan off the heat, allow to cool for 4–5 minutes then drizzle the caramel over the paper in squiggles, pyramids or latticed triangles. Allow to harden, peel off and use as required.

Variation

Toffee Meringue with Caramel Shards and Banana

Put one or two sliced bananas (tossed in a little freshly squeezed lemon juice) on top of the toffee filling.

Coffee Marjolaine Cake

Serves 8–10

If you make the cake several days in advance, it will have softened and be much easier to cut. It should be kept in the fridge, covered, at least overnight.

Meringue
75g (3oz) almonds
4 organic egg whites
250g (9oz) icing sugar

Coffee Butter Cream
110g (4oz) granulated sugar
8 tablespoons water
4 organic egg yolks
300g (101/2oz) butter
coffee essence to flavour (we use Irel)

Decoration
175–225g (6–8oz) flaked almonds, toasted

Cover 4 baking sheets with silicone paper. Draw out 4 circles, approx. 20cm (8in) diameter, on the paper.

Preheat the oven to 150°C/300°F/gas 2.

Blanch and skin the almonds. Chop or grind in a food processor so that they are slightly coarse and gritty (not ground to a fine powder). Follow the Master Recipe until the mixture forms stiff dry peaks. Fold in the almonds. Divide the meringue between the four circles on the silicone paper, spread neatly – about 5mm (1/4in) thick.

Bake immediately for about 1 hour or until the discs are quite crisp and will peel off the paper easily. Allow to get quite cold.

Next make the coffee butter cream: put the sugar and water into a small saucepan and stir over a gentle heat until dissolved.

Remove the spoon and bring to the boil. Boil gently until 106–113°C/233–236°F is reached or until the syrup is at 'thread' stage. Whisk the egg yolks in a bowl until pale and fluffy. Gradually pour the hot syrup over the egg yolks, whisking all the time. Continue until the mixture is thick and light.

Cream the butter and gradually beat into the egg mixture. Flavour with coffee essence. Keep aside. Toast the flaked almonds and set aside to cool.

To assemble the Marjolaine, sandwich the four circles of meringue together with Coffee Butter Cream. If necessary, trim the edges to neaten (if they are jagged it will be difficult to ice the cake), then spread more butter cream around the sides of the cake and press on the flaked almonds.

Cover the top of the cake with Coffee Butter Cream and sprinkle generously with the remainder of the toasted almonds. Cover and refrigerate until needed.

Coconut Meringue with Pineapple and Cream

Serves 10–12

Fresh mango and cream is another delicious filling for coconut meringue.

Meringue
4 organic egg whites
250g (9oz) caster sugar
150g (5oz) desiccated coconut

Filling
1 ripe pineapple, peeled, sliced, cored and cut into chunks
whipped cream

Follow the Master Recipe until the mixture forms stiff peaks, then fold in the desiccated coconut gently. Use a palette knife to spread the meringue mixture onto the circles and bake for 25–35 minutes or until crisp and dry. Allow to cool in the oven. Sandwich the layers together with fresh pineapple and cream.

Meringue Roulade with Mango and Passion Fruit Sauce
Serves 10

We also fill this roulade with sliced strawberries, fraises des bois, raspberries, loganberries, tayberries, blueberries, kiwi, poached kumquats and pomegranate seeds in season. Serve with a complementary sauce.

Meringue
4 organic egg whites
225g (8oz) caster sugar

Mango and Passion Fruit Sauce
1 large ripe mango
4 passion fruit
1–2 tablespoons freshly squeezed lime juice
1–2 tablespoons caster sugar

Filling
1 large ripe mango peeled and thinly sliced
2 passion fruit
425–600 ml (³/₄–1 pint) whipped cream

Decoration
sweet cicely
whipped cream

Swiss roll tin 32 x 20cm (12 x 8in) lined with tin foil and brushed with non-scented vegetable oil

Preheat the oven to 180°C/350°F/gas 4. First make the roulade. Follow the Master Recipe to achieve a meringue that holds a stiff peak. Spread the meringue gently over the tin with a palette knife, it should be quite thick and bouncy. Bake in the oven for 15–20 minutes. Put a sheet of tin foil on the work top and turn the roulade onto it. Remove the base tin foil and allow the meringue to cool.

Meanwhile make the Mango and Passion Fruit Sauce. Peel the mango, chop the flesh and purée in a food processor. Put into a bowl, add the passion fruit seeds and juice, add freshly squeezed lime juice and sugar to taste. Cover and chill. Slice the mango for the filling into another bowl, add the passion fruit seeds and juice, toss gently.

To assemble: turn the roulade out onto a sheet of silicone paper dredged with icing sugar. Spread two-thirds of the cream over the roulade, cover with a layer of fruit (keeping some back for decoration). Hold your breath and roll up the roulade like a Swiss roll.

Transfer carefully onto a serving dish. Pipe some rosettes of cream onto the top, decorate with some of the reserved fruit. Garnish with sweet cicely, dredge with icing sugar and serve with the sauce.

ABOVE: Meringue Roulade with Mango and Passion Fruit Sauce

Meringue Sweethearts
Pipe plain meringue into little heart shapes with a star nozzle. Sandwich together with melted chocolate.

Meringue Kisses with Chocolate or Cocoa
See page 565

Melanie's Meringue Hearts
See page 565

Brown Sugar Meringues

Serves 10–12

4 organic egg whites
110g (4oz) caster sugar
110g (4oz) soft brown sugar

Filling
200ml (7fl oz) double cream, whipped
4 tablespoons Lemon Curd (see page 511)

Preheat the oven to 110°C/225°F/gas ¼. Line two baking trays with silicone paper. Whisk the egg whites with both the sugars (except 2 tablespoons of caster) until it is so stiff that the mixture will not flow at all when whisk is lifted. Fold in the remaining sugar. Spoon or pipe mixture in rounds the size of a golf ball onto baking trays. Bake for 1½–2 hours or until meringues are dry right through and can be easily removed from the paper (or cook for about 45 minutes if you like your meringues toffee-centred). Allow to cool.

Sandwich pairs with a mixture of whipped cream and lemon curd.

Master Recipe
Frosted Meringue Cake

We started to make this recipe to use up leftover or broken meringues. It became such a favourite on the sweet trolley at Ballymaloe that we now have to make meringues and break them in order to make this cake! It is difficult to write the recipe accurately because it depends on the quantity and size of the broken meringue pieces.

We use about equal volume of lightly whipped cream and broken meringue. For best results the broken meringue should be in biggish chunks – say 2.5–4cm (1–1½in) at least, although you often have to use what you have. Err on the side of having too little rather than too much cream. Mix the broken meringue pieces gently into the whipped cream. Turn into a cake or loaf tin which is lined with clingfilm, smooth over the top and cover tightly. Freeze. To serve: remove from the freezer, put onto a chilled plate and cut into thick slices in one of the following ways:

Variations
Frosted Meringue Cake with Summer Fruit and Coulis

Decorate with rosettes of whipped cream and summer berries – fresh strawberries, raspberries, loganberries, blueberries or blackberries. Decorate with mint or lemon balm leaves, and serve a coulis made of the fruit as an accompaniment.

Frosted Meringue Cake with Chocolate Sauce

Decorate with rosettes of cream, chocolate wafers or caraque and crushed praline, and serve with Chocolate Sauce (see page 599).

Frosted Meringue Cake with Irish Coffee Sauce

Decorate with rosettes of cream, chocolate coffee beans and crushed Praline (page 401), and serve with Irish Coffee Sauce (see page 599).

Chocolate Meringue Extravaganza

Serves about 10

8 organic egg whites
500g (18oz) icing sugar
2 tablespoons cocoa

Icing and Filling
600ml (1 pint) cream
450g (1lb) best-quality dark chocolate
1–2 tablespoons rum or orange liqueur

Preheat the oven to 150°C/300°F/gas 2.

Line 2 or 3 baking sheets with silicone or parchment paper. Draw out 3 ovals (about 30 x 18cm/11 x 7in) on the paper. Check that the bowl is dry and spotlessly clean. Put the egg whites into the bowl and add 450g (1lb) of the icing sugar. Whisk until the mixture forms stiff dry peaks, this may well take 10 minutes. Sieve the cocoa with the remaining 50g (2oz) icing sugar and fold it very gently into the stiff meringue mixture. Spread the meringue with a palette knife over the ovals to a thickness of about 5cm (2in). Put the remainder of the meringue into a piping bag with a 8cm (3in) round nozzle, and pipe into long strips. Bake the ovals and the strips in the oven for about 1 hour or until they lift easily from the paper.

Meanwhile make the chocolate filling: put the cream in a heavy-bottomed, preferably stainless steel, saucepan and bring it almost to the boil. Remove from the heat and add the chopped chocolate. With a wooden spoon, stir the chocolate into the cream until it is completely melted. Transfer the chocolate cream to the bowl of a food mixer and allow it to cool to room temperature. Add the liqueur and whisk until it is just stiff enough to pipe.

Remove the meringue from the oven as soon as it is cooked, peel off the paper and allow it to get completely cold on a wire rack.

Arrange one oval on a large serving dish. Spread a layer of mousse over the meringue, top with another layer, then more mousse and the top layer. Press down gently then cover the whole surface with the remaining mousse. Break the meringue strips into 4cm (1½in) bits and cover the sides and top of the 'cake' with them, they can be stuck on haphazardly or porcupine fashion, one way or the other it will look very dramatic. Refrigerate for 1 hour. Just before serving dredge with unsweetened cocoa and icing sugar. Serve with softly whipped cream.

Ice-creams

The Ballymaloe ice-creams are very rich and very delicious, made on an Italian egg mousse base with softly whipped cream and flavourings added. Ice-creams made in this way have a smooth texture and do not need further whisking during the freezing period. They should not be served frozen hard. Remove from the freezer at least 10 minutes before serving. The other method for making ice-cream is a custard base (see Cinnamon Ice-cream, page 401).

Master Recipe
Ballymaloe Vanilla Ice-cream

Serves 6–8

Make double this amount each time if at all possible, especially if you are using a food processor to whisk the mousse; less and you risk the blades not reaching all of the egg in the bottom of the bowl.

2 organic egg yolks
50g (2oz) sugar
125ml (4fl oz) water
½ teaspoon pure vanilla extract
600ml (1 pint) softly whipped cream (measure the cream whipped)

Put the egg yolks into a bowl and whisk until light and fluffy (keep the whites for meringues). Combine the sugar and water in a small heavy-bottomed saucepan, stir over heat until the sugar is completely dissolved, then remove the spoon and boil the syrup until it reaches the 'thread' stage, 106–113°C/223–236°F. It will look thick and syrupy and, when a metal spoon is dipped in, the last drops of syrup will form thin threads. Pour this boiling syrup in a steady stream onto the egg yolks, whisking all the time. Add vanilla extract and continue to whisk until it becomes a thick creamy white mousse. Fold the softly whipped cream into the mousse, pour into a bowl, cover and freeze.

Variations
Ice-cream Sandwich
A layer of ice-cream between 2 chocolate and hazelnut chip cookies.

Chocolate and Praline Ice-cream Wafers
Sandwich a slice of chocolate ice-cream between 2 chocolate wafers. Dip the sides in crushed Praline (see page 401), freeze and serve as soon as possible.

Fudge Ripple Ice-cream
Swirl Butterscotch Sauce (see page 599) or Toffee Sauce (see page 599) through soft frozen ice-cream.

Ice-cream Parfait
Fill a loaf tin lined with clingfilm with 3 layers of vanilla ice-cream layered with crushed praline powder or with 1, 2 or 3 different ice-creams in layers. Serve cut into slices, sprinkled with extra crushed praline and perhaps a Toffee Sauce (see page 599).

Ballymaloe Vanilla Ice-cream with Espresso (Affogato)
Put a scoop of vanilla ice-cream into a cappuccino cup, pour a shot of espresso over the top and serve immediately.

Seville Orange Marmalade Ice-cream
Add 225g (½lb) chopped Seville orange marmalade to the softly frozen ice-cream and return to the freezer until fully frozen.

Ballymaloe Chocolate Ice-cream

Serves 30 or 15 depending on greed!

We use Callebaut, Valrhona or Green and Black's chocolate.

4 tablespoons sugar
225ml (8fl oz) water
4 organic egg yolks
1 teaspoon pure vanilla extract
1.2 litres (2 pints) whipped cream
110g (4oz) plain chocolate (50–55% cocoa solids)
50g (2oz) unsweetened chocolate

Dissolve the sugar in the water, bring slowly to the boil and simmer until the syrup reaches the 'thread stage' (it will look thick and syrupy and when a metal spoon is dipped in, the last drops will form thin threads).

Meanwhile, whisk the egg yolks until white and fluffy. When the syrup is at the correct stage, pour the boiling syrup gradually onto the egg yolks, whisking all the time. Continue to whisk until the mixture is a thick white mousse.

Melt the two kinds of chocolate in a bowl over simmering water or in a very low oven. Cool slightly, add some of the mousse to the chocolate and stir quickly. Add more and then mix the two mixtures thoroughly. Fold in the softly whipped cream. Freeze until well set.

Variations
Tartufo
Scoop out the chocolate ice-cream into balls. Put onto a tray lined with silicone paper and freeze. Meanwhile melt some chocolate.

Toss the balls of ice-cream in the melted chocolate. Put back onto the tray of silicone paper and dredge with the cocoa powder. Chill and serve.

Ballymaloe Chocolate Ice-cream in Chocolate Cases with Rum Cream
Serves 6

Ballymaloe Chocolate Ice-cream (see page 399)

12 individual Chocolate Cases (see page 559)

Rum Cream
125ml (4fl oz) whipped cream
½ teaspoon caster sugar
½ tablespoon Jamaica rum

Chocolate Caraque (see page 400) or chocolate
  coffee beans
unsweetened cocoa powder

Remove the ice-cream from the freezer for about 10 minutes. Meanwhile chill the chocolate cases. Whip the cream to a soft peak, fold in the rum and caster sugar and continue to whip until stiff enough to pipe. Keep chilled. Spoon the ice-cream into the chocolate cases and smooth over the top. Cover and freeze again. To serve, pipe a large rosette of rum-flavoured cream on top of each chocolate case, sprinkle with chocolate caraque or decorate with a chocolate coffee bean. Sieve a dusting of unsweetened cocoa powder over the top of each. Serve immediately on chilled plates, allowing 2 per person.

How to Make Chocolate Decorations

Chocolate decorations can be used for garnishing and for petit fours. See page 561 for guidelines on melting chocolate.

Chocolate Caraque
There are three ways to make caraque:

1. Melt the chocolate and spread it thinly using a palette knife onto a marble slab. Allow it to set almost completely then, using a sharp knife or a clean paint scraper, shave off long, thin scrolls. Use a slight sawing action and keep your hand upright. This is fun to do but there's quite a lot of skill involved. You'll improve with practice, and you can always eat the rejects!

2. Spread the chocolate in the same way on the back of a baking sheet. When it is almost set but still pliable, use a cheese slice to shave off curls of chocolate. Lay the curls on silicone paper.

3. Take a large block of chocolate and use a clean potato peeler to shave off curls of chocolate from the edge of the block.

Use immediately or store in a covered box until needed.

Chocolate Shapes
Spread an even layer of melted chocolate about 1.5mm (¹⁄₁₆in) thick onto a sheet of silicone paper or a non-stick mat. Allow to cool to the point of setting. Cut into squares, diamonds, triangles and use cutters to stamp out hearts or any fancy shapes that seem appropriate. With some experience one can pipe chocolate freehand into the desired shapes from a piping bag. Beginners should pipe over traced outlines on silicone paper.

Curved Shapes
Curved shapes may be made by spreading melted chocolate over a strip of silicone paper. Leave to cool to the point of setting, then wrap the chocolate-covered paper around flexible card or cut into triangles and wrap around a rolling pin. When the chocolate is completely set, peel off the triangles.

Chocolate Leaves
Choose stiff fresh leaves such as rose, lemon or bay leaves with the stem still attached. Brush some melted chocolate on the underside, being careful not to let it drip onto the other side (or they may break when you try to peel them). Arrange on a sheet of non-stick paper. When set, carefully peel away the leaf, holding onto the stem rather than the chocolate leaf.

Chocolate Mint Leaves
Dip spearmint leaves in chocolate and chill, there's no need to peel the leaves away. Serve chilled as a petit four with coffee.

Ballymaloe Coffee Ice-cream with Irish Coffee Sauce
Serves 6–8

ingredients for Ballymaloe Vanilla ice-cream
  (see page 399)
3 teaspoons instant coffee
½ teaspoon boiling water

Irish Coffee Sauce (see page 599)

Follow the method for Vanilla Ice-cream, until the point you add in the vanilla extract to the mousse. Dissolve the instant coffee powder in just ½ teaspoon of boiling water. Add some mousse to the coffee paste and then fold the two together. Carefully fold in the softly whipped cream. Pour into a stainless-steel or plastic bowl, cover and freeze.

To serve: scoop the ice-cream into a serving bowl or ice bowl. Serve the Irish Coffee Sauce separately.

Cappuccino Ice-cream
Serves 8

ingredients for Ballymaloe Vanilla Ice-cream
  (see page 399)
3 teaspoons espresso coffee powder
½ teaspoon boiling water

150ml (¼ pint) single cream
unsweetened cocoa or drinking chocolate

Chocolate Caraque (see opposite)

Follow the method for Ballymaloe Vanilla Ice-cream, until the point you add in the vanilla extract to the mousse. Dissolve the espresso powder in just ½ teaspoon of boiling water. Add some mousse to the coffee paste and then fold the two together. Carefully fold in the softly whipped cream. Pour into a stainless-steel or plastic bowl, cover and freeze.

Divide the ice-cream between 8 cold-resistant tea or coffee cups (not more than half full). Cover and freeze for 5–6 hours or until set.

To serve, remove the ice-cream from the freezer. Put the cups onto the saucers with a teaspoon for each. Whip the cream until soft and fluffy, and spoon a little over each 'cappuccino'. Dust with chocolate powder and some chocolate shavings or caraque. Serve immediately.

Ballymaloe Praline Ice-cream

Serves 6–8

ingredients for Ballymaloe Vanilla Ice-cream (see page 399)

Praline
110g (4oz) unskinned almonds
110g (4oz) caster sugar

Follow the method for Ballymaloe Vanilla Ice-cream.

To make the praline: put the unskinned almonds with the sugar into a heavy saucepan over a low heat until the sugar gradually melts and turns a caramel colour. DO NOT STIR. When this stage is reached and not before, carefully rotate the pan until the nuts are all covered with caramel. When the nuts go 'pop', pour this mixture onto a lightly oiled Swiss roll tin or a marble slab and allow to get cold. When the praline is quite hard, crush in a food processor or with a rolling pin – the texture should be quite coarse and gritty.

After about 1½ hours, when the ice-cream is just beginning to set, fold in 4 tablespoons of praline powder and freeze again. (If you fold it in too early it will sink to the bottom of the ice-cream.)

To serve: scoop out into balls with an ice-cream scoop. Serve in an ice bowl, sprinkle with the remainder of the praline powder.

Caramel Ice-cream with Caramel Sauce and Bananas

Serves 6–8

2 organic egg yolks
50g (2oz) sugar
125ml (4fl oz) cold water
125ml (4fl oz) hot water
½ teaspoon pure vanilla extract
600ml (1 pint) softly whipped cream

Caramel Sauce (see page 598)

Decoration
2 bananas, sliced

Put the egg yolks into a bowl and whisk until light and fluffy (keep the whites for meringues). Combine the sugar and cold water in a small heavy bottomed saucepan. Stir over a gentle heat until the sugar is completely dissolved, then remove the spoon and boil until the syrup caramelises to a chestnut brown.

Quickly pour on the hot water. Do not stir. Boil gently until it again becomes a smooth, thick syrup and reaches the 'thread' stage, at 106–113°C/223–236°F. It will look thick and syrupy when a spoon is dipped in. Pour this boiling syrup onto the egg yolks. Add the vanilla extract and continue to whisk until it becomes a thick, creamy mousse. Fold the softly whipped cream into the mousse, pour into a bowl, cover and freeze.

To serve: scoop the ice-cream into a chilled bowl or ice bowl. Slice the bananas at an angle and add to the sauce. Spoon over the ice-cream or serve separately.

Caramel Sauce keeps almost indefinitely in a glass jar in the fridge or any cold place. Our Caramel Ice-cream is also divine served in Brandy Snap Baskets (see page 425).

Variation
Caramel Ice-cream with Chocolate, Peanut Shards and Sea Salt

Melt 200g (7oz) dark chocolate in a Pyrex bowl over simmering water. Spread out in a thin layer (3mm (⅛in) on baking paper. Sprinkle with chopped toasted peanuts and add a few flakes of flaky sea salt. Allow to set. Cut into long triangles and serve with the Caramel Ice-cream.

Cinnamon Ice-cream

Serves 12–15

Serve a scoop with a warm apple tart.

1 cinnamon stick, 5–7.5cm (2–3in) in length
475ml (17fl oz) milk
475ml (17fl oz) cream
10 organic egg yolks
225g (8oz) sugar

Grind the cinnamon stick coarsely in a coffee grinder to make about a dessertspoon full.

Put the milk in a saucepan, add the ground cinnamon, and bring slowly to scalding point. Add the cream then allow to cool. Leave to infuse for 10–15 minutes.

Whisk the egg yolks and sugar until white and fluffy, then whisk in the warm infusion. Pour back into the saucepan and cook over a gentle heat until the mixture just coats the back of a spoon. Sieve it, then cool quickly and freeze in an ice-cream maker or sorbetiere, according to the manufacturer's instructions. Or pour in a plastic box, cover and put into the freezer, whisking once or twice during freezing.

Strawberry Ice-cream with Strawberry Sauce

Serves 6–8

Italian ice-creams and sorbets are legendary. If I had to choose just one, it would have to be strawberry.

900g (2lb) very ripe strawberries
225g (8oz) caster sugar
300ml (½ pint) water
juice of ½ lemon
juice of ½ orange
150ml (¼ pint) whipped cream

Strawberry Sauce (see page 599)

Decoration
fresh mint leaves
a few sugared strawberries

Dissolve the sugar in the water, boil for 7–10 minutes, and leave to cool. Purée the strawberries in a food processor, or rub through a sieve. Add orange and lemon juice to the syrup. Stir into the purée, then fold in the whipped cream. Freeze in an ice-cream machine or in a covered bowl in the freezer until slushy. Stir once or twice during the freezing to break up the crystals.

Meanwhile make the Strawberry Sauce. Store in the fridge until ready to serve.

To serve: scoop out the ice-cream into a pretty glass bowl and top with a few sugared strawberries and fresh strawberry sauce. Decorate with mint leaves.

Variation
Double Strawberry Ice-cream
Marinade diced fresh strawberries in a little fraises or cassis liqueur and stir into the ice-cream.

TIP: It's fun to serve any of these ice-creams in ready-made sugar cones.

Summer Ice-cream Bombe with Strawberry Sauce

Serves 12–16

Ballymaloe Vanilla Ice-cream (see page 399)

Blackcurrant Ice-cream
2 organic egg yolks
2 tablespoons sugar
125ml (4fl oz) water
300ml (½ pint) Blackcurrant Sauce
  (see page 599)
600ml (1 pint) whipped cream

Strawberry Ice-cream (see page left)

Decoration
225g (8oz) whole strawberries
whipped cream and fresh mint leaves

Strawberry Sauce (see page 599)

First make the vanilla ice-cream, following the method on page 399. Put it into the freezer for about 10 minutes, so that it becomes icy cold. Line a bowl with the ice-cream in an even layer, put it into the freezer and after about 1 hour take it out and improve the shape if necessary.

Meanwhile make the fruit-flavoured ice-creams, beginning with the blackcurrant: follow the vanilla ice-cream method to the mousse stage, then add the Blackcurrant Sauce. Alternatively, use raw fruit sweetened with Stock Syrup (see page 568) to taste. Taste for sweetness after adding to the mousse, adding more syrup if necessary. Fold in the cream. Set to freeze in another even layer, to cover the frozen vanilla ice-cream.

Next make the Strawberry Ice-cream (see left) and freeze in an ice-cream machine or in the freezer until slushy. Fill the middle of the bombe with the strawberry ice-cream, cover the bowl with a plastic lid or clingfilm, and freeze solid. Leave overnight if possible.

To serve, remove the bombe from the freezer and allow to sit for 10–15 minutes. You may need to dip the bowl quickly into hot water. Decorate with fresh strawberries, rosettes of whipped cream and fresh mint leaves. Serve with Strawberry Sauce.

Spanish Lemon Ice-cream with Crystallised Lemon Peel

Serves 4

This is a fresh, tangy and light ice-cream, made using an easy-peasy but quite different recipe. It is a delight to eat at the end of any meal, winter or summer.

1 organic egg
250ml (9fl oz) milk
150g (5oz) caster sugar
zest and juice of 1 good lemon

Decoration
Crystallised Lemon Peel (see page 515)
fresh mint leaves and borage flowers

Separate the egg, keep the white on one side, and whisk the yolk with the milk. Gradually mix in the sugar. Carefully grate the zest from the lemon on the finest part of a stainless-steel grater. Squeeze the juice from the lemon and add with the zest to the liquid. Whisk the egg white until quite stiff and fold into the other ingredients. Freeze in a sorbetière following the manufacturer's instructions or put in a freezer in a covered plastic container. When the mixture starts to freeze, remove from the freezer and whisk again, or break up the crystals in a food processor. Then put it back in the freezer until it is frozen completely. Meanwhile, chill the serving plates.

To serve: scoop the ice cream into the curls, and arrange on chilled plates or in pretty frosted glass dishes. Decorate with crystallised lemon peel, and, in summer, borage flowers and fresh mint leaves.

Sorbets

Sorbets, water ices or what the Italians call granita, are balm to the soul and palate in hot weather. They are a delicious way to end a meal, but are sometimes used to refresh the appetite between courses. If you have a sorbetière or an ice-cream maker sorbets can be frozen in about 25 minutes. However, you can use the freezer too, in which case you need to be ready to whisk the sorbet every few hours as it freezes in order to break up the ice crystals and keep it smooth. A stiffly beaten egg white, whisked in when the sorbet is almost frozen, keeps it light.

Blackberry and Sweet Geranium Sorbet

Serves 6

450g (1lb) blackberries
110g (4oz) sugar
100ml (3½fl oz) water
4–6 large sweet geranium (pellargonium graveleons) leaves

Put the sugar, water and sweet geranium leaves into a saucepan and bring slowly to the boil. Boil for 3–4 minutes. Allow to cool. Meanwhile, liquidise and sieve the blackberries through a nylon sieve.

LEFT: Sweet geranium

When the syrup is cold, mix with the blackberry purée. Taste – it ought to taste a little too sweet at this stage, but add some fresh lemon juice if it's cloying.

Freeze in a sorbetière for about 20 minutes. Alternatively put into a freezer and when almost frozen stir to break up the crystals with a whisk or in a food processor. Return to the freezer. Repeat this once or twice more.

To serve: put a scoop of sorbet on chilled white plates, decorate with whole blackberries and sweet geranium leaves.

> TIP: if you have a food processor, freeze the sorbet completely in a tray, then break up and whizz for a few seconds in the processor, add 1 lightly beaten egg white, whizz and freeze again. Serve.

Lemon Verbena or Lemon Balm Sorbet

Serves 8

Rory O'Connell served this deliciously fresh sorbet as a starter in Ballymaloe – it just flits across the tongue and scarcely needs to be swallowed. A perfect start, or end, if you prefer, to a late summer meal.

225g (8oz) sugar
600ml (1 pint) cold water
2 large handfuls of lemon verbena or lemon balm leaves, or one of each
freshly squeezed juice of 3 lemons
1 organic egg white (optional)

Put the first three ingredients into a non-reactive saucepan and bring slowly to the boil. Simmer for 2–3 minutes. Allow to get quite cold. Add the lemon juice. Strain and freeze for 20–25 minutes in an ice-cream maker or sorbetière.

Alternatively, freeze the sorbet in a bowl in the freezer. When it is semi-frozen, whisk until smooth and return to the freezer again. Whisk again when almost frozen and fold in one stiffly beaten egg white. Keep in the freezer until needed. Serve in chilled glasses or chilled white china bowls. Decorate with lemon balm and verbena leaves.

Melon Sorbet with Lime Syrup

Serves 6–8 as a starter or a pudding

This sorbet works well either as a starter or a pudding.

1 x 450g (1lb) Charentais or Ogen Melon
1 small lemon
75–110g (3–4oz) caster or icing sugar
pinch of salt

225ml (8fl oz) Stock Syrup (see page 568)
1 lime

Decoration
1 small melon
fresh mint or lemon balm leaves

Cut the melon in half horizontally. Take out the seeds and then scoop out the flesh and purée in a liquidiser. Strain the melon into a bowl through a fine sieve or strainer. Add the lemon juice, sugar and a tiny pinch of salt and whisk to dissolve the sugar. Taste and pour the mixture into an ice-cream maker or sorbetière and freeze. Alternatively, put it in a container in the freezer, covered, whisking as it begins to freeze to break up the ice crystals.

Remove the zest from the lime with a zester, add to the syrup, then add the juice of half the lime.

To serve: quarter the small melon, remove the seeds and cut into thin slices. Arrange 3 or 4 slices on chilled plates. Put a scoop of sorbet beside the melon, spoon a little syrup and zest over the slices and decorate with fresh mint or lemon balm leaves.

Strawberry Sorbet

Use the ingredients for Strawberry Ice-cream (see page 402), omitting the cream.

Blackcurrant Leaf Sorbet

Serves 6

Young blackcurrant leaves have a wonderful flavour. They're at their most aromatic in late spring before the fruit comes.

2 large handfuls of young blackcurrant leaves
225g (8oz) sugar
600ml (1 pint) cold water
juice of 3 lemons
1 egg white (optional)

Crush the blackcurrant leaves tightly in your hand, put into a stainless-steel saucepan with the cold water and sugar. Stir to dissolve the sugar, bring slowly to the boil. Simmer for 2–3 minutes. Allow to cool completely. Add the lemon juice.

Strain and freeze for 20–25 minutes in an ice-cream maker or sorbetière. If you do not have one, simply freeze the sorbet in a bowl in the freezer. When it is semi-frozen, whisk until smooth and return to the freezer again. Whisk again when almost frozen and fold in the stiffly beaten egg white. Keep in the freezer until needed.

Serve in chilled glasses or chilled white china bowls or on pretty plates lined with fresh blackcurrant leaves.

Variation
Elderflower Sorbet

We also use the blackcurrant leaf recipe to make an elderflower sorbet – in late spring, you can substitute 4–5 elderflower heads in full bloom. Try it with Green Gooseberry Compote (see page 391).

Julia Wight's Exquisite Blackcurrant Sorbet

Serves 4

First grow your own blackcurrants, then you will capture all the perfume of this summer fruit.

450g (1lb) fresh blackcurrants
175g (6oz) caster sugar

Purée the freshly picked berries in a liquidiser or mouli-légume. Rub through a sieve (this takes ages), and mix in the sugar. Freeze the mixture in an ice-cream maker or put it in a container in the freezer, covered, whisking as it begins to freeze to break up the ice crystals.

Serve on chilled plates. This looks very fetching decorated with the tiny bunches of berries, dipped first in iced water and then in caster sugar.

Winter Tangerine Sorbet

Serves 10–12

The quantity of sorbet below is enough to fill 10–18 tangerine shells. Clementines, mandarins or satsumas may also be used.

Syrup
225g (8oz) sugar
juice of 1/4 lemon
150ml (1/4 pint) water

20–28 tangerines
juice of 1/2 lemon
icing sugar (optional)

Decoration
vine leaves or bay leaves

First make the syrup. Heat the ingredients over a low heat, until they are dissolved together and clear. Bring to the boil, and boil for 2–3 minutes. Leave to cool.

Grate the zest from 10 of the tangerines, and squeeze the juice from them.

Cut the remaining tangerines so that they each have a lid. Scoop out the sections with a small spoon and them press them through a nylon sieve (alternatively, liquidise the pulp and then strain). You need 850ml (1½ pints) of juice. Add the grated zest, the lemon juice and the syrup to taste. Taste and add icing sugar or extra lemon juice, according to whether more sweetness or sharpness is required. Freeze until firm.

Chill the shells in the fridge or freezer, then fill them with the sorbet. Replace the lids and store in the freezer. Cover with clingfilm if not serving on the same day. Serve on a white plate decorated with vine leaves or bay leaves.

> TIP: If you do not have a sorbetière or ice-cream maker, you can fold half a stiffly beaten egg white into the sorbet to lighten the texture.

Thai Coconut Sorbet

Serves 6–8

125g (4½oz) sugar
150ml (5fl oz) water
1 x 400ml (14fl oz) tin coconut milk (we use Chaokah)
juice of 1 lime or small lemon

First make the sugar syrup. Put the sugar and water into a small saucepan, bring to the boil and simmer for 2–3 minutes. Cool and refrigerate. When the syrup is chilled, whisk in the coconut milk and lime or lemon juice. Taste, then pour the mixture into an ice-cream maker or sorbetière and freeze. Alternatively, put it in a container in the freezer, covered, whisking as it begins to freeze to break up the ice crystals. Serve on chilled plates with fresh pineapple.

Espresso Granita

Serves 6–8

600ml (1 pint) espresso coffee
600ml (1 pint) Stock Syrup (see page 568)
whipped cream

Mix the coffee and Stock Syrup together in a bowl. Put into a plastic container and freeze for a couple of hours until just beginning to freeze at the edges. Whisk the frozen mixture into a liquid. Re-freeze and repeat the whisking every few hours. Meanwhile chill some serving glasses.

Remove from the freezer 10 minutes before serving. Spoon some granita into a chilled glass. Spoon a layer of whipped cream on top, then another layer of granita, more cream and finally granita. Serve immediately.

Raspberry Parfait with Raspberry Sauce

Serves 6

A parfait is a mousse that can be fresh or frozen. The word is used with some poetic license! Raspberries have a high water content so the clever trick in this recipe is to use gelatine to help to cut the ice crystals. Loganberries may also be used.

450g (1lb) fresh raspberries
275g (10oz) sugar
150ml (5fl oz) water
1 teaspoon gelatine
1 tablespoon water
600ml (1 pint) whipped cream

Raspberry Sauce (see page 599)

Decoration
fresh raspberries
mint leaves

1 loaf tin 12.5 x 20.5cm (5 x 8in) approx.

Line the loaf tin carefully with clingfilm. Purée then sieve the raspberries. Dissolve the sugar in the water and boil for 2 minutes. Allow the gelatine to sponge in the water for a few minutes. Place the bowl of gelatine in a saucepan of simmering water until it melts and dissolves fully – there should be no residual granules.

Mix the raspberry purée with the syrup, add a little to the gelatine and then whisk the two together. Fold in the whipped cream, pour into the prepared loaf tin, cover and freeze.

Meanwhile make the Raspberry Sauce and allow to cool.

To serve: turn out the parfait and cut into slices. Serve on chilled plates, drizzled with the Raspberry Sauce. Decorate with fresh raspberries and mint leaves.

Blackcurrant Parfait with Blackcurrant Sauce

Serves 8

This exquisite blackcurrant mousse is rich and intense. It needs softly whipped cream as an accompaniment. Fresh blackcurrants are bursting with vitamin C.

350g (12oz) blackcurrants, fresh or frozen
225g (8oz) sugar
4 organic egg yolks
1½ teaspoons gelatine or 1½ leaves of gelatine
150ml (¼ pint) cream
1 dessertspoon crème de cassis

Blackcurrant Sauce (see page 599)

a little whipped cream, whole blackcurrants and a few lemon balm leaves for decoration

8 x individual moulds or 1 x flan ring, lightly oiled or lined with clingfilm

To make the parfait, put the blackcurrants and sugar in a heavy stainless-steel saucepan and allow the sugar to dissolve slowly before the mixture comes to the boil. Then boil gently for 2 minutes.

Meanwhile whisk the egg yolks until they become a pale lemon-coloured mousse. Whizz the blackcurrant mixture in a food processor then push the mix through a nylon sieve to get a smooth purée. Pour directly onto the egg yolks and whisk up to a stiff mousse.

Put 2 tablespoons of cold water in a small bowl or pint measure, sprinkle over the gelatine, and allow to sponge for a few minutes. Put the bowl into a saucepan of boiling water and allow the gelatine to dissolve, it should be liquid and clear with no trace of granules. (If using leaf gelatine, cover the leaves with cold water for 10 minutes or so, discard the water and then dissolve the softened leaves in 2 tablespoons of water in the saucepan.)

Meanwhile lightly whip the cream. When the gelatine has dissolved, blend carefully with the blackcurrant mousse (Add a little of the mousse mixture to the gelatine first and then fold this into the remainder of the mousse.) Finally add the crème de cassis and fold into the lightly whipped cream. Turn the mousse into the mould or into moulds. Allow for 2–3 hours for the small moulds to set in the fridge, 4–5 hours for the large one.

Prepare the Blackcurrant Sauce. If the purée you obtain is very thin, use 1 teaspoon gelatine to set 225ml (8fl oz) of sauce, then allow to cool before you add the water. For this dessert, we sometimes pour some of the thick blackcurrant purée before the water has been added over the top of the parfait to make a shiny top.

To serve: pour a little Blackcurrant Sauce onto the base of 8 white plates, if the mousses are in individual moulds. Turn out a mousse into the centre of each plate. Decorate the sauce by piping on cream and 'feathering' it with the tip of a knife if desired. Pipe a little rosette of cream on top of the mousse, put a whole blackcurrant in the centre and decorate with lemon balm leaves. Serve with softly whipped cream.

Passion Fruit Mousse with Sugared Strawberries

Serves 12

10 passion fruit
2 leaves of gelatine (or 2 teaspoons powdered gelatine)
2 tablespoons water
300ml (½ pint) cream
60g (2½oz) caster sugar

Decoration
450g (1lb) strawberries, caster sugar and mint leaves
Strawberry Sauce (see page 599), optional

12 individual ramekins or soufflé dishes, brushed with non-scented vegetable oil

Halve the passion fruit and scoop out the pulp and seeds. Purée in a food processor (not a liquidiser, as this will crush the seeds) then strain through a nylon sieve.

Soften the leaves of gelatine or sponge the powdered gelatine in the water for a few minutes, then dissolve fully over a pan of hot water.

Add some of the passion fruit pulp to the gelatine then stir both mixtures together thoroughly. Chill, stirring from time to time. Whip the cream until fairly stiff but not grainy, then add the sugar. Fold carefully into the passion fruit mixture, just as it begins to set. It should be a smooth creamy mixture.

Spoon the mixture into the ramekins or soufflé dishes and chill for 1–2 hours before serving. Meanwhile slice the strawberries and sprinkle with caster sugar.

To assemble: ease the mousses gently out of the moulds (dip bases into hot water for a few seconds if necessary). Place each mousse in the centre of a white plate, decorate with sugared strawberries and fresh mint leaves. Drizzle with Strawberry Sauce if using.

Pannacotta

Serves 6–8

Means cooked cream – keep it wobbly!

600ml (1 pint) double cream
1–2 vanilla pods, split lengthways
50g (2oz) caster sugar
scant 2 teaspoons gelatine
2 tablespoons water

6–8 moulds 75–125ml (3–4fl oz), lightly brushed with non-scented vegetable oil

Put the cream into a heavy-bottomed saucepan with the split vanilla pods and sugar. Put on a low heat and bring to the 'shivery' stage.

Meanwhile, sponge the gelatine in the water and put the bowl in a saucepan of simmering water until the gelatine is fully dissolved. Add a little of the cream to the gelatine, then stir both mixtures together. Remove the vanilla pods, then pour into the moulds. When cold, cover and refrigerate until set, preferably overnight.

Serve with summer berries, fruit salad with sweet geranium leaves, Green Gooseberry Compote, Apricot and Cardamom Compote (see page 391), or simply a dark, almost bitter, Caramel Sauce (see page 598).

Variation
Pannacotta with Espresso
Make the Pannacotta. Pour into cups or small bowls. Cover and chill. When ready to serve, pour a shot of espresso over the top of the Pannacotta. Serve immediately.

Ballymaloe Crème Brûlée

Serves 4–6

The ultimate custard! It was created in Trinity College, Cambridge and is a universal favourite. I like to eat it with a compote of fruit – perhaps poached apricots with sweet geranium leaves.

Custard
2 large organic egg yolks
½ tablespoon sugar
300ml (½ pint) double cream (see note below)
½ vanilla pod (optional)

Caramel Topping
110g (4oz) sugar
75ml (3fl oz) water
125ml (4fl oz) whipped cream (optional)

4–6 white shallow-eared dishes (or ramekins)

Make the custard the day before the crème brûlée is needed. Mix the egg yolks with the sugar. Heat the cream with the vanilla pod to the 'shivery' stage but do not boil. Pour the cream slowly onto the egg yolks, whisking all the time. Return to the saucepan and cook on a medium heat, stirring until it is thick enough to coat the back of a spoon. It must not boil. Remove the vanilla pod, pour into the serving dishes and chill overnight. Be careful not to break the skin or the caramel may sink later.

The following day, make the caramel. Put the sugar and water in a saucepan and heat until the sugar is dissolved. Bring to the boil and cook until it caramelises to a chestnut brown colour. Remove from the heat and immediately spoon a thin layer of caramel over the top of the custards. Allow to get cold and pipe a line of whipped cream around the edge to seal the joint where the caramel meets the side of the dish. Serve within 12 hours, or the caramel will melt.

To eat, crack the top by knocking sharply with the back of a serving spoon.

Note: Two yolks only just set the cream. Be sure to use big eggs and measure your cream slightly short of the 300ml (½ pint). The cream takes some time to thicken and usually does so just under boiling point. If the custard is not properly set, or if the skin which forms on top while cooling is broken, the caramel will sink to the bottom of the dish. If there are cracks in the custard, freeze the pudding for 1–2 hours before spooning on the hot caramel.

Variations

Blow Torch Method

The alternative way to make the topping is to sprinkle the custard with a layer of white caster sugar or pale demerara sugar, spray with a film of cold water, then caramelise with a kitchen blow torch. This results in a light thin sheet of caramel.

Crème Brûlée with Praline Topping

Instead of the caramel topping, sprinkle finely crushed Praline (see page 401) over the chilled custard not more than 30 minutes before serving.

Star Anise Crème Brûlée

Add 6 star anise to the cream instead of the vanilla pod. Heat very slowly and infuse for 15 minutes before removing.

Crème Caramel with Caramel Shards

Serves 6

Custard
600ml (1 pint) full-cream milk
vanilla pod or ½ teaspoon pure vanilla extract, optional
4 organic eggs
55g (2oz) caster sugar

Caramel
225g (8oz) sugar
150ml (5fl oz) water

Caramel Shards (see page 396)

1 x 12.5cm (5in) Charlotte mould or 6 x 7.5cm (3in) soufflé dishes

Preheat the oven to 180°C/350°F/gas 4.

To make the custard put the milk into a saucepan over a medium heat and add the vanilla pod if using. Bring to just under boiling point, then leave to cool. Allow to infuse for 6–10 minutes.

Meanwhile, make the caramel. Put the sugar and water into a heavy-bottomed saucepan and stir over a gentle heat until the sugar is fully dissolved. Bring to the boil, remove the spoon and cook until the caramel becomes a golden brown or chestnut colour (do not stir or shake the pan). If sugar crystals form around the side of the pan, brush them down with cold water. Coat the bottom of the Charlotte mould or soufflé dishes with the hot caramel. (When the caramel is ready, it must be used immediately or it will become hard and cold.)

Whisk the eggs, caster sugar and vanilla extract (if used) until thoroughly mixed but not too fluffy. Pour the cooled milk onto the egg mixture, whisking gently as you pour. Strain and pour into the prepared moulds, filling them to the top.

Place the mould or moulds in a bain-marie of simmering water, cover with a paper lid and bake in the oven for about 1 hour for a Charlotte mould and about 35 minutes for individual dishes. Test the custard by inserting a skewer in the centre – it will come out clean when the custard is fully cooked.

Cool and turn out onto a round, flat dish or individual plates. Pour the remaining caramel around and serve with a little softly whipped cream. Decorate with Caramel Shards.

Srikhand

Serves 6–8

One of Alison Henderson's delish recipes.

1kg (2¼ lb) Greek-style yoghurt, or homemade yoghurt (see page 435)
generous pinch of saffron strands
450g (1lb) caster sugar
¼ teaspoon roughly crushed cardamom seeds
2 tablespoons pistachio nuts

Spoon the yoghurt onto a large square of muslin, tie the ends into a knot and hang over a bowl, leaving it to drip overnight. Next day, tip the drained yoghurt into a bowl. Infuse the saffron in a little warm water and then stir it into the yoghurt together with the cardamom seeds and the caster sugar. Mix well, cover and chill. Scatter the pistachio nuts over the pudding and serve with a bowl of mixed berries.

Carrigeen Moss Pudding

Serves 4–6

Carrigeen moss is bursting with goodness. I ate it as a child but never liked it as it was always too stiff and unpalatable. Myrtle Allen changed my opinion. Hers was always so light and fluffy. This is her recipe, it's the best and most delicious. We find that visitors to the country are fascinated by the idea of a dessert made with seaweed and they just love it. The name comes from 'little rock'.

scant 7g (¹⁄₄₀oz) cleaned, well dried carrigeen moss (1 semi-closed fistful)
850ml (1½ pints) milk
1 organic egg
1 tablespoon caster sugar
½ teaspoon pure vanilla extract or a vanilla pod

Soak the carrigeen in tepid water for 10 minutes. Drain and put the carrigeen into a saucepan with milk and vanilla pod if used. Bring to the boil and simmer very gently with the lid on for 20 minutes.

At that point and not before, separate the egg, put the yolk into a bowl, add the sugar and vanilla extract and whisk together for a few seconds, then pour the milk and carrigeen moss through a strainer onto the egg yolk mixture, whisking all the time. The carrigeen will now be swollen and exuding jelly. Rub all this jelly through the strainer and beat it into the milk mixture. Test for a set in a saucer as one would with gelatine.

Whisk the egg white stiffly and fold or fluff it in gently. It will rise to make a fluffy top. Serve chilled with soft brown (Barbados) sugar and cream and or a fruit compote.

Master Recipe
Darina Allen's Bread and Butter Pudding

Serves 6–8

Bread and butter pudding is the most irresistible way of using up leftover white bread – this is a particularly delicious recipe. Cinnamon or mixed spice may also be used but nutmeg is our favourite.

12 slices good-quality white bread, crusts removed
50g (2oz) butter, preferably unsalted
½–1 teaspoon freshly grated nutmeg
200g (7oz) sultanas
4 large organic eggs, lightly beaten
450ml (16fl oz) cream
225ml (8fl oz) milk
1 teaspoon pure vanilla extract
175g (6oz) caster sugar
pinch of salt
1 tablespoon granulated sugar, for sprinkling

Garnish
softly whipped cream

1 x 20.5cm (8in) square pottery or china dish

Butter the bread and arrange 4 slices, buttered side down, in a single layer in the dish. Sprinkle the bread with freshly grated nutmeg and half the sultanas. Arrange another layer of bread, buttered side down, over the fruit, and sprinkle the remaining nutmeg and sultanas on top. Cover with the remaining bread, again buttered side down.

In a bowl, whisk the eggs, add the cream, milk, vanilla extract, sugar and a pinch of salt. Pour the mixture over the bread through a fine sieve. Sprinkle the sugar over the top and let the mixture stand, covered loosely, at room temperature for at least 1 hour or chill overnight.

Preheat the oven to 180°C/350°F/gas 4.

Place in a bain-marie – the water should go half way up the sides of the baking dish and bake in the middle of the oven for about 1 hour until the top is crisp and golden. Serve warm with softly whipped cream.

Variations
Gooseberry and Elderflower Bread and Butter Pudding

Follow the Master Recipe, substituting Gooseberry and Elderflower Compote (see page 391) for the sultanas. Reserve a little of the compote to serve with the pudding.

Rhubarb Bread and Butter Pudding

Slice 450g (1lb) red rhubarb into 2cm (½in) pieces, put into a dish and sprinkle with sugar leave to macerate for an hour. Follow the Master Recipe, substituting the rhubarb for the sultanas. Serve with extra rhubarb compote (see page 524).

Irish Barmbrack and Butter Pudding

Follow the Master Recipe, using 12 slices yeast barmbrack instead of the Panettone.

Brioche Bread and Butter Pudding

Follow the Master Recipe, spreading the brioche with apricot jam and adding a little apricot brandy to the cream.

Panettone Bread and Butter Pudding

Follow the Master Recipe, substituting Panettone for the white bread and brandy or eau de vie in place of the vanilla extract.

Toast and Marmalade Pudding

Smother leftover toast with butter and marmalade. Omit the fruit and nutmeg and proceed as above.

Mincemeat Bread and Butter Pudding

Omit the butter. Spread a layer of Ballymaloe Mincemeat (see page 511) over bread. Serve hot on hot plates.

Chocolate Fudge Pudding

Serves 6–8

Chocolate puddings run neck and neck with apple tarts as people's favourite desserts. This one is wickedly rich with a melting texture. It should be moist in the centre, so don't overcook it, or it will be dull.

150g (5oz) best-quality chocolate
150g (5oz) unsalted butter
1 teaspoon pure vanilla extract
150ml (5fl oz) warm water
110g (4oz) caster sugar
4 organic eggs
25g (1oz) self-raising flour
pinch of cream of tartar

1.5 –1.7 litre (2½–3 pint) capacity pie dish or 7 individual 7.5cm (3in) ramekins, well greased with butter

Preheat the oven to 200°C/400°F/gas 6.

Break up the chocolate into small pieces and melt with the butter in a very low oven or in a bowl over hot but not simmering water. As soon as the chocolate is melted remove from the heat and add the vanilla extract and stir in the warm water and caster sugar. Continue to mix until it is smooth. Separate the eggs and add the yolks to the chocolate mixture, then sift in the flour, making sure that there are no lumps. Whisk the egg whites with the cream of tartar until they form stiff peaks, and gently fold into the chocolate mixture and pour into the pie dish or ramekins.

Put the dish or dishes in a bain-marie of hot water and bake for 10 minutes, then lower the heat to 170°C/325°F/gas 3 for a further 20–30 minutes (ramekins need only 5–10 minutes at the lower heat). The pudding should be firm on top but still soft and fudgy underneath. Dust the top with sifted icing sugar and serve hot or cold with softly whipped cream.

LEFT: Kumquat Toffee Pudding

Sticky Toffee Pudding
Serves 6–8

225g (8oz) chopped dates (deglet noor or even
  block dates are fine)
300ml (½ pint) hot black tea
110g (4oz) unsalted butter
170g (6oz) caster sugar
3 organic eggs
225g (8oz) self-raising flour, sifted
1 teaspoon bicarbonate of soda (bread soda)
1 teaspoon pure vanilla extract
1 teaspoon espresso coffee

Toffee Sauce (see page 599)

*20.5cm (8in) springform tin with removable
  base*

Preheat the oven to 180°C/350°F/gas 4.

Soak the dates in the hot tea for 15
minutes. Brush the cake tin with oil and
line the base with oiled greaseproof paper.

Cream together the butter and sugar until
light and fluffy. Beat in the eggs, one at a
time, and then fold in the flour. Add the
sifted bicarbonate of soda, vanilla extract
and coffee to the date and tea mixture and
stir this into the other mixture. Turn into the
prepared tin and cook in the oven for 1–1½
hours or until a skewer comes out clean.

About 10 minutes before the end of
cooking time, make the Toffee Sauce.

To serve: pour some hot sauce on to a
serving plate. Put the Sticky Toffee Pudding
on top, and pour more sauce over. Put the
remainder into a bowl to serve with the
pudding as well as softly whipped cream.

Variation
Kumquat Toffee Pudding
Put a tablespoon of drained Kumquat
Compote (see page 391) in the bottom of
the tin or individual ramekins. Top with
the pudding mixture. Bake for 20–25
minutes. Serve with the Toffee Sauce.

Chocolate Mousse
Serves 8–10

Rich, sinful, and really good! Make sure
your chocolate has a high percentage of
cocoa solids. Use milk chocolate if you
prefer, or a mixture of milk and dark.

225g (8oz) best-quality dark chocolate
10g (½oz) unsalted butter
150ml (¼ pint) water
1 tablespoon Jamaican rum, optional
6 small or 4 large organic eggs

ramekins or Chocolate Cases (see page 559)

Break the chocolate into small pieces, put
in a bowl with the butter and water and
stir gently over a low heat until melted
and completely smooth. Leave to cool,
then whisk in the rum, if using. Separate
the eggs and add the yolks to the mixture.

Whisk the egg whites and fold them in. Beat
for 5–6 minutes: this makes the mousse
smooth and silky and it will thicken towards
the end. Turn into ramekins or Chocolate
Cases. Set for 5–6 hours or overnight.

Serve with a rosette of cream and a little
unsweetened cocoa powder.

Tiramisu
Serves 8

The name means pick-me-up – not surprising really, considering the amount of booze involved! This is a fairly recent Italian pudding, which seems to have originated in Venice but is now served in restaurants all over Italy, and always tastes different. We've had rave reviews for this version that is very easily put together.

250ml (8fl oz) strong espresso coffee (if your freshly made coffee is not strong enough add 1 teaspoon of instant coffee)
2 tablespoons brandy
2 tablespoons Jamaica rum
85g (3oz) dark chocolate
3 organic eggs, separated
4 tablespoons caster sugar
255g (9oz) mascarpone cheese
unsweetened cocoa (Dutch process)
38–40 boudoir biscuits

25.5cm x 20cm (10 x 8in) dish with low sides or 1lb loaf tin, 20.5 x 10cm (8 x 4in), lined with clingfilm

Mix the coffee with the brandy and rum. Roughly grate the chocolate (we do this in a food processor with the pulse button). Whisk the egg yolks with the sugar until it reaches the 'ribbon' stage and is light and fluffy. Then fold in the Mascarpone a tablespoon at a time. Whisk the egg whites until they form stiff peaks and fold gently into the mascapone mixture. Now you are ready to assemble the Tiramisu.

Dip each side of the boudoir biscuits one at a time into the coffee mixture and arrange side by side in the dish or tin. Spread half the mascarpone mixture gently over the biscuits, sprinkle half the grated chocolate over the top, then add another layer of soaked biscuits and finally the rest of the Mascarpone. Cover the whole bowl or loaf tin carefully with clingfilm or better still slide it into a plastic bag and twist the end. Refrigerate for at least 6 hours – I usually make it the day before I use it. Just before serving scatter the remainder of the chocolate over the top and dredge with unsweetened cocoa. Delicious served with a glass of chilled Italian dessert wine, for example Vin Santo. Tiramisu will keep for several days in a fridge, but make sure it is covered so that it doesn't pick up 'fridgie' tastes.

Note: Mascarpone is a delicious and rich creamy cheese which originated in Lodi in Lombardy. It is often served instead of cream with fruit and pastries and is of course an essential ingredient of tiramisu. You can make your own (see page 434) or buy it ready-made.

Variation
Frosted Tiramisu
Freeze the Tiramisu in a loaf tin. Serve with Irish Coffee Sauce (see page 599).

Sue Cullinane's Banoffee Pie

Banoffee Pie is none the worse for being prepared a day in advance.

2 x 400ml (14fl oz) tins condensed milk
75g (3oz) butter
225g (8oz) digestive biscuits
6–8 bananas, depending on size
juice of 1 lemon
425ml (3/4 pint) double cream
3 tablespoons coffee essence or Tia Maria
toasted flaked almonds

32cm (12in) loose-based tin, lightly oiled with non-scented vegetable oil

Put the unopened tins of condensed milk into a saucepan, keep covered with water and simmer for 3 hours (it is worth doing a few extra for the next time you make this!).

Melt the butter in a pan over a gentle heat. Crush the biscuits (put them in a plastic bag and use a rolling pin) and add to the butter. Line the base of the tin with the biscuit mix and leave to set.

Open the tins of milk and spread the toffee contents over the biscuit base. Slice the bananas, toss in freshly squeezed lemon juice and arrange on top of the toffee.Whip the cream, add the coffee essence or Tia Maria. Spread over the bananas. Cover lightly and refrigerate to set. Serve sprinkled with the toasted almonds.

Variation
Baby Banoffees
Make individual banoffee in tiny sundae glasses.

Master Recipe
Sweet Crêpe Batter

One of the great convertibles: great for a stand-by dish.

170g (6oz) white flour, preferably unbleached
good pinch of salt
1 dessertspoon caster sugar
2 large organic eggs plus 1 or 2 egg yolks
scant 425ml (15fl oz) milk, or for very crisp, light delicate pancakes, milk and water mixed
3–4 dessertspoons melted butter

Sift the flour, salt, and sugar into a bowl, make a well in the centre and drop in the eggs. With a whisk or wooden spoon, starting in the centre, mix the egg and gradually incorporate the flour. Add the liquid slowly and beat until the batter is covered with bubbles. (If the crêpes are to be served with sugar and lemon juice, stir in an extra tablespoon of caster sugar and the finely grated rind of half a lemon.)

Let the batter stand in a cold place for an hour or so – longer will do no harm. Just before you cook the pancakes stir in 3–4 dessertspoons melted butter. This will make all the difference to the flavour and texture of the pancakes and will make it possible to cook them without greasing the pan each time.

Crêpes with Orange Butter

Serves 6 – makes about 12 pancakes

This crêpe recipe is very nearly as good as those Crêpes Suzette they used to serve with a great flourish in posh restaurants when I was a child. They are, though, half the bother and can be made for a fraction of the cost.

Sweet Crêpe Batter (see left)

Orange Butter
175g (6oz) butter
3 teaspoons finely grated orange rind
200g (7oz) icing sugar

freshly squeezed juice of 5–6 oranges

20.5cm (8in) non-stick crêpe pan

Follow the batter recipe. Next make the orange butter. Cream the butter with the finely grated orange rind. Then sift in the icing sugar and beat until fluffy.

When you are ready to eat, heat the pan to very hot, pour in just enough batter to cover the base of the pan thinly, swirling the batter around to get it even. Loosen the crêpe around the edge, flip over with a spatula, cook for a second or two on the other side, and slide off the pan onto a hot plate. The crêpes may be stacked on top of each other and peeled apart later. If you have several pans it is perfectly possible to keep 3 or 4 pans going in rotation, but this is only necessary if you need to feed the multitudes.

To serve: melt a blob of the orange butter in the pan, add some freshly squeezed orange juice and toss the crêpes in the foaming butter. Fold in half and then in quarters to make fan shapes. Serve 2 per person on warm plates, spooning the buttery orange juices over the top. Repeat until all the crêpes and butter have been used.

Note: A tablespoon of orange liqueur e.g. Grand Marnier or Orange Curaçao is very good added to the orange butter if you are feeling extravagant!

> TIP: The crêpes will keep in the fridge for several days and also freeze perfectly. If they are to be frozen, put a disc of silicone paper between each for ease of separation.

Variations

Rosalie's Crêpes with Toffee Sauce and Bananas

Follow the Master Recipe to make the batter. To serve: fold 2 warms crêpes into a fan shape and arrange on a warmed plate. Top each portion with half a sliced banana and hot Toffee Sauce (see page 599). Put a dollop of cream or ice-cream alongside and serve immediately.

Joshua's Crêpes

From my gourmet grandson! Follow the Master Recipe to make the batter. Spread each pancake with nutella using a palette knife. Roll into a Swiss roll and eat as is or cut into little rings. For a more grown-up version serve crêpes with Chocolate Sauce (see page 599) and toasted hazelnuts.

Master Recipe
Apple Crumble

Serves 6–8

Crumbles are the ultimate comfort food. Vary the fruit according to the season; use plums or apricots in autumn. In summer you can use soft fruit, such as peaches and raspberries, in which case there is no need to pre-cook the fruit base.

700g (1½lb) Bramley Seedling cooking apples
35–50g (1½–2oz) sugar
1–2 tablespoons water

Crumble
50g (2oz) butter
110g (4oz) white flour, preferably unbleached
50g (2oz) caster sugar

1.2 litre (2 pint) capacity pie dish

Stew the apples gently with the sugar and water in a covered casserole or stainless-steel saucepan until about half cooked. Taste and add more sugar if necessary. Turn into a pie dish. Allow to cool slightly while you make the crumble. Preheat the oven to 180°C/350°F/gas 4.

Rub the butter into the flour just until the mixture resembles coarse breadcrumbs, then add the sugar. Sprinkle this mixture over the apple in the pie dish. Bake for 30–45 minutes or until the topping is cooked and golden. Serve with whipped cream and soft brown sugar, or try stirring a little Amaretto into your cream.

Variations

Blackberry and Apple Crumble

Substitute three-quarters apple to one-quarter fresh or frozen blackberries for apples.

Rhubarb Crumble

Use the same weight of rhubarb as in the apple recipe, and stew with just sugar – no water – until half cooked and proceed.

Rhubarb and Strawberry Crumble

Stew two-thirds rhubarb with the sugar, stir in one-third strawberries, and proceed.

Gooseberry and Elderflower Crumble

Stew green gooseberries with white sugar and 2 elderflower heads tied in muslin. After stewing, remove elderflowers and proceed as above.

Variations on the Crumble

Add 25g (1oz) oatflakes, sliced hazelnuts or nibbed almonds to the crumble. A teaspoon of ground cinnamon or mixed spice is also a delicious addition.

Lemon Meringue Pie

Serves 6

110g (4oz) white flour
pinch of salt
50–75g (2–3oz) butter
1 organic egg yolk (keep white aside for meringue) about 2 tablespoons cold water

Lemon Curd (see page 511)

Meringue
2 organic egg whites
110g (4oz) caster sugar

18cm (7in) round tin with a pop-up base

Preheat the oven to 180°C/350°F/gas 4.

First make the pastry. Sieve the flour with the salt, cut the butter into cubes and rub into the flour with the fingertips. Keep everything as cool as possible; if the fat is allowed to melt the finished pastry may be tough. When the mixture looks like coarse breadcrumbs, stop. Whisk the egg yolk and add the water. Take a fork or knife, (whichever you feel most comfortable with) and add just enough liquid to bring the pastry together, then discard the fork and collect it into a ball with your hands; this way you can judge more accurately if you need a few more drops of liquid. Cover with clingfilm and chill for half an hour if possible.

Line the flan ring and chill again for 15–20 minutes, line with paper and fill with dried beans. Bake blind for 25 minutes. The pastry case must be almost fully cooked. Remove the paper and beans, paint with a little lightly beaten egg white and put back into the oven for about 5 minutes.

Meanwhile make the Lemon Curd and pour into the pastry case. Next make the Meringue – whisk the egg whites in a perfectly clean dry bowl, until they begin to get fluffy, then add the half the sugar and continue to whisk until they form stiff peaks, fold in the remaining sugar and either pipe or spread it over the lemon mixture with a spoon. Turn the oven down to 130°C/250°F/gas ½ and bake for about 1 hour until the mixture is crisp on the outside. Alternatively set the oven to 200°C/400°F/gas 6 and cook for just 7 minutes. This will result in a meringue which is slighly coloured, crisp on the outside and soft underneath – another delicious option. Serve warm or cold.

Variation
Mile High Lemon Meringue Pie
Double the quantity of meringue and pile into a cone or pyramid on top of the tart.

Peach and Raspberry Crisp

Serves 8

A few summers ago I spent some time at Zingermann's Deli in Ann Arbor in Michigan. Ari Weinzweig sent me a recipe for this delicious pud.

900g (2lb) peaches
350g (¾lb) raspberries
1 tablespoon cornflour

Crisp
110g (4oz) plain white flour
225g (8oz) brown sugar
350g (¾lb) oat flakes
¼ teaspoon freshly ground nutmeg
¼ teaspoon ground cinnamon
110g (4oz) butter, melted
lasagne-type dish, 25 x 24cm (10 x 9in)

Preheat the oven to 180°C/350°F/gas 4.

Put all the dry ingredients for the Crisp into a bowl, add the melted butter and mix until crumbly. Slice the fruit into a bowl. Sprinkle with cornflour and mix well. If the fruit is unusually tart you may need a little sugar. Top with an even layer of crumble – a generous 1cm (½in) thick. I use about 450g (1lb) and keep the rest for another time or to use with another fruit.

Bake in the oven for 30–40 minutes or until the topping is crisp and fruit tender. The juices should bubble up around the edges. Serve with softly whipped cream.

Pastry Making

Pastry making is a magical process. You start off with more or less the same ingredients – flour, fat and something to bind it with – and what you end up with depends entirely on how you treat these ingredients. Most pastry falls into the following categories:

Shortcrust
Can be savoury or sweet – **sweet shortcrust** simply has sugar added. **Rich sweet shortcrust** pastry is made with extra butter. Our '**break all the rules**' pastry (see Cullohill Apple Pie, page 416) is made by the creaming method so people who are convinced they suffer from hot hands don't have to worry about rubbing in the butter. Alison Henderson's pastry (Cherry Pie, page 416) is even easier as it's just whizzed together in a food processor.

Pâte Sucrée or French Flan Pastry
In this recipe, egg yolks are used as opposed to whole eggs – this produces a different textured pastry. Pâte Brisée is the savoury version.

Puff Pastry
Has many layers – supposedly 729! It is used for vol-au-vents and feuilletée. See page 456 for recipe.

Flaky Pastry
This is more economical to make than puff pastry because it uses a quarter butter to flour rather than equal quantities. It is suitable for all dishes both sweet and savoury where you might use puff pastry, except perhaps vol au vents or feuilletée.

Filo Pastry
A paper-thin pastry that is used for both sweet and savoury dishes. A similar pastry is used for Strudel (see page 420).

Choux Pastry
Used for éclairs and profiteroles – see page 459 for recipe.

Sweet Shortcrust Pastry

For rich sweet shortcrust, simply increase the quantity of butter to 150–175g (5–6oz).

225g (8oz) plain white flour, spelt or sifted wholemeal flour
1–2 tablespoons caster or icing sugar
110g (4oz) butter
water or beaten organic egg mixed with a little water

Keep everything as cool as possible; if the fat is allowed to melt, the finished pastry may be tough. Sift the flour into a large bowl with the sugar. Cut the butter into cubes and rub into the flour with your fingertips. When the mixture looks like coarse breadcrumbs, stop. Take a fork or a knife – whichever you feel most comfortable with – and add just enough water or egg with a little water to bring the pastry together, then discard the fork and collect the pastry into a ball with your hands. This way you can judge more accurately whether you need a few more drops of liquid. Although rather damp pastry is easier to handle and roll out, the resulting crust can be tough and may well shrink out of shape as the water evaporates in the oven. Drier and slightly more difficult-to-handle pastry will give a crisper, 'shorter' crust.

Cover the pastry with clingfilm and leave to rest in the fridge for a minimum of 15 minutes. This will make the pastry much less elastic and easier to roll.

Note: Pastry made with:
110g (4oz) flour will line a 15–18cm (6–7in) flan ring
175g (6oz) flour will line a 23cm (9in) flan ring
225g (8oz) flour will line a 25.5–30.5cm (10–11in) flan ring

See page 112 for more tips on how to line a flan ring.

Pâte Sucrée or French Flan Pastry

The French make pastry directly on the worktop. For savoury tarts, pâte brisée is used which is exactly the same recipe but without the sugar.

110g (4oz) plain white flour
tiny pinch of salt
50g (2oz) butter, unsalted
50g (2oz) caster sugar
2 organic egg yolks
2 drops of pure vanilla extract

Sieve the flour with a pinch of salt on to the table or marble slab, make a well in the centre, and in this place the other ingredients. Using the fingertips of one hand, work the butter, sugar and yolks together until mixed; then quickly draw in the flour. Toss up between your fingers until it becomes quite sandy. Gather up into a ball then work with the heel of the hand. Gather up and work again and then repeat once more (3 times in all). Wrap in a polythene bag or paper and chill for at least 1 hour before using.

Preheat the oven to 190°C/375°F/gas 5.

Bake the pastry until it is a pale biscuit colour. Be careful not to overcook because if this pastry gets too brown it will be bitter, hard and unappetising.

Flaky Pastry

For this pastry, the method must be carefully followed and the pastry rolled correctly. Butter is the most suitable fat. All ingredients should be chilled. Flaky pastry can be kept wrapped in the fridge for 1–2 days or it can be frozen. This pastry gives a very good flaky result, and is suitable for all dishes both sweet and savoury where you might use puff pastry, except perhaps vol-au-vents or feuilletée.

350g (12oz) strong white flour
pinch of salt
225g (8oz) butter
125ml (4fl oz) cold water, approx. (if using strong flour more water may be needed)

Sieve the flour and salt into a bowl. Divide the butter into four equal parts. Rub one part of this into the flour and mix to a firm dough with the cold water. Cover with clingfilm and allow to rest for 15–20 minutes in the fridge.

Roll out into a strip about 20.5cm (8in) wide, and dot tiny pieces of a second portion of the butter on two-thirds of the pastry. Fold in three, being careful to align all the edges. Turn the pastry 90 degrees (so that it looks like a book) and roll out, pressing it away from you. Fold in three again, cover and leave to rest again for 15–20 minutes in the fridge.

Roll out as before, dot tiny pieces of the third portion of butter on two-thirds of the strip, again fold in three carefully. Roll, fold in three, and rest as before. Then add the final portion of butter, roll out once more, fold in three again. If the pastry still appears streaky roll it one more time. Cover and leave to rest in the refrigerator for at least 20–30 minutes.

Wrap in clingfilm or greaseproof paper if not using immediately.

Master Recipe
Frangipane and Pear Tart

Serves 8–10

Also known as Normandy Tart, this is certainly one of the most impressive of the French tarts. It is wonderful served warm but is also very good cold and it keeps for several days. Splash in a little kirsch if you are using pears and calvados if you are using dessert apples.

Sweet Shortcrust Pastry (see page 413)

Frangipane
100g (3¹/₂oz) butter
100g (3¹/₂oz) caster sugar
1 organic egg, beaten
1 organic egg yolk
110g (4oz) almonds ground (for best results peel whole, blanch and grind yourself)
25g (1oz) flour
2 tablespoons kirsch if using pears or calvados if using apples

Poached Pears
6 pears
225g (8oz) sugar
600ml (1 pint) water
a couple of strips of lemon peel and juice of ¹/₂ lemon

Apricot Glaze
175g (6oz) apricot jam
juice of ¹/₄ lemon
a little water

23cm (9in) diameter flan ring or tart tin with a removable base

Preheat the oven to 180°C/350°F/gas 4.

Make the pastry. Roll it out, line the tart tin with it and prick lightly with a fork. Flute the edges and chill until firm. Bake blind for 15–20 minutes.

Next make the frangipane. Cream the butter, gradually beat in the sugar and continue beating until the mixture is light and soft. Gradually add the egg and egg yolk, beating well after each addition. Stir in the ground almonds and flour and then add the kirsch or calvados. Pour the frangipane into the pastry case spreading it evenly.

Next prepare the pears. Bring the sugar and water to the boil with the strips of lemon peel in a non-reactive saucepan. Meanwhile peel the pears thinly, cut in half and core carefully with a melon baller or a teaspoon, retaining the good shape. Put the pear halves into the syrup, cut-side uppermost, add the lemon juice, cover with a paper lid and the lid of the saucepan. Bring to the boil and simmer until the pears are just soft - the tip of a knife or skewer should go through without resistance. Drain the pears well and when they are cold cut them lengthwise into very thin slices. Arrange the slices around the tart on the frangipane, pointed ends towards the centre. Arrange a final half pear in the centre.

Turn the oven up to 200°C/400°F/gas 6. Bake the tart for 10–15 minutes until the pastry is beginning to brown. Turn the oven down to 180°C/350°F/gas 4 and continue cooking for a further 15–20 minutes or until the fruit is tender and the frangipane is set in the centre and nicely golden.

Meanwhile make the apricot glaze. (Apricot glaze is invaluable to have made up in your fridge - it would always be at hand in a pastry kitchen and is used to glaze tarts which contain green, orange or white fruit, e.g. kiwi, grapes, greengages, peaches, oranges, apples or pears. It will turn you into a professional at the flick of a pastry brush!). In a small saucepan (not aluminium), melt jam with the lemon juice and enough water to make a glaze that can be poured. Push the hot jam through a nylon sieve and store in an airtight jar. Reheat the glaze to melt it before using. The quantities given above make a generous 300ml (10fl oz) glaze.

When the tart is fully cooked, paint generously with apricot glaze, remove from the tin and serve warm or cold with a bowl of softly whipped cream.

Note: Poached pears are also delicious on their own or with homemade vanilla ice-cream and chocolate sauce – in which case you have Poires Belles Helene, one of Escoffier's great classics).

Variations
Frangipane and Cherry Tart
Substitute 450g (1lb) stoned cherries for pears. Once the frangipane has set in the centre stud the cherries into the tart. Omit the apricot glaze.

Frangipane and Apricot Tart
Substitute ripe apricots for pears in the above recipe. Arrange apricot halves on the frangipane, cut side uppermost, and pop a peeled almond in the centre of each apricot. Brush the tart generously with

apricot glaze when cooked. Ripe peaches or nectarines may be used in the same way.

Seville Orange Tart

Spread a thick layer of Seville orange marmalade in the base of the tart shell. Substitute Grand Marnier for Kirsh in the frangipane. Bake in the usual way and glaze with marmalade minus the bits. Serve with a blob of crème fraiche.

Blueberry or Raspberry Tart

Press fresh blueberries or raspberries or a mixture of berries into the frangipane before baking in the usual way. Glaze with apricot glaze.

Lattice Bakewell Tart

Make a little extra pastry. Line the tin and spread with a layer of homemade Raspberry Jam (see page 504) and then pour in the frangipane. Omit the pears and substitute raspberry jam for apricot jam in the recipe for apricot glaze. Decorate the top with a lattice of pastry. Dredge with icing sugar before serving.

Medjool Date Tart

Barry McNamara, a student on the 12 Week course did this delicious variation on the basic Normandy Pear Tart. He substituted 1 teaspoon Orange Blossom water for Kirsch in the frangipane and reduced the sugar to 50g (2oz). He used 12 stoned and halved Medjool dates and arranged cut side down in the frangipane.

Pear and Mincemeat Frangipane Tart

Spread 3 tablespoons of Ballymaloe Mincemeat (see page 511) over the pastry base and top with the poached pear slices. Spread the frangipane mixture evenly over the pear and bake.

Rory O'Connell's Date Tart

Serves 8–10

Make this – it's divine!

Pastry
200g (7oz) butter, chopped
25g (1oz) caster sugar
1 tablespoon milk
275g (10oz) white flour

Filling
15 fresh Medjool dates, halved and pitted
7 organic egg yolks
100g (3½oz) caster sugar
about 700ml (1¼ pints) single cream
½ vanilla pod, split lengthwise

23cm (9in) flan tin with a loose base

For the pastry, combine the butter, sugar, and milk in a food processor and process until butter is in small pieces. Add flour and process until mixture just comes together. Gently knead pastry on a lightly floured surface to form a smooth ball. Cover with clingfilm and refrigerate for 2 hours.

Preheat the oven to 200°C/400°F/gas 6.

Roll out the pastry on a lightly floured surface and line the flan tin. Cover and refrigerate for 30 minutes.

Place the tart shell on an oven tray, lined with baking paper and filled with dried beans or rice and bake for 10 minutes. Remove paper and beans and bake for a further 10 minutes, or until golden.

Remove from the oven and turn down the heat to 180°C/350°F/gas 4.

Place the dates on the pastry in two circles. Cream the egg yolks and sugar until light and fluffy, then stir in the cream and seeds from the vanilla pod. Pour this cream mixture into the tart shell to cover the dates, then bake for about 30 minutes or until just set. Cool to room temperature before serving.

Sally Clarke's Hazelnut and Chocolate Tart

Serves 8

Sweet Shortcrust Pastry (see page 413)

Filling
200g (7oz) hazelnuts
75g (3oz) best-quality dark chocolate
75g (3oz) butter, unsalted
150g (5oz) caster sugar
2 organic eggs, beaten
1 teaspoon orange zest
25g (1oz) plain white flour
40ml (1½fl oz) freshly squeezed orange juice

1 x 23cm (9in) flan ring or tart tin

Preheat the oven to 180°C/350°F/gas 4.

First make the pastry. Roll it out, line the tin with it and prick lightly with a fork. Cover using greaseproof or silicone paper and weigh down with baking beans. Bake blind for 15–20 minutes.

Put the hazelnuts on a baking sheet and bake until the skins start to flake away. Rub off the skins with a cloth and chop the hazelnuts roughly.

Chop the chocolate into small pieces.

Cream the butter with the caster sugar until light and fluffy. Add 1 egg. Lightly beat in the orange zest, flour, orange juice, hazelnuts and chocolate, adding the remaining egg last.

Spread this mixture in the cooked pastry case and bake for 20–25 minutes. Serve when cool. It should be slightly soft in the centre.

Cullohill Apple Pie

Serves 8–12

This tart was a favourite of patrons of my family's pub, the Sportsmans Inn in Cullohill, Co. Laois. The 'break all the rules' pastry can be used for a variety of fruit tarts. It can be difficult to handle when first made and benefits from being chilled for at least an hour, or preferably overnight.

225g (8oz) butter
50g (2oz) caster sugar
2 organic eggs
350g (12oz) white flour, preferably unbleached

700g (1½lb) Bramley Seedling cooking apples
150g (5oz) sugar
2–3 cloves

egg wash, made with an organic egg
caster sugar, for sprinkling

1 rectangular tin 18 x 32 x 2.5cm (7 x 12 x 1in)
  or 1 round tin 23cm (9in) in diameter

First make the pastry. Cream the butter and sugar together by hand or in a food mixer. Add the eggs and beat for several minutes. Reduce the speed and mix in the flour. Turn out onto a piece of floured greaseproof paper, flatten into a round, wrap and chill overnight if possible.

Preheat the oven to 180°C/350°F/gas 4.

Roll the pastry to a thickness of about 3mm (⅛in). Use a little less than two thirds of the pastry to line the tin. Peel and dice the apples and place into the tin. Sprinkle with sugar and add the cloves. Cover with a lid of pastry, seal the edges and use the leftover pastry to decorate the top. Brush with egg wash and bake in the oven for 45–60 minutes until the apples are tender. When cooked, cut into squares, sprinkle lightly with caster sugar and serve with whipped cream and Barbados sugar.

Ivan Ward's Apple and Ginger Pie

Proceed as for the Master Recipe, omitting the cloves and adding 1–2 tablespoons freshly grated ginger to the apples.

Californian Three-stone Pie

1kg (2¼lb) apricots, peaches and nectarines, mixed
225g (8oz) sugar
3 tablespoons cornflour or flour

Use the above for the filling: stone and slice the fruit into a bowl, sprinkle with sugar and flour and toss well. Proceed as in the Master Recipe.

Alison Henderson's Cherry Pie

Serves 6

225g (8oz) flour
1 teaspoon baking powder
75g (3oz) caster sugar
grated zest of ½ a lemon (scrub the lemon before you grate it)
pinch of salt
110g (4oz) unsalted butter, chilled and diced
1 organic egg plus 1 organic egg yolk
700g (1½lb) stoned cherries
sugar, to taste

Put the flour, baking powder, caster sugar, lemon zest, salt and butter into the food processor. Whizz for a few seconds, add the egg and egg yolk and stop processing as soon as the mixture comes together: it will be a softish dough. Scrape out of the bowl, divide in two, and flatten out each piece on large flat plates and chill for several hours.

Meanwhile stone the cherries and preheat the oven to 180°C/350°F/gas 4. Roll one piece of pastry into a 25cm (10in) round and put on a greased baking tray. Pile the cherries onto the pastry, keeping a rim of about 2.5cm (1in) around the edge, sprinkle with sugar.

Roll out the other piece of pastry into a 24cm (9in) round, brush the underside of the 24cm (9in) round with water or lightly beaten egg white and pop on the top. Fold the bottom edge over and seal well with your fingers or a fork.

Brush the surface with beaten egg white and sprinkle with sugar. Bake in the oven for 10 minutes and then reduce the temperature to 170°C/325°F/gas 3 for a further 40 minutes or until the tart is golden and cooked through. Serve warm or cold with a bowl of softly whipped cream and soft brown sugar.

Tuscan Plum Tart

Serves 10–12

We ate this gorgeous tart in a little restaurant outside Chianti. It's a real wow for an autumn party and so easy to make. You need a pan that can be used in the oven as well as on the stove.

275g (10oz) sugar
150ml (5fl oz) water
900g (2lb) plums
150g (5oz) soft butter
175g (6oz) sugar
200g (7oz) self-raising flour
3 organic eggs

1 x 25cm (10in) sauté pan or a cast-iron frying pan

Preheat the oven to 170°C/325°F/gas 3.

Put the sugar and water into the pan. Stir over a medium heat until the sugar dissolves, then cook without stirring until the sugar caramelises to a rich golden brown.

Meanwhile halve and stone the plums. Arrange cut side down in a single layer over the caramel.

Put the butter, sugar and flour into a food processor. Whizz for a second or two, add the eggs and stop as soon as the mixture comes together. Spoon over the plums, spread gently in as even a layer as possible.

Bake in the oven for about 1 hour. The centre should be firm to the touch and the edges slightly shrunk from the sides of the pan. Allow to rest in the pan for 4–5 minutes before turning out. Serve with crème fraîche or softly whipped cream.

Caramelised Banana Tart

Serves 6–8

Rich and sticky, another delicious pudding for chilly days. This one was inspired, as on many occasions, by a recipe from Sue Lawrence.

Base
75g (3oz) butter
45g (1½oz) soft brown (Barbados) sugar
45g (1½oz) caster sugar
3–4 bananas
a little freshly squeezed lemon juice

Topping
1 ripe banana, mashed
2 tablespoons crème fraîche
1 teaspoon pure vanilla extract
150g (5oz) caster sugar
75g (3oz) butter
2 organic eggs
175g (6oz) self-raising flour

1 flameproof and ovenproof sauté pan 25 x 5cm (10 x 2in) deep or a similar heavyweight tin

Preheat the oven to 180°C/350°F/gas 4.

Melt the butter in the sauté pan or heavy tin, add the sugars and stir well to dissolve. Slice the bananas and arrange in concentric circles over the base. Squeeze a little freshly squeezed lemon juice over the bananas.

Next make the topping. Mash the banana, and add the crème fraîche and vanilla extract. Cream the butter, add the caster sugar and beat until light and fluffy. Add the eggs one at a time and continue to beat well. Gently fold in the flour and banana mixture alternately. Spread the topping evenly and carefully over the bananas.

Bake in the oven for 45–50 minutes or until golden brown and fully cooked.

Allow to rest in the dish for 5–10 minutes before turning out onto a warm serving plate so that the bananas are uppermost. Be careful of the hot juices.

Serve warm with softly whipped cream or crème fraîche.

LEFT Caramelised Banana Tart

Tarte Tatin

Serves 6–8

The ultimate French apple tart. The Tatin sisters ran a restaurant at Lamotte-Beuvron in Sologne at the beginning of the last century. This tart, which some say they created accidentally, is a triumph – soft, buttery caramelised apples (or you can use pears) with crusty golden pastry underneath. It is unquestionably my favourite French tart! One can buy a special copper tatin especially for this tart.

1.25kg (2³/₄lb) Golden Delicious, Cox's Orange
   Pippin or Bramley Seedling cooking apples
175g (6oz) Puff Pastry (see page 456), Pâte
   Sucrée (see page 413) or Sweet Shortcrust
   Pastry (see page 413)
110g (4oz)) unsalted butter
225g (8oz) caster sugar

a heavy 20cm (8in) tatin mould or copper or
   stainless-steel sauté pan with low sides

Preheat the oven to 220°C/425°F/gas 7 for puff pastry or to 180°C/350°F/gas 4 for shortcrust.

Roll out the pastry into a round slightly larger than the mould or pan. Prick it all over with a fork and chill until needed.

Peel, halve and core the apples. Melt the butter in the pan, add the sugar and cook over a medium heat until it turns golden – the colour of fudge. Put the apple halves in upright peeled side down, packing them in very tightly side by side. Replace the pan on a low heat and cook until the sugar and juice are a dark caramel colour. Hold your nerve otherwise it will be too pale. Put into the oven for about 15 minutes.

Cover the apples with the pastry and tuck in the edges. Put the pan back into the oven until the pastry is cooked and the apples are soft – about 25–30 minutes. For puff pastry reduce the temperature to 200°C/400°F/gas 6 after 10 minutes.

Take out of the oven and rest for 5–10 minutes or longer if you like. Put a plate over the top of the saucepan and flip the tart on to a serving plate. (Watch out, this is a rather tricky operation because the hot caramel and juice can ooze out – do it quickly and confidently). Reshape the tart if necessary and serve warm with softly whipped cream.

Tarte Française

Serves 4

The secret of a successful Tarte Française is tightly packed, neatly overlapping rows of fruit – be generous with both fruit and glaze. The jam is the only sweetener in the dish so do be liberal. In the autumn a tart can be made with a combination of dark fruits, which looks spectacular – blueberries, raspberries, figs, damsons, dark plums, redcurrants, blackcurrants and blackberries. Use redcurrant jelly to glaze red and black fruits.

175g (6oz) Flaky Pastry (see page 413) or
   Puff Pastry (see page 456)
egg wash, made with an organic egg

Filling
A mixture of fruit:
2 oranges
75g (3oz) black grapes
2 bananas
1 kiwi fruit
1 red plum

Apricot Glaze (see page 509)

Preheat the oven to 220°C/425°F/gas 6.

Roll out the pastry into a rectangle about 25 x 20cm (10 x 8in). It should be about 3mm (¹/₈in) thick. Prick lightly all over. Cut a border 2cm (³/₄in) wide from the remaining pastry, to exactly fit the rectangle. Brush the outside edge of the rectangle with a little beaten egg and put the border on top.

Flour the blade of a knife and use this to 'knock up' the sides of the pastry: what you are doing is slightly separating the leaves of the pastry horizontally so that the edges will flake during cooking.

Mark a pattern on the border of the pastry case with the back of the knife. Try not to cut through the pastry.

Brush the pastry border carefully with egg wash. Don't let it drip over the side or it will prevent the pastry from rising. Bake in the oven for 15–20 minutes or until golden brown then reduce the temperature to 180°C/350°F/gas 4. Leave to cool on a wire rack.

Segment the oranges, cut the grapes in half and remove the pips. Peel and slice the bananas. Stone the plums and cut into small neat segments. Peel and slice the kiwi fruit.

Arrange the fruit in contrasting rows on the pastry as neatly as possible. Brush generously with apricot glaze. Serve with a bowl of softly whipped cream.

Open French Apple Tart

Serves 8–12 (Makes about 12 tartlets or two open tarts 20cm/8in in diameter)

225g (8oz) Flaky Pastry (see page 413) or Puff
   Pastry trimmings
3 or 4 cooking apples, e.g. Bramley or Grenadier
2 tablespoons sugar, approx.
1 dessertspoon butter

Preheat the oven to 220°C/425°F/gas 7.

Line pie plates or patty tins with pastry rolled thinly, about as thick as a coin for tartlets, slightly thicker for tarts. Thinly peel and quarter the apples, then cut into slices 3mm (¹/₈in) thick, keeping a good even shape. Arrange them on the pastry in overlapping slices. Sprinkle liberally with sugar and dot with pieces of butter. Bake for about 15 minutes. The juice of the apples will caramelise the sugar.

Remove from the tins immediately, otherwise they will stick fast as the caramel cools. Serve with softly whipped cream.

Ballymaloe Flaky Fruit Tart

Virtually every night at Ballymaloe House there's a warm fruit tart on the sweet trolley. You can use the Flaky Pastry or the pastry used for our Cullohill Apple Pie to make tarts with whatever fruits are in season: some of our favourites are:

Rhubarb and Strawberry
Green Gooseberry and Elderflower
Apple and Mincemeat
Apple and Raspberry
Apple and Loganberry
Apple and Mixed Spice
Peach and Raspberry
Plum
Damson
Apricot

Mary Risley's Rustic Peach Tart with Summer Berries

Serves 6–8

A freeform rustic tart.

Pastry
225g (8oz) plain white flour
1 tablespoon caster sugar
110g (4oz) butter, cut into 1cm (½in) dice
cold water or beaten organic egg to mix

Filling
75–110g (3–4oz) caster sugar
2 generous tablespoons cornflour
700–900g (1½–2lb) ripe peaches or nectarines, peeled and sliced 1cm (½in) thick
110g (4oz) fresh blueberries
110g (4oz) fresh raspberries or loganberries
1 tablespoon, approx, caster sugar for sprinkling

1 x 23cm (9in) pie plate or tart tin

First make the pastry. Sieve the flour into a bowl and add the sugar. Rub in the cold butter. When the mixture resembles coarse breadcrumbs, add just enough water or beaten egg to bind. Knead lightly to bring the mixture together. Cover with wax or silicone paper and rest in the fridge for at least 20 minutes.

Roll out the pastry on a lightly floured surface into a 35cm (14in) round. Line the pie plate or tart tin base with it but do not trim it. Put the plate over a bowl to allow the edge to hang down, chill for 30 minutes in the fridge.

Just before baking preheat the oven to 230°C/450°F/gas 8 and prepare the filling. Mix the sugar with the cornflour. Toss in the peaches or nectarines. Allow to sit for 5 minutes and no more, tossing occasionally. Stir the blueberries and raspberries gently into the peaches.

Pour the fruit and the juices onto the chilled pastry and distribute it evenly. Fold the overhanging edge to cover the outer portion of the filling, leaving a 12.5cm (5in) opening of exposed fruit in the centre of the pie. Brush the pastry with water, and sprinkle with a little sugar.

Bake in the oven for 20 minutes. Reduce the temperature to 180°C/350°F/gas 4 and bake for a further 30–35 minutes. Serve warm or cold with softly whipped cream.

Master Recipe
Winter Apple Pie

Serves 8–10

This pie uses a scone dough which cooks on top and is then inverted for serving.

1.1kg (2½lb) apples
225–250g (8–9oz) granulated sugar
1–1½ teaspoons ground cinnamon or mixed spice

Scone Dough
325g (11oz) flour
20g (¾oz) caster sugar
1 heaped teaspoon baking powder
pinch of salt
50g (2oz) butter
1 organic egg
150–180ml (5-6fl oz) full cream milk, approx.
egg wash, made with an organic egg

23 x 5cm (9 x 2in) round tin (we use a heavy stainless-steel sauté pan which works very well, if you don't have a suitable pan par-cook the apples slightly first)

Preheat the oven to 230°C/450°F/gas 8.

Peel and core the apples and cut into chunks. Put into the base of a tin or sauté pan, and sprinkle with the sugar and cinnamon or mixed spice. Put the sauté pan onto a low heat while you make the scone dough.

Sieve all the dry ingredients into a bowl. Cut the butter into cubes and rub into the flour until the mixture resembles coarse breadcrumbs. Whisk the egg with the milk. Make a well in the centre of the dry ingredients, pour in the liquid all at once and mix to a soft dough. Turn out onto a floured board and roll into a 23cm (9in) round about 2.5cm (1in) thick. Place this on top of the apple and tuck in the edges neatly. Brush with a little egg wash. Bake in the oven for 15 minutes, then reduce the temperature to 180°C/350°F/gas 4 for a further 30 minutes until the top is crusty and golden and the apples soft and juicy.

Remove from the oven and allow to sit for a few minutes. Put a warm plate over the top of the sauté pan, turn upside down onto the plate but be careful of the hot juices. Serve warm with soft brown sugar and cream.

Variations
Apple and Mincemeat Pie
Omit the cinnamon or mixed spice and put a layer of mincemeat – about 225g (8oz), see page 515 – on top of the apples.

Rhubarb Pie
Follow the Master Recipe, substituting rhubarb (and sugar to taste), for the apples.

Plum Pie
Substitute plums (and sugar to taste), for the apples.

Elsa Schiller's Apple Strudel

Makes 2 strudels – serves 12–14

Strudel can be served cold but the pastry softens, so in my opinion apple strudel is best served fresh from the oven. The pastry for strudel is very similar to filo.

Pastry
350g (12oz) flour
pinch of salt
1 organic egg
½ teaspoon oil e.g. sunflower or groundnut
½ teaspoon vinegar
150ml (5fl oz) lukewarm water

Filling
900g (2lb) cooking apples (Bramley Seedling or
    Grenadier)
110g (4oz) sultanas
75–110g (3–4oz) caster sugar
1 teaspoon ground cinnamon
grated rind of 2 lemons or 1 orange and
    1 lemon
50g (2oz) chopped walnuts
50g (2oz) ground almonds
50g (2oz) butter, for brushing strudel

Sieve the flour and salt into a bowl, add the egg, oil and vinegar and enough warm water to mix to a smooth pliable dough. Knead for 8–10 minutes then cover and rest for 30 minutes in a warm kitchen.

Preheat the oven to 230°C/450°F/gas 8.

Meanwhile, prepare the filling. Peel the apples, cut into quarters, remove cores and cut into thin slices. Mix with the sultanas, caster sugar, cinnamon, lemon and orange peel and chopped walnuts.

Divide the pastry into two, keep one piece covered. Spread a tablecloth over the work surface. Flour it well. Roll out one half of the pastry as thinly as possible with a rolling pin, then stretch into an oblong shape as gently as possible with floured hands. Do not hurry – do this gradually, and eventually you should be able to see your hand through the pastry. Try not to have any holes if possible. When the rectangle of pastry is as near as possible to 90 x 60cm (3 x 2ft) cut off the thick edges and let the pastry harden slightly for about 15 minutes. Brush with melted butter, sprinkle with half the ground almonds, lay half the filling over two-thirds of the pastry. Roll up the narrow end so that the outside of the strudel is wrapped in several layers of pastry. Pinch the ends of the roll together and cut off any excess pastry.

Make the second strudel in the same way. Transfer the strudels to a buttered baking sheet and shape into a crescent. Brush with melted butter and cook for 10 minutes in the hot oven. Reduce the temperature to 200°C/400°F/gas 6 and cook for a further 20 minutes. Brush with melted butter 3 or 4 times during cooking.

When the strudels are cooked dust with icing sugar and serve immediately with a bowl of softly whipped cream and soft brown sugar.

Steamed Puddings

Suet and steamed puddings were once great winter favourites. My mother made 3 or 4 different kinds which we adored as children. She got the recipes from her mother, who cooked the same for her. Make sure you use a large enough pan, and put an inverted saucer on the bottom of it to keep the pudding basin out of direct contact with the base. Cover the basin with a double layer of greaseproof paper or foil and make a pleat or gusset in the paper across the centre of the basin – this allows for expansion. Tie down firmly with string. The pan must have a tight-fitting lid, and you need to check during the cooking time to make sure the water doesn't boil dry.

Canary Pudding

Serves 4

110g (4oz) butter
110g (4oz) caster sugar
2 organic eggs
a few drops pure vanilla extract
175g (6oz) flour
½ tablespoon baking powder
3–4 tablespoons raspberry jam

12.5cm (5in) pudding basin

Have the butter at room temperature. Put it with the sugar into a bowl and beat until white and creamy using a wooden spoon or electric mixer.

Beat the eggs with the vanilla extract and add gradually to the creamed butter and sugar. Beat well. If preferred the eggs may be broken and beaten into the mixture one at a time. A little sieved flour may be added between each addition of egg if liked.

Fold in the remainder of the flour using a metal spoon, adding a little water if necessary to make a dropping consistency. Add the baking powder mixed with the last addition of flour.

Grease the pudding basin and spread the raspberry jam over the sides and bottom. Put the mixture on top of the jam, and cover with a double layer of greaseproof paper or foil, tied tightly with string, and steam for about 1½ hours. Turn to a hot dish and serve with Raspberry Jam Sauce.

Raspberry Jam Sauce

3 tablespoons raspberry jam
rind and juice of ½ organic, unwaxed lemon
75g (3oz) sugar
150ml (5fl oz) water

Put the sugar and water in a saucepan and heat slowly until the sugar has dissolved. Then boil rapidly until the syrup feels tacky between finger and thumb. Add the rind and juice of the lemon. Add the jam, stir until smooth, then sieve to remove the pips.

Variation
Kumquat Pudding

Follow the method for Canary Pudding (see opposite), substituting Kumquat Marmalade (see page 510) for the Raspberry Jam. Serve with Kumquat Compote (see page 391).

Steamed Valencia Pudding
Serves 4

50g (2oz) sultanas or 75g (3oz) stoned Lexia or Muscatel raisins
110g (4oz) butter
grated rind of 1 organic, unwaxed lemon
110g (4oz) caster sugar
2 organic eggs
110g (4oz) self-raising flour
pinch of salt
about 75ml (3fl oz) milk

12cm (5in) pudding basin, buttered

Line the sides of the basin with the sultanas or split raisins (split side against the basin), arranging them in a pattern if you like. Cream the butter and when soft add the lemon rind and sugar. Beat until light, pale and fluffy. Gradually add the eggs, beating well between each addition.

Fold in the sifted flour with salt, and add enough milk to make the mixture just loose enough to drop from a spoon. Turn into the pudding basin. Cover with a double layer of pleated greaseproof paper or foil and tie down. Steam for 2 hours. Turn out and serve. Serve with Homemade Custard (Crème Anglaise), see page 598.

RIGHT: Elsa Schiller's Apple Strudel

Crawford Café Rice Pudding

Serves 4–6

Few restaurants serve rice pudding nowadays. This is the version served both at Ballymaloe and the Crawford Café, part of the Crawford Art Gallery in Cork, on chilly autumn and winter days. I promised a fan of the Crawford Café that I would include the recipe in this book. As ever, timing is everything. If it has to sit in the oven for ages before being served it will be dry and dull and you'll wonder why you bothered.

50g (2oz) pearl rice (short-grain rice)
25g (1oz) sugar
knob of butter
600ml (1 pint) full fat milk

1 x 600ml (1 pint) capacity pie dish

Preheat the oven to 180°C/350°F/gas 4.

Put the rice, sugar and a little knob of butter into a pie dish. Bring the milk to the boil and pour over. Bake for 1–1½ hours. It's quite tricky to catch it at exactly the right stage. The skin that forms on top should be golden, the rice underneath cooked through and have soaked up the milk but still be soft and creamy underneath. Time it, so that it's ready just in time for dessert. Serve with cream and soft brown sugar.

Sticky Rice with Mango

Serves 4–6

In rice-growing countries it is not considered strange to eat rice for a main course and then again for dessert. Thais serve this dish as a dessert and also as a sweet snack at any time of the day.

400g (14oz) of white glutinous rice
285ml (10fl oz) coconut milk
pinch of salt
2 tablespoons caster sugar
300ml (10fl oz) water

4 small or 2 large ripe mangoes
lime juice and sugar

Decoration
mint sprigs

Soak the rice in cold water for an hour, then drain. Put the rice into a saucepan with the coconut milk, salt and sugar and water. Stir and bring to the boil, simmer gently, uncovered until all the liquid has been absorbed by the rice – about 8–10 minutes. Remove from the heat, cover the saucepan and leave it to stand for 5 minutes. Transfer the rice to a steamer or double saucepan and steam for 15–20 minutes.

To serve: peel and cube the mango, sprinkle with lime juice and a little sugar if necessary. Put a portion of rice in the middle of each dessert plate and arrange the mango around it. Decorate with mint.

Indian Rice Pudding

Serves 4

Kheer is a generic term for creamy rice puddings served all over India. Sometimes fruit and nuts are added and in southern India they add slivers of coconut.

150g (5oz) broken Basmati rice (this gives a
    better, sticky texture to the pudding)
600ml (1 pint) semi-skimmed milk
3 tablespoons ground almonds
150ml (5fl oz) evaporated milk
sugar, to taste
2 tablespoons chopped pistachio nuts (unsalted)
½ teaspoon freshly ground green cardamom

Put the rice and milk in a heavy saucepan and bring gently to the boil. Simmer for about an hour or until soft and mushy. Add the ground almonds and evaporated milk to the rice. Stir until thick, creamy and unctuous.

Add the pistachios and sugar to taste. Sprinkle over the cardamom powder and stir well. Serve chilled or warm, depending on the weather. It's delicious warm on a winter's evening.

Spiced Pan-roasted Pear Cake

Serves 8–10

The incorrigible Antony Worrall-Thompson is one of our favourite guest chefs – this goodie came from him.

200g (7oz) soft brown sugar
110g (4oz) unsalted butter, cut in four
175g (6oz) plain flour
250g (9oz) caster sugar
2 teaspoons cinnamon
1¼ teaspoons baking powder
½ teaspoon salt
2 large organic eggs
150ml (5fl oz) sunflower oil
1 pear, coarsely grated
1 tablespoon peeled and grated ginger
4 pears, peeled, cored and cut into 6

1 round tin 23cm (9in) in diameter and 6cm
    (2½in) high

Preheat the oven to 180°C/350°F/gas 4.

Sprinkle brown sugar over the bottom of the cake tin. Add the butter to the tin. Place the tin in the oven until butter melts (about 5 minutes).

Mix the flour, sugar, cinnamon, baking powder and salt together. Beat in the eggs and oil. Mix in the grated pear and ginger. Remove the cake tin from the oven and whisk the butter and sugar until the sugar dissolves.

Arrange the pear slices in the tin. Pour the batter over the pears and bake until the cake is springy to the touch and a skewer comes out clean – this takes about 1 hour.

Allow to cool slightly; loosen the edges of the cake with a knife and turn out onto a hot plate. Serve warm with softly whipped cream or Homemade Vanilla Ice-cream (see page 399).

Christmas Ice-cream Bombe with Butterscotch Sauce

Serves 12–16

This scrumptious Christmas Bombe is made up of layers of three homemade ice-creams. It may be made several weeks ahead and is perfect for those who dislike Christmas Pudding.

Ballymaloe Chocolate Ice-cream (see page 399)
Ballymaloe Praline Ice-cream (see page 401)
Ballymaloe Coffee Ice-cream (see page 400)

300ml (½ pint) whipped cream
crystallised violets and angelica
sprig of holly

Butterscotch or Chocolate Sauce (see page 599)

2.4 litre (4 pint) capacity stainless steel or
*   enamel pudding bowl or two loaf tins*
*   12.5 x 20.5cm (5 x 8in)*

First make the Chocolate Ice-cream.

Put the pudding bowl into the freezer for about 10 minutes, so that it will be icy cold. Line the bowl with the Chocolate Ice-cream in an even layer, put it into the freezer and after about 1 hour take it out and improve the shape if necessary.

Meanwhile make the Praline Ice-cream. Add an even layer of Praline Ice-cream to the Chocolate Ice-cream in the bowl. Leave the centre free to fill with Coffee Ice-cream. Freeze for about 1 hour.

While the bombe is freezing, make the Coffee Ice-cream. Fill the Coffee Ice-cream into the centre of the bombe, cover the bowl with a plastic clip-on lid or clingfilm and freeze solid. Leave overnight if possible.

To serve, unmould the bombe and decorate with rosettes of whipped cream and crystallised violets and angelica or a sprig of holly. Serve with Butterscotch or Chocolate Sauce.

Jo Bettoja's Christmas Semi-Freddo with Raisins and Marrons Glacés

Serves 10–12

75ml (3fl oz) Jamaica rum
75g (3oz) good-quality raisins
4 organic eggs
50g (2oz) caster sugar
1 teaspoon pure vanilla extract
450g (1lb) chestnut purée
200g (7oz) marrons glacés, roughly chopped
400ml (14fl oz) double cream

Decoration
Chocolate Caraque (see page 400)
6–8 marrons glacés, whole
whipped cream
sprig of holly
icing sugar

2.4 litre (4 pint) pudding bowl, lined with
*   double thickness of cling film*

Put the rum and raisins into a little saucepan, warm the rum almost to boiling point then turn off the heat and allow the raisins to plump up and cool in the rum. Meanwhile, separate the eggs and keep the whites on one side. Beat the yolks with the caster sugar and vanilla extract until light and fluffy, stir in the chestnut purée, cold raisins, the rum and marrons glacés. Mix gently but thoroughly.

Refrigerate while you whip the cream softly and whisk the egg whites stiffly. Fold the whipped cream into the rum and raisin mix, then fold in the beaten egg whites. Gently pour into the lined bowl. Cover and freeze for at least 8 hours, or overnight.

To serve: turn out onto a chilled serving dish, remove the paper, decorate with whipped cream, whole marrons glacés, chocolate caraque and top with a sprig of holly (wrap the stem in tinfoil) and dredge with icing sugar.

Marrons Glacés with Sweet Cream and Crystallised Violets

By the end of October the cafes and food shops in Turin are selling beautiful marrons glacés (candied chestnuts). They are arranged on little gold trays decorated with crystallised violets. The Italians eat these chestnuts and violets for dessert on a bed of crème Chantilly and the combination is divine. Look for them in specialist food shops during Christmas and enjoy them this simple but very delicious Piedmontese way!

To make crème Chantilly, stiffly whip 300ml (10fl oz) double cream, and fold in 1 tablespoon caster sugar and ½ teaspoon pure vanilla extract.

Mrs Hanrahan's Sauce

Serve with Christmas pudding, mince pies or other tarts. This recipe is so delicious that people ask to have more pudding just so that they can have an excuse to eat lots of sauce. This makes a large quantity but the base will keep for several weeks in the fridge, so you can use a little at a time, adding whipped cream to taste.

110g (4oz) butter
225g (8oz) Barbados sugar (moist, soft,
*   dark brown sugar)*
1 organic egg
62ml (2½fl oz) medium sherry
62ml (2½fl oz) port

1.2–1.4 litres (2–2½ pints) lightly whipped
*   cream*

Melt the butter, stir in the sugar and allow to cool slightly. Whisk the egg and add to the butter and sugar with the sherry and port. Refrigerate. When needed, add the lightly whipped cream to taste.

Ballymaloe Mincemeat Crumble Tart

Serves 8–10

The yummiest way to use up leftover mincemeat after Christmas, but of course you can make it any time of the year. This is adapted from a delicious Nigel Slater recipe.

Crumble Topping
110g (4oz) plain flour
¼ teaspoon baking powder
75g (3oz) chilled butter, diced
75g (3oz) caster sugar
25g (1oz) flaked almonds

Cake
110g (4oz) softened butter
110g (4oz) soft brown sugar
2 organic eggs
½ teaspoon pure vanilla extract
2 tablespoons milk
175g (6oz) plain flour
pinch of salt
1 level teaspoon baking powder

550g (20oz) Ballymaloe Mincemeat (see page 515)
icing sugar

22cm (8½in) springform tin, buttered

Preheat the oven to 180°C/350°F/gas 4.

First make the topping. Put the flour, baking powder, butter, and caster sugar into a food processor. Whizz for a few seconds until the mixture resembles coarse crumbs. Tip into a bowl and stir in the almonds.

Next make the cake mixture. Cream the butter with the sugar, beat in the eggs, add the vanilla extract and milk. Fold in the flour, salt and baking powder. Spoon the mixture into the tin. Spread the mincemeat over the mixture. Sprinkle the crumble topping over the mincemeat. Bake for 45–50 minutes until golden. Allow to cool slightly before removing the tin. Dredge the cake with icing sugar. Serve warm on hot plates with softly whipped cream.

ABOVE: Brandy Snaps

Ballymaloe Mince Pies with Irish Whiskey Cream

Makes 20–24 mince pies

Rich Sweet Shortcrust Pastry
225g (8oz) plain flour
110–175g (4–6oz) butter
1 dessertspoon icing sugar
a little beaten organic egg or egg yolk, and water to bind

450g (1lb) Ballymaloe Mincemeat (see page 515)
egg wash, made with organic egg

Irish Whiskey Cream
225ml (8fl oz) whipped cream
1 teaspoon icing sugar
1–3 tablespoons Irish whiskey

shallow bun tins, greased

Make the shortcrust pastry in the usual way (see page 413), and leave to relax for 1 hour in the fridge.

Preheat the oven to 180°C/350°F/gas 4.

Roll out the pastry until quite thin, stamp out into rounds 7.5cm (3in) diameter and line the greased shallow bun tins. Put a good teaspoonful of mincemeat into each tin, damp the edges with water and put another round on top. Use any scraps of pastry to make leaves and holly berries for the top of the pies, then egg wash. Bake the mince pies for about 20 minutes in the oven. Allow them to cool slightly, then dredge with icing or caster sugar.

To make the cream: fold the sugar and whiskey into the whipped cream and serve with the warm mince pies. You could also serve with Mrs Hanrahan's Sauce (see page 423).

Brandy Snap Baskets
Makes 12

Brandy snaps may be stored in an airtight tin for several days. Do not use a fan oven or the mixture will spread.

110g (4oz) butter
110g (4oz) caster sugar
4 tablespoons golden syrup
juice of ½ lemon
110g (4oz) white flour, sifted
large pinch of ground ginger

clean small jars to use as moulds

Preheat the oven to 180°C/350°F/gas 4. Line a baking sheet with silicone paper.

Over a low heat, gently melt the butter with the caster sugar and golden syrup in a pan, then take off the heat and stir in the flour, lemon juice and ginger. Allow to cool.

Drop generous tablespoon-size blobs of the mixture onto the baking tray spaced well apart. They should spread into a 12.5–15cm (5–6in) circle. Bake for 5–6 minutes or until lacy and golden.

Meanwhile have the jars upturned ready to use as moulds. Leave the brandy snaps to cool for a minute or so, then lift quickly off the tray with a spatula. Shape over the upturned jars to form baskets. Cool on a wire rack. Do one tray at a time or they will harden before you have time to shape them. Fill with Caramel Ice-cream (see page 401), sliced bananas and Butterscotch Sauce (see page 599).

Brandy Snaps
Follow the recipe above and roll round the handle of a wooden spoon while still warm. Slide off as soon as they harden and cool on a wire rack. Fill with brandy-flavoured whipped cream.

Brandy Snap Petit Fours
Drop level half-teaspoonfuls of the mixture onto the baking sheet and cook as above. Roll around a pencil or skewer.

ABOVE: Brandy Snap Baskets

Christmas Fruit Salad

Serves 10

175g (6oz) sugar
225ml (8fl oz) water
juice and zest of 2–3 limes
1 large or 2 small melons (I use two Ogen
    or Galia)
225g (8oz) seedless green grapes
4 small juicy pears
4 passion fruit
4 bananas
1 pomegranate

Put the sugar and water into a saucepan, bring to the boil, and cook for 2 minutes. If the pears are under-ripe, poach them for a few minutes in the syrup. Transfer to a large bowl, stir in the lime juice and zest and allow to cool.

Halve the melon, remove the seeds, and scoop the flesh into balls with a melon baller. Add the melon balls to the syrup and scrape any remaining melon flesh into the bowl also. Discard the rind. Peel the grapes and add to the bowl.

Peel the pears, cut in quarters, remove the core and slice lengthways. Add to the bowl. Cut the passion fruit in half, scoop out the seeds, and add to the bowl. Slice in the banana. Cut the pomegranate in half around the equator, carefully remove the jewel-like seeds from the membrane, and add to the fruit salad. Leave to macerate for at least 1 hour. Serve chilled.

Christmas Fruit Salad with Kumquats and Star Fruit

Thinly slice the kumquats and star fruit (carambola) into thin rounds. Divide the syrup in half and poach each fruit individually. Star fruit will take about 10 minutes, kumquats about 15–20 minutes. Chill, add the lime zest and juice and then add the remainder of the fruit.

LEFT: Myrtle Allen's Plum Pudding

Myrtle Allen's Plum Pudding with Brandy Butter

Serves 8–10

Making the Christmas Puddings (from *The Ballymaloe Cook Book* by Myrtle Allen):

The tradition that every member of the household could have a wish, which was likely (note, never a firm promise) to come true, was, of course, a ruse to get all the children to help with heavy work of stirring the pudding. I only discovered this after I was married and had to do the job myself. This recipe, multiplied many times, was made all at once. In a machineless age, mixing all those expensive ingredients properly was a formidable task. Our puddings were mixed in an enormous china crock which held the bread for the household for the rest of the year. My mother, nanny and the cook took it in turns to stir, falling back with much panting and laughing after a few minutes' work. I don't think I was really much help to them.

Christmas puddings should be given at least 6 weeks to mature. They will keep for a year. They become richer and firmer with age, but one loses the lightness of the fruit flavour. We always eat our last plum pudding at Easter. If possible, prepare your own fresh beef suet – it is better than the pre-packed product.

175g (6oz) shredded beef suet (or use the
    vegetarian substitute)
175g (6oz) sugar
200g (7oz) soft breadcrumbs
225g (8oz) currants
225g (8oz) raisins
110g (4oz) candied peel
1–2 teaspoons mixed spice
pinch of salt
2 tablespoons flour
50ml (2fl oz) flesh of a baked apple
3 organic eggs
50ml (2fl oz) Irish whiskey

1.8 litre (3 pint) capacity pudding bowl,
    greased

Mix the dry ingredients thoroughly. Whisk the eggs and add them with the apple and whiskey. Stir very well indeed. Fill the pudding bowl. Cover with a round of greaseproof paper or a butter-paper pressed down on top of the pudding. Put a large round of greaseproof or brown paper over the top of the bowl, tying it firmly under the rim. Place in a saucepan one-third full of boiling water and simmer for 10 hours. Do not allow the water to boil over the top and do not let it boil dry either. Store in a cool place until needed.

On Christmas Day: boil for 1½–2 hours before serving. Serve with Brandy Butter or Rum Butter.

Variation
Fried Plum Pudding

Leftover plum pudding is delicious cut into thick slices and fried very gently in a little butter. Serve with Mrs Hanrahan's Sauce (see page 423).

Brandy Butter

75g (3oz) butter, preferably unsalted
75g (3oz) icing sugar
2–6 tablespoons brandy

Cream the butter until very light, add the icing sugar and beat again. Then beat in the brandy, drop by drop. If you have a food processor, use it: you will get a wonderfully light and fluffy butter.

Variation
Rum Butter

Substitute 3–4 tablespoons Jamica rum for the brandy and proceed as above.

cheese

cheese

One of the most exciting developments on the Irish food scene over the past 20 years has been the emergence of an Irish farmhouse cheese industry. Prior to that, we were a nation of Calvita eaters (a hugely processed cheese wrapped in tin foil). This new industry, made up of passionate, spirited and incredibly dedicated people, has greatly assisted the evolvement of the image of Irish food both at home and abroad.

At Ballymaloe House we have a cheese trolley every night, on which we proudly serve five or six (sometimes more) Irish farmhouse cheeses for our guests to taste. It is part of our menu so they do not have to choose between cheese and dessert, and they seem to love to hear about the local cheesemakers who now make prize-winning cheeses.

Just as all wine starts with a bunch of grapes, so all cheese starts with milk. It can be cow milk, goat milk, sheep milk, buffalo milk or even camel milk – the diversity is truly amazing. Milk sours and curdles naturally, so cheese (like many other things) was discovered by accident. There are various theories – some say it was Arab nomads who made the discovery when carrying milk in a bag made from a calf stomach...

Most cheese is now made from pasteurised milk – a controversial subject. Connoisseurs of good cheese believe that a truly great cheese can only be made from un-pasteurised milk; the natural bacteria contributing to the cheese's unique character and flavour. On the other hand, food technologists argue that when milk is pasteurised it becomes sterile, enabling cheesemakers to introduce exactly the starters they desire and so be in complete control of the quality. The issue is certainly not black and white – a skilled cheesemaker can make superb cheese starting with pasteurised milk, whereas a less skilled or knowledgeable operator can manage to make a poor quality product with raw milk. In Europe the farmhouse cheesemakers are under continuous pressure to pasteurise their milk. Several organisations including the Slow Food Movement and the Euro Toque Association of Chefs are battling to save the raw milk cheeses and to safeguard our right as consumers to have the choice.

At the school we teach our students the rudiments of cheese making and how to make a cottage cheese. Each day one of the students looks after the cheeseboard for lunch. They learn how to care for cheese and label it, so that the other students can become familiar with their names. Most Irish cheeses are named after the townland where they are made, or after an Irish saint, e.g. St. Tola and St. Killian. They are made from cow, goat or ewe's milk – Milleens, Gubbeen, Durrus, Baylough, Cashel Blue, Desmond, Ardsallagh, Kerry, Knockalara, Cooleney, Coolea, Abbey Blue, Killorglin, Ardrahan, Lavistown, Boilie... there are over 80 to choose from.

One of the highlights of the term is when we take the students to visit a farmhouse cheesemaker's. They meet the cheesemakers themselves and see the process from beginning to end. This gives them a greater understanding and appreciation, not only of the of the sheer hard work that goes into making a farmhouse cheese, but also of the passion and dedication involved.

A Plate of Irish Farmhouse Cheeses

The Irish farmhouse cheesemakers are a charismatic lot, mostly women with just a few exceptional men. I feel truly grateful to these artisanal producers who spend long hours making and nurturing their cheese to ensure that each cheese develops to its full peak of perfection. It is sheer joy to talk to them about their produce. Many speak of their cheese fondly as though they were their children – sometimes good, sometimes naughty. Veronica Steele, who is considered to be the matriarch of the farmhouse cheesemakers, refers to her small Milleens as her 'little dotes'.

Many of the Irish farmhouse cheeses are available outside Ireland in specialist cheese shops. Some, however, are not exported, so when you come to Ireland seek them out and taste these wonderful cheeses that are sweeping the boards at all the top cheese shows worldwide.

Types of Cheese

Every cheese is different – the nature of the paste, rind and veins, and the size of the holes are all clues to its quality and condition. Many cheeses now carry an Appellation d'Origine so it's worth reading the label carefully. Sometimes the rind of the cheese itself is stamped, for example Parmigiano Reggiano, Gruyère and Emmenthal. If it is a French cheese, the label will also tell you if the cheese is made in a farmhouse (*fermier*) or a factory (*laitier*) and whether it is made from pasteurised or unpasteurised milk (*lait cru*). It will also indicate the type of milk used and the fat content.

Soft Cheeses

Very soft cheeses must be kept refrigerated and should be eaten within two days. These cheese are uncooked and unripened – e.g. cottage cheese, curd cheese, fromage frais, fromage blanc, quark, Petit Suisse and Camargue and Puzol. Cream cheese, such as mascarpone is, as the name implies, made from cream rather than milk.

Soft spreadable cheeses include Coulommiers, Explorateur, Taleggio, Brie and Camembert. These cheeses are sprayed with a mould (*Penicillium candidum*) which develops into a bloomy white rind.

Semi-soft cheeses are slightly firmer, often crumbly, springy in texture, but still moist – e.g. Gorgonzola, Cashel Blue, St Paulin, Reblochon, Munster, Gubbeen and Durrus. The distinctive rind of the latter comes from a culture of *Breyibacterium linens*.

Semi-hard cheeses form the largest cheese family. They can be sliced easily. Cheddar types include Cheddar, Cheshire, Caerphilly, Wensleydale, Double Gloucester and Stilton, and Raclette. Gouda types include Gouda and Edam. Gruyère types are Gruyère, Comté, Fontina, Jarlsberg and Appenzell.

Hard Cheeses

These are pressed to produce a dense cheese which may be sliced when young but needs to be grated when old. Grana-type cheese, Parmesan (Parmigiano Reggiano), Grana Padana, Pecorino Romano, mature Gruyère and Emmenthal, Mature English Cheddar, Aged Gouda, Desmond and Gabriel.

Buying Cheese

Wherever feasible buy a whole cheese in perfect condition. Alternatively, buy a freshly cut piece of cheese rather than a prepacked section. Cheese should be cut cleanly with a wire or a special cheese knife and wrapped in cheese paper, greaseproof or tin foil – not clingfilm. Unless you can trust your cheesemonger implicitly, it is vital that you know a little about the character of the cheeses, as with wine. This knowledge comes from lots of tasting and accumulated experience. Meanwhile, find a reputable shop which has a wide selection of cheese in good condition. This is not always easy because many shops either have a very poor selection, or else they stock far too many

cheeses without having the turnover to justify it, meaning that many of the cheeses are past their best.

Storing Cheese

For perfection, cheese (other than very fresh soft cheese) should be stored in a cool larder or cheese cupboard. If you do store cheese in a fridge, keep it in the warmest part and remove a few hours before serving to allow it to come back to room temperature. Hard or semi-hard cheese needs high humidity or they will dry out. All other cheese should be wrapped individually in its own wrapping or in greaseproof paper or tin foil. Clingfilm is not good for wrapping cheese. Blue cheese, particularly those without a thick rind, should be wrapped closely in silver or gold foil otherwise the blue mould (*Penicillium roquerfortii*), which is very prolific, will spread into other cheese in the fridge.

Do not keep any cheese in a warm kitchen for long – soft cheese tends to liquefy and harder cheese sweats and become oily. Despite the fact that some manufacturers recommend freezing, it is better not to freeze cheese unless it is a stop gap measure.

A Cheese Board

Cheese may be served on a timber board, marble slab or a flat basket covered with fresh vine or fig leaves. Choose 3–5 cheeses in perfect condition (a mixture of mild, medium and strong).

Accompaniments to Cheese

Many restaurants serve celery, grapes, lettuce, tomato roses and various other garnishes with cheese. There is a recent trend in Australia and the US to serve a cheese course – a cheese plate with nuts, dried fruit, relishes, a little salad and some crackers or flavoured breads. At Ballymaloe we feel that all one needs to serve with cheese in perfect condition is fresh crusty homemade bread or simple cheese biscuits.

Homemade Butter

When I was a little girl, my Great Aunt Lil made butter in an electric churn almost every day, from the rich ripened cream separated from the milk in the the Alfa-Laval separator. When the butter was made we washed it, sprinkled on salt and patted it into little butter pats and butter balls with wooden butter hands. Nowadays one only usually makes butter by accident when one overwhips cream!

600ml (1 pint) cream
salt to taste (optional)

Put the cream into the spotlessly clean stainless-steel bowl of a food mixer. Whisk as fast as possible until the cream whips to a soft peak. Continue and quite soon there will be a sloshing sound and when you look into the mixing bowl you will see little globules of butter and lots of watery milk. Strain through a cold sterilised sieve. Save the buttermilk for soda bread and wash the butter under a cold tap. Using chilled wooden butter hands, pat the butter and continue to wash to ensure that no milk remains trapped in the butter, as this would sour and taint the butter. Sprinkle with salt and mix evenly through.

Form into slabs of 110g (4oz), 225g (8oz) or 450g (1lb). Alternatively, make into little balls.

Note: Butter may be salted or unsalted. Most American and Continental butter is unsalted, while English and Irish butter tends to be salted.

See also Clarified Butter and Ghee, page 105.

Master Recipe
Homemade Cottage Cheese

Yields 450g (1lb) cheese

Rennet is a natural extract from the lining membrane of a calf's stomach; it was first produced in bottled form by a chemist in Denmark in 1876. It is used in cheese-making and is also essential to junket. Seek out non-GM rennet. This cottage cheese is very different from the pasty white cottage cheese made commercially.

2.4 litres (4 pints) full cream milk
1 teaspoon liquid rennet

good-quality muslin or cheesecloth

Put the milk into a spotlessly clean stainless steel saucepan. Heat it very gently until it is barely tepid. Add the rennet, stirring it well into the milk (not more than 1 teaspoon, as too much will result in a tough acid curd). Cover the saucepan with a clean tea towel and the lid. The tea towel prevents the steam from condensing on the lid of the pan and falling back onto the curd. Put aside and leave undisturbed for 2–4 hours by which time the milk should have coagulated and will be solid.

Cut the curd with a long sterilised knife first in 1 direction then the other until the curd is cut into squares. Heat gently until the whey starts to run out of the curds. It must not get hot or the curd will tighten and toughen too much.

Ladle into a muslin-lined colander over a bowl. Tie the corners of the cloth and allow to drip overnight. Next day the curd may be used in whatever recipe you choose.

Variation
Cottage Cheese with Herbs
Follow the Master Recipe and add some chopped dill or a mixture of freshly chopped herbs to the cheese. Season, and add a little cream if desired.

Coeurs à la Crème with Summer Fruits

Serves 4

A most exquisite summer pudding. Also delicious with a Kumquat Compote (see page 391), or Green Gooseberry Sauce (see page 597). You may use 1 large mould or individual moulds. In France, they are traditionally heart-shaped. The moulds must be well-perforated to allow the cheese to drain.

225g (8oz) unsalted cream cheese or homemade
*   Cottage Cheese (see left)*
300ml (½ pint) softly whipped double cream
2 tablespoons caster sugar
2 organic egg whites, stiffly beaten
summer berries: fraises des bois, strawberries,
*   raspberries, loganberries, blackberries,*
*   redcurrants, blueberries*
300ml (½ pint) cream, softly whipped
caster sugar

Garnish
mint leaves

Press the cheese through a fine nylon sieve and blend it gently with the double cream. Stir in the sugar and lightly but thoroughly fold in the stiffly beaten egg whites. Turn the mixture into muslin-lined heart-shaped moulds. Stand them on a wide plate, cover with a large plastic bag and leave in the refrigerator overnight to drain.

Just before serving, turn the cheese hearts out on to white plates, top with mint leaves and scatter summer fruits around the cheese hearts. Serve with softly whipped cream and caster sugar, and a Strawberry Sauce (see page 599), Raspberry Sauce (see page 599) or Blackcurrant Sauce (see page 599).

Note: If you have not got the traditional heart-shaped moulds, make Coeurs à la Crème in a muslin-lined bread basket or even a sieve.

RIGHT: Coeurs à la Crème with Summer Fruits

Put the yoghurt cheese with all the other ingredients in a stainless steel or Pyrex bowl. Mix well. Taste for seasoning and add a little sugar if necessary. Cover and refrigerate for at least 1 hour. If some liquid accumulates, discard it before serving.

As an alternative the herbs used in this recipe, try adding freshly chopped mint, dill or marjoram and a drizzle of olive oil. Sea salt and smoked paprika is also good.

Yoghurt and Cardamon Cream

250ml (8fl oz) milk
200g (7oz) caster sugar
200ml (7fl oz) cream
½ teaspoon cardamon seeds, ground
3 rounded teaspoons powdered gelatine
450ml (15fl oz) natural yoghurt

Put the milk, sugar and cream into a stainless steel saucepan with the ground cardamon and stir until the sugar has dissolved and the mixture is warm to the touch. Remove from the heat and leave to infuse.

Meanwhile dissolve the gelatine – sponge the gelatine in 4 tablespoons of cold water in a small bowl for a few minutes. Put the bowl into a saucepan of simmering water until the gelatine has melted and is completely clear. Add a little of the infused milk mixture and stir well and then mix this into the rest. Beat the yoghurt lightly with a whisk until smooth and creamy, then add into the cardamon mixture. Pour into a wide serving dish and allow to set for several hours, preferably overnight.

Serve with Orange and Kiwi Salad or Kumquat Compote (see page 391).

Yoghurt with Honey and Toasted Hazelnuts

Serve a portion of chilled natural yoghurt per person. Just before serving drizzle generously with really good honey and sprinkle with toasted hazelnuts.

Homemade Crème Fraîche

Crème fraîche, with its ripened flavour, is easy to make at home and keeps well.

450ml (16fl oz) rich cream
225ml (8fl oz) cultured buttermilk

Put the cream and the buttermilk into a stainless-steel saucepan. Warm gently to 30°C (85°F). Pour into a Pyrex bowl and cover with clingfilm pierced in several places.

Leave at room temperature for 6–8 hours until it thickens and tastes characteristically acidic. Cover and refrigerate.

Homemade Mascarpone

1.2 litres (2 pints) rich cream
¼ teaspoon cream of tartar

Heat the cream gently to 180°C (350°F) stirring every now and then. Remove from the heat, add the cream of tartar and stir for 30 seconds, then pour it in to a Pyrex bowl. Stir for 2 minutes.

Line a small bread basket or a sieve with cheese cloth or muslin and allow to drip in a cold place overnight or covered in the fridge. Use as required, or keep in the refrigerator in a tightly covered, clean container for up to a week.

Soft Yoghurt Cheese with Chives and Parsley

Makes enough for 4–6

Be sure that the chives and parsley are thoroughly dry before chopping them.

450g (1lb) whole milk yoghurt
pinch of salt
½ teaspoon very finely sliced chives
1 teaspoon finely chopped parsley
lemon balm or chervil and a little garlic
  (optional)
sugar, to taste

good-quality muslin or cheesecloth

Follow directions for making soft yoghurt cheese on the opposite page. Let the cheese drip overnight.

How to Make Yoghurt

Yoghurt can be made from unpasteurised milk if it is thoroughly boiled and allowed to cool to lukewarm before use. Skimmed or low-fat milk may be used but the resulting yoghurt lacks flavour. The boiling is to destroy unwanted bacteria in the milk which could interfere with the bacterial action of the yoghurt bacilli (*Lactobacillus bulgaricus* and *Streptococcus thermophilus*). Use natural yoghurt for the starter culture.

600ml (1 pint) full cream milk (boiled or sterilised)
2 teaspoons live natural yoghurt

Warm the milk until lukewarm (or cool it to lukewarm if it has been boiled). It should be around 42°C (108°F). Stir in the yoghurt. Pour it into a Pyrex bowl, cover with clingfilm, and put into a warm, draught-free place until set. It usually takes about 14 hours at 24–29°C/78–85°F for the yoghurt to set. Refrigerate once it is ready.

Remember to keep back 2 teaspoons of your bowl of yoghurt as the starter for the next batch. Yoghurt keeps for up to a week refrigerated.

Note: Yoghurt can be set in a warm airing cupboard or near an Aga or a radiator, and in a vacuum flask with a wide neck or an insulated ice bucket. Or it can be made in a bowl set in a larger bowl of warm water, standing in the sink with the hot tap dripping steadily into the outer bowl to keep the water warm. An earthenware pot with a lid, wrapped up in a warm blanket and put near a radiator will also do the job.

The aim is to provide steady, even warmth to allow the bacillus to grow. The cooler the temperature, the longer the yoghurt will take, but too high a temperature will kill the bacillus and yoghurt will not form. The yoghurt will become slightly sour if left for too long in the warmth.

How to Make Soft Yoghurt Cheese (Called Labna in the Arab World)

Whole-milk yoghurt makes a rich, creamy cheese. You may, if you prefer, substitute skimmed-milk yoghurt but I never would! This cheese keeps for up to a week in the refrigerator.

1. Line a strainer with a triple thickness of cheesecloth. Place it over a bowl. Spoon in the yoghurt.

2. Now tie the 4 corners of the cheese cloth to make a loose bundle.

3. Suspend the bundle or bag of yoghurt over a bowl so that it can drip for 3–8 hours, as your recipe requires.

4. Remove the cheesecloth. Refrigerate until needed in a covered plastic container. Add fresh herbs or spices – do this before you refrigerate it.

Paneer with Tomato and Chilli Sauce

Serves 4

A fresh curd cheese made in India, paneer is a prime source of protein for Buddhists, Jains and Hindu Brahmins. It is found extensively in the north but less often in the south where cows are not so prevalent. Paneer can be kept for up to 4 days in the fridge. The most common vegetable dish on our Indian restaurant menus is Matar Paneer – peas and cheese in tomato sauce.

1.8 litres (3 pints) milk (not low fat)
3–4 tablespoons lemon juice or white wine
 vinegar

Tomato and Chilli Sauce (page 591)
chopped fresh coriander
Indian flatbread, to serve

Bring the milk to the boil in a large saucepan; just as it begins to rise in the pot, add 3 tablespoons of lemon juice or vinegar. Stir and turn off the heat – the milk should start to curdle immediately. If it doesn't, bring to the boil again and add another tablespoon of lemon juice or vinegar, stir, and turn off the heat as before.

Put a large sieve or strainer over a deep bowl, line it with a double thickness of muslin or cheese cloth, pour the curds and whey into the muslin-lined strainer allowing the whey to drain away. Gather up the ends of the muslin and put it into a mould with holes. Cover with a plate and weight it down.

Alternatively, just put the cheese onto a board, cover with another board and weight down for about 3–4 minutes. It is then ready to be used or served.

Meanwhile make a little Tomato and Chilli Sauce. Add a little chopped fresh coriander as well.

To serve: slice the cheese into 5mm (¼in) slices and spoon a little sauce on top. Serve with hot crispy Indian flatbread.

ABOVE: Blue Cheese with Honey

Ballymaloe Cheese Biscuits

Makes 25–30 biscuits

We serve these biscuits with our Irish farmhouse cheeses in the restaurant. They keep for several weeks in an airtight tin and also freeze well.

110g (4oz) brown wholemeal flour
110g (4oz) white flour, preferably unbleached
½ teaspoon salt
½ teaspoon baking powder
25g (1oz) butter
1 tablespoon cream
water as needed, about 5 tablespoons

Preheat the oven to 150°C/300°F/gas 2.

Mix the brown and white flour together and add the salt and baking powder. Rub in the butter and moisten with cream and enough water to make a firm dough. Roll out very thinly to 2mm (¹⁄₁₆in). Prick with a fork. Cut with 6–8cm (2½–3in) round cutter. Put onto a lightly greased baking sheet and bake in the oven for about 45 minutes or until lightly browned and quite crisp. Cool on a wire rack.

Blue Cheese with Honey

Serve each guest a section of good-quality blue cheese such as Cashel Blue. Pass around a bowl of pure Irish honey, for drizzling over each helping.

Mary Jo's Cheese Straws

Makes 24–28

225g (8oz) puff pastry
organic egg wash
40g (1½ oz) grated Parmesan or 50g (2oz)
 grated Gruyère
pinch cayenne pepper
40g (1½ oz) flaked almonds or finely chopped
 almonds

Preheat oven to 200°C/400°F/gas 6

Roll the puff pastry to 3mm (⅛ in) thickness in approximately a 20 x 40cm (8 x 16in) rectangle. Trim the edges and brush with egg wash. Sprinkle the cheese and a little cayenne pepper over the lower half length of pastry. Fold over the upper half of the pastry and seal the edge.

Brush the top with the egg wash and sprinkle over the almonds. Lightly roll with a rolling pin to secure almonds. Chill.

Cut into 1cm (½in) wide sticks. Twist and place on baking trays lined with bakewell paper. Bake in the oven until puffed and golden (approximately 15 minutes). Hold in a cool oven (100°C/200°F/gas ¼) until crispy.

Marinated Mozzarella on Rocket Leaves

Serves 4

We can't hope to get the wonderful, fresh, tender, hand-rolled mozzarella that one finds in Italy; however, we can now get buffalo Mozzarella in plastic pouches still in a pool of whey (hugely different from the blocks of Danish mozzarella used for the mass pizza market). Unfortunately, there are far fewer buffaloes in Italy than there used to be and a lot of the milk is being replaced by cow's milk.

Mozzarella can be greatly improved by marinating in good extra-virgin olive oil and perhaps some fresh herbs and chilli or even chilli flakes. Smoked mozzarella has a golden skin and is fun for a change. This makes a lovely starter or light supper dish.

125ml (4fl oz) extra-virgin olive oil
1 fresh chilli, diced or pinch red pepper flakes
crushed garlic (optional)
2 balls mozzarella
marjoram or torn basil leaves
salt and freshly ground pepper
rocket leaves
focaccia
cherry tomatoes

Put the oil into a small saucepan, add the chilli flakes and garlic and warm gently for a few minutes, then allow to cool.

Slice the cheese thickly or dice into 2.5cm (1in) cubes. Put into a shallow dish, scatter some herbs over the cheese and season with salt and pepper. Pour the chilli oil over the top and allow to marinate for several hours, or cover and keep in the fridge for several days.

To serve: put a bed of rocket leaves on a plate, and top with a few slices of marinated mozzarella. Serve with chargrilled focaccia and maybe a few tiny cherry tomatoes, fresh or roasted quickly on the branch.

Goat's Cheese in Olive Oil (Queso de Cabra en Aceite)

Shepherds have traditionally made delicious mild and cured cheeses from goat's milk. They preserve some of the surplus in oil, which keeps cheese fresh. The oil can be strained and used as a dressing or drizzled over bruschetta or toast.

8 small goat's cheeses, with a diameter of
  about 5cm (2in)
4 sprigs thyme
4 sprigs rosemary or annual marjoram
1 tablespoon fennel seeds
1 tablespoon black peppercorns
500ml (16fl oz) olive oil
1 teaspoon chilli flakes

Put the goat's cheese in a sterilised kilner glass jar and tuck the herbs and peppercorns in between. Add enough oil to cover completely. Seal and leave for 1 month before eating. The oil can be used afterward to dress salads.

Note: If the cheese is large roll 25g (1oz) pieces into balls. For extra excitement, make an indent in the centre and press an annual marjoram leaf into each ball, cover with cheese and preserve as above.

Tartiflette

Serves 4–6

Rich but delicious! A speciality from Savoie in France.

extra-virgin olive oil
150g (5oz) chopped, smoked streaky bacon or
  lardons
a little butter
1kg (2¼lb) potatoes, sliced 5mm (¼ inch) thick
1 onion, thinly sliced
salt and freshly ground pepper
1 Reblochon
300ml (10fl oz) crème fraîche

Preheat the oven to 220°C/425°F/gas 7.

Heat a little olive oil in a frying pan and fry the bacon until it starts to crisp.

Gently fry the sliced potato and onion in some butter and a dash of olive oil. Add salt and pepper. When the potatoes are cooked but not brown, place them in an oven-proof gratin dish and sprinkle with the bacon or lardons. Slice the Reblochon in half, horizontally, to make two thin discs. Lay it on top of the potatoes, rind uppermost. Cover with crème fraiche. Place in the oven for approximately 30 minutes.

Enjoy with a green salad and a glass of dry white wine (preferably from Savoie).

Saganaki – Greek Fried Cheese

Serves 6–8

Greek Fried Cheese is cooked in a little round aluminium frying pan called a saganaki. It can be made with various hard cheeses, such as haloumi, Kefalotiri, Parmesan, and even Gruyère. It must be served piping hot; Greek waiters occasionally run to get it to the customer while it is still bubbling.

225g (8oz) hard cheese
butter or olive oil
lemon juice, freshly squeezed
freshly ground pepper
crusty white bread

Cut the cheese into slices, about 1cm (½in) thick. Have some white crusty bread ready on the table. Melt a little butter or olive oil in a small frying pan, put in a few slices of cheese, reduce the heat and let the cheese cook for 1–2 minutes until it begins to bubble. It should not brown. Sprinkle with a few drops of lemon juice and some freshly cracked pepper, rush to the table and eat with crusty white bread.

Note: The cheese can also be dipped in beaten egg and breadcrumbs before frying.

Mozzarella with Fresh Lemon Leaves

Serves 6 as a starter

Lots of garden centres sell Meyer lemon trees nowadays. Buy one and not only enjoy the fruit but also use the fresh leaves in cooking as you would Kaffir lime leaves. Goat's cheese and haloumi may also be used in this simple recipe.

2 balls fresh buffalo mozzarella
sea salt and freshly cracked pepper
16 fresh lemon leaves
extra-virgin olive oil
1 lemon

Carefully slice the mozzarella into 1cm (1/2 inch) slices. Heat a cast iron grill pan. Season the mozzarella with salt and pepper. Cover both sides of the mozzarella with fresh lemon leaves.

Lift carefully onto the hot grill pan. Cook for 45 seconds to one minute on each side. Carefully lift onto a hot plate, serving 2 slices per person with a segment of lemon and a good drizzle of extra-virgin olive oil (lemon oil would be even better). You'll need some crusty bread.

TIP: Lemon leaves can be used to make a delicious infusion. They are also wonderful finely shredded and added to soups, vegetables, fresh cream or curd desserts.

Fundido con Chistora

Serves 4

Artisan meat curing wizard Fingal Ferguson makes a delicious chistora (thin chorizo sausage) which I use for this recipe.

4 earthenware dishes (terracotta) 11.5 x 5cm (4 1/2 x 2in)
225g (8oz) quesa fresca or mozzarella
150g (5oz) chistora

Preheat the oven to 250°C/475°F/gas 9.

Slice the chistora into 2.5cm (1in) lengths. Divide the cheese and chistora between the dishes. Place in the oven for 6 minutes.

As soon as the cheese is melted, serve immediately with lots of hot crusty bread.

Reblochon en Croûte

Serves 4

Reblochon is a cheese with an orange rind from Haute-Savoie in France. In the Middle Ages, the peasants of the region asked the Carthusian monks of La Combe du Reposoir monastery to bless their chalets and offered cheese as the reward. Since the Revolution, Reblochon has been marketed throughout France. This cow's milk cheese is renneted and put into cloth-lined moulds, then brine-washed. The chip-board disks prevent the cheese from becoming soggy. Gubbeen cheese also works well in this recipe.

1 whole Reblochon cheese, ripe and ready to eat
a couple of sprigs of thyme
freshly cracked pepper
110g (4oz) Puff Pastry (see page 456)
organic egg wash

Preheat the oven to 230°C/450°F/gas 8.

Remove the timber disc from the base of the cheese. Make small slashes in the cheese and push a sprig of thyme into each cut. Sprinkle the cheese with pepper.

Roll out the puff pastry to a sufficient size to be able to wrap the cheese completely. Seal the edges and lightly brush the top with the egg wash. Decorate with a few pastry leaves if you want to make it look a little fancier.

Place on a baking tray and cook in the oven for 10 minutes. Reduce the temperature to 180°C/350°F/gas 4 for a further 15–20 minutes or until the pastry is crisp and golden.

To serve: cut into 4 wedges and serve immediately with warm crusty bread and a green salad.

Raclette

Serves 6

Raclette cheese is produced throughout Switzerland, and this way of cooking it originated in the canton of Valais. The 6kg (13 1/2lb) wheels of cheese were cut in half and melted over an open wood fire, and then scraped onto the plates. If you own a raclette stove with little invididual pans and have a chunk of delicious raclette cheese, this is one of the easiest and most delicious ways to entertain and is great fun for a dinner party.

500–700g (18–24oz) raclette cheese

6–12 potatoes, freshly boiled
lettuce
pickled onions and gherkins (optional)
sea salt and freshly ground pepper

Put the raclette stove in the centre of the table and turn on the heat.

Cut the cheese into very thin slices (about 5mm (1/4in) and put a slice on to each little pan. Put on the stove.

Meanwhile serve freshly boiled and seasoned potatoes and crisp lettuce leaves on hot plates. Just as soon as the cheese melts, each guest spoons the melting cheese over the potatoes and puts another piece on to melt.

Swiss Cheese Fondue

Serves 4

The two cheeses that make this great Swiss dish are emmenthal and Gruyère. Emmenthal comprises nearly 45 per cent of Swiss cheese production, and wheels can average 80kg (180lb) or more. It is thought to have been made since the thirteenth century and the holes are caused by a second fermentation process (that other cheeses don't go through), which gives it a nutty and distinctive flavour.

Gruyère, named after Count de Gruyère of the medieval town of Gruyère in western Switzerland, has an entirely different taste and texture and is a great cooking cheese, with its sharp, honest flavour. The holes are few and small.

A fondue set is obviously an advantage but not essential. The fondue pot is called a coque and the stove called a réchaud.

275g (10oz) Gruyère
275g (10oz) emmenthal
1 garlic clove, cut in 2
300–400ml (10–14fl oz) white wine
1 tablespoon Kirsch
1 tablespoon cornflour
freshly ground pepper
pinch of nutmeg
600g (1¼lb) good, crusty white bread, cubed

Rub the cut faces of the garlic clove around an earthenware fondue dish. Pour in the wine and heat to just simmering point, then add the cheese, and stir constantly with a wooden spoon.

When the mixture is bubbly but not burning, stir in the cornflour blended with the Kirsch. Add the pepper and nutmeg and continue stirring.

Transfer to a fondue stove on the table. Serve with the bread. Take care not to let the fondue burn. Make sure it is always being stirred.

Ballymaloe Cheese Fondue
Serves 2

Myrtle Allen's Cheese Fondue recipe made from Irish Cheddar can be made any time. It's a great favourite at Ballymaloe – a meal in itself, it can be made in minutes and is loved by adults and children alike. It is great fun for a party because you must kiss the gentleman or lady on your right if you drop your bread into the pot... so choose your spot carefully!

2 tablespoons dry white wine
2 small garlic cloves, crushed
2 teaspoons Ballymaloe Country Relish or Apple and Tomato Chutney (see page 512)
2 teaspoons freshly chopped parsley
175g (6oz) mature Cheddar cheese, grated
crusty white bread

Put all ingredients except the bread into a small saucepan or fondue pot and stir. Just before serving put over a low heat until the cheese melts and begins to bubble.

Put the pot over the fondue stove and serve immediately with fresh French bread or cubes of ordinary white bread crisped up in a hot oven.

Melted Vacherin Mont d'Or
Serves 4–8

Made in France, near the border with Switzerland, Vacherin can be made from 15th August until 31st March from cow's milk, and is one of the most succulent of cheeses. Bark and cheese are sealed together by bathing in brine, and the resinous perfume permeates the cheese as it ripens. Scrape any residue of cheese from the bark when you slice it.

This gorgeous winter cheese comes from the Massif du Mont d'Or in France near the Swiss border. The French and Swiss battled over the origin for years and years, but the Swiss have now conceded.

We always look forward to the arrival of the first vacherin in Iago in the Cork Market in late autumn. The cheese comes in a wooden box bound by a band of spruce bark. It is wonderful served with crusty bread or with a green salad and charcuterie, gutsy salamis, prosciutto or smoked duck.

Preheat the oven to 230°C/450°F/gas 8. Put the covered box in the oven for 20–30 minutes or until warm and melting. Serve hot in the box with boiled potatoes and a green salad.

Melted Gubbeen or Reblochon Cheese with Winter Herbs
Serves 6–8

1 baby Gubbeen or Reblochon
freshly chopped thyme
1 large or 2 small garlic cloves, finely chopped
freshly ground pepper

Preheat the oven to 180°C/350°F/gas 4.

Cut a square of tin foil, approximately 30.5cm (12in). Split the cheese in half around the equator. Put the base onto the centre of the tin foil, and sprinkle the cut surface generously with chopped thyme, garlic and some freshly ground pepper.

Top with the other part of cheese. Gather up the edges but allow a little vent for the steam to escape. Bake in the oven for 20–30 minutes or until soft and melting.

Open the parcel. Lift off the rind and serve the soft, herby melting cheese on slices of hot crusty bread.

Melted Camembert with Celery Sticks and Breadsticks
Serves 6–8

So simple and much more delish than it sounds.

1 camembert, semi-ripe
18–24 celery sticks
18 breadsticks (see page 487)

Preheat the oven to 180°C/350°F/gas 4.

Just before serving, unwrap the camembert and put it back into its wooden box. Cover and staple the box if necessary so it doesn't come apart in the heat. Put in the oven for 10–12 minutes or until soft, molten and warmed through.

Serve with celery sticks and breadsticks for dipping.

cakes & biscuits

cakes & biscuits

Cooks seem to divide naturally into those who enjoy savoury cooking best, and those who love to bake. Forced to choose, I would plump for the latter. The basic ingredients for cakes and pastries are few – butter, sugar, eggs and flour, and yet skilled chefs are able to create a myriad af delightful tastes and textures. Although baking is most definitely an art form it is also an exact science – you can't just throw in a tablespoon of this or a fistful of that at random; for success and consistency you need to measure accurately and follow a recipe precisely.

There are three basic types of cake: **whisked cakes** (fatless sponges e.g. angel food cake); **creamed cakes** (sponges which include fat e.g. fruit cake) and **molten method cakes** (sponges which use melted ingredients e.g. panforte). Some cake recipes are made by a mixture of two methods, such as whisked up sponge. Biscuits also fall into three basic method techniques: **rubbing in** (e.g. shortbread), **creaming** (e.g. lemon squares) and **molten methods** (e.g. brandy snaps). Once again, many (e.g. toffee squares) use a combination of two or three techniques.

Ingredients

As ever, always choose the finest ingredients for the most delicious end result. The fat adds moistness and improves the shelf life of cakes and biscuits – butter (use unsalted or salted butter as the recipe indicates) gives the best results and flavour. Margarine and other shortenings can be used, producing a light texture but very little flavour. Olive oil is used in some Tunisian, Greek and Moroccan recipes. Use medium-sized, organic eggs, stored at room temperature. Duck eggs are particularly good for sponge cakes. Caster sugar is most commonly used in cakes. Golden caster gives colour and a slightly richer flavour. Icing sugar is used for icings and decoration. Most cake recipes use plain flour. Self-raising flour should only be used where specified – do not substitute it for

plain flour. Sift the flour to increase the lightness of your cakes. Nuts and coconut add moistness and improve the keeping quality of cakes and biscuits.

Preparation and Baking

When choosing tins, always buy good-quality, heavy-gauge tins. Use the exact size of tin stated in a recipe, (or adjust the cooking time accordingly). If tins are very light, tie a layer of brown paper around the outside to protect heavy cakes (e.g. fruit cake) that require a long cooking time. It is well worth taking the time to grease and line a cake tin so that the cake will unmould easily – use good butter or oil to do this (poor-quality fat or oil can ruin the flavour). Use a brush to apply the melted butter evenly to the base and sides of the tin. Dust with flour and shake off any excess. For whisked and creamed cakes, the base of the tin should be lined with greaseproof or silicone paper. Loaf tins need to be lined for cakes and ginger-bread. Greaseproof paper is often of poor quality, so I recommend using silicone paper. I also prefer to use a conventional oven for most cakes and biscuits as those cooked in a fan-assisted oven become stale more quickly.

To test for 'doneness', press the centre gently with your fingertips – when fully cooked it should be the same texture as the outer edge. Alternatively, insert a skewer or toothpick into its centre. If it comes out clean with no trace of stickiness, then the cake is done. Most cakes benefit from standing for a few minutes before being turned out. Cool cakes and biscuits on a wire rack so they don't get soggy underneath. Allow heavy fruit cakes to cool in the tin first.

Keeping Qualities

Rich fruit cakes like Simnel or Christmas Cake keep very well in an airtight tin. Banana Bread, Tunisian Orange Cake and Ballymaloe Barmbrack also keep brilliantly.

Darina Allen's Christmas Cake with Toasted Almond Paste

This makes a moist cake, which keeps very well. I have a passion for almond paste so I 'ice' the cake with almond icing and decorate it with heart shapes made from the almond paste. Then I brush it with beaten egg yolk and toast it in the oven – simply delicious!

110g (4oz) glacé cherries
50g (2oz) whole almonds
350g (12oz) best-quality sultanas
350g (12oz) best-quality currants
350g (12oz) best-quality raisins
50g (2oz) ground almonds
110g (4oz) homemade Candied Peel
  (see page 515)
zest of 1 orange
zest of 1 lemon
5 tablespoons Irish whiskey
225g (8oz) butter
225g (8oz) pale brown sugar
6 organic eggs
275g (10oz) plain white flour
1 level teaspoon mixed spice
1 large or 2 small Bramley apples, peeled, cored
  and grated

23cm (9in) round, or 20cm (8in) square tin, lined
  with brown paper and greaseproof paper, with
  an outer collar of brown paper to come half as
  high again as the height of the tin.

Preheat the oven to 180°C/350°F/gas 4.
Note: it's very important that you use a conventional oven for this cake.

Wash and dry the cherries. Cut in 2 or 4 as desired. Blanch the almonds in boiling water for 1–2 minutes, rub off the skins and chop them finely. Mix the dried fruit, whole almounds, ground almonds, candied peel and grated orange and lemon zest. Add about half of the whiskey and leave for 1 hour to macerate.

Cream the butter until very soft, add the sugar and beat until light and fluffy. Whisk the eggs and add in bit by bit, beating well between each addition so that the mixture doesn't curdle. Mix the spice with the flour and stir in gently. Add the grated apple to the fruit and mix in gently but thoroughly (don't beat the mixture again or you will toughen the cake). Put the mixture into the prepared cake tin. Make a slight hollow in the centre, dip your hand in water and pat it over the surface of the cake: this will ensure that the top is smooth when cooked. Lay a sheet of brown paper over the top of the tin. Put into the oven for 1 hour, then reduce the heat to 170°C/325°F/gas 3 and bake for another 2–2½ hours. Test in the centre with a skewer – it should come out completely clean when the cake is cooked. Pour the rest of the whiskey over the cake and leave to cool in the tin.

Next day, remove from the tin. Do not remove the lining paper but wrap in extra greaseproof paper and tin foil until required. The cake keeps for weeks or even months at this stage.

Almond Paste

450g (1lb) caster sugar
450g (1lb) ground almonds
2 small organic eggs
drop of pure almond essence
2 tablespoons Irish whiskey

Sieve the caster sugar and mix with the ground almonds. Beat the eggs, add the whiskey and almond essence, then add to the other ingredients and mix to a stiff paste. (You may not need all of the egg.) Sprinkle the worktop with icing sugar, turn out the almond paste and work lightly until smooth.

To brush on the cake
1 organic egg white, lightly beaten

Glaze
2 organic egg yolks

Remove the paper from the cake. To make life easier, put a sheet of greaseproof paper onto the worktop; dust with some icing sugar. Take about half the almond paste and roll it out on the paper: it should be a little less than 1cm (½in) thick. Paint the top of the cake with the lightly beaten egg white and put the cake, sticky-side down, onto the almond paste.

Give the cake a 'thump' to make sure it sticks and then cut around the edge. If the cake is a little 'round shouldered', cut the almond paste a little larger. Pull away the extra bits and keep for later to make hearts or holly leaves. With a palette knife press the extra almond paste in against the top of the cake to fill any gaps. Then slide a knife underneath the greaseproof paper and turn the cake right way up. Peel off the paper.

Preheat the oven to 220°C/425°F/gas 7.

Next, measure the circumference of the cake with a piece of string. Roll out 2 long strips of almond paste to half that length: trim both edges to the height of the cake with a palette knife. Paint both the cake and the almond paste lightly with egg white. Press the strips against the sides of the cake: do not overlap or there will be a bulge. Use a straight-sided water glass to even the edges and smooth the join. Rub the cake well with your hand to ensure a nice flat surface. Roll out the remainder of the almond paste about 5mm (¼in) thick. Cut out heart shapes, paint the whole surface of the cake with some beaten egg yolk, and stick the heart shapes at intervals around the sides of the cake and on the top. Brush these with egg yolk also.

Carefully lift the cake onto a baking sheet and bake in the oven for 15–20 minutes or until just slightly toasted. Remove from the oven, allow to cool and then transfer onto a cake board.

Note: as I'm an incurable romantic, my Christmas Cake is always decorated with hearts, but you may feel that holly leaves and berries made of almond paste would be more appropriate for Christmas. You can, of course, decorate it any way that takes your fancy.

Myrtle Allen's White Christmas Cake

This cake with its layer of crisp frosting is a delicious alternative for those who do not like the traditional heavy fruit cake. It is best made not more than a week before Christmas. Good for those of us who leave things until the last moment!

150g (5oz) butter
200g (7oz) flour
pinch of salt
¼ level teaspoon baking powder
1 teaspoon lemon juice
1 teaspoon Irish whiskey
75g (3oz) ground almonds
6 organic egg whites
225g (8oz) caster sugar
75–110g (3–4oz) green or yellow glacé cherries
50g (2oz) finely chopped homemade Candied Peel (see page 515)

American Frosting (see page 447)
Crystallised Flowers (see page 452), angelica or Christmas decorations

round cake tin, 18cm (7in) in diameter, 8cm (3in) deep

Preheat the oven to 170°C/325°F/gas 3.

Line the tin with greaseproof paper. Cream the butter until very soft, sieve in the flour, salt and baking powder, then add the lemon juice, whiskey and ground almonds. Whisk the egg whites until quite stiff; add the caster sugar gradually and whisk again until stiff and smooth. Stir some of the egg white into the butter mixture and then carefully fold in the rest. Lastly, add the chopped peel and the cherries. Pour into the prepared tin and bake for about 1½ hours. Allow to cool, cover and ice the next day.

Ice the cake with the American Frosting. Decorate with Christmas decorations or crystallised violets and rose petals, and angelica.

Simnel Cake

Simnel was originally a spiced bread, probably introduced to Ireland by Elizabethan settlers in the sixteenth century. In and around the Dublin Pale, there was a tradition that the mistress of the house provided the ingredients for the maid-servants to bake a plum cake, iced with almond paste, to take home on Mothering Sunday, the Sunday before Lent begins. In the funeral scene in *Ulysses*, James Joyce describes hawkers selling simnel cakes outside Glasnevin Cemetery in Dublin. Were they smaller then or was he merely using poetic licence?

Use the same ingredients for Christmas Cake (page 443). Follow the method until the mixture is prepared. The first difference from the Christmas cake recipe is that you should put ½ of the cake mixture into the prepared tin, then roll out about ½ of the almond paste into a 22cm (8½in) round, place this on top of the cake mixture and cover with the remaining mixture. Cook as for the Christmas Cake.

When you are ready to finish the cake, preheat the oven to 220°C/425°F/gas 7. Roll out ⅔ of the remainder of the almond paste into a 23cm (9in) round. Brush the cake with a little lightly beaten egg white and top with the almond paste. Roll the remainder of the paste into 11 little balls.

Score the top of the cake with 4cm (1½in) squares, brush with beaten egg or egg yolk, stick the 11 'apostles' around the outer edge of the top, brush with beaten egg. Toast in the oven for 15–20 minutes or until slightly golden. Decorate with an Easter chicken, if you like.

TIP: Remember to use organic eggs whenever possible.

Rum and Raisin Walnut Cake

One of our favourite cakes – it keeps for ages and goes well with coffee.

175g (6oz) raisins
6 tablespoons rum
275g (10oz) butter
175g (6oz) caster sugar
4 organic eggs
50ml (2fl oz) milk
1½ teaspoons pure vanilla extract
275g (10oz) plain white flour
1 level tablespoon baking powder
50g (2oz) walnuts, shelled

23cm (9in) loose-based round tin, lined with greaseproof paper

Preheat the oven to 180°C/350°F/gas 4.

Soak the raisins in the rum for 30 minutes. Drain and save the rum. Cream the butter, add the caster sugar and beat until light and fluffy. Separate the eggs, and add the egg yolks, 1 by 1. Beat well between each addition. Add the rum, milk and vanilla. Mix the flour and baking powder together and fold into the base mixture bit by bit.

Whisk the egg whites in a spotlessly clean bowl until stiff and fluffy. Fold into the cake mixture one third at a time, adding the raisins and chopped nuts with the last addition of egg white.

Pour into the prepared tin and cook in the oven for 45–60 minutes, or until the top is golden and the centre set and firm. Allow the cake to cool in the tin, invert, remove from the tin, invert again and cool on a wire rack.

Porter Cake

Porter cake made with the black stout of Ireland is now an established Irish cake, rich and moist with 'plenty of cutting'. Either Guinness, Murphy or Beamish stouts can be used, depending on where your loyalties are.

450g (1lb) plain white flour
pinch of salt
1 level teaspoon baking powder
225g (8oz) caster sugar
1 level teaspoon freshly grated nutmeg
1 level teaspoon mixed spice
225g (8oz) butter
450g (1lb) sultanas
50g (2oz) Candied Peel (see page 515)
50g (2oz) glacé cherries
300ml (½ pint) porter or stout
2 organic eggs

20 x 7cm (8 x 3in) round cake tin, lined with greaseproof paper

Preheat the oven to 180°C/350°F/gas 4. Sieve the flour, salt and baking powder into a bowl, and add the sugar, nutmeg and spice. Rub in the butter. Add the fruit, then mix the porter with the beaten eggs, pour into the other ingredients and mix well. Turn into the lined tin and bake for about 2 hours in the oven. Allow to cool in the tin, wrap in silicone paper and keep for several days before cutting to allow the cake to mature.

BELOW: Porter Cake

Ballymaloe Barmbrack

This is the teabrack that that they can't take off the menu at Ballymaloe House. It lasts for ages in a tin.

225g (8oz) sultanas
225g (8oz) currants or 225g (7oz) currants plus
   25g (1oz) cherries
350ml (12fl oz) strong, cold tea
1 beaten organic egg
200g (7oz) sugar
215g (7 ½ oz) self-raising flour
1 level teaspoon mixed spice

13 x 20cm (5 x 8in) loaf tin, lined with silicone
   paper

Soak the fruit in the tea overnight.

The next day preheat the oven to 180°C/350°F/gas 4.

Add the beaten egg, sugar, flour and mixed spice to the fruit mixture. Pour into the prepared tin and bake in the oven for 1½ hours. You may need to cover the top with greaseproof paper while cooking to protect the it.

When cooked, brush the top with Stock Syrup (see page 568) and allow to cool on a wire rack. Cut into slices and serve with butter.

Almond or Hazelnut Praline Cake

Another favourite Ballymaloe cake. Praline is a seventeenth-century French invention, a caramelised sugar and nut mixture, which can be ground or pounded to a powder. Almond and hazelnuts are the most commonly used nuts, although in America, pecans are used widely, particularly in Creole cooking.

Praline
175g (6oz) skinned hazelnuts or unskinned
   almonds
175g (6oz) sugar

Cake
150g (5oz) butter
175g (6oz) caster sugar
3 organic eggs
175g (6oz) white flour
1 level teaspoon baking powder
1 tablespoon milk

Praline Buttercream
7 tablespoons water
9 tablespoons sugar
5 organic egg yolks
225g (8oz) unsalted butter
1 teaspoon pure vanilla extract

2 x 20cm (8in) sandwich tins

First make the Praline. Put the sugar into a sauté pan, and sprinkle the nuts evenly over the top. Put the pan over a low heat until the sugar turns a caramel colour. Do not stir but carefully rotate the saucepan until the nuts are covered with caramel. When the nuts start to 'pop', pour the mixture onto an oiled marble slab or a baking sheet lined with silicone paper. Cool. Crush to a coarse, gritty powder with a rolling pin or in a food processor.

Preheat the oven to 190°C/375°F/gas 5.

Brush the cake tins with melted butter and line the base of each with a round of greaseproof paper. Brush the paper with melted butter also and dust the base and sides with flour.

Cream the butter. Add the caster sugar and beat until light and fluffy. Add in the eggs one by one, beating well between each addition. Sieve the flour and baking powder and stir in gradually. Add two tablespoons of the Praline powder. Mix lightly. If the mixture is a little stiff, add a few tablespoons of milk to moisten.

Divide equally between the two prepared tins. Bake for 25 minutes. Allow to cool in the tin for a few minutes before turning out and cooling on a wire rack. Reinvert after a few moments so as not to mark the top of the cake.

Meanwhile, make the Praline Buttercream. Put the water and sugar in a saucepan and bring to the boil, stirring only until the sugar dissolves. Let the syrup boil to the 'thread stage' 106–113°C/223–236°F. Beat the yolks for one minute with an electric beater, and add the hot syrup very gradually. Continue beating until the syrup has all been added and the mixture is almost cool. Still whisking, add the butter in small pieces. Add the vanilla extract. Stir in 4 tablespoons fine Praline powder.

Split each cake in half. Spread with Praline Buttercream. Sandwich the two cakes together. Ice the top and sides with the remaining buttercream. Sprinkle Praline all over the surface of the cake.

TIP: To skin hazelnuts, put the hazelnuts in a fairly hot oven; after 5–10 minutes the skins will loosen. Remove and rub off the loose skins in a clean tea towel.

Coffee Cake

Serves 8–10

Another splendid cake that keeps well.

225g (8oz) butter
225g (8oz) caster sugar
4 organic eggs
225g (8oz) white flour
1 teaspoon baking powder
4–5 tablespoons coffee essence (we use Irel)

Coffee Butter Cream (see right)
Coffee Glacé Icing (see right)

Decoration
hazelnuts or chocolate coffee beans

2 x sandwich tins, 20cm (8in) in diameter

Preheat the oven to 180°C/350°F/gas 4.

Brush the tins with melted butter, dust with flour and line the base of each with a disc of greaseproof paper. Brush with melted butter.

Cream the butter until soft, add the caster sugar and beat until pale and light in texture. Whisk the eggs. Add to the mixture, bit by bit, beating well between each addition. Sieve the flour with the baking powder and stir gently into the cake mixture, finally adding in the coffee essence. Mix thoroughly.

Spoon the mixture into the prepared sandwich tins and bake for about 30 minutes in the oven. When the cakes are cooked, the centre will be firm and springy and the edges will have slightly shrunk from the sides of the tin.

Allow to rest in the tin for a few minutes before turning out onto the wire rack. Remove the greaseproof paper from the base, then reinvert so the top of the cakes don't get marked by the wire rack. Cool the cakes on the wire rack. When cold, sandwich the cakes together with Coffee Buttercream and ice the top with Coffee Glacé icing. Decorate with caramelised hazelnuts or chocolate coffee beans.

Coffee Butter Cream Filling

50g (2oz) butter
110g (4oz) icing sugar, sieved
1–2 teaspoons coffee essence (we use Irel)

Beat the butter with the icing sugar and the coffee essence.

Coffee Glacé Icing

225g (8oz) icing sugar
scant 1 tablespoon coffee essence (we use Irel)
about 2 tablespoons boiling water

Sieve the icing sugar into a bowl. Add the coffee essence and enough boiling water to make it the consistency of thick cream.

Walnut Cake with American Frosting

Even though it is very laborious, we quite often crack open the walnuts ourselves for this cake, to ensure that they are fresh and sweet. Shelled walnuts turn rancid easily so taste one to be sure they are still good.

200g (7oz) plain white flour
a pinch of salt
2½ level teaspoons baking powder
75g (3oz) very fresh walnuts, shelled
75g (3oz) butter
225g (8oz) caster sugar
½ teaspoon pure vanilla extract
2 organic eggs
125ml (4fl oz) milk

Filling
50g (2oz) butter
110g (4oz) icing sugar
a few drops of pure vanilla extract

American Frosting
1 organic egg white
225g (8oz) granulated sugar
4 tablespoons water

Decoration
5 or 6 walnut halves

3 x round 18cm (7in) sandwich tins

Preheat the oven to 190°C/375°F/gas 5.

Brush the tins with a little melted butter and line the base of each with a round of greaseproof paper. Brush the paper with melted butter also and dust the base and edges with flour.

Sieve the flour with a pinch of salt and the baking powder. Chop the walnuts roughly.

Cream the butter, and gradually add the caster sugar and the vanilla extract. Separate the eggs, add in the yolks and keep the whites aside until later. Add the walnuts to the creamed mixture. Fold the flour and milk alternately into the mixture.

Whisk the egg whites until they are stiff. Stir a little into the cake mixture and then fold the rest in gently. Divide between the 3 tins and smooth over the tops. Bake in the oven for about 20 minutes or until firm to the touch. Turn out of the tins onto a wire rack. Remove the greaseproof paper and allow to get completely cold.

Meanwhile, for the filling, cream the butter and add the sieved icing sugar and vanilla extract. When the cake is cold, sandwich the 3 layers together with butter cream.

The delicious frosting is a little tricky to make, so follow the instructions exactly. Quick and accurate decisions are necessary in judging when the icing is ready and then it must be used immediately.

Bring a saucepan of water large enough to support a Pyrex mixing bowl to the boil. Whisk the egg white until very stiff in the Pyrex bowl. In another pan, dissolve the sugar carefully in the 4 tablespoons of water and boil for about 1½ minutes until the syrup reaches the 'thread stage' (106–113°C/223–236°F). It will look thick and syrupy and, when a metal spoon is dipped in, the last drops of syrup to drip off will form a thin thread. Pour this boiling syrup over the stiffly beaten egg white, whisking all the time. Sit the bowl in the saucepan of simmering water. Continue to whisk over the water until the icing is snow white and very thick (this can take up to 10 minutes).

Spread quickly over the cake with a palette knife. It sets very quickly at this stage, so speed is essential. Decorate with 5 or 6 walnut halves.

Coconut Macaroon Cake

This cake has an irresistible crispy topping – the crumb is moist, and rich with coconut and almonds, so it will keep well, stored in an airtight tin.

Cake
225g (8oz) butter
225g (8oz) caster sugar
4 organic eggs and 1 organic egg yolk
¼ teaspoon pure vanilla extract
225g (8oz) plain white flour
½ level teaspoon baking powder
25g (1oz) ground almonds
25g (1oz) desiccated coconut

Macaroon Topping
1 organic egg white
10g (½oz) desiccated coconut
25g (1oz) ground almonds
75g (3oz) caster sugar
¼ teaspoon pure vanilla extract
75g (3oz) flaked almonds

cake tin with sides about 5cm (2in) high and
    diameter of 20cm (8in), lined with
    greaseproof paper

Preheat the oven to 180°C/350°F/gas 4.

Cream the butter, add the sugar and beat until light and fluffy. Whisk the eggs and egg yolk and add gradually, beating well between each addition. Add the vanilla extract. Mix the dry ingredients well and stir in gently. Turn into the prepared tin.

For the topping, whisk the egg white lightly and fold in the coconut, ground almonds, sugar and vanilla. Spread carefully over the cake mixture in the tin. Sprinkle with flaked almonds and bake in the oven for about 1½ hours. Cool in the tin, then on a wire rack.

Note: Pure vanilla extract is labelled as such and comes from the cured pods of the vanilla, a tropical plant and member of the orchid family. It is amber in colour and vastly superior in flavour than vanilla flavouring or essence. It is also more expensive but buy it if you can.

Aunt Florence's Orange Cake

When my Aunt Florence brings a present of this delicious cake in a tin, lots of people suddenly emerge out of the woodwork pleading for a slice. Without question, it is the best orange cake any of us has ever eaten.

225g (8oz) butter
225g (8oz) caster sugar
zest of 1 orange, finely grated
4 organic eggs
225g (8oz) plain white flour
1 level teaspoon baking powder
1 tablespoon orange juice, freshly squeezed

Orange Butter Filling
110g (4oz) butter
225g (8oz) icing sugar
zest of 1 orange, grated
1 tablespoon orange juice, freshly squeezed

Orange Glacé Icing
275g (10oz) icing sugar
orange juice, freshly squeezed

Candied Orange Peel (see page 515)

2 x 20cm (8in) round cake tins, or
    1 x 30cm (12in)

Preheat the oven to 180°C/350°F/gas 4.

Grease and flour the cake tins. Line the base of each with silicone paper.

Cream the butter and gradually add the caster sugar. Beat until soft and light and quite pale in colour. Add the orange zest. Add the eggs 1 at a time, beating well between each addition. Sieve the flour and baking powder and stir in gradually. Mix all together lightly; then stir in the orange juice.

Divide the mixture evenly if using 2 tins, hollowing it slightly in the centre. Bake the in the oven for 35 minutes or until cooked. Turn out onto a wire tray and allow to cool.

Meanwhile, make the filling. Cream the butter; add the icing sugar and orange zest. Beat in the orange juice bit by bit.

To make the icing, simply squeeze the juice from an orange and add enough to the icing sugar to make a spreadable icing.

When the cakes are cold, split each one in 2 halves and spread with a little filling, then sandwich the pieces together. Spread icing over the top and sides and decorate the top, if you like, with little diamonds of candied peel. This cake keeps very well – as long as you hide it well enough!

> TIP: If the butter and sugar are not creamed properly, and you add the eggs too fast, the mixture will curdle, resulting in a cake with a heavier texture.

Tunisian Orange Cake

Sophie Grigson introduced us to this cake on her course here at the school. It is a real goodie and keeps for not just days but weeks.

50g (2oz) slightly stale white breadcrumbs
200g (7oz) caster sugar
100g (3½oz) ground almonds
1½ level teaspoons baking powder
200ml (7fl oz) sunflower oil
4 organic eggs
zest of 1 large unwaxed orange, finely grated
zest of ½ unwaxed lemon, finely grated

Citrus syrup
juice of 1 unwaxed orange
juice of ½ unwaxed lemon
75g (3oz) sugar
2 cloves
1 cinnamon stick

cream, Greek yoghurt or crème fraîche

round tin, 20(8in) in diameter, 5cm (2in) deep

Line the base of the tin with a round of greaseproof paper. Grease and flour the tin.

Mix the breadcrumbs with the sugar, almonds and baking powder. Whisk the oil with the eggs, pour into the dry ingredients and mix well.

Add the orange and lemon zest. Pour the mixture into the prepared tin. Put into a cold oven, and turn on with the heat set to 180°C/350°F/gas 4.

Bake for 45–60 minutes or until the cake is golden brown. A skewer inserted into the centre should come out clean. Allow to cool for 5 minutes before turning out onto a plate.

Meanwhile, make the citrus syrup. Put all the ingredients into a stainless steel saucepan and bring gently to the boil, stirring until the sugar has dissolved completely. Simmer for 3 minutes. While the cake is still warm, pierce it with a skewer. Spoon the hot syrup over the cake. Leave to cool. Spoon excess syrup back over the cake every now and then until it is all soaked up.

One can remove the cloves and cinnamon stick but we like to leave them on top of the cake. Serve with crème fraîche or thick Greek yoghurt.

BELOW: Tunisian Orange Cake

Julia Wight's Carrot Cake

This recipe for carrot cake is by far the best one I know and was given to me by a dear friend. You can use either the cream cheese icing or the glaze as a topping. It keeps for ages.

200g (7oz) wholemeal flour
3 level teaspoons mixed spice
1 level teaspoon bread soda
110g (4oz) soft brown sugar
2 large organic eggs
150ml (5fl oz) sunflower oil
grated rind of 1 orange
200g (7oz) grated carrot
110g (4oz) sultanas
55g (2oz) dessicated coconut
55g (2oz) walnuts, chopped

Cream Cheese Icing
125g (5oz) cream cheese
75g (3oz) icing sugar
75g (3oz) butter
grated rind on 1 orange
toasted flaked almonds or pumpkin seeds for decoration (optional)

Glaze
85g (3oz) soft brown sugar
juice of 1 small orange
1 tablespoon lemon juice

23 x 12 x 5cm (9 x 5 x 2in) loaf tin, lined with silicone paper

Preheat the oven to 180°C/350°F/gas 4.

Put the flour, spice and bread soda into a bowl and mix well. Whisk the eggs with the sugar and oil in another bowl until smooth. Stir in the dry ingredients, and add the orange rind, grated carrot, sultanas, coconut and walnuts. Pour into the lined tin. Bake in the oven for 1³/₄–2 hours until well risen and firm to the touch.

If using cream cheese icing, mix all the ingredients for the icing together and spread over the top of the carrot cake.

If using the glaze, mix the sugar with the orange and lemon juice in a bowl. While the cake is still warm, prick the top with a skewer, pour the glaze over the cake and leave in the tin to cool.

Note: This cake can also be made in a 18 x 8cm (7 x 3in) round tin which needs to be lined and will only take 1 hour in the oven.

Elizabeth Mosse's Gingerbread

Makes 2 loaves

450g (1lb) flour
¹/₂ teaspoon salt
1¹/₂ teaspoon ground ginger
2 teaspoon baking powder
¹/₂ teaspoon bread soda
225g (8oz) soft brown sugar
340g (³/₄lb) treacle
170g (6oz) butter, cut into cubes
300ml (¹/₂ pint) milk
1 organic egg, beaten
1 fistful of sultanas (optional)

2 loaf tins, 23x 12 x 5cm (9 x 5 x 2in), lined with silicone paper

Preheat the oven to 180°C/350°F/gas 4.

Sieve the flour, salt, ground ginger, baking powder and bread soda into a bowl and mix together.

Gently warm the brown sugar and treacle with the cubed butter and then add the milk. Allow to cool a little and stir into the dry ingredients. Add the beaten egg and the sultanas if desired. Mix very thoroughly and make sure that there are no little lumps of flour left.

Bake in one or two lined loaf tins for about 1 hour. This gingerbread keeps very well.

Californian Polenta Cake with Summer Berries

Serves 8

This creation, made famous by another of our guest chefs, John Ash of Fetzers Winery in California, keeps very well and is also delicious served with Rosemary Syrup (see page 568).

225g (8oz) unsalted butter, softened
225g (8oz) caster sugar
225g (8oz) ground almonds
1 teaspoon pure vanilla extract
3 organic eggs
zest of 2 unwaxed lemons, finely grated
110g (4oz) polenta flour
¹/₂ teaspoon baking powder
pinch of salt

450g (1lb) summer berries, e.g. strawberries, raspberries, red currants, loganberries
225ml (8fl oz) crème fraîche or yoghurt (we use Ardsallagh goat's milk yoghurt or thick ewe's milk yoghurt)

springform tin, 20cm (8in) in diameter

Preheat the oven to 170°C/325°F/gas 3.

Butter and flour the cake tin. Cream the butter, add the caster sugar and beat until pale and fluffy. Stir in the ground almonds and pure vanilla extract. Beat in the eggs, one at a time. Fold in the lemon zest and a squeeze of lemon juice. Mix the polenta, baking powder and salt together and stir in gently.

Fill into the prepared tin and bake in the preheated oven for 40–45 minutes or until rich golden brown on top and cooked through in the centre. Cool on a wire rack. Serve with summer berries and crème fraîche.

Note: If you cannot find unwaxed citrus fruit, wash and dry the skin well.

Yoghurt Cake – Chalet Girls' Salvation

Serves 10–14

This recipe works at high altitude – creative chalet girls ring the changes in a myriad of ways, depending on the tins and ingredients available in their store cupboard or fruit bowl. This recipe does not work at sea level!

1 small carton of yoghurt, natural or flavoured (use the yoghurt carton as a measure)
1 carton caster sugar if flavoured yoghurt (1½ cartons if using natural yoghurt)
1 carton sunflower oil
3 cartons plain white flour
4 organic eggs
2 teaspoons baking powder
½ teaspoon pure vanilla extract or a couple of drops almond essence if using plain yoghurt (optional)

20cm (8in) round tin, or 450g (1lb) loaf tin, lined and greased

Preheat the oven to 180°C/350°F/gas 4.

Whizz all the ingredients in a food processor or by hand. Pour into the tin. Bake for 40–50 minutes. Cool on a wire rack. Split in half and fill with jam and cream and dust with icing sugar.

Variations

Lemon Yoghurt Cake

Add the zest and juice of 2 lemons to the basic mix. When cooked, prick the cake with a skewer and pour the juice of 1 more lemon mixed with a tablespoon of caster sugar over the cake.

Coffee Yoghurt Cake

Add 1 tablespoon of instant coffee mixed with 2 teaspoons of hot water to the basic mix. Ice with either Coffee Butter Cream or Coffee Glacé Icing (see page 447) and scatter the top with chopped walnuts.

Chocolate Yoghurt Cake

Add 2 tablespoons unsweetened cocoa to the basic mix. Ice with Chocolate Icing (see page 454).

Note: dried fruit (e.g. chopped dates, raisins or cherries) and extra nuts (hazelnuts, pecans etc.) may be added to any of the above variations.

Swiss Roll

110g (4oz) plain flour
4 organic eggs
110g (4oz) caster sugar
2 tablespoons warm water
1 teaspoon pure vanilla extract
6 tablespoons Raspberry Jam, warmed (see page 504)

Swiss roll tin, 25 x 38cm (10 x 15in)

Preheat the oven to 190°C/375°F/gas 5. Line the tin with greaseproof paper cut to fit the bottom of the tin exactly. Brush the paper and sides of the tin with melted butter, then dust with flour and caster sugar.

Sieve the flour. Put the eggs and caster sugar into a bowl over a saucepan of simmering water. Whisk the mixture until it is light and fluffy. Take it off the heat and continue to whisk until the mixture is cool again. (If using an electric mixer, no heat is required.) Add the water and vanilla extract. Sieve in about one-third of the flour at a time and fold it into the mousse, using a large metal spoon.

Pour the mixture gently into the tin. Bake in the oven for 12–15 minutes. It is cooked when it feels firm to the touch in the centre. The edges will have shrunk in slightly from the sides of the tin.

Lay a piece of greaseproof paper on the worktop and sprinkle it evenly with caster sugar. Turn the Swiss roll tin over onto the sugared greaseproof paper. Remove the tin and greaseproof paper from the bottom of the cake.

While the cake is still warm, spread it sparingly with Raspberry Jam. Catch the edge of the paper nearest you and roll up the Swiss roll away from you.

Variations

There are many delicious fillings to try in a Swiss Roll. If you are using whipped cream or fresh fruit (or any ingredient that will not do well being spread on a warm cake) roll the cake without the filling and, when cool, unroll and add the filling.

Mashed banana with lemon juice and whipped cream

Melted chocolate and whipped cream

Fresh strawberries or raspberries, mashed with a little sugar, and whipped cream

Other homemade jam and whipped cream

Crystallised Flowers

The art of crystallising flowers simply takes patience and a meticulous nature – the sort of job that drives some people around the bend but that others adore. If it appeals to you, the work will be well rewarded as they look and taste divine.

organic egg whites
caster sugar

1. Use freshly picked, strong-textured leaves, and small flowers such as primroses, violets, apple blossom and violas.

2. The caster sugar must be absolutely dry, so to be quite sure, sieve and dry it out in a Swiss roll tin in a low oven, 140°C/275°F/gas 1, for about 2 hours.

3. Break up an egg white slightly with a fork. Using a thin paintbrush, brush the egg white very carefully over part of the petal and into every surface. Pour the caster sugar over the flower or leaf with a teaspoon. Arrange carefully on silicone paper to ensure a good shape. Allow to dry overnight in a warm dry place, (close to an Aga or over a radiator). If properly crystallised these flowers will last for months, even years, provided they are kept dry. We store them in a covered pottery jar or a tin box.

4. Remember to do lots of leaves as well as flowers so one can make attractive arrangements – mint, lemon balm, wild strawberry, salad burnet or marguerite and daisy leaves work well.

Master Recipe
Great Grandmother's Cake

125g (4¹/₂oz) butter
175g (6oz) caster sugar
3 organic eggs
175g (6oz) flour
1 teaspoon baking powder
1 tablespoon milk

Filling
225g (8oz) Raspberry Jam (see page 504)
300ml (10fl oz) whipped cream

caster sugar, to sprinkle

2 x 18cm (7in) sponge cake tins

Preheat the oven to 180°C/350°F/gas 4. Grease and flour the tins and line the base of each with a round of greaseproof paper.

Cream the butter and gradually add the caster sugar. Beat until soft and light and quite pale in colour. Add the eggs one at a time, beating well between each addition. Sieve the flour and baking powder and stir in gradually. Mix all together lightly and add the milk to moisten.

Divide the mixture evenly between the 2 tins, hollowing it slightly in the centre. Bake for 20–25 minutes or until cooked. Turn out onto a wire tray and allow to cool. Sandwich together with homemade Raspberry Jam and whipped cream. Sprinkle with sieved caster sugar. Serve on an old-fashioned plate with a doyley.

Variation
Lemon Victoria Sponge

Follow the Master Recipe, but include the grated zest of 1 lemon when creaming the butter.

homemade Lemon Curd (see page 511)

Icing
350g (12oz) icing sugar
4–5 tablespoons boiling water

Decoration
Crystallised Violets (see left)

Split the cakes in half and spread on a little lemon curd to sandwich them together.

Sieve the icing sugar into a bowl and add enough boiling water to mix to a fairly stiff coating consistency. The icing should hold a trail when dropped from a spoon but gradually find its own level. Put the rest of the lemon curd into a piping-bag, fitted with a fine writing nozzle or use a paper nozzle.

Spread the icing smoothly and evenly over the top and sides of the cakes, using a warm palette knife. While it is still wet, quickly pipe lines with the lemon curd, about 2.5cm (1in) apart, across the top of the cake. Then draw the tip of a skewer or pointed knife through the coloured lines, at right angles, going in opposite directions each time, this is called feathering and may be done in lines or in a circular spider web pattern. Alternatively, decorate the cake with crystallised flowers and leaves.

Whisked-up Sponge
Serves 6–8

When the first edition of this book was published, a fan from Tipperary telephoned me to express her disappointment that there was no whisked-up sponge in the book... this one is for you!

3 organic eggs
225g (8oz) caster sugar
75ml (3fl oz) water
140g (5oz) plain white flour
1 teaspoon baking powder

Filling
cream with fresh fruit (e.g. strawberries,
*   raspberries, loganberries, gooseberries,*
*   kumquats), fruit compote, or homemade jam*

2 x 20cm (8in) sandwich tins, greased
*   and floured*

Preheat the oven to 190°C/375°F/gas 5.

Separate the egg yolks from the whites. Whisk the yolks with the sugar for 2 minutes in a food mixer and then add in the water. Whisk until light and fluffy – about 10 minutes. Gently fold the sieved flour and baking powder into the mousse in batches.

Whisk the egg whites until they hold a stiff peak. Fold them into the mousse.

Divide between the two prepared tins and bake in the oven for 20 minutes. Remove from the tins and cool on a wire rack.

Sandwich the cakes together with whipped cream and any of the above fillings. Sprinkle a little icing sugar over the top before serving on a pretty plate with a paper doyley.

Basic Genoise Sponge
Serves 4

This is the type of sponge that is used as the base for many gâteaux in France.

110g (4oz) flour
50g (2oz) butter
4 organic eggs
110g (4oz) sugar

For Flavouring
½ teaspoon vanilla extract, or grated rind of
 1 lemon or orange, or 1 teaspoon orange
 flower water
1–2 teaspoons coffee essence (we use Irel)

23cm (9in) round genoise cake tin, with 5cm
 (2in) high sides that slope outwards

Brush the inside of the cake tin with a little melted butter. If you like, line the base with a circle of greaseproof paper that exactly fits, and butter it also. Leave it for a few minutes and then sprinkle the tin with flour, discarding the excess.

Preheat the oven to 180°C/350°F/gas 4.

Sieve the flour well. Clarify the butter (see page 105). Put the eggs in a large bowl, and gradually whisk in the sugar. Put the bowl

over hot, but not boiling water, for 8–10 minutes, or until the mixture is light and thick enough to make a distinct figure of 8 when the whisk is lifted. Take the bowl from the heat, add the chosen flavouring and continue beating until cooled.

Sieve the flour over the mixture in three batches, folding each batch as lightly as possible with a wooden spatula or metal spoon. Just after the last batch, pour the cooled, clarified butter around the side of the bowl and fold in gently and quickly (because the whisked mixture quickly loses volume after the butter is added).

Pour the mixture into the prepared tin and bake in the oven for 35–40 minutes, or until the cake shrinks slightly from the side of the tin and the top springs back when lightly pressed. Turn it out on a rack to cool.

Chocolate Mousse Gâteau
Serves 6–8

This is a real labour of love but it's got the wow factor.

For the Genoise
100g (3½oz) flour
25g (1oz) cocoa powder
1½ level teaspoons baking powder
pinch of salt
50g (2oz) unsalted butter
4 organic eggs
150g (5oz) sugar
½ teaspoon pure vanilla extract

For the Chocolate Mousse
275g (10oz) dark dessert chocolate, chopped
6 organic eggs, separated
175g (6oz) unsalted butter
1 teaspoon pure vanilla extract or
 2 tablespoons Grand Marnier liqueur

Chantilly Cream
425ml (15fl oz) double cream
2 tablespoons sugar

1 teaspoon pure vanilla extract
Chocolate Caraque (see page 400)

23cm (9in) Genoise cake tin

Preheat the oven to 180°C/350°F/gas 4.

Prepare the cake tin (see left). Sieve the flour with the cocoa, baking powder and salt and make the genoise mixture following the basic recipe (see left). Add the vanilla extract. Pour the mixture into the prepared tin and bake in the oven for 35–40 minutes or until the mixture springs back when lightly pressed with a fingertip. Cool on a wire rack. The cake can be baked ahead and kept in an airtight container for 2–3 days or it can be frozen.

For the Chocolate Mousse, melt the chocolate in a pan over hot water or in a very cool oven and stir until smooth. Beat the egg yolks one by one into the hot mixture so that it thickens slightly. Beat in the butter and vanilla extract or liqueur. Allow to cool slightly. Whip the egg whites until stiff, add a spoonful of the tepid chocolate mixture to them and fold the two together as lightly as possible, the warm mixture will lightly cook and stiffen the whites. Leave to cool at room temperature, not in the fridge, otherwise the mousse will harden and become difficult to spread.

Make the Chantilly Cream: mix the sugar into the double cream and add the vanilla extract.

To assemble the Gâteau, split the genoise into 3 layers. Spread the chocolate mousse on the bottom layer. Place the second layer of genoise on top and spread it with two thirds of the Chantilly cream, reserving the remaining cream for decoration. Top with the third layer and spread the remaining mousse on the top and sides of the cake.

Decorate the top and sides with chocolate caraque or curls and Chantilly cream.

Garden Café Chocolate Mousse Cake

3 organic eggs
250 g (8oz) caster sugar
6 tablespoons water
110g (4oz) white flour
25g (1oz) cocoa
1 level teaspoon baking powder

Chocolate Ganâche
300ml (½ pint) cream
225g (8oz) best-quality dark chocolate, finely chopped

Chocolate Decorations (see page 400)

2 sandwich tins, 20cm (8in) in diameter

Preheat the oven to 190°C/375°F/gas 5.

Line the bases of the tins with a round of greaseproof paper, then grease and flour. Separate the eggs. Whisk the yolks and sugar for 2 minutes. Blend in the water. Whisk until firm and creamy, about 10 minutes. Sift in the flour, cocoa and baking powder. Beat the egg whites in a separate bowl until they form stiff peaks. Fold them in very gently. Divide the mixture between the two tins and bake in the oven for about 30 minutes. Cool on a wire rack.

Meanwhile make the Chocolate Ganâche. Put the cream in a heavy, preferably stainless steel, saucepan and bring it almost to the boil. Remove from the heat and add the chopped chocolate. With a wooden spoon, stir the chocolate into the cream until it is completely melted.

Transfer the chocolate cream into the bowl of a food mixer and allow to cool to room temperature. Whisk until it is just stiff enough to pipe (do not over-whisk or it will curdle and separate).

Sandwich the cakes together with whipped cream or Ganâche. Spread Ganâche all over the top and sides of the cake. Pipe 8 or 9 rosettes of Ganâche on top of the cake and decorate with curls of chocolate. Dredge with unsweetened cocoa.

Ballymaloe Chocolate Almond Gâteau

An incredibly rich cake. Use the best chocolate you can buy: Valrhona, Menier, Suchard or Callebaut. We use Lesmé Belgian chocolate at Ballymaloe. Enjoy a small slice with a cup of espresso. This cake keeps really well if one can resist.

110g (4oz) best-quality dark chocolate
2 tablespoons red Jamaica rum
110g (4oz) whole almonds
110g (4oz) butter, preferably unsalted
110g (4oz) caster sugar
3 organic eggs, separated
1 tablespoon caster sugar
50g (2oz) plain white flour
50g (2oz) whole almonds or best quality ground almonds

Chocolate Icing
110g (4oz) best quality dark chocolate
2 tablespoons red Jamaica rum
110g (4oz) unsalted butter

Decoration
Crystallised Violets (see page 452)
toasted flaked almonds

2 x 18cm (7in) sandwich tins

Preheat the oven to 180°C/350°F/gas 4.

Grease the tins and line the base of each with greaseproof paper. Melt the chocolate with the rum on a very gentle heat. Bring a small saucepan of water to the boil and add the almonds. Bring back to the boil for 2–3 minutes. Test one to see if the skin is loose. Drain and peel, and discard the skins. Grind in a food processor; they should still be slightly gritty.

Cream the butter, and then add the caster sugar, beating until light and fluffy. Beat in the egg yolks one by one. Whisk the egg whites with a pinch of salt until stiff. Add 1 tablespoon of caster sugar and continue to whisk until they reach the stiff peak stage. Add the melted chocolate to the butter and sugar mixture and then add the almonds. Fold in a quarter of the egg white mixture followed by a quarter of the sieved

flour. Fold in the remaining egg white mixture and flour alternately until they have all been added.

Divide the mixture between the two prepared tins and make a hollow in the centre of each cake. Bake in the oven for 19–25 minutes.

IMPORTANT: The cake should be slightly underdone in the centre. Sides should be cooked but the centre a little unset. Allow to cool for a few minutes in the tins, turn out gently onto a wire rack, remove the paper and allow to get cold.

For the Chocolate Icing, melt the chocolate with the rum in a Pyrex bowl over a low heat. Beat in the unsalted butter a tablespoon at a time. Beat occasionally until cool. If the icing liquefies, put it into the fridge to firm up, then whisk until stiff.

When the cake is completely cold, fill and ice with the Chocolate Icing. Pipe any remaining icing around the top and decorate with flaked almonds and crystallised violets.

Chocolate Chestnut Cake

This is a very rich and decadent cake. The chestnuts add a unique flavour and depth to the chocolate, with a smooth-as-velvet finish. It keeps well for several days. Super chef, Jeanne Rankin, made this cake when she came to the school – we just love it.

110g (4oz) dark chocolate, chopped
200g (7oz) unsweetened chestnut purée
4 organic eggs, separated
200g (7oz) caster sugar

Icing
75g (3oz) best-quality chocolate
1 organic egg yolk
1 tablespoon butter
1 tablespoon rum (optional)
10g (½oz) caster sugar
75ml (3fl oz) double cream, softly whipped
extra cream to serve

20cm (8in) loose-based tin

ABOVE: Ballymaloe Chocolate Almond Gâteau

Preheat the oven to 180°C/350°F/gas 4.

Grease the tin liberally. Melt the chocolate in a Pyrex bowl over a saucepan of hot, but not boiling, water. Pass the chestnut purée through a mouli or a food processor to loosen its texture. It tends to be very compressed straight out of the tin, and you will be able to mix it into the other ingredients better if this is done.

Place the 4 yolks, and ²/₃ of the sugar into the bowl of a mixer, and beat at high speed for 3–5 minutes, until it is very light and fluffy. By hand, whisk the egg whites until they are firm and shiny, and whisk in the rest of the sugar. Continue to whisk for another 30–60 seconds, until they are glossy and stiff. Add the chestnut purée to the yolk mixture and mix in at low speed. Fold in the melted chocolate. Once it is well incorporated, fold in the egg whites by hand.

Pour into the greased springform, and place in the centre of the oven for 30–40 minutes, until a toothpick inserted into the centre comes out clean. Remove from the oven and cool before taking out of the tin.

To make the icing, melt the chocolate, and while it is still warm, stir in the egg yolk and butter. Whisk for 1 minute, and then set aside. Whisk the rum, if using, and sugar into the cream, and fold it all in to the chocolate mixture, a bit at a time. With the aid of a spatula, spread the icing on the top and the sides of the cake. Allow to set in the fridge for at least 1 hour before serving. Serve with a dollop of cream.

Angel Food Cake with Rosewater Cream and Summer Berries

A very delicious way of using up spare egg whites.

125g (4½oz) plain white flour
160g (5½oz) caster sugar
pinch of salt
7 large organic egg whites
1 level teaspoon cream of tartar
1 teaspoon rosewater

For decoration
icing sugar
rose petals, if available
summer berries – raspberries, strawberries,
  blueberries, loganberries, fraises des bois
Rosewater Cream (see right)

23 x 8cm (9 x 3in) round cake tin, greased
  and floured

Preheat the oven to 180°C/350°F/gas 4.

Put 2 tablespoons of caster sugar aside. Sieve the flour with the remainder of the caster sugar and a little pinch of salt. Put the egg whites into a large bowl, whisk slowly at first until foamy, add the cream of tartar and whisk again. Slowly add the reserved caster sugar and beat until the egg whites hold soft peaks. Add the rosewater, then fold in the flour and sugar ⅓ at a time.

Pour the mixture gently into the greased tin, and bake in the oven for 30–35 minutes or until firm and slightly golden. A skewer should come out clean when inserted into the cake. Leave to cool for 20–30 minutes in the tin. Turn out onto a wire rack to cool.

Serve the cake dusted with icing sugar accompanied by summer berries and Rosewater Cream.

Rosewater Cream

425ml (¾ pint) whipped cream
1 teaspoon rosewater, or to taste
a little caster sugar

Mix the whipped cream, rosewater and sugar gently together.

Puff Pastry
Makes about 1¼kg (2¾lb)

Homemade puff pastry takes a little time to make but it is more than worth the effort for the wonderful flavour that bears no relation to the commercial equivalent. It's essential to use butter. It should have 729 layers!

450g (1lb) chilled flour (use strong flour if
  possible)
pinch of salt
300–350ml (10–12fl oz) cold water
squeeze of lemon juice (optional)
450g (1lb) butter, firm but pliable

Sieve the flour and salt into a bowl and mix to a firm dough with water and a squeeze of lemon juice. This dough is called détrempe. Cover with greaseproof paper or clingfilm and rest for 30 minutes in the refrigerator.

Roll the détrempe into a square about 1cm (½in) thick. Unwrap the butter and shape into a slab roughly 2cm (¾in) thick. If the butter is very hard, beat it (still in the wrapper) with a rolling pin until pliable but not sticky. Place in the centre of the dough and fold the dough over the edges of the butter to make a neat parcel.

Make sure your chilled marble slab or pastry bench is well-floured, then flatten the dough with a rolling pin, and continue to roll out into a rectangle about 45cm (18in) long and 15cm (6in) wide (this is approximate so don't get into a fuss if it's not exactly that measurement). Fold neatly into 3 with the sides aligned as accurately as possible. Seal the edges by pressing with a rolling pin.

Give the dough a one-quarter turn (90°): it should now be on your pastry bench as though it was a book with the ends facing north/south. Roll out again, fold in 3 and seal the edges with the rolling pin. Cover with clingfilm or greaseproof paper meticulously and rest in the fridge for 30 minutes.

The pastry has now had two rolls or 'turns'. Repeat the process 2 more times, giving the dough 6 rolls altogether with a 30 minutes rest in the fridge between every 2 turns. Chill for at least 30 minutes before using.

Note: Each time you start to roll the pastry place it on the worktop with the ends north/south as if it were a book. In hot weather it may be necessary to chill the pastry slightly longer between rollings.

Gâteau Pithivier
Serves 8

My brother, Rory O'Connell, does a delicious Chocolate Gâteau Pithivier, adding 110g (4oz) of chopped chocolate to the filling.

half quantity Puff Pastry (see left)

Filling
110g (4oz) ground almonds
110g (4oz) caster sugar
35g (1½oz) melted butter
2 organic egg yolks
2 tablespoons cream
2 teaspoons rum (optional)
egg wash made with 1 beaten organic egg and
  a tiny pinch of salt

Glaze
icing sugar

Preheat the oven to 230°C/450°F/gas 8.

Divide the pastry in half, roll out thinly, and cut into 2 circles about 25cm (10in) in diameter. Put 1 onto a damp baking sheet and chill; also chill the other piece.

Mix all the filling ingredients together in a bowl until smooth. Put the filling onto the pastry base, leaving a rim of about 2.5cm (1in) free around the edge. Brush the rim with beaten egg or water and put on the lid of pastry. Press it down well around the edges.

Make a small hole in the centre, brush with egg wash and leave for 5 minutes in the refrigerator. With the back of a knife, nick the edge of the pastry 12 times at regular intervals to form a scalloped edge with a rose petal effect. Mark long curving lines from the central hole outwards to designate formal petals. Be careful not to cut through the pastry – just score it.

Bake for 20 minutes in the oven, then lower the heat to 200°C/400°F/gas 6 and bake for about 30 minutes. While still hot dredge heavily with icing sugar and return to a very hot oven or pop under a grill for an instant or two and no longer – the sugar will melt and caramelise to a dark brown glaze. Serve warm or cold with a bowl of softly whipped cream.

Note: Gâteau Pithivier is best eaten warm, but it also keeps well and may be reheated.

Mille-feuille
Serves 8

A labour of love, but so delicious…

225g (8oz) Puff Pastry (see left)
about 110g (4oz) Redcurrant Jelly
  (see page 508)
300ml (10fl oz) whipped cream
300ml (10fl oz) Pastry Cream (see page 460)
2–3 tablespoons Kirsch
225g (8oz) raspberries or strawberries
icing sugar

Garnish
mint or lemon balm leaves

Preheat the oven to 220°C/425°F/gas 7.

Roll out the pastry into a very large, thin rectangle about 40 x 85cm (16 x 34in). This pastry should be no thicker than a coin. Transfer to baking sheet. Prick all over with a fork. Cover the baking tray or trays with a second tray and bake – this sounds rather bizarre but it prevents the puff pastry from rising too much or unevenly. Chill for 30 minutes. Then bake in the oven for another 20 minutes and then reduce the heat to 180°C/350°F/gas 4 until brown.

Remove from the oven and while it is still warm cut the pastry into 3 neat equal sized strips, about 12 x 25cm (5 x 10in). Reserve the trimmings of cooked pastry for later. Dredge the 3 pieces of pastry heavily with icing sugar and place under a hot grill. Allow the sugar to caramelise. Remove from under the grill and repeat the process on the other sides of the pastry. Allow to cool completely.

To assemble the mille-feuille, place one of the pastry strips on a board and brush lightly with slightly warmed redcurrant jelly. Mix the pastry cream with the stiffly whipped cream, and flavour with kirsch. Put into a piping bag. Pipe half of this mixture onto the first layer of pastry. Cover with a layer of raspberries or sliced strawberries, (reserve a few whole for decoration). Now brush the second piece of pastry with redcurrant jelly, put on top of the first, and pipe the remaining pastry cream mixture on top of it. Place the last piece of pastry on top.

Dredge the top of the pastry with icing sugar. Crush the leftover pastry trimmings with your hands and push them onto the ends of the cake. They will stick to the pastry cream. Finally score the top of the cake with a red-hot skewer in a criss-cross pattern. Decorate with rosettes of cream and fresh strawberries or raspberries. Place on a serving dish and serve. Use a serrated knife to slice.

Feuillitée of Summer or Autumn Berries
Serves 4

Puff Pastry (see page 456)
Pastry Cream (see page 460)
kirsch
cream
strawberry, raspberries, loganberries,
  blueberries, blackberries or a mixture
organic egg wash

Garnish
mint or lemon balm leaves
icing sugar

Preheat the oven to 250°C/475°F/gas 9.

Roll out the pastry to 2cm ($^3/_4$in) thickness, and stamp into 9–10cm ($3^1/_2$–4in) rounds with a cutter. Sprinkle a few drops of water onto a baking sheet. Turn the rounds upside down and place on the damp sheet. Brush with egg wash in both directions. Take a 6–8cm ($2^1/_2$–3in) cutter, and press down halfway into the pastry. Lightly score the edges and the lid into a pattern with the back of a knife. Rest for 10–15 minutes in a fridge.

Bake the rounds in the oven for 10 minutes, then reduce the temperature to 200°C/400°F/gas 6 until fully cooked. A few minutes before the end of cooking time, remove the pastry lid, scoop out the uncooked pastry in the centre and continue to cook for a few minutes more. Cool on a wire rack.

To assemble, lace the pastry cream well with kirsch, mix in some stiffly whipped cream (about $^1/_2$ cream to $^1/_2$ Pastry Cream).

Put the pastry cases onto 4 serving plates, two-thirds full with the pastry cream mixture. Top generously with berries, pop the lid on top and decorate with lemon balm or mint leaves and dredge with icing sugar.

Master Recipe

Jalousie

Serves 4–5

225g (8oz) Flaky Pastry (see page 413) or
    Puff Pastry (see page 456)
5–6 tablespoons apricot jam
1 organic egg white, beaten until frothy
granulated sugar (for sprinkling)

Preheat the oven to 220°C/425°F/gas 7.

Roll out the dough into a 20 x 32cm
(8 x 12in) rectangle. Trim the edges neatly
and cut in half lengthways. Place one piece
of pastry on a dampened baking sheet.
Fold over the other piece lengthwise and,
with a sharp knife, cut across the fold at
5mm (¼in) intervals to within 1cm (½in)
of the outer edge, like the teeth of a comb.

Spoon the jam filling down the centre of
the uncut piece of dough to within 2.5cm
(1in) of the edges. Brush the edges with
cold water and set the cut rectangle on top
with the fold in the centre. Open out the
folded dough and press the edge down
onto the lower piece. Trim the edges to
neaten them and chill the Jalousie for
10–15 minutes.

Bake the pastry in the oven for 25–30
minutes or until puffed and browned.
About 5–10 minutes before the end of
baking, brush the Jalousie with the beaten
egg white, sprinkle generously with sugar
and continue baking until golden brown.
Alternatively, when the Jalousie is cooked,
dredge heavily with icing sugar and put
under the grill to glaze.

Serve the Jalousie hot, or slide it onto a
rack to cool and serve at room
temperature. It is best eaten the day it is
baked, or it can be frozen, baked or
unbaked.

Variations

Jalousie may also be filled with apple
purée, frangipane or a mixture of
homemade mincemeat and apple purée; or
savoury fillings such as cheese, salmon
and mushrooms.

Almond Filling for Jalousie

75g (3oz) whole skinned almonds
75g (3oz) unsalted butter
75g (3oz) caster sugar
75g (3oz) Candied Orange Peel (see page 515)
¼ teaspoon grated orange zest
1 large organic egg
1 teaspoon kirsch

Preheat the oven to 180°C/350°F/gas 4.

Toast the almonds for 10 minutes, cool and
grind to a slightly gritty powder in the food
processor. Cream the butter, and add the
almonds, sugar, orange zest and peel,
beaten egg and kirsch. Mix well, and fill
the centre of a puff pastry tart or jalousie.

Sacristains

Makes about 35

**These French pastry twists can also
be made as savoury sacristains by
replacing the sugar with grated Parmesan
cheese.**

Flaky Pastry (see page 413) or Puff Pastry
    (see page 456)
1 organic egg, beaten to mix with a pinch of
    salt (for glaze)
110g (4oz) almonds, finely chopped or sliced
200g (7oz) sugar

Preheat the oven to 220°C/425°F/gas 7.

Make the Flaky or Puff Pastry dough and
chill thoroughly. Roll out to a very thin
rectangle and trim the edges. Brush the
pastry with egg glaze. Sprinkle with half
the almonds, then with half the sugar.
Turn the pastry over. Brush the other side
with egg glaze and sprinkle with the
remaining almonds and sugar. Cut the

pastry into 12.5cm (5in) strips, then
crossways into fingers 2cm (¾in) wide.
Twist them several times and place on a
greased baking sheet. Press the ends down
firmly so that they do not unroll during
baking.

Chill for 15 minutes. Bake the pastries in
the oven for 8–12 minutes or until puffed
and brown.

Note: Be very careful as they burn easily.

Transfer to a rack to cool. Strips can be
sandwiched together with cream and
raspberry jam and served for afternoon tea.

Eccles Cakes

Makes 10

**Originally Eccles cakes were filled with
blackcurrants and mint leaves. Now they
are similar to Banbury cakes, without the
candied peel. Make them round or oval in
shape.**

225g (8oz) Flaky Pastry (see page 413) or
    Puff Pastry (see page 456)
110g (4oz) currants
110g (4oz) Candied Peel (see page 515)
1 teaspoon orange zest, grated
50g (2oz) melted butter
50g (2oz) granulated sugar

extra granulated sugar for tops

Preheat the oven to 220°C/425°F/gas 7.

Roll out the pastry to 3mm (⅛in) thickness
and cut with an 8cm (3in) round cutter.
Mix the remaining ingredients together.

Place 1 teaspoon of the filling in the centre
of each round, pinch the sides into the
centre, turn over and roll out until the fruit
is just coming through. Brush with cold
water, dip the top in granulated sugar and
slit the tops with a knife 2 or 3 times. Bake
for 15 minutes.

Moroccan Snake
Serves 10–15 people

One of the glories of Moroccan confectionery, great for a party. Keeps well.

Filling
450g (1lb) ground almonds
350g (12oz) caster sugar
1 tablespoon freshly ground cinnamon
75–125ml (3–4 fl oz) orange flower water

1 packet best-quality filo pastry

75–110g (3–4oz) melted butter
organic egg wash
icing sugar to dust

Preheat the oven to 180°C/350°F/gas 4.

To make the filling, put all the dry ingredients together in a bowl. Add enough orange flower water to form a paste.

To assemble: lay one sheet of filo on the worktop and brush it with melted butter. Take a handful of the paste and make into a snake about 2.5cm (1in) thick. Lay this along the long side of the sheet of filo, about 2.5cm (1in) from the edge. Roll up and bend into a 'snail'. Put a sheet of greaseproof or silicone paper on a baking sheet and put the snail into the centre of the baking sheet. Continue with the rest of the filo and almond paste. Press the ends together to seal the joints and continue to make the snakes until all the filling is used up.

Brush with egg wash and then with melted butter. Bake in the oven for about 30 minutes or until crisp and golden. Slide off the baking tray and cool on a wire rack. Dust with icing sugar and perhaps a little cinnamon. Wonderful warm or cold.

Master Recipe
Choux Pastry

150g (5oz) strong white flour
pinch of salt
225ml (8fl oz) water
110g (4oz) butter, cut into 1cm (1/2in) cubes
4–5 organic eggs depending on size

Sieve the flour with the salt onto a piece of greaseproof paper. Heat the water and butter in a saucepan until the butter is melted. Bring to a fast rolling boil, and remove from the heat. (**Note:** Prolonged boiling evaporates the water and changes the proportions of the dough.)

Immediately the pan is taken from the heat, add all the flour at once and beat vigorously with a wooden spoon for a few seconds until the mixture is smooth and pulls away from the sides to form a ball. Put the saucepan back on a low heat and stir for 1/2 minute or until the mixture starts to fur the bottom of the saucepan. Remove from the heat and cool for a few seconds.

Meanwhile break one egg into a bowl and whisk it. Add the remaining eggs to the dough, one by one, with a wooden spoon, beating thoroughly after each addition. Make sure the dough comes back to the same texture each time before you add another egg. When it will no longer form a ball in the centre of the saucepan, add the beaten egg little by little – use just enough to make a mixture that is very shiny and drops reluctantly from the spoon in a sheet.

Note: you may not need all of the reserved egg. If too much is added, the dough cannot be shaped. (Choux pastry dough should just hold its shape when piped.)

Although the dough puffs up better if used immediately, choux pastry can be stored for up to 8 hours before baking. Rub the surface with butter while the dough is still warm so it doesn't form a skin. When cool, use as required or cover tightly and keep in the fridge until needed.

Chocolate or Coffee Eclairs
Makes 20

Choux Pastry (see left)

Creme Chantilly
300ml (1/2 pint) whipped cream
1/2–1 tablespoon icing sugar
2–3 drops pure vanilla extract

Chocolate Icing (see page 454) or
   Coffee Glacé Icing (see page 447)

silicone paper

Preheat the oven to 220°C/425°F/gas 7.

Make the choux pastry in the usual way. Line a baking sheet with silicone paper and sprinkle with a few drops of cold water. Fill the choux pastry into a piping bag with a 2cm (3/4 in) round eclair pipe. Pipe the dough into 8–10cm (3–4in) strips, 4cm (11/2in) apart to allow for expansion.

Bake immediately in the oven, for 15 minutes then reduce the heat to 200°/400°F/gas 6, for a further 15–20 minutes or until they are crisp and golden. Remove from the oven, make a hole in the side of each éclair to allow the steam to escape, return to the oven and bake for about 5 minutes more. Remove to a wire rack.

Meanwhile make the chosen icing or icings. Make the Chantilly Cream by sweetening the whipped cream to taste with icing sugar and a dash of vanilla extract, put into a piping bag with a small nozzle. As soon as the éclairs are cold, fill them with cream through the hole where the steam escaped (they can be split lengthways and filled that way, too).

Dip the tops in the icing and put onto a wire rack over a tray to catch the drips. Serve within 1 or 2 hours of being made.

Note: sometimes instead of icing éclairs, we dip them in caramel and cool on oiled trays or silicone paper.

Choux Puffs

Pipe 1–2 blobs of Choux Pastry (see page 459) for each puff, onto a baking tray. Flatten the tops with a wet teaspoon, brush with egg wash and bake for 20–25 minutes at 220°C/425°F/gas 7.

Lemon Curd Eclairs or Choux Puffs

Makes 12–15

12–15 éclairs or Choux Puffs (see above)
Lemon Curd (see page 511)
300ml (1/2 pint) whipped cream
Crystallised Lemon Peel (see page 515)

Split the éclairs or choux puffs in half. Mix the cream with the lemon curd to taste – you will not need all the lemon curd, save the rest for another use. Cover and keep refrigerated. Fill the éclairs or choux puffs with lemon cream. Drizzle the remains of the lemon curd on the plate. Put an éclair or a choux puff on top. Decorate with crystallised lemon peel and a sprig of mint.

Chocolate Profiteroles

Serves 8–10

Profiteroles are simply choux puffs filled with a mixture of Pastry Cream and Chantilly Cream or just Chantilly Cream.

Choux Puffs (see above)
Pastry Cream (see right)

Chantilly Cream
150ml (1/4 pint) double cream, whipped with
 1 level tablespoon icing sugar
a few drops of pure vanilla extract

Chocolate Sauce (see page 599)

Croque en Bouche

A spectacular French wedding cake consisting of a pyramid of profiteroles dipped in caramel. It is often decorated with spun sugar and silver decorations.

Crème Patissière (Pastry Cream)

Pastry Cream is the most common filling for sweet choux pastries. Be sure to cook it thoroughly – uncooked, it has an unpleasant taste of raw flour. It is also often spread in tart shells and topped with fruit, or spread between layers of sponge cake.

6 organic egg yolks
110g (4oz) sugar
35g (1 1/2oz) flour
425ml (15fl oz) milk
pinch of salt
vanilla pod

Beat the egg yolks with the sugar until thick and light. Stir in the flour.

Scald the milk by bringing it just to the boil with the salt. Add the vanilla pod to the hot milk, cover the pan and leave to infuse for about 10–15 minutes. Remove the vanilla pod and reheat the milk to boiling point. Whisk the boiling milk into the egg mixture, return to the pan and whisk over a gentle heat until boiling.*

Cook the cream gently, whisking constantly for 2 minutes or until the cream thins slightly, showing the flour is completely cooked. Take it from the heat, transfer to a bowl, and rub a piece of butter over the surface to prevent the formation of a skin. Cover with clingfilm and let it cool. Use as directed in the recipes.

* Be sure that the Pastry Cream is smooth before letting it boil. If lumps form as it thickens, take the pan from the heat and beat until smooth.

Important points:
If the finished cream is too thick, simply thin it with a little milk.

Take special care in keeping Pastry Cream, as lightly cooked egg yolks spoil fairly rapidly. Refrigerate as soon as it is cool and do not keep for longer than a day or two. Thick Pastry Cream can be frozen, but thin cream made with a minimum of flour will separate on freezing.

Crème St. Honoré (Light Pastry Cream)

To make approx. 600ml (1 pint)

300ml (10fl oz) milk
vanilla pod or pure vanilla extract
3 small organic eggs
110g (4oz) sugar
25g (1oz) flour

In a heavy saucepan, bring the milk just to the boil, with a small piece of vanilla pod in it, or add a few drops of vanilla extract afterwards.

Separate 2 of the eggs. Whisk the yolks and the whole remaining egg with the sugar until light in colour. Stir in the flour and then pour on the milk, return to the saucepan and stir over a gentle heat until it comes to the boil. Allow it to boil for 2 minutes, still stirring all the time. (I find a little wire whisk better than a wooden spoon for this operation.) Whisk until the pastry cream is thick. Transfer to a bowl.

Whisk the egg whites stiffly in a clean bowl, and fold into the pastry cream while still warm. Allow to cool before using.

RIGHT: Jane's Biscuits

Jane's Biscuits
Makes 25

A great little recipe because it is quick and its formula of 2/4/6 is easy to remember. The flavour is quite different if you use unsalted butter, but still delicious.

50g (2oz) caster sugar
110g (4oz) butter
175g (6oz) white flour

Preheat the oven to 180°C/350°F/gas 4.

Put the flour and sugar into a bowl and rub in the butter as for shortcrust pastry. Gather the mixture together and knead it lightly. Roll out to 5mm (1/4in) thick. Cut into rounds with a 6cm (2½in) cutter or into heart shapes. Arrange on silicone paper on a baking tray and bake for 10–15 minutes until pale brown.

Remove and cool on a rack. Serve with fruit fools, compotes and ice creams.

Fork Biscuits
Makes 45–50 biscuits

Freshly ground cinnamon, ginger or chocolate chips can be a delicious addition to these biscuits but they're delicious just as they are too. This is the first biscuit recipe the students make.

225g (8oz) soft butter
110g (4oz) caster sugar
275g (10oz) self-raising flour, sifted
grated zest of 1 lemon or orange

Vanilla Sugar (see below)

Cream the butter, add in the sugar, flour and zest, and mix just until it all comes together. Alternatively, place all four ingredients in the bowl of a food mixer and mix slowly until all the ingredients come together. At this stage the dough can either be used right away or put in the deep freeze or kept in the fridge for up to a week.

Preheat the oven to 180°C/350°F/gas 4 when about to cook.

Bring the dough up to room temperature and form into small balls the size of a walnut. Flatten them out onto a baking sheet using the back of a fork dipped in cold water. Allow plenty of room for expansion. Bake in the oven for about 10 minutes. Sprinkle with vanilla sugar. When cold, store in an air tight container.

Vanilla Sugar
Fill a glass jar with caster sugar and put a couple of vanilla pods into the sugar. It stops the vanilla pods drying out too much and makes a wonderful, fragrant sugar. The flavour comes through in around a week. We get fragrant vanilla pods from Mexico. You can use the vanilla pod a couple of times if you wash and dry it.

Sablé Stars

Makes about 40, depending on the size

A French biscuit, originally from Normandy. Sablés can be eaten plain, with fresh berries, or simply stuck together with a little jam and cream; savoury sablés are also made, using cheese.

175g (6oz) plain white flour
75g (3oz) icing sugar
tiny pinch of salt
150g (5oz) unsalted butter
1 organic egg yolk

Sieve the flour and icing sugar into a bowl and add a tiny pinch of salt. Rub in the butter and the egg yolk. Press the mixture together, wrap in clingfilm and rest for 30 minutes in the refrigerator. Alternatively make in a food processor but stop the machine just as soon as the mixture comes together.

Preheat the oven to 150°C/300°F/gas 2. Roll out the pastry into a 3mm (1/8in) thick sheet and stamp into stars or heart shapes with a cutter. Carefully lift onto a baking sheet lined with silicone paper. Bake for about 15–20 minutes until they are pale golden in colour. Cool on a wire rack.

Sprinkle with sieved icing sugar and serve with fruit salads, ice creams, mousses etc.

Shortbread Stars with Strawberries and Cream

Makes about 25

These may be cut tiny or quite large. Raspberries, loganberries, fraises des bois are all delicious fillings.

Jane's Biscuit mixture (see page 461)

strawberries
whipped cream
sugar
tiny mint or lemon balm leaves

Preheat the oven to 180°C/350°F/gas 4.

Make the biscuit mixture. Roll out to 5mm (1/4in) thick on a lightly floured surface. Stamp out into star shapes. Bake in the oven until pale brown, about 8–12 minutes, depending on thickness. They should be pale golden – be careful, they burn easily. Remove and cool on a rack.

To assemble: put a star on a plate and pipe a little sweetened cream onto the biscuit. Add a few slices of strawberry, then pipe another tiny blob of cream. Top with another biscuit. Pipe a little cream in the centre and decorate with mint leaves or lemon balm. Dredge lightly with icing sugar. Repeat with the others and serve as soon as possible.

Shortbread Hearts with Strawberries and Cream

Use a heart-shaped cutter and proceed as above. Perfect for Valentine's Day or as a little surprise when you want to say 'I love you' or simply to bring on a proposal!

Aunt Alice's Biscuits

Serves 30

Mary Dowey, who edited several of my books, gave me this lovely recipe.

110g (4oz) butter
1 tablespoon golden syrup
150g (5oz) white flour
200g (7oz) brown sugar
75g (3oz) porridge oats
1/2 teaspoon bicarbonate of soda (bread soda), sieved

Preheat the oven to 200°C/400°F/gas 6.

Melt the butter and syrup together in a small saucepan over a gentle heat. Put all the other ingredients into a bowl, pour over the butter and syrup liquid and mix well.

Make the mixture into small balls and space them out on baking trays. Bake in the oven for about 10 minutes or until golden brown. Cool on a wire rack.

Orange Tuiles

Makes about 20

These light crisp biscuits look impressive, are easy to make and are great with ice-cream and mousses. They will soften if they are kept in a moist atmosphere so, as soon as they are cold, store in an airtight tin. They are shaped like curved tiles, hence the name (tuile is French for tile).

2 organic egg whites
110g (4oz) caster sugar
50g (2oz) butter
50g (2oz) plain flour
zest of 1 unwaxed orange, grated

Preheat the oven to 190°C/375°F/gas 5.

Line a baking sheet with silicone paper. Whisk the egg whites until quite stiff and add the caster sugar. Continue to whisk until smooth and glossy.

Melt the butter, and add it to the egg white mixture by degrees, together with the sifted flour. Fold in the orange zest. Spread out teaspoonfuls, well apart, on the baking sheet and bake for about 5–6 minutes, until pale brown. Drape the tuiles over a rolling pin to make them round. Cool on a wire rack.

Coupelles or Langues de Chats

Makes 8 'containers', 9cm (3 1/2 in) diameter

These crisp little biscuit cups are simple to make and charming as containers for ices, fruits and dessert creams. They are made from the French egg white batter called langues de chats because it is usually baked in flat cat's tongue shapes. Here the batter is spread in thin discs on baking sheets and as soon as the edges have browned in a hot oven, they are removed one by one and pressed into a teacup, where they immediately crisp into shape. This recipe is adapted from Mastering the Art of French Cooking by Beck, Bertholle and Child.

50g (2oz) butter

75g (3oz) caster sugar

zest of 1 lemon or orange, grated

2 organic egg whites

45g (1³/₄oz) plain flour

tasteless salad oil

2 baking sheets about 35 x 45cm (14 x 18in),
  buttered and floured

a vol au vent cutter, pot lid, or saucer about
  12.5cm (5in) in diameter

a rubber spatula

2 large tea cups or small bowls about 12.5cm
  (5in) in diameter at the top and 5cm (2in) at
  the bottom, and 6cm (2¹/₂in) deep.

Preheat the oven to 220°C/425°F/gas 7.

Set a rack in the middle of the oven. Butter and flour the baking sheets, and then with the cutter and point of the rubber spatula, mark 4 circles on each. Lightly oil the cups or bowls, and set them at a convenient place near the oven.

Beat the butter, sugar and lemon or orange zest in the bowl with an electric mixer or wooden spoon until pale and fluffy. Pour in the egg whites and mix for a few seconds, only just enough to blend. Place the flour in a sieve or sifter and shake it over the batter, rapidly folding it in with a rubber spatula. Place 2 teaspoons of the batter in the centre of each of the 4 circles on the baking sheets. Using the back of the spoon, smear the batter out very thinly to fill the circles (less than 1mm/¹/₁₆ in) thick). Place in the middle of the oven, set the timer for 5 minutes, and bake until biscuits have browned lightly, nearly to the centre, or in large splotches. Form biscuits on a second sheet while these are baking.

As soon as they are done, set the baking sheet on the open oven door so that the biscuits stay warm and pliable – they crisp immediately they cool and then cannot be moulded. Working rapidly, slide the long side of spatula blade under 1 biscuit to scrape and lift it off the baking sheet, turn it upside down over 1 of the oiled cups or bowls, and press into the cup with your fingers.

Rapidly remove a second biscuit from the sheet and press into the second cup. Immediately take the first biscuit out of the first cup – they crisp in seconds – and place on a wire rack. Rapidly mould the third biscuit, and finally the fourth (they will be fragile, so handle with care).

Close the oven door and wait for a few minutes for temperature to return to 220°C/425°F/gas 7 and bake and mould second sheet of biscuits,

Note: If this is the first time you have done this type of biscuit, experiment with 1 or 2 first so that you will understand the system of baking, removing and moulding; they are easy to do as soon as you know what to expect.

Biscuits will stay crisp for several days in dry weather if stored in an airtight container. For longer storage, freeze them. Spoon sorbet, ice cream or fruits into the biscuit cups just before serving. For fruit sorbets or ice cream, such as strawberry, save some of the fruit to decorate the top of each serving.

Mother-in-Law's Tongues

Makes 18–20

250g (9oz) plain white flour

100g (3¹/₂oz) caster sugar

100g (3¹/₂oz) butter

2 organic egg yolks

50–75g (2–3oz) bitter marmalade or lemon or
  lime marmalade

9 x 7cm (3¹/₂ x 3in) oval cutter

Preheat the oven to 180°C/350°F/gas 4.

Put the flour, sugar and diced butter in a food processor. Pulse a few times, and then add the egg yolks and a drop of water – just enough to bring the dough together.

Turn out, flatten into a round and wrap in greaseproof paper. Rest in the fridge for about 30 minutes.

Flour the worktop and roll out the dough to a thickness of 5mm (¹/₄ inch). Stamp out ovals with the cutter. Transfer to a baking sheet. Spoon a small blob of bitter marmalade into the centre of each oval. Pinch the long ends together so they meet in the centre to cover the marmalade.

Bake for 10–15 minutes in the oven. When golden, transfer to a wire rack. Dust with icing sugar when cool.

Note: Sweeter jams e.g. raspberry or blackcurrant can of course be used for 'sweeter' mother-in-laws!

Macaroons

Makes 24–36

These lovely old-fashioned macaroons are easy to make and keep for ages. Originally the macaroon came from Italy, but the French brought it to fame and it became the custom for French nuns to make these and offer them to visitors with a glass of wine. Amaretti, mandorla and pinoccate are all forms of Italian macaroons.

110g (4oz) ground almonds

175g (6oz) caster sugar

2 small organic egg whites

¹/₄ teaspoon pure almond extract

a little granulated sugar

24–26 blanched almonds

Preheat the oven to 180°C/350°F/gas 4. Line 2 baking trays with silicone paper.

Put the almonds and sugar in a bowl. Whisk the egg whites lightly and mix into the dry ingredients, a little at a time. Add the almond extract and beat well to make a fairly smooth, stiff mixture. Spoon the mixture onto the trays in lumps the size of a walnut.

Sprinkle with sugar and decorate each with an almond. Place in the oven and bake for 10–15 minutes, or until just firm. Cool for a few minutes, then lift off the tray and cool on a wire rack.

Carol Fields' Biscotti

Makes 60–72

Carol Fields' books are redolent with the flavours of Italy and baking is her passion. This recipe is from *Italy in Small Bites*.

50g (2oz) raisins
6 tablespoons Cointreau or Curaçao
5 organic eggs
450g (1lb) sugar
1 teaspoon pure vanilla extract
200g (7oz) unblanched almonds, toasted and roughly chopped
450g (1lb) plain white flour
1½ teaspoons bicarbonate of soda (bread soda), sieved
pinch of salt

Swiss roll tin, 30 x 45cm (12 x 18in)

Preheat the oven to 180°C/350°F/gas 4.

Soak the raisins in the liqueur for 20 minutes and then drain, reserving the liqueur.

Separate the eggs and beat the yolks with all but 2 heaped tablespoons of the sugar until thick and pale. Beat in the reserved liqueur and the vanilla extract.

In another bowl, beat the egg whites until they just hold stiff peaks, and slowly add the 2 tablespoons of sugar, beating until they hold stiff peaks.

Whisk ¼ of the egg whites into the yolk mixture to lighten it, then fold in the remaining whites delicately but thoroughly, and finally fold in the drained raisins and the nuts.

Mix together the flour, bicarbonate of soda and salt. Using a rubber spatula, fold the flour mixture into the egg mixture one quarter at a time.

Butter the Swiss roll tin. Gently spread the mixture to cover the base of the tin as evenly as possible. Bake for 20–22 minutes, until pale golden. Remove from the oven and leave to cool until comfortable to handle (about 10 minutes). Ease out of the pan onto a cutting board and use a serrated knife to cut into 4cm (1½in) strips. Cut the strips into 2cm (¾in) wide slices.

Arrange them on the Swiss roll tin, cut side down, and return them to the oven to bake for another 7–8 minutes on each side, until pale golden. Cool on racks.

Anzac Cookies

Makes around 34 cookies, depending on size

These biscuits commemorate the Australian and New Zealand participation in the two World Wars and are traditionally made by the Antipodean contingent in my publisher's office in a competition in April (around Anzac Day).

150g (5oz) plain flour
50g (2oz) porridge oats
50g (2oz) desiccated coconut
150g (5oz) caster sugar
½ teaspoon baking powder
150g (5oz) butter
2 tablespoons golden syrup

Preheat the oven to 150°C/300°F/gas 2.

In a large bowl stir together the flour, oats, coconut, sugar and baking powder. In a small saucepan combine the butter and syrup and cook the mixture over a moderately low heat, stirring until the butter is melted. Pour the butter mixture into the flour mixture and combine the mixture well.

Make into small balls and put them 5cm (2in) apart on baking sheets and flatten them slightly with the back of a fork dipped in water. Bake the cookies in the middle of the oven for 15 minutes or until they are golden.

Let the cookies cool slightly on the baking sheet, then transfer them with a spatula to a rack, and let them cool completely.

Pecan Puffs

Makes about 30

110g (4oz) butter
2 tablespoons caster sugar
½ teaspoon vanilla extract
150g (5oz) pecans, finely ground
150g (5oz) plain white flour, sifted

icing sugar

Preheat the oven to 150°C/300°F/gas 2.

Cream the butter, add the sugar and beat until soft and light. Mix the nuts in with the butter and sugar, and add the flour and vanilla extract. Pinch off teaspoonfuls of the mixture and roll into balls. Place well apart on greased baking sheets. Bake for 30 minutes or until pale and golden.

Remove from the oven. Handle very carefully as they will be fragile, brittle and very hot. Cool on a wire rack, dredge with icing sugar and store in an airtight container.

Chocolate Chip Cookies

Makes about 36–40, depending on size

The quintessential American cookie, now much-loved the world over.

225g (8oz) butter
200g (7oz) brown sugar
175g (6oz) caster sugar
2 eggs, beaten
1 teaspoon pure vanilla extract
350g (12oz) plain white flour
1 level teaspoon baking powder
1 level teaspoon bicarbonate of soda (bread soda)
pinch of salt
150g (5oz) chocolate chips
110g (4oz) chopped nuts

Preheat the oven to 180°C/350°F/gas 4.

Cream the butter, add the sugars and beat until light and fluffy. Add the egg a bit at a time and then the vanilla extract. Mix the dry ingredients together and fold them in. Lastly, add the chocolate chips and chopped nuts.

Divide the mixture into 7g (¼oz) pieces for teeny weeny cookies, or 25g (1oz) for medium cookies or 50g (2oz) for American-style cookies on a baking sheet. Remember to allow lots of room for spreading. Bake for about 8–10 minutes, depending on size.

Cool for a few minutes in the tray and then transfer to wire racks. Store in an airtight container.

Isobel Burnett's Ginger Biscuits
Makes 20–30

When you are about to eat these round, crackly-topped, aromatic biscuits, make a wish, crack the biscuit on your elbow and, if it splits into 3 pieces, your wish will come true! If it cracks into more or less than 3 pieces it's a great excuse to have another one! They keep for ages in an airtight container.

350g (12oz) plain white flour
½ level teaspoon ground ginger
½ level teaspoon bicarbonate of soda
150g (5oz) butter
175g (6oz) golden syrup
150g (5oz) sugar

Preheat the oven to 180°C/350°F/gas 4.

Sieve the first three ingredients together into a bowl and rub the butter into them.

Meanwhile heat the syrup lightly in a small saucepan until runny. Add the sugar and mix well. Add to the dry ingredients and mix well. Roll the mixture into walnut sized balls and arrange them on a tray lined with silicone paper. Bake for 15–20 minutes. Leave on the tray for 2–3 minutes, then lift off with the long side of a spatula and cool on a rack.

Master Recipe
Shortbread

Makes 24–32, depending on size

For some reason it has become a tradition at Kinoith always to have shortbread in the Aga. Many years ago when I was attempting to hide the shortbread from the children who seemed to devour it as fast as it was made, I discovered quite by accident that it keeps beautifully for days in the coolest oven in our 4 door Aga. Now not only the children, but all our friends know where to look.

Shortbread is an ancient Scottish recipe particularly associated with Christmas and Hogmanay. It comes in all shapes and sizes and sometimes the edges are fluted. This shortbread has a more granular texture than Jane's Biscuits.

350g (12oz) plain white flour
110g (4oz) caster sugar
75g (3oz) ground rice
good pinch of salt
good pinch of baking powder
275g (10oz) butter
Vanilla Sugar (see page 461) or caster sugar
  for sprinkling

Swiss roll tin, 25 x 38cm (10 x 15in)

Preheat the oven to 140–150°C/275–300°F/gas 1–2.

Sieve the dry ingredients into a bowl. Cut the butter into cubes and rub it in until the whole mixture comes together. Spread evenly into the Swiss roll tin. Bake for 1–1½ hours in the oven. The shortbread should be pale golden but fully cooked through. Cut into squares or fingers while still hot.

Sprinkle with Vanilla Sugar or caster sugar and allow to cool in the tin.

Variations
Cumin Shortbread

Follow the Master Recipe, adding 2 teaspoons of freshly roasted cumin seeds, ground to a powder, to the dry ingredients.

Poppy Seed Shortbread

Follow the Master Recipe, adding 1–2 tablespoons of poppy seeds to the dry ingredients. Cut into 10cm (4in) rounds and serve sprinkled with caster sugar.

Coconut and Walnut Bars

Makes 24–32

Shortbread Mixture
175g (6oz) butter
250g (9oz) plain white flour
75g (3oz) caster sugar

Nut Layer
2 organic eggs
few drops pure vanilla extract
1 tablespoon plain white flour
110g (4oz) Barbados sugar and 110g (4oz)
  caster sugar or 225g (8oz) soft brown sugar
pinch of salt
¼ level teaspoon baking powder
110g (4oz) desiccated coconut
110g (4oz) walnuts, chopped

Swiss roll tin, 20 x 30cm (8 x 12in), greased

Preheat the oven to 180°C/350°F/gas 4.

Prepare the shortbread mixture: crumble the butter into the flour, add the sugar and turn into the Swiss roll tin. Press flat with the back of a spoon. Partially bake in the oven for 15–20 minutes, until pale golden.

Next, prepare the nut mixture: beat the 2 eggs until light. Add the vanilla extract, flour, sugar, salt, baking powder and coconut. Beat until smooth. Lastly, stir in the nuts and pour over the partially cooked shortbread base. Continue cooking in the oven for 20–30 minutes. Cool a little and cut into fingers.

Chocolate Peanut Butter Squares

Makes about 24

Sue Lawrence is one of the most talented bakers. This recipe is inspired by one from her book, *Sue Lawrence On Baking*. She, in turn, was inspired by the Village Bakery in Melmerby, Cumbria.

200g (7oz) white self-raising flour
75g (3oz) plain flour, sifted
225g (8oz) soft dark brown sugar
110g (4oz) butter, softened
110g (4oz) peanut butter, sugar-free
2 organic eggs, beaten

Topping
150g (5oz) chocolate, milk or plain, broken
  into pieces
75g (3oz) peanut butter
50g (2oz) desiccated coconut

greased Swiss roll tin, 20 x 30cm (8 x 12cm)

Preheat the oven to 180°C/350°F/gas 4.

Mix the flours, sugar, butter, peanut butter and eggs together. Spoon into the Swiss roll tin and level off the top with a spatula. Bake in the oven for 25 minutes, or until the edges are just firm and the centre is still slightly soft. Cool for 5–10 minutes.

Meanwhile prepare the topping: melt the chocolate in a bowl set over a pan of simmering water. Stir in the peanut butter and coconut. Spoon over the biscuit base, carefully smoothing the surface. Cut into squares and allow to cool in the tin for about 20 minutes. Then transfer to a wire rack and leave to become completely cold before hiding away in an airtight tin.

Lemon Squares

Makes 24

170g (6oz) soft butter
170g (6oz) caster sugar
2 organic eggs
170g (6oz) self-raising flour

Icing
freshly grated rind of 1 lemon
freshly squeezed juice of 1–2 lemons
110g (4oz) caster sugar

25 x 18 cm (10 x 7in) Swiss roll tin, well greased

Preheat the oven to 180°C/350°F/gas 4.

Put the butter, caster sugar, eggs and self-raising flour into a food processor. Whizz for a few seconds to amalgamate. Spread evenly in the well-buttered tin. Bake in the preheated oven for about 20–25 minutes, until golden brown and well risen.

Meanwhile mix the ingredients for the icing. As soon as the cake is cooked, pour the icing over the top and leave to cool. Cut into squares. Leave the biscuits in the tin until serving.

Brownies
Makes 16

A great American favourite – the relatively large amount of sugar gives brownies their delicious and characteristic crust.

50g (2oz) best-quality dark chocolate
100g (3½oz) butter
200g (7oz) caster sugar
2 organic eggs, lightly whisked
½ teaspoon vanilla extract
75g (3oz) white flour
½ teaspoon baking powder
pinch salt
110g (4oz) chopped walnuts

square tin, 20cm (8in)

Preheat the oven to 180°C/350°F/gas 4.

Melt the chocolate in a bowl over a pan of gently simmering water or in a low oven. Cream the butter and sugar and beat in the eggs, vanilla extract and melted chocolate. Lastly stir in the flour, baking powder, salt and chopped nuts. Spread the mixture in the tin and bake in the oven for about 30–35 minutes. Cut into 5cm (2in) squares for serving.

Banana Nut Brownies
Makes 16

Moist, rich and delicious. Can be an irresistible nibble or a gorgeous pud with a blob of crème fraîche.

175g (6oz) butter, cut into pieces, plus extra for greasing
300g (10oz) light muscovado sugar
175g (6oz) dark chocolate, broken into pieces
100g (4oz) hazelnuts, toasted and chopped
3 organic eggs, beaten
2 ripe bananas, mashed
100g (4oz) self-raising flour, sieved
1 teaspoon baking powder, sieved

20 x 30cm (8 x 12in) Swiss roll tin, lined with silicone paper

Preheat the oven to 180°C/350°F/gas 4.

Melt the butter in a sauté pan on a gentle heat and add the sugar and chocolate, stirring until melted and smooth. Remove the pan from the heat.

Stir in the nuts, beaten eggs and mashed banana. Mix well, then add in the sieved flour and baking powder. Pour the mixture into the prepared tin. Bake for 30 minutes until firm in the centre. Cool in the tin, then turn out and cut into squares.

BELOW: Brownies

Caramelised Almond Squares
Makes 24

175g (6oz) flour
25g (1oz) caster sugar
110g (4oz) butter
drop of pure vanilla extract
1 organic egg yolk or ½ a whole egg, beaten

Topping
175g (6oz) flaked almonds
75g (3oz) butter
45g (1¾oz) light brown sugar
3 tablespoons set honey
1 tablespoon cream

20 x 30cm (8 x 12in) Swiss roll tin, greased

Preheat the oven to 180°C/350°F/gas 4.

Put the flour and sugar into a bowl, rub in the butter, add the vanilla extract and bind with the egg yolk or beaten egg. Press into the greased tin. Prick the pastry and bake for 10–15 minutes, or until golden. Remove from the oven, and cool in the tin for a few minutes.

Next make the topping: put all the ingredients except the cream into a saucepan and cook together over a low heat until they are a pale straw colour. Stir in the cream and cook for a few more seconds. Spread this topping over the cooked base and bake until the topping is a deep golden brown colour – anything from 8–20 minutes, depending on the length of time the topping ingredients were cooked for originally.

Allow to cool in the tin for 10 minutes, then remove to a wire rack to cool completely. Cut into squares about 5cm (2in).

Apple and Raisin Squares
Makes 12–16

225g (8oz) self-raising flour
225g (8oz) rolled oats
1 teaspoon bicarbonate of soda (bread soda)
225g (8oz) butter
225g (8oz) sugar
2 tablespoons golden syrup
2 dessert apples, peeled, cored and finely chopped
110g (4oz) raisins

23cm (9in) square tin, greased and lined

Preheat the oven to 180°C/350°F/gas 4.

Mix the flour, oats and bicarbonate of soda together. Melt the butter, sugar and golden syrup together in a small saucepan over a gentle heat and add to the mixture. Press half the mixture into the tin. Mix the apple with the raisins and sprinkle over the mixture in the tin. Then spread the remaining oat mixture on top. Bake for 30 minutes. Leave to cool for 5 minutes and then cut into squares and transfer to a wire rack.

Master Recipe
Flapjacks
Makes 24–32

These nutritious flapjacks keep very well in a tin. Children love to munch them with a banana. Don't compromise – make them with butter, because the flavour is immeasurably better.

Oats come from the berry of a cultivated grass. Oatmeal is obtained by grinding oats after the husk has been removed and it comes in three grades – fine (used mostly in oatcakes and scones), medium and coarse (used mostly in porridge, soups, black and white puddings, haggis, and here).

350g (12oz) butter
1 tablespoon golden syrup
1 teaspoon pure vanilla extract
225g (8oz) caster sugar
450g (1lb) rolled oatmeal

25.5 x 38cm (10 x 15in) Swiss roll tin, use half the recipe for a 23 x 33cm (9 x 13in) tin

Preheat the oven to 180°C/350°F/gas 4.

Melt the butter, and add the golden syrup and vanilla extract. Stir in the caster sugar and oatmeal and mix well. Spread into the Swiss roll tin and bake in the oven until golden and slightly caramelised – about 30 minutes. Cut into 24–32 squares while still warm.

Variations
Follow the Master Recipe adding one or a mixture of the following: unsweetened desiccated coconut, chocolate chips, raisins, chopped dried apricots, chopped hazelnuts, chopped walnuts, sunflower seeds, pumpkin seeds.

Oatmeal and Banana Crunch
For an instant pudding, cover a flapjack with slices of banana, put a tiny dollop of cream on top and eat. Simply delicious!

Oatmeal and Apple Crumble
Loose crumbs may be scattered over some stewed apple for an instant crumble.

Toffee Rice Krispies
Makes 24

These don't need baking and so are good to make with children.

175g (6oz) butter
1 slab toffee, 5 x 10cm (2 x 4in)
1 packet marshmallows
1 x 375g (13oz) box Rice Krispies

Grease 2 small Swiss roll tins. Melt the butter, toffee and marshmallows together in a saucepan and add the rice krispies. Mix well and pour into the tins. Cool and cut into fingers.

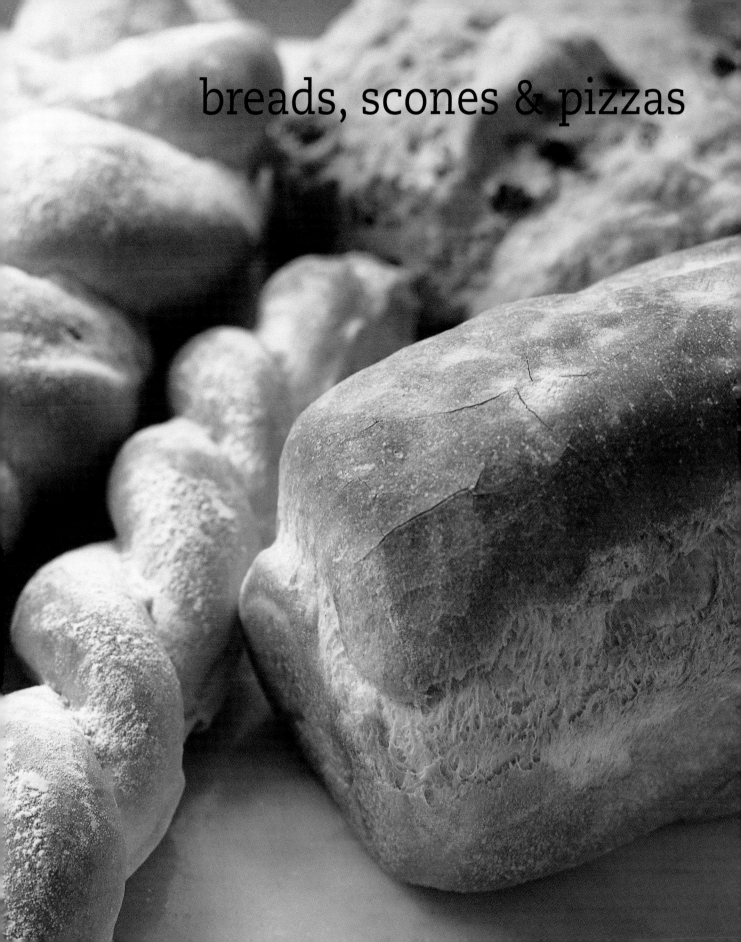

breads, scones & pizzas

breads, scones & pizzas

Every day at the school we make all sorts of bread including yeast, soda and sourdough breads, flat breads and pizza. We all adore baking – I've baked nearly my entire life and to this day I still get a buzz every time I take a loaf of bread out of the oven! Of all the many skills and techniques we teach at the school, teaching people how to make bread is the one that seems to give the most satisfaction and pleasure.

Once you've learnt the basics of bread-making (and lost your fear of yeast) you can play around with exciting flavours; olives, sun-dried tomatoes, caramelised onions... and you'll realise how forgiving breads can be. They take very little effort, and one can fit them into virtually any schedule by carefully choosing a place for the dough to rise. A cooler place or even the fridge will slow the fermentation, and warmer places will speed up the process (just remember cold doesn't kill yeast whereas heat over 40–50°C does.)

We can only fit so many bread recipes into this cookery book, which means I can only give a tiny taste of the bread-making possibilities (just enough to whet your appetite). However my husband, Tim, is also passionate about bread-making and has written *The Ballymaloe Bread Book* (Gill and Macmillan) – seek it out for more temptations!

Flour

In Ireland, we have wonderful flours, some roller-milled and others stoneground. The resulting flour with flakes of bran and wheatgerm is perfect for our soda breads. Flour varies enormously from country to country, so making bread is always a matter of trial and error until you find a flour to suit your needs for a particular bread recipe.

Wheat Flour

This is the flour most commonly used for bread because of its high gluten content. Gluten is the protein in wheat that allows the dough to become elastic. The more gluten, the more it will rise.

White flour is made from wheat that has had its outer casing of bran and the inner centre of wheatgerm removed. It is very fine and can be bought bleached or unbleached. The more refined and processed the flour, the less flavour and vitamins it will have. Some white flours are enriched with B vitamins. **Strong** or **Baker's flour** is made from hard wheat. The best varieties come from North America and have a very high gluten content. This makes it suitable for use in puff, flaky and choux pastry, pizza and yeast breads. It produces a light, well-risen loaf and is used by professional bakers. **Plain white** or **household flour** is a general, all-purpose flour suitable for soda breads, cakes, biscuits and scones as it does not have the high gluten content of strong flour. It is generally made from soft European wheat. **Self-raising flour** is usually made from soft wheat, which has a raising agent added. It is not used in yeast cookery. Buy in small quantities and store in a dry place. It loses its oomph quite quickly.

Wholemeal/wholewheat flour is milled from the whole wheat grain so it includes the bran and wheatgerm. Bread made from wholewheat is more nutritious because it includes more B vitamins and fibre. Some wholemeal flour is stoneground by the ancient method of milling between stone rollers. This flour is less processed than the flour made by modern milling methods. The texture is slightly coarser and sometimes needs more yeast to rise the bread.

Bran is the outer husk of the wheat grain. It can be added to bread and provides roughage, but has little in the way of flavour or nutrition. **Wheatgerm** is the 'living' part of the wheat grain from which new plants can grow. It's usually extracted from the grain during flour making. Wheatgerm is full of B vitamins and can be eaten on its own or added to breakfast cereals or breads. As it goes rancid easily, buy it in small quantities and keep it refrigerated.

Other Flours

Spelt is an ancient variety of wheat, but higher in protein and with a greater concentration of vitamins and minerals. It is also low in gluten and makes a digestible substitute for wheat flour. **Rye** is a grass grown extensively as a grain, and is also a member of the wheat tribe. Rye bread is typically denser than bread made from wheat flour, and is often darker in colour and stronger in flavour. It is also higher in fibre than many common types of bread. Other flours include **rice**, **corn** and **potato** flour.

Raising Agents

There are two basic types of raising agent: biological ones (such as yeast) and chemical ones (like baking powder).

Yeast is a living organism – a one-celled plant of the fungus family. Given the right conditions, i.e. warmth (approximately 35°C/95°F), food and moisture, it reproduces amazingly fast, giving off bubbles of carbon dioxide which puff up the dough, making it light and aerated. It can be bought in three forms – **fresh** (or compressed), **dried** and **fast-acting** yeast.

We prefer to use **fresh yeast**, but it can be difficult to obtain, especially in small quantities. If you buy a kilo (2¼lb) at a time, however, it can be frozen in small pieces so that you can thaw them when needed. Use as soon as the yeast has defrosted. It will keep, wrapped, in the fridge for at least a week.

Dried yeast (often called 'active' dried yeast) is bought in granular form, often in a tin. You need half, or less than half, the weight specified for fresh yeast. It keeps fresh for six months in a cool, dry place. Bread made with dried yeast tends to have a more yeasty taste and a slightly heavier texture.

Fast acting, or rapid rise yeast is a variation on dried yeast. It is finer in texture and rises the bread in approximately half the time giving a good flavour. Stir directly into the dry ingredients. Knead and prove the dough just once.

Baking powder consists of an acid (cream of tartar) and an alkali (bicarbonate) in correct proportion. Corn flour or rice flour is included to create bulk and to absorb moisture. Action starts immediately when the mixture is moistened, so it is essential to add it last and get the cake or scones into the oven immediately.

Bicarbonate of soda is used for soda breads, scones or other mixtures. The lactic acid in the milk acts on the bicarbonate of soda to produce CO_2, which raises the bread. **Measure bicarbonate of soda meticulously** – a level teaspoon means just that (use a knife to level off the spoon). Too much soda will not make the bread rise more, it will simply result in a bread that has a strong flavour, the smell of soda, and a greenish-brown tinge to the crumb. Store bicarbonate of soda in a screw top jar. It keeps for years.

Cream of tartar is used in some batters and reacts with bicarbonate of soda to raise the mixture. If sour milk is not available for soda bread, use ordinary milk but add 1 teaspoon of cream of tartar, as well as the bicarboante of soda, to each 450g (1lb) of flour.

Baking Bread

In our experience, traditional soda breads and most yeast breads (with the exception of the Ballymaloe Brown Yeast Bread) are best baked in a conventional oven. Wet doughs, such as the Simply Nutritious Loaf and the Ballymaloe Brown Yeast Bread benefit from the drying heat of a fan oven, but may also be baked in a conventional oven. We also have a wood-burning oven at the school (that came as a kit from an Italian firm) and it gives fantastic results.

Bread should sound hollow when cooked. Test it by tapping lightly with the finger tips over all the top and bottom. It should sound the same both in the centre and at the sides. With a round loaf the centre is the last part to cook, so be quite sure that the bread sounds hollow when tapped there. Cutting a cross in soda bread enables it to open out in the centre and thus cooks more evenly.

Scones

Scones can be made from most bread mixtures – crunchy- or sugar-topped, square or round, sweet or savoury, seeded or plain… there are endless varieties. They are very quick to assemble and cook in almost the same amount of time that it will take to heat a bowl of soup.

Pizza

Pizzas have undergone a sea-change since chefs such as Alice Waters and Wolfgang Puck in California rescued us from predictable pizzas. There are just a few pizza recipes in this book, but let your imagination run wild with different combinations of ingredients. Keep in mind, too, that pizzas are not only savoury. A banana, strawberry and chocolate spread pizza makes an unusual and delicious feast! The thing to remember is that there must be a balance between the base and topping – very often the base is too thick and heavy.

Simply Nutritious Wholemeal Bread

Makes 1 loaf

This is a more modern version of Soda Bread, and couldn't be simpler; just mix and pour into a well greased tin. It is the first bread we teach students to cook to take the mystery out of breadmaking – even a child could cook this bread. It keeps well for several days and is also great toasted.

400g (14oz) stone ground wholemeal flour
50g (2oz) white flour, preferably unbleached
1 tablespoon bran
1 tablespoon wheatgerm
1 level teaspoon bicarbonate of soda (bread soda), sieved
1 teaspoon salt
1 teaspoon soft dark brown sugar
1 organic egg
1–2 tablespoons groundnut or sunflower oil, unscented
425ml (15fl oz) buttermilk or sour milk
sunflower or sesame seeds (optional)

22 x 12 x 5cm (9 x 5 x 2in) loaf tin

Preheat oven to 200°C/400°F/gas 6.

Put all the dry ingredients including the sieved bicarbonate of soda into a large bowl and mix well. Whisk the egg, add the oil and most of the buttermilk. Make a well in the centre of the dry ingredients and pour in the liquid, mix well and add more buttermilk if necessary. The mixture should be soft and slightly sloppy. Pour into an oiled tin and bake for 60 minutes, or until the bread is nice and crusty and sounds hollow when tapped. Cool on a wire rack.

> TIP: Always use a large, wide bowl when making bread so that you can mix comfortably with big generous movements. This results in a lighter bread.

Master Recipe
White Soda Bread

Makes 1 loaf

Soda bread only takes 2 or 3 minutes to make and 20–30 minutes to bake. It is another of my 'great convertibles'. We have had the greatest fun experimenting with different variations and uses. It's also great with olives, sun-dried tomatoes or caramelised onions added – the possibilities are endless. Flour varies from country to country and our soft Irish flour is perfect for soda bread. Buttermilk also varies in texture, so you may need slightly more or less.

450g (1lb) plain white flour, preferably unbleached
1 level teaspoon salt
1 level teaspoon bicarbonate of soda (bread soda)
about 600ml (1 pint) sour milk or buttermilk

Preheat the oven to 250°C/475°F/gas 9. Sieve the dry ingredients. Make a well in the centre. Pour in all of the milk at once. Using 1 hand, with your fingers stiff and outstretched like a claw, stir in a full circular movement from the centre to the outside of the bowl in ever-increasing circles. The dough should be softish, not too wet and sticky. When it all comes together, turn it out onto a well-floured work surface. **Wash and dry your hands.**

Tidy it up and flip over gently. Pat the dough into a round about 4cm (1½in) deep. Cut a deep cross on the loaf and prick in the four corners. Bake in the oven for 15 minutes, then turn down to 200°C/400°F/gas 6 for 30 minutes until cooked. If you are in doubt, tap the bottom of the bread: when it is cooked it will sound hollow. Cool on a wire rack.

Note: soda breads are best eaten on the day they are made but are still good for a day or so more.

> TIP: Seek out plain dairy, cooking or kosher salt. Avoid free-run salt, which includes chemicals.

Variations
White Soda Bread with Herbs

Follow the Master Recipe, adding 1–2 tablespoons of freshly chopped herbs (rosemary, sage, thyme, chives, parsley or lemon balm) to the dry ingredients.

White Soda Bread with Cumin

Follow the Master Recipe, adding 1–2 tablespoons of freshly roasted cumin seeds to the flour.

Seedy Bread

If you like caraway seeds, this is a must, delicious served for afternoon tea. Follow the Master Recipe, adding 1 tablespoon of sugar and 2–3 teaspoons of caraway seeds to the dry ingredients.

> TIP: All soda breads should be put into a fully preheated oven as soon as they are made otherwise they will be heavy and not rise fully.

Spotted Dog

Makes 1 loaf

Spotted Dog is also called railway cake in some parts of the country: 'a currant for each station'. This bread is one of the great homely foods of our family. It has always been a favourite with my children – freshly made on a Sunday morning for our picnics on the cliffs at Ballyandreen, or relished with delight when eaten with lashings of butter, jam and steaming mugs of hot chocolate after a winter walk on Shanagarry strand. It is also a staple in our 'pre-weighed repertoire'; made on our family boating trips on the Shannon and given as a parting gift to the many boats we met on the way.

450g (1lb) plain white flour, preferably unbleached
1 level teaspoon bicarbonate of soda (bread soda)
1 level teaspoon salt

1 dessertspoon sugar
75–110g (3–4oz) sultanas
1 organic egg
350ml (12fl oz) buttermilk

Preheat the oven to 220°C/425°F/gas 7.

In a large mixing bowl, sieve the flour and the bicarbonate of soda and add the salt, sugar and fruit. Mix well by lifting the flour and fruit up in your hands and then letting them fall back into the bowl through your fingers. This adds more air and therefore hopefully more lightness to your finished bread. Now make a well in the centre of the flour. Break the egg into the bottom of your measuring jug and add the buttermilk to the 400ml (14fl oz) line – the egg is part of your liquid measurement. Whisk briefly to blend, and pour most of this milk and egg into the flour. Using one hand, with the fingers open and stiff, mix in a full circle drawing in the flour from the sides of the bowl, adding more milk if necessary. The dough should be softish, not too wet and sticky.

The trick with Spotted Dog like all soda breads is not to over-mix the dough. Mix it as quickly and as gently as possible thus keeping it light and airy. When the dough all comes together, turn it out onto a well-floured work surface. **Wash and dry your hands.** With floured fingers, roll lightly for a few seconds – just enough to tidy it up. Pat the dough into a round, pressing to about 5cm (2in) in height.

Place the dough on to a baking tray dusted lightly with flour. With a sharp knife, cut a deep cross on it, letting the cuts go over the sides of the bread. Prick with a knife at the 4 angles as, according to Irish Folklore, this is to let the fairies out!

Cook in the oven for 10 minutes, then turn the oven down to 200°C/400°F/gas 6, for 35 minutes or until cooked. If you are in doubt about the bread being cooked, tap the bottom: if it is cooked it will sound hollow. Serve freshly baked, cut into thick slices and smeared with butter and jam. Spotted Dog is also really good eaten with cheese.

Spotted Puppies

In the window of E.A.T. in New York on St. Patrick's weekend I spied lots of little spotted puppies – they were selling like the proverbial hot cakes. Make the Spotted Dog as above. Divide the dough into 6 pieces, shape each piece into a little round loaf. Cut a cross on top and bake for about 20 minutes. Cool on a wire rack.

Stripy Cat

While Paul and Jeanne Rankin were teaching a class at the Cookery School, Timmy showed their daughter how to make Spotted Dog and when she had mastered that, she tried the next batch with chocolate chips and this was the delicious result. She called it Stripy Cat.

Follow the Master Recipe, adding 75g (3oz) of roughly chopped best quality dark chocolate to Spotted Dog recipe in place of sultanas. This is good made into scones also.

Note: the chocolate's very hot when it comes out of the oven so handle very carefully.

BELOW: Stripy Cat

'Focaccia' with Red Onion, Olives and Rosemary

Makes 1 loaf

Here we use White Soda Bread as a base for Focaccia – it sounds sacrilegious but tastes delicious. White Yeast Bread dough may of course be used instead.

1 quantity White Soda Bread dough
  (see page 474)

extra-virgin olive oil
10 black olives (Kalamata or Gaeta), stoned
75g (3oz) red onion, finely chopped
about 1 tablespoon freshly chopped rosemary
sea salt

23 x 32cm (9 x 12in) Swiss roll tin

Preheat the oven to 250°C/475°F/gas 9.

Follow the recipe for White Soda Bread. Brush the tin generously with olive oil. Roll the dough quickly into a rectangle and press gently into the tin. Brush the surface generously with olive oil, dot with black olives and thin wedges of onion. Sprinkle with rosemary and flakes of sea salt, and bake in the oven for about 15 minutes or until brown and crisp and golden on top. Brush with a little extra olive oil. Cool on a wire rack and serve while they are still warm.

Gluten-free White Soda Bread

Makes 1 loaf

Coeliacs can also enjoy delicious soda bread and scones if they follow Rosemary Kearney's recipes.

275g (10oz) rice flour
110g (4oz) tapioca flour
50g (2oz) dried milk powder
1 scant level teaspoon bicarbonate of soda
  (bread soda), sieved
1 heaped teaspoon gluten-free baking powder
1 teaspoon salt

1 heaped teaspoon xanthan gum
2 tablespoons caster sugar
1 organic egg, lightly beaten
225–300ml (8–10fl oz) buttermilk

Preheat the oven to 230°C/450°F/gas 8.

Sieve all the dry ingredients together into a large bowl and mix well. Lightly whisk the egg and buttermilk together. Make a well in the centre and pour in most of the egg and buttermilk at once.

Using 1 hand, mix in the flour from the sides of the bowl, adding a little more buttermilk if necessary. The dough should be softish, not too wet and sticky. When it comes together, turn it out onto a rice floured board and knead very gently for a few seconds.

Transfer to a baking sheet sprinkled with a little rice flour. Pat the dough into a round 4cm (1½in) deep and cut a deep cross in it. Bake in a hot oven for 5 minutes and then reduce the heat to 180°C/350°F/gas 4 for a further 25 minutes or until cooked. If you are in doubt, tap the bottom of the bread: if it is cooked it will sound hollow.

Note: This soda bread is best served the day it is made. However, it is lovely served toasted the next day. If there is any bread left over, I whizz it in a food processor and keep the gluten-free bread crumbs in the freezer for a future use.

Scones

Makes 15–20 depending on size

Any soda bread recipe can be made into scones of different sizes. Follow either the **White Soda Recipe** (see page 474) or the **Gluten-free Recipe** (see left). Preheat the oven to 250°C/475°F/gas 9 for scones made from White Soda Bread Dough and to 230°C/ 450°F/gas 8 for scones made from Gluten-free Soda Bread dough. Flatten the dough to about 2.5cm (1in) and cut into scones with a knife or scone cutter. Bake for 20 minutes.

Herb Scones

Add 1–2 tablespoons of freshly chopped herbs (rosemary, sage, thyme, chives, parsley or lemon balm) to the dry ingredients.

Cheddar Cheese Scones

Make the soda bread dough. Cut or stamp into scones, brush the top of each one with egg wash and then dip into grated Cheddar cheese. Bake as for soda scones, or use to cover the top of a casserole or stew (see Shanagarry Chicken Casserole, page 280).

Cheddar Cheese and Thyme Leaf Scones

Add 2 tablespoons of thyme leaves to the dry ingredients and proceed as above.

> TIP: It is better not to put the cheese into the dough as this makes the bread heavier. Reduce the heat to 220°C/ 425°F/gas 7 and then 180°C/350°F/gas 4 or the cheese may burn on top.

Rosemary and Olive Scones

Add 1½ tablespoons of chopped fresh rosemary and 2 tablespoons roughly chopped stoned black olives to the dry ingredients.

Rosemary and Raisin Scones

Substitute 3oz (75g) whole raisins for olives in the above recipe.

Rosemary and Sun-dried Tomato Scones

Add 1–2 tablespoons of chopped rosemary and 2 tablespoons of chopped sun-dried tomatoes to the dry ingredients.

Olive Scones

Flatten the soda bread dough into a 4cm (1½in) square. Dot the top with whole olives. Brush generously with olive oil, sprinkle with sea salt, and cut into square scones.

Sweet Scones

See pages 494–495

Chilli Scones

Add ½–1 tablespoon chilli powder to the flour.

Chilli and Cheddar Cheese Scones

Add 1–2 chopped green chillies to the flour. Brush the top of the scones with egg wash then dip into grated Cheddar cheese and proceed.

Teenie Weenies

Makes about 40

Follow the Master Recipe for White Soda Bread or Gluten-free White Soda Bread, and flatten the dough into a round just less than 2.5cm (1in) thick and stamp out into teeny weeny scones using a 4cm (1½in) cutter. Add chopped fresh herbs such as rosemary or thyme, or olives, to the dry ingredients to make delicious little herb scones. Brush the tops with egg wash and dip in grated cheddar cheese for yummy cheddar teeny weenies. Bake for 8–15 minutes at 230°C/450°F/gas 8.

Crunchy Tops

Makes 7 scones

These crunchy-topped scones join together in the cooking make an appetising loaf. We've used a selection of toppings here, but use just one if that seems more appropriate to your meal.

White Soda Bread (see page 474) or Gluten-free White Soda Bread dough (see page 476)

organic egg wash or buttermilk
sunflower seeds, sesame seeds, kibbled wheat, caraway seeds, poppy seeds, oat flakes and grated cheese

a round tin, well greased with butter or olive oil; 23cm (9in) in diameter and 4cm (1½in) high
7.5cm (3in) scone cutter

Preheat the oven to 230°C/450°F/gas 8.

ABOVE: White Soda Scones

Pat the dough into a round about 4cm (1½in) wide and stamp out 7 scones with a 7.5cm (3in) scone cutter. Brush the top of each scone with egg wash or buttermilk and dip in the seeds of your choice. Arrange side by side in a well-greased tin.

Bake for 15 minutes, then reduce the temperature to 200°C/400°F/gas 6 and bake for a further 15 minutes. Remove from the tin and replace in the oven for a further 5–8 minutes or until fully cooked. If you are in doubt, tap the bottom of the bread. When it is cooked it will sound hollow. Allow to cool on a wire tray.

Brown Soda Bread
Makes 1 loaf

Always cook breads in a fully preheated oven, but bear in mind that ovens vary so it may be necessary to adjust the temperature accordingly.

600g (1lb 4oz) brown wholemeal flour, preferably stone-ground
600g (1lb 4oz) plain white flour, preferably unbleached
2 teaspoons salt
2 teaspoons bicarbonate of soda (bread soda), sieved
about 850ml (1½ pints) sour milk or buttermilk

Preheat the oven to 230°C/450°F/gas 8.

Mix all the dry ingredients together in a large wide bowl, make a well in the centre and add all of the sour milk or buttermilk. Using one hand, stir in a full circle starting in the centre of the bowl working towards the outside of the bowl until all the flour is incorporated. The dough should be soft but not too wet and sticky. When it all comes together (a matter of seconds), turn it out onto a well-floured board. **Wash and dry your hands.** Roll the dough around gently with floury hands for a second, just enough to tidy it up. Flip over and flatten slightly to a depth of about 5cm (2in).

Sprinkle a little flour onto a baking sheet and place the loaf on top of the flour. Cut a deep cross on the loaf, prick in the four corners to let the fairies out, and bake in the oven for 15–20 minutes, then reduce the heat to 200°C/400°F/gas 6 and cook for a further 20–25 minutes or until the bread is cooked. (In some ovens it is necessary to turn the bread upside down on the baking sheet for 5–10 minutes before the end of baking.) The loaf will sound hollow when tapped. Cool on a wire rack.

Variations
Rich Brown Soda Bread
Add 25g (1oz) fine oatmeal, 1 egg and 25g (1oz) butter for a richer soda bread dough.

Lighter Brown Soda Bread
If a lighter bread is preferred, use 600g (1¼lb) white flour and 450g (1lb) brown wholemeal flour.

Brown Soda Scones
Make the dough as above. Form it into a round and flatten to 4cm (1½in) thick. Stamp out into scones with a cutter, or cut with a knife. Bake for about 30 minutes.

Kibbled Wheat Scones
Follow the Recipe. Brush the top of the scones with egg wash or buttermilk, dip in kibbled wheat and proceed.

> TIP: Use the cutter as efficiently as possible so that only the minimum amount of dough needs to be rerolled. The less the dough is handled or rolled the lighter the scones will be.

Master Recipe
Ballymaloe Brown Yeast Bread
Makes 1 loaf

This much loved bread is Myrtle Allen's version of the Doris Grant loaf. When making yeast breads, remember that yeast is a living organism. In order to grow, it requires warmth, moisture and nourishment. The yeast feeds on the sugar and produces bubbles of carbon dioxide which cause the bread to rise. Too much heat (over 50°C/140°F) will kill yeast. Have the ingredients and equipment at blood heat. White or brown sugar, honey, golden syrup, treacle or molasses may be used. Each will give a slightly different flavour to the bread. At Ballymaloe we use treacle. The dough rises more rapidly with 75g (3oz) yeast than with 50g (2oz) yeast.

We use a stone-ground wholemeal flour. Different flours produce breads of different textures and flavour. The amount of natural moisture in the flour varies according to atmospheric conditions. The quantity of water should be altered accordingly. The dough should be just too wet to knead – in fact it does not require kneading. The main ingredients – wholemeal flour, treacle and yeast – are highly nutritious.

Dried yeast may be used instead of baker's yeast. Follow the same method but use only half the weight given for fresh yeast and allow longer to rise. Fast-acting yeast may also be used; follow the instructions on the packet. From start to finish, this bread takes 1½ hours to make but the time you are working on it is only a couple of minutes.

450g (1lb) wholemeal flour or 400g (14oz) wholemeal flour plus 50g (2oz) strong white flour
1 teaspoon salt
1 teaspoon black treacle
425ml (15fl oz) water at blood heat (mix yeast with 150ml (5fl oz) lukewarm water)
25g (1oz) fresh yeast
sesame seeds (optional)

13 x 20cm (5 x 8in) bread tin, greased with sunflower oil

Preheat the oven to 230°C/450°F/gas 8.

Mix the flour with the salt. The ingredients should all be at room temperature. In a small bowl or Pyrex jug, mix the treacle with 150ml (5fl oz) of water and crumble in the yeast.

Sit the bowl for a few minutes in a warm place to allow the yeast to start to work. After about 4 or 5 minutes it has a creamy, slightly frothy appearance.

When ready, stir and pour it, with all the remaining water, into the flour to make a loose dough. The mixture should be too wet to knead. Put the mixture into the greased tin. Sprinkle the top of the loaves

RIGHT: Brown Soda Bread

with sesame seeds if you like. Cover the tin with a tea towel to prevent a skin from forming and leave to rise.

Just before the bread comes to the top of the tin, about 10–15 minutes depending on the temperature of the kitchen, remove the tea towel and pop the loaf in the oven for 50–60 minutes or until it looks nicely browned and sounds hollow when tapped. It will rise a little further in the oven. This is called oven spring. If, however, the bread rises to the top of the tin before it goes into the oven it will continue to rise and flow over the edges.

We usually remove the loaf from the tin about 10 minutes before the end of cooking and put it back into the oven to crisp all round, but if you like a softer crust there's no need to do this.

Variations
Back to Front Bread
Follow the Master Recipe, reversing the proportion of white flour and wholemeal flour which make up the 450g (1lb) of flour. This makes a lighter bread, which we discovered by accident when a student with a hangover couldn't read! The result is delicious.

Russian Village Bread
Tim and I enjoyed several bread courses at the Village Bakery in Cumbria with Andrew Whitley. Andrew makes many Russian breads, one with coriander seeds on the top and bottom. On our return we experimented with our Brown Yeast Bread, and although it is not as complex as Andrew's Sourdough version, it is still very delicious.

Follow the Master Recipe, using 400g (14oz) wholemeal flour, 50g (2oz) rye flour and 50g (2oz) strong white flour. Brush the tin with sunflower oil, sprinkle a layer of whole coriander seeds over the base of the tin and another layer over the top of the bread before baking.

Frank's 'Pumpernickel' Bread
Makes 1 loaf

Frank McLaughlin, a student from Montreal in Québec, Canada, loved to experiment with our bread recipes. One day he majored on the treacle and produced this fantastic dark bread, reminiscent of pumpernickel but a fraction of the work.

450g (1lb) wholemeal flour
1 teaspoon salt
300ml (½ pint) water at blood heat
125ml (4fl oz) black treacle
25g (1oz) fresh yeast
sesame seeds (optional)

Preheat the oven to 230°C/450°F/gas 8.

Mix the flour with the salt and warm it very slightly (in the cool oven of an Aga, or in a gas or electric oven when starting to heat). In a small bowl, mix the treacle with 150ml (5fl oz) water and crumble in the yeast. Put the bowl in a warm position such as the back of the cooker. In about 5 minutes the mixture will have a creamy and slightly frothy appearance on top.

When ready, stir it well and pour it, with most of the remaining water, into the flour to make a wettish dough. The mixture should be too wet to knead. Put the mixture into a loaf tin and sprinkle with sesame seeds if you like them.

Put the tin back in the warm place and put the tea towel over it. In 10–15 minutes the loaf will have risen to twice its original size. Remove the tea towel and bake the loaf in the oven for 45–50 minutes, or until it sounds hollow when tapped.

We usually remove the loaf from the tin about 10 minutes before the end of cooking and put it back into the oven to crisp all around, but if you like a softer crust there's no need to do this.

> TIP: Brush the pan of the scales with oil before measuring treacle, golden syrup or honey; it just slides off into the pan or bowl.

Savoury Muffins
Makes 12–14

225g (8oz) plain white flour
2 teaspoons baking powder
½ teaspoon salt
pinch of cayenne (optional)
2 organic eggs
225ml (8fl oz) milk, buttermilk, yoghurt or sour cream
10g (½oz) caster sugar
75ml (3fl oz) sunflower oil

225ml (8fl oz) grated cheese (a mixture is good e.g. Gruyere, Cheddar even a little leftover camembert or blue cheese)

Preheat the oven to 200°C/400°F/gas 6.

Mix the flour, baking powder, salt and cayenne in a bowl. In another bowl, whisk the eggs with the milk, yoghurt or sour cream. Pour the liquid into the dry ingredients and stir to barely combine (don't overmix or the muffin will be heavy and tough). Gently fold in the tasty bits. Spoon into muffin cases and bake for 20 minutes or until pale golden. Cool on a wire rack. Best served warm.

Variations
Swap the grated cheese in the above recipe for the same quantity of any of the following (or create your own!).

Chopped spring onions and crispy bacon

Chopped chorizo, Kabanos sausage, cooked ham or streaky bacon lardons

Roasted peppers, basil, a little goat's cheese and marjoram

Chopped rosemary and raisin

Ballymaloe White Yeast Bread

Makes 2 loaves, 450g (1lb)

This basic white yeast bread dough is multi-purpose. It takes about 5 hours from start to finish, but for much of that time the bread is rising or baking so it's not 'your time'. In reality, the time spent kneading and making is about 20 minutes. Once you've made it, shape it in loaves or use it for plaits, rolls, twists or for pizza bases.

20g (³/₄oz) fresh yeast
425ml (15fl oz) water, more as needed
25g (1oz) butter
2 teaspoons dairy salt
10g (¹/₂oz) sugar
700g (1¹/₂lb) strong white flour

poppy seeds or sesame seeds for topping (optional)

Preheat the oven to 230°C/450°F/gas 8.

Mix the yeast with 150ml (5fl oz) lukewarm water until dissolved. Put the butter, salt and sugar into a bowl with 150ml (5fl oz) of very hot water, stir until the sugar and salt are dissolved and the butter melted. Add 150ml (5fl oz) of cold water. By now, the liquid should be lukewarm or blood temperature, so combine with the yeast.

Sieve the flour into a bowl, make a well in the centre and pour in most of the lukewarm liquid. Mix to a loose dough adding the remainder of the liquid, or more flour or liquid if necessary. Turn the dough onto a floured board, cover and leave to relax for approx. 5 minutes. Then knead for about 10 minutes or until smooth, springy and elastic (if kneading in a food mixer with a dough hook, 5 minutes is usually long enough).

Put the dough in a bowl. Cover the top tightly with clingfilm – yeast dough rises best in a warm, moist atmosphere. If you want to speed up the rising process put the bowl near your cooker, or a radiator, or close to an Aga. Rising time depends on the temperature; however, the bread will taste better if it rises more slowly. When the dough has more than doubled in size, knead again for about 2–3 minutes or until all the air has been forced out – this is called 'knocking back'. Leave to relax again for 10 minutes.

Shape the bread into loaves, plaits or rolls, transfer to a baking sheet and cover with a light tea towel. Allow to rise again in a warm place, this rising will be shorter, only about 20–30 minutes. The bread is ready for baking when a small dent remains when the dough is pressed lightly with the finger. Brush with water and sprinkle with flour. Sprinkle with poppy or sesame seeds if using.

Bake in the oven for 30–45 minutes depending on size. The bread should sound hollow when tapped underneath. Cool on a wire rack.

> TIP: If you are using tins, brush well with oil before putting in the dough.

Variation

Ballymaloe Plaits

Take one quantity of white yeast bread dough after it has been 'knocked back', divide into three equal pieces. With both hands roll each one into a rope; thickness depends on how fat you want the plait.

Then pinch the three ends together at the top, bring each outside strand into the centre alternately to form a plait, pinch the ends and tuck in neatly. Transfer onto a baking tray. Allow to double in size. Egg wash or mist with water and dredge with flour. This makes a very large plait. Divide the dough in 2 or 4 for smaller plaits.

Rolls and Other Shapes

Makes 12–15 rolls

Though they are sometimes made with a bread dough rich with butter and eggs, rolls can be made from any bread dough. Rolls also cook faster than bread, and can be served straight out of the oven, while bread must cool before it can be sliced. You can get 12–15 rolls from the amount of dough used for 1 loaf.

Preheat the oven to 190°C/375°F/gas 5.

General directions for rolls:
Form about one loaf's worth of bread dough into a log shape; the log should be 4–5cm (1¹/₂–2in) in diameter and is formed by rolling the dough between hands and bread board. Cut the log into equal-sized pieces.

Shape into one or more of the following types of rolls or some other shape. Allow to rise for 20 minutes. Brush with egg wash, sprinkle with poppy or sesame seeds and bake in the oven for about 25 minutes until nicely browned.

Plain Rolls

Take 10g (¹/₂oz) or 25g (1oz) pieces of dough, flatten and roll into rolls; place on a greased baking sheet sprinkled with corn meal.

Clover Leaf Rolls

Divide sections into 3 pieces. Shape each into a ball. Place three balls in a greased muffin cup.

Snail or Spiral Rolls

Roll each section into a length about 15cm (6in) long. Coil it up and place in greased muffin cups.

Flower Rolls

Flatten a 25g (1oz) piece of dough into a circle, divide into 6 but keep attached to the centre.

Butterhorns or Crescents

Instead of shaping the dough into a log, roll out in a circle about 5mm (¼in) thick. Brush with melted butter. Cut into 8–12 wedges. Roll up, starting from the wide end. Twist to form a crescent. Place on a greased baking sheet.

Knots

Roll a 25g–50g (1–2oz) piece of dough into a rope, tie into a loose knot and allow all the rolls or shapes to rise before baking.

Sunflower Bread

Makes 1 loaf

450g (1lb) White Yeast or Soda Bread dough
  (see page 481 or 474)
cornmeal

Roll the dough into a round, about 20cm (8in). Sprinkle a baking tray with cornmeal, transfer the dough onto the baking tray. Allow the yeast dough to rest for about 5 minutes. Brush with water and sprinkle with cornmeal. Press a 7.5cm (3in) cutter or small glass into the centre of the dough. With a pastry cutter or knife divide the dough into half, quarters, eighths, sixteenths. Give each 'petal' a quarter turn so part of the cut side faces upwards. Allow to rise to double size.

Preheat the oven to 230°C/450°F/gas 8. Bake for 10–15 minutes, then reduce heat to 180°C/350°F/gas 4 until crusty and golden. Cool on a wire rack.

Rosemary and Raisin Buns

Makes 12

450g (1lb) White Yeast Bread dough (half recipe)
50g (2oz) raisins
2 tablespoons extra-virgin olive oil
1 tablespoon freshly chopped rosemary
olive oil
organic egg wash

Preheat the oven to 180°C/350°F/gas 4. Soak the raisins in hot water for about 20 minutes.

Make the dough in the usual way, cover and allow to rise to double in size. Knock back.

Gently heat the olive oil in a frying-pan, add the drained raisins and the finely chopped rosemary, stir-fry for 1–2 minutes. Allow to cool.

Roll out the dough into a rectangle about 30 x 20cm (12 x 8in). Sprinkle the rosemary, raisins and oil over the dough. Fold in the long edges and roll into a Swiss roll. Cut into 8 pieces. Allow to rise on a lightly oiled baking sheet. When puffy and about double in size, brush gently with egg wash. Bake in the oven for 20–25 minutes. Cool on a wire rack.

Flowerpot Bread

White yeast bread can be baked in well-seasoned flowerpots. Oil well before using.

Bean-can Breads

Bake the dough in well-greased bean cans.

Pizza Dough

Makes 6 pizzas

Substitute 2–4 tablespoons of olive oil for butter and 50g (2oz) rye flour for 25g (1oz) white flour in the White Yeast Bread recipe and proceed as for the recipe.

Preheat the oven to 250°C/475°F/gas 9.

Divide the dough into 6 equal pieces or more. Roll out as thinly as possible into rounds 25–30cm (10–12in) in diameter or your chosen size. Spare dough can be shaped into rolls, loaves and plaits. Sprinkle some semolina onto a pizza paddle and place the dough on top. Cover with your chosen topping and bake for 9–11 minutes.

How to Cook Pizzas and Get a Well Browned Bottom!

I experimented a lot with different ovens to get the best result or at least the result that I'm happy with and I found I had to cook a different way in each oven. For all types of oven, preheat well ahead to maximum temperature – 250°C/475°F/gas 9.

Here at the cookery school we have a wood burning oven, which unquestionably makes the best pizzas. In just 1½ minutes, the thin crust bubbles up and is ready to eat – everyone adores them. The challenge is to achieve a similar result in a domestic oven. The faster the thin-crust pizzas cook the more delicious they are.

In gas or electric ovens with elements at the sides, I get best results by preheating a good heavy baking sheet in the oven on a high shelf. I slide the pizza from the paddle directly onto the baking sheet – a 25–30cm (10–12in) pizza 3–5mm (⅛–¼in) thick has a crusty base and bubbly golden top in 9–11 minutes. In a fan oven, I put in a wire rack and cover it with four 20 x 20cm (8 x 8in) quarry tiles, which I preheat for at least 20 minutes. This gives an excellent result in a similar length of time.

In my 48-year-old Aga, I preheat the baking sheet in the centre of the hot oven and slide the pizza directly on to it. Heat varies from Aga to Aga so some people may find it better to cook lower down in the oven.

If you don't have a pizza paddle, use a flat baking tray with no lip in its place. It's a bit more tricky, and if you plan to make pizzas often, I'd recommend investing in a pizza paddle.

Nettle and Ricotta Pizza

Makes 1

1/6 recipe Pizza Dough (see page 482)
a little cornmeal
200g (7ozs) fresh young nettles
1 garlic clove, slivered or finely chopped
35g (1½oz) fresh mozzarella, roughly grated

sea salt and freshly ground pepper
extra-virgin olive oil
1oz (25g) ricotta or Ardsallagh goat's cheese

Preheat the oven to 475°F/250°C/gas 9 and place a heavy baking sheet in the oven.

Stretch or roll the dough into a thin round. Sprinkle a little cornmeal onto a paddle. Lay the pizza on top and brush with olive oil. Sprinkle with garlic and mozzarella. Top with a mound of young nettles. Mist generously with water, season with salt and pepper and top with a few blobs of ricotta or goat's cheese. Cook for 7–8 minutes depending on the intensity of the heat. Remove from the oven, drizzle with extra-virgin olive oil and serve immediately with a few flakes of sea salt sprinkled over the top.

Pizza Margherita

Makes 1; serves 1–2

Possibly the most traditional and universally popular pizza in Italy, it was apparently named in the last century in honour of Margherita, the pizza-loving Queen of Italy.

1/6 recipe Pizza Dough (see page 482), about
  200g (7oz) dough

175g (6oz) mozzarella cheese*
3 tablespoons olive oil
4 tablespoons Tomato Fondue (see page 200)
1 dessertspoon freshly chopped annual
  marjoram
1 tablespoon freshly grated Parmigiano Reggiano

semolina, if using a pizza paddle

Preheat the oven to 250°C/475°F/gas 9.

Roll out the pizza dough in the usual way. Grate the mozzarella and sprinkle with the olive oil. Sprinkle a little semolina all over the surface of the pizza paddle and put the pizza base on top. Spread the mozzarella over the base to within 2cm (3/4in) of the edge. Mix the marjoram through the Tomato Fondue and spread over the top. Sprinkle with the Parmesan. Bake in the fully preheated oven for 10–12 minutes or until the base is crisp and the top bubbly and golden. Serve immediately.

* The best mozzarella available in Italy, particularly around Naples, is made from the milk of the water buffalo. Its texture and flavour are sensational and quite different from the mozzarella made with cow's milk, Fior di latte, and altogether different from the mozzarella available outside Italy. However I have had great success with Marcella Hazan's wonderful tip to improve the flavour of mozzarella for cooked dishes. She suggests grating it on the largest part of a grater and then sprinkling it with olive oil, 1 tablespoon to every 50g (2oz); mix well and leave to steep for 1 hour.

Pizza with Caramelised Onions, Blue Cheese and Rosemary

Makes 1, serves 1–2

This is one of my great favourites, but it does take a little longer to make than some of the others.

1/6 recipe Pizza Dough (see page 482), about
  200g (7oz)
4 onions, thinly sliced
2–3 tablespoons olive oil
50g (2oz) Gorgonzola or Cashel Blue cheese
1 teaspoon finely chopped fresh rosemary

semolina, if using a pizza paddle

First make the caramelised onions because they take a long time to cook. (They are so delicious with steaks or even on toast that it's worth cooking 2–3 times the recipe and keeping them in the fridge.) Heat the olive oil in a heavy saucepan, toss in the onions and cook over a low heat for whatever length of time it takes for them to soften and caramelise to a golden brown – about 30–45 minutes.

Preheat the oven to 250°C/475°F/gas 9. Roll out the dough as thinly as possible into a round 25–30cm (10–12in) in diameter.

Sprinkle some semolina on to the pizza paddle and place the dough on top. Cover the surface of the dough to within 2cm (3/4in) of the edge with caramelised onions. Crumble the blue cheese and scatter over the top, then sprinkle with chopped rosemary. Drizzle with a little olive oil and slide off the paddle into the fully preheated oven. Bake for 10–12 minutes and serve immediately.

Pizza with Potato, Onion Marmalade and Wild Mushrooms

Makes 4 pizzas; serves 4–8

1/2 recipe Pizza Dough (see page 482), about
  600g (1¼lb)
4 large 'floury' potatoes, such as Golden
  Wonder
1 organic egg yolk
225ml (8fl oz) creamy milk
50g (2oz) butter

4 tablespoons Onion Marmalade (see page 513)
110–225g (4–8oz) wild mushrooms
2 tablespoons finely chopped tarragon, thyme
  or marjoram
olive oil
salt and freshly ground pepper
rocket leaves
Parmigiano Reggiano
black olives

Preheat the oven to 250°C/475°F/gas 9.

First make the pizza bases and place on parchment paper. Cook the potatoes in boiling, salted water until tender and then mash with the egg yolk, milk and butter. Brush the edges of the pizza bases with olive oil and spread each base with the potato purée. Next spread the Onion Marmalade. Sauté the mushrooms in a little olive oil, season with salt and pepper and herbs and divide between the pizzas. Place the pizzas on preheated baking sheets in a hot oven and bake for 8–12 minutes until the bases are crisp and the topping is bubbling. Serve with rocket, olives and Parmesan shavings.

Pizza with Broccoli, Mozzarella and Garlic Slivers

Makes 1, serves 1–2

This is one of my favourite pizzas, originally made for me by an American student Erin Thomas.

1/6 recipe Pizza Dough (see page 482), about 200g (7oz)
110g (4oz) calabrese or green broccoli
2 tablespoons olive oil
2–3 garlic cloves, cut into thin slivers
75g (3oz) mozzarella, grated
10g (1/2oz) Parmigiano Reggiano, grated (optional)
sea salt

Preheat the oven to 250°C/475°F/gas 9.

Cook the broccoli florets in boiling salted water until al dente.

Roll out the dough as thinly as possible into a round 25–30cm (10–12in) in diameter. Sprinkle some semolina onto the pizza paddle and place the dough on top. Brush the surface of the dough with olive oil. Sprinkle on the slivers of garlic,

arrange the broccoli on top and sprinkle with Mozzarella and a little Parmesan if liked. Drizzle with olive oil and season with sea salt. Slide off the paddle onto a hot baking sheet. Bake for 10–12 minutes and serve immediately.

Variations

Tuna and Tomato Pizza

Spread some Tomato Sauce on the pizza base. Sprinkle some tuna on top, followed by some grated cheese, mozzarella and Parmesan. Criss-cross the top with anchovies and dot on a few olives. Bake for 10–12 minutes in a preheated oven 230°C/450°F/gas 8. Garnish with basil leaves and serve.

Pizza Quattro Formaggio

Spread the pizza base with Tomato Sauce. Sprinkle grated Parmesan on one quarter, grated Gruyère on another, crumbled blue cheese e.g. Gorgonzola, Stilton, Cashel Blue or Chetwynd on the third quarter and mozzarella on the fourth quarter and bake in the usual way.

Other Pizza Toppings to Try

Piperonata (see page 199), mozzarella, and marjoram

Piperonata (see page 199), mozzarella and pepperoni

Mozzarella, Tomato Fondue (see page 200), black olives, basil oil

Mozzarella, rocket and a drizzle of olive, truffle or chilli oil

Tomato Fondue (see page 200), anchovies, black olives, mozzarella, basil oil

Tomato Fondue (see page 200), Mushroom à la Crème (see page 201) and crispy bacon

Aubergines cooked in olive oil, roasted red peppers and marjoram

Mushroom à la Crème (see page 201), crispy streaky bacon, marjoram

LEFT Pizza with Caramelised Onions, Blue Cheese and Rosemary

Sliced garlic, sliced fresh chilli, mozzarella, marjoram and Tomato Fondue (see page 200)

Pan-grilled aubergine and pesto

Pesto, mozzarella and rocket

Roast tomatoes, aubergine slices, mozzarella and fresh roughly torn herbs

Onion Marmalade (see page 513), Gorgonzola, rosemary and whole garlic cloves

Roast tomatoes, deep-fried capers, smoked salmon, red onion rings and a drizzle of mango chutney

Sautéed mushrooms with garlic, marjoram and a drizzle of truffle oil

Tomato Sauce (see page 591), red onion, chorizo, goat's cheese, thyme leaves

Tomato Sauce, Mozzarella, Parma ham, rocket

TIP: Pop a few rolled out, uncooked pizza bases into the freezer. You can take one out, put the topping on and slide it straight into the oven.

Garden Café Pizza Dough

Makes 8 x 25cm (10in) pizzas

This recipe is so quick and easy that by the time your tomato sauce is bubbling in the oven your pizza base will be ready for its topping. This dough also makes delicious white yeast bread which we shape into rolls, loaves and plaits.

700g (1½lb) strong white flour
½ level teaspoon salt
10g (½oz) sugar
50g (2oz) butter
1 packet fast-acting yeast
2–4 tablespoons olive oil
350–400ml (12–14fl oz) lukewarm water

In a large, wide mixing bowl sieve the flour and add in the salt and sugar. Rub in the butter and fast-acting yeast, mix all the ingredients thoroughly. Make a well in the centre of the dry ingredients, add the oil and most of the lukewarm water and mix to a loose dough – you can add more water or flour if needed.

Turn the dough onto a lightly floured work top, cover and leave to relax for about 5 minutes. Then knead the dough for about 10 minutes or until smooth and springy (if kneading in a food mixer with a dough hook, 5 minutes is usually long enough). Leave the dough to relax again for about 10 minutes. Shape and measure into 8 equal balls of dough, each weighing about 150g (5oz). Lightly brush the balls of dough with olive oil.

If you have time, put the oiled balls of dough into a plastic bag and chill. The dough will be easier to handle when cold but it can be used immediately. On a well floured work surface, roll each ball into a 25cm (10in) disc.

Tuscan Piadini

Makes 8

225g (8oz) white flour
½ teaspoon salt
1 tablespoon extra-virgin olive oil
9–10 tablespoons lukewarm water

Sieve the flour and salt together in a bowl. Make a well in the centre and add the olive oil and enough water to mix to a dough. Knead for 3–4 minutes until smooth and silky. Put onto a plate, cover with an upturned bowl and rest for 20 minutes.

Heat a heavy iron pan. Divide the dough into 8 pieces and roll each piece into a thin round about 15cm (6in) across. Slap one onto the hot and slightly oiled pan. Cook for 2–3 minutes or until it starts to brown on one side. Turn over onto the other side and continue to cook for another ½–2 minutes. Serve warm whilst continuing to cook the others.

Mediterranean Pizza Pie

Serves 1–2

We love these pizza pies. You can have lots of fun experimenting with fillings.

375g (13oz) White Yeast Bread dough
  (see page 481)
1 aubergine, sliced, de-gorged and chargrilled in
  olive oil, cut into slices
1 courgette, chargrilled in olive oil and sliced
2 small red peppers, roasted, peeled and sliced
salt and freshly ground pepper
extra-virgin olive oil
5 or 6 basil leaves
1 tablespoon marjoram

Preheat the oven to 230°C/450°F/gas 8.

Divide the dough in half, roll both pieces into circles. Put one on a baking tray, arrange the vegetables, sprinkle with marjoram, seasoning between each layer. Brush the edge with water. Lay the other piece of dough on top and seal the edges.

Brush with water and bake for 25–30 minutes. Brush with olive oil and serve. It may be necessary to reduce the temperature to 200°C/400°F/gas 6 after 20 minutes if the pie looks like burning. Serve warm or cold.

Calzone

Serves 1 very hungry person or 2 people who feel sharing is fun!

Calzone originated in Apulia, the high heel of Italy. Basically it is a covered pizza baked in the shape of a turnover or half moon. Again there are many fillings one can use. Here is one we enjoy.

1/6 recipe for White Yeast Bread dough (see page
  481), about 200g (7oz)
50g (2oz) goat's cheese, crumbled
50g (2oz) mozzarella, roughly grated, soaked in
  1 tablespoon olive oil if possible
1 teaspoon finely chopped parsley
1 teaspoon finely chopped annual marjoram

45g (1³/₄oz) cooked ham or crispy bacon
  (optional)
2 tablespoons Piperonata (see page 199), or
  Pesto, or Tapenade

semolina, if using pizza paddle
olive oil, for brushing

Preheat the oven to 250°C/475°F/gas 9.

Mix all the ingredients for the filling together. Roll the dough very thinly into a 30cm (12in) round. Sprinkle the paddle, if using it, with semolina, put the dough on top and spoon the filling over the bottom half to within 2cm (³/₄in) of the edge. Brush the edge with water, fold over the rest of the dough and seal the edge by crimping with your fingers. Brush the top with cold water and slide into the fully preheated oven.

Bake for 20–30 minutes. Brush with olive oil when baked and serve with a Rocket and Cherry Tomato Salad (see page 221). A steak knife is a good idea for cutting it.

Ham and Cheese Sfinciuni

Serves 8–10

1/2 recipe White Yeast Bread dough (see page 481)
olive oil
175–225g (6–8oz) cooked ham, thinly sliced
150g (5oz) mozzarella, grated
45g (1³/₄oz) Parmigiano Reggiano
1–2 tablespoons freshly chopped parsley

33 x 23cm (13 x 9in) Swiss roll tin

Preheat the oven to 250°C/475°F/gas 9. Make the dough in the usual way. Knock back and rest for a few minutes.

Divide the dough in half. Roll 1 piece into a rectangle the same size as the tin. Brush the tin with olive oil and spread the dough over the base. Cover with slices of ham, sprinkle with a mixture of mozzarella and Parmesan cheese and finally the parsley. Spread the filling right out to the edges

and corners. Roll out the remainder of the dough and cover the filling, pressing down gently at the edges. Brush with egg wash and bake in the oven for 15–20 minutes and then reduce the temperature to 200°C/400°F/gas 6 for a further 5–10 minutes. Serve warm, cut into squares.

Panzarotti

Makes 16

450g (1lb) White Yeast Bread dough
  (see page 481)
4 very ripe tomatoes, peeled, seeded and
  chopped
salt and freshly ground pepper
1 teaspoon sugar
4 teaspoons freshly chopped marjoram
50g (2oz) buffalo mozzarella, grated
1–2 tablespoons freshly grated Parmigiano
  Reggiano

Preheat the oven to 230°C/450°F/gas 8.

Divide the dough into 25g (1oz) pieces, shape into rolls and allow to relax for a few minutes. Roll into circles less than 5mm (¼in) thick. Spread about ½ teaspoon of chopped tomato, seasoned with salt, pepper and sugar, onto the dough. Sprinkle with a little marjoram and ½ teaspoon Parmesan. Brush the edge of the circles with water, fold over into a half-moon shape. Seal with your fingers or press with the tines of a fork.

Bake for 15–20 minutes or until they are golden brown. Alternatively, deep-fry a few at a time until golden on both sides. You will need to turn them over halfway through cooking. Drain on kitchen paper. Serve immediately.

TIP: Dried yeast may be used instead of baker's yeast. Follow the same method but use only half the weight as given for fresh yeast. Allow longer to rise.

Focaccia

Makes 1 or 4 pieces (see recipe)

The classic Italian flat bread; great to nibble before dinner but also good served with a selection of olives or roasted vegetables as a starter, and great for sandwiches.

1 quantity Pizza Dough (see page 482) made
  with all strong white flour
olive oil and sea salt

Preheat the oven to 230°C/450°F/gas 8.

Roll out your dough, you can either roll it into 1 large disc or 4 smaller discs. The discs need to be about 1cm (½in) thick. Put onto an oiled baking sheet and make indentations all over the surface with your fingers. Brush liberally with olive oil and sprinkle with sea salt. Allow the Focaccia to rise again. Put it into the oven and bake for 5 minutes. Then reduce temperature to 200°C/400°F/gas 6 and bake for a further 15–20 minutes.

Variations
Focaccia with Rosemary
Follow the Master Recipe and sprinkle 2 teaspoons of finely chopped rosemary over the oil and then sprinkle with sea salt and proceed and bake as above.

Focaccia with Sage
Follow the Master Recipe and knead 2 teaspoons of finely chopped sage into the dough before rolling it out.

Focaccia with Black Olives
Follow the Master Recipe, adding 1–2 tablespoons of pitted black olives to the top of the dough. A teaspoon of chopped marjoram or thyme leaves is also a delicious addition here.

Breadsticks

Makes millions

Crusty breadsticks are all the rage, the more rustic looking the better – great with soups, salads or just to nibble.

1 quantity Ballymaloe White Yeast Bread
  dough (see page 481)
sea salt, chopped rosemary, crushed cumin
  seeds, sesame seeds, poppy seeds, ground
  black pepper, chilli flakes, grated Parmigiano
  Reggiano

When the dough has been knocked back, preheat the oven to 220°C/425°F/gas 7. Sprinkle the work surface with coarse sea salt or your chosen flavouring.

Pull off small pieces of dough, 10–25g (½–1oz), roll into very thin, medium or fat breadsticks with your hands. Roll in your chosen 'sprinkle'. Place on a baking sheet. Repeat this process until all the dough is used. Bake in a preheated oven for 8–15 minutes, depending on size, until golden brown and crisp. Cool on a wire rack.

Note: Breadsticks are usually baked without a final rising but for a slightly, lighter result let the shaped dough rise for about 10 minutes before baking.

Variations
Tuscan Breadsticks – *Sgabei*
Makes 30–32 (depending on size)

Completely addictive – utterly irresistible!

450g (1lb) White Yeast Bread dough
  (see page 481)
sea salt
olive or sunflower oil, for frying

Make the dough in the usual way, knead, allow to rise, knock back and rest for 5–10 minutes. Keep covered. Heat the oil in a deep fryer to 190°C/450°F. Pull off 7g (¼oz) pieces, roll into thin bread sticks with your finger tips. Cook a few at a time in the hot oil and after a minute, when they are puffed and golden on one side, turn over

onto the other side and continue to cook for another 1½ minutes or until cooked through. Drain on kitchen paper, sprinkle with sea salt and eat as soon as possible with hot Garlic Butter (page 588), Chilli Pepper Oil (page 227) or sweet chilli sauce (available from Asian grocers) to dip.

Sgabei with Cheese
Pull off 50g (2oz) pieces of bread dough. Roll into fat breadsticks. Deep-fry in hot oil for 4–5 minutes, turning halfway through. Drain on kitchen paper, slit along the side and fill with Taleggio or Stracchino cheese and eat as the cheese melts – yummy!

Anchovy Breadsticks
Break off 10g (½oz) pieces of bread dough, roll out, and flatten. Lay one or two anchovies along one side, pinch to cover, roll again and deep-fry as above.

Wiggly Worms
Shape a very thin breadstick which has been rolled in finely grated parmesan cheese into a wiggly worm.

Ciabatta

Makes 4 loaves (each about the width of a hand and the length of the arm from wrist to elbow)

The students love to make this recipe from *The Italian Baker* by Carol Field.

'Ciabatta' means slipper in Italian; one look at the short stubby bread will make it clear how it was named. Ciabatta is a remarkable combination of rustic country texture and elegant and tantalising taste. It is much lighter than its homely shape would indicate, and the porous chewy interior is enclosed in a slightly crunchy crust that is dusted with flour.

The dough should be made in a mixer. I have made it by hand but wouldn't recommend it unless you are willing to knead the wet, sticky mass between your hands. You can't work it on the table because the natural inclination is to add lots of flour to this very sticky dough and pretty soon you wouldn't have a Ciabatta. Resist the temptation to add flour and follow the instructions. The dough will feel utterly unfamiliar and probably a bit scary. And that's not the only unusual feature – the shaped loaves are flat and look definitely unpromising; even when they are puffed after the second rise, you may feel certain you've done it all wrong. Don't give up – the loaves rise nicely in the oven.'

Biga (or Starter – made 12–24 hours ahead)
7g (¼oz) fresh yeast
400ml (14fl oz) warm water at room
  temperature
500g (1lb 2oz) plain white flour

Ciabatta
7g (¼oz) fresh yeast
125ml (4fl oz) warm milk
300ml (10fl oz) warm water
1 tablespoon olive oil
475–600ml (17–20fl oz) Biga
500g (1lb 2oz) plain white flour
20g (¾oz) salt

To make the Biga: stir the yeast into 50ml (2fl oz) of the warm water and allow to stand until creamy, about 10 minutes. Stir in the remaining water and then the flour, 1 cup at a time. Remove to a lightly oiled bowl, cover with clingfilm and allow to rise at room temperature for 12–24 hours. It will more than double in volume and be wet and sticky. It will also have a very strong fermented smell when ready.

To make the Ciabatta: Measure out 475–600ml (17–20fl oz) of the Biga. Save the rest for the next batch. Stir the yeast into the milk in the bowl of an electric mixer and allow to stand until creamy, about 10 minutes. Add the water, oil and measured Biga and mix with the paddle until blended. Add the flour and salt and mix for a further 10 minutes. Change to the dough hook and mix for 15–25 minutes at high speed, or until the dough is stringy and pulling away from the sides of the bowl (this stage is essential for the final shaping of the dough).

Place the dough in an oiled bowl, cover with clingfilm, and allow to rise until doubled in size, about 1¼ hours. The dough should be full of air bubbles, very supple, elastic and sticky.

Cut the dough into 4 equal pieces on a well-floured surface. Roll up each piece into a cylinder, then stretch each into a rectangle, about 25 x 10cm (10 x 4in), pulling with your fingers to get it long and wide enough.

Generously flour 2 baking trays. Place 2 loaves, seam-side up, on a tray. Dimple the loaves vigorously with your fingertips or knuckles so that they won't rise too much. The dough will look heavily pockmarked, but it is very resilient so don't be concerned. Cover loosely with dampened towels, and let rise until puffy but not doubled: 1½–2 hours. The loaves will look flat and definitely unpromising but don't give up for they will rise more in the oven.

Preheat the oven to 220°C/425°F/gas 7. Bake for 20–25 minutes, dusting with flour and spraying 3 times with water in the first 10 minutes. Cool on a wire rack.

Master Recipe
Green or Black Olive Bread
Makes 4 loaves

Olive bread is made in many of the Mediterranean countries with many variations on the theme. In Provence, the olives are left whole but in Greece they are pitted and then chopped.

900g (2lb) strong white flour
1 teaspoon salt
6 tablespoons olive oil
50g (2oz) fresh yeast or 25g (1oz) dried yeast
2 teaspoons sugar
400ml (14fl oz) warm water (approx.)
275g (10oz) green or black olives pitted and
  chopped – yields about 225g (8oz)
2 tablespoons olive oil, for greasing

Put the flour and salt in a bowl with the olive oil. Mix the yeast with the sugar and 150ml (5fl oz) of the water. Leave for 3–4 minutes in a warm place until the yeast starts to work. Pour this mixture into the flour, add the remaining water and mix to a pliable dough. Knead for about 10 minutes or until the dough is smooth and elastic, then knead in the olives.

Put 1 tablespoon of oil into the bowl and turn the dough in it to grease the surface and prevent a dry crust forming. Cover the bowl with a damp cloth or cling film and leave the dough to rise in a warm place for about 1½ hours or until it doubles in bulk. Knock back the dough by kneading for 3 or 4 minutes and then divide it into 4 balls.

Place the balls on an oiled baking tray, pressing them down gently or shaping them in any way you like. Let the dough rise again, covered with a damp cloth, for about 1 hour or until it has doubled again.

Preheat the oven to 230°C/450°F/gas 8.

Brush the loaves with water to soften the crust and bake for about 30 minutes or until they sound hollow when tapped on the bottom – cooking time depends on the size of the loaves. Brush with the remaining olive oil and cool on a wire rack.

Variations
Olive and Rosemary Bread
Follow the Master Recipe, adding 2 tablespoons chopped rosemary with the olives. Bake in tins or as round loaves.

Walnut and Raisin Bread
Follow the Master Recipe, omitting the olives and kneading in 225g (8oz) walnuts and 50g (2oz) raisins and allow to rise. Bake in loaf tins or as round loaves.

Herb Bread
Follow the Master Recipe, adding 4 tablespoons of finely chopped fresh mixed herbs (rosemary, sage, thyme, chives, parsley, lemon balm) to the dough with the yeast.

Sicilian Semolina Bread

Makes 2 loaves

This bread, which comes from the hill town of Erice in Sicily, is made from durum semolina flour and is shaped into an extravagant variety of forms. Mafalda, the most common one, looks like a snake curled back and forth with a baton laid over it. If it is made without the baton it's called scaletta or little ladder. The shape that looks like a pair of slightly askew glasses is in homage to Santa Lucia, the patron saint of vision. All the loaves have a crunchy golden crust with a sesame seed topping.

20g (³/₄oz) fresh yeast or 2¹/₂ teaspoons
   dried yeast
50ml (2fl oz) warm water
1 tablespoon olive oil
1 teaspoon sugar
175ml (6fl oz) water at room temperature
365g (12¹/₂oz) durum flour or very fine
   semolina, as used for pasta
110g (4oz) unbleached all-purpose flour
2 teaspoons salt
10g (¹/₂oz) sesame seeds

Dissolve the yeast in the warm water in a large mixing bowl, add the oil, sugar and water. Mix the flours and salt in a bowl, add the liquid and mix to a dough, allow to rest for a few minutes, then knead for 8–10 minutes by hand or 5 minutes by machine. Put the dough into a lightly oiled bowl, cover tightly with clingfilm, and leave to rise until doubled in size, about 2¹/₂ hours. The dough should be springy and blistered but still soft and velvety.

Punch the dough down, knead it briefly, and let it rest for 5 minutes. Flatten it with your forearm into a square. Roll it into a long, fairly narrow rope, about 50–55cm (20–22in) long – the dough should be very elastic. Cut the dough in half and mould into your chosen shape.

Put the loaves onto floured silicone paper or oiled baking sheets. Brush the entire surface of each loaf lightly with water and sprinkle with sesame seeds; pat the seeds very gently into the dough. Cover with a cloth and allow to rise until doubled in size, 1–1¹/₂ hours.

Preheat the oven and a baking sheet to 220°C/425°F/gas 7. Sprinkle the baking sheet with cornmeal just before sliding the loaves onto it. Bake for 10 minutes, spraying the bread with water at 3 intervals throughout the baking. Reduce the heat to 200°C/400°F/gas 6 and bake for 25–30 more minutes. Cool on racks.

Baguettes

Makes 2–4 baguettes (depending on size)

This dough may also be shaped into round loaves or rolls.

450ml (16fl oz) lukewarm water (do not use
   the hot tap)
10g (1¹/₂ oz) fresh yeast or 5g (¹/₄ oz) dry yeast
very small pinch of sugar
700g (1¹/₂ lb) strong white flour
2¹/₄ teaspoons salt

Put the tepid water into a mixing bowl. Crumble in the yeast, add sugar, stir gently and leave for 4–5 minutes for the yeast to sponge. When the mixture looks creamy and slightly bubbly, stir in the flour and sprinkle with salt. Cover with a tea towel and allow to rest for 15–20 minutes. (This allows the flour time to absorb the moisture). Knead by machine for 5–6 minutes or by hand for 10–15 minutes.

Put into a pottery bowl. Cover with clingfilm and allow to rise in a warm place for 1¹/₂ hours or until doubled in size. Knock back and allow to rise again for about 1 hour. (This second rising may be omitted if time will not permit.)

Preheat the oven to 230°C/450°F/gas 8. Shape the dough into baguettes. Leave to rest between the pleats of a floured tea towel and let rise in a warm place until light and doubled in size (20–45 minutes). Transfer to a baking tray. Slash with a sharp blade, mist with water and bake for 20–30 minutes.

Arnaud's Pitta Bread

Makes 8–10

25g (1oz) fresh yeast
325ml (11fl oz) lukewarm water
450g (1lb) strong flour
2 teaspoons salt

Crumble the yeast into 125ml (4fl oz) of the water. Leave for 10 minutes until the yeast is dissolved. Sieve the flour and salt into a bowl, add the yeast and the rest of the water. Stir by hand until well mixed. The dough should not be too dry. Knead the dough until it is very smooth and elastic. If too sticky, add flour while kneading. Transfer the dough into an oiled bowl and oil the whole surface of the dough. Cover and leave to rise in a warm place for 1–1¹/₂ hours or until more than doubled in volume.

Knead the dough again until smooth. Roll into a thick log and cut with a floured knife into 8–10 equal-sized pieces. Roll each piece into smooth balls. Place onto a floured surface, cover and leave to rise for about 30 minutes or until double again.

Preheat the oven to the highest setting. Heat the baking sheets. Roll the balls to about 15cm (6in) circles about 5mm (¹/₄in) thick. Bake 2 at a time – 2 per baking sheet. Bake for about 3 minutes until just browning and puffed. Leave to cool on wire racks if not using immediately. They can be frozen but will not be as good as fresh.

Sometimes, one or two will not puff enough to make a pocket – they are still fine to eat.

Rye and Caraway Seed Bread

Makes 1 loaf or 3 small loaves

350g (12oz) strong white flour
150g (5oz) dark rye flour
1 teaspoon salt
20g (3/4oz) caraway seeds
7g (1/4oz) fresh yeast
300ml (1/2 pint) lukewarm water
45g (11/2oz) butter
poppy seeds (optional)
organic egg wash

12 x 20cm (5 x 8in) loaf tin

Preheat the oven to 230ºC/450ºF/gas 8.

Crumble and mix the yeast with the water. Mix the flours, salt and caraway seeds in a bowl and add the yeast with extra warm water if necessary to make a soft but not sticky dough. Add the butter and knead until smooth, about 10 minutes. Cover and leave to rise in a warm place.

Punch down and shape into 1, 2 or 3 round or oval loaves. Cover and allow to rise again for about 30 minutes until well-risen. Alternatively, place in the well-oiled loaf tin.

Brush with egg wash, sprinkle with poppy seeds and slash the top in a cross with a sharp knife or baker's blade. Bake for 40–45 minutes for a loaf in a tin or until the bread sounds hollow when knocked underneath. Small loaves will take 25 minutes. Cool on a wire rack.

Granary Loaf

Makes 1 loaf

Granary flour is a mixture of malted wheat and rye, with a proportion of wholewheat kernels. Some people find the malt flavour rather strong, so you can mix a proportion of plain or strong white flour with the granary meal. Homemade granary bread stays fresh and moist for an unusually long time.

600g (11/4lb) granary flour or 450g (1lb) granary flour and 110g (4oz) strong white flour
1 rounded teaspoon salt
20g (3/4oz) yeast
about 300ml (1/2 pint) lukewarm water
1 teaspoon black treacle (optional)
2 tablespoons light olive oil
1 tablespoon kibbled wheat (optional)

12 x 20cm (5 x 8in) loaf tin

Preheat the oven to 230ºC/450ºF/gas 8.

Mix the flours with the salt. Mix the yeast with tepid water, treacle and oil, add to the flour and mix to a dough; it will be very lithe and pliable. Knead for a few minutes, then form it into a ball, cover it and leave to rise in the usual way. When the dough has at least doubled in bulk and is puffy, knock it back and knead for 2–3 minutes.

Put the dough into the well-oiled loaf tin, cover and leave for about 30 minutes until it has filled the tin and is beginning to rise above the rim. Brush lightly with water and sprinkle with kibbled wheat, if using. Bake in the oven for about 25 minutes, reduce the heat to 200ºC/400ºF/gas 6 for the remaining time: approx. 20 minutes. Remove from the tin and allow to cool on a wire rack.

Note: For a crisper crust on the base, the bread may be removed from the tin and replaced in the oven 10 minutes before the end of cooking time.

Ballymaloe Spelt Bread

Makes 1 loaf

Spelt is an ancient variety of wheat that originated in the Persian Gulf 5000 years ago. There are even references to spelt flour in the New Testament! It was grown throughout Europe for centuries, however high cost production meant that spelt production had virtually ceased in Britain by the Second World War. In recent years there has been a huge increase in popularity as more and more organic farmers look for disease-resistant crops. Although it belongs to the same family as common wheat, it has a different gene structure so it is higher in protein and has a greater concentration of vitamins and minerals. It is low in gluten and makes a digestible substitute for wheat flour for those who are gluten intolerant.

450g (16oz) spelt flour
1 teaspoon salt
1 teaspoon black treacle or molasses
400ml (14floz) lukewarm water
20g (3/4oz) fresh non-GM yeast
sunflower oil
sesame seeds (optional)

13 x 20cm (5 x 8in) loaf tin

Preheat the oven to 230ºC/450ºF/gas 8.

Mix the flour with the salt in a large mixing bowl. In a small bowl or Pyrex jug, mix the treacle with 140ml (5fl oz) of the water and crumble in the yeast. Put the bowl in a warm place for a few minutes to allow the yeast to start to work. Grease the bread tins with sunflower oil. Meanwhile, check to see if the yeast is active. After about 4 or 5 minutes it should have a creamy and slightly frothy appearance on top.

When ready, stir and pour it, along with the remaining water, into the flour. Mix with your hand in a full circular movement to make a loose, wet dough. The mixture should be too wet to knead. Put the mixture into the greased tin. Sprinkle the top of the loaf with sesame seeds.

Put the tin in a warm place somewhere close to the cooker or near a radiator perhaps. Cover the tin with a tea towel to prevent a skin from forming. Just as the bread comes to the top of the tin (20–45 minutes), remove the tea towel and pop the loaf into the oven for 50–60 minutes or until it looks nicely browned and sounds hollow when tapped.

The bread will rise a little further in the oven. This is called "oven spring". If the bread rises to the top of the tin before it goes into the oven, it will continue to rise and will flow over the edges and stick to them.

We usually remove the bread from the tin about 10 minutes before the end of cooking and put it back into the oven to crisp all round, but if you like a softer crust there's no need to do this. Cool on a wire rack.

Ballymaloe Sourdough Starter

When making sourdough bread you must not use tap water which is likely to contain chlorine, but instead use pure spring water. Your starter must always have a pleasant smell and must not be allowed to get too warm – it grows best at comfortable room temperature. If it is too thick to beat easily, add a little more water. The flavour will grow more complex with use and age.

Day 1
Choose a large jar that will hold at least 2 litres (3½ pints). Put 50ml (2fl oz) barely tepid pure spring water and 50g (2oz) bread flour in the jar. Mix well, cover and set aside at room temperature overnight.

Day 2
Add 50ml (2fl oz) water and 50g (2oz) bread flour. Mix well, cover and leave overnight at room temperature.

Day 3
Add 50ml (2fl oz) water and 50g (2oz) bread flour. Mix well, cover and leave overnight at room temperature.

Day 4
Add 50ml (2fl oz) water and 50g (2oz) bread flour. Mix well, cover and leave overnight at room temperature.

Day 5
Add 50ml (2fl oz) water and 50g (2oz) bread flour. Mix well, cover and leave overnight at room temperature.

Day 6
Add 50ml (2fl oz) water and 50g (2oz) bread flour. Mix well, cover and leave overnight at room temperature.

The starter dough is now ready for use. You should have enough (450ml) to follow the bread recipe. It's best to use it right away but it can be stored in a covered jar in the fridge indefinitely (it will need to be refreshed or fed before use). The more you use the starter for making bread, the stronger it becomes.

Ballymaloe Sourdough Bread

It takes roughly 24–36 hours to make a loaf of sourdough bread from start to finish. The sourdough starter is not as powerful as commercial yeast so it takes longer to prove, which produces bread with a more complex flavour and nutritional content.

450ml (16–20fl oz) sourdough starter (see recipe above)

Night before
Add 225ml (8fl oz) water (blood temperature) and 225g (8oz) strong white flour to the sourdough starter. Mix well, cover and allow to stand at room temperature overnight.

Next morning
The sourdough will look puffy and very much alive. Add 225ml (8fl oz) water and 225g (8oz) strong white flour, cover, and allow to stand for 5–6 hours at room temperature. It will have increased in size and be light and bubbly in appearance.

Transfer 450–600ml (16fl oz) of this mixture into another bowl, cover, and save for next batch of bread (keep refrigerated).

Put the remainder into a large mixing bowl (almost 850ml) and add:

75–175ml (3–6fl oz) water at room temperature
700g (1½ lb) strong white flour
1 tablespoon wheat germ
1 tablespoon rye flour

Mix well. Cover the bowl with clingfilm or a damp cloth for 20 minutes. Sprinkle with 2½ teaspoons dairy salt (no chemicals). Knead by machine for 6 minutes or by hand for 15 minutes. Check for consistency and continue to knead for another 5 minutes – the dough should be slightly sticky. Cover and allow to rise until light (6–8 hours at room temperature). Knock back. Shape into two 900g (2lb) loaves. Dust with flour and put into a banneton or napkin-lined bread baskets. Cover or slip the baskets into large plastic bags. Refrigerate overnight.

Next morning
When the dough seems ready, remove from the fridge and allow to return to room temperature (about 1–1½ hours).

Meanwhile, preheat the oven to 230°C/450°F/gas 8. Gently turn the dough onto a baking tray. Slash the top with a sharp blade and sprinkle (mist) with water. Bake for about 40 minutes or until the lobes sound hollow.

This treasured leaven, given care and use, will provide you with you a lifetime of amazing bread.

Handkerchief Bread
Makes about 24

When we stayed in the Leela Hotel in Mumbai in India the chefs made many wonderful flat breads. This one particularly intrigued me. We tried it with well-rested White Yeast Bread Dough.

1 x White Yeast Bread recipe (see page 481)

Make the dough in the normal way; knock back. Heat a wok or Indian wok karhai on a hot flame. Take 50g (2oz) dough, roll it out into a very thin round. The Indian chefs start with a rolling pin, but then spin it around their heads, pizza-style! Roll one piece as thinly as possible, allow it to rest for a few minutes while you start to roll out another piece. Then go back to the first and roll it so thinly that one could almost read through it.

Slap it onto the hot upturned karhai. It will bubble and blister almost immediately. Turn over onto the other side, then fold in the sides and fold in three or four to make a little parcel like a folded handkerchief. Serve immediately.

Moroccan Bread
Makes 2 loaves

In Morocco, they knead with clenched fists; I did my best to learn from the cooks in La Gazelle d'Or in Taroudant but eventually reverted to my own method! This recipe is based on one from Paula Wolfert's book *Good Food from Morocco*.

25g (1oz) fresh yeast or 7g (¼oz) packet
  active dry yeast
1 teaspoon granulated sugar
lukewarm water
500g (18oz) white flour
150g (5oz) fine wholemeal flour
2 teaspoons salt
1 teaspoon sesame seeds
1 tablespoon aniseed
225ml (8fl oz) lukewarm milk
cornmeal or polenta

Preheat the oven to 200°C/400°F/gas 6.

Put the yeast into a small bowl with the sugar and 2 tablespoons of lukewarm water, stir and leave in a warm place until the yeast starts to bubble. Mix the flours with the salt and spices in a large mixing bowl. Make a well in the centre. Add the yeast, pour in the milk and enough lukewarm water to form a stiff dough. Since flours differ in their ability to absorb moisture; it is difficult to give a precise amount. Turn the dough out onto a lightly floured board and knead hard. It will take anywhere from 10–12 minutes to knead the dough thoroughly; it should be smooth and elastic.

In an electric beater with a dough hook, knead for 7–8 minutes at slow speed. When the dough is smooth and elastic, shape into two balls and rest for 5 minutes on the board.

Lightly grease a mixing bowl. Transfer the first ball of dough to the greased bowl and form into a cone shape by grasping the dough with one hand and rotating it against the sides of the bowl, held by the other hand. Turn out onto a baking sheet that has been sprinkled with maize flour. Flatten the cone with the palm of the hand to form a disc about 12.5cm (5in) in diameter with a slightly raised centre. Repeat with the second ball of dough. Cover loosely with a damp towel and let rise for about 2 hours in a warm place. To see if the bread has fully risen, poke your finger gently into the dough – the bread is ready for baking if the dough does not spring back.

Using a fork, prick the bread around the sides 3 or 4 times and place on the centre shelf of the oven. Bake for 12 minutes, then lower the heat 150°C/300°F/gas 2 and bake for 30–40 minutes more. When done, the bread will sound hollow when tapped on the bottom. Remove and let cool. Cut into wedges just before serving.

Note: At the Gazelle d'Or they also cooked a flattened circle of the dough on a griddle until browned on both sides. This is absolutely delicious with fresh butter and honey. They also kneaded thyme into the dough and and brushed the circles with oil and cooked them on a griddle for lunch; they called them Berber breads.

How to Cook Poppadoms

Poppadoms come in a packet, you'll be glad to hear! There are several flavours – from chilli, to peppercorn to garlic, but I like the plain ones best. I also favour the brands in the simple cellophane packets rather than those with fancy packaging. They can be cooked in various ways: deep-frying is best. Cook in sunflower oil for a few seconds, and when they have expanded to almost double their size, drain well on kitchen paper. If your deep fryer is not large enough, cook them in halves or quarters or even strips.

Alternatively, cook under the grill or in a microwave but note that they don't expand so much when cooked this way.

Look out for mini pappads or poppadoms, which are great for canapé bases or just for nibbling.

Poppadoms with Toppings
Serves 4

We were served poppadoms with various toppings in both Mumbai and Kerala. They came instead of bread but would make a perfect simple starter or a delicious nibble to go with drinks. You may want to go easy on the chilli powder although they are, in fact, very spicy in India.

8 cooked poppadoms
2 very ripe tomatoes, peeled
8 teaspoons finely diced red or white onion
chilli powder
coriander, freshly chopped

Dice the tomato flesh very finely, add the tiny onion dice and sprinkle a little over each poppadom. Dust with a little chilli powder and freshly chopped coriander leaves. Serve immediately.

Kelley's Sweet Hot Corn Bread
Makes 1 loaf

One of my students, Kelley Ryan-Bourgoise from Los Angeles, gave me this terrific recipe for cornbread.

350g (12oz) yellow cornmeal
375g (13oz) plain white flour
150g (5oz) sugar
1½ teaspoons salt
1½ tablespoons baking powder

8 tablespoons melted butter
350ml (12fl oz) buttermilk
100ml (3½fl oz) milk
2 beaten organic eggs
tabasco, to taste

100ml (3½fl oz) corn kernels (canned is fine)
75g (3oz) Cheddar, grated
60g (2½oz) green onion, chopped
2 tablespoons freshly chopped coriander

Preheat the oven to 220°C/425°F/gas 7.

Combine the cornmeal, flour, sugar, salt and baking powder in a bowl.

In another bowl, whisk together the butter, buttermilk, milk and eggs and add tabasco to taste. Combine both mixtures together and fold in the remaining ingredients.

Pour the mixture into a square baking tin, big enough to let the mixture come two-thirds of the way up the side of the tin. Bake for 20 minutes or until golden brown and a toothpick inserted into the centre comes out clean.

Cut into squares, butter and eat while still warm.

Pretzels
Makes 10–12

In the German Christmas market they make huge pretzels with ham, cheese and tomato – delicious.

1 Ballymaloe White Yeast Bread dough recipe
(see page 481)
organic egg wash
sea salt

poppy seeds, sesame seeds, grated cheese for
sprinkling

Preheat the oven to 230°C/450°F/gas 8. Mix and knead the bread dough and leave it to rise until doubled in size.

Knock back. Divide the dough into pieces about 110g (4oz) weight. Roll each piece into a thin rope, about 60cm (2ft) long and 1cm thick. To shape the pretzels: form each piece of dough into a loose horseshoe shape with the ends pointing towards you. Take the ends, and cross them over twice and rest both ends on the edge of the loop of dough.

Transfer each one onto a greased baking sheet. Cover and allow to rise in a warm place for about 10 minutes. Glaze gently with a light egg wash and sprinkle with coarse crystals of sea salt and poppy seeds, sesame seeds or grated cheese, if using. Bake the pretzels for about 15 minutes or until golden brown. Transfer to a wire rack and serve warm or cold.

Sea Salt Crackers
Makes about 30

450g (1lb) White Yeast Bread dough (see
page 481), about ½ the recipe
1–2 tablespoons extra-virgin olive oil
1–2 tablespoons Maldon sea salt

3 baking trays

Preheat the oven to 230°C/450°F/gas 8. Divide the dough in 3 pieces and roll out as thinly as possible.

Knead, roll, rest for 1–2 minutes and then roll again. We bake these crackers on the upturned base of the baking trays so the edges don't get in the way.

Brush the tray with olive oil.* Lay the sheet of paper-thin bread dough on top. Brush with olive oil and prick with a pastry pricker or fork. Cut into 4 strips lengthways with a pastry wheel or knife and then cut into 5cm (2in) diamonds (smaller if you wish). Sprinkle with flakes of sea salt. Bake for 3–6 minutes in the oven. They will bubble up and shrink apart in the oven. As soon as they are crisp and golden, lift off and transfer to a wire rack to cool. Store in an airtight container.

Variation
Rosemary Crackers
Proceed as above to*. Sprinkle with ½ tablespoon finely chopped rosemary evenly over the oil. Lay the dough on top. Sprinkle with salt and more finely chopped rosemary. Cut into 3 strips lengthways, then into 4 across to make 12 large squares (36 for 3 trays). Bake as above and cool on a wire rack. Store in an airtight container.

Master Recipe
Tortillas de Harina de Trigo (Flour Tortillas)
Makes about 25 tortillas, 23cm (9in) in diameter

Wheat flour tortillas are usually larger than corn tortillas and they come from northern Mexico, where maize does not grow so easily. They are made with animal fat (usually lard), salt and plain white flour (I use butter and get a very good result). Cooked on a hot griddle, they must be very pliable and soft for storage. For most purposes, flour tortillas can be used instead of corn tortillas and many people prefer them. They can be used in the same way but are never eaten cold.

To freeze flour tortillas, put a sheet of silicone or greaseproof paper between each one as they tend to stick together, especially when frozen. They defrost easily if left at room temperature for 30 minutes.

450g (1lb) plain white flour
1 dessertspoon salt
75g (3oz) lard, vegetable shortening or butter
about 225ml (8fl oz) warm water (at body temperature)

Heat a heavy frying pan (without greasing it) on a moderate heat until a drop of water will sizzle in it.

Sieve the flour and salt together in a bowl and rub in the butter as you would for shortcrust pastry. Slowly add the warm water – the amount may vary with the type of flour used. Knead the dough on a floured board with floured hands until it is no longer sticky. Keep the dough covered with a warm, damp cloth.

Take about 25g (1oz) dough at a time and knead for a few seconds, folding it back on itself to trap air. Now make it into a little ball and flatten it. Place the flattened ball on a floured board, and roll it out with a floured rolling pin until it is so thin that you can see the board through the pastry. Cut into 18–23cm (7–9in) rounds. Slap a tortilla straight onto the pan, cook for 30 seconds on one side, then turn over and cook for 15–30 seconds on the other.

Remove, cover with a tea-towel and keep them warm or store in a tortilla basket if you have one. If you need to warm up a lot of tortillas together, wrap 6 tortillas in tin foil and reheat them in a moderate oven (180°C/350°F/gas 4) for 15 minutes.

Variations

In the farmer's market in St. Paul in Minnesota, a Mexican stallholder offered a whole range of flavoured tortillas, even chocolate, which he insisted would be delicious with ice-cream and hot chocolate sauce. Try adding cayenne pepper, freshly chopped herbs (thyme, chives, coriander or parsley), or sun-dried tomatoes to the flour; or tomato or spinach purée to the water in the recipe above. For sweet tortillas, add sweetened cocoa or ground cinnamon to the flour.

Tortilla Chips

Cut the tortilla into 6 pieces and deep-fry for a few seconds.

To shallow-fry: cover the base of a heavy bottomed frying pan with 2.5cm (1in) of cooking oil. When the oil is hot, fry one tortilla at a time for about 20 seconds. Remove from the oil and drain on absorbent kitchen paper until required.

To deep-fry: heat the oil in a deep fryer to 200°C/400°F. Immerse the tortilla and fry for 1–1½ minutes. Remove from the oil when they are light gold, as they keep browning after they have been removed. Drain on kitchen paper.

Master Recipe
Mummy's Sweet White Scones

Makes 18–20 scones using a 7.5cm (3in) cutter

I regularly meet people on the street who make these, having watched me make them on the television in Ireland and they love the crunchy topping.

900g (2lb) plain white flour
pinch of salt
50g (2oz) caster sugar
3 heaped teaspoons baking powder
175g (6oz) butter
3 organic eggs
425ml (15fl oz) milk, to mix

For Glaze
organic egg wash
granulated sugar, for sprinkling

Preheat the oven to 250°C/475°F/gas 9.

Sieve all the dry ingredients together in a large wide bowl. Cut the butter into cubes, toss in the flour and rub in the butter. Make a well in the centre. Whisk the eggs with the milk, add to the dry ingredients and mix to a soft dough. Turn out onto a floured board.

Knead lightly, just enough to shape into a round. Roll out to about 2.5cm (1in) thick and cut or stamp into scones. Put onto a baking sheet – no need to grease.

Brush the tops with egg wash and dip each one in granulated sugar. Bake in the oven for 10–12 minutes until golden brown on top. Cool on a wire rack.

Serve split in half with homemade jam and a blob of whipped cream or just butter and jam.

Variations
Fruit Scones

Follow the Master Recipe, adding 110g (4oz) plump sultanas when the butter has been rubbed in. Continue as in the Master Recipe.

Lexia Raisin Scones

Follow the Master Recipe, adding 110g (4oz) lexia raisins to the basic recipe and continue as in the Master Recipe.

Cherry Scones

Follow the Master Recipe, adding 110g (4oz) of quartered glacé cherries to the basic mixture when the butter has been rubbed in. Continue as in the Master Recipe.

Craisin (Dried Cranberry) or Dried Cherry Scones

Follow the Master Recipe, adding 110g (4oz) of craisins or dried cherries. Continue as in the Master Recipe.

Crystallised Ginger Scones

Follow the Master Recipe, adding 110g (4oz) chopped crystallised or drained ginger in syrup to the dry ingredients and continue as in the Master Recipe.

Candied Citrus Peel Scones

Follow the Master Recipe, adding 110g (4oz) best-quality candied orange and lemon peel to the dry ingredients after the butter has been rubbed in, coat the citrus peel well in the flour before adding the liquid.

Cinnamon Scones

Follow the Master Recipe, adding 4 teaspoons of ground cinnamon to the dry ingredients in the basic mixture. Mix 1 teaspoon of ground cinnamon with 50g (2oz) granulated sugar. Dip the top of the scones in the sugar mixed with the cinnamon. Bake as in the Master Recipe.

Poppy Seed Scones

Follow the Master Recipe, adding 4 tablespoons of poppy seeds to the dry ingredients after the butter has been rubbed in. Proceed as in the Master Recipe. Serve with freshly crushed strawberries and cream.

Chocolate Chip Scones

Follow the Master Recipe, adding 110g (4oz) best-quality dark chocolate, chopped, to the dry ingredients after the butter has been rubbed in and proceed as in the Master Recipe.

Orange or Lemon Scones

Add the grated rind of one orange or lemon to the Master Recipe. Sandwich together with Lemon Curd (see page 511) or serve with Orange or Lemon Butter (see below).

Scones with Orange or Lemon Butter

Serve the freshly baked scones with orange butter.

Orange or lemon butter
175g (6oz) butter
3 teaspoons orange or lemon zest, finely grated
200g (7oz) icing sugar

Cream the butter with the finely grated rind. Add the sifted icing sugar and beat until fluffy.

TIP: Scone mixture may be weighed up ahead – even the day before. Butter may be rubbed in but do not add raising agents or liquid until just before baking.

Coffee and Walnut Scones

Makes 18–20 scones, using a 7.5cm (3in) cutter

In the US, scones are rarely eaten with butter or cream so be generous with the icing.

900g (2lb) flour
pinch of salt
50g (2oz) caster sugar
3 heaped teaspoons baking powder
175g (6oz) butter
3 organic eggs
2–3 tablespoons coffee essence
about 425ml (15fl oz) milk, to mix
150g (5oz) walnuts, coarsely chopped

Coffee Icing
450g (1lb) icing sugar
scant 2 tablespoons coffee essence
about 4 tablespoons boiling water

First preheat the oven to 250°C/475°F/gas 9.

Sieve all the dry ingredients together. Rub in the butter and add the walnuts. Make a well in the centre. Whisk the eggs and coffee essence with the milk, add to the dry ingredients and mix to a soft dough. Turn out onto a floured board. Knead lightly, just enough to shape into a round. Roll out to about 2.5cm (1in) thick and stamp into scones. Put onto a baking sheet. Bake in a hot oven for 10–15 minutes until golden brown on top. Cool on a wire rack.

To make the coffee icing: sieve the icing sugar into a bowl. Add coffee essence and enough boiling water to make it the consistency of thick cream. Spread each scone generously with coffee icing. Allow to set.

Rosemary Kearney's Gluten-free Sweet White Scones

Makes 15 scones, using a 6cm (2½in) scone cutter

Rosemary Kearney, a past student and teacher at the School, teaches an excellent one-day course on gluten-free cooking for coeliacs every year. She has been a coeliac all her life.

275g (10oz) rice flour
50g (2oz) tapioca flour
4 teaspoons gluten-free baking powder
2 teaspoons xanthan gum
1 level teaspoon salt
4 tablespoons caster sugar
110g (4oz) butter
2 organic eggs
125–175ml (4–6fl oz) natural yoghurt
organic egg wash

Preheat the oven to 250°C/475°F/gas 9.

Sieve all the dry ingredients together into a large bowl and mix well. Rub in the butter. Lightly whisk the eggs and natural yoghurt together. Make a well in the centre and add to the dry ingredients. Mix to a soft dough, adding a little more natural yoghurt if necessary.

Turn out onto a rice-floured board and knead lightly, just enough to shape into a round. Roll out to about 2.5cm (1in) thick and stamp into scones using a 6cm (2½in) cutter. Put on a rice-floured baking sheet and brush with a little egg wash.

Bake in a hot oven for approx. 10 minutes, until golden brown on top. Cool on a wire rack.

Serve split in half with homemade Raspberry Jam (see page 504) and a blob of whipped cream.

Walnut and Cinnamon Buns

croissant dough (see page 528)
melted butter
cinnamon
sugar
chopped walnuts
Caramelised Walnuts (see page 564)

Preheat the oven to 200°C/400°F/gas 6.

Roll the dough into a rectangle. Brush with melted butter and sprinkle with sugar, cinnamon and chopped walnuts.

Roll up, cut into 5cm (2in) pieces and allow to rest on a baking tray. When the buns have doubled in size, brush with egg wash, put a spoonful of caramelised walnuts on top and bake for 30–35 minutes or until fully cooked, slightly caramelised and deliciously sticky.

Master Recipe
Brioche
Makes 15–20 individual brioches or 2 large ones

Brioche is the richest of all yeast doughs and absolutely irresistible to eat. Some recipes can be intimidating but this very easy version works well and I've designed it so that the dough can rise overnight in the fridge and be shaped and baked in the morning. In France, brioche is traditionally baked in fluted tins but it can, of course, be baked in any size or shape, either free-form or moulded. The individual 'brioches à tête', which literally means brioches with a head, are usually eaten warm for breakfast with butter and homemade jam. The dough can also be used for all sorts of 'grand' recipes – anything from Saucisson en Brioche to a whole fish encased in brioche dough – Saumon or Loup de Mer en Croûte for example. Pretty impressive!

LEFT: Brioche

25g (1oz) fresh yeast (or use half quantity of dried yeast)
50g (2oz) caster sugar
65ml (2½fl oz) tepid water
4 organic eggs
450g (1lb) strong white flour
large pinch of salt
225g (8oz) soft unsalted butter
organic egg wash
1 beaten organic egg

Dissolve the yeast and sugar in the water, add the beaten eggs and pour into a mixing bowl. Add the flour and salt and mix to a stiff dough either by hand or with the dough hook of an electric mixer. When the mixture is smooth, beat in the butter in small pieces. The finished dough should have a silky appearance. Place it in an oiled bowl, cover and rest it overnight in the fridge.

Next day
Preheat the oven to 180°C/350°F/gas 4. Knead the dough lightly, weigh into 50g (2oz) pieces and roll it into balls or divide in half for large brioches. With the side of your hand, make a deep indent into each ball of dough slightly off-centre. Put the dough (heavy end first) into well-buttered brioche moulds and with a floured index finger, push the 'little hat' towards the centre, leaving it just protruding above the body of the dough.* This classic technique takes practice and skill; if it seems too difficult just form them into a roll or cheat by pushing the floured handle of a small wooden spoon down through the hat into the base, this helps to anchor it firmly.

Brush the top of each brioche with egg wash and allow them to prove in a warm place until doubled in size (though not too warm because of the high butter content). This should take 45 minutes–1½ hours.

Gently brush the brioches once again with egg wash and cook in the oven for 20–25 minutes. Large brioches will take 40–50 minutes to cook. A skewer inserted into the centre should come out clean. Serve with butter and homemade Strawberry Jam.

* They can be frozen at this stage.

Chocolate Chip Brioche
Add 110g (14oz) chopped dark chocolate when the bread is being knocked back.

Cheese Brioche
Makes 1 loaf

This is really scrummy, particularly when eaten warm.

½ quantity brioche dough
75–110g (3–4oz) Gruyère, coarsely grated
organic egg wash

23 x 12.5 x 5cm (9 x 5 x 2in) loaf tin

Make the dough as per Master Recipe. Next day, preheat the oven to 200°C/400°F/gas 6.

Knead half of the cheese into the dough after it has been knocked back. Put it into a well-buttered loaf tin and brush with egg wash. Allow to double in size, egg wash again, sprinkle with the remainder of the cheese and bake for 15 minutes, then reduce the temperature to 180°C/350°F/gas 4 for approx. 25–30 minutes. Remove from the tin and cool on a wire rack.

Croissants
See page 528

Pain au Chocolat
See page 529

Basic Bun Dough
Makes about 32

Bun dough is the basis for doughnuts, bath buns, currant buns, hot cross buns, Chelsea buns, iced whirls, etc.

900g (2lb) strong white flour
75g (3oz) caster sugar
pinch of salt
175g (6oz) butter
2 organic eggs
50g (2oz) yeast
300–425ml (½–¾ pint) water at blood temperature

Dissolve the yeast in a little water at blood temperature. Sieve the flour, sugar and salt into a bowl. Rub in the butter and then add the eggs. Add the yeast and enough water to obtain a fairly soft dough. Cover and rest the dough for 10 minutes. Knead well until the dough becomes firm and springs back when pressed with a finger (5–10 minutes). Put into a deep Pyrex or pottery bowl, cover with clingfilm and allow to rise until it doubles in size. Knock back by kneading well for 2 or 3 minutes, rest briefly and shape as desired.

Water Icing

Mix icing sugar with boiling water. It should be a reasonably thick liquid that can be brushed onto the buns.

Bun Wash

Make a syrup with 600ml (1 pint) water, 450g (1lb) sugar, boil for 2 minutes. Bun wash keeps very well.

Bath Buns

450g (1lb) Bun Dough
110g (4oz) sultanas
50g (2oz) candied peel
grated rind of 1 lemon
1 organic egg for egg wash
50g–75g (2–3oz) nibbed or coarse sugar

Knead the sultanas, peel, sugar and lemon rind into the bun dough. Roll into a thick cylinder and break off into 16 equal pieces. Place them on a baking sheet, flatten slightly and brush them with egg wash. Dip the tops into nibbed sugar and allow to prove in a warm moist atmosphere until double their size.

Bake at 230°C/450°F/gas 8 for 10 minutes and brush with bun wash after baking.

Chelsea Buns

450g (1lb) Bun Dough
50g (2oz) melted butter
110g (4oz) sultanas
110g (4oz) candied peel
50–75g (2–3oz) brown sugar
grated rind of 1 lemon
1 teaspoon mixed spice or cinnamon

Roll the bun dough into a rectangle 25 x 40cm (10 x 16in) and brush with the melted butter. Sprinkle the buttered dough with the sultanas, peel, brown sugar, lemon rind and mixed spice. Roll into a fairly tight cylinder, brush with melted butter and divide into 16 pieces. Place them face down on a lightly greased 2.5cm (1in) deep four-sided tray, fairly close together. Egg wash the tops and leave to rise in a warm and moist place until doubled in size. By then all the buns should be touching each other.

Bake at 200°C/400°F/gas 6 for about 20–30 minutes. Remove from the oven when cooked and, while still hot, brush with bun wash and dust with icing or caster sugar. Cool on a wire rack.

Variation
Easter Ring

450g (1lb) Bun Dough
12 diamonds of angelica
6 cherries
25g (1oz) flaked almonds

Make as for Chelsea buns and roll into a cylinder, Then transfer to a baking tray and form into a circle. Pinch the edges together to seal. Cut down half way in eight places and twist so the cut surface is facing upwards. Brush with egg wash, allow to rise to double size. Preheat oven to 220°C/425°F/gas 7. Bake for 15 minutes, then reduce temperature to 200°C/400°F/gas 6, until fully cooked.

Transfer to a wire rack and brush with bun wash while still hot.

Then ice the top with white icing, it will drip down over the sides. Decorate with cherries, diamonds of angelica and toasted flaked almonds.

Iced Whirls

Divide 450g (1lb) bun dough into 8 x 50g (2oz) pieces. Form each piece into a roll and pull to about 25cm (10in) long. Roll up from one end and seal with egg wash. Place on a greased baking tray and leave to rise until double in size. Egg wash and bake for about 15 minutes. Brush the top with bun wash and then ice with fondant or water icing.

Hot Cross Buns
Makes about 16

Nowadays, Hot Cross Buns are traditionally eaten in Ireland on Ash Wednesday and on Good Friday. This practice would have been frowned on in the past when these were strict fast days and the people would scarcely have had enough to eat, let alone spicy fruit-filled buns.

25g (1oz) fresh yeast
75g (3oz) caster sugar
225–300ml (8–10fl oz) tepid milk
450g (1lb) strong white flour
75g (3oz) butter
¼ teaspoon freshly ground cinnamon
¼ teaspoon freshly grated nutmeg
1–2 teaspoons mixed spice
2 organic eggs
75g (3oz) currants
50g (2oz) sultanas
25g (1oz) chopped peel
110g (4oz) shortcrust pastry (see page 112) or a paste made from flour and water, a little melted butter and sugar
organic egg wash made with milk, sugar and 1 egg yolk

Preheat the oven to 220°C/425°F/gas 7.

Dissolve the yeast with 1 tablespoon of the sugar in a little tepid milk.

Put the flour into a bowl, rub in the butter, add the cinnamon, nutmeg, mixed spice and the remainder of the sugar. Mix well. Whisk the eggs and add to the milk. Make a well in the centre of the flour add the eggs, yeast and most of the milk and mix to a soft dough – add more milk if needed.

Leave for 2–3 minutes, then knead until smooth. Add the currants, sultanas and chopped peel and continue to knead until the dough is shiny. Cover the bowl with clingfilm and allow it to rise in a warm place until it doubles in size.

Knock back by kneading for 3–4 minutes, rest for a few minutes, shape in 35g (1½oz) buns. Put them onto a baking sheet, egg wash and mark each with a cross.

If you are using shortcrust pastry, roll out thinly, and cut into narrow strips 5cm (2in) long. Carefully put a cross of shortcrust pastry on to each bun. Allow the buns to rise to double the size. Egg wash again carefully.

Alternatively, allow to double in size, then slash the top with a sharp blade and pipe the top with a liquid cross on top. I make the liquid by mixing the flour, butter, water and sugar together and filling a paper piping bag. Carefully glaze with egg wash.

Bake in the oven for 5 minutes, then reduce the heat to 200°C/400°F/gas 6 for a further 10–15 minutes or until golden. Cool on a wire rack.

Cinnamon Rolls
Serves 4–5

450g (1lb) Bun Dough
10–25g (½–1oz) melted butter
50g (2oz) brown sugar
1 teaspoon ground cinnamon
organic egg wash

Preheat the oven to 190°C/375°F/gas 5. Roll out the Bun Dough to a rectangle about 5mm (¼in) thick. Brush with melted butter. Sprinkle with sugar, cinnamon and raisins if used. Roll up from the long side. Cut into pieces 4cm (1½in) square and place flat on a greased baking sheet. Allow to rise until double in size, approx. 20–30 minutes. Brush with egg wash. Bake in the oven for 20 minutes or until cooked through.

Variation
Pecan Nut Rolls
Serves 4–6

Preheat the oven to 180°C/350°F/gas 4. Prepare the recipe for cinnamon rolls as above (omitting the sugar in the filling). Use a 23 x 23 x 5cm (9 x 9 x 2in) tin. Cover the bottom of the pan with a thick layer of honey, and sprinkle on 75–110g (3–4oz) of chopped nuts (walnuts, pecans or others). Place cut rolls next to each other on top of this mixture. Allow to rise until double in size, about 20–30 minutes, and bake for about 30 minutes. Turn the rolls upside down onto a serving plate.

Hallowe'en Barmbrack
Makes 2 loaves

The word barm comes from an old English word *beorma*, meaning yeasted fermented liquor. Brack comes from the Irish word brac, meaning speckled – which it is, with dried fruit and candied peel. Hallowe'en has always been associated with fortune-telling and divination, so various objects are wrapped up and hidden in the cake mixture – a wedding ring, a coin, a pea or a thimble (signifying spinsterhood), a piece of matchstick (which means that your husband will beat you!).

450g (1lb) strong white flour
½ level teaspoon ground cinnamon
½ level teaspoon mixed spice
¼ level teaspoon ground nutmeg
pinch of salt
25g (1oz) butter
20g (¾oz) fresh yeast
75g (3oz) caster sugar
300ml (½ pint) tepid milk
1 organic egg
225g (8oz) sultanas
110g (4oz) currants
50g (2oz) chopped candied peel
1 tablespoon sugar

Ring, matchstick, dried pea, piece of cloth, all wrapped in greaseproof paper

All utensils should be warm before starting to make barmbrack. Sieve the flour, spices and salt into a bowl, rub in the butter. Mix the yeast with 1 teaspoon of sugar and 1 teaspoon of tepid milk, leave for 4–5 minutes, until it becomes creamy and slightly bubbly. Add the rest of the sugar to the flour mixture and mix well. Pour the tepid milk and the beaten egg onto the yeast mixture and add to the flour. Knead well either by hand or in the warmed bowl of an electric mixer set with the dough hook at high speed for 5 minutes. The batter should be stiff but elastic. Fold in the dried fruit and chopped peel, cover with a cloth and leave in a warm place until the dough has doubled in size. Knock back again for 2–3 minutes and divide into two portions. Grease 2 x 18cm (7in) loaf tins and put one portion in each tin. Add the ring, stick, pea and piece of cloth. Cover again and leave to rise for about 30–60 minutes.

Preheat the oven to 180°C/350F/gas 4. Bake for about 1 hour until golden.

Glaze the top with the sugar dissolved in 2 tablespoons of boiling water, put back into the oven for 2–3 minutes. Turn out to cool on a wire tray. When cool, serve cut into thick slices, buttered.

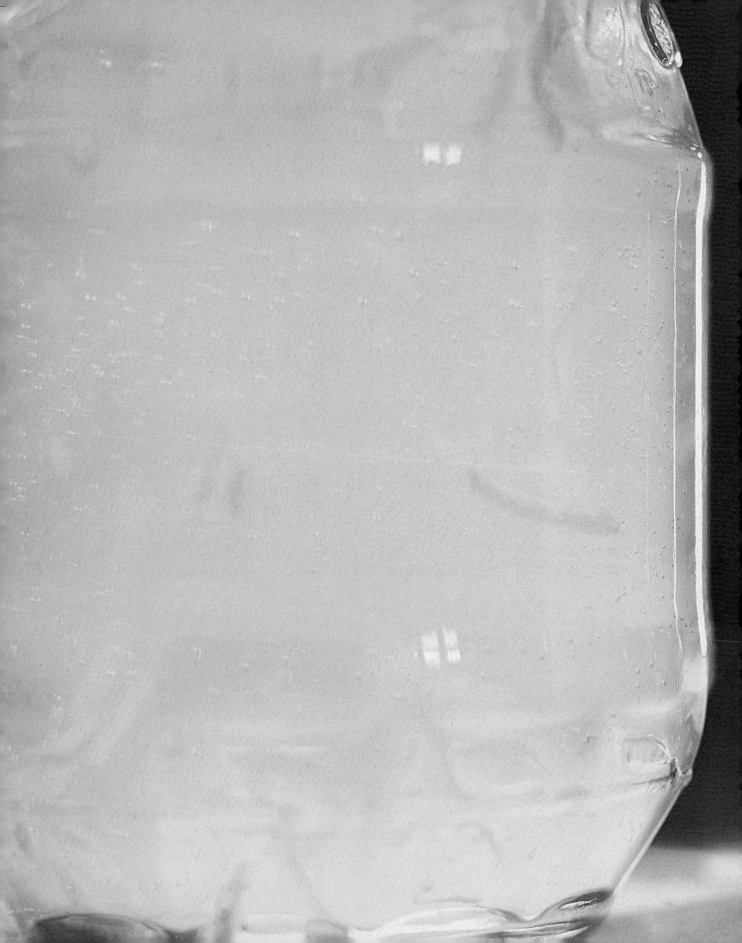

jams & preserves

Taking the Mystery out of Jam Making

As a child I lived in an Irish country village and I vividly remember life before electricity. Without fridges or freezers preserving was essential. In the soft fruit season Mummy made lots of jam – enough to last the family through the winter. The process was quite a performance – jam pots everywhere with vast mountains of fruit and sugar and the inevitable sticky saucepans. We would spend our day at school eagerly looking forward to going home to taste the new season's preserve on Mummy's freshly made scones. For me, jam making was a huge annual and not something to be undertaken lightly!

Years later, shortly after I arrived at Ballymaloe House, my (now) mother-in-law Myrtle Allen announced very matter-of-factly, late one night as she went around checking the fridges, 'We ought to make these strawberries into jam; they won't last till the morning'. I couldn't believe my ears! It was almost midnight... was she completely mad? Memories of the mammoth jam-making sessions of my childhood came flooding back to me; but I was new and anxious to impress, so I just asked how I could help. Before I knew what had happened the jam was made! As we began to fill and cover the jam jars, I realised Myrtle's secret. It is easy to make jam, provided you make it in small quantities and often.

Whenever you have fruit left over, it can easily be made into jam – even just one punnet of raspberries or strawberries. Jams or conserves are made with cut or whole fruit, marmalade is made with citrus fruit, and jelly is made from strained fruit juice. Jams, marmalades and jellies are all made by boiling fruit with sugar to setting point. Fruit contains acid, pectin and sugar, and these need to be in the correct proportions to set – preserves need a minimum of 60 per cent sugar to prevent mould forming after bottling.

Pectin

Pectin, a mucilaginous substance, is the setting agent in jams. It is found in the skin, seeds and core of fruit. Acidic or very slightly under-ripe fruit has a higher pectin content than fully ripe fruit. Blackcurrants, plums, gooseberries, cooking apples and redcurrants all have a high pectin content, whereas blackberries, strawberries and raspberries have low pectin levels. For this reason redcurrant juice, lemon juice, cooking apples or the reduced juice of cooking apples are added to some jams to help them set.

Average Composition of Fruits

Fruit	Solids	Sugar	Acid	Pectin
Blackcurrants	19.9%	6.4%	3.5%	1.1%
Plums	13.7%	7.4%	1.6%	0.8%
Gooseberries	11.1%	3.5%	2.2%	0.8%
Apples	14.3%	7.6%	1.1%	0.75%
Redcurrants	16.2%	4.8%	2.5%	0.7%
Blackberries	18.7%	5.1%	0.8%	0.5%
Strawberries	11.1%	5.5%	0.9%	0.5%
Raspberries	14.1%	3.6%	1.7%	0.5%

People ask me if it's necessary to use jam-making sugar (sugar with an artificial pectin). My view is that if you have good-quality fruit, you won't need artificial pectin, and if the fruit is not of a good enough quality, you shouldn't bother to make jam with it at all. I find that jam sugar affects the character, flavour and keeping quality of the jam.

Equipment

A shallow, wide, heavy, stainless steel **preserving pan** of 9 litres (17½ pints) capacity is perfect for jam making but is not essential. Choose your widest saucepan with low sides for fast evaporation. A **sugar thermometer** is a failsafe way to discover when the jam has reached setting point (105°C/220°F). A **jam funnel** is very useful for avoiding drips when filling jars – they are cheap and

worth seeking out if you make preserves on a regular basis. A **jellybag** (a conical cloth bag that can be suspended over a bowl to allow fruit juice to drip through) is also worth having for jelly-making. You could use a pillowcase or glass-cloths, but this can be a messy operation. Treat yourself to a jellybag – they last for years.

Containers

Containers for preserves must always be sterilised. Glass jars can be placed in a moderate oven at 180°C/350°F/gas 4 for 10 minutes, or put into boiling water for the same period and then dried upside down in an oven. The lids must also be boiled. If recycling jars, remove all the labels and wash thoroughly before sterilising. Glass jars are sold in various sizes – 450g (1lb) used to be a standard, but now it is more common to find jars of 200g (7oz), 350g (12oz), 500g (18oz) or 750g (1lb 10oz).

Other Preserves

There are many traditional ways of preserving food using natural preservatives such as salt, sugar, vinegar and spices. Aside from jam- and jelly-making, there is drying, salting, curing, smoking, pickling, preserving in fat or alcohol, spicing, crystalising, candying, and cheese and butter-making. Chutnies, confit, fruit syrups, ketchup, salami, sausages, patés and potted meats are all preserved foods.

A couple of years ago, chefs wouldn't be seen dead making chutneys (not macho enough!) but now it's all the rage. Chutneys and relishes are made from vegetables, fruit or a combination of the two and dried fruit is often included. If you make them with white malt vinegar, you should leave them to mellow for two weeks before eating. We sometimes use wine vinegar instead of malt. Flavoured vinegars, such as tarragon, are too strong and tend to dominate.

Guidelines for Making Delicious Jam

1. Fruit must be freshly picked, dry and unblemished. Top-quality fruit makes top-quality jam.

2. If the fruit is picked slightly under-ripe, it contains more pectin and so will set better.

3. Jam made from fruit picked while wet is likely to go mouldy in a short time.

4. Make jam in small quantities – it will reach setting point in a few minutes (the faster the jam is made, the fresher it tastes).

5. Ideally you should use a preserving pan for jam making. Failing that, choose a wide pan with sides at least 22cm (9in) deep.

6. Sugar acts as a preservative in jams, so it is important to use the correct amount - too little and the jam may ferment, too much and crystallisation may occur.

7. Citrus fruit peel, blackcurrants, gooseberries etc. must be thoroughly softened before sugar is added (sugar has a hardening effect on fruits).

8. Sugar must be completely dissolved before the jam comes to the boil (otherwise the jam will crystallise at the top of the jar). For this reason, it is better to add heated sugar, which dissolves more quickly. Stir with a wooden spoon until the 'gritty feeling' disappears.

9. Fruit should be simmered until the sugar is added, but from then on, it is best to boil as fast as possible until setting point is reached (it should read 105°C/220°F on a thermometer).

10. Test for setting frequently so that the jam is not allowed to overcook: put 1 teaspoonful on a cold plate and leave in a cool place for a few minutes – if the jam wrinkles when pushed with the finger, it has reached setting point.

11. If necessary, skim near to the end of cooking – or, if there is only a little scum, dissolve it by stirring in a lump of butter after the jam has reached setting point.

12. Make sure the jam jars are spotlessly clean, inside and out, and sterilise them in the oven before filling.

13. Fill the jars to within 3mm (⅛in) from the top to allow for shrinkage on cooling (use a jam funnel to avoid drips).

14. Press a round of waxed or silicone paper onto the surface of the jam immediately after filling (waxed side next to the jam).

15. Wet the cellophane paper on one side and stretch over the pot, securing with an elastic band. Label clearly with the date and type of jam, and store in a dry, airy cupboard.

Master Recipe
Raspberry Jam

Makes about 3 x 450g (1lb) pots
Season: mid summer

This is the first recipe I show my students to take the mystery out of jam making. It takes just 5, maybe 6 minutes to reach setting point. In fact, it is possible to make a batch of scones and, while they are baking, make some jam – remember, you can make jam with as little as even a punnet of fruit, just using equal quantities of sugar.

900g (2lb) fresh raspberries
900g (2lb) white sugar (use 110g/4oz) less if the fruit is very sweet)

Wash, dry and sterilise the jars in a moderate oven (180°C/350°F/gas 4), for 10 minutes. Heat the sugar in the same oven for 5–10 minutes. Put the raspberries into a wide stainless steel saucepan and cook for 3–4 minutes until the juice begins to run. Bring the raspberries to boiling point and add the hot sugar. Stir over a gentle heat until fully dissolved. Increase the heat and boil steadily for about 5 minutes, stirring frequently.

Test for a set. Remove from the heat immediately. Skim and pour into sterilised jam jars. Cover immediately. Hide the jam in a cool place or else put on a shelf in your kitchen so you can feel great every time you look at it! Anyway, it will be so delicious it won't last long.

Variations
Raspberry and Cassis Preserve
Follow the Master Recipe, and add 4 tablespoons of cassis to the jam just before potting.

Raspberry and Blackberry Jam
800g (1¾lb) raspberries
110g (4oz) fresh blackberries

Follow the Master Recipe using the above proportion of blackberries to raspberries.

Raspberry and Loganberry Jam
450g (1lb) raspberries
450g (1lb) loganberries

Follow the Master Recipe, using the above proportion of loganberies to raspberries.

Loganberry Jam
Follow the Master Recipe and substitute loganberries for raspberries.

Tayberry Jam
Follow the Master Recipe and substitute tayberries for raspberries.

Boysenberry Jam
Substitute boysenberries for the raspberries in the Master Recipe.

Strawberry Jam

Makes about 3kg (7lb)
Season: mid summer

Homemade strawberry jam can be sensational but only if the fruit is a good variety. It is one of the most difficult jams to set because strawberries are low in pectin, so don't attempt it if your fruit is not perfect. Redcurrants are very high in pectin and their bitter-sweet taste greatly enhances the flavour.

1.8kg (4lb) unblemished organic strawberries (El Santa or Rapella if available)
1.6–1.8kg (3¾–4lb) granulated sugar
150ml (¼ pint) Redcurrant Juice (see right) or the juice of 2 lemons

First prepare the Redcurrent Juice (see right) using about 450g (1lb) fruit to obtain 150ml (¼ pint) of juice.

Put the strawberries into a wide stainless steel saucepan with the redcurrant juice. Use a potato masher to crush about 90 per cent of the berries, leaving the rest intact. Bring to the boil and cook the crushed strawberries in the juice for about 2–3 minutes. Warm the sugar in a low oven and add it to the fruit and stir over a gentle heat until the sugar is dissolved. Increase the heat and boil for about 10–15 minutes, stirring frequently. Skin, test and pot into sterilised jars.

Note: This jam sticks and burns very easily so be careful.

Redcurrant Juice
Put 450g (1lb) redcurrants (they can be fresh or frozen) into a stainless steel saucepan with 175ml (6fl oz) of water. Bring to the boil and simmer for about 20 minutes. Strain through a fine sieve. This juice can be frozen for use another time if necessary.

Mummy's Strawberry Jam

Makes about 3.2kg (7lb)

Mummy discovered this 'overnight' recipe by accident! Strawberry jam can be difficult to set but with this method we find that it sets much more easily.

1.8kg (4lb) unblemished organic strawberries (El Santa or Rapella if available)
1.6–1.8kg (3¾-4lb) granulated sugar (not caster or jam sugar)
juice of 2 lemons

Put the strawberries into a large saucepan with the lemon juice and sugar. Stir and allow to stand, covered, overnight.

The next day, use a potato masher to crush most of the berries, leaving the rest intact. Bring to the boil, stirring occasionally and cook over a gentle heat until the sugar has dissolved. Increase the heat and boil for about 10–15 minutes stirring frequently. Skim, test and pot into sterilised jars. Cover and store in a cool dry cupboard.

Note: This jam sticks and burns very easily so be careful.

Rhubarb and Ginger Jam

Makes 8 x 450g (1lb) jars
Season: late spring, early summer

This delicious jam should be made when rhubarb is in full season and not yet thick and tough.

1.8kg (4lb) trimmed rhubarb
1.8kg (4lb) granulated sugar
grated zest and juice of 2 unwaxed lemons
25–50g (1–2oz) fresh ginger, peeled and bruised
50g (2oz) preserved stem ginger in syrup, chopped (optional)

Wipe the rhubarb and cut into 2.5cm (1in) pieces. Put it in a large bowl and layer with the sugar, then add the lemon zest and juice. Leave to stand overnight. Next day, put it into a wide, stainless steel saucepan, add the bruised ginger tied in a muslin bag and stir continuously over a low heat until the sugar is dissolved. Then boil rapidly until the jam sets, which takes about 10 minutes. Stir in the chopped stem ginger, if using, at the end of the cooking time. Remove the bag of fresh ginger and then pour the jam into hot clean jars, cover and store in a dry airy cupboard.

Elderflower and Green Gooseberry Jam

Makes 6 x 450g (1lb) pots
Season: late spring

Gooseberries should be tart and green and hard as hail stones – as soon as the elderflowers are in bloom in the hedgerows search for the gooseberries under the prickly bushes or seek them out in your local greengrocer or farmers' market. This jam should be a fresh colour, so be careful not to overcook it.

1.3kg (3lb) green gooseberries
600ml (1 pint) water
5–6 elderflower heads
1.6kg (3½lb) sugar

Wash the gooseberries if necessary. Top and tail them and put into a wide, stainless steel preserving pan with the water and elderflowers tied in muslin. Simmer until the gooseberries are soft and the contents of the pan are reduced by one third, about 30 minutes. Remove the elderflowers and add the warm sugar, stirring until it has completely dissolved. Boil rapidly for about 10 minutes until setting point is reached. Pour into hot sterilised jars.

Blackcurrant Jam

Makes 3.6–4kg (8–9 lb) jam
Season: late summer

1.8kg (4lb) fresh or frozen blackcurrants
1.2 litres (2 pints) water
2.2kg (5lb) white granulated sugar

Remove the stalks from the blackcurrants, put the fruit into a greased preserving pan, add the water and cook until the fruit begins to break. Put the sugar into a stainless steel bowl and heat it for almost 10 minutes in a preheated oven at 150°C/300°F/gas 2. (It's vital that the fruit is soft before the sugar is added, otherwise the blackcurrants will taste hard and tough in the finished jam.) Add the sugar and stir over a gentle heat until the sugar is dissolved. Boil briskly for about 20 minutes, stirring frequently. Skim, test and pot.

Master Recipe
Victoria Plum Jam

Makes 2.6–3kg (6–7lb)
Season: autumn

1.8kg (4lb) Victoria or Opal plums
1.3–1.8kg (3–4lb) sugar (taste the plums – if they are very sweet use minimum)
600ml (1 pint) water

Wash the plums and remove the stones. Save the stones and tie in a muslin bag. Put the sugar into a moderate oven (180°C/350°F/gas 4) to heat for about 10 minutes. Grease the stainless steel preserving pan, put in the plums, bag of stones and water, and cook until the plums burst. Add the hot sugar, stir until it has completely dissolved. Turn the heat to maximum and boil until the jam will set, about 15–20 minutes. Discard the bag of stones. Test, skim and pot into hot sterilised jars.

Greengage Jam

Follow the Master Recipe and substitute greengages for plums.

Damson Jam

Makes about 4–4.5kg (9–10lb)
Season: autumn

Damson jam has always been a great favourite of mine. As a child, my school friends and I used to collect damsons every year in a field near the old castle in Cullohill. First we ate so many we almost burst – the rest we brought home for Mummy to make into damson jam. The preserving pan is greased to prevent the fruit from sticking to the bottom.

2.6kg (6lb) damsons
2.6kg (6lb) sugar
850ml (1½ pints) water

Pick over the fruit carefully, wash and drain well, discarding any damaged damsons. Put the damsons and water into a greased, stainless steel preserving pan and stew them gently until the skin breaks. Heat the sugar in a low oven, add it to the fruit and stir over a gentle heat until the sugar is dissolved. Increase the heat and boil steadily, stirring frequently. Skim off the stones and scum as they rise to the top. Test for a set after 15 minutes boiling. Pour into hot sterilised jars and cover.

Blackberry and Apple Jam

Makes 9–10 x 450g (1lb) jars
Season: autumn

All over the countryside every year, blackberries rot on the hedgerows. Think of all the wonderful jam that could be made – so full of Vitamin C. This year, organise a blackberry picking expedition and take a picnic. You'll find it's the greatest fun, and when you come home, one person can make a few scones while someone else is making the jam. The children could be kept out of mischief and gainfully employed drawing and painting homemade jam labels, with personal messages like 'Lydia's Jam – keep off!' , or 'Grandma's Blackberry Jam'. Then you can enjoy the results of your labours with a well-earned cup of tea. Blackberries are low in pectin, so the apples help the set as well as adding extra flavour. A few lemon-scented geranium leaves enhance the flavour of this jam.

900g (2lb) cooking apples
2.2kg (5lb) blackberries
2kg (4lb) sugar (use 225g/8oz less if
    blackberries are sweet)

Wash, peel, core and slice the apples. Stew them until soft with 300ml (½ pint) water in a stainless steel saucepan. When soft, remove from the heat and beat to a pulp.

Pick over the blackberries, and cook until soft, adding about 150ml (¼ pint) water if the berries are dry. If you like, push them through a coarse sieve to remove the seeds. Heat the sugar in a slow oven for 10 minutes.

Put the blackberries into a wide stainless steel saucepan or preserving pan with the apple pulp and the heated sugar, and stir over a gentle heat until the sugar is dissolved.

Boil steadily for about 15 minutes. Skim the jam, test it for a set and pot into warm, sterilised jars.

Peach or Nectarine and Sweet Geranium Jam

Makes 2 x 450g (1lb) jars
Season: summer

900g (2lb) nectarines or peaches, peeled, stoned
    and sliced (the nectarines needn't be peeled)
350g (12oz) sugar
juice of 1 unwaxed lemon
3–4 sweet geranium leaves

Put the fruit and sugar into a small, stainless steel saucepan and add the lemon juice and geranium leaves. Bring to the boil over a medium heat, stirring constantly. Cook until the fruit is soft, which takes about 15 minutes. Test for a set. Pour in sterilised jars, cover and store in a cool, dry place.

Julia Wight's Fresh Apricot Jam

Makes about 2.6kg (6lb)
Season: summer

This is a lovely golden preserve which keeps well. The flavour of apricots straight from the tree comes through in Julia's simple recipe. The kernels give a delicious almond flavour to the jam. Apricot jam can also be made with dried fruits.

1.6kg (3½lb) whole fresh apricots to yield
    1.3kg (3lb) fresh apricots when stoned
1.3kg (3lb) sugar
juice of 2 unwaxed lemons

Halve the apricots and remove the stones, keeping a few kernels to add to the finished jam. In a large bowl, layer the apricots and sugar, finishing with a layer of sugar and leave in a cool place overnight.

Put the lemon juice in a large saucepan and add the fruit and sugar. (If the fruit is lacking in juice, you could add about 300ml (½ pint) water with the lemon juice.)

Bring to the boil very slowly. Make sure that all the sugar has dissolved, then simmer for 30–40 minutes, stirring occasionally. Add blanched and halved kernels half way through the simmering.

Test for a set and allow the jam to cool slightly before potting into hot, sterilised jars.

Making Jellies

We make 2 types of jellies: with and without water.

For jelly-making, the fruit must be cooked before the juice is extracted. Apples and pears, for example, should be washed, any blemishes or bruises removed and then chopped. There is no need to peel or discard the cores as they add pectin and flavour.

Cover the fruit with water and cook on a medium heat, stirring occasionally until soft and pulpy. Pour into a jelly bag and allow to drip over a bowl overnight or at least for a few hours. Resist the temptation to squeeze the jelly bag or the jelly will be cloudy. Jellies may be flavoured with all manner of herbs and spices. Quince or japonica may also be added to make up a proportion of the fruit.

Redcurrants are very high in pectin. Redcurrant Jelly may be made as above but a more intensely delicious jelly is made by the quick method on page 508. The method may also be used for blackcurrants but add 600ml (1 pint) water to reduce the intensity.

Master Recipe
Crab Apple or Bramley Apple Jelly

Makes 2.7–3kg (6–7lb)
Season: autumn

2.4kg (5½lb) crab apples or windfall cooking apples or a mixture
2.6 litres (4½ pints) water
2 unwaxed lemons
sugar

Wash the apples and cut them into quarters – do not remove either the peel or core. Windfalls may be used, but make sure to cut out the bruised parts. Put the apples into a large saucepan with the water and the thinly pared zest of the lemons. Cook until reduced to a pulp, (about ½ hour). Turn the pulp into a jelly bag and allow to drip until all the juice has been extracted – usually overnight.

Measure the juice into a preserving pan and allow 450g (1lb) sugar to each 600ml (1 pint) of juice. Warm the sugar in a low oven.

Squeeze the lemons, strain the juice and add it to the preserving pan. Bring to the boil and add the warm sugar. Stir over a gentle heat until the sugar is dissolved. Increase the heat and boil rapidly without stirring for about 8–10 minutes. Skim, test and pot immediately.

Variations
Apple and Lemon-scented Geranium Jelly
Follow the Master Recipe, adding 6–8 large leaves of sweet geranium while the apples are stewing and put a fresh leaf into each jar as you pot the jelly.

Apple and Clove Jelly
Follow the Master Recipe, adding 3–6 cloves to the apples as they stew and put a clove in each pot. Serve on bread or scones.

Apple and Mint Jelly
Follow the Master Recipe, adding 4–6 large sprigs of fresh mint to the apples while they are stewing and 6–8 tablespoons of finely chopped fresh mint to the jelly just before it is potted. Serve with lamb as an alternative to mint sauce.

Apple and Rosemary Jelly
Follow the Master Recipe, adding 2 sprigs of rosemary to the apples as they stew and put a tiny sprig into each pot. Serve with lamb.

Apple and Elderberry Jelly
Follow the Master Recipe, adding a fist or 2 of elderberries to the apple and continue as above. Up to half volume of elderberries can be used. A sprig or two of mint or sweet geranium or a cinnamon stick enhances the flavour further.

Apple and Marjoram Jelly
Follow the Master Recipe, adding 4–6 large sprigs of fresh marjoram to the apples while they are stewing and add 3–4 tablespoons of finely chopped fresh marjoram to the jelly just before it is potted.

Apple and Chilli Jelly
Follow the Master Recipe, adding 2 tablespoons of chilli flakes to the apples. Vary the amount according to how hot you like things.

Apple and Cranberry Jelly
Follow the Master Recipe, adding 450–900g (1–2lb) cranberries to the apples.

Apple and Jalapeño Jelly
Follow the Master Recipe, adding 2–4 jalapeño chillies to the strained juice.

Apple and Sloe Jelly
Follow the Master Recipe, adding a fist or two of sloes to the apples.

Sloe and Crab Apple Jelly

Makes 2.7-3.1kg (6-7lb)
Season: autumn

Every year we still collect sloes in the time-honoured way and spend lengthy sessions around the kitchen table, pricking the sloes with a darning needle to make sloe gin (see page 574) in order to spread a little good cheer to all our friends. The remainder we use in this delicious jelly – an excellent accompaniment to lamb, mutton or venison.

1.8kg (4lb) sloes
1.8kg (4lb) crab apples or Bramley Seedlings, (take out any bad bits but the stalk and pips all go in)
water to cover
sugar – allow 450g (1 lb) to every 450g (1lb) fruit

Pick over the sloes and place in a large saucepan. Check the apples for bad bruises, core, cut into quarters or eights and add to the sloes. Cover with water and bring to the boil, cooking until the apples are reduced to a pulp and the sloes burst. Turn the pulp into a jelly bag and allow to drip until all the juice has been extracted – usually overnight.

The next day, measure the juice into a preserving pan and allow 450g (1lb) sugar to each 600ml (1 pint) of juice. Warm the sugar in a low oven. Bring the juice to the boil and allow to reduce by about half – about 5–6 minutes. Add the sugar and stir over a gentle heat until it has dissolved. Increase the heat and boil rapidly for about 15 minutes until the setting point is reached. Pour into sterilized jars, cover and seal immediately.

Medlar Jelly

Season: autumn

Medlars are a bizarre looking fruit of the malus family. Use one-third firm medlars and two-third barely softened or bletted fruit when making the jelly.

1.3kg (3lb) medlars
water to cover
2 strips of lemon peel
sugar
tiny piece of cinnamon stick
2 cloves

Wash the medlars, cut them into quarters and place in a large saucepan with the water and the lemon peel. Bring to the boil, cover and cook until reduced to a pulp (about 20–30 minutes). Turn the pulp into a jelly bag and allow to drip until all the juice has been extracted. Don't squeeze the jelly through the bag or the juice will be cloudy.

The next day, measure the juice into a preserving pan and allow 450g (1lb) of sugar to every 600ml (1 pint) of juice. Warm the sugar in the in a moderate oven. Bring the juice to the boil and add the warm sugar, stirring over a gentle heat until it is dissolved. Then increase the heat, add the spices and boil rapidly without stirring for about 8–10 minutes until setting point is reached. Pour into hot, sterilized jars and cover immediately.

Serve with game, pork, coarse patés or with cream cheese hearts.

Redcurrant Jelly

Makes 3 x 450g (1lb) pots
In season: summer

Redcurrant jelly is delicious and a versatile product to have in your larder. It has myriad uses: used like jam on bread and scones, served as an accompaniment to roast lamb, bacon or ham, good with rough pâtés and game, and invaluable as a glaze for red fruit tarts.

This recipe is a particular favourite of mine, not only because it is fast to make and results in a delicious, intensely-flavoured jelly, but because you can use the leftover pulp to make a fruit tart; double value from the redcurrants. Unlike most other fruit jellies, no water is needed in this recipe.

900g (2lb) redcurrants
900g (2lb) granulated sugar

Remove the strings from the redcurrants either by hand or with a fork. Put the redcurrants and sugar into a wide, stainless steel saucepan and stir continuously over a medium heat until they come to the boil.

Boil hard for exactly 8 minutes, stirring only if they appear to be sticking to the bottom. Skim carefully. Turn into a nylon sieve and allow to drip through. Do not push the pulp through or the jelly will be cloudy. You can stir it gently once or twice just to free the pulp from the bottom of the sieve. Pour immediately into hot, sterilised pots.

Redcurrants are very high in pectin so the jelly will start to set just as soon as it begins to cool.

Fruit Glazes

Fruit glazes are essential in the pastry section of a restaurant kitchen – they are brushed over fruit tarts to enhance the flavour and to give a shiny appearance. Apricot glaze is used for yellow and green fruit such as apricots, peaches, nectarines, grapes, kiwi fruit and orange segments. Redcurrant jelly, with its bitter, sweet flavour, makes a delicious glaze for red and black fruits, such as strawberries, raspberries, loganberries, boysenberries, tayberries, blackberries, blueberries and blackcurrants.

Fruit glazes keep for several weeks. They should be stored in sterilised jars, as for jams.

Apricot Glaze

Makes about 300ml (½ pint)
Season: summer

Apricot glaze is used to glaze orange or green fruits such as peaches, nectarines, oranges, grapes and kiwi, particularly in fruit tarts.

350g (12oz) Julia Wight's Fresh Apricot Jam (see page 506)
juice of ¼ lemon or 2 tablespoons water

In a small stainless steel saucepan, melt the apricot jam with 1–2 tablespoons of juice or water. Push the hot jam through a nylon sieve and store in a sterilised, airtight jar.

Melt and stir the glaze before use, if necessary.

Redcurrant Glaze

Makes a generous 300ml (½ pint)
Season: summer

This is immeasurably better if you start off with homemade redcurrant jelly; remember it only takes 8 minutes to make! Use it to glaze red fruits.

350g (12oz) Redcurrant Jelly (see left)
about 1 tablespoon water (optional)

In a small stainless steel saucepan, melt the Redcurrant Jelly and add the water only if it needs thinning out. Stir gently, but do not whisk or it will become cloudy. Cook for just 1–2 minutes – the jelly will darken if cooked for longer. Store any left over glaze in an airtight jar and reheat gently to melt it before use.

Making Marmalade

When you are making marmalade, be it orange, lemon or lime, you should always wash the fruit beforehand to remove any deposits and grime on the skin. Cut around the equator of the fruit, squeeze out all the juice and save the seeds. Remove the peel carefully, and slice and chop it to the thickness you are after. Then remove the pulp (but not the pith) with a sharp spoon. Tie the seeds and the pulp up in a muslin bag and boil with the peel in a mixture of water and the juice.

The peel must be soft and the liquid reduced to between a third and half its original volume before you add the sugar. If you add the sugar too soon, it will have a hardening effect upon the peel and no amount of cooking will soften it; it will in fact become more like candied peel. Also, if there is too much liquid the marmalade will take far longer to set, losing its fresh taste. It will become dark and more bitter in flavour, but some people actually prefer this. You can also make a darker marmalade by adding molasses to the recipe.

ABOVE: Marmalade on toast

Old-fashioned Seville Orange Marmalade

Makes 3.2kg (7lb)

Seville and Malaga oranges come into the shops after Christmas and are around for 4–5 weeks.

900g (2lb) Seville oranges
2.4 litres (4 pints) water
1 lemon
1.8kg (4lb) granulated sugar

Wash the fruit, cut in half and squeeze out the juice. Remove the membrane with a spoon, put with the pips, tie them in a piece of muslin and soak for half an hour in cold water. Slice the peel finely or coarsely, depending on how you like your marmalade. Put the peel, orange and lemon juice, bag of pips and water into a non-reactive bowl or saucepan overnight. Next day, bring

everything to the boil and simmer gently for about 2 hours until the peel is really soft and the liquid is reduced by half. Squeeze all the liquid from the bag of pips and remove it.

Add the warmed sugar and stir until all the sugar has been dissolved. Increase the heat and bring to a full and rapid rolling boil until setting point is reached. Test for a set, either with a sugar thermometer (it should register 110°C/225°F), or with a saucer. Put a little marmalade on a cold saucer and cool for a few minutes If it wrinkles when you push it with your finger, it's done. Stir well and immediately pot into hot sterilised jars. Cover immediately and store in a cool dry place.

Note: The peel must be absolutely soft before the sugar is added, otherwise when the sugar is added it will become very hard and no amount of boiling will soften it.

Seville Orange Marmalade Made with Whole Oranges

Makes 5.6–6.6kg (13–15lb)
Season: late winter

You'll find Seville and Malaga oranges in the shops for just a few short weeks after Christmas. Buy what you need and make the marmalade while the oranges are fresh if possible. If not, just pop them into the freezer as this recipe works brilliantly for frozen oranges and it's not even necessary to defrost them. Some recipes slice the peel first but in this one the whole oranges are boiled and then the peel is sliced.

Use bitter oranges; marmalade demands bitterness and the flavour of the rind is quite different from that of the sweet orange. The word 'marmelade' derives from marmelo, which is the Portuguese word for quince. Mary Queen of Scots frequently demanded orange preserves, which she had tasted in France, and it is believed that 'marmelade' could also be a corruption of 'marie-melade'.

2kg (4½lb) Seville or Malaga oranges
5.4 litres (9 pints) water
4.4kg (9lb) sugar

Wash the oranges. Put them in a stainless steel saucepan with the water and put a plate on top to keep them under the surface of the water. Cover with the lid of the saucepan, simmer gently until soft; about 2 hours. Cool and drain, reserving the water. (If more convenient, leave overnight and continue the next day.)

Warm the sugar in a moderate oven (180°C/350°F/gas 4) for 10 minutes.

Put your chopping board onto a large baking tray with sides (so you won't lose any juice) and cut the oranges in half and scoop out the soft centres. Slice the peel finely. Pop the pips into a muslin bag and put the escaped juice and sliced oranges in a large, wide, stainless steel saucepan with the reserved marmalade liquid. Bring to the boil and add the warm sugar, stir over a brisk heat until all the sugar is dissolved. Boil fast until setting point is reached. Pot in sterilised jars and cover at once.

Note: With any marmalade it's vital that the original liquid has reduced by half or, better still, two-thirds before the sugar is added, otherwise it takes ages to reach a set and both the flavour and colour will be spoiled. A wide, low-sided, stainless steel saucepan is best for this recipe, 35–40cm (14–16in) wide. If you don't have one around that size, cook the marmalade in 2 batches.

Orange, Lemon and Grapefruit Marmalade

Makes about 4.5 kg (10lb)
Season: winter

Homemade marmalade is always a welcome present, particularly at Christmas, because quite often people have just run out of the previous year's marmalade. This tangy 3-fruit marmalade can be made at times when Seville oranges aren't in the shops. It is made from orange, lemon and grapefruit, so may be made at any time of the year.

2 sweet oranges and 2 grapefruit, weighing
*   1.3kg (3lb) altogether*
4 unwaxed lemons
3.6 litres (6 pints) water
2.6kg (6lb) sugar

Wash the fruit, cut each in half and squeeze out the juice. Remove the membrane with a sharp spoon, set aside. Cut the peel in quarters and slice the rind across rather than lengthways. Put the juice, rind and water in a bowl.

Put the pips and membrane in a muslin bag and add to the bowl. Leave overnight. The following day, simmer the fruits in a stainless steel saucepan with the bag of pips for 1½–2 hours until the peel is really soft. Cover the pan for the first half an hour. The liquid should be reduced to between a third and a half of the original volume.

Meanwhile, warm the sugar in a moderate oven (180°C/350°F/gas 4) for about 10 minutes. Then remove the muslin bag and discard. Add the warmed sugar to the soft peel and stir until the sugar has dissolved. Bring to the boil and keep concentrating until it reaches setting point, about 8–10 minutes. Pour into sterilised jars and cover while hot.

Note: If the sugar is added before the rind is really soft, the rind will harden and no amount of boiling will soften it.

Variation
Ginger Marmalade
Follow the Master Recipe, adding 175–225g (6–8oz) of peeled and finely chopped fresh ginger to the recipe. Demerara sugar gives a fuller flavour and a darker colour.

Kumquat Marmalade

Makes 3 x 450g (1lb) jars
Season: winter

I first tasted this in Australia in the Regent Court off Potts Point in Sydney, one of my favourite places to stay in the world and certainly the best breakfast.

900g (2lb) kumquats
1.5 litres (2½ pints) water
1.3kg (3lb) sugar

Slice the kumquats thinly crossways. Collect the seeds and put them in a small bowl with 225ml (8fl oz) of the water; allow to stand overnight. Put the kumquats in a larger bowl with the remaining water, cover and allow to stand overnight.

Next day, strain the seeds, saving the liquid (this now contains the precious pectin, which contributes to the setting of the jam); discard the seeds.

Put the kumquat mixture into a large saucepan with the reserved liquid from the

ABOVE: Lemon Curd

seeds. Bring to the boil, reduce the heat and simmer, covered, for 30 minutes or until the kumquats are very tender.

Warm the sugar for 10 minutes in a low oven. Add the warm sugar to the kumquats and stir until fully dissolved. Bring to the boil and cook rapidly with the lid off for about 15 minutes. Test for a set. Pour into hot sterilised jars.

No-cook Marmalade

Makes 8 x 350ml (12fl oz) jars
Season: all year round

If you use organic fruit for this recipe, you will really notice the difference.

5 oranges, roughly chopped and discarding as many pips as possible
1 lemon, roughly chopped
1 grapefruit, roughly chopped
sugar, the combined weight of the above fruit, minus 110g (4oz)

Put all the ingredients into a liquidiser and whizz together. Then transfer to a sterilised jar and cover. This fresh-tasting marmalade will keep in the fridge for approximately 3 weeks.

Ballymaloe Mincemeat

Makes about 3.2kg (7lb)
Season: winter

This recipe has been passed down in Myrtle Allen's family.

2 cooking apples, such as Bramley Seedling
2 lemons
450g (1lb) beef suet or butter, chilled and grated
110g (4oz) mixed peel (preferably homemade)
2 tablespoons orange marmalade
225g (8oz) currants
450g (1lb) raisins
225g (8oz) sultanas
900g (2lb) Barbados sugar (moist, soft, dark-brown)
60ml (2½fl oz) Irish whiskey

Core and bake the whole apples in a moderate oven (180°C/350°F/gas 4) for about 45 minutes. Allow to cool. When they are soft, remove the skin and mash the flesh into pulp. Grate the rind from the lemons on the finest part of a stainless steel grater and squeeze out the juice. Add the other ingredients one by one and, as they are added, mix everything thoroughly. Put into jars, cover with jam covers and leave to mature for 2 weeks before using. This mincemeat will keep for a year in a cool, airy place.

Short-time Preserves

Lemon or lime curd are what we call short-time preserves because they have a short shelf life. They are much more perishable than jam, so they should be used within a few weeks; they are best kept in the refrigerator as well. They can be made all year round, in a matter of minutes.

Master Recipe
Lemon Curd

Makes 2–3 pots

50g (2oz) butter
110g (4oz) caster sugar
finely grated zest and juice of 2 large, unwaxed lemons
2 organic eggs and 1 egg yolk (set the white aside for meringue)

On a very low heat, melt the butter, add sugar, lemon juice and rind and then stir in the well-beaten eggs. Stir carefully over a gentle heat until the mixture coats the back of a spoon. Draw off the heat and pour into a bowl (it will thicken as it cools).

Variations
Lime Curd

Substitute 4 limes for the lemons in the Master Recipe. You may need to add a little more sugar. It will be an odd colour.

Elderflower Lemon Curd

In late spring, you can gather elderflowers – eight heads are sufficient for this quantity. Don't pick them until you are ready to make the curd, as they quickly turn brown. Use a fork to pull the creamy flowers from the stalks and add with the sugar. This version is truly divine – an annual treat – and makes a quick dessert served with crème fraîche, meringues and strawberries.

Chutneys

Another wonderful, age-old method of preserving vegetables and fruit. Vinegar is the most essential ingredient in chutneys and preserves because it inhibits the growth of contaminating micro-organisms. Salt and sugar are other essential preservatives. Spices add flavour.

Chutneys can be made from vegetables, fruit, or both vegetables and fruit mixed. Dried fruit, such as raisins or sultanas, are frequently included. In India, mango chutney is made from the green mango but there are also a myriad different bitter pickles, which are a favourite condiment. Chutneys and pickles should not be confused with relishes, which are simply a mixture of chopped fruit and vegetables.

The fruit and vegetable used for pickling must always be young and firm: nice crunchy baby onions, beetroot, gherkins and cauliflower florets. Shredded cabbage can also be pickled as in Sauerkraut. Vegetables for pickles are usually salted or brined first to remove any excess moisture. This will enable them to absorb more vinegar, and will result in a firmer, crunchier pickle. Use plain dairy or kosher salt.

Spicy Apple Chutney

Makes 6–8 x 450g (1lb) pots
Season: autumn

1.8kg (4lb) cooking apples (use Bramley Seedling or Grenadier)
450g (1lb) onion, peeled and finely chopped
450g (1lb) sultanas
900g (2lb) granulated sugar
1.2 litres (2 pints) white malt vinegar
25g (1oz) salt
2 teaspoons mustard seed
1 teaspoon ground ginger
½ teaspoon curry powder
½ teaspoon cinnamon
½–1 level teaspoon ground cloves

Peel and cut the apples into quarters, remove the core and chop finely.

Put all the ingredients into a wide stainless steel saucepan. Simmer gently until soft and pulpy, stirring frequently. Cook, uncovered for 1½–2 hours until very thick and dark brown. (It should be reduced to about a third of the original volume.)

Allow to mature for about two weeks before using. Wine vinegar is less fierce but obviously more expensive.

Apple and Tomato Chutney

Makes 10 x 450g (1lb) pots
Season: summer and autumn

3.1–3.6kg (7–8lb) ripe tomatoes, peeled and chopped
450g (1lb) onions, chopped
450g (1lb) eating apples, peeled and chopped
1.3kg (3lb) sugar
850ml (1½ pint) white malt vinegar
2 tablespoons salt
2 teaspoons ground ginger
3 teaspoons freshly ground pepper
3 teaspoons all spice
4 garlic cloves, crushed
1 level teaspoon cayenne pepper
225–350g (8–12oz) sultanas

Prepare all the ingredients and put into a large, wide, stainless steel saucepan. Bring to the boil. Simmer steadily until reduce and slightly thick – about 1 hour (time will depend on the width of the saucepan).

Pour into hot, sterilised jars and cover. Allow to mature for 2 weeks before using.

Red Pepper Chutney

Makes 8–9 jars

225g (½lb) onions, finely chopped
4 tablespoons olive oil
450g (1lb) very ripe red peppers, seeded and chopped into small dice
½ teaspoon salt
½ teaspoon powdered ginger or grated root ginger
½ teaspoon all spice
½ teaspoon mace
½ teaspoon nutmeg
450g (1lb) very ripe tomatoes, peeled and chopped
1 garlic clove, chopped
110g (4oz) raisins
225g (8oz) white sugar
150ml (¼ pint) white wine vinegar

Sweat the onions in the olive oil in a tall, narrow, stainless steel saucepan until softened and then add the peppers, salt and spices. After 10 minutes, add the tomatoes, garlic, raisins, sugar and vinegar. Bring to the boil and simmer very gently for about 1¼ hours until it looks thickish. Pour into hot, sterilised glass jars and store in a cool, dry place. Good with spiced beef or cold meats or coarse pâtés.

Fresh Fruit and Mint 'Chutney'

Makes 1 pot

25g (1oz) raisins
1 orange
1 eating apple e.g. Cox's Orange or Golden Delicious
2–3 tablespoons freshly chopped mint
½–1 fresh chilli, deseeded and diced (optional)
juice of 1 lemon
sugar and a pinch of salt

Pour boiling water over the raisins and leave aside to plump up for approx. 1 hour. Cut the peel and the pith off the orange and dice. Remove the core from the apple and dice.

Put into a serving bowl with the mint and add the chilli and raisins. Add a little lemon juice, sugar and salt to taste. Serve with curry or spiced dishes.

Fresh Mint Chutney
See page 594

Onion Marmalade

Makes 450ml (¾ pint)

This superb recipe is especially delicious with pâtés and terrines, game and poultry. It is also wonderful served warm, particularly with pan-grilled monkfish or even a lamb chop. It will keep for months.

700g (1½lb) white onions, peeled and
  thinly sliced
110g (4oz) butter
160g (5½oz) caster sugar
1½ teaspoons salt
1½ teaspoons freshly ground pepper
7 tablespoons sherry vinegar
250ml (scant ½ pint) full-bodied red wine
2 tablespoons cassis

Melt the butter in the saucepan and hold your nerve until it becomes a deep, nut brown colour – this will give the onions a delicious, rich flavour but be careful not to let it burn. Toss in the onions and sugar, salt and pepper and stir well. Cover the saucepan and cook for 30 minutes over a gentle heat, stirring from time to time with a wooden spatula.

Add the sherry vinegar, red wine and cassis. Cook for a further 30 minutes uncovered, stirring regularly. This onion jam must cook very gently (but don't let it reduce too much). When it is cold, skim off any butter which rises to the top and discard. Pot up as for jam.

Variation
Red Onion Marmalade
Use red onions instead of white.

Janie's Green Tomato Jam

Makes 2 small jars
Season: beginning and end of tomato season

This recipe was given to me by Janie Suthering to solve the issue of my green tomato glut, which happens every year when the weather turns colder and the tomatoes ripen more slowly. Delicious with cold meats and pâté.

500g (18oz) green tomatoes, sliced
450ml (16fl oz) water
300g (11oz) granulated sugar
finely grated zest and juice of 1 unwaxed lemon

Place the tomatoes in a large pan with the water. Bring to the boil and then simmer, covered, for 50–60 minutes until tender. Add the remaining ingredients and stir over a gentle heat until the sugar is dissolved. Then turn up the heat and boil rapidly without stirring for 10–12 minutes or until setting point is reached. Pot immediately.

Tomato and Chilli Jam

Makes 3 pots

This zingy jam, inspired by Peter Gordon, is great with everything from fried eggs to cold meat. Terrific on a piece of chicken breast or fish or spread on bruschetta with goat's cheese and rocket leaves.

500g (1lb 2oz) very ripe tomatoes
2–4 red chillies
4 garlic cloves, peeled
about 2.5cm (1in) piece fresh ginger, peeled and
  roughly chopped
30ml (1fl oz) fish sauce (nam pla)
275g (10oz) golden caster sugar
100ml (3½fl oz) red wine vinegar

Peel the tomatoes and cut them into a 1cm (½in) dice. Put the chillies, garlic, ginger and fish sauce in a blender and whizz. Put the purée, sugar and vinegar into a stainless steel saucepan, add the tomatoes and bring to the boil slowly, stirring occasionally. Cook gently for 30–40 minutes, stirring every now and then to prevent sticking. When cooked, pour into hot, sterilised glass jars. Allow to cool, then store in the fridge.

Mango Relish
See page 92

Pickled Kumquats with Orange Slices

Makes 1–2 x 450g (1lb) jars
Season: winter

This delicious pickle comes from *Jane Grigson's Fruit Book*. Jane sweetly gave me permission to print it in *Simply Delicious Christmas* and we also have it here. It is delicious served with cold ham, goose, duck or pork.

1 large orange
225g (8oz) kumquats
275g (10oz) sugar
225ml (8fl oz) white wine vinegar
5cm (2in) piece of cinnamon stick
8 whole cloves
2 blades of mace

Scrub the orange well and rinse the kumquats. Cut a slice off the top and bottom of the orange down as far as the flesh and discard those 2 pieces of peel. Cut the rest of the orange into slices and put them in a wide, stainless steel saucepan with the kumquats. Cover generously with cold water. Bring to the boil, cover and simmer until the orange slices are tender, about 20–30 minutes. The kumquats may be ready before the orange slices so watch them if they show signs of collapsing.

Meanwhile, in a stainless steel saucepan dissolve the sugar in the white wine vinegar, add the cinnamon, cloves and mace, and stir until it comes to the boil. Drain all the liquid off the oranges and set aside in case you need it. Put the kumquats and oranges into the vinegar syrup and, if necessary, use some of the cooking liquid to cover the fruit. Simmer until the orange slices look transparent and slightly candied, about 10 minutes.

Arrange the fruit in a wide-mouthed, sterilised glass jar. Pour the boiling syrup over and cover tightly (not with a tin lid). Label and leave to mature for 3–4 weeks before use.

Beetroot and Ginger Relish

Makes 1 litre (1³/₄ pints)

This sweet-sour relish is very good with cold meats and coarse country terrines.

450g (1lb) raw beetroot, peeled and grated
225g (8oz) onions, chopped
50g (2oz) butter
3 tablespoons sugar
salt and freshly ground pepper
30ml (1fl oz) sherry vinegar
125ml (4fl oz) red wine
2 teaspoons freshly peeled and grated ginger

Sweat the onions slowly in butter until they are very soft, then add the sugar and seasoning. Add the rest of the ingredients and cook gently for 30 minutes. Serve cold. This relish keeps for several weeks.

Pickled Beetroot

Serves 5–6

Most pickled beetroot is far too vinegary. This is sweet and delicious but does not keep indefinitely.

450g (1lb) cooked beetroot, (see page 178)
225g (8oz) sugar
450ml (16fl oz) water
1 onion, peeled and thinly sliced (optional)
225ml (8fl oz) white wine vinegar

Dissolve the sugar in water and bring to the boil. Add the sliced onion, if using, and simmer for 3–4 minutes. Add the vinegar, pour over the peeled, sliced beets and leave to cool. It should keep for 1–2 weeks in the fridge.

Sweet Cucumber Pickle

Serves 10–20

900g (2lb) cucumber, thinly sliced and unpeeled
3 small onions, thinly sliced
350g (12oz) sugar
2 level tablespoons salt
225ml (8fl oz) cider vinegar

Combine the cucumber and onion slices in a large bowl. Mix the sugar, salt and vinegar together and pour over the cucumbers. Place in a tightly covered container in the fridge and leave for at least 4–5 hours or overnight before using. It should keep for up to a week in the fridge.

Chilli and Red Pepper Relish

Makes 2–3 pots

25g (1oz) green chillies, de-seeded and chopped, or 2–3 depending on size
1 red pepper, deseeded and cut in 2cm (³/₄in) dice
2 x 400g (14oz) tins chopped tomatoes
1 clove of garlic, crushed
2 teaspoons caster sugar
2 teaspoons soft brown sugar
1 tablespoon white wine vinegar
2 tablespoons water
salt and freshly ground pepper

Put the chillies, pepper, tomatoes and garlic into a stainless steel saucepan with the sugar, vinegar and water. Season and simmer for 10 minutes until reduced by about half. Store in a tightly sealed container. Keeps for weeks in the fridge.

Add the sherry vinegar, red wine and cassis. Cook for a further 30 minutes uncovered, stirring regularly. This onion jam must cook very gently (but don't let it reduce too much). When it is cold, skim off any butter that rises to the top and discard. Pot up as for jam.

Mustard Fruits

These crystallised fruits are delicious served with cold meats.

500ml (18fl oz) cold water
500g (18oz) sugar
a few strips of organic lemon zest (alternatively scrub the rind first before paring)
500g (18oz) fruit (e.g. pears, figs, peaches, apricots), peeled
50ml (2fl oz) honey
125ml (4fl oz) verjuice
2 tablespoons mustard seeds, lightly crushed
1 teaspoon fennel seeds
1 small cinnamon stick
3–4 cloves

Put the sugar, water and lemon rind into a stainless steel saucepan over a medium heat and stir until the sugar dissolves. Bring to the boil, add the peeled fruit and simmer until tender. Remove the fruit, add the honey, verjuice, mustard seeds and spices to the syrup. Bring back to the boil and reduce to a thick syrup (be careful not to allow it to caramelize). Meanwhile, pack the fruit into sterilized jars, then cover with the hot syrup and close the jars immediately. Cool and store in a cool place or the fridge for a few days before eating. It keeps for months.

Julia Wight's Quince Paste

This paste is absolutely delicious served with a spoonful of soft goat's cheese and a leaf of sweet cicely or rose geranium. Julia also loves quince paste with Stilton or Cashel Blue (Irish farmhouse cheese).

quinces
sugar

2 Swiss roll tins, 23 x 30cm (9 x 12in)
mouli-légume

Preheat the oven to 100°C/200°F/gas ¼.

With a cloth, rub the down off the skins of as many quinces as you can pack into a large earthenware jar. Do not add any water. Cover the pot and place in a low oven for about 4 hours until the fruit is easily pierced with a skewer. Quarter the fruit, remove the core and any blemishes, and put the pieces through a mouli-légume using the biggest disc. (If you do not have one, buy one!)

Weigh the quince pulp and add three parts of sugar to every four parts of pulp. Cook the mixture in a preserving pan over a medium heat, and stir continuously with a wooden spatula until the mixture becomes rich in colour and it stops running together again when the spatula is drawn through the mixture. Line 2 Swiss roll tins with baking parchment, fill with the paste and leave overnight to get quite cold.

The following day, dry the tins of paste out in a low oven (100°C/200°F/gas ¼) for about 4 hours until it is quite firm. Check it is ready by lifting a corner of the paste – it should be solid all the way through. When the paste has cooled, cut into four strips, wrap in baking parchment and store in an airtight container. It will keep for about 4 months, but is best eaten when freshly made, cut into 2.5cm (1in) squares as a sweetmeat.

Claudia Roden's Preserved Lemons

Lemons preserved traditionally in salt and lemon juice take at least a month to mature, so we often use the recipe Claudia Roden introduced us to when she came to the Cookery School – these preserved lemons may be used immediately.

8 lemons
8 tablespoons salt
2 litres water (depending on the size of the saucepan and the lemons)

With a sharp knife, make 8 fine and superficial incisions into the lemon skins from one end of the lemon to the other. Put the lemons in a large pan with salted water to cover. Put a smaller lid on top of them to keep them down as they float, and boil for about 25 minutes or until the peels are very soft. When cool enough to handle, scoop out the flesh, pack the skins into a glass jar and cover with sunflower or light vegetable oil.

Crystallised Lemon or Orange Peel

We always have lots of crystallised lemon, orange and lime peel in a jar to decorate tarts, scatter on mousses or just to nibble.

2 unwaxed lemons or oranges
300ml (10fl oz) Stock Syrup (see page 568)
25–50g (1–2oz) caster sugar

Peel the lemons very thinly with a swivel top peeler, being careful not to include the white pith. Cut the strips into a fine julienne. Put into a saucepan, cover with cold water and simmer for 5 minutes. Drain, refresh in cold water, cover with fresh water and repeat the process. Put the julienne into a saucepan with the syrup and cook gently until it looks translucent or opaque. Remove with a slotted spoon and allow to cool on silicone paper or a cake rack. When cold, toss in the caster sugar

and allow to dry in a cool place. It can be stored in a jar or airtight tin for weeks or sometimes months.

Homemade Candied Peel

5 oranges, lemons or grapefruit (or a mixture)
850ml (1½ pints) water
1.3kg (3lb) sugar
1 teaspoon salt

Cut the fruit in half and squeeze out the juice. Reserve the juice for another use, perhaps Homemade Lemonade (see page 569). Put the skins into a large bowl (not aluminium, because the acid in the lemon reacts with the citrus and taints the taste), add salt and cover with cold water. Leave to soak for 24 hours.

Next day, throw away the soaking water, put the peel in a saucepan and cover with fresh cold water. Bring to the boil, cover and simmer very gently until the peel is soft, up to 3 hours. Remove the peel and discard the water. Scrape out any remaining flesh and membranes from inside the cut fruit, leaving the white pith and rind intact. (You can do the next step the following day if more convenient.)

Dissolve the sugar fully in the water, bring it to the boil, add the peel and simmer gently until it looks translucent; this will take 30–60 minutes. Remove the peel, drain and leave it to cool. Boil down the remaining liquid until it becomes thick and syrupy but before it turns to a caramel. Remove from the heat and put the peel in again to soak up the syrup. Infuse for 30 minutes.

Fill the candied peel into sterilised glass jars and pour the syrup over. Cover and store in a cold place or in the fridge. Alternatively, cool the peel on a wire rack and pour any remaining syrup into the centres. Finally, pack into sterilised glass jars and cover tightly. It should keep for 6–8 weeks or longer under refrigeration.

breakfast

breakfast

Every year we teach an 'Irresistible Breakfast' course at the cookery school and every year the message is the same – breakfast can be the dullest of meals or a real feast; it all depends on the care with which you source your produce, right down to the freshly roasted and ground coffee, good tea made with tea leaves or a cup of steaming rich hot chocolate.

Guests love breakfast at Ballymaloe House. It starts with freshly made breads – Brown Soda Bread, Ballymaloe Yeast Bread, Spotted Dog, breakfast scones – no sliced bread. The toast is made from Ballymaloe White Yeast Bread cut into generous slices, served still with the crusts on, a forgotten flavour. Turn to the jams and preserves chapter (see page 500) to find recipes for delicious homemade marmalades and jams. We serve honeycomb at the beginning of the new season – I have a few beehives at the end of the orchard that Michael Wolfe and our son Toby look after. Our apple blossom honey is particularly delicious, so is the heather and wild flower honey. Seek out and support a local beekeeper, and serve the honey proudly.

The Great Irish Breakfast

In Ireland, the traditional breakfast is a huge fry up. It used to be eaten every day, but nowadays most people save it for a weekend or holiday treat. Here, more than ever, the quality of the raw materials can make the difference between an average meal and a sensational feast.

Despite the fact that Ireland is famous for its ham and bacon, the flavour of real bacon as we knew it as children is difficult to find, although a few passionate pioneers have started to cure and smoke bacon in the traditional way – let us hope this trend continues. Seek them out and serve their products to your family and friends. Good-quality, traditionally cured bacon won't ooze salt and nitrates when cooked. People love sausages but avoid those flavoured with too many herbs and garlic for breakfast. Juicy sausages and good black and white pudding are easier to find as more butchers make their own. Ripe tomatoes are delicious in summer (don't bother to serve them in winter). Small flat mushrooms are also delicious, and if you are fortunate enough to have a few wild mushrooms in the autumn, serve those as a special bonus. Eggs must be really fresh, free-range, and better still, organic as well.

Other Options

Of course the great big fry up, though delicious when all the ingredients are good, is not the only option for breakfast.

Nothing compares with a bowl of Macroom oatmeal porridge in the winter or some Ballymaloe strawberry muesli in the summer. The range of breakfast cereals nowadays is mesmerising yet I've never found one that I craved – many are unbearably sweet. Homemade crunchy granola and nut and grain muesli are delicious, healthy and so easy to make. Proprietary brands tend to be heavy on oatmeal and bran and light on the more expensive grains and dried fruits.

Smoothies are also great for breakfast, just whizz up some yoghurt, banana, wheatgerm, maybe a mango and a few raspberries – a whole meal in a glass. You can certainly go to work on one of these. Compôtes of seasonal fruit are also a delicious part of a breakfast menu and a winter breakfast fruit salad with lots of juicy prunes and apricots provides plenty of roughage in a delicious way. I also love thick unctuous natural yoghurt made from sheep's, goat's or cow's milk – several delicious organic yoghurts are now available. Always read the label carefully, as some yoghurts are made from milk powder and some contain the artificial sweetener aspartame.

For a very nutrious and protein-packed breakfast, try kippers and other fish. Muffins, French toast and croissants are other tempting alternatives, and steaming pain au chocolat with freshly brewed coffee is irresistible.

I've had some of the best breakfasts of my life in the US (usually in diners rather than posh hotels) - great American pancakes, hash browns, huevos al ranchero, oatmeal…. Then there's the memorable breakfast of congee that I ate in a neighbourhood restaurant in Hong Kong, dosa and idli appam in India and rice noodles in Vietnam….

Fresh Fruit Juice
The term 'freshly squeezed orange juice' – one of the most abused terms in the English language – should not be applied to juice that was squeezed days earlier in a huge machine and sold in plastic containers in the shops and supermarkets. Freshly squeezed juice – pure and simple – comes from a citrus fruit cut in half, juiced either manually or on a citrus fruit juicer that does not press the zest from the skin into the juice. Drink it as soon as possible to benefit from all those vitamins. Citrus fruit juices oxidise quickly when exposed to the air and it soon tastes inferior. If you absolutely must squeeze orange juice the night before, put it into a dark glass bottle, fill right to the top, seal tightly and keep in the fridge - it will still taste very good. A single juicy orange is sufficient for one person although

occasionally, if the oranges are small, you may need two. Citrus fruit should feel heavy for their size – they are best and juiciest during the citrus fruit season in winter. Don't just serve orange juice ad nauseum even if it is freshly squeezed. Become a little more adventurous and serve mandarin, tangerine, pink grapefruit, blood orange or experiment with a mixture of citrus juices. For a special brunch, mix blood orange juice with Champagne, sparkling wine or Prosecco. For apple juice, you'll need a juice extractor, then the fun begins – all kinds of juices are possible.

Don't Skip Breakfast
More and more people are missing breakfast, especially during the week when they have less time. Don't be tempted to skip breakfast. Your body needs refueling after a night's sleep and eating breakfast will supply you with the energy you need to start the day off productively. The digestive system is also at its most efficient in the morning and eating something at this time will provide some of the fibre and essential vitamins and minerals needed to fulfil your daily quota.

Skipping breakfast because you are on a diet is equally not advisable. It might make you feel virtuous for a while, but it often results in overeating later and increasing the appetite. There's no evidence to support the idea that skipping meals will help you lose weight.

Oatmeal Porridge

Serves 4

Virtually every morning in winter I start my day with a bowl of porridge. Search out a stoneground oatmeal which has the most delicious toasted nutty flavour. At Ballymaloe, we use Macroom oatmeal stoneground by Donal Creedon in the last stone-grinding mill in Ireland.

160g (5¹/₂oz) oatmeal
1 litre (1³/₄ pints) water
1 level teaspoon salt

To Serve
single cream or milk
soft brown sugar

Bring the water to the boil and sprinkle in the oatmeal gradually, stirring all the time. Put over a low heat and stir until the water comes back to the boil. Cover and simmer for 15–20 minutes, stirring occasionally.

Add the salt and stir again. Serve with single cream or milk and soft brown sugar melting over the top.

> TIP: Leftover porridge can be stored in a covered container in the fridge – it will reheat perfectly next day.

Pinhead Oatmeal Porridge

Serves 4

160g (5¹/₂oz) pinhead oatmeal
1 litre (1³/₄ pints) water
1 level teaspoon salt

To Serve
single cream or milk
soft brown sugar

Soak the oatmeal in 250ml (9fl oz) of cold water. Meanwhile, bring the rest of the water to the boil and add the oatmeal. Put over a low heat and stir until the water comes to the boil. Cover and simmer for 15–20 minutes, stirring occasionally.

Stir in the salt. Cover again and leave in a warm spot overnight; the oatmeal will absorb all the water. Reheat and serve with single cream or milk and soft brown sugar.

Granola

Makes 20 servings

A toasted grain cereal that always goes down well at breakfast time.

350g (12oz) honey
225ml (8fl oz) sunflower oil
450g (1lb) oat flakes
200g (7oz) barley flakes
200g (7oz) wheat flakes
110g (4 oz) rye flakes
150g (5oz) seedless raisins or sultanas
150g (5oz) hazelnuts or cashew nuts, split and roasted
25g (1oz) sunflower seeds, toasted
50g (2oz) dried apricots, chopped
50g (2oz) chopped dates (optional)
75g (3oz) wheatgerm and/or millet flakes

To Serve
bananas, sliced

Preheat the oven to 180°C/350°F/gas 4.

Mix the oil and honey together in a saucepan and heat just sufficiently to melt the honey. Mix all the flakes together and then pour in the honey/oil mixture. Spread thinly on 2 baking trays.

Bake in the oven for 20–30 minutes, turning frequently, making sure the edges don't burn. It should be just golden and toasted, not roasted!

Cool and mix in the raisins or sultanas, nuts, toasted seeds, apricots, dates (if using) and wheatgerm. Store in a screw-top jar or a plastic box for 1–2 weeks. Serve with a sliced banana.

> TIP: Buy wheatgerm in small quantities from a shop with a high turnover. Store in the refrigerator and use up quickly.

Master Recipe
Ballymaloe Apple Muesli

Serves 2

4 tablespoons rolled oats
3 tablespoons water
2 large dessert apples e.g. Cox's Orange Pippin
1 teaspoon honey

Measure out the water into a bowl and sprinkle the oatmeal on top. Let the oatmeal soak up the water while you grate the apples, using the largest side to grate the apple coarsely, skin and all. Pick out the pips.

Stir the honey into the oatmeal and then stir in the grated apple. Taste; if it needs a little more honey add it; this depends on how much you heaped up on the spoon earlier on.

Divide it between 2 bowls. Have one yourself and give the other to your favourite person that morning. It tastes delicious just like that but will taste even scrummier if you sprinkle over a little soft brown Barbados sugar and runny cream.

Variations

Apple and Hazelnut Muesli

Follow the Master Recipe, adding about 1 tablespoon of chopped hazelnuts.

Raspberry Muesli

Follow the Master Recipe and use raspberries and loganberries instead of apples.

Strawberry Muesli

Follow the Master Recipe, but as soon as strawberries come into season, mash some fresh ones and use instead of apples.

Blackberry Muesli

Follow the Master Recipe and, in autumn, pick a few fresh blackberries and add to your apple muesli.

Ballymaloe Nut and Grain Muesli

Makes 12 servings

This recipe, bursting with goodness, was given to me by my sister-in-law Natasha Harty. It keeps in a screw-top jar for several weeks.

8 Weetabix
200g (7oz) oat flakes
35g (1½oz) bran
55g (2¼oz) fresh wheatgerm
55g (2¼oz) raisins
60g (2½oz) sliced hazelnuts or a mixture of cashews and hazelnuts
60g (2½oz) soft brown sugar
2 tablespoons Lecithin* (optional)

Crumble the Weetabix in a bowl, add the other ingredients and mix well. Store in an airtight container. Keeps for 2–3 weeks in a cool place. Serve with fresh fruit and fresh creamy milk.

*Available from chemists or health food shops, Lecithin comes from soya beans. It is rich in phosphatidyl choline, an important nutrient in the control of dietary fat, which helps the body to convert fats into energy rather than storing them as body fat. Check that it is GM-free.

Orange, Mint and Grapefruit

Serves 4

2 oranges
2 grapefruit
1 tablespoon caster sugar
2 tablespoons freshly chopped mint

Garnish
4 sprigs of mint

Peel and carefully segment the oranges and grapefruit into a bowl (see page 73). Add the sugar and mint; taste and add more sugar if necessary. Chill. Serve in pretty bowls or arrange the segments of orange and grapefruit alternately on the plate in a circle and pour a little juice over the fruit. Garnish with fresh mint.

LEFT: Oatmeal Porridge
BELOW: Ballymaloe Nut and Grain Muesli

Mango, Blueberry, Pomegranate and Kiwi Salad
Serves 4

Great for breakfast or dessert.

2 mangoes, peeled and chopped into cubes
1 pomegranate, deseeded
2 kiwis, peeled and diced
½ punnet of blueberries
1–2 tablespoons sugar
juice of ½ lemon or lime

Put the prepared fruit into a bowl with the sugar and lemon or lime juice. Toss gently and serve.

Melon with Raspberries and Mint
Serves 4

1 ripe melon, Ogen or Charentais
225g (8oz) fresh raspberries
2 tablespoons caster sugar
1 tablespoon freshly chopped mint

Cut the top off the melon; scallop the edges if you like. Discard the seeds, scoop out the melon with a melon baller and sprinkle the flesh with the sugar and mint. Mix with the raspberries and fill into the melon shell or pretty white bowl. Cover and chill, serving within 1 hour so that the fruit keeps its shape.

Melon with Sweet Cicely
Serves 4

1 very ripe melon, Ogen, Charentais or Galia or
   better still a mixture of all three
2 tablespoons caster sugar
juice of ½–1 lemon
1 tablespoon freshly snipped sweet cicely

Cut the melons in half, discard the seeds and cut the flesh into generous cubes. Put into a bowl and sprinkle with sugar and lemon juice. Sprinkle sweet cicely over the top and serve very well chilled.

Papaya with Lime
Serves 4

A delicious breakfast compote. Ripe mangoes are also wonderful served in this way.

3 ripe papayas
2 limes

Peel the papaya, cut it in half and remove the seeds. Cut the flesh into 8–10mm (⅓–½ in) chunks. Sprinkle with lime juice. Lime zest may also be sprinkled over the top.

Winter Breakfast Fruit Salad
Serves 8

This can be made ahead and kept in the fridge; we love it and often eat it as a winter dessert with a few pistachio nuts or toasted almonds added.

200g (7oz) prunes
175g (6oz) dried apricots
1 small handful of raisins
grated zest of ½ lemon
1–2 tablespoons runny honey
225ml (8fl oz) orange juice
3–4 bananas

Soak the prunes and apricots overnight in boiling water to cover. Next day, put them in a casserole with the raisins and lemon zest.

Mix the honey with 4 tablespoons warm water and enough of the fruit-soaking water to cover the prunes and apricots. Bring to the boil and simmer for about 35 minutes.

Allow to cool and keep in the refrigerator. Just before serving, add a little fresh orange juice and some sliced bananas to each bowl. Serve with pouring cream. Keeps for 1–2 weeks in a screw-top jar in the fridge.

Poached Plums
Serves 4

Something amazing happens when you poach plums in a simple syrup. Plums that were dull and almost inedible are transformed into a delicious compôte. Use blood plums or opal plums in season.

200g (7oz) sugar
225ml (8fl oz) cold water
450g (1lb) fresh plums, stoned

Put the sugar and water into a saucepan and bring slowly to the boil. Add the plums; cover and simmer until the plums are soft and bursting. Turn into a bowl and serve chilled with pouring cream.

Variations
Poached Plums with Lemon-scented Geranium Leaves
Follow the recipe above, adding 4–6 large geranium leaves with the sugar and water.

Poached Apricots with Lemon-scented Geranium Leaves
Substitute apricots for plums in the recipe above. Puréed and mixed with softly whipped cream, this makes a divine fool.

Ginger Pear Compote
Makes about 450ml (16fl oz)

Great with pancakes, waffles, French toast and ice cream… It is also good served like apple sauce as an accompaniment to roast pork, duck or smoked bacon.

900g (2lb) ripe pears, peeled and cut into 1cm
   (½in) chunks

125ml (4fl oz) water
50ml (2fl oz) sugar
3 tablespoons lemon juice
1–1½ tablespoons freshly grated peeled ginger

Put the pears, water, sugar, lemon juice
and ginger into a stainless steel saucepan.
Cover and bring to a simmer. Uncover and
cook, stirring occasionally, until the pear
is tender and the sauce has thickened
slightly – about 25 minutes, depending
on the ripeness of the pears. Serve hot or
cold. It will keep in the fridge for 2–3 days.

Rhubarb Compote
Serves 4

450g (1lb) red rhubarb (we use Timperley
  Early)
450ml (16fl oz) Stock Syrup (see page 568)

Cut the rhubarb into 2.5cm (1in) pieces.
Put the cold syrup into a stainless steel
saucepan, add the rhubarb, cover, bring to
the boil and simmer for just 1 minute (no
longer or it will dissolve into a mush). Turn
off the heat and leave the rhubarb in the
covered saucepan until cool. A few
strawberries sliced into the cooked
compôte make it extra delicious.

Variation
Rhubarb and Banana Compote
Slice 1 or 2 bananas into the cold compote.

RIGHT: Poached Plums

Apple and Sweet Geranium Compote

8 medium-sized eating apples, such as
  Golden Delicious
175g (6oz) sugar
2–3 strips of lemon rind
juice of 1½ lemons
4 large sweet geranium leaves

Peel, quarter, core and slice the apples into 5mm (½in) segments. Put them into a stainless steel or enamel saucepan. Add the sugar, lemon rind and juice and the sweet geranium leaves. Cover with a greaseproof paper lid and the lid of a saucepan; cook on a gentle heat until the apples are soft but not broken.

Breakfast Smoothie

Serves 2–4

2 bananas
300ml (10fl oz) natural yoghurt
300ml (10fl oz) milk or soya milk
1 tablespoon honey
2 tablespoons crushed ice (optional)

Put all the ingredients into the blender and whizz. Taste and serve immediately.

Variations

Use whatever fruit you have and like – a handful of strawberries or raspberries, mango, papaya...whatever is in season. Also experiment with different types of yogurt and if you're feeling naughty, add a scoop of ice-cream.

Laura's Power Smoothie

Add 100g (3½ oz) rolled oats to the above if you have an energetic day ahead.

How to Make a Delicious Cup of Tea

First buy best-quality tea leaves; tea bags do not make such good tea, and tend to be more wasteful, particularly for single cups.

Fill the kettle with cold, fresh water. When the water has come to the boil, pour a little into a teapot. Swirl the water around in the pot until the pot feels warm. Discard the water, and add the tea leaves. Traditionally, you should allow 1 teaspoon of tea per person, plus one for the pot, but add more or less, depending on how strong you like your tea. Bring the water back to the boil. Pour instantly over the tea leaves, fill and cover the pot. Cover and allow to 'draw' for 3–4 minutes before serving.

Perhaps it's my imagination but tea always seems to taste better from a china cup rather than a mug. Keep the tea pot covered with a tea-cosy if available.

Proper Breakfast Kippers

Serves 2

The Woodcock Smokery in West Cork produce the very best kippers I have ever tasted. I like them cooked for breakfast by what I call the jug method.

2 undyed kippers
Maitre d'Hôtel Butter (see page 588)

Garnish
2 segments of lemon
2 sprigs of parsley

Put the kippers head downwards into a deep heatproof jug. Cover them with boiling water right up to their tails. Leave for 2–3 minutes to heat through.

Lift them out carefully by the tail and serve immediately on hot plates with a pat of Maitre d'Hôtel Butter melting on top. Garnish each with a segment of lemon and a sprig of parsley.

Pan-grilled Mackerel with Maître d'Hôtel Butter

Serves 4

8 fillets very fresh mackerel
seasoned flour
small knob of butter

Maître d'Hôtel Butter (see page 588)

Garnish
segment of lemon
parsley

First make the Maître d'Hôtel Butter.

Heat the pan-grill. Dip the fish fillets in flour which has been seasoned with salt and freshly ground pepper. Shake off the excess flour and then spread a little butter with a knife on the flesh side of the fish, as though you were buttering a slice of bread rather meanly.

When the pan-grill is quite hot but not smoking, place the fish fillets butter-side down on the grill; the fish should sizzle as soon as they touch the pan. Turn down the heat slightly and let them cook for 4–5 minutes before turning them. Cook on the other side until crisp and golden.

Serve on a hot plate with some slices of Maître d'Hôtel Butter and a segment of lemon. The butter may be served directly on the fish or, if you have a pretty shell, place it at the side of the plate as a container for the butter. Garnish with parsley.

Note: Fillets of any small fish are delicious pan-grilled in this way. Fish under 900g (2lb) such as mackerel, herring and brown trout can also be grilled whole on the pan. Fish over 900g (2lb) can be filleted first and then cut across into portions. Large fish 1.8–2.6kg (4–6lb) can also be grilled whole. Cook them for about 10–15 minutes on each side and then put in a hot oven for another 15 minutes or so to finish cooking.

Kedgeree
Serves 6–8

Kedgeree immediately conjures up images of country house breakfasts which were often a veritable feast.

450g (1lb) wild salmon, freshly cooked (see page 232), or 225g (8oz) salmon and 225g (8oz) cooked smoked haddock
225g (8oz) white long-grain rice
3 hardboiled organic eggs
140ml (¼ pint) cream
45g (1½oz) butter
3 tablespoons freshly chopped parsley
1½ tablespoons freshly chopped chives
salt and freshly ground pepper
pinch of cayenne pepper

First cook the salmon and leave to cool.

Meanwhile, cook the rice in boiling salted water, for about 10 minutes until cooked. Hard-boil the eggs, cooking in boiling salted water for 10 minutes. Drain off the water and run under a cold tap to stop the cooking. Peel.

Remove the bones and skin from the fish and flake into small pieces. Heat the cream and butter in saucepan and add the parsley and chives. As soon as it bubbles, add the rice, flaked fish and roughly chopped hard-boiled eggs. Season well with salt, freshly ground pepper and a pinch of cayenne. Mix very gently. Taste, correct the seasoning if necessary, pile into a warm dish and serve with freshly baked bread or hot buttered toast.

Hot Potato Cakes with Crème Fraîche and Smoked Salmon
Serves 8

900g (2lb) unpeeled 'old' potatoes
25g–50g (1–2oz) butter
50g (2oz) flour

1 tablespoon chopped parsley, chives and lemon thyme, mixed (optional)
salt and freshly ground pepper
creamy milk
seasoned flour
clarified butter (see page 105), for frying
crème fraîche
110g (4oz) smoked salmon
2 tablespoons freshly snipped chives

Cook the potatoes in their skins, pull off the peel and mash right away, adding the butter, flour and herbs. Season with lots of salt and pepper, and add a few drops of creamy milk if the mixture is altogether too stiff. Mix well. Taste and correct the seasoning. Shape into potato cakes 2.5cm (1in) thick. Dip in seasoned flour. Fry the potato cakes in clarified butter until golden on 1 side, then flip over and cook on the other side, for about 4–5 minutes – they should be crusty and golden. Serve on very hot plates. Put a dollop of crème fraîche on top of each potato cake. Top with slivers of smoked salmon and sprinkle with chives. Serve immediately.

Alternative Serving Suggestions
1. Use smoked mackerel or trout instead of smoked salmon.
2. Serve hot crispy bacon instead of salmon.
3. Serve smoked eel and dill instead of salmon and chives.

The Great Irish Breakfast

If you are cooking for more than 3 people, it is essential to have 2 or more pans.

Rashers

For me, fried rashers have the best flavour. Grilling seems to intensify the salt and harden poor-quality bacon. Buy fat bacon rashers. Remove the rind. Have the pan quite hot and add a tiny dash of oil. Cook the rashers until quite crisp on one side before turning; if there is a pool of milky liquid on the rashers dab this off with kitchen paper. Turn down the heat slightly, if necessary. Cook until crisp on the second side. Drain on kitchen paper and keep warm. Pour off the bacon fat and reserve. Wash the pan before frying another batch of rashers or eggs.

Sausages

Buy good-quality pork sausages and use them quickly. Oil the pan with just a few drops of oil. Cook them over a medium heat, turning every few minutes until they are uniformly brown. Drain on kitchen paper and keep warm.

Mushrooms

Flats have most flavour. Keep them whole or slice them. Have your pan very hot, melt a little butter and toss in the sliced mushrooms, sprinkle with salt and freshly ground pepper and cook through, for only 2–3 minutes. The most important point here is to have a very hot pan and not to cook too many at a time. A squeeze of lemon juice will help to keep mushrooms white if that's what you want. If you cook too many mushrooms together or if you have a cool pan, the mushrooms will be soggy and wet.

Tomatoes

Choose very dark red, ripe but firm tomatoes. Slice across in the middle and arrange cut side up on an ovenproof plate. Sprinkle with salt, pepper and sugar and

put a tiny blob of butter on each. Bake in a moderate oven, 180°C/350°F/gas 4, for 5–10 minutes. Alternatively you could just fry them over a low heat turning once. Ripe tomatoes can be delicious baked whole at 180°C/350°F/gas 4 for 10–15 minutes until they are soft.

Black and White Pudding

Choose good quality puddings, preferably in natural casings, not in plastic. Cut into slices and fry for 3–4 minutes on each side in a little butter or bacon fat over a medium heat, or grill.

Fried Eggs

Choose very fresh eggs, preferably free-range and organic. See page 102 for frying instructions.

Kidneys

Peel the fat and membrane from the kidneys. Cut in half and remove the centre core. Wash and dry well, dip in a little seasoned flour and cook gently in a frying pan in a little melted butter. Serve hot.

Ulster Fry

An Ulster Fry also includes fried potato brad or fadge and very delicious it is too.

Fadge or Potato Bread
Serves 8

In Ulster, people are passionate about fadge. It can be cooked on a griddle, in a frying pan or in the oven.

900g (2lb) unpeeled 'old' potatoes e.g. Golden Wonder or Kerr's Pinks
2 tablespoons flour
1 organic egg
25–50g (1–2oz) butter
creamy milk
seasoned flour
salt and freshly ground pepper
bacon fat, butter or olive oil, for frying

Cook the potatoes in their jackets, pull off the skins and mash right away. Add the beaten egg, butter and flour. Season with lots of salt and freshly ground pepper, adding a few drops of creamy milk if the mixture is too stiff. Taste and correct the seasoning. Shape into a round 2.5cm (1in) thick and then cut into eighths. Dip each section in seasoned flour. Bake in a moderate oven 180°C/350°F/gas 4 for 15–20 minutes. Alternatively, cook on a griddle over an open fire or fry in bacon fat or melted butter on a gentle heat. After about 4–5 minutes, when the fadge is crusty and golden on one side, flip over and cook on the other side. Serve with an Ulster Fry or just on its own on hot plates with a blob of butter melting on top.

Scrambled Eggs
See page 102

Poached Eggs
See page 99

Molettas
See page 139

Popovers
Makes 8

A popover is a browned bulbous pastry with a steaming hot, eggy inner lining and hollow centre, meant to be pulled apart and smeared in butter. At the Popover Café in New York, everything is served on a popover base. One can even have them sent by overnight delivery to anywhere in the US, in a long stem flower box with a jar of fudge chocolate topping or strawberry preserve!

225g (4oz) plain flour
210ml (7½fl oz) milk
2 organic eggs, lightly beaten
1 tablespoon butter, melted (optional)

muffin tin, well-greased

Preheat the oven to 220°C/425°F/gas 7. Put the muffin tin in the oven to heat it.

Sieve the flour into a bowl, make a well in the centre, and pour in the milk and the lightly beaten eggs. Mix to a smooth batter. Whisk really hard until the surface is covered with air bubbles. If possible, leave to stand in a cold place for about 1 hour.

Stir in the melted butter, if using, and beat again. Pour the batter into the hot muffin tins so that they are just over half full. Bake in the oven for about 10 minutes, then reduce the heat to 180°C/350°F/gas 4, and bake for a further 15–20 minutes (or until the popovers are well risen, crisp and golden brown).

Variations
Popovers with Strawberry Butter

Dredge the popovers with icing sugar and serve on a plate with a little bowl of strawberry butter. To make the butter whizz 110g (4oz) unsalted butter with 50g (2oz) strawberry jam in a blender.

Popovers with Marmalade Butter

You can also replace the strawberry jam with marmalade to make a delicious marmalade butter. See pages 509–511 for homemade marmalade recipes and follow the directions above.

LEFT: The Great Irish Breakfast

Popover Café Eggs Benedict

Serves 8

The Eggs Benedict at Popover Café are particularly memorable – served on huge popovers that look as though they are on steroids!

Popovers (see page 527)

Hollandaise Sauce (see page 581)

8 organic eggs
8–16 rashers bacon

Make the popovers and the Hollandaise Sauce. Then cook the bacon until crisp and poach the eggs (see page 99). Split the popovers in half, turn the top half upside down and put on top of the base so that it forms a container for the poached egg and pieces of crispy bacon. Coat generously with Hollandaise Sauce and serve immediately.

Breakfast Burrito

Makes 2

A breakfast burrito will set you and your pals up for the day.

2 large flour tortillas
Scrambled Egg with Chorizo (see page 102)
50g (2oz) grated Cheddar
refried black beans (Frijoles de Olla – Mexican Beans, see page 139)
Tomato and Coriander Salsa (see page 592)
salt and freshly ground pepper
sour cream, to serve
fresh coriander leaves, to serve

Wrap the tortillas in tin foil and warm in a moderate oven (alternatively heat for a few seconds on each side in a hot pan). Meanwhile prepare the scrambled eggs.

Just before you assemble the burrito, sprinkle a small handful of cheese over the centre of the warm tortilla. Top with half the scrambled egg. Add a generous tablespoon of refried black beans and a tablespoon of Tomato and Coriander Salsa. Fold over the two sides and roll into a sausage-like wrap.

Transfer to a warm plate, spoon a generous portion of sour cream on top, and scatter generously with Tomato and Coriander Salsa and fresh coriander leaves.

Children's Breakfast Menu

One can have lots of fun doing children's breakfast dishes and you'll be rewarded with lots of smiling faces – both parents and children! Special children's crockery and cutlery may also be used; Beatrix Potter, Bunnykins etc.

Boiled Eggs with Children's Names
Use either lead pencil or water-resistant markers to paint funny faces or names. Serve with soldiers of toast.

Mini Breakfast
Little streaky rashers, cocktail sausages, cherry tomatoes, fried bantam or quail's eggs.

Toast with a Face
Use scrambled egg as a base, cherry tomatoes for eyes, cocktail sausages for eyebrows and nose and streaky rashers for the mouth.

Tiny Breakfast Pancakes
Make Buttermilk Pancakes (see below) in small sizes.

Croissants

Makes 16

Sadly, one now has to search in France to find really good buttery croissants – the quintessential French breakfast. For years I thought croissants were the most complicated thing on earth to make, particularly as the first recipe I tried came from Julia Child's wonderful book, *Mastering the Art of French Cooking*, and covered 10 pages! That dampened my spirits for a while but eventually, undaunted, I came up with this version which I find gives terrific results for the minimum amount of effort. Use the very best unsalted butter. This recipe can be left to rise in a fridge overnight and the uncooked croissants can also be frozen so you can bake one at a time for a real breakfast treat.

150ml (¼ pint) milk
25g (1oz) sugar
150ml (¼ pint) water
10g (½oz) yeast
450g (1lb) strong white flour
pinch of salt
275g (10oz) unsalted butter

egg wash made with 1 beaten organic egg

Heat the milk and dissolve the sugar in it, then add the water. Allow the liquid to cool to tepid before pouring it onto the yeast. Stir until dissolved.

Sieve the flour into a bowl and add a pinch of salt. Rub in 50g (2oz) of the butter. Add the yeast liquid and mix to a dough. Knead until smooth, by hand or in a food mixer with a dough hook – about 8–10 minutes by hand or 5 minutes in a machine. Cover with pure clingfilm and leave in the fridge for 2 hours.

Beat the remaining butter into a thin layer between sheets of greaseproof paper or clingfilm with a rolling pin. Roll out the dough into a rectangle, put the butter on 1 half of the rectangle 2.5cm (1in) from the edges all around and fold the other half over it.

Roll out the dough into another rectangle, fold in 3 (as for puff or flaky pastry) keeping all the sides aligned, cover and rest for 30 minutes in the fridge.

With the open ends facing from your tummy button, roll out the pastry again, and fold in 3 as before. Cover and leave in a fridge until next day; roll and fold in 3 once again.

Finally roll out the pastry 5mm (¼in) thick, 35cm (14in) wide and as long as possible (usually about 55cm (22in). Trim the edges. Cut into half lengthways and then divide each stip into equilateral triangles with each side about 15cm (6in). You will have 2 smaller triangles left over at either end.

Preheat the oven to 220°C/425°F/gas 7.

Start at the base of each triangle and roll it as tightly as possible towards the tip. Place the croissants on a baking sheet with the tip tucked underneath. Egg wash each and put them in a warm place to prove for 30–45 minutes. When they have doubled in size, egg wash again very carefully.

Bake the croissants for 10 minutes, then reduce the temperature to 180°C/350°F/gas 4 for 10 minutes until the croissants are crisp, golden and brown on the bottom. Serve with homemade jam.

Croissants may be filled with all kinds of things, from almond paste, cheese, garlic butter and chocolate to almost any sort of sandwich filling.

Pain au Chocolat

Roll the croissant dough as above. Cut into three strips instead of two. Divide the strips into 9 x 12.5cm (3½ x 5in) pieces. Arrange 2 strips of chocolate on the centre of each one about 4cm (1½in) apart. Cover with one piece of dough, brush the edge with water and barely overlap with the other piece. Transfer to a baking sheet and allow to rise. Egg wash again. Preheat the oven to 220°C/425°F/gas 7 for 10 minutes. Put in the pains au chocolat, then reduce the temperature to 180°C/350°F/gas 4 for 10 minutes or until they are crisp and golden brown on the bottom. Cool on a wire rack and serve.

Note: Seek out the strips of chocolate specially made for pains au chocolat.

Variation
Teeny Weeny Pains au Chocolat
In Italy, all the cafés carry tiny pains au chocolate croissants for those who long for a daily treat but find the classic size too damaging for their waistline.

Brioche
See page 497
Serve with homemade jams.

Chocolate Chip Brioche
See page 497

BELOW: Croissants

How to Make Perfect Coffee

Choose the blend of coffee beans that most appeals to your taste, low, medium or high roast. Store in a screw top jar or tin. Fill the kettle with **cold** water and bring to the boil. Meanwhile, grind the coffee.

The texture will depend on the coffee-making method being used. It should be ground very fine if you are making espresso and a little less fine for the filter method and coarser still for the cafetière and jug methods.

The Jug Method (My Favourite)

Bring the cold water to the boil. Pour a little into a delph or pottery jug to scald it. When the pot feels warm, discard the water. Add the freshly ground coffee and fill the pot with the water. The water should be **just off the boil**. Wait for 3–4 minutes, stir, cover. Serve with a strainer.

The Filter Method

Bring cold water to the boil. Meanwhile, put a filter paper into the filter and rest over a coffee jug. Fill about half way with finely ground coffee. When the water comes to the boil wait for 10 seconds and then pour the water quickly over the coffee. Allow to gradually drip through. (It's best to scald the pot here also.)

The Cafetière Method

Bring cold water to the boil as before. Remove the plunger. Scald the pot. Discard the water, add the coffee. Fill the pot about 3/4 full, put the plunger into the pot. Allow to sit for 3–4 minutes then stir. Slowly push the grinds to the bottom of the pot with the plunger. Do not force before the coffee is ready. When the coffee is ready, the plunger will push down easily.

The Espresso Method

Fill the filter container with finely ground coffee, usually high roast. Fill the base with cold water. Fit the coffee container into the base and screw on the top. Put on the heat, within a few minutes, the water will boil and the steam will saturate the coffee. Wait until it has all come through. Serve.

French Toast (or Eggy Bread)

Serves 4

French toast is so good that you forget how economical it is. The French don't call this French toast. They call it *pain perdu* or 'lost bread', because it is a way to use up leftover bread you would otherwise lose – the only bread you've got on the baker's day off. French toast is actually better if the bread is a little stale or sliced and dried out overnight.

3 organic eggs
2 tablespoons milk or cream
salt to taste
6 slices bread (preferably a dense homemade type; typically white, but try rye or wholewheat too)
4 tablespoons butter
icing sugar

Stir the eggs, milk and salt briskly with a fork until well blended.

Strain the mixture through a sieve into a shallow bowl in which you can easily dip a slice of bread. Dip both sides of each slice of bread in the batter and place the slices on a piece of waxed paper.

Melt half of the butter in a frying pan big enough to hold 3 slices at once. Fry the bread over a medium heat until very lightly browned, turning once.

Keep the cooked slices warm in an oven while frying the other 3 in the remaining butter. Serve warm, sprinkled with icing sugar.

French Toast with Bananas and Maple Syrup or Honey

Serves 1

1 organic egg
2 tablespoons milk
1 teaspoon sugar
1 banana
2 slices white bread
Clarified Butter (see page 105)

Garnish
1 banana, sliced
best-quality natural yoghurt, chilled
maple syrup or honey
1 tablespoon roughly chopped walnuts

Whisk the egg in a bowl with the milk and add the sugar. Mash the banana well with a fork and add to the mixture. Alternatively, whizz the whole lot together in a liquidiser or food processor. Pour onto a plate and dip both sides of the bread into it.

Melt a little clarified butter in the pan, fry the bread over a medium heat and, when golden on one side, turn over onto the other. Put on a hot plate, top with banana slices and a dollop of yoghurt. Drizzle with maple syrup or honey and scatter with a few chopped walnuts. Serve immediately.

Master Recipe
Buttermilk Pancakes with Crispy Bacon and Maple Syrup
Serves 10

450g (1lb) plain white flour
1 teaspoon bicarbonate of soda (bread soda)
large pinch of salt
25–50g (1–2oz) sugar
1 organic egg
600ml (1 pint) buttermilk
20 hot crispy streaky bacon rashers
maple syrup or runny honey

Mix the dry ingredients together in a bowl, make a well in the centre and add the egg and enough buttermilk to make a batter of a dropping consistency (it usually takes the full measure).

Drop 1 large tablespoonful into a hot non-stick pan and cook for 1–2 minutes on 1 side before turning over; the pancakes are ready to turn when the bubbles burst. Flip over gently and cook until golden on the other side.

To serve: put 1 pancake on a hot plate, spread with butter and drizzle with maple syrup or honey and top with another buttered pancake. Put a few pieces of hot crispy bacon on top. Serve more maple syrup or honey as an accompaniment.

Variations
Buttermilk Pancakes with Sour Cream and Jam
Serve hot pancakes with jam and sour cream.

Buttermilk Pancakes with Marmalade and Clotted Cream
Serve hot pancakes with marmalade and clotted cream.

Puffy Pancake with Honey and Berries
Serves 2–4

5 organic eggs
2 tablespoons caster sugar
2 tablespoons white flour
½ teaspoon salt
125ml (4fl oz) milk
1 teaspoon pure vanilla extract
25g (1oz) butter

To Serve
icing sugar
450g (1lb) mixed fresh berries
runny honey

25cm (10in) non-stick frying pan

Preheat the oven to 230°C/450°F/gas 8.

Separate the eggs. Mix the caster sugar, flour and salt in a bowl. Make a well in the centre and drop in the egg yolks and vanilla extract. Whisk in the milk gradually. Whisk the egg whites in a large bowl (spotlessly clean and free of grease) and fold gently into the batter mixture.

Melt the butter in a non-stick frying pan over a medium heat. Pour all of the fluffy batter into the pan.

Transfer to the oven and bake for 8–10 minutes or until set underneath and puffy on top. Slide onto a warm plate. Dredge the top with icing sugar and serve with summer berries, fresh mint leaves and a drizzle of honey or maple syrup. It's also delicious with crispy bacon and Cheddar.

Classic Waffles
Makes about 8

Totally yummy! You'll need a waffle iron – I took the plunge and invested in an electric one a few years ago and it's dreamy; easy to use and never sticks. Ordinary waffle irons are much less expensive – just remember to season before using (by greasing with oil and heating) or they will be infuriatingly sticky!

225g (8oz) white flour
pinch of salt
4 teaspoons baking powder
2 tablespoons caster sugar
2 organic eggs
350ml (12fl oz) milk, warmed slightly
125 ml (4fl oz) vegetable shortening, melted
75g (3oz) butter, melted

Put all the dry ingredients into a bowl. In another bowl, whisk the eggs well and stir in the warm milk. Pour the egg mixture into the flour mixture and stir gently. Add the melted butter and beat until well blended.

Heat the waffle iron until very hot. Pour a ladle full of batter into the waffle iron and cook until golden and crisp.

Sprinkle with icing sugar and serve hot in a myriad of ways. Great with any combination of fresh fruit, whipped cream, chocolate or toffee sauce, chopped nuts (add to waffles 30 seconds before they have finished cooking)...

Variation
Cornmeal, Buckwheat or Rye Flour Waffles

Substitute 50g (2oz) cornmeal, buckwheat flour, or rye flour for 50g (2oz) of the white flour called for in the basic recipe.

Heavenly Hots
Makes about 30 hot cakes

4 organic eggs
½ teaspoon bread soda
25g (1oz) plain white flour
½ teaspoon salt
3 tablespoons caster sugar
450ml (16fl oz) sour cream

Whisk the eggs in a bowl. Add all the other ingredients and mix well.

Heat a heavy pan and melt a little clarified butter. Drop dessertspoons of batter into the pan, allowing space for them to spread. When bubbles rise and burst on top, turn over and cook for a few more seconds.

Serve right away.

Ginger Muffins
Makes about 10

Almost our favourite muffin recipe, this is adapted from Marion Cunningham's *The Breakfast Book*.

110g (4oz) unpeeled ginger root, cut into chunks
175g (6oz) caster sugar
110g (4oz) butter
zest of 2 lemons
2 organic eggs
225ml (8fl oz) buttermilk
275g (10oz) white flour
½ teaspoon salt
½ teaspoon bicarbonate of soda (bread soda)

Preheat the oven to 200°C/400°F/gas 6.

Grease 1 tray of muffin tins or line with non-stick muffin cases. Whizz up the ginger in a food processor then put it into a saucepan with a couple of tablespoons of sugar over a medium heat until the sugar melts. Allow to cool.

Cream the butter, add the remaining sugar and the lemon zest, then add the eggs one by one and beat well between each addition.

Next stir in the buttermilk and ginger mixture and blend well. Finally, stir in the flour, salt and bicarbonate of soda until just mixed. Fill the greased muffins tins with the batter, and bake for 30–40 minutes in the oven. Serve warm.

Chocolate and Orange Muffins
Makes 24 muffins

The beauty of these tasty muffins lies in the fact that the batter can be kept in the fridge for 30 days, so you can bake a few muffins fresh each day. This is Dervilla Whelan's delicious version.

2 organic eggs
325g (11oz) soft brown sugar
400ml (14fl oz) milk
1 teaspoon vanilla essence
350ml (12fl oz) sunflower oil
155g (5½oz) sultanas
75g (3oz) bran
375g (13oz) plain flour
½ teaspoon salt
2½ teaspoons bicarbonate of soda (bread soda)
175g (6oz) chocolate chips
zest of 5 oranges

Preheat the oven to 200°C/400°F/gas 6.

In the bowl of an electric mixer, beat the eggs and brown sugar. Add in the milk, vanilla essence, sunflower oil, sultanas, bran, flour, salt and bicarbinate of soda. Mix until completely blended. The mixture will be a very wet, gloopy batter but don't worry.

Take the bowl off the mixer and gently stir in the chocolate chips and the grated orange zest. Line the muffin trays with muffin cases and fill with the mixture leaving about 1cm (½in) below the rim. Bake for approximately 30 minutes until risen and spongy to the touch.

Toby's Hot Chocolate
Serves 4

This is the hot chocolate that my son Toby makes; the flavour of 'proper' hot chocolate is a revelation if you've never tried it before.

110g (4oz) best-quality dark chocolate
60ml (2½fl oz) water
600ml (1 pint) milk
1–2 teaspoons sugar
4 large teaspoons whipped cream
grated chocolate

Put the chocolate and water into a heavy saucepan and melt on a very low heat. Meanwhile, bring the milk almost to the boil in a separate saucepan. When the chocolate has melted, pour on the milk, whisking all the time; it should be smooth and frothy. Taste and add some sugar. Pour into warmed cups, spoon a blob of whipped cream on top and sprinkle with a little grated chocolate.

barbecues

536   DARINA ALLEN'S COMPLETE COOKERY COURSE

barbecues

Cooking over an open fire is the world's oldest cooking method – somehow it seems to re-awaken our primordial instincts. Even those who wouldn't normally be caught dead in an apron feel an urge to grab the tongs when they see a barbecue! Barbecueing means less fuss, more fun and (when one gets the hang of it) more flavour too. It's all about easy, casual entertaining – unwinding with friends and family, while the steaks sizzle and the chicken wings crisp over glowing embers.

You certainly don't need a lot of fancy equipment to get started. I've cooked many an outdoor feast in the most basic circumstances – a circle of stones, a fire and a wire rack will get you started. The skills one needs to learn are: how to light the fire, how to judge when the heat is right for cooking, and where to position the food in relation to the source of heat.

Choosing a Grill
First choose your grill – use something really basic until you learn how to control and manage the fire.

Foil Barbecue – the most basic type which comes ready-made and can be dumped in the bin after use (make sure that it's damped down and totally dead first). This type is perfect for picnics and for people with a tiny garden or patio.

Hibachi – sturdy, portable, cheap and easy to carry. Perfect if you're cooking for small numbers, with the advantage of adjustable grill levels. Can even be positioned in the centre of a table out of doors.

Free-standing Barbecue – wagon/kettle-grill types, with or without wheels. Some have a folding base which makes them easy to pack away and transport in the boot of a car.

Webber-Type Grill – has many possibilities – with this type of barbecue you can cook whole joints of meat (slow-cooked lamb, pork, chickens, ducks) or even pizza. Try barbecuing your Christmas turkey for a change – completely delicious.

Build your own - buy a kit and build a barbecue at home. Choose a spot carefully, taking wind, hanging branches, children, pets and proximity to the kitchen into consideration.

Which Fuel?
You can use **charcoal timber**, or **charcoal bricks** in grills. Purists insist on **wood** or **charcoal**, but if you like to barbecue on the spur of the moment, then you should consider a an **electric** or **gas-powered barbecue**. Here you have push-button control, so if you don't want to get involved with charcoal and frantically fanning flames, this could be the answer.

Lighting the Barbecue and Fuel
Unless you have a gas-powered barbecue, the most important thing is to get your barbecue lit in time. This could be anything between 15 and 45 minutes before you intend to start cooking, depending on the kind of fuel you're using. Never use firelights, paraffin, methylated spirits, petrol, diesel or lighter fuel to light your fire – it can be incredibly dangerous.

Charcoal
There are two types of charcoal: the first will be ready to cook on within 15 minutes, but it burns off quite quickly. The second is slower-burning and has better staying power, but takes longer to reach the cooking stage. Charcoal briquets take the longest of all (up to 45 minutes), but then they last for ages and they hold their heat very well. Charcoal is ready for cooking when it turns light grey

and ashy, not before. Don't be tempted to begin cooking while there are flames still licking around the grill – this usually results in uncooked but blackened and charred food.

Wood

I love wood barbecues. We have a great tradition of breakfast barbecues on the cliffs of Ballyandreen, and when barbecueing on the beach, collecting drift wood for the fire is all part of the experience (although I do cheat by bringing some kindling and newspaper in the back of the car, so I can get it started while others collect the wood!). Make sure there's no glue or paint on the wood, as these will release toxins when burnt. Woodchips (apple, hickory or oak) add different smokey flavours to the food. Soak in cold water for a good hour or so before putting them directly onto the hot embers.

Cooking

Before you start barbecuing, make sure that you're organised with tongs, seasoning and dishes ready to go. Barbecues are laid-back affairs, but will only seem effortless if you've organised yourself a little first.

The fundamental principle of barbecuing is **controlling the heat**. You do this by raising or lowering the grill. The larger the pieces of meat the further they should be from the heat source. Sear thick steaks, chicken legs and larger cuts of meat over the high heat for a few minutes before transferring it to the edges of the grill, where the heat is lower. Searing will seal the meat, so that the juices remain inside during further cooking on a low heat. Smaller pieces of food (chicken paillarde or lamb chops) can be within 10–12.5cm (4–5in) of the coals. It is difficult to gauge if chicken legs and wings are properly cooked through. Because of the risk of salmonella and campylobacter, it is definitely worth pre-cooking chicken drumsticks a little

first – this may sound like cheating, but it's better to be safe, particularly if you are using intensively produced meat. I like to buy organic chicken.

As you cook, fat will drip off the meat and onto the coals, producing flames. Damp these down by spraying a little water on the coals. Avoid basting with too much oil or marinade as well, as this can also cause flames to leap up. Keep turning the meat so it does not stick, burn or dry out. Most burgers, chops and so on should be ready within 20 minutes, but do check before serving. Fish and seafood will be much quicker.

Marinating

Marinades are fun to experiment with, and can be an excellent way to improve the flavour of meat, but they are not essential. If you start off with good-quality fish and meat, you shouldn't have to do very much to it. For a simple marinade, all you need is extra-virgin olive oil, sea salt, a few herbs and perhaps a little lemon or lime juice, vinegar or red wine. You need only marinade for 10–15 minutes, and be particularly aware not to leave meat in an acidic marinade for too long as it can be counter-productive and toughen it. A word of warning: avoid marinades with tomato or honey as they tend to burn. It's a better idea to baste the meat with sauce once it's cooked.

Food for Barbecues

Barbecues were traditionally carniverous affairs, with perhaps the odd green salad or baked potato on the side. This is far from the case now. There are some exceptionally tasty vegetarian and non-meat options to try: vegetable kebabs and parcels, quesadillas, bruschetta, stuffed flat mushrooms, goat's cheese wrapped in vine leaves, coal-baked potatoes, prawns and fish.

Remember that people's appetites increase when they eat outdoors, and of course all those lovely aromas of cooking food will make them hungrier still. Keep your guests' hunger at bay with some fingerfood – this will also ensure that they're not completely sozzled if you get your timing wrong and the cooking takes longer than expected! As a rough guide, allow per person:

3–4 portions of 'main' courses, e.g. kebabs, steak, burgers, sausages or fish parcels
2–3 portions of salads or vegetable dishes, e.g. baked potatoes, salads or vegetable parcels
1–2 portions of dessert
3–4 drinks (provide soft drinks as well...!)

Try to have some standby food on hand, such as extra sausages (which can be frozen later if they're not used) and bananas or tomatoes which can be wrapped in streaky bacon.

Hygiene and Safety

When cooking outdoors take sensible precautions:

1. Keep all food refrigerated (or cool) until it's needed.
2. Keep cooked and uncooked meat separate and use different implements and serving dishes to avoid cross-contamination.
3. Wash your hands after touching uncooked meat.
4. Position your barbecue on a flat heat-proof surface away from overhanging trees and shrubs. Once you light it, don't move it.
5. If you are barbecuing at night, make sure there's good lighting around the cooking area.
6. Never leave the barbecue unattended.
7. Always keep a fire extinguisher at hand. A plant mister is handy to keep flames down.
8. NEVER use a barbecue indoors.
9. Damp down the barbecue completely before you empty out the ashes, and allow it to cool before moving it.

Olive Oil Marinade for all Meats and Fish

Makes about 300ml (10fl oz)

250ml (8fl oz) extra-virgin olive oil
2–4 garlic cloves, crushed
4 tablespoons freshly chopped herbs, such as
    parsley, thyme, mint, chives, rosemary and sage
salt and freshly ground pepper

Optional Extras
1–2 teaspoons finely grated orange zest
2 tablespoons finely chopped shallots

Combine the ingredients, and season with salt and pepper.

Basic Marinade for Chicken and Lamb

Makes about 300ml (10fl oz)

150ml (5fl oz) extra-virgin olive oil
50ml (2fl oz) lemon juice
lots of salt and freshly ground pepper

Optional Extras
1 grated onion and a good sprinkling of
    cinnamon
3 garlic cloves, crushed
3 sprigs tarragon, thyme or rosemary
1/2–1 teaspoon lemon zest
1/2–1 teaspoon freshly grated ginger

Mix all the ingredients together, taste and correct the seasoning.

Olive Oil and Ginger Marinade for Pork and Chicken

Makes about 8 tablespoons

4 tablespoons extra-virgin olive oil
1–2 tablespoons freshly peeled and chopped
    ginger
4 garlic cloves, chopped
2 tablespoons orange rind

Combine all the ingredients and mix well.

Spicy Chicken Marinade

Makes about 10 tablespoons

1 tablespoon ground cumin seeds
1 tablespoon ground paprika
1 teaspoon cayenne pepper
1 tablespoon ground turmeric

1 teaspoon freshly ground pepper
2 teaspoons salt
3 garlic cloves, crushed
5 tablespoons lemon juice
2–3 tablespoons sunflower oil

Mix the cumin, paprika, cayenne, turmeric, black pepper, salt, garlic, lemon juice and oil in a bowl. Rub this mixture all over the chicken pieces. Put in a bowl, cover, then keep in a cool place for at least 3 hours.

Yoghurt Marinade for Chicken and Lamb

Makes 600ml (1 pint)

425ml (15fl oz) natural yoghurt
4 tablespoons extra-virgin olive oil
2 large garlic cloves, crushed
2 tablespoons freshly chopped mint leaves
freshly ground pepper

Optional Extras
1–2 tablespoons freshly roasted and ground
    cumin or 1–2 tablespoons ground coriander
    seeds, or a mixture of both

Mix all the ingredients together, taste and correct the seasoning.

Barbecue Sauce for Chicken, Lamb, Pork or Sausages

Makes about 225ml (8fl oz)

4 tablespoons extra-virgin olive oil
2 garlic cloves, crushed
110g (4oz) onion, finely chopped
1 x 400g (14oz) tin chopped tomatoes

salt and freshly ground pepper
7 tablespoons tomato purée
7 tablespoons red or white wine vinegar
4 tablespoons pure honey
4 tablespoons Worcestershire sauce
2 tablespoons Dijon mustard

Heat the oil in a frying pan, add the garlic and onion, and sweat gently for 4–5 minutes. Add the tomatoes and juice, cook for a further 4–5 minutes, then season with salt and pepper. Purée in a liquidiser or food processor. Pour back into a clean pan, add the remainder of the ingredients and bring to the boil over a medium heat and simmer for 4–5 minutes. Use as a basting sauce, marinade or accompaniment.

Note: Don't marinade for longer than 15–20 minutes or the meat will be inclined to burn easily.

Chicken Breasts with Roasted Red Pepper, Tomato and Basil Salsa

Serves 4

450g (1lb) organic skinless chicken breasts
2 teaspoons runny honey
2 tablespoons lemon juice
1 tablespoon tomato ketchup or Hot Chilli
    Sauce (see page 592)
1/2 teaspoon ground roasted cumin
1/2 teaspoon salt

Roasted Red Pepper, Tomato and Basil Salsa
    (see page 592)

Cut each chicken breast into 4 or 5 strips. Mix the honey, lemon juice, tomato ketchup and cumin in a bowl. Add the chicken and toss until all the pieces are coated, then marinate in the fridge for 1–2 hours.

Light the barbecue. Just before cooking, add the salt to the marinated chicken and toss well. When the barbecue is really good and hot, grill chicken pieces 15cm (6in) from the heat for 5–7 minutes each side, depending on thickness. Cook far enough from the flame otherwise the honey will burn. The chicken must cook through but still be juicy. Serve with Roasted Pepper, Tomato and Basil Salsa.

Asian Chicken and Lettuce Rolls
Serves 4

This was one of our favourite recipes when Antony Worrall Thompson did a guest chef appearance at the Cookery School recently.

400g (14oz) organic chicken, minced
1 red chilli, de-seeded and finely diced
2 spring onions, finely chopped
1 garlic clove, crushed
1 teaspoon freshly grated ginger
1 teaspoon sesame oil
salt and freshly ground pepper
25g (1oz) water chestnuts, chopped
2 tablespoons freshly chopped coriander
2 tablespoons cashew nuts, chopped
1 carrot, finely diced
2 tablespoons oyster sauce
2 teaspoons clear honey
16–20 Cos lettuce leaves

200g (7oz) brown Basmati rice, to serve
lime wedges, to serve

In a bowl, mix the chicken with the chilli, spring onions, garlic, ginger and sesame oil. Heat a large, non-stick frying pan over a medium heat and cook the mince mixture for about 5 minutes, breaking the meat up with the back of a fork until golden brown. Season with salt and pepper.

Add the water chestnuts, coriander, cashews, carrot, oyster sauce and honey, stirring to combine and continue to heat until the chicken is cooked through. Taste and correct the seasoning.

Serve the mince with the lettuce leaves (each diner rolls the parcels themselves), cooked rice and lime wedges to squeeze – delish.

Sweet Chilli and Ginger Chicken Paillardes
Serves 4

8 organic chicken breasts, butterflied (see page 272)

Marinade
3 garlic cloves, crushed
2 chillies, seeded and finely chopped
1 tablespoon freshly grated ginger
6 tablespoons honey
3 tablespoons soy sauce
6 tablespoons lemon juice

Mix all the ingredients for the marinade together. Dip the chicken paillardes in the marinade, cover and allow to marinate in the fridge until the barbecue is ready (at least 30 minutes).

Grill over medium heat for 2–3 minutes on each side (not too close to the coals). Serve with a salad of lettuce and fresh herbs.

Chicken with Lemon and Ginger
Serves 6

6 organic chicken breasts

Marinade
juice of 1 lemon
2 garlic cloves, crushed
1½ teaspoons freshly grated ginger
1 teaspoon finely grated lemon zest
125ml (4fl oz) extra-virgin olive oil
salt and lots of freshly ground pepper

Mix all the marinade ingredients in a bowl, and marinate the chicken breasts in a shallow dish for half an hour. Prepare the barbecue or heat a char-grill to medium heat. Dry off the chicken breasts with kitchen paper and brush them with a very little olive oil. Grill for about 5 minutes on each side. Heat the marinade in a small pan until just simmering. Serve the

chicken on very hot plates with a little of the marinade and a green salad with rocket and cherry tomatoes.

Chicken Burgers
Serves 6

A great recipe from Bonnie Stern, well-known TV chef in Toronto. Wrap the burgers in caul fat if available; it is vital to cook the chicken burgers thoroughly but not to let them dry out – they should still be good and juicy. Serve with Teriyaki Sauce (see page 591).

450g (1lb) boneless, skinless chicken breasts
1 organic egg
50g (2oz) fresh breadcrumbs
1 garlic clove, crushed
1 teaspoon freshly grated ginger
2 tablespoons freshly chopped coriander or parsley
1 teaspoon freshly chopped tarragon
2 tablespoons chopped chives or spring onions
salt and freshly ground pepper
caul fat (optional)
6 hamburger buns or pitta breads
mixture of crisp lettuce and salad leaves

Mince the chicken breasts finely or cut them into cubes about 1cm (½in) thick, put them into a food processor fitted with the steel knife and pulse until finely chopped.

Put the chicken into a bowl, add the beaten egg, breadcrumbs, garlic, ginger, coriander, tarragon and chives, and season with salt and pepper. Mix well.

Shape the mixture into 6 burgers. Wrap in caul fat, if using. Cover and refrigerate until ready to cook. Brush with olive oil.

Light the barbecue or preheat a pan-grill. Grill the burgers for 3 minutes on each side. Keep turning and brushing with the Teryaki Sauce every 2 minutes for about 8–10 minutes or until the burgers are fully cooked through. Serve in hamburger buns or pitta bread with shredded lettuce, salad leaves and tomato and cucumber slices.

Chicken Thighs with Honey and Mustard

Serves 10

10 organic chicken thighs

Marinade
4 garlic cloves, crushed
6 tablespoons honey
2 tablespoons Dijon mustard
2 tablespoons wholegrain mustard (moutarde de meaux)
2 tablespoons lemon juice
salt and lots of freshly ground pepper

Score the chicken skin with a sharp knife to allow the marinade to penetrate evenly. I prefer to cook the thighs on the bone for extra flavour but feel free to remove if you wish.

In a large bowl, mix all the marinade ingredients together and then dip the thighs until they are well coated. Transfer to the fridge and marinate for at least an hour. Light the barbecue.

When the barbecue is at optimum heat, lay the thighs at a distance of about 8–9cm (3–3¹/₂in) from the coals, turning regularly because the honey burns easily. Allow at least 5 minutes on each side to cook, perhaps more if they are still on the bone. When there is no trace of pink close to the bone the chicken thighs are cooked. Serve with a tomato salad and a mixture of organic salad leaves.

Chinese Duck Breast with Sea Salt and Five Spice Powder

Serves 4

4 duck breasts

2 teaspoons Chinese five spice powder
1 teaspoon sea salt (Maldon or Halen Mon)
¹/₂ teaspoon freshly ground pepper

Sauce
50ml (2fl oz) tomato ketchup
50ml (2fl oz) Hoisin sauce
1 tablespoon honey
1 tablespoon soy sauce
¹/₄ teaspoon Chinese five spice powder
2 tablespoons rice wine vinegar

Trim the excess skin off the duck breasts and score the skin at 1cm (¹/₂in) intervals with a sharp knife. Mix the five spice powder with the salt and pepper and sprinkle over both sides of the duck. Light the barbecue.

Meanwhile, make the sauce. Mix all the ingredients in a saucepan and warm gently over a low heat.

Cook the duck breasts skin side down on the barbecue over a low heat, about 15cm (6in) from the coals, for 6–7 minutes or until the skin is nearly crisp. Then turn over and cook for a few more minutes on the other side. It's nice to serve them ever so slightly pink with the Asian sauce.

Souvlakia – Kebabs

Serves 6–8

The word comes from souvla, meaning skewer or spit in Greek. Delicious little chunks of lamb threaded onto skewers and barbecued on a grill or open fire are sold everywhere throughout the country, even on street stalls. You will need plain wooden skewers. Pork or chicken can be cooked in the same way but should not be served pink, rather, cooked a little further from the fire and well done. Beef is much juicier if not cooked too long.

900g–1.1kg (2–2¹/₂lb) leg or shoulder of lamb
125ml (4fl oz) olive oil
juice of 1–2 lemons
2 tablespoons marjoram, mint, thyme or rosemary
12 or so bay leaves (optional)
sea salt and freshly cracked pepper

Trim the meat of any fat or sinew and cut into 2.5cm (1in) cubes. Mix the olive oil with the lemon juice, chosen herb and pepper. Toss the lamb in the marinade. Cover and refrigerate for an hour or so.

Heat the barbecue to very hot. Thread about 6 pieces of meat onto each skewer, season with sea salt; a few pieces of bay leaf can also be threaded on but it's not essential. Grill the meat, basting every now and then with the marinade until it is dark and crusty on the outside, but still tender and juicy inside. Lamb may be served pink. Serve immediately with a salad or perhaps some olives and radishes and a dollop of Tzatziki (see page 69).

Master Recipe
Lamb Chops with Marjoram

Allow 2–3 chops per person and 4 if greedy!

lamb chops
marjoram
olive oil
freshly ground pepper and sea salt

Trim the chop of excess fat and score the back fat. Chop the marjoram. Take a flat dish large enough to take the chops in a single layer, brush the base with olive oil and sprinkle with some marjoram. Season the chops on both sides with pepper, and place them on top of the marjoram.

Sprinkle some more marjoram on top and drizzle with olive oil. Marinate for 1 hour or more. Drain off any excess oil and season well with sea salt. Grill on a griddle 15cm (6in) from the hot coals for 10–15 minutes depending on the thickness and degree of doneness required. Baste frequently with the oil and serve immediately.

ABOVE: Hamburgers with Avocado Sauce

3 tablespoons soy sauce
1 tablespoon dry sherry
2–3 tablespoons hoisin sauce

2lb flank steak

Mix the marinade ingredients in a wide dish. Coat the beef and leave to marinate in the fridge for 1 hour. Light the barbecue or preheat a pan-grill.

Lift the steak from the marinade and drain well. Cook on a hot barbecue or very hot pan-grill for 4–5 minutes on each side. Allow to rest and cool slightly for 3–4 minutes before carving on a slant and across the grain, into thin slices.

Hamburgers with Avocado Sauce

Serves 4–8

Homemade hamburgers cooked on the barbecue are just so different from anything you would buy in a high street burger bar. It is quite worth the effort. We wrap the burgers in caul fat as this bastes them and helps to keep them from crumbling.

homemade Hamburgers (see page 347)

Avocado Sauce
2 ripe avocados
3–4 tablespoons lime or lemon juice
1 tablespoon olive oil
1 tablespoon freshly chopped coriander or
   flat-leaf parsley
sea salt and freshly ground pepper

Wrap the hamburgers in caul fat, if using, and cook them 15cm (6in) from the coals for 5–8 minutes on each side, turning once.

Next make the avocado sauce: scoop out the flesh from the avocados and mash with a fork. Add the lime juice, olive oil, coriander, salt and pepper to taste. Serve with the hamburgers.

Note: The hamburgers are also good served with **Tomato and Chilli Jam** (see page 513), **Tomato and Coriander Salsa** (see page 592), or **Mushroom à la Crème** (see page 201).

Variations
Lamb Chops with Rosemary
Follow the Master Recipe, substituting chopped rosemary for the marjoram.

Pork Chops with Sage
Use 1 good-sized chop per person and sage instead of marjoram.

Pork Chops with Olive Oil and Fennel Seeds
Follow the Master Recipe, using 1 good-sized chop per person and 1 tablespoon of crushed fennel seeds instead of marjoram.

Anne Rossiter's BBQ Flank Steak

Serves 4–6

Beef flank steak is much less expensive than sirloin or fillet. It can be tough but it has superb flavour and texture if cooked properly and Anne claims this marinade makes flank steak taste like fillet.

Marinade
1/2 tablespoon sugar
1 teaspoon five-spice powder
4 garlic cloves

Barbecued T-Bone Steak or Rib Steak

T-bone or rib steaks, 5–6cm (2–2¹/₂in) thick
salt and freshly ground pepper
olive oil

toothpicks soaked in cold water
Béarnaise Sauce (see page 586)
Horseradish or Garlic Mayonnaise (see
  page 584)

Trim the excess fat off each steak, leaving between 5mm (¹/₄in) and 1cm (¹/₂in). Score in several places (keep the excess pieces of fat to grease the griddle of the barbecue). If necessary, secure the tail of each steak with a toothpick which has been soaked in water.

Just before cooking, brush each steak with a very little olive oil and season generously with salt and pepper. Set the rack 10–15cm (4–6in) above the hot coals to preheat it, grease the griddle with some of the excess fat and sear the steaks for 1–2 minutes on each side on the hottest part of the barbecue. Then turn onto the fat for a minute to brown it. Move the steak to a cooler part of the barbecue or raise the grid 2.5–5cm (1–2in) higher. Continue to grill until the beef is cooked to your taste. Allow a further 12–15 minutes for rare, 16–20 minutes for medium and 25–30 minutes for well done.

This is a rough guide; it's best to judge by feel. If the meat feels soft when pressed with the tongs it is rare, if springy it is medium but if it feels quite firm and stiff it is well done.

Transfer the steak to a carving board; allow to rest for 10 minutes, then remove the toothpick and discard. Cut the meat off the bone and cut across the grain into 5mm (¹/₄in) thick slices. Serve immediately on hot plates with Béarnaise Sauce and Horseradish or Garlic Mayonnaise.

Barbecue Spare Ribs

There are dozens of variations of this recipe; every Chinese chef would have his very own favourite recipe for barbecue ribs. Some call for the ribs to be par-boiled prior to being cooked, others for the ribs to be roasted in a tin foil parcel. This recipe, from Naranjan McCormack, is one that I have found to be very successful and simply delicious. It is of course a very popular starter in many restaurants in the West. When serving barbecued ribs as a starter, always provide a finger bowl as the only way to enjoy these ribs is to eat with your fingers!

2 racks pork spare ribs
1 teaspoon freshly grated ginger
2 garlic cloves, crushed
1 tablespoon dry sherry
¹/₄ level teaspoon freshly ground nutmeg
a pinch of Chinese 5-spice powder
2–3 heaped tablespoons hoisin sauce
2 tablespoons honey

Garnish
lettuce, peppers and slices of lemon

Using a sharp knife, slice the rack of ribs into individual pieces. If the ribs are rather small then you would be advised to slice the ribs into twos, otherwise the meat on the ribs tends to dry out a little on the barbecue.

Place the spare ribs, ginger and garlic together in a very large bowl and add the sherry, nutmeg and the 5-spice powder and mix together. Then add the hoisin sauce and mix thoroughly.

Cook on the barbecue or alternatively line a large roasting tin with tin foil, leaving it to extend generously out over both ends. Layer the spare ribs into the roasting tin and fold over the tin foil, making a loose parcel. Roast the pork spare-ribs in a preheated oven at 200°C/400°F/gas 6 for approx. 1 hour.

Then open out the tin foil parcel and baste the ribs. Leave the foil open and return the ribs to the oven for about 10 minutes. Then glaze the ribs with the honey and return to the oven for another 5–10 minutes. Serve hot, garnished with lettuce, peppers and lemon slices or wedges.

Sweet Sticky Pork Chops
Serves 10

10 organic pork chops

Marinade
9 tablespoons soy sauce
5 tablespoons tomato ketchup
6 tablespoons Hoisin sauce
4 tablespoons rice wine or medium sherry
3 tablespoons honey
3 tablespoons soft dark brown sugar
1 tablespoon lemon juice

Mix all the marinade ingredients in a bowl. Pour ³/₄ of the marinade into a large, shallow dish and dip the pork chops, coating thoroughly on each side. Cover and transfer to the fridge until the barbecue is ready.

Grill over a medium heat (not too close to the coals) for 3–4 minutes on each side, depending on the thickness of the chops. Drizzle the remainder of the marinade over the top to glaze and serve with a green salad.

Black Pudding with Golden Delicious Apple Sauce

Serves 12 for canapés, 4–6 as a starter

12 slices best-quality black pudding, about 1cm
   (1/2in) thick
olive oil
1 tablespoon wholegrain mustard
1 teaspoon honey

Golden Delicious Apple Sauce (see page 597)

First make the Apple Sauce.

Brush the slices of black pudding with olive oil. Barbecue until crisp on both sides. Mix the grainy mustard with the honey. Put a dollop on the top of each piece of black pudding and serve with Golden Delicious Apple Sauce.

Bananas Wrapped in Streaky Bacon

bananas
thin streaky bacon rashers

Peel the bananas and cut into chunks about 5–6cm (2–2¹/₂in) long (depending on the width of the rasher). Wrap each piece in bacon and secure with a cocktail stick which has been soaked in cold water. (Toss the bananas in lemon juice if prepared ahead.) Cook on the barbecue 10–15cm (4–6in) from the coals for 5 minutes.

Wire-rack Salmon with Dill Butter

Serves 10–20

Fish works brilliantly on the barbecue provided you put it in a fish cage for ease of turning. However, you can do a perfectly good job with a Heath-Robinson solution using two wire cake racks.

1–2 sides of wild salmon, unskinned
sea salt and freshly ground pepper
olive oil or melted butter

Dill Butter
110–225g (4–8oz) butter
4–8 tablespoons freshly chopped dill

Sprinkle the salmon generously with sea salt up to an hour before cooking.

Light the grill or barbecue.

When the barbecue is ready, lay the fish skin-side down on the wire rack. Brush the flesh with oil or melted butter and sprinkle with freshly ground pepper. Put the other wire rack on top. Lay on top of the barbecue, 15–20cm (6–8in) from the heat, and cook for 10–15 minutes on the skin side. Turn the entire cage over and continue to cook for 5–6 minutes or until just cooked through. The exact time will depend on the thickness of the fish.

Meanwhile, melt the butter and stir in the freshly chopped dill.

To serve, spoon the Dill Butter over the salmon as it is served.

Butterflied Prawns with Chilli and Ginger

Serves 4

Isaac's restaurant in Cork serves these as a starter. Customers complain every time they try to take them off the menu!

24 Dublin Bay prawns or tiger prawns
   (uncooked)
salt and freshly ground pepper

chilli and ginger sauce (available in Asian stores)
   or sweet chilli sauce with added fresh ginger

Garnish
coriander leaves
4 segments of lemon

First 'butterfly' the prawns. Remove the head from the prawns, leaving the tails on, and split lengthways. Remove the intestine (see page 254). Open them out flat, keeping them attached at the tails. Place in a large bowl and season with salt and pepper.

Just before cooking, douse with chilli and ginger sauce and toss well. Barbecue on both sides for 4–6 minutes and, when cooked, transfer to a plate and serve immediately garnished with fresh coriander leaves and a segment of lemon.

Barbecued Prawns with Tartare Sauce

Serves 4

Tiger prawns may also be used; try tossing them in sea salt and harissa first.

24 jumbo Dublin Bay prawns, whole and
   uncooked
olive oil
sea salt
Tartare Sauce (see page 585)

Toss the prawns in the oil and season with sea salt. Barbecue the prawns whole, turning from side to side until cooked through. Serve in their shells with Tartare Sauce.

Chargrilled Quesadillas

Quesadillas work incredibly well on the barbecue. You might want to assemble them beforehand so they can be lifted easily onto the grill or you could lay out a pile of ingredients on a large board so that guests can make their own. Follow the quesadilla recipes on page 91 and serve with big bowls of Tomato and Coriander Salsa (see page 592), Guacamole (see page 593) and sour cream as accompaniments.

Chargrilled Bruschetta

Bruschetta is delicious cooked on the barbecue. Follow the recipe on page 66, but chargrill the bread on both sides on the barbecue. Preheat the oven to 220°C/425°F/gas 7.

Chargrilled Pizza Margherita

Makes 1

Possibly the most traditional and universally popular pizza in Italy. As this pizza is basically cheese and tomato it is crucial that your tomato sauce has a really super flavour.

140g (5oz) Garden Café Pizza Dough
    (see page 485)
4 tablespoons Isaac's roasted tomato 170g
    (6oz) mozzarella cheese
3 tablespoons extra-virgin olive oil
sauce or very ripe tomatoes
1 dessertspoon freshly chopped annual marjoram
1 tablespoon freshly grated Parmigiano
    Reggiano

Roll out the pizza dough to 33cm (12in) rectangle or circle, about 5mm (1/4in) thick. Brush both sides with olive oil. Gently place the dough on the grid in the centre of the barbecue, directly over the heat for 2–4 minutes, until the bottom of the crust is well marked and browned. Turn upside down.

Slice mozzarella, sprinkle with the olive oil and arrange over the cooked side of the crust, within 2cm (1in) of the edge. Spread Isaac's roasted tomato sauce over the top. Sprinkle with the freshly grated parmesan and season very well with salt and freshly ground pepper. Return the pizza to the centre of the cooking grate and cook with the lid closed until the bottom is well browned, the toppings are warm and the cheese is bubbly (about 5–10 minutes). Sprinkle the freshly chopped marjoram on top and serve immediately.

Isaac's Pizza Sauce

450g (1lb) very ripe tomatoes, halved
6 garlic cloves, unpeeled
1 tablespoon balsamic vinegar
2 tablespoons extra-virgin olive oil
sprinkle of salt, pepper and sugar

Put the tomatoes on a roasting tray, seeds facing up in a single layer. Put the garlic, vinegar, oil, salt, pepper and sugar over the tomatoes. Roast in a hot oven until the tomatoes are completely soft. Mouli all the ingredients, taste and correct the seasoning.

Baked Potatoes with Dill and Yoghurt Sauce

Serves 16

Of course these potatoes can equally be baked in a hot oven, but the flavour of potatoes cooked in the coals is just so delicious that it is worth the bother.

16 large 'old' potatoes

Dill and Yoghurt Sauce
450ml (16fl oz) sour cream or fromage blanc
2 teaspoons Dijon or grainy mustard
225ml (8fl oz) natural yoghurt
6 tablespoons freshly chopped dill
1/2 teaspoon salt
sugar to taste

Scrub the potatoes well, prick them in 3 or 4 places with the tip of a knife. Wrap them in tin foil and bury in the hot coals of a barbecue for 45–60 minutes. Meanwhile, mix all the ingredients together for the sauce. To serve, cut a cross in the top of each potato and spoon in some dill and yoghurt sauce.

Goat's Cheese in Vine Leaves

Serves 6

12 large fresh vine leaves
6 rounds of goat's cheese, or use feta, Gruyère, emmenthal, Cheddar or mozzarella, cut into 5 x 1cm (2 x 1/2in) pieces

Blanch and refresh the vine leaves quickly and dry with kitchen paper.

To assemble: take a vine leaf and put a piece of cheese in the centre of the 'veiny' side. Fold over the edges to make a parcel, put the parcel on a second vine leaf and wrap tightly with the seam underneath. Grill on the barbecue until the cheese starts to melt inside, about 5 minutes on each side. Unwrap and eat with crusty bread. The leaves may be eaten or discarded.

Barbecued Spring Onions

Serves 6

18 large spring onions
3 tablespoons olive oil
sea salt and freshly ground ppper

Wash the spring onions, trim the root ends and cut into 15cm (6in) lengths. Drizzle with oil, season with salt and pepper and toss onto the barbecue. Cook over a medium heat until golden on 1 side, turn and allow to cook on the other side.

Flat Mushrooms with Garlic and Fresh Herbs

Makes 15–20

15–20 flat mushrooms, depending on size
150ml (5fl oz) extra-virgin olive oil
2 tablespoons chopped herbs, such as thyme, parsley, chives and marjoram
2–4 large garlic cloves
sea salt and freshly ground pepper

Arrange the mushrooms on a flat tray and sprinkle with the olive oil, herbs and garlic; leave for 15–30 minutes, turning occasionally. Place gill-side up on the barbecue. Season and grill for 6 minutes or until cooked through. Serve as they are, or with Garlic Butter (see page 588).

Flat Mushrooms with Asian Chilli Dressing
Serves 8

Another Antony Worrall-Thompson brainwave.

8 flat mushrooms
4 tablespoons extra-virgin olive oil
1 teaspoon sesame oil

Dressing
4 tablespoons olive oil
2 teaspoons soy sauce
2 tablespoons dry white wine
1/2 red chilli, de-seeded and chopped
2 garlic cloves, finely sliced
1 teaspoon honey
1 1/2 tablespoons freshly chopped mint
2 tablespoons roughly chopped coriander leaves
1 teaspoon orange zest (optional)
salt and freshly ground pepper

Remove the stalks from the mushrooms. Mix the olive and sesame oils, brush over the mushrooms and season. Cook them gill-side up on the barbecue for 5–6 minutes until cooked through.

Meanwhile, make the dressing: put the olive oil, soy sauce, wine, chilli, garlic and honey in a small saucepan, bring to the boil and cook until reduced a little, then remove from the heat. Add the mint, coriander and orange zest. Season with salt and pepper.

When the mushrooms are cooked, arrange them on a large serving plate and spoon the dressing over. Serve warm or cold.

RIGHT: Fruit Kebabs

Master Recipe
Fruit Kebabs
Makes 16 kebabs approx.

8 peaches or nectarines
8 apricots
24 cherries
16 strawberries
4 bananas
fresh lemon juice
orange liqueur (Cointreau or Grand Marnier)
175–225g (6–8oz) caster sugar
whipping cream

Cut the peaches or nectarines and apricots into halves, discarding the stones, and keep the strawberries and cherries whole. Peel the bananas and cut into large chunks, about 2cm (3/4in) long and sprinkle with a little lemon juice. Mix the fruit in a bowl, sprinkle with orange liqueur, and macerate for about 15 minutes.

Thread the fruit onto skewers. Roll in caster sugar and barbecue for 5–8 minutes or until they start to caramelise. Serve immediately with a little softly whipped cream. For real excitement, pour some of the liqueur over each kebab, set it alight and serve immediately. Otherwise just drink the marinade with the kebabs later on!

Variation
Cut Apple Kebabs

dessert apples, cut into large chunks, or quarters, sprinkled with lemon juice

Just before cooking, toss in or paint with melted butter, sprinkle with caster sugar and thread onto skewers. Grill for 5–8 minutes or until golden and caramelised.

Note: The fruit can also be cooked in tin foil papillotes on the barbecue.

finger foods

finger foods

Wow! Haven't canapés come a long way. When I was little, a neighbour gave a cocktail party and I was so intrigued and exalted that I went round to help her prepare the food. I was amazed to find little chunks of cheese and grapes on cocktail sticks sticking out of a melon. I thought it was the most exciting and sophisticated thing I'd ever seen.

Since those days, Lorna Wing and others have well and truly liberated us from all those predictable canapés. We can now let our imagination run riot and come up with delicious little bites, from teeny weeny portions of fish and chips to mini poppadoms, sushi and shepherd's pie!

Canapés are most often served with drinks at cocktail parties and at occasions such as weddings and funerals. More and more people are entertaining by serving larger canapés, served one by one, over a period of perhaps an hour. These may include hamburgers in buns, Thai fish cakes, wontons, spring rolls, lamb lollipops... Many canapés may be used as starters, too.

Presentation

Finger food is often fiddly to present and even more difficult to eat – especially if you have a glass of wine in one hand. Use your imagination to come up with creative ways of serving. Chinese porcelain spoons are an attractive solution, particularly if your canapé needs to be served with a little sauce. Delicious morsels may be threaded onto skewers or satay sticks to make perfect, easy-to-eat finger food. Sprigs of woody herbs, such as rosemary and sage, make creative alternatives to the usual cocktail sticks and skewers.

Tiny cardboard boxes are good for crispy croquettes and raita; shot glasses for liquid canapés; tin or plastic sand buckets with crumpled paper are great for fish and chips. Oyster shells, scallop shells and egg cups are other options. Tiny cups with saucers are perfect for serving portions of hot or cold soup.

Attractive serving platters are vital for presentation. You can use china, plastic, rushes, baskets, sushi and split cane mats, slate and galvanised tin plates. Be careful that they are not too heavy or the server will be exhausted from carting them around. Balsa wood circular boxes that large bries are sold in are also terrific. Virginia creeper leaves, vine leaves and even fig leaves are also very effective. Now that we have a banana tree in the garden, we love to serve finger food on its shiny, green leaves.

Don't forget to provide cocktail sticks, serviettes and suitable containers for your guests to discreetly deposit their used cocktail sticks, bones and pips into.

What To Serve and When

At a drinks party, start by serving savoury canapés with your cocktails, wine or champagne. About two-thirds of the way through the evening, you may want to switch to a good dessert wine and replace your savoury selection with sweet canapés such as petits fours, little lemon tartlets and glazed strawberries. Variety and balance are essential. If the situation allows, serve both hot and cold canapés, and balance meat dishes with vegetarian.

Choose the canapés carefully so you have a contrast of flavours and texture – some mild, some hot and spicy, some perennial favourites. You may also want to balance expensive canapés which include prawns or lobster with a less extravagant but delicious and ever-popular favourite like Irish Cheddar Cheese Croquettes (see page 551) with Ballymaloe Relish.

Suggested Bases and Toppings

Here is a list of bases that we regularly make and use. The bases can be combined with all sorts of toppings, so let your imagination run riot. Don't forget to season, and taste, taste, taste!

White bread or croutons 2.5–4cm (1–1½in) round or square

Round, square or diamonds of brown yeast bread or pumpernickel

White or brown cheese biscuits

Tiny pieces of Melba toast

Water biscuits

Cucumber sliced into 5mm (¼in) rounds

Tiny tartlet shells

Tiny poppadoms

Tiny pittas

Savoury drop scones

Crostini

Crostini cups

Round toasts and heart toasts

Corn griddle cakes

Hot potato cakes

Prawn crackers

Raggedy filo tartlets

Tiny rosettes of smooth pâtés (such as Chicken Liver or Crab Pâté) can be piped onto little biscuits or pieces of Melba Toast. Tartlets can be filled with any quiche mixture and cooked at the last minute. Potato cakes served with a little smoked salmon or warm smoked trout garnished with dill and crème fraîche is another morish canapé.

For an Eastern flavour, spoon a little Mint Chutney (see page 594), Mango Relish (see page 92) or Spicy Aubergine (see page 552) onto miniature poppadoms, or top prawn crackers with spicy toppings or salsas.

One of the problems with canapés is that they often need to be assembled at the last moment. If they are prepared too far in advance they can become tired, limp and soggy. This is particularly true when using porous bases such as prawn crackers. Put the toppings on at the last possible minute otherwise they will melt through and do as much preparation as possible: arrange the bases on serving trays and have the garnish ready to go.

Quantities

Finger food should be bite-sized for easy eating and handling. On the whole you will need to allow 6 or 7 canapes per person. However, if your guests are coming straight from work they may be very hungry so allow 7 to 9 helpings per person and think about making the portions more substantial. If guests have already eaten, 5 or 6 each will be adequate.

In case of emergency, you may want to keep some really good-quality cocktail sausages on hand. They are quick to prepare and are very tasty tossed with grainy mustard and honey. These can be produced if it looks like the food might run out. Ballymaloe Brown Bread and Smoked Salmon (see page 556) is another fantastic standby.

Finger-food Etiquette

Surprisingly, not everyone seems to realise that it is bad manners to double-dip. To circumvent this, cut crudités into single bite-size pieces.

Olives

There are many sorts of olive; Greece is famous for its almost almond-shaped blue-black Kalamatas, and Italy has the Gaeta olives, all black and wrinkled. Spain comes in with tasty green Manzanillas and the French with Picholines and Niçoise. Olives can be cured in many ways – including dry, oil, lye, brine and water. They can be pitted and then stuffed – often with capers, anchovies or pimientos. They can be also be seasoned with a variety of flavourings such as garlic or cumin seeds.

Green or Black Olive Purée

Serve with goat's cheese.

225g (8oz) green or black olives, stoned
125ml (4fl oz) extra-virgin olive oil

Put the stoned olives and oil in a food-processor and pulse to purée coarsely. Transfer to a sterilised jar. Pour a layer of extra-virgin olive oil over the top. The purée will keep, covered in a fridge, for 1–2 weeks.

Note: Pouring a thin layer of olive oil over foods in jars – such as olive purée or tomato purée – makes the food last longer by excluding the air.

Marinated Olives

Serve with drinks or as part of an antipasti.

350g (12oz) black olives, Kalamata or Niçoise
1 teaspoon chilli flakes
1/2–1 teaspoon cumin, freshly crushed
lemon juice, freshly squeezed
125ml (4fl oz) extra-virgin olive oil

Mix the ingredients into a bowl and allow to marinade for at least 15 minutes.

Marinated Black or Green Olives

Marinated olives are served in all Greek tavernas; each has its own version.

225g (8oz) olives (Kalamata, Vollos, Moroccan Picholine, Tunisian Salhi)
1 garlic clove, crushed
1/2 teaspoon hot paprika
1 tablespoon sherry or red wine vinegar
pinch of ground cumin
2 tablespoons extra-virgin olive oil

Mix all the ingredients together and store in a jar. This way the olives will keep for several months.

Roasted Almonds

Preheat the oven to 180°C/350°F/gas 4.

Put dry whole, unpeeled, almonds onto a baking tray, and roast for about 10–15 minutes until golden and crisp. Toss in a little olive oil and sea salt, and leave to cool.

Spicy Fruit and Nuts
Serves 6–8

Delicious little spicy eats to serve with drinks.

4 tablespoons extra-virgin olive oil
1/2 teaspoon freshly ground coriander
1/2 teaspoon freshly ground cumin
120g (41/2oz) dates, stoned
60g (21/2oz) dried apricots
60g (21/2oz) almonds, whole, unblanched
60g (21/2oz) cashew nuts
60g (21/2oz) hazelnuts, halved
60g (21/2oz) pecans, halved
finely grated rind of 1 lemon or lime
1 red chilli, de-seeded and finely chopped
salt and freshly ground pepper

Heat the oil in a frying pan over a medium heat. Sprinkle in the coriander and cumin, stir, and then add all the dried fruit and nuts. Toss until they begin to change colour. Remove from the heat and add the lemon or lime zest, and chilli. Mix thoroughly, season to taste and serve.

Edamame with Sea Salt
Serves 4–8

These fresh soya beans in their pods are one of our favourite nibbles – they are not widely available fresh but can be found frozen and then cooked in minutes.

1.2 litres (2 pints) water
3 teaspoons sea salt
450g (1lb) edamame

Bring the water to the boil, add the salt and the edamame beans. Bring back to the boil, cook for 3–4 minutes. Taste – if cooked sufficiently they should have a slight bite. Drain and sprinkle with sea salt. Serve cold.

Greek Salad Kebabs
Makes 20

1/2–1 crisp cucumber, cut into cubes
20 cherry tomatoes
20 Kalamata olives
6 spring onions, cut into 2.5cm (1in) chunks
110g–150g (4–5oz) Feta or Knockalara ewe's milk cheese, cut into cubes

Dressing
3 tablespoons extra-virgin olive oil
1 tablespoon lemon juice, freshly squeezed
2 tablespoons annual marjoram, chopped
sprigs of flat-leaf parsley
salt, freshly cracked pepper and sugar

20 or so satay sticks

Thread a piece of cucumber, tomato, olive, spring onion, and a chunk of feta onto one end of a satay stick. Arrange on a round plate with the salad towards the centre. Just before serving, whisk the dressing, sprinkle over each kebab and serve immediately.

Parmesan Crisps

Makes 8–12 nibbles or serve on starter salads

8 tablespoons grated Parmesan

1 sheet silicone paper

Preheat the oven to 180°C/350°F/gas 4. Draw circles about 10cm (4in) in diameter on the silicone paper. Carefully fill the circles with the Parmesan. Spread the cheese in an even layer out to the edges of the circle. Cook in the moderate oven for 5–8 minutes until golden and bubbly. Remove from the oven and allow to cool on the tray.

Place gently onto a wire wrack. The disks may also be moulded into shapes just before they get cold. Store in an airtight container.

Note: Be careful not to over-cook or they will taste bitter.

Irish Cheddar Cheese Croquettes

Makes 50–60, depending on size

We get into big trouble if these crispy cheese croquettes are not on the Ballymaloe lunch buffet every Sunday. They are loved by children and grown ups, and are a particular favourite with vegetarians.

425ml (15fl oz) milk, infused with a few slices
   of carrot and onion
1 small bay leaf, 1 sprig of thyme and
   4 parsley stalks
225g (8oz) Roux (see page 580)
2 organic egg yolks
225g (8oz) mature Cheddar, grated
1 tablespoon chopped chives (optional)
salt and freshly ground pepper

seasoned flour
beaten organic egg
fine dried breadcrumbs
Tomato and Chilli Jam (see page 513) (optional)

Put the cold milk into a saucepan with the carrot, onion and herbs and bring slowly to the boil. Simmer for 3–4 minutes, turn off the heat and allow to infuse for about 10 minutes if you have enough time.

Strain the flavourings, rinse them and add to a stockpot if you have one on the go. Bring the milk back to the boil and whisk in the roux bit by bit; it will get very thick but persevere. (There always seems to be too much roux but you need it all so don't decide to use less.) Season with salt and pepper. Cook for 2 minutes on a gentle heat, then remove from the heat. Stir in the egg yolks, cheese and chives. Taste and correct seasoning. Spread out on a wide plate to cool.

When the mixture is cold or at least cool enough to handle, shape it into balls about the size of a golf ball weighing about 25g (1oz) each. First roll in seasoned flour then in beaten egg and then in breadcrumbs, and chill until firm. Bring them back to room temperature before cooking otherwise they may burst. Just before serving, heat a deep fryer to 150°C/300°F, cook the cheese croquettes until crisp and golden. Drain on kitchen paper and serve hot with a green salad and Sweet Chilli Jam or a good tomato chutney.

Note: Cooked cheese croquettes can be kept warm in an oven for up to 30 minutes. They can also be frozen and reheated in an oven.

Pollenza Bocconcini

I came across these pollenza in Piedmont, northern Italy, where several cafés on the main street served them as an aperitif.

oil for deep-frying
fresh breadcrumbs or a mixture of breadcrumbs
freshly grated Parmesan
bocconcini
flour, seasoned with a pinch of cayenne pepper or smoked paprika
beaten organic egg

Heat the oil in the deep fryer to 190°C/375°C. Mix an equal amount of breadcrumbs and grated Parmesan. Toss the bocconcini in the seasoned flour, then in the beaten egg and finally in the breadcrumb and Parmesan mixture. Deep-fry a few at a time. Drain on kitchen paper and serve immediately. Delicious on their own or with a dipping sauce.

Indian 'French Toast'
Serves 4

4 thickish slices of good white bread
3–4 organic eggs
rock or sea salt
1 small onion, finely chopped
1 green chilli chopped
4 tablespoons of freshly chopped coriander
oil for frying

First lightly toast the bread (in Calcutta it was chargrilled over charcoal). Whisk the eggs in a flattish dish and then add the salt, onion, green chilli and coriander. Dip one slice of bread into the egg, turning it over to make sure it is saturated on both sides. Heat the oil in a pan and then slap a slice of bread into it. Cook until crispy on both sides. Cut into quarters, sprinkle with rock salt and serve.

Melted Camembert with Celery Sticks and Breadsticks
See page 439

Gorgonzola and Fig Toasts
Makes 16

16 x crostini (see page 67)

110g (4oz) Gorgonzola
4 fresh figs (2 if large), cut into small wedges
16 wild rocket leaves

Spread each freshly cooked crostini with a little lump of Gorgonzola, top with a wedge of fresh fig and garnish with a little rocket leaf. Arrange on a platter and serve as soon as possible.

Torino Aperitivo
Makes 48 mini sandwiches (3–4 per person)

In Italy 'aperitivo' is very popular, especially in the north. An offering with the pre-dinner drink, it can be as small as a few potato chips and olives to an elaborate buffet including hot dishes and sometimes pizza. The latter is becoming an attraction in itself as many more bars aggressively compete for the 'aperitivo' crowd.

8 slices of good-quality white bread
soft butter or Tapenade (see page 301)

Filling
mozzarella
salt and freshly ground black pepper
radicchio
mayonnaise
freshly chopped flat-leaf parsley

satay sticks

Spread the bread with butter or tapenade. Top with a slice of mozzarella and season with salt and pepper. Add a leaf of radicchio to provide a delicious bitter note. Pop the other slice of bread on top and press down. Make some more sandwiches in the same way, experimenting with different fillings. I recommend mozzarella, tomato and basil, tuna mayonnaise, diced celery and chopped parsley, saucisson…

Spread the top of the sandwich with mayo and dip in the chopped parsley. Remove the crusts and cut into 6 squares. Thread 3 or 4 mini sandwiches, preferably with different fillings, onto a satay stick and serve with a glass of chilled white wine or prosecco.

Crostini with Spiced Aubergine
Makes about 24

For this dish, I do think it makes a difference to salt the aubergines before cooking.

Spiced Aubergine Topping
2 aubergines
1 teaspoon salt
50ml (2fl oz) olive oil
1 large onion, finely chopped
4 ripe tomatoes, skinned and coarsely chopped
sugar
½ teaspoon ground cumin
½ teaspoon ground allspice
pinch of cayenne pepper
2 garlic cloves, crushed
2 tablespoons raisins
1 heaped tablespoon fresh mint, chopped
1 heaped tablespoon fresh coriander, chopped

24 crostini, 5mm (¼in) thick (see page 67)

Garnish
natural yoghurt and fresh mint leaves (optional)

Cut the aubergines into 1cm (½in) cubes. Put them in a colander and sprinkle with a little salt. Mix together with your hands and leave to drain for 20–30 minutes. Meanwhile, heat 3 tablespoons of the olive oil in a pan and fry the onions until golden. Add the tomatoes, a pinch of sugar and the spices. Stew gently for 5–10 minutes, then stir in the garlic and take off the heat. Stir in the raisins.

Tip the aubergines into a clean tea towel and gently squeeze them dry. Put the remaining olive oil in your largest frying pan and heat until smoking.

Add the aubergines and stir-fry briskly until thoroughly golden and cooked through. Stir in the onion and tomato mixture, and the fresh herbs. Tip into a bowl and leave to cool. Taste for seasoning and add more if necessary. Spoon a little spiced aubergine onto each warm crostini. Top with a little blob of yoghurt and a sprig of mint if you fancy.

Anchovy and Mustard Sticks

Makes about 25

225g (8oz) Puff Pastry (see page 456)
Dijon mustard
about 24 anchovies, drained
egg wash made from 1 beaten organic egg
2 tablespoons grated Parmesan cheese

Preheat the oven to 180°C/350°F/gas 4.

Roll the pastry into 2 rectangles, 3mm (1/8in) thick. Trim the edges. Smear one piece of pastry with mustard, then arrange 4 rows of anchovies in lines lengthways about 2.5cm (1in) apart. Put the other sheet of pastry on top and seal. Refrigerate just before cooking. Egg wash the pastry, sprinkle with grated Parmesan, cut into 1cm (1/2in) wide strips widthways and bake for 15–20 minutes or until crisp and golden.

Anchovy and Sesame Seed Straws

Omit the mustard from the recipe above and replace the Parmesan with 2 tablespoons sesame seeds.

Filo Triangles

Makes 30–50 depending on size

filo pastry
melted butter

Filling of Your Choice
1 x Mushroom à la Crème (see page 201)
1 x Piperonata (see page 199)
1 x Scallops Mornay (see page 252)

Preheat the oven to 230°C/450°F/gas 8.

Cut a sheet of filo into 7.5cm (3in) strips lengthways. Put the strips on top of each other. Brush the top one with melted butter. Put 1 dessertspoon of your chosen filling at the front edge. Wrap the pastry around and then fold over and over into a triangle; seal the edge with melted butter. Repeat with the others until all the filling is used up.

Brush with melted butter and bake in the oven for 15–20 minutes. Arrange on a warmed plate and serve immediately.

Briouates

Makes about 25

Moroccan briouates are little stuffed parcels of paper-thin pastry deep-fried in oil. My favourite fillings are minced meat, prawn and chicken. If you prefer not to fry, you can bake them in the oven for 30 minutes at 180°C/350°F/gas 4.

The pastry leaves (*ouarka*) are so difficult and time consuming that I substitute filo instead. The traditional shapes are triangles, rectangles and cigars. This recipe comes from Claudia Roden's *Mediterranean Food*, which I love.

225g (8oz) filo pastry sheets
1 organic egg yolk, beaten
sunflower oil for deep-frying
icing sugar (optional)
cinnamon (optional)

Filling for Briouates de Kefta (minced meat pastries)
350g (12oz) lean minced beef
1/2 large onion, finely chopped
small bunch of coriander, finely chopped
small bunch of parsley, finely chopped
1 teaspoon cinnamon
pinch of ground ginger
salt
pinch of cayenne (optional)
3 tablespoons sunflower oil
4 organic eggs, lightly beaten

Mix together all the filling ingredients except the eggs, then transfer the mixture to a frying pan. Cook gently for a few minutes, stirring until the moisture evaporates and the meat separates. Drain off the fat, then add the eggs and stir until they are a slightly scrambled consistency.

Cut the filo sheets into rectangles about 12.5cm (5in) wide and stack them on top of each other. Take a sheet of pastry and put a heaped teaspoon of filling at one end and fold into a triangle. Stick the loose edge down with a little egg yolk. Fry in hot oil (180°C/350°F) until crisp and golden. Drain on kitchen paper and serve sprinkled with icing sugar and cinnamon if wished.

Haloumi Triangles

Makes about 15–20

4 filo pastry sheets
50g (2oz) butter, melted

Filling
110g (4oz) haloumi cheese, grated
110g (4oz) ricotta
1 organic egg
1 tablespoon finely chopped mint, parsley and chives
lots of freshly ground black pepper and sea salt
a little salt

To Serve
sweet chilli jam
Fresh Tomato sauce (see page 591) or salsa

Keep the filo covered with a damp cloth. Mix the ingredients for the filling together and correct the seasoning. Preheat the oven to 180°C/350°F/gas 4.

Cut each sheet of filo into four strips. Arrange the strips on top of each other to prevent them from drying out. Brush the top strip with melted butter and put a generous teaspoon of filling onto one end. Turn over and over into a triangle. Brush with melted butter. Repeat with the others.

Bake in the oven for 10–12 minutes. Serve with sprigs of fresh mint and a fresh tomato sauce or sweet chilli jam.

Filled Pretzels

Make larger pretzels (see page 493) and cook in the usual way. Split the pretzels horizontally, keeping them attached at the back. Fill with anything you fancy – tomato, brie and rocket; saucisson, Provolone and watercress

Crispy Potatoes with Sweet Chilli Sauce and Sour Cream

Serves 16

700g (1½lb) potatoes
salt
sweet chilli sauce
sour cream

Scrub the potatoes and cook in boiling salted water until tender. Drain and cool. Cut into wedges. Deep-fry in hot oil until crisp and golden. Drain on absorbent kitchen paper. Season with salt. Serve immediately with a bowl of sweet chilli sauce and sour cream on each plate.

Note: Rustic Roast Potatoes may also be used (see page 181).

Potato Wedges with Pappadew Pepper Dip

Serves 8 (makes 24-32 potato wedges)

4–8 old potatoes (depending on size)
extra-virgin olive oil
salt and freshly ground pepper

Pappadew Pepper Dip
6 pappadew peppers, drained
300ml (10fl oz) sour cream
1 tablespoon freshly chopped chives
2 tablespoons freshly chopped flat-leaf parsley
   or coriander
freshly cracked pepper
sea salt to taste

Preheat the oven to 200°C/400°F/gas 6.

Scrub the potatoes well. Cut into quarters or eighths lengthwise depending on size. The pieces should be chunky rather than skinny. Put into a roasting tin, drizzle with a little olive oil, toss to coat and sprinkle with salt. Roast for 20–30 minutes and drain on kitchen paper.

Meanwhile chop the pappadew peppers coarsely. Stir into the sour cream with the freshly chopped herbs and season with freshly cracked pepper and sea salt.

Avocado, Red Onion and Coriander Salsa on Mini Poppadoms

Makes 25

Best made close to serving time, but if you must make it ahead, don't season until just before serving.

1 avocado
3 very ripe tomatoes, de-seeded and diced
1 small red onion, finely diced
½–1 green chilli, finely diced (optional)
2 tablespoons coarsely chopped fresh coriander
juice of 1 lime, freshly squeezed
pinch of sugar (optional)
salt and freshly ground pepper

25 mini poppadoms (see page 492)
vegetable oil for deep-frying

Peel and stone the avocado and cut it into dice similar in size to the tomato. Put into a bowl with the onion, chilli and coriander, add the freshly squeezed lime juice, season with salt and pepper and toss gently.

Taste and add a pinch of sugar if necessary. Heat the oil to 180°C/350°F and deep-fry the poppadoms. Drain on kitchen paper.

Just before serving, spoon the salsa onto the poppadoms.

Quesadillas

See page 91

Rillettes of Fresh and Smoked Salmon on Cucumber Slices

Serves 30–40, or as a starter

The texture of this pâté should resemble that of pork rillettes, where the meat is torn into shreds rather then blended.

10g (½oz) butter
175g (6oz) smoked salmon
1 tablespoon water
175g (6oz) butter, softened
175g (6oz) salmon, freshly cooked
salt and freshly ground pepper
pinch of nutmeg
lemon juice to taste
1 cucumber

Garnish
sprigs of chervil, fennel and chives

Melt the butter in a low saucepan and add the smoked salmon and water. Cover and cook for 3–4 minutes or until it no longer looks opaque. Leave to get quite cold.

Cream the softened butter in a bowl. With 2 forks, shred the fresh and smoked salmon and mix well together. Add to the softened butter, still using a fork (do not use a food-processor). Season with salt, pepper and nutmeg. Taste. Add lemon juice as necessary.

Cut the cucumber into scant 5mm (¼in) thick slices. Arrange on a plate or flat basket and put a dollop of soft salmon pâté on top of each slice. Garnish with a sprig of chervil, fennel or some cheeky chives. Sprinkle with chive or fennel flowers too, if you have them.

Variations

Chicken Liver Pâté (see page 80), Salmon Pâté and Smoked Mackerel Pâté (see page 78) make great finger food, piped onto slices of cucumber or tiny pieces of Melba toast (see page 78).

RIGHT: Rillettes of Fresh and Smoked Salmon on Cucumber Slices

Prawns with Sage Leaves
Makes 20

10 rashers (slices) of streaky bacon
20 sage leaves
20 raw Dublin Bay prawns, de-veined and
    peeled
20 button mushrooms
oil for deep-frying
Rouille (see page 55)

20 cocktail sticks

Remove the rind from the bacon, cut each rasher in half crossways and with the back of a knife, stretch each rasher. Place 1 sage leaf on each prawn, then wrap a piece of bacon around each one.

Thread a mushroom, then a prawn on to each of 20 cocktail sticks. Heat the oil over a medium heat and deep fry the skewers until the bacon is golden and the prawns are pink. Drain on kitchen paper and serve hot with Rouille.

Oyster Shooters
Makes 24–28

These were all the rage at drinks parties in Australia when I went to *Tasting Australia* in Adelaide.

600ml (1 pint) mirin
400ml (14fl oz) sake
2 tablespoons Japanese rice vinegar
1½ tablespoons soy sauce
1½ tablespoons wasabi powder
24–28 oysters

24–28 shot glasses

Put the mirin and sake into a sauté pan, bring to the boil and allow to flambé. When the flames die down, turn off the heat, pour into a Pyrex measuring jug and leave to cool.

Add the vinegar, soy sauce and whisk in the wasabi powder. Cover and chill in the fridge overnight.

Just before serving, open the oysters and put one into each shot glass. Cover with chilled liquid (leaving the sediment behind in the measure). Serve immediately.

Tiny Triple Decker Smoked Salmon Sandwiches
Makes 24

butter
12 slices Ballymaloe Brown Yeast Bread (see
    page 478)
12 thin pieces of smoked salmon
freshly ground pepper
juice of 1 lemon

To Garnish
sprigs of fennel or dill

Butter the slices of bread and make a double-decker sandwich with the smoked salmon. Season each layer with pepper and a few drops of lemon juice, then butter the top of the sandwich. Trim a slice of smoked salmon to fit the top exactly, and press down onto the butter. Then trim off the crusts and cut the sandwiches into 6 tiny squares. Garnish each with a tiny sprig of fresh fennel or dill and serve.

Variations
Ballymaloe Brown Bread and Smoked Salmon
For a simpler version, simply butter slices of Ballymaloe Brown Yeast Bread, roll each piece of salmon into a loose rosette, and put a little drained Cucumber Pickle (see page 514) in the centre. Place on top of the bread and continue with the rest. Garnish with chervil and wild garlic flowers if available. Serve.

Good-quality salami can be used instead of smoked salmon; add a little chopped parsley to the butter for the bread.

Rory O'Connell's Fish Kebabs
Makes 20–30

1 red pepper, cut into 1cm (½in) dice
1 green pepper, cut into 1cm (½in) dice
1 medium onion, cut into 1cm (½in) dice and
    sweated in 25g (1oz) butter
150g (5oz) black sole fillet, cut into 1cm (½in)
    dice
150g (5oz) salmon, cut into 1cm (½in) dice
olive oil for frying
salt and freshly ground pepper
1 tablespoon chopped chives

Thread cocktail sticks with the above. Just before serving, fry them gently in a little olive oil, then season and sprinkle with chopped chives. Serve immediately.

Pigs in Blankets
Makes 8

Pigs in blankets are usually sausages in bacon but we like to use the name for these yummy little sausage rolls. We use chipolatas.

8 really good sausages, cooked
350g (12oz) puff or flaky pastry, chilled
1 organic egg, beaten with 1 tablespoon milk
    or water

Preheat the oven to 230°C/450°F/gas 8.

Roll the chilled pastry to a thickness of 4mm (¹⁄₁₆in), and cut into 2.5cm (1 in) strips. Wrap each cooked sausage in the pastry, allowing it to overlap slightly each time. Lay on a baking tray and chill. Egg wash each one just before baking for 10–12 minutes or until crisp and golden.

Parma Grissini

Roll a half slice of prosciutto di Parma around the end of a breadstick or grissini (see page 487). Delicious.

Parma Parcels

Makes about 20

10 slices Parma ham
about 20 balls of ripe melon
20 long chives

If the slices of Parma ham are large
enough, cut them in half. Put 1 large melon
ball into the centre of a piece of ham,
gather up the edges to enclose the filling
and tie with chives. Cover and chill until
ready to serve.

Teeny Yorkshire Puddings with Rare Roast Beef and Horseradish Sauce

Makes about 28

ABOVE: Teeny Yorkshire Puddings with Rare
Roast Beef and Horseradish Sauce

Chargrill a thick sirloin steak to medium
rare, rest and thinly slice just as needed to
make these delicious puds. You will need
1 or 2 muffin trays with tiny 4cm (1½in)
openings.

110g (4oz) plain flour
2 organic eggs
300ml (½ pint) milk
10g (½oz) butter, melted

sunflower oil for greasing the tins
Horseradish Sauce (see page 587)
175–225g (6–8oz) rare roast beef

To Garnish
rocket or flat leaf parsley leaves

Preheat the oven to 230°C/450°F/gas 8.

To make the batter: sift the flour into a
bowl, make a well in the centre and drop
in the eggs. Using a small whisk or wooden
spoon, stir continuously, gradually drawing
in flour from the sides, and adding the
milk in a steady stream at the same time.
When all the flour has been incorporated,
whisk in the remainder of the milk and
the cool melted butter. Allow to stand for
1 hour.

Heat the patty tins in the oven, grease with
sunflower oil and half fill with batter.

Bake in the preheated oven for 15 minutes
or until crisp, golden and bubbly. Remove
from the tins and cool on a wire rack.

To serve: fill each pudding with a tiny
dollop of Horseradish Sauce. Top with a
thin sliver of rare roast beef. Garnish with
a sprig of flat-leaf parsley or a rocket leaf.
Serve soon – best freshly cooked.

Variation

We also do these with pink lamb, a little
Apple and Mint Jelly (see page 507) and
watercress .

Spicy Chicken Wings

Serves about 10

Chicken wings have become a great
favourite; there are lots of delicious
marinades one can use – freshly chopped
herbs and olive oil are perfect also.

900g (2lb) chicken wings

Marinade
1 tablespoon Szechwan peppercorns, toasted
* and ground*
1 tablespoon crushed garlic
3 tablespoons grated ginger
3 tablespoons finely grated orange zest
4 spring onions, finely chopped
1 red chilli, finely chopped
2 tablespoons honey
2 tablespoons soy sauce
450ml (16fl oz) sunflower oil
125ml (4fl oz) sesame oil
salt and freshly ground pepper

Combine all the marinade ingredients in a
large bowl. Add the chicken wings and toss
in the marinade until well coated. Allow to
marinate for at least 4 hours or better still
overnight.

Preheat the oven to 180°C/350°F/gas 4.

Spread the chicken wings on 1 or 2
roasting tins and cook in the oven, turning
several times, for about 35 minutes. Serve
just as they are or with Red Chilli
Mayonnaise (see page 585).

Ginger and Sesame Chicken Wings

Serves about 10

In our house we squabble over the chicken wings; for me they are the tastiest part with perhaps the oyster pieces at the base of the legs a close runner up. Tossed in a little olive oil, freshly chopped herbs and sea salt and roasted until crisp and golden, they are lip-smackingly good. Alternatively, try this recipe – irresistible too, and easy to remember: 2 of everything.

50g (2oz) untoasted sesame seeds
900g (2lb) chicken wings

Marinade
50ml (2fl oz) honey
50ml (2fl oz) red wine
50ml (2fl oz) soy sauce
2 teaspoons freshly grated ginger

Mix all the marinade ingredients together. Boil for 2–3 minutes in a small saucepan. Add the sesame seeds and leave to get cold.

Separate the wings into joints if attached and discard the pinion (see page 279).

Marinate the wings for a few hours or better still overnight. Preheat the oven to 200°C/400°F/gas 6, bring the wings to room temperature and then cook for 30–45 minutes. Serve hot or at room temperature.

Thai Curry Chicken Morsels

Makes 30

These gorgeous morsels look great served on Chinese soup spoons.

450g (1lb) skinless and boneless chicken breasts, cut into 30 even-sized pieces
25g (1oz) butter
45g (1³/₄oz) fresh root ginger, peeled and finely chopped
2 garlic cloves, crushed
¼ teaspoon green peppercorns
1 stalk lemongrass, finely chopped
2 red chillies, finely chopped
1 teaspoon homemade Chicken Stock (see page 36)
½ teaspoon lime juice, freshly squeezed
½ teaspoon ground coriander
400ml (14fl oz) coconut milk (Chaokoh)
2 teaspoons freshly chopped coriander leaves
salt and freshly ground pepper

Melt the remaining butter in the pan, sauté the ginger, garlic, peppercorns, lemongrass and chillies. Add the chicken stock, lime juice and ground coriander. Gradually stir in the coconut milk, bring to the boil, then reduce the heat and simmer for about 4 minutes. Add the chicken cubes and cook for a further 4–6 minutes.

Stir in the coriander leaves and season to taste. Place a morsel of chicken on a chinese soup spoon. Spoon some sauce over the top and garnish with coriander leaves.

Alternatively, spike with cocktail sticks and arrange on a serving dish. Spoon the sauce over the chicken or serve separately as a dipping sauce. The chicken pieces may also be reheated in the sauce and served hot.

LEFT: Ginger and Sesame Chicken Wings

petit fours

Ballymaloe Fudge

Makes about 96

Ivan Allen, my father-in-law, could never resist Ballymaloe fudge at the end of a meal, no matter how good the dinner had been. We remember him every time we eat a piece of fudge.

225g (½lb) butter
1 x 410ml (14½oz) tin evaporated milk
200ml (7fl oz) water
900g (2lb) light brown sugar or caster sugar
3 teaspoons pure vanilla extract

23 x 33cm (9 x 13in) Swiss roll tin

Melt the butter in a heavy saucepan over a low heat. Add the milk, water, sugar and vanilla extract and stir with a whisk until the sugar is dissolved. Turn up the heat to simmer, and stir constantly until it reaches the soft ball stage. To test, put a blob of the fudge into a bowl of cold water. It should be firm but malleable.

Pull the saucepan off the heat, put the base of the saucepan into cold water, and stir until the fudge thickens and reaches the required consistency. Pour into a swiss roll tin and smooth out with a spatula. Allow to cool and then cut before completely cold.

Note: Evaporated milk is made by heating milk slowly in a strong vacuum to reduce the temperature at which it boils. Most of the water content evaporates and this thickened 'milk' is then sterilised when the temperature is rapidly raised. Condensed milk is evaporated milk which has been sweetened to preserve it.

Chocolate Cases

Makes 8–10

110g (4oz) best-quality dark chocolate
20 chocolate paper cases – use bun or sweet cases

Melt the chocolate until smooth in a very low oven or in a bowl over simmering water. Put 2 paper cases together and spread melted chocolate evenly over the inside of the paper case with the back of a teaspoon. Check that there are no 'see through' patches when you hold them up to the light; if there are, spread a little more chocolate in that area. Stand the paper cases upright to dry. Chill until they set hard, then carefully peel the paper off the cases (it is a good idea to do a few extra cases to allow for accidents).

Note: Chocolate cases can now be bought in supermarkets. The quality of the chocolate has improved so much that they are perfectly acceptable. The paper cases or bon bon cases can be bought from a newsagents or specialist kitchen shop.

Suggested Fillings

Bailey's Chocolate Cases
Fill the chocolate cases with Bailey's Cream liqueur – enjoy!

Sue's Hazelnut Whirls
Fill the chocolate cases with 1 toasted hazelnut. Pipe a rosette of Ganache (see right) on top. Dust with unsweetened cocoa powder.

Tiramisu
Fill the cases with Tiramisu (see page 410).

Ballymaloe Chocolates

Makes 24–30

24–30 chocolate cases (see left)

Chocolate Ganache
150ml (¼ pint) cream
110g (4oz) best-quality dark chocolate, roughly chopped
¼–½ tablespoon rum or orange liqueur (optional)

Decoration
Crushed Praline (see page 401) or crystallised violets or unsweetened cocoa powder

First make the Chocolate Cases (see left). Make a few extra cases to allow for accidents or thefts!

Next make the Chocolate Ganache: put the cream in a heavy, preferably stainless steel saucepan and bring it almost to the boil. Remove from the heat and add the chocolate. With a wooden spoon, stir the chocolate into the cream until it is completely melted. Transfer the chocolate cream to the bowl of a food mixer and allow it to cool to room temperature. Add the liqueur and whisk until it is just stiff enough to pipe. (Careful: it splits very easily if you overwhisk.)

To assemble: using a piping bag and a 8mm (³/8in) star nozzle, pipe a rosette of the mixture into peeled Chocolate Cases. Decorate each one with a little crushed praline or a crystallised violet leaf or a dusting of unsweetened cocoa powder.

Chocolate

According to legend, it was the god, Quetzalcoatl, who first taught the Aztecs how to make chocolate from the beans of the wild cocoa tree, *Theobroma Cacao* – *Theobroma* meaning 'food of the gods'. When we started the Ballymaloe Cookery School in the early eighties, it was still difficult for the general public to buy good cooking chocolate and we had to buy enormous quantities at a time in order to get the top-quality chocolate we wanted to use. Nowadays many brands of good chocolate are available such as Lindt, Menier, Suchard, Lesmé, Callebaut and Valrhona. Chocolate varies enormously in flavour. Different brands not only taste different but react differently in recipes, so experiment and choose a chocolate or chocolates to suit your taste and recipes. Working with chocolate is a fascinating art which requires skill and patience.

Melting chocolate

Chocolate needs to be melted with great care. It burns easily and is then irretrievable. This is the method we use: Break the chocolate into even-sized pieces. Put into a Pyrex bowl over a saucepan of water, and bring slowly to almost simmering point. Turn off the heat immediately and allow the bowl to sit over the saucepan. The water must not boil as the chocolate softens. Stir occasionally. Do not allow even a drop of water to get into the chocolate or the chocolate will block or seize. If this happens no amount of stirring will remedy the situation, however, if a few drops of vegetable oil or clarified butter are added it will loosen the mixture to the extent that it can be blended with other ingredients.

Note: If you need a large quantity of chocolate, do it in batches. Chocolate may also be melted in the microwave in a Pyrex or plastic bowl. Different brands melt at different rates.

Types of Chocolate

Unsweetened Chocolate

Unsweetened chocolate is just that – a cocoa mass with just a little cocoa butter added. The percentage varies from brand to brand. It keeps well and gives chocolate dishes a wonderfully expensive taste. Available in specialist shops and well worth seeking out.

Dark Chocolate

Bittersweet or semi-sweet chocolate. This must contain at least 34 per cent cocoa solids (cocoa mass and cocoa butter). The higher the percentage of cocoa solid, the better quality the chocolate. Check the label, many good brands of chocolate bars now have cocoa solids from 50–70 per cent. As a general rule, the higher the amount of cocoa solids the darker and more bitter the chocolate will be. Seek out Valrhona, Lindt, Menier, Suchard or, at least, Bourneville which will have approximately 34 per cent cocoa solids.

Milk Chocolate

Made from cocoa mass and milk which is usually added in condensed or dried form. It must contain at least 10 per cent cocoa mass and at least 12 per cent milk solids. Both dark and milk chocolate can have fruit, nuts, ginger, coffee and nut pastes added. It can be substituted for dark chocolate in most recipes but the flavour will be different.

White Chocolate

White chocolate is not strictly speaking chocolate. It contains no cocoa mass, it is merely a mixture of cocoa butter, sugar and flavouring. Buy the best quality otherwise it will be difficult to melt. Store in airtight containers; if it picks up moisture from the air it will be impossible to melt properly and may crack.

Chocolate-flavoured Coverings or Confectionery Coatings

A sweetened combination of vegetable fat instead of cocoa butter, flavouring and sometimes low-fat cocoa powder and/or dry milk solids. Understandably, it does not taste as good as chocolate and is much less expensive. It also comes in a variety of pastel colours.

Couverture

This is the chocolate of choice for most food professionals and pastry chefs. Couverture is a *quality* rather than a *type* of chocolate, with at least 32 per cent cocoa butter. Quality varies from one brand to another; some have a much higher cocoa butter content and have been conched for 2 or even 3 days. The best melt beautifully and are perfect for moulding, coating and hand dipping. Converture is sold through wholesalers and speciality kitchen shops.

Chocolate Drops

These are graded pieces of chocolate designed to stay whole while baking. Good for biscuits, cakes and desserts.

Tempering Chocolate

Some chocolate (e.g. couverture) need to be 'tempered' to stabilise the high cocoa butter content. Electric tempering machines are available but it can be done by hand. The chocolate is first heated to 43C°/110°F and then cooled to 26°C/80°F, then heated once more to 40°C/90°F before use. When chocolate is tempered it will cool with a perfect sheen.

Cocoa Powder

Cocoa powder is derived from cocoa mass or cocoa liquor which has almost all the cocoa butter removed. The pressed cake is then ground into a powder called cocoa.

Dutch Process Cocoa

Cocoa that has been alkalised. During manufacturing an alkali in the form of a soluble salt, such as potassium carbonate, neutralises the natural acidity of the cocoa bean thereby raising the pH level. Dutch process cocoa is usually darker in colour than 'natural' cocoa, and the latter has a stronger, more chocolatey flavour.

Ballymaloe Chocolates and Cream

Serves 10

10 Chocolate Cases (see page 559)
whipped or pouring cream

First make the Chocolate Cases, allow to cool and set. When they are hard, carefully peel off the paper.

To serve: arrange the chocolate cases on a plate, fill with a rosette of whipped cream or pouring cream. Your guests can drop the cream-filled chocolate cups into their coffee and allow them to melt or alternatively they may just pour in the cream and eat the chocolate – delicious either way.

Ballymaloe Chocolates with Grapes and Kirsch

Makes about 12–14 chocolates

12–14 Chocolate Cases (see page 559)

12 small seedless green grapes
6 tablespoons Stock Syrup (see page 568)
1 tablespoon Kirsch

First make the Chocolate Cases.

Peel the grapes. Put them into a small bowl, pour over the syrup and Kirsch and leave to macerate for about 10 minutes. Put a grape into each chocolate case and pour over the syrup. Serve as soon as possible, certainly within 2 hours.

Note: Best-quality dark chocolate should be melted very gently to avoid destabilising the formulation and making it look whitish on the outside. It can become hard and grainy if melted too fast. Always buy the best-quality chocolate you can afford.

Ballymaloe Chocolates with Banana, Walnuts, Rum and Raisins

Makes 12

Jamaica rum is quite different in colour (dark versus clear) and flavour from Bacardi rum, and should be used in all these recipes.

12 Chocolate Cases (see page 559)

2 tablespoons raisins
1–2 teaspoons Jamaica rum
2 round tablespoons banana (diced to about the same size as raisins)
2 level tablespoons chopped walnuts

Cover the raisins with hot water and allow to swell for 2 hours. Drain, then mix the plumped-up raisins, rum, banana and walnuts together. Taste, fill into little chocolate cases and serve in sweet papers.

Mary Jo's Chocolates

Makes about 50

Even though these homemade chocolates are a little fiddly, believe me, when you taste them you will reckon it was worth every minute!

300ml (½ pint) cream
225g (8oz) best-quality dark chocolate, roughly chopped
½–1 tablespoon rum or orange liqueur

For Coating the Chocolates
225g (8oz) best-quality dark chocolate
2 tablespoons flavourless oil (peanut or sunflower)

Put the cream in a heavy, preferably stainless steel saucepan and bring it almost to the boil. Remove from the heat and add the chocolate. With a wooden spoon, stir the chocolate into the cream until it is completely melted.

Transfer the chocolate cream to the bowl of a food mixer and allow it to cool to room temperature. Add the liqueur and whisk until it is just stiff enough to pipe. Using a piping bag and a 8mm (³⁄₈in) plain nozzle, pipe the mixture into small blobs onto a tray lined with silicone paper.

Smooth the top of the chocolates with your finger or better still, a teaspoon dipped regularly in iced water. Put the tray in the fridge to allow the chocolates to set.

Meanwhile, gently melt the chocolate to coat the chocolates, and stir in the oil. When the refrigerated chocolates have become quite cool, with the help of 2 forks dip them into the melted chocolate and coat them evenly. Place on a wire tray and allow to set. The chocolates are now ready to be served or may be decorated further by dribbling the top with more melted chocolate.

Store in a covered container in a cool place. They are best eaten on the same day but will in fact keep for 3 or 4 days.

Agen Chocolate Prunes

Makes 22

From Agen, a town in Aquitaine in the south of France, these are the aristocrat of prunes; soft and melting. Guaranteed to convert even the most ardent prune hater. You can also do these with dried apricots.

225g (8oz) best-quality dark chocolate
22 Agen prunes, stoned

Melt the chocolate gently in a Pyrex bowl over barely simmering water. Turn off the heat just as soon as the water comes to the boil – the chocolate will gradually melt in the hot bowl. Dip the prunes one at a time into the chocolate. Shake off the excess chocolate and allow to set on a baking tray covered with silicone paper.

Ballymaloe Chocolate Truffles

Makes 30–40

175g (6oz) best-quality dark chocolate
50g (2oz) unsweetened chocolate
1 tablespoon Jamaica rum
75g (3oz) unsalted butter
2 tablespoons cream
75g (3oz) praline, finely crushed
melted chocolate and unsweetened cocoa
 powder for finishing

Melt both chocolates over a gentle heat to a thick cream with the rum. Take off the heat, stir in the butter bit by bit, then add the cream and praline. Put small teaspoonfuls onto waxed or greaseproof paper. When set, have the melted chocolate ready. Put a little on the palms of the hands and lightly roll the truffles between them. Toss into a bowl of unsweetened cocoa powder. Brush off the surplus and put on racks to dry (see illustrations above).

LEFT: Ballymaloe Chocolate Truffles

Fruit and Nut Clusters
Makes 24

150g (5oz) best-quality dark chocolate
3 heaped tablespoons hazelnuts, shelled and
   toasted
3 heaped tablespoons raisins

Melt the chocolate in a Pyrex bowl very
gently over simmering water or in a very
low oven. Stir in the hazelnuts and raisins.
Drop clusters onto a baking tray with a
teaspoon. Allow to set in a cool place. Put
into dark brown sweet papers.

Caramelised Walnuts
Makes 20

40 walnut halves
75g (3oz) marzipan

Caramel
200g (7oz) sugar
125ml (4fl oz) water

Sandwich the walnut halves together with
marzipan. Dissolve the sugar for the
caramel in the water. Bring to the boil and
cook until it caramelises to a chestnut
brown colour. Remove from the heat and
use to coat the walnuts. Allow them to
harden on an oiled Swiss roll tin, in a dry
place. Serve in petit four cases.

Marzipan Dates
Makes 28

Use up any scraps of almond paste for
these dates. The best dates, in my
opionion, are Medjool dates from north
Africa. They are fat and juicy with thin
skin and have less fibre than many of the
other dates.

28 fresh Medjool dates
110g (4oz) almond paste or marzipan (see page
   443)
caster sugar
pistachio nuts, finely chopped (optional)

Split one side of the date and remove the
stone. Roll a little piece of marzipan into
an oblong shape and fit it neatly into the
opening. Smooth the top and roll the
stuffed date in sugar. Repeat the procedure
until all the dates and marzipan are used
up. Dip in finely chopped pistachio nuts, if
you like.

Chocolate-dipped Strawberries
Makes as many as are in the punnet!

1–2 punnets strawberries
110g (4oz) white chocolate
110g (4oz) dark chocolate

Melt both chocolates carefully in separate
bowls in a very low oven or over
simmering water. Hold each strawberry by
the calyx and dip it into the melted
chocolate about three-quarters of the way
up. Allow to drain slightly and place it on a
baking tray lined with silicone paper or tin
foil to set. Arrange on a white plate.

Glazed Fruits

Use un-hulled strawberries, cherries with
their stalks, grapes, segments of tangerine
or clementine or physalis.

225g (8oz) sugar
125ml (4fl oz) water

Dissolve the sugar in the water in a heavy
saucepan. Bring to the boil and cook to a
light caramel. Carefully dip the fruits into
the caramel to glaze them lightly. Put them
immediately onto silicone paper or onto an
oiled surface where the glaze will set hard.
Keep in a dry place and serve in individual
petit four cases within 1 hour.

Strawberry Amandine
Serves 24

150g (5oz) peeled almonds
175g (6oz) caster sugar
45g (1³/₄oz) candied angelica
1–2 egg whites
12 fresh strawberries

24 petit four cases

Grind the almonds in a food-processor
with the sugar. Cut some of the angelica
into little sticks, to resemble strawberry
stalks, and put aside until later. Chop the
remaining angelica finely and mix with the
almonds and sugar. Moisten the mixture
with enough egg white to make a paste.

Wash, hull and dry the strawberries.
Sprinkle a board with caster sugar. Take a
ball of paste for each strawberry and
flatten on the board into a round about
5cm (2in) across, 3mm (¹/₈in) thick.

Place a strawberry in the middle of each
and mould the paste around. Cut in half,
place the reserved angelica sticks in at one
end to resemble stalks and serve in petit
four cases. Serve within 4 hours.

Lemon Curd Tartlets

Preheat the oven to 250°C/475°F/gas 9. Fill
tiny petit four pastry cases with a blob of
Lemon Curd (see page 511), and pipe a
rosette of meringue on top. Bake in the
oven for 60 seconds.

Candied Peel Dipped in Sugar or Chocolate

Cut freshly made Candied Peel (see page
515) into 0.5–1cm (¹/₄–¹/₂in) thick slices and
roll it in caster sugar and serve with coffee.
Alternatively dip one end of Candied
Orange Peel in melted dark chocolate,
allow to set and serve.

Meringue Kisses with Chocolate or Cocoa

Makes about 40

2 organic egg whites
125g (4½oz) icing sugar

Decoration
110g (4oz) dark chocolate or 25g (1oz)
unsweetened cocoa

Preheat the oven to 150°C/300°F/gas 2. Line several baking trays with silicone paper.

Make the Meringue mixture (see page 394). Put the mixture into a piping bag with a tiny rosette nozzle. Pipe tiny rosettes onto baking trays. Bake in the oven for 30–45 minutes or until the meringue nests will lift easily off the paper. Turn off the oven and allow them to cool in the oven.

Arrange the 'kisses' on a plate and dredge with unsweetened cocoa powder. You could also dip the spiky tops of the meringue in melted chocolate and allow it to set before serving.

Melanie's Meringue Hearts

Makes 20–25

Adorable little heart-shaped meringues, perfect for wedding finger food or buffets.

Meringue mixture (see page 394)

whipped cream
silver dragees (balls)

Preheat the oven to 150°C/300°F/gas 2. Make the meringue mixture and pipe into tiny heart shapes before baking on trays lined with silicone paper.

Allow to cool before decorating each with a piped rosette of cream and a silver dragee.

Coconut Kisses

Makes about 35

2 organic egg whites
110g (4oz) caster sugar
100g (3½oz) desiccated coconut
40 hazelnut halves (optional)

Decoration
unsweetened cocoa (optional)
whipped cream (optional)

Preheat the oven to 150°C/300°F/gas 2. Line 2 baking trays with silicone paper.

In a spotlessly clean bowl whisk the egg whites with the caster sugar until very stiff, then gently fold in the desiccated coconut.

Drop teaspoonfuls of the mixture onto the baking trays. Pop a hazelnut on top of each one, if you like. Cook in the oven for 15–20 minutes or until crisp and dry. Allow to cool on the tray. Dredge some with unsweetened cocoa and leave some plain.

Almond and Orange Blossom Filo Fingers

Makes about 28

225g (8oz) filo pastry sheets
75g (3oz) unsalted butter, melted
225g (8oz) ground almonds
110g (4oz) caster sugar
3 tablespoons orange blossom water

Decoration
icing sugar

Preheat the oven to 180°C/350°F/gas 4.

Cut the sheets of filo into 4 rectangles and put them on top of each other so that they do not dry out. Brush the centre of each rectangle with melted butter.

Mix the ground almonds with sugar and orange blossom water. Put 1 teaspoon of the filling at the end of each rectangle. Roll up into a cigar shape, folding the longer

sides in over the filling midway. Brush with melted butter and bake in the oven for 20–30 minutes, or until slightly coloured. Serve cold, sprinkled with icing sugar.

Note: These pastries may be deep-fried instead. The oil should not be too hot and they only need a few minutes until they are lightly coloured. Filo pastries may be made in 2 shapes, cigars or triangles. If the pastries are filled with spinach they are sometimes made into snail shapes but the triangular shape is also used.

Tuiles d'Amandes

Makes about 15–20

25g (1oz) butter
110g (4oz) caster sugar
3 organic egg whites
50g (2oz) flour
1½ tablespoons nibbed or flaked almonds
few drops of pure vanilla extract

Preheat the oven to 220°C/425°F/gas 7.

Beat the butter and sugar together. Blend in the egg white carefully. Sift the flour over the mixture and add the almonds and a few drops of vanilla extract. Gently mix until a smooth batter is obtained. With a teaspoon, smooth the batter into 10cm (4in) rounds quite thinly onto a baking tray lined with silicone paper.

Place in the oven and cook for about 10 minutes until golden brown. Remove immediately from the oven and, with a flexible metal spatula, transfer to a tuile tray or lay them over a rolling pin. They will set very quickly and should be light and brittle. It is a good idea to bake just 2 tuiles first to see if the thickness and the size of the tuile is correct. If the batter proves to be too thick it can be thinned out with a little extra egg white.

drinks

Every evening in Ballymaloe there's a special children's tea at 5.30pm. The children choose what they'd like to eat and this is served with lots of homemade lemonade – exactly the same lemonade that Myrtle originally devised for her children to take to school instead of fizzy drinks. Now the students make this and many variations on the theme everyday at the school. These drinks are so quick to make and refreshing. The basic syrups keep for ages in the refrigerator and can also be frozen. We also make refreshing non-alcoholic drinks from the leftover syrups of compotes such as rhubarb and strawberry, gooseberry, elderflower, plum and apricot by diluting them with water and lemon juice if necessary and adding lots of ice. We're also into fancy ice cubes, so we pop all sorts of things into the icetrays – herb leaves, flowers and berries.

Iced Water

Jugs of iced water are essential at the table but think before you drop in slices of any old lemon; if you must add lemon, use unwaxed ones. I personally find it's not always an improvement – a sprig of fresh mint, lemon balm, sweet cicely or sweet geranium is my preferred addition.

Flavoured Ice Cubes

Use herb leaves such as mint, lemon balm, lemon verbena, sweet cicely or sweet geranium; edible flowers such as borage, violas and marigold petals; and berries such as cranberries, fraises des bois and raspberries.

Fill ice trays with water and put a leaf, flower or berry into each ice cube. Use in drinks or in homemade lemonade.

Star Anise Ice Cubes
Pop a piece of star anise into each cube of an ice tray. Fill with water and freeze.

Festive Ice Cubes
At Christmas put cranberry or pomegranate seeds into ice cubes.

Master Recipe
Stock Syrup
Makes 800ml (28fl oz)

450g (1lb) sugar
600ml (1 pint) cold water

Dissolve the sugar in the water over a gentle heat and bring to the boil. Boil for 2 minutes, then allow it to cool. Store in the fridge until needed.

Variations
Try the following flavoured stock syrups:

Rosemary Syrup
Follow the Master Recipe, adding 2 sprigs of rosemary to the pan with the sugar and water. Strain when cool, before storing. Use this as the basis of lemonades or fruit compotes.

Sweet Geranium Syrup
Follow the Master Recipe, adding 6–8 sweet geranium leaves to the pan with the sugar and water. Strain when cool, before storing.

Lavender Syrup
Follow the Master Recipe, adding 1–2 tablespoons of lavender to the sugar and water in the pan. Strain when cool, before storing.

Mint Syrup
Follow the Master Recipe, adding 4–6 sprigs of fresh mint, preferably spearmint, to the sugar and water in the pan. Strain when cool, before storing.

Lemongrass Syrup
Follow the Master Recipe, adding 2 stems lemongrass to the sugar and water in the pan. Strain when cool, before storing.

Elderflower Syrup

6 heads of elderflowers
175g (6oz) caster sugar
600ml (1 pint) cold water
zest and juice of 2 unwaxed lemons

Put the sugar and water into a saucepan over a medium heat. Stir until the sugar dissolves. Add the elderflowers, bring to the boil for 5 minutes, remove from the heat and add the zest and juice of the lemons. Leave aside to cool. Cover and leave to infuse for 24 hours. Strain and bottle. Dilute as desired.

Rose Hip Syrup
Makes 1.2 litres (2 pints)

This syrup is bursting with vitamin E. Use either wild rose hips (Rosa cavina) or the hips of Rosa rugosa. Serve with ice cream or use as the basis for a drink.

900g (2lb) rosehips
2.6 litres (4½ pints) water
450g (1lb) sugar

Bring 1.8 litres (3 pints) of water to the boil. Meanwhile chop or mince the rosehips and immediately add them to the water. Bring back to the boil. Remove from the heat and leave to infuse for 15 minutes.

Strain through muslin or a fine nylon sieve. Put the pulp back into the saucepan, add another 850ml (1½ pints) of water and bring back to the boil. Leave to infuse again as before, and strain. Pour all the juice into a clean saucepan and reduce, uncovered, to 850ml (1½ pints). Add the sugar, stir until dissolved and allow to boil for 5 minutes.

Pour the syrup into sterilised screw-cap bottles and seal titghtly. It will keep for months.

ABOVE: Homemade Lemonade

Homemade Lemonades

If you keep some chilled Stock Syrup made up in your fridge all these fresh fruit drinks are simplicity itself to make. They contain no preservatives so they should be served within a few hours of being made. Many different types of citrus fruit maybe used.

Master Recipe
Orange and Lemonade
Makes about 2 litres (3½ pints)

4 lemons
2 oranges
about 450ml (16fl oz) Stock Syrup (see left)
about 1.5 litres (2½ pints) water

Garnish
sprigs of fresh mint or lemon balm

Juice the fruit and mix with the stock syrup, adding water to taste. Pour into glasses, add an ice cube or two, garnish with sprigs of fresh mint or lemon balm and serve.

Variation
Limeade
Makes about 1 litre (2 pints)

5 limes
300ml (½ pint) Stock Syrup (see left)
700ml (1¼ pints) water
ice cubes

Garnish
sprigs of fresh mint or lemon balm

Follow the method of the Master Recipe, using limes instead of lemons and oranges. Taste and add more water if necessary.

Rosemary Lemonade
Makes 4–6 glasses

A delicious, thirst-quenching lemonade inspired by The Herb Farm in Seattle.

juice of 3 lemons, freshly squeezed
225ml (8fl oz) Rosemary Syrup (see opposite)
700ml (1¼ pints) water

Mix the lemon juice with the Rosemary Syrup and water. Add a little more syrup or water if necessary.

Lemongrass Lemonade
Serves about 6

If you want to have access to exotic ingredients in a rural area the only solution is to grow them yourselves. We've been growing lemongrass for several years and now have so much that we can afford to use it in all sorts of delicious ways. This is a wonderfully refreshing drink.

3 lemons
850ml (1½ pints) water
225ml (8fl oz) Lemongrass Syrup (see left)

Juice the lemons. Mix the juice, water and the cold Lemongrass Syrup in a jug. Mix well, taste and add more water if necessary. Serve chilled.

Blackcurrant Leaf Lemonade
Serves about 6

2 large handfuls of young blackcurrant leaves
600ml (1 pint) water
225g (8oz) granulated sugar
juice of 3 freshly squeezed lemons
700–850ml (1¼–1½ pints) still or sparkling
   water
ice cubes

Crush the blackcurrant leaves tightly in your hand (this helps to bring out the flavour), then put them into a stainless steel saucepan with the water and sugar. Stir to dissolve the sugar and bring to the boil slowly. Simmer for 2–3 minutes, then set aside to cool completely. When cold, add the lemon juice and the still or sparkling water. Taste and add more water if necessary. Serve chilled with lots of ice.

Ginger and Limeade with Star Anise Ice Cubes
Makes 8–10 glasses

125ml (4fl oz) lime and/or lemon juice, freshly squeezed
1 tablespoon finely grated fresh, peeled ginger
175g (6oz) sugar
450ml (³/₄ pint) water

Mix the lime juice with the ginger in a bowl. Put the sugar and water into a saucepan and bring to the boil, stirring constantly to dissolve the sugar. Let the syrup boil for 30 seconds, then allow it to completely cool. Add to the lime-ginger mixture. Cover and chill thoroughly.

Serve with star anise ice cubes (see page 568) and dilute with water to taste.

Agua de Jamaica (Rosella Drink)
Serves 4

In Mexico, the bright red flower sepals of the hibiscus are used to make drinks. The plant is known in Mexico as *Flor de Jamaica* and elsewhere as rosella sepals. In Egypt hibiscus tea is served widely. We buy them dried in the markets and you can buy them in Latin American or Mexican shops.

1 litre (1³/₄ pints) water
50g (2oz) dried rosella sepals
a little granulated sugar

Put the water and dried rosella in a large saucepan. Bring to the boil over a moderate heat. Allow to boil gently for 1 minute, remove from the heat and leave to stand for 15 minutes. Stir in a little sugar, sweetening to taste. Strain into a jug, cool, and then cover and chill very well. Serve ice-cold in tall tumblers with lots of ice.

Fresh Tomato Juice
Serves 5

This is only worth making when you have very well-flavoured vine-ripened tomatoes. We make it in late summer when our tomatoes have really developed an intense flavour.

450g (1lb) very ripe tomatoes, peeled and halved
1 spring onion with a little green leaf or 1 slice onion, 5cm (2in) in diameter and 5mm (¹/₄in) thick
3 large basil or mint leaves
2 teaspoons white wine vinegar
1 tablespoon olive oil
125ml (4fl oz) cold water
1 level teaspoon salt
1 teaspoon sugar
a few grinds of black pepper

Liquidise the ingredients together, then strain through a nylon sieve. Best when freshly made and better not kept for more than 8 hours. Serve unadorned in tall glasses.

Elderflower Sparkler
Makes about 4.5 litres (8 pints)

This magical recipe transforms perfectly ordinary ingredients into a delicious sparkling drink. Elder is common in hedgerows and has wonderfully fragrant flowers; pick in full bloom. Freeze heads of elderflower for up to 3 months.

2 heads of elderflowers
600g (1¹/₄lb) sugar
2 tablespoons white wine vinegar
4.5 litres (8 pints) cold water
1 lemon

Remove the peel from the lemon with a swivel top peeler and juice the lemon. Put the elderflower heads into a bowl with the lemon peel, lemon juice, sugar, vinegar and water. Leave for 24 hours, then strain into strong screw-top bottles.

Lay them on their sides in a cool place. After 2 weeks the elderflower should be sparkling and ready to drink. Despite the sparkle this drink is non-alcoholic.

Saudi Champagne
Serves 8

75g (3oz) sugar
6 lemons
125ml (4fl oz) water
1 dessert apple
1 litre (1³/₄ pint) apple juice
1 litre (1³/₄ pint) sparkling water
lots of fresh mint leaves

Put the sugar and water into a saucepan, and stir over a medium heat until the sugar dissolves and the water comes to the boil. Boil for 1–2 minutes. Cool.

Meanwhile, juice the lemons and put into a jug. Cut the apple into thin slices and cut each slice into 3 pieces. Add to the lemon juice with a bottle of apple juice and lots of mint leaves (tear some of them).

Just before serving, add the sparkling water and some ice cubes.

Homemade Ribena
Makes about 4.5 litres (8 pints)

This concentrated blackcurrant cordial packed with vitamin C is delicious diluted with sparkling or plain water or sparkling wine – it keeps for several months in a cool place. My sister-in-law Hazel Allen gave me this recipe.

1.1kg (2¹/₂lb) blackcurrants
2.6kg (6lb) sugar
4 litres (scant 7 pints) water
225ml (8fl oz) white wine vinegar

Boil the blackcurrants and water together in a stainless steel saucepan for 15 minutes. Strain and add the sugar to the liquid. Add the white wine vinegar. Boil for 3 minutes. Pour into sterilised bottles and seal well.

LEFT: Ginger and Limeade with Star Anise Ice Cubes

Sharbat (Apple Milk Drink)

For 2–4 people

2 red eating apples
2 tablespoons granulated sugar or 2 teaspoons rosewater or orange-flower water
500ml (18fl oz) cold milk
shaved ice (optional)

Peel, core and cube the apples. Put into a liquidiser with the sugar, orange-flower water and milk. Whizz at high speed for 15 seconds. Serve, with shaved ice, if desired, in small glasses.

Lassi

In India we came across many different Lassi, some sweet and some salty. They can be drunk with meals or as a refreshing beverage on a hot afternoon. The yoghurt is rich and wonderful in India, so don't dream of using low-fat yoghurt!

Salty Lassi

Serves 2

175ml (6fl oz) natural yoghurt
350ml (12fl oz) water and ice mixed
good pinch of salt
1 tablespoon fresh mint leaves (optional)

Whizz in a blender for a few seconds. Serve in chilled glasses.

Sweet Lassi

Serves 2

175ml (6fl oz) natural yoghurt
350ml (12fl oz) water and ice mixed
1–2 tablespoons caster sugar
¼–½ teaspoon rose water or kewra.

Whizz all the ingredients in a blender. Pour into chilled glasses and serve immediately.

Laxshmi's Lassi

Serves 1

Laxshmi Nair from Mumbai, whose family own the Leela Palace Hotel (where we spent a wonderful few days on a food trip) made this delicious and refreshing drink.

75ml (3fl oz) best quality plain yoghurt
175ml (6fl oz) water and ice mixed
½ green chilli, de-seeded and chopped
2 curry leaves
4 fresh mint leaves
pinch of salt

Put everything in a liquidiser and whizz for a few seconds. Serve in a tall glass.

Leela's Lassi

Serves 1

Leela Palace Hotel's chefs gave me this recipe.

tiny pinch saffron stamens
1 tablespoon water
225ml (8fl oz) plain yoghurt
1 tablespoon pistachio nuts
1 teaspoon sugar
1 teaspoon mint

Put the saffron stamens in a tiny bowl with 1 tablespoon of water and soak for 10–15 minutes. Then put everything except the saffron in the liquidiser. Pour into a tall glass and drizzle the saffron over the top.

Smoothie Classic

Serves 2

Smoothies and slushies, now all the rage, are clearly influenced by the lassi of India, and the sherbets of Morocco. This could be the granddaddy of all smoothies, developed in America and now sweeping Europe and Australia.

225ml (8fl oz) orange juice
1 punnet strawberries, hulled and quartered
2 fresh bananas, frozen and sliced
honey to taste

Pour the orange juice into a blender. Add the strawberries and bananas. Blend until smooth. Add a little honey to taste.

Tropical Smoothie

Makes 2 large drinks or 4 dessert servings

You can serve this as a dessert or a drink. Served right out of the food processor or blender, it's a delicious dessert sorbet; served in a glass with a straw it makes a refreshing cooler (add an extra 125ml/4fl oz orange juice right away if you are serving it as a drink). This recipe comes from More Heartsmart by Bonnie Stern

1 banana, sliced
75g (3oz) strawberries, sliced
75g (3oz) mango, cubed
125ml (4fl oz) orange juice
1 tablespoon honey, or more to taste
1 tablespoon lemon juice

Spread the banana, strawberries and mango on baking sheet and place in the freezer. Freeze until solid (about 2 hours). Place frozen fruit in food processor or blender. Add the orange juice, honey and lemon juice. Purée until smooth. Serve in dessert dishes with a spoon or in a glass with a straw.

Hawaii Slushie

Makes 2 large drinks or 4 pudding servings

You can serve this as a pudding or a drink.

1 banana
1 peach
150g (5oz) strawberries, sliced
150g (5oz) mango, cubed
125ml (4fl oz) orange juice
1 tablespoon honey or syrup, or more to taste
1 tablespoon lemon juice

Peel the banana and cut into chunks. Spread the banana, peach, strawberries and mango on a baking sheet and put into the freezer. It will take about 2 hours to freeze solid.

Place the frozen fruit in a liquidiser or blender. Add the orange juice, honey or syrup and lemon juice and whizz until smooth. Serve in a tall glass with a straw.

Fruit Punch

Makes about 30 glasses

900g (2lb) sugar
4 sweet geranium leaves (optional)
2.4 litres (4 pints) water
4 mandarins or clementines, peeled and thinly
  sliced
10 oranges
6 lemons or 4 lemons and 2 limes
4 bananas
275g (10oz) small seedless grapes
1.2 litres (2 pints) ginger ale
600ml (1 pint) cold strained tea
2.4 litres (4 pints) soda water

Garnish
sprigs of fresh mint or lemon balm

Put the sugar and sweet geranium leaves (if using) into a saucepan, cover with cold water and bring to the boil and simmer for 5 minutes. Allow to cool slightly, then add the peeled and thinly sliced mandarins or clementines. Juice the oranges, lemons and limes. Remove the sweet geranium leaves from the cold syrup and add the fruit juice, grapes and sliced bananas.

 Chill thoroughly, then add the ginger ale, cold tea and soda water. Just before serving, add lots of ice. A large punch bowl with sprigs of fresh mint or lemon balm floating on top looks very decorative.

ABOVE: Fruit Punch

Prosecco

A glass of chilled Prosecco is my favourite aperitif, either on its own or with a dash of elderflower cordial or fresh fruit purée (strawberry, raspberry or mango). A dash of blood orange juice or ruby grapefruit juice makes a very refreshing drink during the citrus fruit season in winter. Even just dropping a few fresh berries into the glass, without the purée, is a lovely touch.

Bucks Fizz

Also known as 'mimosa' in the US. Perfect for a special brunch. Pour some freshly squeezed orange juice into Champagne flutes and top with Champagne or sparkling white wine.

Frozen Lemon Vodka
Serves 10

225g (½lb) Spanish Lemon Ice-cream
 (see page 402), or bought lemon ice-cream
½ bottle vodka, chilled
tonic water

Chill 10 small tumblers for at least 1 hour before serving. Scoop out 10 small balls of lemon ice cream and place one in the bottom of each of the glasses. Pour over a shot of vodka and top up with tonic water to taste.

Limoncella (Lemon Liqueur)
Makes 1.5 litres (2½ pints) of delicious dynamite!

5 ripe, unwaxed lemons
450ml (¾ pint) vodka
450g (1lb) sugar
450ml (¾ pint) water

fine sieve or piece of cheesecloth

Remove the peel from the lemons with a swivel top peeler. Put the zest in a large glass jar or bottle capable of holding 1.5 litres (2½ pints). Pour the vodka over the top, cover and allow to stand in the sun for 8 days for the flavour to be extracted from the ingredients.

To make the limoncella: put the sugar and water into a saucepan. Bring to the boil, stirring to dissolve the sugar, simmer for 10 minutes, then set aside to cool.

Pour the lemon-flavoured vodka through a fine sieve or cheesecloth, discard the zest, and then pour the strained liquid back into the jar.

Stir in the sugar syrup. Mix well and leave for at least 10–15 days before drinking. Serve chilled as an aperitif. Better still if you can resist, keep it for several months before drinking, it will taste exquisite.

Sunset Stripper
Serves 4

125ml (4fl oz) tequila
6 tablespoons triple sec
6 tablespoons Cointreau
6 tablespoons fresh lime juice
125ml (4fl oz) fresh pineapple, diced and chilled

Place all the ingredients in a liquidiser and whizz until smooth. Serve in tall glasses.

Peachy Fizz
Serves 4–6

300ml (10fl oz) orange juice, freshly squeezed
150ml (5fl oz) peach schnapps
1 bottle sparkling wine
1 peach, peeled and thinly sliced
a few raspberries
mint leaves

Mix the orange juice and peach schnapps together. Add the sparkling wine at the last moment, followed by peach slices, a few raspberries and the mint leaves. Pour into chilled glasses and add ice if you wish.

Campari and Pink Grapefruit Juice
Serves 1

1 measure of Campari
pink grapefruit juice, freshly squeezed
ice cubes with mint leaves or pomegranate seeds

Choose a tall glass. Put in the ice cubes first, followed by Campari, and then fill with pink grapefruit juice.

Sea Breeze
Serves 1–2

75ml (3fl oz) cranberry juice
75ml (3fl oz) pink grapefruit juice
40ml (1½fl oz) vodka
lemon or lime slices

Mix the first 3 ingredients together in a jug and pour into tall glasses. Serve with lots of ice and a slice of lemon or lime.

Isaac's Ultimate Bloody Mary
Serves 10

3 tablespoons Worcestershire Sauce
1 teaspoon Tabasco sauce
1 teaspoon celery salt
5 tablespoons lemon juice, freshly squeezed
1 tablespoon orange juice, freshly squeezed
1 teaspoon horseradish, grated
1 teaspoon shallot, very finely chopped
1.8 litres (3 pints) tomato juice, fresh or tinned
2 tablespoons dry sherry
300ml (½ pint) vodka

Garnish
celery stalks

Blend everything but the vodka in a liquidiser. Strain the mixture through a fine sieve then stir in the vodka. Serve in glasses over ice and garnish with a stick of celery.

Damson or Sloe Gin
Makes enough to fill a 2 litre kilner jar

Damsons are wild plums (sometimes called bullaces), in season in autumn and less tart than sloes. Sloes are little tart berries that resemble tiny purple plums, and grow on prickly bushes in hedgerows or on top of stone walls. They are in season as the leaves fall from the trees.

850ml (1½ pints) damsons or sloes
350g (12oz) unrefined white sugar
1.2 litres (2 pints) gin

Wash and dry the damsons or sloes. Prick in several places, with a clean darning needle. Put them into a sterilised glass kilner jar, add the sugar and pour in the gin. Cover and seal tightly. Shake every couple of days to start with and then every now and again for 2–3 months, by which time it will be ready to strain and bottle.

Damson or sloe gin will improve on keeping so try to resist drinking it for few a few months – should be perfect by Christmas.

Sloe Gin and Tonic
Need I say more! Delicious.

Mulled Red Wine
Serves 4–6

One of the easiest ways to entertain friends in winter is to serve mulled wine.

110g (4oz) sugar
1 bottle of good red wine
thinly pared zest of 1 lemon
a small piece of cinnamon bark
a blade of mace
1 clove

Put the sugar into a stainless steel or cast-iron saucepan, pour the wine over and add all the other ingredients. Heat slowly, stirring to make sure the sugar is dissolved. When hot but not scalding, serve in wine glasses with a wedge of lemon in each if desired.

Christmas Punch

3 bottles of red wine
250g (9oz) sugar
3 cloves
1 cinnamon stick about 12cm (5in)
grated zest and juice of 1 lemon
grated zest of 1 and juice of 2 oranges
300ml (½ pint) Jamaican rum

Put all the ingredients except the orange and lemon juice into a stainless steel saucepan. Warm gently. Then add the juice, leave over the heat for 1–2 minutes and then serve warm (but not hot) in tall tumblers.

Master Recipe
Hot Port
Serves about 8

50g (2oz) sugar
225ml (8fl oz) good port
225ml (8fl oz) water
1 orange, quartered
1 small cinnamon stick
a blade of mace
8 cloves

Put the sugar into a stainless steel or cast-iron saucepan and pour the port and water over. Stud the orange with the cloves and add to the saucepan with the cinnamon and mace. Heat slowly, stirring to make sure the sugar is dissolved. When it is hot but not boiling, serve in glasses with a wedge of orange in each one if you like.

Hot Rum
Use rum instead of port in the above recipe.

Irish Whiskey Punch
Serves 1

This most warming beverage is guaranteed to restore your spirits if you feel a cold coming on! Even if you don't try it anyway – nothing could be more comforting to sip by a roaring fire on a winter's evening.

75ml (3fl oz) Irish whiskey
1 segment of lemon
3 or 4 cloves
2 teaspoons sugar
boiling water

Put the whiskey and sugar into a robust glass. Stick the cloves into the segment of lemon and add; fill to the top with boiling water, stir to dissolve the sugar and serve immediately.

Doreen Costine's Gaelic Coffee
Serves 1

Gaelic coffee always puts me in mind of my father-in-law, who always managed to end up with a white moustache as he carefully sipped it, much to the general hilarity of his grandchildren!
Doreen Costine demonstrates how to make the most irresistible velvety Gaelic coffee to our students on every 12 week course.

Sláinte agus saol agat – health and long life to you!

2 teaspoons soft brown sugar
1 measure Irish whiskey
strong black coffee
softly whipped cream

Warm a medium-sized wine glass with hot water. Pour out the water and put the sugar and whiskey into the glass. Add the coffee and stir well. Pour the cream out of a jug over the back of a spoon onto the top of the coffee. The cream should float at the top, so don't attempt to stir. The hot whiskey flavoured coffee should be drunk through the cold cream – one of the very best Irish traditions!

Frappuccino
Serves 2

225ml (8fl oz) strong, fresh Espresso coffee, chilled
1 tablespoon caster sugar
225ml (8fl oz) crushed ice cubes
3 tablespoons double cream

Pour the coffee, sugar and crushed ice into a blender or food processor. Whizz until light and frothy. Stir in the cream, pour into 2 glasses and serve immediately.

Claudia Roden's Turkish Coffee

Serves 1

1 very heaped teaspoon pulverised coffee beans
1 heaped teaspoon sugar, or less to taste
1 small coffee cup water

Although it is more common to boil the water and sugar alone first and then add the coffee, it is customary in my family to put the coffee, sugar and water in the kanaka or pot (a small saucepan is not successful), and bring them to the boil together. By 'very heaped teaspoon' of coffee I mean, in this case, so heaped that it is more than 2 teaspoons. A level teaspoon of sugar will make a 'medium' coffee.

Bring to the boil. When the froth begins to rise, remove from the heat, stir, and return to the heat until the froth rises again. Then remove, give the pot a little tap against the side of the stove, and repeat once again. Pour immediately into little cups, allowing a little froth (wesh) for each cup. (Froth is forced out by making your hand tremble as you serve). Serve very hot. The grounds will settle at the bottom of the cup. Do not stir them up or drink them.

Try flavouring the coffee with a few drops of orange blossom water, cardamom seeds (called heil) or a little cinnamon, adding the flavouring while the coffee is still on the stove.

Herb Teas and Infusions

We make fresh herb teas or infusions a lot. I've got a particular aversion to the little tea bags that are frequently used. If you have fresh herbs all you need to do is pop a few into a pot and pour on the boiling water. Infinitely more delicious. I'm very wary about ordering herb tea in a restaurant for this reason, but one Paris restaurant I dined in recently served herb infusions in the most delightful way. The waiter came to the table with several china bowls of fresh herbs on a silver salver. With tiny silver tongs he put the guest's chosen herb into a little china teapot, poured on boiling water and served it with flourish. Exquisite.

Bring fresh cold water to the boil. Scald a china tea pot, take a generous pinch of fresh herb leaves (such as lemon verbena, rosemary, sweet geranium, lemon balm, spearmint or peppermint) and crush them gently in your hand. The quantity will depend on the strength of the herb and how intense an infusion you enjoy. Put them into the scalded water. Pour the boiling water over the leaves, cover the teapot and allow to infuse for 3–4 minutes. Serve immediately in china cups.

Master Recipe
Moroccan Mint Tea

Serves 4

2 teaspoons Chinese green tea
4 tablespoons chopped mint, preferably
    spearmint
850ml (1½ pints) water
sugar, to taste

To decorate
4 lemon slices (optional)
4 small mint sprigs

Heat a teapot with boiling water. Add the tea and mint to the pot and fill it with boiling water. Allow to infuse and stand for 5 minutes.

Pour the tea through a strainer into warmed glasses or small cups. Add sugar to taste (remember, in Morocco, tea is supposed to be very sweet) and decorate each glass or cup with a lemon slice, if liked, and a sprig of mint.

Variation
Iced Mint Tea

Follow the Master Recipe, adding the sugar to the pot with the tea and mint. After steeping, pour the tea through a strainer over cracked ice so it cools quickly. Serve in cold glasses with ice cubes, decorated in the same way.

Mulled Apple Juice

Serves 8–16 depending on the size of glass

1 orange preferably unwaxed and organic
8 whole cloves
750ml (1 ¼ pints) pure apple juice
750ml (1 ¼ pints) water
85g (3oz) golden caster sugar
3 small cinnamon sticks
6 star anise
½ teaspoon freshly grated nutmeg

Wash the orange in warm water and stud it with the whole cloves, aiming to have 2 cloves in each segment of the orange. Then cut into 8 segments and divide each segment in half.

Pour the apple juice and water into a stainless steel saucepan, add the sugar and spices and then the orange segments. Heat gently. Taste and add more sugar if necessary.

Serve with a slice of orange in each glass.

Mexican Hot Chocolate

Serves 1

225ml (8fl oz) water or milk or a mixture
35g (1½oz) Mexican or any unsweetened
    (bitter) chocolate

Put the water or milk in a saucepan together with the chocolate and slowly bring to a simmer over a low heat. Stir until the chocolate has melted, and then continue to heat gently for 4–5 minutes to blend the flavours. Pour the chocolate into a jug and beat with a molinillo until frothy. If a molinillo is not available, use a whisk or an electric mixer. Pour the chocolate into a mug and serve at once.

RIGHT: Mexican Hot Chocolate

sauces

A complementary sauce, judiciously made and served can turn a simple meal into a feast. Equally a sauce that is too abundant or luscious can make a meal seem hopelessly rich and cloying.

Many of the sauces in this chapter are what we refer to as 'Mother' sauces. Once you have mastered the initial recipe a myriad of 'daughter' sauces can be made by adding some other ingredients to the basic recipe.

The classic sauces such as mayonnaise, hollandaise, bearnaise and beurre blanc are still much loved and it's well worth mastering them. Mayonnaise in particular seems like a mystery to many people but I show students on every course how to make it by hand in less than five minutes – it is so fast to make that one would scarcely have found one's car keys to go to the village to buy it! Hollandaise sauce is also very quick to make and can transform a piece of fresh fish into a feast.

Fresh tasting salsas and pestos are gaining in popularity and diversity and people are also becoming more adventurous with salad dressings and flavoured oils and vinegars.

Roux

Roux is used as a thickener in flour-based sauces and occasionally in gravies. Make in small or large quantities – it's brilliant to have some on hand. Roux can be stored in a cool place and used as required or made up on the spot if you prefer. It will keep at least a fortnight in the fridge.

110g (4oz) butter
110g (4oz) white flour

Melt the butter, add the flour, combine, and cook for 2 minutes on a low heat, stirring occasionally.

ABOVE: Roux

White Sauce

Makes 600ml (1 pint)

This method is a marvellously quick way to make White Sauce or Béchamel if you already have Roux prepared.

600ml (1 pint) milk (not low fat)
50g (2oz) Roux (see left)
salt and freshly ground pepper

Bring the milk to the boil, thicken with roux and season. This simple white sauce can be the basis of a number of flavoured sauces.

Mother Sauce
Béchamel Sauce

Makes 300ml (½ pint), serves 3–4 approx.

To make a classic Béchamel one starts by making Roux in a saucepan, and then gradually adding in the milk, whisking all the time to avoid lumps. However, if you already have Roux prepared it's faster, and equally good, to simply whisk Roux into boiling milk to the required consistency.

300ml (½ pint) milk (not low fat)
a few slices of carrot
a few slices of onion
small sprig of thyme
small sprig of parsley
3 peppercorns
35g (1½oz) Roux (see left)
salt and freshly ground pepper

Put the cold milk into a saucepan with the carrot, onion, peppercorns, thyme and parsley. Bring to the boil, simmer for 4–5 minutes, remove from the heat and leave to infuse for 10 minutes.

Strain out the vegetables and herbs, bring the milk back to the boil and whisk in the roux to thicken to a light coating consistency. Allow to bubble gently for 4–5 minutes. Season with salt and pepper, taste and correct the seasoning if necessary.

Daughter Sauces
Parsley Sauce

Serve with boiled bacon, ham, poached fish... Follow the recipe for White or Béchamel Sauce until thickened with roux to a light coating consistency. Then add 25–50g (1–2oz) freshly chopped parsley and simmer on a very low heat for 4–5 minutes. Taste and correct the seasoning.

Mornay Sauce or Cheddar Cheese Sauce

The classic sauce for cauliflower cheese, leek gratin... Follow the recipe for Béchamel or White Sauce until thickened with roux to a light coating consistency. Add 110g (4oz) mature Cheddar and ¼ teaspoon mustard, preferably Dijon. Season with salt and freshly ground pepper, taste and correct the seasoning if necessary.

Egg and Parsley Sauce

Serve with vegetables or smoked haddock. Add 2 roughly chopped hard-boiled eggs plus 2 tablespoons of finely chopped parsley to 600ml (1 pint) Bechamel Sauce. You can also add ½–1 tablespoon of finely chopped chives.

Gluten-free Bechamel Sauce

Makes 600ml (1 pint)

A recipe from Rosemary Kearney.

600ml (1 pint) milk
few slices of carrot and onion
3 peppercorns
sprig of thyme
4 parsley stalks
50g (2oz) butter
25g (1oz) cornflour
25g (1oz) rice flour
salt and freshly ground pepper

Put the cold milk into a saucepan with the carrot, onion, thyme, peppercorns and parsley. Bring to the boil, simmer for 4–5 minutes, remove from the heat and cool. Strain out the vegetables.

Melt the butter in a saucepan and stir in the flours over a low heat. Pour in the milk, whisking continuously and allow to thicken. Season if necessary.

Onion Sauce

Serves 8–10

Also known as Sauce Soubise, this sauce is great with roast lamb or pan-grilled lamb chops. Onion sauce is a forgotten flavour which makes a welcome change from the more usual mint jelly.

3 onions, about 450g (1lb) in weight, thinly sliced or finely chopped
50g (2oz) butter
½ teaspoon salt
¼ teaspoon freshly ground pepper
½ tablespoon flour
300ml (½ pint) milk or 250ml (9fl oz) milk and 50ml (1fl oz) cream

Melt the butter over a gentle heat, add the onions and cook in a covered saucepan on a low heat until really soft but not coloured (up to 1 hour). Season. Stir in the flour, add the milk, and simmer gently for a further 5 minutes. This sauce keeps for 3–4 days covered in the fridge.

Onion and Mint Sauce

Add 2–3 tablespoons freshly chopped mint to the Onion Sauce above before serving.

Mother Sauce
Velouté Sauce

Makes 600ml (1 pint)

This 'mother sauce' can be made with veal, chicken or fish stock. A velouté is usually enriched either with a liaison of egg yolks and cream or with butter just before serving. It is very good with fish, poultry, veal, vegetables and eggs.

600ml (1 pint) well-flavoured Veal, Chicken or Fish stock (see page 36)
Roux (see page 580)
salt and freshly ground pepper

Bring the stock to the boil, gradually whisk into the roux, then bring back to the boil whisking all the time. Season. Simmer for 5–10 minutes, until the flavour and consistency are as required.

Daughter Sauces
Sauce Supreme

Serve with chicken. Add 2 tablespoons of cream to the Master Recipe made with Chicken Stock. Season, whisk in 50g (2oz) butter just before serving.

Mushroom Sauce

Serve with chicken, veal or fish. Add 110g (4oz) sliced or finely chopped, sautéed mushrooms to a Sauce Supreme before whisking in the butter.

Sauce Aurore

Serve with fish, pork, sweetbreads and eggs. Add 2 tablespoons of concentrated Tomato Purée (see page 50) to a basic Velouté Sauce. Season, and whisk in 50g (2oz) butter just before serving.

Mother Sauce
Hollandaise Sauce

Serves 4–6 (depends what it is served with)

Hollandaise is the mother of all the warm emulsion sauces. The classic version is made with a reduction but, with our superb Irish butter, we rather favour this version which is both easy and delicious. Like mayonnaise it takes less than 5 minutes to make and transforms any fish into a feast. You don't need a double boiler or any special equipment, just a good heavy-bottomed saucepan and a little whisk. Once the sauce is made it must be kept warm, although the temperature should not go above 180°F/350°C or the sauce will curdle. A thermos flask can provide a simple solution on a small scale, otherwise put the sauce into a porcelain, Pyrex or plastic bowl in a saucepan over hot but not simmering water.

Hollandaise Sauce cannot be reheated absolutely successfully so it's best to make just the quantity you need. If, however, you do have a little left over, use it to enrich other sauces, enliven a fish pie, or beat it into mashed potato.

2 organic egg yolks
1 dessertspoon cold water
110g (4oz) butter, diced
1 teaspoon lemon juice, to taste

Put the egg yolks in a heavy stainless-steel saucepan on a low heat, or in a bowl over hot water. Add water and whisk thoroughly.

Add the butter bit by bit, whisking all the time. As soon as one piece melts, add the next. The mixture will gradually thicken but if it shows signs of becoming too thick or slightly scrambling, remove from the heat immediately and add a tablespoon or two of cold water. Do not leave the pan or stop whisking until the sauce is made.

Finally add the lemon juice to taste. If the sauce is slow to thicken it may be because you are excessively cautious and the heat is too low. Increase the heat slightly and continue to whisk until the sauce thickens to coating consistency.

TIP: If you are making Hollandaise Sauce in a saucepan directly over the heat, it should be possible to put your hand on the side of the saucepan at any stage. If the saucepan feels too hot for your hand it is also too hot for the sauce. If you are making Hollandaise for the first time keep a bowl of cold water close by so you can plunge the bottom of the saucepan into it if it becomes too hot.

Daughter Sauces
Cucumber Hollandaise

¼ cucumber, peeled and cut into tiny dice
5g (¼oz) butter
1 teaspoon finely chopped fennel (herb)
salt and freshly ground pepper

Follow the Master Recipe. Pour the Hollandaise into a bowl and keep warm over hot but not boiling water. Melt the butter and toss the cucumber in it for 1–2 minutes. Add to the sauce with the fennel.

Sauce Maltaise (Maltese Sauce)

This is particularly good with asparagus. Cut the zest of half a Seville orange into needle-like shreds, blanch in boiling water for 1–2 minutes, drain and add to 300ml (½ pint) Hollandaise Sauce. Add the juice of half the orange, taste for seasoning and serve.

Sauce Mireille

Serve with eggs, asparagus, fish, artichoke hearts, Jerusalem artichokes or offal. Add 1½ tablespoons Tomato Purée (see page 50) and ½ teaspoon finely chopped basil to 300ml (½ pint) Hollandaise Sauce. Taste for seasoning.

Sauce Noisette

Serve with poached eggs, broccoli, asparagus... Use *beurre noisette* rather than ordinary melted butter to make the Hollandaise: cook it over medium heat until nut brown, then proceed as in Master Recipe.

Sauce Moutarde

Serve with eggs and fish or vegetables. Add 1–2 teaspoons Dijon mustard to 300ml (½ pint) Hollandaise Sauce.

Sauce Mousseline

Serve with asparagus, fish, chicken or sautéed sweetbreads. Add 4 tablespoons stiffly whipped double cream to 300ml (½ pint) Hollandaise Sauce. Taste for seasoning.

TIP: If using unsalted butter, all these sauces will need a pinch or two of salt.

Quick Hollandaise Sauce

There is an even faster way to make great Hollandaise. Using the same ingredients as for Hollandaise Sauce, melt the butter and heat until it foams. Then gradually pour into the eggs, whisking all the time until it thickens to a light coating consistency. Taste for seasoning. One can use the same method using a blender or food processor.

Light Hollandaise Sauce

Following either the Master Recipe or the above recipe, whisk 2 tablespoons of water into the sauce to lighten.

Bretonne Sauce

Serves 4–6 (depends what served with)

A really delicious sauce to serve with prawns (see page 254) or poached mackerel.

50g (2oz) butter, melted
2 organic eggs yolks
1 teaspoon Dijon mustard
2 teaspoons white wine vinegar
1 tablespoon chopped parsley, or a mixture
  of chervil, chives, tarragon and fennel

Melt the butter and allow to boil. Put the egg yolks into a Pyrex bowl, add the mustard, wine vinegar and herbs. Mix well. Whisk the hot melted butter into the egg mixture little by little so that the sauce emulsifies. Keep warm by placing the bowl in a saucepan of hot but not boiling water.

Mother Sauce
Sauce Beurre Blanc

Makes about 225ml (8fl oz)
Serve 2–3 tablespoons per person

This classic French butter sauce was the darling of the nouvelle cuisine era. In the restaurants of the Loire, its place of origin, it would traditionally be made with fine local butter and Muscadet wine and served with pike from the river. It is so versatile, many variations on the master recipe are possible – hence beurre blanc is another mother sauce. As people become more conscious of rich foods, though, this sauce is no longer a 'must have' on every menu. That said, try a little with freshly poached fish – it really is exquisite.

3 tablespoons dry white wine
3 tablespoons white wine vinegar
1 tablespoon finely chopped shallots
pinch of ground white pepper
1 tablespoon double cream
175g (6oz) unsalted butter, diced
salt, freshly ground pepper
lemon juice, freshly squeezed

Put the first four ingredients into a stainless-steel saucepan over a medium heat. Bring to the boil and reduce down to about a tablespoon. Add 1 generous tablespoon of cream and reduce again until the cream begins to thicken. Whisk in the chilled butter a piece at the time, keeping the sauce just warm enough to absorb the butter. Season with salt, taste and add a little lemon juice if necessary. Keep warm until needed – either transfer to a Pyrex bowl over a saucepan of hot but not boiling water, or put it in a Thermos flask.

Daughter Sauces
Sauce Beurre Rouge
Serve with fish or meat. Substitute 3 tablespoons red wine and 3 tablespoons red wine vinegar for the white wine and white wine vinegar in the Master Recipe.

Orange Beurre Blanc
Serve with John Dory or whiting. Add the finely grated rind of one organic or unwaxed orange to the Master Recipe. If you cannot find organic oranges, scrub the skin well before using the zest.

Sauce Beurre d'Anchois
Serve with beef, fish or vegetables. Add 2 finely chopped anchovies to the Master Recipe.

Saffron Beurre Blanc
Serve with fish and shellfish. Soak a good pinch of saffron in the cream. Add to the reduction and continue as in the Master Recipe.

TIP: Beurre blanc can curdle if the pan gets too hot. If this should happen put 1–2 tablespoons of cream into a clean saucepan, reduce to about half, then vigorously whisk in the curdled mixture, little by little. Serve as quickly as possible. The flavour will be a little softer, so you may need a little more lemon juice to sharpen it up and cut the richness.

Rosemary Butter Sauce
Serve with sole, turbot or crab claws. Add 1 tablespoon of freshly chopped rosemary to the reduction and continue as in Master Recipe.

Shrimp Butter Sauce
Serve with fish mousse or baked plaice, lemon sole or turbot. Add 110g (4oz) peeled cooked shrimps to the Master Recipe.

Lobster Butter Sauce
Serve with fish mousse or poached or baked fish. Add 110g (4oz) diced cooked lobster to the Master Recipe.

Crab Butter Sauce
Serve with fish. Add 110g (4oz) cooked crab meat to the Master Recipe.

Sauce Beurre Rouge

Orange Beurre Blanc

Sauce Beurre d'Anchois

Saffron Beurre Blanc

Beurre Blanc

Oyster Butter Sauce

Serve with baked sole or fish mousse.
Heat 10g (½oz) butter in a frying pan,
add 8 freshly opened oysters. Cook for 2–3
minutes, just until the edges are starting to
curl, add a squeeze of lemon juice, and add
to the Master Recipe.

Ginger Beurre Blanc

Delicious with John Dory. Add 2.5cm (1in)
cube of fresh green ginger, peeled and cut
into small dice, to the wine, vinegar and
shallots and follow the Master Recipe.

Mother Sauce
Mayonnaise

Makes 350ml (12fl oz), serves 8–10

Mayonnaise is the 'mother' of all the cold
emulsion sauces, so once you can make it
you can make any of the daughter sauces
by just adding some extra ingredients.
The quality of mayonnaise depends totally
on the quality of the egg yolks, oil and
vinegar used. A little mustard helps
the emulsion. If you use poor-quality
ingredients the mayonnaise will be bland.

Many mayonnaise recipes call for olive oil,
but extra-virgin olive oil will be too strong
for most tastes. We use 7 parts sunflower
or groundnut oil and 1 part extra-virgin
olive oil, or 6 to 2 for a more distinct olive
flavour. If you use the best quality, you
can also make it with all vegetable oil. If
you would rather use all olive oil you may
want to choose pure olive oil, rather than
extra-virgin.

Homemade mayonnaise does not have
preservatives added like commercial
brands, but will keep perfectly for at least
a week depending on the freshness of the
eggs. I've happily eaten mayonnaise 3
weeks after I've made it, but then I know
exactly where the eggs come from.

2 organic egg yolks
¼ teaspoon salt
¼ teaspoon Dijon mustard or pinch of English
  mustard
1 dessertspoon white wine vinegar
225ml (8fl oz) oil (sunflower, groundnut or
  olive oil or a mixture, 7:1 or 6:2)

Put the egg yolks into a medium-sized
Pyrex bowl with the mustard, salt and
the white wine vinegar. Put the oil into a
measure. Take a whisk in one hand and
the oil in the other and drip the oil onto
the egg yolks, drop by drop whisking at the
same time. Within a minute you will notice
that the mixture is beginning to thicken.
When this happens you can add the oil a
little faster, but don't get too confident or
it will suddenly curdle because the egg
yolks can only absorb the oil at a certain
pace. Taste and add a little more seasoning
and vinegar if necessary.

If the mayonnaise curdles it will suddenly
become quite thin, and if left sitting the oil
will start to float to the top of the sauce.
Should this happen you can quite easily
rectify the situation by putting another
egg yolk or 1-2 tablespoons of boiling
water into a clean bowl, then whisk in the
curdled mayonnaise, a half teaspoon at a
time until it re-emulsifies.

Serve with cold cooked meats, fowl, fish,
eggs and vegetables.

Daughter Sauces
Aïoli or Garlic Mayonnaise

Add 1–4 crushed garlic cloves (depending
on size) to the egg yolks just as you start to
make the mayonnaise. Add 2 teaspoons
freshly chopped parsley at the end and
taste for seasoning.

Roasted Garlic Aïoli

1 head organic garlic
extra-virgin olive oil
homemade Mayonnaise (see left)
2 tablespoons freshly chopped parsley
1 tablespoon freshly chopped chives

Preheat the oven to 200°C/400°F/gas 6.

Cut the top off the head of garlic to expose the cloves. Take a square of tin foil and place the head of garlic in the centre. Drizzle with about a tablespoon of extra-virgin olive oil, then gather up the edges and twist to seal. Cook the garlic in the oven until tender (about 45 minutes). Remove from the oven, and when cool enough to handle squeeze the soft garlic pulp from the skins, crush, and add to the mayonnaise with the freshly chopped parsley and chives. Taste and correct the seasoning.

Chilli Basil Mayonnaise

Add a good pinch of chilli powder to the egg yolks when making Garlic Mayonnaise, omit the parsley and add basil instead. Great with salads and sandwiches.

Basil Mayonnaise

Pour boiling water over 10g (½oz) basil leaves, count to three, drain immediately and refresh in cold water. Chop and add to the egg yolks and continue to follow the Master Recipe.

Tomato and Basil Mayonnaise

Add 1–2 tablespoons of concentrated Tomato Purée (see page 50) to Basil Mayonnaise.

Dill Mayonnaise

Add 2–3 tablespoons of freshly chopped dill to the Master Recipe. Particularly delicious with poached salmon or sea trout.

> TIP: To crush garlic, put the whole clove of garlic on a board, preferably one that is reserved for garlic and onions. Tap the clove with the flat blade of a chopping knife to break the skin. Remove the skin and discard. Then sprinkle a few grains of salt onto the clove. Again using the flat blade of the knife, keep pressing the tip of the knife down onto the garlic to form a paste. The salt provides friction and ensures the clove won't shoot off the board.

Spicy Mayonnaise

Add 1–2 teaspoons Ballymaloe Tomato Relish and 1 teaspoon of chilli sauce to a cupful of basic Mayonnaise.

Roasted Red Pepper or Red Chilli Mayonnaise

Add the puréed flesh of 1–2 roasted red peppers, or 1 teaspoon of roasted, peeled and diced red chilli to the basic Mayonnaise or mild Aïoli (see left). Taste and correct the seasoning. Serve with cold meat, spiced chicken or goujons of fish.

Piquillo Pepper Mayonnaise

Add 2 chopped piquillo peppers and 2 tablespoons chopped rocket or coriander to the mayonnaise. Good with cooked shrimps, prawns, hake or trout.

Wasabi Mayonnaise

Add 2–4 tablespoons of Wasabi paste to the eggs instead of mustard.

Rémoulade Sauce

homemade Mayonnaise (see left)
2 teaspoons Dijon mustard
1–2 tablespoons capers, chopped
1–2 tablespoons pickled gherkins, chopped
3 tablespoons freshly chopped parsley
2 teaspoons freshly chopped tarragon
4 anchovy fillets, chopped

Follow the Mayonnaise Master Recipe, then add all other ingredients. Serve with deep-fried plaice, sole, monkfish or Fritto Misto.

Orly Sauce

Follow the Mayonnaise Master Recipe, then add concentrated homemade Tomato Purée (see page 50) to taste. Serve with deep-fried fish, for example plaice or lemon sole.

Andalouse Sauce

Follow the Mayonnaise Master Recipe, then add concentrated homemade Tomato Purée (see page 50) and chopped sweet red peppers. Serve with chicken, salads and fish.

Mustard and Dill Mayonnaise
Serves 8–10

Serve with gravlax, soused mackerel or herring. Using sugar here may seem surprising, but it balances with the mustard and vinegar to produce a great flavour.

2 organic egg yolks
2 tablespoons French mustard
1 tablespoon white sugar
150ml (¼ pint) groundnut or sunflower oil
1 tablespoon white wine vinegar
1 tablespoon finely chopped fresh dill
salt and white pepper

Whisk the egg yolks with the mustard and sugar in a medium-sized glass bowl, drip in the oil drop by drop whisking all the time until the mixture has emulsified, then add the vinegar and dill.

Horseradish Mayonnaise

Following the recipe above, substitute 1 heaped teaspoon of chopped parsley and 1 heaped teaspoon of chopped tarragon for the dill, and add with 1 tablespoon of freshly grated horseradish. Serve with cold rare roast beef or carpaccio.

Dijon and Grainy Mustard Cream
Serves 8

225ml (8fl oz) crème fraîche
1 tablespoon Dijon mustard
1 tablespoon grainy mustard
2 tablespoons flat-leaf parsley, chopped
2 teaspoons lemon juice, freshly squeezed
sea salt and lots of freshly ground pepper

Mix all the ingredients together and season to taste. (Alternatively, for a warm sauce, warm the cream before adding the rest of the ingredients.)

Tartare Sauce

Serves 8–10

A classic tartare sauce is great with deep-fried fish, shellfish or fish cakes. Tartare sauce will keep for 5–6 days in a fridge. Omit the parsley and chives if you wish to keep it for longer than a day or two.

2 hard-boiled organic egg yolks
2 raw organic egg yolks
¼ teaspoon Dijon mustard
1 tablespoon white wine vinegar
350ml (12fl oz) sunflower or groundnut oil or 300ml (10fl oz) of either plus 50ml (2fl oz) olive oil
salt and freshly ground pepper
1 teaspoon chopped capers
1 teaspoon chopped gherkins
2 teaspoons chopped chives or chopped spring onions
2 teaspoons chopped parsley
chopped white of the 2 hard-boiled eggs

Sieve the hard-boiled egg yolks into a bowl, and add the raw egg yolks, mustard and 1 tablespoon of wine vinegar. Mix well and whisk in the oil drop by drop, increasing the volume as the mixture thickens.

When all the oil has been absorbed, add the other ingredients – capers, gherkins, chives or spring onions and parsley. Then roughly chop the hard-boiled egg white and fold in gently. Season and add a little more vinegar or a squeeze of lemon juice if necessary.

Cheat's Tartare Sauce

A quick version can be made by adding the extra ingredients into homemade Mayonnaise at the end.

Mother Sauce
Béarnaise Sauce

Serves 8–10

One of the great classics. Use French rather than Russian tarragon if you can find it. Serve with beef, grills, fish and eggs.

4 tablespoons tarragon vinegar
4 tablespoons dry white wine
2 teaspoons finely chopped shallots
pinch of freshly ground pepper
1 tablespoon water
2 organic egg yolks, preferably organic
about 110–175g (4–6oz) butter, salted or unsalted depending on what it is being served with
1 tablespoon freshly chopped French tarragon leaves

If you do not have tarragon vinegar to hand, use a wine vinegar and add some extra chopped tarragon. Boil the first four ingredients together until completely reduced and the pan is almost dry but not browned.

Add 1 tablespoon of cold water immediately. Pull the pan off the heat and allow to cool for 1 or 2 minutes. Whisk in the egg yolks and add the butter bit by bit over a very low heat, whisking all the time. As soon as one piece melts, add the next piece; it will gradually thicken. If it shows signs of becoming too thick or slightly 'scrambling', remove from the heat immediately and add a little cold water if necessary. Do not leave the pan or stop whisking until the sauce is made. Finally add 1 tablespoon of freshly chopped French tarragon and taste for seasoning.

If the sauce is slow to thicken it may be because you are excessively cautious and the heat is too low. Increase the heat slightly and continue to whisk until the sauce thickens to a coating consistency. It is important to remember, however, that if you are making Bearnaise Sauce in a saucepan directly over the heat, it should be possible to put your hand on the side of the saucepan at any stage. If the saucepan feels too hot for your hand it is also too hot for the sauce. Another good tip if you are making Béarnaise Sauce for the first time is to keep a bowl of cold water close by so that you can plunge the bottom of the saucepan into it if it becomes too hot. Keep the sauce warm in a bowl over warm water or in a thermos flask until you want to serve it.

Daughter Sauces
Sauce Choron (Tomato Béarnaise)

Add 1½ tablespoons concentrated homemade Tomato Purée (see page 50) to 300ml (½ pint) Béarnaise Sauce. Serve with steak, fish, eggs or vegetables.

Sauce Foyot (Béarnaise with Meat Glaze)

Add 1 teaspoon meat glaze to 300ml (½ pint) Béarnaise Sauce. The sauce should be the colour of café au lait. Serve with steak.

Sauce Paloise (Mint Béarnaise)

Substitute chopped fresh mint for the tarragon. Serve this variation with lamb.

Béarnaise au Poivre Vert (Green Peppercorn Béarnaise)

Omit the chopped tarragon from the Béarnaise Sauce. Instead add 1 level tablespoon of drained and crushed green peppercorns to every 300ml (½ pint) of sauce. Serve with steak, lamb or salmon.

Béarnaise Butter

Leftover Béarnaise Sauce will solidify when it cools. It'll still be delicious so serve it as a butter melted over the top of your steak.

Mother Sauce
Ballymaloe Cream Sauce

Serves 8

This undisputably rich sauce is one of our most requested recipes. It is truly delicious, but I'm sure I don't have to tell you to eat it sparingly. You can add freshly snipped herbs to the basic sauce, or follow one of the variations below.

150g (5oz) butter
225ml (8fl oz) cream
salt and freshly ground pepper

Put the cream into a small saucepan and gently reduce to about 4 tablespoons or until it is in danger of burning. Then whisk in the butter bit by bit as though you were making a Hollandaise sauce. Thin with warm water if necessary and keep warm in a Pyrex bowl. Taste and correct the seasoning and add chosen flavouring.

Daughter Sauces
Red Pepper Sauce
Serve with poached fish, monkfish, sole, turbot or plaice. De-seed a red pepper and dice the flesh into 3mm (⅛in) cubes. Sweat gently in a teaspoonful of butter in a tiny covered saucepan until soft (it's really easy to burn so turn off the heat after a few minutes and it will continue to cook in the pan). Stir into the basic sauce.

Spinach Butter Sauce
Add 50g (2oz) cooked spinach, chopped into 2.5cm (1in) pieces, to the Mother Sauce. Thin with fish stock if necessary. Serve with trout or salmon.

Tomato and Basil Sauce
Add 4 ripe firm tomatoes, peeled, diced and seasoned with salt, pepper and sugar, along with 10–15 freshly chopped basil leaves to the Mother Recipe. Serve with pan-grilled chicken breasts or fish.

Horseradish Sauce
Serves 8–10

Can be mild or hot depending on your preference.

2–6 tablespoons horseradish root, scrubbed,
  peeled and grated
1 teaspoon wine vinegar
1 teaspoon lemon juice
¼ teaspoon mustard
¼ teaspoon salt
freshly ground pepper
1 teaspoon sugar
225ml (8fl oz) softly whipped cream

Put the grated horseradish into a bowl with the vinegar, lemon juice, mustard, salt, pepper and sugar. Fold in the softly

whipped cream but do not overmix or it will curdle. It keeps for 2–3 days but cover it tightly so it does not pick up other flavours in the refrigerator.

Horseradish Cream
Follow the method above but use double cream (unwhipped). Use immediately – it should be pouring consistency.

Tomato and Horseradish Sauce
Enough for 8–10 people

Serve with cooked shrimps as a dipping sauce.

6 tablespoons best-quality tomato ketchup
1 tablespoon fish sauce (nam pla)
1 tablespoon freshly grated horseradish
sugar to taste

Mix the tomato ketchup with the fish sauce and the horseradish, then add sugar to taste.

Sauce Gribiche
Serves 6–8

Wonderful with pan-grilled fish or chicken breast.

2 organic egg yolks
175ml (6fl oz) sunflower or groundnut oil
salt and pepper
1 tablespoon red wine vinegar
2 hard-boiled eggs, peeled and finely chopped
1 tablespoon capers, finely chopped
2 sprigs of tarragon, finely chopped
1 tablespoon flat-leaf parsley, finely chopped

To make the gribiche, put the egg yolks in a small bowl with a pinch of salt and pepper. Gradually whisk in the oil as for mayonnaise. When all the oil is incorporated, add the vinegar, chopped hard-boiled eggs, capers and chopped herbs. Taste and correct seasoning.

Flavoured Butters

Flavoured butters are literally made in minutes. They are great to serve with pan-grilled or barbecued meat, fish and vegetable dishes. For all the recipes below, the flavoured butters can be rolled into butter pats or formed into a log, wrap in greaseproof paper or tinfoil, screwing each end so that it looks like a cracker. Refrigerate to harden. It will keep for 2–3 weeks.

Master Recipe
Maitre d'Hôtel Butter (Lemon and Parsley Butter)

110g (4oz) butter
2 tablespoons finely chopped parsley
a few drops of lemon juice, freshly squeezed

Cream the butter and add in the parsley and a few drops of lemon juice.

Variations
Garlic Butter

Add 3–5 crushed garlic cloves to the Parsley Butter. Serve with pan-grilled steaks and anything else you fancy.

Herb Butter

Substitute a mixture of chopped fresh herbs – parsley, chives, thyme, fennel, lemon balm… for the parsley in the recipe for Parsley Butter.

Mint or Rosemary Butter

Substitute 2 tablespoons of finely chopped mint or 1–2 tablespoons of rosemary for the parsley. Serve with roast or pan-grilled lamb.

Wild Garlic Butter

Substitute 2 tablespoons of chopped wild garlic leaves, and perhaps some flowers, for the parsley.

Nasturtium Butter

Substitute 3 tablespoons of chopped nasturtium flowers (red, yellow and orange) for the parsley.

Lemon Butter

Cream the butter, add the lemon rind of 1 unwaxed lemon then and beat in the juice of the lemon very gradually.

Mustard and Parsley Butter

Add 1 tablespoon of finely chopped parsley and 1 tablespoon Dijon mustard.

Provençale Butter

Spread this butter over cooked mussels on the half shell, dip in white breadcrumbs and pop under the grill for yummy garlicky Moules Provençales. Also good slathered on mushrooms, tomatoes or snails!

2 large garlic cloves
2 tablespoons freshly chopped parsley
1 tablespoon olive oil
75g (3oz) soft butter

Peel and crush the garlic and pound it in a mortar with the finely chopped parsley and olive oil. Gradually beat in the butter (this may be done either in a bowl or a food processor).

Grainy Mustard Butter

This is particularly good with pan-grilled mackerel or herring.

110g (4oz) butter
1 tablespoon Dijon mustard
2 teaspoons approx. grainy mustard
1 tablespoon chopped parsley, optional

Cream the butter, then add the mustards and the parsley, if using.

Chilli and Coriander Butter

110g (4oz) butter
1 red or green chilli, seeded and finely chopped (we use Jalapeno or Serrano)
1 tablespoon chopped coriander or marjoram
freshly ground pepper
a few drops of lime or lemon juice

Cream the butter, then add the chilli and fresh herbs. Season with freshly ground pepper and lime or lemon juice.

Olive and Anchovy Butter

110g (4oz) butter
2–3 anchovies
6 black olives, stoned
about 2 teaspoons freshly chopped parsley

Whizz all the ingredients together in a food processor, or chop ingredients finely and mix with the butter.

Sage Butter

Serve with ravioli or lamb's liver.

110g (4oz) butter
12–16 finely chopped fresh sage leaves

Melt the butter. When it foams, add the fresh sage leaves. Allow to bubble for 1–2 minutes. Toss in cooked ravioli and serve.

Master Recipe
Classic Pesto
Makes 2 small jars

The best pesto is made in a pestle and mortar, but you can also make it in a food processor. It can be difficult to get enough basil; if you have trouble try one of the variations using different herbs – different but still delicious. Pesto keeps for weeks in the fridge. Store in a jar, covered with a layer of olive oil

110g (4oz) fresh basil leaves
150ml (5fl oz) extra-virgin olive oil
25g (1oz) fresh pine nuts (taste when you buy to ensure they are not rancid)
2 large garlic cloves, peeled and crushed
50g (2oz) freshly grated Parmesan (preferably Parmigiano Reggiano)
salt, to taste

Whizz the basil with the olive oil, pine nuts and garlic in a food processor or pound in a pestle and mortar. Remove to a bowl and fold in the Parmesan. Taste and season. Pour into sterilised jars. Cover with a layer of olive oil. Screw on the lid and store in the fridge. Pesto also freezes well but for best results don't add the Parmesan until defrosted.

Variations
Pesto without Parmesan
Omit the cheese and store as above.

Rocket Pesto
Substitute basil in above recipe with rocket leaves.

> TIP: Each time you use some pesto, clean the top and sides of the jar and make sure the pesto is covered with a layer of extra-virgin olive oil before replacing in the fridge. Otherwise the pesto will darken and go mouldy where it is exposed to the air.

Master Recipe
Parsley Pesto
Makes 2 small jars

When basil is less aromatic and scarce, use parsley to make pesto. Other fresh herbs e.g. mint and coriander are also delicious. Use one or a mixture of several – experiment and taste.

25g (1oz) freshly chopped parsley, leaves only
1–2 garlic cloves, peeled and crushed
35g (1½oz) freshly grated Parmesan (preferably Parmigiano Reggiano)
25g (1oz) pine nuts
75ml (3fl oz) extra-virgin olive oil
salt (essential to bring out the flavour)

Put all the ingredients except the oil into the food processor. Whizz for a second or two, add the oil and a little salt. Taste and correct seasoning. Pour into a sterilised jar. Cover with oil, seal and refrigerate.

Variations
Rosemary and Parsley Pesto
Add 1–2 teaspoons freshly chopped rosemary with the parsley in the Master Recipe. Serve with lamb, pan-grilled chicken breasts, portobella mushrooms, aubergine…

Mint and Parsley Pesto
Add 1–2 teaspoons fresh mint with the parsley in the Master Recipe.

Kale Pesto
Serves 12–16

450g (1lb) fresh kale, leaves
1 clove garlic, crushed
½ teaspoon sea salt
75–150ml (3–5fl oz) extra-virgin olive oil

Strip the kale from the stalks and wash well. Put all the ingredients in a food processor and whizz to form a thick paste.

This can be made ahead and stored in a covered jar in the fridge for several days. If you prefer a mellower flavour, blanch the kale in boiling salted water for 3–4 minutes, refresh and drain well and proceed as above. Serve on freshly cooked crostini.

Coriander Pesto
Makes 2 small jars

50ml (2fl oz) light olive oil or groundnut oil
1 spring onion, white and green parts, coarsely chopped
1 garlic clove, coarsely chopped
1 tablespoon pine nuts, toasted
1½ teaspoons lemon or lime juice
50g (2oz) coriander sprigs with short stems
50g (2oz) flat-leaf parsley, large stems removed
salt
cayenne pepper

Mix everything except the salt and pepper in the blender. Add salt and a few pinches of cayenne, purée until smooth. Taste and correct the seasoning.

Wild Garlic Pesto

Try this in early summer, when you can buy wild garlic leaves.

50g (2oz) wild garlic leaves
25g (1oz) pine nuts
1 garlic clove, peeled and crushed
175–225ml (6–8fl oz) extra-virgin olive oil
35g (1½oz) freshly grated Parmesan (preferably Parmigiano Reggiano)
salt and sugar, to taste

Whizz the wild garlic, pine nuts, garlic and olive oil in a food processor or pound in a pestle and mortar. Remove to a bowl and fold in the Parmesan. Taste and season. Store in a sterilised covered jar in the fridge.

Roasted Red Pepper Pesto

Makes 2 small jars

Serve on warm olive oil fried crostini or as a sauce for pasta with extra Parmesan.

2 large fresh red peppers
5 anchovy fillets
1 tablespoon extra-virgin olive oil
½ dried red chilli or a pinch of red pepper flakes
sea salt and freshly ground pepper

Roast the peppers over a chargrill, under a radiant grill or in a hot oven. When they are well charred, transfer to a bowl, cover with clingfilm and leave until cool enough to handle. The skin should peel off easily. Split the peppers and remove the seeds. DO NOT WASH or you will lose the precious sweet juices. Chop the peppers roughly. Put with all the other ingredients into the bowl of a food processor. Pulse for a few seconds until the mixture has a slightly chunky texture.

Sun-dried Tomato Pesto

Makes 2 small jars

75g (3oz) 'Sun-dried' Tomatoes (see page 188)
1–2 garlic cloves, crushed
50g (2oz) freshly grated Parmesan (preferably Parmigiano Reggiano)
25g (1oz) pine nuts
75ml (3fl oz) extra-virgin olive oil
salt

Whizz all ingredients except the oil for a couple of seconds in a food processor. Add the oil and a little salt. Correct seasoning. Store in sterilised jars in the fridge.

Variation
Mint and Sun-dried Tomato Pesto

Add 50g (2oz) fresh mint leaves or 25g (1oz) parsley and 25g (1oz) mint leaves to the above recipe.

Pistou

Makes 2 small jars

Pistou is a 'cousin' of the Italian pesto (it contains no pine kernels) and can be used in a similar way.

5 large garlic cloves
about 30 fresh, large basil leaves
50g (2oz) freshly grated Parmesan (preferably Parmigiano Reggiano)
6 tablespoons extra-virgin olive oil

Peel and crush the garlic well or pound in a mortar. Then add the basil and continue to pound to a paste. Stir in the Parmesan, mix well and then add in the oil drop by drop.

Tapenade

Makes 2 small jars

Tapenade is a paste made from olives and anchovies. Its strong gutsy flavour can be an acquired taste, but it soon becomes addictive. Serve with crudités, bruschetta, crostini, lamb or pasta.

50g (2oz) anchovy fillets
110g (4oz) stoned black olives (Kalamata)
1 tablespoon capers
1 teaspoon Dijon mustard
1 teaspoon lemon juice, freshly squeezed
freshly ground pepper
3–4 tablespoons extra-virgin olive oil

Whizz up the anchovy fillets in a food processor with the olives, capers, mustard, lemon juice, and pepper. Alternatively, use a pestle and mortar. Add the olive oil as you mix to make a coarse or smooth purée as you prefer.

Black and Green Tapenade
Use a mixture of black and green olives in the above recipe.

Olive and Sun-dried Tomato Tapenade

Makes 2 small jars

Serve on crostini, with goat's cheese, with pan-grilled chicken breasts or lamb chops.

175g (6oz) stoned black olives, (Niçoise or Kalamata
375g (13oz) stoned green olives, try Picholine
¼ cup sun-dried tomatoes

1 tablespoon capers
1 garlic clove, crushed
2 anchovy fillets
6–8 basil leaves
1 teaspoon thyme leaves
2 teaspoons freshly chopped flat-leaf parsley
1 teaspoon marjoram
125ml (4fl oz) extra-virgin olive oil

Put all the ingredients except the oil into a food processor and pulse for a few seconds. Add the olive oil slowly and continue to pulse. The texture should be coarse. Store in a sterilised jar or plastic container, sealed with a layer of olive oil. Cover and store in the fridge. Keeps for 1–2 weeks.

Master Recipe
Tomato Sauce
Makes 450ml (16fl oz)

A good tomato sauce is a terrific accompaniment to all sorts of dishes besides pasta. I find it invaluable to have in the fridge or freezer as a standby. Use it on pizza, or with polenta, courgettes or courgette flowers. Serve hot or cold. It is wonderful with the Provençal Terrine.

25g (1oz) butter
2 tablespoons extra-virgin olive oil
1–4 garlic cloves, according to taste, peeled and chopped
1 medium onion, finely chopped
900g (2lb) very ripe tomatoes, peeled and chopped, or 2 x 400g (14oz) tins Italian tomatoes, chopped
salt, freshly ground pepper, sugar

Melt the butter, add the olive oil and toss in the chopped garlic. Cook for 1–2 minutes or until pale golden. Add the onion and cook for 1–2 minutes before adding the tomatoes. Season with the salt, pepper and a little sugar.

Cook fast for 15–20 minutes if you want a fresh-tasting sauce, or more slowly for up to 1 hour if you prefer it more concentrated. Purée through a mouli-légumes. Taste and correct the seasoning.

Variations
Tomato Sauce with Basil or Annual Marjoram
Add 1–2 tablespoons freshly chopped basil or annual marjoram to the Master Recipe.

Tomato Sauce with Balsamic Vinegar
Add 1–2 teaspoons of balsamic vinegar to the Master Recipe just before serving. It intensifies the flavour of the sauce quite magically.

Creamy Tomato Sauce
Bring the tomato sauce back to the boil (with or without herbs) and add 125ml (4fl oz) double cream. Allow it to bubble for 1–2 minutes then serve at once.

Tomato and Chilli Sauce
Serves 4–6

Serve with Onion Bhajis (see page 188).

25g (1oz) green chillies (2–3, depending on size), de-seeded and chopped, or 1 large red pepper, de-seeded and cut in 5mm (¼in) dice
200g (14oz) tinned chopped tomatoes
1 garlic clove, crushed
1 dessertspoon caster sugar
1 dessertspoon soft brown sugar
1 tablespoon white wine vinegar
2 tablespoons water
salt and freshly ground pepper

First make the sauce: put the chillies, garlic and tomatoes into a stainless steel saucepan with the sugar, vinegar and water. Season, and simmer until reduced by half.

Hot Chilli Sauce
Serves 4–6

If you want some real excitement in your life, serve this as an accompaniment to your curry. We use this as a basis for chilli con carne as well.

4–5 fresh chillies or 6–7 small dried chillies
1 large red pepper
1 large onion, chopped
2 garlic cloves
salt

If the chillies are dried, soak for about an hour, then split in half and wash out the seeds. Cut the chillies and pepper in half and wash out the seeds.

Purée with the other ingredients in a food processor. You may need 1-2 tablespoons of cold water if the mixture is too dry. Season to taste with salt. This sauce can be stored in a covered container for a few days, or frozen for much longer.

Note: Salt brings up the flavour of chillies so don't forget to put it in.

Teriyaki Sauce
Makes 1 litre

300ml (10fl oz) sake
300ml (10fl oz) mirin
225g (8oz) soft brown sugar
300ml (10fl oz) soy sauce
1 tablespoon grated ginger
½ teaspoon dried chilli flakes (optional)

Heat the ingredients together until the sugar is dissolved. Remove from the heat and allow the flavours to develop for half an hour. Strain and set aside.

Pixie's Peanut Sauce
Serves 6–8

6 tablespoons peanut butter
3 tablespoons light soy sauce
6 tablespoons dark soy sauce
6 tablespoons tahini (sesame seed paste)
125ml (4fl oz) dark sesame oil
2 tablespoons medium sherry
125ml (4fl oz) hot water

Put all the ingredients except the hot water into a food processor. Whizz until smooth. Thin with hot water to a light coating consistency. This keeps indefinitely in the fridge.

Tomato and Coriander Salsa

Serves 4

This sauce is ever present on Mexican tables. Serve with nachos, quesadillas, tostadas, Mexican scrambled eggs...

4 very ripe tomatoes, chopped
1 tablespoon onion, chopped
1 clove garlic, crushed
½–1 chilli, finely chopped
1–2 tablespoons freshly chopped coriander
juice of ½ lime
salt, freshly ground pepper and sugar

Mix all the ingredients together, and seaon with salt, pepper and sugar.

Roasted Red Pepper, Tomato and Basil Salsa

Add peeled, seeded and chopped roasted red pepper and replace the coriander with basil in the above recipe.

Parsley and Chilli Salsa

Serves 8

This salsa doubles as a pasta sauce; serve with a sprinkle of toasted breadcrumbs.

6 garlic cloves, finely chopped
2–3 large red chillies, seeded and finely chopped
100g (4oz) flat-leaf parsley, finely chopped
extra-virgin olive oil
sea salt and freshly ground pepper

Mix the garlic and the chillies together, then the flat-leaf parsley, lots of olive oil, a little sea salt and freshly ground pepper.

Coriander, Parsley and Chilli Salsa

Use 50g (2oz) flat-leaf parsley and 50g (20z) fresh coriander leaves instead of only flat-leaf parsley.

Tomato and Avocado Salsa

Serves 4

1 avocado, peeled and chopped
2 ripe tomatoes, chopped
1 tablespoon spring onion, chopped
1 garlic clove, crushed
1–2 chilli peppers, chopped
¼–½ teaspoon lightly roasted cumin seeds, crushed
1–2 tablespoons roughly chopped fresh coriander
salt and freshly ground pepper
juice of 2 limes, freshly squeezed

Mix all the ingredients in a bowl, taste and correct the seasoning.

Avocado and Coriander Salsa

Serves about 8

2 avocados, diced
4 spring onions, finely chopped
1 garlic clove, crushed
a drizzle of extra-virgin olive oil
1–2 tablespoons coarsely chopped coriander
squeeze of lemon juice
salt, freshly ground pepper and sugar to taste

Put all the ingredients into a bowl. Season with salt, pepper and sugar. Mix gently.

Salsa Verde

Makes 2 small jars

Serve with pan-grilled beef, lamb, chicken, liver, aubergines or goat's cheese.

2 bunches Italian flat leaf parsley
zest and juice of 1–2 lemons
3 cloves garlic, crushed
2 teaspoons freshly grated horseradish
1½ tablespoons salted capers, rinsed
extra-virgin olive oil
salt and freshly ground pepper

Put the parsley leaves, lemon zest, garlic, horseradish and capers in a food processor. Process in an on/off method until the mixture is finely chopped. (Alternatively, chop on a wooden board with a knife or mezzaluna.) Add the freshly squeezed lemon juice and enough olive oil to make a moist salsa. Season to taste with salt and pepper.

Watermelon Salsa

Serves 6–8

225g (8oz) watermelon, seeded and diced
2 tablespoons red onion, chopped
2–3 tablespoons freshly chopped coriander leaves
1 tablespoon jalapeno pepper, diced
½ teaspoon salt
1–2 garlic cloves, crushed
2 tablespoons lime juice, freshly squeezed

Mix all the ingredients in a stainless steel bowl. Taste and allow to stand for 15 minutes.

Tomatillo Salsa

Serves 6

The tomatillo is a small, spherical green or green-purple fruit surrounded by a paper-like husk. It is the key ingredient in fresh and cooked Latin American green sauces. Serve with tacos, quesadillas and spicy sausages.

5 or 6 fresh tomatillos
1–3 chillies, chopped
25g (1oz) onion, chopped
1 garlic clove, crushed
good pinch of salt
1–2 tablespoons coarsely chopped coriander

Remove the papery husks from the tomatillos. Wash. Put into a small saucepan, cover with cold water, and add a good pinch of salt. Cook until the fruits are soft and the skins tender – about 18–20 minutes, depending on size. Tomatillos float, so don't forget to turn them over during cooking otherwise the tops can be undercooked. Simmer rather than boil to prevent them from bursting.

Meanwhile grind the chillies, onions, garlic, coriander and salt, preferably with a coarse pestle and mortar. If you don't have one, use a food processor or blender (although the resulting purée will be more watery).

When the tomatillos are tender, drain and reserve the cooking liquid. Grind them with the chilli mixture, or alternatively blend everything together to a coarse purée. Add about 4 tablespoons of the cooking water to thin the sauce to a medium consistency. Taste, season with salt and allow to stand for about half anhour to allow the flavours to develop.

Bagna Cauda
Serves 4–6

This is one of the great specialities of the Piedmont area in Northern Italy. A great dip for raw vegetables.

175ml (6fl oz) olive oil
5 cloves garlic, crushed
14 anchovies fillets, chopped ·
110g (4oz) butter

Heat the oil gently in a small pot, add the garlic and cook until soft but not brown. Add the anchovies and stir over a low heat until dissolved. Add in the butter and serve from the pot, keeping warm on a spirit lamp or over a night light.

Anchoïade
Makes 300ml (10fl oz)

Serve with crudités or just slathered on toast, bruschetta, or warm pitta bread. Anchoïade is also great with a simple pan-grilled chicken breast.

110g (4oz) tinned anchovy fillets (weight out of tin)
2 garlic cloves, chopped
2 teaspoons thyme leaves
1 tablespoon freshly chopped basil leaves
1 tablespoon Dijon mustard
1 tablespoon red wine vinegar
lots of freshly ground pepper
300ml (½ pint) olive oil

Whizz all ingredients together except the oil in a food processor. Add the oil very gradually. Taste, and add a little more oil if necessary. Store in a covered jar in the fridge.

Salmoriglio
See page 243

Guacamole

Serves 4

1 ripe avocado
1 garlic clove, crushed (optional)
1–2 tablespoons lime or lemon juice,
1 tablespoon extra-virgin olive oil (optional)
1 tablespoon freshly chopped coriander or
    parsley
sea salt and freshly ground pepper

Mash the avocado flesh with a fork, then add the garlic, lime or lemon juice, olive oil, coriander or parsley and salt and pepper to taste. Place a sheet of plastic on the surface of the guacamole to cover, otherwise it may discolour.

Alison Henderson's Aubergine Raita

Serves 6–10

1 large aubergine
600ml (1 pint) natural yoghurt
1 large garlic clove, crushed
salt
1 teaspoon turmeric
1 tablespoon oil, plus extra for frying
1 dessertspoon cumin seeds
1 teaspoon ground paprika

Slice the aubergines into rounds about 5mm (1/4in) thick and set aside. Heat enough oil in a frying pan so that it comes halfway up the sides. When the oil is hot put in slices of aubergine a few at a time, frying them on both sides until nice and crisp. Set aside to drain on kitchen paper.

Pour the yoghurt into a bowl and stir in the crushed garlic and salt to taste. Add the slices of aubergine and sprinkle with the cumin seeds and paprika. Serve with lamb, couscous or Indian lamb dishes.

Cucumber and Coriander Raita

Serves 6–8

This cooling relish is good served with spicy food.

1/4 medium-sized cucumber
1/2 tablespoon onion, chopped
1/2 rounded teaspoon salt
1/2–1 tomato, diced
1 tablespoon chopped coriander or
    1/2 tablespoon parsley and 1/2 tablespoon mint
150ml (1/4 pint) plain yoghurt
1/2 teaspoon whole cumin seeds
salt and freshly ground pepper

Peel the cucumber if you prefer, cut in half and remove the seeds. Cut into 5mm (1/4in) dice. Put into a bowl with the onion, sprinkle with salt and allow to de-gorge for 5–10 minutes. Drain, and add with the diced tomato and chopped herbs to the yoghurt. Heat the cumin seeds, crush lightly and add. Taste and correct seasoning. Chill before serving.

Pomegranate Seed Raita

Serves 4–6

I ate this and the Beetroot and Mustard Seed Raita at the Bangala in Karakudi (Tamil Nadu, South India).

150ml (5fl oz) of natural yoghurt
1 fresh pomegranate
1 tablespoon olive oil
1 teaspoon black mustard seeds

Split the pomegranate in half around the equator, then hold the halves over a container and tap vigorously with the back of a wooden spoon – the seeds will dislodge and fall into the dish. Add the yoghurt. Heat the olive oil in a saucepan, add the mustard seeds, and as soon as they start to pop pour into the yoghurt mixture and stir. Season with salt to taste.

Beetroot and Mustard Seed Raita

Serves 6–8

110g (4oz) beetroot, peeled and freshly grated
225ml (8fl oz) natural yoghurt
1 teaspoon black mustard seeds
salt

Mix the beetroot with the natural yoghurt in a bowl. Heat a frying pan, add the mustard seeds, and as soon as they start to pop remove and crush lightly. Add them to the yoghurt and beetroot and season with salt.

Banana and Cardamom Raita

Serves 6

Try this with curries and spicy dishes.

25g (1oz) raisins or sultanas
10g (1/2oz) blanched slivered almonds
3–4 green cardamom pods
100ml (31/2fl oz) natural yoghurt
2 tablepoons cream
2 tablepoons sour cream
1 dessertspoon pure honey
2 firm ripe bananas
pinch of salt

Pour boiling water over the raisins or sultanas, leave for 10 minutes. Toast the almonds (watch them, as they burn really easily). Remove the cardamom seeds from their pods, and crush in a pestle and mortar.

Mix the yoghurt with the creams and cardamom seeds, add the honey, taste and add more if needed. Add the raisins and toasted almonds. Slice the bananas, season with a pinch of salt and add to the yoghurt base. Turn into a serving bowl and scatter with toasted almonds, chill for an hour if possible.

Fresh Mint Chutney

Serves 8–10

This fresh chutney is often served in India with curries. It is good with grilled fish or roast lamb as an alternative to mint sauce. It also makes a really yummy dip for poppadoms. Surprisingly, even though it is uncooked, this chutney will keep for several days in a covered jar or plastic container in the fridge.

1 large cooking apple (we use Grenadier or
  Bramley Seedling), peeled and cored
large handful of fresh mint leaves, Spearmint
  or Bowles
50g (2oz) onions
25–50g (1–2oz) caster sugar (depending on
  tartness of apple)
salt and cayenne pepper

Whizz all the ingredients in a food processor, season with the salt and a little cayenne.

Ballymaloe Mint Sauce

Serves 4

5g (¼oz) sugar
5g (¼oz) finely chopped fresh mint
3–4 tablespoons boiling water
1 tablespoon white wine vinegar or lemon juice

Put the sugar and freshly chopped mint into a bowl. Add the boiling water and vinegar or lemon juice. Allow to infuse for 5–10 minutes. Serve with spring lamb.

Gravy

Makes 600ml (1 pint), serves 10

Gravy should be made in the roasting tin so that you utilise all the flavour of the caramelised meat juices on the bottom of the tin. The meat can be resting while you make the gravy. Be sure to use a flameproof roasting pan.

600ml (1 pint) stock (preferably homemade
  Beef Stock, see page 36)
Roux (see page 580), optional
salt and freshly ground pepper, to taste

Spoon the fat off the roasting tin. Pour the stock into the remaining cooking juices and heat on the top of the stove. Boil for a few minutes, stirring and scraping well to dissolve the caramelised meat juices on the pan (I find a small metal whisk ideal for this). Thicken very slightly with a little roux if you like (years ago flour would have been sprinkled over the fat in the tin). Taste and add salt and pepper if necessary. Strain and serve in a warm gravy boat.

Onion Gravy

Serves 4–6

Serve with roast beef or lamb's liver.

8 onions, about 900g (2lb) in weight, thinly
  sliced
2 tablespoons water
600ml (1pint) homemade Beef Stock
  (see page 36)

Put the sliced onions into a pan with the water and cook very slowly, stirring every now and then. The sugar from the onions will slowly caramelise and become brown and sweet-tasting. This process can take up to an hour.

Add the stock and simmer for a further 15–20 minutes. Serve in a warmed gravy boat.

Bread Sauce

Serves 6–8

I love Bread Sauce but if I hadn't been reared on it I might never have tried it – the recipe sounds so dull. Quatre épices is a French product made from equal amounts of ground white pepper, cloves, nutmeg and ginger. Serve with roast turkey, chicken or guinea fowl.

600ml (1 pint) milk
75–110g (3–4oz) soft white breadcrumbs
2 onions, peeled and stuck with 6 cloves each
50g (2oz) butter
salt and freshly ground pepper
2 good pinches of ground cloves or quatre
  épices
75–125ml (3–4fl oz) double cream

Put all the ingredients except the cream in a small, deep saucepan and bring to the boil. Season with salt and pepper.

Cover and simmer gently on a very low heat or cook in a low oven 170°C/325°F/gas 3 for 30 minutes. Remove the onion and add the cream just before serving.

Correct the seasoning and add a little more milk if the sauce is too thick. Serve hot.

Cumberland Sauce

Serves 8–10

Serve with cold ham, turkey, chicken, guinea fowl, game or rough pâtés.

1 orange, unwaxed
1 lemon, unwaxed
225g (8oz) Redcurrant Jelly (see page 508)
3–4 tablespoons port
pinch of cayenne pepper
pinch of ground ginger

With a swivel-top peeler, remove the peel very thinly from the orange and half of the lemon (make sure there is no white pith). Shred into julienne strips, cover with cold water, bring to the boil and simmer for 4–5 minutes. Strain off the water and discard it, then refresh the peel under cold water. Strain and keep it aside. Squeeze the juice from the fruit and put it into a stainless steel saucepan with the jelly and spices. Allow it to melt down. Then add the peel and port to the sauce. Boil it rapidly for 5–10 minutes. Test like jam by putting a little blob on a cold saucer. When it cools it should wrinkle slightly. Cumberland Sauce may be served right away or it may be potted up and kept until needed, like jam.

Minted Nuoc Cham
Makes 1 jar (serves 6–8)

This recipe, given to me by ace cook Alison Henderson (who runs the café at Ballymaloe House) is an unusual combination of mint and peanuts. Serve with spicy dishes.

3 tablespoons sugar
3 tablespoons boiling water
1/3 cup fish sauce (nam pla)
juice of 1 lime, or more, to taste
3 tablespoons freshly chopped mint
1 tablespoon freshly chopped coriander
freshly chopped hot chilli, to taste
1 tablespoon crushed roasted peanuts

Combine the sugar and water in a small pan and stir until the sugar is dissolved. Allow to cook for 5 minutes, then add the other ingredients. Serve immediately.

Tamari and Lime Sauce
Serves 4

6 tablespoons of tamari
3 tablespoons lime juice, freshly squeezed

Mix the tamari with the lime juice. Serve with hot oysters.

Balsamic Syrup
Makes approx. 110ml (4fl oz)

Chefs love to drizzle this balsamic reduction around their salads and starters. You don't need to use very expensive vinegar.

225ml (8fl oz) balsamic vinegar

Put the balsamic vinegar into a small stainless-steel saucepan over a low heat. Allow to reduce to about half its original volume – take care not to let it reduce too much. It will thicken as it cools. Store in a bottle with a drizzle spout – it will keep for several weeks.

Harissa
Makes 2 small jars

Harissa is the fiery blend of red chillies, garlic and spices that adds life to dishes. It is used during the preparation of dishes, and appears in small bowls on the table. It originated in Tunisia although it is now used throughout Morocco and Algeria as well.

2 red peppers, roasted and skinned
25g (1oz) fresh red chillies, chopped, seeds retained
1–2 garlic cloves, crushed
1/2 teaspoon coriander seeds, toasted
2 teaspoons caraway seeds
olive oil
salt

Put the red peppers, the chillies and their seeds, garlic, coriander and caraway seeds and a pinch of salt in a food processor or blender and mix together, adding enough olive oil to make a thick paste.

Pack the harissa into a small, clean, dry jar and pour a layer of oil over the top. Cover with a tight-fitting lid and keep in the refrigerator.

Fire and Brimstone Sauce
Makes 2 small jars

This sauce is great to serve with pan-grilled chicken, pork or lamb. We also use it as a dipping sauce for all kinds of fried food, especially chicken or fish goujons.

2–4 red chillies, serrano or jalapeno
4 garlic cloves, crushed
225g (8oz) apricot jam
5 tablespoons white wine vinegar
good pinch of salt

De-seed and roughly chop the chillies, then whizz all the ingredients in a food processor. This sauce keeps for up to 2 weeks in a covered jar in the fridge.

Salad Dressings
See pages 226–227

Vermouth Sauce with Periwinkles or Shrimps
Makes 300ml (1/2 pint), serves 10–12

Vermouth sauce is delicious with many fish, particularly turbot, seabass, sole, brill and plaice. It may of course be served without the addition of periwinkles. Cooked shelled shrimps may also be added to the sauce at the end.

salted water – 175g (6oz) salt to every 2.3 litres (4 pints) water
fresh live periwinkles (buy a pint: you need 50–110g/2–4oz periwinkles when removed from their shells)
1 shallot, finely chopped
75g (3oz) unsalted butter
2 tablespoons dry white wine
1 tablespoon dry Vermouth (Noilly Pratt)
150ml (1/4 pint) homemade white Fish Stock (see page 37)
150ml (1/4 pint) double cream
a little lemon juice

Bring the water to the boil, and the periwinkles. Bring back to the boil, then strain off the water and allow the periwinkles to get cold. Meanwhile sweat the shallot in 50g (2oz) butter until soft. Add the wine and vermouth and reduce by half to remove the taste of alcohol. Add the fish stock and again reduce by half. Now add the cream and reduce the sauce carefully to a light coating consistency.

Finally mount the sauce with 25g (1oz) butter, swirling the pan all the time to incorporate the butter. Check seasoning and add a little lemon juice to sharpen the sauce.

Remove the cooled periwinkles from the shells with a pin, and add to the sauce just before serving.

Bramley Apple Sauce

Serves 10

The trick with apple sauce is to cook the fruit in a covered pan on a low heat with very little water. Serve with roast goose, duck, pork, and anything else you fancy.

450g (1lb) cooking apples, e.g. Bramley Seedling or Grenadier
1–2 dessertspoons water
50g (2oz) sugar, depending on how tart the apples are

Peel, quarter and core the apples. Cut the quarters in half and put in a stainless-steel or cast-iron saucepan with sugar and water. Cover and put over a low heat. As soon as the apple has broken down, beat into a purée, stir and taste for sweetness. Serve warm.

Note: Apple Sauce freezes perfectly, so make more than you need and freeze in tiny, plastic cartons. It is also a good way to use up windfalls.

Golden Delicious Sauce

Use Golden Delicious instead of Bramleys, but you will need to reduce the sugar, as these are dessert apples. Serve with Black Pudding (see page 543).

Cranberry Sauce

Serves about 6

Cranberry Sauce is delicious served with roast turkey, game and some coarse pâtés and terrines.

175g (6oz) fresh cranberries
4 tablespoons water
75g (3oz) granulated sugar

Put the cranberries in a heavy stainless-steel saucepan with the water – don't add the sugar yet as it tends to toughen the skins. Bring to the boil, cover and simmer until the fruit pops and softens (about 7 minutes). Remove from heat and stir in the sugar until dissolved. Serve warm or cold.

Variations
Cranberry and Orange Sauce

Use freshly squeezed orange juice instead of water and add the grated rind of half an unwaxed orange to the above recipe.

Cranberry and Ginger Sauce

50ml (2fl oz) cider vinegar
110g (4oz) sugar
½ teaspoon freshly peeled and finely grated ginger
1 large garlic clove, crushed
good pinch cayenne pepper
salt and freshly ground pepper
Cranberry Sauce (see left)

Put the vinegar, sugar, ginger, garlic and cayenne into a small saucepan and cook for 5-6 minutes, or until reduced by half. Add the Cranberry Sauce. Season, taste and correct.

Note: Cranberry Sauce will keep in the fridge for a week to 10 days.

Green Gooseberry Sauce

Serves 8–10

A delicious sauce to accompany pan-grilled mackerel, goat's cheese and roast pork with crackling.

275g (10oz) fresh green gooseberries
approx. 175ml (6fl oz) Stock Syrup, to cover (see page 568)
knob of butter (optional)

Top and tail the gooseberries, put into a stainless-steel saucepan, and barely cover with Stock Syrup. Bring to the boil and simmer until the fruit bursts. Taste. Stir in a small knob of butter if you like but it is very good without it.

Redcurrant Sauce

Serves 4–6

A simple, delicious sauce which is unbelievably quick to make. It goes well with lamb, guinea fowl, ham and pâté de campagne.

150g (5oz) redcurrants
150g (5oz) sugar
125ml (4fl oz) water

Remove the strings from the redcurrants (see tip below). Put the sugar and water into a saucepan, stir over a medium heat until the sugar dissolves, and then bring to the boil. Toss in the redcurrants, bring back to the boil, and cook uncovered for 4–5 minutes or until the redcurrants burst. Serve hot or cold.

This keeps for several weeks in a covered jar in the fridge and may be reheated gently.

TIP: Redcurrants freeze brilliantly, so you can make this at any time of year. Put them into the freezer in a punnet or a plastic bag. Once they are frozen, shake the bag and the berries will fall off their strings – much easier than painstakingly removing the stings from fresh berries.

Sweet Sauces

Crème Anglaise (Custard Sauce)

Serves 15–20

This basic sauce is usually flavoured with vanilla but can be made with any number of other flavourings, such as lemon or orange rind or mint. It is used in many recipes, including ice-cream, though in that case the proportion of sugar is much higher than usual because unsweetened cream is added during the freezing.

600ml (1 pint) full-fat milk
vanilla pod or alternative flavouring
6 organic egg yolks
50g (2oz) sugar

Bring the milk almost to the boil with the vanilla pod, if using. Beat the egg yolks with the sugar until thick and light. Whisk in half the hot milk and then whisk the mixture back into the remaining milk. Cook over very low heat, stirring constantly with a wooden spoon, until the custard thickens slightly. Your finger should leave a clear trail when drawn across the back of the spoon. Remove from the heat at once and strain. Cool, cover tightly and chill. The custard can be kept for up to 2 days in the fridge.

Lemon Custard Sauce

Stir 110g (4oz) Lemon Curd (see page 511) into 300ml (½ pint) of Crème Anglaise.

Chocolate Sauce

Serves 6–8

Serve with ice-cream, profiteroles...

50g (2oz) plain chocolate
25g (1oz) unsweetened chocolate
175ml (6fl oz) Stock Syrup (see page 568)
rum or pure vanilla extract

Melt the chocolate in a bowl over simmering water or in a low oven. Gradually stir in the syrup. Flavour with rum or vanilla extract.

Master Recipe
Caramel Sauce

Serves 8–10

225g (8oz) sugar
75ml (3fl oz) cold water
225ml (8fl oz) hot water

Dissolve the sugar in the cold water over a gentle heat. Stir until all the sugar has dissolved, then remove the spoon and continue to simmer until the syrup

caramelises to a chestnut colour. If sugar crystals form during cooking, brush down the sides of the pan with a wet brush, but do not stir. Remove from the heat, pour in the hot water and return to the heat until the caramel dissolves and the sauce is quite smooth. Allow to get cold. Delicious with ice-cream.

Variation
Caramel Cream Sauce
Use 225ml (8fl oz) double cream in place of the hot water.

Rich Caramel Sauce

Serves 10–12

Serve with ice-cream, roast bananas, pancakes....

300g (10oz) sugar
125ml (4fl oz) water
1 teaspoon pure vanilla extract
110g (4oz) butter, cut in cubes
180ml (6fl oz) cream

Put the sugar and water in a saucepan and stir over a medium heat until the all the sugar has dissolved. Without any further stirring allow the sugar to caramelise and form a rich, chestnut coloured caramel. Remove from the heat and add the vanilla extract. Whisk in the butter and cream. Cool.

Butterscotch Sauce or Toffee Sauce

This irresistible sauce is delicious with ice-cream, but is even better with sliced bananas. It will keep for several weeks stored in a screw-top jar in the fridge.

110g (4oz) butter
175g (6oz) dark soft brown Barbados sugar
110g (4oz) granulated sugar
275g (10oz) golden syrup
225ml (8fl oz) double cream
½ teaspoon pure vanilla extract

Put the butter, sugars and golden syrup into a heavy-bottomed saucepan and melt gently on a low heat. Simmer for about 5 minutes, remove from the heat and gradually stir in the cream and the vanilla essence. Put back on the heat and stir for 2–3 minutes until the sauce is absolutely smooth. Serve hot or cold.

Irish Coffee Sauce

Serve with ice-cream or parfaits.

225g (8oz) sugar
75ml (3fl oz) water
225ml (8fl oz) coffee
1 tablespoon Irish whiskey

Put the sugar and water in a heavy-bottomed saucepan, stir until the sugar dissolves and the water comes to the boil. Remove the spoon and do not stir again until the syrup turns a pale golden caramel. Then add the coffee and put back on the heat to dissolve. Allow to cool and add the whiskey.

Coffee Sauce

Omit whiskey in the above recipe and serve with coffee ice-cream.

Irish Mist Sauce

Substitute Irish Mist for Irish whiskey in the recipe for Irish Coffee Sauce.

Strawberry Sauce
Serves 10–12

Serve with ice-cream or a meringue roulade or Coeurs à la Crème (see page 432).

450g (1lb) fresh strawberries
75g (3oz) icing sugar
lemon juice, freshly squeezed

Clean and hull the strawberries. Purée with the sugar and strain through a nylon sieve. Taste and add freshly squeezed lemon juice if necessary. Store in the fridge.

Raspberry Sauce
Serves 6–8

225g (8oz) raspberries
Stock Syrup to taste (see page 568)
lemon juice (optional)

Liquidise the raspberries with some syrup. Strain through a nylon sieve and sharpen with lemon juice if necessary. Store in the fridge.

Loganberry Sauce
Serves 6–8

Serve with ice-cream or a meringue roulade or Coeurs à la Crème (see page 432).

225g (8oz) loganberries
Stock Syrup (see page 568) to taste
lemon juice (optional)

Add some syrup to the loganberries. Liquidise and sieve, taste, and sharpen with lemon juice if necessary. Store in the fridge.

Rhubarb Sauce
Serves 6

Serve warm with roast pork or with ice-cream or Bread and Butter Pudding.

450g (1lb) red rhubarb cut into 2.5cm (1in) pieces
110g (4oz) sugar
Redcurrant Jelly (see page 508), optional

Put the rhubarb into a stainless-steel saucepan, add the sugar and toss around. Leave for 5–10 minutes until the juice from the rhubarb starts to melt the sugar. Cover the saucepan, put on a gentle heat and cook until soft. Taste and add a little more sugar if necessary. It should not be too sweet but should not cut your throat either. If you have really good redcurrant jelly stir in a spoonful at the end, otherwise leave it out.

Blackcurrant Sauce
Serves 8–10

Very good, served either warm or cold with vanilla or blackcurrant ice-cream or Pannacotta (see page 406).

225g (8oz) blackcurrants, topped and tailed
225ml (8fl oz) Stock Syrup (see page 568)
125–150ml (4–5fl oz) water

Pour the syrup over the blackcurrants and bring to the boil, cook for 3–5 minutes until the blackcurrants burst. Liquidise and pour through a nylon sieve. Allow to cool. Add the water.

Mango and Passion Fruit Sauce
Serves 4–6

1 large ripe mango
4 passion fruit
1–2 tablespoons lime juice, freshly squeezed
1–2 tablespoons caster sugar

Peel the mango, scrape the flesh from the stone and purée in a food processor. Put in a bowl with the passion fruit seeds and juice, add the lime juice and sugar to taste. Cover and chill. Serve with ice-cream.

Pineapple Sauce
Serves 4–6

Serve with ice-cream or Yoghurt and Cardamon Cream (see page 434).

225ml (8fl oz) fresh pineapple, chopped
1/2–1 tablespoon caster sugar
lime or lemon juice to taste
1 tablespoon freshly chopped mint (optional)

Whizz the first three ingredients in a food processor to create a coarse puree. Taste and add more sugar or citrus juice as needed. Turn into a bowl and add mint if using.

Oven Temperatures

Celsius*	Fahrenheit	Gas	Description
110°C	225°F	mark ¼	cool
130°C	250°F	mark ½	cool
140°C	275°F	mark 1	very low
150°C	300°F	mark 2	very low
170°C	325°F	mark 3	low
180°C	350°F	mark 4	moderate
190°C	375°F	mark 5	mod. hot
200°C	400°F	mark 6	hot
220°C	425°F	mark 7	hot
230°C	450°F	mark 8	very hot
250°C	475°F	mark 9	very hot

* For fan-assisted ovens, reduce temperatures by 10°C

Volume

5ml	1 teaspoon
10ml	1 dessertspoon
15ml	1 tablespoon
30ml	1fl oz
50ml	2fl oz
75ml	3fl oz
100ml	3½ fl oz
125ml	4fl oz
150ml	5fl oz (¼ pint)
200ml	7fl oz (⅓ pint)
250ml (¼ litre)	9fl oz
300ml	10fl oz (½ pint)
350ml	12fl oz
400ml	14fl oz
425ml	15fl oz (¾ pint)
450ml	16fl oz
500ml (½ litre)	18fl oz
600ml	1 pint (20fl oz)
700ml	1¼ pints
850ml	1½ pints
1 litre	1¾ pints
1.2 litres	2 pints
1.5 litres	2½ pints
1.8 litres	3 pints
2 litres	3½ pints

Weight

10g	½oz
20g	¾oz
25g	1oz
50g	2oz
60g	2½oz
75g	3oz
100g	3½oz
110g	4oz (¼lb)
150g	5oz
175g	6oz
200g	7oz
225g	8oz (½lb)
250g (¼kg)	9oz
300g	10½oz
275g	10oz
350g	12oz (¾lb)
400g	14oz
450g	1lb
500g (½kg)	18oz
600g	1¼lb
700g	1½lb
800g	1lb 12oz
900g	2lb
1kg	2¼lb
1.1kg	2½lb
1.3kg	3lb
1.5kg	3lb 5oz
1.6kg	3½lb
1.8kg	4lb
2kg	4½lb
2.2kg	5lb

Measurements

3mm	⅛in
5mm	¼in
1cm	½in
2cm	¾in
2.5cm	1in
3cm	1¼in
4cm	1½in
5cm	2in
6cm	2½in
7.5cm	3in
9cm	3½in
10cm	4in
12.5cm	5in
15cm	6in
18cm	7in
20cm	8in
23cm	9in
25cm	10in
28cm	11in
30cm	12in

American Cup Measures

Butter, Margarine, Lard

25g (1oz)	2tbsp	¼ stick
100g (3½oz)	8tbsp	1 stick

Liquids

225ml (8fl oz)	1 cup

Golden Syrup, Treacle, Clear Honey

350g (12oz)	1 cup

Sugar

Caster and granulated

225g (8oz)	1 cup

Moist brown

200g (7oz)	1 cup

Icing sugar

125g (4½oz)	1 cup

Breadcrumbs

Fresh

50g (2oz)	1 cup

Dried

110g (4oz)	1 cup

Cheese

Grated cheese

110g (4oz)	1 cup

Diced Cheddar

175g (6oz)	1 cup

Parmesan

150g (5oz)	1 cup

Cream cheese

225g (8oz)	1 cup

Dried Fruits

Currants, raisins and sultanas

150g (5oz)	1 cup

Apricots

150–175g (5oz–6oz)	1 cup

Prunes

175g (6oz)	1 cup

Glacé cherries

125g (4½oz)	1 cup

Nuts

Almonds, whole and shelled

150g (5oz)	1 cup

Almonds, flaked

110g (4oz)	1 cup

Ground nuts

110g (4oz)	1 cup

Hazelnuts

150g (5oz)	1 cup

Walnuts and pecans

110g (4oz)	1 cup	

Chopped nuts

110g (4oz)	1 cup

Flour

110g (4oz)	1 cup

Cornflour

25g (1oz)	¼ cup

Oats

Rolled oats

100g (3½oz)	1 cup

Oatmeal

175g (6oz)	1 cup

Pulses, Rice and Grains

Haricot beans

200g (7oz)	1 cup

Kidney beans

25g (1oz)	1 cup

Rice, uncooked

200g (7oz)	1 cup

Rice, cooked and drained

165g (5½oz)	1 cup

Semolina, ground rice and couscous

175g (6oz)	1 cup

Split peas, lentils

225g (8oz)	1 cup

Vegetables

Beansprouts

50g (2oz)	1 cup

Cabbage, shredded

75g (3oz)	1 cup

Onions, chopped

110g (4oz)	1 cup

Peas, shelled

150g (5oz)	1 cup

Potatoes, peeled and diced

165g (5½oz)	1 cup

Potatoes, mashed

225g (8oz)	1 cup

Spinach, cooked purée

200–225g (7–8oz)	1 cup

Tomatoes

225g (8oz)	1 cup

Fish

Fish, cooked and flaked

225g (8oz)	1 cup, packed

Prawns, peeled

175g (6oz)	1 cup

Refrigerator Storage

Meat, Poultry and Fish

Raw meats

Joints	3 days
Bacon	7 days
Chicken	2 days
Fish	1 days
Minced meat	1 day
Offal	1 day
Raw sliced meat	2 days
Sausages	3 days

Cooked Meats

Casseroles	2 days
Fish	1 day
Ham	2 days
Joints	3 days
Sliced meat	2 days

Dairy Produce

Cheese, hard	7–14 days
Cheese, soft	2–3 days
Eggs, raw	2 weeks
Eggs, hard-boiled	2 days
Milk	4–5 days

Tinned foods	2 days*
Cooked vegetables	2 days
Coked potatoes	2 days
Freshly squeezed fruit juice	1 day

Always transfer tinned foods, once opened, into a clean, dry container with a lid.

Freezer Storage

Meat and Poultry

Beef, lamb, pork and veal	4–6 months
Chicken, turkey and venison	10–12 months
Duck, goose and rabbit	4–6 months
Ham and bacon joints	3–4 months
Minced beef	3–4 months
Offal	3–4 months
Sausages and sausage meat	2–3 months

Fish

Oily fish	3–4 months
Shellfish	2–3 months
White fish	6–8 months

Dairy Produce

Butter, unsalted	6–8 months
Butter, salted	3–4 months
Cheese, hard	4–6 months
Cheese, soft	3–4 months
Cream	6–8 months
Ice-cream	3–4 months
Milk, skimmed	3–4 months
Milk, semi-skimmed	3–4 months

Fruit and Vegetables

Fruit juice	4–6 months
Fruit	8–10 months
Mushrooms and tomatoes	6–8 months
Most vegetables	10–12 months
Vegetable purées	6–8 months

Bread	2–3 months
Bread dough	2–3 months
Cakes	4–6 months

Highly seasoned dishes	2–3 months
Ready-prepared dishes	4–6 months

contact addresses

Ardsallagh Goats Products Ltd.
www.ardsallaghgoats.com

Woodstock
Carrigtwohill
County Cork
Ireland
Tel: + 353 21 4882336
Email: jane@ardsallaghgoats.com

Ballymaloe Country Relish (Hyde Ltd.)
www.ballymaloecountryrelish.ie

Courtstown Pk
Little Island
County Cork
Ireland
Tel: + 353 21 4354810
Email: hyde@ballymaloe.com

Ballymaloe Cookery School
See page 640

Ballymalloe House
www.ballymaloe.ie

Shanagarry
County Cork
Ireland
Tel: + 353 21 4652531
Email: res@ballymaloe.ie

Bord Bia – Irish Food Board
www.bordbia.ie

Dublin Head Office
Clanwilliam Court
Lower Mount Street
Dublin 2
Ireland
Tel: + 353 1 668 5155

The Bread Bakers' Guild of America
www.bbga.org

3203 Maryland Avenue
North Versailles
PA 15137
USA
Tel : + 1 412 823 2080
Email: info@bbga.org

CáIS – The Irish Farmhouse Cheesemakers' Association
www.irishcheese.ie

C/o Cooleeney Farmhouse Cheese
Moyne
Thurles
County Tipperary
Ireland
Tel: + 353 504 45112
Email: cooleeney@eircom.net

Certified Farmers' Markets (UK)
www.farmersmarkets.net

PO Box 575
Southampton
Hampshire
SO15 7BZ
Tel: + 44 845 4588420

Clonakilty Black Pudding Co.
www.clonakiltyblackpudding.ie

16 Pearse Street
Clonakilty
West Cork
Ireland
Tel: + 353 23 34835
Email: sales@clonakiltyblackpudding.ie

Coolea Farmhouse Cheese
Dick Willems

Coolea
Macroom
County Cork
Ireland
Tel: + 353 26 45204
Fax: + 353 26 45204
Email: cooleacheese@eircom.net

Euro-Toques International
(European Community of Chefs)
www.euro-toques.org

Gubbeen Farmhouse Products
www.gubbeen.com

Gubbeen Smoke House
Tel: + 353 28 27824
Email: smokehouse@gubbeen.com

Gubbeen Cheese
Tel: + 353 28 28231
Fax: + 353 28 28609
Email: cheese@gubbeen.com

Heirloom Seeds
www.heirloomseeds.com

PO Box 245
West Elizabeth
PA 15088-0245
USA
Tel: + 1 412 384 0852
Email: mail@heirloomseeds.com

IACP – International Association of Culinary Professionals
www.iacp.com

304 West Liberty Street – Suite 201
Louisville
Kentucky 40202
USA
Tel: + 1 502 581 9786
Fax: + 1 502 589 3602
Email: iacp@hqtrs.com

Jobs for Cooks
www.jobsforcooks.com
Email: info@jobsforcooks.com

Irish Farmers' Markets
www.irishfarmersmarkets.ie

Aughrim
County Wicklow
Ireland
Tel: + 353 1 87 6115016
Email: info@farmersmarkets.ie

Macroom Oatmeal Mills
Donal Creedon

Massytown
Macroom
County Cork
Ireland
Tel: + 353 26 41800
Fax: + 353 26 41800

Mandy's Irish Shops

830 Garrett Lane
Tooting
London
SW17 0NA
Tel: + 44 208 767 9942

161 High Road
Willesden
London
NW10 2SG
Tel: + 44 208 459 2842

Smoked Salmon (Bill Casey)
Shanagarry
County Cork
Tel: + 353 21 4646955

Soil Association
www.soilassociation.org

South Plaza
Marlborough Street
Bristol
BS1 3NX
Tel: + 44 117 314 5000
Email: info@soilassociation.org

Ummera Smoked Products
www.ummera.com

Inchybridge
Timoleague
County Cork
Ireland
Tel: + 353 23 46644
Fax: + 353 23 46419
Email: info@ummera.com

To get involved in the organic and local food movement the following websites are a great start. They are full of information about how to find local and organic food suppliers near you, organic box schemes, recipes, family events and much more!

UK
www.sustainable.ie

Ireland
www.whyorganic.org

glossary

Acidulated water: Cold water with lemon juice or vinegar added to it to stop the discolouration of certain fruits and vegetables. Add 1 teaspoon of lemon juice or vinegar to every 300ml (1/2 pint) water.

Agar agar: Vegetarian equivalent of gelatine, made from seaweed.

à la carte (F): 1) Menu from which the customer can choose dishes. 2) Dishes cooked to order.

à l'Anglaise (F): Served in an English style.

à la crème (F): A dish accompanied by cream or cooked in a cream-based sauce.

al dente (I): An Italian cooking term referring to perfectly cooked pasta that has a barely discernible bite.

alla, à la (I/F): Used to describe a certain style of cooking.

Allumettes (F): Thin strips of vegetables.

Amandine (F): Cooking with or coating with almonds.

Antipasti (I): Italian hors-d'oeuvre served either hot or cold.

à point (F): Used to describe meat that is medium-cooked.

Arachide oil: Groundnut oil.

Arrowroot: Fine white starch, ground from the root of an American plant of the same name. Used to thicken sauces.

Aspic: A clear jelly made from the cooked juices of meat or fish.

Au gratin (F): Cooked food, covered with a sauce, breadcrumbs or grated cheese, and butter, then browned under the grill.

Bakewell paper: Brand name of non-stick silicone paper.

Baking blind: Baking a pastry case without the filling inside. The case is usually lined with greaseproof paper and filled with dried beans to prevent the pastry from puffing up. This process ensures a crisp pastry case.

Bain-marie (or water bath): 1) A deep container, half-filled with hot water, in which delicate foods such as custards or fish mousses are cooked in their moulds or terrines to protect them from direct oven heat. Cooking in a bain-marie produces a gentle, steamy atmosphere which reduces the risk of curdling. 2) A container that holds several pans, used to keep food warm during restaurant service.

Barbados sugar: Soft, dark brown sugar that has been treated with molasses.

Barbecue: Cooking over red hot coals, normally charcoal. Apple or hickory chips can be added for flavour.

Barding: Wrapping meat, game or poultry which is low in fat with thin slices of bacon or pork fat to prevent it from drying out while roasting.

Basting: Spooning roasting juices over meat during cooking to moisten and add flavour.

Beating: Beating food with a wooden spoon, hand whisk or electric mixer to introduce air, making food lighter or fluffier.

Binding: The addition of eggs, cream, melted fat or roux to a dry mixture to hold it together.

Blanching: Briefly boiling food – 1) To loosen the skin from nuts, fruit and vegetables.

2) To kill enzymes and set the colour of food before freezing. 3) To remove strong or bitter flavours.

Blanquette (F): Poultry, veal or rabbit stew in a creamy sauce.

Blender: An electronic mixer whose blades reduce ingredients to a smooth consistency.

Blending: Achieving a smooth consistency through the use of a spoon, beater, or liquidiser.

Blini, Bliny (R): Buckwheat and yeast pancake traditionally served with caviar and sour cream.

Boiling: Cooking in liquid at a temperature of 100°C (212°F).

Boning: Removing the bones of meat, poultry, game or fish.

Bouquet garni: A small bunch of fresh herbs used to flavour stews, casseroles, stocks or soups, usually consisting of parsley stalks, a sprig of thyme, perhaps a bay leaf and an outside stalk of celery (removed before serving).

Bourguignon (F): In the Burgundy style, i.e. cooked with red wine.

Braising: Browning in hot fat and then cooking slowly in a covered pot with vegetables and some liquid.

Brine: Salt and water solution used in pickling and preserving.

Brioche (F): Slightly sweetened soft bread made of rich yeast dough.

Brochette (F): Skewer used for grilling chunks of meat, fish and vegetables under a grill or over charcoal.

Broiling (US): American term for grilling.

Browning: Searing the outer surface of meat to seal in the juices.

Brûlée (F): Describes a dish such as cream custards with a caramelised sugar glaze.

Butterfly: To slit a piece of food horizontally almost, but not quite, through, so that when it is opened out it resembles butterfly wings. This technique is often applied to a leg of lamb, large prawns and thick fish fillets, so that they cook faster.

Canapé (F): Small tasty mouthful served as an appetiser.

Cannelloni (I): Large tubes of pasta which are then stuffed.

Capers: The unopened flower buds of a Mediterranean shrub, usually pickled and used as a garnish or flavouring.

Caponata (I): Sicilian dish of aubergines, celery, onions, tomatoes, onions, capers and black olives.

Carbonnade (F): Beef and beer stew.

Casserole (F): 1) Cooking pot with lid, made from ovenproof earthenware, glass or metal. 2) Slow-cooked stew of fish, meat or vegetables.

Cassoulet (F): Stew of haricot beans, pork, lamb, goose or duck, sausage, vegetables and herbs; cassoulets come from south-west France.

Chantilly (F): Whipped cream, slightly sweetened and flavoured with vanilla.

Charlotte: 1) Hot, moulded fruit pudding made of buttered slices of bread, filled with fruit and cooked with apricot jam. 2) Cold, moulded dessert consisting of sponge fingers and filled with cream and fruit, or a cream custard set with gelatine. 3) A plain

mould for Charlottes or other desserts.

Chiffonade (F): Shredded herbs or salad leaves used as a garnish.

Chilling: Cooling food in a fridge, without freezing it.

Chining: The separation of ribs from the backbone to make carving a joint of meat easier.

Chinois (F): 1) In the Chinese style. 2) A conical-shaped sieve with a fine mesh.

Chorizo (S): Smoked pork sausage originally from Spain.

Chowder (US): Fish dish containing sweetcorn, halfway between a stew and a soup.

Clarified butter: Butter cleared of impurities and water by heating slowly.

Clarifying: 1) Clearing fats by heating and filtering. 2) Clearing consommés and jellies with beaten egg white.

Cocotte (F): Small ovenproof dish used for baking individual egg dishes.

Coddling: Cooking slowly in simmering water, particularly of egg cookery.

Colander: Perforated metal or plastic bowl used to drain liquids.

Compote (F): Dessert of fresh or dried fruit cooked in syrup – usually served cold.

Concassé (F): Roughly chopped, usually applies to the flesh of tomatoes.

Conserve: Fruit preserved by boiling with sugar and used like jam.

Coquille (F): 1) Scallop. 2) Shell-shaped ovenproof dish used to serve fish, poultry or game.

Cornflour/cornstarch: Finely ground flour from cornmeal, used for thickening sauces or puddings.

Corn syrup (US): Syrup derived from maize, used in baking and confectionery.

Coulis: A thin purée soft enough to pour, usually made of vegetables or fruit.

Creamy milk: When one of our recipes calls for creamy milk, we mean a mixture of one-third cream to two-thirds milk. Creamy milk is often used in soups or sauces when full cream would be too rich.

Crème (F): Applied to fresh cream, butter and thick creamy soups.

Crème brûlée (F): Cream custard with caramelised topping.

Crème caramel (F): Cold moulded egg custard with caramel topping.

Crème fraîche (F): Cream that has matured but not soured.

Creole: Cooked in a Caribbean style.

Crêpe (F): Thin pancake.

Crêpes Suzette (F): Pancakes cooked in an orange sauce and flambéed in alcohol.

Croquettes (F): Cooked foods moulded into small shapes, dipped in egg and crumbs, then deep-fried.

Croûstade (F): Small, crispy fried or baked bread or pastry shape filled with a savoury mixture.

Croûtes (F): 1) Pastry covering meat, fish and vegetables. 2) Slices of bread or brioche, spread with butter or sauce, then baked until crisp.

Curd: Semi-solid part of milk, produced by souring.

Curdle: The separation of different elements of a food. Cold emulsion sauces such as mayonnaise may curdle if oil is added too quickly. Acid such as lemon juice will curdle milk. A cake mixture can curdle if eggs are added too fast.

Cure: To preserve meat or fish by salting, smoking or drying.

Dairy salt: A finely ground pure salt added to butter and margarine.

Dariole: Small, cup-shaped mould used for making jellies, puddings and creams.

Daube (F): Stew of braised meat and vegetables.

Deep-frying: Frying food by submerging it in hot oil.

De-glaze: Adding wine, cream or stock to dilute pan juices and make gravy.

De-gorge: Sprinkling vegetables (such as cucumber or aubergines) with salt to draw out juices or excess moisture.

De-grease: To remove grease from the surface of the liquid. If possible, the liquid should be chilled so that the fat solidifies. Otherwise, skim off the fat with a large metal spoon, then trail strips of kitchen paper on the surface to remove the remaining globules.

Dice: Cut into small cubes.

Dough: Mixture of flour, water, milk and/or egg, sometimes enriched with fat, which is firm enough to knead, roll and shape.

Drawing: To remove the intestines from poultry.

Dredging: Sprinkling sugar or flour over food.

Dress: To pluck, draw and truss poultry or game.

Dressing: 1) Sauce for a salad. 2) Stuffing for meat or poultry.

Dripping: Fat that drips from meat, poultry or game during roasting.

Dusting: Sprinkling lightly with flour, sugar, spice or seasoning.

Eclair (F): Cigar-shaped choux pastry bun filled with whipped cream and topped with chocolate.

Egg wash: Raw egg beaten with water or milk and brushed onto raw tarts, pies, buns and biscuits to produce a shiny, golden glaze when cooked.

Emulsion: A mixture of two insoluble liquids, e.g. oil and water.

En croûte (F): Food encased in pastry.

En papillote (F): Food wrapped, cooked and served in oiled or buttered paper or foil to prevent loss of flavour and conserve moisture.

Entrée (F): Main course.

Escalope: A thin slice of meat, beaten flat and shallow-fried.

Estoufado (GR): 1) Greek cooking pot 2) Greek stew typically containing chicken or rabbit, onions and cinammon.

Fermentation: Chemical action caused by enzymes. Intentional effervescence occurs when yeast is used to raise bread; accidental effervescence occurs in preserves or pickles that ferment when incorrectly prepared.

Fines herbes (F): A finely chopped mixture of fresh parsley, chervil, tarragon and chives. Traditionally used in French cookery.

Flake: 1) Separating cooked fish into individual flaky slivers. 2) Grating chocolate or cheese into small slivers.

Flambé: Food flamed in a pan using burning brandy or other alcohol.

Florentine: 1) Of fish and eggs, served on a bed of buttered spinach and coated with a cheese sauce. 2) Thin petit-four biscuit made of nuts, glacé fruit and chocolate.

Foie gras (F): The preserved liver of specially fattened goose or duck.

Folding in: Using a large, metal spoon or spatula to mix one ingredient or mixture into another very gently so as not to knock out the air.

Fondue (Sw): Melted cheese and white wine dish into which diners dunk cubes of bread. Chocolate fondue and fondue Bourguignon are other versions.

Fool: Cold dessert of fruit purée and whipped cream.

Freezing: Solidifying or preserving food by chilling it and storing at -18°C.

Fricassée (F): White stew of chicken, rabbit, veal or vegetables fried in butter, then cooked in stock and finished with cream and egg yolks.

Frost: 1) To coat a cake with sugar icing. 2) To dip the rim of a glass in egg white and caster sugar, then chill in a fridge until set.

Fumet (F): Concentrated broth or stock made from fish, meat or vegetables.

Galette (F): 1) A flat pastry cake. 2) A flat potato cake either mashed or sliced.

Gelatine: Transparent protein derived from animal tissue and bones which melts when hot and forms a jelly on cooling. See also *agar agar*.

Genoise (F): A rich sponge cake made from eggs, sugar, flour and melted butter, then baked in a tin.

Ghee (In): Clarified butter, usually made from the milk of the water buffalo originating in India. Often used in meat dishes, it has a distinctive, nutty taste.

Giblets: Edible internal organs of poultry and game including the liver, heart and gizzard.

Gill: Liquid measure, equivalent to a ¼ pint (5fl oz).

Gizzard: The muscular stomach of a bird in which food is ground.

Glacé (F): Glazed, iced or frozen.

Glace de viande (F): 1) Meat glaze or residue in the bottom of a pan after frying or roasting meat. 2) Concentrated meat stock.

Glaze: Brushing food with milk, beaten egg, sugar syrup, or jelly after cooking to produce a glossy finish.

Gluten: A protein in flour that is developed when dough is kneaded, making it elastic.

Gnocchi (I): Small dumplings made from semolina, potatoes or choux pastry.

Goujon (F): A term used for little strips of fish or meat about the size of a small fish called a gudgeon.

Goulash (H): Beef and onion stew flavoured with tomato and paprika.

Granita (I): Water ice.

Gravy: 1) Juices drained from roasted meat and poultry. 2) A sauce derived from these juices made by boiling up with either stock or wine and often thickened with flour.

Griddle: A flat, metal plate used for baking cakes and breads on top of the stove.

Grill pan: A heavy cast-iron pan, with a ridged bottom, either round or rectangular.

The ridges mark the food attractively while keeping the meat or fish from direct contact with the fat. A heavy pan gives a good, even heat.

Grissini (I): Breadsticks.

Groats: De-husked, often milled grain, especially oats.

Groundnut oil: Peanut oil.

Hanging: Suspending meat or game in a cool, dry place until it becomes tender.

Haricot vert (F): Green bean.

Hash: Dish of leftover chopped meat, potatoes or other vegetables, fried together.

Herbs: Plants without a fibrous stem, used to add flavour when cooking.

Hors-d'oeuvre (F): Hot or cold appetiser served at the beginning of a meal.

Hulling: Removing the green stems from strawberries, raspberries etc.

Icing: Sweet coating for cakes.

Infusing: Steeping herbs, tea leaves or coffee in water or other liquid to extract the flavour.

Irish coffee: Coffee with a shot of whiskey and a topping of thick cream.

Jaggery: Brown, unrefined lump sugar made from cane sugar or palm sap.

Joint: 1) Prime cut of meat for roasting. 2) To divide meat into individual pieces.

Jugged: Meat dishes stewed in a covered pot, e.g. jugged hare.

Julienne: A term used when vegetables or citrus fruits are cut into very fine, thin

matchsticks or 'needle-shreds'. A recipe will sometimes indicate the size required. Generally a julienne of vegetables or citrus fruits is used as a garnish, but sometimes a much larger julienne may be used as a vegetable or as part of a salad.

Junket: Curds mixed with cream, sweetened and flavoured.

Jus (F): Juices from roasting meat used as gravy.

Kebab (T): Meat cubes marinated and grilled on a skewer with vegetables.

Kedgeree (In): Dish of cooked meat or fish, rice and eggs, often eaten for breakfast or lunch.

Kosher: Food prepared in accordance with Orthodox Jewish Law.

Kosher salt: So called because it is used to help extract the blood from meats, thereby making them kosher. The grains are larger than regular table salt and are free of additives. Many chefs also prefer the flavour.

Langouste (F): Clawless crawfish, almost lobster size, found in warm, coastal waters.

Langue de chat (F): Flat, finger-shaped crisp biscuit served with cold desserts.

Lard: Purifed pork fat used in deep-frying, roasting meats and in pastry making.

Larding: Threading strips of fat through lean meat using a specially designed needle, to prevent meat that is naturally low in fat from drying out when roasting.

Lasagne (I): Square or rectangular sheets of fresh or dried pasta that form the base of the Italian dish of the same name.

Leaven: Ingredients such as yeast that cause dough to rise.

Légumes (F): 1) Vegetables. 2) Plants with a seed pod such as peas and beans.

Lentils: Seeds of a legume, soaked and used in soups, stews and purées.

Liaison (F): Mixture used to thicken a sauce or stew.

Lyonnaise (F): In the Lyons style, usually with onions.

Macaroni (I): Short, hollow tubes of pasta.

Macerate: To soak fruit in syrup or other liquid so that it will absorb flavour and in some cases become more tender.

Mandolin: A kitchen implement made of stainless steel or wood, with adjustable blades used for slicing vegetables into various shapes.

Marinade: Blend of oil, wine or vinegar, herbs and spices used to add flavour to meat.

Marinate: To steep in marinade.

Marinière (F): 1) Mussels cooked in a white wine and vinegar sauce then served half open. 2) Fish cooked in white wine and then garnished with mussels.

Medallions (F): Small circular cuts of meat, fish and pâté.

Meringue (F): Whisked egg white blended with sugar, spooned or piped on top of sweet pies or into shapes and then baked at a very low temperature until crisp.

Meunière (F): Fish cooked in butter, seasoned, and then sprinkled with parsley and lemon juice.

Milanese (I): Milan-style escalopes, coated in egg and breadcrumbs, seasoned with grated Parmesan cheese, and then fried in butter.

Mirabelle (F): 1) Small yellow plum, used in a tart filling. 2) A liqueur made from the fruit.

Mirepoix (F): Mixture of finely diced vegetables and ham which, when fried in butter, is used as a base for brown sauces or stews.

Mocha: 1) High-quality coffee served after dinner. 2) A blend of coffee and chocolate flavours.

Mouler (F): To grind soft food into a purée, or dry food into a powder.

Moules (F): Mussels.

Moussaka: Middle-eastern dish of aubergines, minced meat and tomatoes, topped with cheese sauce or savoury custard.

Mousse: Light, cold dish, either sweet or savoury, whose ingredients may include cream, whipped egg white and gelatine.

Navarin (F): Stew of lamb and vegetables.

Neapolitan (I): 1) In the style of Naples. 2) Ice-creams and sweet cakes in colourful layers of flavour.

Niçoise (F): In the style of Nice, i.e. cooked with tomatoes, onion, garlic and black olives.

Noodles: Flat ribbon pasta made from water, flour and sometimes egg.

Normande (F): In the Normandy style, i.e. cooked with cider and cream.

Nouilles (F): Noodles.

Offal: Edible internal organs of meat, poultry and game.

Orzo (I): A small pasta grain resembling rice in appearance, which may be used in a variety of dishes, hot and cold.

Osso bucco (I): Dish of braised veal shank containing marrow bone, prepared with tomatoes and wine.

Oyster meat: In poultry, there are two succulent ovals of meat along both sides of the backbone, level with the thigh.

Paella (S): A traditional Spanish dish of saffron rice, chicken or shellfish, named after the traditional pan in which it is cooked.

Palette knife: A blunt knife with a rounded tip and flexible blade – useful for spreading meringue etc.

Palm sugar: A form of sugar available in cakes or lumps produced by boiling the sap of various palms.

Paneer (In): An Indian fresh cheese curd.

Panettone (I): Cake-like bread containing raisins, served at Christmas.

Panko crumbs: Japanese breadcrumbs.

Paper lid: When sweating vegetables for the base of a soup or stew, we quite often cover them with a butter wrapper or a lid made from greaseproof paper which fits the saucepan exactly. This keeps in the steam and helps to sweat the vegetables.

Paprika (H): Ground, hot, sweet red pepper, either natural or smoked.

Par-boiling: Boiling for a short while to partially cook food.

Parfait (F): Frozen or fresh dessert made from whipped cream and fruit purée.

Parmentier (F): Used to describe dishes containing potatoes.

Pasteurising: Method of sterilising milk by heating it to 60–82°C (140–180°F) to destroy the bacteria.

Pastry: Dough made with flour, butter and water, then baked or deep-fried until crisp.

Pastry wheel: Small, serrated metal wheel for cutting or fluting pastry.

Pasty: Small pastry pie with a savoury filling.

Pâté (F): Smooth or coarse savoury mixture; the latter is baked in a terrine or a pastry covering. It is occasionally served warm but usually cold.

Pearl barley: De-husked barley grains, used in soup.

Pectin: Gelling agent which occurs naturally in fruit and vegetables. Sets jellies and jams.

Percolator: A coffee pot that filters water through ground coffee.

Perdrix (F): Partridge.

Petits fours (F): A catch-all word for dainty little sweetmeats usually served at the end of a meal with coffee or occasionally at the end of a drinks party with dessert wine.

Petit pois (F): Tiny young green peas.

Pickle: To preserve meat or vegetables in a brine or vinegar solution.

Pilaf (T): Middle-Eastern dish of cooked rice mixed with spiced, cooked chicken, meat or fish.

Pimento: Green or red pepper.

Pipe: To decorate various dishes by forcing mashed potato, meringue, icing or savoury butter through a forcing bag fitted with a nozzle.

Piquant (F): Hot, pungent and appetising.

Pith: The white lining that attaches the rind to the fruit in citrus fruits.

Pizzaiola (I): Meat or chicken cooked in red wine, tomato sauce and flavoured with garlic.

Plat du jour (F): Dish of the day.

Poaching: Cooking food in simmering liquid, just below boiling.

Polenta (I): Cornmeal, made from dried and ground maize.

Potage (F): Thick soup.

Praline (F): Sweet consisting of nuts caramelised in boiling sugar and then ground to a paste.

Preserving: Keeping food in good condition by boiling in sugar, pickling in salt, refrigerating or using chemicals.

Pressure cooking: A method of cooking at specific levels of pressure. The higher the pressure, the higher the temperature at which water boils. Cooking food with liquid in this fashion means that the steam created by the liquid is sealed in under increasing pressure, cooking the food in less time than conventional methods of steaming.

Prosciutto (I): Raw smoked ham, served finely sliced, e.g. Parma, Serrano, Pate Negra.

Provençal (F): In the style of Provence, e.g. cooked with garlic and tomatoes.

Pudding: 1) Boiled or baked sweet dessert. 2) Boiled suet crust which is filled with meat, poultry or fruit. 3) A catch-all word for desserts.

Pulp: 1) Soft, fleshy tissue of fruit or vegetables. 2) To reduce food to a soft mass by crushing or boiling.

Purée (F): 1) Sieved raw or cooked food. 2) Thick vegetable soup passed though a blender or food processor.

Quenelles: (F) Light savoury dumpling, either meat or fish, used as a garnish.

Quiche (F): Open pastry tart filled with a savoury mixture.

Ragout (F): Stew of meat and vegetables.

Ramekins: Individual ovenproof dishes.

Ratafia: 1) Flavouring made from bitter almonds. 2) Liqueur made from fruit kernels. 3) Tiny maracoon.

Ratatouille (F): Mediterranean stew of aubergines, onions, peppers and tomatoes cooked in olive oil.

Ravioli (I): Small, savoury-filled pasta pillows, boiled and served with a flavoured butter, sauce or grated cheese.

Reducing: Concentrating a liquid by boiling and evaporating excess liquid.

Refreshing: Cooling hot food quickly, often vegetables or shellfish, either by placing it under cold running water or by plunging it into iced water, thus stopping it from cooking and setting the colour.

Relish: Sharp or spicy sauce made with vegetables or fruit which adds a piquant flavour to other dishes, usually served as an accompaniment.

Rendering: Slow cooking of meat tissues and trimmings to obain fat.

Rennet: Extract from the stomach lining of calves, used as a coagulating agent in the production of cheese curd.

Rice paper: Glossy, white edible paper made from the pith of a tree grown in China.

Rigatoni (I): Ridged macaroni.

Rillettes (F): An item of French charcuterie which is normally made of pork but can also be made of duck, rabbit or other meat.

Risotto (I): Savoury rice, fried and then cooked in stock or tomato juice, then finished with cheese.

Rissole: Small roll or patty made from cooked minced meat.

Roasting: Cooking in the oven with radiant heat, or on a spit over an open flame.

Roe: 1) Soft roe – milt of the male fish. 2) Hard roe – eggs of the female fish. 3) Coral roe – eggs of shellfish, coral colour when cooked.

Rôtisserie (F): Rotating spit used for roasting or grilling meat or poultry.

Roulade (F): A savoury roll of meat or sweet, as in chocolate cake or meringue.

Roux (F): A mixture of equal parts butter and flour, this is a basic liaison which is used as a thickening agent.

Saganaki (Gr): Small, round aluminium frying pan used to fry and serve piping hot cheese.

Saignant (F): Used to describe meat that is underdone.

Salamander: Metal plate on handle that can be heated and placed over food to brown it.

Salami (I): Spiced meat sausage, sold fresh or smoked.

Sauté (F): To fry food rapidly in hot fat.

Scald: 1) To heat milk or cream to just below boiling point. 2) To plunge fruit or vegetables in boiling water to remove their skins.

Scallion (US): Young onion or spring onion with an undeveloped bulb used either in salads or as a garnish.

Scallop: Edible mollusc with white flesh and orange roe or coral. The fluted, deep shell is used for serving the scallops and other foods.

Scallopini (I): Small escalopes of veal, weighing approximately 40g (1¹/₂oz) and measuring about 7.5cm (3in) square.

Schnitzel (G): Veal slice; see escalope.

Scoring: 1) Cutting gashes in the surface of food. 2) Making a pattern of squares or diamonds on pastry crust.

Searing: Browning meat rapidly over a high heat to seal in the juices.

Seasoned flour: Flour seasoned with salt and pepper.

Sifting: Passing flour or sugar through a sieve to aerate and remove lumps.

Silicone paper: A non-stick parchment paper which is widely used for lining baking trays, cake tins etc. It may be used several times over and is particularly useful when making meringues or chocolates because they simply peel off the paper.

Silver dragee: Edible silver balls used for decoration on cakes and petits fours.

Simmering: Cooking in liquid just below boiling point.

Singe: To flame duck or geese quickly to remove all traces of feathers and down after plucking.

Skewer: Metal or wooden pin which holds meat or fish together when cooking.

Skimming: Removing cream from the surface of milk, or fat or scum from jam or broth.

Smoking: Curing food, such as fish or bacon by exposing it to warm or cold wood smoke over a period of time.

Sorbet (F): Water ice made with fruit juice or purée.

Soufflé (F): Baked dish consisting of a sauce or purée thickened with egg yolks into which stiffly beaten egg whites are folded.

Soufflé dish: Straight-sided circular dish used for cooking and serving soufflés.

Sousing: Pickling food in brine or vinegar.

Spit: Revolving skewer on which meat, poultry or game is roasted or grilled.

Spring-form mould: Baking tin with hinged sides which release the cake or pie when opened.

Sponge, to: A term used when working with powdered gelatine. The gelatine is sprinkled over a specified amount of liquid and left to sit for 4–5 minutes. During this period, the gelatine soaks up the water and becomes 'spongy' in texture. Gelatine is easier to dissolve if it is sponged before melting.

Starch: Carbohydrate obtained from cereal or potatoes.

Steaming: Cooking food in a tightly sealed container over simmering water.

Steeping: 1) Soaking in liquid until saturated with a soluble ingredient. 2) Soaking meat in water to remove excess salt.

Sterilising: Eliminating bacteria by heating food to a high temperature.

Stewing: Cooking food slowly in a covered pan or casserole.

Stir-frying: Cooking small pieces of food rapidly in very little fat, tossing constantly over high heat, usually in a wok.

Straining: Separating liquids from solids by passing them through a muslin sieve.

Strudel (G): Thin leaves of pastry dough, filled with fruit or savoury mixtures, rolled and then baked.

Stuffing: A savoury mixture of bread or rice, herbs, fruit or minced meat used to fill fish, meat, poultry and vegetables.

Suet: Fat around beef or lamb kidneys.

Sumac: A coarse, brick-red powder used in Mediterranean or Middle-Eastern cooking to give a citrus lift to salads, flatbreads, fish and meats.

Sweat: To cook vegetables in a little fat or oil over a gentle heat in a covered saucepan, until they are almost soft but not coloured.

Syrup: A sweet liquid made by boiling sugar with water or fruit juice.

Table d'hôte (F): Meal of three or more courses at a fixed price.

Tagine: 1) Shallow, round, earthenware, glazed pot with a tall conical lid that traps steam in during cooking and prevents stews from drying out. 2) Moroccan-style stew cooked in a tagine pot.

Tagliatelle (I): Thin, flat egg noodles.

Terrine (F): 1) Earthenware pot used for serving and cooking pâté. 2) Coarse pâté.

Timbale (F): 1) Cup-shaped earthenware or metal mould. 2) Dish prepared in such a mould.

Truffles: Expensive delicacies, these rare mushroom-like fungi are black or white in colour and have a delicate taste.

Trussing: Tying a bird or joint of meat in a neat shape with skewers and string before cooking.

Turnover: Sweet or savoury pastry made by folding a circle or square of pastry in half to form a semicircle or triangle.

Unleavened: Bread made without a raising agent, which when baked is thin and flattish, also referred to as flatbreads.

Unsweetened chocolate: Chocolate which does not contain any sugar. If it is unobtainable, use ordinary chocolate but adjust the amount of sugar accordingly or substitute 3 tablespoons of unsweetened cocoa and 15g (1/2oz) unsalted butter for every 30g (1oz) unsweetened chocolate.

Vanilla sugar: Sugar flavoured with vanilla by enclosing it with a vanilla pod in a closed jar or combining with a vanilla pod in a liquidiser.

Velouté (F): 1) Basic white sauce made with veal, chicken or fish stock. 2) Soup of creamy consistency.

Vermicelli (I): Very thin strands of pasta.

Vinaigrette (F): Mixture of oil, vinegar, salt and pepper often flavoured with herbs.

Vinegar: A clear acidic liquid obtained by fermenting wine, cider or malt beer.

Vol au vent (F): Light flaky case of puff pastry.

Wafer: Thin biscuit made of rice flour, served with ice-cream.

Waffle: Batter cooked on a hot, greased waffle iron to a crisp biscuit.

Wheatgerm: The living germ or 'embryo' of the wheat grain. Usually extracted from the grain during milling because it is more perishable than the rest of the grain. It is highly nutritional and may be eaten on its own or added to cereals or breads. It should be bought in small quantities and stored in the fridge.

Whey: Liquid separated from curd when milk curdles, used in cheese making.

Whisk: Looped wire utensil used to beat air into cream, eggs or batters.

Xanthan gum: A natural product produced by fermenting sugar using a natural bacteria Xanthamonas campestris. It is classified as a stabliser.

Yeast: Fungus cells used to produce alcoholic fermentation, or as a rising agent in dough.

Yoghurt: Curdled milk which has been treated with harmless bacteria.

Zabaglione (I): Dessert made from egg yolks, white wine or marsala and sugar, whisked together in the top of a double boiler over boiling water until thick and foamy.

Zest: Coloured oily outer skin of citrus fruit, which can be grated to add flavour to food or liquid.

Zester: Small tool for scraping off zest.

Key to abbreviations in glossary

F	French	G	German
Gr	Greek	H	Hungarian
I	Italian	In	Indian
R	Russian	S	Spanish
Sw	Swiss	T	Turkish
US	American		

index

This edition published in 2007
by Kyle Cathie Limited
122 Arlington Road
London NW1 7HP
general.enquiries@kyle-cathie.com
www.kylecathie.com

First published in Great Britain in 2001

Text © Darina Allen 2001, 2007
Photography © Ray Main 2001, Peter Cassidy 2007
Design © Kyle Cathie Limited 2007

ISBN 978-1-85626-729-8

The publishers would like to thank Mick and
Gill Hodson for their help.

A CIP cataloguing in publication record for this
title is available from the British Library.

10 9 8 7 6 5 4 3 2

Project editor: Jennifer Wheatley
Design: Geoff Hayes
Photography: Ray Main, Peter Cassidy (see below)
Copy editors: Vicki Murrell, Laura Wheatley
Home economists: Janie Suthering, Linda Tubby
(see below)
Production: Sha Huxtable and Alice Holloway
Index: Alex Corrin
Repro: Scanhouse Singapore

Photographs by Peter Cassidy, with food
preparation by Linda Tubby, appear on pages
1, 62–63, 70, 94–95, 120–121, 127, 156, 202–203, 224,
227, 256, 279, 314–315, 332–333, 339, 349, 350–351,
380–381, 409, 470–471, 477, 516–517, 534–535, 541,
546–547, 566–567, 578–579

Printed and bound in Singapore by
Tien Wah Press

THE BALLYMALOE COOKERY SCHOOL

'When you step through the little wooden side gate and into the courtyard of Ballymaloe Cookery School you enter a different, some say magical world. A world where the loudest sounds are the sounds of the countryside and maybe, if the windows are open, the quiet chatter and gentle clatter of people at work in a kitchen. A world where the whole emphasis is on food – growing it, preparing it, cooking it, eating it and, crucially, enjoying it.'
Darina Allen

Set in the middle of ten acres of organic market gardens, orchards and greenhouses which are, in turn, surrounded by a hundred acres of organic farm, the Ballymaloe Cookery School in Shanagarry, County Cork is a mecca with international renown for those with a passion for food who recognise that the best cooking comes from using the best ingredients. Darina's mission is to help people feel that cooking is not a mystery, and to give them confidence, and the courses at Ballymaloe are for everyone, from those who wish to pursue a professional culinary career to enthusiasts who want to explore a passion.

12-week Certificate We are now running the highly-regarded Ballymaloe Certificate Course three times a year. The course embraces all aspects of cookery from basic principles to advanced professional techniques. In addition to a thorough grounding in cookery, Ballymaloe students are exposed to a total food experience and the 12 weeks will equip you with the skills, confidence and inspiration to boost your career or simply to revitalise your approach to cooking. The course covers:
• every aspect of the Ballymaloe style of cooking
• French classic, regional and modern innovatory styles
• menu planning
• food costing
• food hygiene
• an opportunity to see the Ballymaloe House restaurant kitchen in operation
• excursions to specialist, local food producers
• an opportunity to learn the principals of organic gardening and farming

Short Courses We offer a variety of short courses of varying duration. The $2^1/_2$ and 5 day courses combine demonstration and practical sessions. Before booking your course, please visit our web site where you will find extra information on all aspects of the cookery school and courses.

Forgotten Skills Courses We also offer a series of short courses for those who would like to learn forgotten skills – a beginners guide to bee-keeping, growing organic vegetables, making butter, yoghurt and homemade cheese, smoking your own meat and fish, foraging for wild foods, how to keep a few chickens… all endangered skills which contribute to a convivial lifestyle and are a vital part of our traditional food culture.

Afternoon Cooking Demonstrations Every week day, open to the public.

Bespoke Courses We can offer a variety of courses tailor-made for your group for team building, incentive schemes, hen parties or special celebrations. Courses can combine elements of cooking, gardening and farming.

Ballymaloe Cookery School, Shanagarry, Co. Cork, Ireland
Tel: +353 (0) 21 4646 785 Fax: +353 (0) 21 4646 909
email: info@cookingisfun.ie
www.cookingisfun.ie